T0316403

Bread, Politics and Political Economy in the Reign of Louis XV

Illustration 1. Map of France in the eighteenth century showing provinces and customs divisions. Necker, *Compte-rendu* (Paris, 1781).

Bread, Politics and Political Economy in the Reign of Louis XV

Second Edition

Steven L. Kaplan

Foreword by Sophus A. Reinert

ANTHEM PRESS

Anthem Press
An imprint of Wimbledon Publishing Company
www.anthempress.com

This edition first published in UK and USA 2015
by ANTHEM PRESS
75-76 Blackfriars Road, London SE1 8HA, UK
or PO Box 9779, London SW19 7ZG, UK
and
244 Madison Ave. #116, New York, NY 10016, USA

First edition published in the Netherlands by Martinus Nijhoff Publishers, 1976; re-released
by Springer Science+Business Media B. V., 2013. The author gratefully acknowledges the
devolution of publishing rights.

British Library Cataloguing-in-Publication Data
A catalogue record for this book is available from the British Library.

Library of Congress Cataloging-in-Publication Data
A catalog record for this book has been requested.

ISBN-13: 978 0 85728 510 2 (Hbk)
ISBN-10: 0 85728 510 6 (Hbk)

Cover image: *The Golden Legend* by René Magritte, 1958, © 2015 C. Herscovici / Artists Rights
Society (ARS), New York

This title is also available as an ebook.

TABLE OF CONTENTS

List of Illustrations — vii

Foreword to the Second Edition by Sophus A. Reinert — ix

Acknowledgements — xv

List of Abbreviations — xvii

Introduction — xix

Chapter I. The Police of Provisioning — 1

Chapter II. The Regulations and the Regulators — 52

Chapter III. The Origins of Liberty — 97

Chapter IV. The Response to Liberalization: Theory and Practice — 164

Chapter V. Forcing Grain to Be Free: The Government Holds the Line — 215

Chapter VI. The Reforms and the Grain Trade — 252

Chapter VII. Paris — 300

Chapter VIII. The Royal Trump — 344

Chapter IX. The Government, the Parlements, and the Battle over Liberty: I — 408

Chapter X. The Government, the Parlements, and the Battle over Liberty: II — 451

Chapter XI. From Political Economy to Police: The Return to Apprehensive Paternalism — 491

Chapter XII. Policing the General Subsistence, 1771–1774 — 555

Chapter XIII. The King's Grain and the Retreat from Liberalization — 614

Conclusion — 677

Bibliography — 703

Index — 751

LIST OF ILLUSTRATIONS

1. Map of France — frontispiece

2. Itinerant market-bakers — *facing page* 130

3. The making of the *mercuriale*: the measurers' register — 131

4. Grain passport — 146

5. Grain arrivals and sales: the porters — 147

6. Grain-to-bread cycle — 480

7. Paris bakeshop — 481

8. Economic milling — 496

9. Leprévost and the famine plot — 497

10. The *Bagarre* by Galiani — 608

11. The international grain market at Marseilles — 609

FOREWORD TO THE SECOND EDITION

The Political Economy of Subsistence

"Let Them Eat Baklava" was the title of a recent article in *The Economist* about how rising food prices help explain unrest and revolution in much of the Middle East during the so-called Arab Spring of the early 2010s.[1] The venerable London magazine saw no need to explain the jocular title; the story on which it draws—a sovereign suggests luxury desserts as a substitute for basic food—long ago became the stuff of legend. Indeed, it might be the world's best-known anecdote about the politics of food: reacting to news that the people of Paris could not afford bread on the eve of the French Revolution, Queen Marie Antoinette exclaimed, "Let them eat cake!" The cartoonish evil of the scenario might help explain its enduring appeal in spite of scholars long ago having debunked it, noting, for example, that already Jean-Jacques Rousseau's *Confessions*, written when Marie Antoinette was still a young girl, had mentioned "a great princess who was told that the peasants had no bread, and who responded: 'Let them eat brioche.'"[2] As a historical trope, a cruel ruler taunting her famished subjects lies somewhere beyond the realm of simple memes or urban legends, being timeless and prevalent enough that countless variations of it, dating at least as far back as the Eastern Jin Empire in fourth-century China, have received the classification number AaTh 1446 in the influential Aarne-Thompson typology of folktales.[3] Although apocryphal, or rather *because* apocryphal, it speaks to the sprawling and often undigested array

---

1   "Let them Eat Baklava," *The Economist*, 17 March 2012. For analysis, see Jane Harrigan, *The Political Economy of Arab Food Sovereignty* (Basingstoke: Palgrave Macmillan, 2004).

2   Jean-Jacques Rousseau, *Confessions*, trans. Angela Scholar (Oxford: Oxford University Press, 2000), 262. This popular misconception regarding Marie Antoinette was influentially attacked by Antonia Fraser, *Marie Antoinette: The Journey* (New York: Anchor, 2002), 135. Fraser's argument was effectively translated onto the big screen by Sofia Coppola and, in this particular scene, a strikingly gothic Kirsten Dunst in *Marie Antoinette* (Columbia Pictures, 2006). On such evil, though he does not use this particular example, see Chuck Klosterman, *I Wear the Black Hat: Grappling with Villains (Real and Imagined)* (New York: Simon and Schuster, 2013).

3   On the polyvalence of this tale and its scholarship, see Véronique Campion-Vincent and Christine Shojaei Kawan, "Marie-Antoinette et son célèbre dire: deux scénographies et deux siècles de désordres, trois niveaux de communication et trois modes accusatoires,"*Annales historiques de la Révolution française*, no. 327, (2002): 29–56, building on Antti Aarne and Stith Thompson, *The Types of the Folktale: A Classificaiton and Bibliography*, 2nd edition (Helsinki: Suomalainen Tiedeaktatermia, 1961), 424.

of thoughts and emotions—from incredulity through consternation to righteous rage—that food can evoke across time and space. Disentangled from the particular circumstances of Marie Antoinette and the dawning of a particular Revolution, this infamous trope speaks to far deeper transhistorical processes. The incomprehension between rulers and subjects to which it testifies, the sometimes opaque wall between popular and elite politics, strikes at the very core of human coexistence. Material inequality is a polyvalent and often poorly understood force in any society, conducive simultaneously to emulation and jealousy, to social progress and disintegration, but food is somehow different. Food is so conspicuous because it is, by nature, existential.[4]

The book being republished here, almost forty years after its initial appearance, remains the most thoughtful and rigorous reconstruction of the political economy of subsistence in eighteenth-century France and, arguably, anywhere. No scholar has done more to unpack the real and symbolic importance of bread, in France and elsewhere, in the past and the present, than Steven L. Kaplan. Though his *Bread, Politics and Political Economy in the Reign of Louis XV* has often been lauded as magisterial, it was merely the opening salvo in what would eventually become a tetralogy if not a heptalogy of often massive tomes dedicated to analyzing and explaining what Kaplan would later call the "breadways" of French history.[5] To a naïve modern reader, this might seem like an easily circumscribed task, even in a bread-obsessed country like France. Yet Kaplan's mastery, not only of the historian's art, but also of its craft, makes of the "bread nexus" a lens through which to view practically all aspects of society, from popular culture to high theories of

---

4   An old argument made from a variety of ideological perspectives, for good examples of which see Ferdinando Galiani, *Dialogues sur le commerce des bleds* (Paris: N.P., 1770); Frances Moore Lappé and Joseph Collins, *Food First: Beyond the Myth of Scarcity* (Boston: Houghton Mifflin, 1977); and Peter M. Rosset, *Food is Different: Why We Must Get the WTO Out of Agriculture* (London: Zed Books, 2006).

5   The main arc of analysis could be seen to consist of Steven L. Kaplan, *Bread, Politics and Political Economy in the Reign of Louis XV* (The Hague: Martinus Nijhoff, 1976); idem, *The Famine Plot Persuasion in Eighteenth-Century France* (Philadelphia, PA: The American Philosophical Society, 1982); idem, *Provisioning Paris: Merchants and Millers in the Grain and Flour Trade During the Eighteenth Century* (Ithaca, NY: Cornell University Press, 1984); and idem, *The Bakers of Paris and the Bread Question 1700–1775* (Durham, NC: Duke University Press, 1996), though his edition of Ferdinando Galiani, *La Bagarre: Galiani's "Lost" Parody*, edited with an introduction by Steven L. Kaplan (The Hague: Martinus Nijhoff, 1979), his *Good Bread is Back: A Contemporary History of French Bread, the Way it is Made, and the People who Make It*, trans. C. Porter (Durham, NC: Duke University Press, 2006), and *Le pain maudit: Retour sur la France des années oubliées, 1945–1958* (Paris: Fayard, 2008) obviously partake in the same project. For ego-textual reflections on this project, see Steven L. Kaplan with Jean-Philippe de Tonnac, *La France et son pain: Histoire d'une passion* (Paris: Albin Michel, 2010) and, more obliquely, Steven L. Kaplan, "The 1960's: Was Braudel a Turning-Point?," *Review, a Journal of the Fernand Braudel Center* XXIV, no. 1 (2001): 185–210. See also *The Stakes of Regulation: Perspectives on Bread, Politics and Political Economy Forty years Later* (London: Anthem, 2015). On breadways, see idem, *The Bakers of Paris*, p. 16 and *passim*.

political economy: a trenchant, conscious example of what a Lucien Febvre or a Fernand Braudel might have called a "total history."[6] The volume indeed straddles diverse historiographical traditions that all too seldom communicate: the high and the low, the intellectual and the socio-economic, theory and practice, focused textual analysis and broad archival wisdom.[7]

Fundamentally, *Bread, Politics and Political Economy in the Reign of Louis XV* grapples with the politics, economics and culture of subsistence in the century leading up to the French Revolution. It centers on the ravages of chronic food insecurity, the nature of governmental regulation, the relationship between incessant policing of every aspect of the grain trade—from the planting of seeds to the sale of baked loaves—and emerging theories of political economy, and, most particularly, on the radical nature and consequences of dangerously flawed reforms adopted from 1763 onward to liberalize the grain trade. The immediate inspiration for these reforms was the extremely successful work (both in theoretical terms and with regard to public relations) of a sect of political economists known as the Physiocrats, named for their advocacy of "Physiocracy," or "the rule of nature." The roots of the modern discipline of economics lie deep in Physiocracy, invariably mentioned in scholarly work and mainstream media as the beginning of "scientific" economics.[8]

Grain regulation was not a peripheral issue in the larger enterprise of political economy; it cut to the core of French society and contemporary notions of the social contract—not the ideal social contract theorized by the likes of Jean-Jacques Rousseau, but the tacit and continuously renegotiated relationship between citizen and authority, subject and sovereign. The Hungarian social scientist Karl Polanyi asserted that all economies are by necessity embedded in wider social and cultural matrices, and that modern societies are subject to destabilizing shocks when excessive faith in nature's supposedly self-regulating proclivities creates disorders that in turn generate counter-movements to safeguard the social fabric.[9] As Kaplan demonstrates, Enlightenment France represents an exemplary

---

6   On the "bread nexus," see Kaplan, *Bakers of Paris*, p. 9. On "total history," see among others Fernand Braudel, *The Mediterranean and the Mediterranean World in the Age of Philip II*, vol. II, trans. Siân Reynolds (Berkeley: University of California Press, 1995), 1238; and, generally, Geoff Eley, *A Crooked Line: From Cultural History to the History of Society* (Ann Arbor: University of Michigan Press, 2005), 37.

7   On the difficulty of repeating such projects today, see the similarly interdisciplinary Michael Sonenscher, *Work & Wages: Natural Law, Politics & the Eighteenth-Century French Trades*, with a new preface (Cambridge: Cambridge University Press, 2011), xx.

8   On Physiocracy and its recent scholarship, see Sophus A. Reinert, *Translating Empire: Emulation and the Origins of Political Economy* (Cambridge, MA: Harvard University Press, 2011), 176–81.

9   Karl Polanyi, *The Great Transformation: The Political and Economic Origins of Our Time*, with a foreword by Joseph E. Stiglitz and a new introduction by Fred Block (1944; repr., Boston: Beacon Press, 2007). On Polanyi's theory, see among others Fred Block and Margaret R. Somers, *The Power of Market Fundamentalism: Karl Polanyi's Critique* (Cambridge, MA: Harvard University Press, 2014), 10.

case of these dynamics. The idea that the king was "victualer of last resort" was sacrosanct in much of Europe, and the Physiocratic project was revolutionary in freeing people from such conceptual paternalism in favor of a radically new cosmology based on private property and a "natural order" of self-interested and, crucially, self-regulating market transactions.[10] Grain prices were to move freely according to the dictates of supply and demand, and, in a country characterized by great regional variety in agricultural output, food was to find its own way to where it was needed most.

The theoretical tenets and reformist zeal of Physiocracy strikingly prefigure the general direction taken by the economics profession in the decades leading up to the current crisis: indeed, the dramatic and wide-ranging reforms of 1763 represent the original "shock doctrine," the ur-case of radical overnight market liberalization for the explicit purpose of increasing future growth, no matter the short-term costs.[11] However, the consequences of real dearth—bad harvests in many regions—were amplified in the echo chamber of subsistence anxiety, with disastrous results in a context that was simply unready for liberalization, even in crude infrastructural terms. The reform measures quickly led to negative supply shocks as grain failed to materialize when and where necessary, provoking surging prices as well as speculation and generating widespread unrest, suffering, riots and a deadly delegitimation of royal sovereignty that would explode, under similar circumstances, in the years of the Revolution.

As Kaplan observed, later scholars have nonetheless treated the Physiocrats well and been "warmly sympathetic to their enterprise." Though that assessment still largely holds true among professional economists, *Bread, Politics and Political Economy in the Reign of Louis XV* represents a historiographical turning point, inspiring much subsequent work more attentive to the real-world consequences of economic ideas and reforms.[12] Yet there is no revanchism here, no vilification; instead it offers a remarkably even-handed exposition of how and why different actors proposed dramatically divergent policies in the face of very real challenges, and why even the best of theoretical intentions—individual freedom and economic development—might come to naught, and indeed become downright destructive, when faced with the merciless complexities of real life. Many scholars have since traced the failures of the Physiocratic "shock doctrine," the emergence and eventual victory of the so-called Antiphysiocrats and

---

10 Kaplan, *Bread, Politics*, 7.

11 The literature on modern "shock doctrines" is extensive; see for an iconic example Naomi Klein, *The Shock Doctrine: The Rise of Disaster Capitalism* (New York: Picador, 2007).

12 Kaplan, *Bread, Politics*, 115, note 43. For more recent arguments downplaying their centrality to the Enlightenment and the history of political economy, not to mention their ostensible success, see John Shovlin, *The Political Economy of Virtue: Luxury, Patriotism, and the Origins of the French Revolution* (Ithaca, NY: Cornell University Press, 2007), 3–4; Paul Cheney, *Revolutionary Commerce: Globalization and the French Monarchy* (Cambridge, MA: Harvard University Press, 2010), 6.

the degree to which the historical experiences of the eighteenth century inspired a more Fabian mainstream of political economy acutely aware of the dangers of radicalism and the comparative virtues of gradual reforms on the British model. But they stand squarely on Kaplan's shoulders.

It is not merely rhetorical to observe that *Bread, Politics and Political Economy* may be more timely today than when it was first published. Having long enjoyed subsistence safety—even subsistence overabundance—in large parts of the Western world, we have come to take it for granted. In many countries today, the problem is not that people don't eat enough but that they eat too much, and we find ourselves unfit to face the cruel, de-civilizing dynamics of hunger and unrest. Yet after this long period of seemingly increasing food security, the world suddenly seems more complicated again; even its most advanced market societies have had to learn once more that supply and demand for crucial goods and services do not always reach ideal equilibria in emergencies, and that the veneer of civilization can be fatally thin in the face of nature's fury.[13] Indeed, questions of subsistence, security and political economy, and most crucially of our relationship to nature and the right role for government, are now more central to our preoccupations than they have been since World War II. And by most accounts, large parts of the world are again—or still—facing great uncertainty regarding climate, resources and the most basic access to food and water.[14] A more historically-grounded awareness of past experiences can help us navigate our uncertain future, and Kaplan's *magnum opus* remains our most rigorous reconstruction of precisely such a moment.

Social disintegration has been hunger's constant companion throughout the ages, from the ancient world through the great man-made famines of the nineteenth and twentieth centuries. The Stoic philosopher Seneca, after all, warned of "the general revolution that follows famine," because "a hungry people neither listens to reason, nor is appeased by justice, nor is bent by any entreaty."[15] And even when dearth and famine have failed to foment revolution, they have invariably been vehicles of trauma and the destruction of social bonds, even descending to the unfathomable point, in such settings as Stalinist Russia and Maoist China, of familial cannibalism.[16] To think about the political economy of subsistence is

---

13 For the case of buses to facilitate escape from New Orleans during Hurricane Katrina, for example, see the essays in Cedric Johnson, ed., *The Neoliberal Deluge: Hurricane Katrina, Late Capitalism, and the Remaking of New Orleans* (Minneapolis: University of Minnesota Press, 2011).

14 For an impressionistic sample, see Brahma Chellaney, *Water: Asia's New Battleground* (Washington, D.C.: Georgetown University Press, 2013); Ian Christoplos and Adam Pain, eds., *New Challenges to Food Security: From Climate Change to Fragile States* (Milton Road: Routledge, 2015).

15 Seneca, *De brevitate vitae*, 18.5, in Seneca, *Moral Essays*, vol. II, trans. John W. Basore (Cambridge, MA: Harvard University Press, 1932), 349.

16 See, among endless others, Peter Garnsey, *Famine and Food Supply in the Graeco-Roman World: Responses to Risk and Crisis* (Cambridge: Cambridge University Press, 1988); Emma C. Spary, *Feeding France: New Sciences of Food, 1760–1815* (Cambridge: Cambridge University Press, 2014), 270; Christine Kinealy, *The Great Irish Famine: Impact, Ideology, and Rebellion* (Basingstoke: Palgrave

to think about the nature of society, and one can ask for no better guide to these abundant fields than Kaplan, whose *Bread, Politics and Political Economy* is among those all-too-rare works that transcend their subject matter to speak to perennial problems of human history. It will continue to offer food for thought for many years to come.[17]

Sophus A. Reinert
Harvard Business School

Macmillan, 2001), 27; Mike Davis, *The Late Victorian Holocaust: El Niño Famines and the Making of the Third World* (London: Verso, 2000); Orlando Figes, *A People's Tragedy: The Russian Revolution, 1891–1924* (London: Penguin, 1998), 15 and *passim*; Timothy Snyder, *Bloodlands: Europe Between Hitler and Stalin* (New York: Basic Books, 2012), 50–55 and *passim*; and Yang Jisheng, *Tombstone: The Great Chinese Famine 1958–1962*, trans. Stacy Mosher and Guo Jian; ed. Edward Friedman, Guo Jian and Stacy Mosher (New York: Farrar, Straus and Giroux, 2012).

17 For Kaplan's own take on his first book, and on much of the relevant scholarship since its publication in 1976, see *The Stakes of Regulation*, a sort of companion volume to the second edition of *Bread, Politics and Political Economy*.

ACKNOWLEDGEMENTS

For helping me to crystalize issues at the outset of this project, I am indebted to Professors Franklin Baumer, Harry Miskimin, and Henri Peyre of Yale University and Professors David Bien of the University of Michigan, François Billacois, formerly of the University of Paris-X, Darline Levy of Barnard College, and Jeffry Kaplow of the University of Paris-VIII. I am grateful to my teachers and friends at the ex-Sixième Section of the Ecole Pratique des Hautes Etudes in Paris for their guidance and for the rigorous demands they made upon me: Professors Louis Bergeron, François Furet, Pierre Goubert, and the late Jean Meuvret. Professors Robert R. Palmer and Peter Gay of Yale University provided me with useful comments on an earlier version of this work. I talked about it endlessly with my former colleague Mack Walker, now of the Johns Hopkins University; I am deeply obliged to him and to my colleagues Daniel Baugh, Michael Kammen, and Dominick LaCapra for their probing criticism and helpful suggestions. It is not enough for me to thank Professor Charles C. Gillispie of Princeton University for his illuminating remarks on an early draft; he has been my mentor and friend since my freshman year of college. Near the end of my task I benefitted from the wise counsel and encouragement of Professor M. C. Brands of the University of Amsterdam.

To the *chartistes* and to the *huissiers* of more than two score libraries and archives scattered throughout France who indulged my curiosity and my persistence, I am delighted to express my appreciation. Among the curators, for special kindness, I must mention Yves-Marie Bercé and Odile Krakovitch of the Archives Nationales, Jean Dérens of the Bibliothèque Historique de la Ville de Paris, and François Avril of the Bibliothèque Nationale. The staffs of the Yale and Cornell Libraries labored cheerfully to fulfill all my exotic requests; I am beholden to Hendrik Edelman of Cornell for facilitating my work in myriad ways.

My research would not have been possible without the generous support of Yale University, the Alliance Française, the Western Societies Program of Cornell, and Cornell University. The History Department of Cornell contributed funds for microfilming. The typing, heroically and skillfully accomplished by Mrs. Lina Hood, was financed by the Humanities Faculty Research Grants Committee and the Office of Academic Funding of Cornell. Mary Ann Quinn and Nan E. Karwan were zealous and perspicacious research aides.

This book is dedicated to my wife, an eighteenth century specialist and a devoted friend, who did not hesitate to *mettre la main à la pâte*.

LIST OF ABBREVIATIONS

(This is not a complete listing of archival sources; for that, see Bibliography)

Parisian Archives and Libraries

Archives de l'Assistance Publique	AAP
Archives des Affaires Étrangères	Arch. AE
Archives du Département de la Seine et de la Ville de Paris	Archives Seine-Paris
Archives Historiques de l'Armée	Arch. armée
Archives Nationales	AN
Bibliothèque de l'Arsenal	Arsenal
(archives de la Bastille)	mss. Bastille
Bibliothèque Historique de la Ville de Paris	BHVP
Bibliothèque Nationale	BN
Collection Joly de Fleury	Coll. Joly
manuscrits français	mss. fr.
manuscrits nouvelles acquisitions	mss. n. a.

Departmental Archives

A.D. Bouches-du-Rhône	A.D. B-du-R.
A.D. Calvados	A.D. Cal.
A.D. Charente-Maritime	A.D. C-M.
A.D. Côte d'Or	A.D. C d'O.
A.D. Eure-et-Loir	A.D. E-et-L.
A.D. Gironde	A.D. Gir.
A.D. Haute-Garonne	A.D. H-G.
A.D. Hérault	A.D. Hér.
A.D. Ille-et-Vilaine	A.D. I-et-V.
A.D. Indre-et-Loire	A.D. I-et-L.
A.D. Loire-Atlantique	A.D. L-A.
A.D. Puy-de-Dôme	A.D. P-de-D.
A.D. Seine-Maritime	A.D. S-M.

Administrative and Institutional Titles

Controller-General	CG
Intendant	IN.
Lieutenant General	LG
Parlement	Parl.
Procurator General	PG
Subdelegate	SD

INTRODUCTION

I

Modern times has invented its own brand of apocalypse. Famine is no longer one of the familiar outriders. The problems of material life, and their political and psychological implications, have changed drastically in the course of the past two hundred years. Perhaps nothing has more profoundly affected our institutions and our attitudes than the creation of a technology of abundance. Even the old tropes have given way: neither dollars nor calories can measure the distance which separates *gagne-pain* from *gagne-bifteck*.[1]

Yet the concerns of this book seem much less remote today than they did when it was conceived in the late sixties. In the past few years we have begun to worry, with a sort of expiatory zeal, about the state of our environment, the size of our population, the political economy and the morality of the allocation of goods and jobs, and the future of our resources. While computer projections cast a Malthusian pall over our world, we have had a bitter, first-hand taste of shortages of all kinds. The sempiternal battle between producers and consumers rages with a new ferocity, as high prices provoke anger on the one side and celebration on the other. Even as famines continue to strike the Third World in the thermidor of the green revolution, so we have discovered hunger in our own midst. The historian of pre-industrial

---

1 Although the French have substantially reduced their bread consumption, nutrition experts still accuse them of eating too many cereal calories. Michel Cépède, "Le Régime alimentaire des Français," in *Encyclopédie française*, ed. by G. Berger (Paris, 1955), XIV, 14. 42. 4. The Paris bakers, drawing with fine discrimination on the popular medical literature, claim on the the contrary that consumers eat too much meat and not enough bread. The most engaging source for this point of view is Pierre Poilâne, 8, rue du Cherche Midi, Paris 6ᵉ.

Europe has always been able to find analogies and metaphors in press reports from Asia and Africa about "famine plots," crowds pillaging storehouses, governments promulgating draconian measures against food hoarders and speculators, and famished consumers obdurately rejecting unfamiliar staple substitutes. Now the historian experiences the same eerie feeling of déjà-vu when he reads front-page articles in the *New York Times* about monstrous international wheat deals. Now that scarcity looms as part of our future, it is easier to make the case that it is also a heritage of our past—a heritage worth knowing, if not commemorating. Though we are not terrified by the same fears that obsessed our ancestors, we now have a keener sense of the burdens of subsistence and survival.

The subsistence problem dominated life in old-regime Europe in a merciless and unremitting way. No issue was more urgent, more pervasively felt, and more difficult to resolve than the matter of grain provisioning. Cereal-dependence conditioned every phase of social life.[2] Grain was the pilot sector of the economy; beyond its determinant role in agriculture, directly and indirectly grain shaped the development of commerce and industry, regulated employment, and provided a major source of revenue for the state, the church, the nobility, and large segments of the Third Estate. Subsistence needs gave cereal-dependence its most telling expression. The vast majority of people in the Old Regime derived the bulk of their calories from cereals, in bread or some other form. Never did the old proverb "a man is what he eats" hold truer. Because most of the people were poor, the quest for subsistence preoccupied them relentlessly; the study of how they dealt with their never-ending subsistence problem tells us a good deal about who and what they were.

Grain dependence was an obsession as well as a servitude because the cereals economy was an economy of scarcity and uncertainty. The dread of shortage and hunger haunted this society. The line separating critical from ordinary times was perilously thin and protean. The menace of crisis never disappeared, for it was impossible to predict, assure, or apportion the harvests, or to evade the consequences of nature's caprices or of human vice or error. Cereal dependence produced a chronic sense of insecurity, which

---

2 The fact that in *ordinary* times the bulk of the population had to spend about 50 percent of its income on the bread ration and in critical times virtually all of it is one striking measure of this dependence. See Labrousse's works, cited below in note 6 and Georges Lefebvre, *Études orléanaises* (Paris, 1962), I, 218.

caused contemporaries to view their world in terms that may strike us as lugubriously overdrawn.[3] This dependence generated fears and attitudes which had a powerful reality of their own, apart from the "objective" reality of, say, harvest results. Indeed, these fears and attitudes helped to make prices, to determine trade patterns and practices, and to prompt governmental action. Eighteenth-century administrators and writers insisted emphatically on the distinction to be made, in terms of *cause*, between a "real" dearth and a dearth "of opinion," but they could not deny that the *effects* were very much the same in the two cases.

While cereal dependence reinforced the deep cleavages in society between the haves and the have-nots, the consumers and the producers, and the city and the countryside, the subsistence obsession also forged curious ties of solidarity between the governors and the governed. The government, at all levels, worried about the food supply as earnestly as the consumers. Subsistence was the chief common interest that attached them to each other; their shared anxiety to deal successfully with the subsistence problem served as a sort of mutual guarantee of fidelity and responsibility. A particularly disastrous harvest, or a series of short crops, in addition to setting the ration and price of survival, unleashed a terrible multiplier effect, producing widespread disorder: social, economic, and psychic. The government strained to do everything in its power to avert this kind of disarray, or at least to limit its depredations. It nervously tracked the phases of the harvest cycle, as if vigilance, like some rite of propitiation, were itself a mode of prophylaxis. The ministry gathered data on the planting immediately following the harvest; it waited impatiently through the course of the winter until the spring began to betray "appearances" and the serious wagering on the likelihood of a good crop could begin; it agonized as the tension mounted during the *soudure*, that seemingly interminable period, sometimes a month, sometimes as many as three or four, which marked the time after the supply of "old" grain had become scarce and before the new crop was ready to be taken. Meanwhile,

---

3 Staff of life and symbol of salvation, grain was also, in the eyes of several eighteenth century social critics, the mark of bondage and misery. S.-N.-H. Linguet, *Réponse aux docteurs modernes* (London, 1771), parts I and II, 158–90; Linguet, *Du Pain et du bled* in *Oeuvres*, VI (London, 1774), *passim;* Linguet, *Annales politiques, civiles et littéraires du 18ᵉ siècle*, VII (Nov. 1770), 169–78; L.-S. Mercier, *Tableau de Paris* (Amsterdam, 1783) VI, 124 and *passim*.

On the anguish over tomorrow's subsistence, see the illuminating remarks of Robert Mandrou, *Introduction à la France moderne: essai de psychologie historique, 1500–1640* (Paris, 1961), 21, 34–35.

regional and local agencies of government took various measures designed to meet their own provisioning requirements.

Nor were subsistence doubts fully allayed even by a good harvest, for there were still perils and delays to face. A "good" harvest crudely measured in terms of visible output did not necessarily mean high-quality, high-yield grain. Freshly-cut grain (and, to a lesser degree, new flour) could not be used immediately for consumption, except at the risk of endangering the health of consumers or producing unpalatable bread—a terrible provocation. In some seasons, atmospheric calm, flooding, freezing, or low water resulted in a secondary form of subsistence crisis—a flour crisis, for in these conditions the millstones could not convert grain, however abundant it was, into usable foodstuff.

It would be wrong to give the impression that subsistence was purely a function of meteorological accidents, before or after the harvest.[4] Ideal weather, from September through August and beyond, was not by itself a guarantee of subsistence. There was still a vast distance to traverse between the fields and the tables of consumers. This was the space (and the time) covered by the process of distribution. Distribution was an even more delicate and complex matter than production, for it was contingent upon many more variables—economic, administrative, legal, geographical, historical, technological, social, psychological, and political. Distribution depended upon modes of transporation and communication links, conservation techniques, market systems, the organization of the grain and flour trades, the degree of integration and commercialization of the milling and baking industries, the brokerage function, the development of credit institutions, local foodways, the availability

---

4 Although weather was an admittedly capricious, irresistible, and politically neutral force, superbly equipped to absorb consensual blame, it rarely functioned as a credible scapegoat for dearth in the Old Regime. Public officials were more favorably disposed to a non-naturalistic explanation because acknowledging publicly that a dearth was due to natural calamity was tantamount to confessing that it was beyond control. Authorities believed that such an avowal of helplessness would exacerbate difficulties by reinforcing the disaster cues received by the public. Moreover, the consumers and many officials believed deeply in the natural abundance of France, even as they dreaded the recurrence of scarcity. Given the inordinate richness of French arable, *ceteris paribus*, dearths *should not* have erupted as often as they did. This attitude nurtured a conspiratorial turn of mind: the conviction that dearths were more often than not *un*natural in their origins, the result of evil-doings along the path of distribution. See, in this regard, the vain efforts of the comte de St.-Priest to persuade a band of Parisian women early in the Revolution that the dearth was the product of bad weather and that "... the king was no more capable of making wheat grow than of making it rain...." *Mémoires*, ed. by baron de Barante (Paris, 1929), II, 14–15.

of food surrogates, local social structure and employment patterns, relationships between town and country, competition for hinterland, local and regional "custom" in legal and socioeconomic terms, the implantation and operation of overlapping or rival police jurisdictions, the collective subsistence memory of the community, local attitudes toward commerce, the conventional understanding of the law, the degree of interest of regional and central administrators in local affairs—the list could be extended generously.

Though the subject is far from exhausted, it has been many years since historians have seriously studied provisioning in the eighteenth century.[5] There are a number of reasons for this neglect. First of all, the evidence: it is elusive and scant, despite the overwhelming presence of the subsistence problem in the Old Regime. Moreover, it tends to focus on the pathological experiences, the record of deviation rather than the chronicle of what was normal (though, to be sure, the boundary separating them is not always clearly marked). We can learn a good deal about times of catastrophe but it is much more difficult to see what happened in the ephemeral years which left no monuments to their passage. The inherent bias of the evidence reinforces the indifference that historians often manifest toward the study of the banalities of everyday life. Understandably, the subsistence problem has generally acquired importance, from the historian's vantage point, in the breach, when it leads to one sort of disaster or another. It is no accident that the subsistence question has most often been investigated in the context of the French Revolution.

---

5 The most important contributions in recent years have been made by Richard Cobb. They pertain almost exclusively to the Revolutionary period. See below, note number 14. When Jean Meuvret's thesis on agricultural and subsistence problems in the seventeenth century appears it will render invaluable service to those interested in grain questions. Despite the handful of pioneering studies which appeared in the early part of this century (e.g., J. Letaconnoux, *Les Subsistances et le commerce des grains en Bretagne au XVIIIe siècle* (Rennes, 1909); Charles Desmarest, *Le Commerce des grains dans la généralité de Rouen à la fin de l'ancien régime* (Paris, 1926); Louis Viala, *La Question des grains et leur commerce à Toulouse au 18e siècle* (Toulouse, 1909); Pierre Lefèvre, *Le Commerce des grains et la question du pain à Lille de 1713 à 1789* (Lille, 1925)), there is still a great deal of work to be done on the grain trade and the entire bread nexus on the local level. The standard work on the grain trade on a national scale, G. Afanassiev, *Le Commerce des céréales en France au 18e siècle* (Paris, 1894), though it contains much useful information, is often misleading or erroneous, sketchy, superficial or tendentious in interpretation, and badly dated. A. P. Usher's *The History of the Grain Trade in France 1400–1700* (Cambridge, Mass., 1913) is extremely suggestive but it is a very rapid survey. For Paris, Léon Cahen's articles—too numerous to cite here—mark a beginning. But here too the bulk of the work remains to be done.

Secondly, given its very character, eighteenth-century France invites attention elsewhere, particularly during the long reign of Louis XV. It was a century of extraordinary national efflorescence in virtually every domain. France was the richest, the most populous, and among the most cohesive states in Europe. Culturally, the French exercised an astonishing hegemony, throughout the Western world and in some instances beyond. If domestic politics were often turbulent, nevertheless there were remarkably few social repercussions: compared to the seventeenth century, the eighteenth century seems placid. Economically, this was an era of expansion and vitality, especially after 1730. And it seemed less noteworthy that the poor—the bulk of the population—remained poor or became poorer than that certain segments of society enjoyed heady prosperity. Historians of the eighteenth century are always gazing beyond, diverted if not transfixed by the great moments which mark the end of the epoch. Quite naturally, they have tended to concentrate on the portents of change and the innovations rather than on the familiar and the immutable.

Finally, the conceptual and methodological framework which has had the greatest influence on the shape of historical inquiry into eighteenth-century France during the past generation—the brilliant Labroussean model, derived from exhaustive studies of grain prices—has ironically deflected attention away from subsistence-type problems.[6] It has encouraged surrender to the historiographical tyranny exercised by the Revolution, reducing the Old Regime to a mere prelude. It has also given primacy to the "long-run" view. Skillfully employed, the long-run approach is a superb analytical tool. But it is capable, too, of obscuring and distorting historical reality. Subsistence and provisioning are questions of short-run determination and significance. In the long-run perspective, it is hard to take stock of day-to-day problems of survival; they are overlooked, averaged out, or grouped and subsumed under certain clinical rubrics and treated more or less casually as predictable and tiresome accidents, spasms, or outliers. In complicity with the disdain for the "event" which has accompanied it, the

---

6 C. E. Labrousse, *Esquisse du mouvement des prix et des revenus en France au 18ᵉ siècle* (Paris, 1933) and *La Crise de l'économie française à la fin de l'ancien régime et au début de la révolution* (Paris, 1944); Fernand Braudel and Labrousse, eds., *Histoire économique et sociale de la France*, Vol. II: *Des Derniers temps de l'âge seigneurial aux préludes de l'âge industriel (1660–1789)* (Paris, 1970).

long-run approach can generate an abstract, homogenized social history devoid of flesh and blood and unconvincing despite its scientific cachet.[7]

Labrousse's pioneering achievements helped to inspire interest in historical demography, a field which has made stunning conquests in the short time that it has existed. The ardor of the demographic historians has tended to bolster a certain long-run insouciance. On the one hand, demographers are interested in individuals and events—the vital events of birth, death, etc. On the other hand, these historians are understandably impatient to make sense of the long-term transformations which imperceptibly yet radically modify the character of society. One of their foremost teachers and forebears, the late Jean Meuvret, was perhaps the first to suggest the changing nature of demographic crises, from the murderous crises of the grim seventeenth century to the "larvated" crises of the far less Malthusian eighteenth century. For Meuvret, a "revolution" separated the two worlds, though neither he nor his followers have succeeded in clearly defining and ranking the causes of this putative revolution.[8]

The implications, however, are plain: for whatever reasons, subsistence problems were far less acute under Louis XV than they had been under his immediate predecessors. Indeed, it is now even possible to infer that subsistence was no longer really an issue for the men of the Enlightenment and the flourishing "phase A." No one has since questioned the claim that the era of famines ended in 1709. One economist, with the slogans of May 1968 reverberating in his mind, has marked 1709 as the beginning of the age of the "society of consumption."[9] Historical demographers of the "young school"— Dupâquier at their head—now confidently contend that "nobody died of hunger any more in France after 1710," an assertion which

---

7 There is some evidence, though it is not without ambiguity, that the "event" is making a discreet comeback in French scientific circles. See the special number of *Communications*, 18 (1972).

8 Jean Meuvret, "Les Crises de subsistances et la démographie de la France d'ancien régime," *Population*, I (Oct.–Dec. 1946), 643–50; Meuvret, "La Géographie des prix des céréales et les anciennes économies européennes: prix méditerranéens, prix continentaux, prix atlantiques à la fin du 17e siècle," *Revista de Economia*, IV (June 1951), 64; Meuvret, "Les Mouvements des prix de 1661 à 1715 et leurs répercussions," *Journal de la société de statistique de Paris*, LXXXV (May–June 1944), 109–19; Labrousse, *Crise*, 182–84; Marcel Reinhard, "Les Répercussions démographiques des crises de subsistances en France au 18e siècle," *Actes du 81e Congrès des Sociétés Savantes*, Rouen et Caen, 1956 (Paris, 1956), 67. Armand Husson crudely anticipated Meuvret's conclusions. *Les Consommations de Paris* (Paris, 1875), 180–81.

9 Jean Fourastié in l'*Express* (9–15 Feb. 1970), 70–71.

continues to trouble some old hands like Pierre Goubert, Meuvret's leading student, and some new ones like Michel Morineau and Georges Frêche.[10]

There are a number of points to be made about the findings of the demographic school. Firstly, as I suggested above, the history of the subsistence problem is not coterminous with the history of subsistence crises, for the former was chronic and omnipresent rather than spasmodic. Secondly, until there is more evidence, and until we have a better understanding of the relationship between scarcity on the one hand and morbidity and mortality on the other, it is premature to pronounce the eclipse of even the "killing" subsistence crisis. Thirdly, mortality is not always a reliable or sufficient measure for the significance or acuity of a subsistence crisis. Subsistence crises can have a seismic impact on individuals, communities, and institutions without claiming lives on a massive scale. The demographic test should not be the sole litmus for the existence of a subsistence crisis.

Fourthly, we must place the results of demographic research in historical context; we must not allow the total picture of the past which it retrospectively constructs to distort our vision of what actually happened at any given point in time. We know, for example, all the naïveté which Maxime du Camp required to write: "Contemporary testimonies unanimously show that the whole eighteenth century was but

---

10 Jacques Dupâquier, "Sur la population française au 17ᵉ et au 18ᵉ siècles," *Revue historique*, CCXXIX (Jan.–Mar. 1968), 66 and *passim* and his extremely provocative "De l'Animal à l'homme: le mécanisme autorégulateur des populations traditionnelles," *Revue de l'Institut de Sociologie* (1972), no. 2, 177–211. Cf. Voltaire's similar opinion, setting the eclipse of killing subsistence crises even earlier. *Petit écrit sur l'arrêt du conseil du 13 septembre 1774* (Jan. 1775) in *Oeuvres complétes de Voltaire*, ed. by Beaumarchais, *et al.* (Kehl. 1784–89), XXX, 541; J.-B. Briatte, a philosophe interested in the problem of poverty, attacked Voltaire ("the philosophe adulator of power and opulence") for claiming that the "horrible famines" of 1709 and 1740 did not kill ("this consoling lie"). *Offrande à l'humanité* (Amsterdam, 1780), 132n. In the present-day controversy, Goubert, if he is not frankly in the Briatte camp, nevertheless has serious reservations about the Voltaire-Dupâquier position. See Goubert's contribution in Braudel and Labrousse, eds., *Histoire économique et sociale*, II, 3–84 and "Un Quart de siècle de démographie historique: bilan et réflexions," *Hommage à Marcel Reinhard* (Paris, 1973), 315–23. See also Morineau's iconoclastic work, cited in note 15 below and Frêche's mass of granite, *Toulouse et la région Midi-Pyrénées au siècle des lumières (N.p., 1974–75)*. A recent study which argues for the extinction of killing crises (they "died mysteriously with the second decade of the eighteenth century"), but for the proliferation of misery is Olwen H. Hufton, *The Poor of Eighteenth Century France, 1750–1789* (Oxford, 1974), 13–15. Pierre Chaunu also charts out a moderate (but vigorous!) position on this issue. *Histoire, science sociale* (Paris, 1974), 346–47.

one long dearth."[11] Yet there is no doubt that many contemporaries perceived their world in this way. From this psychological perspective, it would be pointless to belabor the significance of the shift from one demographic "régime" to another or to insist upon the reduction of amplitude of price oscillations, for there is little indication that contemporaries received the news. Without the benefit of moving averages and a comparative framework, they were much less likely to be impressed by the advent of new times than we are today. In this sense, regardless of the global balance sheets of the demographic historians, we will still be able to acknowledge the validity of the portraits painted by Michelet and Taine of the extreme precariousness of "popular" life.

Finally, within the *problématique* of the demographic school, there remain a number of crucial unanswered questions. One I mentioned above: why did the "old demographic régime" give way to a new one? Historians have hinted at many possible explanations, none of which has yet been rigorously tested: better hygiene and medicine, less harsh climate, better transportation, innovations in technology, improvements in market organization and linkage, the emergence of a more refined style of warfare, changes in the nature of diseases and perhaps also in the characteristics of their carriers and the susceptibilities of their hosts, development of new food tastes and variation of diet, improved administrative practices, and progress in agriculture.[12]

Among these, the question of agricultural production and productivity has received the most careful attention in recent years. Unless it can be shown that agriculture progressed (in one sense or another) significantly in the eighteenth century, it will be extremely difficult to account for the population growth, which is universally acknowledged. To be sure, historians no longer write about a "demographic revolution,"

---

11 Maxime du Camp, *Paris, ses organes, ses fonctions et sa vie dans la seconde moitié du 19ᵉ siècle* (Paris, 1869–75), II, 23.

12 See Goubert in Braudel and Labrousse, eds., *Histoire économique et sociale*, II, 55–84; Labrousse in *ibid.*, 694–95; Pierre Léon, *Économies et sociétés pré-industrielles, 1650–1780* (Paris, 1780), II, 221–22; Jean Meyer, *La Noblesse bretonne au 18ᵉ siècle* (Paris, 1966), I, 488n; Louis Henry, "The Population of France in the 18th Century," in *Population and History*, ed. by D.V. Glass and D.E.C. Eversley (London, 1965), 448; Karl F. Helleiner, "The Population of Europe from the Black Death to the Eve of the Vital Revolution," in *The Cambridge Economic History of Europe*, IV, ed. by E.E. Rich and C.H. Wilson (Cambridge, 1967), 92–93; F. Braudel and F. Spooner, "Prices in Europe from 1450 to 1750," in *ibid.*, 395–96. Cf. François Lebrun, *Les Hommes et la mort en Anjou aux 17ᵉ et 18ᵉ siècles* (Paris, 1971), 368 and Joseph Ruwet, *et al.*, *Marché des céréales à Ruremonde, Luxembourg, Namur, et Diest aux 17ᵉ et 18ᵉ siècles*, Recueil de Travaux d'Histoire et de Philologie (Louvain, 1966), 43.

but it is generally accepted that the population of France on the whole advanced by between one-fifth and two-fifths in the course of the century. (Nor can one even here dispose of "causes" with absolute certainty: were mortality changes alone responsible for this increase?)[13] The best recent scholarship on agricultural production points to a differential scheme of growth, varying from thumping development in certain areas to stagnation in others, but with a generally positive balance-sheet for the kingdom as a whole.[14]

At the same time, Michel Morineau has challenged the sanguine portrait of a decidedly "modern" eighteenth century which breaks with the past in demographic and economic terms. He is not at all convinced that the eighteenth century witnessed the emergence of a new demographic regime, he rejects the idea of an agricultural

---

13 Though the analysis is not yet complete, it is likely that Louis Henry's I.N.E.D. study will show that population growth was faster and greater in the eighteenth century than we have supposed. Perhaps the next generaton of historians will again feel authorized to write about a "demographic revolution"!

14 E. Le Roy Ladurie, "Première esquisse d'une conjoncture," in J. Goy and Le Roy Ladurie, eds., *Les Fluctuations du produit de la dîme: conjoncture décimale et domaniale de la fin du moyen âge au 18ᵉ siècle* (Paris, 1972), 367–74. See also Labrousse in Braudel and Labrousse, eds., *Histoire économique et sociale*, II, 696–97; E. Le Roy Ladurie, "L'histoire immobile," *Annales: économies, sociétés, civilisations*, XXIX (May–June 1974), 673–692; E. Le Roy Ladurie, "Pour un modèle de l'économie rurale française au 18ᵉ siècle," *Cahiers d'histoire*, XIX (1974), 5–27; B.H. Slicher van Bath, "Eighteenth Century Agriculture on the Continent of Europe: Evolution or Revolution," *Agricultural History*, XLIII (Jan. 1969), 173–79; André J. Bourde, *Agronomie et agronomes en France au 18ᵉ siècle* (Paris, 1967), I, 20–21 and II, 1572–85; J.-C. Toutain, *Le Produit de l'agriculture française de 1700 à 1958* in *Cahiers de l'I.S.E.A.*, supplement, no. 115 (1961); Le Roy Ladurie, "Les Comptes fantastiques de Gregory King," *Annales: économies, sociétés, civilisations*, 23rd year (Sept.-Oct. 1968), 1086–1102; Robert Mandrou, *La France aux 17ᵉ et 18ᵉ siècles* (Paris, 1967), 124–25; Jean Bastié, *La Croissance de la banlieue parisienne* (Paris, 1964), 82; Marc Bloch, "Transformations techniques," *Journal de psychologie normale et pathologique*, XLI (Jan.-March 1948), 107; A. Moreau de Jonnès, "Statistique des céréales de la France. Le blé, la culture, sa production, sa consommation, son commerce," *Journal des économistes*, IV (Jan.–March 1843), 129–66, 309–19. Léon Cahen, who did such remarkable work on material culture, took a markedly pessimistic view of French agriculture ("The production of grain is on the average deficient."). "Le Pacte de famine et les spéculations sur les blés," *Revue historique*, CLII (May–June 1926), 35. Cole and Deane saw little evidence for a rise in output per head. W.A. Cole and Phyllis Deane, "The Growth of National Incomes," in H.J. Habakkuk and M. Postan, eds., *The Cambridge Economic History of Europe* (Cambridge, 1966), VI, part I, 5–6, 11. Richard Cobb, the leading authority on subsistence questions in the revolutionary period, has steadfastly maintained that throughout the eighteenth century the subsistence problem was above all a problem of distribution rather than production. "Le Ravitaillement des villes sous la terreur; la question des arrivages," *Bulletin de la Société d'Histoire Moderne*, 53rd year (April–June 1954), 8–12; *Terreur et subsistances, 1793–95: Études d'histoire révolutionnaire* (Paris, 1965); and *The Police and the People: French Popular Protest, 1789–1820* (Oxford, 1970).

revolution along with the notion of a demographic one, he persists in attributing significant "mortalities" to recurring subsistence crises, and he questions the now classical dichotomy between a somber seventeenth century and a dynamic eighteenth century.[15] Recently, too, it seems that Labrousse has retreated slightly from his earlier position, maintaining now that the Malthusian race between population and agriculture in the eighteenth century ended in what looks very much like a tie.[16]

A great deal of research in this domain is just coming to fruition. Louis Henry's massive retrospective survey at the Institut National d'Études Démographiques and Jacques Dupâquier's pioneering investigations at the École des Hautes Études en Sciences Sociales (the *ci-devant* Sixième Section) will clarify our notions about population. We will know considerably more about production and productivity after the second round of the tithe studies—this one of international scope—conducted by Emmanuel Le Roy Ladurie and Joseph Goy of the E.H.E.S.S. Georges Frêche promises a vast publication on the *mercuriales*; it is to be hoped, too, that he and Michel Morineau will continue to challenge the conventional definitions and methods. Several of Pierre Goubert's students are engaged in regional inquiries—on the model of *Beauvais* one trusts; and Goubert himself is preparing Jean Meuvret's long-awaited "thesis" for publication.

To complement this work on supply and demand, we urgently need a series of studies on the distribution side of the subsistence problem. Shockingly little is known about the grain and flour trades even in metropolitan areas. Nor have the baking and milling industries fared any better.[17] Attention must also be addressed to the police of provisioning, market organization, public victualing, and the dearths and crises of the eighteenth century. No one will be able to deal confidently with the subsistence question until this solid foundation is erected on the local and regional scales.

---

15 Michel Morineau, "Y a-t-il eu une révolution agricole en France au 18ᵉ siècle?" *Revue historique*, CCXLII (April–June 1968), 299–326 and more fully in *Les Faux-Semblants d'un démarrage économique: agriculture et démographie en France au 18ᵉ siècle* (Paris, 1971), 67–68, 86, *passim*. See also his "Réflexions tardives" in Goy and Le Roy Ladurie, eds., *Dîme*, 331. It seems to me less important to catalogue Morineau's methodological crimes and interpretive inconsistencies—as many reviewers have done—than to take note of the enormous heuristic value of his contribution.

16 Labrousse in Braudel and Labrousse, eds., *Histoire économique et sociale*, II, 697–98.

17 I am completing monographs on the bakery and the bread problem in eighteenth century Paris and on the grain and flour trades and the milling industry in the Paris region.

II

This book deals with the subsistence problem in the 1760's and 1770's when the concerns of politics and of provisioning dramatically intersected at the national as well as the grassroots levels. There are two major focuses of analyses. The first, which I call liberalization, is a radical reform of the grain trade undertaken in 1763–64. The second is a severe subsistence crisis which jarred the entire kingdom in the last decade of the reign of Louis XV. The aim of this book is to explain the genesis of the reforms and the crisis, examine their relationship, and assess the profound impact they had upon French life.

The main theme of liberalization is the shift from control to freedom, from intervention to laissez-faire, from police to political economy. I consider the liberal laws of 1763–64 to be among the most daring and revolutionary reforms attempted in France before 1789. Renouncing a stewardship it had exercised, so it seemed, from time immemorial, the royal government broke an unwritten covenant with consumers and proclaimed that subsistence was no longer its overriding responsibility. The consumers lost their privileged identity as *the* people even as grain lost its privileged status in commerce and public life. The politico-moral claims of the people were superseded by the natural rights of proprietors in the esteem of the king. Subsistence became a matter for the individual to work out on his own.

Trapped in a political, economic, and fiscal cul-de-sac, the government conceived the grain reform as a gateway to a new age. It assigned itself a new role and endorsed values alien to the corporate ethos of the Old Regime. Liberalization was not merely an experiment in (a theoretically) free market economy, though in this regard alone it was of enormous significance. It was a crucial stage in the transformation of the relations between state and society, the governors and the governed, the individual and the collectivity, political power and economic power, producers and consumers, the public sector and the private sector. Liberalization was the story, on the one side, of an avid appetite for change based on an exciting and liberating view of the future free from the barbarities and stupidities of the past, and, on the other, of passionate resistance, not to change per se, but to a specific kind of change that seemed to strike at the very heart of the public interest and promised a future replete with uncertainties and insecurities. The crisis which engulfed liberalization was a crisis in the process of modernization—a crisis at once political, socioeconomic, administrative, intellectual, and moral.

This crisis began as a subsistence crisis; its course of development is my other chief preoccupation. It was marked by the most serious and widespread eruption of disorder in the long reign of Louis XV. The consumer-people became desperate as prices doubled and tripled, supplies became scarce, wages lagged behind prices, unemployment spread, and "panic terror," as contemporaries called it, set in. Though they were startling in their incidence and intensity, the reactions of the consumers threatened by shortage and hunger were more or less predictable. What jolted the royal government was the response of the police. In a sense, the police rioted, too. They rioted against the liberal reforms which tied their hands and which they blamed for the acuity of the subsistence difficulties. The police and the people formed the nucleus of a powerful, albeit disparate, coalition of opposition to liberalization which crystallized between 1765 and 1768. Ultimately, several of the parlements took the lead in the campaign against the liberal reforms, even as several other parlements had been at the head of the liberal lobby. Just at the moment when historians usually emphasize the unity of the sovereign courts, on this crucial issue they were deeply divided. Similar fissures appeared in the community of philosophes; traumatized by the crisis, many philosophes found that they could not support liberty in all its avatars.

The sixties have always been known to historians as a decade of crisis, but for different reasons than the ones I have proposed. In the standard view, the crisis was the Brittany Affair and the dénouement was the "coup d'état" mounted by Chancellor Maupeou. Without denying the importance of the constitutional issue, I suggest that the standard view requires major revisions.[18]

Throughout the troubles in the four or five years following the reforms, the ministry did not flinch in its commitment to liberalization. Rarely in the course of the Old Regime had a government shown greater determination to defend a highly controversial innovation. At first, the ministry blithely denied that there was a genuine provisioning problem; later, it argued that the difficulties would resolve themselves, provided public officials refrained from taking action (save to

---

18 Obscured as a result of the traditional emphasis on the constitutional issue and the recent tendency to locate a surge of prosperity in the post-war years, the crisis of liberalization has also been eclipsed by the flourishing historiographical cult of Turgot. See, for example, the serious misapprehensions about the liberalization experience and the crisis of the late sixties and early seventies in an otherwise fascinating piece by Pierre Vilar, "Motín de Esquilache et crises d'ancien régime, *Historia Iberica* (1973), 11–13.

repress disorders). An exception was made in favor of Paris, for which a special fund of king's grain had been constituted. Ironically, the assistance that the government tried to organize for the benefit of the capital provoked charges that the government was secretly speculating on the people's hunger under the cover of liberty. Liberalization helped to give shape to what came to be called the "famine pact." Though the famine plot persuasion was nothing new, liberalization gave it a corrosive political edge. It seriously compromised the liberal ministries of the sixties and continued to undermine public confidence in the king and in public authority until the end of the Old Regime.

A deepening economic crisis, proliferating disorder, persistently short crops, and an ever-burgeoning public opposition compelled the government to abandon liberalization in 1770. De-liberalization, however, did not abruptly stem the crisis. Nor was the police restoration a smooth, uniform process throughout the realm. Gradually, tranquility returned to much of the kingdom in the next few years. The Midi, bastion of liberal strength, suffered the last violent spasms in 1773. Inclined to a moderate position and not wholly unsympathetic to the liberal thesis, Terray, the new Controller-General, found himself increasingly obliged to take an authoritarian, interventionist stand. To combat dearth, he finally countenanced all the classical police tactics: market constraints, declarations, requisitions, and so on. The king's grain operation expanded prodigiously in his hands; largely as a result of this massive intervention on the supply side, the famine plot accusations continued to stigmatize the government and discredit king and kingship.

Nevertheless, experience convinced Terray that laissez-faire and a monarchical system resting upon a society of orders were essentially incompatible. Economically alluring, the sociopolitical costs of liberalism were prohibitive in his estimation. Terray perceived the subsistence problem in national terms and devised a model of control and coordination that was as audacious in conception as it was unworkable in practice.

Louis XV died in mid-1774, a king no longer beloved by his subjects, in part because of his betrayal of their subsistence interests. With the nomination of the administrator-philosophe Turgot to replace Terray, liberalism was assured another chance. Turgot's hopes, however, went up in the smoke of the Flour War, really the last battle in a struggle that had begun more than a decade before.

The first two chapters of this book investigate the police tradition and the subsistence mentality. They discuss the relations between the police and the people and the assumptions that each made about subsistence. They deal with the police apparatus of control as well as the police ideology, with the actual way in which the police functioned as well as the role theoretically prescribed for them. Against this background, it will be easy to understand why the liberal reforms embodied such a drastic departure from the past. The following chapter looks back to the intellectual, political, and socioeconomic roots of liberalism and the liberty movement.

Chapter four traces the beginning of the crisis that united the police and the people against the royal government and the liberty lobby. The fifth chapter focuses on the tenacious refusal of the liberal ministry to give ground on the new reforms. Chapter six attempts to gauge the impact of liberalization upon the grain trade. Chapter seven scrutinizes the effects of the crisis on Paris. In the hope of neutralizing Paris while the rest of the kingdom assimilated liberalization, the government provided the capital with large doses of the king's grain. This victualing operation, its organization, and its political significance are the subjects of chapter eight. Resistance to liberalization continued to develop as the subsistence troubles deepened and spread. By the end of 1767, a number of parlements began to press for a sweeping modification of the liberal legislation. At the same time, other parlements rushed to the defense of the reforms. Chapters nine and ten treat this clash and the repercussions it had in the marketplaces, the salons, and the corridors of Versailles.

The last three chapters consider the restoration of the police way, or what I have called de-liberalization. With extreme reluctance, in the face of a generalized economic crisis, the government renounced the reforms. Terray's appointment as Controller-General marked the end of a decade of liberal ministries. Chapter eleven examines the state of the kingdom in 1770 and Terray's plans for dealing with subsistence problems in the short run as well as the long run. In addition, it evokes some of the connections between the grain question on the one hand and the Brittany affair and the Maupeou coup on the other. Chapter twelve studies Terray's efforts to implement his subsistence policy throughout the kingdom in the years 1771–74. Even as the government abjured liberalization, so many philosophes turned their fire on its intellectual patrons, the physiocrats. The last part of this chapter looks into the "grain quarrel"—a debate which turned not on airy postulates, but on the grim facts of the national crisis. Chapter thirteen concentrates on the king's grain operations under Terray's management. It closes with the ascension of a new king, who anxiously groped for a new beginning in public affairs, and with the advent of a new Controller-General who believed deeply in the principles of 1763–64.

Chapter I

THE POLICE OF PROVISIONING

I

At every level of administrative life, public officials expended enormous amounts of time, energy, and money in dealing with the subsistence question. Virtually everyone who practiced or wrote about public administration, or what was commonly called "police" in the Old Regime, considered provisioning to be among its paramount concerns. "The abundance of grain," intoned Colbert, "is the thing to which we must pay the most attention in the police." A hundred years later his eulogist, Necker, wrote that "the subsistence of the people is the most essential object which must occupy the administration." Dupont, physiocracy's chief merchandiser and a mordant critic of what he believed to be the Colbert-Necker continuum of policy, remarked ironically on the "abundance" of the subsistence subject and deplored the fact that it dominated so much of public business: "nothing can better prove to you that this branch of Administration is truly the first of all [of them] than the multitude of Laws, Regulations, *Arrêts* of Parlements, Ordinances of Judges, Ordinances of Municipalities, Ordinances of intendants or royal agents which have come into place in all times on the matter of the provisioning of grain."[1]

Management of food supply was directly or indirectly connected with some of the policies we associate with the growth of the state.

---

1 Colbert cited by Jacques St.-Germain, *La Reynie et la police au grand siècle, d'après de nombreux documents inédits* (Paris, 1962), 261; Necker to Sartine, 14 Feb. 1778, AN, F^{11}* 1, fol. 238; P.-S. Dupont de Nemours, *Analyse historique de la législation des grains depuis 1692 à laquelle on a donné la forme d'un rapport à l'Assemblée Nationale* (Paris, 1789), 51. Cf. Nicolas Delamare, *Traité de la police*, 2nd. ed. (Paris, 1729), II, the richest single source for questions of subsistence administration; N.-T.-L. Des Essarts, *Dictionnaire universel de police* (Paris, 1786–90), I, 328–29 and II, 193. For a perspective on modern provisioning problems, see Paul Leblond, *Le Problème de l'approvisionnement des centres urbains en denrées alimentaires en France* (Paris, 1926).

To sustain cities, huge supplies of food had to be wrenched from the countryside (and partly because of the difficulty of provisioning them, old-regime governments tried to limit the size of certain urban centers). To promote industrial development and enable France to compete internationally—so Colbert maintained—an easy and sure subsistence had to be provided for the working population. On a more general plane, without regard to particular economic or political doctrines, an easy subsistence seemed to serve the public interest. A sufficiently nourished people would produce more (goods and children), earn more, buy more, and pay more taxes, and thereby enhance national prosperity and strength. To support an army, the government had to marshal regular stocks of food. Food management was a bewilderingly complex business and it generated many conflicts of interest, between various public institutions such as the armed forces or hospitals and the society at large, between cities and hinterland, between competing regions, etc. The state itself was often a party to these disputes, which it was supposed to mediate. Its *missi dominici* dispatched to displace local, seignorial, or old-time royal officials in the exercise of police and justice inherited responsibilities for provisioning which they could not renounce.

The state had many other reasons for wanting to create and expropriate part of an agricultural surplus. Whether subsistence considerations shaped the development of fiscal policy or not, fiscal policy affected the government's ability to control the food supply. Direct taxation promoted the commercialization of agriculture, forced peasants into the market, and helped make grain supply visible and available. Partly in order to facilitate provisioning, the government sporadically endeavored to eliminate the labyrinth of fiscal (and feudal) excrescences which hindered market transactions and impeded the circulation of goods. The state encouraged investment in agriculture with an eye toward increasing national wealth yet, in deference to subsistence demands, when cultivators sought to shift, say, from grain to wine in response to market incentives, it prohibited the move. Decisions about the floating population and public assistance policy in general were always made in reference to the subsistence situation in the cities and the countryside.

Connections like these underline the intimate relationship between the management of subsistence and the development of the state. They suggest that by the beginning of the early-modern period the state was already deeply enmeshed in the regulation of production, consumption, and distribution. But the extraordinary urgency which administrators at all levels, not just the agents of the central state, attached to the question of subsistence was the result above all of their overriding concern for social stability. The growth of the state itself generated forces of instability, but the concern for "tranquility," as contemporaries called it, was neither peculiar to France nor to the Old Regime.

The policy of provisioning as a means of social control had been practiced, in one form or another, since the beginning of urban civilization. It was not, at least in the French case, the product of a particularly cynical view of man, society and polity. It was based upon the familiar conviction, informed by a rapid reading of the history of the plebs and the state, that the failure to assure an adequate food supply could jeopardize the political and social structure of the kingdom. Nicolas Delamare, author of the most influential treatise on "police" in the Old Regime, drew the lesson from antiquity. The Roman experience taught that hunger caused depopulation and moral and physical deterioration and—far worse—threatened to "excite the greatest revolts, the most dangerous seditions." In the same vein, the author of an essay on "the history of subsistence," written in the early 1770's, argued that dearths "preceded, prepared, and caused" grave and sometimes lethal disorders in the empires of Rome, Constantinople, and China. "Everywhere," he warned, "you will see subsistence gives the first start to revolutions." Necker was the first major public figure in the Old Regime who dared articulate these fears in detail and make the case for social control in terms of a full-blown model positing the inherent fragility of social organization and the ineluctability of class conflict, but many of his assumptions and conclusions were drawn from the common stock of administrative or police thought.[2]

The police theory of containment assumed that the state was not only menaced, from within, by magnates and their clans, religious minorities, mutinous constituted bodies, and other fractions of society, but that it was vulnerable, too, in its relations with the mass of people, the vast majority of whom saw themselves above all as consumers. As a rule, the people "submitted" provided their elementary needs were more or less satisfied. When the people felt their existence to be

---

2 Delamare, *Traité de la police*, II, 566; *Journal de l'agriculture, du commerce, des arts et des finances* (Jan. 1772), 48; Necker, *Sur la législation et le commerce des grains* (Paris, 1775).

threatened, however, their threshold of tolerance plummeted. They not only became enraged by prolonged periods of shortage, soaring prices, and extreme and unusual misery, but they became resentful of burdens which in other circumstances they ignored or reluctantly accepted. When the people took on this mood, they could be contained only with the greatest difficulty. When the routine of daily life was disrupted, the government could not carry out its business. In the worst of circumstances, it found itself submerged in chaos.

Implicit in this view was the idea that the government which *exposed* itself by dereliction or insouciance to this kind of menace deserved what it reaped, for the people should not have to be put to this sort of terrible test. To be sure, there were other sources of popular disorder, such as excessive or novel fiscality, military or militia conscription, and the abrogation of certain customary franchises. Yet none of these was as permanent and as pervasive a prod to disruption, none caused such profound disaffection toward the state and society, and none aroused the people to such a pitch of fury as threatened subsistence. Ultimately, the government, not the people, had to answer for this sort of breach of tranquility. In the absence of order, government could not endure and society could not hold together. The "prerequisite" for order, in the words of an eighteenth-century intendant, was "to provide for the subsistence of the people, without which there is neither law nor force which can contain them."[3]

This is not to suggest that this simple model of containment guided all decisions made by the government, though the further one moves from the center the more compelling it becomes and the more nearly it describes the instincts of local authorities for whom social control was a firsthand, visceral matter. The ministers, if not the *échevins* and the royal procurators, did not believe that they could govern by bread alone or that what worked for antiquity would function well in what they self-consciously felt to be a modern state and society. State policy had its own imperatives aside from social control or solicitude for the hungry. Yet the exigencies of social control, and ultimately the concern for survival, placed serious constraints on the freedom of the state to elect certain strategies for its own development and for the growth of society. The subsistence preoccupation influenced social and economic policy in obvious ways, but perhaps its most important implications were in

---

3 Bertier de Sauvigny, "Observations sur le commerce des grains," BN, mss. fr. 11347, fol. 228.

the end political. The state committed itself to the consumer interest. The consumer interest embraced the overwhelming majority
of the population. It included not only the laboring people of
the cities, but vast numbers of peasants, workers, and craftsmen
inhabiting the countryside.

The commitment to the consumer interest was symbolized by the
king and embodied in the idea of the king as father-to-his-people.
Probably every king would have liked to see himself regarded as
father to his people; the history of kings shows that the paternal metaphor was a slogan for all seasons. In France, however, it acquired
at least one specific and consistent meaning. In the Old Regime it
was widely believed that the king had a duty to safeguard the existence and therefore the subsistence of his subjects. The origin of the
notion is obscure, though eighteenth-century commentators traced
it as far back as the time of Charlemagne.[4] Whether it began as a
sincere statement of royal intention or as a device for propaganda,
it was taken very seriously by both the kings and the people. The
fatherly monarch was, *d'office*, by his own proclamation and by universal anticipation and acclaim, the supreme victualer. What more
solemn duty could a father have than to make it possible for his children to enjoy their daily bread? Though it never found expression
in the coronation oath or achieved the fundamental stature of, say,
the salic law, the commitment to subsistence–the social contract of
subsistence–became, informally, a responsibility and an attribute of
kingship. It was not merely something the king did for his people; it
was something he was expected and in some sense required to do.
The people counted on royal intervention and took the measure of
a king partly in terms of his fatherly success. Morally and politically,
the king was highly motivated to play the role well. Royal paternalism and the policy of social control were two sides of the same coin;
both dealt with the relationship between the ruler (or his deputies)
and the ruled. But whereas social control spoke the chilling language
of *raison d'état* and stressed the checks placed upon the people and
the supremacy of the interests of the state, this brand of paternalism exuded the compassion characteristic of familial ties, emphasized
not the constraints upon the subjects but their claims upon the State,
not the prerogatives of the government but its obligations, and found

---

4 F. Aubert, "Réflexions sur le commerce des grains," (1775), BN, mss. n.a. 4433, fol. 33;
Leprévost de Beaumont, "Additions," Arsenal, mss. Bastille 12353. Cf. Ambroise Morel,
Histoire abrégée de la boulangerie en France (Paris, 1899), 45.

its rationale in the very nature of the royal mission, consecrated by tradition and religion.

If the medieval myths of the princely *héros nourriciers* no longer had currency in the Old Regime, still the idea of linking kingship and subsistence elicited enduring support.[5] The theoretician of absolutism and divine monarchy, Bossuet, argued that the king's responsibility to assure subsistence was the "foundation" of all his claims on his subjects.[6] His master, Louis XIV, did not always practice what Bossuet preached, but he understood the significance of the charge and he performed the victualing part self-consciously and convincingly. "I entered personally into a very detailed and very exact knowledge of the needs of the peoples and the state of things," he proudly told the dauphin, in reference to the millions he spent importing grain during the great dearth in the early 1660's; "I appeared to my subjects as a veritable *père de famille*, who makes provision for his house and shares the food equitably with his children and his servants." If Parisians forgave Louis XIV for some of his brutal excesses, it was at least in part because he had been their "pharaoh."[7]

Though the Enlightenment raised probing questions about its validity, this conception of governmental responsibility found influential adherents in the eighteenth century. Montesquieu asserted that the state owed its citizens "an assured subsistence"; in this he differed little from the author of *Politics Drawn from the Holy Scriptures*, though he hardly shared Bossuet's view of Louis XIV as the ideal of kingship incarnate. The imperious human right to existence, which the radical social critics Mably and Linguet claimed the Sovereign was bound to guarantee, had more in common with the old vision of the providential and liturgical vocation of kingship than with the new conception of the rights of man that was beginning to emerge in the second half of the eighteenth century. In a crude essay submitted to the government during the subsistence troubles of the 1770's, a petitioner contended that "if by divine right the peoples owe a tribute to their Sovereign, there is one [tribute] perhaps equally indispensable

---

5 Jacques Le Goff, *La Civilisation de l'occident médiéval* (Paris, 1967), 292–93.

6 Jacques St.-Germain, *La Vie quotidienne en France à la fin du grand siècle* (Paris, 1965), 191.

7 Cited by P. Bondois, "La Misère sous Louis XIV: la disette de 1662," *Revue d'histoire économique et sociale*, XII (1924), 61–62, 78; *Le Magasin pittoresque*, 43rd year (1875), 110. See also Edme Béguillet, *Description historique de Paris et de ses plus beaux monumens....* (Paris, 1779), I, 66–67; Pierre Clément, *Portraits historiques* (Paris, 1855), 189–92; George Rosen, *Madness in Society* (New York, 1969), 167ff.

due them and that would be that which would act to guarantee them against dearth." Another memorandum, composed at about the time of the Flour War by a lawyer and knight of the order of St. Louis, declared that, among the "obligations" which a "father owes to his children," the "necessity to furnish the essential food, which is bread" stood first. Writing at a time when the king's authority to undertake provisioning came under sharp attack, Desaubiez, author of a treatise on "Public Happiness," insisted that royal grain supplying was a "sacred right of the crown." Nor were the women who marched on Versailles in October 1789 engaged in an act of irrational fury: their view of the king as baker-victualer of last resort had a long tradition.[8]

Although Louis XV did much to discredit it, the paternalistic idea and the expectations it engendered remained very much alive at the end of the Old Regime and the traditional connection between king/ government and subsistence went on to trouble the revolutionary leaders. The wistful, consoling vision of a king-provider served as a major theme in counter-revolutionary popular propaganda. On a number of occasions Parisians besieged the bakers shouting slogans of a mood similar to that of the southern Italians who revolted in the mid-nineteenth century to the nostalgic refrain "the king fed us."[9] Beset by serious subsistence problems and unable to devise new methods to deal with them, the revolutionaries were haunted by the specter of the old-regime victualing state whose successes they simultaneously exaggerated, denounced, and envied. Indeed, if one were to study prerevolutionary France through the eyes of a Creuzé-Latouche, one would believe that "under the Old Regime the government itself furnished Parisians with bread," a grave distortion of fact but a revealing

---

8 J. Hecht, "Trois précurseurs de la sécurité sociale au 18ᵉ siècle," *Population*, XIV (Jan.-March 1959), 73; André Lichtenberger, *Le Socialisme au XVIIIᵉ siècle; étude sur les idées socialistes dans les écrivains français du XVIIIᵉ siècle avant la révolution* (Paris, 1895), 91 (the relevant passage from the *Esprit des lois* is in book XXIII, chapter 29); S.-N.-H. Linguet, *Du Pain et du bled* in (*Oeuvres* (London, 1774), VI, 67 and *Annales politiques, civiles et littéraires du dix-huitième siècle*, VII, 203–204; D.-Z. [Desaubiez], *Le Bonheur public* (London, 1782), 146; "Essay sur le moyen d'établir des greniers d'abondance" (30 May 1771), AN, F¹¹ 265, fol. 7; F. Aubert, "Réflexions," BN, mss. n.a. 4433, fols. 20–21, 24, 27.

9 C. Tilly, "Collective Violence in European Perspective," in H. Graham and T. Gurr, *Violence in America: Historical and Comparative Perspectives. A Report to the National Commission on the Causes and Prevention of Violence* (N.Y., 1969), 17; AN, AF¹² 1470 (16, 17 Apr. 1793). Cf. Colfavru, "Question des subsistances," *La Révolution française*, V (July-Dec. 1883), 330. Cf. an anonymous pamphlet of 1791, "Sous un roi nous avions du pain."

acknowledgement of the legacy and the memory of the traditional provisioning policy.[10]

If the old-regime governments did supply bread, of course, as Creuzé-Latouche pointedly added, it was not for wholesome motives. The bread was tainted, and the revolutionaries heaped scorn upon Frenchmen who would still succumb to its blandishments. "The Ministry in the Old Regime," explained an essayist in 1792, "afraid of the people in the big cities, tried to give them cheap bread in order to hold them in a sort of lethargy...." Parisians of the Old Regime sold out to the government, Manuel contemptuously remarked in his *Police Unveiled*; in return for bread, they offered their "cadaverous tranquility." "If the Old Regime bought your silence," asked another revolutionary in 1791, "must you not, now that you are free, repulse far from you everything which can recall your servitude?"[11]

II

For the sake of its own conservation and in pursuit of its interests, for the well-being and peace of society, to meet its traditional, quasi-contractual obligations, and for still other reasons which we touched upon, the state intervened in subsistence affairs and encouraged or condoned in most instances the intervention of other public authorities not acting expressly upon its instructions. But what forms did this intervention take? Extended to its logical extreme, the government's promise to give "its first attention ... to procuring an easy and convenient subsistence" for the people would imply that it was prepared actually to furnish consumers with grain or bread.[12] In fact, this was not at all the government's intention, nor indeed did the public expect it. To be sure, in dire emergencies, Louis XIV turned the Louvre into a bakery, Louis XV commissioned great bankers and a legion of petty merchants to buy and sell grain in his name, and municipalities throughout the kingdom undertook a large part of

---

10 *Archives parlementaires, recueil complet des débats législatifs & politiques des chambres françaises* (Paris, 1898), LIV, 683.

11 *Ibid.*; Pierre Manuel, *La Police de Paris dévoilée* (Paris, 1794–95), I, 10; "La Cherté du pain," (1792), AN, T 644[1-2]; "Mémoire présenté par M. de Monchanin déposé au Secrétariat de la Municipalité, 30 Octobre 1791...," AN, F[10] 215–216.

12 *Arrêt du Conseil*, 5 Sept. 1693 cited by Cherrière, "La Lutte contre l'incendie dans les halles, les marchés et les foires de Paris sous l'ancien régime," in *Mémoires et documents pour servir à l'histoire du commerce et de l'industrie en France*, 3rd series, ed. by J. Hayem (Paris, 1913), 107.

the supply burden. But the government was victualer only in the last resort. It had no desire to go into the grain, flour and baking business. Its refusal reflected a realistic appraisal of the limits of its power and its resources. The government simply was not equipped to handle the primary food trade, nor could it hope to marshal the capital and mount and maintain the leviathan machine that would be necessary to undertake day-to-day provisioning operations on the scale of a kingdom as vast as France.

This keen sense of its own incapacity, coupled with a desire not to frighten off those persons whose profession and social function it was to deal in grain and flour, induced the government not only to eschew ordinary trading activities, but also to refrain from establishing organizations of "abundance" on the model of Joseph's Egypt, sixteenth-century Venice, or contemporary Geneva. "Most nations," wrote the farmer-general Claude Dupin, "have placed themselves on guard against the disastrous events of dearth and of excessive abundance by means of magazines which cause grain to disappear when there is too much and from where it resurfaces when it is lacking...." "We alone," he complained, "who have the glory to possess the wisest regulations in the Universe on other matters, have remained far behind our neighbors on this one which is nevertheless the most important, since the wealth or poverty and even the life of all the Subjects depend upon it."[13] For all its anxiety about subsistence, the state never elaborated a master-plan for lean years or fat. Directly on the supply side, the government intervened as most Frenchmen lived, *au jour le jour*, sometimes massively, sometimes selectively, and always reluctantly. On the municipal level, the state encouraged the institutionalization of foresight, without, however, offering any serious material incentives for the establishment of granaries. A plan to mobilize all the convents and monasteries in the kingdom into a network for funding grain storage never received serious implementation outside the Paris area, and not even the capital could count on a modest state-sponsored reserve until the second half of the eighteenth century.[14]

---

13 Dupin, "Mémoire sur les bleds," (1748), BN, mss. n.a. 22777, fols. 155, 167. Cf. the anonymous memoir to the IN. of commerce de Montaran: "The means of assuring bread do not seem to stir interest until we are at the point of not finding any more ... the defect is ordinarily only perceived at the moment of need." 19 June 1784, AN, F¹¹ 294–95. See also P. Macquer, *Dictionnaire portatif des arts et métiers* (Paris, 1766), I, 564.

14 On the Parisian "community" granary system see Degand to Hérault, 14 Sept. 1728, Arsenal, mss. Bastille 10274; AAP, Délibérations du Bureau de l'Hôtel-Dieu, #97, 9 Jan. 1728 and

The characteristic expression of government intervention was regulation. The burden of public authority was not to feed the people but to make sure they would be fed. This distinction implied a fairly simple division of social labor. Cultivators grew the grain; it was their responsibility, aided by a host of commercial agents, to market it. It was up to the government to make sure that it reached the public in "due time," in good condition, and at a price accessible to the bulk of the consumers. Authorities stalked grain from the time it was seeded until the bakers transformed it into bread. They kept track of all the agencies of the grain and flour trade, in the countryside, on the roads, at the inns, in the marketplace. They labored to preserve the customary division of hinterland, to protect the channels of provisioning, and to keep the supply optimally visible and reassuringly ubiquitous. By so doing they expected by and large to be able to prevent major disruptions in the flow of grain, serious shortages, and excessive rises in prices.

Except in certain maritime and frontier areas, public authorities throughout the kingdom depended upon the nation's own production to meet provisioning needs. They expected fluctuations and sometimes failure here and there, but they believed that "abundance," in the words of one Controller-General, was the "natural state" of affairs. Her rich arable land was France's granary of abundance. Certain observers estimated that a "common" year yielded at least one-third and often one-half more than the kingdom required. Others claimed that France harvested three times its annual needs in wheat and that even a "bad" year furnished enough to nourish the people. Public officials on the whole tended to be more cautious and their attitudes varied considerably from place to place and level to level, but few doubted that provisioning was for the most part a matter of "good police."[15] When they could not,

---

#98, 20, 23, 30 Dec. 1729; BN, Coll. Joly 1428, fols. 168–87; Assemblée de police, 8 March 1736, BN, mss. fr. 11356, fols. 297–98. On the effort by Machault to establish a granary system by linking military and civilian victualing at the end of the forties, see "Extrait d'un mémoire sur les bleds communiqué par M. de Machault à M. Pâris-Duverney…" and Pâris-Duverney, "Extrait de l'avis de M.P.D. sur le mémoire précédent," AN, F^{12} 647; Dupont, *Analyse … rapport*, 92–98; Marcel Marion, *Machault d'Arnouville: étude sur l'histoire du contrôleur-général des finances de 1749 à 1754* (Paris, 1891), 429–30. For granary or dearth-prevention plans after mid-century, see below chapters eight and thirteen.

15 M. Reneaume, "Sur la manière de conserver les grains," *Mémoires de l'Académie des Sciences* for 1708 (Paris, 1709), 76; H.-L. Duhamel du Monceau, *Traité de la conservation des grains* (Paris, 1753), iv; Antoine A. Parmentier, *Le Parfait boulanger, ou Traité complet sur la fabrication et le commerce du pain* (Paris, 1778), 118; Claude Dupin, *Mémoire sur les*

for one reason or another, prevent dearths or price rises by regulation, they repressed and redressed. They punished cultivators and merchants for violating the rules governing the trade ("contravening the police") more or less severely according to the gravity of the crime; they went after "hidden" supplies in the name of the law when they believed owners were willfully withholding them from consumption; often they set the price of bread and sometimes the prices of grain and flour; much less frequently they intervened on the wage side, for it was prices rather than wages which fixed public attention throughout the Old Regime. "Police" was the means by which government sought to assure the subsistence of the people. As a rule, government, central and local, undertook ordinary supply tasks only when "police" by itself could no longer deal with the situation.

Before we explore the ways in which provisioning was a police matter, we ought to take note of the word "police" itself, for it was a much more important and versatile expression in the Old Regime than it is for us today. By police we commonly mean today a branch of government, one of whose primary missions is the enforcement of law. To some extent that applies here; we are dealing with a wide range of public officials, operating at many different levels of government, who performed this and other tasks. Commonly, in the Old Regime as today, the police were associated with the business of repression, inspiring as a result respect from some segments and dread and hatred from other portions of society. During the Old Regime, however, the police as an agency of administration were responsible for an extraordinary scope of public functions, ranging from the regulation

---

bleds (1748), BN, mss. n.a. 22777, fol. 155; Claude J. Herbert, *Essai sur la police générale, sur leurs prix et sur les effets de l'agriculture* (London, 1755) in *Collection des économistes et des réformateurs sociaux de la France*, ed. by E. Depitre (Paris, 1910), 40; Regnaud, "Histoire des événements arrivés en France …," BN, mss. fr. 13734, fol. 180n; Laverdy to First President Miromesnil of Normandy, 8 March 1768 in *Correspondance politique et administrative de Miromesnil*, ed. by P. Le Verdier (Rouen and Paris, 1899–1903), V, 107; Etienne François, duc de Choiseul, *Mémoires*, ed. by J.-L. Soulavie (Paris, 1790), I, 45–50; E. Chevalier, "Mémoire sur les moyens d'assurer la diminution du pain… (n.p., 1793), 9; F. Aubert, "Réflexions simples et pratiques sur le commerce des grains" (1775), BN, mss. n.a. 4433, fol. 165; "Histoire de ce qui s'est passé au sujet des bleds en 1725," Bibliothèque de l'Arsenal, Recueil Fevret, ms. 3308; "Mémoire sur la police des grains" (ca. 1758), BN, mss. fr. 14296, fol. 181. Cf. C. Benoist, "Compte rendu," *Revue historique*, XXXVII (May–Aug. 1888), 194; J.-C. Colfavru, "La Question des subsistances en 1789," *La Révolution française*, V (July–Dec. 1883), 391; and Augustin Rollet, *Mémoire sur la meunerie, la boulangerie et la conservation des grains et des farines* (Paris, 1846), 133–34n.

of both wet-nurses and prostitutes, to the control of guilds and prisons and the enforcement of rules pertaining to the observance of religious holidays, the cleaning and lighting of streets, and the production and sale of a host of goods and services. In other words, they were concerned with every aspect of daily life, moral and material, not just the affairs of deviance and disorder.[16] The relations between the police and the people, even in a large city, were intimate and much can be learned about urban life from studying them. Although it is generally believed that those relations were strained, they were often symbiotic, instrumentally if not sentimentally; people were willing to differentiate among the myriad police functions and react selectively.

The universality of the police function derived from another sense which the word had in pre-modern times. Under the Old Regime police meant managing and maintaining the life of the community, as Plato was understood to have defined it. It embraced, in the words of one writer, "everything which treats of the public good." Indeed, it *was* the public good, for it was an end as well as a means, an ideal type as well as a method for achieving it, a political as much as an administrative notion. As noun, verb, and adjective, it was used to describe the way in which social and civil life should be organized. It was also a measure of the progress of civilization, for nations without a police were viewed as barbarous. States with a vicious or imperfect police perished quickly, while those with a "good police" endured. Without proscribing growth or change, police implied a social process which tended inevitably toward equilibrium and continuity. The vocation of police, according to one jurist, was to assure that "harmony and concord" prevailed among citizens.[17]

---

16 See, for example, the tables of contents in the four volumes of Delamare, *Traité*; Des Essarts, *Dictionnaire*, I through VIII; Jacques Peuchet, ed., *Collection des lois, ordonnances et règlements de police depuis le XIIIe siècle jusqu'à l'année 1818* (Paris, 1818–19). I through VIII; Edme de la Poix de Fréminville, *Dictionnaire ou traité de la police générale des villes, bourgs, paroisses et seigneuries de la campagne* (Paris, 1758).

17 Léopold Pelatant, *De l'organisation de la police* (Dijon, 1899), 10; F. Olivier-Martin, *Cours d'histoire du droit public. La Police économique* (Paris, 1944–45), 13–15; Marc Chassaigne, *La Lieutenance générale de police de Paris* (Paris, 1906), 24; Goyon de la Plombanie, cited by Simone Gout, *Henri de Goyon de la Plombanie, économiste périgourdin* (Poitiers, 1933), 105; BHVP, mss. series 142 or Bournon 459; J-B. Dénisart, *Collection de décisions nouvelles et de notions relatives à la jurisprudence actuelle* (Paris, 1777), III, 529. Cf. Robert H.I. Palgrave, ed., *Dictionary of Political Economy* (London, 1894–99), III, 124; Vivien, "Police," in C. Coquelin and Guillaumin, eds., *Dictionnaire de l'économie politique* (Paris, 1873), II, 376–78; Charles Musart, *La Réglementation du commerce des grains au XVIIIe siècle: la théorie de Delamare, étude économique* (Paris, 1922), 39 and *passim*; article "Police," Diderot, *et al.*, *Encyclopédice*, XII, 911;

For the working police, the *commissaires*, the lieutenants, and their counterparts, police was above all a concrete program of action. Commissaire Delamare tried to place the full range of options, strategies, precedents, and laws, along with explicit instructions on how to use them in different circumstances, at the disposition of all public authorities in his mammoth *Traité de la Police* published during the last years of Louis XIV. Although Delamare self-consciously tried to give the notion of police a more "limited sense" than it had before in order to make it as widely accessible and as clearly understood as possible, his work is a staggering monument to the range, complexity, and pretension of the police enterprise. Schooled in Delamare yet sensitive to the fashions of his own times, the Parisian Commissaire Lemaire, writing in 1770, was led to define police as "the *science* of governing men...."[18]

Such a notion of police did not thrive in the climate of the Enlightenment. Police, for many philosophes, epitomized what was wrong with government in the Old Regime, and the idea of a scientific police must have struck them as ludicrous or grotesque. They saw police not as a general method of governing or as a loosely-defined commitment to the public good, but as an elaborate defense of and apology for a specific and pernicious system of rule. They equated police with Tradition, which they rightly saw as one of their most resourceful enemies. Police was the political pretext and the administrative mechanism that authorities used to diminish and enslave men. Prohibition and constraint were its leitmotivs and its very pervasiveness was a mark of corruption and abuse. To be sure, the critics of police were not hostile to law and order, but to the spirit of the laws and the nature of the order which the police of France embodied and symbolized. In this sense all police was *basse police*. For many philosophes, as we shall see, there was no difference between the police which terrorized merchants and monitored or requisitioned grain,

---

Pierre Richelet, *Dictionnaire de la langue françoise ancienne et moderne* (Lyon, 1759), III, 197; the definition of the abbé Fleury, cited in Jean Egret, *Le Parlement de Dauphiné et les affaires publiques dans la deuxième moitié du dix-huitième siècle* (Grenoble, 1942), I, 122; the definition of Malesherbes cited by Pierre Grosclaude, *Malesherbes et son temps* (Paris, 1964), II, 404; the use of the word police by the abbé Coyer, *Chinki, Histoire cochinchinoise qui peut servir à d'autres pays* (London, 1758), 94; and the use of the term by eighteenth century German writers and jurists: Albion Small, *The Cameralists* (Chicago, 1909), 328, 436–39, 505ff.

18 Delamare, livre 1, titre 1, cited by Pelatant, *De l'organisation*, 11; A. Gazier, ed., "La Police de Paris en 1770," 27–28.

on the one hand, and the police which burned books and deprived men of their freedom, on the other.

At the end of the Old Regime a writer in the *Encyclopédie Méthodique* noted that the historical concept of police had lost its old meaning and had become "hardly respectable." He blamed its demise on jurists in the service of the system who used the concept of police to justify and perpetuate ingrained errors instead of reestablishing it on rational principles and adapting it to the needs and the ideas of the age. The revolutionaries cared even less than the philosophes for making fine distinctions on this matter. For them the "old police" meant the regime of "spies, *lettres de cachet*, bastille" and associated evils. Reviling the police *en bloc* was one thing, however, and destroying it *en bloc* quite another. The revolutionaries found it considerably easier to raze the Bastille than to do without some of the less ostentatious institutions and practices which characterized the "policed state" of the Old Regime.[19]

III

The hallmark of a "well-policed state," according to the old-regime specialists in this matter, was its "police of provisioning" or "grain police." This police took priority over all others because it concerned the "common," "urgent," or "first" needs of the citizenry and because it was the key to maintaining "good order" or "public tranquility."[20] In order to understand this police we must first examine its organization and then the apparatus of controls, with special reference to the provisioning of Paris. Remember that by "police" we mean two things at once: the exercise of a certain kind of authority, in this instance authority over provisioning, and the agencies which exercised this authority, regardless of their nominal charges or titles. For the sake of clarity we shall begin at the top, with the caveat, however, that the view from the summit and

---

19 "Discours Préliminaires," *Encyclopedie méthodique*, jurisprudence, police et municipalités (Paris, 1789), IX, cx, cxii–cxiii, cxxxix–cxliv; Prudhomme, *Révolutions de Paris*, #7(22 Aug. 1789), 7.

20 Des Essarts, *Dictionnaire*, I, 328–29; Duchesne, *Code de la police ou analyse de règlements de police* (Paris, 1767), 261; Macquer, *Dictionnaire des arts et métiers*, I, 564; Béguillet, article "Abondance," *Encyclopédie (Supplément)*, I, 30; Dumas, "Mémoire sur le commerce des grains au 18ᵉ siècle," *Bulletin du Comité des Travaux Historiques et Scientifiques, Section des Sciences Économiques et Sociales* (for 1891) (Paris, 1892), 86; A. Clément, article "Approvisionnement," *Dictionnaire de l'économie politique*, ed. by Coquelin and Guillaumin, I, 61. This theme permeates Delamare's *Traité*.

center invariably distorts the focus, for it implies much more coherence in the organization and operation of the police than actually existed.

The king exercised the supreme police power in the land. Royal legislation devised or reaffirmed the general rules which were meant to govern the provisioning trade throughout the realm. The monarch invested officials at the regional and local levels with authority specifically to enforce these rules and, more broadly, to assure the provisioning of their areas. On an irregular basis, several of the royal councils, especially the Councils of *Dépêches* (interior) and Commerce (which had a sporadic existence) reviewed the state of subsistence in the kingdom, discussed proposals for legislation, entertained petitions from individuals and institutions concerning the grain trade, and adjudicated disputes.[21] In periods of dearth, which required extraordinary measures of relief, the king became personally involved.

The king's chief deputy for matters of provisioning (and indeed for all domestic affairs) was the Controller-General.[22] His was a sort of super-ministry which embraced virtually everything pertaining to the economy, finance, public works, public assistance, and general administration. Mercier hardly exaggerated when he wrote that "the history of the reign of Louis XIV and of Louis XV could be [read] in its entirety in the history of the Controllers-General."[23] For most of his business, the Controller-General circumvented the councils, preferring to "work" directly with the king or in intimate ministerial committees. His recommendations were carefully

---

21 For the royal council, see the excellent thesis of Michel Antoine, *Le Conseil du Roi sous le règne de Louis XV* (Paris, 1970).

22 There is no modern scholarly study on the Contrôle-Général comparable to Antoine's work on the royal council. Montyon's *Particularités et observations sur les ministres des finances les plus célèbres depuis 1660 jusqu'en 1791* (Paris, 1812) is piquant but heavily dated and tendentious. Henri de Jouvencel's *Le Contrôleur-Général des finances sous l'ancien régime* (Paris, 1901) is better than most law theses, but is still of very limited utility. Paul Viollet, *Le Roi et ses ministres pendant les trois derniers siècles de la monarchie* (Paris, 1912) is of little service. For the most part, one is obliged to rely on primary materials (for example, in the G⁷ series in the AN), on general histories of the eighteenth century such as L.-E.-A. Jobez, *La France sous Louis XV* (Paris, 1864–73) which, despite its age, remains one of the most useful, or on specialized studies of royal finances which tend to focus on only one aspect, albeit a vital one, of the Controller-General's activities. Among the latter are Marcel Marion, *Histoire financière de la France depuis 1715* (Paris, 1914–17); Charles Gomel, *Les Causes financières de la révolution française: les ministères de Turgot et Necker* (Paris, 1892); and René Stourm, *Les Finances de l'ancien régime et de la révolution* (Paris, 1885) and *Bibliographie historique des finances de la France au 18ᵉ siécle* (Paris, 1895).

23 Mercier, *Tableau de Paris* (Amsterdam, 1782–1788), II, 142. Cf. *ibid.*, VIII, 237–238, 242.

prepared in his bureaus, "these little kings of France," as they were called by the physiocrat Baudeau, who hated "bureaucratie" with all the ardor of a Maoist on the rue d'Ulm.[24] Among these bureaus was the "grain department," also known as the bureau of subsistence or the department of abundance. Managed by an intendant of finance or commerce and staffed by clerks who provided a continuity of expertise by surviving frequent ministerial changes, this bureau collected data on production, consumption, and prices and assessed the mass of information on subsistence, which the minister needed to make his decisions.[25]

The Controller-General tried to anticipate deficits and surpluses and facilitate regional distribution of supplies. In emergencies, he coordinated regional and local efforts to cope with dearth and organized relief operations. He was interested in every aspect of the grain trade and the provisioning police and he kept track of them through the enormous correspondence he maintained, not only with the intendants of the generalities who were directly responsible to him, but with myriad lesser officials as well.

Yet, despite his omnicompetence, and to some extent because of it, the Controller-General had little influence in day-to-day provisioning affairs. In part, this was a matter of voluntary restraint, for the government conceived of subsistence as a preeminently local problem. Its policy was to leave provisioning to the grain trade under the supervision of local authorities who were encouraged to resolve subsistence problems on their own. But this policy itself reflected the government's inability to deal with this vast and infinitely complex business from the center. France was too big and too diverse, the royal administration was too small, too jerry-built, and too ill-equipped, particularism was too deeply entrenched, and communications too slow and uncertain to afford the minister real control. The information he received was characteristically incomplete, of uneven quality, and often tendentious. Frequently it arrived too late and the

---

24 "Chronique secrète de Paris sous le règne de Louis XVI," *Revue rétrospective*, III (1834), 62, 72. The historiographer of France, Duclos, described the same phenomenon as "conocratie." *Ibid.*, 79. Cf. Gournay, cited by F. M. Grimm, *et al.*, *Correspondance littéraire, philosophique et critique*, ed. by M. Tourneux (Paris, 1877–82), VI, 30 and Mirabeau, cited by G. Weulersse, *La Physiocratie à la fin du règne de Louis XV* (Paris, 1959), 84–85, 91.

25 On the grain department, see the *Almanach royal* for virtually any year in the eighteenth century. See also Labrousse, *Esquisse*; the F[11] series in the AN; and works devoted to individuals who played a prominent role in the department such as Trudaine de Montigny.

orders in reply were often stale once they reached the field where they sometimes met with a lukewarm reception and an indifferent execution. Moreover, the vast scope of his ministry seriously reduced the Controller-General's effectiveness. Overwhelmed with pressing responsibilities in many different domains, he was rarely able to delve deeply into the intricacies of provisioning. The "presumptuous *commis*" of the grain bureau, whom Baudeau accused of "governing the kingdom," were few in number and confined to technical matters with no authority to deal with police questions in the minister's behalf. The field administrators were the real protagonists in the police of provisioning. The Controller-General played the role of *deus ex machina*, keeping vigil from above and swooping down upon the stage when the drama required his intervention.

A survey of the police must also include the Secretaries of State, colleagues of the Controller-General in the ministry, though their part was generally quite modest.[26] In addition to specific ministerial duties based on a functional division of labor (war, marine, foreign affairs, etc.), each secretary was supposed to exercise a general stewardship over the administration of a block of generalities or provinces. His responsibilities in this capacity were not precisely defined. Except in territorial matters that had a direct bearing upon his ministerial interests (e.g., the ports and the secretary of the marine, the frontier fortresses and the secretary of war), the secretary habitually ceded authority for the management of provincial affairs to the Controller-General. Officially, the secretary "dispatched" royal will to the regions in his department, but he also served as a conduit and sometimes as a spokesman for provincial opinion in the king's councils. He registered the fears of provincial officials over prospective shortages, their complaints against encroachment upon their supply zones or other practices they perceived as threatening, and their desires for assistance from the center. In consultation with the Controller-General, the secretary tried to promote distribution

---

26 On the Secretaries of State there is also a severe paucity of useful literature. For want of any alternatives, see Comte H. Luçay, *Des Origines du pouvoir ministériel en France: les secrétaires d'état jusqu'à la mort de Louis XV* (Paris, 1881) and A. Dumas, "l'Action des secrétaires d'état sous l'ancien régime," *Annales de la Faculté de Droit d'Aix-en-Provence*, new series, No. 47 (1954), 5–92. See also the O¹ series in the AN and scattered materials in the Maurepas papers at Cornell, in the AN (257 AP) and at the BHVP (mss. 719–21, letters between the Secretary for Paris and the Lieutenant General of Police, to be supplemented by A. de Boislisle, ed., *Lettres de M. de Marville, Lieutenant Général de Police, au Ministre Maurepas* (Paris, 1896–1905)).

within his jurisdiction, prevent conflicts between institutional and civil provisioning, and encourage cooperation among the authorities in the field.

As a rule, the Secretary for the Royal Household had in his sphere the department of Paris which, in the words of Mercier, "is a sort of kingdom [in itself] given the fact that the Government of the Capital has a very great influence and that it extends far abroad."[27] Although he did not deal directly with the Parisian provisioning trade, he kept a close eye on the subsistence situation, for he was personally responsible to the king for the tranquility of the capital. He supervised the capital's municipal and police administrations and served as liaison both between the Parisian authorities and the central government and between the Parisian authorities and the host of public servants, from the intendants to the local officials, who exercised police powers in the vast area that Paris claimed as its hinterland.

The intendants of the *généralités* constituted the first line of royal police in the field. The crucial role they played in the development of the administrative monarchy and the astonishing range of their activities are too well known to warrant rehearsal here.[28] The intendant was deeply involved in the police of provisioning, though it must not be imagined that he achieved on the level of the *généralité* a procrustean control which eluded the Controller-General on the national scale. The same constraints that inhibited the minister at Versailles hampered the intendant. Assisted only by a small corps of subdelegates and inspectors, the intendant was dependent upon a staggering array of local officials, each of whom retained considerable autonomy, for the conduct of the grain police. Unless they were

27 Mercier, *Tableau de Paris*, IX, 34–38. See also William Mildmay, *The Police of France* (London, 1763), 43–44; R. Darnton, ed., "The Memoirs of Lenoir, Lieutenant of Police of Paris, 1774–85," *The English Historical Review*, LXXXV (July 1970), 549. Cf. Malesherbes, who found the post "boring." Grosclaude, *Malesherbes*, I, 343.

28 On the intendants and their powers, see Charles Godard, *Les Pouvoirs des intendants sous Louis XIV* (Paris, 1901); P. N. Ardashev, *Les Intendants de province sous Louis XVI* (Paris, 1909); H. Fréville, *L'Intendance de Bretagne* (Rennes, 1953); V. R.Gruder, *The Royal Provincial Intendants: A Governing Elite in 18th Century France* (Ithaca, 1968); Maurice Bordes, *D'Étigny et l'administration de l'intendance d'Auch (1751–67)* (Auch, 1957); Bordes, "Les Intendants de Louis XV," *Revue historique*, CCXXII (1960), 45–62; Bordes, "Les Intendants éclairés de la fin de l'ancien régime," *Revue d'histoire économique et sociale*, XXXIX (1961), 57–83. Cf. the perspicacious remarks of Sénac de Meilhan, himself an intendant: "For a long time, the intendants, led by public opinion, have sought more to distinguish themselves by their tenderness for the Peoples and by useful works than by their subservience to the ministerial wills." *Du Gouvernement, des mœurs, et des conditions en France avant la révolution* (Paris, 1814), 102–103.

perplexed by a special problem, afraid to make a decision likely to be controversial, or locked in conflict with a public or private party, the local authorities had little reason to solicit instructions from the intendant or anyone else. Aside from certain local idiosyncracies, their police was fashioned from the common fund of rules which had remained substantially unchanged for generations. Based on his assessment of the harvest and the diagnosis of needs which his subdelegates, scattered throughout the province, helped him make, the intendant *recommended* a more or less strict application or enforcement of those rules. With the aim of unifying control procedures or eliminating abusive practices, he sometimes issued interpretive ordinances which clarified the meaning or redefined the terms of the existing laws and customs. The intendant could also influence policy by systematically favoring the officials who followed his line in the frequent disputes that erupted among police authorities. Occasionally he caused local sentences or statutes of which he disapproved to be quashed, impugned the claim of a locality to its hinterland, or, in drastic situations, peremptorily suspended local self-government.

The intendant exercised his greatest leverage, however, not by punishing recalcitrant subordinates or expropriating control of individual markets, but by regulating the circulation of grain across time and space. He had the power to ease and speed the flow of grain within the province or impede its movement. He could nullify the permission to trade granted by lesser authorities or issue licenses which they had denied. Although he could not always prevent interceptions and requisitions of grain, he could nullify them and demand exemplary compensation or condone them, selectively or generally. In certain circumstances, the intendant took it upon himself to prevent the "export" of supplies outside the boundaries of his jurisdiction. A decision such as this affected other *généralités* and invariably aroused the ire of their intendants. Intendants often clashed bitterly over matters of policy and jurisdiction; want of solidarity and mutual understanding were not defects peculiar to the local police in the Old Regime.[29] A king's man par excellence, the intendant was charged with the mission of enforcing the royal will. Yet he was also responsible for the well-being of his *généralité*. He faced a cruel dilemma when the former struck

---

29 See, for example, the attitude of the intendant of La Rochelle, who ardently supported the idea of free internal circulation, but refused to tolerate the export of grain from his generality to Bordeaux in 1759. Courteille to IN., 12 Jan. 1759, C. 191, A.D. C-M.

him as contrary to the latter. The subsistence issue often generated this divergence and the intendants demonstrated that they were no less skilled than local officials in the discreet disobedience of royal instructions.

Of all the *missi dominici*, the intendant of the Paris *généralité* was least competent and least inclined to defy royal authority, largely because of his propinquity to Versailles. He also had the least influence in provisioning affairs because his jurisdiction did not include the city of Paris—the capital was subject to no intendant—and because the police of the capital exercised extensive authority in the hinterland.[30]

The police powers that we have considered so far emanated directly from the king and fit logically into a pyramidal hierarchy which extended from the center apex to the more than thirty *généralités*. There was, however, yet another major police authority, exercised on the regional scale by the thirteen sovereign courts called parlements. Though royal in origin, the parlements owned a generous measure of institutional and constitutional independence—infinitely more than any of the other police agencies—and they functioned to a large degree outside the royal hierarchy. The parlements' police role cannot be understood in terms of some grand political design. The narrow political prism through which we habitually view parlementary life has obscured the extremely important administrative role played by the courts and exaggerated the extent to which the parlements can be seen as a single-minded force. The parlements exercised a sort of parallel police vis-à-vis royal administration, sometimes complementing it, sometimes supplanting or challenging it. When a parlement favored a royal measure—and that one court did is no warrant to believe that the other parlements followed suit—it not only registered the act expeditiously, but it served as a far more vigorous and effective watchdog for its execution than the agents of the royal administration. In some parlements, the First President and *Gens du Roi*, whom the king appointed by commission, had particularly cordial relations with the central government. The First President of the Parlement of

---

30 On the Paris intendancy, see Robert Conte, *L'Administration de la généralité de Paris à la fin du règne de Louis XIV, 1681–1715* (Lille, 1926); Jacques Phytallis, *et al.*, *Questions administratives dans la France du 18ᵉ siècle* (Paris, 1965), 195; M. Barroux, *Le Département de la Seine et de la Ville de Paris: notions générales et bibliographiques pour en étudier l'histoire* (Paris, 1910), 178. The papers of the Bertier de Sauvigny, who did a great deal to reinvigorate the intendancy in the second half of the century, are quite useful. AN, 80 AP.

Provence exemplified the intimacy of the connection in the extreme, for he was also intendant of the *généralité*.

The parlements are better known, however, for taking issue with royal authority. The most spectacular cases, upon which we need not dwell, involved the refusal to register royal legislation. They resulted in a direct confrontation between crown and courts. But there were many other less conspicuous points of opposition concerning more prosaic matters which were only incidentally related to the political resurgence of the parlements in the eighteenth century. Without throwing down the gauntlet, the parlements could deform or dilute royal legislation by formal ordinances and informal instructions of interpretation. Sitting as a civil and criminal court, a parlement could thwart royal intentions by finding in favor of parties who were indicted or convicted for putatively illicit acts. As in the first half of the seventeenth century, though generally with less éclat, the parlements struggled with the intendants and other royal officials for authority over many issues, including control of the grain trade and other police business. The courts dared to annul the actions of royal officials, issue contradictory measures, or, through the offices of the Procurator General, one of the *Gens du Roi*, instruct local police officials to follow a given line. Many of the *Gens du Roi* were deeply attached to their companies and unwilling to rubber-stamp royal decisions. One does not need to rely upon singular figures like La Chalotais to make the point (though it is worth noting that on certain issues, the freedom of the grain trade for example, the Breton Procurator General warmly supported the crown). As faithful a royal servant as Miromesnil, First President at Rouen and future Keeper of the Seals, often apologized for the recalcitrance of his fellow magistrates.[31]

For our purposes, however, it is just as important to note the rivalry among the parlements for jurisdiction and police control as it is to take account of the competition between the royal administration and the parlements. Shared political ambition was no more a guarantee of parlementary solidarity on issues affecting them unequally than common service in the elite corps of *maîtres des requêtes* assured cooperation among the intendants. The Parlements of Paris and Rouen fought for many years over rights to hinterland. Neighboring parlements angrily protested every time a court declared an embargo on the shipment of

---

31 See the *Correspondance politique et administrative de Miromesnil*, ed. by P. Le Verdier, especially volumes 4 and 5.

grain outside its jurisdiction, or *ressort*. It is well known that the provincial parlements resented the pretensions to superiority flaunted by
the Paris court; the argument over the proper locus of the court of
peers is probably the most famous example of this jealousy. Yet the
most sustained and widespread friction resulted not from sensational
political issues, but from conflicts over administrative jurisdictions.
The Paris Parlement was itself the largest provincial parlement. The
other sovereign courts viewed its vast *ressort* an as irritant and a menace. It encompassed areas which had closer geographical, economic,
and cultural ties with the nearby provincial parlements than with the
Paris-based court. Even when it did not actually overstep its bounds,
the Paris Parlement made decisions that directly affected regions in
the other parlementary *ressorts*.

We have already noted in passing some of the levers by which
the parlements exercised their police. The most familiar are the
captious tactics by which the courts subverted laws, by overt opposition and by more subtle devices (judicial decisions, filibustering,
inadequate publicity, etc.), or remolded them to conform to their
own needs or views. Much of this was a matter of adaptation
rather than obstruction, for the crown gave the courts fairly wide
latitude in the interpretation and implementation of the bulk of
royal legislation. Less well known is the authority which the parlements possessed to enact quasi-legislative decrees called *arrêts de
règlement*.[32] In this capacity they acted on their own initiative and
in their own terms rather than in reaction to measures taken by
the central government. Unless the king's council decided to quash
their regulatory decrees on grounds that they contradicted new
or existing royal legislation, they had "force of law" within each
ressort. They dealt with a sweeping range of issues affecting public, private, and criminal law, as well as police affairs. The acts
by which the Paris Parlement limited bakers in a dearth period
to the making of only two sorts of bread and by which the Dijon
Parlement placed an embargo on the removal of grain outside its
jurisdiction were *arrêts de règlement*. Whereas the rights of registration and remonstrance gave the parlements significant political

---

32 A. Esmein, *Cours élémentaire d'histoire du droit français* (Paris, 1898), 538–39; F. Olivier-Martin,
   Cours d'histoire du droit public, (Paris, 1945–46), 165–67; Germain Martin, *Les Associations ouvrières
   au 18ᵉ siècle* (Paris, 1900), 56. Olivier-Martin's students began to catalogue and inventory the
   arrêts de règlement in the thirties. Their work remains extremely incomplete; much of it is
   unpublished.

influence, this quasi-legislative power to render *arrêts* enabled the sovereign courts of justice to function as authentic regional governing institutions.

Another powerful instrument of parlementary police, which we tend to overlook, is the juridico-administrative apparatus directed by the Procurator General. It was particularly important in the Parlement of Paris whose Procurator General commanded great prestige and whose jurisdiction stretched over a third of the kingdom.[33] The Procurator had *substituts,* or deputies, in scores of towns and hamlets scattered throughout the *ressort.* These deputies, often called royal procurators (*procureurs du roi*), functioned as local officers of justice and police as well as representatives of the *Gens du Roi.* The *substituts* regarded the Procurator General as their protector and as the authority to whom they were ultimately accountable. Many of them corresponded with him regularly, keeping him closely informed on general affairs such as the state of the market and the price of grain, as well as on matters of justice. They often solicited his advice and instructions for the proper conduct of affairs; he was supposed to keep them posted on changes in laws, regulations, and procedures and he gave them specific orders either in his capacity as a superior police official himself or as the spokesman for the court. The *substituts* constituted an extraordinary network of grassroots intelligence and enforcement. In many instances the Procurator General was better informed than the intendants and even than the Controller-General, and better placed than they to see his commands executed.

As long as the Procurator General behaved like a faithful king's man, the central government did not begrudge him his enormous administrative influence. The parlements made excellent use of his network for conducting investigations and diffusing their propaganda as well as their *arrêts.* Intermediary between the crown and the sovereign companies, the Procurator felt intense pressure from each side during the eighteenth

---

33 I do not know of any studies specifically devoted to the Procurator General and his administrative role. The best sources are in manuscript: the Joly de Fleury Collection at the BN, the surviving minutes of the ordinary police assemblies (BN, mss. fr. 11356), and the parlementary or X series at the AN, especially the Conseil Secret. On the general functions of the Procurator, see E.D. Glasson, *Le Parlement de Paris, son rôle politique depuis le règne de Charles VII jusqu' à la révolution* (Paris, 1901), 2 vols., J. Shennan, *The Parlement of Paris* (Ithaca, 1968), and sporadic references in F. Olivier-Martin, *Histoire du droit français des origines à la révolution* (Paris, 1951). On the foremost dynasty of Procurators of Paris, see the informative but unimaginative work of Paul Bisson de Barthélémy, *L'Activité d'un Procureur Général au Parlement de Paris à la fin de l'ancien régime: les Joly de Fleury* (Paris, 1964).

century. The Procurator of the Paris Parlement and the Controller-General cooperated closely, especially on provisioning affairs, until the 1760's. When the Controller-General suspected that the Procurator was out of sympathy with his position, he did not hesitate to go over his head and deal directly with the *substituts*. How flattered a modest *substitut* must have felt to be courted by two of the most powerful men in France!

The Paris Procurator General was also the organizing force behind the informal "assembly of police," which met sometimes once a month, sometimes once a week, to discuss all matters pertaining to the administration of the capital.[34] Composed of the First President, the Lieutenant General and the Prévôt des Marchands as well as the Procurator, it took a special interest in subsistence questions. The Lieutenant General reported on the state of public opinion, the situation in the Halles, or central markets, the conduct of the bakers, and the conditions in the markets and the farms of the nearby hinterland; the Prévôt told his colleagues about the port markets and the river trade; and the Procurator passed on data from his *substituts* on the harvests, stocks, and market conditions throughout the *ressort*. The officials assessed the situation and tried to decide upon a common course of action (or inaction). Decisions did not come easily, for the Prévôt and the Lieutenant were bitter rivals, and both of them resented the "tutelage" which the First President, in the name of parlement, pretended to exercise over them. On balance, the assembly of police seems to have been fairly successful in coordinating general policy for the police of provisioning, at least during the first half of the reign of Louis XV, the only period for which the minutes of the meetings survive.

The parlements practiced what was called the "grand police."[35] To the abbé Véri, a critic of parlementary officiousness, this was nothing more than a convenient pretext, "a passport" for "interfering" in all

---

34 See the minutes of the assemblies, BN, mss. fr. 11356, plus references to meetings and discussions in Arsenal, mss. Bastille, 10875 and 10270 (Bourlon to Hérault, 12 Oct.1725); BN, mss. fr. 21651 (Delamare papers), fols. 285–86; BN, Coll. Joly 1117, fol. 219; Coll. Joly 1118, fols. 180–81; Coll. Joly 1310, fol. 2.

35 On the parlements' *grande police*, see Glasson, *Parlement de Paris*; Shennan, *Parlement of Paris*; Olivier-Martin, *Police économique* and *Histoire du droit français*; Egret, *Parlement de Dauphiné* and *Louis XV et l'opposition parlementaire* (Paris, 1970); J.-L. Gay, "L'Administration de la capitale entre 1770 et 1789," *Mémoires de la Fédération des Sociétés Historiques et Archéologiques de Paris et de l'Ile-de-France*, VIII–XII (1956–61).

the affairs to which their "caprice" leads them. His sarcasm aside, Véri was not very wide of the mark. The straightforward definition given by a prominent jurist emphasized the open-ended nature of this power. The grand police, wrote Dénisart, was the authority of the parlement to take action "on its own" on matters "which interest essentially the public order and the public good."[36] Provisioning fitted this criterion admirably and elicited close attention from many of the sovereign courts. The Rouen Parlement, for example, in the 1750's and sixties not only published general instructions for a strict enforcement of the traditional grain police, but also issued specific orders for "visits" to private granaries in search of clandestine hoards and for investigations of suspected merchants. As early as the fourteenth and fifteenth centuries, the Paris Parlement punished millers who sold bad quality flour and passed measures for the fixation of the price of bread. The Paris court claimed to be "the first protector of the capital" and competed with the king for recognition as its material providence. Visitors to the Parlement's chambers were invited to view the portrait of a former first president who earned the sobriquet "the baker" for having spent a large part of his personal fortune to import grain for Parisians during a severe dearth.[37]

It would be absurd, however, to reduce the police of Paris subsistence to a popularity contest. It was an extremely delicate and onerous responsibility with which both the crown and the Parlement were loath to trifle. Still, it would be naive to pretend that they were disdainful of Parisian opinion or that they did not sometimes mix police and politics. Thus, for example, a contemporary observer characterized the Parlement's decision to parade the relic of Sainte Geneviève in the midst of serious shortage and disorder in June 1725 as a "mischievous" action, "a vengeance of the parlement" against the crown, presumably for having forced the registration of a fiscal package, including the new fiftieth tax, in a *lit de justice* several days before. Apparently the Parlement's aim was to emphasize the misery of the people and its solicitude for their lot in juxtaposition to the fiscal cupidity of the

---

36 Abbé J.-A. de Véri, *Journal de l'abbé de Véri*, ed. by B. Jehan de Witte (Paris,1928–30), I, 213; Dénisart, *Collection de décisions*, III, 530.

37 E. Boutaric, ed., *Actes du Parlement de Paris* (Paris, 1863–67), I, lxii; Guy Lemarchand, "Les Troubles des subsistances dans la généralité de Rouen," *Annales historiques de la révolution française*, 35th year (Oct.–Dec. 1963), 419–20; H. Monin, *L'État de Paris en 1789, études et documents sur l'ancien régime à Paris* (Paris, 1889), 287; Pierre Vinçard, *Les Ouvriers de Paris, alimentation* (Paris, 1863), 3–4.

crown, which not even a dearth could temper. According to another observer during a subsistence crisis fifteen years later, the ministry ordered a forced reduction in the price of Parisian bread in order to steal a march on the Parlement, which was rumored—erroneously as it turned out—to be preparing some sort of subsistence remonstrance. A year later, with the situation still grave, the Parlement invoked the "high prices" and "the calamity common to all classes [*conditions*]" to protest the levying of the *dixième*. In 1740–41, as in all the other subsistence crises of the eighteenth century, rumors and suspicions swirled about, implicating public officials including ministers and magistrates in various maneuvers designed to produce high profits on grain at the cost of public suffering. Although the Parlement was reported to be under heavy public pressure to launch an independent investigation to expose the "speculators" and "monopolists"—an inquiry which, regardless of outcome, would have sparked new rumors and undermined confidence in the royal government—it refused.[38]

In 1752, during another brief period of soaring prices and mushrooming suspicions of speculative plots, the marquis d'Argenson allegedly learned from parlementary informants that the court would "seriously investigate that which concerns the *cherté* of grain and go all the way to the source, which involves M. de Machault [Controller-General and then Keeper of the Seals]." The lawyer Barbier confirmed the fact that "everyone is half-persuaded that there are frauds concerning grain." Here was a chance for the Parlement to embarrass and discredit the government, for according to d'Argenson, to be sure not a wholly disinterested witness, "the people was, in advance, very grateful" to the Parlement for its "patriotic démarches." In fact, the abbé de Vougny, a forty-seven year old counselor in the *Grand'Chambre* (and not, as the stereotype would have us believe all parlementary hotheads to be, a young Turk from the *Enquêtes*), wanted to denounce the grain perfidies in the Parlement and demand a debate and an inquiry. His impassioned appeal won no support, in large measure because the magistrates

---

38 Mathieu Marais, *Journal et mémoires sur la régence et le règne de Louis XV*, ed. by de Lescure (Paris, 1863–68), III, 198, 202; Gazetins, 18–19 October and 27–28 November 1740, Arsenal, mss. Bastille 10167, fols. 161, 185; remonstrances of 6 Sept. 1741, J. Flammermont, ed., *Remontrances du Parlement de Paris au 18ᵉ siècle* (Paris, 1888–98), I, 379–83. But note the rumors implicating the Procurator General and the magistrates in maneuvers alleged to be responsible for the dearth in 1740: Gazetins, 25, 28–29 Sept. 1740, Arsenal, mss. Bastille 10167, fols. 142–43, 167.

were preoccupied with the ongoing Unigenitus affair, but doubtless also because the idea of such an inflammatory action frightened them.[39]

"There's smut in wheat," runs a Middle Western American
adage, "but there's dirt in politics." In eighteenth-century France,
wheat politics were among the dirtiest politics. On balance, however, at least till the sixties, the restraint of the government and
the Parlement of Paris and their efforts to avert political confrontation on grain questions are much more striking than the skirmishes
recorded above. By tacit accord, it was their wish that subsistence
remain a non-partisan issue. Political rivalry between crown and
Paris Parlement had no perceptible effect on the provisioning of
Paris and, until the sixties, there were virtually no differences in
their conception of the proper police.

Even at the highest levels, the police of provisioning was neither a
highly centralized nor a rationally organized affair. Though they shared
a common concern and in many cases followed the same general
program of regulation and intervention, the regional and provincial
authorities were divided by jurisdictional and institutional rivalries and,
in some cases, by personal and political animosities. Their powers and
claims overlapped, their downward lines of authority crisscrossed, and
their control over their field subordinates was never certain. They were
divided, too, by interest and this was the cruelest division of all, for in
the worst of circumstances, it meant a struggle for subsistence which
set off *généralité* against *généralité*, *ressort* against *ressort*. The ideal of the
police was fraternal as well as paternal. In a well-policed state, the
regions gifted with a surplus were supposed to rush to the assistance of
those areas in deficit. From the center, the Controllers-General labored
to encourage these exchanges; this was perhaps their most important
single police responsibility, and in the eighteenth century they exercised
it with mixed success. One of the most serious charges that its critics

---

39 E.-J.-F. Barbier, *Chronique de la régence et du règne de Louis XV* (Paris, 1857), V, 313–314; R.-L. de
Voyer, marquis d'Argenson, *Journal et mémoires du marquis d'Argenson*, ed. by E.-J.-B. Rathery
(Paris, 1859–67), VII, 286, 325–26. In 1752, as later in 1768, the Rouen Parlement preceded
the Paris court in its exposure of dubious grain "maneuvers." D'Argenson, *Journal et mémoires*,
VII, 278. Yet several months after reporting on the popularity of the Paris Parlement with
the people for the stand it took on the grain question, d'Argenson noted public resentment
against the magistrates for failing to deal effectively with high prices. *Journal et mémoires*, VII,
446. On the magistrate who denounced the alleged maneuvers to the Paris court in 1752,
see F. Bluche, *L'Origine des magistrats du Parlement de Paris au 18ᵉ siècle* in *Mémoires de la Fédération
des Sociétés Historiques et Archéologiques de Paris et de l'Ile-de-France*, V–VI (1953–54), 411.

made against the police of provisioning on the regional and provincial scale was that it fostered the very sort of reactionary particularism that the modern state was dedicated to eradicating.

IV

Particularism took its most extreme form at the local level where authority for the police of provisioning was widely diffused and fragmented in a crazy quilt of unintegrated, poorly defined, and overlapping jurisdictions. Virtually every public official dealing with administrative and/or judicial affairs, no matter how humble his origins or functions, "held" some sort of grain police. In addition, below or beyond these local authorities, myriad specialized officers such as grain measurers and porters and market stewards, and a host of more or less private individuals such as *engagistes* of the royal domain or less mighty seigneurs, lay or ecclesiastical, noble or bourgeois, who owned or farmed market "rights" or related tolls and duties, all claimed or exercised some sort of police power.[40]

The leading figures in the police of a given community are easy to identify—though we think of them as petty officials, they loomed large in the lives of the citizenry—but the cast of characters, the attributions of function, and the system of recruitment vary from place to place and make it difficult to conceive of a typical structure.[41] Mayors, *échevins*, *capitouls*, *jurats*, *prévôts*, lieutenants of police, commissaires of police, procurators (royal and fiscal), and others shared or vied for the police in different towns and hamlets and villages. The common aim of these officials was to assure that their communities enjoyed a sufficient supply of grain at a reasonable price. By applying royal legislation, parlementary *arrêts* and local statutes, by issuing their own regulations, by rendering or causing to be rendered

---

40 BN, mss. fr. 12595, fols. 472–503. Cf. Missonnet report, BN, Coll. Joly 1112, fol. 18.

41 See, for example, Provins in the Brie: Lobinod to PG of the Paris Parl., 28 July 1725, BN, Coll. Joly 1117, fol. 102.

For an excellent account of local authorities and their relations with their superiors, see Jean Ricommard, *La Lieutenance générale de police à Troyes au 18ᵉ Siècle* (Troyes, 1934). Also relevant is his "Les Subdélégués des intendants aux 17ᵉ et 18ᵉ siècles." *Information historique*, 24th year (Sept.–Oct. 1962), 139–48; (Nov.–Dec. 1962), 190–95; 25th year (Jan.–Feb. 1963), 1–8. Another useful treatment of local police can be found in Maurice Bernard, *La Municipalité de Brest de 1750 à 1790* (Paris, 1915).

criminal, civil and police sentences, by monitoring and registering transactions, and by exhorting and threatening the parties involved, the local authorities sought to control the flow of grain, stocking, selling, and buying, on and off the marketplace. In principle, the officials of each community were supposed to cooperate among themselves, respect the needs and rights of their neighbors, and act in harmony with the wishes of their various superiors.

In fact, however, officials within the same community often quarreled among themselves and clashed with their superiors, and communities fought one another. Conflicts arose over the competition for supplies and over jurisdictional rivalries, two questions that were usually, though not necessarily, closely related. The competition for subsistence characteristically took the form of a dispute over rights of jurisdiction, administrative and moral. Did a big community have priority, regardless of the circumstances, over a small one? Could a major city (say, Paris) expropriate supplies which "belonged" to one of the little towns in its metropolitan supply network when that town found itself inadequately provisioned? Could a community forbid "foreigners" from entering its market or its hinterland? Could it force merchants to sell grain and sell it at a fixed price?

Sometimes officials used the subsistence issue as a pretext for administrative aggrandizement, but it is not usually difficult to tell when the struggle was genuine, that is, when the communities urgently needed the supplies and the contest for power was subsidiary to the competition for grain. The communities fought over the grain itself, the control of the supply zones, the allegiance of merchants, the legitimacy of certain regulations and the validity of sentences pronounced against individuals. Feuds developed with the police of one place intercepting grain bound for another or punishing a merchant enrolled somewhere else in order to avenge an affront and take an eye for an eye, or since it is a question of cereals, an ear for an ear. In some instances a confrontation mobilized the inhabitants of a community, more or less spontaneously or in response to cues from the police. Disorder was the ultimate weapon of the police authorities in their efforts to maintain public order.

Tensions over jurisdictions were not epiphenomenal byproducts of price oscillations or grain shortages. They were woven into the very fabric of a system that diffused authority broadly and clouded the lines of authority in uncertainty. Rivalry was one of the motors of the system and mutual mistrust was the fuel on which it ran. The tensions fed on every issue of authority, precedence, perquisites, and patronage. Sometimes, they were brought to the surface by the competition for subsistence itself or by the competition to determine *who* would exercise the police of provisioning, the control of which could be profitable as well as prestigious. On other occasions, they resulted in bitter rows which had nothing to do with subsistence, but incidentally complicated or crippled the efforts to police the provisioning trade and assure a regular supply. On the local level, as on the regional or national scale, conflicts erupted horizontally (between "peer" or approximately equal officials) and vertically (officials against their superiors or subordinates): between jurisdictions within the same community (for instance, the conciliar municipality against the lieutenant of police), between officials dependant on different jurisdictions (the procurator and the subdelegate) or in a general way between representatives of central and local authority or between hometown officials and outsiders.

It is not surprising that *intra*-community rivalries often erupted during dearths when common action was most urgently needed, for it was precisely then, under stress, that the old administrative patterns broke down and new initiatives had to be taken. In September 1725, for example, the *substitut* at Vitry and the subdelegate quarreled violently over strategy to combat rising prices. The Controller-General characterized the dispute as one of many caused "by jealousy of authority and of function, which is only too common in small towns...." In the same year at Versailles, the police commissaire Narbonne and the royal procurator Regnier were "en froid," partly due to a disagreement on grain policy, partly because Regnier claimed the "glory" for containing a riot, an achievement that Narbonne said was his. At the same time the subdelegate based at Poissy denounced the *prévôt* for "jealousy of métier" and "little knowledge of the public interest" as manifested in his conduct of the grain police. In 1740 Guillemin, procurator of Châlons-sur-Marne, sharply criticized the municipality for a draconian measure that prohibited the exodus of grain and bread from the city. "The market is free to everyone," he declared, "and if it is permitted to buy merchandise which is sold in the city, can it be prohibited to take it away?" The *prévôt* of the *échevinage* responded by physically assaulting Guillemin in the public marketplace.[42] At Calais it was the

---

42 Dodun to PG, Sept. 1725, BN, Coll. Joly 1117, fol. 185; Pierre de Narbonne, *Journal de Pierre de Narbonne* (Versailles, 1955), 124, 127; Legrand to Hérault, LG of Police of Paris, 15 Dec. 1725, Arsenal, mss. Bastille 10371; Guillemin to Joly de Fleury, 15 Nov. and 4 Dec. 1740, BN, Coll. Joly 1123, fols. 196, 204–205.

municipality that took what one might call, somewhat tremulously, the liberal stance. While it purchased grain abroad and in the interior for sale to the public, the municipality believed that the best way to assure abundance was to guarantee "a complete liberty in the sale of grain on the markets." The lieutenant of police and his *huissiers* did not, however, share its faith in free exchange and effectively sabotaged the policy of the town fathers by harrassing sellers, examining and verifying goods, and forcing the price. That the lieutenant also interfered with the shipment of grain to Paris—a service adroitly rendered by the municipality—probably sealed his fate with the Controller-General Orry, who recommended that he be suspended from his functions for six months.[43]

Inter-community subsistence rivalry understandably reached its peak during dearths, but even in good times, relations sometimes remained troubled. This is most strikingly illustrated by the recurrent clashes between Paris and the multitude of towns and villages in the borderless expanse surrounding it. A great many factors, of course, besides subsistence contributed to this chronic strain. On one level, it can be viewed in terms of the familiar struggle between city and countryside common to virtually all societies through many different stages of development.[44] The city was the seat of power and wealth. It was the embodiment of privilege. It obtained exemptions from or dilutions of a plethora of burdens, which almost everyone outside had to bear. City dwellers controlled much of the countryside through ownership of land, capital, and the production instruments of rural industry. In the eighteenth century, moralists and political economists frequently portrayed the city as tyrannical, egotistical, vulturous, and decadent. In their view, the city wantonly drained the countryside of all its riches without the slightest regard for its well-being.

---

43 Petition of mayor and *échevins*, BN, Coll. Joly 1123, fol. 133; Orry to PG, 20 Oct.1740, *ibid.*, fol. 150.

44 See S.P. Huntington, *Political Order in Changing Societies* (New Haven, 1968),72–78 and *passim*. We need studies of the notion of the city, the tension between city and country, and the process by which a provincial, especially someone of rural origins, becomes Parisianized (a special case of becoming urbanized) in the Old Regime. The impact of the change in material culture and habit alone must have been jarring for a newly-arrived Parisian. In rural France, for example, it was perfectly normal for a peasant or a rural worker to consume secondary grains. But in the capital even the poor people ate a wheaten bread.

On the provincial dislike of Parisians, see Louis Chevalier, *Les Parisiens* (Paris, 1967), 13–15 and *passim*.

On another level, however, the conflict was not merely between a city, not even a particularly mighty city, and the countryside, but between Paris, city *sui generis*, and the rest of France.[45] The antinomy Paris-France or Paris-province—where everything outside the capital is known, almost pejoratively, as provincial—forms one of the great and enduring themes of French history, and the Revolution, which is sometimes credited with sinking the abyss between them, only modernized it and gave it vast new dimensions. Regional power, one of the most passionately debated political issues in the France of the late 1960's and the 1970's, has roots deep in the Old Regime. Mercier's wry "supposition," which he knew would be considered "bizarre, frantic, extravagant," still seems fresh:

> If all the orders of the state assembled, having recognized after a mature examina-tion that the capital exhausts the kingdom, depopulates the countryside, retains far from it the great proprietors, ruins agriculture, hides a multitude of bandits and useless artisans, corrupts morals little by little, postpones the epoch of a govern-ment more formidable abroad, freer and happier; if all the orders of the state, I say, everything considered and reviewed, ordered the whole city to be burned after having previously given the inhabitants a year's warning, what would be the result of this great sacrifice made for the fatherland and for future generations? *Would it in fact be a service rendered to the provinces and the kingdom?* I leave it to you, reader, to study and decide this interesting problem.[46]

The grain trade, a matter of life and livelihood, gave the old-regime strug-gle between Paris and the provinces its most visceral expression. Perceived as Babylon by critics like the abbé Coyer who condemned it for "suck-ing the blood" of the provinces, Paris loomed as a new Rome in the eye of commentators on subsistence questions. The chemist and physician Malouin deplored Paris' short-sighted, selfish provisioning policy which worked "to the detriment of the countryside because it places [the people of the provinces] in dearth." This approach, he warned,

> contributed to the ruin of Rome & of its empire. Rome's grain provisions were immense. It was the provinces of the empire which were obliged to furnish these sup-plies, as tributaries; which exhausted them.

---

45 Though the epic battles over grain opposed Paris to the rest of France, the provinces regularly fought against each other for the control of provisioning terrain. See, for example, Machault to IN. of Alençon, 23 May 1750, C. 90, A.D. Orne; Parl, of Bordeaux to Louis XV, c. fall 1748, C. 1439, A.D. Gir; Bertin to IN. of Burgundy, 26 July 1760, C. 80, A.D. C d'O.

46 L.-S. Mercier, *Tableau de Paris*, IV, 309–310.

The sovereigns of Rome, noted the journalist-philosophe Linguet, "favored its provisioning by the most odious violence" and "watched famine desolate the provinces without misgivings, provided it did not extend to the Capital." Paris does not "devour" the "entire kingdom," noted Mercier judiciously, only that part of it within a range of 40 leagues. The "sacrifices" which the central government imposed upon France in favor of Paris, wrote the physiocrat Dupont, "are the object of the jealousy of the whole kingdom." While certain revolutionaries chided Parisians for having tamely submitted to the blandishments of the old-regime victualers, the counter-revolutionary essayist Rivarol reproached the old government for "its predilection and its profusions for the capital which always ate cheaper bread than the provinces and always at the expense of the royal treasury." Revolutionaries, too, sounded the theme that Paris could not expect to play the "monster" in the new regime as it had in the old.[47]

Paris owed its privileged position in the competition for subsistence to the conviction held by the government that "outcries of need there would be more dangerous than anywhere else and would set a fatal and contagious example."[48] Political experience had demonstrated well before the eighteenth century that it was cheaper to take risks with provisioning in the provinces than in the capital. Paris was considered highly vulnerable because of the immensity of its population—contemporary estimates ran as high as a million though historians today prefer a figure between six and 700,000 around the mid-century point—and

---

47 Abbé G. Coyer, *Essai sur la prédication* (Paris, 1781), 15; P.-J. Malouin, *Description des arts du meunier, du vermicellier et du boulanger*, new edition, ed. by J.-E. Bertrand (Neuchâtel, 1771), 429; Simon Linguet, cited by abbé André Morellet, *Théorie du paradoxe* (Amsterdam, 1775), 99–100; P.-S. Dupont de Nemours, *Analyse*, 182; Rivarol, cited by Léon Biollay, *Études économiques sur le XVIIIᵉ siècle. Le pacte de famine; l'administration du commerce* (Paris, 1885), 60; Du Vaucelles in AN, F¹⁰215–216. Cf. J.-J. Rousseau, "De l'économie politique," in *Œuvres complètes*, ed. by A. Houssiaux (Paris, 1852), I, 602 and H.E. Jacob, *Histoire du pain depuis six mille ans* (Paris, 1958), 89.

48 Mercier, *Tableau de Paris*, IV, 203. On the special urgency of provisioning Paris and on the vulnerability of the capital and the volatility of its population, see: Delamare, *Traité*, II, 828; remonstrances of Paris Parl., 2–4 March 1776, Flammermont, ed., *Remontrances*, III, 300; Regnaud, "Histoire des événements arrivés en France depuis 1772...," BN, mss. fr. 13734; d'Argenson, *Journal et mémoires*, ed. by Rathery, VII, 81; anonymous memoir to CG, 1784, AN, F¹¹ 294–95; Marc Bloch, "Les Aliments du Français." in *Encyclopédie française*, ed. by G. Berger (Paris, 1955), 14.42.10.Cf. Max Weber, *The City*, ed. and trans, by D. Martindale and G. Neuwirth (Glencoe, Ill., 1958), 73; Max Beloff, *Public Order and Popular Disturbances, 1660–1714* (London, 1938), 129 and *passim*.

potentially volatile, among other reasons, because the vast majority of its inhabitants led a marginal and uncertain life and were more likely to react collectively and violently to threats to their subsistence than to any other stimulus.[49] Paris was the historical capital of the kingdom and, even after the government shifted to nearby Versailles, it remained the nerve-center of the realm. Given the scale and intensity it could achieve, a Parisian uprising, it was believed, could overturn the government.

"As long as the bread of Gonesse is not lacking," wrote Mercier, "the commotion will not be general; but if Gonesse bread lacks for two consecutive markets, the revolt will be universal."[50] Mercier took

---

49 For estimates that place the population under 600,000, see: A.-J.-P. Paucton, *Métrologie, ou traité des mesures, des poids et des monnaies* (Paris 1780), 482 (589,000); William Mildmay, *The Police of France* (London, 1763), 125–26 (between 492,000 and 580,000); N.-F. Dupré de Saint-Maur, *Essai sur les monnaies* (Paris, 1746), 48–55 (under 600,000); Messance cited in *Journal économique* (Feb. 1766), 82 (576,630); Armand Husson, *Les Consommations de Paris*, 2nd ed. (Paris, 1875), 27 (under 600,000); B. Gille, "Fonctions économiques de Paris," in *Paris: fonctions d'une capitale*, Colloques, Cahiers de Civilisations (Paris, 1962), 131 (500,000 in 1789); J. Dupâquier, "Sur la population française au 17ᵉ et au 18ᵉ siècles," *Revue historique*, (Jan.–March 1968), 54n (500,000 at the beginning of the century); P. Goubert in F. Braudel and E. Labrousse, eds., *Histoire économique et sociale de la France* (Paris, 1970), II, 73 (not much above 500,000 at end of century).

For estimates between 600,000 and 800,000, see: Délibérations du Bureau de l'Hôtel de Ville, 3 May 1775, AN, H* 1876, fols. 127–29 (700,000–800,000); E. Béguillet, *Description historique*, I, 36–41 (over 700,000); article "Paris," in Diderot, *et al.*, *Encyclopédie* XI, 944 (700,000); M. Brion, *État actuel de la France* (Amsterdam, 1774), 36 (750,000); Mercier, *Tableau de Paris*, I, 60 (700,000); Arrêté sur les subsistances, 27 Sept. 1791, Conseil Général de la Commune de Paris, AN, T 644¹⁻² (700,000).

For estimates over 800,000: Délibérations du Bureau de l'Hôtel de Ville, Aug. 1755, AN, H* 1866 (1,000,000); Gazier, ed., "La Police de Paris en 1770," 30 (1,000,000); Béguillet, *Description historique*, I, 164n and *Traité des subsistances*, 658–60n (over 800,000); J. Rutledge, *Le Babillard* (5 Aug. 1778), 291 (1,000,000); Des Essarts, *Dictionnaire*, I, 332 (1,000,000).

On the Paris population, see also L. Cahen, "La Population parisienne au milieu du 18ᵉ siècle," *Revue de Paris*, 26th year (1 Sept. 1919), 146–70 and J. Kaplow, "Sur la population flottante," *Annales historiques de la révolution française*, 39th year (Jan.–March 1767), 1.

On the government's preoccupation with the size of the capital and its efforts to limit further growth, in part for reasons of police and subsistence, see the letters patent of April 1672, the royal Declarations of July 1724 and Jan. 1726, and the letters patent of July 1766. AN, G⁷ 446–447 and Q¹ 1099 159ff.: Archives Seine-Paris, 2AZ 2 47 pièce 3f; *Recueil général des anciennes lois françaises depuis l'année 420 jusqu'à la révolution de 1789*, ed. F.-A. Isambert (Paris, 1821–33), XXI, 273–75; L.-E.-A. Jobez, *La France sous Louis XV*, II, 373–74; Albert Babeau, *Paris en 1789* (Paris, 1892), 8.

50 Mercier, *Tableau de Paris*, XII, 136. Mercier echoed the Cardinal de Retz who remarked that the Parisian Fronde could not endure because the bourgeois of the capital could not do without their *pain de Gonesse*, an unusually savory white wheaten loaf

some poetical liberties with the facts, for the contribution of the Gonessiers in his time was relatively modest and the allure of their bread had declined over the years. On the other hand, it was not at all farfetched to anticipate an explosion if the usual supply of bread at the Wednesday and Saturday markets in the sixteen marketplaces of the capital failed. Voltaire joked that Paris needed only "bread and circuses" to flourish, but Delamare took the Roman lesson seriously, and his successors in the police felt confident about their ability to keep peace in Paris only when they could steadily assure the provisioning of the markets and occasionally provide "aliments to divert the people" as well.[51] Its enormous size made Paris logistically difficult as well as politically urgent to provision. Without the special administrative advantages that the capital enjoyed, suggested the author of a dictionary of police, "one would have trouble imagining that there are sources capable of meeting the needs of this vast pit."[52] Finally, authorities believed that it was important for there to be "a secret and invisible hand"—the police, not self-interest!—in the provisioning of the capital because Paris served as a regulator market, setting a price standard which had an impact, like Parisian fashion and Parisian outcries, far beyond the limits of the city.[53]

Although the protests of the provinces were sometimes exaggerated— "it is necessary to complain," Voltaire allowed, "so that you are drained

---

made by the "forains" or itinerant bakers of the village of Gonesse located northeast of Paris. *Mémoires du Cardinal de Retz*, ed. by Petitot in *Collection des mémoires relatifs à l'histoire de France* (Paris, 1825), XLIV, 274. Cf. Voltaire to Imbert, 21 Jan. 1771 in *Œuvres complètes*, ed. by Moland, XV, 331 (#8185) and Delamare, *Traité*, II, 823.

51 Voltaire to François de Chennevières, 22 Oct. 1760 in *Voltaire's Correspondence*, ed. by T. Besterman, vol. 37, p. 156 (#7823); Voltaire to Suzanne Necker, 6 Feb. 1770, *ibid.*, vol. 74, p. 81 (#15144); Delamare, *Traité*, II, 600; Bachaumont, *Mémoires secrets*, XXIV, 176–77 (22 Aug. 1772). Cf. Béguillet, *Description historique*, I, 28n.

Yet Lenoir was correct in claiming that "there had been few popular insurrections in Paris as long as the old ordinances were strictly observed." Lenoir, "Essai sur la guerre des farines," in R. Darnton, "Le Lieutenant de Police Lenoir, la guerre des farines et l'approvisionnement de Paris à la veille de la révolution," *Revue d'histoire moderne et contemporaine*, XVI (Oct.–Dec. 1969), 612. Mercier felt that Parisians were on the whole a tranquil people, yet he noted that once the populace became agitated, it was likely to explode, with terrible violence. *Tableau de Paris*, VI, 26–30 and XII, 6–8. Cf. Prudhomme's claim, written of course from the perspective of 1789, that the people "rose up" frequently and violently because of subsistence problems during the Old Regime. *Révolutions de Paris*, no. 7 (22 Aug. 1789), 2.

52 Des Essarts, *Dictionnaire*, I, 329.

53 PG Daguesseau fils to CG, 24 Feb. 1709 in A. de Boislisle, ed., *Correspondance des contrôleurs généraux des finances avec les intendants des provinces* (Paris, 1874–97), III, 102; Gazier, ed. "La Police de Paris en 1770," 116.

a little less"—they had a solid basis in fact.[54] The Paris provisioning machine was a juggernaut; when it spared towns and villages, the reason was inefficiency, not solicitude. Over centuries, the city extended its hinterland in all directions. It encroached upon areas which had traditionally served the needs of Rouen, Orléans, Reims, Troyes, Bourges, Dijon, and other towns at an even greater remove. Once Paris staked out a region as its turf, it tried, with considerable success, to shut out competitors. Yet to assure its access to areas which it could not wholly appropriate, the capital opportunistically espoused the cause of free internal circulation and preached a rhetoric of solidarity of city and hinterland.[55] Absorbed by their own task, Parisian authorities evinced little sympathy for local subsistence needs and the problems that the local police faced. Often, without taking the trouble to investigate, they imputed a delay or an obstruction, which hindered the flow of grain, to local ill will and malicious design. Even as the provincials tended to regard the Parisians as parasites, so the Parisian police, like the *sans-culottes* of the Revolution, tended to see the provincials as "egotists" capable of the most horrid crimes of *lèse-*Paris.[56]

The Parisian authorities were determined to see the capital provisioned. That the producing areas might suffer did not matter. Paris disdained what a parlementary commission called "this ancient principle [which "the peoples bear in their heart"] that grain is first reserved to the province where it is born." The textbook authority on Parisian imperialism, Delamare, conceded that "natural equity" spoke strongly in favor of local claims, but equity had to be weighed against other demands. Throughout the Old Regime (and afterwards), there were tensions of the sort that developed at Châlons-sur-Marne in 1740, which suggest the nature of the problem. The news that buyers for Paris would soon descend upon that town with official commissions from the Paris municipality "cast alarm in all the minds." "The trouble," wrote

---

54 Voltaire, article "Blé ou bled" (1770), *Dictionnaire philosophique* in *Œuvres complètes*, ed. by Moland, XVIII, 11.

55 See, for example, CG to IN. of Burgundy, 12 Sept. 1725, AN, G⁷ 34. When circulation was interrupted, Paris faced serious problems. See BN, mss. fr. 16741, fols. 9–11; CG to Legendre, 21, 31 August and 27 Sept. 1709, in *Correspondance des contrôleurs généraux*, ed. by Boislisle, III, 204; d'Argenson to CG, 27 Dec. 1698, cited by R. Conte, *L'Administration de la généralité de Paris à la fin du régne de Louis XIV* (Paris, 1926), 149.

56 R. Cobb, *Terreur et subsistances 1793–1795: Études d'histoire révolutionnaire* (Paris, 1965), 217–19; Cobb, *Les Armées révolutionnaires* (Paris, 1961–63), II, 368, 395–96, 438.

the *substitut*, "is universal, I don't know of any remedy to contain a populace of ten to 11,000 men who have no bread at all and who will watch [Parisians] take away that on which they seem to have the right to count." Paris, he asserted, "has many resources which a Province cannot find; if Paris draws this year from Champagne, *it is to put the knife at the throat of all the people of this country.*"[57]

Provincial opposition to Parisian exactions took several forms. Popular resistance was often the most effective and always the most worrisome to the central government. It ranged in scope from a simple demonstration in the marketplace or before the house of an official to mass armed attacks on grain warehouses or on wagon convoys and boats. Generally spontaneous, with simple demands for immediate gratification, the eruptions were affirmations of the intensely felt right of the community to its subsistence. The popular rising was a political act by which the population expressed its dissatisfaction with the management and protection of local interests and protested against changes in market organization or violations of conventional patterns of distribution that had developed over the years. Frequently, field authorities shared the resentment of the people and on occasion made common cause with the insurgents, covertly or openly. Popular intervention occurred throughout the Old Regime—at Joigny in 1693 where a troop of women armed with billhooks marched against a Paris-bound grain convoy; at Nogent-sur-Seine in 1725 where a vigilante group patrolled the marketplace and expelled Paris buyers; at Montlhéry in 1728 where "the populace" forced a Paris merchant "to cede part of his purchases at the same price at which he had bought" and the procurator vigorously defended their action; at Versailles in 1740 where a crowd shouting "kill the bastards" intercepted a flour train led by Paris bakers en route to the capital; and at scores of other places during the second half of the eighteenth century, including the revolutionary years.[58]

---

57 Chambre des Enquêtes, "Mémoire" (Aug. 1771), BN, Coll. Joly 1111, fol. 145; Delamare, *Traité*, II, 823; Guillemin to PG, 4 Oct. 1740, BN, Coll. Joly 1123, fols. 177–78.

58 Factum for J. Roger, BN, mss. fr. 21642, fol. 369; St.-Germain, *La Reynie*, 266; Herlaut, "La Disette de pain à Paris en 1709," *Mémoires de la Société de l'Histoire de Paris et de l'île-de-France*, XLV (1918), 17,18; Abbott P. Usher, *The History of the Grain Trade in France*, 6, 192; Petition to Hérault, May 1728 and royal procurator to Hérault, 18 May 1728, Arsenal, mss. Bastille 10274; 23 August 1740, AN, Y 11227; 14 July 1740, AN, Y 15047; BN, mss. fr. 11356, fol. 424. Cf. the English experience in R.B. Rose, "Eighteenth Century Price Riots and Public Policy in England," *International Review of Social History*, VI, part 2 (1961), 287.

Resistance was not only popular but administrative, and Paris encountered it on all levels. Until Colbert succeeded in disciplining them, the neighboring parlements, especially the court at Rouen, boldly challenged Parisian inroads. The intendants formed an obdurate and resourceful bulwark against the demands of the capital. When they could not entirely isolate or insulate their *généralités*, they did not hesitate to lie, stall, wrangle with superiors, contest the claims of colleagues, and bargain to reduce the burdens imposed upon them. Toward the end of the reign of Louis XIV, the Lieutenant of Police d'Argenson complained to the Controller-General that the intendants were not faithfully enforcing the regulations governing the provisioning of Paris. He ultimately found it more expeditious to do the job himself by dispatching commissaires like Delamare. Serving as a sort of super-intendant with his own "subdelegates," Delamare led armies of occupation into Champagne, Burgundy, the Orléanais and elsewhere in 1693–94, 1698, and 1709–10.[59] The Paris police lieutenants during the reign of Louis XV, confident of support from Versailles and conscious of their mounting prestige and influence, tended to deal directly with intendants, to send them what amounted to orders, and to rebuke them when necessary. In 1725 the intendants of the *généralités* surrounding the capital offered no hospitality to Paris merchants seeking grain and allowed their subdelegates to harass them. The Controller-General countered by imposing grain-for-Paris quotas on these intendancies under a program personally supervised by the Paris police chief. Intendants on the path of foreign grain bound for the capital were severely reprimanded for diverting those supplies for local usage. In the forties, the Controller-General Orry, himself a former intendant, requisitioned grain for Paris and other destinations and monitored the conduct of the intendants through extra-administrative channels.[60]

---

59 Bondois, "La Disette de 1662," *Revue d'histoire économique et sociale*, XII (1924), 107; d'Argenson to CG, 25 Jan. 1699 cited by Conte, *L'Administration de la généralité de Paris*, 147; St.-Germain, *La Vie quotidienne*, 201. On Delamare's missions, see Delamare, *Traité*, II, 855–59, 877, 880–85, 906–917; BN, mss. fr. 21598, fols. 409–11; BN, mss. fr. 21635, fols. 37–39; BN, mss. fr. 21642, fol. 74; BN, mss. fr. 21645, *passim* and 21646, fols. 77–78, 236, 261; BN, mss. fr. 21643, fol. 174; Clément, *Portraits*, 195; Usher, *Grain Trade*, 305–309; Germain Martin, "Les Famines de 1693 et 1709 et la spéculation sur les blés," *Bulletin du Comité des Travaux Historiques et Scientifiques, Section des Sciences Économiques et Sociales* (1908), 158–59.

60 BN, Coll. Joly 1116, fols. 50–58; Warmet to Hérault, 8 Oct. 1725, Arsenal, mss. Bastille 10270, fol. 199; Doubleau to Hérault, 28 Dec. 1725, Arsenal, mss. Bastille 10271; Marquet to CG, 13 April 1726, Arsenal, mss. Bastille 10273; De Gasville to Joly, 21 Aug. 1725, BN, Coll. Joly 1117, fols. 82–83; Arsenal, mss. Bastille 10270, fol. 296.

The resistance most difficult to prevent or repress, because it was so scattered, came predictably from the local police. In defense of their supply and their jurisdiction, they protested vehemently against Parisian intrusion, commandeered Paris-bound grain, and hampered Paris dealers in countless ways. They invoked current royal legislation which, if understood literally without regard to dispensations made for Paris, often seemed to favor their cause. They pointed to local precedents which in non-subsistence matters were generally respected by higher authorities. They also justified recourse to supra-legal emergency measures in the name of the *salus populi*, a doctrine which their superiors denounced as casuistry. In some instances, to thwart Parisian buyers, they used their authority informally, making it difficult for the offended parties to document their complaints. In other cases, they issued ordinances which they knew would buy time until news of them doddered to the center where the royal council (or a parlement on the regional level) could eventually review and quash them.

The nature of the issues that opposed the local and the Parisian police changed very little over the years. In 1725 the police at Soissons and Vitry-le-François refused to permit licensed merchants "for the provisioning of Paris" to ship the grain they purchased to the capital. Enraged by the arrogance of these local authorities—"it is against all the rules that a city of the kingdom billets itself off against all the others"—the Controller-General, without scruple for consistency, insisted that "the liberty of commerce" be maintained and that Parisian buyers receive not merely equal but preferential treatment. Similarly, he castigated a subdelegate at Bourges for allowing a Paris dealer to be "insulted and threatened by the people" and for failing to "support her and furnish her all the necessary help." The Paris Procurator General acted in the same fashion to prevent the local officials from "troubling" Paris merchants. Hérault, the Paris police chief, accused the *bailli* of Versailles of trying to stop Versailles bakers from bringing their bread to the Paris markets. Jealous of the success of the Versailles market in attracting flour merchants, Hérault sent an agent on a secret mission to "engage them to prefer Paris." Of the fifty-two *substituts* who replied to a parlementary questionnaire of 1788, twelve blamed grain removals for Paris as a major cause of the dearth.[61]

---

61 CG to Orry, 29 July 1725, AN, G⁷ 34; CG to SD at Bourges, 12 Sept. 1725, *ibid.*; BN, Coll. Joly 1117, fol. 29; bailli of Versailles to LG, 12 Sept. 1725, Arsenal, mss. Bastille 10270; Cleret to LG, 1 Dec. 1725, Arsenal, mss. Bastille 10271; Regnault to Joly, 17 Dec. 1738, BN, Coll. Joly 1119, fols. 196–97; BN, Coll. Joly 1111, fol. 67, 1123, fol. 135, 1112, fols. 5, 66,

Opposition to Paris was not a unifying force; the towns and villages of the provinces battled among themselves even as each continued to resist the capital. We have already indicated the sorts of issues and the tactics that characterized these conflicts. They did not vary much from place to place, within or outside the Parisian sphere of influence. Beyond the reach of Paris, other centers of metropolitan demand played a role similar to that of Paris, albeit on a more modest scale. Even within the Paris zone, the larger towns tried to lord it over the lesser communities in imitation of the way the capital colonized its hinterland. Ironically, within the Paris zone, it was not uncommon for a town in open conflict with the capital to invoke its solidarity with Paris in order to justify its encroachment on other communities. The police of the Brie market-town of Provins, for example, sought to repel Parisian incursions while at the same time they moved against neighboring communities on the grounds that Provins was a vital link in the all-important Parisian supply system.[62]

In fact there were many towns like Provins which had an ambiguous attitude toward Paris, for they alternately suffered (usually in bad times) and benefited (usually in "normal" years) under its aegis. When they were not competing for subsistence, these towns were competing for clients: *laboureurs*, *blatiers* (petty grain traders), grain and flour merchants, millers, and bakers. They competed for Parisian patronage even as they suffered Parisian oppression. For the concentration of Parisian demand on the markets was, in many cases, the chief source of income in such towns, and employment depended almost entirely on the vitality of the grain market. Town fathers and influential seigneurs lobbied with Parisian officials against rival towns in the hope of securing certain most-favored-market privileges. Just as the invasion of Parisian buyers in the Hurepoix town of Montlhéry sparked a defensive riot against the outsiders in the dearth year 1725, so the news that this market-town would be put off limits to Parisian buyers incited a popular uprising in 1737 in favor of the outsiders.[63]

1130, fols. 234–35 and 240–41. For a case during the Revolution, see AN, BB 3 81 A (15 July 1793).

62 On Provins, see Delamare, *Traité*, II, 826; BN, mss. fr. 21645, fol. 376; Lobinod to PG, 28 July 1725 and Paulfry to PG, 6, 18 Aug. 1725, BN, Coll. Joly 1117, fols. 102–105; PG to LG, Aug. 1725, Arsenal, mss. Bastille 10270; Missonnet to PG, 6 June 1752, BN, Coll. Joly 1112, fol. 7. Cf. A. A. Parmentier, *Le parfait boulanger*, 123.

63 Delamare, *Traité*, II, 823–24; Marchais to LG, 3 Dec. 1725, Arsenal, mss. Bastille 10271; petition of inhabitants to Cardinal Fleury, ca. 1737, BN, Coll. Joly 1314, fol. 30; Sentence of 11 Jan. 1737, BN, mss. fr. 21635, fols. 64–65; 4 Feb. 1737, AN, Y 11224.

In bad times, inter-community rivalry resulted in a war of prohibitions; in good times, it produced a war of indulgences. To make their market more attractive, the officials of Etampes, a market-town set in the rich wheatlands of the Beauce, relaxed the police regulations and tolerated informal and covert trading practices that were against the law—national, Parisian, and local. For fear of losing clients, other markets responded with an equally permissive attitude. The breakdown of controls alarmed the Parisian police, who feared that it would upset the orderly provisioning of the capital, as much as it delighted Parisian buyers and local sellers. Parisian commercial pressure and Parisian police pressure worked at cross-purposes and posed a dilemma for local authorities. The royal procurator of Dourdan complained that when he rigorously enforced the rules recommended by the Paris police, buyers and sellers fled his market in order to trade in places which showed "more tolerance." Arguing that it was unfair to force him into actions which ruined his market while strengthening those of rival towns, he appealed to the Procurator General to require *all* the local police to enforce the rules with the same diligence. Etampes responded to Parisian criticism in the same vein. "Would you please," an official asked the Procurator General, "order your *substituts* to execute the Declarations of the King in the other markets [as well?]"[64]

Across the breadth of the kingdom and the span of a century, it is easy to compile a long list of local and regional administrative conflicts. But it is difficult to measure their incidence and impact through time and space. On balance, it seems clear local affairs were not in a perpetual state of disorder. Surely in most respects local life in the eighteenth century was far less chaotic than it had been a century earlier. All that can be safely said about local administration is that it was more or less incoherent in organization and erratic in performance. In most places it functioned well enough to pass all the major tests, despite occasional lapses into anarchy. In many places, it resulted in a permanent atmosphere of cold war among officials and jurisdictions. But chronic cold war itself generated conventions and compromises by which officials managed to get along. The tensions in the system had salutary as well as deleterious effects. They kept officials alert and stirred emulation among them. Administrators checked each others' excesses and pretensions and from these encounters a rough balance of power and division of labor sometimes emerged.

---

64 Odile to PG, 19 Oct. 1738 and Montulle to PG, 13 Nov. 1738, BN, Coll. Joly 1119, fols. 108, 118.

In this way administrative rivalry was not a wholly dysfunctional principle of administrative operation. The Controller-General (or, on a different scale, the intendant) manipulated these rivalries to his advantage, playing one official off against another, using the reports of one to verify those of another, and so on. The central government was not strong enough to implant itself decisively and permanently at the base, but it was far too powerful and prudent to permit any genuine, long-term independence of action. Subsistence, however, required constant attention and the central government simply could not intervene everywhere at once. The responsibilities of provisioning placed great strains on a flawed structure. It placed the greatest burdens on the bottom, where the structure was weakest.

V

The style and operation of the local police depended upon the personnel as well as the structure of administration. Large-scale prosopographic studies of local administration have not yet been undertaken. Fragmentary data suggest a wide range of variation among officials in family background, social origin and status, fortune, modes of recruitment, etc.—not only among different classes of officials (say, mayors, judges, commissaires, and procurators,) but also within the same categories (i.e., the *substituts* of a substantial town and of an unobtrusive hamlet). Some officials were "notables" or even nobles (albeit usually "incomplete"), while others were simple bourgeois; some had considerable education, while others had little formal schooling or training for public service; some municipalities were dominated by merchants, others by lawyers, still others by landowners or mixed elites, while in some places the municipal government per se was of little consequence in day-to-day administration; some posts were venal, others non-venal but practically hereditary, still others filled by commission, cooptation, or some semblance of election.

Diverse pressures played upon the local police agent of whatever stripe. He was concerned about his career and he understood that obedience was the virtue his superiors esteemed most highly, yet he knew that his chances for advancement were probably slim and he could not afford to overlook the incentives for disobedience. When he needed advice or authorization he found the system frustrating and demoralizing, but when he wished to act on his own account he took refuge in its complexity and unwieldiness. On the one hand, he was ferociously jealous of his authority and, even if he sympathized with a given decision or policy (say, to fix the price of grain), he was tempted to oppose it vehemently if it infringed upon his competence, menaced his autonomy, or issued from a tainted source. On the other hand, he was as a rule extremely solicitous of the interests of what we shall call his constituency, though not always for the purest motives, and he hesitated to act (or not to act) without carefully assessing the likely effect on "his" public opinion. Finally, his personal affairs, obligations to his benefactors and clients, and his business connections doubtless also entered into his reckoning.

The quality and the personnel of the local police of provisioning came under stinging attack in the eighteenth century. Ministers, intendants, and parlementarians at various times expressed impatience with the fecklessness, the obtuseness, the indifference, the overzealousness, or the insubordination of these local authorities. The harsh portrait of the local police as a band of benighted, brutish, and undependable subalterns fashioned by the physiocrats in their onslaught against the regulatory regime in the sixties and seventies was not an original canvas; they merely elaborated upon what must be considered the semi-official picture.[65]

The Paris police had little sympathy with their counterparts in the hinterland and they often cited misconduct as a pretext for intervening in local affairs. On the one hand, as we shall later see, Paris denounced them for indiscreet, excessive, and presumptuous action; on the other, they stood accused of a lack of zeal, firmness, and sense of mission. One Paris agent in 1725 deplored the "negligence" of the judges at Provins and the prolonged absence of the lieutenant of police who "liked his pleasure too much." Another decried their indolence and their apathy toward their duties: "I talked [about the situation] several times to these officers who told me that things were going quite smartly... [a] reply which made me laugh." At Auneau, reported still

---

65 On the physiocratic attitude, see: Mirabeau, *La Philosophie rurale, ou économie générale et politique de l'agriculture* (Amsterdam, 1763), II, 113, 246; "Suite de l'explication de plusieurs défauts de la police actuelle des grains en Angleterre...," *Gazette du commerce, de l'agriculture, et des finances* (25 April 1767), 320; *Journal économique* (June 1768), 261 and (April 1769), 177; Roubaud, *Représentations aux magistrats* (London, 1769), 66; Baudeau, *Avis au peuple sur son premier besoin* (Paris, 1768), 158; Condorcet, *Le Monopole et le monopoleur* in *Collection des principaux économistes*, ed. by E. Daire and G. de Molinari (Osnabruck, 1966; orig. 1847), XIV, 465; *Ephémérides du citoyen*, (1769), I 62.

another correspondent of the Lieutenant General of Paris, the police was "very badly observed" in large measure because the fiscal procurator was "very inattentive." "The officers charged with the police in these markets [around the capital] could, if they so wished, prevent the augmentation of the price of grain as we do at Paris," wrote the commissaire Duplessis, a colleague of Delamare; "a bit of vigor or of good will on their part would be necessary, that is what they lack." In 1740 the Paris police received similar complaints about the conduct of the royal procurators at Dourdan, St. Arnoult, Rambouillet, and Auneau. Towards the end of the fifties Poussot, the inspector of police assigned to the Halles, urged that the intendant of Paris be asked to review meticulously the behavior of the local officials responsible for the grain police. "It is sure," he maintained, "that the majority fail in their duty and in the fervor which they must have...."[66]

Even those high-placed officials who were generally well-disposed towards grass-roots administrators scorned their ignorance. One royal procurator, for example, whose father and grandfather had also been *substituts* at Joigny, submitted a series of earnest memoirs recommending reform in the system of tax collection and the administration of justice as well as the suppression of useless offices. Commenting on the projects and their author, the secretary of the Paris Procurator General noted that he was a person "who might have zeal, but who has neither logic nor expression; he knows neither how to write nor how to think; the whole thing is not worth the trouble of reading."[67]

On balance, it was less the "lack of enlightenment" of the local officials than their devotion to material "self-interest" that troubled their Parisian critics.[68] Throughout the seventeenth and eighteenth centuries local authorities were repeatedly accused, by unjaundiced witnesses as well as by their professional adversaries, of engaging in surreptitious and illicit grain trading, and manipulating police regulations in order to further their personal ventures. Included in this indictment were not only the officials formally charged with police responsibilities, but a

---

66 Lobinod to PG, 22 Aug. 1725, BN, Coll. Joly 1117, fols. 110–11; Bourlon to LG, 13 Dec. 1725, Arsenal, mss. Bastille 10271; Marchais to LG, 14 Dec. 1725, mss. Bastille 10271; Duplessis to PG, 5 June 1726, BN, Coll. Joly 1118, fols. 155–56; (?) to Marville, 23 Sept. 1740, mss. Bastille 10027; 29 March, 7 April 1760, mss. Bastille 10141; Foucaud, "Mémoire concernant les abus … dans le commerce du bled" (July–August 1725), BN, Coll. Joly 1117, fols. 236–37.

67 BN, mss. fr. 8128, fols. 135, 158.

68 Foucaud to PG, 18 Oct. 1740, BN, Coll. Joly 1121, fols. 265–66.

multitude of other officials, many of whom had family, political, and business connections with them: officers of the *minages* (grain-measuring stations), measurers at the markets, collectors of royal, ecclesiastical and seignorial impositions, clerks and lawyers attached to the courts.

Although many of them were entangled in everyday grain commerce, the officials aroused the greatest resentment for speculating in time of dearth. In 1630 the extraordinary General Assembly of Police learned that "officiers" in the countryside were hoarding and dealing in grain. In the early 1660's evidence reached Paris that officials at Châlons-sur-Marne, Vitry-le-françois, Soissons, and Coulommiers were associated with grain merchants or personally involved in the traffic. In 1693–94 Colmet, receiver of the domain at Bray and a commissioner for the powerful Paris grain dealer Jean Roger, bought, sold, and stored grain with the help of his wife, collector of tolls at the local bridge, who was well placed to follow the movement of grain to and from market. Several years later, the Parisian Lieutenant General of Police d'Argenson denounced two receivers of the *taille* at Châteaudun and several municipal officials at Etampes for regrating, that is, buying and reselling illegally. "Grain is in the possession of those who govern," he lamented, "and their interest will always predominate." Delamare in 1709 urged the Paris police agents on mission in the countryside to pay special attention to the activities of local authorities who "quite commonly undertake a sort of grain commerce." Among those he accused were the president of the election of Rozoy, the fiscal procurator of Coulommiers, and the president of the presidial at Melun.[69]

Charles Foucaud, an itinerant agent who collected intelligence in the supply zone for the Paris police, found numerous examples of regrating and engrossing by local authorities between the mid-twenties and early forties. "All the justice of the place, right up to the Lieutenant-General," reported a commander of the *maréchaussée* [rural constabulary] in reference to Rozoy-en-Brie, "is mixed up in regrating." "Almost all the officers" in the Vitry area, a *substitut* claimed, "do this commerce secretly, buying whole granaries." In 1748 a grain merchant formally filed a complaint with the Châtelet, the Parisian criminal, civil, and police

---

69 BN, mss. fr. 21641, fol. 130; Bondois, "Disette de 1662," *Revue d'histoire économique et sociale*, XII (1924), 85; Usher, *Grain Trade*, 77, 306; La Reynie to Delamare (?), 15 July 1694, BN, mss. fr. 21642, fols. 309–10; Palez to LG, 9 Oct. 1698, BN, mss. fr. 21643, fols. 385–86; St.-Germain, *Vie quotidienne*, 202; BN, mss. fr. 21646, fols. 78, 238–61; Delamare, *Traité*, II, 925; BN, mss. fr. 21645, fols. 88, 210, 258, 423.

court, against the fiscal procurator of Rambouillet for illicit speculations. The Procurator General Joly de Fleury marveled at the story of
the officer of the *poids le roy* [measuring station] at Vitry who traded
extensively in grain as well as hemp, wool, candles, *mercerie*, and *épic-
erie*. The physiocrats reviled the local police for their venality as well
as their stupidity, but one of their own, Letrosne, was apparently both
an officer of municipal police at Orléans and a grain speculator.[70] A
correspondent of the intendant of Languedoc complained that the
city fathers of Toulouse "steeped their hands in the iniquities and
maneuvers" of the grain dealers. Themselves proprietors or *fermiers* in many instances, the local authorities in Brittany and Picardy
commonly entered the grain trade, in their own names and through
intermediaries.

For many years one Sieur Bedel served the busy market of Pont
Sainte-Maxence as royal procurator and juror-grain measurer while
simultaneously engaging in grain traffic and acting as broker for flour
and grain dealers. In 1774 the grain trader Gayard accused Bedel
of masterminding an "odious maneuver" aimed partly against him.
Gayard's plaintive account of his inability to win redress underscores
the enormous influence exercised by local merchant-police:

> that [Bedel] being royal procurator at the seat where the litigation took place, he was
> supposed to take charge of and enforce the police on the fact of grain, and that far
> from demanding respect for the laws so wisely established, he was on the contrary the
> first law-breaker, misleading the judge and the parties in whose name he wished to
> force the delivery of the grain… in order to appropriate for himself the price without
> having furnished the value.[71]

---

70 Foucaud, "Récapitulation," ca. July 1725, BN, Coll. Joly 1117, fol. 231; Marchais to LG, 21
    June 1726, Arsenal, mss. Bastille 10273; Domballe to PG, 25 Oct. 1725, BN, Coll. Joly 1116,
    fol. 280; Marchais to LG, 14 Dec. 1725, mss. Bastille 10271; AN, Y 11235 (18 Oct. 1748);
    Joly de Fleury to Lecler du Brillet, 24 Oct. 1749, BN, mss. fr. 21632, fol. 211; C. Bloch,
    "Le Commerce des grains dans la généralité d'Orléans (1768)," *Études sur l'histoire économique
    de la France* (Paris, 1900), 35. For other examples, see: Foucaud to LG (?), 17 Nov. 1739,
    mss. Bastille 10277; Anon, to Marville, 23 Sept. 1740, mss. Bastille 10027; Missonnet to PG,
    12 June 1752, BN, Coll. Joly 1112, fol. 93; mss. Bastille 10141 (10 March 1760); De Vandour
    to St.-Priest, 21 April 1773, C. 2914, A.D. Hér.; IN. of Brittany to Terray, ca. May 1774,
    C. 1653, A.D. l-et-V.; reply of IN. to *enquête*, Oct. 1773, C. 86, A.D. Somme.
71 Archives Seine-Paris, 23 June 1774, D4B⁶ 52–3196. On illicit traffic by public officials, see
    also Madame d'Epinay to abbé Galiani, 20 Jan. 1771 in F. Nicolini, ed., *La Signora d'Epinay e
    l'abate Galiani, Lettere inedite* (Bari, 1929); Egret, *Parlement de Dauphiné*, I, 189; *Révolutions de Paris*,
    no. 3 (26 July–1 Aug. 1789), 41; Robert Forster, *The Nobility of Toulouse in the Eighteenth Century:
    A Social and Economic Study* (Baltimore, 1960), 75.

The alleged cupidity of local officials manifested itself in still another way. The grain trade regulations required the Paris bakers, unlike the merchants, to conduct all their grain-buying exclusively at the markets and to do the purchasing themselves, not through agents. The same rules strictly prohibited the millers from engaging in grain trade and the mealmen from selling their flour off the markets. The aim of these controls was to prevent a confusion of function among the principals of the provisioning trade and the bread industry, to enable the police to keep track of supplies and suppliers, and to force a large segment of the traffic onto the public market, especially the Paris Halles, which the police believed to be declining in importance toward the middle of the century. In order to enforce these controls, the Paris police required the bakers to procure an attestation from one of the officials at the market where they purchased their grain indicating the amount purchased and the date of the transaction. As part of the mandatory declaration which they had to make upon bringing their merchandise into the capital, the bakers, or the millers who converted the grain for them, or their drivers, had to present the certificate for examination. The bakers, millers, and flour dealers all found the restrictions on their freedom extremely irksome. The bakers relished the liberty to scour the countryside for the best buy and the best quality or to spare themselves the travail of purchasing and transporting by delegating the task to millers. The millers enhanced their chances in the competition for baker clients by agreeing to purchase the grain—which in effect made them flour merchants—and the flour traders wanted to be able to prepare flour on speculation and deliver it directly to the bakers' shops without bothering to stop at the market.

With the collusion of the local officials who, for a price, supplied fraudulent or blank certificates covering fictitious sales in the names of real or imaginary bakers, the bakers, millers, and flour dealers were able to evade the regulations. In November 1749, for example, two Paris grain measurers, part of a corps of sometime venal officers who exercised important police functions on the markets, ports, streets, and on the periphery of the city, challenged a baker transporting 16 sacks of unbolted flour to show the certificate authenticating the purchase of the flour or of the wheat from which the flour was made. The baker, Bontems, from the faubourg St. Antoine, produced a certificate from Meaux which the measurers denounced as "fraudulent" because the information concerning date and amount appeared in fresh ink and in a hand different from the one which signed and filled in the other formalities.

The certificate, they charged, was issued in blank and "not for purchase made upon the market."[72]

In another incident several years later the measurers stopped
the driver of the flour dealer Sorel, who was carting ten sacks of
bolted flour to the widow Massy, mistress baker in the Marais.
The certificate displayed by the driver, bearing the imprint of the
Versailles *poids le roy* and the signature of Girard, police clerk, was
blank. Seizing the flour, the measurers denounced "three formal
violations of the regulations of police": the first committed by
Sorel, who sold flour without exposing it on the market; the second by the widow Massy, for buying off the market; "the third
and the most considerable" by the official Girard, who "delivers
certificates in blank for money, [certificates] that the millers and
flour merchants fill out in the name of such-and-such a baker...
that occasions a clandestine commerce, which is very prejudicial
to the provisioning of the city of Paris, and contemptuous of all
the ordinances." The Pont Sainte-Maxence market (where Sieur
Bedel served) had a reputation for providing spurious certificates.
In the early thirties, the Paris police lieutenant Hérault fined its
royal procurator 1,500 *livres*, an enormous sum, for issuing such
documents, and thirty years later, Poussot charged that three-
quarters of all certificates from Pont were "false."[73]

A case that occurred in 1761 illustrates the extent to which the
distribution of fraudulent papers and the illicit trading practices of
bakers had become the "usage." Confronted by two measurers at
7 a.m. at the barrier of Chaillot, the baker Leduc, driving a wagon
with 17 *septiers* of wheat, confessed that he had no certificate. Cheerfully, without any sense of self-incrimination, Leduc recounted that
after buying the grain at a farm, he stopped at the nearby Rambouillet market to pick up the necessary documents. The officers there,
however, refused to issue him papers. Their rigidity—the measurers
called it probity—surprised him, for in the past, he said,

> Every time that he had purchased grain in the farms either on the Rambouillet side or
> on the Dammartin side [respectively southwest and northeast of Paris] and elsewhere,
> he had been in the habit of taking certificates from the nearest market.[74]

72 AN, Y 9622 (28 Nov. 1749).
73 AN, Y 11241 (17 Aug. 1754) and Y 9539 (6, 17 May 1758); Arsenal, mss. Bastille 10141
    (10 March 1760 and 8 April 1761).
74 AN, Y 9539 (11 Sept. 1761).

Generally the Paris police were the market modernizers and the local officers the defenders of antiquated forms of market organization. In these instances, albeit for wholly unworthy motives, the local police of the hinterland were on the side of flexibility and change.

Much of the evidence presented here for local police corruption and incompetence is tendentious and heavily biased in favor of a single region. Yet it seems clear that a considerable number of officials at one time or another betrayed their public trust and broke the laws by engaging in a trade from which they were explicitly banned and by using their police authority to personal advantage. Perhaps a larger number of local officials, more circumspect or less brazen, were guilty of what our public servants fastidiously call a conflict of interest. While the central government "destituted" and punished culpable officials now and then, it never found a systematic method for policing and purging the local police. Local administration was too atomized and too inaccessible to subject to thorough reform. Moreover, in a system built upon privilege, favor, venality, fiscality, hereditary succession, nepotism, "usage," and neo-feudal fidelities, and in which the idea of bureaucracy hardly existed and the boundaries separating public and private enterprise remained obscure, corruption was a difficult thing to define and locate. Then, as now, it was a phenomenon of degree and circumstance. Often it was tolerated where it did not do great damage. Issuing false documents, despite the self-serving hyperbole of the Paris police, was unlikely either to jeopardize the provisioning of the capital or enable these white collar (or black-robed) brigands to lead an opulent existence. For the most part, the local officials who practiced grain speculation were petty nuisances, not robber-barons in the mold of a Fouquet.

Then again, such activities might have had a more subtle and profound impact on public opinion than on public administration. They prepared certain portions of the public to lend credence to grave suspicions that circulated, especially in times of dearth, implicating the highest officials in the kingdom in conspiracies to reap huge profits by manipulating the supply of grain. These charges found their most shocking expression in the so-called *pacte de famine*, a plot denounced publicly for the first time in the late sixties, but they appeared in various forms throughout the eighteenth century, commanding widespread belief and heaping discredit upon the leading figures of the central government. Viewed upon the background of the local experience, which taught many people to expect to find local authorities involved in secret grain trafficking, it is easier to understand the willingness of Frenchmen to believe that more highly placed officials, with far greater appetites and powers, could launch massive, illicit speculations on grain. The idea that government could have some sinister connection with the provisioning trade had solid local roots.

Nor can the local police be fairly assessed without considering the extremely difficult conditions under which they operated. The confusion of the system afforded them real advantages but, as I suggested, it victimized them as well. Often they had no clear idea of where they fit, of how they *should* function, and to whom they should or should not defer. If they were insular, unsophisticated, or excessively wedded to the past, frequently it was because they were not kept abreast of changes in law, procedures, and policies—the fruit of the neglect and contempt of their superiors as well as of systemically poor communications. Although it is impossible to say how often such gaps occurred, the case of Lanson, fiscal procurator of a small market-town near Chartres, graphically illustrates the danger of isolating and abandoning the local forces of order. "In the two years that I have been fiscal procurator at Auneau," he wrote, "I have neither seen nor received any old or new regulations on the matter of grain." He learned *"from common rumor"* that it was forbidden for grain to be sold by sample. After consultation with the judge at Auneau, Lanson wrote his own ordinance prohibiting such transactions on pain of a hundred *livres* fine and requiring all grain to be exposed for sale in sacks on the open market. He worried, however, about the wisdom and legitimacy of his initiative and about how to handle such situations in the future. His letter to the Procurator General Joly de Fleury is a pathetic and revealing plea:

> As I have no Regulations in my hands at all, I very humbly implore Your Grandeur to please address them to me [as soon as possible]… if it pleases Your Grandeur, when there will be new Edicts, *Arrêts* or Regulations on the matter of the police, have a copy sent to me ....[75]

If the local police were demoralized and easy prey to lassitude or venal temptation, it was partly because their superiors ignored their hunger for recognition and recompense for service rendered. Demonchu, procurator at Compiègne, must have seemed ludicrous with his

---

75 Lanson to PG, 9 Dec. 1738, BN, Coll. Joly 1119, fols. 53–54. Cf., on the communications gap, Odile to PG, 29 Nov. 1738, *ibid.*, 108–109; Morin at Nogent-le-Rotrou to IN. of Alençon, 13 Oct. 1773 and Soalhat of Sées to same, 20 Oct. 1773, C. 89, A.D. Orne.

puffed-up sense of importance ("I am a magistrate," he emphasized), his pompous manner ("It is in dispensing justice exactly and filling his function with distinction that he [a procurator] must pay his court [*faire sa cour*]; it is in his bureau and on the tribune that one must find him diligent, not in the antichambres of the great."), and his reformist ardor ("It is indecent that justice is sold for the price of money."). But Demonchu, doubtless like many other local officials with pride and a certain dose of ambition, believed that he served the public and the government well and that he deserved something more than the 117 *livres* he earned in *gages* ("all my work is free"), most of which was devoured by the *dixième, capitation,* and *paulette.* To "reanimate the courage" of the police, he urged—in vain—that the local magistrates be salaried and that a special "order," akin to the honors accorded military achievement, be created to pay homage to outstanding officials.[76]

---

76 BN, mss. fr. 8128.

Chapter II

THE REGULATIONS
AND THE REGULATORS

The police were structurally fragmented and often divided by interest and ambition, but they shared a number of basic ideas about the provisioning question. This chapter deals with the police view of the grain trade and the ways in which the police translated their attitudes into action. It is the story of persistence rather than change, of an overwhelming sense of continuity informed by a belief that things— at least subsistence things—are at bottom always the same. The police clung to the old ways because they were proven ways. Yet it would be a mistake, I argue, to infer from the immobility and the tone of police regulations that the police operated in a mindless, mechanical, and timeless fashion. On the other hand, there were limits to flexibility and adaptability. The police were wholly unprepared for the radical innovations that they had to face in the 1760's when the government turned against the multisecular tradition of regulation.

I

The rules developed to govern the grain trade were based upon the tenet that grain was essentially *unlike* any other commodity commonly exchanged and thus must be treated differently. As an item of "first necessity" and ultimately a matter of life or death for millions of consumers, grain could not be legitimately compared with goods whose exchange merely complemented subsistence or enhanced pleasure. As a rule, in other sorts of commerce, shortage, tardiness, deception in transaction, or other defects and vices caused inconvenience only to individuals and never in lethal doses. In the grain trade, however, "the least error almost always affects the public," threatening the entire community at its most vulnerable point.

Given its special nature, those who undertook to deal in grain, the police believed, assumed solemn responsibilities toward society.[1]

Since society depended entirely on grain commerce for its subsistence in ordinary times, the police viewed the trade as a kind of public service. They made demands and imposed restrictions upon grain traders that other merchants escaped. The grain merchant had obligations to the public that would sometimes require him to resist the promptings of his self-interest, which the police recognized as his chief source of motivation. He had to be satisfied with a "just and legitimate gain" based upon his investment, his labor, and the energy with which he served the public rather than on the cunning with which he manipulated supply and demand factors. There was no room in the grain trade for dealers "corrupted by *amour-propre* and immoderate cupidity for a sordid profit." Certain customs and laws in the Old Regime violated property rights as defined by the absolutist standards whose consecration the Revolution first began. Implicit in the police conception of the grain trade was the notion that the grain held by a merchant (or cultivator) was not perfectly and exclusively his own to dispose of as he saw fit. As the primary source of subsistence, grain was a "common good" upon which society had certain claims. The police, as guardians of the commonwealth, stood ready to enforce those claims according to the needs, not of social justice (though there are hints that some police officials thought of it in this way), but of social tranquility.[2]

The grain merchants gave the police little reason to believe that they would honor those claims voluntarily and the police made little effort to conceal their distrust of the merchants. In part the police attitude reflected the low esteem in which commerce was generally held. Commerce never overcame the stigma attached to it by moralists and theologians. "To fornicate," the canon law proclaims, "is always forbidden to anyone, but to trade is sometimes allowed and sometimes not." The indulgence which certain medieval doctors and their followers accorded trade did little to modify the deeply-rooted and widely-held idea that there was something odious about the trader. The merchant remained the prototype of the liar who menaced the

---

1 Delamare, *Traité*, II, 619, 796.

2 *Ibid.*, II, 775; Gazier, ed., "La Police de Paris en 1770," 117; La Reynie to CG, 13 July 1695 in *Correspondance des contrôleurs-généraux*, ed. by Boislisle, I, 397. Cf. E. F. Heckscher, *Mercantilism* (London, 1935), II, 271–74; Emile Coornaert, *Les Corporations en France avant 1789* (Paris, 1941), 143.

well-being and the bonds of solidarity of society. In the popular religious literature, the merchant always stood last in the order of salvation, if indeed there was to be a place for him at all. The classics taught the kingdom's future elite that Mercury, god of merchants, was also god of thieves.[3]

Although mercantilist doctrine portrayed the merchant as a benefactor of the state, most Frenchmen continued to see commerce as a dishonorable profession well into the eighteenth century. In his *English Letters*, Voltaire deplored the "disdain" which commerce aroused in France, inhibiting social and economic progress. The abbé Coyer encountered the same attitude in his efforts to induce the nobility to undertake certain kinds of commerce. The principles upon which French society was stratified invited the merchant to despise himself and produced a constant hemorrhage of successful men out of business and into professions or estates, which brought dignity.[4]

The reputation of the grain merchants, whose commerce concerned the public more than any other, was particularly execrable (a distinction they shared with mealmen and millers, as Daudet's tales evocatively suggest). The merchants and their supporters blamed the police for creating the stereotype of the grain-trader-criminal in their ordinances and sentences and for teaching the people to regard merchants as their born enemies. The police rejoined that the traders' image was the fruit of their own perfidy and that the people needed no lessons from the authorities in perceiving villainy in their midst.[5]

The police view of the merchants was deeply ambivalent. On the one hand, provisioning was fundamentally a commercial operation and traders were absolutely necessary in order to fulfill this public

---

3 R. de Roover, "The Scholastic Attitude toward Trade and Entrepreneurship," *Explorations in Entrepreneurial History*, n.s., I (Fall 1963), 76; Roover, "Scholastic Economics: Survival and Lasting Influence from the 16th Century to Adam Smith," *Quarterly Journal of Economics*, LXIX (1955), 179–80; G. Bollème, "Littérature populaire et littérature de colportage au 18e siècle," in F. Furet, ed., *Livre et société dans la France du 18e siècle* (Paris, 1965), I, 78–79. Cf. Mandrou, *Histoire de la France aux 17e et 18e siècles*, 163; Le Goff, *Occident médiéval*, 437; R. Cobb, *Les Armées révolutionnaires*, I, 188–189.

4 Voltaire, *Lettres philosophiques* in *Œuvres complètes*, ed. by Moland (Paris, 1877–1885), XXII, 110–111; G.-F. Coyer, *La Noblesse commerçante* (London, 1756).

5 See, for example, Prior-consuls of St. Malo, Mémoire, Feb. 1762, C. 3911, A.D. I-et-V. and Letter of the Grenoble Parl. to the king, 26 April 1769, B. 2314, fol. 111, A.D. Isère. For the physiocratic portrayal of the police, see chapter one above and especially chapters nine and ten below. Cf. the speech of Creuzé-Latouche, 8 Dec. 1792, *Archives parlementaires*, LIV, 679 and J.-B. Biot, *Lettres sur l'approvisionnement de Paris et sur le commerce des grains* (Paris, 1835), 58–59.

mission. On the other hand, the police could not help themselves from thinking that this traffic, like usury, tended to recruit men of contemptible character who harbored evil designs. For it was in the nature of commerce to speculate and who but vicious men would speculate on the subsistence of their fellow-citizens? The international *négociant* dealing in precious metals or other goods was a man without a country, but the grain trader was a man without a conscience. Grain merchants, as a sixteenth-century statute noted, were often motivated only by "rapacity and avarice, having neither God, charity or salvation before their eyes...." Their aim was "to profit from public misfortune" and they did not hesitate to promote such misfortune by maneuvers which fomented "panic terror amongst the people." They were "justly suspect" because they had "no views other than their [own] interests."[6]

The salient trait of the evil grain dealer was his "avidity." A local police official writing in 1725 explained what he meant by this stricture. Instead of selling, the merchants buy grain and hide it away in order to drive the price up. They offer it for sale "only when they wish" and often they sell it to men who are their own agents in order to keep it from the people. These merchants, "real rogues," were the "cause of the *cherté*" in the provisioning crown (as the hinterland was called) around the capital.

Throughout the Old Regime, the police and the people frequently blamed shortages and outbreaks of high prices on merchants.[7] Commissaire Delamare's analysis of the origins of the subsistence crisis of 1692–93 captures the themes of the scenario. In the spring of 1692 a blight ruined half of the prospective harvest. The situation did not alarm the authorities, for a half year's crop combined with ample stocks of old grain appeared to cover needs. "But," reported Delamare,

---

6 Cited by Molinari, article "Céréales," in Charles Coquelin and Guillaumin, *Dictionnaire de l'économie politique* (Paris, 1873) I, 303.

7 Reneaume, "Sur la manière de conserver les grains," 76; Lepoupet to LG of Police, 30 Oct. 1725, Arsenal, mss. Bastille 10271; "Mémoire" (1725), mss. Bastille 10270, fol. 374; BN, mss. fr. 21647, fol. 9; Daguesseau to CG, 24 Feb. 1709, *Correspondance des contrôleurs-généraux*, ed. by Boislisle, III, 102; Narbonne, *Journal*, 460; La Reynie to Delamare, 24 July 1693, BN, mss. fr. 21639, fol. 161; Louis Thuillat, *Gabriel Nicolas de la Reynie, premier Lieutenant Général de Police de Paris* (Limoges, 1930), 84–111; St.-Germain, *La Reynie*, 270; Lemarchand, "Troubles," *Annales historiques de la révolution française*, 35 (Oct.–Dec. 1963), 409; Trennin to PG, 26 Oct. 1768, BN, Coll. Joly 1142, fol. 154; Dépêches, 31 May 1770, AN, O¹* 446, fol. 124. For a striking expression of police suspicion of grain merchants, conditioned of course by the terrible circumstances of the hour, see the acts of the *Chambre des Blés* of 1709, AN, X²ᵇ 1090.

since only a pretext is necessary to determine evil-intentioned Merchants, always avid
for gain, to exaggerate matters pertaining to a dearth, they did not fail to profit from
this one; they were immediately observed resuming their ordinary style and putting
into use again all their bad practices for making the price of grain go up; associations,
dashes into the Provinces, false rumors spread about, monopolies through purchases
of all the grain, overbidding in the markets, down payments on grain still uncut or in
the barns and granaries, retention in the magazines; thus the whole commerce was
reduced to a certain number among them who made themselves its master.[8]

The most serious and damaging charge leveled against the merchants
was that they engaged in monopolistic activities, a vague and sweeping
indictment derived from Roman, canonical, and patristic sources and
richly embroidered in the fabric of French jurisprudence from earliest
times. One of the major aims of the corporate structure of the Old
Regime and one of the chief justifications for its labyrinthine regulations was the prevention of monopoly (though this sometimes entailed
the creation of official monopolies in the sense that we understand the
word). Monopolies did not occur exclusively in grain; the police often
denounced their presence in the commerce of wine, wood, and other
goods. But because it involved the subsistence of the people, monopoly
in grain preceded the other kinds in importance.[9]

Instinctively, the police and the public linked the onset of dearth
and suffering with the existence of monopolies. In hard times, the
monopolist was ubiquitous. The revolutionaries excoriated the *monopo-
leurs* in the same breath with the most unregenerate *malveillans* and the
term survived as a general description and epithet in its loose, protean
sense well into the nineteenth century, especially in the socialist vocabulary of exploitation. Throughout the Old Regime the police tirelessly hunted monopolists. Mercier, who considered them "assassins,"
arranged to ban them from his utopia. Linguet proposed erecting gal-
lows in every major marketplace to punish and deter them. Monopoly
was an abomination because it was a social crime; blindly and indifferently, it struck down thousands of innocent people. The authorities never defined the term with precision because the phenomenon

---

8 Delamare, *Traité*, II, 866. Cf. *Ibid.*, 855, 879.
9 Roover, "Monopoly Theory Prior to Adam Smith: A Revision," *Quarterly Journal of Economics*,
   LXV (Nov. 1951), 492–524; John W. Baldwin, "The Medieval Theories of the Just Price,"
   Transactions of the American Philosophical Society, XLIX, part 4 (1959), 1–92; Roman Piotrowski,
   Cartels and Trusts, Their Origin and Historical Development from the Economic and Legal Aspects
   (London, 1933), 281–82; Coornaert, *Corporations*, 249; AN, H 2192, fol. 50; BN, mss. fr.
   11356, fol. 345. See also A. de Tarde, *L'Idée du juste prix* (Paris, 1907).

could take very different forms in different circumstances. "Monopoly" did not so much describe the *modus operandi* of a crime as it did its effect. Practices deemed monopolistic in a period of stress might conceivably pass for reasonable mercantile operations in a more tranquil moment. An action was not intrinsically monopolistic; it became monopolistic to the extent that it menaced the public interest or caused inconvenience and woe.[10]

Virtually any "bad maneuver" qualified as a monopoly. Charlemagne denounced as monopolists "those who by tricks, surprises, and other unjust means amass goods with the aim of a shameful gain." In 1660 the Paris Parlement censured for "monopoly" several merchants who scoured the countryside buying at any price and withheld grain from the market in secret hoards. The first Parisian Police Lieutenant, La Reynie, used the term to account for any untoward incident in the markets. For example, when the price of grain in the supply zone "suddenly increased substantially *without any reason*" in 1693 he blamed a handful of monopolists whose machinations were hardly original: they constituted hoards, spread "false rumors," uttered "seditious discourses," and endeavored in other ways to drive up prices. Eighty years later the official sense of monopoly had not changed: it characterized an insolent, almost treasonous posture, a willful disregard of the law and the state of affairs, and a series of maneuvers that tended to make grain scarce, inflate prices, and propagate fear. In these instances the "monopolies" were "exercised" by *laboureurs* and *fermiers* in the markets of Gonesse and Choisy, near Paris, and in Pontrieux in Brittany.[11]

---

10 AN, H * 1874, fol. 17 (29 Aug. 1770); *Journal politique* (Sept. 1770), first quinzaine, 57; *Mercure historique et politique*, 81 (July 1726), 104; BN, mss. fr. 21642, fols. 1ff.; Madame d'Epinay to Galiani, 29 Oct. 1770 in *Lettres de l'abbé Galiani à Madame d'Epinay*, ed. by Eugène Asse (Paris, 1882), I, 162–63; Prudhomme, *Révolutions de Paris*, #3 (26 July 1789), 41; Lettres patentes, 12 Nov. 1768, BN, mss. fr. 6680, fol. 186; Cobb, *Armées révolutionnaires*, II, 339; Jean Dubois, *Le Vocabulaire politique et social en France de 1869 à 1872* (Paris, 1962); Linguet, *Réponse aux docteurs modernes* (1771) cited by G. Weulersse, *La Physiocratie à la fin du règne de Louis XV*, 158; L.-S. Mercier, *Tableau de Paris*, III, 198 and *L'An 2440, rêve s'il en fût jamais*, 145; Necker, *De L'Administration des finances en France* (n.p., 1784), III, 226–230; L.-J. Bourdon-Desplanches, *Lettres à l'auteur des observations sur le commerce des grains* (Amsterdam, 1775), 25–26; C.E.D. Roonptsy (R.-A. de Pellisery), *Le Caffé politique d'Amsterdam* (Amsterdam, 1776), II, 2–3, 11.

11 *Mercure Suisse* (Sept. 1740), 74–75; BN, mss. fr. 14295, fol. 12; BN, mss. fr. 21641, fol. 177; La Reynie to Delamare, 28 July 1693, BN, mss. fr. 21642, fol. 190; ordonnance, 27 July 1694, BN, mss. fr. 21643, fols. 13–14, 28–29; Dépêches, to CG, 26 June 1776, AN, O¹ 416; SD to IN. of Brittany, 17 April 1789, C. 1715, A.D. I-et-V.

In many cases monopoly implied conspiracy: the premeditated design of a number of collaborators. But monopolies were often the work of individuals reacting to market conditions. Monopoly did not necessarily connote bigness of enterprise or breadth of offense; two brothers, humble *laboureurs*, committed monopoly simply by ceasing their normal monthly deliveries to the Paris Halles, and three bakers who independently sold their bread at an "exorbitant price" were judged culpable of "a marked monopoly, prejudicial to the citizens." Of course the larger the monopoly, the more dreadful it was likely to be. Visions of behemoth grain monopolies furtively run by bankers like Samuel Bernard or Isaac Thellusson or by "societies" like the Indies Company tormented the collective consciousness throughout the eighteenth century. Monopoly associated with shortage was not merely a crime; it was a general explanation for disaster on a scale which all men could seize. By denouncing monopoly Frenchmen proclaimed the innocence of nature and the guilt of men: dearth "was not so much caused by lack of grain as by the nasty maneuvers of certain monopolists."[12]

In almost every monopoly arraignment the police accused the merchant(s) of "illicitly," "illegitimately," or "criminally" forcing prices up.[13] Again, it is worth noting that the merchant was not condemned for his trading practices per se; in other conditions the same techniques might elicit no reprobation. What made them illicit and dangerous was the effect they had on the price structure at a given moment. When merchants drove the price above a certain level, which varied in time and space and depended upon such factors as the "ordinary" price and wage scale, the elasticity of demand, and the likelihood of harvest recovery, they wronged the whole society. Implicit in the notion of monopoly and stemming from the same moralistic tradition was the idea of a just price. Lieutenants general of police, commissaires, inspectors, grain measurers, and local officials repeatedly invoked the "just price," which they construed as their obligation to assure. Their conception was a relativistic and empirical one that sprung from no

---

12 Sentence, 28 June 1727, BN, mss. fr. 21633, fols. 283–84; Sentence, 20 Aug. 1728, BN, mss. fr. 21640, fol. 158. For examples of the accusations implicating Bernard and the Indies Company, see: "Histoire de ce qui s'est passé au sujet des bleds en 1725," Arsenal, mss. 3308; Gazetins, 15 Nov. 1725, Arsenal, mss. Bastille 10155, fol. 126; Gazetins, 23 March 1726, mss. Bastille 10156, fol. 121; Gazetins, 29–30 Sept. 1741, mss. Bastille 10167, fol. 333.

13 *Mercure Suisse* (Sept. 1740), 75–76; extrait des registres du Parl. de Dauphiné, 12 July 1768 in *Mercure historique* (Sept. 1768), 288–89.

coherent theory of social or commutative justice. The just price was a price which would neither "disgust" merchants nor "wound" consumers. It was predicated upon an ideal of moderation, which tended to vary with the circumstances. A price was thought just when merchants settled for a moderate profit and the bulk of the people, who lived in a state of chronic misery, did not suffer immoderately, that is to say, more than they did usually. In untroubled moments, the just price was simply the current price (as the theologians had recommended), fixed by common estimation rather than imposed by merchant maneuvers or governmental fiat.[14]

In a dearth, which grotesquely distorted standards of moderation, the just price became much more difficult to define. For most police officials, it no longer bore any relation to the current price, which was warped by the effects of monopoly, panic, or inclement weather. For many authorities, the just price now became, the price of social stability, the price that would still be accessible to the majority of the population. In the midst of a crisis, few administrators believed that the just price could be attained without some form of governmental intervention. In some parts of the kingdom, this action took the form of price "taxation" or fixation by local officials. In the Paris area, more commonly, it involved all-azimuth war against the monopolies by means of closer surveillance, intimidation and harassment, and competitive buying and selling by governmental suppliers.

Critics of police ideology and practice disputed the conventional representation of monopoly. Upon examination, they argued, monopoly

---

14 On the theory of the just price, see: Baldwin, "The Medieval Theories," 7–78; Roover, "Scholastic Economics," *Quarterly Journal of Economics*, LXIX (1955), 168–69; Roover, "Monopoly Theory," *Quarterly Journal of Economics*, LXV (1951), 492ff.; Roover, "The Concept of the Just Price: Theory and Economic Politics," *Journal of Economic History*, XVIII (Dec. 1958), 418–34; E.A. J. Johnson, "Just Price in an Unjust World," *International Journal of Ethics*, XLVIII (Jan. 1928), 165, 169–71; Alfred des Cilleuls, *Le Socialisme municipal à travers les siècles* (Paris, 1905), 38; B. Bailyn, *The New England Merchants in the Seventeenth Century* (New York, 1964), 20–21. For the sense that the notion had in the eighteenth century, see: La Reynie to Delamare, 5 March 1694, BN, mss. fr. 21643; *Journal économique* (Jan. 1754), 98; Missonnet to Joly, 6 May 1754, BN, Coll. Joly 1113, fol. 122; Arsenal, mss. Bastille 10141 (20 Jan. 1760); Gazier, ed., "La Police de Paris en 1770," 117; AN, Y 9474 (24 Aug. 1771); SD of Valenciennes, "Observations sur l'arrêt du conseil d'état du Roy du 14 juillet 1770," C. 6690, A. D. Nord; Diderot, *et al.*, *Encyclopédie*, XIII, 392. Cf. Turgot's view in which the "just price" was always supposed to be the true market price, whether times were troubled or not. In his sense the just price was the natural price, or what the *économistes* called the *bon prix*. See "Lettres sur le commerce des grains," 30 Oct. and 2 Dec. 1770 in *Œuvres*, ed. by Schelle, III, 267, 315–16; Turgot to IN. of Alençon, 16 July 1775, C. 90, A.D. Orne; déclaration du Roi, 5 Feb. 1776, BN, Coll. Joly 1111, fol. 48.

turned out to be a manifestation of popular fear and an outlet of popular frustration rather than an objective reality. Hungry people, remarked one observer, find a strange consolation in blaming their distress on monopolists. Under the stress of shortage, everyone's "first thought is to believe in monopoly," noted the abbé de Véri. Monopoly is a "war cry," commented the *Journal d'Agriculture, du Commerce, des Arts et des Finances*, which people instinctively shriek when put upon by high prices. Herbert, the leading exponent of free grain trade before the physiocrats, likened the belief in monopolies to Charlemagne's exorcism of the evil grain-devouring demons. We ought to be ashamed, he suggested, in an age of Enlightenment, that our anxieties and, far worse, our jurisprudence, still give credence to gothic "prejudices" and spectral "phantoms." Addressing the Convention in 1792, Creuzé-Latouche similarly compared the monopoly preoccupation with "the ancient popular visions of sorcerers and ghosts."[15]

According to their critics, the police found it useful to cultivate the monopoly obsession. It diverted popular hostility away from the government and it gave them added leverage in dealing with recalcitrant merchants. If by monopoly we mean "exclusive sale, the control of which a single party has seized," asked a commentator in the seventies, then how can we accuse a host of independent traders competing against one another of engaging simultaneously in monopoly?[16] The muddled notion of monopoly exasperated the eminent lawyer Target:

> Monopoly! the people see only this monster ... when the government makes purchases, they cry out monopoly; when individuals form magazines, they cry out monopoly; when one preaches an absolute general liberty, a full and entire competition, they reply to you: Oh! My God, monopoly! Apropos exportation, apropos importation, apropos the King's grain, apropos the grain of the subjects, apropos commerce, stagnation, competition, privileges, liberty, slavery, always it is monopoly! If one takes grain to a province which lacks [or] if one lets it languish, the humanity which

---

15 Véri, *Journal*, ed. by J. de Witte, I, 150; *Journal de l'agriculture, du commerce, des arts et des finances* (Sept. 1772), 17; C.J. Herbert, *Essai sur la police générale des grains*, ed. by E. Depitre (Paris, 1910), 4; *Archives Parlementaires*, 8 Dec. 1792, LIV, 682. Cf. "Observations de Dampierre de la Salle (1770), BN, mss. n.a. 22777, fol. 249 and "Deuxième avis des députés du commerce" (1764), BN, mss. fr. 14295, fol. 26. For a similar view, see Tolosan, *Mémoire sur le commerce de la France et de ses colonies* (Paris, 1789), 85.

16 "Observations de Dampierre de la Salle," BN, mss. n.a. 22777, fol. 249.

comes to its aid is a monopoly [and] the indifference which neglects it is a monopoly! Alas! ... let us try to have some clear ideas about the words which we use.[17]

Although the adversaries of the police assailed the common conception of monopoly, they nevertheless agreed that certain kinds of monopoly frequently occurred in the grain trade and were often the true cause of dearth. While they did not define the notion with any more rigor than their opponents—they viewed it from a purely commercial rather than a social perspective and subsumed under the heading monopoly any practice that served to restrain trade in any way—they had no doubts whatsoever about what caused it. Unlike the police, who argued that the tendency toward monopoly was inherent in the "very nature" of the grain trade, these critics maintained that this tendency was inherent in the nature of the controls and regulations that governed the trade. The police not only used the image of monopoly to manipulate the people and the merchants, but they created the very conditions which make monopoly possible. "They engender monopoly," the physiocratic journalist Roubaud charged, "and then they torment themselves in order to wipe it out; and the regime which they use to destroy it is the very same one which produces it." "It is the legislative precautions against monopoly," argued a writer in the *Journal Economique*, "which cause the terrible monopoly which could starve us all."[18]

The critics were not calling the police criminal accomplices of the monopolists, though they pointed out that subaltern officials frequently engaged in rascally grain dealings. Rather, they contended that monopoly was in the nature of the police system because the system was based upon grants of exclusive privilege and special favors and the imposition of arbitrary controls and other servitudes that stifled competition, trammeled exchanges, and violated natural rights. "To constrain the grain trade," as a reviewer in the *Journal de Trévoux* dryly put it, "is to place in the State a source of dearth and of monopoly." It followed, then, that the only sure remedy for monopoly was the dismantling of the entire police apparatus. A "total liberty" of trade featuring "the most free and extensive competition" was the

---

17 G.-J.-B. Target, *Observations sur le commerce des grains, écrites en décembre, 1769* (Amsterdam, 1775), 31–32.

18 N. Baudeau, *Première introduction à la philosophie économique, ou analyse des états policés* (Paris, 1771), 84; Roubaud, *Représentations aux magistrats* (London, and Paris, 1769), 56; letter to the editor, probably by the marquis d'Argenson, *Journal économique* (May 1754), 81.

radical solution recommended by these critics whose drive against the police regime we shall have occasion to deal with again later. "Liberty and monopoly are so contrary," epitomized the *Journal Economique,* "that they cannot exist together."[19]

The police of course took a very different position: monopoly was the fruit of liberty run amuck; unregulated competition crushed small traders and concentrated commerce in the hands of a few; "total" liberty would produce chronic dearth and disorder. Yet their view of liberty was not flatly negative. Long before the great debates on the grain trade in the second half of the eighteenth century, the police were aware of the advantages of the liberal market model. They themselves believed that an unencumbered market system was, at least in principle, the most efficient and economical vehicle for the distribution of supplies. They felt that competition was one of the surest ways to keep prices at a reasonable level. They knew that "liberty was the soul of commerce," the medium most congenial to commercial enterprise. Nor did the architects of controls ever forget that provisioning was a fundamentally commercial operation and that commerce simply could not function without a certain amount of freedom of action.[20]

The problem was fixing the proper dosage. The police never for a moment imagined that "police" and liberty were antithetical notions. The liberty, which they considered tonic and salutary, had serious limitations and necessarily operated in conjunction with rules and restraints. They viewed liberty not as a right derived from nature, but as a concession granted by society on a conditional basis. This liberty was contingent, never absolute—contingent upon the good faith of the merchants, upon local supply conditions, and ultimately upon the pleasure and the sapience of local authorities. From this perspective, the polar opposite of police was not liberty but "license" or "libertinage," words meant to convey moral degeneration and perversion as well as

---

19 *Journal de Trévoux* (April 1754), 804; Condorcet, *Le Monopole et le monopoleur* in *Collection des principaux économistes,* ed. by Daire and Molinari, XIV, 468, 470; *Journal économique* (June 1768), 261; "Mémoire sur l'exportation et l'importation des grains," BN, mss. fr. 14296. See also similar views of Nicolas Baudeau, *Avis au peuple sur son premier besoin* (Amsterdam and Paris, 1768), 130; Roubaud, *Représentations aux magistrats,* 122–23; Condillac, *Le Commerce et le gouvernement* (1776), in *Collection des principaux économistes,* ed. by Daire and Molinari, XIV, 417–20; D'Argenson, *Mémoires et journal inédit du Marquis d'Argenson, Ministre des affaires étrangères sous Louis XV,* ed. by marquis d'Argenson (Paris, 1857–58), V, 36.

20 Delamare, *Traité,* II, 775. Cf. Heckscher, *Mercantilism,* II, 271–74; Coornaert, *Les Corporations,* 143. For eighteenth century uses of the word "liberty," see Ferdinand Brunot, *Histoire de la langue française des origines à 1900* (Paris, 1930), VI, 129.

chaos in trade. Experience taught the police that sooner or later unbridled or excessive liberty gave way to license, which resulted in antisocial crimes such as monopoly. If liberty meant nothing more than the right of an owner to dispose of his property unconditionally as he saw fit, it was inadmissible to the police, for it denied society any convincing guarantee that public needs would be met.[21]

Liberty, police-style, was supposed to be a filter rather than a sieve, but it was no easy matter to set the gauge correctly. The police disagreed among themselves on the optimal doses and the appropriate conditions for application. As much as they worried about license and monopoly, the authorities were also aware that over-police might destroy commerce. In order to assure provisioning, the police endeavored to "excite" and to "contain" the grain trade at the same time, two strategies that were often in flagrant contradiction and always in uneasy tension.[22]

II

To enable and, if necessary, to compel commerce to perform its victualing services, the police relied upon a large body of regulations. They were an amalgam of royal laws, parlementary *arrêts*, local statutes, and lessons discriminately gleaned from the testing ground of past experience ("There occurring nothing new under the sun," wrote Delamare, "... it is primarily in past events that we can draw the rules of prudence and conduct for the present, and for the future."[23]), and

---

21 *Journal économique* (May 1752), 121–27; L. Viala, *La Question des grains*, 29–30.
22 AN, K 908.
23 Delamare, *Traité*, I, préface. Delamare's multi-volume *Traité* was the most important work on and of police in the Old Regime. Foreign princes kept it in their libraries, local officials and jurists based their sentences and codes on it, and Parisian magistrates expressed astonishment when they could not find a piece of information within its thousands of folio pages. The highest administrative and judicial officials in eighteenth century France continually referred to the *Traité* and to the Delamare mss. (much of which is preserved today in the BN) and often consulted his collaborator, Lecler, a lawyer and procurator in the Admiralty Court. See Bondois' useful but unimaginative assessment, "Le Commissaire Nicolas Delamare et le *Traité de la police*," *Revue d'histoire moderne*, X (Sept.–Oct. 1935), 313–51; Musart, *La Réglementation du commerce*, 33–36; Desmaze, *Châtelet*, 198–99. For examples of use in the eighteenth century, see: *Mercure de France* (Jan. 1743), 120; Délibérations, Hôtel de Ville, 22 May 1758, AN, H * 1867, fol. 436; BN, Coll. Joly 2432, fol. 324; *Code Duchesne*, vii; Joly to Lecler, 7 Dec. 1738, BN, mss. fr. 21636, fol. 339; Joly to Lecler, 24 Oct. 1749, BN, mss. fr. 21632, fol. 211; Grimperel note, March 1768, AN, Y 13396; A. Zahorski, "L'État et la

modernized and adapted to meet local needs. The only regulations that can usefully be considered from a national or regional standpoint are those concerned with the movement of grain across provincial and international frontiers. They were also the only ones which were more or less frequently modified by actual changes in the law rather than informal adjustment. Since they were the most visible and the most sweeping in breadth, they gave the French grain police a reputation for desultoriness at the top, accompanying its reputation for both rigidity and capriciousness at the bottom.[24]

As a rule, the export of grain was forbidden on the grounds that it jeopardized the subsistence of the French people. Throughout the Old Regime, however, the government accorded numerous provisional, partial, short-term, and individual authorizations to export, subject to revocation without notice and dependent upon such factors as harvest circumstances, the remaining stock of old grain, the conservability of new grain, the state of public opinion, and the influence of individual courtiers and regional grain lobbies.[25] Since occasional exportation did not represent a threat in their eyes, it was never an issue of importance for the bulk of the provisioning police.

Legislation devoted to internal grain circulation also varied frequently during the Old Regime, but its significance is more difficult to assess.[26] Although it occasionally subjected interprovincial grain commerce

---

modernisation de l'administration urbaine," in P. Francastel, ed., *Utopie et institutions au 18ᵉ siècle, le pragmatisme des lumières* (Paris, 1963), 189; M. L'Héritier, "Le Despotisme éclairé de Frédéric II à la révolution française," *Bulletin of the International Committee of Historical Sciences* (Paris, 1937), IX, 181–225. There remains an important book to be written on Delamare.

24 See, for example, Véron de Forbonnais' complaint on the caprice of national grain legislation. *Recherches et considérations sur les finances de France depuis 1595 jusqu'en 1721* (Liège, 1758), I, 291.

25 See, for example, the *arrêts du conseil* of 6 Dec. 1735, 10 Jan., 24 April and 18 Sept. 1736, 17 April 1737, etc.

26 See Afanassiev, *Commerce des céréales,* whose treatment differs fundamentally from mine. Paris, as I indicated, had a vested interest in the freedom of internal circulation (see, for example, the remarks due probably to commissaire Lemaire in Gazier, ed., "La Police de Paris en 1770," 117). Although the customs barriers and the jungle of fees and duties on rivers, roads, and bridges—the marketplace "droits" are another problem—seriously hampered trade in most places, neither the Paris police nor the merchants serving the capital complained of their existence, in part because the areas ordinarily subject to Parisian commerce were not thickly overgrown with these obstacles and in part because the exemptions from paying these fees which the government accorded in times of dearth to Paris-bound grain and flour may have become permanent. See the *arrêt du conseil* of 22 Dec. 1725, BHVP, no. 92218 and the *arrêt* of Dec. 1740, *Mercure historique et politique,* 109 (Dec. 1740), 700. Cf. Conte, *L'Administration de la généralité de Paris,* 147.

to the issuance of licenses and sometimes prohibited the transfer of grain from one part of the kingdom to another in response to special circumstances, characteristically, the government favored "free" circulation in the interior as a function of the interplay of supply and demand. Yet the measures it took to promote internal trade were generally weak and half-hearted and bespoke its reluctance to jar established habits and patterns of trade. They were vague and hortatory, without a specific program of action and machinery for enforcement; they were not vigorously publicized; tacitly or expressly, they provided for countless exceptions; they paid little attention to the natural, customary, privileged, and fiscal obstructions to communication; and they were powerless to reduce the physical cost of transportation, the chief economic impediment to large-scale, long-distance trade in the interior.

In ordinary times, the government left effective control of grain circulation in the hands of the intendants. Regardless of the law, intendants whose generalities were chronically short of grain tended to be fervent (one-way) free traders, while intendants of the most fertile regions acted magnanimously toward their neighbors in surplus years and parsimoniously in deficit periods. But even if France had had a more compelling, better integrated national makeup and the police and the public had been willing to renounce their special subsistence claims, it seems probable that the grain trade would have remained overwhelmingly intra-regional and local until the age of the railroad, steamboat, and telegraph. In day-to-day business, the general regulations governing internal and external circulation had little bearing on the police of provisioning.

The regulations that mattered most to the police concerned the operation of the local grain trade. The purpose was to organize the commercial process into a reliable, orderly provisioning system. Instead of allowing the trade to chart its own course, the police undertook to give it a secondary structure, supple enough to accommodate market forces, yet designed to stabilize its composition, its loci of activity, its patterns of exchange, and the rhythm of supply. If the grain trade assimilated this graft, the controls embedded in the structure would become simple commercial conventions and the suppliers would be spared more violent forms of police correction. The controls were meant to define the primary and extraordinary crowns of the supply area, to establish clear-cut lines of supply, and to keep them open at all costs. They aimed at forcing grain into commerce as rapidly as possible, keeping it visible and moving, and directing it to market through the hands of as few middlemen as possible, where it would be sold quickly and openly at a reasonable price. In return for a firm commitment to furnish the market steadily with grain, the regulations offered the suppliers certain facilities of exchange, and competitive advantages vis-à-vis "foreign" dealers.[27] But the consumers were the chief beneficiaries of the regulatory structure. In a confrontation with the supplier, without benefit of police mediation, the authorities believed that the consumer would be trampled. Without rules, the owners of grain would impose impossible conditions. The regulations were social contrivances aimed at redressing a social imbalance that menaced the peace and well-being of the community.

Like the police who interpreted and enforced them, the regulations differed from place to place despite common sources and strong substantive resemblances. To understand how they worked, one would have to view them in the peculiar context of each community's subsistence system, a task clearly beyond our compass. We can, however, identify some of the most important regulations which governed the Parisian provisioning system and which had close parallels throughout the kingdom.

The first rule of the trade, virtually universal in application, required all persons who wished to deal in grain to register with the police. Paris-based traders furnishing the Halles (which received all land-borne grain and almost all flour) enrolled at the Châtelet, and those serving the ports signed the books of the Hôtel de Ville. The majority of merchants supplying Paris resided in the hinterland (they commonly took the title "merchant for the provisioning of Paris" and sometimes the name "forain" or itinerant merchant) and registered with the clerk of the police in the locality in which they primarily operated. The police in Paris and in the provisioning zones exchanged information in order to keep track of new entries and verify the claims made by the merchants outside their home communities. The Prévôt des Marchands usually issued formal written commissions to his merchants (rarely more than thirty at a given moment, most of whom lived on the same street in Paris) and to their "commissioners" or buying agents in the hinterland to facilitate their dealings.

---

27 The value of the "protection" which merchants "for the provisioning of Paris" enjoyed from the Parisian police authorities and the central administration should not be underestimated. See, for example, AN, H * 1864, fols. 205–206 (16 Dec. 1751); Marville to Joly, 22 Aug. 1740, BN, Coll. Joly 1124, fol. 213; Sentence of Bureau de l'Hôtel de Ville, BN, F 23720, p. 207 (imprimé) and *arrêt* of Paris Parl., 17 Jan. 1742, BN, F 23673, fol. 136 (imprimé); Des Essarts, *Dictionnaire*, I, 331.

In presenting themselves to the police, all the merchants had to declare, in addition to name and address, the places where they made their purchases, the names of their correspondents, the location of their storehouses or magazines, the anticipated scale of their commerce, and the usual place of destination (Paris in our example, though a "forain" could also be expected to supply his hometown). Informally, the police investigated the moral character, business capacity, and reputation of the enrolled merchants. "All this knowledge carefully established," wrote Delamare, "it is not difficult to make them [the merchants] obey and to engage them to contribute to the replenishment of abundance." Legally, the merchant could hide nothing; theoretically, the police could trace him at any moment, examine his situation, and pressure him to increase his service or modify it in a publicly useful fashion. The police viewed marked deviations in the pattern and cadence of a merchant's trade with suspicion and concern. They considered undeclared dealers as dangerous monopolists whose only motive in evading registration was to commit crimes against society. Although the police frowned upon partnerships or associations ("societies") for fear that they would lead to efforts to manipulate supply and price, they tolerated them provided the parties informed authorities of their commercial relations and signed contracts before notaries.[28]

The regulations barred certain persons from the grain trade in any capacity and severely limited the kinds of commerce which others could perform. Nobles could not become grain traders because the profession was incompatible with their quality and status. As cultivators and rentiers of the soil, however, they could market the grain they harvested or received as revenue. This distinction invited evasion, but very few nobles in the Paris area became directly involved in the capital's provisioning trade, and it seems likely in any case that the police would have tolerated, if not welcomed, their presence so long as they remained unobtrusive and followed the other rules. Public officials and judges were explicitly excluded from the grain trade on the grounds that it would conflict with their administrative and judicial responsibilities.

The police prohibited *laboureurs* and *fermiers* from dealing in grain: they could only sell their own production and only buy for seed upon demonstration of need. The authorities feared that regular participation in grain traffic would divert these cultivators from their

---

28 Delamare, *Traité*, II, 227, 823.

primary role as producers and that the *laboureurs* would abuse the permission to buy by forming secret hordes easily masked in their farms. And, although the police did not want a few giants to dominate the trade, neither did they wish to see it atomized into "an infinity of small proportions" difficult to detect and mobilize. Similarly, the regulations permitted bakers to buy grain and flour "for the exercise of their profession" but expressly proscribed them from conducting any "commerce," that is, from buying for purposes of resale (regrating) because prices might thereby be driven up. Millers were strictly forbidden to buy or sell grain (except that which they received as tolls) for their own account or as agents for others. The police felt that the license to trade would give the miller too much leverage in the provisioning chain and would distract him from the crucial task of manufacturing public and baker flour. In practice, the *laboureurs* frequently took the title of merchant, especially in times of shortage, in response to speculative opportunities, and the millers would have found it difficult to stay in business had they faithfully conformed to the rules.[29]

To bring order and regularity to the provisioning trade, officials throughout the kingdom counted most heavily on the rule that required *all* transactions to take place on the public marketplaces. "Nothing is more important," proclaimed the Code Duchesne, "than to maintain the ban on selling elsewhere." Elsewhere usually referred to the farms and granaries of the *laboureurs* (and country inns as well) where merchants could conduct business without regard to market customs or prices, take possession of all grain immediately available, and make down-payments on future purchases or on grain which the *laboureurs* would continue to keep in their own storehouses—all of which practices were illegal. To prevent hoarding or engrossing, the *laboureurs* were not permitted to stock their grain production for more than two years, a limitation reinforced by the constraints of crude conservation technology, and merchants could not amass grain at all except to prepare shipments for market. Nor could merchants or other persons intercept provisions on the way to market (forestalling) or buy grain in the market with the intention of reselling it in

---

29 Des Essarts, *Dictionnaire*, I, 17; Gazier, ed., "La Police de Paris en 1770," 118; BN, Coll. Joly 1111, fol. 174; BN, mss. fr. 21640, fol. 64 and 21644, fol. 165. The English authorities also banned millers from grain traffic. See R. A. MacCance and E. M. Widdowson, *Breads White and Brown, their Place in Thought and Social History* (London, 1956), 13 and Richard Bennett and John Elton, *History of Corn Milling* (London, 1898–1904), III, 169.

the same market or nearby, immediately or shortly after purchase (regrating). *Laboureurs* and merchants planning to sell had to transport their grain in its physical entirety to market for exchange; sales based on examination of samples carried in pouches were forbidden. All transactions had to take place formally in public view on the *carreaux*, not in the taverns surrounding the marketplace or other private locations, and secrecy was considered *prima facie* evidence of illicit intention. All eligible buyers had to have the opportunity to bid for goods, and parties to a prospective deal were expected to show signs of "bargaining," that is, proof that they had not prearranged the transaction and that the price agreed upon resulted from genuine haggling.[30]

The grain (or flour), like the merchant who bought it, had to be registered and had to have a passport, a *lettre de voiture*, or a certificate of purchase. The buying merchant informed the market police (or, in many cases, the measurers exercising police functions) of the amount, price, and quality of the merchandise he purchased and received a receipt which he had to present to the authorities at its destined market. Officials at the market of purchase in the supply zone kept a copy for their records or forwarded it to the Paris police to enable them to double-check the merchant. Depending upon the gravity of the offense, the circumstances involved, and the past record of the dealers, the police punished violations of trading regulations with the confiscation of goods and equipment (including animals, wagons, and even boats), fines, and, in extreme cases (recidivism or an abuse deemed particularly odious or inopportune), jail sentences and interdictions from the profession.[31]

The aim of the mandatory market was to flush all supplies out of the countryside. If they could concentrate all of the available supply in a single place and assemble buyers and sellers to engage in open exchanges, the police believed they could prevent artificial shortages and violent price oscillations, satisfy subsistence needs in a regular,

---

30 Declaration of 19 April 1723, BN, Coll. Joly 1829, fols. 302–303; Archives Seine-Paris, D5Z carton 9: Des Essarts, *Dictionnaire*, I, 19, 330, 402; Delamare, *Traité*, II, 790–97; Fréminville, *Dictionnaire*, 72; *Code Duchesne*, 99; Mildmay, *The Police of France*, 99; Diderot, *et al.*, *Encyclopédie*, XIV, 34–35; BN, Coll. Joly 1312, fol. 117; Des Cilleuls, *Socialisme*, 53, 324. Cf. the English attitude toward regrating: Beloff, *Public Order*, 69, 73 and Donald G. Barnes, *A History of the English Corn Laws from 1660 to 1846* (London, 1930), 39, 81–83.

31 The "regime" under which "Paris" merchants operated differed from the general conventions in a number of ways. For example, on the one hand they were invariably fined more heavily than others for the same offenses and on the other they were excused from certain obligations (e.g., procuring *lettres de voiture*) which were mandatory for other merchants.

predictable fashion, establish a climate of "just balance" between buyers and sellers, and guarantee the quality of goods. If all exchanges took place on the market, the police would have a fairly clear notion of the magnitude of the supply in relation to local and metropolitan demand and sufficient information to assess the performance of the traders. The market made the supply highly visible. The police insisted on the need "to keep the universal mass of this wealth in the greatest possible evidence" not only in order to set a just price but also to reassure the consumers. "The people," noted an Advocate General of the Paris Parlement, "as a matter of fact, never is satisfied that there is abundance except when it *sees* the Halles, the markets well-provisioned." When the market lacked grain, the police strained their ingenuity devising ploys to create the impression of continuing plenty.[32]

The marketplace at which the police labored so intensely was not simply a concourse of buyers and sellers. It was an institution, like the church or the law courts, with which it shared certain characteristics. It was a place for celebrating festivals and punishing criminals, the point from which authorities frequently broadcast news and propaganda, and a permanent forum in which people found sociability, established reputations, defended (or impugned) honor, shared ideas, and gave expression to grievances. The market was the vital center of police activity because there, the grain trade most dramatically revealed itself to be a social and political as well as a commercial matter.

If he registered with the police, eschewed all clandestine business, restricted his operations to the market, constituted no hoards, and suborned no other buyers or sellers into illicit traffic, the merchant complied with the requirements to which the police attached the most significance. Still, there were other obligations which followed from and complemented the first-line prohibitions. Many took the form of rules instituted by local police in scores of markets in the Parisian supply zone. They concerned strictly local needs and preoccupations: access to the market, days and hours of sale, priorities for buying, the system for measuring grain and flour and recording sales, arrangements for loading and delivery, and limitations on quantity of purchase. Many of these regulations were meant to shield the local market from metropolitan demand, favor local dealers over Parisian merchants,

---

32 Gazier, ed., "La Police de Paris en 1770," 117; speech of Advocate General of Paris Parl., 5 July 1763, in *Recueil des principales lois relatives au commerce des grains* ... (Paris, 1769), 59–61. Cf. Cobb, *Police and People*, 268 and Roubaud, *Représentations aux magistrats*, 461.

commissioners, and bakers, and, above all, satisfy the needs of resident consumers. Parisian authorities had an ambivalent attitude toward these local controls. In order to win the cooperation of the zone police in maintaining a steady flow of grain to the capital, they tolerated many local idiosyncracies and vexations. If, however, local law and custom began seriously to impede traffic and hamper provisioning operations, they intervened to quash them through royal, parlementary, or municipal channels, or by means of informal pressure from high-ranking officials.[33]

Certain regulations regarding supply practices and market conduct were peculiar to the capital, though in some cases they were imitated elsewhere. The police created a sort of de-commercialized zone extending for a radius, first of eight and later of ten leagues (36 and 45 kilometers), around Paris in which no merchants or bakers could purchase any grain, even in the marketplaces. The aim was to force the Paris-provisioning merchants to look beyond the close hinterland and extend the supply zone deep into the countryside, compelling the zone *laboureurs* themselves to make the journey to the capital. The producer-*laboureur*, from the police perspective, was the ideal supplier, for by eliminating the middle-man he reduced the cost of the grain. "The inconvenience of the trip [a grain wagon could cover approximately eight leagues in a single day] and the rush to return home," noted Delamare candidly, "induce the *laboureurs* and the others who bring their own grain to the Market to relax on the price, and there results a kind of fixation which obliges the merchants to do likewise." Or, in the words of another official, the *laboureur* finds it in his interest to set a "reasonable" price which "then serves as the *Standard* for the course of the market and as remedy against the monopolies of the merchants." The de-commercialized zone formed the first "crown" of the Parisian supply system. Theoretically, all the grain produced therein and not consumed locally had to reach the capital. Once it entered this zone, grain from outside could not turn back but had to proceed to the capital.[34]

---

33 See, for example, the cases of the Paris (Grève) grain merchants Jauvin (at Crécy and Meaux) and Armet (at St. Dizier). BN, Coll. Joly 1123, fols. 81, 287, 290–91, 302; 1313, fols. 86–100; 1130, fols. 227–37, 247–53.

34 Delamare, *Traité*, II, 621–22; BN, Coll. Joly, 1116, fol. 247. In the seventeenth century the police envisioned extending the de-commercialized zone to 20 leagues. BN, mss. fr. 21644, fol. 10. Many provincial towns maintained a two-league forbidden sector. See Conte, *L'Administration de la généralité de Paris*, 146 and Afanassiev, *Commerce des céréales*, 75.

Nor were the *laboureurs* the only suppliers to be incommoded by the rules governing sale on the markets and ports within Paris. To "rush" the merchant and engage him to offer his grain at what one high official called the "natural price," the regulations enjoined him to sell his entire stock within three market days (which meant usually within a calendar week, though bakers could purchase grain or flour on any day). Regardless of the price at the end of the third market day, he had to dispose of his grain. Despite changes in the current price, on the second and third market days he could not ask more than he had initially demanded on the first offering. Instead of storing unsold grain as the merchants would have preferred, the police seized it and arranged for its sale through a broker on the ports or at the Halles. Finally, to discourage the suppliers from losing interest in returning to Paris regularly, the police required them to keep the ports and markets "sufficiently furnished" on pain of fines, exclusion from the trade, or worse. Delamare referred specifically to the "obligations" of the merchants and the "contract" they had with the public. The police expected them to come at least once and preferably twice a month and more often in difficult times, when "so instructed."[35]

III

The historian must not let himself be intimidated or misled by this elaborate array of regulations and prohibitions any more than the grain merchant did. If it is impossible to understand the grain trade without examining the regulations, it is equally impossible to understand it without taking a step beyond them. Heavily armed with weapons from their legal and administrative arsenal, the police knew when to hold their fire. Delamare himself envisaged a differential police of grain: a police for periods of abundance, one for middling years, another for dearth, and still another for famine.[36]

During the normal years—most of the eighteenth century—the Paris police adopted a posture of benign neglect. To be sure, the police neither repudiated procedures which had become fully assimilated to commercial practice nor condoned blatantly illicit activities considered to be dangerous, but they refrained from enforcing many of the regulations

---

35 Gazier, ed., "La Police de Paris en 1770," 121–22; BN, Coll. Joly 1312, fol. 117; BN, mss. fr. 21549, fols. 5, 6; Delamare, *Traité*, II, 618; *Code Duchesne*, 105, 121.

36 Delamare, *Traité*, II, 794.

with rigor and they permitted others to lapse into virtual desuetude. The traditional controls, especially the mosaic of rules locating all commercial activity in the markets, Joly de Fleury, the Procurator General of Paris, informed the intendants and his *substituts*, "are not strictly executed in times when there is no dearth to fear." Although the central government had insisted on the uninterrupted application of the old system of constraints as recently as April 1723 in a royal Declaration which was widely disseminated, the "usage," said Joly de Fleury, was to ignore it. To a local official who earnestly complained of violations of the 1723 law, he urged caution and restraint:

> You must exhort and engage, as much as you can, the grain merchants to furnish the markets; you could not even be blamed for threatening [them] sometimes. But when grain is at a reasonable price, you must resort to judicial pursuits only with a great deal of circumspection and with precautions and you must do it only after having carefully investigated the abuses and after having received my reply on the action that can be taken.[37]

In another letter he described the traditional prohibitions, in terms which a physiocrat could not have reproached, as "regulations which hamper the grain trade…." "I do not know," the Procurator General wrote yet another of his *substituts*, "if in the present circumstances … it is not more prudent to *close your eyes* to what transpires." When the harvests are good, he added, we must make a greater effort to favor "the liberty of the grain trade."[38] Although he did not shy away from using force on most matters, Joly frequently counseled the local provisioning police to avoid the "authoritarian ways" whenever possible. Remember that Joly was not mouthing slogans or affecting an enlightened pose for purposes of a public debate or a parlementary remonstrance. In intimate administrative correspondence, the official

---

37 BN, Coll. Joly 1130, fols. 156–57 and 2418, fol. 177; Joly to fiscal procurator of Charly, 23 Nov. 1757, Coll. Joly 1107, fols. 6, 7.

38 Letters of PG to two local procurators, BN, Oct. 1739, Coll. 1107, fols. 8, 9. See also Letaconnoux, *Le Commerce des grains en Bretagne*, 87–88, 91–93; P. Binet, *La Réglementation du marché*, 43; Musart, *La Réglementation du commerce des grains*, 64; L. Cahen, "A Propos du livre d'Afanassiev: L'Approvisionnement de Paris en grains au début du XVIIIᵉ siècle," *Bulletin de la Société d'Histoire Moderne*, 22nd year (5 March 1922), 162; Dénisart, *Collection de décisions nouvelles*, I, 263; Jean Meyer, *La Noblesse bretonne au 18ᵉ siècle* (Paris, 1966), I, 521; A.-P. Floquet, *Histoire du parlement de Normandie* (Rouen, 1940–42), VI, 414–19. Two of the severest critics of the old system. Lemercier de la Rivière and the revolutionary leader and physiocratic sympathizer Creuzé-Latouche, both conceded that the police regime seemed to be substantially more moderate in the eighteenth century than it had been in earlier times. Lemercier, *L'Intérêt général de l'état* (Paris, 1770) and Creuzé's speech, 8 Dec. 1792, *Archives parlementaires*, LIV, 679.

who embodied the idea of police in the eyes of judges and procurators throughout the kingdom was promoting a strikingly loose construction of the law and a remarkably subdued, indulgent line to follow in the grain police.

Whether they self-consciously followed Joly's line or arrived there by their own wiles, there is no question that many local authorities practiced a seasonally lenient police. Bertier, intendant of Paris, observed with consternation that the police of grain seemed to hibernate all year long in normal times.[39] The Parisian lieutenants of police, as we have seen, complained frequently about the lackadaisical attitude of local officials. The dossiers of prohibition, repression, and punishment are easier to find because they are thicker and they tend to cluster, but the archives of the Châtelet, the municipal Bureau (the little that is left), the *maréchaussée*, and the Parlement are replete with examples of tolerance for or inattention to patently illegal activities (normally called "crimes" or "abuses"), such as surreptitious transactions, sample selling, regrating, purchases via unauthorized intermediaries, shipments without passports, and hoarding. Unfortunately the data are too discontinuous and heterogeneous to be plotted on a curve against grain prices. On such a curve one would expect to find a significant positive correlation between price stagnation and police lethargy, though it should be noted that low prices often induced the suppliers to stay away from the markets and thus pricked the police back into action.

Throughout the kingdom as well as in the Paris area, officials, in the words of the Controller-General Bertin, "ordinarily shut their eyes" provided the supply situation was untroubled. They reserved their "rigor" for "preventing abuses in times of dearth." "It is important in moments of *cherté* to hold severely to the execution of the regulations which prohibit all persons from selling grain in their granaries, with the injunction to furnish the public markets," wrote Levignen, intendant of Alençon, "but in periods of abundance and tranquility there is no disadvantage in relaxing the stringency of the prohibitions." His subdelegates confirmed that the "usage" in their localities was to overlook violations in normal times. Nor was the

---

39 Bertier de Sauvigny to PG, 13 June, 11 July 1760 (?), BN, Coll. Joly 1130, fols. 158–59, 162–63; Bertier de Sauvigny, "Observations sur le commerce des grains," (1763), BN, mss. fr. 11347, fols. 226 and *passim*. See the similar warning by the first LG of Police against a police of occasional neglect. La Reynie to CG, 13 July 1695, *Correspondance des contrôleurs-généraux*, ed. by Boislisle, I, 396.

market obligation insisted upon in the Soissonnais save, significantly enough, in those markets frequented by merchants buying for Paris, where it was applied only to traders *not* committed to the provisioning of the capital. According to the intendant of Brittany, off-market transactions were "always" tolerated in his generality. Conceiving the mandatory market law of 1723 as a psychological device meant "to frighten" and "to disconcert" potential monopolists—"a sort of ostentatious display of rigor", the parlementaires of Aix claimed that magistrates who registered it never intended a strict enforcement and the local police "never executed [it] seriously."[40]

Laxity or permissiveness, however, was sporadic and rarely indiscriminate. It would be wrong to imagine that under the cloak of every police official there beat a heart of laissez-faire. The point is not that the police of the grain trade was a myth; rather the myth, immortalized by the critics of the regime, is that the police was inexorable, iron-handed and tropismatic, or that the grain trade was relentlessly oppressed and trod under foot. Doubtless the authorities had a keener sense of their own self-restraint and solicitude than the merchants and grain owners who still had to live with great uncertainty about the future, comply with many vexatious rules, and face inconsistencies in police attitudes in different places as well as different times. But the merchants appreciated and profited from the distinctions made between law and usage and had as little or as much trouble anticipating major changes in police orientation as they had in forecasting weather and predicting the harvest.

The manner in which they treated the mandatory market requirements, the keystone in the regulatory arch, best illustrates the flexibility of the Paris grain police. On the one hand, they demanded that local authorities oblige the cultivators and dealers of the area to obey the market rule in order to expose the local supply to the full intensity of metropolitan demand. On the other hand, for the same purposes of promoting abundance and facilitating the operations of the suppliers, the Paris police authorized merchants trading specifically for the provisioning of the capital to buy in the barns and granaries

---

40 Bertin, "Mémoire à consulter sur la liberté du commerce des grains," 1761, C. 69, A.D. I-et-V. and C. 2420, A.D. B-du-R.; Levignen to Bertin, Aug. 1761, C. 89, A.D. Orne; SD of Verneuil and SD of Falaise to Levignen, 14 Aug. 1761, C. 89, A.D. Orne; IN. of Soissons to Bertin, 19 Aug. 1761, AN, K. 908; IN. of Brittany to Terray, ca. May–June 1774, C. 1653, A.D. I-et-V; Parl. of Aix to Louis XV, 21 Nov. 1768, B. 3677, A.D. B-du-R. Cf. the IN. of Montauban to Terray, 16 Dec. 1771, AN, F^{11} 223.

of the *laboureurs* in contravention of the law. The promulgation of the royal Declaration of April 1723, however, alarmed the Paris suppliers, for it seemed to invite all police officials, without exception, to repress off-market transactions in all times. Despite "verbal and written permissions to buy in the countryside, in the farms, houses, and anyplace else" which they received from the Paris police, the merchants who openly traded off the markets were harassed by certain hinterland officials who issued summonses, levied fines, or seized their merchandise. The Parisian police almost invariably managed to have these sentences quashed and the goods restituted but the merchants complained that the insecure atmosphere stifled their commerce and that the remedies were too slow and cumbersome. Instead of short-term relief, they demanded a durable solution.[41]

The leading group of Parisian merchants made a strong case that the "liberty" to buy in the countryside "which we have always enjoyed" was of "an absolute necessity in order to procure and maintain the abundance of grain in Paris." The market organization of the hinterland, they suggested, was inadequate to serve the capital. If they were bound to the market, the rhythm of Paris supply would be considerably slackened and the prices would mount—that is to say, the obligatory market rule would produce the very consequences it was supposed to prevent. Normally, contended the merchants, the *laboureurs* took their time in bringing grain to market; in some seasons, they did not come at all. Furthermore, most zone markets were held only once a week. Forced to await the day of the market, the merchant could never buy enough grain in a single session to fill a boat and would thus be compelled to camp in the market for several weeks. This caused him to waste time and added significantly to his costs, which were further increased by the exaction of market fees and the obligation to bid competitively against other buyers for the market stock.[42]

---

41 "Mémoire pour les marchands de bled pour l'approvisionnement de Paris," BN, Coll. Joly 1428, fols. 38–48; assembly of police, 10 May 1731, BN, mss. fr. 11356, fols. 157–58. The most vigorous opponents of the off-market tolerance were the local zone police who claimed that it depleted the local supply, raised prices and discriminated unfairly against merchants whose destination was not the capital. Other objections came from persons with a material vested interest in the sanctity of the marketplace—farmers or owners of *minage* and other market "rights" (*droits*). They lobbied strenuously and always in the name of the common good and a "bonne police" to prohibit practices which diminished turnover at the market. See, for example, the violent denunciations of merchant "license" by the comte de Rochebrune, baron of Bray, an important Brie market-town. BN, mss. fr. 21635, fols. 244–45.

42 "Mémoire pour les marchands de bled," BN, Coll. Joly 1438, fols. 38–48. Cf. an earlier "Mémoire concernant le commerce des grains" (ca. 1725), Coll. Joly 1116, fols. 266–69.

Although habitually skeptical of special pleading by the provisioning interest groups, the police in this instance clearly sympathized with the merchants' argument. They hesitated, however, to recommend a statutory abrogation of the mandatory market rule, for they were loath to abandon a control that they believed to be extremely useful in difficult times. Also, they feared that merchants outside the Paris system, and the public generally, would misapprehend the limited scope and significance of the projected changes in the law. Finally, after years of deliberation, in September 1737, a shrewdly phrased royal declaration expressly "maintained" the merchants regularly supplying the capital in the "faculty" of buying outside the market without, however, exempting them from conforming to the mandatory market rule when the Paris police chose to enforce it. Since it virtually guaranteed them immunity from constraint except in periods of disorder, the declaration delighted the merchants.[43]

The significance of this case lies partly in the fact that the decision did not please everyone in the Parisian police administration. The police remained divided on the wisdom of granting concessions. The market tolerance violated a rule "reiterated since the Capitularies of Charlemagne," remarked one agent, and it created a "Monopoly" spirit which emboldened the merchants to buy up all the supplies with a view toward driving the price up. Missonnet, another agent charged with encouraging Paris provisioning from a base in the hinterland, was convinced that purchases made by Parisian merchants and commissioners at the farms served only to reduce the circulating supply, boost prices, and encourage "abuses." Along with Foucaud, the operative who toured the provisioning crowns for the Paris police, Missonnet favored a return to exclusive market transactions.[44] It appears that police authorities in closest contact with the hinterland and the markets tended to be less liberal about grain trade rules than their superiors who never left Paris except to go to Versailles. Whether this rigidity resulted

43 Assemblies of police, 22 June, 30 Nov. 1730 and 10 May 1731, BN, mss. fr. 11356, fols. 127, 138, 157–58; 11 Mar. 1734, 30 June 1735, BN, Coll. Joly 1428, fols. 63, 65; Lecler to PG, 25 April 1736 and 16 Dec. 1736, Coll. Joly 1428, fols. 72–73; BN, mss. fr. 21640, fol. 63.

44 "Mémoire contre la Déclaration du 9 septembre 1737," BN, mss. fr. 21635, fols. 168–69; Missonnet to PG, 31 July, 30 Oct. 1752 and 2 April 1753, BN, Coll. Joly 1112, fols. 114, 192–93, 220; Foucaud to PG, April 1757, BN, Coll. Joly 1113, fols. 240–41.

from a fair-minded, first-hand assessment of conditions or from a myopic perspective and an appetite for authority is a question that remains to be answered.

Another set of attitudes tended to inhibit the rigorous execution of provisioning trade rules. The police, especially at the highest levels, did not have a blind confidence in the efficacy of the regulatory approach. On occasion, they acted on the premise that so-called precautionary regulations were more likely to provoke than to prevent the evils they confronted, in much the manner that some persons shun the umbrella for fear that it will incite rain. Or, to use the image which the police found most congenial, they feared that the remedy of regulation might prove worse than the disease. Though they remained vigilant, in normal times the police relaxed the rules. Because Parisians, and, indeed, the vast majority of Frenchmen, were deeply apprehensive about subsistence and therefore in permanent expectation of disaster, the police believed that any official suggestion in the form of preemptive or restrictive measures would raise the probability of occurrence in their minds. Anxieties thus created might cause "murmurs," "seditions," pillaging, consumer hoarding, and other antisocial behavior. At certain moments in the eighteenth century the authorities esteemed that the unintended disorganizing and disruptive consequences of energetic regulation and intervention were prohibitively costly.

In these instances, the attitudes of the police engendered a policy of inertia for the sake of discretion. This does not mean, to be sure, that the police stood by and did nothing at critical junctures. But the paralysis of discretion tended to sap the initiative of the highest officials, confuse their subordinates in the field, and postpone or dilute action which might have been more effective if it had been taken earlier or more lustily. At its worst, the reasoning of the police was timid and circular; it revealed a lack of administrative imagination, or perhaps too much of it, and a grievous incapacity to deal with public opinion. In times such as these, the police, not the people, proved to be the great "trembleurs" of the Old Regime. Indecisiveness and Micawberism masquerading as sang-froid were rarely to be found at the local level; they were as peculiar to the police at the top as impulsive outbursts of authority were to the police at the bottom. At its best, the discretion argument bespoke a genuine sensitivity to the psychological elements which help transform a dearth or any other threatening situation into a social and political crisis and an awareness of the dangerous side-effects of government intervention.

Examples of the paralysis of discretion abound in the eighteenth century. In 1708, despite the demands of several intendants and evidence of a short crop, the Controller-General refused to rescind a permission to export that the government had granted, for fear of frightening the people and causing an "artificial" price rise. Yet by not acting to stem the outflow, he risked public vilification for provoking a *real* price rise and for failing to preserve the national subsistence. In the beginning of the following year, perhaps the worst in the century, Daguesseau fils, the Procurator General of the Paris Parlement, wrote: "It is certain that some remedies must be brought to bear but since the matter is *so delicate* that the remedies often only aggravate the illness, it is only tremulously that one can propose several of the precautions that it appears that one could take to reassure the spirit of the people and calm their nervousness a little." Daguesseau might have taken his inspiration from Delamare who warned that "... it would often be dangerous to expose to the public everything that there is to fear, & that an alarm given too precipitately could cause grain to become scarce or rise in price & produce several other bad effects." In 1710 the police decided not to publish an *arrêt* meant to dissuade people from pillaging grain convoys in order not "to renew the sad ideas of dearth," that is, in order not to incite them to pillage grain convoys![45]

Similar incidents occurred during the reign of Louis XV. In 1723 the Controller-General Dodun urged administrators to eschew the heavy-handed "authoritarian way" in dealing with the dearth: "The éclat that the regulations cause amplifies the alarm of the peoples and causes the grain supply to contract...." The assembly of police in 1730 instructed the Lieutenant General of Vitry not to enforce the grain rules strictly "because that would be to sound the alarm and maintain the high prices." For many years the assembly delayed asking the king for a declaration clarifying the status of the Paris-provisioning merchants in part because "any new law on this subject would cause it to be

---

45 CG to IN. of Languedoc, 24 Aug., 1 Sept. 1708, in *Correspondance des contrôleurs-généraux*, ed. by Boislisle, III, 12; Daguesseau fils to CG, 24 Feb. 1709, *ibid.*, III, 102; Delamare, *Traité*, II, 809; BN, mss. fr. 21634, fol. 280. Cf. similar attitudes in England, Sylvia Thrupp, *A Short History of the Worshipful Company of Bakers of London* (London, 1933), 33; and the remarks of Linguet on the urgency for, but difficulty of attaining, discretion, *Annales*, VII (Nov. 1779), 233. Arthur Young condemned the French police for taking action on subsistence matters which provoked "alarm." *Travels in France during the years 1787, 1788 and 1789*, ed. by Jeffry Kaplow (Garden City, N.Y., 1969), 106. Cf. *ibid.*, 376–77, 380, 474.

believed that we fear a dearth." Similarly, for fear of generating "too much alarm," the assembly refused in 1738, on the eve of a great dearth, to issue a "general regulation" of discipline for the grain trade or to authorize coercive measures to force grain out of hiding. In the same year the intendant of Orléans rebuffed insinuations that he was not showing sufficient industry in the campaign to find grain for the capital. One wonders whether his explanation, that he moderated his zeal because "... these sorts of searches [for grain] cast alarms and fears in the spirits which usually cause the augmentation [of prices]," was very convincing in Paris. In 1772 an experienced royal procurator of Melun, who had served as a subdelegate for a quarter century, wanted to extend an investigation sponsored by the Parlement into every parish in his jurisdiction in order to amass data on population, taxes, and subsistence. The Procurator General vetoed his plan on the grounds that it would "stir anxiety, cause éclat, inspire distrust, fears, and complaints; and that is precisely what must be avoided."[46]

The dangers of inaction and benign neglect worried a number of police authorities. In 1760, Bertier, the intendant of Paris, warned against the bad example that police inertia set for the people. If we tolerate clandestine grain transactions, he wrote sarcastically, "at least it would be useful to *appear* to pay attention from time to time" to the law. If we never enforce the law in normal times, he argued, we will have no credibility in the merchant community or with the public when we want to insist upon its execution in a crisis. Finally, if we do implement it in an emergency after years of indifference, it will stir a great "sensation" and inevitably arouse alarms. And if we are confident that it will arouse alarms, the intendant hinted, we will probably not want to enforce it. Such was the cycle of indulgence, inattention, conditioning, and rationalization in the management of police affairs.[47] In 1771, a memoir prepared for the Procurator General took a step away from the discretion syndrome:

---

46 CG to First President of Rennes Parl., 4 July 1725 and to d'Angervilliers, 21 Oct. 1725, AN, G⁷ 34; assemblies of police, 30 Nov. 1730, 27 Nov., 4 Dec. 1738, BN, mss. fr. 11356, fols. 137, 369, 371; Baussau to CG or Hérault, 26 Nov. 1738, Arsenal, mss. Bastille 10275; PG to Cadot, 5 Jan. 1772, BN, mss. fr. 8128, fol. 191. Cf. Controller-General Laverdy's reproach to the First President of the Rouen Parlement for stirring popular fear by meeting too conspicuously with the intendant of the province. To Miromesnil, 10 May 1768, in *Correspondance Miromesnil*, ed. by LeVerdier, V, 193.

47 B. de Sauvigny to PG, 13 June, 11 July 1760 (?), BN, Coll. Joly 1130, fols. 158–59, 162–63.

Nothing being more delicate without doubt than the matter of subsistence, a measure of éclat taken inopportunely can cause much ill; but absolute silence is also very dangerous. Between doing too much and doing nothing at all there is a middle position to take: it consists of acting with prudence in favorable circumstances.[48]

Middle ground is extremely difficult to find and occupy. Administrators are inclined to believe they are there when they oscillate, more or less evenly, between extremes. In 1725, for example, the Controller-General Dodun preached, on the one hand, a low-profile approach to the problem of rising prices in order to avoid alarming the public and, on the other hand, he realized that "… in avoiding precautions for fear of making the public anxious, we expose ourselves to seeing the markets go empty which is a greater evil than the anxiety that we wish to avoid."[49] Invariably, at some point in the development of a crisis, or what passed for one, the police reached Dodun's conclusion. The famous "murmur," the key variable in the simplistic police model of public opinion, was a treacherous index of popular feeling, for it was difficult to tell whether it came from the stomach or from the mind, whether it was a product of dearth (in which case it was probably too late or pointless to apply a strategy of discretion) or of the fear of dearth (in which case it might still make sense to suppress cues likely to reinforce the fear). Past a certain point, alarm was no longer the chief preoccupation; assuring an adequate supply of grain and flour became the overriding problem, even at the cost of enhancing short-run anxieties. Once the police agreed among themselves that a situation was critical and unlikely to prove ephemeral, they spared no effort and overlooked no useful control in coming to grips with it. When conditions were normal, or when they were irregular and the authorities half-hoped and half-expected that they would remain so only temporarily, the discretion syndrome operated most effectively to liberalize the police of the grain trade.

Another indication of the determination of the Paris police to use their authority judiciously and to allow the grain trade considerable latitude was their rejection of price-fixing, or *taxation*, as it was called. They did not, of course, abstain from trying to influence the price. Indeed, all their efforts aimed not merely at assuring a regular supply but assuring it at a reasonable or just price. In the Paris

48 "Mémoire" (1771), BN, Coll. Joly 1111, fol. 147.
49 Dodun to PG, 29 July 1725, AN, G⁷ 34.

markets and in the zone, there were, as we have seen, a number of regulatory constraints on the price-making machinery. To encourage merchants and *laboureurs* to lower their prices, the police entreated, hounded, wheedled, and threatened, and sometimes punished a few harshly as an example for the others. At certain times the government marketed grain belonging to the religious communities and hospitals or to the king in order to depress the current price. But the Paris police never applied a *taxation* policy to grain and flour in any systematic way and they rarely resorted to it at all.

Price-fixing was often proposed, for it seemed to follow logically from the regulations which the police imposed on commerce and from their deep mistrust of merchants. Moreover, it appeared to be a relatively straight-forward way to implement the police theory of price justice, and it was a technique which had Roman and biblical pedigrees and was still practiced in a number of French and European towns. In Paris itself, the prices of certain goods, such as wood, candlewax, meat, and hay were subject to fixation. "Nothing seems easier than to fix the price of grain," noted Delamare, "it is an expedient which comes easily to mind because it appears at first to be a prompt remedy to pressing ills & it is this pretended advantage which gives birth to this speculative proposition as many times as we have this misfortune to be afflicted with dearth." But every time the idea received a hearing—in 1630, 1662–63, 1709, the police turned it down.[50]

The police rebuffed price-fixing not from scruples about violating the property rights of merchants and *laboureurs*—the physiocrats and doubtless the dealers themselves regarded *taxation* as "theft"— but because they considered it unwise, unfeasible, and much less simple than generally supposed.[51] Delamare viewed price-fixing as a "specious remedy ... rather an evil than a remedy." The purpose of police control was to contain and excite commerce, not eradicate it. Price-fixing would be disastrous because, Delamare contended, it would "stop the circulation of grain and destroy the principle of all the commerces which is that of gain." In a dearth it was especially important to stimulate a "free trade"

---

50 Delamare, *Traité*, II, 922–34; BN, mss. fr. 21647, fols. 64–74; Bondois, "Disette de 1662," *Revue d'histoire économique et sociale*, XII (1924), 53–118; P.-J. Malouin, *Description et détails des arts du meunier, du vermicellier, et du boulanger, avec une histoire abrégée de la boulangerie et un dictionnaire de ces arts* (Paris, 1761), 270.

51 *Ephémérides du citoyen* (Aug. 1767), cited by G. Weulersse, *Le Mouvement physiocratique en France de 1756 à 1770* (Paris, 1910), I, 538; François Lacombe (d'Avignon), *Le Mitron de Vaugirard, dialogues sur le bled, la farine, et le pain, avec un petit traité de la boulangerie* (Amsterdam, 1777), 41.

between surplus and deficit areas and to attract supplies from abroad. Police pressure by itself could not produce these results: "the hope of profit," the primary motive for commercial activity, had to be kept alive. Although he showed no indulgence for merchant abuses, Delamare was no partisan of what he called a "forced commerce." Within certain bounds, commerce had to be free if it was to fulfill the subsistence needs of the capital. Price-fixing upset the delicate balance between freedom and regulation upon which the Paris trade was based.

Even if price controls were adopted, Delamare argued, it would be virtually impossible to implement them in a reliable, intelligent fashion. One could not devise a system pliant enough to take account of the great diversity of weights and measures and commercial customs in different regions, the different qualities of grain, the relative scarcities in different places, and the varying costs of transportation. Nor could one amass and keep up to date the vast amount of data on the whereabouts of the grain and the merchants and *laboureurs* that would be necessary for such an operation.[52]

During the reign of Louis XV, practitioners and the theorists of good administration, both of whom considered problems from within a framework highly favorable to state intervention, decried price-fixing on the same grounds as Delamare. Trained by Delamare, commissaire Duplessis, in charge of the department of the Halles during the dearth of 1725–26, proved that he had learned his lessons well. In the midst of the crisis, he urged an "entire liberty of commerce." Only liberty would keep supplies flowing into the capital. Although he anxiously wanted to see a diminution of both the grain and flour prices in January 1725, he told the Procurator General that "it must come on its own, you know better than anyone that everything which is forced produces a bad effect."[53]

More than thirty years later, another police officer assigned to the Halles, inspector Poussot, wrote in the same vein that "the more liberty is established between seller and buyer, the more the Halles will be furnished and consequently this abundance will of itself cause a

---

52 Delamare, *Traité*, II, 923–34; BN, mss. fr. 21647; fols. 64–74; St.-Germain, *Vie quotidienne*, 208–209. Cf. the remarks attributed to the banker-victualer Samuel Bernard, cited by A. de Boislisle, "Le Grand hiver et la disette de 1709," *Revue des questions historiques*, LXXIV (1903), 505.
53 Duplessis to PG, 2, 5 Jan., 21 Sept. 1726, BN, Coll. Joly 1118, fols. 5, 8–9, 206–207.

[price] diminution." Intensely interested in the revitalization of the Halles market, he claimed that a "fixed price" drove away buyers and sellers and made the *carreau* a desert. Similarly, the Controller-General Dodun, hardly the most enlightened or liberal finance minister in the eighteenth century, viewed the question in terms of stimulating provisioning as well as trade. "Nothing is in fact more dangerous," he cautioned, "than to undertake to fix the price of grain and of bread when one is not sufficiently supplied." "It is better," he added, "even for the people to pay more dearly for their grain and to have some than to lack totally as a result of the effort to procure it [for them] more cheaply ... the liberty of the price and the *cherté* itself attracting large numbers of merchants ... soon abundance by itself causes the price to fall." Turgot could not have put it any better.[54]

On an ad hoc basis the police occasionally fixed prices or used pressure tactics to influence prices that bordered on price-fixing. In 1725 Lieutenant of Police Hérault set the price—probably a simple maximum rather than a qualitative schedule—on flour at the Halles. The millers and mealmen complained bitterly that the established price was too low to sustain their commerce. Partly in order to appease them, Hérault authorized his agent at Pontoise, one of the major flour entrepôts in the zone, to fix the price of wheat despite the orders of the Controller-General to "allow liberty of the price" in the markets around Paris. Hérault imposed the price in a desperate effort to hold down bread prices. But a decline in flour arrivals, plus the objections of the ministry and his own commissaire Duplessis, apparently persuaded Hérault to loosen his grip at the end of the year. Yet four years later, when he felt that the going price was excessive, the Lieutenant General again fixed the "head" price of the flour. A police official at

---

54 Arsenal, mss. Bastille 10141 (28 Sept., 16, 26 Oct. 1759); Dodun to PG and First President of Rennes Parl., 1 July 1725, AN, G⁷ 34. Subsistence commentators outside the government, who were not in principle hostile to government intervention in provisioning affairs, rejected grain price-fixing as "impracticable," "senseless," and fatal to commerce. Camus, "Mémoire sur le bled," *Journal économique* (Nov. 1753), 155; J. Necker, *Sur la législation et le commerce des grains*, 282–83; Galiani, "Memoir to Lieutenant General of Police Sartine," ca. 1770, in *Lettres*, ed. by Asse, I, 416; Doumerc to PG, 17 Feb. 1789, BN, Coll. Joly 1111, fols. 203–205. For the eighteenth century argument in favor of price-fixing, see: Delamare, *Traité*, II, 930–34; "Mémoire concernant la fixation du prix du bled," BN, Coll. Joly 1111, fols. 158–67; Couet de Montbayeux to PG, 11 Nov. 1725, BN, Coll. Joly 1117, fols. 248–50; Therbaud, "Moyens pour empêcher l'augmentation...," July 1739, BN, Coll. Joly 1120, fol. 33; anonymous memoirs, ca. 1725, Arsenal, mss. Bastille 10270, fols. 313–14, 374–75; Narbonne, *Journal*, 309.

Versailles, whose mealmen ordinarily furnished Paris, protested that the set price "seriously disconcerted" the flour merchants and made it impossible for them to supply Paris because the cost of wheat, which remained unfixed, absorbed the entire price of flour. "It is not," he said apologetically, as if he were embarrassed for being too soft on traders, "that I am unaware of how much the cupidity of men is great, how much it is necessary to contain it, but the great point [after all] is not to go lacking [for flour]…"[55]

I have found no other example of outright grain or flour price-fixing in Paris during the reign of Louis XV. The police generally insisted on respect for "the current." If a merchant, *laboureur* or baker tried to force up the current, he was liable to prosecution for monopoly. In threatening or troubled times, the police tried to shape the current price by pressuring merchants and *laboureurs* and by selling government grain in the open market. In the short run—for a market day or two—the police could arbitrarily hold the line against an upsurging current price. But once a new level clearly declared itself, the police ventured to strike at the sources of the price rise rather than to annul it by ukase.

Temperate, tolerant, flexible—however far one wishes to go in rehabilitating or demythologizing the police of provisioning, the fact remains that it was a police regime: a regime of prohibitions and constraints, of permissions rather than permissiveness. Less rigid and oppressive than often imagined, it was still officious and forbidding. If the authorities frequently overlooked the rules in easy times, in hard times they often enforced them vengefully, as if to atone for their indulgence, or discarded them in favor of a new set of brutal expedients including household searches and seizures, requisitions, imposition of quotas, and profit controls. If the critics of the police system exaggerated its oppressiveness by focusing on the extraordinary episodes of police intervention, it was after all not so unreasonable because the dearth experience was the ultimate test and it left the deepest imprint on the minds of traders, officials, and consumers. Even in times called normal, it was the prospect of dearth, of tomorrow, which preoccupied everyone. Good times were merely truces; if the police withdrew, they

---

55 Cleret to Hérault, 5, 10, 15 Oct. 1725, Arsenal, mss. Bastille 10270, fols. 224, 248, 315; CG to d'Angervilliers, 25 Nov. 1725 and to Hérault, 22 Nov. 1725, AN, G⁷ 34; Regnier to Hérault, 21 June 1729, mss. Bastille 10275; Anon. to Marville, 1740, mss. Bastille 10027, fols. 391–92; Laurent to Hérault, May 1726, mss. Bastille 10273.

remained coiled to strike. For they believed that the grain trade was too important to be left to the grain traders. Whatever the defects of the police system, the authorities, who were not unaware of them, felt that without it provisioning would be jeopardized.

IV

Allowing generously for local, regional and social variations, a subsistence calendar for the eighteenth century would show five cycles, each from ten to twenty years in length, of relative ease interrupted by episodes of severe troubles.[56] If one takes as criteria harvest failures or markedly short crops, the doubling or tripling or the wild fluctuation of prices above normal levels, unusual proliferation and deepening of distress among the laboring poor and the marginal population, pronounced social unrest on a collective scale, violent disruption of the provisioning trade, and in some instances and some places, far-reaching economic dislocation and demographic repercussions, then we can point to subsistence crises, in the Paris area and through a considerable portion of the kingdom, in 1709, 1725–26, 1738–42, and 1765–75. There were, in addition, in the late forties and fifties some threatening moments for the capital and some grave difficulties for some of the outlying provinces. These were the times of maximal police intervention on all levels. Government, central and local, interceded directly on the supply side, spending millions on the purchase of domestic and foreign grain. For the suppliers (including producers as well as intermediaries), they were years of quick profits and speculative dreams, but also of inquisition, abuse, and sometimes commercial failure. The police trailed them, inspected them, and goaded them mercilessly, and consumers occasionally subjected them to popular forms of summary justice.

Each of these crises was occasioned by what Delamare defined as a *disette*, or dearth: "a famine commenced," that is, a situation in which

---

56 For "lists" of dearths and famines of extremely unequal value, see *Dictionnaire de Trévoux* (1771), III, 375; Husson, *Les Consommations de Paris*, 180; Molinari, "Céréales," in Coquelin and Guillaumin, eds., *Dictionnaire de l'économie politique*, I, 322; Morel, *Boulangerie*, 39–40; Andre Schlemmer, *Le Blé et le pain* (Brevannes, n.d.), 6–7; "Famines et disettes," *Magasin pittoresque*, 10th year (1842), 166–67; E. Levasseur, *Les Prix. Aperçu historique* (Paris, 1893), 105. See also François Vincent, *Histoire des famines à Paris* (Paris, 1946); Michel Cépède and Maurice Lengellé, *L'Economie de l'alimentation* (Paris, 1964); Michel Cépède and Hugues Gounelle, *La Faim* (Paris, 1967); and Cornelius Walford, *The Famines of the World, Past and Present* (London, 1879).

grain was in short supply, "rare" as well as "dear." By the commissaire's standard, the eighteenth century knew no famine, for a famine "is nothing other than a dearth consummated to its last extreme," a total absence of supplies.[57] In the contemporary hierarchy of hard times, the first stage, at once the most common and most fluid, was called *cherté*. It meant a period of extremely variable duration in which prices had already climbed above the level conventionally deemed normal and might go still higher. Although it often gave way to dearth, *cherté* did not necessarily imply a physical shortage of supply. Nor was it considered to be a truly critical situation. The police derived a certain amount of comfort from being able to categorize a given problem as a *cherté*, for it gave them some breathing space before they committed themselves to a definite course of action. Turgot and the physiocrats always insisted that *cherté* did not mean "penury" of grain and thus was not a harmful or alarming phenomenon.[58] Exasperated by what he considered to be precious, academic distinctions, Linguet, who wrote extensively about subsistence, argued that for the "people" a *cherté* was "absolutely equal" to a famine since bread was out of their reach in both instances. Using Linguet's cost-of-living measure, every year was a trying year for large segments of the population in the eighteenth century.[59]

It is worth noting that despite the unmistakable signs of crisis that characterized each of the episodes mentioned above, there were no universally acknowledged dearths in the century before the Revolution—not even the legendary "grand hyver" of 1709. By that I mean that some of the men who dealt with subsistence problems in the eighteenth century, as well as some who wrote about them, were not convinced that these dearths were "real." They conceded that some so-called dearths resembled real dearths in their immediate consequences, but they contended that no genuine grain shortages were involved. The most vocal debunkers were the physiocrats, who were also the most determined critics of the police regime. "Everyone knows that the one in Paris in 1725 was artificial," wrote Lemercier de la Rivière. Roubaud concurred and added 1740 to the list of "phony dearths."

---

57 Delamare, *Traité*, II, 794; "Mémoire joint à l'avis des Députés du Commerce" (1764), BN, mss. fr. 14295, fol. 64.

58 Edgar Faure, *La Disgrâce de Turgot* (Paris, 1961), 230.

59 Linguet, *Annales*, VII (Nov. 1779), 204, 224. Cf. *Année littéraire*, IV (1768), 98–99; remonstrances of 2–4 March 1776 in Flammermont, ed., *Remontrances*, III, 303; F. Gohin, *Les Transformations de la langue française pendant la deuxième moitié du 18ᵉ siécle* (Paris, 1903), 127.

Quesnay and Dupont both believed that most dearths were "dearths of opinion" rather than "real dearths." Even Galiani, who reviled the physiocrats, claimed that "dearth is, for three quarters [of the cases], a malady of the imagination."[60]

What is interesting is that the police did not dispute this assessment. As suggested earlier, the police were habitually disinclined to blame dearth upon natural shortage. The staunchly traditionalist intendant Bertier wrote that dearth "is almost never real" and the Code Duchesne echoed this attitude. But whereas the physiocrats ascribed these dearths, in the words of Condorcet, to "bad laws," the police blamed them, in the words of Delamare, "on the malice of men" or, as Bertier put it, "on the avidity of some and on the fear and fermentation of others." The physiocrats held the police responsible for causing the false dearth while the police blamed themselves only for not having held the line rigorously enough beforehand. Both sides agreed that fears and anxieties ("opinion") played a major part in the difficulties but whereas the police saw no difference between "real" needs and needs which "exist only in opinion," the physiocrats maintained that while appeasing opinion, police action heightened anxieties by suggesting the possibility of real shortage. Naturally the physiocrats' idea that dearth was unreal led them to deprecate the gravity or the urgency of the situation, whereas police tended to view dearth as a potential social crisis regardless of its origins. In fact, an artificial dearth could be even more serious than a real one, for if the people learned that they were suffering shortage in the midst of abundance they were likely to react furiously. It was precisely in cases of false dearth that disagreement was most pronounced: the police believed that their methods would be extremely effective and their critics believed that they would be both harmful and futile. To concede that dearths were normally real would have required both sides to modify their basic positions. Thus, by reinforcing the notion that dearths were artificial, both the police and their adversaries invited the

---

60 Roubaud, *Représentations aux magistrats*, 412; Lemercier de la Rivière, *L'Intérêt général*, 269; Dupont, *Analyse ... rapport*, 29; Quesnay, "Grain," in Diderot, *et al.*, *Encyclopédie*, VII, 825; Galiani, memoir to Sartine in *Lettres*, ed. by Asse, I, 420. Cf. *Journal économique* (Nov. 1768), 521; Condillac, *Le Commerce et le gouvernement*, in *Collection des principaux économistes*, ed. by Daire and Molinari, XIV, 329; and Turgot, who conceded the "reality" of the 1740 dearth, *Œuvres*, ed. by Schelle, III, 339.

public to believe that either there was something wrong with the grain trade or something wrong with the government, or both.[61]

There are some indications that the police regime was generally milder during the reign of Louis XV than it had been under Louis XIV. None of Louis XV's Lieutenants General of Police was as suspicious of merchants as La Reynie or as mistrustful of bakers as d'Argenson had been. Nor did they brutalize the hinterland as mercilessly as those two Lieutenants General. Although these signs of moderation may very well be the result of general changes in the political, economic, and military conditions rather than a specific revulsion against authoritarian methods, it is possible that individual police officials in the reign of Louis XV were influenced by some of the critical currents we associate with the Enlightenment. A great deal continued to depend on the personal styles and attitudes of different Controllers-General, Lieutenants General, and others in authority. Machault thought more seriously about dearth prevention than Dodun; Sartine was more interested in subsistence problems than Marville. However, prior to the 1760's, the police of provisioning, at least in the Paris area, did not undergo any profound transformations, either in day-to-day regulation or in strategies for dearth, real or artificial.

The ministers of Louis XV seem to have intervened more readily and more decisively on the supply side than their predecessors had. Perhaps the most striking aspects of the campaigns against the dearth in 1725 and 1740 were the operations for the purchase of "king's grain," grain purchased by the government or under its sponsorship for use especially in Paris and surrounding markets. Prior to the reign of Louis XV Paris had no emergency reserve system at all. In 1725 Hérault, the Lieutenant of Police, marshaled the hundreds of religious and hospital "communities" in and around the capital into a crude granary network which served Paris, on a very limited basis, until the

---

61 Condorcet, *Le Monopole et le monopoleur*, in *Collection des principaux économistes*, ed. by Daire and Molinari, XIV, 467; Delamare, *Traité*, II, 795–96; Bertier de Sauvigny, "Observations," BN, mss. fr. 11347, fol. 229; *Code Duchesne*, 103; L.-J. Bourdon-Desplanches, *Projet nouveau sur la manière de faire utilement en France le commerce des grains* (Brussels, 1785). 110; Lenoir, "Vivres, subsistances et approvisionnements," Lenoir papers, Bibliothèque municipale d'Orléans, ms. 1421; Terray to Esmangart, 12 Nov. 1773, C. 1439, A. D. Gir. For the persistence of the distinctions between real and artificial subsistence crises and their relation to the plot mentality, see *Révolutions de Paris*, #18 (7–14 Nov. 1789) and #61 (20–27 Aug. 1791), and R. Cobb, "Le Ravitaillement des villes sous la terreur: la question des arrivages," *Terreur et subsistances*, 211–192.

seventies. With the same aim in mind, the Controller-General Machault tried to launch a larger reserve scheme based on military provisioning in the fifties. Although he was unsuccessful, his efforts indirectly led to the establishment of a permanent king's grain fund which did give the Parisian police a modest safety valve of a kind that they never had before.

In the second half of the eighteenth century, the Paris police became deeply involved in the technological side of the subsistence question. They sponsored experiments in milling and baking to improve yield and quality, and they paid serious attention to foodways and to the development of new forms of bread and of wheaten-white bread surrogates. Future investigation will probably also show that police methods changed across the century in response to changes in the structure of the provisioning trade. There is strong evidence that the flour trade was displacing the grain trade as the major vehicle of Parisian supply; that the quondam grain barons of the port of the Grève were losing interest (and perhaps losing money) in the grain trade even as their alleged protectors in the Hôtel de Ville were losing influence; that the brokerage system was more important in 1750 than it had been half a century earlier; that the most powerful Paris bakers were more deeply enmeshed in grain and flour purchasing operations than their fathers and grandfathers had been. The impact of some of these changes was reflected in the resurgence of the Halles as the center of Parisian provisioning after mid-century; the consequences of others have yet to be charted.[62] Yet despite many signs of *aggiornamento*, the fundamental disposition of the police and their conception of their task did not change. Although the police read Delamare more critically in 1760 than in 1710, they still looked to him for their basic texts.

V

By a Declaration of May 1763 and an Edict of July 1764, the government of Louis XV broke radically with the provisioning tradition.[63] The king renounced the old police, the entrenched

---

62 The evidence for these claims is too scattered to cite here. It forms the basis of my forthcoming study, "The Paris Grain and Flour Trades in the Eighteenth Century."

63 The bulk of the following discussion is based upon an analysis of the texts of the two reform laws. Isambert, ed., *Recueil*, XXII, 393; *Recueil*, 30–33, 58–63.

priorities, and the very premises upon which the provisioning policy had been based. He proclaimed an era of liberty in which grain would be freed from the controls which had inhibited its movement, spied on its whereabouts, and governed the conditions of its exchange. The first of these liberal measures, the May Declaration, is best known for the freedom which it accorded grain to circulate interprovincially without passports or permissions. We have seen that the principle of liberty of internal movement was not alien to the police tradition. Officials viewed it, however, not as an imperative precondition for trade but as an allowance to be made in discretionary fashion depending upon the circumstances and the advantages it portended for a given moment and place. Good times usually meant a relatively untrammeled flow of grain; real, imagined, or anticipated difficulties tended to generate an obstructionist and xenophobic stance that reflected not merely subsistence anxiety, but the lessons of an intensely parochial world characterized by primitive communications, a multitude of different customary laws, collective traditions, and weights and measures, and a constricted sense of community.

The liberty of circulation postulated in the May Declaration defied established practice in two ways: it deprived officials of the freedom to mete out liberty as they saw fit and it imposed the principle as a uniform, integrative law of the land, a "general" law of the sort that French governments rarely succeeded in enforcing until the time of Napoléon.[64] It proclaimed a national market where none had existed before, based upon an identity of purpose in a single national community which most contemporaries could not yet discern. The May Declaration represented the finest expression of a form of enlightened kingship, which manifested itself intermittently in the Europe of *lumières*: the exercise of central authority to eradicate popular habit, administrative caprice, and widespread parochialism; the use of a grand prohibitive law to prohibit prohibitive laws; absolutism in the service of liberalism.

---

64 Historians have paid much more attention to the promulgation of (therefore, to the aspiration for) general or national laws than to their execution. Careful investigation of implementation would probably raise serious questions about the efficacy of the administrative monarchy and the meaning of centralization. See P. Goubert's perceptive remark in E. Labrousse and F. Braudel, eds., *Histoire économique et sociale*, II, 571. Often local officials did not receive word of important royal and parlementary *arrêts* or *lettres* until many months after publication. See, for example, Coueseau to the PG of the Paris Parl., 20 July 1769, BN, Coll. Joly 1146, fol. 15. Sometimes word of new legislation did not reach certain sections of the kingdom at all. See G. Afanassiev, *Le Commerce des céréales*, 154. See also below, chapter one.

By itself, the injunction against interference with grain circulation would have proven insufficient to effect a truly free commerce
in the interior. It afforded an impersonal and negative type of independence to a commodity; because it did not deal with the men who
traded in grain, it left them subject to a wide range of constraints.
Far more significant than the freedom proclaimed for grain was the
blanket invitation bestowed upon all citizens, of whatever quality
or conditions, including nobles and *privilégés*, to engage in this commerce "as it will seem to please them." This permissive immunity
breathed real iconoclasm into the liberal measures. For in the past
it had not been so much the grain as the owner and the trader
who were "prisoner" of the police nexus.[65] The declaration utterly
destroyed the system of controls. By granting everyone a mandate
not merely to trade but to deal anonymously, clandestinely, and/or
in association, to transact business off the markets, and to stockpile
limitlessly, it made it practically impossible for the police to operate. Explicitly, the declaration forbade officials to subject dealers to
"any formalities," such as registration of names and addresses and
declarations of amounts purchased and destination. To promote
greater facility of movement, another article prohibited "subjects"
who owned or farmed rights of *péage, passage, pontonage,* or *travers*—
the major customs barriers—to demand payment on any grains,
flour, or legumes. A similar measure, in the precarious form of an
arrêt du conseil, had been promulgated in 1739 in the midst of a grave
dearth. In many places it was simply ignored by officials unwilling
to join the issue with the influential interests who stood to lose revenue as a result of the law. In other areas it provoked wearisome
litigation which postponed execution indefinitely or open warfare in
the marketplaces between consumers who claimed—incorrectly—
that the *arrêt* freed them from paying *all* fees, not just transit tolls,

---

65 Michelet made the wheat-as-prison image famous in his *Histoire de France, Œuvres complètes*
(Paris, ed. Flammarion, n.d.), XVI, 192. Herbert used it in his pioneering treatise in favor of
liberty, *Essai sur la police générale des grains,* ed. by E. Depitre (Paris, 1910), 33. Necker employed
it in his *Sur la législation et le commerce des grains,* 176 and Galiani also adopted it in the *Dialogues
sur le commerce des bleds* (1770), ed. F. Nicolini (Milan, n.d.), 159. Simon Linguet, too, viewed
wheat as "trapped in the prisons," not of a tyrannical police, as Michelet contended, but of
the oppressive "opulence" of a perverse and disequilibrated society. *Du Pain et du bled,* 37.
Similarly, for L.-S. Mercier, wheat was the "bourreau" and man the victim. *Tableau de Paris,*
IV, 132. Voltaire saw the city, center of opposition to liberalization, as archetypal "prison."
"Voltaire à l'auteur des *Représentations aux magistrats,*" July 1769 in *Mercure de France* (Aug.
1769), 134.

and the owners of the *droits* who threatened to "demolish" the markets in retribution. By giving the abolition project the form of "a permanent law," Bertin expected that "it would be recognized in all the courts and generally enforced." In fact it proved as controversial in the sixties as it had a quarter century earlier, especially in those regions, such as the Bordelais and lower Normandy, where tolls were numerous and owners exacting. Diversely interpreted, contested, mired in a labyrinth of legal niceties, and subsequently modified, the clause did not give commerce the sort of thrust for which the ministry hoped.[66]

The last two articles, inspired by very different concerns, delimited the ambitions of the declaration. One extended the new law to its logical conclusion by abrogating all previous legislation and regulations contrary to it. The other pledged, "for the present time," to maintain in force all the rules heretofore elaborated for the provisioning of Paris.

The May Declaration treated the grain trade as a national affair; the Edict of July 1764, by permitting the export of grain and flour, added an international dimension. It marked, in the words of a distinguished Breton magistrate, the entry of France into "the common market of Europe."[67] Habitually, in times of stress and shortage, Frenchmen of all conditions blamed illicit traffic abroad as a major cause of hardship. When a climate of fear and uncertainty enveloped the kingdom, modest convoys of grain were reported as huge caravans, small barges became leviathan ships, while agitated witnesses spoke of plots and maneuvers to plunder the countryside and starve the people.[68] Sensitive to these anxieties, and cognizant of the real material threat which inopportune exports could pose, government policy, as we have seen, had always been circumspect and variable. In periods of dearth, it often proscribed grain exporting on pain of death. Henri IV underlined the link between kingship and subsistence by making unauthorized

---

66 Orry to IN. of Alençon, 17 Nov. 1739 and SDs of Falaise and Argentau to IN., 28 Nov. and 4 Dec. 1739, C. 89, A.D. Orne; Bertin to IN., 4 July 1761, C. 89 and 13 April 1762, C. 90, *ibid.* For a discussion of the limitations of this article and the effects of the maintenance of the "droits de marché," see Afanassiev, *Commerce*, 153–58; Georges Weulersse, "Les Physiocrates et la question du pain cher au milieu du dix-huitième siècle, 1756–1770," *Revue du dix-huitième siècle*, I (Jan.–March 1913), 180.

67 La Chalotais, charge to the Parl. of Rennes, 20 Aug. 1764, cited by D-Z [Desaubiez], *Le Bonheur public*, 36.

68 For an example of this syndrome, see Gazetins, 5 May 1729, Arsenal, mss. Bastille, 10159, fol. 155.

exportation a crime of "lèse-majesté."[69] In times of relative ease, the government issued new instructions, sometimes as frequently as every six months, licensing exportation through certain provinces, certain ports, or certain individuals for limited durations.

The July Edict introduced a fundamentally different approach. It established "free" or open exportation as the rule and interdiction as the exception. It named 27 ports as points of embarkation and—this was one of several mercantilist remnants in the liberal legislation—required traders to use French ships captained by nationals and manned by crews composed of at least two-thirds Frenchmen. Article seven imposed a negligible one-half percent duty on the value of exports. Export by land could take place at all border points where the General Farm maintained collection bureaus. Whenever the price of grain at the port or town of sortie passed 12 *livres* 10 *sous* the quintal (30 *livres* the Paris *septier* or approximately twice the average national price of the early sixties) during three consecutive markets, exportation would automatically cease from that point until the royal council specifically decided to reinstitute it by issuing a new piece of legislation. The edict also allowed traders of all nations to import grain and flour in national or foreign bottoms upon payment of a 1% duty on wheat and a 3% levy on all other cereal types. Merchants who re-exported foreign wheat within one year and flour and other grains within six months did not have to pay these fees. Finally, the July law reaffirmed the critical innovations concerning internal trade contained in the May Declaration.

The liberal legislation dealt with the grain trade, not from the perspective of subsistence and distribution, which had been the traditional focus of concern, but from that of agriculture. In its myopic solicitude for the consumers, the old system was now said to have discriminated against the producers, "this precious portion of our Subjects," and to have neglected the land "whose product is the most real and surest source of the wealth of a state." The king determined to redress the balance by offering the producers—the "owners" and *"fermiers"*—"special signs of the care we take of their interests." The May and July laws aimed at reinvigorating French agriculture. In concrete terms,

---

69 "Mémoire joint à l'avis des Députés du Commerce" (ca. pre-July 1764), BN, mss. français, 14295, fol. 45. Cf. Dupont de Nemours, *Analyse ... Rapport*, 32; Edme Béguillet, *Traité des subsistances* (Paris, 1780), 362; Pierre Lefèvre, *Le Commerce des grains à Lille*, 176. For traditional policy towards exportation, see Afanassiev, *Commerce des céréales*, 187–204; Musart, *Réglementation du commerce*, 77; Delamare, *Traité*, II, 776.

the king's favor meant the powerful incentive of higher prices in order to indemnify the cultivators for their labors, compensate the proprietors for their investments, and induce the landed interests to expand and intensify the exploitation of the realm's most productive resource. The new laws would promote the circulation of grain and legitimize their quest at home and abroad for a more profitable return.

According to this new approach to subsistence, the higher cost to consumers would represent, in the long run, a reasonable premium on the best possible insurance policy against scarcity and suffering. For only a revitalized, ambitious agriculture and an unfettered commerce could create a situation of permanent and widely diffused abundance, and only a "free and entire competition" in the marketplace could prevent the abuses of monopoly. Consumers who assimilated this lesson in political economy would have no cause for anxiety. Moreover, they would enjoy the largesse of an unlimited importation, which would deter grain from reaching a price "onerous to our Peoples." To the weak-willed and the worriers "who would not yet feel sufficiently the advantages that liberty must procure," the king conceded, not as a matter of principle, but as a sop, the 30 *livres* price ceiling above which exportation would cease.

For the moment, Paris was allowed to retain a special status. Qualifying articles reiterated in the Edict of 1764 maintained the capital's traditional provisioning police. In principle the Parisian authorities could do what they had always done to assure a regular supply for the capital. But the legislation did not indicate the specific modalities by which the city would be quarantined. Presumably it could be isolated in time and space and cut off from its multiple hinterlands simply by royal command. Prudential and political considerations prompted the government to apply this temporary double standard. Implicitly, the government conceded that the transition from prohibition to liberty would involve certain risks and adjustments. The ministry did not want the success or failure of the reform to pivot on this massive and unpredictable variable represented by the capital. Paris neutralized, the reform would have the opportunity to establish itself firmly in the rest of France. At some future date, Paris could be integrated into a national system of liberty. Nor was this the only ransom that the government was willing to pay in order to deliver the grain in the rest of the kingdom from captivity. Informally, outside the context of the reform legislation, it offered positive tribute to Parisian anxieties. In case of need, the capital had first call upon the large stock of king's grain and flour stored in depots near the city, which the government arranged to purchase by the contract which later became known as the Pact of Famine.

By the liberal decrees, Louis XV estranged himself unequivocally from the past and dissociated his reign from the policies which it had inherited and faithfully executed for almost a half century. The king repudiated the over-government and excessive rigor of his predecessors which he held responsible for agricultural lethargy and commercial demoralization. Nor was the old police merely vexatious and inordinate; grounded on false precepts, it was bound to stumble and miscalculate. The old system was niggardly, pessimistic, suspicious, and prohibitive; the new mood would be generous, sanguine, trusting, and permissive. Oblivious to the social utility of economic egotism, the police approach stunted growth and initiative; liberty, through the harmonious concourse of self-interests and in conformity with "the order established by divine providence," would release constructive energies and encourage progress. In place of a quixotic multiplicity of restrictive laws, which mistook simple mills for hideous monopolies and proved ineffective even in face of real abuses, the king proposed a self-disciplining commerce animated and regulated by the purgative forces of competition. The hubris that impelled the police to intervene in every affair would cede to a sophisticated administrative humility informed by an understanding of natural law.

At the same time it dismantled the police apparatus, the liberal legislation desacralized grain. Grain lost the privileged status with which custom, liturgy, and the terror of hunger had invested it. The May and July laws distinguished grain from any other merchandise only insofar as it represented the paramount source of national wealth. Styling his measures as "solemn and perpetual," the king made it patently clear that he viewed them as neither tentative nor experimental. Agriculture and commerce required security and confidence in order to bear fruit; Louis assured merchants and cultivators that there would be "no return" to the old ways.

The government labored mightily to keep the pledge it made in the king's name. But before examining the impact of liberalization and the problems it posed, let us inquire into its origins.

Chapter III

THE ORIGINS OF LIBERTY

A dramatic innovation, liberalization, I shall argue, took shape directly from the needs and circumstances of the early 1760's. Yet insofar as it embodied a certain vision of public administration and economic life—a theory of political economy—it had an ample critical tradition upon which to draw. It is beyond the scope of this chapter to sketch a history of the development of political arithmetic or political economy in the Old Regime, though such a study, fully integrated into the context of political, economic, and social change, is sorely needed. Nor can it attempt to do for the idea of liberty what Mauzi did for "happiness" and Ehrard for "nature," though such an undertaking, too, would be of great value. I wish only to suggest that liberalization had an important intellectual as well as political and economic preparation, leaving it to others to pursue these connections in detail. I have already discussed on several occasions the critics of the police. Most of them were part of what became the movement for liberalization. I refer to all persons who favored a fundamental reform of the police in the direction of greater liberty as liberals. By liberalism I mean to indicate nothing more than those political, economic, and social ideas that informed the attitude of the grain trade reformers and their allies. To others, too, I leave the task of charting out the links between this grain-centered liberalism of the Old Regime and the Liberalism which triumphed in the nineteenth century.

I

Like many of the notions that became preoccupations of the Enlightenment, the liberal idea crystallized during the reign of Louis XIV. It appeared in several versions in the anti-mercantilist,

Christian-agrarian, and utilitarian currents which traversed the kingdom in the second half of the seventeenth century.[1] Already the landowners were plotting the political resurgence and the revenge taken in prices and profits which the eighteenth century would allow them. A large part of the merchant community rejected Colbertism on grounds that would become familiar to eighteenth century reformers.[2] Political dissenters criticized the methods of government for their arbitrariness and their oppressiveness—that is, for their excessive police in all domains of life: administration, religion, and foreign policy as well as the economy. At the turn of the century, when Delamare began to codify the principles of good police, Boisguilbert, the archetypal *officier*-reformer, assailed the regulatory apparatus and ascribed the generalized economic, financial, and human catastrophes which marked the last years of Louis XIV to benighted government policy. Ardent partisan of free trade, he enunciated the fundamental liberal proposition that low prices spelled agricultural ruin and national depression and that high prices were the only cure for high prices.[3] Neglected in his own time, in the second half of the eighteenth century his stature rose as sharply as the rent on land. Niggardly with praise, the *économistes* ranked him as one of their few authentic precursors.[4]

The regency is often celebrated as a period of revulsion for the fiercely regimented style of the classical world. It is better known for its libertinage than for its philosophy, but it is worth noting that John Law postulated liberty of commerce as a precondition for agricultural development, which he tied to his grand scheme for increasing the gross national product.[5] His collaborator, Jean-François Melon, espoused a modulated free trade policy in the interior contingent upon

---

1 See L. Rothkrug, *Opposition to Louis XIV: The Political and Social Origins of the French Enlightenment* (Princeton, 1965).

2 The English example made a deep impression on the merchant community. See the remarks of Turgot, "Lettres sur le commerce des grains," 30 Oct. 1770 (#1), *Œuvres*, ed. by G. Schelle (Paris, 1913–1923), III, 270. Cf. Donald G. Barnes, *A History of the English Corn Laws from 1660 to 1846* (London, 1930).

3 See his *Détail, Factum* and *Traité des grains* (1696–1707). Cf. Marguerite Leblanc, *De Thomas More à Chaptal. Contribution bibliographique à l'histoire économique* (Paris, 1961), 20; Henri Curmond, *Le Commerce des grains et l'école physiocratique* (Paris, 1900), 28–34; André J. Bourde, *Agronomie et agronomes en France au dix-huitième siècle* (Paris, 1967), I, 129–30; Labrousse in Labrousse and Braudel, eds., *Histoire économique et sociale*, II, 368–69.

4 Le Mercier de la Rivière, *L'Intérêt général de l'état*, 236–37; A. Morellet, *Réfutation de l'ouvrage qui a pour titre: Dialogues sur le commerce des bleds* (London, 1770), 301.

5 Bourde, *Agronomie*, I, 161; Labrousse in E. Labrousse and Braudel, eds., *Histoire économique et sociale*, II, 370.

the sufficiency of supply and subject to evaluation by an elaborate central data-collecting agency. Albeit philosophically "very superficial," his achievement, observed Diderot, "... and it is not a small merit, is to have been the first in recent times to stir up economic matters."[6]

In the 1740's, buoyed by the English example and alarmed by evidence of agricultural stagnation, Claude Dupin, one of several eighteenth century farmers-general who labored publicly for reform, composed a vigorous *Mémoire sur les Blés*. He denounced the unfraternal and "cowardly" attitude of intendants who sealed off their provinces as if "surrounded by enemies" and argued that a global free trade policy founded on a belief in national social solidarity would preserve France from both "the horror of sterility" and "the burdens of superfluity" by maintaining a price acceptable to consumers and producers. Dupin's "projet d'édit," which he submitted to two Controllers-General, stopped short of authorizing an absolute liberty. He subjected merchants to constant police surveillance, imposed a sliding cut-off ceiling on exports, and proposed import bounties when the price surpassed 24 *livres* the two hundred pound sack. Orry, a tough-minded interventionist minister, apparently manifested genuine interest in the financier's plan. His ephemeral *Arrêt du Conseil* of September 1743, however, lamely endorsed interprovincial grain movement only when undertaken in compliance with "the different regulations made in the different provinces."[7]

The next Controller-General, Machault, also gave the project serious consideration. His biographer strained apologetically to portray him as a forward-looking statesman whose avid liberal ambitions were thwarted by unfavorable circumstances.[8] Viewed in broader perspective, it is clear

6 Diderot, 15 Nov. 1769, in F. M. Grimm, *Correspondance littéraire, philosophique et critique par Grimm, Diderot, Raynal, etc.*, ed. by Maurice Tourneux (Paris, 1877–82), VIII, 372; Georges Weulersse, *Le Mouvement physiocratique en France (1756–1770)* (Paris, 1910), I, 17–21.

7 C. Dupin, "Mémoire sur les bleds," BN, mss. n.a. 22777, published in 1748 and reprinted in the *Journal économique*, Feb. and March 1760; *Journal de Trévoux* (April 1754), 821–28; Orry to IN. of Alençon, 2 Oct. 1743, C. 89, A.D. Orne; Afanassiev, *Commerce des céréales*, 106. Tessier, in the *Encyclopédie méthodique*, credited Dupin with being "the first [who] wrote in favor of the liberty of this commerce" but remarked that he argued with "so much timidity and circumspection that his work would suffice to demonstrate to what extent we were then removed from true principles." Article "Commerce des grains," *Encyclopédie méthodique*, Agriculture (Paris, 1793), III, 355.

8 Marcel Marion, *Machault*, 425, 429. For a similar opinion, see E. Levasseur, *Histoire des classes ouvrières ... en France* (Paris, 1901), II, 578n. Cf. G. Schelle, *Vincent de Gournay* (Paris, 1897), 43 and "Extrait d'un mémoire sur les bleds communiqué par

that Machault faced the same imbroglio which bedevilled intelligent administrators throughout the century. Ideally, he would have preferred to rely solely on an unencumbered grain trade to provision the realm; police control and government operations were onerous and costly. But on numerous occasions he found commerce unequipped and unwilling to perform the mission. Faced with imperious demands, he felt obliged to intercede.[9]

On the one hand, Machault affirmed with considerable ardor "that it is of the greatest importance to maintain full liberty in the grain trade, never to chance impairing it in the slightest...." On the other hand, "since this unlimited liberty, lacking fixed and wise rules, could give rise to the most dangerous abuses," the Controller-General felt that "it is of an equal importance to take quite specific measures which, *without impairing the liberty of trade*, will restrict its exercise within the boundaries prescribed by different regulations and prevent this unlimited liberty from serving as a pretext for disorders and monopolies." Among the measures he had in mind were merchant registration, mandatory market transactions, monitoring of circulation by intendants, and regular searches of granaries in order to stamp out hoarding. As if to reassure himself, Machault emphasized that none of this "could ever be considered as a blow against liberty of trade." Appalled by the glaring contradictions, the next generation of reformers viewed Machault's position as an astonishing act of self-parody and -deception at best and as an access of hypocrisy at worst. Schooled in the same prudential tradition as the Controller-General, administrators perceived no inconsistency in his dual commitment to freedom and regulation. Precisely in order to make "free circulation" socially useful, Machault wanted to "direct" the activities of merchants, to establish uniform control procedures throughout the realm, to match supply and demand in time and space, and, on occasion, to intervene on the supply side, in the short run with government grain purchases and in the long run with publicly-sponsored

---

M. de Machault, contrôleur-général à Mr. Pâris Duverney ...," AN, F[12] 647. D'Argenson's estimation is harsh but not wholly without merit. See his *Journal et mémoires*, ed. by E.J.B. Rathery (Paris, 1859–67), III, 340 (10 July, 1750).

9 On the circumstances of Machault's interventions, see "Additions," Arsenal, mss. Bastille, 12352; Michel Lhéritier, *L'Intendant Tourny* (Paris, 1920), I, 391–404, 411–414; Pierre Clemént and Alfred Lemoine, *M. de Silhouette, Bouret, les derniers fermiers-généraux du XVIIIe siècle* (Paris, 1872), 155–64; Marcel Marion, "Une Famine en Guyenne (1747–48)," *Revue historique*, XLVI (May–Aug. 1891), 247ff.; Dupont, *Analyse ... rapport*, 90ff.

granary organizations. In a word, he regarded liberty not as an alternative, but as an adjunct to the police way.[10]

Between 1748 and 1751, the Age of Enlightenment produced some
of its greatest monuments: The *Esprit des Lois*, the *Discours*, and the first
installments of the *Encyclopédie*. In 1753 Claude-Jacques Herbert, a
middle-rank public servant at Bordeaux alert to the changing mood
of the times, published a treatise which argued forcefully for a central
place for political economy and the grain question in particular in the
movement *of lumières*. Offering his *Essay on the General Police of Grain, on
its Prices, and on the Effects of Agriculture* as a contribution to "the happiness of people," he dedicated it to his friend Maupertuis and invoked
the patronage of Locke and Newton, both of whom had at some point
dealt with "Economic Subjects."[11] The *Essay*, which enjoyed six editions
in the next four years, was the most detailed and cogent critique yet
written on the public administration of the grain commerce. The *économistes* of the sixties and seventies borrowed heavily from Herbert, generally without attribution; he charted out the lines of reasoning which
they refined, amplified, or incorporated into their more ambitious
systems.[12] Herbert wrote with none of their truculence; his approach
was self-consciously sober and judicious. Nonetheless, the essay read
as a searing indictment of the police, a sort of anti-Delamare in which
Herbert turns the ponderous innocence of the commissaire to his own
advantage.[13] A glance at Herbert's *Essay* thrusts into relief the major
points of contention between the police and the liberals.

Herbert charged that Delamare misused history and misunderstood
the significance of the past for present needs. The commissaire's infatu-
ation with remote Rome was one source of police sophistry. "But these
laws so necessary to the Romans," Herbert asked, "are they applicable to our present situation?" Within our own past, he wrote, there
was a time, in the age of Saint Louis, when the police of grain was
simple, clear, and restrained. Ever since, despite occasional flashes

---

10 Machault to IN. of Rouen, 12 Dec. 1751, C. 103, A.D. S-M. His reflections were prompted
    by the subsistence alarm of 1751 which he attributed in large measure to trader "cupidity"
    and "maneuvers."

11 Herbert, *Essai*, ed. by Depitre, iii–iv.

12 Though there is no sure way to measure its influence, Herbert's *Essai* was certainly more
    widely known in the sixties by local officials and notables than any of the works of the
    économistes. See, for example, the "Mémoire" (1762) of the prior-consuls of St. Malo,
    C. 3911, A.D. I-et-V.

13 See, for example, the discussion of Delamare's work, Herbert, *Essai*, ed. by Depitre, 23, 40,
    passim.

of light, it seems "the more we wanted to perfect this Police the more we strayed from the right path." The proof of the failure of the police Herbert drew from Delamare himself and from Dupré de St. Maur's price series in which "one could read ... a part of the History of our Monarchy." Characteristically, when the police intervened in the bleak years they drove rising prices higher, frightened off or dried up the sources of supply, and prolonged public suffering. In addition to exacerbating present difficulties, the police regulations compromised future prospects, for they gravely damaged agriculture by making cultivation economically unattractive.[14]

In Herbert's judgment, a fatal confusion of priorities misled the police. To be sure, the aim of the grain trade was to feed the nation as well as to enrich it. But in order to assure the success of this mission, agriculture had to be protected and rewarded. The land is our "common mother" and agriculture furnishes the "most real" source of our wealth and well-being. The government, Herbert admonished, must realize that "the severe police of grain never caused an ear to grow."[15] A good subsistence police would consist of stimulating increased production while leaving the rest to a free commerce. The current English example in this regard was far more relevant than the Roman. A liberal policy has enabled English agriculture and trade to flourish while ours has languished, though "our peasants work more cheaply than the English [and] our land is generally better [and] easier to work." Nor have we "... seen England afflicted by any dearth or any marked *cherté*" as a result of this policy of letting men pursue their own interests in the most favorable conditions.

The Enlightenment was so exhilarating because it told men that they could find within themselves the seeds of progress and happiness. In order to release these progressive energies, men had to be freed of artificial internal and external constraints. Self-interest was the psychological foundation of all human activity and the proper agency for this emancipation. "It is the destiny of humanity," Herbert intoned, "to be highly motivated only by personal interest." The police shared this view, but drew from it stark conclusions which prompted them to see interest as a potentially antisocial force in need of constant discipline. On the contrary, Herbert argued, the sum of all interests was inevitably congenial, and their interplay socially concordant and profitable:

14 *Ibid.*, 2–3, 33, 74. Cf. *ibid.*, 25–29.
15 *Ibid.*, 1, 32, 44, 51, 103.

"needs and interests govern the Universe; unite these wellsprings; and men by a natural instinct will direct themselves in concert towards the objectives of their needs and their country."[16]

Needs and interests, in Herbert's reckoning, invariably find their own equilibrium. When government undertakes to satisfy the one and curtail the other, it undermines the balance and hurls the system into disarray. Nor could government, inspired by the best intentions, fulfill the needs as rapidly, economically, and neatly as private individuals. The dynamics of greed excluded elements of risk, waste, and inefficiency. In pursuit of their interests men performed prodigies of public service. For the police to insist upon an ideal of disinterest, at least in matters of commerce, was to deprive men of their most powerful incentive to do good and to deny society the benefits of social organization. "The Ordinances," concluded Herbert, "conduct little grain to the market; it is interest which brings them there."[17] Left unimpeded, the multiplicity of interests, through competition, will generate their own rules and snuff out abuses. Appetite for profit will propel grain wherever there is need and rivalry for clients will assure the public of a reasonable price and suitable quality.

The first step in the process of police reform must be demystification. The fetishistic attitude toward grain, along with all the "phantoms" accused of subtilizing it, had to be exorcised. Grain must be frankly treated as an "object of commerce" and its dealers as simple merchants. Herbert deplored the factitious distinctions that the law had made between good trade and bad, usurious and honest, covert and open. There was only one sort of trade, that by which businessmen tried to make as large a profit or sustain as little loss as possible. Lurid scenarios of merchant turpitude written into police codes served only to dissuade the ablest men from entering the commerce and to discredit the entire profession in the eyes of the public.[18] Rehabilitated, the grain trade had to be opened to everyone without distinction and without any formal obligations to register and report to authorities. No restrictions of any kind would hamper interior circulation. In the name of "family" cohesion and "public utility," France would cease to be shamefully "at war with herself." Open communication from province

---

16 *Ibid.*, 7, 57.

17 *Ibid.*, 95. Cf. *ibid.*, 21.

18 *Ibid.*, 14–15, 50, *passim.* Cf. Grimm's concurrence, despite his general lack of sympathy with grain liberalism. *Correspondance littéraire*, ed. by Tourneux, III, 100–104 (Oct. 1755).

to province would attenuate *cherté* in sterile areas, temper the discouragement of glut in surplus regions, and generally equalize prices throughout the realm. On exportation, this precious boon to agriculture, Herbert took a cautious and somewhat evasive stand. Experience will instruct and embolden us, he suggested; for the moment, he foresaw a general permission to export only in "the time of a superfluous abundance."[19]

In Herbert's estimation, nothing impeded reform so much as the tacit pact of collaboration which bound together the police and the people. Over the course of the years, they developed a lamentable symbiosis which reinforced their attitudes towards the subsistence question to the detriment of reason, prosperity, and good habits of government. From the earliest times, ignorance and dread underlay suspicion of the grain trade and malaise over provisioning. Instead of combating these primitive instincts, the police indulged them; instead of exposing popular prejudices, they wrote them into law. The police cultivated a constituency of fear and rationalized brutal interventions in the grain trade by the need to contain a frightened population. The police codes conditioned the public to expect authorities to provide for its well-being at any cost. "But it is dangerous for the people and for the State," warned Herbert, "to maintain bread at too low a price." Overly cheap bread maimed the state by reducing its revenue and drying up the sources which produced it and it corrupted the people and threatened the social order by encouraging "idleness, the mother of vice," and engendering "the race of beggars." Consumers had to learn that the entire economy depended upon the pilot grain sector, that their interests were the same as those of the producers, and that this solidarity precluded discriminatory treatment geared to assure them a "too easy subsistence." "Opinion is the queen of the world," noted Herbert, reciting one of the Enlightenment's favorite aphorisms. The old police, "timid and fickle" like the people, had to bear the responsibility for shaping the popular mentality on the grain issue. The "new police" had to begin by re-educating the nation in the school of "absolute liberty."[20]

None of the liberals ever devised a convincing strategy for waging the battle for mass opinion. Herbert himself aimed at winning adherents among the highly literate and informed who could influence the course of public affairs. On the whole, his *Essay* received a warm

---

19 *Ibid.*, 15, 31–32, 61.
20 *Ibid.*, 4–5, 7, 10, 29, 91, 95–96, 108.

reception. Two of the foremost *mauvaises langues* of the century, d'Argenson and Grimm, heaped praise upon the author. The marquis judged the liberal spirit of the work "in my taste" because it confirmed his contention that "to govern better, one must govern less." Grimm, the editor of the *Correspondance Littéraire*, who later became one of the most stinging adversaries of *économiste* dogma and bombast, lauded the *Essay* for the clarity and vigor of its language and its great good sense. Herbert revealed "the contradiction of our laws, their perpetual conflict, and the evils which result from them" and he rescued grain dealers from the gratuitous opprobrium which dishonored them. Writing many years later, Grimm viewed the *Essay* as the first salvo in the "combat" which, "à force de brochures," led to the liberal legislation of 1763–64. The propagandists who followed Herbert merely repeated his ideas, "but this very repetition was necessary in order finally to achieve so salutary a project." In a joyful but dubious analogy, an anonymous correspondent of the *Journal Economique* proposed to crown Herbert "the second Joseph of our fertile Egypt."[21]

The most auspicious applause came from an unlikely source, the *Journal de Trévoux*, a periodical not notorious for its hospitality to iconoclastic propaganda. The editors confessed that they did not undertake to publicize Herbert on their own humble initiative:

> We give notice to our readers that a number of very distinguished persons who have influence in the Government wanted the two works., extracts of which have just been presented [the *Essay on the General Police* and Dupin's *Mémoire* of 1742] to *make some impression on the public*. It is that which inspired us to enter this important discussion.

Even with a quasi-official imprimatur, the editors felt uneasy with Herbert's assault on traditional government. A fastidious reading of the text revealed to them a fortunate distinction which reassured them on Herbert's purpose. On first sight Herbert "appears to oppose the laws received among us regarding the general Police of grain," but "at bottom" he quarreled with "the disadvantages of the letter" rather than with their guiding "spirit." Herbert was an amiable critic of good will, not a hostile subversive. He impugned neither the "intentions" of the law nor "the sentiments of our Princes for their Subjects." He demonstrated "only that we have not entered the route consonant with the public needs and with the desire that we had to satisfy them."

---

21 D'Argenson, *Mémoires*, ed. by Rathery, IV, 168 (Feb. 1754); Grimm, *Correspondance littéraire*, ed. by Tourneux, III, 100–104 (Oct. 1755); *ibid.*, VI, 30 (July 1764); Letter to the Editor, *Journal économique* (May 1754), 80–82.

Once they discovered an appetite for change, traditionalists showed remarkable ingenuity in making the reform menu palatable. The editors of the *Journal de Trévoux* distorted the recipe but they devoured the *pièce de résistance.* "To disturb the grain trade," they averred, "is to place in the State a source of dearth and monopoly."[22]

In 1754, five months after the *Journal de Trévoux* launched this trial balloon at its urging, the government issued an *arrêt du conseil* proclaiming the liberty of internal circulation and authorizing exportation by two southern ports.[23] Given the sequence of events, it would be tempting to view this legislation as a resounding victory for liberalization at the highest levels, the fruit of the collaboration of a ministry predisposed to reform, a handful of propagandists led by Herbert, and an influential liberal clique, animated perhaps by the intendant of commerce Vincent de Gournay, which had the government's ear.[24] To sustain such a view, however, one would have to make an artful distinction, as the editors of the *Journal de Trévoux* did, between the elusive spirit and the actual letter of the law. For the letter was flatly pedestrian and conventional, resembling a number of earlier laws of occasion meant to promote communications in the interior and to relieve specific areas of burdensome surpluses. The *arrêt* suppressed the obligation to obtain passports or permits for interprovincial trade, a requirement very frequently ignored in good times. It did not touch the crazy quilt of police regulations and controls which governed the trade at the grass roots. Prefaced by no declaration of principles and published without fanfare, the *arrêt* enjoyed little resonance and gradually died of inanition. Local police, if they knew of its existence, remained blithely indifferent and the intendants executed it without conviction.[25] The form of legislation chosen to convey the act deprived it of the prestige and

---

22 *Journal de Trévoux* (April 1754), 802–804, 810.

23 See copies of the *arrêt* in C. 80, piece 22, A.D. C d'O and C. 89, A.D. Orne. Cf. CG to IN. of Champagne, 29 Sept. 1754, C. 418, A.D. Marne.

24 Marion argues unconvincingly that the liberal spirit pervaded the ministry under Machault. *Machault,* 433–35. Skeptical of Marion's claims, Schelle believed that Gournay, backed by the new Controller-General Moreau de Séchelles, was the moving force of liberalization in many different domains. *Gournay,* 74–76. Dupont later included Herbert on the select list of Gournay's disciples. Léonce de Lavergne, *Les Economistes français du dix-huitième siècle* (Paris, 1870), 174 and Schelle, *Gournay,* 238.

25 On the indifference of authorities, even at the highest provincial level, to the enforcement of the *arrêt,* see the complaints of the Controllers-General Peirenc de Moras and Bertin. Moras to IN. of Rouen, 31 Jan. 1757, C. 104, A.D. S-M.; Moras to IN. of Provence, 23 June, 25 July 1757, C. 2420, A.D. B-du-R.; Bertin, "Mémoire à consulter

authority it needed to be successful and suggested that the government did not consider it to be a crucial affair. The *arrêt du conseil* was not an "immutable law;" not enveloped in letters patent and thus "unknown to the parlements," it was incommensurate with the task of transforming the police of grain.[26]

Intrinsically banal, the *arrêt* of 1754 acquired significance only isofar as it followed closely behind the liberal propaganda offensive. If it is to be construed as a response to such pressure, rather than as an act of circumstance prompted by a series of unusually good harvests, it must still be seen less as a sign of the political strength of the expanding liberal camp than as a measure of its continuing weakness. If the government sought a way to gratify liberal opinion and benefit owners of surplus grain without engaging any serious political or social risk, then the *arrêt* was shrewdly conceived. To be sure, the *arrêt* heartened liberal commentators not so much for its substance, which inspired virtually no discussion, as for its symbolical quality. They saw it as a personal "triumph" for Herbert, specifically crediting his *Essay* with having "occasioned" it.[27] This attitude bespeaks an idealized conception of reform which was widely held in the Age of Enlightenment and to which many historians, searching for the connection between philosophy and politics, have since subscribed. The basic idea was that the government, albeit susceptible to change, lacked the imagination and the will to generate it. The plan and the impetus had to come from

---

sur le libre commerce des grains," 1761, C. 2420, A.D. B-du-R. On the other hand, the intendant of Burgundy, Joly de Fleury, tried vainly to enforce the law in the late 1750's, but the Dijon Parlement adamantly refused to cooperate. Indeed, on the grounds of a threatened scarcity in 1759, the magistrates brazenly flouted the royal legislation by imposing an embargo on the shipment of grain outside the Burgundian *ressort*. Though this measure incensed the Controller-General Silhouette, he esteemed that it would be inopportune for the king's council to annul the parlementary *arrêt* "in the current circumstances." His decision must have demoralized the intendant even as it encouraged the Parlement to pursue its autonomous course. IN. to CG, 10 Oct. 1759 and CG to IN. 13, 19 Oct. 1759, AN, H 187.

26 Forbonnais [?], "Mémoire sur la police des grains," (April 1758), BN, mss. fr. 11347; Bertin to Turgot, Sept. 1774, cited by Weulersse, *Mouvement*, II, 210-lln; Bertier de Sauvigny, "Observations sur le commerce des grains" (1765), BN, mss. fr. 11347, fol. 224; Montaudouin de la Touche, *Supplément à l'essai sur la police générale des grains ...*, ed. by Depitre, (Paris, 1910), 149; *Journal encyclopédique*, VIII (1 July 1759), 49.

27 *Journal de commerce* (Brussels, Sept. 1759), 84; Savary des Bruslons, *Dictionnaire portatif de commerce* (Copenhagen, 1761), III, 137; *Journal de Trévoux* (Oct. 1755), 2598–99; *Journal encyclopédique*, VIII (1 July 1759), 48–49. Cf. *Journal économique* (Aug. 1755), 113. In the aftermath of a family financial disaster, Herbert committed suicide in 1758. Grimm, *Correspondance littéraire*, ed. by Tourneux, III, 482 (March 1758).

outside. First the case had to be put before the public. If it passed the test, and in addition proved technically feasible, the government could reasonably be expected to receive it with favor. In this view the courtier-intellectual played the higher role of citizen-intellectual. In less progressive times, ministers had made decisions and afterward commissioned books and pamphlets to popularize and justify them. Now patriots wrote books, mobilized enlightened opinion, and presented the government with a program and a pretext to act.

In Herbert's sober estimation, liberty had not yet won the day. For the idea that liberty was "dangerous" still commanded support in the kingdom.[28] Muffled by the peal of acclaim for the *Essay*, several strains of criticism played on the perils of liberalization. The reviewer in the *Journal des Sçavans* admired Herbert's earnestness but warned against his method of analysis and the side-effects of the remedy he proposed. Without specifically articulating his fears, he sensed something sinister in Herbert's approach, the seed of a powerful disintegrating force reaching far beyond our "alimentary code." Laws and rules which seem defective when torn from their context may prove to be "very wise" when viewed as part of a larger scheme:

> Everything holds together in a well-regulated Government and to reason about it correctly one must see the ensemble of its different parts and the bond which they have with one another.[29]

This appeal to the whole and the cohesion of a complex and intricate design became the refuge of beleaguered conservatism in the Age of Enlightenment. But it should be remembered that the argument enjoyed a certain philosophical respectability—Montesquieu used a nuanced version of it—and it served a school of system-building philosophes who became the chief proponents of the liberal spirit in the sixties and seventies. Vague and portentous, this objection is interesting precisely because it raises the specter, not of famine and suffering and the immediate risks which seemed to make liberalization dangerous, but of the long-run political implications that lurked beneath the surface, an aspect of the problem which did not receive sustained consideration until the following decade. Just as Herbert questioned the relevance of dated historical and cultural models, so the reviewer in the *Journal des Sçavans* challenged the applicability of the contemporary foreign examples upon which the author of the *Essay* drew. Different nations

---

28 "Avertissements" to the 1755 edition in *Essai*, ed. by Depitre, v.
29 *Journal des sçavans* (April 1754), 366–77.

not only had different resources and interests; they possessed different constitutions. Was liberty compatible with the French system of government? The *Journal de Trévoux* reconciled Herbert's reform plans with the traditional aims of government. It approved his onslaught against unfounded "prejudices": "it is to destroy them that this excellent work was written." But, it cautioned, "why destroy everything?" Herbert's tendency to categorize all "privileges" and "exemptions" as "abuses" alarmed the editors and prodded them to wonder whether he did not extend the cutting edge of his logic too far.[30]

The *Journal Economique*, purging its conscience before its total conversion to the liberal cause, published several pieces sharply critical of Herbert's reform program. Herbert strenuously denied that the grain trade was inherently flawed and given to deceptions which mangled the public interest. He treated monopolies as byproducts of police controls which liberty would dissipate or as imaginary bogeys contrived by authorities to conceal their ineptitude and embraced by a susceptible populace in search of scapegoats. "To that we reply," wrote a commentator in the *Journal*, "that monopolies of grain are neither a chimera nor a prejudice." Perpetrated by cunning men who operated clandestinely, they "produce the greatest evils." It was the urgent business of authorities to pursue them relentlessly and expose their maneuvers.[31]

Another critic writing for the *Journal* took particular exception to the notion that "everyone indistinctly should have a hand in the commerce of grain." Such a policy would invite social disorder, confusion of roles, and conflicts of interest. The hierarchy of orders which assured social stability also had functional value. It guaranteed that jobs would be well done. An open grain trade would encourage men to abandon their professions in search of windfall lucre without regard for public needs and for proper care of their merchandise. Nobles would be tempted to derogate and judges to associate themselves with merchants for whose conduct they were responsible. Under such conditions, "monopoly" and "usury" would flourish.[32]

Anxious to avoid an unseemly polemic, Herbert did not respond directly to these objections. But the debate that was brewing served his purposes. Flushing defenders of the traditional system from their redoubt of impassive silence, it would compel them to justify their

---

30 *Ibid.; Journal de Trévoux* (Oct. 1755), 2604, 2622.
31 *Journal économique* (Feb. 1754), 116–119.
32 *Ibid.*, (Aug. 1755), 113–118.

position publicly. In the preface to a new, enlarged edition of the *Essay*, Herbert called for a strenuous campaign of propaganda to expose their errors at every turn and to disseminate "economic knowledge" among the profane.[33]

Criticism from the enlightened left surprised and nettled Herbert more than disapprobation from the benighted right. In 1756 Montaudouin de la Touche, a specialist in commercial affairs and member of a prominent shipping family, published an article rebuking Herbert for his "excessive prudence" and "timidity," the very qualities for which the latter reproached the traditionalists. Montaudouin represented the mood of unconditional and impatient liberalism reminiscent of Boisguilbert, which would find its fullest expression in the next decade. He assailed Herbert for his lack of faith, for betraying his own principles, and for abandoning the "entire liberty" which he pretended to espouse.

The crucial issue was exportation. Herbert recoiled at the thought of granting unlimited and irrevocable authorization. In order to protect France from pillage and uncertainty, he advocated either duties on shipments abroad or a sliding price ceiling which would automatically cut off exportation at certain junctures. Beneath Herbert's fleshy liberalism, Montaudouin detected the sallow bones of neo-mercantilism and "a residue of respect for old prejudices." Herbert did not understand that the nations of the world were "like a great family formed by commerce." The power of self-interest transcended national boundaries; the solidarity of individuals merged imperceptibly with the harmony of nations. Ideally situated in the middle of Europe, and endowed with extraordinary natural abundance, a free-trading France would become the breadbasket and entrepôt of the continent. A niggardly, partial liberty would leave the kingdom vulnerable to dearth. Only a total liberty promised a total cure.[34]

---

33 Preface to the 1759 edition of the *Essai*, ed. by Depitre, vii.

34 *Supplément à l'essai sur la police générale des grains*, ed. by Depitre, 149–54 and *Réplique à la lettre précédente, ibid.*, 159–64. The latter appeared in the *Journal de commerce* (Brussels, Oct. 1761), 68–82.

In the sixties, when the most vocal exponents of economic liberalism consolidated their efforts under Quesnay's aegis, Montaudouin again found himself constrained to demur. His position underscores the ambiguities in the physiocratic argument. He deeply resented Quesnay's contention that commerce was a sterile occupation, that merchants were vagabond aliens, and that agriculture was the sole source of national wealth. See his "Observations sur le commerce," with Quesnay's peremptory notations in *François Quesnay et la physiocratie* (Paris: Institut National des Études Démographiques, 1958), II, 879–883.

In a pointed rebuttal, Herbert deplored Montaudouin's doctrinaire approach, political naiveté, and carping attitude. In order to effect political change, Herbert believed it was necessary to win public confidence. At all costs, he wanted to avoid "alarming" citizens and ministers with his proposals:

> It is not by a peremptory tone that one persuades; one must have discretion and care and conform to the standard manner of thinking in order to scandalize no one, and obtain first the easiest to arrive [later] at the most difficult.

Nor was it merely a tactical regard for sensibilities that motivated Herbert's program. Unbounded exportation genuinely worried him. It would imperil the nation's subsistence. In his lust for liberty, Montaudouin "confused … times of penury with those of plenty." The national interest demanded a flexible export policy responsive to changing conditions. Learned in commerce, Montaudouin ignored the rudiments of government. Insouciantly, "he admits of no preparation, forms no doubt, [foresees] no difficulty with total liberty."[35] Herbert's cautious attitude in general, and his stand on exports in particular, sharply distinguished his brand of liberalism from that of his successors in the grain liberation movement.

II

Herbert deserves credit for sparking the liberal effervescence of the fifties but he was not alone in a wilderness. Concurrently, or shortly afterwards, a host of writers began to give shape to the publicity campaign which the author of the *Essay* so ardently desired. In these formative days, the criteria for militancy were still generously defined. Although Montaudouin's purist stance presaged a deep fissure which would soon develop in the liberal camp, for the moment it was possible to rally men of diverse ideas around a commitment to overthrow the old regime of grain. Forbonnais, later excommunicated by the ultras, roundly denounced traditional police principles as "against the order of nature." He decried the policy of treating grain exclusively from the vantage point of consumers to the neglect of producers and traders. He called for a "just equilibrium" of their interests, which meant a sweeping liberalization of trade in the interior aligned with a

---

35 "Lettre à M. de Boissy au sujet des observations sur le livre de l'essai sur la police générale des grains," in Depitre edition of *Essai*, 155–58 and *Journal de commerce* (Oct. 1761), 58–68.

general permission to export subject to suspension when prices jeopardized the balance.[36] The agronomist Duhamel du Monceau eschewed general theories but unequivocally condemned "popular prejudices" against the freedom to stock and exchange grain which victimized in the first instance the cultivator:

> The public ... never finds the price of grain low enough: it seeks to make us consider without distinction any reserve as criminal; it pushes the injustice to the point of refusing the *fermier* the honest profit which is due him.

This mentality, he believed, led ineluctably to the "decadence" of agriculture.[37]

The *Journal de Commerce*, edited by a future physiocrat, focused on the plight of the *négociant* whose calling was stifled by the police. Unlike the cultivator who works mechanically and instinctively, the cosmopolitan merchant "meditates, he weighs, he measures, he calculates, he combines ideas, he discusses principles ... he foresees Abundance, Dearth, War & Peace." Freedom of the grain trade would liberate his syncretic "genius," which contained elements of Locke, Newton, Richelieu, Cromwell, and Colbert. Convinced of the pragmatic nobility of commerce, the abbé Coyer inveighed against a policy of suspicion of trade and disdain for agriculture: "one would say that we are hearing in our turn the awful voices of the Evil Spirits who devoured grain under the reign of Charlemagne." "Is it grain that you want?" he asked. Then "render it more useful to the *laboureur* by the liberty of exporting so that he is assured of its sale, so that he never fears abundance." A *lieutenant des chasses* at Versailles, Leroi, one of the many bridges between Encyclopedism and physiocracy, found it "astonishing" that France "followed false measures for such a long time" and urged a policy of internal and external liberty.[38]

---

36 François Véron de Forbonnais, *Éléments du commerce* (Paris, 1754), cited by Depitre in his edition of Herbert, *Essai*, xxv–xxx. See also Forbonnais' *Recherches et considérations sur les finances de la France depuis 1595 jusqu'à l'année 1721* (Basel, 1758), II, 160–61 in which he condemns the police excesses, such as the ban on stockage, which stifle the grain trade, but in which he also criticizes the idea of a "total liberty." On Forbonnais' contemporary reputation, see M.-F. Pidansat de Mairobert, *Journal historique de la révolution opérée dans la constitution de la monarchie françoise* (London, 1776), II, 191 (21 Oct. 1771).

37 Duhamel du Monceau, *Traité de la conservation des grains* (Paris, 1753), xxi–xxiii. On Duhamel's work, see *Gazette de l'agriculture, du commerce, des arts et des finances* (7 Aug. 1770), 582–583.

38 *Journal de commerce* (Sept. 1759), 37–38, 54, 56; G. Coyer, *Développement et défense du système de la noblesse commerçante* (Paris and Amsterdam, 1757), 94–95; Article "Froment," in Diderot, *et al.*, *Encyclopédie* (Paris, 1757), VII, 336.

In the same decade Plumart de Dangeul, the Chevalier de Vivens, Pinczon du Sel des Monts, O'Heguerty, Goudar, Piarron de Chamousset, Mirabeau, and Abeille were among the critics who struck one or another of the liberal chords.[39] Nor was freedom of the grain trade the only liberalizing current of the fifties. In a kindred spirit, administrators like Gournay and Trudaine, seconded by a band of energetic pamphleteers, assailed the guild structure, controls placed on manufacture, prohibitions against enclosure, internal customs barriers, and a congeries of other restraints placed on domestic and foreign commerce.[40]

The man with whom the destiny of the liberal theory would be most closely associated posed his candidacy for ideological leadership of the movement in the last years of the fifties. François Quesnay, a peasant's son who rose to membership in the Academy of Sciences and to the place of confidant and physician to Madame de Pompadour, followed the path of a number of eminent European philosophes who shifted quite naturally and fruitfully from medicine to other forms of scientific investigation and therapy.[41] In volumes VI and VII of the *Encyclopédie*, Quesnay published two articles on political economy. "Fermiers" dealt with the practice and the significance of agriculture and "Grains" developed the same themes and included the first enumeration of the "Maxims of Economic Government," which became the catechism of his followers.

Quesnay saw himself not as "a dreamer of philosophy" but as an analyst with practical cures. Not satisfied merely to enlighten the public, he wanted to influence the king and his council.

---

39 Plumart de Dangeul, *Remarques sur les avantages et les désavantages de la France et de la Grande-Bretagne par rapport au commerce et aux autres sources de la puissance des états* (Leyden, 1754); François de Vivens, *Observations sur divers moyens de soutenir et d'encourager l'agriculture principalement dans la Guyenne* (1756–1761); Pinczon du Sel des Monts, *Considèrations sur le commerce de Bretagne* (Rennes, 1756); Pierre-André O'Heguerty, *Essai sur les intérêts du commerce* (The Hague, 1754); Ange Goudar, *Les intérêts de la France mat entendus, dans les branches de l'agriculture, de la population, des finances, du commerce, de la marine et de l'industrie* (Amsterdam, 1756); *Journal économique* (Jan. 1760), 6; *Journal de commerce* (Feb. 1759); *Journal encyclopédique*, VIII (1 July 1759), 47–58; Abeille, *Corps d'observations de la Société d'Agriculture, de Commerce, et des Arts établie par les États de Bretagne* (Rennes, 1760 for 1757 and 1758).

40 For an important recent work dealing with one such "economic" movement, the campaign against the *exclusif*, see Jean Tarrade, *Le Commerce colonial de la France à la fin de l'ancien régime* (Paris, 1972), I, 223ff.

41 For Quesnay's life, see J. Hecht, "La Vie de François Quesnay," *François Quesnay et la physiocratie*, 211–94. For the medical nexus and metaphor in the Enlightenment, see Peter Gay, *The Enlightenment: An Interpretation* (New York, 1969), II, 12–23.

He conceived the famous *Tableau Economique* as a clear and schematic expression of the principles of his new science, written in the tough-minded language of "interest" and geared to attract official attention. In an incredible *mise-en-scène* representing the king accosting Philosophy, Quesnay arranged to have Louis XV himself run the first edition of the *Tableau* on the private royal printing press. Whether the exercise imprinted the zig-zag and its complicated linkages on the king's mind or merely amused him is a matter of conjecture. The experience, however, amply demonstrated the extraordinary opportunity for reaching the summit of authority which Pompadour's patronage assured Quesnay. And the *Tableau*, despite its opacity, won an audience beyond the corridors of Versailles.

With the doctrinal foundation laid, Quesnay began to recruit proselytes. At about this time he established amicable relations with Gournay and Turgot, sympathizers rather than disciples, and he converted the parlementaire Lermercier de la Rivière, whom Quesnay thought was admirably suited to become minister of finance. The pretentious "Ami des Hommes," Mirabeau, Quesnay's most important early pupil, came to him "no more *économiste* than his cat."[42] They collaborated on a number of works, including the *Théorie de l'Impôt* (1760) which Mirabeau hoped would make him prime minister, but which instead cost him a brief sojourn in jail for affronting the farmers-general and criticizing the management of royal finances. By the mid-sixties, Quesnay and the *économistes* acquired a journal, established a public lecture course in "economic arithmetic," gained a score of new adherents, the most enterprising of whom were Dupont, Letrosne, and the abbé Baudeau, and achieved international notoriety and quasi-institutional status. To their friends, they were a "school," a forum of educators devoted to the dissemination of the principles of good government; to their adversaries, they formed a "sect," a clique of shallow zealots who preached a gospel of nonsense and disorder.

Between the late fifties and the mid-sixties, Quesnay and the *économistes* transformed the liberal critique into an ideology, or, as they preferred to have it, into a science. Pioneer liberal propaganda had been a mélange of audacity and diffidence, pugnacity and accommodation, captious denigration and constructive suggestion. Even at its best, it was fragmented, disjointed, and incomplete. Rarely did it venture beyond the single issue of grain; it failed to develop the

---

42 Hecht, "Quesnay," *François Quesnay et la physiocratie*, 256.

germ of the potent liberal theory into a coherent, global conception of political economy. Quesnay dramatically enlarged the perspective by redefining the methodological premises and philosophical bases of the argument and connecting it to a sweeping program of economic, social, and political reform. Physiocracy, as Dupont baptized it, was a *system*, ontologically, as it emerged from the nature of things, and politically, in terms of the kinds of solutions it imposed. It was a science to the extent that it elaborated a universally valid method, combining rational analysis, empirical diagnostics, and model-making in the pursuit of immutable laws which explain social and economic relations and make policial decision-making intelligible.

For a proper discussion of the physiocratic doctrine, the reader must be referred to the prolific specialized literature which extends from Marx to the erudition of modernization.[43] In brief let us note that the physiocratic conception resulted from a study of the "natural order" which convinced them that the "imprescriptible," "inviolable," and "holy" right of property and the concomitant power to dispose of property with "absolute" and "total" liberty were the formative principles, anterior to all manner of social life, from which all relations and activities developed. Everything in the "moral" order derived from the "physical" world which was nature's peculiar domain. Their integral, dynamic analysis of economic mechanisms demonstrated

43 The best recent work on physiocracy is warmly sympathetic to their enterprise: R. L. Meek, *The Economics of Physiocracy* (Cambridge, Mass., 1963). Georges Weulersse's classic *Le Mouvement physiocratique en France (1756–70)* (Paris, 1910), 2 vols., is brilliant, exhaustive and still invaluable after more than sixty years' wear. See also Léonce de Lavergne, *Les Economistes français au dix-huitième siècle* (Paris, 1870); G. Schelle, *Dupont de Nemours et l'école physiocratique* (Paris, 1888); Michel Bernard, *Introduction à une sociologie des doctrines économiques des physiocrates à Stuart Mill* (Paris, 1963); Henri Curmond, *Le Commerce des grains et l'école physiocratique* (Paris, 1900); Joseph A. Schumpeter, *History of Economic Analysis* (New York, 1954); and the essays and bibliography in *François Quesnay et la physiocratie*, I. Among the *économiste* sources upon which my considerations are based are: Nicolas Baudeau, *Avis au peuple sur son premier besoin* (Amsterdam and Paris, 1768), premier traité, 72–73; P.-J.-A. Roubaud, *Représentations aux magistrats*, 379, 395, 398; Mirabeau, cited by Weulersse, *Mouvement*, II, 37; Dupont, cited in *ibid.*, I, 214; "Observations sur les effets de la liberté … par l'Auteur des Ephémérides," *Journal économique* (Aug. 1770), 348; Dupont, *Analyse … rapport*, 12; Quesnay, article "Fermier," Diderot, *et al.*, *Encyclopédie*, VI, 534–35 and article "Grains," *ibid.*, VII, 830–31; *Ephémérides du citoyen*, II (1767), 22, 33, and IX (1768), 83–84; *Nouvelles éphémérides*, I (1775), 30–31; J.A.N. de C. Condorcet, *Lettre d'un laboureur de Picardie à M. N****, auteur prohibitif (Paris, 1775), in E. Daire and G. de Molinari, eds., *Collection des principaux économistes* (1847; reprint: Osnabruck, 1966), XIV, 485; Quesnay, *Physiocratie*, ed. by Dupont (Paris, 1767); G. Weulersse, *La Physiocratie à la fin du règne de Louis XV*, 80.

that the land was the unique source of national wealth. The discovery of nature's laws showed men the range of their options—what they could do through positive law—and the scope of their errors—what they must undo in order to make the best use of their lives, individually and collectively. As a consequence of their study, the *économistes* proposed ideas for changes in economic policy, financial administration, modes of political participation, education, and the structure of society.

Virtually all of the major threads of their thinking converged on the question of the grain trade. They argued that grain was a commodity like any other, that the traditional, invidious police amounted to theft, and that real abundance and low prices were mutually exclusive and contradictory ambitions. Liberalization represented the precondition and the take-off stage for their program to renew agriculture and revitalize the management of public affairs.

Thanks to Quesnay's enduring charisma and the energy of the *économistes*, a relentless surge of propaganda appeared, rehearsing over and over again their favorite themes. Overbidding their predecessors and preempting the center stage, they expropriated the liberal argument and recast it in their own image. They became so intimately identified with the liberal critique that it seemed to be something of their own creation. Turgot, who shared many of their ideas without adopting their posture, noted with alarm and annoyance the tendency to confound the issue and the party of its most visible partisans:

> I am well aware that those who for some time have written or spoken against the liberty of the grain trade affect to regard this opinion as exclusively that of several writers who have given themselves the name of *économiste* and who may have prejudiced a part of the public against themselves by the air of sect which they have quite blunderingly assumed and by a tone of enthusiasm.[44]

But Turgot gave their enemies too much credit. The *économistes* themselves fostered the confusion and relished the role of intellectual vanguard. Sure of their science and doctrinaire by temperament as well as by conviction, they found moderation no virtue and left little margin for discussion. While they broadened the objectives and responsibilities of liberty, they narrowed the base of possible consensus. They changed the test for adherence to liberal principles from a simple litmus to a difficult rorschach. Their inflated style was easy prey for

---

44 Turgot, "Lettres sur le commerce des grains," 30 Oct. 1770 (#1), *Œuvres*, ed. by Schelle, III, 270.

caricature, but it was their ideological rigidity which cost them most dearly. It repelled many potential sympathizers who were unwilling to take physiocracy *en bloc*. Purged by the *économistes* for nonconformity and excoriated by their adversaries as fellow-travelers, they lapsed ineffectually into the tepid limbo between the two camps. To be sure, not everyone who publicly endorsed liberty embraced physiocracy. But it became, as Turgot discovered, increasingly difficult to accept the one while abjuring the other.

The price of ideological coherence was also heightened vulnerability. As pendant to its added strength, the liberal argument exposed many more flanks to attack. In addition to provoking new enmities, physiocracy breathed life into the inert, unreconstructable opposition. Embarrassed and on the defensive during the period of low-key liberalism, the incorrigibles returned to the attack against the *économistes*. In response to ultraliberalism, their brand of relative extremism again seemed reasonable. A great debate ensued, buffeting both the political and the intellectual establishments, dividing ministers, magistrates, and philosophes. Later we shall have occasion to consider it more carefully. In anticipation, it is worth noting that it was not a rhetorical and stylized rendition of the quarrel between the ancients and the moderns nor a recondite scholastic dispute over fine points of doctrine. The debate turned specifically on the political, social, and economic impact of liberalization on the French nation and it was fiercely argued in practical as well as theoretical terms in this age whose triumph it was to bridge the gulf between these perspectives.

To suggest that physiocratic thought, by itself, would not have caused such a seismic stir is not to demean its originality but to underscore both its precocity and its concrete political ambitions. Physiocracy became significant in its own time only after the idea of liberty moved from the rarefied air of Quesnay's *entresol* to the volatile atmosphere of the marketplaces. The royal legislation of 1763–64 contributed more to *économiste* notoriety than all their apothegms, paradigms, and preciosities.

There is no way to gauge the achievement of the Herberts and the Quesnays in arousing and educating public opinion on the liberty issue. But the furor of interest in all matters pertaining to the economy, not only the grain trade, which erupted at this time suggests that their work was as much a symptom as a cause of this growing sophistication. In 1763 the *Journal Economique* noted with satisfaction that "the genius of the nation today seems turned almost entirely to the side of the economy." Voltaire commented on this vogue in the *Dictionnaire philosophique*, dating its origin "at about 1750." During these years, Linguet wrote, a metamorphosis occurred, transforming the "philosophical insect" into the "economist insect."[45]

To be sure, it had been developing in larva for a long time. It emerged in the fifties and sixties as the Enlightenment reached maturity, accelerating in pace and expanding in scope to encompass all the dimensions of human activity. The *Encyclopédie* epitomizes this omnivorously curious and critical spirit; it treats the economy as a subject of practical, universal, and urgent concern in scores of articles. The ubiquitous example of the English, in commerce and agriculture as well as in government, stimulated inquiry into economics. Indeed, the accomplishments of England in war and peace, thrust into high relief in the decade of the Seven Years' War, had a traumatic impact on the French. Anglomania was suitably cosmopolitan for philosophic taste but it masked a sense of profound disarray and provoked a bout of intense introspection. Enthusiasm for England soured rapidly; even at its most buoyant, admiration had implied national humiliation and infirmity. Nevertheless, tracts on political economy and treatises on husbandry, planting and conservation crossed the channel regularly in response to growing French demand.

Fiscality was one form of economic discourse which everyone understood. The attempts of Machault, Silhouette, and Bertin to reform finances and restructure the tax system focused public attention on the state of the economy and confirmed the idea, promoted by the critics, that fundamental change was necessary. The parlementary opponents of these reforms tried to refute them substantively—economically; they rarely contested the need for reforms per se and in fact painted a gloomier picture of the economy than the ministers. Perhaps, too, there is something to Voltaire's sally that the nation turned to the clinical problems of production, investment, circulation, and exchange because it was "fed up with verses, tragedies, comedies, operas, novels, romantic stories and even more romantic moral reflections, and theological disputes on grace and on the convulsions...."[46] Political economy found a congenial mood in which to flourish after mid-century. School of

---

45 *Journal économique* (Jan. 1763), 11; Article "Blé ou bled," (1770), *Dictionnaire philosophique*, in *Œuvres complètes*, ed. by Moland, XVIII, 7; *Réponse aux docteurs modernes* (1771), cited by Weulersse, *Mouvement*, II, 683.
46 Article "Blé ou bled," *Dictionnaire philosophique*, in *Œuvres*, ed. by Moland, XVIII, 11.

citizenship and utility, it channelled the passion of the French into the prosaic and the concrete.

The fifties were the halcyon years of agronomy and agromania. A profusion of tracts, pamphlets, manuals, and catechisms appeared ranging in subject from specialized studies of black vetch and druidic potions to augment seed productivity to broader frescoes of rural life redolent of Olivier de Serre's classical *Théâtre d'agriculture*. "So much has been written on this matter [grain and agriculture]," wrote Voltaire, "that if a *laboureur* planted as much weight in grain as we have of volumes on this product, he could aspire to the most ample harvest...."[47] Duhamel du Monceau, chemist-naturalist and consultant to the naval ministry, collected and synthesized a vast amount of material which, combined with his experiments in the laboratory and in the field, formed the basis for a French science of agronomy.[48] A throng of popularizers rewrote the technical treatises in simple, didactic language in an effort to reach deeply into the rural world. They importuned cultivators to abandon pernicious and dated practices and tried to instill in them an enhanced sense of their worth by insisting that agriculture was the nerve of the state and that no other profession merited more esteem. The Patriarch of Ferney himself symbolized the fresh prestige which agriculture enjoyed. "Besides, I have become *laboureur*, vintner and shepherd," he confided in a letter of December 1758; "that is worth a hundred times more than being a man of letters in Paris."[49]

Through the complicity of the government and local notables, agricultural societies with central coordinating and branch bureaus sprung to life in the provinces.[50] Soon afterward the government

---

47 *Ibid.*, 7. Cf. Bourde, *Agronomie*, I, 369ff. and *passim*; Simon Linguet, *Canaux navigables* (Amsterdam and Paris, 1769), 152; P.-J.-B. Legrand D'Aussy, *Histoire de la vie privée des français* (1783), ed. by de Roquefort (Paris, 1815), I, 30.

48 Duhamel du Monceau: *Éléments d'agriculture* (Paris, 1762), 2 vols.; *Traité de la culture des terres, suivant les principes de M. Tull, anglois* (Paris, 1750–61), 6 vols.; *École d'agriculture* (Paris, 1759).

49 Voltaire to Joseph Saurin, 27 Dec. 1758, *Voltaire's Correspondence*, ed. by T. Besterman (Geneva, 1953–1965), XXXIX, 269 (#7294).

50 See Bertin's call for the organization of "assemblies of agriculture" aimed at "perfecting agriculture" by drawing upon the "local knowledge" and "practical skills" of farmers, notables, administrators, etc. Circular to INs., 22 Aug. 1760, AN, F¹² 149 and Bertin to IN. of La Rochelle, 28 March, 11 May 1761, C. 195, A.D. C-M. According to a report prepared for Bertin's "Department of Agriculture," by the mid-sixties there were 18 societies established in 21 generalities with 2000 active members. AN, K 906. There is some evidence that these estimations may have been conservative. On the societies, see: E. Labiche, *Les Sociétés d'agriculture au XVIIIᵉ siècle* (Paris,

invested a secretary of state with responsibilities closely resembling the tasks of a minister of agriculture and promoted, through legislation and propaganda, the clearing of new land and the rationalization of production. Seminars called agricultural assemblies met periodically and agricultural *fêtes* celebrated the rural awakening. A priest with a reputation for "profane" language scandalized the Académie Française by preaching a sermon on "holy agriculture."[51] Lesser literary academies did not hesitate to incorporate the topic into their agendas for discussion and prize competitions.

Dosed heavily with salon sensibility, sometimes excessively sentimental and patronizing in attitude, and largely based in urban centers, agromania aroused the skepticism of many observers who challenged its authenticity, or at least doubted its efficacy.[52] But it should not be forgotten that the shortest route to the countryside, then as now, often passed through Paris. Eighteenth-century agronomists did not succeed in revolutionizing French agriculture in terms of organization, production, or technology. The publicists, however, by challenging the habit of neglect and indifference to agriculture, thrust it into the forefront of national preoccupations. They made themselves the moral representatives of the single largest constituency in the kingdom and made rural France—or rather the agribusiness elite that dominated it—a powerful, self-conscious political force in the last decades of the Old Regime.

The sixties were preeminently the economic years: the decade of "economic bread," "economic milling," "economic industry," "economic invention." But the focus of interest shifted from technology to policy, from agronomy to political economy. The élan and the ambitions of the improvers and reformers seemed to be in fundamental contradiction to traditional patterns of managing the commonweal. The first stage in the process of reform had been reached. Ignorance was no

---

1908); P. S. Lavergne, *La Société d'agriculture de Paris* (Paris, 1859); Mauguin, *Études historiques sur l'administration de l'agriculture en France* (Paris, 1876–77); Louis Passy, *Histoire de la Société nationale d'agriculture de France* (Paris, 1912), I.

51 Legrand d'Aussy, *Vie privée*, I, 30–31; E. Regnault, *Christophe de Beaumont, Archevêque de Paris (1703–81)* (Paris, 1882), II, 306; abbé Mery, *L'Ami de ceux qui n'en ont point ou système économique, politique et moral* (Paris, 1767), 93ff. Cf. Bourde, *Agronomie*, I and II.

52 Voltaire to Pierre Rousseau, 11 July 1759, *Voltaire's Correspondence*, ed. by Besterman, XXXVI, 213 (#7668); Weulersse, *Mouvement*, II, 152. Cf. *Année littéraire* (1770), VI, 99 and Arthur Young, *Travels in France*, ed. by J. Kaplow, 100. Some of the severest strictures against "cabinet" agromania came from the agromaniacs themselves. See, for example, the Montpellier magistrate P.-F. de Rosset's *L'agriculture, poème* (Paris, 1774), vi.

longer an insuperable barrier to progress. The necessary knowledge, practical and theoretical, was available. The major obstacle to implementation, apart from the inertia of entrenched habit, was political. Partisans of change looked to the government to create the conditions in which innovations could bear fruit. The government had to clear the law codes of dead weights and blockages even as enterprising farmers had to clear the land of hedges and stumps before it could be reclaimed and rendered fertile. The doctrine of the "Tableau économique," the minutes of the "economical assemblies," and the vision of an "economical monarchy" were all concerned with politics.[53] Reformers from all the different economic camps—those devoted to agronomy, to foreign commerce, to manufacture, or to the grain trade—agreed that the next step was an affair of state.[54]

The government was inured to petitions from economic groups seeking to promote their interests through official patronage. Typically, however, these supplicants sought exclusive privileges and other concrete advantages geared to their specific enterprises. In the sixties the most vocal demands came from broader-based citizen-groups seeking not particular permissions and concessions but general enabling acts opening new economic frontiers to all comers. Liberty was the leitmotif of all the petitions: in its broadest and least controversial form, freedom to pursue one's interests and to profit from new skills and methods of business; in its explicitly political form, as it concerned, for example, the Herberts and the Quesnays, freedom from the constraints of a noxious police regime. The agriculturalists and the liberals found considerable sympathy in official quarters. The ministry itself helped to channel the fashionable enthusiasm of the fifties into the nettlesome pressure groups of the early sixties. A liberty lobby, supported by elements within virtually all the parlements, the provincial estates, the agricultural societies, the chambers of commerce, the burgeoning economic press (the *Journal Economique*, launched in 1751, set the trend in journalism, to be followed by the *Journal de Commerce*, the *Gazette du Commerce, de l'Agriculture, et des Finances*, the *Journal de l'Agriculture, du Commerce, des Arts, et des*

---

53 Compare the common roots of Letrosne's narration of the birth of "economic science" and the St. Malo *prior-consuls'* call for "a good economic government." Letrosne, *Discours sur l'état actuel de la magistrature et sur les causes de sa décadence* (Paris, 1764), 72; Supplique des prieur-consuls, 1762, C. 3911, A.D. I-et-V.

54 On the passion for a practical and indeed a *political* approach to agricultural renewal, see the *mémoires* addressed to Bertin in the early sixties. AN, K 906.

Finances, and the *Ephémérides du Citoyen*), and a large body of land-owners, merchant-cultivators, and businessmen (*négociants* in the lead) emerged determined to influence royal decisions.

The liberty lobby, perhaps the most remarkable example of sustained civic insurgency in old-regime politics, merits a separate investigation beyond the bounds of this study. Its activists are familiar to us for what they wrote in their periodicals, brochures, and petitions—there is considerable truth in the *économiste* Letrosne's remark that "it is to the liberty of the pen that we owe the granting of exportation"—and for what they said in their assemblies.[55] But the bulk of their supporters—the "interests" of the "productive nation" which they represented—we know only inferentially and indirectly, through notarial records such as leases, marriage contracts and after-death inventories, personal account-books and commercial registers, the collection logs of *fermiers seigneuriaux* or *gros décimateurs*, and so on. There is no doubt that the landowners whom the physiocrats styled "proprietary class" and the farm operators and grain growers who ordinarily disposed of substantial marketable surpluses (as well as the merchants, moneychangers, brokers, and ship-owners, without direct ties to the land, who specialized in grain exchanges) ardently favored the liberal policies which promised to increase their rents and/or their profits. The "class" of proprietors cut across all the orders in its recruitment, resided in the towns or in the countryside (or both), and drew much of its wealth from its *fermages*. It is estimated that they comprised no more than 5 to 8% of the population but that they owned at least 50% of the land and almost all the rents, *métayages*, tithes, and seignorial rights.[56] The merchant-cultivators were an extremely diverse group, who produced and often stocked grain and depended for their income primarily upon the profits they derived from their market dealings rather than on *fermages*. Their number, like that of the commercial auxiliaries in the towns and ports, has not been satisfactorily estimated. More numerous than the "proprietors," they were still a small, albeit powerful, minority of the nation.

In retrospect, we know that the eighteenth century, especially the second half, was the "golden age" of the proprietor and to a great

---

55 G.-F. Letrosne, "Lettre sur les avantages de la concurrence des vaisseaux étrangers pour la voiture de nos grains," *Journal de l'agriculture, du commerce et des finances* (July 1765), 47.

56 E. Labrousse in Labrousse and Braudel, eds., *Histoire économique et sociale*, II, 473–87.

extent of the owner of grain surpluses as well. Prices—of rents and of grain, among many other items—began to rise in the thirties and continued to mount, despite cyclical reverses, through the whole century. Preoccupied with the present and the immediate past, the agricultural-commercial elite at mid-century had no clear image of a burgeoning favorable trend. On the contrary, they had a gloomy memory of the travails of their fathers and grandfathers and a bitter personal taste of painfully low prices during several years in each of the decades of the century. No platform could have been better geared to capture their suffrage than the demands put forth by the liberal spokesmen. Prices, incidentally, not only affected the attitude of this mighty socioeconomic elite toward liberalization but toward other political questions as well. For example, the sluggishness of prices in the early sixties, which reduced their revenues, sharpened their opposition to the heavy royal fiscal demands and thus also intensified their support of the parlements. At the same time, it stimulated their appetite for liberty.

The lobby derived its greatest strength from its many institutional bases: the provincial estates, parlements, societies of agriculture, chambers of commerce, and cultural academies provided the corporate and individual cadres for the movement. They gave form and direction to the propaganda, harangued the king, and besieged the intendants with advice and memoirs.[57] They gave the lobby a semblance of organization; the agricultural societies and the chambers of commerce, and perhaps the parlements as well, corresponded with one another and coordinated their action.[58] Implanted throughout the realm, the lobby had particular influence in the west, throughout the south, and in the southeast. Toulouse, for example, was the nexus of one of the most militant pressure groups: the Estates, the Parlement, the diocesan assemblies, and the Chamber of Commerce joined forces in a common front. Similarly, in Brittany, members of the Estates, the Parlement, and

---

57 In some instances, the intendants themselves seemed to have joined forces with the lobby. See IN. of Brittany to CG, 23 Nov. 1763, C. 1648–49, A.D. I-et-V.; H. Fréville, *L'Intendance de Bretagne*, II, 189–94; IN. of Rouen to CG, 7 Sept. 1761, C. 103, A.D. S-M.

58 On the operation of branches of the societies of agriculture, on the connections among them, and on their keen interest in liberalization, see D. 14, A.D. Aisne; C. 139, A.D. Somme; Société d'Agriculture of La Rochelle to Bertin, 25 July 1764, C. 198, A.D. C-M.; Société d'Agriculture de Rouen, "Mémoire," April 1763, AN H 1507; Société d'Agriculture d'Auch, "Mémoire concernant l'indispensable nécessité de l'exportation," March 1775, AN, H 72–73; Letaconnoux, *Les Subsistances et le commerce des grains en Bretagne*, 238.

the Society of Agriculture (where Abeille and Montaudouin were active) led the liberal campaign, seconded by local notables and administrators, especially from maritime districts, companies of international traders, bankers and *armateurs*, and the biggest lay and ecclesiastical seigneurs.[59] The arguments they used are familiar: a mélange of Herbert and Quesnay contrived both to conceal and to justify an urgent appeal in behalf of local and regional interests. The prior-consuls of St. Malo, like the *co-députés* of Vannes and Tréguier and the commercial agents of Toulouse, deplored the ruin of agriculture, the burden of idle abundance, the lack of outlets, the difficulty of paying taxes and meeting other obligations in a climate of economic stagnation, the tyranny and inutility of police, and the failure to keep pace with the English ("our natural and irreconcilable enemies," according to the Malouins, who clung to certain old-fashioned ideas which embarrassed more enlightened liberals). They were confident that a full liberty, including freedom to export, would dramatically reverse their fortunes.[60]

The briefs for liberty that reached the king were more elaborate and sophisticated. The deputies of commerce, the lobby's national agents at Versailles, presented a memoir in favor of exportation meant to convince men of different epistemological persuasions by "the *evidence* of the principles" as well as by "proofs of fact." The highlight of their dissertation was a tendentious historical allegory which purported to show that liberty to trade interprovincially and to export abroad

---

59 See Robert Forster, *The Nobility of Toulouse in the Eighteenth Century: A Social and Economic Study* (Baltimore, 1960); Georges Frêche, "Etudes statistiques sur le commerce céréalier de la France méridionale au dix-huitième siècle," *Revue d'histoire économique et sociale* XLIX, (1971), 211ff; Emile Levasseur, *Histoire des classes ouvrières*, II, 579; petitions of *négociants*, 1758, C. 1666, A.D. I-et-V.; Royou to IN. of Brittany, 2 May 1763, C. 1648–49, A.D. I-et-V.; La Chalotais, speech of 20 Aug. 1764, C. 1648–49, A.D. I-et-V.; juge-consuls of Nantes, Mémoire, April 1763, C. 775, A.D. L-A.; Letaconnoux, *Les Subsistances et le commerce des grains en Bretagne*, 201–205; Jean Meyer, *La Noblesse bretonne au dix-huitième siècle*, I, 580–82. Cf. *ibid.*, 518–26; Gaston Rambert, *Histoire du commerce de Marseille* (Paris, 1954–1966), IV, 339; Roubaud, *Représentations*, 36; *Journal économique* (Feb. 1764), 55–56; P. de St.-Jacob, *Les Paysans de la Bourgogne du Nord* (Paris, 1960), 337ff.

60 "Supplique" of *prior-consuls* of St. Malo, 1762, C. 3911, A.D. I-et-V.; Memoir of *co-députés* of Tréguier, 30 Jan. 1758 and memoir of *co-députés* of Vannes, 7 Feb. 1758, C. 1666, A.D. I-et-V.; *députés du Commerce* of Toulouse, "Mémoire sur la liberté de l'exportation," 1762, C. 2908, A.D. Her. Because they all flocked to the standard of liberalization, it should not be imagined that the different interest groups which comprised the liberty lobby shared a common position on all related issues. The "total liberty" of the Malouins, for instance, allowed for the exclusion of foreign bottoms, a policy abhorrent to many grain-hoarding lords and *négociants*.

was "the primitive and fundamental law of the French Monarchy" with roots deeply embedded in the earliest national past. Prohibitive police was a modern, seventeenth-century innovation. Despite the heroic efforts of Sully, "the restorer of France," to choke it in embryo, the police imposter, masquerading in the dress of tradition and the public interest, profited from the disorders of the times to insinuate itself everywhere with its train of financial abuses and economic depredations. Although this might reassure conservatives, the important point ultimately was not that the police way was a deviation from the past but that it was the "principal cause" of the "decline" and "destruction" of French agriculture and, in addition, the "source of monopoly and the cause of dearths." The result was disastrous for producers and consumers as well as for the governors of the state because agriculture was "the principal source of wealth" and killing dearths were virtually impossible in a regime of full liberty.[61]

Not bound by the conventions of public discourse, a self-styled Marseilles businessman-trader bespoke in truculent terms a feeling that was doubtless widespread in the grain lobby. It was time for the king to make a choice between a "nervous people"—the consumers—which wants to be coddled, and the dynamic elements in society which account for the "strength" of the nation. It is not the job of the active and productive groups to be "purveyors" to the masses and consequently to suffer infringements on their liberty. The maxim "Salus populi suprema lex esto" is "only respectable if it is salutary to the [interest of the] nation." "Laisses-nous [sic] faire," exhorted the merchant.[62]

III

Rumors that the government was moving toward a major reform of the grain trade began to circulate widely in the middle of the Seven Years' War.[63] To the partisans of liberty, the arrêt of 1754 was a source of frustration and dissatisfaction. Officially, the government sustained the fiction that, in the words of one minister, "the freedom of grain

---

61 "Mémoire joint à l'avis des Députés du Commerce" (ca. 1764), BN, mss. fr. 14295. Cf. "Avis des Députés du Commerce sur le libre commerce des grains" (26 Oct. 1769), AN, F¹² 715.
62 "Lettre d'un négociant sur la nature du commerce des grains" (Marseille, 8 Oct. 1763), BN, mss. fr. 14296, fols. 50–51.
63 Anonymous memoir, "Commerce intérieur et extérieur des blés" (ca. 1761), BN, mss. fr. 11347, fols. 213–216.

circulation in the interior of the kingdom is generally established."[64] But no one at Versailles disputed the existence of the yawning gap between law and fact denounced by traders, publicists, and lobbyists. The Controllers-General of the late fifties repeatedly deplored the failure of officials at all levels to implement and respect the *arrêt*. "I ask you, Monsieur," wrote Moras to the intendant of Provence in one of many such instructions dispatched in these years, "to give the most positive orders so that in the future there will not exist under any pretext any difficulties in the breadth of your department for the free export [i.e., circulation] of grain in the interior of the kingdom."[65] Yet the *arrêt* itself was substantively vague and the hortatory letters from the ministry addressed none of the tangled and prickly questions which a genuine effort to execute it would have raised. On the grounds that their generalities were not "sufficiently abundantly supplied," intendants continued to interfere with circulation; on the grounds that "precautions" were necessary, as always, "to prevent abuses," local authorities counteracted the modest dose of liberty accorded by the *arrêt*. Supporters of the liberal cause within and outside the government became convinced that the *arrêt* of 1754 was neither powerful nor precise enough, legally and politically, to effect real changes. They agreed, as the Controller-General Silhouette remarked in 1759, that "a new law was necessary."[66]

Writer, critic, translator, traveler—in a word, philosophe—Etienne de Silhouette came to the ministry amidst giddy expectations for a period of enlightened administration. Though he served for less than a year and faced the enormously demanding task of managing an international war, he prepared a remarkable number of reform projects, which aroused violent controversy.[67] Immediate fiscal problems engrossed him above all, yet Silhouette was deeply interested in the grain question. Convinced that agricultural development was the key to sustained prosperity as well as "the foundation of our finances"

---

64 CG Boullongne to de Brou (?), 20 Jan. 1759, C. 103, A.D. S-M. Cf. the very similar position of the IN. of finance Courteille to IN. of Bordeaux, 18 June 1762, C. 1425, A.D. Gir.

65 Moras to de la Tour, 23 June and 25 July 1757, C. 2420, A.D. B-du-R. Cf. Moras to de Brou, 31 Jan. 1757, C. 104, A.D. S-M.

66 Silhouette to IN. of Rouen, 12 July 1759, C. 103, A.D. S-M. Cf. the IN. of Franche-Comté to Bertin, 2 April 1762, C. 496, A.D. Doubs.

67 On Silhouette's career, which merits a fresh and comprehensive examination, see M. Guillaumat-Vallet, *Le Contrôleur-général Silhouette et ses réformes en matière financière* (Paris, 1914) and C. J. Mathon de la Cour, *Collection des comptes-rendus ... concernant les finances de France depuis 1758 jusqu'en 1787* (Lausanne, 1788), 27–48.

and that conventional regulatory policy stymied agricultural growth, this Controller-General resolved to introduce a larger and more compelling measure of freedom into the grain trade than the previous legislation had allotted. Since "present circumstances do not permit me to do everything that I would desire in favor of agriculture [e.g., to institute exportation in a permanent form]," wrote Silhouette, "I will restrict myself for the time being to proposing a project for a declaration concerning internal commerce."

Though he fell from power before he could translate it into law, Silhouette's project is of interest, both for its boldness and for its reticence. It contained two important articles, each the product of somewhat contradictory preoccupations. The first prohibited "all our officers under any pretext whatsoever from stopping the transport of grain and flour from one place to another within the same province or from one province to any other in our kingdom." In form and in spirit this was a major advance upon the *arrêt* of 1754; it anticipated one of the critical elements in the law which eventually liberated the grain trade in 1763. In his commentary, however, Silhouette made it clear that he was not hostile, in principle, to all forms of control. To be sure, he sharply reproved the parochialism of the local police, who did not hesitate to compromise "the effect of a general good" (free circulation) in order to satisfy their short-term provisioning needs. Yet it was not the idea of intervention that Silhouette deplored; it was the fact that their intervention was ill-conceived or, as he put it, "unenlightened." It was bound to be, by the very nature of things, for the view from the field was inevitably myopic, biased, and uninformed by broader concerns or a larger data base. Like Machault and other state-makers, Silhouette had a horror of local pretensions to political autonomy, of local administrative initiatives, and of local idiosyncracies of all kinds. He was a nationalizer: if there were to be rules, they were to be uniform throughout the realm; if there was to be regulation of the grain trade, it would emanate exclusively from the center, for only the royal government was "in a position to know everyone's needs." While he struck a blow against local police authority, Silhouette reserved the right to police the grain trade as he saw necessary.

The second article expressed the Controller-General's ambivalence more starkly. The first part of it was a portentous innovation, in the manner of the future liberal reforms: it opened the trade to all comers and authorized apparently unlimited stocking. In other words, it set the stage for the drastic transformation of the very character of grain commerce. But, as if he were alarmed by the implications of these changes, Silhouette recoiled in the second part of the article from the laissez-faire strategy. He required all transactions to occur exclusively upon the public markets. The exigencies of provisioning still had considerable sway over this reformer's mind; regardless of the needs of agriculture, Silhouette still wanted a visible, dependable supply. Though his record hardly suggests that he lacked daring, the Controller-General was unwilling to risk in 1759 what his successor Bertin ventured four years later. Like Machault, Silhouette believed that a certain kind of liberty and a certain kind of police were compatible and indeed complementary.[68]

Silhouette's project reflected uncertainties about the grain trade that were still widely felt. Many of the intendants favored some form of liberalization of the regulatory apparatus in order to promote commerce and agriculture but a considerable number probably shared the circumspection of the intendant of Amiens who supported a generous internal liberty provided the ban on off-market dealings was explicitly maintained. "The provisioning of the public marketplaces must at all times be encouraged," argued this intendant, "because that is the surest means of establishing the tranquility of the people."[69]

Social control considerations were not, however, paramount in everyone's reckoning. Acutely critical of Silhouette's project, Feydeau de Brou, the intendant of Rouen, submitted a counter-proposal which called for a much stronger and more coherent measure of liberty. Feydeau was not an intransigent liberal militant. He respected Silhouette's prudent approach; on pragmatic grounds, he agreed that it was wise to relegate the export question to another time. Yet he believed that the Controller-General permitted so many ambiguities to subsist in the projected law that the liberty of 1759 would register no more impact than had the liberty of 1754. By trying to hedge his bets, Silhouette was not giving liberty a chance. There was no need to worry about tracking grain and merchants and staging encounters of supply and demand. "Interest alone will always keep the merchants on the surest route," Feydeau maintained, "and for provisioning [one can] depend entirely on liberty." Silhouette's retention of the exclusive market rule irreparably flawed his project. The obligation to go to authorized,

---

68 Silhouette to IN. of Rouen, 12 July 1759, C. 103, A.D. S-M.; Silhouette to IN. of Rouen, 15 April 1759 and to IN. of Amiens, 6 April 1759, C. 104, *ibid.*; Silhouette to IN. of Alençon, 9 June 1759, C. 89, A.D. Orne.

69 IN. to CG, 6 April 1759, C. 105, A.D. S-M.

public markets (public markets, Feydeau acidly pointed out, which were often "owned" and/or operated for a substantial profit by private parties who basked in the "image of public good" with which the law imprinted their enterprise) severely limited the size, range, and vigor of the grain trade. It dulled competition, bloated costs, and discouraged the formation of magazines since merchants who could not freely dispose of their goods would not stock for speculative purposes. The market system protected by the law was archaic and irrational; markets were insufficient in number, haphazardly located, and absurdly programmed into weekly schedules which bore little relation to commercial needs. The aim of the law, continued the Rouen intendant, should be to "multiply the places and times" of transactions, thereby modernizing market organization and stimulating commerce.

The mandatory market rule was symptomatic of a larger problem concerning the exercise of police powers and the relations between the rulers and the ruled to which Feydeau called attention. Few observers had such a lucid sense of the requirements for a successful liberalization and of the difficulties the reform would encounter. Liberating grain alone was not enough in Feydeau's view; at the same time it was urgently necessary to free public officials at all levels of authority from the obligation of managing the grain trade by shackling their hands firmly and permanently. One of the chief reasons why the *arrêt* of 1754 failed was because it made liberty of circulation "entirely depend on us and on our subdelegates whose prejudices can still be deep and difficult to vanquish." By prohibiting the police unequivocally from interfering with any aspect of the grain trade, the government could, after a fashion, conquer their prejudices. But behind these "prejudices" stood a force of extraordinary compulsion which suggested that officials were not wholly free to act as they saw fit. For as long as the police were considered "responsible in the eyes of the people for abundance or for dearth," they could not, without enormous risk and difficulty, avert their eyes from the grain trade. Thus Feydeau insisted that the law on liberty had to announce loudly and clearly to the people that provisioning was no longer a police matter and it had to place the police, morally and politically as well as juridically, in a position in which they could not be "forced" to take the action demanded by their own prejudices or by the people.

Though he should have known better, the intendant of Rouen apparently believed that a stroke of legislation could effect this transformation. To make sure that the message got across, Feydeau's proposal specifically forbad the police to demand declarations, confine trade to markets, impede circulation anywhere in the interior, bar anyone from the trade, interfere with stocking, fix the price of grain or flour or otherwise mediate exchanges between buyers and sellers, and visit granaries to inspect and inventory supplies. From a strictly practical point of view, without regard for doctrine, the intendant of Rouen meant to show Silhouette that liberty and police were mutually contradictory and destructive notions. In addition to its conceptual defects, the Controller-General's project was out of joint with the times. For the "public" in Feydeau's estimation had in recent years made striking advances in "enlightenment"; it was now ready for a more potent dose of liberty than Silhouette prescribed. My law would be no more difficult to get registered than yours, claimed the intendant; your law risks setting back the cause by "rejuvenating and fortifying prejudices" which we have already begun to overcome.[70]

Silhouette suffered disgrace before he had the opportunity to implement his project (and before he had a chance to mark grain reform with his ill-starred cachet). His successor, Bertin, did not reach the ministry on the strength of a towering reputation. "Two-bit wine," his senior colleague in foreign affairs, Choiseul, styled him, an appreciation which never became highly controversial in Bertin's time.[71] On the whole, historians have been more generous in their assessment, praising Bertin for his perspicacity, firmness, and administrative skill.[72] Whether his nomination to the Contrôle-Général at a time when the voices of liberalism were becoming increasingly influential represents a happy coincidence or signifies Versailles' sympathy for those reformist tendencies remains subject to debate.[73] Bertin had always been keenly interested in agriculture, as a proprietor as well as a public official. While serving as

---

70 IN. to CG, 1 Aug. 1759, C.103, *ibid.*

71 N. Baudeau (?), "Chronique secrète de Paris sous le règne de Louis XVI," (7 June 1774), *Revue rétrospective*, III (1834), 75. Yet cf. the favorable estimation in M.-F. Pidansat de Mairobert, *L'espion anglais, ou Correspondance secrète entre mylord all'eye et mylord all'ear* (London, 1784), I, 100–101.

72 Guy Caire, "Bertin, Ministre physiocrate," *Revue d'histoire économique et sociale*, XXXVIII (1960), 257–84; Bourde, *Agronomie*, II, 1088–1090; Léonce de Lavergne, *Economistes*, 446–47. Cf. G. Bussière, "Bertin," *Bulletin de la Société Historique et Archéologique du Périgord*, XXII (1905), 216–44, 381–418; XXXIII (1906), 72–113, 211–43, 311–31; XXXIV (1907), 53–83, 272–314, 373–388, 451–66; XXXV (1908), 274–313, 437–64; XXXVI (1909), 133–62, 210–81; and Weulersse, *Louis XV*, 12.

73 Bourde insists that Bertin's appointment marked a clear desire on the part of the government to promote new ideas. *Agronomie*, II, 1097–99.

Illustration 2. "Foreign" baker supplying the twice-weekly bread market. *The Baker's Cart* by Jean Michelin (1656). The Metropolitan Museum of Art, Fletcher Fund, 1927.

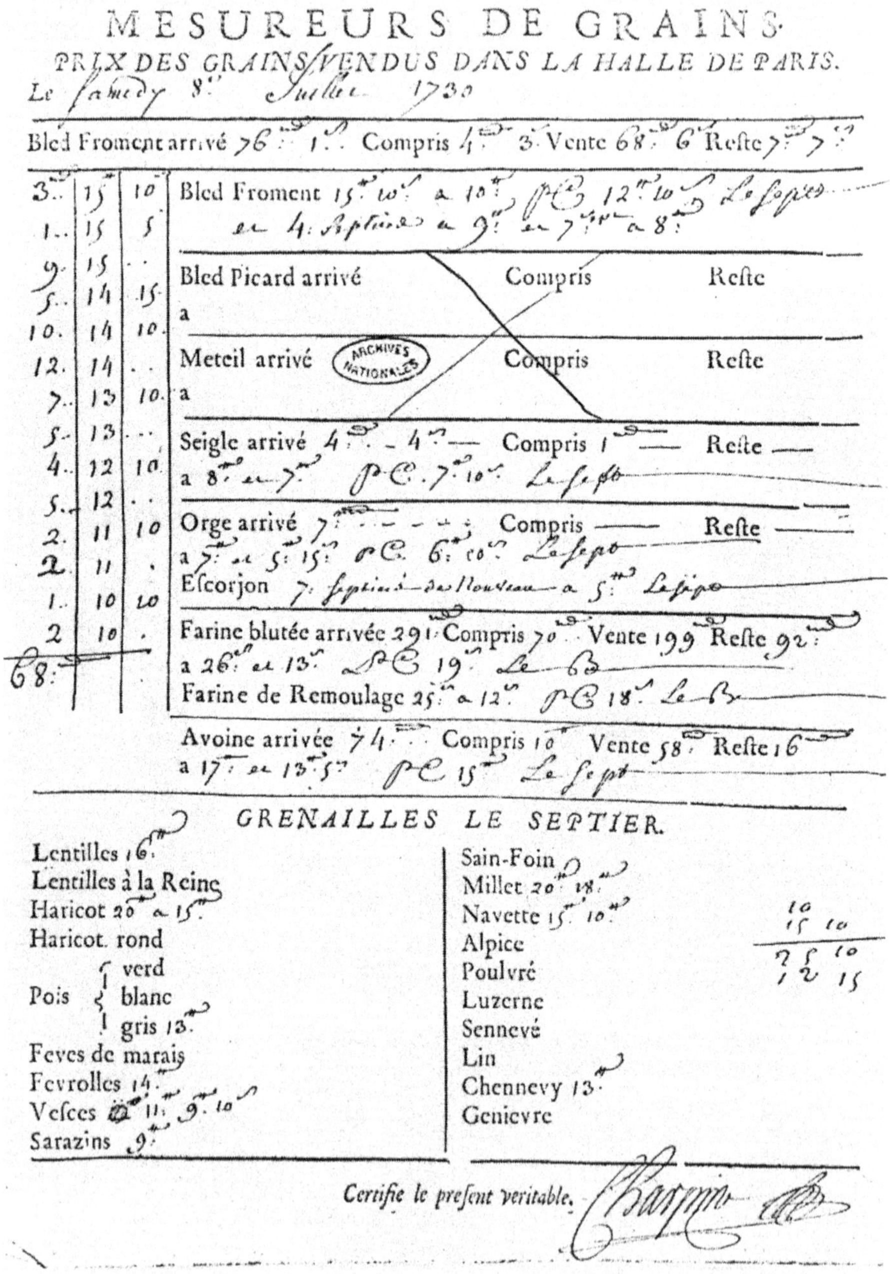

Illustration 3. Example of the record of grain and flour arrivals, sales, and prices kept by the Paris market administration. Archives Nationales.

intendant at Lyons, he cultivated Gournay, who shared with him his radical notions of political economy. As a protégé of Madame de Pompadour, it was assumed that Bertin continued his education with Quesnay and regarded the nascent physiocratic view with favor. At the ministry, he drew his closest advisers from liberal, agronomist, and *économiste* circles: Abeille, Baudeau, Dangeul, Dupont, Morellet, Daniel Trudaine, Turgot, and the marquis de Turbilly.[74]

On the other hand, it is worth noting that his carreer was perfectly conventional and his ascension more or less predictable. Son of an enterprising provincial parlementaire who owned ironworks and ships, he served a classic apprenticeship as lawyer, councillor, and President of the Grand Conseil, master of requests and intendant in Roussillon and Lyons. His views were judged sufficiently orthodox to win him the delicate post of Lieutenant General of Police of Paris in the year that Damiens assaulted the king. Considered one of the most difficult charges in the kingdom, the *lieutenance* put the appointee's fortitude and talents to the most rigorous test and tended to mark him *prima facie* as a "dur." It was widely believed that the king named him Controller-General for his quality as a "policeman" to restore the order disrupted by the "remedies" prescribed by "doctor" Silhouette, son-in-law of a renowned physician. Before Pompadour integrated Bertin into her patronage system, he had been the favorite of the Secretary of State St. Florentin, scion of one of the oldest and least progressive ministerial dynasties in the kingdom. And, if he surrounded himself with liberals and reformers, he named as his official propagandist J. N. Moreau, historian of the "cacouacs" and mordant critic of the philosophes.[75]

Bertin became Controller-General in late November 1759, an extremely difficult time when the government was pressed by urgent

---

74 Bussière, "Bertin," *Bulletin ... Périgord*, XXV (1908), 274–75 and XXVI (1909), 211–12, 215; Bourde, *Agronomie*, II, 1099. According to J. Peuchet, an almost-contemporary student of old regime administration, "Bertin was [a member] of the *économiste* sect...." *Mémoires tirés des archives de la police de Paris* (Paris, 1838), II, 162. On Bertin and the "Chinese" spirit, see Charles L. Chassin, ed., *Les Elections et les cahiers de Paris en 1789* (Paris, 1889), IV, 122–23.

75 François Bluche, Les *Magistrats du grand conseil au XVIIIe siècle, 1690–1791* (Paris, 1966), 53; M. Prévost, "Bertin," in R. d'Amat and M. Prévost, eds., *Dictionnaire de biographie française* (Paris, 1954), VI, 244–45; Bourde, *Agronomie*, II, 1083; E.J.F. Barbier, *Chronique de la régence*, VII, 207–208 (Nov. 1759); Jacob-Nicolas Moreau, *Mes souvenirs*, ed. by C. Hermelin, I, 78, 80. Cf. Y. Durand, ed., *Mémoires de J.-J. de Laborde, fermier général et banquier de la cour* in Annuaire —*Bulletin de la Société de l'Histoire de France* (1968–69), 158 which emphasizes Bertin's total dependence on Pompadour.

wartime fiscal needs and censured by the parlements in increasingly strident and vitriolic terms for extortionate, wasteful, and illegal practices. At the cost of major political concessions, Bertin won approval for the bulk of the emergency measures he proposed. Despite his preoccupation with finances and the mutinous attitude of the courts, he indicated from the beginning that he would seek a liberalization of the grain trade regime "at the right moment." He shared the assessment of the intendant of Rouen that the "enlightened" portion of the nation was ready for such a major reform and he was persuaded, on the basis of his analysis of the economy, that the kingdom needed it. Bertin moved with conviction but without precipitation; no doctrinaire, his determination to promote agricultural prosperity was tempered by a keen sense of the political and social risks inherent in grain reform.[76]

Memoirs "from everywhere" on the grain question flooded Bertin's offices and the royal council. Their central theme was that agriculture was mired in stagnation as a result of recurrent gluts, sustained low prices, and lack of outlets and that this stagnation threatened the well-being of the kingdom. "It appears be be generally desired," the Controller-General reported, "that the Government encourage agriculture by giving the grain trade a liberty which is capable of raising the price." In a circular letter soliciting the opinions of intendants and other administrators, Bertin left no doubt that his government planned to respond positively to this desire. He invited no criticism of the premises upon which the government view rested. The only matter to be discussed was how much and what sort of liberty would be accorded. A universal liberty, applicable in all spheres, was from the start out of the question. The first taboo enveloped the Paris provisioning system. Since "it is essential not to give the least anxiety on an object of this nature," even if "abuses" are detected, "for the present" they are to be studied rather than remedied. Similarly, consideration of the freedom to export would be postponed "for the present time." Like Silhouette, Bertin envisioned a two-stage reform in which the delicate and complex export issue would not even be raised until the trade had adjusted to the new regime. (Liberal stalwarts, of course, argued that Bertin's prudential segregation of the export question was self-defeating, for no workable adjustment could occur until exporting was allowed.)

---

76 Marcel Marion, *Histoire financière*, I, 209; E. Glasson, *Le Parlement de Paris*, II, 258–62; Léon Biollay, *Le Pacte de famine*, 95.

Allowing for these two exceptions, however, Bertin intimated that he was ready to go further along the road to liberty than any of his predecessors had dared: to dismantle the entire regulatory apparatus as it applied to internal commerce. In order to determine whether the administrative corps shared his thinking, he asked them whether they favored freeing merchants from all formalities, barring certain "qualities" of persons from trading, increasing or restricting the number of merchants, allowing stocking, dispensing traders from transacting business on the public markets, and sparing grain the imposition of all road, river, and bridge tolls (*péages*).[77]

We have not been able to unearth a large enough number of replies to Bertin's questions to venture a global evaluation of administrative opinion. But we have a sampling sufficiently rich to suggest the range and type of attitudes encountered. From his intendancy in the Limousin, Turgot drafted a long, rambling memoir in which he rehearsed the main themes of the liberal doctrine (citing, doubtless to make a point, Gournay rather than Quesnay) instead of answering Bertin's queries. Though he did not explicitly criticize Bertin's plan, Turgot revealed that he favored a far more comprehensive liberalization than the Controller-General envisioned, a "total liberty" including freedom to export. He hinted that a reform short of this might not succeed in rescuing agriculture, wresting the grain trade from "paltry" hands and passing it on to capitalist entrepreneurs, and saving France from both the "horrors" of famine and glut.[78]

The intendants of Brittany and Bordeaux seem to have shared Turgot's enthusiasm for a stronger measure.[79] The Chamber of Commerce of Marseilles also pledged itself to press for "a complete liberty" permitting unlimited exports, stockage, off-market business, and trade by all persons regardless of quality. Yet, despite their plea to "laissez agir," the Marseillais, worried about the ability of the police

---

77 Bertin to de la Tour, 1 Aug. 1761 and "Mémoire à consulter sur la liberté du commerce des grains," C. 2420, A.D. B-du-R. Cf. Bertin to INs. of Brittany (C. 69, A.D. I-et-V.), Alençon (C. 89, A.D. Orne), Rouen (C. 103, A.D. S-M.). Franche-Comté (C. 496, A.D. Doubs), and Caen (C. 2619, A.D. Cal.). Originally Bertin envisaged a completely separate declaration dealing exclusively with the problem of tolls and duties on grain in transit. See Bertin to Boisemont, 4 July 1761, C. 6690, A.D. Nord and Vedier to Premion, 15 July 1761, C. 775, A.D. L-A.

78 Turgot draft letter in *Œuvres*, ed. Schelle, II, 122–28.

79 H. Fréville, *L'Intendance de Bretagne* (Rennes, 1953), II, 189–94; Boutet to Courteille, 18 June 1763, C. 1426, A.D. Gir. Cf. the confident assertion of the intendant of Hainaut that Bertin's project was really superfluous, given the fact that liberty already reigned in his *généralité*. Boisemont to Bertin, 16 July 1761, C. 6690, A.D. Nord.

to monitor "the state of provisioning," asked the Controller-General to require merchants to declare the whereabouts of their storehouses and the destination points of their shipments.[80] Levignen and De Gourgues, intendants of Alençon and Montauban, took positions at the opposite extreme from their counterparts in the Limousin, the Bordelais and Brittany. Levignen denied that prices were too low and felt that exportation should be "entirely prohibited" in order to protect consumers. De Gourgues cautioned Bertin that "by revoking the old laws he was opening the door to still greater abuses." Both intendants favored retaining the old system of internal trade for its flexibility, which enabled authorities to relax controls in good times and apply them sternly in periods of stress.[81]

At the bottom as well as at the top of royal provincial administration, opinion ran the gamut from zealous liberalism to outright hostility to serious grain reform. Like the intendants who solicited their views, we are particularly interested in the attitudes of the subdelegates because they were in relatively close touch with the day-to-day problems of grain trading and provisioning. Seven subdelegates in the generality of Alençon replied to Bertin's questions. On one side stood the subdelegate at Argentan, a self-proclaimed disciple of Herbert, whom he believed had already published "all that could best be said on this matter." There was "nothing to fear" in introducing liberty; indeed, only liberty could stimulate production and thus strike at "the real cause of dearth."[82] Bourdon of Lisieux staked out this same terrain, albeit

---

80 Chamber of Commerce to IN. of Provence, 26 Sept. 1761, C. 2420, A.D. B-du-R.

81 Levignen to Bertin, ? Aug. 1761, C. 89, CD. Orne; De Gourgues to Terray, 16 Dec. 1771, AN, F[11] 223. Levignen followed the *avis* of his subdelegate from Bernay almost word for word. SD to Levignen, 22 Aug. 1761, C. 89, A.D. Orne.

De la Corée, the intendant of Franche-Comté, expressed even stronger reservations in a commentary on the draft version of the liberalizing law which Bertin circulated the following spring. He insisted on the urgency of "reconciling" liberty with "the precautions necessary to prevent abuses and especially monopolies." In his estimation, there was as much need "for publicity as for liberty" in the conduct of the trade. While he endorsed interprovincial freedom of circulation, he favored mandatory declarations and market exchanges. To Bertin, 29 April 1762, C. 496, A.D. Doubs.

82 To IN., Aug. 1761, C. 89, A.D. Orne.

In his extremely thoughtful letter, this subdelegate pointed to two matters which would later be of considerable significance. The first was a remarkably rarefied issue for a minor official to join. It concerned the political implications of the fact that England, the nation whose "hundred years of success" with liberty was supposed to be a powerful incentive for the French to adopt their system, had a "republican constitution." The lesson drawn by the subdelegate was not that liberty was therefore ill-suited for France, which boasted "a monarchical constitution." Rather, he suggested, since a monarchical constitution accorded far more authority to the central government

with considerably less eloquence than his colleague from Argentan.[83] Three other subdelegates answered all of Bertin's questions in the liberal sense, yet each official had some reservations about the reform. The "total liberty" conceived by the first of this triumvirate, the subdelegate of Alençon, allowed for full-scale police intervention in "critical times," that is, precisely when the liberals argued that police interference was historically and theoretically most pernicious.[84] The other two administrators, in addition to opposing export on the grounds that "it would necessarily cause the people to suffer," also challenged some of the basic liberal ideas. The subdelegate of Verneuil suggested that the "pretended abundance" which the liberals deplore as a burden "does not always have as much reality" as they would like us to believe. His colleague from Sées attacked the idea that price conditions determined how much land the *laboureurs* would sow in marketable grain; regardless of yesterday's or today's price, the *laboureurs* will always plant "as much as possible" in the "hope of a price increase" tomorrow.[85]

Finally, two subdelegates, preoccupied above all with the needs of consumers, advised against the sort of liberalization which Bertin imagined. Afraid that "an entire liberty" would be "dangerous," the first wanted off-market exchanges to be strictly prohibited and grain owners obliged to supply the public on a regular basis. There was no question in his mind that local grain was to be used for local use and that the business of the grain trade was to serve the consuming public. The second official predicted that there would be "troubles

---

than a republican constitution, it would be even easier for France to adopt the liberal system and adjust it to its needs than it had been for England. *In fine*, this was the whole theory of enlightened despotism scaled to practice. Far less interesting as political theory, the second point raised by the subdelegate had much greater practical political significance. Though he sincerely believed in the liberal doctrine, he was haunted by the fear that the new system would call into existence huge companies which would force individuals out of the trade and corner the market. Without any fastidious concern for doctrinal coherence, the subdelegate simply wanted them banned from the grain trade (along with "excessively rich seigneurs"). Such a populist fear coming from a local official sympathetic to liberalization should have served as a warning to the government. The specter of monster companies cast a shadow across the whole liberal experience.

83 To IN., 24 Aug. 1761, *ibid.*

84 To IN., 16 Aug. 1761, *ibid.* This subdelegate, like his colleague at Argentan, also worried about the tyranny of grain trading companies.

85 To IN., 14 and 17 Aug. 1761, *ibid.* Cf. the attitude of the two Provençal procurators who also favored liberalization on the one hand but worried about its disequilibrating effects on the other. Bonnet and Rostolun to IN., 31 Aug. 1761, C. 2420, A.D. B-du-R.

and popular riots" if exportation were ever allowed. Nor was he serene about the prospects of free internal circulation. To check the "abuses" inherent in the trade, he recommended the maintenance of most of the traditional controls, especially the laws of 1567, 1577, 1699, and 1723 which fixed transactions on the open markets and authorized the police to constrain grain owners to furnish supplies.[86] On the whole it is perhaps more remarkable to find two local-level officials eagerly committed to the liberal position and three others generally favorable to reform than to encounter two partisans of the police system in which they all had been trained. Nevertheless, the Controller-General could not have remained insensitive to the fact that opinion within the administration was divided and still evolving at all levels.

Though Rouen's Feydeau de Brou unhesitatingly endorsed Bertin's reform plan since it closely approximated the proposal he had made to Silhouette, he was nevertheless a bit less sure of himself now than he had been in 1759. He warned the Controller-General that it would require considerable political skill to bring off the reforms. The intendant claimed that he needed time to work on a number of the Rouen parlementaires who still nurtured "prejudices" contrary to liberty. Nor should the minister entertain the thought of doing without parlementary registration. Without the magistrates' approbation, Feydeau candidly reminded Bertin, no law could pretend to be "permanent" and have a "general bearing." Moreover, given the public confidence enjoyed by the sovereign courts, the people would never believe that there was "no contradiction" between liberalization and "the general welfare" unless the parlements announced their approval.[87] This assessment of parlementary influence was written not by a propagandist paid to puff the robe but by the agent of royal absolutism in the province. Feydau foresaw how deeply the magistracy would be involved in the unfolding story of liberalization.

Though Bertin felt that "the circumstance is [now] favorable to make a decision" when he circulated his memoir in the summer of 1761, almost two more years elapsed before the promulgation of the May law. The demands of war, finances, and related matters may have diverted the Controller-General's attention from the reform project. But it also

---

86 To IN., 2 and 22 Aug. 1761, C. 89, A.D. Orne. The subdelegate-general of Brittany apparently had similar fears for the fate of consumers. See Fréville, *L'Intendance de Bretagne*, 191.

87 IN. to Bertin, 7 Sept. 1761, C. 103, A.D. S-M.

appears that Bertin realized that he had underestimated the political difficulties which the passage of the measure entailed. He wanted to prepare his case more carefully in the royal council, where there were rumblings of uncertainty, in the administration, in the sovereign courts, and in the elusive domain called public opinion. On the one hand, he encouraged the liberal lobby and the "economic" press to maintain their pressure and he barraged the intendants with reformist propaganda. On the other, he emphasized, in the council, in ministerial committees, and in the Bureau of Commerce, the safeguards that the law would contain.

In April 1762 Bertin sent a draft version of the future May Declaration to the intendants, the parlements, the societies of agriculture, and to other public figures and institutions. He introduced it in a covering letter far more aggressive in tone than the memoir-questionnaire which had circulated the previous summer. This former Lieutenant General of Police attacked the police far more sharply than he had before, depicting them as inflexible, nervous, intemperate, undiscriminating, and blustery rather than supple, stolid, moderate, judicious, and discreet. He blamed agricultural stagnation and the underdevelopment of the grain trade squarely upon the police. Nor could the police justify their practices on the grounds that they were necessary to prevent dearth, for the record indicated that they had achieved little success in this domain. "The only means of encouraging agriculture and creating thereby a constant abundance," concluded Bertin, "was to leave liberty to the internal trade and assure the cultivators a price proportionate to their works."

Yet, despite his conviction that the new liberty and the old police could not coexist, the Controller-General was unwilling to venture a total liberty as the liberals would have liked; instead, he would avoid instituting any change which "could, by its novelty, give rise to some untoward revolution." Thus, Bertin refused to change his mind about Paris and about exports; the draft declaration contained articles maintaining the old rules in the capital and the general prohibition against exports save by special license. Paris remained the "*noli me tangere* of the affair," even at the risk of limiting the freedom of a large number of traders, because it was simply too dangerous to tamper with the city's provisioning system given the "extent" and the "nature" of its population. Nor could free exportation be envisioned until the government assessed the impact of liberalization upon the domestic provisioning trade in order to make certain that grain necessary for subsistence would not escape abroad. Bertin never overcame his deep skepticism about the wisdom of an unlimited authorization to export. Later, he vainly opposed the efforts of his successor to implement this policy.[88]

Bertin's legislative proposal of 1762 consisted of a preamble explaining the motives that inspired the king to break radically with the police tradition and eight articles spelling out the new ground rules (and anti-rules) for the conduct of trade in the interior. The first three clauses opened commerce to all comers, abolished the registration requirements and the bans on stockage and off-market exchanges, guaranteed unimpeded circulation in the interior, prohibited the police from interfering with the trade in any way, and dispensed buyers or sellers from paying road, river, or bridge tolls on their grain. The next three articles reaffirmed the old prohibitive policy on exports and instituted controls to prevent coastwise and frontier traders from engaging in fraudulent exportation under the cover of free internal circulation. Codifying the special status of the capital, the seventh article exempted Paris from conforming to any of the changes stipulated in the previous clauses. By declaring void all previous legistation and regulations contrary to the new law, the eighth and last article formally interred the corpus of law that perpetuated the police tradition.

On the whole reactions to Bertin's proposal must have been reassuring, for the declaration which finally appeared a year later in May 1763 followed the draft law exactly, save for the complete suppression of articles four, five, and six. Though there was a certain amount of criticism from those who opposed liberalization, the most vocal objections appeared to come from the liberal camp. The prior-consuls of

---

88 Bertin circular to INs., P Gs., etc., 13 April 1762, AN, F^{12} 149; Bertin to Levignen, with draft of law, 13 April 1762 and Bertin to Levignen, 25 May 1762, C. 90, A.D. Orne; Biollay, *Le Pacte de famine*, 91–103; Caire, "Bertin," *Revue d'histoire économique et sociale*, XXXVIII (1960), 267; Musart, *Réglementation du commerce des grains*, 18. Yet Bertin was resolutely opposed to issuing "individual licenses," the common practice before liberalization. If there was to be a liberty to export, it had to be "general." Bertin to IN. of La Rochelle, 3 May 1761, C. 189, A.D. C-M.

In early 1763 Bertin had the government publish two measures allowing the uncontrolled export of flour (first *farine de minot* and then all flour) and grain except for wheat and méteil, a hybrid crop of wheat and rye. The Controller-General willingly made these concessions to the liberals because he knew that they would have little bearing upon the provisioning situation. In addition, he allowed specific areas burdened with surpluses to export for limited periods. See, for example, B 2314, fol. 89, A.D. Isère.

St. Malo, for example, claimed to be "infinitely surprised" by the Controller-General's draft version:

> It is very distressing that the overly tender love of the Sovereign and of his ministers for the People prevents them from abrogating completely and forever this timorous and uncertain police which has almost destroyed our Agriculture.[89]

In response to charges that he had gone too far, Bertin had only to point to overdrawn reproaches such as this to prove that his position was essentially moderate.

The issue which excited the ire of the Malouins as well as of the deputies of commerce and other liberals was exportation. Perhaps it was in part to placate them that the Controller-General dropped articles four, five, and six from the final version of the law. By passing over the export question in silence the government was likely to provoke less discontent among the liberals than by announcing explicitly that it had examined and rejected the possibility of permitting exports. The export renunciation formula of the 1762 draft suggested that no change was probable for some time to come whereas the absence of any statement of intention in the May Declaration seemed to intimate that a decision to extend liberty to exportation could follow in the very near future. Surely the liberals also applauded the disappearance of the articles requiring coastwise and frontier traders to obtain passports for their shipments and discharge visas upon delivery.[90] Had these controls survived authorities could have used them to hamper internal trade on the pretext of preventing clandestine exportation. In fact, traders appear to have profited from the opportunities for illicit exporting in the fourteen months which elapsed between the May Declaration and the July Edict. The failure to provide for such controls and to re-dedicate the government to a no-export policy reinforced the suspicions of those who felt that Bertin's ostensibly moderate stand was an illusion.

Bertin, the architect of the May Declaration, had no time to ponder the significance of his success. Another issue surged to the forefront, overshadowing the grain reform at the very moment of its

---

89 Prior-Consuls of St. Malo to Estates of Brittany (?), ca. summer 1762, C. 3911, A.D. I-et-V. Cf. the opinion of the deputies of commerce, "Commerce intérieur et extérieur des blés," BN, mss. fr. 11347, fols. 213–16.

90 The Bretons were especially sensitive to restrictions on coastwise trading, for much of their "internal" grain trade took place by water. Though coastwise trading was not explicitly mentioned in the final version of the May Declaration, Bertin assured them that such trade was "free" subject to the continued use of *acquits à caution*. Bertin to Damilly, 3 Aug. 1763, C. 774, A.D. L-A.

promulgation. In order to deal with the immediate problems of winding down the war and meeting pressing civil as well as military obligations, the Controller-General asked the royal council for a series of fiscal measures prolonging the multiple *vingtièmes*, levying them on the basis of a new assessment of landed wealth, and imposing, in addition, a number of new taxes and tax supplements. Bertin's proposals aroused such furious resistance from the sovereign courts that Louis XV felt obliged to dismiss him from office in late November 1763. In his stead the king named Laverdy, a member of the Paris Parlement and son of a celebrated lawyer. Politically obscure and suspected of entertaining extravagant Jansenist sympathies, Laverdy had a sufficiently solid judicial reputation to excite genuine hope for a successful administration. In large measure, these expectations rested on Laverdy's promise to make peace with the parlements. In return for a number of extraordinary concessions, including a royal invitation to the sovereign courts to participate in the elaboration of fiscal policy, the renunciation or dilution of most of Bertin's tax program, and effusively conciliatory pronouncements by the king, Laverdy won a fiscal accord likely to tide the government through the rest of the decade.[91]

Within months after he came to power, the new Controller-General turned his attention to the grain question. Whereas Bertin's contacts and his career in the field predisposed him to take a special interest in the matter, there was nothing in Laverdy's parlementary background to suggest what his attitude would be. Professionally, he was best known for being "an indefatigable worker." His private life was hardly less dreary than his public career. Married to the daughter of a wealthy cloth merchant (a "Colbertist" choice!), Laverdy lived simply ("bourgeoisement"), frequenting neither the masked balls and gaming tables nor the salons. About his ideas we know little more than that his distrust of "philosophy" was firmly rooted. The point is worth remembering, for Laverdy's conversion to the new political economy would soon prove that it was possible to join the Enlightenment without making any concession to "philosophy," or at least not admitting to any.[92] Weeks before she died and deprived the liberal cause of a powerful ally,

---

91 *Nouvelliste suisse* (Dec. 1763), 540; Bachaumont, *Mémoires secrets* (London, 1780–1786), II, 44 (13 April 1764); Marion, *Finances*, I, 214–30; Glasson, *Parlement de Paris*, II, 280–92; Moreau, *Souvenirs*, ed. by C. Hermelin, I, 144.

92 *Journal de Barbier* (Dec. 1763), VIII, 119–22; Pidansat de Mairobert, *L'Observateur anglois* (London, 1778), I, 277.

Madame de Pompadour hinted at the course the new Controller-General would take by presenting him with a portrait of Sully, an unmistakable, highly political symbol of reform. At the same time the appropriate verses, flat and fustian, circulated in Paris:

> Of the shrewd and wise *Sully*
> there remains only the image
> Today this great personage
> is recalled to life in *Laverdy*.[93]

The Sullyist position at the beginning of 1764 was best expressed by the *économiste* Letrosne:

> The Declaration of 25 May 1763 razed these interior barriers erected by timidity, maintained for such a long time by habit, so favorable to monopoly, and so dear to the eyes of arbitrary authority. *But there still remains to take the most essential step.*[94]

The "essential step" was the "constant and irrevocable grant of exportation," the necessary complement to internal liberty without which agriculture would not revive, the "common price of Europe" would not be attained, abundance would not become a blessing as well as a certainty, and the revenues of the state and the prosperity of the citizenry would not grow. Laverdy shared Letrosne's view of the urgency of taking this step and he believed, moreover, that the time was ripe to do so. Though a canvass of administrative opinion which he conducted in early 1764 revealed that there were still pockets of dissent, the general mood seemed to be favorable to some form of general authorization to export. The May Declaration generated a certain momentum for reform; it became, according to Laverdy's predecessor Bertin, who felt uncomfortable with it, an irresistible "enthusiasm," reinforced by an excellent harvest in 1763 and superb "appearances" for 1764.[95]

Laverdy did not, however, take precisely the giant step that Letrosne and other liberals demanded: a "total" freedom to export without limits. He feared that such a decision would alienate moderate opinion, cause widespread alarm, and precipitate changes too brusquely. Though he called upon two of the leading liberal spokesmen in the kingdom, Turgot and Dupont, to help draft what

---

93 Bachaumont, *Mémoires secrets*, II, 44 (13 April 1764).
94 G.-F. Letrosne, *Discours sur l'état actuel de la magistrature et sur les causes de sa décadence* (n.p., 1764), 68.
95 Biollay, *Le Pacte de famine*, 112.

became the July 1764 Edict, the Controller-General rejected their advice that no conditions be placed on the permission to trade in the interior or abroad.[96] Instead he insisted that the law contain a mechanism for cutting off exports automatically when the price reached thirty *livres* the Parisian *septier*. (With equal determination he repulsed Bertin's plea that the price ceiling be set at twenty-five *livres* or less.) Any general permission to export was in itself an awesome innovation, Laverdy reasoned, and the liberals themselves admitted that thirty *livres* was well above the "common price of Europe" to which they sought to adjust French agriculture. Though they rejoiced sincerely in the promulgation of the July Edict and supported Laverdy zealously during his tenure in the ministry, the *économistes* never forgave him for the barrier he raised against absolute liberty in 1764 even as they continued to reproach Bertin for his qualmishness in 1763. Years later, well after the first great battle over liberalization had been lost, the *économistes* took their revenge. Dupont officially purged Laverdy from the roll of liberal authenticity that he drew up. In favoring the step to exportation, the Controller-General, he wrote, had been "more swept along than convinced."[97] But if the policy he pursued with unstinting energy and stubborn resolution during the four and one half years following the passage of the July Edict is a fair measure of his conviction, then it is impossible to fault his commitment to the liberal reforms.[98]

The Controllers-General Bertin and Laverdy played the leading roles in the preparation and passage of the liberalizing measures. But a word must be ventured about the position taken by the Foreign Minister Choiseul who is supposed to have been the preponderant figure in a government memorable neither for ministerial coherence nor stability.[99]

---

96 *Œuvres de Turgot*, ed. by Schelle, II, 405–406. Cf. J. Nio, *Turgot et la liberté du commerce* (Bordeaux, 1928), 98–99.

97 Dupont to Prince Carl Ludwig, 1773, *Carl Friedrichs von Baden Brieflicher Verkehr mit Mirabeau und Dupont*, ed. by C. Knies (Heidelberg, 1892), II, 136.

98 On this point I take issue with Weulersse who deplored Laverdy's lack of "convictions" and "firmness of character" to which he partially ascribed the failure of the reforms. *Mouvement*, II, 216.

99 Lebrun wrote that Choiseul then "reigned" at court. *Opinions, rapports, et choix d'écrits politiques de C.-F. Lebrun*, ed. by A.-C. Lebrun (Paris, 1829), 16. Abbé Georgel claimed that Choiseul had "all the powers of prime minister without having the title." *Mémoire pour servir à l'histoire des événements de la fin du dix-huitième siècle* (Paris, 1820), I, 96. Cf. *ibid.*, 173. Apparently Choiseul did not have close personal or political relations with either Controller-General Bertin or his successor Laverdy. See Jacob-Nicolas Moreau, *Mes souvenirs*, ed. by C. Hermelin (Paris, 1898–1901), I, 80, 118, 143–144, 185, 216 and II, 53.

Choiseul's intelligence and range impressed contemporary observers. He had a "prompt, penetrating" mind, according to one acquaintance; another esteemed that he was "capable of rather big ideas" despite an air of frivolity and a pronounced distaste for the details of governing.[100] Although he detested Doctor Quesnay, his obligations to Madame de Pompadour, his patroness, compelled him to treat the *économistes* sympathetically. The abbé Morellet, a busy philosophe who toiled in their camp, characterized Choiseul as "protector of the liberty of the grain trade," but noted that he was hostile, more for temperamental than ideological reasons, to philosophy in general and physiocracy in particular.[101]

Wisps of evidence from the mid-sixties indicate that he worried about provisioning, kept himself informed on grain trade affairs, and intervened on occasion with local and provincial authorities.[102] In *Mémoires* attributed to him, composed well after his disgrace, Choiseul defined his attitude toward liberalization without, however, divulging the stand which he had taken in the royal council in the period preceding the liberal reforms. While the view he expressed here is consistent with our other information about him, his sharply critical assessment of the way the government handled liberalization suggests that he had dissociated himself from this policy-making, leaving it to the controllers-general in whose domain it naturally belonged.

Choiseul saw no reason why merchants should not have an "entire liberty" to export grain. Aware of the fears of consumers, he argued that they must understand that, if grain were short and dear in France, "exportation is null, for one will always prefer to sell at home and save on the transport." But the decision to liberalize *should have* been based "purely" on grounds of "fact" and "calculation," or incontrovertible data comparing average annual grain production to the number of "mouths there are in France which eat bread." The government in the early sixties forsook simplicity and clarity and invited misunderstanding and disputation by tying its reforms to an elaborate theory.

---

100 Abbé de Véri, *Journal*, ed. by J. de Witte, I, 53; Pierre Besenval, *Mémoires de M. le Baron de Besenval* (Paris, 1805), I, 316–24.

101 Weulersse, *Mouvement*, I, 116–17; Abbé Morellet, *Mémoires de l'abbé Morellet de l'Académie Française sur le dix-huitième siècle et sur la révolution* (Paris, 1821), I, 186. Cf. J. Nio, *Turgot et la liberté du commerce* (Bordeaux, 1928), 97.

102 Letters to Choiseul, 4, 13 Sept. 1765, AN, F^{12} 150. Galiani claimed to have presented his "system" of grain trade reform to Choiseul (rather than to the Controller-General) in 1763–64. Galiani to Suard, 15 Dec. 1770, *Lettres*, ed. by Eugène Asse (Paris, 1882), I, 88.

"On this issue," charged Choiseul, "metaphysics serves only to muddle the mind and the matter."

This error in preparation, according to Choiseul, led to another in public relations which proved fatal. Through its supporters, the government undertook to expose and justify its position publicly, a "beautiful and honest" but terribly "expensive" gesture which violated a fundamental rule of government: "the administration must neither write nor allow to be written anything on affairs which might excite the mind of the peoples." The official defense provoked a stormy debate which in turn produced a "doubt" (Choiseul did not explicitly concede that the "doubt" may have arisen endogenously). "This doubt," he reasoned, "in matters of the substance of first necessity, turns quite naturally into terror;" and the terror, in this instance, generated widespread resistance to the new laws. Choiseul's critique was a lesson in the pitfalls of mixing enlightenment and absolutism in uncertain portions and without regard for the other elements in the recipe. "I therefore think," he concluded, "that, principally on the issue of grain as in affairs of [religious] dogma, one must give only the decisions & conserve, in the sanctuary of the administration, the motives which determine [policy] as well as the means put into effect to prevent and repair the disadvantages of the law."[103]

Whether it was possible in the 1760's to run government, introduce profound changes in administration, and manipulate, dismiss, or disregard public opinion in the chaste manner that Choiseul suggested remains open to question. We shall have occasion shortly to take the measure of the foreign minister's analysis of the government's failure in managing the grain issue. First we must examine the "motives" that "determined" the government of which Choiseul was a part to venture a reform which obviously entailed such great risks.

IV

Why did the government undertake this radical new departure in liberalization in 1763–64? The most obvious answer, widely endorsed by contemporaries and which seems to befit a government constrained to follow a policy of opportunistic empiricism, is best described as the thesis of circumstances. Even enemies of the reform conceded that conditions were strikingly propitious for change. The salient fact was the

---

103 Duc de Choiseul, *Mémoires*, ed. by Soulavie, I, 43–45, 50–51.

price of grain, product of three unusually bountiful harvests in succession. Despite its pronounced anxiety over the new measures, the Parisian municipality was unable to remember a single below-average harvest in the past "ten or twelve years" and noted that the prices have recently been "on a very low footing, even at Paris."[104] The average annual price of wheat in France, calculated on the basis of official reports in Parisian *septiers*, fell from 18.37 *livres* in 1760 to 15.60 in 1761, 15.48 in 1762, and 14.88 in 1763. For the same years the prices reported in Paris were 17.85 *livres*, 13.75, 13.80 and 13.05.[105] The prices paid by the Hôpital Général, which habitually purchased top quality wheat in the provisioning zones of the capital, ranged from 18.25 (January–April) to 22.60 (May–June) in 1760; 12.50 (November) to 18.20 (February–April) in 1761; and 13.45 to 14.60 in 1762.[106] These figures suggest a clear-cut, short-term downward movement. The impression they made on contemporaries, not only large grain producers burdened with substantial, unremunerative surpluses, but upon administrators, field and center, was dramatic. It was generally agreed that prices were abnormally low and that there was considerable margin for a socially innocuous and economically productive upward turn.

For pessimists, however, the thesis of circumstances could cut another way. Such was the rhythm of life in a cereals-dominated economy that a fortunate spate of excellent harvests could cause a different sort of consternation, for it could be interpreted to mean that a series of bad or mediocre years were in store. Moreover, still other circumstances militated against any major political innovation. France had just suffered a humiliating and costly defeat in a war whose demoralizing and disorganizing economic and social effects have never received adequate attention from historians. At the same time, the parlements violently resisted the ministry's fiscal designs. Michelet and R. R. Palmer both used the word "revolutionary" to describe the developing situation.[107]

---

104 "Mémoires et avis de Messieurs du Bureau de la Ville" (prior to July 1764), BN, mss. fr. 14296, fol. 29.

105 Ernest Labrousse, *Esquisse*, I, 104, 113. Cf. the monthly prices reported in the *Journal économique* from 1756 to 1766 and the "Table du plus beau froment vendu dans les marchés de Paris" in Béguillet, *Traité des subsistances*, 799–800. Béguillet contended that the "current price" did not vary dramatically in the course of the century. The prices he reported for the years in question—16 *livres* 16 *sous*, 15 1. 18 s., 16 1. 1 s., and 15 1. 17 1/2 s.—are significantly higher than those published by Labrousse.

106 AAP, 105, liasse 9, nos. 1 and 2.

107 Michelet, *Histoire de France*, XVI, 124–25; R.R. Palmer, *The Age of the Democratic Revolution*, (Princeton, 1959), I, 86–99. Cf. H. Martin, *The Decline of the French Monarchy*, trans. by M.L. Booth (Boston, 1866), 203 and Moreau, *Souvenirs*, ed. by C. Hermelin, I, 28.

The failure of the climate of post-war uncertainty and political volatility to deter reform and the fact that previous ministries, in times when low prices converged with domestic and international peace, had never dared to envision such reform, suggest that other factors, not encompassed in a "circumstantial" explanation, were at work. Stagnating prices fashioned one seam in a complex web; they were a necessary but not a sufficient condition to motivate liberalization.

Another explanation, which also emerged from contemporary comment, a product of the unwitting complicity of the *économistes* and their adversaries, can be called the thesis of conspiracy. Although the friends of Quesnay were by no means entirely satisfied with the legislation of 1763–64, they were delighted to acknowledge spiritual paternity. They intimated that it would not have been realized without their pressure and they let it be known that Dupont and Turgot actually collaborated in drafting it.[108] Not till late in the decade, in the midst of serious political and social troubles, did their attitude toward the achievement become somewhat captious and detached.

Their critics, however, generously insisted on placing credit where it was due. In their view the king was not a convert but a captive. They played a variation on the venerable theme in the literature of oblique political dissent which exculpated the prince by blaming his counselors. The pernicious "doctrine" of the *économistes*, in the words of Mably, "infected" the ministry. "A part of the ministry," wrote Linguet, "[had] become pupil and proselyte of the flour fanaticism of which I have spoken." The *économistes*, "with their unfortunate brochures," charged Mercier in his gay and mordant *Tableau*, "have struck the people with a calamity for which equitable history will not fail to reproach them." They have no right to deny responsibility, he added: "it was in their name and following their books that this great commotion was given to the grain trade." In milder tones, Galiani characterized them as the "promoters" and "instigators" of the reform; with their swaggering claims of expertise, their "poise" and "assurance," they "convinced" the government to make the changes. In similar fashion, highly placed royal officials and magistrates traced the reforms to the "speculative" writings of the friends of Quesnay. According to Béguillet, the *économistes* "wrested, as it were, from the paternal goodness of the Sovereign the famous law of exportation which

---

108 Schelle, *Dupont*, 24; Turgot, *Œuvres*, ed. by Schelle, II, 48.

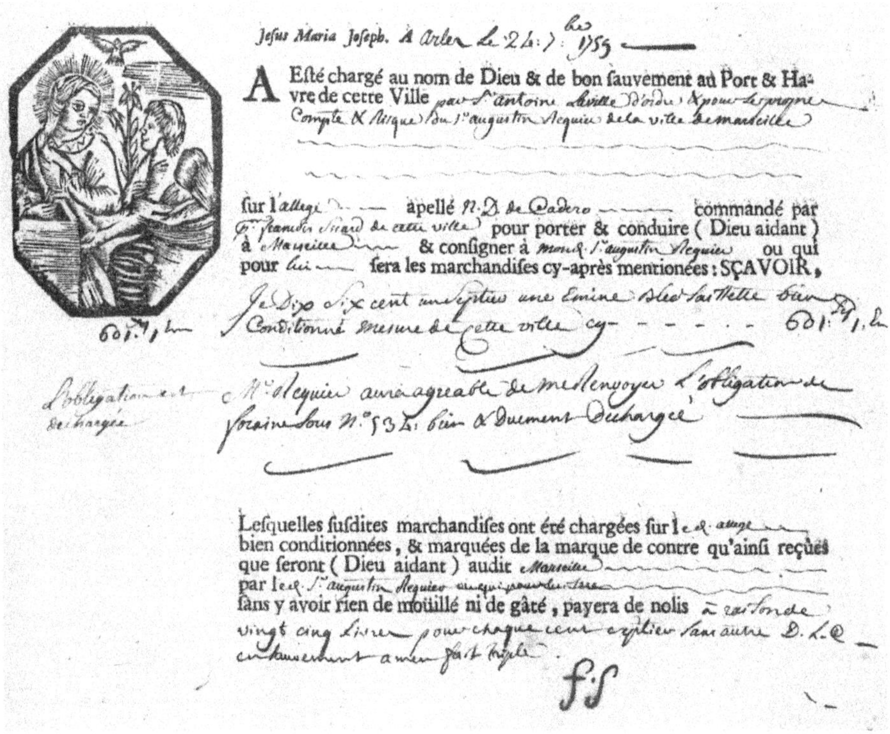

Jesus Maria Joseph. A Arles le 24. 7bre 1759

A Esté chargé au nom de Dieu & de bon sauvement au Port & Havre de cette Ville par Sr antoine ... pour le propre Compte & Risque du Sr augustin Requier de la ville de Marseille

sur l'allege apellé N. D. de ... commandé par ... de cette ville pour porter & conduire (Dieu aidant) à Marseille & consigner à mond. Sr augustin Requier ou qui pour lui sera les marchandises cy-après mentionées : SÇAVOIR,

Je dix six cent un septier une Emine bled ... Conditionné mesure de cette ville cy - - - - 601 ...

601 ...

Mr Requier aura agreable de me renvoyer l'obligation de foraine sous No. 532 bien & duement deschargée

l'obligation est deschargée

Lesquelles susdites marchandises ont été chargées sur le d. allege bien conditionnées, & marquées de la marque de contre qu'ainsi reçues que seront (Dieu aidant) audit Marseille par le d. Sr augustin Requier ... sans y avoir rien de mouillé ni de gâté, payera de nolis à raison de vingt cinq livres pour chaque cent septier sans autre ...

Illustration 4. One type of passport required for the transit of grain. Private collection.

Illustration 5. Officials supervising the reception and sale of grain at the Paris ports. Grands Moulins de Paris.

gave such terrible jolts to the State."[109] In almost the same words, the *économiste* Roubaud inverted the formula, claiming that it was not the reform which was extorted from a besieged king but the "restrictions" annexed to it which were "in a way wrested" from a philosopher-prince devoted to the principle of unconditional liberty:

> His wish was for complete competition, for the greatest liberty, the general and indefinite liberty. But by a paternal condescension, he wished to leave *no anxiety to those* who might *not yet* have sufficiently felt the *advantages which liberty must procure*.[110]

Based on a consensus of opinion composed of partisans and adversaries of the liberal reforms, the conspiratorial thesis, or its polemical counterpart, the thesis of a True Believer-king, has strong claims to credibility. Even if we did not know that two militants had a direct hand in writing the preambles, some of their key phrases are transparently liberal or physiocratic. Having already printed *économiste* tracts in his craft shop at Versailles, the king could reasonably be expected to publish the new laws on the same political economy press. Madame de Pompadour energetically promoted the connection between Quesnay and the king. Political economy, to be sure, is not bedroom philosophy but there is no cause other than an instinctive distrust of anecdotal history and a certain lack of imagination to discount this intimate channel of influence. The *économistes* themselves viewed her death as a blow to their party.[111]

When post-Revolutionary defenders of the old order sought to trace the origins of subversion, they habitually pointed to the stunning triumphs of the enlightened literati, outsiders and mavericks unfamiliar with public affairs and excluded from all the meeting-houses except the salon, classic refuge for reverie and libertinage. But, as we have seen, many of the most telling critiques of royal

---

109 Béguillet, *Traité des subsistances*, 797; Abbé de Mably, *Du Commerce des grains* (1755), in *Collection complète des œuvres de l'abbé Mably*, ed. by Arnoux (Paris, an III), XIII, 298; Linguet, *Annales*, VI (1779), 303; Mercier, *Tableau*, VI, 228, 232–233; Galiani, *Dialogues sur le commerce des bleds*, ed. by Fausto Nicolini, 88, 133. Cf. Charles Desmarest, *Le Commerce des grains dans la généralité de Rouen à la fin de l'ancien régime* (Paris, 1926), 111–12; Marion, *Finances*, I, 242n; Henri Martin, *Histoire de France* (Paris, 1860), XVI, 232. For a contrary view, argued rather simplistically, see René Girard, *L'Abbé Terray et la liberté du commerce des grains, 1769–1774* (Paris, 1924), xxiv.
110 Roubaud, *Représentations*, 39. His italics.
111 Schelle, *Dupont*, 27–28. For another, more subtle variation on the "conspiracy" theme, this one involving Quesnay, La Chalotais, and one of the king's lesser mistresses, see below, chapter 11.

policy emanated from within, or nearly within, the public administration: from financial, municipal, and royal officials and *commis* of
the ministries. If, by the sixties, the highest councils were "infected"
with liberalism, it was less the product of infiltration than of spontaneous generation. The government secreted its own reformers, men
who benefited enormously from the critical methods and insights
of the philosophes but who came to their liberalism personally
and professionally, as a result of their own participation in public
administration. The ministries did not have to send their officials
to the salons for an education; the salons recruited in the bureaus.

Bertin's government, it was noted, counted more than a half-
dozen liberal or *économiste* counselors. Doubtless some were merely
quondam consultants or transient hangers-on. Others, however,
such as Trudaine de Montigny, were solidly entrenched in the royal
bureaucracy. Highly placed in the Contrôle-Général, Trudaine fils
enjoyed an extraordinary administrative apprenticeship at the side
of his father, "the great Trudaine," provincial intendant, intendant
of finances, master-road-builder, and close collaborator of Vincent
Gournay. From the beginning of his career he had to deal with concrete problems of commercial and industrial organization, agricultural growth, and state regulation of and investment in the economy.
He visited ports and mines, studied navigation and engineering, practiced mathematics, chemistry, agronomy, and natural science. To prepare for reforms which firsthand examination convinced him were
necessary, he immersed himself in legal history in order to be able to
tell his future adversaries: "I know better than you these laws which
you reproach me with desiring to destroy; and it is because I know
them that I would like to change them." A man of many interests,
he was sufficiently worldly to earn passing censure for "dissipation"
and versatile enough to write poetry and translate Lessing as well as
compose preambles for Controllers-General from Bertin to Turgot.[112]
His critics felt he was too intellectual, overly given to "theory"; the
duc de Croy solemnly warned Turgot in the mid-seventies against
adopting "a system à la Trudaine."[113] Croy specifically referred to

112 Ernest Chouillier, "Les Trudaine," *Revue de Champagne et de Brie*, XIV (1883), 19–23, 131–36,
    208–210; Grandjean de Fouchy, "Eloge de M. de Trudaine," *Histoire de l'Académie Royale
    des Sciences* (Paris, 1780 for the year 1777), 70–93; Denis Diderot, *Correspondance*, ed. by
    Georges Roth (Paris, 1955–1970) IV, 306; Weulersse, *Mouvement*, I, 118, 204; Mauguin,
    Etudes historiques sur l'administration de l'agriculture en France (Paris, 1876–77), I, 336.
113 Bachaumont, *Mémoires secrets*, X, 193 (8 Aug. 1777); Duc de Croy, *Journal
    inédit du Duc de Croy, 1718–1784*, ed. by Vicomte de Grouchy and Paul Cottin

Trudaine de Montigny's grain trade policy which, along with his well-known sympathy for Quesnay's group, gave him a reputation as an *économiste*. Trudaine regarded the battle for liberalization as his greatest challenge; he campaigned vigorously for the reform measures of 1763–64, believing them to be "the salvation of the kingdom and of mankind." In the following years his struggle to enforce and preserve these reforms against the hostility of "most" of the nation inspired by "the most absurd and the most popular prejudices" was, in his own words, also the "source of my great troubles." It compromised his health and nearly broke his spirit.[114]

The conspiratorial thesis, whether it is meant to flaunt or to flay physiocracy, is as superficial and misleading as it is engaging. On the one side, it begs the perplexing question of the relationship of old-regime politics to *lumières* or, rather, reduces it to caricatural simplicity. On the other, it implicitly posits a factitious dichotomy between ideas (the reserve of thinkers) and administration (the domain of ministers and *commis*) thereby denying the government any possiblity of intellectual originality. Both sides exaggerate the malleability and underestimate the nerve of the government. There was indeed a rendez-vous between policy and doctrine in the sixties. It was, however, the ministers, not the doctrinaires, who set the time, the place and the conditions. Physiocracy, to be sure, made its influence felt in a multitude of ways. But it is worth remembering, with Turgot, that physiocratic thinking antedated physiocracy. In a number of areas, particularly tax reform and, to a lesser extent, the regulation of manufacture, the royal government took *quasi-économiste* positions before the time of Quesnay. Nor did the ministries of the sixties show serious interest in the other major economic and political reforms dictated by physiocratic doctrine. Politically, the government sought to avoid the extremist stigma attached to the *économistes*. For obvious reasons it tried to promote the idea that it was above doctrine even as it was above party. The government wanted to project a reputation for independence

---

(Paris, 1906–07), III, 139. Trudaine shared with Turgot a remarkably similar background and a close friendship. Turgot to Dupont, 20 Aug., 1 Dec. 1769, *Oeuvres*, ed. by Schelle, III, 61, 72 and II, 64–65.

114 Grandjean de Fouchy, "Eloge de Trudaine," *Histoire de l'Académie Royale des Sciences* (Paris, 1780 for the year 1777), 80; Chouillier, "Les Trudaine," *Revue de Champagne et de Brie*, XIV (1883), 209–210; Trudaine to Sartine, 13 Sept. 1768, Archives Seine-Paris, 3 AZ 10, pièce 6; Weulersse, *Mouvement*, I, 77–78, 119. Trudaine allegedly refused the Controller-Generalship at this time. Bachaumont, *Mémoires secrets*, IV, 191 (19 Jan. 1769).

and sobriety of the sort which enabled one prominent journalist, who had no love for philosophy, to characterize its attitude toward the grain question as a "middle position" between opposing camps.[115]

Ostensibly the *économistes* gave the government encouragement and confidence, but whether in fact they gave more than they received remains an open question. The government provided them with extraordinary protection, promoted their journal, found posts for their votaries, and probably financed some of their tracts.[116] It used the *économiste* school to serve its own needs: it benefited from the impact of physiocratic propaganda upon certain segments of public opinion without incurring responsibility for their affronts or extravagances. On the question of agricultural and commercial policy the interests of the government and the aims of the liberals converged. The point of confluence was a common perception of the state of the economy and its potential for expansion. This analysis was the fruit of the field experience of the Bertins and the Trudaines, the reports of subdelegates and intendants, the accounting books of landowners, and the successes of other nations such as England. Quesnay's *Tableau*, like the liberal reforms, resulted from it; the "zig-zag" did not produce it. That this view, in addition to reflecting economic realities, also stood in conformity to natural law was a kind of unearned intellectual increment from which the government profited, significantly, but incidentally.

Liberalization was above all an economic policy whose goal was to increase the wealth and power of the state by making the nation more prosperous and industrious. That does not mean that the government was indifferent to the political and the philosophical implications of liberalism as a doctrine. As a broadly conceived approach to governing and as a political posture, rather than as exclusive and irrefragable dogma, the theory of liberalism appealed to the government in a number of ways. Liberal theory argued, first of all, that the perennial state of impoverishment of the king—which made him vulnerable to political blackmail and tempted him to lean too heavily on the tax-paying, overwhelmingly rural public—was not simply or even primarily a result of careless and inefficient management, prodigality, and corruption. It had more profound causes than generally supposed, connected with the

---

115 *Année littéraire*, I (1770), 290.

116 Diderot in Grimm, *Correspondance littéraire*, ed. by M. Tourneux, VIII, 373 (Nov. 1769); Bachaumont, *Mémoires secrets*, XIX, 171–72 (18 April 1770); Weulersse, *Mouvement*, I, 209.

very structure of the economy and the society and unsusceptible to short-run, make-shift resolution. The government found it strangely reassuring to learn that a grave and chronic problem had deeper roots than expected. This line of reasoning offered the king a shelter from immediate pressure, applied particularly by the parlements, by suggesting, on the one hand, that fundamental reforms were the only way to remedy the situation—a prospect unlikely to enamor the sovereign courts—and, on the other, that such measures required long, painstaking preparations—a claim virtually impossible to refute. It challenged royal critics to discuss public policy on an entirely new plane. As a pledge of good faith, the king presented the reform of 1763–64 as the first thrust in the new departure.

The advantage of this diversionary approach was that it seemed, unlike myriad previous ones, to be part of a logical, consistent whole. In this respect, as the vehicle for a systematic attitude toward problem-solving, liberal theory found a warm welcome in the ministry, especially among the professional public servants surrounding the Controller-General and the top officials at the sub-ministerial level. These men were disgusted and demoralized by years of half-hearted cosmetic measures, of equivocation and capitulation, and of brusque changes of personnel at the highest levels. Liberal theory promised to replace a frustrating, sometimes humiliating politics of expedients and ploys with a coherent and enlightened politics built on principles—principles drawn from nature and sanctioned by (Cartesian) insight and (Newtonian) observation. It gave them a stronger case and a brighter prospect for sustained policy than they ever had before and a fresh enthusiasm for serving the king.

While it buoyed ministerial morale, liberalism, as an officially endorsed idea, had a potentially grander purpose. The new political economy offered the king a chance to insert his reign into the mainstream of the Enlightenment and to reply positively to critical strictures from right to left. It had all the makings of a counter-ideology, a progressive alternative to subversive philosophy and equally dangerous parlementarianism. It invited the king to take the offensive and reassert the moral leadership which critics charged he had sacrificed in favor of vapid routine, debauchery, and oppression. Although more often than not they did a mediocre job in cultivating it, the king and his ministers were seriously concerned about their reputation. They were jealous of the popularity of the parlements and envious of the prestige which accrued to the intellectuals; and they frankly avowed their impotence to muzzle either group. The liberal posture meant an opportunity to steal a march on the parlements and gain a foothold in the camp of the philosophes through the informal coalition with the *économistes*.

Physiocracy contributed the rudiments to the liberal royal ideology. Stripped of its most excessive tendencies (including Lemercier de la Riviére's "legal despotism," which embarrassed Dupont and other politically-sensitive *économistes* because it *seemed* to be naked confirmation of the parlement's most apocalyptic premonitions) and interpreted not according to the letter but following the moderate spirit in which Quesnay and Mirabeau construed it (a modulated and selective hostility to "privilege," a disavowal of certain imprudences of encyclopedism, a respect for rank and ritual, etc.), physiocracy was compatible with royal scruples. It met the essential criteria for reason-in-government without promoting irreligion, immorality or disaffection. Instead of history and fundamental law—muddled areas of controversy—it called upon the irresistible and impartial arbitration of nature and physical law. Physiocracy in this form rejected the fragmentation of sovereignty and the claims of the intermediary bodies, but it prescribed limits on kingship and envisioned an alternative system of national political participation. Eminently practical, it fashioned a politics geared to interest as well as to principles: the interests of the elites in all three Estates whose wealth was predominantly landed and agricultural. A sanitized, palatable, and supple ideology, the new political economy placed the king and his government unequivocally on the side of liberty, law, and progress.

Politically, the liberal ideology implied two strategies, two wagers: one concerned the king's relationship with the nation at large while the other involved his attitude toward the parlements. Addressed specifically to the rural world, the liberal reform was an overture for support and confidence as well as a program for growth. In the sixties the government rediscovered this other France, the kingdom of the majority, preponderant demographically and economically, superior quantitatively and, according to liberal evaluation, qualitatively too. The reform laws were a frank and contrite avowal of the king's neglect of the agricultural realm. They seemed to confirm the charge, commonly adduced by liberal and parlementary critics alike, that the government's only interest in the countryside had been in levying heavier and heavier taxes. It was as if the king realized that he had fallen out of touch with the nation and sought in a single, dramatic stroke to make amends and to link the fate of government policy with the destiny of rural France.

Partisans of the policy did not hesitate to see it as a rebuke to urban haughtiness, the beginning of the end of a Parisocentric preoccupation with luxury, manufactured goods, the court, salons, convulsions, *rentes*, and indolence. During the battle over liberalization, they characterized the opposition as spurious and marginal precisely because it seemed to emanate primarily from the cities. Nor did Louis scruple to remind the Paris magistrates who protested against the reform that he was king of all the people, not merely patron of the capital. Rhetorically, the liberal laws had a fundamentalist air: a return to first principles and to the bond with the bone and sinew of the nation, this "precious" part of the people. Despite *économiste* claims, however, the bone and sinew of the countryside, buyers for the most part, more gravely menaced by high prices than by low, had more in common with the urban laboring poor than with the substantial *laboureurs*, the managerial *fermiers*, and the other comfortable landowners. It was the latter rather than the former who clamored for liberty and whose dominant socioeconomic position in the countryside (and, for that matter, in the cities) made the reform policy an alluring political gamble. Styled as a bounty for the rural nation, liberalization was sure to be an immense pork barrel for the privileged and the proprietary interests.

The significance of the liberal posture for royal-parlementary relations will emerge more clearly in the course of our discussion of the crisis which erupted after the promulgation of the laws of 1763–64. It is an extremely complex question because it intersects with another crisis, one of a constitutional order, which seethed in the sixties. In the constitutional view, the sixties witnessed a great battle between the forces of light and the forces of darkness. The king, cast almost as an underdog, sought to rationalize his administration by reaffirming his supreme authority. The parlements are seen as forming a united front of hectoring obstructionism and obscurantism, devoted single-mindedly to the defense of privilege in all its manifestations. From the perspective of the liberal reforms, however, the lines and issues of confrontation are less clear-cut. The defense of royal prerogative was not the king's paramount concern in this matter; his stance was modest and placatory rather than imperious. Liberalism was not the uncontested touchstone of enlightenment; this affair plunged the philosophes into profound disaccord. The parlements were bitterly divided within and among themselves and their positions do not fit easily into the conventional categories of motivation and purpose. Liberalization wrought strange alliances. La Chalotais, who was hardly a perfect king's man, espoused the royal cause, yet the Brittany Parlement, despite its attachment to the Procurator General, changed its mind on liberalization in mid-stream. The Parlements of Toulouse and Grenoble, which opposed the government's fiscal measures in 1763 with such violence, remained staunch supporters of the liberal laws. Though stained with the blood of the Calas, the Toulouse magistrates earned the encomiums of the philosophe-*économistes* for the ardor with which they preached the law of nature. Rouen categorically renounced the new political economy after mid-decade but it joined the liberal Parlements of Languedoc, Dauphiné, and Provence in a proto-Girondin uprising in 1768 against the privileged status of Paris. The Paris court, incidentally, also drew provincial ire for its jurisdictional claims in the D'Aiguillon affair.[117] Whether the *union des classes* was a convincing political hypothesis upon this background is difficult to say.

The liberal ideology had a more subtle bearing on royal-parlementary rapport. The reform of 1763–64 hinted at ground for a possible understanding between king and courts based on a new style of governance. Like all laws, these measures were formally the product of his "full power" and "certain science." But the tone and substance of the texts belied the formula. In part they were an autocritique of self-sufficient absolutism, absolutism which depended singularly on its own sagacity for instruction. By the same token they cast doubt on the reliability of fundamental law, the congeries of precedents to which the parlements insisted the king must cede. The source of royal inspiration for the reform was natural law—neutral terrain between absolutist prerogative and parlementary pretension. The king stood in relation to it less as legislator than as executor. Voluntarily, the king assumed

---

117 This is a summary statement of a position I will develop in the course of the book. The major indicators are: La Chalotais, speech of 20 Aug. 1764, cited by DZ [Desaubiez], *Le Bonheur public*, 36; *Journal économique* (Aug. 1768), 352; *Mercure historique*, CLXV, 281–95; *Éphémérides du citoyen* (1768), VIII, 145–58 and (1769), I, 199–212, II, 138–96, III, 182–198, V, 236–39, VI, 261–62, VII, 118; Bachaumont, *Mémoires secrets*, XIX, 9 (Aug. 1768), XIX, 73–74 (19 May 1769), XIX, 143 (22 Dec. 1769); "Discours prononcés à la clôture de la 8ᵉ année des assemblées économiques chez Monsieur le Marquis de Mirabeau," 13 May 1774 in Knies, ed., *Correspondance Dupont*, II, 199; J. Letaconnoux, *Les Subsistances et le commerce des grains en Bretagne*, 41, 87–88, 91; L. Viala, *La Question des grains et leur commerce à Toulouse*, 72–75; Jean Egret, *Le Parlement de Dauphiné, I, 161–91;* Girard, *Terray*, 17–18; Afanassiev, *Commerce des céréales*, 178–80.

a humble pose. The liberal posture endowed kingship with a new and fashionable image. The bloated and blustery prince of the interventionist administrative monarchy reappeared as the lean and unobtrusive king who governs less in order to govern better.

In return for this streamlined model of rational monarchy the parlements would be expected to give up their party spirit. If both sides submitted to it in good faith, natural law would mediate their quarrels and neither party would lose face. King and parlements would collaborate to make fundamental law and positive law uniformly congruent with natural law. Cooperation would be assured provided the parlements agreed with the king's conception of natural law.

Theoretically, from this relationship, a set of rules of governance would emerge. The parlements would be able to deal with a monarch who did not act capriciously or willfully. The king, by making his authority hostage to nature's law, would win immunity from political contestation. Over the years the parlements had developed a "broad program of constitutional liberalism."[118] Insistent, however, on preserving a world honeycombed with privileges, they fashioned a political and legislative liberalism denuded of any social implications. Now the king postulated a radically different version of liberalism, a socioeconomic and executive liberalism surely corrosive of privilege but steadfastly opposed to sharing political power. In the long run, parlementary liberalism more than anything else undermined the prestige of the monarchy and thereby destroyed the court's own raison d'être. At the end of the sixties, the voice of royal liberalism was stifled by the very grain crisis it helped precipitate. The parlements could not agree upon a common position and the king ultimately recoiled in the face of grave disorders. With the failure of the *coup de nature*, the crown resorted to the *coup de force*. At the end of the decade the king abjured the liberal posture and at the same time dissolved the old parlementary system. Curiously, the government did not again experiment with political economy until the parlements of nostalgia were recalled to life in the mid-seventies.

The circumstantial and conspiratorial/ideological theses, originally stated by contemporaries, suggested a number of ways to account for liberalization. Another view, which also surfaced at the time, can be called the thesis of fiscality. Although it ultimately nurtured yet another bogey-man theory, the idea of linking fiscality with the grain

---

118 Palmer, *Age*, I, 99.

question or with any other object of royal policy was a perfect commonplace. The vast majority of Frenchmen conceived of the state
above all as tax collector. Taxation, perhaps even more than justice,
was the most salient manifestation of the presence of the government in the kingdom. Since the state was chronically short of funds
and applied all its cunning to augment its resources, it could undertake virtually no act free of the taint of fiscal motive. Suspicion and
innuendo were rife, not merely because vocal hostility to taxation was
one of the few direct political actions within the grasp of the mass of
people, but also because administrative organization reinforced the
notion that all the agencies of government were in the service of the
fisc. Blurred and overlapping institutional perimeters invited distrust.
In the financial administration, where several concurrent bureaucra-
cies operated, no visible frontier separated public function from private enterprise. The intendant's fiscal responsibilities obscured and
overshadowed his police and judicial duties. At the highest levels, it
hardly seemed accidental that the intendants of finance were the officials in charge of the grain and subsistence department and that the
head of the bureau of impositions supervised agrarian reform.

Since grain was the chief measure of wealth as well as the predominant form of subsistence, the obsession with fiscality often thwarted
efforts to facilitate distribution on a regional or national scale. Intendants exaggerated or invented reports of scarcity in order to win
rebates on taxation. Conditioned to expect fiscal reprisals, lower-level
officials and cultivators leagued to resist royal and parlementary data-
collecting projects. The sincerity of the Controller-General seemed
dubious when he appealed to his subordinates to press the *taille* levy
vigorously in order to force grain on depleted markets and spare consumers anguish. Nor did the manner in which the government handled
grain policy tend to clear the odor of fiscality. It was widely believed
that the government sold authorizations to export for limited periods
to the highest bidders. In times of emergency, it seemed significant that
the government turned to the farmers-general, to old style financiers
like Samuel Bernard and the new magnates of the private bank like
Isaac Thellusson to undertake enormous purchases of foreign grain.

Somewhat mysterious and remote at the olympian heights of the
center, the marriage of fiscality and provisioning was garishly celebrated at the marketplaces. Consumers chafed at the multitude of
taxes and duties which encumbered foodstuffs and goods while sellers
had to pay petty ransoms for permission to dispose of their goods. A

panoply of minor officials mediated exchanges in return for obligatory honorariums. Many of these inspectors and controllers rendered
important services to the police and the public, but the others, whose
venal posts were created for purely fiscal reasons, served to discredit
their colleagues.

A long line of commentators, beginning in the late sixties and continuing through the Revolution, ascribed the liberal reforms to fiscal
or parafiscal motives. The parlements had made fiscal criticism their
speciality. It was not merely their bête noire; it was the one issue that
gave them the greatest leverage and sustained their political ambitions. Before the sixties, the courts took the tack that a reduction of
the *taille* would provide the surest stimulation to agriculture. Liberalization jarred their unity but did not dull their fiscal consciousness.
Two distinguished Paris magistrates, the Presidents Lepelletier and
Hocquart, sitting in the Assembly of General Police in 1768, warned
that behind the desire to foster higher prices lay a scheme to increase
taxes, especially the *vingtièmes*. Their colleagues at Rouen shared the
same idea: the wealth to be generated by liberalization would be nothing more "than a pretext to raise taxes." In its famous remonstrances
against Turgot's edicts in 1776, the Paris Parlement recalled the liberal measures of '63–'64 as acts of fiscal desperation. Financially
exhausted, the ministry sought to prepare the ground for new tax
incursions and simultaneously increase the product of the old impositions by pushing up the price of grain, land, and leases.[119] Hinting
both at fiscal and venal motives, Galiani had the President in his *Dialogues* remark cryptically: "some believe it [liberty] to be a financial
speculation, others a means of facilitating the collection of the *tailles*
...." The philosophe Mably viewed liberalization as a pretext for fiscality, nothing more than a "new tax." An article in the *Moniteur* in
the fall of 1789 suggested that the aim of liberalization, in addition
to "brigandage," was to double the production of the *vingtièmes*. A
farmer and correspondent of several societies of agriculture writing a
few years later in a pamphlet on "the means to assure a diminution of
[the price of] bread and prevent dearths" echoed the same interpretation. Nor were these admonitions and innuendos simply political red
herrings. On the morrow of liberalization, in the Edict of November 1771 extending the life of the two *vingtièmes* and establishing

119 *Recueil*, 184, 229; Anonymous, "Mémoire," (1771), AN, F[11] 264; remonstrances, Parl. of
    Rouen, 25 Jan. 1769, Conseil Secret, A.D. S-M.; remonstrances 2, 4 March 1776, in Jules
    Flammermont, ed., *Remontrances*, III, 298.

still other *droits*, the government itself justified the increased tax bite in terms of the sustained price rise of the sixties and the added value it gave to land and produce.[120]

Although it cannot pretend by itself to account for liberalization, the thesis of fiscality correctly points to one of the cardinal preoccupations of the government in the sixties. Repeated failure to restructure the tax system, extend its base, and rationalize assessment and collection finally persuaded the government to change its approach. Alarmed and wearied by the rising tenor of fiscal criticism, much of it aimed at the ministry and the crown rather than at the privileged elites, the government sought to divert attention away from finances. In 1763 it accepted a dubious and jerry-built compromise with the parlements, an accord which could only be justified by the government's desire to buy a breathing space no matter what the price. At the same time an *arrêt du conseil* imposed a ban of silence on the discussion of fiscal affairs by prohibiting all publications concerning that subject. Determined to postpone but not to abandon fiscal reform, the government launched its policy of liberalization, which turned the focus on incentives rather than on impositions, on the positive question of wealth rather than the negative matter of taxes.

There is no doubt, however, that the Controllers-General, like Doctor Quesnay, envisaged the anticipated expansion of the GNP as a surrogate for and a prelude to fundamental fiscal reform. In the short run, the general increase in production and productivity would automatically augment tax revenue along existing bases. Later, it was imagined, under the tonic influence of prosperity, a structural reform could be more easily effected. Bertin stressed the fiscal component in liberalization, reminding intendants that low prices prevented cultivators from meeting tax obligations. Laverdy assured the intendant of Tours that "it will not be long before you see in the payment of taxes" one of the first benefits of liberalization. Four years later, in a report to Louis XV, the Controller-General explicitly tied the decision to free the grain trade to the increasingly "cruel" financial situation of the state. Writing in the next decade, a high ministerial official

---

120 Galiani, *Dialogues*, ed. by Nicolini, 236; Mably, *Du Commerce des grains*, cited by Weulersse, *La Physiocratie sous les ministères de Turgot et de Necker (1774–1781)* (Paris, 1950), 152; *Moniteur* (Sept.–Oct. 1789), cited in P.-J.-B. Buchez, *Histoire de l'Assemblée Constituante* (Paris, 1845 [1846]), II, 66–67; "Mémoire sur les moyens d'assurer la diminution du pain, de prévenir les disettes...," par Etienne Chevalier, cultivateur à Argenteuil et correspondant de plusieurs sociétés d'agriculture (Paris, n.d., ca. 1793); Isambert, *et al.*, eds., *Recueil des anciennes lois françaises*, XXII, 540.

described the desire to "make the king's revenues more abundant" as one of the chief "principles which directed the administration from 1763 through 1768."[121]

Among the champions of liberalization, the deputies of commerce did not blush to raise the fiscal issue as a solid argument in their favor. Merely by increasing the kingdom's resources, they claimed, exportation would simultaneously reduce the burden on the people and swell royal income.[122] Other liberals went a step further, linking the success of liberalization with the implementation of major fiscal reforms in the kind of multi-stage process envisaged by the government. By reinvigorating agriculture and restoring prosperity, the Procurator General La Chalotais told the Rennes court, liberalization will make possible "a plan of taxation based on true and unique principles," that is, on the physiocratic assumption of the exclusive productivity of the land.[123] For the Parlement of Dauphiné, liberalization marked "the most memorable epoch" in the reign of Louis XV because it was both the beginning of and the precondition to "the regeneration of the body politic." Without the liberty of the grain trade there was "no reform possible." In its wake, however, the Parlement told the king, landed income will be increased, "leading us by degrees to a simpler and more equitable plan of contributions to public expenses and thus preparing the total replacement of the [current] fiscal regime."[124] These grand ideas were comfortably remote and hypothetical, but we are not obliged to discount them merely because they were pronounced by parlementaires. They were not rhetorical devices aimed at persuading the ministry to introduce the reforms; the new laws were already on the books. They dealt with too controversial and delicate a matter to be interpreted simply as gestures to gratify the government or as spontaneous effusions of enthusiasm.

From another perspective, this parlementary position could be construed as a solemn warning to the government: liberalization is

121 Bertin to IN. of Alençon, 13 April 1762, C. 90, A.D. Orne; Laverdy to Lescalopier, July 1764, C. 94, A.D. I-et-L.; Biollay, *Pacte de famine*, 109–110; St.-Prest, memoir, Sept. 1773, C. 1441, A.D. Gir.

122 *Députés du commerce*, "Deuxième supplément au premier mémoire," (1764), BN, mss. fr. 14295, fols. 1–6. Cf. the similar attitude of the Besançon Parlement, 4, 7 Aug. 1764, B. 2173, A.D. Doubs.

123 Address of 20 Aug. 1764, C. 1648–49, A.D. I-et-V. Doubtless La Chalotais was alluding, *inter alia*, to what the Rouen magistrates denounced as "the cadastre, Sire, this plan terrifying for your peoples [which] was proposed *with the economic system*." Remonstrances, 25 Jan. 1769, Conseil Secret, A.D. S-M. My emphasis.

124 Letter to the king, 26 April 1769, B. 2314, fols. 89, 103, A.D. Isère.

your last best chance for genuine reform. But if this is so it is less significant for the threat, which was already the ministry's working premise, than for the willingness to talk seriously, albeit vaguely, about eventual and necessary fiscal reforms. Still, when the intoxication with liberal-style reform began to wear thin, the liberals did not shy from attempting a sort of fiscal blackmail as a lever for tightening the resolve of the king to maintain liberalization. Without the continued permission to export, warned the Estates and the Parlement of Languedoc, the province would not be able to meet the present tax schedule or entertain the possibility of an increment.[125] Overshadowed by broader economic and political considerations, fiscality nonetheless lurked in the atmosphere of the liberal reform.

The thesis of fiscality had another side which bore a conspiratorial visage and which had serious political significance. In its broad outlines, it was not peculiar to the sixties. In this view the king stood accused of speculating in grain. In its mildest form, however, the gravity of the charge was mitigated by ascribing the monarch's motives to fiscality rather than to personal venality. In 1752 the marquis d'Argenson reported the news that the king was manipulating the grain trade to force prices up in order to increase his tax revenue. A warm partisan of liberty and lean government, his analysis of this episode is interesting, for it reveals the enormous complexity of the grain/subsistence issue and the tension between fine theory and hard social fact. D'Argenson deplored "this bad principle ... which has it that grain must always be at a certain price to enable the farmer to pay his master and the King." Inverting the "false" and "dangerous" physiocratic formula that abundance and low prices mean misery, he argued that "the greatest abundance and the cheapest price for necessary foods is the best of principles ...."[126] D'Argenson, in this instance, censured the king for erroneous policy, not perfidy.

Elsewhere in his *Mémoires*, however, d'Argenson implicated a number of ministers—he skirted the issue of direct royal responsibility—in vast schemes to corner the grain market and profit from public misery. In the sixties, Leprévost de Beaumont, a lay ecclesiastical official, detected similar sinister designs to which he gave the portentous name of *Pacte de Famine*, or famine plot. The story of the *Pacte* will be told later; here it is imperative to note that Leprévost specifically

---

125 Anon., "Mémoire," 8 Aug. 1773, AN, F¹¹ 265; Weulersse, *Mouvement*, II, 249.
126 D'Argenson, *Mémoires*, ed. by Rathery, VII, 285 (27 Aug. 1752).

linked the alleged *Pacte* to the liberal reforms of 1763–64. He, too, claimed to be a champion of liberty, an admirer of Sully, a believer in the primacy of landed-wealth. But he became convinced that liberalization was introduced as an elaborate cover for illicit and shameful speculations:

> Everything here is thought out and disposed as carefully as possible in order to try to conciliate in some fashion the public interest with the renewal of the clandestine Pacts and sub-pacts of Famine ....[127]

It was devilishly clever, he acknowledged, to conceal monopoly in the very acts devised to extirpate it.

The importance of Leprévost's interpretation as a clue to the impression "pacte" allegations made on public opinion cannot be overestimated. Tales of odious speculation had circulated for generations. Self-proclaimed muckrakers, jealous outsiders, and dearth-syndrome paranoids had, over the years, exposed various plots at all levels of public and private life. What gave credibility to the *Pacte* and enabled Leprévost to crystallize widely-shared suspicions, what transformed it from a fugitive calumny into a political issue that endured until the end of the nineteenth century, was the reform of the grain trade. All the pieces seemed to fit neatly together. If the king had trafficked in grain in the past, he had done it modestly. Now it was as if he transferred his infamous trysting-place from the Parc aux Cerfs to the Tuileries gardens. Under the guise of philosophy and the common good, he abolished all police controls on circulating grain in order to favor the maneuvers of the cabalists and he devised legislation meant to veil the export of the people's grain which he planned either to sell or to store at the nearby isles of Jersey for resale at a later time in France at inflated prices. The specter of the *Pacte* prowled the streets, demoralized merchants, haunted the parlements, unnerved the *économistes*, and embarrassed and worried the government.

The thesis of conspiracy coupling liberalization and the *Pacte* enjoyed great vogue during the Revolution. Creuzé-Latouche, addressing the Assembly in 1792, described the liberal reform as a vicious deception:

> Louis XV was engaged in the grain monopoly for his own profit; thus he wished first of all to cover his agents with the shield of the law ... then they destroyed this same liberty by attributing it exclusively to themselves.[128]

---

127 Arsenal, mss. Bastille, 12353.
128 *Archives Parlementaires* (8 Dec. 1792), 679. Cf. Pierre Manuel, *La Police dévoilée* (Paris, an II), vol. I.

Buffered from the events by two decades, a liberal like Creuzé could argue righteously that liberty never received an honest test during the Old Regime. Obviously the earnest liberals of the sixties, allies of the king, could not exploit this thesis in the same way—at least not openly. The opposition, however, used it to advantage, not so much to besmirch the king as to discredit the principle of unconditional liberty which led ineluctably—witness the *Pacte*—to heinous crimes of libertinage.

Finally, there was a royal thesis, a self-proclaimed motive for reform which Louis XV brandished with particular fervor. Liberalization was not introduced merely because it was right, necessary and natural. No less instrumental was the fact that it was enormously popular. It was not imposed from above; the king depicted the laws as a response to an extraordinary demand addressed to him "from everywhere." Although it was the special vocation of royal sapience to lead the people to the truth, in this case Louis cheerfully conceded that he followed the tide of opinion. In the debates in the royal council which preceded the reform it was reported that the dauphin, seconded by his father, spoke in behalf of the liberty "party" which represented "approximately 12,000,000 Frenchmen."[129] To be sure, the gesture of deference to opinion was a self-protective, political act. If the reform aroused controversy, it would be known in advance that it was a program coveted by the nation itself, and for which the nation would have to bear responsibility. The government did not scorn this occasion to improve its public relations and to present the monarch as an enlightened and benevolent prince highly sensitive to the feelings of his people.

But the appeal to opinion was not a nervous demagogic pirouette, in the parlementary style, or a hollow boast. It was a sign of strength rather than of weakness. For the popularity of the liberal project was incontestable. Opponents of the legislation later openly acknowledged that it came about "at the request of all the Nation," that the king undertook it"… in order to conform, as it were, to the desires of his subjects."[130] Commentators who agreed on nothing else concurred that a feisty "enthusiasm" for liberty billowed across the kingdom in the early sixties. The government nurtured this sentiment, invited pressure and petition, and took them as incentives and sanctions for action.

---

129 Grimm, *Correspondance littéraire*, ed. by Tourneux, VI, 29–30 (July 1764). There are no clues to indicate how the dauphin arrived at this figure.

130 *Recueil*, 113, 161–162.

Although the ground had been prepared in many ways, liberalization was still a sensational event, for it marked a decisive rupture with one of the great monarchical traditions. Favorable harvest circumstances and such political issues as the end of the war, the expulsion of the Jesuits, and the fiscal vendetta helped to mask its significance. The government invested great hopes in liberalization, both in the short and long runs. A highly influential and vocal segment of public opinion vigorously supported the ministry and hoped it would move still further in the direction of liberalization and reform. In 1763–64, everything seemed to augur well for the new policy. The problem now was to implement the legislation—everywhere save in Paris—as rapidly and as unobtrusively as possible. If the police apparatus could be quickly dismantled and the new system firmly entrenched without any serious accidents while the mood of the nation remained calm, then liberalization could begin to bear its promised fruits immediately. Whether the mood of the nation would remain calm, however, depended upon forces beyond the control of the ministers and the political economists.

Chapter IV

THE RESPONSE TO LIBERALIZATION: THEORY AND PRACTICE

The explosion of joy and gratitude that followed the promulgation of the liberal measures seemed to confirm the royal claims. The May Declaration elated the *Journal économique*. In it the editors rediscovered the prince whose proud sobriquet had once been "the well-beloved": they hailed "the august monarch that heaven gave for master to this great kingdom" and characterized him as "so justly cherished by all his people." They regarded the declaration as a genuine triumph but they esteemed it more for what it portended than for what it actually was likely to achieve. It was "a first step," the "forerunner" of an "unlimited" freedom which the king would not deny the nation. La Chalotais, the Procurator General of the Rennes Parlement, asked the councillors to view the Declaration not "as a simple law of interior police but as a Blessing of the Monarch," as one of those momentous acts which provide for "the happiness of peoples." More than the measure itself, it was the certainty that it "will undoubtedly be followed by a complete and general liberty to export" that enraptured the Breton magistrate.[1]

The eagerly awaited July Edict, despite its limitations, generated a wave of exultation. While the *laboureurs* shed happy "tears" in the fields, the effusions of the journalists were no less lachrymose: "At last we see the dawn of the beautiful day for agriculture for which we have sighed for so long."[2] In the Toulouse area, proprietors, parlementaires and local administrators celebrated the victory. "The liberty to export our grain ... has become an immutable law which will render dear the memory of the prince who issued it and the

---

1 *Journal économique* (Feb. 1764), 55–57; *ibid.*, (Sept. 1763), 391; Speech of La Chalotais, 6 July 1763, C. 1648–49, AD. I-et-V. See the similar remarks in the provincial edition of the *Gazette du commerce* (16 July 1763), 146.

2 *Journal économique* (Nov. 1764), 492.

citizen-minister who inspired it," declared a representative of the Toulouse Chamber of Commerce.[3] La Chalotais, whom the *Correspondance littéraire* considered to be the only magistrate in the kingdom with "the ideas and the tone of a statesman,"[4] judged the edict to be "in conformity with the wish of the Nation which provoked it, with that of the Estates of the provinces, with experience which is the mistress of man, with the sentiment of Henry the Great and the illustrious Sully, with the opinion of all those who examined this question in an unprejudiced and disinterested manner." Henceforth there would be no reason to fear either dearths, or "what was almost as terrifying," the superabundance of harvests.[5] Buoyed by its success, the liberty lobby continued to ask for an "absolute" and "indefinite" liberty throughout the decade of the sixties. During the next few years king and government clung tenaciously to the idea that liberty was a truly popular policy despite growing evidence of an angry and widespread reaction.[6]

This chapter deals with the origin and the nature of the first stages of the reaction against liberalization. First, I show that, despite the lack of extensive opposition in the early sixties to this radical new policy, a number of individuals and institutions expressed serious reservations about liberalization. This early critique of liberalism anticipated many of the major arguments which later took shape against the reform and the reformers. Second, I consider the relationship between liberalization and the great political issues of the hour which the parlements turned stunningly to their advantage. From the very beginning, there was some hesitation in several of the sovereign courts about the wisdom of the reform measures.

The bulk of the chapter is devoted to the reaction in the field—the complaints of the consumers and of the police. The people responded to the burgeoning subsistence crisis of the middle sixties in very much the same way that earlier generations had reacted to soaring prices, scarcity, and fear. It is not so much the kinds of popular riots and

---

3 Cited by G. Frêche, "Etudes statistiques," *Revue d'histoire économique et sociale*, XLIX (1971), 214.

4 *Correspondance littéraire*, ed. by Tourneux, VI, 124 (Nov. 1764).

5 Speech of La Chalotais, 20 Aug. 1764, C. 1648–49, A.D. I-et-V. Cf. Dz [Desaubiez], *Le Bonheur public*, 24–49.

6 Though the liberals stressed its nation-wide popularity, there is some evidence that liberalization was not universally celebrated, not even in the beginning. See the remark of the intendant of Champagne who was personally a believer in "total liberty"—at least in the beginning. Rouillé to SDs, 4, 24 Aug. 1764, C. 418, A.D. Marne.

demonstrations that are striking as their incidence and intensity. Equally important and far more singular in my estimation were the reactions of the local authorities—reactions not only to grave subsistence problems but to liberalization. The new departure in grain policy, I argue, alienated and crippled the police; I try to explain why. The *Fronde* of the police as much as the popular riots in the towns and marketplaces placed liberalization in jeopardy.

I

In the early sixties there was no organized and powerful force which opposed the liberty movement, no vocal anti-lobby. Potential adversaries found no leader around whom to rally; the king, natural candidate to raise a defense of established ways, had deserted with his government to the reform side. Nor was there an influential constituted body, corps, or company of national or regional stature prepared to marshal resistance; the parlements, the best-equipped institutions for such opposition, seemed to be either won over or disarmed by the liberals. There appeared to be little ground for political bickering on an issue which united crown and courts in deep embrace. Face to face, potential opponents did not discover any glaring differences between themselves and the liberals. The latter came from the city and the countryside, the north and the south, the government and the salons, and from a broad spectrum of professions. Generally they were men of some substance, a quality which distinguished them from the population at large but not from the sort of men with whom they would debate political economy and public administration.

Unlike the reformers, their potential antagonists had neither a solid notion of precisely what they were to be against nor a clear idea of exactly what they were to defend. After all, the reformers took pains to show that their projects were fully consonant with national traditions; the parlements attested to their legal legitimacy; the savants demonstrated their scientific pedigrees; and the king vouchsafed that they were without risk and in the public interest. These references suggested that liberalization could turn out auspiciously. In any case, the limitations sagely built into the laws served as collateral against error. It seemed premature to assail the reform before it actually took effect, in conditions which posed no immediate socioeconomic risks, and at a time when other matters, especially those of a fiscal nature, had greater claims on public attention. Liberty was not the sort of issue which anyone relished attacking abstractly, as an evil in itself; nor was police control a policy for which men found it easy to apologize in the abstract, as a good in itself. Later, a formidable opposition to liberty did arise—well after the liberal laws had gone into effect—forged not by the prospect of liberty, but by what were perceived to be its measurable results.

The failure to mount an effective resistance, however, did not mean that the liberal position went entirely unchallenged in the early sixties. A number of magistrates, bureaucrats, and writers dissented, expressing specific reservations about one part or another of the projected liberalization or more diffuse and serious doubts about its likely effects, accompanied in some cases by veritable intimations of doom. The issue divided the king's own council; the monarch averted a stalemate by openly siding with the ministerial group against a bloc of worried "old wigs" [sic] whose experience in public affairs taught them circumspection.[7] The father of the 1763 reform, Bertin, who remained in the government after his gentle disgrace from the Contrôle-Général toward the end of 1763, tried vainly to play a moderating role in the preparation of the second phase. "I did everything in my power," he confessed, to lower the export ceiling in the July Edict from 30 to 25 livres but he was overwhelmed by the "enthusiasm" of the moment.[8]

Firmly advocating maintenance of the traditional system of export by exception, the Bureau of Commerce, which exercised quasi-conciliar functions, voiced a theme which all the dissenters shared: unchecked exporting was dangerous for it defied a deeply ingrained "national prejudice" and it exposed the nation to dearth and hardship.[9] The Lieutenant Criminel of the Châtelet predicted that if grain exports were allowed in 1764 "it would be a fatal thing." In a kindred tone, a correspondent of the Journal de Commerce et d'Agriculture warned of disaster should the decision to authorize exports coincide with a bad harvest. An anonymous memorialist argued that it would be particularly dangerous to permit exportation in the first years after the end of the Seven Years' War when the domestic demand, swelled by returning soldiers and by renewed orders from the colonies, would place unbearable pressure on the supply. For this writer, however, the real issue was not the timing but the principle of the decision. "Physics

---

7 *Correspondance littéraire*, ed. by Tourneux, VI, 29, 30 (July 1764).

8 Cited by Biollay, *Pacte de famine*, 111–12.

9 *Ibid.*, 108–109. Cf. Afanassiev, *Commerce des céréales*, 217–18, whose treatment is superficial and tendentious.

is useless without experience," he lectured the physiocrats; "theory can illuminate and perfect practice without ever replacing it." Experience showed that abundance could never be excessive in a nation as large as France; so great and incalculable were its needs that it could never afford to be without a potential surplus, "a provision of precaution."[10]

The intendant of Paris, Bertier de Sauvigny, subscribed to the notion that it was the responsibility of the government to make sure that the people were fed. He questioned not only the revision of the export rules but the wisdom of tampering with any of the old police regulations. "Since 1709," he noted with satisfaction, "we parried every major dearth and the French people never lacked subsistence." The renunciation of police control, in Bertier's mind, would jeopardize public order and social harmony and undermine respect for authority. Grimm recorded an instructive encounter between the intendant and Abeille, civil servant, agronomist, and sometime *économiste*, in which Bertier expressed his pessimism candidly. The latter "perorated pompously on the dangers of this liberty."

> 'They [the government] moved very quickly,' he said. 'When the riots break out in Paris, when my windows and those of the Lieutenant of police are broken, it will be too late to remedy the evils of this free and dangerous commerce.' 'Set your mind at rest,' Abeille told him, 'that is precisely what will not happen.' 'Once you deny the facts,' replied the intendant, 'there is no longer any use in arguing.'[11]

In early 1764 the Parisian municipality submitted a memoir to the government which somehow managed to pass as a cautious endorsement of Laverdy's liberalizing plans. It is significant because it proposed a series of restrictions whose effect would have been to render the reform legislation meaningless and because it attacked the liberal approach so stormily. If agriculture needs the "encouragement" of exportation, the city fathers conceded, there could be no time "more favorable than the present." But they took issue first with the pessimistic liberal assessment of the state of agriculture in France and second with the idea that liberalization would be the most effective incentive. According to the

---

10 Testard du Lys, Lieutenant Criminel, in *Recueil*, 139; "Lettre concernant la liberté du commerce des grains," *Journal de commerce et d'agriculture* (Jan. 1762), 71; "Commerce intérieur et extérieur des blés," BN, mss. fr. 11347, fols. 213–16. Cf. similar strictures in Girade, "Cinquième mémoire contre la concurrence dans le fret...," *Journal de l'agriculture, du commerce, et des finances* (June 1766), 167, 170–171.

11 Bertier de Sauvigny, "Observations sur le commerce des grains," (prior to May 1763), BN, mss. fr. 11347, fol. 229 and *passim*. Cf. "Questions et réponses," *ibid.*, fols. 247–48, and *Correspondance littéraire*, ed. by M. Tourneux, VI, 124 (Nov. 1764).

municipality, the *laboureur* had "far greater need" of tax relief, a prescription frequently suggested by parlementaires and philosophes alike which the government could neither fill nor refute.[12] Even if we grant, the city fathers continued, that agriculture must have more outlets, "... it would be neither prudent nor wise to accord it an unlimited liberty." Liberty must be "restrained and subject to rules" because "in good public economy as in private we must assure ourselves of bread before we think about enriching ourselves." The "people" have a claim on the "grain of the kingdom." When they see it sent abroad, "they enter into fury [and] the riots and revolts become difficult to appease."

This was the heart of the issue for the municipality and a measure of the gulf between the police and liberal positions. The liberals emphasized wealth, profits, production, agriculture, commerce. For the elders of the largest city in France, it was a different question, "doubtless the most interesting by the importance of the objects which it embraces and the most delicate by its consequences which it is possible to raise in the administration of a State like France; it is a question of nothing less than the Subsistence of the People."[13]

To make liberalization safe, the city fathers had several recommendations wholly out of character with the government's new mood. First, freedom to export should only be granted when there exists a certifiable surplus. Not surprisingly, the municipality evaded the matter of defining exactly what constituted a surplus in this huge, populous, and unevenly rich nation. Nor was it sanguine about obtaining the vast amount of detailed information on production, consumption, and distribution necessary in order to make accurate judgments. To deal with these questions the city fathers suggested the creation of a new, collegial "general bureau" of grain, despite the fact that the Contrôle-Général already had an intelligence system of which it was proud. The proposal amounted to a censure of Laverdy, for it implied that the government was technically ill-prepared to undertake liberalization and that it was acting more on faith than on hard data. Clearly the

---

12 See, for example, the argument of Joly de Fleury that a tax reduction would be a greater stimulus to growth than a price rise and Grimm's warning that tax reform was a prerequisite for rural prosperity. Koly's speech to Parl., 25 May 1763, *Recueil*, 43–44 and *Correspondance littéraire*, ed. by Tourneux, VI, 31 (July 1764).

13 Registres du Bureau de l'Hôtel de Ville, Feb. 1764, AN, H * 1870, fols. 374–84; Jollivet de Vannes, *procureur du roi et de la ville*, to Saint Florentin (?), 29 Jan. 1764, AN, O¹ 361; "Mémoire et avis de Mrs. du Bureau de Ville" (1764), BN, mss. fr. 14296.

municipality wanted exports to be authorized only exceptionally, under the strictest controls and for limited periods of time in specially appointed places as it had always been in the past.

The second recommendation of the city fathers specifically concerned Paris. The liberals hoped that in the projected phase two of liberalization all the remnants of the police regime would be swept away, especially the Parisian apparatus. The procurator of the municipality replied, on the contrary, that liberalization would require authorities to "augment the precautions for Paris" because it enhanced the vulnerability of consumers. Lacking a formal organization of abundance, Paris lives nervously from "day to day" wholly dependent upon commercial avenues of supply. The "slightest shortage" and the "least increase of prices," argued the procurator, provoke a panic mentality which threatens explosions whose "dangers are boundless." The mere announcement of a general permission to export will send a quiver of anxiety coursing through the capital. Merchants and *laboureurs* who normally supply Paris will find the temptation to profit from the new outlets irresistible, the city official prophetically noted, and the pattern of provisioning will be seriously disrupted. To forestall these dire consequences it was not enough simply to preserve the traditional police of the capital; it had to be strengthened and extended. To make it impossible for suppliers to circumvent Paris, exports from the major ports of Le Havre, Rouen, and Nantes should be prohibited, thereby sharply reducing the potential for centrifugal traffic on the Seine and Loire. To insulate Paris from liberalization, the procurator thus proposed not merely a quarantine around the capital but a *cordon sanitaire* around half the kingdom yoked exclusively to the Paris provisioning system.

Finally, the city fathers reproached the liberals for their doctrinaire attachment to "their system," for their distortion of history for political purposes (apotheosis of Sully, vilification of Colbert), and for other intellectual defects which became standard themes in the critique of liberalism which developed during the next ten years. The municipality made its most astute and original remarks in regard to the use of England as an example to follow. Contrary to the liberal conception, it contended, English grain policy was neither the only nor the best reason for English growth and prosperity. Moreover, England was not an appropriate model for France, not only for the usual geophysical and commercial reasons but because of a political distinction which shaped the temperament and the values of the citizenry.

The municipality sensed that there was an intimate connection between the British form of government and the more or less liberal policy vis-à-vis the grain trade. England was a special case for its peculiar constitution engendered a feeling of participation and "patriotism" which drastically reduced the hiatus between public and private interests. Neither political economy nor social ethics operated independently of the political system. French institutions did not promote a natural and ineluctable accommodation of general and personal interests; on the contrary, they required explicit and diligent mediation. Given the striking differences between the two governments, the municipality concluded, there is no reason to puzzle that the liberalism which admirably suited the one would fail egregiously to fit the other. The implication was arresting: for liberalism to work in France, major political changes would be necessary. It was left for Galiani and the anti-*économistes* at the end of the decade to transform this argument into a precise warning: liberalism was a politically as well as a socially subversive program.

Joly de Fleury, Advocate General of the Paris Parlement and scion of the famous high robe dynasty, pronounced the most resolute and sophisticated critique of the liberal movement in this early period. He foreshadowed many of the arguments favored in the later years by the opposition party, which accorded him nearly heroic stature for his sibylline insights and his courage in resisting the tide of opinion.[14] Joly's status and the circumstances of his demurrer gave his opinions a significance far greater than those of the intendant, uttered privately or within the administration, or those of the municipality, whose resonance was limited. Joly addressed the parlement, a quasi-public forum, in behalf of the "public ministry" whose voice he embodied. As a "king's man," with one foot within and one foot outside the parlement, his "conclusions" were carefully weighed by the magistrates. In July 1763, in defiance of the royal will, he encouraged the court to question the merits of the first of the new grain laws. That the magistrates endorsed the reform despite the powerful case against it made by Joly suggests that liberalism, in one way or another, had made deep inroads into the sovereign court.

"It is extremely dangerous," admonished Joly, "to run experiments on such a delicate matter and on one over which opinion, or if you wish,

---

14 See, for example, the statements of President Lefebvre and Advocate General Séguier in the Assembly of General Police, Nov. 1764, *Recueil*, 114, 242.

the prejudices of the people, have so much sway." Naturally the people were hypersensitive to a question upon which "their life depends." For over 200 years the old structure of police, codified in 1567 and 1577 and renewed in 1699 and 1723, has worked remarkably well. Recently, a "new system" arose. It claimed that "these laws are imperfect, ... that they are contrary to the progress of agriculture, and that all these laws made with the aim of favoring the consumer have become too unfavorable to the cultivator and the dealer." This "strange system" shocked the Advocate General. No doctrine could be more incendiary; nothing was more likely to "cast alarm among the people." Henceforth grain was to be denied any privileges or rights of asylum:

> They want to subject the commerce of a good so necessary to life to the same principles to which is subjected that of things less useful and even superfluous.

Joly did not dispute the contention that the old laws offered special protection to the consumers. On the contrary, he assumed that there was a fundamental opposition of interests between consumers and producers and he argued that since, in the nature of things, the strong always command the weak, it was the responsibility of the government to favor the have-nots. He rejected, however, the liberal suggestion that the tension between consumers and producers was really a contest between city and country. This equation was a false, politically-motivated device which aimed to polarize feelings and divide the nation. In fact, the majority of the people in rural France were consumers like their brethren in the cities:

> the artisans, the vintners, the *manœuvriers*, the poor who inhabit the countryside are not less desirous that bread be cheap.

A recipe for social disorganization, Joly de Fleury esteemed, was built into the liberal program. First of all there will be a deadly lag between the augmentation of the price of grain and the compensatory increase in wages during which time the poor will suffer. Even after they begin to respond to the upward movement, wages will not rise in proportion to the surge in prices. Employers will either cut back on jobs or will profit from the clamor for work by holding wages down. The net result will be an increase in misery and social strain and instability, too dear a price to pay for whatever advantages agriculture might derive. Agriculture, in any case, was not suffering as desperately as the liberals liked to imagine. The real "principle of discouragement" in the countryside was onerous taxation, not depressed prices. A reduction of this burden would do more for rural France than an augmentation in prices, with far less incidental damage.

Joly heartily approved the goal of promoting internal circulation; this was the purpose, too, he claimed, of all the old laws. But the prospect of opening the trade to everyone he found "frightening." He feared that the men who controlled the crop (*laboureurs*) would form "monopolies" with men who marshalled "influence and authority" (nobles and officers) and those who concentrated capital (financiers). Joly was particularly concerned about maintaining the sanctity and the centrality of the marketplace. The psychological role played by the market was as important as its purely economic function. Unless grain was visible, the people were uneasy.

If the suppliers cooperated, they could count on police indulgence. Joly insisted that it was a calumny and a misconception to depict the police as an impassive machine relentless in all seasons. Stringent laws remained on the books in case of emergency; in normal times, the police "tempered" the formal rules or neglected to enforce them. Occasionally, the Advocate General conceded, an overzealous local official violated the tacit convention by executing the letter of the law. Such outbursts of assiduity, however, were exceptional and the victims could easily petition for relief.

To eliminate caprice and make the system more predictable, Joly was willing to consider some sort of formal safeguards or institutionalized cues. One possibility would be to insert a clause in the basic police legislation making it operative only after prices reached a certain level. Joly ventilated this idea casually, without real conviction. "Perhaps," he reflected, "all sides considered, it would be better yet to leave things in their present state, to prevent abuses, to contain those who prosecute the Declaration of 1723 with too much rigor and no discernment, and to live as we have lived." Closing his case, fittingly, with a citation from Delamare and a warning against exportation, the next innovation on the horizon, the Advocate General beseeched the king for a *new law* which would contain some of the features of the May Declaration (freedom of interprovincial circulation, elimination of duties and tolls which swelled the price of bread, etc.) and many of the traditional regulations (primacy of market sales, restrictions on the right to enter the grain trade, etc.).[15]

Although they were primarily concerned with the projected impact of liberalism, these vanguard critics vigorously contested a number

---

15 Joly de Fleury, speech to Parl., 5 July 1763, *Recueil*, 33–57.

of reformist assumptions about the present state of France. The most significant part of the argument turned on the conditions of French agriculture and placed in relief the tension between political and psychological needs on the one side and the perception of socioeconomic realities on the other. The liberals argued, often in shrill, alarmist tones, that the kingdom faced "imminent ruin" in the early sixties. To be sure, agriculture had been mired in "lethargy" for a long time. (Keeping their historical options open, the liberals never said precisely how long.) But in recent years, it showed evidence of a precipitous decline; it had passed beyond the stage of languor to "decadence," "desolation," "destruction," and "profound misery." Signs of crisis allegedly abounded: massive rural depopulation, striking diminution of land under cultivation, technological stagnation, a loss of half of the nation's "real revenue," and increases in indolence, mendicancy, and crime. The smashing defeat in the war, which could be seen as a symptom of decay, further weakened the state and the economy. For this baleful situation, the liberals blamed the policy that pandered to the cities and the industries. The "restoration" of France would begin with the abolition of the prohibitive regime.[16]

The critics retorted by accusing the liberals of cultivating a gratuitously despondent mood and painting an excessively bleak picture of the state of affairs for political reasons. Joly de Fleury, we have seen, charged them with "exaggerating" and generally misrepresenting the plight of rural France which, he suggested, had far more to do with the structure of land distribution and fiscality than with prices and police. The Paris municipality derided the liberal legend of a golden age when grain moved freely across frontiers, every parcel of arable was under cultivation, and sober peasants paid close attention to improvement and growth. On the whole, argued

---

16 "Mémoire joint à l'avis des Députés du Commerce," "Premier supplément au premier mémoire," and "Deuxième supplément au premier mémoire," BN, mss. fr. 14295; "Avis des députés du commerce sur le libre commerce des grains," AN, F^{12} 715; Roubaud, *Représentations*, 345–46 and *Récréations économiques ou lettres de l'auteur des Représentations aux Magistrats à M. le chevalier Zanobi, principal interlocuteur des "Dialogues sur le commerce des blés"* (Amsterdam and Paris, 1770), 105–106; Voltaire, *Siècle de Louis XIV,* in *Oeuvres complètes*, ed. by Moland, XIV, 523; Weulersse, *Mouvement*, I, 317–32. On the consequences of the war, which no one faced squarely, see the remarks of the king entered into the minutes of the Conseil Secret of the Parl., 11 Jan. 1769, AN, X^{1B} 8957; the representations of the Rouen Parl. (May 1768), in P. LeVerdier, ed., *Correspondance Miromesnil*, V, 210–211n; Voltaire, *Précis du siècle de Louis XV*, in *Oeuvres complètes*, ed. by Moland, XV, 373–75; remonstrances, 24 June and 9 Aug. 1763, in Flammermont, ed., *Remontrances du Parlement de Paris*, II, 349–50, 360, 362.

the city government, land is better cultivated today and more of it is under cultivation than ever before. Land left untilled is either too costly and difficult to reclaim or too remote from roads and rivers. The sepulchral air of the liberal propaganda itself sowed demoralization and invited men, contrary to every social instinct, to welcome bad years.

In July 1763 the *Journal économique* published a trenchant refutation of the thesis that "France is in decadence and in the old age of her power." Agriculture had expanded considerably since the death of Louis XIV; as evidence of both increased production and productivity, the author cited the soaring prices of leases. He deplored the "widespread mania" to denigrate France and contended that economically and demographically the kingdom betrayed unmistakable signs of vitality. Several years later, Forbonnais skillfully exposed the Quesnayesque vision of erstwhile agricultural splendor as a fiction and attributed liberal moroseness to hypochondria. Galiani disposed of the decadence thesis in similar fashion, arguing that the kingdom was "very flourishing" and that the recovery of marginal lands would have little effect upon agriculture.[17]

By drawing the lines so sharply on the state-of-the-nation issue, both sides ensnarled themselves in contradictions and ambiguities. The critics, with the parlementaire Joly in the forefront, assailed the liberals for contriving a crisis, by hyperbole and distortion, to further their political ends. Yet the parlements, especially the Paris court, must bear greater responsibility than any other group for propagating an image of an exhausted, depleted, and shipwrecked France in the years before liberalization. The leitmotif of remonstrance after remonstrance was "universal ruin," "prostration," "discouragement," coupled with a plea for "renewal" or "liberation" from suffering. The portrait of misery drawn by the parlements and other sovereign courts was strikingly similar to the tableau of decadence drawn by the liberals. It contained rubrics for rural depopulation,

---

17 Joly de Fleury, speech to parl., 5 July 1763, *Recueil*, 39–40; "Mémoire et avis de Mrs. du Bureau de Ville," BN, mss. fr. 14296; "Réflexions sur l'état actuel du royaume, relativement à l'agriculture et à la population," *Journal économique* (July 1763), 296–305; J. Hecht, "La Vie de Quesnay," in *François Quesnay et la physiocratie*, I, 255; Galiani, *Dialogues*, ed. by Nicolini, 135, 139, 240. Cf. the retrospective view of the Paris Parlement, remonstrances, 2–4 March 1776 in Flammermont, ed., *Remontrances du Parlement de Paris*, III, 295 and the critique of Mirabeau by S.-A.-C. de Saint-Supplix, *Le Consolateur* (Brussels and Paris, 1763).

desertion of land, exhaustion of resources, discouragement of agriculture, and proliferation of beggary.[18] In other circumstances, Joly de Fleury might very well have accepted the liberal crisis analysis, provided it was not linked causally with the grain question. Upon the background of parlementary insurgency, Joly's position seemed neither consistent nor convincing.

Although it appeared to serve their interests admirably, the state-of-the-nation question posed far more serious problems for the liberal camp. While awaiting the felicitous results expected from liberalization, the government had to provide for its immediate financial needs. If it adopted an overly pessimistic posture on the state of the nation, it undercut its own demands for more or continued supplementary taxation. To counterpoise the gloomy mood which it helped inspire, it took pains to sponsor rebuttals to the sensational *Antifinancier* essay which also argued, outside the context of the grain debate, that France was spent.[19] Similarly uneasy, the *économistes* sometimes strained to explain how a depressed and underdeveloped agriculture was regularly able to produce "excessive abundances" and how it would be able to support France's immediate entry into the "European common market."[20] Towards the end of the sixties, the crisis analysis continued to embarrass them. In the course of only a few years they had called attention to signs of agricultural advance everywhere. A brusque and extensive regeneration, however, implied a widespread and effective implementation of the reform laws which the *économistes*, as we shall see, claimed never came to pass.[21]

In the sixties, the grain question, along with the defeat in war and the chronic fiscal dilemma, offered the occasion for a probing appraisal of the state of the kingdom. But the issue was never clearly or frankly explored. Divergent ideological and political pressures within each camp further muddled a debate already marred by the

---

18 See, for example, Flammermont, ed., *Remontrances du Parlement de Paris*, II, 326–27, 349–50, 360, 362–63, and Glasson, *Parlement de Paris*, II, 282, 291.

19 Marion, *Histoire financière*, I, 222.

20 See, for instance, *Ephémérides du citoyen* (1768), IX, 83.

21 Turgot to Condorcet, 6 April 1772, *Correspondance inédite de Condorcet et de Turgot, 1770–1779*, ed. by Charles Henry (Paris, 1883), 81; "Observations sur les effets de la liberté du commerce des grains, par l'Auteur des Ephémérides du citoyen," *Journal économique* (July 1770), 330ff; Baudeau, *Avis au premier besoin*, 1er traité, 39 and "Lettres à un Magistrat du Parlement de Paris ...," *Nouvelles éphémérides économiques* (1775), I, 23; G. Weulersse, "Les Physiocrates et la question du pain cher au milieu du dix-huitième siècle," *Revue du dix-huitième siècle*, I (Jan.-March 1913), 181 and *Louis XV*, 70; Turgot, "Septième lettre sur le commerce des grains," 2 Dec. 1770, in *Oeuvres*, ed. by Schelle, III, 341.

polemical clash between them. The arguments perplexed Frenchmen as sensitive as Voltaire, who throughout this period was unable to make up his mind about the reform or the reformers. In one place he wrote solemnly of the "profound misery" of agriculture while in another he decried the overwrought despair of the liberals.[22]

The debate over the meaning and significance of "decadence" and the proper role of agriculture led to a decisive break with the belief in abundance that was so deeply ingrained in the national self-image.[23] It was, however, the men of tradition, the party of the police, not the non-conformist liberals who broke the faith. The liberals remained squarely within the abundance persuasion, though they interpreted abundance as a simple economic variable rather than as a gauge of providential favor. Some of them tried to "prove" it, laboriously applying the statistics of Vauban and his epigones; most of them simply accepted it as a notorious donnée, confirmed by history and experience.[24] On one level they relied upon it to build confidence in their program by showing that a kingdom as abundant as France had nothing to lose and everything to gain from a policy of liberalization and exportation. If all the arteries of communication and commerce were opened, there would be more than enough grain to go around. With a different purpose in mind, the liberals considered this chronic abundance not as a blessing but as a plague. They condemned it as "excessive," "onerous,"

---

22 Voltaire, *Siècle de Louis XIV* in *Oeuvres complètes*, ed. by Moland, XIV, 523; article "Agriculture" cited by Weulersse, *Mouvement*, I, 222.

23 For evidence of the belief in abundance, see Duhamel du Monceau, *Traité de la conservation des grains*, iv, 6; Herbert, *Essai*, ed. by Depitre, 40; M. Reneaume, "Sur la manière de conserver les grains," *Mémoires de l'Académie des Sciences, 1708*, 76; François Aubert, "Réflexions simples et pratiques sur le commerce des grains" (1775), BN, mss. n.a. 4433; Anonymous, "Histoire de ce qui s'est passé au sujet des bleds en 1725," Arsenal, Recueil Fevret, mss. 3308; A. A. Parmentier, *Le Parfait boulanger*, 118; Regnaud, "Histoire des événements arrivés en France depuis 1772...," BN, mss. fr. 13734, p. 180. For the dissenting view, see the trenchant "Mémoire sur les bleds" (n.d., ca. 1750) of Pâris-Duverney, AN, F^{12} 647 ("Il n'est plus vrai qu'une récolte suffise à la consommation de trois années ... on ne peut nier que dans les 10 années comprises en 1740 et 1750 [*sic*], chacune l'une portant l'autre, n'ait donné demie récolte.").

24 See, for example, "Premier supplément au premier mémoire des Députés de Commerce," BN, mss. fr. 14295, fols. 4–7; Quesnay, articles "Grains" and "Fermier," *Encyclopédie*, VII, 813 and VI, 533; memoir of the deputies of commerce of Toulouse to CG (1762), C. 2908, A.D. Hér.; *arrêté*, Parl. de Dauphiné, 12 July 1768, C. 2420, A.D. B-du-R.; Letter addressed by Dauphiné Parl. to Louis XV, 26 April 1769, B. 2314, fol. 107, A.D. Isère; Letrosne, *Discours sur l'état actuel de la magistrature et sur les causes de sa décadence* (Paris, 1764), 60n; Condorcet, *Sur la liberté de la circulation des subsistances*, in *Oeuvres*, ed. by A.C. O'Connor and M.F. Arago (Paris, 1847), X, 360–361; Henri Curmond, *Le Commerce des grains et l'école physiocratique*, 165–66.

and "pernicious"; it was unsound and unhealthy, for it depressed agriculture, made future dearths inevitable, and distributed its largesse unevenly across space and time. This abundance Quesnay deplored as a condition of "misery," for it meant plenty at low prices. For Baudeau it was no less destructive in its overall socioeconomic effects than a scarcity. In its place the liberals wanted to establish a viable abundance of prosperity linked to profit and expansion, measured not in terms of the ratio of French production to French consumption but according to the universal indices of supply and demand. Thus the liberals were able to maintain a reassuring faith in abundance and at the same time to expose it as a flawed and vulnerable condition.[25]

The defenders of the police in the early sixties took issue with the liberals on both aspects of the question. Challenged to put the national belief in abundance to the test by endorsing the reform laws, they backed off and abjured it. They rejected the idea of abundance with painful reluctance, for unlike the liberals, they thought that abundance was unconditionally a good thing. Since they believed that the purpose of agriculture was first of all to nourish, it struck them as paradoxical and sophistical to construe plentiful harvests as beacons of woe and symptoms of stagnation. The problem was not with abundance but with the idea of it: it was patriotic and comforting but it was thoroughly misleading. The intendant Bertier came to regard the abundance persuasion as a myth that no longer served the public interest. "Let us not fool ourselves," he admonished; the kingdom simply does not produce the quantity of grain claimed by the mongers of abundance. Joly and other commentators adopted the same tough-minded stance. Neither history nor experience confirms the idea of abundance; on the contrary, they are replete with lessons which warn us against complacency.[26]

In the seventies a growing band of writers spoke out publicly against it. Struck by the recurrent scourges of dearth and the unremittingly

---

25 Herbert, *Essai*, ed. by Depitre, 18; Quesnay, article "Fermier," *Encyclopédie*, VI, 534 and *passim*; "Premier supplément au premier mémoire des Députés de Commerce," BN, mss. fr. 14295, fol. 61; Baudeau, *Avis au premier besoin*, l^er traité, 33; *Journal économique* (June 1768), 262.

26 B. de Sauvigny, "Observations sur le commerce des grains," BN, mss. fr. 11347, fol. 231; Joly de Fleury, speech to Parl., 5 July 1763, *Recueil*, 39; "Mémoire et avis de Mrs. du Bureau de Ville," BN, mss. fr. 14296, fols. 22–23; Anonymous, "Commerce extérieur," BN, mss. fr. 11347, fols. 215, 220–21. Cf. the similar positions of the intendant of Hainaut and one of his subdelegates. SD of Avesnes to Taboureau, Oct. 1773 and Taboureau to CG, 4 Aug. 1774, C. 6690, A.D. Nord.

precarious nature of daily life, Galiani, Necker, and Béguillet, three of the most vocal antiphysiocrats, cast serious doubts on the abundance idea.[27] The intendant of Picardy flatly stated that "...abundant harvests do not produce nearly as much as has always been believed."[28] Simon Linguet heaped scorn on the "tantalus" myth, a nostrum contrived by the haves to contain the have-nots: "abundance exists only for him who has a share in it."[29] When Turgot, its last great hope, acceded to the Controller-Generalship in 1774, liberalism, too, gave up the abundance idea. Or rather, Turgot shattered it for them in a pithy and momentous sentence in the preamble to the *arrêt du conseil* of 13 September 1774: "Now then, the common year of production cannot be above the habitual consumption."[30]

But the abundance persuasion died hard. It invited belief for it seemed to temper the travail of living. The idea reappeared again and again, through the time of the Revolution and beyond, espoused by Pangloss-Pluchistes who believed in a cleverly providential universe, by political economists whose arithmetic calculations always seemed incontrovertible, and by police officials, too, who found it less complicated to combat the vices of men than the inconstancy of nature.

It is important to emphasize how much more difficult it was for the early critics of liberalism at the very beginning of the sixties to break with abundance than it was for their successors a decade later. After assailing the liberals for despairing of the state of the nation in the short run, they themselves posited a proto-malthusian view of the world far more pessimistic in its implications. France was rich and fertile but much less fortunate as a rule than the liberals suggested. Times of genuine abundance, that is to say, of subsistence ease, were relatively rare. It was cynical to consider this kind of abundance a "surcharge," a "burden," or a sign of "decadence." It was a respite, a

---

27 Galiani, *Dialogues*, ed. by Nicolini, 125–27, 132, 139, 141; J. J. Spengler, *French Predecessors of Malthus; A Study in Eighteenth Century Wage and Population Theory* (Durham, N.C., 1942), 332; Béguillet, *Traité des subsistances*, 357–58, 435, Cf. similar ideas in the article "Disette," *Encyclopédie méthodique*, Jurisprudence, Police et Municipalités (Paris, 1791), X, 32 and Vernuit, "Réflexions d'un citoyen sur les disettes du bled en France ..." (ca. an I), AN, F[10] 215–216.

28 Reply to inquiry from CG, Oct. 1773, C. 86, A.D. Somme.

29 Linguet, *Annales*, VII (Nov. 1779), 205. Cf. *ibid.*, 198–99.

30 *Arrêt du Conseil*, 13 Sept. 1774, in BN, Coll. Joly 1111, fol. 36. Writing some years later, Tolosan condemned a group of English agronomist-writers—did he have, *inter alia*, Arthur Young in mind?—for sustaining the misleading abundance persuasion by their "exaggerations" regarding the capacity of French agriculture. *Mémoire sur le commerce de la France*, 5.

fleeting moment of serenity for which the nation should be grateful, for every year, regardless of the preceding one, was a test and a trial.[31]

II

Why the parlements were not more responsive to the objections raised against the liberal legislation in 1763–64 is not easy to explain. The fears and reservations of Joly and the others touched upon issues to which the magistracy had always been acutely sensitive. Nor did the political climate seem propitious, at least in the beginning, for a joint enterprise sponsored by the king and the courts. The exigencies of war had somewhat tempered parlementary dissidence, but the dispute over the Jesuits led to stormy exchanges and Bertin's fiscal edicts inspired a paroxysm of furious resistance in several provincial capitals in 1763.[32] Almost at the very moment that the king promulgated the first of the liberal measures in May, he imposed a *lit de justice* upon the Paris court, which replied by denouncing him as an inept tyrant.[33] If the government counted on liberalization to mollify the parlements or derail their opposition to the fiscal measures, then it badly miscalculated, for the sovereign courts adamantly held out until the king was ready to capitulate. The parlements most effusively sympathetic to liberalization were also the ones which combatted the fiscal legislation most violently. Rather than a favor granted by a loving king to the nation, as the liberal press liked to put it, liberalization may very well have been a concession by the magistracy to a defeated and humiliated monarch. Conceivably, the Paris Parlement's tardy but crucially important registration of the May Declaration in 1764 was part of a bargain which resulted in the withdrawal of the most obnoxious fiscal measures and the appointment of the Parisian magistrate Laverdy to the Contrôle-Général. In any case, it should not be forgotten that the grain reform became law at a time when the parlements appeared to be, in the words of a contemporary observer, "the master of public affairs."[34]

---

31 "Commerce intérieur et extérieur des bleds," BN, mss. fr. 11347, fols. 213–214; "Mémoire et avis de Mrs. du Bureau de Ville," BN, mss. fr. 14296, fol. 22.

32 M. Marion, *Histoire financière*, I, 201–230; Glasson, *Parlement de Paris*, II, 237–346; Palmer, *Age*, I, 86–99.

33 Remonstrances, 31 May 1763, in Flammermont, ed., *Remontrances du Parlement de Paris*, II, 339ff; E.-J.-F. Barbier, *Chronique de la régence*, VIII, 73 (May 1763).

34 Moreau, *Souvenirs*, ed. by C. Hermelin, I, 128.

The liberal publicists were especially proud of their contingent of parlementary allies whose support seemed to be the best riposte to the charge that the reformers were dangerous speculators. To underscore the ideological nature of the alliance, the liberal press published manifestoes of doctrinal orthodoxy from parlements and parlementaires and editorialized on the community of views which bound together enlightened magistrates, ministers, and *économistes*. Given the robe's odious reputation for egotism and opportunism, historians have always felt embarrassed about treating parlementary eloquence in ideological terms. Parlementary ideas are rarely examined for what they have to say but rather for what they have to hide. It is generally assumed that parlementary discourse serves merely to rationalize corporate advantage of one kind or another and thus is disingenuous or beside the point. Liberal ideology, however, obviates nagging doubts about sincerity by making self-interest a civic virtue when properly understood. That is not to suggest that self-seeking was the major cause of parlementary adherence to the new political economy; rather, it is to note that material gain was a powerful and appropriate motive and that solidarity with the reformers fits the conventional image of the parlements much more neatly than opposition to them.

We do not have the elements to test a model of economic determinism for explaining parlementary attitudes toward liberalization akin to the one developed by Charles Beard.[35] Crudely applied on a collective and regional level, such a model might help to suggest why some of the parlements—Toulouse is probably the best example—ardently espoused liberalization; it would be of much less use, however, in trying to account for the inconstancy, the indifference, and the hostility within many of the others. In neither case could it adequately measure the influence of the different constituencies and pressure groups in each jurisdiction.

Emphasis on the desire to profit from higher grain prices, higher rents, and economic expansion tends to obscure other areas where parlementary and *économiste* thinking seemed to converge. Both cherished the right of property: characteristically, each group justified its most extreme and controversial positions by reference to this supreme authority. Both viewed property as the best guarantee of personal liberty and

---

35 I am thinking, of course, about *An Economic Interpretation of the Constitution of the United States* (New York, 1913).

the source of social stability. A physiocrat might have composed the remonstrance in which the Rouen Parlement defended property as a right anterior to all forms of social and political organization.[36]

Although they entertained different conceptions of the rule by law, both the parlements and the *économistes* detested the arbitrary exercise of power in any form. Neither had any affection for the extension of the royal bureaucracy, albeit for different reasons. The liberal denunciation of vexatious, uninformed, and tyrannical local police authorities was redolent of the parlementary onslaught against similarly noxious fiscal agents.[37] The parlements often expressed the same warm solicitude for rural France mingled with a suspicion of the city for which the *économistes* were known.[38] Both found the world of finance, *traitants*, and sly and rapid fortunes repugnant.[39] Both feared that the present tax system would permanently ruin the economy and they joined in deploring government waste and extravagance.

Like the liberals, the parlementaires saw themselves as a party of economic reform, focusing specifically on fiscal management. They decried prodigality, inefficiency, the endless multiplication and the gratuitous duplication of posts, the failure to keep proper accounts, "shadowy" decision-making, "mysterious" forms of tax collection, and abuses in expenditure.[40] They called for a general house-cleaning, a spirit of frugality and retrenchment, and a regular "publicity" to restore public confidence. All of these goals were familiar to Quesnay and Mirabeau. Both groups, as we have previously shown, impressed upon the public the idea that France was teetering on the brink of doom. In the early sixties a parlementaire interested in charting out common ground with the liberals would discover that they shared a belief in a number of fundamental principles, a critical attitude toward numerous aspects of administration, and a desire for regeneration and renewal. Since the grain reform addressed itself to these issues as well as to the matter of agricultural profit, many magistrates found it hard to resist.

---

36 H. Martin, *Histoire de France*, XVI, 227–28; Michelet, *Histoire de France*, XV, 123–24.

37 M. Marion, *Histoire financière*, I, 215–217. Cf. the explicit analogy between grain and fiscal police in the deliberations of the Estates of Languedoc, Dec. 1768, C. 2411, A.D. H-G.

38 Remonstrances, 19 May 1763, in Flammermont, ed., *Remontrances du Parlement de Paris*, II, 327.

39 Remonstrances, 4 Sept. 1759, 20 Jan. 1760, 19 May 1763, *ibid.*, II, 231, 277, 325–26.

40 Remonstrances, 4 Sept. 1759, 20 Jan. 1760, 24 June 1763, 4 Sept. 1763, 1 Dec. 1768, 21 Jan. 1770, *ibid.*, II, 229–31, 277, 349, 412–13 and III, vii–viii, 75–77.

The liberal reforms elicited a warm welcome in most of the sovereign courts. The Parlement of Provence registered the May Declaration as soon as it arrived, at the end of June, without debate. In the next five weeks the magistrates of Toulouse, Grenoble, Bordeaux, Dijon, Lille, and Rennes followed suit. As often happened in the legislative process in the Old Regime—more often than historians who read only the remonstrances are aware—one of the courts made its registration conditional upon the inclusion of an explanatory rider concerning its peculiar regional needs and the government accepted it without hesitation. In this instance the Bretons, much of whose trade was seaborne, wanted to make it explicitly clear that the freedom granted internal circulation in the Declaration also applied to coastwise commerce. Not as a condition of its approbation but as a collective wish, the Dauphinais urged Louis XV to extend the new liberty to include exports. Although the king "approved the principles of His Parlement," the government was not yet ready to take this second giant step. Pointing to "the fear that so rapid a change might impair the provisioning of the kingdom," the Controller-General Bertin cautioned that before opening the ports and frontiers the ministry would wait until "the liberty accorded by the Declaration of 25 May last" produced a solid base of "abundance."[41]

It is hardly surprising to learn that these same parlements registered the July Edict with uncommon dispatch the following summer.[42]

---

41 Parl. of Provence, 30 June 1763, B. 3676 and B. 3422, fols. 251–253, A.D. B-du-R.; Parl. of Toulouse, 13 July 1763, B. 1953, fol. 235, A.D. H-G.; Bordeaux Parl. registers for 29 July 1763 and I-B 49, fol. 184 (1 Aug. 1763), A.D. Gir.; Parl. of Dijon, 2 Aug. 1763, B. 12134, fols. 247–48, A.D. C d'O.; Parl. of Rennes, 4 Aug. 1763, C. 1648–49, A.D. I-et-V.; Bertin to Berulle, First President of Grenoble Parl., 26 April 1769, B. 2314, fols. 88–89, A.D. Isère. It is puzzling that in the broadside versions of the May and July laws which the Rennes Parlement had published, the articles regarding the maintenance of the Paris police regime were excluded. Was the omission intentional? If so, was it because the articles seemed irrelevant or because the magistrates desired not to publicize the fact that the capital retained its special privileges? This matter, we shall see, had major political and economic significance throughout the kingdom. The Rennes examples are the only bowdlerized copies of the liberal laws that I found.

42 Provence, 2 Aug. 1764, B. 3676, B. 3475, and B. 3433, fols. 688–694, A.D. B-du-R.; Bordeaux, 17, 20 Aug. 1764, B. 1470, I B 51, fols. 14–17 and I B 52, fols. 18–20, A.D. Gir.; Toulouse, 8 Aug. 1764, B. 1953, fols. 308–310, A.D. H-G. Though they welcomed the July Edict enthusiastically as soon as they received it, the magistrates of Metz delayed registration until the end of November, apparently in order to impose several "conditions" regarding the levying of duties and fees on grain entering, leaving, and passing through Lorraine and the Barrois. See the registres secrets, 14 Aug. and 26 Nov. 1764, B. 458 and the deliberations of 29 Nov. 1764, B. 38, A.D. Moselle.

Though liberals everywhere proclaimed that it was a moment to be grateful, at least two of these parlements expressed a feeling widely held in the liberal camp: the July law was excellent but it could still be improved. To their registration, the Dijon magistrates appended the "supplication" that the king "lift as soon as possible the limitations placed on the full liberty of grain exportation... ."[43] The Parlement at Rennes asked for a revision of the law to allow for an automatic re-opening of exports in ports where the price had triggered the closing mechanism once the price fell below the ceiling barrier for three consecutive markets; for exports by ships and crews of any nationality in order to maximize profit opportunities and economize on costs; for embarkation from any Breton port rather than only the six stipulated in the law; and for the suppression of all duties on imported and exported grain.[44] These were, it should be emphasized, requests rather than demands; their tone was profoundly respectful and patient. None of these proposals was anathema to the government. On the contrary, it was very likely that the ministry would adopt them as soon as it felt that conditions permitted and it was probably not unhappy to have such a plea, emanating, as it liked to believe, "from the nation," on the record. The Parlements of Dijon, Besançon, and Rennes also urged the government to dispel an ambiguity in the May Declaration which enabled many kinds of *octrois* and other *droits* to subsist by abolishing *all* internal duties and fees attached to grain transit in the interior—this despite the fact that a number of magistrates in each court owned or farmed some of them.[45]

---

43 Dijon Parl., 4 Aug. 1764, B. 12134, fols. 455–58, A.D. C d'O. Cf. Pierre de St.-Jacob's description of the Parlement as "physiocratic" in attitude. *Les paysans de la Bourgogne du Nord au dernier siècle de l'ancien régime* (Paris, 1960), 348, 350.

44 Parl. of Rennes, 22 Aug. 1764, C. 1648–49, A.D. I-et-V. In response to complaints that the ad valorem duties levied on imports and exports by the July Edict provoked confusion and "contestations" because of the changing value of the commodities, the government did not abolish them as many of the parlements desired but converted them to fixed amounts per hundred-weight. See the letters patent of 7 Nov. 1764 either in C. 2420, A.D. B-du-R. or Archives des Affaires Étrangères, France 1361, fols. 335–36.

45 Parl. of Rennes, 7 Feb. 1766, C. 1648–49, A.D. I-et-V.; Dijon Parl., 5 May 1764, B. 12134, fols. 403–405. Cf. the similar though less militant stand taken by the Bordeaux court. *Arrêt* of 23 Nov. 1763, A.D. Gir.

As a result of the sweeping statements of suppression in the May Declaration, it was initially assumed that all internal duties (save market *droits*) were abolished. Many duties, however, were owned by estates, municipalities, and religious and assistance institutions which bitterly complained about the loss of revenue. See, for example, the

Yet it is not true, as the *Mercure de France* later claimed, that all of the parlements registered the liberal reforms with spontaneous acclamation.[46] There may well have been a considerable amount of antagonism *within* the parlements considered above and those whose manuscript "secret councils" were not investigated first-hand.[47] There was in fact serious hesitation and hostility in Rouen and Paris. Significantly, only the May 1763 Declaration on internal liberty caused these Parlements to agonize. The Paris court routinely registered the July 1764 Edict on exportation and Rouen endorsed it with an unwonted exuberance which embarrassed the Controller-General Laverdy.[48] But after many months of delay and discussion the May Declaration barely squeezed through the Paris Parlement by "two or three votes"; the Rouennais subjected it to a year's "prudent study" before they finally assented.[49]

Both houses regarded the first of the liberal laws with far more consternation than the second. The May Declaration, in the words of the First President of the Normandy court, introduced "principles diametrically opposed to those of the past."[50] This law virtually abolished the police of grain and made the trade a free-for-all. It was not merely a prerequisite for exportation; it went far beyond the conditions necessary to allow exports. It determined the character which exportation would have and assured that it would generate a pervasive multiplier

"Mémoire" of the Bordeaux city fathers, C. 1426, A.D. Gir. As a result of intense lobbying, the government issued interpretive legislation which "provisionally" exempted from the suppression the *droits* owned by the above-mentioned groups. See the letters patent of 5 March 1764, Archives des Affaires Etrangères, France 1361, fol. 66; B. 2173, fol. 140, A.D. Doubs. Cf. the Flanders Parlement which asked for indemnification of all toll and fee owners in its act registering the May law. Bertin to IN., 16 Sept. 1763, C. 6690, A.D. Nord.

46 *Mercure de France* (Aug. 1769), 128.

47 According to the historian of the Besançon court, "liberty" was the dominant economic notion of the magistrates. Though he does not deal specifically with liberalization, he shows how the province's peculiar geography caused it to resist obdurately the mandatory market law of April 1723 and to regard the right to export as part of its "natural liberty." F. Prost, *Les remontrances du Parlement de Franche-Comté au 18e siècle* (Lyon, 1936), 121–122. Though it approved the liberal reforms, events later compelled it, along with several other courts that hailed liberalization in the beginning, to reassess its stand.

48 Rouen, *Conseil Secret* (1963), 4 May, 9 Aug. 1764, A.D. S-M. Cf. Terray to the Comte de Périgord, 25 Nov. 1772, C. 2912, A.D. Hér.

49 LeVerdier, ed., *Correspondance Miromesnil*, III, xxxviii; Rouen Parl., Conseil Secret (1763), 22 March 1763, A.D. S-M.; A. Floquet, *Histoire du Parlement de Normandie*, VI, 421–23; Desmarest, *Commerce des grains ... Rouen*, 116–17; *Recueil*, 57. Cf. the remarks of the First President of the Paris Parl., *Recueil*, 104.

50 Miromesnil to Laverdy, 10 May 1768, in LeVerdier, ed., *Correspondance Miromesnil*, V, 183.

effect throughout society. The May Declaration seemed to be much less easily reversible than the July Edict; exportation remained contingent and self-restrictive whereas internal liberty was unconditional and unlimited. Although the export question caused a much greater public stir, these Parlements viewed it as something of an anticlimax.

Five years after the fact, at the height of its semi-public campaign *against* liberalization, the Rouen Parlement claimed that its hesitation over the May Declaration had been based on "the fear of abuses" perverting the provisioning trade.[51] Nor was the magistrates' memory self-serving, not at least on this point, for the First President of the court, a friend of the reform, confirmed their self-analysis. But he blamed their fears, and thus their resistance, on the magistrates' lack of sophistication in "economic matters" which left them prey to "the old prejudices." For many months after the Parlement first received the legislation the First President toiled vigorously to "combat" their retrograde ideas by distributing liberal propaganda and meeting with recalcitrant members.[52] When they overcame their prejudices and finally registered the law, the magistrates did so on the impeccably liberal grounds that "dirt-cheap prices" threatened to "ruin" agriculture. Significantly, once they decided to risk the transformation of the grain trade which the May Declaration implied, they *immediately* asked the king for a law permitting exports, for their newly-acquired sophistication in economic matters taught them that such a measure would make the May Declaration work more efficiently and strengthen powerfully the incentives which liberalization offered to agriculture.[53]

In Paris there was enormous pressure from the government, but it is not clear what forms it took. If Joly's fears could be shown to be "groundless," there was still the more diffuse horror of brusque change of any kind: inverting the liberal crisis argument, it could be claimed that France was "too fatigued to suffer great commotions" precisely because she was in "imminent peril."[54] The appointment of Laverdy may have been instrumental in winning some votes. As a gesture of parlementary solidarity, certain magistrates may have felt it proper to cede to the urgent importunities of their provincial confreres. Perhaps the government also used its classic arsenal of material and moral

---

51 Lettre et supplication au roi, 29 Oct. 1768, *Conseil Secret*, A.D. S-M.
52 Courteille to IN. of Rouen, 9 Jan. 1764, C. 103, A.D. S-M.
53 *Conseil Secret* (1763), 22 March, 13 April 1764, A.D. S-M.
54 "Observations" (1771), BN, Coll. Joly 1109, fol. 211 and remonstrances, 9 Aug. and 4 Sept. 1763, in Flammermont, ed., *Remontrances du Parlement de Paris*, II, 409–411.

inducements in its quest for support. Presumably the liberals had a genuine footing within the parlements, but its size, locus, and influence are unknown. The rapporteur of the May Declaration bespoke the gnawing distrust of many magistrates who acquiesced in its passage:

> Let us try it; if, as there is every reason to fear, experience proves the disadvantages of this new legislation, we will go back to the old laws.[55]

The words were prophetic and so was the choice of the counselor to recite them, the abbé Terray, future Controller-General.

III

Men do not give free reign to nature in social life, remarked the Chevalier in Galiani's *Dialogues sur le commerce des bleds*, unless the "sea" is calm and the "wind" is stable: "Sailors never talk of letting the sails go at the mercy of the winds except when they see a grand tranquility."[56] The sea was not perfectly calm, but the social climate of France was on the whole favorable when the navigators of the ship of state freed the grain trade and entrusted nature with its police. There was, to be sure, considerable political agitation in the early sixties, but it did not reach deeply into society; it affected the daily lives of very few Frenchmen. Fundamental law could not displace subsistence as the chief object of popular concern and the marketplace rather than the palace of justice remained the best place to test public feeling. Years of good harvests and moderate-to-low prices had produced a situation of relative quiescence which not even the pressure of war or fiscality could seriously disturb. The indifference of the consuming public to the grain reforms in 1763 and 1764 did not surprise contemporary observers. "Do you think," asked one, "that when bread is only 2 *sols* 6 *deniers* at the market the people have something to say?"[57] Without general internal peace and subsistence ease, liberalization would have been unthinkable.

This tranquility, however, did not endure and, as the circumstances changed, the people proved that they had a good deal to say. Already in 1764, while the *Journal économique* warmly welcomed the new era of liberal politics and derided "the chimerical fear of falling into dearth,"

---

55 *Recueil*, 57. Cf. Anon., "Mémoire" (1771), AN, F[11] 264.
56 Galiani, *Dialogues*, ed. by Nicolini, 224.
57 Anon., "Mémoire" (1771), AN, F[11] 264.

malaise over grain movements and exportation detonated riots in Caen and Cherbourg and in Tallard in the Dauphiné.[58] These troubles were not isolated, idiosyncratic episodes. During the next six years riots and *émotions* erupted throughout the kingdom, especially in the northern half (the south would have its share in the early seventies). Although he found them tiresome and redundant, the *économiste* Dupont conceded that they were "perpetual."[59] I have counted over sixty within the jurisdictions of the Parlements of Paris and Rouen between 1765 and 1768; elsewhere there are scores of others to be noted.[60] Though the rhythm

---

58 *Journal économique* (Nov. 1764), 492; Lamoignon to Miromesnil, 24 Dec. 1764, in LeVerdier, ed., *Correspondance Miromesnil*, III, 429; introduction, *ibid.*, V. xiii. "Women of the little people" spearheaded the rising at Caen, intercepting grain and forcing its sale at the market below the current. C. 2664, A.D. Cal. According to the municipality of Cherbourg, the mutineers there were "a troop of *canaille*" impelled to attack a grain boat from "fear of a future dearth." Letter of 14 Dec. 1764, C. 2680, A.D. Cal. B. 2315, fols. 116–20, A.D. Isère.

59 Dupont, *Analyse ... rapport*, 105–106, 108.

60 1765: Abbeville, Caen, Blois, Orléans, Sablé, Cosne, Cognac, Sancerre, Bléré, Angers, Châtellerault, Avoise, Montrésor, and elsewhere in the Touraine and the Orléanais; 1766: Amiens, Tonnère, St. Dizier, Bourges, Vitry, Sens, Bar-sur-Aube, Beaufort; 1767: Coulommiers, Rebais, Tournan-en-Brie, Crécy-en-Brie, St. Denis, La Ferté-Gaucher, Montlhéry, Corbeil, Rozoy, Troyes; 1768: Brevant, Joigny, Abbeville, Carentan, Beaufort, Bléré, Mamers, La Ferté-Bernard, La Flèche, Pithiviers, Malesherbes, Villaines-le-Jubel, Châlons-sur-Marne, Compiègne, Belleville, Montereau, Rozoy, Rouen, Fécamp, Magny, Pont-l'évêque, Elbeuf, Darnétal, Maromme, La Bouille, Gournay, Bourgthéroulde. Laverdy (?) to Lescalopier, 18 Aug. 1765, AN, F^{12} 150; C. 2664, A.D. Cal.; CG to Choiseul, 4 Sept. 1765, F^{12} 150; CG to Cypierre, 13 Sept. 1765, *ibid.*; CG to Perceval, 13 Sept. 1765, *ibid.*; CG to PG, 19 Nov. 1765, BN, Coll. Joly 1131, fol. 5; CG to PG, 4 Dec. 1765, *ibid.*, fol. 9; Prevost (Angers) to PG, 25 Aug. 1765, *ibid.*, fol. 15; royal procurator at Blois to PG, 31 Aug. 1765, *ibid.*, fols. 28–29; CG to PG, 21 Aug. 1765, *ibid.*, fol. 131; fiscal procurator at Cosne to PG, 25 Aug. 1765, *ibid.*, fols. 106–107; CG to PG, 13 Sept. 1765, *ibid.*, fols. 92–93; CG to IN. of Touraine, 15, 19, 28 Aug. 1768, C. 94, A.D. I-et-L.; IN. to CG, 10 Sept. 1768, *ibid.*; Haberty to IN., 4 Sept. 1765, *ibid.*; Cypierre to intendant's secretary, 9 Sept. 1765, *ibid.*; Choiseul to IN., 2 Oct. 1765, *ibid.*; Coll. Joly 1132, *passim*, especially CG to PG, 7 Oct. 1766 and 15 Jan. 1767, fols. 12, 246; SD Masson to IN. of Champagne, 9 Sept., 7 Oct. 1766, C. 299, A.D. Aube; IN. of Touraine to CG, 30 June 1766, C. 96, A.D. I-et-L.; Coll. Joly 1133, fols. 9–16, 30, 43ff; Coll. Joly 1134, fols. 128–169, 175–76, 197; ? at Coulommiers to PG, 22 Nov. 1767, Coll. Joly 1135, fols. 74–75; Fasquel to PG, 29 Nov. 1767, *ibid.*, fol. 76; petition of Sieur Montgolfier, *ibid.*, fols. 80–81; CG to PG, 7 Dec. 1767, *ibid.*, fol. 82; reports from Crécy, La-Ferté-Gaucher, Rebais, Coulommiers, and Montlhéry, *ibid.*, fols. 130–132, 201, 225, 85–86; Laurent to PG, 19 Oct. 1767, *ibid.*, fol. 152; Nauvin to PG, 1 Dec. 1767, *ibid.*, fol. 163; *officiers* of Troyes to PG, 2 June 1767, *ibid.*, fols. 175ff; CG to PG, 22 June 1767 and 12 July 1767, *ibid.*, fols. 179–181; reports from Abbeville, Beaufort, Belleville, Bléré, Châlons-sur-Marne, and Compiègne, Coll. Joly 1140, fols. 7, 36, 57–58, 61, 95, 170; reports from Montereau and Rozoy-en-Brie, Coll. Joly 1142, fols. 2–6, 84; C. 1908, A.D. Aube; St. Florentin to B. de Sauvigny, 18 Nov. 1768 and dispatch to same, 4 Oct. 1768, AN, O^{1*} 410; Hardy's Journal, 28 March and 5 June 1768, BN, mss. fr. 6680,

of disturbances abated the following year, it rebounded violently in 1770 and continued to jar many parts of France through 1775.[61] After years of repose, the marketplace became the Saint-Médard of the sixties and seventies.

These risings shared a number of traits in common. They occurred in substantial towns as well as in more modest bourgs and hamlets. They struck towns located on or near rivers more frequently than those remote from water transportation. Most of the towns were entrepôt markets integrated more or less formally into a larger chain of provisioning serving a metropolitan center or feeding river traffic to the coast. For the most part the disturbances were indigenously and spontaneously generated, albeit the geographical and commercial relations of the towns sometimes suggested a process of contagion and emulation. Panic and rising prices were both causes and effects, although in the beginning the former often seemed to precede and prime the latter. In normal times there was a relatively high tolerance for the physical displacement of grain and flour. In time of anxiety there was a distortion of perspective and a new threshhold of alarm became established. Grain movements which once passed imperceptibly now aroused resentment and fomented resistance. Opposition to what contemporaries called "removals" [enlèvements] and "exportation" of grain (which in this context meant nothing more than the transfer of grain from one community for use elsewhere, within the kingdom or abroad) was the form which these risings characteristically took. As long as grain seemed to be available, it was merely a question of intercepting it and diverting it to the market, in most cases for relatively orderly distribution by sale to local consumers. When the grain seemed to disappear from circulation, consumers felt more desperate and helpless. Instead of lying in wait for grain which might never pass by, they went after it wherever they believed it to be hidden. In the latter

---

fols. 152 and 165; Gazette à la main par Marin, Lettres Ossolinski, 28 March 1768, BHVP, ms. 625, fol. 127; C. 2667, A.D. Cal.; Laverdy to Miromesnil, 27 March 1768, in LeVerdier, ed., Correspondance Miromesnil, V, 133–34; Trudaine de Montigny to Miromesnil, 13 May 1768, ibid., V, 200; IN. of Champagne to Bertin, 25 July 1768, C. 413, A.D. Marne; CG to IN. of Touraine, 5 June 1768, C. 94, A.D. I-et-L.; royal procurator of Bléré to IN., 21 June 1768, ibid.; Durangouin, lieutenant in maréchaussée, procès-verbal, 27 June, 1 Aug. 1768, ibid.; Brissard to IN., 25 July, 7 Aug. 1768, ibid.; SD of Pithiviers to IN. of Orléanais, 30 June 1768 in C. Bloch, Le Commerce des grains dans la généralité d'Orléans d'après la correspondance inédite de l'intendant Cypierre (Orléans, 1898), 44.

61   For a fuller discussion of the disruption of the early seventies, see below, chapter twelve.

case more than in the former, the public demanded that the grain price be fixed at a level within general reach.

In all these riots and *émotions*, women played a strikingly prominent role. "Women distinguished themselves the most" in these events, noted Dupont dryly.[62] They led the assault on merchant storehouses in the fall of 1765 at Auray in Brittany. In November 1765 most of the participants in a mutiny near Abbeville aimed at preventing the removal of grain were women, some of whom carried knives. During the following year, women led similar riots near Amiens and at Tonnerre. In 1767 a large gathering of women marched against the *laboureurs* of Montlhéry, women excited the crowd to action against the exporters at Provins, and a "seditious" band of females with rocks hidden under their aprons invested the marketplace at La Ferté-Gaucher. A woman detonated an anti-export riot at Troyes in June 1767 which mobilized several thousand people; according to one report, all sixty persons arrested in the rising were women. The "movement" which led to the pillaging of the grain storehouses at Rouen in March 1768, a witness reported, "was caused almost uniquely by women." At St. Brieuc in Brittany, women tried to burn the vessels preparing to sail abroad with cargoes of grain. At Belleville, women formed barricades to obstruct the passage of grain convoys. An "assembly of women" at Compiègne in the summer of 1768 did not disband until troops arrived while at Bléré and Châlons authorities reported that the women were the most difficult group to appease. In the course of the next two years women captured grain wagons at Dijon and diverted them to the *halle*, cut the wheels off the carts at Auxonne to halt outbound traffic, thwarted the departure of a grain ship at Boulogne, and caused tumultuous disorder at the markets of Dammartin, Lagny, and St. Germain. At Vitry-le-François a woman sparked a riot by assaulting the lieutenant of police to whom the crowd assigned ultimate responsibility for the dearth.[63]

---

62 Dupont, *Analyse ... Rapport*, 105.
63 IN. of Brittany to SD Dumener, 16 Sept. 1765, C. 1679 A.D. I-et-V.; IN. of Amiens to CG, 20 Nov. 1765, BN, Coll. Joly 1131, fols. 7–8; Jan. 1766, Coll. Joly 1133, fols. 9–16; 12 Nov. 1766, *ibid.*, fols. 175–176; 4 June 1767, Coll. Joly 1135, fols. 130–131; 6 Oct. 1767, *ibid.*, fol. 225; 2 June 1767, Coll. Joly 1136, fols. 175ff; Paillot to PG, 19 June 1767, C. 1908, A.D. Aube; Lettres Ossolinski, 28 March 1768, BHVP, ms. 625, fol. 127; 1 June 1768, Coll. Joly 1140, fols. 57–58; 10 June 1768, *ibid.*, fol. 170; Hardy's Journal, 5 June 1768, BN, mss. fr. 6680, fol. 165; IN. of Champagne to Bertin, 25 July 1768, C. 413, A.D. Marne; Armier to CG, 18 June 1768, C. 94, A.D. I-et-L.; Bacalan to Langlois, June 1769, AN, F¹²* 153; CG to Amelot, 15 May 1770, *ibid.*, fol. 211; CG to First President, Dijon Parl., 19 May 1770, *ibid.*, fol. 213; CG to Amelot, 20 May 1770, *ibid.*; 23 July 1770, BN, Coll. Joly 1149,

Undaunted by the fear of violent confrontation, these bands of women never hesitated to back their demands with force. But they were furies who sought a primitive justice, as they construed it, of a material and distributive sort rather than an exemplary vengeance. They often pillaged but just as frequently they offered a price for the merchandise they appropriated. On occasion the women brutalized officials and traders, but they were rarely wantonly cruel. It would be absurd to characterize their riots as orderly but as a rule they did not produce more violence than was necessary to achieve the goals which the women had announced at the outset, unless there was unusual provocation. What transformed a grain-directed demonstration of women at Troyes in 1767 into a punitive raid on the personal property of a wealthy bourgeoise was the latter's tender suggestion that "if they [the insurgents] had no bread with which to nourish their children they had only to eat them." The episode at Metz in 1774 in which a group of women slaughtered the keeper of the grain warehouse and threatened the intendant Calonne with the same fate was exceptional.[64]

The generous participation of women in these riots made a deep impression on local authorities. They took it as a sign of the gravity of the situation; in their minds, it gave the risings a certain legitimacy. Only very powerful forces of fear and misery could draw women from the hearth to the crossroads and marketplaces. Women, remarked Mercier, have become noted for their part in Parisian insurrections: "but it is necessary first that the Halles be concerned, otherwise they remain

---

fols. 123–24; CG to Bertier de Sauvigny, 1 Aug. 1770 and CG to La Vrillière (St. Florentin), 9 Aug. 1770, AN, F¹² 153; Aug. 1770, BN, Coll. Joly 1150, fols. 33–36; Lettres Ossolinski, Oct. 1770, BHVP, ms. 628, fol. 93; 6 Nov. 1770, Coll. Joly 1111, fol. 141; 6 Nov. 1770, Joly 1153, fol. 25.

According to a contemporary witness, women took a major part in the Flour War revolts of May 1775. "As we all know," he added, "[women] are more dangerous than men in these sort of crises." François Métra, *Correspondance secrète, politique et littéraire* (London, 1787–90; reprint Geneva, 1967), I, 321 (3 May 1775). For other subsistence risings in which women played a decisive role, see A. P. Usher, *The History of the Grain Trade in France, 1400–1710* (Cambridge, Mass., 1913), 310; Herlaut, "La Disette de pain à Paris en 1790," *Mémoires de la Société de l'Histoire de Paris*, XLV (1918), 10, 13; "Chronique" (20 Feb. 1743), *Revue rétrospective*, V (1834), 240; Letaconnoux, *Bretagne*, 326; G. Dumay, ed., *Une Émeute à Dijon en 1775* (Dijon, 1886), 19, 21; Guy Lemarchand, "Les Troubles de subsistances dans la généralité de Rouen," *Annales historiques de la révolution française*, 35th year (Oct.–Dec. 1963), 401–27; Max Beloff, *Public Order and Popular Disturbances, 1660–1714* (Oxford, 1928); J.-P. Gutton, *La Société et les pauvres* (Paris, 1970), 87.

64 Paillot to IN. of Champagne, 1 July 1767, C. 1908, A.D. Aube; Hardy's Journal, Oct. 1774, BN, mss. fr. 6681, fol. 425.

calm." In the disturbances provoked by parlementary affairs, "they don't sound a word." For an official in the Touraine the participation of women in a riot in the summer of 1768 was proof itself that "the people are dying of hunger." One woman whom he questioned went to five bakeshops without finding any bread. "This will make many people thieves despite themselves," he glumly predicted.[65]

Moheau, the pioneer demographer and sociologist, was not surprised that "women are more audacious and enterprising than men" in popular risings:

> different reasons have been given for it; but there is one which is constant and appreciable, it is that they are more wretched.

Moheau was more interested in describing and accounting for their general condition—exploitation by convention and discrimination by law founded on "a ridiculous and atrocious division of function"—than in pinpointing the factors which mobilized them to collective action.[66] Too little is known about the social composition of these groups of women to warrant conjecture about their precise motives. It is not clear if they were predominantly wage-earners themselves, if they were married or single, if they were housewives and mothers as well as partial providers, and if they participated with the approbation and support of their husbands, brothers, fathers, and sons. The authorities tended to concede that in times of suffering and hunger, the women had an imperious responsibility to fulfill.

In most of the cases the rioters, men and women, blamed their distress first of all on the merchant: anyone engaged, professionally or opportunistically, in the traffic of grain. The fact that the harvest might be patently bad or the supply notoriously short in a given area no more justified the maneuvers of the traders than it made the concomitant rise in prices palatable. In the popular etiology of dearth, the naturalistic or supernaturalistic explanation—some form of divine wrath and/or meteorological accident—was never by itself sufficient. Even in the midst of obvious scarcity, the consumers of each village, bourg, and town stubbornly believed that if the grain "of the place" were properly used and honestly apportioned, there would be enough, albeit barely, for everyone at prices which would be onerous but accessible.

---

65 Mercier, *Tableau de Paris*, XII, 136; Armier to IN., 18 June 1768, C. 94, A.D. I-et-L.

66 Moheau, *Recherches et considérations sur la population de la France* (1778), ed. by R. Gonnard, *Collection des économistes*, No. 10 (Paris, 1912), 282–83.

Dearth was testing time for the merchant when he could not hide his true intentions as he passed before the citizenry sitting as an ad hoc vigilance committee. It was perfectly reasonable to hold the merchant accountable in the midst of *cherté* when the whole community stood at his mercy, for in ordinary times he largely escaped scrutiny and rarely failed to profit from his relative inconspicuousness. What passed for shrewd trading in normal periods became immoral and culpable speculation during a moment of stress. The public accused the merchants of removing or "exporting" grain with regard only to their own profit and of withholding it and exchanging it clandestinely in order to drive up prices and sap the will of the community.

In September 1765 crowds at Auray and Vannes beset traders who made substantial purchases for the purpose of diverting it for sale elsewhere. At Bourges toward the end of the year the populace denounced the merchants to the authorities as "jobbers." In several towns in the Brie late in 1767 "the people, imagining that the merchants were cause of the augmentation of prices, hurled themselves against those who do this trade or whom they suspected of doing it [and] roughed them up very gravely...." In the summer of 1768 at Abbeville the populace seized a grocer rumored to be "a hoarder and starver of the people." At Beaufort the crowd threatened to administer summary punishment to a grain merchant who came to pick up grain he had purchased on commission. At Bléré the inhabitants marched against "several foreign merchants"—strangers to the land, men who did not usually deal in the area, aroused passionate hostility—who allegedly siphoned off supplies before they reached the local market. A brawl broke out "between the people and the traders" at the market of Mamers, the former forcing the latter to unload their horses and empty their sacks. Amidst rumors of hoarding and maneuvers, a crowd at Châlons-sur-Marne besieged the homes of several grain traders, breaking windows and "demanding bread in a great outcry." Consumers at St. Dizier, also in Champagne, threatened in 1770 to burn the storehouse of one of the town's biggest export merchants if he did not "abandon [his] grain at the discretion of the people." At the same moment a "troop of people" at Reims invaded merchant storehouses as well as conventual granaries in search of hoards. Nocturnal transport, like the presence of strangers, seemed *prima facie* proof of wrongdoing. At Montereau, in the spring of 1768, the tocsin sounded in response to the news that several merchants were removing stocks under the cover of dark:

That caused a sensation among the inhabitants of the place who assembled in force but several shots fired by the conductors of the convoy forced them to withdraw.[67]

The rioters ascribed their suffering to the avid, profiteering merchants, but ultimately they held the public authorities responsible for the irregular and threatening situation.[68] When spontaneous and direct pressure upon the traders failed to win tangible, immediate redress, the insurgents expected the police to intervene. Indeed, some of the *émotions* seemed to have aimed not so much at humbling the merchants as at making a point to the constabulary and providing it with a pretext for action. The grain riot was not always or exclusively an act of desperate frustration; it was a primitive political gesture, the only form of expression available to the bulk of consumers, and its demands were usually modest and straightforward: the constant availability of grain (or bread) at a price within the means of the majority of the laboring poor. The riot involved certain risks, but they were not entirely unpredictable and if they frequently seemed worth taking it was because more often than not they resulted in an improvement in the collective lot of the village or town. In the most favorable circumstances, the police would preempt or dissipate the riot by requisitioning supplies and/or readjusting the price of grain as a measure of general interest and social control founded on the vague but widely shared premise that private property had public obligations. In the most adverse situations, local authorities, almost invariably aided and goaded by outside hands, would crush the rising with a smart display of rigor generally followed by a program of appeasement and containment geared primarily to satisfy subsistence needs and only incidentally to protect the liberty and property of the suppliers.

In the sixties the riot often became a medium of collaboration between the police and the people. In some instances the police

---

67 IN. of Brittany to CG, 17, 20 Sept. 1765 and SD Dubodan to IN., 18 Sept. 1765, C. 1670, A.D. I-et-V.; CG to Rouillé, 10 July 1770, AN, F^{12} 153; Lieutenant of police and *échevins* to IN., 12 July 1770, C. 414, A.D. Marne; De Saint-Père to Joly, 10 April 1768, BN, Coll. Joly 1142, fol. 6. Cf. the intendant of Champagne's repeated complaint against indiscriminate "removals." To CG, 20 June 1767, C. 1908, A.D. Aube. For the other sources for this paragraph, see above, note number 60.

68 E. P. Thompson has brilliantly described a similar attitude on the part of English consumers in terms of a still regnant "moral economy." See "The Moral Economy of the English Crowd in the 18th Century," *Past & Present*, 50 (Feb. 1971), 76–136. In this same regard, Martin Needler's "representational" violence category is extremely suggestive. *Political Development in Latin America: Instability, Violence and Evolutionary Change* (New York, 1968), 46–55.

responded rapidly to signals from the people and together they were able to avert bloody confrontations. This sort of joint undertaking developed out of what might be called the "pre-riot." The pre-riot was more than the mere premonition of a disturbance (though the police, as we shall remark, used the putative fear or prospect of revolt as a justification for intervention), but less than a full-dress upheaval mobilizing large numbers of people for the performance of violent actions. It was the first stage of a riot that achieved its aims precociously and smothered on its success. Its most commonly denounced symptoms were incendiary speeches and seditious "bruits," unusual public gatherings, individual acts of exemplary defiance meant to inspire collective emulation, etc. At this critical point the police took dramatic steps designed to reassure the people and improve the subsistence situation. Some officials may indeed have welcomed the pre-riot—or, as their critics charged, perhaps even incited or organized it—for it afforded them a relatively inexpensive opportunity to take decisive action under the cover of emergency authority.

Thus, for example, a pre-riot at Chartres in January 1768 led the police to commandeer supplies from millers and mealmen. In the "critical circumstance" of the fall of 1768, which found the market of Brie-Comte-Robert barren, the royal procurator "believed that in order to prevent a popular rising he had to order and publish that grain would be drawn from the storehouses, which was done, and it was observed immediately that the market increased by more than thirty *muids* which not only checked the considerable augmentation of price which would have taken place but even caused it to fall somewhat." Later that year the authorities at Montargis in similar circumstances forced merchants to appear on the market. At Bar-sur-Aube in May 1770 the police and the people together prevented the removal of grain earmarked for Besançon. Not long afterward in the Bordelais the officers of Libourne, moved by the "desperation" of the people, visited private granaries in search of supplies, enjoined merchants to declare stocks, "and opposed the circulation of grain passing through their city." Simultaneously at Reims, in view of growing signs of disorder, the authorities met in a "general assembly of police" which placed a de facto embargo on grain outflow, took steps leading to requisition, and organized public purchases and charitable distributions. This pre-riot ended in an outburst of joyful relief and fraternization: "the people and the lowest people gathered in a crowd around the police commissaires and universally applauded the measures taken by the general assembly."

Though the anti-dearth measures in all these cases were announced in the name of the police, their striking feature was that they were the fruit of some sort of common undertaking with consumers. The victims of such action pointedly denounced the league between the police and the people. The intendant of the Orléanais, despite his sympathy for frustrated officials and hungry citizens, warned his superiors of the dangers of tolerating a situation in which the people, "upheld by the police," virtually made subsistence policy.[69]

The most common type of complicity between the police and the people in the riots of the sixties and seventies was *taxation populaire*, or collective price-fixing, a fugitive social contract ratified openly in the marketplace. In response to popular demands for a just price, often backed by violent demonstrations, the authorities declared a fixed price at which all grain offered for sale or captured and brought to market would be distributed, usually for cash, though credit arrangements were occasionally made. Sometimes the police took the lead in assigning the price, mobilizing supplies, and supervising distribution; when, in other instances, the people took the initiative, intercepted grain, announced a price, and organized the sales, the police intervened merely to confirm faits accomplis. Less frequently, price-fixing took the form of a negotiated transaction in which suppliers, under pressure, ceded to consumer demands, tempered by police mediation, by lowering their prices significantly in what amounted to a ransom paid in the hope of salvaging their well-being and most of their property.[70]

In June 1767 a riot erupted at La Ferté-Gaucher, a market-town near Provins in the Paris provisioning zone. "The people are persuaded," reported the *substitut*, that the increase [in the price] of wheat was caused only by the grain merchants, factors, millers, and *blatiers*. "In this occasion," he continued, "I believed I had to [on the one hand] placate the anger of the people and on the other protect the life of these unfortunates who are perhaps innocent ... and in consequence I forced the *laboureurs* to give wheat for the price I fixed."[71] Next month, not far away

---

69 Ordonnance, 5 Jan. 1768, B. 3958, fol. 47, A.D. E-et-L.; royal procurator to PG, 1 Oct. 1768, BN, Coll. Joly 1146, fols. 28–29; Cypierre to T. de Montigny, 2 Nov. 1768 published by C. Bloch, *Correspondance inédite de l'intendant Cypierre*, 147; Laroi to IN. of Champagne, 11 May 1770, C. 299; A.D. Aube; procurator Lesbarat to IN. of Bordeaux, Aug. 1770 and Terray to same, 21 July 1770, C. 1431, A.D. Gir.; Lieutenant of police to IN. of Champagne, 12 July 1770, C. 414, A.D. Marne.

70 See, for example, the riots at Bléré and Châlons-sur-Marne in the summer of 1768. Fiscal procurator to IN. of Touraine, 18 June 1768, C. 94, A.D. I-et-L. and IN. of Champagne to Bertin, 25 July 1768, C. 413, A.D. Marne.

71 BN, Coll. Joly 1135, fols. 130–32.

at Crécy-en-Brie, "revolt was ready to break out." To calm the agitation, the lieutenant general of police visited the market personally and promised to have suppliers deliver grain in priority to the consumers of the community at a "reasonable price."[72]

On a Sunday night in the late spring at Troyes, following a week in which little grain appeared on the market and bread prices rose substantially, a small crowd intercepted a grain convoy leaving the city for Burgundy. Guards protecting the wagons were beaten and the grain was placed by collective decision "in depot" in a nearby inn. Their ranks quickly swelled by hundreds of newcomers, the rioters led a torch-lit march on the houses of dealers and of "bourgeois" known for speculation and for maintaining stocks. Though some grain was pillaged, witnesses testified that the "largest quantity [was] removed and put in storage in the inns to be sold on the market." Apparently the police did not appear on the scene that night. Their critics charged that "they hid themselves out of fear," but the authorities claimed that they were simply overwhelmed by thousands of "artisans" rendered "furious" by "the fear of famine." The next day, as the rioters continued to draw fresh recruits and multiply their expeditions against granaries, the mayor and the police officers joined the riot, putting themselves "at the head of the people in order to calm them [and] tolerating despite themselves some acts of violence in order to prevent far greater ones." The police placed the seized grain for sale at almost 50 percent below what had been the current price and lowered bread by six *deniers* the pound. The police, not the people, broke down the doors of the shops of several bakers who refused to yield to the new schedule and led the crowd to the storehouses of several suspected hoarders in order to force the sale of their grain at the fixed price.[73]

Shortly afterward at Corbeil, an important entrepôt in the Paris hinterland, "a crowd of people" shouting for wheat converged on the market where "there was not a single grain" to be found. The problem here was more delicate than elsewhere because Corbeil served as the major storage center for king's grain destined to aliment the Paris Halles. Marching to the royal magazines, the crowd threatened to "pillage and remove the grain by force." The royal manager offered to sell them grain at a price the rioters deemed too high and of a quality that they found suspect.

---

72 *Ibid.*, fols. 85–86.
73 Patris (?) to IN. of Champagne, 2, 3 June 1767; municipality to IN., 2 June 1767; Paillot to IN., 9 June, 1 July 1768, C. 1908, A.D. Aube.

The police authorities intervened, "and the Public having asked to set the tax," they convoked an expert, a local miller "well regarded in this city," to set an honest value. The miller reported what the going price had been at nearby markets, found the quality of the royal grain to be significantly inferior, and recommended a price that satisfied the police and the public but enraged the manager of the Corbeil stockhouses.[74]

According to the royal procurator of Meaux in the summer of 1770, the combined effect of the prolonged dearth and "a vice of commerce" which diverted grain from the market was "terrible." The gaping "disproportion" between need and supply was "breaking up the households of workers and country folk," reducing honest men to mendicancy, and threatening to provoke a wave of crime. Every day more and more people milled about the marketplace aimlessly and uneasily. One morning in the third week of July a horde of hungry consumers "made themselves masters of the sale and of the price of the grain." Obviously sympathetic to the crowd, the procurator coolly described the posture assumed by the authorities:

> Thus despite all the coordinated attention and vigilance of the police, the *maréchaussée* [the rural gendarmerie] and the subdelegate [of the intendant], it was necessary, while appearing to command, to cede to the populace and engage the grain-sellers to give their goods at forced discounts in order to prevent pillage.[75]

Throughout the Brie "considerable seditions" erupted in which "the people forced the *laboureurs* to sell them grain at a price they set themselves." Failure to placate "this famished people," noted the fiscal procurator of Faremoutiers, might have produced a "bloody revolt." Several months later, at St. Germain-en-Laye on the other side of the capital, "to put a stop to the tumult," the police commissaire distributed flour "at the price which the mutineers demanded."[76]

Consumers viewed price-fixing not as a concession but as a right which the force of circumstances periodically authorized them to invoke, a concrete disposition of the right to existence which it was the state's business to guarantee. Doubtless many police officials shared this belief (indeed, many critics of the police charged that they inculcated it, often for unworthy motives). Other officials resorted to

---

74 BN, Coll. Joly 1135, fols. 60–63.
75 Canelle to PG, 21 July 1770, BN, Coll. Joly 1151, fols. 55–56.
76 Cordenier to PG, 23 July 1770, *ibid.*, fols. 52–53; BN, Coll. Joly 1111, fol. 141; Coll. Joly 1153, fols. 25–26; Coll. Joly 1156, fols. 14–15.

price-fixing because it was an accepted, traditional emergency measure which could be practiced exceptionally "without establishing precedent" and because it was a relatively simple, rapid, and inexpensive vehicle of social control. It was not, however, a remedy for all occasions. To be successful, price-fixing had to be applied relatively early in the course of a disturbance by agents in whom the public had confidence. In a number of cases an angry or suspicious crowd spurned tardy offers of official arbitration or, moved by other subsistence grievances, rejected the set price solution as inadequate or irrelevant. Nor was price-fixation of much use either in a situation of near-absolute grain scarcity or one in which the impoverished and the unemployed, with virtually no means to buy, composed the mass of the population at risk. Unless it was accompanied by a willingness to mobilize suppliers and pursue them, if necessary, into their grain redoubts, price-fixing could prove to be positively harmful even in the short run. Imposed in a heavy-handed manner, it could drive away frightened traders and desolate the marketplace. Imperceptibly, fixation could lead to a policy of intense local protectionism which could seriously disrupt commerce, inconveniencing neighbors, provoking retaliatory embargoes and boycotts, and compromising the flow of grain toward the metropolitan market.

It would be extravagant to pretend that as a rule the authorities collaborated with or capitulated to the crowd. The actions of authorities depended on a congeries of factors: the season of the year; the size of the market and its location; the experience of the officials; the nature of their public posts and their private interests; their attitude toward liberalization; their relationship with the public; the armed forces at their disposal; their assessment of the significance of the disturbance, the mood of the insurgents, and the validity of popular demands; the conduct of the suppliers; the prospects for relief; and the likely reaction of their superiors. In the late sixties the police seem to have resorted to price-fixing with remarkable frequency; in some instances they clearly relished the opportunity to take the initiative and impose a solution.

Yet it must not be forgotten that there were also cases where the police tried energetically to forestall price-fixing, where the consumers wrested their price by force rather than by collusion, and where the fixed price was the trophy of a pyrrhic victory which the authorities allowed the people to claim only as a balm for their wounds. At Vannes in 1765 the police conceded a fixed tariff to the crowd at the market (possessed by "a spirit of vertigo") reluctantly and only until they were able to organize an armed repression. Similarly, in the summer of 1768 at Châlons-sur-Marne and at Bléré in the Touraine, the rioters extorted the price by violence and intimidation. Two years later at Rebais, an important Brie market, the clamor for price-fixation was muffled as a direct result of the presence of outside forces interposed by order of the intendant in conjunction with the Controller-General. Forewarned of the danger of "movements on the subject of the rising prices of grain," Bertier de Sauvigny dispatched a detachment of troops to the town. A former soldier named Rousselot presented a demand that "a price be put on the grain." Asked to identify himself and explain his behavior,

> he replied only with invectives and challenged [the troops] to put him in prison in the hope of being supported by the populace which appeared at the instant to give itself over to murmurs and even to threats; but the officer commanding the troops having arrested him and ordered his soldiers to load their arms, this firm stand contained the people.

Ostensibly because he distrusted local justice and wanted "to make a more prompt example" of this crime, the intendant requested a *lettre de cachet* to incarcerate Rousselot in the Parisian prison of Bicêtre.[77]

IV

The local police officials in the field did not conceal their uneasiness over the deepening subsistence crisis and their misgivings about government policy. Significantly, they did not focus upon harvest failure as the primary source of unrest, although there was considerable empirical evidence to support such an hypothesis and the allure of a clinical explanation which largely absolved human agencies from responsibility. Nor did the central government betray any interest on this line of analysis, not at least until the end of the decade, for a public admission of disaster would have been hard to reconcile with its determination to pursue liberalization. The immediate causes to which the local police ascribed the upheavals of the sixties were abrupt grain exports and removals, bristling resentment against grain traders, prolonged penury, misery, and high prices. But they also described a general state of mind, a pervasive and terrible anxiety—they called it an "agitation" or

---

77 IN. of Brittany to CG, 17 Sept. 1765, C. 1670, A.D. I-et-V.; royal procurator of Bléré to IN., 18 June 1768, C. 94, A.D. I-et-L.; IN. of Champagne to Bertin, 25 July 1768, C. 413, A.D. Marne; CG to La Vrillière, 28 July 1770, AN, F¹² 153, fol. 377.

"fermentation"—and a state of socioeconomic anarchy, both of which they linked to the new liberal regime.

The dismantling of the regulatory apparatus worried, baffled, and sometimes shocked these administrators. Very few of them simply turned their backs on the new legislation, although it was often tempting and prudent to claim ignorance. Rather, they confronted it, tried to deal with it, and found that it provoked for them a crisis of conscience as well as one of authority. For it seemed perilous and wrong-headed to undermine the public order and well-being by abandoning the grain trade to a concourse of self-interests. Despite its imperfections, the old system created for the community a semblance of solidarity and a sense of accountability and it frequently managed to reduce the margin of unpredictability and temper the consequences of accidents. Now wheat that habitually furnished a given market succumbed to strange blandishments. New dealers proliferated in grain commerce, brandishing the liberal code as if it were a special royal patent, thereby exacerbating the standard dearth-syndrome fears of plots and maneuvers. Ordinary people, with neither criminal proclivities nor anti-social motives, rose up in insurrection. A refrain of frustration and anomie arose from the police, chanted by the intendant as well as the fiscal procurator of the bourg: "our hands are tied"—what should we do?[78] Many of the disturbances of the sixties were police as well as popular revolts, riots for rather than against an apparently dated version of the *chose publique*. In this sense popular behavior and administrative attitude constituted the foundations of a grassroots movement for the recall of the reform measures of 1763 and 1764.

Though a cynical observer might suggest that they were merely contriving pretexts to justify their disobedience, many local authorities appear to have viewed the liberal laws with genuine incredulity. Like the people, the police had certain expectations and beliefs about the conduct of government. There were certain steps which they simply could not believe that the government—personified in their minds by the king himself—would take. "If, by the declaration of 1763," the fiscal procurator of Châtillon-sur-Loire wrote his intendant, "the King seems to have given commerce a certain liberty that it did not have heretofore, *His intention surely was not* to strip the police officers *of the right* they have to prevent grain from being sold anywhere but in the public marketplaces ... the sole precaution

---

78 Dronay to PG, 14 Sept. 1766, BN, Coll. Joly 1134, fols. 197–98.

capable of procuring abundance in the markets and, consequently the *just price* of grain." Similarly, the acting royal procurator at Montargis rejected as "a false interpretation" of liberalization the claim the traders made that the new laws authorized off-market transactions. These were "abuses" which were certainly "contrary to the intentions of His Majesty," for Louis XV "had no less in view [the aim] of providing for the provisioning of the markets and the needs of His people" than of "favoring commerce." A subdelegate in the Hainaut, despite a mass of contrary evidence, persisted in believing that "the intention of His Majesty was never to alter the general police established to procure abundance...."[79]

Departing from the same assumptions as his colleagues in the Orléanais, a Beauce procurator composed an interpretive brief in which he contended that the reform laws did not grant as much liberty as everyone pretended. "The Declaration of 1764 [*sic*]" he argued, "gives liberty of commerce, but it does not give that of buying and of selling grain clandestinely, in the cabarets, on a mere sample."[80] Though in fact the liberal laws authorized all these practices, it was inconceivable to the procurator that this could be. Groping to make sense of the events which were threatening to engulf their community, the municipal officers of Châlons-sur-Marne wishfully predicted that liberalization could not last much longer because it was so violently at odds with the functions of kingship. "It is still true," they reassured themselves, "that the King is the common father to his subjects and that His heart is revolted by the idea that a part of those who have the good fortune to live under His laws be exposed to lacking bread by the impossibility of meeting the price to which grain would be carried by the continuation of exports."[81]

The most common sentiment expressed by the local officials was a mixture of confusion and helplessness. Convinced that there was a mistake in the legislation which could be administratively rectified, that the central authorities lacked information about the true state of affairs, or that, as in the past, exceptions would be readily made to accommodate local peculiarities, they besieged the Procurator General

---

79 Cypierre to T. de Montigny, 18 Oct. 1768 and Montargis police register, Oct. 1768 in C. Bloch, *Correspondance inédite de l'intendant Cypierre*, 135–138, 153–155; SD at Valenciennes to IN., 22 July 1770, C. 6690, A.D. Nord.

80 Procurator of Angerville-la-Gaste to PG (ca. 1770), BN, Coll. Joly 1148, fol. 65. Police officials often confused the Declaration of May 1763 with the Edict of July 1764. Viewing them as parts of a single measure, they tended to overlook (or disdain) distinctions made between internal and external liberty.

81 Châlons municipality to Laverdy, 29 Dec. 1767, C. 413, A.D. Marne.

of the Paris Parlement or their intendants with petitions for clarification and precise instructions. In the fall of 1766 the lieutenant general of police at Vitry-le-François painted a gloomy picture of his town's provisioning situation. A host of merchants descended upon the market, stripping it bare; others prowled the countryside, buying, hoarding, and driving prices up. He complained that the Declaration of 1763, by introducing freedom of trade everywhere, crippled him. Within the terms of the law, he could do nothing, but he knew exactly the sort of measures the circumstances demanded:

> I dare not undertake anything without the authority of My Superiors; consequently, I have the honor of supplicating Your Grandeur to please authorize me to have a sufficient quantity of grain brought to the market to be sold to the people...."

To underline the urgency of the request—it was as close as a petty official could come to threatening the highest authorities—the lieutenant characterized the public mood as combustible: "already underhand cabals are forming which menace fire, mutilation of [grain and flour] sacks, and obstruction of the departure of grain from this city."

Four years later the situation had not substantially changed. Without effective powers of police, the city officials could do nothing to allay misery or prevent revolt. Faced with an "extremely urgent" predicament, the royal procurator, in a laborious letter, asked Joly de Fleury for authorization to use old-fashioned constraints, boldly hinting that whatever his response the force of circumstances would compel the city fathers to defy the liberal regime:

> We will soon be reduced to having no more bread if you do not have the kindness to support the officers of police. We cannot do otherwise than to interdict the transport of grain; we no longer have any choice. In 1768 the Parlement overturned a Sentence of the lieutenant of Police of this city which condemned to a fine several individuals who had refused to bring grain to the market. *We respect the arrêt without being able to understand it.* Nevertheless, Monseigneur, we cannot take any other course, we are forced to do it in order to avoid some excess of the people.[82]

In 1767 the police at Mantes told the Procurator General that they no longer knew how to fulfill their functions. Liberalization seriously dislocated commercial exchanges in this busy market port. In execution of the laws, the police suspended prohibitions on buying, selling, and regrating, a throng of newcomers entered the grain trade, and

---

82 Deballidart to PG, 6 July 1770, BN, Coll. Joly 1152, fol. 175.

consumers lost the right to satisfy their needs before the merchants entered the market. Persuaded that the *cherté* and misery of the times were a direct result of the new system, the Mantes authorities wanted to know if there were any loopholes in the reform laws. Are all "prosecutions of evil-doers forbidden?" they inquired.[83] The liberal laws perplexed the lieutenant general of Dreux. Have they changed all the old rules and definitions? he wondered. Does the "great liberty" of 1763 permit the purchase and resale of grain at the same market, a price-swelling practice rigorously prohibited according to traditional ways? Do I treat men who commit such abuses as "Monopolists"? queried the lieutenant.[84] Do we understand correctly, asked the municipality of Angers, that "according to the current System of the Council it must no longer be a question [for the police] of taking measures to assure the subsistence of the people?"[85]

The fiscal procurator of Tournan in the Brie testified to the success of liberalization from the point of view of the suppliers. "Ever since the Declaration of the King which allows freedom of trade," he reported, "all the merchants, *blatiers*, and regraters have believed themselves to be authorized to no longer follow the regulations of police...." In order to parry the dearth the procurator argued that it was "of an indispensable necessity" to enforce those rules.[86] Although he understood that it was a "delicate matter," the procurator of another Brie town wanted to know in writing whether, in order to maintain public order, he could (1) compel merchants and *laboureurs* to supply the market, (2) visit and inspect the storehouses of dealers, and (3) fix the price of grain.[87] A Breton subdelegate warned of serious disorders unless the police were rearmed to combat the "avarice" to which the new laws have given a "total freedom."[88] Independently, a *bailli* and a subdelegate in Champagne urged the resuscitation of the 1723 Declaration banning trading outside the markets; they saw no other way to deal with exorbitant prices, hoarding, and popular suffering, all consequences of liberalization.[89] Ganneron, royal procurator of Dammartin, a market near

---

83 Chedde to PG, 26 Sept. 1767, BN, Coll. Joly 1146, fols. 143–44.
84 LG of Dreux to PG, 9 Jan. 1769, *ibid.*, fols. 104–105.
85 Mémoire, 1769, C. 96, A.D. I-et-L.
86 Fiscal procurator of Tournan to PG, 22 Dec. 1770, BN, Coll. Joly 1155, fol. 18.
87 Cordenier (Faremoutiers-en-Brie) to PG, 23 July 1770, BN, Coll. Joly 1151, fols. 52–53.
88 Pravalon of Lannion to IN., 6 Oct. 1768, C. 1652, A.D. I-et-V.
89 Lenoir (Arcis-sur-Aube?) to IN., 25 Sept. 1766 and Masson to IN., 9 Sept. 1768, C. 299, A.D. Aube.

Paris, watched helplessly as the suppliers traded privately and irresponsibly, inflated the prices, and created a situation likely to produce "famine," crime, and unspeakable hardships. "Because the Declaration of the King binds my hands," he wrote, inviting Joly to untie him, "I can do nothing without new orders."[90]

The high station of Cypierre, intendant of the *généralité* of Orléans, gave him hardly more freedom of initiative than the petty provincial police. He also found his "hands tied" at the very moment that circumstances demanded energetic intervention.[91] Cypierre's case is instructive, for he was politically and ideologically sympathetic to the liberal cause and he had been among the first within the upper reaches of public administration to solicit exportation. In principle, he continued to favor liberty, but as the chief officer responsible for public order in his province, he could not accept the presumably short-run costs of transition from the old regime to the new. He wanted the freedom to temper liberty—at least momentarily—with the kinds of precautions geared to reestablish orderly and overt exchanges at the public markets.[92]

The boldest critics amongst the police spoke out forthrightly in condemnation of the liberal system. The new laws were social, economic, and political disasters. Bertinière, *substitut* at Melun, held them directly responsible for the extensive dearth and disorder: "The unhappy circumstance to which the people find themselves reduced by the brusque *cherté* of grain... is occasioned neither by the lack of grain nor of harvests but by the unique cupidity of evil-intentioned men who on the basis of the general liberty of this commerce buy at any cost in order to hoard." Since 1763 "the grain markets have been filled with nothing but unknown persons" who scour the countryside cornering harvest futures after plundering supplies in the towns. Disdainful of "this pretended liberty," Bertinière called for a return to the "sage dispositions" of old which served as a "brake" on self-interest and a barrier against dearth.[93] Little more than a year after the July Edict a Touraine municipality anxiously reported that prices had climbed 50% above pre-liberal levels, hoarding was widespread, and the markets deserted

---

90 Ganneron to PG, 18 June 1770, BN, Coll. Joly 1149, fols. 118–19.

91 Cited by C. Bloch, "Le Commerce des grains dans la généralité d'Orléans," *Etudes sur l'histoire économique de la France, 1760–1789* (Paris, 1900), 38. For a fuller discussion of Cypierre's thinking, see below, chapter five.

92 *Ibid.*, 36–53. Bloch insists on the "contradictions" in Cypierre's position without, however, trying to understand and explain it.

93 Bertinière to PG, 29 Sept. 1767, BN, Coll. Joly 1136, fols., 124–125.

as grain usually bound for the city drained instead to Nantes, apparently for export abroad. As a consequence the city fathers were ready to renounce "all the advantage" which the new regime promised.[94]

"The *cherté* of grain seems to me to have its origin in the dispositions of the edict of the month of July 1764," wrote the subdelegate of Avesnes in the Hainaut. The decisive test for him was that "the unlimited liberty accorded by this law has made more *malheureux* than *heureux*." The proof could be heard in "the general protest of the provinces," which resounded throughout the realm. Though he was unmistakably a moderate rather than a hothead, who appreciated the need to stimulate a "stagnant" agriculture and who "feared" both the "Scylla" and the "Charybdis" of administrative extremism, this subdelegate could not bring himself to approve the consequences of liberalization. "The frantic license, the avarice, and the cupidity" released by the liberal reforms, he contended, "have broken and shattered all the links and the chains which should naturally bind one part of the nation to the other, that is to say, the proprietors of the land, the cultivators, and the country-folk [on the one side] with the businessmen, the artisans, the workers [*ouvriers*], and the inhabitants of the towns and cities [on the other]." Even as it freed grain, the liberal legislation enslaved the majority of Frenchmen: "Three-quarters of the French nation has become within a year tributary to the other quarter." At least five other subdelegates in the Hainaut agreed with his analysis and demanded, along with him, that limits be placed on the liberty of the trade— limits which would concentrate grain in the markets and illuminate the activities of the traders and owners of subsistence.[95]

Among the adversaries of liberalization at the local police level were officials who had been buffeted by the "economic" winds of the sixties despite their distance from ministerial bureaus and philosophical salons and who had thought seriously about the implications of the reforming current. Viewing the decade in retrospect, Deniloy, a Picard subdelegate, recalled the optimism which the prospect of liberty had aroused even among administrators of his humble rank:

> Never had any law marshalled more good wishes than the declaration [*sic*] of 1764. It was supposed to change the face of agriculture; to procure for us the foreigner's gold by the export of our grain surplus; to revitalize trade ... and to carry abundance as far as the huts of the poor.

94 Mémoire to CG., Sept. 1765, C. 94, A.D. I-et-L.
95 "Réflexions sur l'édit du mois de juillet 1764...," ca. Oct. 1770, C. 6690, A.D. Nord; reports of the SDs of Valenciennes, Cambrai, St. Amand, etc., ca. Oct. 1773, *ibid.*

The results, however, "did not meet expectations." On the contrary, liberalization spelled ruin for "the mass of people." Prices had been "too low" before 1763–64, but soon afterwards they "broke the dike and rose without limits." The "new riches" produced by the swirling grain trade "remained in a small number of hands." For the common citizens, wages fell, unemployment spread, and "epidemics" followed hard upon "the horrors of dearth." To deal with this crisis, the police had to be given "a new life." Had we not lost sight of the essential quality of human nature, Deniloy reflected, we would never have succumbed to the allure of liberty, for "whoever knows the heart of man" will agree that "prohibitive laws are necessary."[96]

In contrast to his colleague from Picardy, Champassais, a subdelegate from the generality of Alençon, had been acutely skeptical of the liberal panacea from the start. "I never adopted the system" whose principles he learned about in "numerous brochures and writings," he recalled. "I foresaw from the very beginning," Champassais claimed, "the dangerous consequences [of liberalization] that we so unfortunately suffer today." Liberty made the grain trade socially "abusive" by "doubling and tripling" the price and thus causing "desperate misery" amongst the people, some of whom were forced to join the ranks of beggars or turn to crime in order to survive. This official had no doubt that only a swift return to the police regime could stem the tide of social disorganization.[97]

Deeply shocked by the consequences of liberalization and the apparent indifference of the government toward them, the royal procurator at Meulan confided in Joly de Fleury:

> I respect and I submit myself to its [the council's] decrees. *But as a good citizen I cannot keep silent* on the effects of the exportation of grain abroad [further along in the letter he makes it clear that he means "extraordinary removals" regardless of ultimate destination] which it was believed necessary to permit in order to encourage agriculture. But, Monseigneur, if this good results, we see that there is born in my opinion a real evil for the public in general.

After the "very abundant" harvest of 1766, everyone in the area agreed that the grain should not sell for more than 12 to 15 *livres* the *septier* (Paris measure). "Yet," reported the procurator "instead of diminishing after the harvest as it usually does, it has increased from one market-day to another." Under the new system, only the public stood to lose.[98]

---

96 Deniloy to IN., 2 Feb. 1772, C. 84, A.D. Somme.
97 Champassais to IN., 12 Oct. 1771, C. 89, A.D. Orne.
98 Royal procurator at Meulan to PG, 17 Oct. 1766, BN, Coll. Joly 1134, fols. 11–12. Italics mine.

For fiscal and other reasons local authorities rarely tended to overestimate their harvest yields, yet many officials in the sixties (and again in the seventies) reported reasonably satisfactory, or even good, crops in the midst of continuing subsistence crises. Nothing seemed to reveal more starkly the artificiality and the criminality of the dearth from which they suffered than the apparent co-existence of soaring prices and substantial supplies.[99] A cherished aim of the physiocrats, *cherté*-in-abundance, was a cruel and unacceptable paradox to the police and the people. It was proof that the shortage was the product of human evil and bad administration rather than unfathomable and intractable hazard. It was this paradox that infuriated the people and frequently drove them to resist. The police implied, for reasons that were in part self-serving, that the people would have been less inclined to violence had they not perceived themselves as victims of a moral and political wrong and conversely more disposed to some form of sullen resignation had the harvest been unequivocally bad and scarcity consequently authentic, inevitable and universal. Though subsistence stress blurs everyone's vision, it is not inconceivable, once we learn more about harvests and collective action on the local level, that we will find that people rioted more, and more violently, in areas where the harvest situation was *believed to be* reasonably good than in places where *natural* desolation was indisputable.

For certain officials the moral and political failure of liberalization was ultimately more compelling ground for objection than functional arguments bearing on social control and the public interest. In one way or another they acknowledged that the people had rights and claims vis-à-vis the government and vis-à-vis property-owners and that the liberal laws had trampled those rights and ignored those claims. From our perspective their stand might seem remarkably audacious or aberrant, for we are not accustomed to locating what appear to be the harbingers of sans-culottic ideology or the remnants of archaic communal solidarity in the lowest echelons of provincial administration in old-regime backwater France. But to the officials who espoused it this position was a commonplace perfectly in harmony with their

---

99 See, for example, the memoir (Dec. 1766) of the *élus généraux* of Burgundy: "The province of Burgundy experiences in a year in which the countryside produced an *abundant harvest* all the hardship of dearth and is on the brink of feeling the horror of famine." C. 3215, fols. 622–25, A.D. C d'O. Cf. Masson to IN. of Champagne, 9 Sept., 7 Oct. 1766, C. 299 and Patris to same, 2 June 1767, C. 1908, A.D. Aube; Deniloy to IN. of Amiens, 2 Feb. 1772, C. 84, A.D. Somme.

world. Like many other towns in the late sixties, Chartres suffered from excessively high prices, grain penury, and generalized "misery" which the municipal officials blamed on the license for "Monopoly" granted by the May Declaration. Even as the partisans of liberty had looked to nature for laws capable of freeing them from the constraints of the positive laws of traditional monarchy, so the police of Chartres invoked a higher law to justify their dissent. Though the May law explicitly rendered internal trade totally free, they argued that there were explicit bonds and obligations from which no piece of legislation could free men. Whatever the law stipulated, the liberty of May must "... always remain subject to the *rules of justice*, subordinated to the *rights of humanity*."[100] Abstract and threadbare to our eyes, this formula nevertheless comes closest to capturing the outraged mood of the consumers at the marketplaces. Put into practical terms by the Chartres police, it meant that they had the responsibility, and by logical extension the authority, to combat the abuse of an unchecked liberty which led to monopoly and then to misery.

In explaining popular disorders, authorities everywhere dwelled on the loathing consumers had to see "the grain naturally destined for their subsistence" slip out of their hands.[101] In the thinking of the subdelegate of Quimper in Brittany, the people had "rights" (*des droits*) over "commodities of first necessity," at least in times when "cherté" threatens to deprive them of their subsistence. "I would dare to say," he continued in a language that is clumsy yet unmistakable in meaning, "that whatever the functions which have regulated property might be, each individual is in the right to say that what is necessary to make up his subsistence cannot be renounced for him by someone else when he cannot procure it by dint of his own work alone." A perspicacious man, the subdelegate was alert to the implications of this doctrine which invested the propertyless with rights and placed limits on the rights of property and the propertied. "These maxims would be dangerous if they were spread among the people," he conceded, "but they are salutary and sacred in the cabinets of Princes and of the persons who govern."[102] That is to say, it was not up to the people themselves to

---

100 B. 3953, fol. 82 (2 Sept. 1768), A.D. E-et-L. My italics. Cf. the reaction of the *économistes*: Roubaud, *Représentations*, 107.

101 Cypierre to T. de Montigny, 1 Sept. 1768, in C. Bloch, *Correspondance inédite de l'intendant Cypierre*, 50. Cf. Masson to IN. of Champagne, 29 May 1770, C. 299, A.D. Aube.

102 Durun (Quimper) to IN., 11 Feb. 1772, C. 1725, A.D. I-et-V.

take consciousness of their rights and lay claim to them. In order to preserve the social order, it was the duty of the police to enforce these rights for the people, preemptively and without fanfare. Riots were evidence of police dereliction, for if the public administrators performed their duties properly, the citizenry would never find it necessary to revolt. Though crudely put, this subdelegate's argument anticipated the ideas of Necker and other exponents of government intervention in provisioning affairs. On the local level, it meant that the police had frequently to serve, in the words of a subdelegate from Champagne, as the "representative" of the people.[103]

By the end of 1768 the outcry of "misery" was universal. In the frontier areas, observed the duc de Croy, the people suffered more than they had in 1709, the memory of whose agonies served as an index of catastrophe for distant generations. "Brittany is abandoned to an all-embracing calamity and exposed to the torments of famine," wrote a commission of the Estates. Lillois compared their hardship to the more recent dearth of 1740 and, faced with serious disorder, the city fathers made "representations" against the liberal laws which "cannot be executed... without occasioning an extreme misery."[104] "How could a man who earns 15 or 16 sols a day," asked Trennin, an official at Versailles, "who only three years ago used 12 to furnish bread [for his family] and for whom today 24 is necessary, regard his condition tranquilly?" "You know, moreover," continued Trennin,

> how much I respect the laws: if a few words escape from me which seem opposed to what the government appears to have thought in 1764, do not accuse me, I beg you, of temerity.

---

103 Gehier (Bar-sur-Aube) to IN., 10 Jan. 1775, C. 299, A.D. Aube.

104 Duc de Croy, *Journal*, ed. by de Grouchy and Cottin, II, 302; Petition of Commissaires des Etats de Bretagne, 1 Oct. 1768, AN, H 543–45; Pierre Lefèvre, *Commerce des grains à Lille*, 53, 184–86. For reports of growing misery in the Hainaut and in Auvergne, see Taboureau to Laverdy, 1 Oct. 1767, C. 6690, A.D. Nord and officers of the bailliage of Aurillac to Moheau, 26 Aug. 1769, C. 906, A.D. P-de-D.

One of the most poignant expressions of desperation came to the surface in a complaint filed with the police by a miller named Jacques Collet from the Parisian suburb of Antony. In late November 1768 he received an anonymous note urging him to place several *septiers* of maslin in a specially prepared cache along a back road for a family plunged "in misery." The awkward hand and style and the phonetic spelling confirm its authenticity:

"Monsieur et madame Collet ge sont tras pauvre homme avec nos anfans et nos famme ge sont au dessespoire ge sont sant pain ... Sis vous voulay nous faire plaisir de nous avance chaqun un septies de Metaille ge vous seron bien oblige vous nous tiray de malleur ge pouvons pas voir mourire de fain nos anfans sis vous aves cet bonte pour nous ge prirons bondieu pour vous ge vous prion nous refusses par ge crain que ge srons pousse a mal fair." AN, Y 18668 (28 Nov. 1768).

Often laws which are the most advantageous in appearance by the motives which caused them to be promulgated, have need of *restrictions, explanations, or modifications.…*

Politically adept rather than merely deferential, Trennin understood the value of affecting a moderate tone. Yet the "modifications" and "restrictions" he sought were sweeping.

Trennin's recommendations could have served as a manifesto of the police reaction. He began with an unequivocal statement of indictment: "It is, however, to the abuses that this Edict [Trennin, like many other officials, assimilated the dispositions of both reform laws to the July Edict] occasioned that one can without lacking the respect due to the authority from which it emanated attribute the *cherté* which makes us groan." By abuses Trennin meant most of the rights with which the reforms had invested traders: the right of anyone to enter the commerce, to deal off the markets, to stock and speculate, to exchange grain without regard for public needs. The liberal laws inflamed the "insatiable avidity" of the dealers who, with "a copy of the Edict in hand," spread disorder wherever they go. Among the "precautions" urgently required, argued Trennin, "it is above all necessary *not* to stifle all the regulations of police which must be exercised on the markets in order to prevent monopoly." Specifically, he asked that "liberty of trade" be maintained on the condition that all dealers register their names, addresses, and location of storehouses; that merchants be forbidden to buy on their home market, a practice which drove up prices and created shortages; that *laboureurs* be prohibited from buying grain in order to resell; that the purchase of "futures" be forbidden; that "in order for exportation not to prejudice the subsistence of the inhabitants" a careful examination be made of the state of the preceding harvests and the prospects for the next and no decisions be reached before the end of the winter season; that the government substantially lower the ceiling above which exports would automatically halt, for the cut-off price became in effect the price of consumption and the current level of 30 *livres* the *septier* was far too high. In sum, voicing a demand seconded by scores of his colleagues throughout the kingdom, Trennin wanted the government to restore to the local police—the men who had to deal with the subsistence problem in the field—all the powers and responsibilities granted to them by "the ordinances anterior to 1763."[105]

---

105 Trennin to PG, 26 Oct. 1768, BN, Coll. Joly 1142, fols. 153–164. Cf. the tough demands of the Burgundy élus. Petition to IN., 26 Nov. 1770, C. 3363, fols. 73–74, A.D. Cd'O.

In a limited but significant way, Trennin's program was implemented from below by a growing number of officials who passed beyond expressions of bewilderment, admonition, and protest to direct action. In addition to price-fixing, the police in places widely scattered throughout the realm intervened by intercepting supplies on the road or preventing their departure from the town or village, requiring all transactions to occur exclusively on the marketplace under public scrutiny, imposing provisioning quotas on merchants or requiring them to appear regularly at the local market in return for permission to trade in the area, compelling dealers to register with authorities, inspecting granaries and private homes suspected of containing hoards, and conducting inventories of all grain held in storage.[106] In a few cases the authorities were constrained to act; they had no taste for bullying merchants or breaking the law. Delighting in their defiance, in a handful of contrasting instances the police staged theatrical entries upon the market-stage. The behavior of some administrators betrayed a bitter resentment over the fact that the liberal regime had undercut their authority to govern locally, without, however, relieving them of the obligation to maintain order.[107] Of the officials who stopped to ponder the significance of their actions, most appear, like Masson of Arcis-sur-Aube, to have suffered an enormous emotional strain and to have worried about their disobedience even when they were sure that what they were doing was necessary and right.[108] Yet the vast majority of interventions were singularly unspectacular and it may very well be that the bulk of the police who undertook them acted unselfconsciously and instinctively, as they always had in times of stress "from time immemorial," oblivious or indifferent to the new laws, like the commissaire of Nogent-le-Rotrou, the syndic of Montrésor, or the judge of Pompiez.[109] Many of them simply did not perceive or acknowledge a dissonance between their conception of their responsibilities and their coercive options on the one hand and the dictates of

---

106 Cypierre to T. de Montigny, 4 Nov. 1768 in C. Bloch, *Correspondance inédite de l'intendant Cypierre*, 151; *Gazette de l'agriculture, du commerce, des arts et des finances* (10 July 1770), 518; Terray to de la Galaizière, 10 July 1770, AN, F^{11} 153; CG to Turgot and CG to Lieutenant of Police of Angoulême, 10 April 1770, AN, F^{12} 154; *arrêts du Conseil* of 12, 19 Aug. 1770, AN, F^{12} 6; CG to IN. of Tours, 9 May 1770 and IN. to officers of Amboise, 11 May 1770, from the personal collection of the author.

107 Royal procurator to PG, 1 Oct. 1768, BN, Coll. Joly 1146, fols. 28–29.

108 Masson to IN. of Champagne, 29 May 1770, C. 299, A.D. Aube.

109 B. 2376, A.D. E-et-L.; Haberty to IN. (?), 4 Sept. 1765, C. 94, A.D. I-et-L.; Bouget to IN. of Bordeaux, 28 June 1770, C. 1431, A.D. Gir.

liberalization on the other. Certainly many of these officials were surprised the first time they received a reprimand from their superiors or notification that one of their sentences had been quashed by a higher jurisdiction.[110]

Given the niggardliness and the heterogeneity of the evidence, it is immensely difficult to generalize about police resistance. Though we have tried to take note of certain similarities of attitude and action which appear to constitute patterns, it was doubtless true in the sixties and seventies, as it was in the good and bad years of the preceding century, that the police of each place had its own peculiar character, that conditions varied widely from place to place depending upon a host of historical, geographical, economic, and sociodemographic variables, and that it is virtually impossible retrospectively to "predict" police conduct. Allowing for qualitative disparities and erratic and idiosyncratic behavior, can one adumbrate a rough chronology and geography of resistance? Police opposition to liberalization broke out as early as the fall of 1764 and in some places—in the south where the liberal regime endured the longest—it erupted as late as 1773–74. North of the Loire, areas close to the main channels of transportation seem to have experienced police dissidence earlier than the more isolated places; the police acted first where the "removals" first disrupted the ordinary train of life, rather than in the areas which suffered the earliest crop failures. Toward the end of the decade one can detect a demonstrator or emulation effect, a sort of contagion of defiance which induced more and more officials to take action. Resistance reached its collective peak in 1770 on the very eve of the end of liberalization, perhaps in anticipation of its demise, as the subsistence-economic crisis lurched to a head.

We know for certain that police resistance was astonishingly widespread, and this fact alone gives it great significance. On this point the exquisitely tendentious contemporary pamphlet and periodical literature, which has misled many historians, converges with a convincing assortment of more nearly neutral sources.[111] It is not yet clear, however, that resistance was sharpest where one might have expected it, i.e., in areas with the most trying subsistence problems, in places

---

110 See, for example, Laverdy to PG, 5 April 1768, BN, Coll. Joly 1142, fols. 56–58 and Petit, fiscal procurator of Rambouillet, to PG, 27 June 1768, *ibid.*, fols. 72–73. Cf. Ricommard, *Troyes*, 292–94.

111 For an example of the polemical literature, see *Gazette de l'agriculture, du commerce, des arts et des finances* (10 July 1770), 517–519 and (26 Jan. 1771), 59.

without relevant crisis experience, in river-towns, in metropolitan regions, etc. Though it seems true that its incidence was considerably lower, at least till the seventies, in the "liberal" segments of the realm (and if this is right, it is more likely to turn out to be a cause rather than a result of regional liberalism), there are no pronounced differences among the "overpopulated cereal lands of the north and east," the "*bocages* of the west," and the "specialized" wine, forest, coastal, and urban-hinterland areas.[112] As a rule, it appears the resistance was easier in the smaller towns and villages than in the major cities (though the Rouen Parlement protected the municipal authorities against pressure from the center) and in the more remote rather than the most accessible places (though in both instances this may simply reflect the relative facility of procuring supplies). It is not easy to say what difference the attitude and influence of the major representatives of royal authority might have made. Two critics of liberalization, Cypierre, the intendant of the Orléanais, which lay in the shadow of Versailles (or Fontainebleau, to be more precise), and De Gourgues, who managed the far-off generality of Montauban, both complained that the police had "their hands tied" by the new laws. But whereas in the Montauban area the police apparently resigned themselves to their incapacitation, albeit grudgingly, in the Orléanais, according to Cypierre himself, they engaged in wholesale subversion.[113] Surely there were intra- as well as inter-regional patterns of resistance. Though his claim will require careful testing, the intendant of Brittany's geography of local interest may prove to be the most promising suggestion to pursue. In his view, those officials "who were placed in the commercial cities breathed nothing but liberty [while] those of the interior spoke only of prohibitions ...."[114]

The revolt of the consumers and the mutiny of the police seriously menaced the prospects for liberalization. Determined not to be intimidated either by the public or by public authorities, the liberal ministry set upon a course of action which precluded compromise or conciliation. The rationale for this policy and some of its results are discussed in the next chapter.

---

112 These are Goubert's regional categories in Braudel and Labrousse, eds., *Histoire économique et sociale*, II, 104–118.

113 Cypierre to T. de Montigny, 16 Oct. 1768 in C. Bloch, *Correspondance inédite de l'intendant Cypierre*, 132–133 and De Gourgues to CG, 16 Dec. 1771, AN, F^{11} 223.

114 IN. of Brittany to CG, June 1774, C. 1653, A.D. I-et-V.

Chapter V

FORCING GRAIN TO BE FREE:
THE GOVERNMENT HOLDS THE LINE

The government responded to the burgeoning unrest—popular revolts and police resistance—with a hard and determined line, starkly re-affirming its commitment to liberalization and to high prices as an express policy of state. Laverdy correctly believed that traditional attitudes toward subsistence constituted the single greatest barrier to change. But, like many self-consciously enlightened ministers and reformers, he neither understood nor sympathized with the workings of popular psychology, nor did he know how to deal with it. Diffusing light, to be sure, was no easy matter; since all men were not equally equipped to seize the truth, often it was necessary to force them to accept it. To re-educate the public, Laverdy saw no alternative to brutal and relentless reconditioning.

Impetuously, the people believed that their right to subsist took precedence over all the rights prescribed by natural law as the basis of social organization. They assumed that it was the solemn duty of the state to intervene when necessary to guarantee their subsistence without regard for so-called natural rights. Such views, in Laverdy's estimation, were erroneous and pernicious; they misconceived the role of the government and its relation to the citizenry and did violence to the soundest principles of political economy. In a word, they were irrational; the Controller-General refused a dialogue with unreason. "The people," he lamented, "hardly used their reason in matters of subsistence."[1] Surely the bulk of police officials who dealt with these problems day to day would have found it singularly fatuous to rebuke the people for being unreasonable when they were hungry, impoverished,

---

1 CG to Cypierre, 7 Sept. 1768 cited by Bloch, "Le Commerce des grains," *Etudes sur l'histoire économique*, 43. Cf. the remark of the liberal First President of the Parlement of Provence: "The multitude never reasons coolly on the matter of subsistence." Draft letter to CG, 8 July 1768, A.D. B-du-R., C. 2420.

or simply anxious. It was the job of the authorities to be reasonable about provisioning; for the public, especially in time of stress, it was virtually impossible to avoid subsistence terror. Insofar as popular fears were often imaginary—a fact which had little bearing upon the clinical state of fright or its consequences—and popular solutions were illegal and myopic, Laverdy would not acknowledge them either as manifestations of a legitimate problem or even as authentic symptoms of a congenital psychosomatic disorder.

To combat and discredit this mentality, Laverdy chose to belittle and insult it with all the sophistry of progressive thinking. It consisted of nothing more than a crazy quilt of "prejudices." "Prejudice" was one of the harshest epithets in the political vocabulary of the Enlightenment; it acquired added force when accompanied by Laverdy's favorite metaphors, light and sight. Their prejudices "blinded the people," not only to the "veritable principles of things," but also to "their true interests." (A decade later, in similar fashion, Turgot explained popular resistance to his liberal program on the grounds that the people are "too little enlightened on their real interests.") In letter after letter, the Controller-General railed against the "old prejudices which still subsist against the liberty of the grain trade." He hated "ignorance" and "prejudice" *en philosophe* for the "obstacles ... always contrary to all sorts of good [which they] opposed to progress."[2]

Though he knew that it had to be done urgently and that it would be enormously difficult, Laverdy had no concrete plan for "breaking the old chain of prejudices." "Surely you feel how important it is," he wrote Lescalopier, intendant of the Touraine, "to prevent the people from giving themselves over to presumptions and prejudices against such a useful law [the July Edict]." But what was the intendant to make of the feeble and nebulous ministerial instructions which left the burden squarely on his shoulders: "I invite you," the letter continued, "to neglect nothing in order to make known to them [the people] all the advantages [of liberalization] and to destroy the false interpretations which might be applied to it." Courteille, one of Laverdy's assistants, hinted to the intendant of Bordeaux that there was nothing to do except insist upon the law until "the people have accustomed themselves to it," until "time and experience prove to them the advantages

---

2 CG to PG, 4 Dec. 1765, BN, Coll. Joly 1131, fol. 9; Laverdy to PG, 23 Oct. 1766, Coll. Joly 1109, fols. 145–46; CG to Miromesnil, 31 Dec. 1767, in LeVerdier, ed., *Correspondance Miromesnil*, V, 70; Turgot to IN. of Alençon, 19 Sept. 1774, C. 89, A.D. Orne.

which must result from it." Laverdy's own instincts were slightly more aggressive, though no less hazy. Only a tough, unbending stance would produce results. "By stiffening against the prejudices of the people," he predicted, "they will gradually weaken and we will succeed in accustoming them to a *bien*," though, he conceded, "they will continue to misjudge [it] for still some time to come." Misjudging it, however, was one thing, and actively opposing it, quite another. The threat of bludgeoning them into submission was the only real incentive the Controller-General offered the people to embrace the liberal program.[3]

Firmly convinced that liberalization was salutary and necessary, Laverdy repulsed the idea that it could be materially responsible for the multitude of riots and disruptions. Rejecting the police analyses which ascribed them to misery, *cherté*, and removals, he attributed the disturbances to the benighted popular mentality. At Abbeville, for example, in 1765, Laverdy claimed that grain was abundant and prices moderate; the rising, therefore, could only have resulted from "the prejudice which exists against the liberty of the grain trade." At Sens a year later, after another revolt which the police blamed on the "export of grain," Laverdy argued that "this fermentation was occasioned only by the ancient prejudices which still subsist against the liberty of the grain trade." In none of the uprisings was there "any motive for fears," only the "frivolous and illusory pretext" for precipitate action.[4] Or, as a liberal journal serenely put it, the riots "are not and *cannot be* the effect of real need" because in a regime of liberty, "the dearth that the enraged minds fear, or feign to fear, is manifestly impossible."[5] Laverdy managed to convince himself that the aroused crowd acted aimlessly, passionately, and whimsically; "blindly," he preferred to say. The irony of the image escaped him. It was precisely the question of visibility which agitated the crowd—the empty market, the loaded boat, the camouflaged caravan, the absence of

---

3 CG to Lescalopier, July 1764, C. 94, A.D. I-et-L.; Courteille to IN., 18 July 1764, A.D. Gir., C. 1426; CG to PG, 11 Nov. 1765, BN, Coll. Joly 1131, fol. 24. Cf. Diderot on the difficulty of reeducating the people on the subsistence question. Diderot to Necker, 10 June 1775, *Diderot Correspondance*, ed. G. Roth and J. Varloot (Paris, 1968), XIV, 146.

4 CG to PG, 4 Dec. 1765, BN, Coll. Joly 1113, fol. 9; CG to PG, 7 Oct. 1766, Coll. Joly 1132, fol. 12; CG to PG, 13 Sept. 1765, Coll. Joly 1131, fols. 92–93; CG to PG, 23 Oct. 1766, Coll. Joly 1109, fols. 145–46; projet de *lettres patentes, ibid.*, fols. 155–58; CG to Miromesnil, 9 Feb. 1768, Le Verdier, ed., *Correspondance Miromesnil*, V, 82; CG to Miromesnil, 27 March 1768, *ibid.*, V, 135.

5 "Supplément aux Journaux de l'agriculture, du commerce, et des finances," Sept. 1765, C. 80, A.D. Somme.

laboureurs—and its goals were specific rather than diffuse, just as its fury was particularistic rather than universal.

Although his contempt for them was sincere, the riots troubled the Controller-General deeply. On the one hand, he made a point of deprecating their significance. A riot at Rebais in 1767, part of a recurring cycle of Brie disorders, he styled a "mediocre event" unworthy of attention; the tumultuous uprising at Rouen the following year, he reduced to "theft and pillage rather than a sedition."[6] On the other, he conceded that the disturbances were "almost universal," and he worried about the "consequences" of risings in which the people "go beyond all the limits and deliver themselves to the most extreme disorders."

Two assumptions, in Laverdy's view, seemed to have emboldened the people. First, that they could riot with "impunity," an expectation encouraged by many police authorities—those at Rouen, for example—who fail to put down popular movements swiftly and mercilessly and who in some instances even seem to sympathize with the insurgents. Second, "the persuasion which the populace of the cities ordinarily shares that the fear of the riots which it might excite will force the King to modify the laws which established liberty." Nothing was "more essential," according to the Controller-General, than to "destroy" these aberrant opinions.[7]

To dispel the idea that consumers could riot without risk, Laverdy instructed and exhorted the police after every episode to repress with dispatch and pitilessness. Repeatedly, he asked for "a few examples of severity," which would serve not only to "contain the people," but also to "destroy those prejudices" which motivated them, presumably by revealing the futility of following their lead. If the repression were to be delayed, the didactic advantages would be lost. "Nothing is more important," Laverdy wrote Joly de Fleury in reference to a riot which took place in the fall of 1766, "than to accelerate the procedures instituted against the principal authors ... examples in such circumstances are of the greatest necessity and when they are deferred, they do not produce nearly the same effect." Moreover, delays threatened the "security" of the grain trade and deterred prospective dealers from engaging in their speculations. Impatient with "the

---

6 CG to PG, 7 Dec. 1767, BN, Coll. Joly 1135, fol. 82; CG to Miromesnil, 19 March 1768, in LeVerdier, ed., *Correspondance Miromesnil*, V, 138.

7 CG to PG, 23 Oct. 1766, BN, Coll. Joly 1109, fols. 145–46; CG to PG, 13 Sept. 1765, AN, F^{12*} 150.

slowness of the official inquiries, the appeals, the forms to which the [ordinary] tribunals are subjected," the Controller-General considered resuscitating a draconian repressive law which had been used before to bypass local jurisdictions. Finally, he abandoned the plan, apparently as a result of the refusal of the Procurator General and the First President to endorse it, on the grounds that it would tend to frighten rather than calm the people and that it discredited the established system of justice.[8]

Soft sentences annoyed Laverdy as much as dilatory ones. Even as he urged the police to show rigor in the streets and marketplaces, so he goaded prosecutors to demand heavy penalties and judges to pronounce them. He followed cases eagerly in all their details, made his expectations clearly known, and bristled with indignation when the results displeased him. In the wake of a massive riot at Troyes, for example, in which the police had failed to deal harshly with the insurgents, Laverdy pressed for a stern judicial reckoning. He was satisfied to learn that the royal procurator and the rapporteur would ask the death penalty for three of the putative leaders and stringent punishment for the others. In anticipation of such a verdict and a hostile popular reaction, extra brigades were sent to reinforce the constabulary. To virtually everyone's surprise, the *présidial* rendered a stunningly mild provisional sentence which could lead to the release of all the prisoners in three months. The Controller-General angrily denounced the verdict and demanded an explanation; "the excesses to which the people have given themselves in this circumstance," he wrote, "require a much more severe punishment."[9]

To disabuse the public of the other notion which prodded it to insurrection—that popular demonstrations would compel the king to renounce liberalization—Laverdy asked officials at all levels of admin-istration to make it plain that nothing could induce the government to waver. Publicize the point, he enjoined them, that the liberal laws are "fixed and invariable," "perpetual and irrevocable." Even if the people did not understand the laws, they must realize that they cannot be changed under any circumstance. On a more sophisticated level,

8 CG to PG, 22 June 1767, BN, Coll. Joly 1136, fol. 179; CG to Joly, 12 July 1767, *ibid.*, fol. 181; CG to bishop of Angers, 13 Sept. 1765, AN, F^{12*} 150; CG to Dupre de Saint-Maur, 13 Sept. 1765, *ibid.*; *Dépêche* to B. de Sauvigny, 10 April 1768, AN, O^{1*} 410, fols. 219–20; CG to PG, 23 Oct. 1766, BN, Coll. Joly 1109, fols. 145–46; PG to CG, 1 Nov. 1766 and anonymous comments, *ibid.*, fols. 149, 152–53; projet de *lettres patentes* and discussion, *ibid.*, fols. 155–61.

9 CG to IN. of Champagne, 5 June, 12 July 1768 and Paillot to IN., 13, 28 June 1768, C. 1908, A.D. Aube.

Laverdy charged the *économiste* Dupont to conduct a permanent propaganda campaign in behalf of liberalization in the periodical press and in pamphlets.[10]

Disdainful of indulgence or compromise on the question of liberty, the Controller-General depended upon the local police to execute the laws with fidelity, if not with ardor. Many of these authorities, however, shared with the public the very prejudices which Laverdy enjoined them to combat. The failure of the police to execute the liberal policy with resolution elicited angry protests, first from merchants and factors directly aggrieved by their actions and later from the *économistes* and other liberal partisans who accused them of outright sabotage of the new regime. Doubtless, scores of cases of police brutality or contrariety went unreported either because the victims did not know how to seek redress or preferred not to become entangled in appeals or because the local authorities, often backed by their superiors, commanded too much influence to suffer challenge.

Complaints reaching the central government usually involved blatant infringement on the liberty of dealers to acquire and dispose of property in grain. An anonymous letter from Châlons-sur-Marne accused local authorities of obstructing grain removals and "fabricating" false reports of merchant treachery and popular unrest to justify their conduct.[11] Sieur Montgolfier, an enterprising Brie grain and flour merchant, who also ran his own mill and furnished Paris with the help of several commissioners, bespoke the irritation and sense of insecurity of many traders. During the summer and fall of 1767 at Rebais, Coulommiers and nearby markets, mobs pillaged his grain wagons, assaulted his agents, and harassed him in his ordinary operations. Nor were there any mitigating cicumstances, he emphasized. Like many other men who have occasion to call upon the law in defense of property—one thinks of Turgot in 1775—Montgolfier hinted that he might have viewed these crimes more sympathetically, if they had truly been inspired by need. But the prices here are no higher than the prices elsewhere (an argument which flattered the merchant's idea of equity while offering the consumer little consolation), grain "abounded," and "those who interfere with commerce and who are guilty of theft ... were not motivated by want of grain."

---

10 CG to PG, 13 Sept. 1765, AN, F[12]* 150; CG to IN. Lescalopier, 28 Aug. 1765, *ibid.*; CG to Lescalopier, (?) Sept. 1765, C. 94, A.D. I-et-L.; *Oeuvres de Turgot*, ed. by Schelle, II, 55 (introduction).

11 Letter to CG, 29 Dec. 1767, C. 413, A.D. Marne.

Against this violence, Montgolfier protested in vain first to the seignorial judges and then to higher authorities. The royal constabulary, the *maréchaussée*, remained a "tranquil spectator of events that it should foresee and prevent." In chorus with Laverdy, the merchant warned that the "continued inaction" of the police served to "authorize" and incite "the perturbers of commerce." "A *négociant*"—Montgolfier saw himself as something more substantial than a common dealer—"might very well undertake to seek punishment for a personal insult or restitution of a given object," he contended, "but it is impossible for him to struggle against a wild populace." He pressed Joly de Fleury, who forwarded the petition to Laverdy, to recall the local police and the *maréchaussée* "to their duty." Otherwise, he gave notice, he would be forced, "along with several other *négociants*, to abandon his enterprise and his commerce."[12]

While the government refused to be blackmailed by popular protests, it was highly sensitive to this sort of threat. At about the same time, at Corbeil, the manager of the royal grain magazines assailed the local "juges de police" for ceding avidly to "the clamors of the people" for price controls and for nurturing the "untoward prejudices" of the crowd.[13] The following year, a Paris grain merchant demanded "justice" after the *substitut* at Montereau arbitrarily requisitioned his wheat for public sale at a price below the going rate.[14] Fearful for his property in light of the irascible mood of consumers, a merchant who had gathered large stocks at Bar-sur-Aube for shipment to Lyons vainly sought guarantees from the local police that they would "engage themselves to authorize his removals [of grain] in case the people tried to oppose him."[15] Belly, an influential business man from Troyes, who introduced several novel marketing techniques in the late sixties, angrily denounced the local police for hectoring his agents, infringing upon his freedom to buy and remove grain, and, most seriously, after their other tactics failed to intimidate him, "exciting the people to riot against him" in the marketplace. While the police charged that the people of the city, "long animated against this dealer," arose spontaneously to defend their interests, Belly sought the "protection" which any enterprise "useful to the public" merited.[16] Elsewhere in

---

12 Nov. 1767, BN, Coll. Joly 1135, fol. 80.

13 Mellinet to PG (?), 26 Sept. 1767, *ibid.*, fols. 62–64.

14 Petitions, March and May 1768, BN, Coll. Joly 1142, fols. 2–3, 12–13.

15 Masson to IN. of Champagne, 29 May 1770, C. 299, A.D. Aube.

16 Belly, "Mémoire historique," ca. June 1770, C. 1908, A.D. Aube; Terray to IN.

Champagne, a leading merchant specializing in military provisioning raved against the authorities at Bar-sur-Aube for supporting efforts to prevent him from removing his grain from the town.[17] In all these instances, the central government clearly supported the plaintiffs.

While the merchant complaints were discreet and dispersed, the liberal camp tirelessly and vehemently exposed the perfidy of the field police. "The inferior police," Roubaud, the *économiste*, wrote, "required to maintain the execution of the Declaration of 1763 and the Edict of 1764, seems to ignore them, & for the sake of the well-being of the people, they aggravate public fears, the *cherté*, and the dearth, by destroying liberty, despite their solemn dispositions." Every judge and officer has "erected himself into interpreter and arbiter of the law" and every day they "violate" the law, "drawing on the old Regulations expressly revoked by the same law." "One of the most disastrous effects of the regulations," noted the liberal Dauphiné Parlement in an *Avis* to the monarch, was "to have habituated the People to hold the Government responsible for *cherté* or dearth." The police, Roubaud argued, intervene in response to popular cues which they themselves inculcated, while the people view such official intervention as a model and sanction for riot, pillage and popular price-fixing. Turgot deplored the tendency of the police in his own jurisdiction to emulate "the people" in their "reasoning" on liberty and the grain question.[18]

The motives of the police, according to the liberals, ranged from guileless ignorance on one extreme to crass venality on the other. In principle, Condorcet believed in the perfectability of all men, including the police, and at least in some cases he was willing to blame their "stupid blunders" on their "lack of knowing what liberty is" rather than on bad will. His friend Turgot shared an interest in educating them, although he was less optimistic about the prospects. From his intendancy in the Limousin, he distributed to local authorities the texts of the reform laws accompanied by a free copy of the *économiste* Letrosne's perfervid apology, *The Freedom of the Grain Trade, Always Useful and Never Harmful.* When he became Controller-General in

---

of Champagne, 27 June 1770, *ibid.*; Bertin to IN., 29 July 1770 and SD Paillot to IN., 11 June 1770, *ibid.*

17 *Directeurs des Vivres* at Besançon to IN. of Champagne, 11 May 1770, C. 299, A.D. Aube.

18 Roubaud. *Représentations*, 39, 80, 93; "Avis du Parlement de Dauphiné ... au Roi," 26 April 1769, in *Ephémérides du citoyen* (1769), VII, 156; Turgot, "Lettre circulaire aux officiers de police dans des lieux où il y a des marchés de grains," 15 Feb. 1766, C. 479, A.D. Haute-Vienne. See also *Journal économique* (April 1770), 173.

1774 and announced his intention to revive the liberal program of the sixties, Turgot rightly warned the intendants that "it is principally the police judges and their subordinate officials who must be [re-]educated" and, if that failed, then, like the people, they must be "contained."[19]

Nor, in Turgot's mind, was police ignorance always innocent, for these officials were also notoriously "mercenary." "It is sufficient for us to say," noted the *économiste* Baudeau, "that several of the subalterns of the provincial administration have made themselves a little Peru from these exclusive privileges...." This "race of public bloodsuckers" derived its income from the dues and fees it collected on market transactions, from fines and penalties it levied, and from a combination of graft, fraud, and extortion. Although they were "decorated with the pretext of assuring provisioning," wrote an essayist in the physiocratic organ, the *Ephémérides du Citoyen*, the "aim" of the old laws was "primarily fiscal." The police insisted on market sales because the market was the theatre of their venal operations. Greed, rather than a genuine concern for the public good, suggested the Dauphiné Parlement, made the police so "jealous of conserving their rights of inspection."[20]

Liberalization menaced the police with the loss of considerably more than their incomes. The new regime displaced them, depriving them of their sense of purpose and undermining their self-esteem and status in the community and beyond. Without rules to enforce, police officials, noted Condorcet, "might just as well be ordinary individuals." Letrosne and Dupont suggested that the police resented more than anything else the idea of being reduced to supernumeraries. They defended their police powers with all the fierce zeal of men fighting for their professional lives. In their work the police depended as much upon moral as upon legal authority; without public confidence they could not be effective. Liberty maimed them, noted the abbé de

---

19 Condorcet to Turgot, 1775, in *Correspondance Condorcet-Turgot*, ed. by Henry, 212; Turgot circular, 15 Feb. 1766, in *Oeuvres*, ed. by Schelle II, 489; Weulersse, *Mouvement*, I, 119; Turgot, "Septième lettre sur le commerce des grains," 2 Dec. 1770, in *Oeuvres*, ed. by Schelle, III, 323. Turgot to IN. of Alençon, 19 Sept. 1774 and Turgot to PG of Rouen Parl., 19 Sept. 1774, C. 89, A.D. Orne.

20 Baudeau, *Avis au premier besoin*, 1ᵉʳ traité, 130–31 and 3ᵉ traité, 181; "De la liberté du commerce des grains," *Ephémérides du citoyen*, (1769), I, 55–56, 77; "Avis du Parlement de Dauphiné ... au Roi," 26 April 1769, B. 2314, fol. 98, A.D. Isère. Cf. Desmarest, *Rouen*, 114 and Afanassiev, *Commerce des céréales*, 153.

Véri; it "snatched from them a cherished part of their influence on the people."[21] "First of all," noted Condorcet,

> there is nothing to gain in protecting absolute liberty, and never has one made himself a reputation by giving the appearance of doing nothing. In the next place, the goal of every honest town officer is the love and the regard of the people of his city.

Likening them to the Roman tribunes who "corrupted the Roman Republic" through grain distributions, the Provence Parlement decried the appetite of the local police to "distinguish themselves in their home-districts," which led them to seek "the esteem of the People by procuring for them a cheap subsistence."[22] The police courted the favor of the people by "sacrificing" to them the grain traders. The desire "to commend themselves to the public," claimed Dupont, was one of the chief reasons for the police—not only the subalterns but the magistrates in several parlements as well—to subvert the liberal regime.[23]

All of their beliefs, Roubaud asserted, conspired to make the police reactionary and demagogic. The police mind was shallow, narrow, and simplistic; it preferred routine to inquiry, habit to analysis. Persuaded that only tradition begets order, the police official "finds in nature which he does not consult only disorder." Piously, he believes in the efficacy of rules and controls; for every problem, without studying its causes, he proposes a standard solution; autonomically, without thinking, he "regulates … in order to regulate." Unschooled in the liberal ethic, he "is convinced that the more the Sovereign governs, the better the people are governed." He conceives of his jurisdiction in "the image of a little State governed by a Despot" and as a result he neither understands nor accepts the new role designed for him in the liberal legislation. The new police, the Estates of Languedoc told the king, must be observers and reporters; instead of "inspecting" and "constraining," they must "watch" and "protect." When merchants like the Sieur Montgolfier seek to purchase, store, and transport their

---

21 Condorcet, *Lettre d'un laboureur* (1775), in *Collection des principaux économistes*, ed. by E. Depitre and G. de Molinari, XIV, 496; Dupont to Prince Carl Ludwig, 1773, in *Correspondance Dupont*, ed. by Knies, II, 136; Weulersse, *Mouvement*, II, 505; abbé de Véri, *Journal*, ed. by de Witte, I, 287 (26 May 1775).

22 Letter to the king, 21 Nov. 1768, B. 3677 and C. 2420, A.D. B-du-R.

23 Condorcet, *Le Monopole et le monopoleur*, in *Collection des principaux économistes*, ed. by E. Depitre and G. de Molinari, XIV, 464; Dupont to Prince Carl Ludwig, 1773, in *Correspondance Dupont*, ed. by Knies, II, 141.

grain, the police must be "invisible." But when traders are victims of popular abuse and assault, the police must rush to their rescue.[24]

Although the liberals overstated their case against the police, it was not entirely wide of the mark. Many of the local officials, as we have seen, deeply resented liberalization, but not always for the sordid or foolish motives that the liberals imputed to them. Doubtless, too, most of the police were guilty of actions which could reasonably pass as parochial, mean, or eccentric. Nor were the *économistes*, despite the increasingly polarized political climate, the only ones to express concern about the police in the late sixties and seventies. The Advocate General Joly de Fleury, who criticized the liberal innovations with such vigor in 1763, conceded that the "subaltern officers" sometimes enforced the laws with excessive and baleful enthusiasm.[25] Two distinguished presidents of the Paris Parlement used epithets such as "ignorant," "arbitrary," and "short-sighted" to characterize the field police and Terray, who was accused of everything except sympathy for the liberals, worried about the "abuses" and "zeal" of these authorities.[26] The government itself launched the idea—which became a basic tenet of the physiocratic apologia—that the police were responsible for the shortcomings of liberalization and for the crisis of the sixties. In letters patent of November 1768, the king admitted that

> We have not yet succeeded in establishing this salutary liberty as firmly as we would have desired; our Declaration of 25 May 1763 has not been executed in its entirety in several provinces of our kingdom, because of fears which have arisen in the minds of a great part of our Subjects, & *principally of those who were specifically charged with its execution.*[27]

Laverdy toiled strenuously to bring the police into line. He had no patience with authorities who demonstrated laxity in dealing with violations of the liberal laws or with disruptions of public order. Horrified at reports of police complicity in several uprisings in Brittany in 1765, he ordered an investigation to determine if the royal procurator involved "is in fact as guilty as he appears to be." To deal with a violent grain riot at Troyes, the local police, according to the subdelegate,

---

24 Roubaud, *Représentations*, 107, 195; "Supplications ... au Roi sur le commerce des grains," Dec. 1768, *Ephémérides du citoyen* (1769), I, 199–212.

25 Speech of 5 July 1763, *Recueil*, 53–54.

26 Presidents Murard and Lefebvre, *ibid.*, 201, 240; F. Dumas, *La Généralité de Tours au dix-huitième siècle* (Paris, 1894), 353.

27 Letters patent, 10 Nov. 1768, *Recueil*, 78–79. My italics.

"found no better expedient for containing the people than approving, as it were, their actions." Vexed to begin with that he had to learn about this uprising from the Procurator General rather than through his own service, Laverdy unsparingly criticized "the weakness that the mayor and the officers of the bailliage showed." Appeasement "merely excited further disorders"; there was no excuse for not using "the greatest firmness." Similarly, Laverdy denounced the police at Bourges for having "contributed indirectly" to provoking a riot by "welcoming to a certain degree the complaints of the people." They also broke the law by fixing the price of grain. The Controller-General's instructions made it plain that they no longer had the broad freedom of action which they had heretofore enjoyed. Their new role was "to limit themselves uniquely to preventing disorder in the markets." In the past it was presumed that market disorder was caused by the traders; the police of markets meant disciplining the dealers and thereby protecting the people. Liberalism inverted this conception, assigning to the police the task of protecting the merchants and disciplining the consumers.[28]

Developing one of the Controller-General's themes, Trudaine de Montigny contended that it would be easy to "put a stop to these popular fermentations." What was needed, in addition to "a few cavaliers of the constabulary" who could be excited to repressive diligence with cash bonuses for merit, was a large measure of "firmness," applied at the first sign of trouble.[29] Too many officials made the fatal mistake of vacillating at the beginning and of listening to the people's complaints as if the people were capable of rational discourse and as if this sort of dialogue could serve any purpose other than

---

28 CG to de Flesselles, 25 Sept. 1765, AN, F[12]* 150; CG to PG, 20 June 1766, BN, Coll. Joly 1133, fols. 94–95; CG to IN. of Champagne, 5 June 1767, C. 1908, A.D. Aube. Cf. de Montigny to Cypierre, 9 Sept. 1768 in C. Bloch, *Correspondance inédite de l'intendant Cypierre*, 66 and the violent grain riot at Tallard in the Dauphiné in May 1764 which mobilized "the whole community." The police "stood in inaction"; they refused to take "the slightest measure to control this furor." This passivity combined with the extraordinary appearance of organization which the riot projected led the militia commander to suggest "a veritable plot." To the ministry's delight, the First President of the Grenoble Parlement personally intervened to direct the repression. B 2315, fols. 116–20, A.D. Isère.

29 Trudaine found this firmness lacking at the highest as well as the lowest levels of field administration. See his rebukes to the intendants of Tours and Champagne for their failure to deal more energetically with the spate of riots in the spring and summer of 1768. To DuCluzel, 17 May, 8 July, 13 Dec. 1768, C. 94, A.D. I-et-L, and to Rouillé d'Orfeuil, 28 July 1768, C. 413, A.D. Marne. For the ideal of rigorous repression which aroused admiration in the ministry, see IN. of Brittany to SDs, 29 Sept. 1768, C. 1670, A.D. I-et-V.

encouraging them to resist. "I know," Trudaine wrote, "that the artisans and workers living within a city are little prepared to grasp these great principles [of liberty], that they react only to the rise in the price of goods without suspecting any cause for it other than [the actions] of those who govern them, whom they still regard as responsible above all for procuring them, subsistance." So, he concluded, there is no point in taking them seriously. The "singular" thing is that the authorities tolerate these public forums. "Seditious" words mark the beginning of riots; those who utter them, Trudaine instructed, should be "arrested on the spot and punished in a manner to serve as examples to the others." He came close to advocating preemptive strikes against the mob-to-be in the volatile marketplaces of the sixties. In this way serious disorders would be prevented and the liberty of the trade would be safeguarded.[30]

The Controller-General accused local authorities throughout the kingdom of taking a gratuitously alarmist posture on the subsistence situation and using the fears which *they* aroused as a pretext for violating the law. "I do not find at all," he wrote in rebuke of the Moulins police, "that the anxieties of the Lieutenant of Police are authorized; I beg you to reassure this officer and to please recommend to him to leave the grain trade the most complete liberty and to deviate under no pretense from the dispositions of the Declaration of 1763 and the Edict of 1764." The police of Craon in Anjou earned the same upbraiding for their lack of confidence in liberty. Under a smokescreen of "exaggerated anxieties," Laverdy wrote the municipal officers of Châlons-sur-Marne, "I see that you are giving the contents of the Declaration of 1763 and the Edict of 1764 interpretations contrary to the spirit of these laws." Instead of trembling in public, he told them, you must set an example for the public by showing confidence in the "true principles" of the reform laws and encouraging "speculators" to stock and to export as they see fit. Laverdy did not conceal his contempt for officials who lost their nerve. The fiscal procurator of St. Denis who panicked over a minor market disturbance showed signs of cowardice; he was "intimidated," esteemed the Controller-General, by his own self-doubts.[31]

Although his will never flagged, it is clear that the Controller-General's campaign to discipline the field police was not entirely successful.

---

30 T. de Montigny to Cypierre, 4 Sept. 1768 in C. Bloch, *Correspondance inédite de l'intendant Cypierre*, 53–55.

31 CG to PG, 5 Oct. 1766, BN, Coll. Joly 1134, fol. 30; CG to IN. DuCluzel, 20 July 1768, C. 96, A.D. I-et-L.; CG to municipality of Châlons, 11 Jan. 1768, C. 413, A.D. Marne; CG to PG, 7 Dec. 1767, BN, Coll. Joly 1136, fol. 165.

There is little question that he failed to anticipate both the depth and the breadth of official disaffection. Once the problem became acute, Laverdy felt it was politically imperative, in order to safeguard the liberal reforms and protect his own position within the ministry, to belittle its significance. He underestimated not so much police attachment to habit as the extent to which this attachment was selective and derived from a rational and empirical approach to their work. He misunderstood not their particularism, but the conditions—structural and circumstantial—which made them impotent as well as unwilling to abjure that particularism. Laverdy lacked the means and the information to deal with this resistance effectively and discreetly. Chronic but only spasmodically manifest, often unreported or brought to light long after the fact, characteristically sober and oblique rather than shrill and defiant, and scattered in scores of tiny cavities throughout the kingdom, each of which had its own peculiarities, this opposition could not be disarmed in a single stroke.

The irony of liberalization is that to have worked it would have required, *inter alia*, a more powerful central government and a better disciplined and more extensive royal bureaucracy. It is ironical because the theorists of liberalism hated bureaucracy and the administrative monarchy bequeathed by Louis XIV. But to liberate France from too much government (or police), they were ready to concede that the central government first had to become stronger (in the physiocratic scheme, the king had to act despotically in order to institute his "legal despotism"). Centralization, then, was a prerequisite for liberalization and, indeed, for all sorts of reforms desired by the liberals. In order to clear the debris, to combat resistance to the new order and nostalgia for the old, the state had to be mighty, almost ubiquitous, and pitiless. The liberal state could not wither away until it became a truly modern state, that is, until it triumphed completely over particularism, feudalism, and other instances of the dispersion of power and authority throughout the kingdom. At least in its first stages, liberalization demanded a highly authoritarian way of governing. For this task neither the ministry of Laverdy nor any government until the Revolution was prepared.

After one of the early episodes of police disobedience, Laverdy vowed to consult the king and council "in the most appropriate methods" to "restore" the officers to their duty.[32] But short of outright

---

32 CG to de Flesselles, 25 Sept. 1765, AN, F¹²* 150.

purges, which would have disrupted public business and spread alarm during a time already marked by social turbulence, there were few sanctions that the Controller-General, at the summit of the absolutist apparatus, could apply. When it learned of specific police sentences which contravened the law, the royal council could formally annul them, but the time lags seriously attenuated the impact, the intervention did not prevent the police from taking similar action in another incident, and the process involved the council in the morass and minutiae of local affairs which it was neither equipped nor keen to handle.[33] Threats and exhortations were commonly rebuffed or dismissed while reprimands were on occasion deflected or diluted before they reached target. The concurrent hierarchies of enforcement and the multiple levels of administration made it difficult to isolate responsibility and coordinate action. Fronts of recalcitrance often coalesced, joining in a common posture royal procurator, town fathers, police lieutenant or judge, subdelegate, and commander of the *maréchaussée* brigade—functionaries whose jealousies and rivalries were traditionally among the surest guarantors of royal control—sometimes backed more or less overtly by the intendant and/or the parlement.

The parlements had a major share in the task of executing the law; at the grassroots, the main burden devolved upon the *substituts* of the Procurator General. Laverdy dealt with the former through the intermediary of the latter, and depended upon him to maintain tight control. Highly skeptical of the wisdom of liberalization, the Paris Procurator did not earnestly use his enormous moral and legal authority to second the Controller-General. Cautious in his relations with Laverdy, he tended to be vague and evasive in his correspondence with his *substituts*. He showed little enthusiasm in conveying the minister's fulminations and he took the liberty in certain instances to ignore or quash matters which Laverdy deemed important.[34] Joly's equivocal stand added to the confusion surrounding the liberal laws. It befuddled those officials who habitually relied on his leadership and encouraged others who, counting on his protection, interpreted his attitude as tacit authorization to follow their own devices. This situation makes it easy to understand Trudaine de Montigny's lament

---

33 See, for example, *arrêt du Conseil*, 12 Dec. 1766 in Des Essarts, *Dictionnaire*, I, 22 and CG to IN. of Caen, AN, F^{12}* 153, fols. 48–52.

34 See, for example, BN, Coll. Joly 1142, fol. 57.

that "it is difficult to stop these police judges when they believe themselves to be especially upheld by the Parlement."[35]

Challenged by the crowd of police from below, Laverdy also had to face defections from the elite of the grand police. Some intendants, such as Lebret of Brittany, Montyon of Auvergne, and Turgot of the Limousin, officially endorsed the ministry's hard-line by ordering local authorities to enforce the liberal legislation faithfully, repress popular movements, and protect commerce, or face "severe" punishment for "negligence." Yet not even Lebret could accept Laverdy's contention that the *cherté* in the first years after liberalization was the product of "a lack of liberty"; on the contrary, the intendant of Brittany frankly blamed the dearth and the "uprisings of the people" on "the liberty which has been accorded for the export of grain."[36] Rouillé d'Orfeuil, intendant of Champagne, had serious difficulties reconciling his sense of administrative necessity with the imperatives of liberty.[37] Despite the changes in the law of the land, De la Corée, intendant of Franche-Comté, remained convinced that it was "the sacred obligation" of merchants "to supply grain at a just and moderate price."[38] De Gourgues of Montauban, La Galaizière of Lorraine, and Taboureau des Réaux of Hainaut were among the other royal commissioners who claimed to have spoken out early and candidly against the dangers of the new system.[39]

Cypierre of the Orléanais was one of the most vigorous critics of liberalization within the corps of intendants. It is worth noting the manner as well as the substance of his dissent. Publicly, he remained a faithful servant of royal policy. "I parade the advantages of complete

---

35 T. de Montigny to IN. of Orléans, 25 Oct. 1768 in C. Bloch, *Correspondance inédite de l'intendant Cypierre*, 144.

36 Lebret to SDs, 29 Sept. 1765 and Lebret draft, 18 Sept. 1765, C. 1670, A.D. I-et-V.; CG to IN. of Bordeaux, 28 Sept. 1766, C.1425, A.D. Gir.; Turgot, "Lettre circulaire aux officiers de police dans des lieux où il y a des marchés de grains," 15 Feb. 1766, C. 479, A.D. Haute-Vienne; Montyon to Mauriac police, 20 March 1770, C. 907 and to municipality of Giat, 10 April 1770, C. 910, A.D. P-de-D.

In parts of the generalities of Rouen and Tours and the area around Troyes, the intendants lacked either the will or the means to control local police authorities. Dumas, *Tours*, 353; Desmarest, *Rouen*, 28; Ricommard, *Troyes*, 292. In Brittany the subdelegates appear to have spearheaded the police revolt. Letaconnoux, *Le Commerce des grains en Bretagne*, 197.

37 IN. to Bertin, 25 July 1768, C. 413, A.D. Marne.

38 De la Corée to CG, Sept. 1770, C. 844, A.D. Doubs.

39 De Gourgues to Terray, 16 Dec. 1771, AN, F^{11} 223; De la Galaizière to Terray, 30 Dec. 1771, AN, F^{11} 223; Taboureau to CG, Nov. 1767, C. 6690, A.D. Nord.

liberty," he assured the ministry; "I censure all the [police] orders which might contradict it."[40] Privately, however, Cypierre bitterly criticized the policy, which reduced him to "inaction," to serving, alongside the lesser authorities, as the helpless "Spectators of the different monopolies." It was an untenable position for him as well as for the police, for it undermined their authority and their credibility. The "victims" of monopoly, the people, wrote Cypierre, "see in *me* the author of their misery because they compare my silence with the firmness that my predecessor M. Barentin showed in similar circumstances, without wishing to understand that the law is no longer the same."[41] Cypierre scoffed at Laverdy's contention that the "evil" was in the "mind"—the intendant's as well as the people's—rather than in the facts. Monopoly was no less real than the misery, unemployment, and disorder one observed wherever one looked. Nor could all the philosophy in the world transform the way people felt about subsistence: "the people will never calmly stand by as their markets are stripped, as grain wagons cross the marketplace with faraway destinations, not as long as they do not have bread."[42]

There was a "general crisis" in his province, the intendant declared. To cope with it, "the police officers must have an authority to act."[43] Everyday "*circumstances force*" the local police to take measures for the general good which are contrary to the law. This dissonance between fact and law generated a kind of anarchy which confused everyone. Cypierre called for a new law, a revision of liberalization incorporating some of the old controls, which would empower the police to deal with

---

40 Cypierre to T. de Montigny, 16 Oct. 1768 in C. Bloch, *Le Commerce des grains dans la généralité d'Orléans d'après la correspondance inédite de l'intendant Cypierre* (Orléans, 1898), 134. It is clear that this attitude of serenity and discretion was not a pose meant for his superior but a professional obligation which the intendant took very seriously. See, for example, Cypierre to bishop of Orléans, 23 Sept. 1768, *ibid.*, 81. This sense of discretion might help to account for the extremely reserved proposal which Cypierre prepared for the Paris General Assembly of Police in Nov. 1768. Mémoire, *ibid.*, 156–159.

41 Cypierre to T. de Montigny, 1, 7 Sept. 1768 and Cypierre to CG, 24 Sept. 1768, *ibid.*, 51, 62, 101. Cf. the strikingly similar complaint of Saint-Priest, intendant of Languedoc:"... and the people, imbued with [the memory of] the power formerly exercised by the intendant in this domain [e.g., provisioning], believe that it is simply up to him to prevent the disorder by putting a stop to exportation; they push the insolence to the point of saying [because of the intendant's failure to act as he was supposed to] that he must be in complicity with the speculators." To CG, 3 Sept. 1766, C. 2908, A.D. Hér.

42 Cypierre to bishop of Orléans, 23 Sept. 1768, C. Bloch, *Correspondance inédite de l'intendant Cypierre*, 86.

43 Cypierre to T. de Montigny, 9 Sept. 1768 and to bishop of Orléans, 9 Oct. 1768, *ibid.*, 69, 117.

dearth and commercial abuses.[44] He claimed to remain an ardent partisan of liberal reform, but "liberty," he said, "demands precautions, that is my refrain."[45] By the fall of 1768 Cypierre considered the situation so serious that he made it known to the Controller-General that he would no longer answer for public order as long as his hands remained tied.[46]

Cypierre's stand embodied all those characteristics that the Controller-General found most reprehensible: a skeptical attitude toward the new political economy, an attachment to many of the old regulations, an indulgent attitude toward the people, and a sympathy for the predicament of the police. As the breach between them deepened, neither man made a convincing effort to understand the position of the other. How seriously could Cypierre take the surprised innocence Laverdy expressed when he wrote: "I do not know why the police judges think that I have tied their hands." What value could Laverdy assign to Cypierre's repeated insistence that "nothing was more essential than maintaining the freedom of trade" and that the liberal laws were "wise" and "salutary"?[47] Trudaine de Montigny chided the intendant for ceding to "the empty clamors of a blind populace," to the "cry of the people," which he likened to their worn denunciations of "pretended sorcerers who caused hailstorms, rains and other misfortunes." In Cypierre's view, however, it was the ministry which was blind for failing to see that while the evocation of sorcery was a matter of "superstition," the "present outcry results from need." He regarded Trudaine's argument that liberty had no sense unless it was absolute as a blueprint for disaster. Trudaine viewed his call for moderation as a trap ("The first chains are presented to us," the Parlement of Provence later wrote, "under the guise of moderation").[48]

Frustrated at his failure to convert Cypierre by gentle persuasion, Laverdy exploded in a bristling reprimand delivered in early September 1768:

---

44 Cypierre in separate letters to bishop of Orléans, CG and Sartine, all on 9 Oct. 1768, *ibid.*, 114, 117, 122.

45 Cypierre to Sartine, 7 Oct. 1768, *ibid.*, 113. Cf. Cypierre to CG, 7, 10 Sept. 1768, *ibid.*, 57, 70; St.-Florentin to Cypierre, 27 Sept. 1768, AN, F^{12}* 150; and Cypierre to Terray, 30 Jan. 1772, AN, F^{11} 223.

46 Cypierre to St.-Florentin, 2 Sept. 1768 in C. Bloch, *Correspondance inédite de Cypierre*, 55–56.

47 CG to Cypierre, 11 Sept. 1768, Cypierre to CG, 15 Aug. 1768, and Cypierre, *Mémoire* (Nov. 1768), *ibid.*, 48–49, 61, 155–159.

48 T. de Montigny to Cypierre, 1, 4 Sept. and 14 Oct. 1768 and Cypierre to T. de Montigny, 16 Oct. 1768, *ibid.*, 49, 53, 130, 133; Parl. of Provence, letter to the King, 10 Nov. 1770, B. 3677, A.D. B-du-R.

I confess to you my great surprise at the letters which you have recently written to M. de Montigny and to me. You speak favorably of the liberty of the grain trade and yet none of the [other] Intendants has yet lodged such violent complaints against the effects of this liberty.

You want me, Laverdy went on, to "authorize you to annul all speculative grain operations [*arrhements*]," but on what grounds? "Am I entitled," asked the Controller-General, "to expect from your administration and the care which you give to your jurisdiction only hearsay and vague terrors which I see supported by no facts?" Why do you think His Majesty issued the May Declaration? Precisely, answered Laverdy, to quash the old laws which you wish to resuscitate and the "prejudices of the people" which you share. At least have the courage to admit, the Controller-General brutally challenged the royal commissioner, that you are our enemy in the campaign for liberalization: "… own up that very far from favoring the liberty of commerce, you [really] think that it can only be harmful to the State."[49]

It is not clear whether Laverdy wanted Cypierre to resign, recant, or merely keep quiet. Doubtless the intendant was not surprised to learn the following week from his friend the Bishop of Orléans that Laverdy was "biased against you" and that he thought "that your head was enraged without reason."[50] Cypierre passionately rejected the charges levelled by the minister:

Do you believe, Monseigneur, that it is having the head enraged to [try to] save the people and prevent them from going to dangerous extremes, to employ such delicate and such discreet means … to bring about a halt to the rise in the price of bread and assure subsistence until the point where the minister, by his superior views and his knowledge of the general state of subsistence, has the time to attend to our representations and tranquilize this department?

Cypierre's conception of his function clashed sharply with the liberal ministry's view of the proper relationship between the government and the public, though it could fairly stand as the administrative credo of the eighteenth century intendant. "An intendant," he wrote,

administrator of his province, must be its first patron and guardian angel; my heart repeats to me every day my lesson and shows me my duties. Report to the

---

49 CG to Cypierre, 7 Sept. 1768 in C. Bloch, *Correspondance inédite de Cypierre*, 58–59.
50 Cypierre to bishop of Orléans, 19 Sept. 1768, *ibid.*, 81–83.

ministers, inform them exactly of the state of things in the department each time that circumstances demand it, confide to them my troubles and my fears when they concern the tranquility and the well-being of the people, obey and execute their orders, that is my mission vis-à-vis the ministers. *But I have other engagements to fulfill vis-à-vis the people* at the same time: to inspire them with confidence, the keystone of administration; use authoritarian means only to make it known to the people that it is used always for their advantage, husband the resources of the people, and make them love the government. That is my profession of faith ....[51]

Cypierre made little effort to avoid a confrontation with the Controller-General; on the contrary, he seems to have decided to provoke one. He believed that there were other highly placed officials, in the field and at the center, who shared his criticism of government policy, and there are some indications that he tried to organize them into an anti-Laverdy faction. He courted the favor of Saint-Florentin, the minister of the royal household, who may indeed have shared some of his reservations about liberalization.[52] He broached his plan for a modification of the reform laws with the powerful Paris police chief, Sartine, whose "manner of thinking on this important article of administration," he believed, would lead him "to back my representations."[53] Through the intervention of the bishop of Orléans, who shared his views and pressed his case at Versailles, he sought the support of Choiseul.[54] It is probable that Cypierre's efforts contributed to the decision announced by Louis XV at the end of September to dismiss Laverdy.

Elated by the disgrace of the Controller-General, the intendant of the Orléanais interpreted it as a vindication of his stance and as a sign that the policy of "unlimited liberty" would soon be changed. But he badly misread the intentions of Laverdy's successor, Maynon d'Invau, perhaps because he expected that Maynon, who came from an intendancy, would inevitably have experienced difficulties and afterthoughts similar to his own. Though Maynon promised him that he "would carefully reflect upon the thoughts you have on the disadvantages of this liberty," the new Controller-General revealed himself to be more inflexible in his liberalism than his predecessor.[55]

51 Cypierre to bishop of Orléans, 23 Sept. 1768, *ibid.*, 83–85.
52 Cypierre to St.-Florentin, 2 Sept. 1768, *ibid.*, 55. Cf. St.-Florentin to Cypierre, 5 Nov. 1766, *ibid.*, 52; Cypierre to T. de Montigny, 7 Sept. 1768, *ibid.*, 64; bishop of Orléans to Cypierre, 19 Sept. 1768, *ibid.*, 82.
53 Cypierre to Sartine, 9 Oct. 1768, *ibid.*, 115.
54 Cypierre to bishop of Orléans, 20 Sept. 1768, *ibid.*, 106. Cf. bishop to Cypierre, 19 Sept. 1768, *ibid.*, 82.
55 Cypierre to bishop of Orléans, 9 Oct. 1768, *ibid.*, 118–119; Maynon to Cypierre, 3 Oct. 1768, *ibid.*, 105.

As a counterweight to Cypierre's rebellion, the liberal ministry in the mid-sixties could take heart from the loyal support of the intendant of Auvergne. His report of his experience with the reform laws was a text-book illustration of the way liberty was destined to work when it was honestly and energetically applied. "The anxieties that the People have shown throughout the breadth of my Generality," he wrote Laverdy in June 1766,

> as a result of the grain *cherté*, are beginning to diminish. I have endeavored in all the letters which I wrote to my Subdelegates and to the officers of Police to make them feel how very dangerous it would be for them to oppose exportation and when several of them departed from the Rules which the Edict of July 1764 prescribed to them, I made them understand how very prejudicial their conduct was to the good of the administration as a result of the fright which it would inspire in the People.

Just as the liberal theorists contended, the intendant showed that *cherté* was a self-curing problem, for the high prices were attracting merchants from surrounding areas to provision the markets of his province. In a reply that was published in the *Gazette du Commerce, de l'Agriculture, et des Finances*, Laverdy congratulated the intendant and took delight in pointing to the moral of the episode: that "… the full and entire execution of the Edict of July 1764 is the surest means of preserving the kingdom from dearth."[56]

Ultimately, dissent from within the corps of intendants posed a far less grave threat to the liberal program than opposition from the other claimants to the grand police, the magistrates of the parlements. Several parlements came out openly against liberalization in the late sixties. The *économistes*—and their most influential confrere in the ministry, Trudaine de Montigny—accused them of setting a fatal example by attacking and discrediting the law, thereby reinforcing popular prejudices and fanning police insubordination. As early as September 1766 the Parlement of Bordeaux deliberated on the *cherté* and listened to vocal criticism of royal policy.[57] The Controller-General struggled vainly to avert an open rupture with Rouen which posed a threat even before the spring riots of 1768 galvanized the Norman opposition.[58] Just as he argued that the people could not see in matters of political

56 *Gazette du commerce, de l'agriculture, et des finances* (28 June 1766), 417 and (5 July 1766), 437.
57 (?) to IN., 23 Sept. 1766, C. 1425, A.D. Gir.
58 CG to Miromesnil, 13 Oct. 1767, in LeVerdier, ed., *Correspondance Miromesnil*, V, 49. Cf. CG to Miromesnil, 8 May 1768, *ibid.*, V, 177–180 and Trudaine de Montigny to Miromesnil, 16 May 1768, *ibid.*, V, 212–13.

economy, so Trudaine could not "tire of deploring the *blindness* of the Magistrates on an object where it is so easy to demonstrate the truth."[59] Obdurate and rancorous—a cynic might say doing business as usual—the Rouen court rankled the government without causing it, solely on the basis of these impertinences, to tremble for the liberal program. It was the attitude assumed by the Paris Parlement, as we shall see, which proved to be the decisive element in turning the tide.

In good conscience, the Controller-General could insist, time and again, that police fears over liberalization were groundless and imaginary, but the incontrovertible fact remained that prices were steadily climbing. Compare, for instance, the average annual prices in the following *généralités* for the years 1763 and 1768 (computed from subdelegate reports and converted to the Paris *septier*):[60]

	1763 (in *livres t.*)	*1768*
Champagne	11.90	21.45
Orléans	12.40	24.80
Tours	14.25	21.90
Soissons	12.55	27.50
Rouen	14.30	30.14
Caen	15.05	25.10
Paris	13	27.90
Paris-city	13.05	27.50

A recent reconstruction of Paris prices based on a four-season average, civil year, for the best quality wheat sold at the Halles reveals the following progression:[61]

$$1763 - 15.88$$
$$1764 - 15.55$$
$$1765 - 18.30$$
$$1766 - 20.40$$
$$1767 - 22.05$$
$$1768 - 32.80$$

While these prices clearly suggest the direction of the short-run movement, they obscure the brusque paroxysms and day-to-day fluctuations which alarmed and confounded consumers and officials and provoked

---

59 Trudaine de Montigny to Miromesnil, 22 May 1768, *ibid.*, V, 221.

60 Labrousse, *Esquisse*, 106–13.

61 M. Baulant, "Le Prix des grains à Paris de 1431 à 1788," *Annales: économies, sociétés, civilisations,* 23rd year (May-June 1968), 520–40. For the behavior of prices in segments of the Parisian supply crowns, see J. Dupâquier, M. Lachiver, and J. Meuvret, *Mercuriales du pays de France et du Vexin français, 1640–1792* (Paris, 1968).

them to act with little regard for yesterday or tomorrow. In the capital, for example, the highest wheat price for the first market of January 1768 was 25.75 *livres*, but in the first week in November the maximum reached 41 *livres*.[62]

Laverdy considered the price rise in two ways, relatively and normatively. In the first mood, he argued, as did many of the *économistes*, that the short-run perspective distorted impressions, that a more generous vista across time would show that the price behavior represented a recovery rather than a prodigious leap forward, and that, in any case, the experts in the bureaus of the Contrôle-Général did not feel that it was out of line with standard economic indicators. In the second vein, which he sometimes joined with the first, Laverdy embraced the upswing with relish or regretted that it was not more pronounced, frankly asserting that such an increase was precisely the aim of his policy. To a fearful lament about "high prices" and their sequellae from Rambouillet in November 1767, the Controller-General curtly replied: "25 *livres* is not at all excessive."[63] Sure of himself, Laverdy similarly disposed of complaints from Vitry against exorbitant prices: "the prices are still very moderate and well below what the interest of proprietors and cultivators would demand."[64]

The new political economy invalidated the old standards of reference to which the police unreasonably clung. "The pretension that wheat should be worth only 12 to 15 *livres* the *septier*," wrote Laverdy, censuring the attitude of the Meulan procurator, "proves how much he who addressed these protests to you is influenced by the ancient prejudices; if his wish were fulfilled, the cultivator would soon be forced to abandon his labors...."[65] For generations, the grain price level has been artificially depressed, retarding agricultural growth and establishing a specious relationship between the cost of grain and of other goods and services, the minister contended. The "principal object" of the liberal legislation "was to procure for the price of grain an augmentation which would excite the emulation of the cultivators and establish a proportion between the value of this commodity and that of all the other things which are consumed and employed every day."[66]

---

62 Price table in BN, Coll. Joly 1136.

63 Petition to PG, 21 Nov. 1767 and CG to PG, 30 Nov. 1767, *ibid.*, fols. 137–40.

64 CG to PG, 24 Sept. 1766, BN, Coll. Joly 1134, fol. 204.

65 CG to PG, 8 Nov. 1766, *ibid.*, fol. 15.

66 CG to PG, 5 Oct. 1766, *ibid.*, fol. 30.

No areas could escape the price increase. Despite the "sensation" that the *cherté* provoked in the capital, "this progression must occur equally in Paris and in the places which surround it." It would be "more dangerous" to curtail the rise because if Paris prices were not "superior" to those in the outlying regions, the capital would be unable to attract any supplies at all. Although he scored the fatalism of police officials who tremulously expected at any moment to be engulfed in a torrent of popular unrest, he recognized a direct relationship between *mercuriale* and mutiny and he seemed prepared to run the sociopolitical risks inherent in liberalization. "The fermentation which has taken place in several spots," he told Joly de Fleury, "was caused only by the augmentation which occurred on the grain prices and which was a necessary result of the liberty and the chief aim of the dispositions which were taken relative to this subject."[67]

From the commercial point of view, the success of liberalization depended upon the willingness of urban and rural businessmen to take bold risks of their own. The abandonment of controls created a climate juridically hospitable to the emergence of a new grain trade, but only the prospect of a sustained higher price level could give merchants the incentives to establish aggressive, large-scale enterprises and diffuse the fruits of liberalization throughout the kingdom. For this reason, despite the disorders and the scarcity which neared their zenith in 1768, Laverdy felt relieved that a brusque and generalized diminution of prices did not take place. "It would have repelled the speculations of commerce," he noted, "and perhaps the losses that the *négociants* would have incurred would have deprived us for a long time of the resources that we have reason to expect from commerce and that we must conserve with the greatest care." Every effort must be extended to reassure the merchants in this delicate transitional stage during which the Controller-General hoped to witness the eclipse of the old style of timid and half-hearted trade by a new form of expansive entrepreneurship.

"Once this type of commerce becomes more firmly rooted and the *négociants* are no longer frightened by events and by the memory of the old prohibitive laws, the prices will find a level whose variations

---

67 CG to PG, 30 June 1766, *ibid.*, fols. 6–7. Cf. the effusively liberal avowal of the "inhabitant of the capital, head of a large family, and thus consumer of a great deal of bread," who nevertheless "wishes with all my heart" for a rise in the price of bread for the sake of the general good of France. "Lettre à l'auteur de la *Gazette du commerce*" (14 Jan. 1764), 29.

will be barely noticeable," the minister blithely predicted, conceding, however, that "we are still distant from this state of abundance and tranquility." Approximately how far away he did not dare to conjecture, but he never tired of reminding his correspondents that a single step backward, a simple gesture of imprudence or impatience, would slow the pace even further.[68] The "level" to which he referred was what the *économistes* called the "right price" *(bon prix)* which would align French prices upon those of the international market and redress the idealized balance between producers and consumers. The attenuation of variations which he foresaw was what the *économistes* meant by "equalization" of prices, the process by which local and regional disparities would gradually diminish in magnitude and extent and prices would tend to become more and more uniform as a national market emerged little by little.

Although the *économistes* did not anticipate that it would be difficult to generate a merchant class commensurate with the needs of liberalization, in their post-mortem assessment of the liberal experience they claimed that the grain trade before 1764 had been highly underdeveloped and that afterward it enjoyed too little time and too little genuine liberty to flourish and fulfill its mission. *Grande culture* in agriculture, *grand commerce* in the grain trade, such was the rationalizing, capitalistic vision of physiocracy. The new grain traders had to be powerful and wealthy men capable of concentrating large amounts of money, establishing extensive networks of exchange, and engaging in efficient and mammoth wholesale operations.[69]

Laverdy had a certain amount of sympathy with the atomized, middling and *blatier*-type traffic of old. Convinced of the social utility of such dispersed, grassroots commerce, he entertained a more merciful conception of competition than the rigorist *économistes*. In permitting the destruction of the small traders, "one would assure the exclusive *[l'exclusif]* in favor of the *grands*, and the exclusive is always the worst [of situations]...."[70] Yet Laverdy clearly perceived the urgency of creating a legion of big-time professional speculators. Indulgent toward the modest merchants, he paid special attention to the *négociants*, who

---

68 CG to Miromesnil, 9 March 1768, in LeVerdier, ed., *Correspondance Miromesnil*, V, 110–111.
69 See, for example, Turgot, "Septième lettre sur le commerce des grains," in *Oeuvres*, ed. by Schelle, III, 323; Roubaud, *Représentations*, 19–21,451–52,454; Weulersse, *Mouvement*, I, 531.
70 CG to Miromesnil, 8 May 1768, in LeVerdier, ed., *Correspondance Miromesnil*, V, 180.

merited the "honor" and "respect" of the nation. In addition to blandishing them with high prices, he endeavored to give them evidence of "the most striking protection."[71] Above all, this meant facility of commerce: freedom from all harassment and intimidation, popular or official; perfect security of property; cooperation from government agencies with no strings attached. Materially, it signified the opportunity to earn substantial profits and morally, it promised government stewardship of the grain merchant reputation (publicity to create a new image for the citizen-speculator, letters of commendation from the king and council for exemplary achievements, etc.).

Finally, this "protection" suggested a new understanding of the functions and methods of commerce and a disinfection of the old terms used to describe it. The proliferation of private grain magazines, a form of hoarding which the police had always regarded as a dangerous abuse, Laverdy viewed with satisfaction as a means of making commerce itself the best guarantee against scarcity. Secrecy was a perfectly legitimate prerogative of commerce. Off-market exchanges were "necessary" for the impulse they gave to grain movement, for the regular rhythm of sales, and for the convenience and morale of merchants. The police could never accept the idea that the grain trade was a purely commercial adventure; for them the notion of grain "speculations" evoked the syndrome of avidity which began with daring clandestine purchases and ended up with monopoly. Laverdy felt that "speculations"—any commercial operation involving an investment, incurring risk, and motivated by a desire for profit rather than by a sense of fear or obligation—were at the very heart of the grain trade, were positively salutary, and merited encouragement rather than mistrust or repression.[72] *Enarrhement*, a practice by which future

---

71 *Ibid.*, V, 177–78. For a concrete instance of the sort of protection and honor Laverdy envisioned, see his letter to the IN. of Rouen, 12 May 1768 and the latter's reply, 3 June 1768, C. 105, A.D. S-M. See also the *arrêt du conseil* of 30 Oct. 1767 which sought to define, encourage, and reward all forms of large-scale wholesale trade. *Recueil général des anciennes lois françaises*, ed. by Isambert, *et al.*, XXII, 470. Turgot, during his ministry, also promised "public marks" of honor to *négociants* who served the kingdom brilliantly. Turgot to IN. of Caen, 15 June 1775, *Oeuvres de Turgot*, ed. by Schelle, IV, 494.

On the stigma attached to grain trading (which "destroys agriculture along with this commerce") and the need to refurbish the image of the grain merchant, especially the *négociant*, see "Lettre à M. l'abbé Roubaud sur la profession du commerçant en grains," *Journal de l'agriculture, du commerce, des arts et des finances* (Dec. 1773), 4–10.

72 Cf. the depiction of "Speculators" as public heroes in the *Gazette du commerce, de l'agriculture et des finances* (28 June 1766), 417.

harvests were cornered in advance, was the sort of speculation that the police strove to eradicate, a classical form of business cunning explicitly and reiteratively prohibited in countless ordinances and sentences. Laverdy, however, cautioned against such a narrow-minded and old-fashioned interpretation. Properly construed, *enarrhement*, like the other opprobrious terms assigned to speculative techniques, cannot mean the same thing in a regime of liberty as it had before. "This word," he wrote, "is equivocal and can comprehend the most legitimate [sort of] commerce as well as the most fraudulent."[73]

One of the most compelling demonstrations of good faith which the government could have made would have been to renounce solemnly the practice of undertaking grain operations itself, directly or through intermediaries. The partisans of liberty argued that the fear of competing with the king, who (in theory) could afford to lose vast sums and who was backed by a giant administrative apparatus, dissuaded the most adventuresome businessmen from speculating in grain. This contract of restraint Laverdy was not yet prepared to sign. In the transitional stages between the police and liberal regimes, he was determined to retain all his options. Moreover, he believed that an activist but discreet government grain role would facilitate the material and psychological process of conversion from the old to the new way, at least insofar as the capital was concerned. Short of a formal promise, however, the ministry publicly affirmed its sincere commitment to laissez-faire. If the kingdom was to be provisioned, it would be serviced "by way of commerce." The government would efface itself as much as possible in order to give "all the freedom" for the trade to thrive.[74]

Repeatedly put to the test, Laverdy proved himself innumerable times to be a faithful supporter of liberalization. Indeed, on balance, he seems to have erred more often by excesses of liberal bullheadedness than by want of devotion to the reforms. The charge, invented by contemporaries and reaffirmed by historians, that the Controller-General, either by duplicity or ineptitude, betrayed the cause cannot be

---

73 CG to Miromesnil, 31 Dec. 1767, in LeVerdier, ed., *Correspondance Miromesnil*, V, 68; CG to Miromesnil, 8 May 1768, *ibid.*, V, 179–80; CG to Miromesnil, 9 March 1768, *ibid.*, V, 110–111. Cf. the Parlement of Provence's rejection of the old definitions which established the "false crimes" of hoarding, monopoly, etc. Letter to the king, 10 Nov. 1770, B. 3677, A.D. B-du-R.

74 See, for example, Trudaine de Montigny to Miromesnil, 10, 23 Feb. and 8, 16 May 1768, in LeVerdier, ed., *Correspondance Miromesnil*, V, 84, 93, 176, 213; CG to IN. of Champagne, 4 Aug. 1768, C. 413, A.D. Marne; CG to IN. of Touraine, 19 June 1768, C. 94, A.D. I-et-L.

sustained.[75] To be sure, there were inconsistencies in Laverdy's management; given the magnitude and complexity of the transformation over
which he presided, it would be astonishing not to discover certain contradictions. Viewed by themselves, some of Laverdy's decisions seem
strangely out of joint and even suspicious. But they are less interesting
for the veneer of credibility which they might lend to the indictment of
the Controller-General than for what they reveal about the difficulties
of executing liberalization.

It is true, for example, that Laverdy occasionally authorized officials to supply a market by constraint and that he sometimes took it
upon himself to compel suppliers to furnish.[76] But it must be remembered that these cases were exceptional. They signified emergencies or
arose from extraordinary conditions in a given time and place. They
bespoke not an infidelity to principle but a refusal to risk and test the
principle when the odds were stacked irreversibly against it. Laverdy's
zeal for liberalization did not wholly stifle his sense of comparative
cost and advantage. He ceded where he felt he had to and where he
could afford it, in derogation of the faith, the better to defend the
policy. Perhaps, in the end, he failed because he did not cede enough.

Laverdy's handling of export affairs, which raised embarrassing
questions about his real intentions, was a product of the same approach.
The export question was so murky and complex that it was bound to
cause embarrassment. Neither the process for the verification of legally
excessive prices (i.e., above the ceiling of 30 *livres* the Paris *septier*), nor
the system for the transmission of signals from the field to the center
and back to the field was carefully rehearsed. Time and space lags, precipitate or dilatory action in one place or the other, wild price fluctuations, innocent error, maneuvers of rival factions—all of these factors
could intervene to produce an inopportune or unjustified embargo or
to postpone a closing urgently and genuinely required. The mechanistic inflexibility of the law was certain to arouse resentment and
stir suspicions, for there was no provision for automatic reopening of
the export points once the price receded.[77] Nor was the government

75 See, for instance, Weulersse, *Mouvement*, II, 216; C. Bloch, "Le Commerce des grains,"
   Etudes sur l'histoire économique, 70; Afanassiev, *Commerce des céréales*, 232–34, *passim;* J. Nio,
   Turgot et la liberté du commerce (Bordeaux, 1928), 70.

76 See, for example, CG to PG, 7 Nov. 1767, BN, Coll. Joly 1135, fol. 161; CG to PG, 28 July 1768,
   Coll. Joly 1136, fol. 142; Biollay, *Le Pacte de famine*, 129; Afanassiev, *Commerce des céréales*, 232.

77 In principle, the export cut-off device in the July Edict was mechanistic and
   inflexible. But we do not know precisely how it went into effect in every instance. In

inclined, once a port had been closed, to risk another bad episode or create a potentially dangerous precedent by reopening it through a special law, a procedure which in any case smacked of the ignominous old system of occasional permissions.

Thus, apart from any willful design, flaws inherent in the system could give rise to instances of ostensible administrative arbitrariness. Such appears to have been the case with the closing of the port of Le Havre. According to the embittered merchants of this city, the government invoked the automatic export suspension clause at a time when the market price stood a full 25% below the prohibitive ceiling. Despite the ministry's promise to favor large-scale commerce, the Le Havre merchants found themselves suddenly "deprived of the fruits of their speculations."[78]

There were other instances when apparently arbitrary measures seemed to reflect, not structural faults in the system, but a conscious decision made by the Controller-General. This is what appears to have been at the origin of the closing of the port of Nantes in early November 1766.[79] Shocked and angered by this decision, the leaders of the city applied immediately for a reconsideration. They reminded Laverdy that they had been among the earliest and most vocal members of the liberal lobby, the Controller-General's surest base of political support. They called attention to the ideal geographical situation of Nantes as a grain entrepôt, to their enormous investment in new ships (38 grain-carrying vessels constructed directly in response to the stimulus of the July Edict), port improvements and granaries, and the obligations which the city's *négociants* had contracted in the international market. Promised that there would "never" be a "return to prohibitive laws," the Nantais now felt deeply betrayed. Even as the international business community would "lose confidence" in the traders of the city, so the Nantais hinted that their confidence in the Controller-General had been severely jarred. They maintained not only that the decision to close exports was economically disastrous,

---

an ambiguous but intriguing letter, Trudaine hinted to the intendant of Bordeaux that a port closing did not occur automatically after 3 consecutive over-ceiling market days, but that it remained a fundamentally *political* decision to be made by the Contrôle-Général. 4 Sept. 1766, C. 1425, A.D. Gir.

78 Communications of 8, 12, 15, 19 Dec. 1766, AN, Marine G 81. Cf. Girard, *Terray*, 20. Yet when Laverdy realized a mistake was made—for example, when as a result of a "malentendu" of the Farmers-General office, export through Dieppe was halted—he immediately rectified it. CG to IN. of Rouen, 7, 22 June 1767, C. 103, A.D. S-M,

79 CG to the mayor of Nantes, 2 Nov. 1766, C. 775, A.D. L-A.

but that it was also wholly unjust. For they claimed that the price rise that the government used as a pretext for imposing the embargo was the result of a plot which aimed at nothing less than "overturning the laws of the kingdom" in order to favor the interests of "monopoly." They characterized the transactions which drove the price above the thirty *livres* per *septier* barrier as "isolated" and "unrepresentative" and they denounced the merchant, Gamier, who made them as a speculator with "evil intentions."[80]

Determined to "unmask the maneuvers," the General Assembly of Commerce of Nantes dispatched a two-man delegation to appeal to the Controller-General in person.[81] En route to Paris, the deputies visited all the major market-towns along the Loire in the hope of "engaging them to join their protests to ours." To their keen disappointment, however, they found that virtually all of the officials they encountered welcomed the closing of Nantes. They met with more sympathy at Orléans where they discussed the plight of their city with one of the best-known defenders of liberalization, the *économiste* Letrosne. He offered to write to Laverdy in their behalf.

The sojourn of the deputies in the capital began auspiciously when another *économiste*, Abeille, who had close ties with both the Breton liberal lobby and the ministry, arranged a meeting with Trudaine de Montigny. Subsequently, however, nothing seemed to go right. The deputies expected Trudaine to greet them warmly and volunteer his support, but he proved to be extraordinarily evasive. Pretending that he had little influence in these matters, Trudaine said that he could do no more than urge Laverdy to receive the delegation. D'Aiguillon, Brittany's most illustrious representative then in Paris, flatly refused to see them—assuredly for reasons that had little to do with the destiny of Nantais commerce. The *Bureau du Commerce*, which had always expressed reservations about liberalization, refused to sponsor the deputies' petition. Citing the high price of grain as more than ample justification for the suspension, Courteille, the head of the grain

---

80 "Mémoire tendant á obtenir la rèvocation de la défense d'exporter des grains du port de Nantes pour l'étranger." C. 774 and Juge-consuls to CG, 20 Nov. 1766, C. 775, *ibid.* Partly out of vengeance, partly in order to give their remonstrances a documentary base, the Nantes police condemned Gamier on 4 December to a 500 *livres* fine for buying above the current price. The royal council quashed the sentence a week later. C. 775, *ibid.*

81 Most of what follows is based upon the report submitted by the two deputies, Kerregan and Millet, to the Nantes assembly of commerce in December 1766. C. 775, *ibid.*

department, rejected out of hand the deputies' contention that the government had been deceived or had acted improperly.

Meanwhile, the deputies set out on their own to uncover clues to the plot. Interviews with officials and businessmen convinced them that the trail from Garnier, the merchant responsible for breaking through the price ceiling at Nantes, led ultimately to Leray de Chaumont, a ubiquitous entrepreneur with excellent political connections with whom we shall become familiar in a later chapter. Deeply involved in the financing and organizing of the royal grain reserve for Paris, Leray also served Laverdy as a counselor for grain affairs.

Armed with a letter of introduction from Montaudouin, himself a Nantes trader and a militant liberal, the Breton deputies did not shrink from confronting Leray himself with their suspicions.[82] Leray tried to place the closing of the port of Nantes in a broader social and economic context. Bad harvests everywhere made various "precautions" necessary. The situation was becoming critical in large segments of the realm. You are partisans of liberty, Leray told the deputies, but remember, "if 800,000 people [in Paris] were to lack bread for six hours, *everything* would blow up." The government acted at Nantes not as the result of a plot, but in order to prevent one in which all the exporting merchants were accomplices. Regardless of the price, Leray argued, the Controller-General has the power to stop exports "because the *négociants* can always find the way to prevent grain from rising above the ceiling in order to allow themselves to export all the kingdom's grain." In fact, Leray contended, the price at Nantes had been far above the statutory limit and the Controller-General's decision was perfectly regular. As for the rumors which linked him with Garnier, Leray pronounced them false. The Nantes deputies made it clear that they believed no part of his story and challenged him, in vain, to show them proof of his assertions.

Finally, towards the end of their second week in Paris, Laverdy agreed to meet the delegation. He received them with a "severe air" and then exploded in a "tirade" against their mission, which he considered illegal and unwarranted. "I am very much disposed against you," the Controller-General informed them. Alarmed by the stir which their private investigation had already caused, he warned them against making further insinuations and spreading ideas which could have "unfortunate consequences." "Have you come here to oppose the

---

82 See Montaudouin's violently anglophobic argument in favor of the immediate reopening of the port of Nantes to exports, C. 775, *ibid.*

law?" he asked them menacingly. "I shall uphold it in the prohibitive part as in the permissive part."

Pointing out that "half" the city of Paris was against grain exports,
the Controller-General seemed to be saying, like Leray de Chaumont,
that there were certain *political* variables which a minister had to take
very seriously. Self-proclaimed protector and promoter of the grain
trade, Laverdy nevertheless sternly reproached the Nantes merchant
community for having "pushed up" prices with "an extravagance
which caused them to mount everywhere prodigiously." This time
they have gone too far; while they are worried about their speculations, the Controller-General reminded the deputies, I am worried
about "the starving of the kingdom." He dismissed with contempt
the delegation's apocalyptic theory about a plot devised to ruin the
interests of Nantes and, along with them, those of French agriculture
and, indeed, of "all humanity."

> Ah, the usual reasons! Everything is always lost, ruined, agriculture, navigation. Well
> then, Messieurs, so you will earn a little less with your 38 [new] ships.

When it did not serve government needs, the special pleading of the
liberty lobby was no more compelling and no less tiresome than that
of any other interest group courting favor.

Throughout the interview, Laverdy oscillated between moods of
irascibility and solicitude. After the long rebuke, an unexpectedly sanguine prediction: the Controller-General felt sure that he would be
in a position within three months to reopen the port for exports. Yet,
after the balm, another fulmination: you are trouble-makers, he told
the deputies; you are to leave Paris immediately because "I am afraid
of your undertakings [here]." Unable to obtain a full hearing or an
inquiry, the deputies left for home bitterly disappointed and more
confident than ever that the ministry was covering up a sordid affair.

The Controller-General officially notified the Nantes municipality that he would accept no further remonstrances.[83] In his letter he
made no allusion to the political argument which he pressed upon
the delegation. He claimed to have based his decision strictly on principle —on the law. To the Nantais contention that the high price was
not a valid indicator of the state of the market because it characterized only a small percentage of transactions, Laverdy replied that

---

83 CG to *Juge-Consuls*, 3, 18 Dec. 1766, C. 775, *ibid.* Cf. *Juge-Consuls* to CG, 9 Dec. 1766, *ibid.*

the suspension price did not have to be the common price: the sale of "just a few holdings" was sufficient to trigger suspension. Yet it soon became clear that this principle was not nearly as invariable as Laverdy pretended, for less than a year later he rejected the intendant of Hainaut's plea for export suspension in frontier areas of that generality on the grounds that "the quantity of grain sold above 12 *livres* 10 *sous* the quintal [the ceiling price, i.e., 30 *livres* the Paris *septier*] is a very small amount in comparison with that which was sold below this price."[84] Despite the Controller-General's optimistic assurance, Nantes never recovered the right to export under the provisions of the July Edict. The only real concession which the merchants obtained was the permission to export grain already contracted for or loaded for departure. On the other hand, despite the dire premonitions of the municipality and the merchant association, the port soon began to prosper from a trade in grain imports, which grew spectacularly in the next few years.

Laverdy's export management helped in still other ways to arouse misunderstanding and mistrust.[85] While encouraging the merchant community, he tried simultaneously to allay the fears of the consumers. For example, on several occasions the ministry spread the rumor—which it knew to be wholly false—that exportation had been officially suspended in the hope that this news would reassure public opinion and thus permit exporters, under the cover of the lull, to speculate in tranquility.[86] But such deceptions were perilous risks

---

84 CG to Taboureau, 16 Nov. 1767, C. 6690, A.D. Nord.

85 Though it did not personally inculpate Laverdy, the Dauphiné Parlement retrospectively charged that "interested parties" plotted to arrange the closings of key ports. In fact, though they differ in scale and object, the Dauphiné accusations are strikingly redolent in tone and even in language of the famine plot denunciations of Leprévost de Beaumont. "The law [the clause in the July Edict dealing with the export ceiling] has become in guilty hands the instrument of monopoly," the magistrates contended. "Liberty," they wrote, "has thus served as a pretext to cover a crime ...." If one did not know that the parlementaires were criticizing the *limits* placed on liberty, which allegedly invited maneuvers and thus further sabotaged liberty, one could easily mistake these remarks for slogans in the campaign *against* liberalization. Specifically, the Dauphiné court charged that a secret agent of an "accredited company" artificially arranged for the closing of the port of Nantes, one of the major centers of export-import traffic in the kingdom, thus dealing the renascent grain trade a terrible blow. *Avis* and letter to Louis XV, 26 April 1769, B. 2314, fols. 112–113, A.D. Isère. The Dauphiné parlementaires claimed that once Nantes was closed to export, the port's utility as an import entrepôt was also destroyed because the prohibitive climate repelled traders. In fact, it seems clear that Nantes' role as an import center continued to grow throughout this period. See D'Agay to CG, 10 May 1770, C. 1718, A.D. I-et-V.

86 Note by Miromesnil, 10 Feb. 1768, in LeVerdier, ed., *Correspondance Miromesnil*, V, 83.

because they had extremely limited short-run returns at best and because they were very rarely convincing. Though they were practiced in the service of liberty, they bore the mark of the prohibitive regime during which the government had often secretly arranged with favored *négociants* to undertake exports when circumstances permitted, free from the glare of publicity and the goad of competition. The whole point of liberalization, as Laverdy understood it, was to put an end to ploys, special covenants, uncertain speculative prospects, and privileged mandarins.

Laverdy's handling of export affairs led to recurrent charges at the end of the sixties that he manipulated port closings either for venal reasons (to facilitate the grain purchases of a quasi-governmental monopoly or a private cabal of powerful dealers) or as a pretext to prepare for a repudiation of liberalization. Though they were without foundation, these imputations impaired the Controller-General's credibility and helped to undermine the liberal reforms. Nothing suggests that he was disenchanted with the July Edict for which he had fought so vigorously in the royal council or that he used the closure clause and the highly charged exportation issue as political instruments to justify his own defection from the liberal camp. He was too intimately identified with liberalization—especially with exportation—to carry off a convincing separation and he believed too deeply in the worth and destiny of the policy to contemplate such a move. He made errors in judgment and he took steps which sorely disappointed his liberal clients. But there is no reason to doubt the sincerity of the remark he made in August 1767 to his close friend Miromesnil: "My personal sentiment would be to render exportation completely [free]."[87]

The accusation to which Laverdy is most vulnerable concerns neither his internal police, nor his export policies, but a matter which had a bearing upon both: his use of the king's grain and his reliance upon various forms of state intervention in the grain trade.[88] Doubtless these activities clashed with the liberal aims (although it is worth noting that his critics argued not from the fact that they did but, according to liberal theory, that they *must have*). The persistence of old style government buying, selling, stocking, subsidizing, and intriguing seemed to these critics to be irrefutable proof that Laverdy did not take his

---

87 CG to Miromesnil, 5 Aug. 1767, *ibid*, V, 9. Cf. Laverdy's sharp condemnation of the efforts of the Bordeaux Parlement to halt exports without regard to the price mechanism of the July Edict. CG to IN. of Bordeaux, 1 Oct. 1766, C. 1425, A.D. Gir.

88 For a discussion of the use of the king's grain in the sixties, see below, chapter eight.

liberalism seriously. From Laverdy's point of view, however, the king's grain and other carefully calculated emergency purchases sponsored by the government provided him with the margin of security and the buffer that he needed in order to effect the transition in political terms as well as in terms of political economy. It was not enough to let right principles do their work; it was necessary, in certain instances, to smooth the way for their triumph with old-fashioned doses of paternalism. A total abandonment of official provisioning would have left Laverdy helpless to bargain, to bribe, to intimidate, and to parry contingencies such as natural disaster or social eruption. In the short run the king's grain would guarantee the success of liberalization; in the long run, the practice would die of ination as it exhausted its usefulness. In the last analysis, Laverdy's critics charged him with having been insufficiently doctrinaire in his prosecution of the reforms, a quality of dubious merit in a high administrator.

The liberal laws of 1763–64 survived longer than their perfervid champion, the Controller-General Laverdy. Much to his astonishment, for he believed himself to be in favor, and to the surprise of the people of Paris, who had enjoyed considerable success over the years in forecasting ministerial changes, Laverdy was disgraced at the end of September 1768.[89] Now there was never an absolute paucity of reasons or pretexts for the cashiering of a Controller-General. It is no exaggeration to say that virtually everyone had a particular motive for desiring the downfall of one of the most conspicuous of ministers. The ouster of a Controller-General was one of the few acts by which the king could please the vast majority of his subjects in a single gesture, without taking into consideration any of their specific grievances. In most previous cases, however—with, for example, Orry or Machault or Silhouette or Bertin—one could safely ascribe the acts of dismissal to concrete causes or singular incidents. But Laverdy, it appears, did not have the satisfaction of knowing exactly why he was displaced. It may be that he was revoked because he failed to improve the financial situation, albeit modern appraisals of his management seem extravagantly harsh ("an extreme incompetence").[90] Or he may

89 Sept. 1768, *Journal et mémoires de Charles Collé*, ed. by H. Bonhomme (Paris, 1868), III, 207 and Alphonse Jobez, *La France sous Louis XV*, VI, 413.

90 This is the judgment of Henri Martin, *Histoire de France*, XVI, 246. Cf. Coquereau ("aussi méprisable par la Bêtise & l'absurdité de son Ministère"), *Mémoires concernant ... l'Abbé Terrai* (London, 1776), 203; Lebrun (Laverdy "messed up everything in a department that he did not know, and obtained neither success nor confidence."), *Opinions, rapports et choix d'écrits politiques*, ed. by A.-C. Lebrun (Paris, 1829), 16–17; M.-F. Pidansat

have fallen victim to enmities he aroused among *rentiers* by his plans for amortization, among municipal oligarchs and puissant lords by his reform of local government, or among parlementaires, his former colleagues, by his projects to rationalize the collection of the *taille* and other taxes and by the support he gave their bête noire, D'Aiguillon. Finally, there is little doubt that a feud with Choiseul contributed to his downfall.[91]

The fact that he left office at the very end of September, in the midst of the increasingly strident confrontation on the issue of the liberal reform between the king and the ministry, on the one hand, and the Paris Parlement and the other critics of the new system in the magistracy and the upper and lower administration, on the other, suggests that his handling of liberalization may have been one of the keys to his disgrace. Insofar as his stewardship of affairs was identified with dearth, soaring prices, and social and administrative disorder, Laverdy had become a liability to the liberal cause. His dismissal deprived the antiliberals of an easy target and enabled the king to dissociate himself and the new ministry from Laverdy's execution of the liberal policy, without repudiating the liberal laws. To judge from Cypierre's reaction, it appears that the government reaped some short-term political advantage from the replacement of the Controller-General. But the ouster must not be construed as a retreat from liberalization, for the king replaced Laverdy with Maynon d'Invau, a *maître des requêtes* who consummated his apprenticeship as an administrator-*économiste* by marrying the sister of Trudaine de Montigny. The latter remained in the ministry to bridge the gap between incoming and outgoing Controllers-General.[92]

Albeit puzzling, the disgrace for Laverdy was mild, accompanied by gifts from the king and an invitation to return to the honorable obscurity from which he had emerged only four years before. Laverdy did not reappear upon the public stage until 1793, when he became the

---

de Mairobert, *Journal historique de la révolution opérée dans la constitution de la monarchie françoise* (London, 1776), I, 386; and especially Marion, *Histoire financière*, I, 226–45, followed by Michel Antoine, *Le Conseil du Roi sous le règne de Louis XV*, 221.

91 Jobez, *La France sous Louis XV*, VI, 407–13; Henri Martin, *Histoire de France*, XVI, 246; Marion, *Histoire financière*, I, 233–45; Maurice Bordes, *La Réforme municipale du contrôleur-général Laverdy* (Toulouse, 1968), *passim*; J.-N. Moreau, *Mes souvenirs*, ed. by C. Hermelin, I, 185.

92 Bachaumont, *Mémoires secrets*, XIX, 29 (21 Oct. 1768); Diderot to Sophie Volland, 26 Oct. 1768, in *Correspondance Diderot*, ed. by Roth, VIII, 203 (# 507); Morellet, *Mémoires*, I, 179; Léonce de Lavergne, *Economistes*, 174.

victim of the collective memory of the people, who still connected him with the grain question, and of the personal vengeance of Leprévost de Beaumont, the man whom he had had arrested for propagating rumors of a "famine pact." Inspired by Leprévost's deposition, the product of a quarter-century's festering reflection in royal prisons such as the Bastille, and the discovery of a pitful of rotten and germinated grain adjacent to Laverdy's château, the Revolutionary Tribunal condemned him to death for master-minding "a plot tending to deliver the Republic to the horrors of famine," a conspiracy which began with the efforts to free the grain trade in the sixties.[93]

The disgrace and execution of Laverdy takes us far in advance of our problem. By 1766, a crisis had declared itself in the kingdom, whether the government wanted to acknowledge it or not—a crisis of grain supply, a crisis of public order and public opinion, and a crisis of authority within the police administration. The government's hard line was based upon the conviction that the subsistence difficulties were ephemeral events which would pass once the nation adjusted itself to the liberal regime. The government had never claimed that liberalization, in the short run, would make subsistence easier, and now it adamantly refused to concede that the reform laws actually operated in a way which made it more difficult than ever before for consumers to procure supplies. In the next chapter, we shall examine the validity of the government's contention, with particular reference to the state of foreign and internal grain trade.

---

93 H. Wallon, *Histoire du tribunal révolutionnaire de Paris* (Paris, 1880), II, 96–97, 101; Maurice Tourneux, *Bibliographie de l'histoire de Paris pendant la révolution française* (Paris, 1890–1906), II, 41–45 and IV, 235; *Bulletin du Tribunal criminel révolutionnaire*, 99–100 (3 frimaire an II).

Chapter VI

THE REFORMS AND THE GRAIN TRADE

A few short years after the proclamation of liberalization, the government found itself faced with a burgeoning subsistence crisis and embroiled in a growing debate on the judiciousness of the reform. The reforms were meant to change the way in which the grain trade was conducted. The May Declaration radically altered the conditions of internal commerce and the July Edict opened the frontiers to exports. Taken together, these measures were supposed to build a stronger, more resilient, and more dependable commercial structure at the same time that they generated powerful incentives for agricultural expansion. In this chapter we shall consider the impact of the reforms on domestic and foreign trade and especially on the customary patterns of provisioning. In addition, we shall examine the way in which partisans and adversaries of the May and July laws explained the relationship between liberalization and dearth.

I

Contemporaries were never able to assess dispassionately the impact of liberalization upon the grain trade and the patterns of provisioning. The proliferation of scarcity, spiraling prices, and disorder polarized feelings toward the reform legislation. The parties to the debate were more interested in ascribing and denying political and moral responsibility for the crisis than in studying the processes of cause and effect. Resentful of the dearth that jarred their serenity, the liberals viewed it as an accident, ill-timed but banal, which bore no intrinsic relation to the implementation of liberalization. On the contrary, they claimed that it was a vindictive legacy of the old police system, for were the liberty perfect in its application, dearth by definition would be impossible. If prices were occasionally excessive, it was due to the persistence of the old prohibitions, to the inclemency of the weather, or to other traditional sources of fluctuation. The opponents of liberalization ridiculed the idea that the reforms and the scarcity were merely coincidental occurrences. After all, the avowed purpose of the laws was to open new markets for the grain trade and to raise prices. The dismantling of controls led directly to the flight of grain and the vertiginous increase in prices to which, in the eyes of the police party, the popular disturbances furnished eloquent testimony.

In one sense modern scholarship incidentally favors the liberal argument, in part because the counter-claim is not readily susceptible to quantitative testing, but more importantly because the experience of the sixties fits comfortably the schema of cyclical and seasonal price behavior which characterizes the Old Regime. By analogy with similar episodes in other times, the price rise of the sixties can theoretically be explained without recourse to exogenous political factors. Bad weather would be the crucial variable. Although a precise geography of differential production, distribution, and demand remains to be drafted, it can be plausibly argued that harvest lapses and disasters were sufficiently pronounced and widespread to occasion a conventional scarcity and *cherté*.[1]

That is not to say, however, even if one accepts this clinically neutral thesis which by itself failed to satisfy either party to the quarrel, that the harvests can account for all the outbreaks of dearth, that liberalization played no role, or that this dearth as a whole was in fact no different from other dearths. The harvest of 1765 does not seem to have been unusually short in most places, while opinion on the severity of the deficits between 1766 and 1768 differs from source to source and place to place.[2] In many cases brusque price augmentations preceded harvest

---

1 Though a number of methodological problems must be resolved in order to make them usable, masses of harvest reports are awaiting scrutiny in the department C series.

2 Assessments of harvest performance varied within the same region or between nearby areas. Reports from the Brie around Melun in 1768 indicated a poor crop, while a writer from the vicinity of Meaux claimed the harvest was "very good." J.M. Desbordes, ed., *La chronique villageoise de Varreddes* (Paris, n.d.), 31. Subdelegations within Picardy differed in wheat production in 1769 by as much as 150 percent. The previous year produced similar variations. États des Récoltes, C. 81, 82, and 84, A. D. Somme. Calculated in fractions and multiples of "the common year"—a normative and somewhat idiosyncratic concept which lends itself reluctantly either to quantification or comparison—these harvest estimates must be used with caution, in conjunction with control data. Clearly certain discrepancies in harvest appreciation were voluntary, the product not of rudimentary and parochial accounting techniques but of political imperatives. Contrast, for example, the optimism of Trudaine de Montigny and the pessimism of officials in the field. C. 413, A.D. Marne.

failures or the intimation of prospective difficulties. Some places experienced *cherté* while they continued to enjoy apparently normal harvests and before they became conscious of trouble elsewhere. In both kinds of examples, the price increases seem to have been related to changes in trading practices. For different purposes, *économistes* and their critics often pointed to the paradox which suffered (allegedly) abundant supplies to coexist with exorbitantly high prices. A critical reading of administrative evidence and impressionistic testimonies strongly suggests that the freeing of the grain trade, if it did not itself provoke *cherté*, exacerbated the short-term oscillations and quickened the cyclical and long-run movement by overturning market habits, modifying the customary flow-patterns of grain, multiplying the number of intermediaries, reducing the local visible supply, encouraging forestalling and regrating, and introducing a whole new dimension of adventure and uncertainty which influenced supply and demand. The last point, concerning the psychological impact of liberalization, is perhaps the most important. For dealers big and small the liberal laws opened a fresh vista of opportunities backed by the assurance of legal security in speculation. For consumers and the police, liberalization engendered the expectation of disaster by making security a matter of private interest. Producers and traders assumed a heady attitude of independence and aloofness; police authorities seemed hamstrung and helpless; consumers felt abandoned and betrayed.

The most sensational issue in the debate on the causes of the dearth was the question of exports. A concrete and theoretically measurable phenomenon, it aroused deep feelings and became, to the chagrin of the *économistes*, the symbol and standard of the entire liberal program. For consumers and for many local officials, who had no interest in political economy, the existence of a law authorizing exports explained

---

Finally, it is worth emphasizing the immediate "physical" consequences of a bad harvest, apart from its broader socioeconomic impact. Usually it meant not only a short crop but a harvest of bad quality. Low quality grain yielded *less* flour as well as less good flour than the same amount of a high quality crop. The flour in turn had lower "baker value," absorbing less water, kneading less well, and proofing less successfully than the same quantity of good flour. Thus a short crop usually produced "multiples of less" through all the stages of transformation. And of course the quality of the bread made it unappetizing and, in some instances—in parts of Bretagne for example in 1768—"unhealthy." See SD at Lannion to IN., 6 Oct. 1768, C. 1652, A.D. I-et-V. Moreover, poor quality grain did not keep well, especially at a time before conservation technology was highly developed and diffused. Bad grain got worse and worse. In a dearth, since dealers knew that they could dispose of it regardless of condition, there were few incentives for "repairing" grain or rushing sales.

everything: shortages, soaring prices, and market dislocation were the direct consequences of the rush to dispose of grain abroad. From this perspective it made no difference that the liberals themselves did not expect a huge outflow of grain or that there were competitive, logistical, and legal limits to the amounts that could be exported. What mattered was that since 1764 grain took to the roads and rivers, merchants and *laboureurs* took to the taverns and granaries, and the government blithely approved practices which it had once prohibited.

Exportation loomed as a mammoth, tentacular pump that voraciously drained the grain from the lifestream of the kingdom. "This big word *exportation*," regretted Dupont in retrospect,

> repeated perhaps too often by the defenders of liberty, although they really demanded only the right to export, which can exist fully without any effective exportation; this big word *exportation* frightened minds little acquainted with what it is all about.[3]

The liberals had presented their case with excessive ardor. They made exportation the *sine qua non* of their program, argued that it must be unlimited (blurring, as Dupont complained, the distinction between right and fact and seemingly predicting that in reality infinite amounts of grain would quit the kingdom), and insisted, at the risk of perplexing an unsophisticated audience, that exportation was "the surest means to prevent scarcity" and "the best precaution against dearth."[4] Voltaire pungently expressed a sentiment that must have been widely felt at the time. Writing in the beginning of 1771 from Ferney where "we are dying of hunger," he asked his friend if he knew the journal called the *Ephémérides du Citoyen*: "It claims that we are lacking bread only because we have not sold enough grain abroad."[5]

---

3 "Observations sur les effets de la liberté du commerce des grains … par l'Auteur des Ephémérides du citoyen," *Journal économique* (July 1770), 332. The fact that many officials and consumers characterized all outward bound trade, regardless of destination, as "exportation" did not help the liberal cause. It is easier to understand the domination of the export issue when one realizes, as one liberal commentator mournfully remarked, that "the greatest number [of people] wholly confound interprovincial circulation with exportation abroad." Anon., "Mémoire sur l'exportation des grains," (Oct. 1768), A 1/3677/, #113, Arch. Armée. References to "the liberty of exportation in the interior" abound in the administrative correspondence. See, for instance, SD at Bernay to IN. of Alençon, 12 Oct. 1773, C. 89, A.D. Orne and IN. of Burgundy to SDs, "Mémoire concernant les grains," ca. Oct. 1771, C. 81, A.D. C d'O.

4 "Premier avis des Députés du Commerce…," (Jan. 1764), BN, mss. fr. 14295, fol. 10; Anonymous, "Mémoire sur l'exportation des bleds" (ca. 1764) BN, mss. fr. 14296, fols. 15–16.

5 Voltaire to Chevalier de Rochefort, 9 Feb. 1771, in *Voltaire's Correspondence*, ed. by Besterman, vol. 78, p. 84 (#15978). Though Voltaire telescoped the liberal growth sequence for the

When it came time to take stock of the crisis, in the late sixties and for many years afterwards, the partisans of liberty tried to focus attention on the data rather than on the rhetoric. They emphasized the crucial distinction, in the words of the Dauphiné Parlement, between "the act" ("unlimited exportation") which did not occur and "the power to act" ("the unlimited liberty to export") which the law guaranteed and which helped to "perfect" the grain trade and Europeanize French prices without draining national supplies. Though they warmly acknowledged that exportation produced "precious" fruits for the kingdom, the magistrates of Aix insisted that it had been nothing more than "a simple metaphysical possibility." The liberals demanded a rigorous accounting of exactly how much grain left France, by which they meant to show that exportation could not have been a significant disruptive factor.[6] With few exceptions, the critics of liberalization disdained fastidious inventories and concentrated their attack on liberal theory and its promised consequences. Implicit in their argument was the assumption that exportation had unequivocally proved itself to be a social disaster, regardless of the statistical indications.

The most common reproach formulated was that the government should have known how very dangerous it was to risk exportation. The objections echoed commissaire Delamare's classical lesson that "it is just to safeguard our own preservation before thinking about that of our neighbor" and that exportation must never be permitted unless we are absolutely sure that there is a "surplus beyond our subsistence needs."[7] Testard du Lys, Lieutenant Criminel of the Paris police and a vehement adversary of the new political economy, categorically denied that the kingdom contained a surplus beyond need prior to liberalization and intimated that France could never safely afford to qualify a residue as disposable. What was left after consumption in the early sixties was not a superfluity but merely a "provision of precaution on which depends tranquility." The social and political value of this treasure far

---

sake of burlesque, he did not wholly denature the liberal reasoning process. "Do you want France to experience a happy superabundance?" asked the Grenoble magistrates. "We must begin," they answered, "by launching a great export trade; the grain which leaves the kingdom will increase the mass of subsistence in the interior by the encouragement of cultivation, of multiple clearings, and by the amelioration of all the land." Parl. to Louis XV, 26 April 1769, B. 2314, fol. 119, A.D. Isère.

6 Parl. of Dauphiné to Louis XV, 26 April 1769, B. 2314, fol. 107, A.D. Isère; Parl. of Provence to Louis XV, 10 Nov. 1770, B. 3677, A.D. B-du-R.

7 Nicolas Delamare, *Traité de la police*, II, 726. Cf. E. F. Heckscher, *Mercantilism*, II, 100.

outstripped whatever material return it could produce in foreign commerce. Testard angrily denounced the idea that this surplus was in some sense a "burden" or an "evil." He made belief in abundance as an unqualified good a test of civic virtue and hinted that the desire for exportation bordered on a sort of moral treason:

> There are few citizens who do not wish for and relish the pleasure of the abundance of grain. To desire, without limits or reserves, the free outflow of grain is to endanger Society.[8]

The abbé Galiani indicted the Edict of July 1764 as one of the chief causes of the crisis of the sixties. Founded on erroneous principles of public administration, it was an invitation for social disorganization. In principle it made sense to seek outlets for excess production. But "the idea alone of the delicateness" of the operation required to separate the surplus from the necessary was "frightening":

> It is a question so to speak of removing the epidermis of the whole of France without touching the skin which is sensitive and which makes one cry, is that possible and isn't it the veritable cause of the eternal squallings of the people as soon as one tampers a little with the grain trade? … But when the operation is in itself difficult, delicate, scabrous, it is impossible not to do damage.

Given the physical difficulties and commercial risks of the grain trade, the diversities in regional supply and demand, and the primitive means of communication and transportation, this putative surplus was socially and politically precious. In practice, Galiani told Diderot, exporting was "lunacy." Given the capricious nature of the supply and the highly inelastic quality of the demand, exportation was not the barter of grain for money, but the patently disadvantageous exchange of grain you now have against grain that you will later have to buy back. For Galiani, the experience of the sixties confirmed the admonition of the grain imprésario and government consultant Pâris Duverney (who was accused of profiting from just such insight) that "ordinarily a grand outflow (exportation) [sic] of grain when it is cheap is followed by a dearth during which one repurchases the same grain very dearly." In addition to transmitting violent shocks through French society, exportation did not even fulfill its self-assigned goals. Instead of stimulating internal circulation, it destroyed it by diverting energy and capital from the center to the periphery where trade was easier and more remunerative. Instead of enriching agriculture, it sated only the middlemen who skimmed off most of the profits and

---

8 *Recueil*, 136–37.

quickened the avidity of the state, which would surely use liberalization as a pretext to raise taxes, thereby devouring the rest.[9]

The future finance minister Necker deplored the innovations of the sixties and held exportation largely responsible for the scarcities and soaring prices. He derided the liberal effort to belittle the importance of real exports:

> The more one insists on the smallness of the exportation occasioned by the Edict of 1764, the more one exposes the major drawbacks of liberty, for one proves that the outflow of a very small quantity of grain is sufficient to cause a prodigious revolution in the prices.

The drain of several hundred thousand *septiers* could jeopardize the lives of millions of people in the last months or weeks before a harvest. The nation which regularly exports will suffer continued depopulation and consequently a steady erosion of power, for men rather than money were the best indicators of strength.[10]

Growth, however, could not be the sole preoccupation of the judicious Legislator in Necker's view. He had to labor to avert social disequilibrium and the threat of conflagration because the interests of the members of society were not identical and would not, as the *économistes* presumed, harmonize spontaneously even when "properly understood." It was the duty of the Legislator to moderate and mediate the "continual shock of interests, principles, and opinions" which beset social life. Surplus grain, "precious" for him as for Galiani, was one of the most effective instruments the Legislator could use to reconcile divergent interests artificially. The surplus served as a balancing agent and the guarantee of a crude form of social equality without which the laboring poor—the majority of consumers—would be in a perpetual state of distress. The surplus "excites the owners to sell in fear of being bypassed, tempers their power, and weakens their natural empire over the buyers." The price rise of the sixties, unaccompanied by a compensatory movement of wages, struck the poor like an enormous "capitation"; indeed, it was worse than a capitation, for its limits were not known in advance. In some places in the kingdom, the price rose 100 percent as a result of exports. The price of grain, Necker insisted, does not rise in direct proportion to the amount diverted

---

9 Galiani, *Dialogues*, ed. by Nicolini, 169, 188, 244–53, 262, 282; Galiani, "Mémoire à M. de Sartine" (ca. 1770), in Asse, ed., *Lettres*, I, 411; Diderot to Sophie Volland, 22 Nov. 1768 in *Correspondance Diderot*, ed. by Roth, VIII, 233; Pâris Duverney, "Extrait des divers mémoires sur les bleds" (ca. 1750), AN, F^{12} 647.

10 Necker, *Sur la législation et le commerce des grains*, 58–64.

away. The model used for projecting the price increase must contain social, political and psychological variables; one must compare the amount lacking not to the mass of grain but to the "surplus necessary to temper the power of the sellers and the alarms of the consumers."[11]

In Necker's paternalistic vision, for the sake of equilibrium the Legislator could "demand some slight sacrifices on the part of the fortunate Citizens." Even more sharply than Galiani, he rejected the idea that property in society was held unconditionally. The owners "owed" the people a "social sentiment." This meant, for example, as Delamare had argued, that they could not deprive their fellow men of the food of "national" grain for profit. Nor was it merely a gesture of altruism in the guise of a moral debt to be paid under threat of governmental reprisal. If the owners understood their own interests and the fragile albeit venerable conventions that guaranteed their rights, they would pay this slight ransom of self-restraint and, by denying themselves the dubious benefits of exportation, appease the consumers. From the Legislator's vantage point, if the cost of promoting agriculture through exportation was the eruption of a "sort of obscure but terrible combat" between haves and have-nots, then it was prohibitively expensive.

Moreover, like the Neapolitan philosophe, the Swiss banker not only suggested that agriculture did not need the incentive of exports given its huge internal market but wondered as well whether exportation did not do agriculture more harm than good. In any case, there was no reason to believe, despite the assurances of the liberals, that what was good for agriculture was best for the nation. Industry and agriculture, for example, were indissolubly linked and interdependent, "branches of the same trunk." Exportation severely penalized industry by inflating its costs and undermining its competitiveness. In sum, "in a country like France, the prohibition to export grain must be the fundamental law," allowing, however, for sale abroad when the prices and circumstances made the risk worthwhile.[12]

The other adversaries of liberalization drew similar conclusions from the experience of the sixties. Amplifying a note sounded by both Galiani and Necker, a writer of "Observations on the Grain Trade in France" challenged the serene cosmopolitanism of the économistes. Events proved that a fertile and large nation like France was often fleeced of its

---

11 *Ibid.*, 1, 21, 26, 52, 65–70.
12 *Ibid.*, 35–49, 86–87, 92–100, 117, 135, 137–50, 175–77, 188–89, 193, 322–24.

abundance in easy times by other states and left to suffer bad times in unfraternal solitude. It was far more important to assure domestic needs than to try to profit from *chertés* abroad.[13] The subsistence specialist Béguillet spoke for "the best organized minds" against the "rash vehemence" of the liberals. The satisfaction of immediate needs and the existence of a surplus were not in themselves sufficient reasons to warrant export. "It has not been realized," noted this advocate of public granaries, "that in voluntarily depriving ourselves of our surplus ... before having placed in reserve a sufficient quantity of grain, we render the life of the people precarious." Invoking the "genius of the Grand Colbert," Béguillet, too, contended that only "the certitude of abundance" and the consumption of the surplus at home at low prices would enable the arts to flourish, manufactures to develop, and the population to grow.[14]

Writing more than a decade after the crisis, Mercier excoriated the "law of exportation," which wrought death and suffering, "devouring the poor at the door of the granaries which crumbled under [the weight of] the abundance of grain" destined for sale elsewhere. The indifference of their moral posture rather than the substance of their political economy aroused his ire against the *économistes*. Even as Necker protested that men are not "x's" in algebra, that their "happiness," which is the goal of good government, cannot be reduced to formulae, so Mercier inveighed against the *Tableau* mentality and the unquantifiable flaw of liberal social science: "It is not enough to be a calculator; one must be a statesman."[15]

The *économistes* continued to believe that only cold "calculations" could put an end to the furor over exportation. In 1768 they circulated figures, based on extracts from the registers of the royal farms, purporting to show "that it is not at all exports to which the grain dearth in France must be attributed because there remains here much more than necessary to nourish all the inhabitants." Average annual exportation in the three years between October 1764 and October 1767 was approximately 800,000 *septiers*. Subtracting annual

---

13 Anonymous, "Observations sur le commerce des grains en France" (ca. 1769), BN, mss. fr. 5682, fols. 89–90. Cf. the similar argument and the attack on the intoxication with the English example which sustained the enthusiasm for exporting in the anonymous "Mémoire sur l'exportation," Oct. 1760, A 1/3677, Arch. Armée.

14 Béguillet, article "Abondance," *Supplément à l'Encyclopédie* (Amsterdam, 1776–1777), I, 31 and *Traité des subsistances*, 802–804.

15 L.-S. Mercier, *L'An 2440. Rêve s'il en fût jamais*, I, 145–46; Necker, *Sur la législation*, 72.

grain imports, the total should be reduced to 600,000 *septiers*, which represents no more than one-sixtieth of the annual harvest. Juxtaposed to this infinitesimal amount, the fears of a massive grain drain are revealed to be "vain and illusory." The "misfortunes of the people" and the "clamors of the ignorant" were thus due to "causes completely foreign" to exportation. They resulted from "blockages occasioned by the lack of circulation" and from "obstacles placed in the way of exportation," that is to say, from an imperfect and hesitant application of liberalization. The events of the sixties merely confirmed the physiocratic dogma that "it is *impossible* that there ever be dearth when there will no longer be any obstruction at any time under any pretext."[16]

In his energetic defense of liberalization, the abbé Roubaud modified these calculations in a downward direction. In the four years 1765 through 1768, an annual average of no more than 500,000 *septiers* left the kingdom (ranging from 600,000 to 700,000 in 1765 to only 200,000 to 300,000 in 1768) which accounted for one-eightieth to one-ninetieth of the average annual harvest or a mere four to five days' national subsistence. In a word, "exportation deprived us of nothing."[17] Several years later, Choiseul affirmed, on the basis of "first-hand knowledge," that the exports of each of the years 1765 and 1766 were at most 1,000,000 *septiers* (a figure probably uncorrected for importation) which amounted to "an imperceptible mass against the consumption and the production of the realm."[18]

Writing in October 1768, the deputies of commerce contested not the authenticity but the comprehensiveness of the statistics drawn from the revenue offices of the royal farms. The farm data indicated a total of about 1,800,000 *septiers* exported (imports subtracted) between October 1765 and August 1768. "This weak exportation," explained the deputies, "being not at all commensurate with the opinion which they formed on the subject, they undertook researches which do not allow them to doubt that these figures albeit faithfully extracted … do not include nearly the totality of the exportation." Of the 615 export offices, 494 were not provided for in the extracts. The deputies suggested that false declarations and fraud were rampant, especially since the offices were hastily organized and manned by agents of the "last order" whose ludicrously low salaries rendered them especially vulnerable to corruption. In addition, given the existence of certain traditional privileges of

16 Bachaumont, *Mémoires secrets*, IV, 78–79 (10 Aug. 1768). My italics.
17 Roubaud, *Représentations*, 230, 232ff.
18 Choiseul, *Mémoires*, I, 53. Cf. Weulersse's reading, *Mouvement*, II, 229.

exemption and the "foreign" status of several provinces, a significant portion of the kingdom escaped monitoring completely. The deputies made no attempt to construct new totals but emphasized repeatedly that exportation was "very considerable," "very extensive," and "very useful to the State."[19]

Outside the liberal camp, as within, opinions were divided. Malisset, the knowledgeable entrepreneur of the royal grain reserve, discounted the significance of actual exportation while his sometime associate, the enormously successful *négociant* Leray de Chaumont, characterized it as "extraordinary" in degree and regretted that it "succored humanity" at the cost of depleting France.[20] Rolland, President of the First Chamber of the Requêtes du Palais, expressed astonishment at the amplitude of the grain outflow. The Lieutenant General of Police Sartine deplored the "sad experience" of excessive exporting. Pointing to extensive deceptions in trading practices, which the official figures did not reflect, Lefebvre, one of the most outspoken Presidents of the Paris Parlement, assailed the liberal claim that real exportation had been insignificant.[21] Other magistrates, however—those who believed that it was a wholesome and beneficial policy—suggested that it had been practiced in moderation.[22]

Evidence from local sources, which must be more fully exploited before a convincing picture emerges, shows that there was heavy export of flour and grain from Le Havre and Rouen to Spain, Portugal, and Italy between 1764 and 1767 and that the demand for exports gave shipbuilding a healthy impulsion.[23] Substantial quantities also passed through the "southern" Atlantic and Mediterranean ports. On the other hand, it is well to remember the technical, geographic, and economic limitations on potential exportation. The difficulty and expense of transportation, which hindered internal circulation, obviously affected prospects for participation in exportation.[24] In light of the critique of the deputies and other indicators, the leading scholarly

---

19 "Avis des Députés du Commerce sur la libre circulation des grains," (Oct. 1768), AN, F^{12} 715.

20 BN, mss. fr. 14295 and AN, F^{11} 1193.

21 *Recueil*, 130, 189, 234–35.

22 *Ibid.*, 160, 192–96 (Clément, *maître des comptes* and Murard, President of the third *Chambre des Enquêtes*).

23 Pierre Dardel, *Navires et marchandises dans les ports de Rouen et du Havre au dix-huitième siècle* (Paris, 1963), 108, 115–16, and *passim* and Weulersse, *Mouvement*, II, 425–26.

24 Labrousse, *Esquisse*, 124–34.

authority on the question estimated total exports (to mid-1768) at 1 or 2 million *septiers* above the farm bureau figure: 3,828,910 to 4,828,910 *septiers* or, allowing for imports, an export balance of 2,795,155 to 3,795,155 *septiers*. Even at this revised evaluation, exportation appears to have been much less "considerable" than the deputies of commerce imagined, although the fact that they felt so certain is significant for our understanding of government decision-making processes, which depended on such expert "avis" as theirs, and of popular reactions to exportation, which were based upon observations little different from those of the deputies. It would be extremely misleading to assess the influence of exportation on the basis of its volume alone, yet it seems clear that total real exports never amounted to much more than one million *septiers* a year or between 1 and 2½% of annual French grain production.[25]

For Dupont, however, no less than for Necker, small material causes could have imposing socioeconomic effects. For Necker the results of exportation were wholly baleful while for Dupont they were spectacularly salutary. With customary hyperbole, the *économistes* claimed that exportation (for Dupont it was "the hope of being able to export at will," for he maintained that real exports were "more than null") transformed agriculture. It made men more laborious, animals more vigorous, and the soil more fertile. It brought thousands of new acres under cultivation,[26] increased production substantially and in some places

---

25 Weulersse, *Mouvement*, II, 227 and Labrousse, *Esquisse*, 123. Cf. Labrousse and Braudel, eds., *Histoire économique et sociale*, II, 373 where Labrousse suggests how the physiocratic design anticipated the modern notion of "marginalism."

26 The debate over the impact of liberalization on land clearing and reclamation has not yet been settled, despite pioneering local studies (e.g., G. Debien, *En Haut-Poitou: défricheurs au travail* [Paris, 1952]) and subtle and judicious syntheses (Labrousse in Braudel and Labrousse, eds., *Histoire économique et sociale de la France*, III, 417–432). The liberals unanimously insisted on the major thrust that liberty gave to land clearing. Their critics scoffed at these claims; they were disinclined to see progress upon a background of widespread misery and dislocation. In any event, they were more likely to ascribe clearing to the major fiscal incentives offered by the government in 1766 than to the grain reforms. Given the highly political nature of the question, it is difficult to take the measure of contemporary testimony. For a number of reasons, which Labrousse reviews, not even the statistical data can be used without extreme care. It seems clear that there was a surge of clearing in the sixties, though its total contribution to French agricultural production appears to have been rather meagre, "in the hundredths," as Labrousse writes. It is, for example, hard to take seriously the Provençal claim that the province, in large part as a result of the recovery of arable, was now self-sufficient, subsistence-wise. Parl. of Aix to Louis XV, 10 Nov. 1770, B. 3677, A.D. B-du-R. Many administrators reported unequivocally that liberalization encouraged clearing and contributed ultimately to larger harvests. See, for example, SD to IN. of

productivity as well, mercifully saved the families of innumerable cultivators from ruin, spurred capital investment in land, livestock and technology, created new jobs, stimulated nuptuality and natality, swelled national wealth, and made it easier for everyone to pay taxes and other obligations.[27]

The change was sudden and profound; depressed and languishing in 1763, within a few years agriculture flourished brilliantly. The magistrates of Provence marveled at "this resurrection of agriculture"; their Dauphiné counterparts called it a "revolution." The Parlement of Aix maintained that this should be taken as "the true thermometer of the success of the new legislation." "Nothing was more striking and immediate than the effect of this [export] law," observed another advocate of liberty; "the income of the cultivator increased all of a sudden, and I saw with my own eyes villages, almost deserted and falling in ruins, rebuilt, in the twinkling of an eye, so to speak...." Years later the liberals of Languedoc looked back upon the sixties as a golden age of expansion, wealth, rising land values, and optimism.[28] The poet of the "Seasons," Saint Lambert, lyricized

> Il fut enfin permis au peuple des hameaux
> De Vendre à l'étranger les fruits de leurs travaux.
> Le Fermier s'enrichit; le Commerce plus libre
> Fit couler sur nos champs l'or du Tage et du Tibre.

Alençon, 25 Oct. 1773, C. 89, A.D. Orne; IN. of Alençon to CG, 25 Jan 1772, AN, F[11] 223. Yet others either reported little clearing because of the extremely marginal land available or acknowledged "much clearing" while questioning its importance in view of the fact that it took place on inferior arable and that it drained capital, fertilizer, and care from proven lands, thus decreasing their yield. SD at Bernay to IN. of Alençon, 12 Oct. 1773, C. 89, A.D. Orne and SD at Bar-sur-Aube to IN. of Champagne, 29 Oct. 1773, C. 299, A.D. Aube. Cf. the data on clearings in C. 265 and C. 266, A.D. P-de-D.

27 "Observations sur les effets de la liberté du commerce des grains ... par l'auteur des Ephémérides du citoyen," *Journal économique* (July 1770), 330–332; Baudeau, *Avis au premier besoin*, 1er traité, 39; Roubaud, *Représentations*, 232–67; Baudeau, "Lettres et mémoires à un Magistrat du Parlement de Paris ...," *Nouvelles éphémérides économiques* (1775), I, 23; *Ephémérides du citoyen* (1770), V, 24 and VII, 231–33 and VIII, 41–50; Dupont to Prince Carl Ludwig, (ca. 1773), *Correspondance Dupont*, ed. by Knies, II, 140; *Journal économique* (April 1769), 176; Turgot to Condorcet, 6 April 1772, *Correspondance Condorcet-Turgot*, ed. by Henry, 81; Weulersse, *Mouvement*, II, 233. Cf. Labrousse and Braudel, eds., *Histoire économique et sociale*, II, 426ff.

28 Parl. of Aix to Louis XV, 2 Nov. 1768 and 10 Nov. 1770, B. 3677, A.D. B-du-R.; Parl. of Dauphiné to Louis XV, April 1769, B. 2314, fol. 109, A.D. Isère; *Arrêté* of Dauphiné Parl., 12 July 1768, C. 2420, A.D. B-du-R.; Anon., "Réflexions sur les principes des parlements...," France 1375, fol. 294, Arch. AE; deliberation of the *commissaires ordinaires*, diocèse de Toulouse, 21 Nov. 1779, C. 977, fol. 70, A.D. H-G.

On paya les impôts sans se croire opprimé;
Tout fut riche et content; et le Roi fut aimé.[29]

As always, however, the *économistes* paid a price for their extravagance. On the one hand, they naturally wanted to show that liberalization had worked just as they had promised it would since Quesnay drew the first "zig-zag." On the other hand, as the reforms came under increasingly sharp attack, their enthusiasm for the dramatic efficacy of liberalization placed them in an awkward position. For instead of affirming their ideological responsibility and resolutely standing their ground on the basis of the positive achievements of liberalization, they wavered and retreated. They began to argue that liberalization was indeed faulty, but in its application, not in its aims or in the consequences that it would have produced had it been unimpeded. The *économistes* had always argued that the reform laws did not fully meet their theoretical demands (those of natural law); now they added that they were not genuinely, rigorously, and universally implemented even as they were drafted. Liberty was restricted, incomplete, and sometimes nonexistent. That is why dearth and disorder occurred. Dupont's small causes argument presupposed that everyone had the opportunity to dispose of his property in grain as he wished. But in response to their critics the *économistes* increasingly implied that neither this opportunity nor the belief in it really existed in large parts of the kingdom.

Once self-defense impelled them to modify their view of liberalization, the logic of consistency suggested that they revise their boastful assessment of its fruits. Could a liberty so infirm have generated a genuine rural renaissance? The abbé Morellet, staunch ally of the *économistes*, reproved their tendency to exaggeration and regretted the damage it did to their case. He admitted that they overstated the effects of exportation upon agriculture; the benfits were neither as "considerable" nor as "prompt" as they pretended.[30] Their arch-enemy Linguet exposed the contradictions in physiocratic reasoning, and condemned them for impudence and imposture. Deriding the idea of a brusque renewal, he contended even more vigorously than Galiani and Necker that liberty had "weakened" French agriculture.[31]

---

29 Cited by Weulersse, *Mouvement*, I, 549n.

30 Morellet, *Réfutation de l'ouvrage qui a pour titre: "Dialogues sur le commerce des bleds,"* 301.

31 Linguet, *Réponse aux docteurs modernes* (London, and Paris, 1771), partie III, 144, 152–55 and *Du pain et du bled*, 174–75. An administrator experienced in grain affairs, Bourdon-Desplanches argued that liberalization hurt agriculture by "diverting"

II

In the debate over the causes of the scarcity and the high prices of the sixties the exportation issue overshadowed all other questions. Remarkably little explicit attention was paid to the matter of internal trade although both parties clearly understood that the problems of internal traffic and exportation were inextricably linked and that the home marketplaces were the theatres of subsistence drama and politics. Obviously the liberty to export would be of limited significance unless internal trade were free and open. The liberals maintained that exportation would have a marvelously tonic effect on internal circulation, increasing its range and velocity and fanning its goods briskly across the kingdom.[32]

In his reading of the process, however, Galiani argued that the two forms of commerce were not symbiotic; exportation would ruin domestic trade even as it destroyed agriculture. It was a mistake to permit exports to become the government's signal preoccupation: "interior commerce is so preferable, of such an importance, of such superior utility to the other that there is no comparison to make between the two." Whereas the liberals, partly in an effort to show that exports for technical reasons could not be as heavy as their critics charged, tended to emphasize the difficulties and risks of export traffic and the special demands of expertise, capital and experience it imposed, Galiani insisted on its facility. Export trade would eclipse internal circulation in importance precisely because it was "infinitely easier." Given a choice, serious businessmen would no longer bother with domestic provisioning because transport abroad was often simpler, cheaper, and speedier than traffic to the center (France, like ancient Rome, would suffer its heartland drained of nourishment), it spared the merchant the petty details involved in a diffuse internal network (tedious collection of accounts

---

attention from the "care of the land" into feverish speculative endeavors. *Projet nouveau sur la manière de faire utilement en France le commerce des grains* (Brussels, 1785), 12–13. Though it is impossible to test Bourdon's hypothesis rigorously, it is undeniable that many *laboureurs*, farmers and other *exploitants* invested greater energies in the trade in the late sixties than they ever had before.

32 To clear the historical, institutional, and psychological debris which littered the pathway of internal circulation a powerful wind was required, the liberals argued, which could only be generated by opening the gates of fortress France to exports. See Parl. of Dauphiné to Louis XV, 26 April 1769, B. 2314, fol. 107 and the remarks of several Dauphinais subdelegates on the stunning new vigor of the trade in the états des récoltes, 1765, II C. 50, A.D. Isère.

payable from a multitude of relatively small buyers, maintenance of a chain of magazines, etc.), it insulated him against official and officious nuisances ("the industry and genius of men have not yet succeeded in establishing Mayors, Echevins, Baillis, and especially Subdelegates on the vast plains of the Ocean"), and it assured greater profits, not only from the sale of huge amounts of grain, but through other commercial and banking opportunities which would certainly arise.[33]

On commercial grounds, Galiani's argument is open to serious dispute; more significant are its political implications. Exportation diverted the grain trade from its primary mission: the fulfillment of national subsistence needs. Other purposes, such as enhancing national wealth, Galiani contended, had to be subordinate and incidental. Moreover, in a country as large and as populous as France, with marked regional differences in climate, soil, and nature and quality of produce, traffic from one province to another—say from one enjoying a surplus to another afflicted with dearth—was a "veritable exportation."[34] At least there was no question that it was so regarded by the bulk of consumers who, from their own spatial and psychological vantage point, denounced every "removal" as an export irrespective of destination.

Ironically, as a result of popular reactions—not because of Galiani's "economic" reasoning—the liberal deputies of commerce esteemed that freedom to export had in fact paralyzed internal circulation instead of promoting it: "*Cherté* having followed Exportation, Exportation engendered inquietude … from which moment any displacement of grain, albeit destined for interior circulation, appeared as a dangerous exportation." No matter where they set out to go, to the frontiers and coasts or to interior markets, merchants were harried and their grain was intercepted. In face of these "prejudices," grain trade became a virtual impossibility by the end of the sixties.[35] The deputies by no means conceded that real exports themselves caused the *cherté* but

---

33 Galiani, *Dialogues*, ed. by Nicolini, 244–50.

34 *Ibid.*, 252–54. Cf. note 3 below. The widespread confusion over the precise meaning of exportation caused serious misunderstandings. In November 1767, for example, the port of Dunkerque was closed to exports because the current price exceeded the legal ceiling during three consecutive markets. "This prohibition," according to the intendant of Flanders, "was misunderstood by the people who confused exports with [internal] circulation...." To enforce their conception of the export suspension, the people blocked and pillaged grain boats and wagons and imposed a virtual embargo on grain removals. Caumartin to Taboureau, 7 Nov. 1767, C. 6690, A.D. Nord.

35 "Avis des Députés du Commerce sur le libre commerce des grains," AN, F^{12} 715.

observed that the public "attributed" it to exports. Whether consumers would have thought or acted any differently in a dearth situation unaccompanied by a highly-publicized liberty to export is questionable. It is worth noting, however, that the deputies, like Galiani, deplored its deleterious effect on the ordinary flow of grain.

For two administrator-magistrates deeply involved in the grain crisis, exportation, real or imagined or potential, analyzed hypothetically or on the basis of first-hand experience, was much less significant than it seemed either to the liberal deputies or to the antiliberal abbé Galiani. To be sure, they agreed that the trade was gravely disorganized, but they refused to ascribe this disruption to exportation. The first, Moreau, the royal procurator at the Paris Châtelet, who made extensive investigative tours through the kingdom in 1767–68, cautioned against the temptation to confuse the issues and draw the wrong conclusions. Exportation provided an incentive and an opportunity for wrecking the channels of provisioning, but it was not the real source of the problem. "All the evil," Moreau contended, "derives from the too extensive liberty of the grain trade." "I believe," he added, "that exportation in itself would never have operated the excessive *cherté* that we suffer if it had not been permitted to buy grain at the home of the *laboureur*; as a consequence of this facility, grain is no longer brought to the markets." The Declaration of 1763, rather than the Edict of 1764, was responsible for the perilous situation of the nation. It invited everyone to become a grain dealer, it authorized sales in the granaries and even in the fields, and it wrought chaos by reducing the whole subsistence question to a matter of profit. If the old regime of regulations had not been abrogated, Moreau suggested, it would have continued to channel supplies to the markets where they were urgently needed and it would have suppressed practices which tended to augment prices. Presumably, then, only grain that was not actually required for domestic consumption would have escaped the honeycomb of controls and reached the exit points.[36]

Reflecting on the crisis several years later, the second of the two officials, the Parisian Procurator General, concurred. Exportation was at best the "secondary cause." The "first cause" was the "overly absolute and too little monitored liberty in the interior commerce." This license made possible "monopolies" and "hoards" without which exports

---

36 Moreau to (?), 2 Oct. 1768, AN, F^{11} 1179.

could not have had a major effect.[37] Exportation preoccupied the liberals because it was the issue that galvanized public opinion and because it was the one on which they felt most vulnerable. For high-ranking judicial officials like Moreau and Joly, however, there was a more fundamental problem of which exportation was merely the most sensational symptom. The scores of protests from local authorities and the myriad popular uprisings testified to its crucial importance. In their estimation the crisis in the grain trade was due above all to the eclipse of the police.

There were less dramatic signs than riot of what the police termed "abuses" in the grain trade which contributed to make grain scarce and dear and which diverted it from the well-tread paths it "ordinarily" followed. "Under the pretext that the trade is now free," according to the fiscal procurator of Rambouillet, "rich Beauce *laboureurs*" purchased grain at the market instead of bringing it for sale there, while the local merchants conducted all their transactions surreptitiously in barns and storehouses. At Vitry-le-François commerce became almost completely furtive, moving from the open market to the country and leaving officials who were once experts ignorant of the true state of affairs. Throughout Brittany dealers began stripping the markets and scouring the countryside in order to prepare hoards for export or regrate at the propitious moment. In similar fashion, traders, like locusts, devastated parts of Picardy and Champagne, leaving in their wake a trail of "removals," which suggested transit abroad. When they failed to intercept supplies on the road, merchants in Auvergne simply outbid consumers in the public market. Deeply-rooted habits were rudely jarred. Bidaux, a *blatier* from Bléré, a town near Tours, who used to transfer grain from meagre village markets to the larger trading centers with clockwork fidelity, now visited the *fermiers* at home, bought in the granaries, and transacted all his business underground. Boureau, an unfortunately-named baker from another town in the Touraine, "goes buying from parish to parish, village to village which means that the markets are not furnished, almost no grain falls to them." An awareness of the significance of the new permissive climate and a certain intoxication with the unfolding vistas of liberty stretched down from the international trading companies of Rouen, which anxiously awaited the first toll of the liberty bell in order to send their agents into the interior and their ships abroad, to the petty dealers

---

37 BN, Coll. Joly 1109, fol. 215.

of the Brie, who believed that the king would soon enact legislation definitively razing the old market-prisons by explicitly authorizing trade by sample and exchanges in private granaries. The same climate fired the popular imagination in quite another way. The discovery of a huge pit of charred grain covered with fresh sand containing between 25 and 50 *muids* on the road between Meaux and Claye nearly caused a riot. The incident struck the people as an example of the sort of terrible maneuvers that merchants engineered in order to keep the markets empty and the prices exorbitant.[38]

Deserted by suppliers, once flourishing markets were dying of asphyxiation. Méry-sur-Seine was almost entirely abandoned. "The *laboureurs* and tradesmen enrich themselves and become very indolent," wrote the *substitut*, "while the Bourgeois and the little people suffer extraordinarily from the *cherté* of grain." At Etampes trading was vigorous but invisible as dealers transacted business over tiny sacks instead of bringing their goods for display and public bargaining. Trading patterns at Arcis-sur-Aube were also violently disrupted, but the results were rather different, at least for the commercial interest. For instead of choking the market, liberalization breathed new life into it, rationalized its operation, and modernized its role. Instead of convening buyers and sellers once a week, as custom ratified by law had previously decreed, the market "is held every day because grain is brought here continually and there are ten buyers at every wagon." Nor was this the only shock administered to Arcis. Before liberalization it had served almost exclusively as an entrepôt for the provisioning of Paris, "but since [1763–64] it has shipped a great deal [of grain] every year by the Canal of Briare [towards the Atlantic or the Mediterranean]; and when Franche-Comté and the elections of Langres and Chaumont are depleted, it supplies them as well." As a consequence of these changes a once modest commerce had grown to "immense sums," according to a knowledgeable subdelegate. This Cinderella-like transformation of Arcis was the liberal dream come true, the proof that all

---

38 Petit to PG, 21 Nov. 1767, BN, Coll. Joly 1136, fol. 137; Salligny to PG, 24 June 1769, Coll. Joly 1144, fols. 111–12; SD report, 4 Sept. 1765 and IN. of Brittany to CG, draft, 17 Sept. 1765, C. 1670, A.D. I-et-V.; report to IN. of Champagne, 29 Dec. 1767, C. 413, A.D. Marne; subdelegation of Amiens, état de récolte, 1768, C. 81, A.D. Somme; IN. of Auvergne to SD, 18 Dec. 1766, C. 7506, A.D. P-de-D.; Haberty to IN. (?) of Tours, 4 Sept. 1765, C. 93, A.D. I-et-L.; C. 103, A.D. S-M.; fiscal procurator of Brie-Comte-Robert to PG, 1 Oct. 1768, BN, Coll. Joly 1146, fol. 28; declaration of Sept. 1766, Arsenal, mss. Bastille 10076.

things would work out for the best in a laissez-faire world. But if liberty and competition brought efficiency and abundance, they also promoted *cherté*. The purpose of the old, policed market system had been to assure abundance while preventing *cherté*: indeed, it was geared specifically to preclude their coexistence. Thus neither the local police nor the consumers applauded these changes. On the contrary, they regarded them as inimical to the public interest and denounced them as the product of merchant crimes.[39]

The "authors" of "maneuvers" and "abuses" varied from place to place. In the Brie, according to a report in which Joly de Fleury placed considerable confidence, the arch-villain was the cultivator-turned-merchant, the *laboureur-maltôtier* who was becoming "as rich as the big financiers." The *laboureurs* appeared publicly uniquely to buy, sold only clandestinely and in great lots, hoarded their stores in magazines hidden in the countryside, and became "masters of the price" wherever they chose to go. "Since 1763," noted Petit of Rambouillet, "the *fermier*, too opulent, has become a grain merchant," hoarding supplies and driving up prices. In Champagne, *laboureurs* sold their crops before the harvest, solicited earnest money in return for keeping their grain off the markets, and hoarded for their own speculative accounts.[40]

Small-time itinerant grain merchants, seeking to expand their commercial horizons, were also considered suspect. The police arrested Antoine Lelièvre, a fifty-two year old veteran grain trader from Etampes, as much for his bravado as for his allegedly illicit operations. He was accused of assembling a large stock of grain, in secret association with two other dealers, constituted by purchases made in the farms and in the markets. Asked by an *exempt* of the *maréchaussée* at Arpajon (who, it is true, had no business asking such a question) whether he had authorization to buy in the market, he replied in an abusive fashion. Reportedly, he expressed delight with the high prices instead of bargaining to resist them and announced with cheerful morbidity

39 Bouquigny to PG, 1 April 1769, BN, Coll. Joly 1146, fols. 150–51; Picard to Sartine, 8 Jan. 1769, AN, Y 12618; Paillot (?) to IN. of Champagne, 23 Oct. 1773, C. 1179, A.D. Aube.

40 BN, Coll. Joly 1135, fols. 180–185; Petit to PG, 1 Sept. 1770, Coll. Joly 1154, fol. 132; Masson to IN. of Champagne, 9 Sept. 1766, C. 299, A.D. Aube. Cf. the desire of the Hainaut subdelegate to ban "rich persons" in general from the grain trade as a means of preventing speculative *chertés*. Report to IN., ca. Oct. 1773, C. 6690, A.D. Nord.

that "it would be necessary this winter to have teeth of gold in order to eat bread."[41]

Catherine Jourdain of Poissy, widow of Claude Leclerc, late "grain merchant for the provisioning of Paris and flour merchant for the provisioning of Paris and Saint Germain," petitioned the Procurator General to quash a warrant for the arrest of her son and business associate who had gone into hiding to escape capture. His trouble began at Mantes where his buying activities aroused the ire of other customers. "The decision having been made to furnish the people a victim," widow Leclerc protested, the police confiscated his grain and pursued him although they knew he was "innocent." She claimed that he was made the scapegoat to satisfy the anxieties and the lust of the crowd. He fled not because he was guilty but because "he knew the animosity of the people of this country [pays] which is always pushed to the extremity." According to his mother, he was a petty dealer, but the authorities charged young Leclerc with being a "monopolist" and a "commissioner for the companies."[42]

Sieur Normant of Montargis, flaunting a permit from the Paris municipality, combed the countryside, intercepting grain at the farms at "a high price" and thus drying up the neighborhood markets. Reports reached the Contrôle-Général that one Simonneau, not noted as a major trader, had purchased the extraordinary amount of 20,000 sacks of wheat in a single month in the area around Nemours and Montereau. "There are in different places," an anonymous correspondent warned the Procurator General, "merchant stores of grain and flour which serve to make famines."[43]

Bakers as well as *laboureurs* and merchants attracted attention for unusual trade practices. Officials at Dammartin and Dreux complained that bakers were undertaking grain commerce on a scale never before witnessed. Paris bakers frequenting Dammartin denounced a local baker turned "merchant-*blatier*" who preempted

---

41 12 Oct. 1768, AN, Y 12617. Cf. the wealthy grain merchant with large magazines who warned in 1768 that "it will be necessary to have teeth of silver to eat bread." BN, Coll. Joly 1142, fol. 98. Diderot, writing about grain and property rights, cited the "farmer of Sully" who said: "I have grain but damn! You need silver teeth to eat it." *Apologie de l'Abbé Galiani* (1770), *Œuvres politiques*, ed. by Paul Vernière (Paris 1963), 121.

42 BN, Coll. Joly 1111, fol. 137.

43 Dispatch to Bignon, *Prévôt des Marchands*, 25 Dec. 1766, AN, O¹* 408, fols. 872–73; dispatch to B. de Sauvigny, IN. to Paris, 15 May 1770, AN, F¹²* 153, fol. 217; 25 July 1770, BN, Coll. Joly 1109, fol. 178.

them by buying on samples and then reselling at a higher price on the same market. The "populace" of Gonesse squalled that they were unable to purchase grain on their own market "because of the avidity of the bakers" who serviced the capital. In the same area a Paris baker bought in a single transaction 500 *septiers* of wheat which was, moreover, three years old and badly worm-eaten. Trudaine de Montigny suspected the Paris bakers and certain prominent grain merchants of the same sort of "maneuvers" and "cabals" which President Mirosmesnil detected at Rouen.[44]

In October 1768 the Paris police arrested a fifty-three year old faubourg Saint Antoine baker named François Gibert for having provoked a "popular rising" at the Montereau market by "purchasing with earnest-money the largest portion of grain [available] at the price demanded of him" and thereby "forcing up the price." Gibert claimed that he bought only fifteen *septiers* and "acquitted himself for the best price he could make." Challenged by the commandant of the *maréchaussée* unit to justify his purchases, he displayed a simple certificate from the Paris police commissaire Lemaire indicating that he supplied the Maubert bread market which he tried to pass off for a special permission from the Lieutenant General of Police. Gibert denied the imposture, admitting only that he said the Lieutenant was surely informed of the role he played in serving the capital's needs. Pressured by the procurator of Montereau to share his purchases with local buyers, Gibert complied. But when he refused to sell below the price he had paid, a band of women assaulted him, upsetting the wig which this proud businessman-baker affected in his commercial traveling. Gibert insisted on his stature as a major figure in the baking industry. It was perfectly legitimate for a baker who "employed three journeymen [garçons] as well as his wife and a servant" and who converted sixty *septiers* a week into bread to make large purchases in the countryside.[45]

Certainly Gibert's activities were no different from the operations of ambitious bakers before and after the decade of the sixties. While the dearth drove many bakers deep into the countryside in pursuit of grain

---

44 Ganneron to PG, 13 June 1769, BN, Coll. Joly 1146, fols. 102–103; LG of Dreux to PG, 9 Jan. 1769, *ibid.*, fol. 105; "Mémoire," 10 May 1768, AN, F¹¹ 1174; letter to Trudaine de Montigny. 3 Dec. 1767, AN, F¹¹ 1174; Miromesnil to CG, 18 March 1768 and Trudaine de Montigny to Miromesnil, 22 March 1768, in LeVerdier, ed., *Correspondance Miromesnil*, V, 120–121, 130.

45 28 Oct. 1768, AN, Y 14095.

and tempted some to speculate for resale (Gibert emphatically denied that he regrated), a great many others, with only marginal means, found their usual sources dried up and were only saved from ruin by police assistance. One observer maintained that, as a result of the *cherté*, bakers who usually went to the field for supplies flocked instead to the Halles where authorities concentrated large doses of the king's grain.[46]

Although they habitually distrusted the more enterprising bakers, the Paris police could not afford to be overly concerned about how the bakers procured their supplies as long as they acted discreetly— Gibert's sin was that he stirred an uproar—and continued to furnish quality bread at the going price. The measurers and porters at the Paris Halles and ports assumed as always a large share of the burden of surveillance of baker grain and flour dealings. The age-old battle between these officers and the bakers persisted, somewhat tempered by the desire of senior officials to avoid any hassles which would reduce baker capability to provide bread. The points of contact (and contention) remained the same: the measurers and porters stalked incoming grain and flour wagons, challenging the bakers and/or suppliers to prove that their merchandise had been legally purchased and the obligatory fees properly paid upon entry. When their goods were sequestered and when they received summonses, many of the bakers protested to higher authorities, appealed in court, or resorted to extra-legal gestures of defiance and evasion. Angry enough to bypass the police and take aim at the summit of the hierarchy, the master baker Pharoux remonstrated to the Contrôle-Général against measurer harassment and attempted extortion. Baker Antoine Chevalier sent his wife to the hearing over the porters' seizure of eleven sacks of bolted flour delivered by his Beaumont miller. By appearing personally to defend him, she succeeded in avoiding a fine and recovering "by grace" one-half of the sale price of the confiscated goods. Not long afterward master baker Boulanger suffered the loss of 12 sacks for a false declaration of amount and origin and in addition a 20 *livres* fine for failing to answer the summons.[47]

Victim of a measurer flour seizure, another master baker appealed immediately to Parlement, not in the first instance to contest the matter of his guilt (although he conceded nothing), but to win the prompt

---

46 "Mémoire" (ca. 1771), AN, F¹¹ 264.
47 Trudaine de Montigny to Sartine, 10 June 1769, AN, F¹²* 153; 14 June 1765, AN, Y 9632; 14 Nov. 1766, AN, Y 9633.

release of the confiscated flour in order to prevent its spoilage and to enable him to meet his pressing obligations for "the furnishing of bread." The high court acknowledged his special role as "baker of Paris"—a status enhanced and a responsibility made heavier by scarcity and high prices—despite the unremitting opposition of the measurers. On similar grounds a mealman applied for the deliverance of a boatload of flour detained for litigation, citing the demand of the bakers who had "an urgent need to bake" in order to satisfy "their obligation to the public." Baker Bonhommet launched his appeal against the market officers spontaneously in the streets—opposition to these petty policemen was perhaps the only issue on which the bakers could count on public support—almost detonating a "popular riot." Refusing to show his certificate of purchase and physically resisting the seizure of his fifteen-sack flour wagon, Bonhommet forced the porters to call the Guard in order to disperse the crowd that had gathered in response to his outcries. In this instance the police showed no sympathy for the baker; Sartine approved the confiscation and ordered the public sale of the flour at the Halles.[48]

The flour trade showed signs of a new vitality and expansiveness. The lingering distinction, already somewhat dim, between miller/flour dealer and grain merchant became increasingly blurred. Liberalization encouraged the millers to dispense with such middlemen as the mealman and the grain dealer and to engage speculatively in grain and flour traffic. More commonly than before and without exaggeration, the miller began to style himself "merchant." In some cases he even dropped the designation miller in favor of the more imposing "merchant of grain and flour living at the mill of X."[49] Merchant millers like the Sieur Aubry from the Meaux area or Claude Hallé of Belleville or Goriot from Pontoise purchased grain directly from the *laboureurs*, converted it to flour, and sold it through brokers at the Halles or directly to Paris bakers, if they felt bold enough to test the vigilance of the porters and measurers.[50] Jacques Pavie's mill at Bretoncelle in Alençon sometimes took on the appearance of a village grain market. Hettard, a Persan miller, only bothered to transform to flour if the grain

48 10 May 1769, AN, X[1B] 9475; 1 Oct. 1765, AN, Z[1H] 449; 7 Feb. 1766, Archives Seine-Paris, 6 AZ 472.

49 See, for example, the mediator's report of 4 Nov. 1769, Archives Seine-Paris, D6B[6] carton 6. Cf. the quasi-hysterical fear of the rise of the capitalist miller-cheater in "Objections sur le commerce des grains" (ca. 1768), C. 2420, A.D. B-du-R.

50 Mediator's report, 18 Dec. 1767, Archives Seine-Paris, D6B[6] carton 5; Archives Seine-Paris, D5B[6] 5367; 17 Dec. 1771, AN Y 9474.

he proffered failed to draw a sufficiently attractive price. Lambert, a super-miller at Pontoise, allegedly amassed "in different places" 18,000 sacks of grain.[51]

An investigation conducted by the Paris Parlement revealed that in 1768 an Etampes miller named La Place had amassed a huge stock of grain drawn from the Orleans and Paris provisioning zones where he had buying agents. Although he displayed large quantities on the market, he sold little because he demanded a price "more dear than the current." When he could not sell he bought, flour as well as grain, outbidding needy consumers. He rebuffed the protests of other merchants, brashly averring that "the trade was today free" and consequently that "he was free at present to make deals as he wished and that he feared nothing." In addition, La Place stood accused of removing grain secretly from the market at night, mixing "rotten and overheated" grain with good wheat, and of disposing of some of it at Montlhéry where he was less well known than at Etampes.[52]

In order to meet the competition of the millers, the mealmen had to broaden and consolidate their businesses. Many flour dealers enlarged the scope of their grain-purchasing activities, others battled for control of the lesser millers who remained artisanal, while still others seem to have been spurred to establish their own mills and secure greater commercial independence and flexibility.[53] Liberalization and the technological innovations in milling stimulated by the liberal reforms reinforced the gradual secular trend towards the eclipse of grain by flour in the trade supplying the capital.[54]

The police perceived a direct connection between the proliferation of abuses in the grain trade and the infiltration of new men into the business: greedy opportunists, merchants equally lacking in skill and probity, men previously excluded from this commerce who exploited their wealth and influence unfairly, and above all men who knew and cared nothing for the conventions, traditions, and responsibilities which were so integral a part of the trade before liberalization. Opening the trade for the first time to all comers, the May Declaration abolished the old eligibility controls and most of the socioprofessional

---

51 29 Feb. 1772, C. 89, A.D. Orne; Procès-verbal, 28 Oct. 1768, BN, Coll. Joly 1140, fol. 48; Coll. Joly 1142, fol. 53.

52 18 April 1769, AN, X[1B] 9434.

53 See, for example, the cases of Raguidet of Gouvieux (9 Feb. 1769, Archives Seine-Paris, DC[6] 116, fol. 8) and Renard of Gonesse and Châtelain of Tillet (20 May 1775, AN, Y 11441).

54 See Malisset's pertinent "Observations" (Jan. 1765), BN, mss. fr. 14295, fol. 161.

incompatibilities (nobles, for example, were specifically authorized to trade; the *Journal économique* exhorted them to engage in such useful and profitable enterprise).[55] According to contemporaries, the result was a remarkable multiplication of new faces in grain and flour commerce recruited from every quality and condition. An "infinity" of individuals suddenly installed themselves in the trade at Rambouillet, in the Brie, in the Beauce, at Orléans, in the Hainaut, at Besançon, Troyes, Bar-sur-Aube, Châlons-sur-Marne, Sézanne, Angers, Noirot, Amiens; at Vitry *gentilshommes* and *curés* participated prominently; Etampes boasted a hairdresser and several domestics; "the smallest *fermiers*" in the Dauphiné began to gamble; "strangers" in droves descended upon the Brittany coast to forage for grain; in the Toulouse area, piddling adventurers with a fistful of change speculated no less avidly than the grand proprietors and big farmers who took a much keener interest in marketing their own crop and acquiring other produce than ever before. The sheer increase in numbers of persons engaged in the trade astonished authorities throughout the kingdom. In Languedoc merchants seemed to "grow by the hundred" while in Champagne their storehouses "multiplied as if by miracle." A great many of the traders were "unknown persons" and the police had no right to inquire into their origins or their intentions.[56]

Although there was only a faint resemblance between the grain fever of the sixties and the reckless speculation and jolting social dislocation of the time of John Law, nevertheless the lives of many men were changed in the sixties as they had been in the Regency by the acquisition of rapid fortunes or a brusque shift in function, status, and self-esteem.

---

55 *Journal économique* (Nov. 1764), 494.
56 "Mémoire" (1771), BN, Coll. Joly 1111, fol. 143; Petit to PG, 27 June 1768, Coll. Joly 1142, fols. 72–73; Coll. Joly 1152, fols. 141–58; Pascaud (?) to Sartine, Sept. 1770, AN H 1669; reports of SDs of Valenciennes, Quesnay and St. Armand to IN. of Hainaut, ca. Oct. 1773, C. 6690, A.D. Nord; de la Corée to CG, 2 Sept. 1770, C. 844, A.D. Doubs; Municipality of Châlons to CG, 29 Dec. 1767, C. 413, A.D. Marne; Masson to IN. of Champagne, 9 Sept. 1766 and Gehier to same, 29 Oct. 1773, C. 299, A.D. Aube; Paillot to IN. of Champagne, 23 Oct. 1773, C. 1179, A.D. Aube; SD at Dourdan to Cypierre, 24 Sept. 1768 in C. Bloch, *Correspondance inédite de l'intendant Cypierre*, 99; enquête de 1773, C. 86, A.D. Somme; Parl. of Dauphiné to Louis XV, 26 April 1769, B. 2314, fol. 110, A.D. Isère; Parl. of Bordeaux, *arrêt* 12 May 1773, C. 1439, A.D. Gir.; draft, IN. of Brittany to CG, 17 Sept. 1765, C. 1670, A.D. I-et-V.; de Vandoul (?) to IN. of Languedoc, 21 and 28 April, C. 2914, A.D. Hér.; C. 2909, A.D. Hér.; Léon Cahen, "Le Pacte de famine et les spéculations sur les blés," *Revue historique*, CLIII (May–June 1926), 37ff.; Weulersse, *Louis XV*, 172; Georges Jorre, "Le Commerce des grains et la minoterie à Toulouse," *Revue géographique des Pyrénées*, IV (1933), 41, 44; Viala, *La Question des grains ... à Toulouse*, 38.

Urbain Guillot, for example, had been a marginal intermediary in a number of different trades. Now he was a "merchant of grain for the provisioning of Paris" operating for his own account and residing proudly on the rue de la Mortellerie, street of the Paris grain mandarins. Cadet Roux of Bourg-la-Reine gravitated quite naturally from the profession of wagon-driver to that of sometime grain and flour merchant. Later he confessed that he was unequipped to practice the commerce for "he never had any knowledge to be able to distinguish the good from the bad quality of the flour." A Sieur Laperde from the Bordelais "exercised several professions in which his conduct was not without reproach." In an effort to recoup his losses, "he threw himself headlong into the grain traffic." Antoine Demolle, a native of Normandy, came to Paris as a servant, left domestic service to become a "grain merchant" at the end of the sixties, and was arrested several years later for stealing from his ex-master.[57]

Another new man drawn into the trade by the lush prospects of the new age, Henry Coquelin, son of a woodworker living in the Paris region, had a remarkable appreciation of the meaning of liberalization and a sense of the ethos it meant to propagate. Although his own commerce was incommensurate with the breadth of his views— he bought and sold on a generally modest level in the Mantes area— he believed that the reform laws were "founded on the help that the Provinces of the Kingdom could expect from the great freedom of circulation and interior commerce of grain." He believed that "by embracing the grain trade he would fashion for himself a situation enabling him to subsist and that he would be useful to the Society of which he is a member." No doubt he was also interested in making money, for in a short time he became known as an artful dealer and at the end of the decade found himself in jail on suspicion of hoarding. Clinging shrewdly to the letter of the law, he adamantly denied practicing any "maneuvers or monopolies contrary to the free circulation of this commerce or prejudicial to the public interest."[58]

Like Coquelin, but with more capital and entrepreneurial imagination, Sieur Belly, a *contrôleur ordinaire des guerres* at Troyes, plunged into the grain trade in the sixties. He, too, celebrated his arrival as a great day for

---

57 Mediator's report, Oct. 1769, Archives Seine-Paris, D6B⁶ carton 5; mediator's report, April 1773, Archives Seine-Paris, D6B⁶ carton 7; SD to IN. of Bordeaux, 24 Jan. 1775, C. 1442, A.D. Gir.; 22 April 1772, AN, Y 10325.

58 Petition to PG, ca. Oct. 1770, BN, Coll. Joly 1151, fol. 33.

the public interest. Unabashedly, he contended that the public would benefit from his enterprise more or less directly in proportion to his profits and that its success, and thus the extent to which it served the public good, hinged upon the liberty he had to manage its affairs. Ambitious and innovative, Belly represented precisely the sort of forward-looking, quasi-industrial commerce which the liberal ministry longed to see flourish. He set out to change habits. In addition to speculating in grain, at considerable financial risk, he experimented with new techniques in milling and marketing, introducing a cheaper type of flour unfamiliar to local consumers and bakers and offering it for sale directly to the public in retail flour stores of a kind that had never before existed. It is not surprising that his style, which in ordinary times would have startled old hands, aroused suspicion and resentment in a period of dearth and insecurity. While Belly claimed to serve the "party of the poor people" by giving them the chance to obtain good quality, inexpensive flour without having to run the usual gauntlet of middlemen, the Troyes police denounced him as a hypocrite and a trouble-maker. Far from serving the public good, he caused the people to "murmur" by producing a flour that nobody wanted because it made a bread with a "dusty" taste and a dark color, using the flour establishment as a cover for abusive commercial practices, and bilking the community for huge profits. For years Belly and the authorities wrangled over the legitimacy as well as the utility of his enterprise. They accused him of buying indiscriminately, without regard for the local "usages" and priorities, without bargaining for the best possible price, and with the aim of gaining a corner on supplies. Time and again Belly replied in the language of liberty: that how he ran his affairs was nobody's business but his own and that according to the law "every citizen has *the right*" to buy and to sell, or not to sell, as he pleased. To defend himself Belly had far greater resources and more leverage than had poor Henry Coquelin. No less a personnage than Bertin offered his protection against the local police. Equally obstinate, the authorities continued to harry Belly's agents, sully his reputation, and predict that the people would one day rise in vengeful fury against him—a self-fulfilling prophecy which finally came true, with the help of the police, in 1770.[59]

A contemporary observer who aptly called himself "Fromant" in honor of his expertise credited the liberal climate with exciting the

---

59 C. 1908, A.D. Aube.

"Capitalists" to enter the trade.[60] Dampierre de la Salle probably referred to the same men when he remarked that "many idle and gluttonous people hurl themselves headlong into this traffic."[61] It was at this time that the Necker family realized substantial gains from "fortunate speculations on grain."[62] The government's efforts to bar from the trade public officials whose participation might compromise the discharge of official business or scandalize public opinion were not successful in some places. A group of merchants at Soissons accused the local police of dominating the commerce. Two commissaires were among the biggest dealers, the wife of a third was a major broker, and the farmer of the market measuring services also had a hand in these operations. The conflict of interest did not trouble a cavalier of the *maréchaussée* in the Brie who became a large-scale trader-by-stealth and encouraged his colleagues to do the same. Elsewhere "those who had the conduct of royal monies"—financial *officiers*—allegedly used their funds and their strategic position to profit from grain manipulations.[63]

The appearance of a host of new men in the trade alarmed the police and contributed mightily, as we shall see, to Terray's decision to restrict the commerce in 1770–71. The wide-open trade degenerated into a frenzy of "cupidity" according to this Controller-General. In the name of profit and self-interest, dealers committed crimes against the general interest. Instead of heightening competition and thus supplying grain more efficiently and at lower cost, the multiplication of "hands" in the trade interposed more and more middlemen, forced prices higher and higher, and made grain less and less visible. Before liberalization, wrote one of Terray's *commis*, the merchants had been "less opulent and consequently more docile and under the hand of the administration." From the police point of view, the main problem with the new men was that they were faceless. Relieved of the requirement to register and identify themselves formally, the traders were able to escape detection. The commerce of a commodity of first necessity, in Terray's

60 Lacombe d'Avignon, *Le Mitron de Vaugirard. Dialogues sur le bled, la farine et le pain*, 3.

61 "Observations de Dampierre de la Salle sur un projet de l'abbé Terray," BN, mss. n.a. 22777, fol. 259.

62 Herbert Lüthy, *La Banque protestante en France de la révocation de l'édit de Nantes à la révolution*, (Paris, 1959–1961), II, 373–74.

63 Cugnet to PG and collective petition, 4 Aug. 1768, BN, Coll. Joly 1142, fols. 126–27; fiscal procurator of Brie-Comte-Robert, 10 Feb. 1769, Coll. Joly 1146, fol. 66; "Mémoire," 8 Aug. 1773, AN, F¹¹ 265; CG to Calonne, 25 Aug. 1770, AN, F¹²* 155. On the entry of "les gens revêtus de charges," see also the IN. of Franche-Comté to Terray, Sept. 1770, C. 844, A.D. Doubs.

estimation, should always be in "known" hands "continually under the eyes of the people and those of the administrators."[64]

III

One must be cautious, however, with the evidence that suggests this phenomenon of "new faces" and links it to liberalization. It is dispersed and fragmentary, albeit copious, and it depends on a mosaic of impressions which, despite their confluence and mutual reinforcement, may themselves be the product of a shared set of perceptions and assumptions characteristic of a dearth experience. *Chertés* in the past, which had nothing to do with liberalization, had always called forth a host of transient speculators and modest adventurers seeking to profit from the circumstances. The heated atmosphere of a dearth often projected mirages which deluded the least naive and best intentioned observers. Traders in scarcity, like the *cherté* in the old adage, "abound," that is to say, they swarm from place to place, often far beyond their normal range where they are unlikely to be recognized or remembered, plundering or succoring. In the sixties merchants had the chance to wander more widely and more freely than ever before. It is not impossible that the strange faces spotted in a dozen different markets belonged to the same man.

There is no doubt that the old pattern of commerce was seriously disrupted and it was tempting then, as it is now when people confront a threatening experience, to ascribe it to outsiders, "foreigners," new men. Yet not everyone agreed that the personnel of the trade had dramatically changed. In the Dauphiné there may have been no significant influx of new dealers or it may have occurred in the first few years after the promulgation of the reforms, thus enabling the apprentice-merchants to appear as old hands by 1771.[65] In 1769 the

---

64 Terray, "Mémoire" (Aug. 1773), cited by Weulersse, *Louis XV*, 179; "Mémoire," 8 Aug. 1773, AN, F¹¹ 265; Leon Cahen, "Le Prétendu pacte de famine. Quelques précisions nouvelles," *Revue historique*, CLXXVI (Sept.–Oct. 1935), 201. In addition to being faceless, reported a Hainaut subdelegate, "half of these new merchants "barely know how to read and write." SD of St. Armand to Taboureau, ca. Oct. 1733, C. 6690, A.D. Nord.

65 IN. Pajot to Terray, 31 Oct. 1771, AN, F¹¹ 223. Yet the Parlement of Dauphiné saw things somewhat differently, stressing the enormous speculative current generated by liberalization. See its letter to the king, 26 April 1769, B. 2314, fol. 110, A.D. Isère. Cf. also the *arrêt* of 23 March 1774 cited by Pierre Rabatel, *Le Parlement de Grenoble et les réformes de Maupeou* (Grenoble, 1912), 147–48.

deputies of commerce argued that popular hostilities were so intense that "almost no one today dares to devote himself to the grain trade." It was an ambiguous remark, to be sure, which, if true, may merely mean that the liberalization-nurtured trade had already peaked.[66] Despite the talk about capitalists, the grain entrepreneur Leray de Chaumont in 1768 called attention to the failure of the liberal reforms to produce or win the allegiance of powerful *négociants* capable of handling the provisioning of Paris.[67] According to Bacalan, a high official on tour in the Lille region in 1768, "the grain trade did not exist there ... the prejudices against this commerce subsist in all their force."[68] The *économistes*, too, lamented the anemic state of the trade at the end of the decade.[69] But the relative paucity of capital concentration and sophisticated organization in the trade does not mean that huge fortunes were not made or that important changes in the nature of commercial practice and the nature of commercial opportunity did not occur. It is possible that the trade remained diffuse precisely because it drew so many dealers who thrived on their own.

There is a lesson to ponder, too, in the Parlement of Dauphiné's remark that "two thirds of the kingdom" was engaged in the grain trade—if by grain trade one means merely the business of selling grain.[70] This is of course a necessary but not usually a sufficient criterion for identifying the trader. Characteristically, grain trading implied, *inter alia*, a certain professional self-consciousness and specialization rather than a casual flirtation, stocking for speculative

---

66 "Avis des Députés du Commerce sur le libre commerce des grains," AN, F^{12} 715.
67 Leray to Trudaine de Montigny (?), May 1768, AN, F^{11} 1194.
68 AN, F^{12} 650.
69 For example, Lemercier de la Rivière, *L'Intérêt général de l'état*, 8, 401–402 and Weulersse, *Mouvement*, II, 218. Cf. *Journal économique* (Feb. 1770), 60.

It is a shame that we cannot recall to the witness stand the merchant who lamented the extreme underdevelopment of the grain trade in France in the first days of liberalization. Encouraged to undertake grain speculation by the Declaration of May 1763, this businessman sent "a man of confidence" to Champagne and Lorraine, where grain was said to be bountiful and cheap, in order to purchase 2–3,000 *septiers* for transshipment to Provence, where grain was said to be rare and dear. The agent reported that a transaction of this magnitude was virtually impossible to undertake given the fractionalized, innerdirected, retail nature of the local grain trade, the paucity of storage facilities, and the lack of means of transport. As a result of the organization of local markets and the attitudes of the inhabitants, who were not accustomed to wholesale grain removals, the Paris dealer concluded that the purchases he envisaged would provoke "panic terrors" and wild price increases despite the real abundance of grain. *Gazette du commerce* (14 Jan. 1765), 27–28.

70 Parl. to Louis XV, 26 April 1769, B. 2314, fol. 117, A.D. Isère.

purposes, and buying for resale. In the harried climate of liberalization, such discriminations are not always easy to make. One must be on the alert not to take every vendor for a dealer merely because he is a stranger flaunting a sack of grain. Finally, it is important to consider the documentation we do *not* have as well as the evidence available. For every new face invented, imagined, or counted twice by overwrought or expectant witnesses, there may well have been another who passed unremarked because he was adept at secrecy and optimally exploited the provisions of the law which assured him anonymity.

One way to discern more clearly the breadth and authenticity of the new commercial activity engendered by the liberal reforms and the crisis of the sixties is to trace the history of the *arrêt du conseil* of 23 December 1770. This law, enveloped in letters patent, required more systematically than ever before that all persons desiring to undertake commerce in grain or flour, and/or form associations for trade with others, declare their names, contracts of partnership, addresses, and location of magazines with local royal authorities. In theory, one should be able to learn, directly and obliquely, a good deal about the state of commerce from the registration lists generated by the law, *provided* that the lists have survived and the *arrêt* was enforced with some enthusiasm. The meager yield from searches in over thirty departmental archives warrants little optimism on the first account, though, given the procedure indicated by the *arrêt*, it is quite possible that extant lists should be sought elsewhere, viz., in communal depots.

On the second account there is ample margin for uncertainty. The *arrêt* of 23 December 1770 was an enormously important piece of legislation which re-introduced a whole series of police controls in addition to the declaration requirement. There are good reasons to believe, as I shall attempt to show later, that this law, or rather several of its clauses, were rigorously enforced in a large part of the realm, especially in the regions north of the Loire. Nor is this surprising; this was the antiliberal law that local authorities avidly craved and they were generally highly motivated to apply it. Moreover, to support their efforts, they could count upon the Contrôle-Général, now lost to the liberals, the bulk of the parlements, and their own consumer-constituents. Yet we also know that political and commercial conditions varied considerably from place to place and that as a result there was no monolithic pattern to which all local authorities conformed. In certain areas, where the sources of subsistence troubles seemed to come from outside the community and where the local dealers had never caused difficulties, the police did not appear to press the matter of registration.[71] In other places the police concentrated on the other controls in the *arrêt* which, in their estimation, made registration merely a supplementary refinement; or they were negligent in the conduct of their administration; or they lacked the capacity to cast their nets widely enough to snare the host of small-scale dealers.[72] Inevitably, too, there arose jurisdictional quarrels which paid homage to the reticence of traders who wanted to avoid registration. The *arrêt* enjoined traders to make their declarations at the nearest *royal* jurisdiction. In some towns, however, there was more than one royal jurisdiction. The contending authorities clashed over the stewardship of the registry in the nastiest sort of administrative war promoted by rival clerks ravenous to claim the twenty *sous* to which each declaration entitled them. Traders resident in seignorial, ducal bailliage, or similar jurisdictions, remote from the citadels of royal authority, enjoyed a certain immunity, though the Procurators General, construing the law loosely, ultimately authorized *any* police power, in the absence of royal jurisdiction, to enroll grain dealers.[73] A subdelegate in the Hainaut complained that registration before a royal jurisdiction was a perfunctory formality without police function. In its stead he proposed obligatory declarations before municipal authorities where merchants would have to confront "a contradictor" rather than a mere clerk.[74]

The weight of the evidence, allowing for local idiosyncracies, suggests that registration was widely practiced. Such a conclusion, however, is almost wholly inferential and it says nothing about the *quality* of enforcement. Obviously the discovery of declaration lists would shed considerable light upon this matter as well as upon the question of the trade itself.

Two such registers, one opened in the capital itself under the auspices of the lieutenant of police and the other in Meaux, an important market town in the Brie, offer a curious albeit tenuous glimpse of the state of

---

71 See, for example, "Résultat des observations des officiers de police des différentes villes de la province de Champagne sur l'exécution de l'arrêt du 23 Dec. 1770," bailliage de Vertus, C. 417, A.D. Marne.

72 See, for exemple, Terray to IN. of Burgundy (?), 22 Nov. 1772, C. 81, A.D. C d'O and SD of Pont Château to IN. of Brittany (?), 25 Feb. 1772, C. 1725, A.D. I-et-V.

73 "Résultat des observations des officiers de police ...," Sézanne, Ruhet, and Fismes, C. 417, A.D. Marne.

74 SD of Avesnes to IN., ca. Oct. 1773, C. 6690, A.D. Nord. Taboureau, the intendant, pressed the campaign for registration with great vigor. Taboureau to SDs, 11 Sept. 1772, C. 6689, *ibid.*

the trade around Paris.[75] It must be borne in mind that registration in these cases was far from exhaustive; that the registrants were unequally garrulous; that there is no truly reliable control or standard of reference against which to measure this data; and that enrollment began in early 1771, well after the government undertook its retreat from liberalization and several years after the time when liberalization and high prices exercised their greatest allure to prospective traders.

The declaration book kept by the Paris police contains approximately 100 names.[76] Forty-seven of the registrants were based in Paris. While only 26 specifically indicated that they were merchants "for the provisioning of Paris," there is no doubt that all of them aimed primarily at furnishing the capital. Thirty—25 men, 4 married women and a widow—dealt exclusively in grain. Seventeen traded in both grain and flour. Of the latter, 6 were millers, at least 4 of whom operated windmills. Of the 2 in the register who appropriated the promising title of *négociant*, 1 seemed to be an occasional grain merchant who dealt on an international scale and kept a warehouse at Rouen while the other had no magazines but supplied the Halles regularly from as far away as Champagne and Burgundy.

Only 3 others appear to have been very substantial businessmen. Mabille, a grain and flour merchant who had operated a flour company under the patronage of Poussot, the police inspector of the Halles in the sixties, maintained 5 magazines on the Oise and near Rambouillet. Jean Honoré Aubert, a merchant afflicted with chronic financial difficulties, drew supplies from Etampes in the south, Meaux in the east, and Pont Sainte-Maxence in the north and expanded his commerce to embrace flour as well as grain. Miller for the Paris General Hospital and son-in-law of the highly regarded modernizing miller César Buquet, Nicolas Rolland registered an "act of society" signed with the marquis de Feuquières, Lieutenant General of the province of Picardy, who promised to invest 30,000 *livres* and the use of 6 mills. Instead of capital,

---

75 Because it was garbled in organization, a third register, for the bailliage of Châteauneuf in A.D. E-et-L. (B. 4777), yielded very little. Sixty-eight traders enrolled. Most were *blatiers*, shifting grain from market to market in small quantities. Most declared a single storehouse. A handful claimed to have "always" been engaged in grain commerce. A few indicated that they had recently undertaken the trade. It is extremely difficult to take the measure of the experience of the majority, for they declared ambiguously that they were "continuing" to deal in grain without revealing anything about their backgrounds. The register from Orléans, surely a gem, must have been destroyed during World War II (C. 83, A.D. Loiret). There is a fragmentary listing for Graisivaudan in the Dauphiné, C. 48, A.D. Isère.

76 AN, Y 9648. Cf. 8 March 1771, Archives Seine-Paris, D5B⁶ 4910.

Rolland contributed "only his talent for milling and for the grain and flour trade." Once the business was launched, the parties agreed to split profits and losses evenly.

At the other extreme of scope and structure of enterprise stood the dame Laval, wife of a clerk in the tax farms, who was hardly more than a *blatière*, affiliated with her sister in an extremely humble traffic. Three other dealers acknowledged commercial associations, 2 between grain merchants and colleagues at La Ferté-sous-Jouarre and Poilly (Auxerre) and 1 linking a grain and flour trader with a Versailles miller and grain dealer. At least 3 grain merchants had agents regularly buying for them in the country (one of whom was a cloth merchant new to the business) and 2 others served as commissioners for merchants based in the provisioning zones.

The 47 Paris-based merchants, operated in all the supply crowns tributary to the capital. Only 14 indicated that they did not maintain storehouses in the field. Seven reported magazines in 3 or more different locations while the average for the entire group was slightly more than 1 per trader. The Brie was the area of choice; the Beauce, the Pays Chartrain, the Hurepoix, the French Vexin, and the Soissonnais were also represented. Although they used river transportation at least part of the way, many of these merchants marketed their goods at the Halles rather than at the ports.

The most striking feature of the group is that almost half of its members appear to be new men—relatively recent recruits to the trade. Of these 22 newcomers, the professions of 19 are definitely known: 4 wine merchants, 2 other kinds of merchants, 2 artisans, 2 innkeepers, 2 clerks, 3 bakers, 3 bourgeois de Paris, and a soldier's wife. This data, like all fleeting references to profession, *état*, *qualité*, and *condition* in police and notarial archives, must be used with circumspection. The register does not reveal whether they have abandoned their stated professions or how long they have been in the provisioning commerce. The internal evidence, however, suggests that most of them have been engaged in the grain and flour traffic long enough to establish patterns of buying and selling, a task requiring at the minimum several months and in some cases perhaps several years. Although it was fairly common to dissemble trade and rank for social, economic, and psychological purposes, there is no plausible reason for so large a proportion of registrants to have falsified their status in this public document.

Ten years earlier it would have been unimaginable for a wig-maker or a tinsmith living in the heart of Paris to petition the police for authorization to engage in the grain trade or to undertake such traffic surreptitiously. In those days the trade was not especially attractive and the police were not notorious for indulging the ambitions of tyros and part-timers. Liberalization seems to have accustomed the police to accepting new recruits, for even after the reaction to the liberal laws set in and Terray moved to put an end to anonymity and uncontrolled speculation, the authorities did not attempt to disqualify anyone who came forward to enroll. In 1770–71 candor became the mark of good faith and the *quid pro quo* for protection; it involved no risks for the registrants. The presence of these 22 newcomers on the police list—it is quite likely in addition that some of the remaining 25 dealers were relatively fresh to the trade—suggests that the trade had opened up considerably since 1763–64 and lends credence to the sometimes harried reports of contemporary observers.

The register also contains declarations from 50 merchants residing in the provisioning crowns around the capital, especially in the Brie and in the St. Denis-Gonesse-Dammartin area. Twenty-six claimed to be engaged exclusively in grain traffic. Only 8 of the 14 millers enrolled specifically indicated that they dealt in both grain and flour, but it is unlikely that the other 6 rigorously eschewed grain exchanges. Eight registrants signed in as merchants of grain and flour while 2 described themselves as simple flour traders. Fifteen of the 50 brandished the title "merchant for the Provisioning of Paris," though virtually all of them were part of the Paris nexus. Seven disclosed that they served as purchasing agents for Paris-based buyers: 4 for bakers (all of whom were millers; after mid-century Paris bakers rarely employed commissioners who could not themselves convert the grain they bought), 2 for grain merchants, and 1 for several religious communities. With the exception of the last, all of them supplied the market as well.

For almost all of these zone merchants, the Halles rather than the ports was the destination point. The vast majority kept storehouses (they averaged slightly more than 1 per dealer; at least 5 merchants had none while 1 maintained 4) but they were much less widely dispersed than those of their Paris counterparts. Approximately 20 percent of the zone registrants could not sign their names, a considerably larger proportion than among the Parisians. None of the 50 was associated with other merchants in his commerce. Most of them seem to have run modest, family-controlled businesses, limited in geographical range and socioeconomic ambition. Arnoult of St. Denis called himself *négociant* and boasted magazines at St. Denis, Dammartin, and Claye but was hardly the sort of merchant-baron to whom the liberals wanted to entrust the fate of the cities. More than anyone else the millers were the grain and flour moguls of this group. Dezobry of St. Denis operated 4 different mills; at least 3 other millers each controlled 2 establishments. Jean-Claude Colas, a Stains miller better known by his sobriquet Valentin, was the creditor of a host of Paris bakers in the late sixties and early seventies. Seven of the 14 millers were also *laboureurs*—that is to say, they had structured a vertically integrated enterprise in which they sowed and harvested grain and sold it, stored it or transformed it into flour.

Strictly speaking, only 7 of the 50 zone merchants were newcomers to the trade: a mercer, a horse-trader, a baker, 2 tavern-keepers, and 2 day-laborers. But it is well to remember that before 1763–64, millers and *laboureurs* were legally prohibited from entering the grain trade. Millers were considered artisans whose function it was to convert grain on demand into flour for bakers and private individuals; they could not openly buy grain on speculation, sell it, or grind it in anticipation of demand. *Laboureurs* were supposed to market their crop as quickly as possible and return to the tillage of the soil; they could not store grain indefinitely or buy grain clandestinely or on the market for purpose of stockage or resale. In the sense that they received legitimation as traders for the first time, millers and *laboureurs* were also new men. Five registrants were merchant-*laboureurs* (or *fermiers* or *receveurs-fermiers*) in addition to the 7 *laboureurs* who were also millers. There is no way to determine how many of the other zone dealers may have begun to deal in grain and flour in the last few years.

The Meaux declaration-book, opened in January 1771, registered traders dealing in a remarkably wide area in and around the Brie in all the major markets including Coulommiers, Tournan, Rozay, Rebais, Lagny, La Ferté-sous-Jouarre, La Ferté-Gaucher, Charly, Lizy, Dammartin, and Provins.[77] The listing contains 165 entries, only 2 of whom represent women. In 114 cases we have a fairly clear indication of the amount of time the merchant has been engaged in grain and/or flour commerce. The average for all 114 is 6.9 years with a range of 1 month to 48 years. Although this dispersion severely limits the utility of the mean, it is hard to resist noting that 6.9 years would take us back to 1764, just after the freeing of internal trade and just before the opening of the export gates. If we were able to establish the significance

---

77 Uncatalogued mss., bailliage de Meaux, A.D. Seine-et-Marne.

of the figure, it would mean that the "average" Meaux-enrolled merchant was a new man in the trade. If we use a more prudent approach and allow prospective merchants a little more time to react to the lure of liberalization or to the commercial opportunities of the sixties, we find that 65% (74) began their grain commerce in 1765 or afterwards and thus were new men. If we take 5 years rather than 6 as the threshold for "newness"—a very conservative baseline—then 51% were fresh to the trade, a figure comparable to the Parisian pattern. Of the 114 merchants, a little more than 25% had 10 years of experience or more in the trade; slightly less than 17% had traded for 15 years or more.

Generally the same caveats that qualified the Parisian data must be used here. We do not know how many traders operated around Meaux and the other areas encompassed in this register before liberalization nor how many entered the trade as new men after the promulgation of the reforms and left before 1771 in failure, in triumph, or in disgust at the reversion to the police system. We have no clear idea of a "normal" turnover rate in the profession. Professional mobility—upward, downward or lateral—may very well have been greater in the grain trade than in lower risk occupations. Nor can we ignore the possibility that a small number of merchants entered the grain trade at the very end of the sixties, not in response to the fever of liberalization, but to the more stable conditions which the revival of the police system presaged. Finally, we cannot say with certainty what percentage of the grain and flour trading community registered. There are some indications that it was high but it must be remembered that the traders had the option to register where they desired. There was probably a good deal of cross-registering and registering away from "home" (in principle, the place which was the center of the trading activities). The failure of the administration to zone the declaration area according to some precise geographical or commercial standard blurs the picture of distribution. All things considered, however, it appears virtually certain that in the Meaux region, too, a substantial number of "new" persons decided to undertake the grain or flour commerce professionally for the first time in the sixties.

Various observations in the register suggest that many of the traders never knew the old regime of regulation and would find it difficult to unlearn trading habits which the police, after January 1771 as before May 1763, considered "abuses" or "crimes." At least a half-dozen registrants casually reported that they ordinarily bought or sold on sample, purchased grain before it was harvested, or bought and resold in the same market. Without any sense of wrong-doing, for instance, Pierre Godard and Pierre Desprez, both of whom began to trade in grain in the late sixties, indicated that they bought in the farms of *laboureurs* and stored their purchases there as well. Neither revealed whether he intended to abandon these practices. On the other hand, Claude Clément the younger, who started trading in 1763 and might have had a fleeting first-hand taste of the old system, acknowledged that he used to buy and sell off the markets but promised henceforth "to conform" to the newly restored rules which required his presence at the markets.

Of the 165 merchants enrolled, 45 or 27% appear to exercise or to have recently exercised another profession or, in some cases, 2 other professions. Seventeen were millers of whom 10 were simple grain/flour merchant-millers, 3 were *laboureur*-grain/flour merchant-millers, and 4 were baker-grain/flour merchant-millers (of the latter, at least 1 seems to have owned considerable amounts of grain-producing land and thus spanned the entire provisioning chain from seed to loaf). In addition to these 4 bakers, 4 others were grain/flour merchant-bakers. Seven merchants were also *laboureurs* not including the *laboureurs* who were also millers. The "other" professions of the 17 remaining merchants—38% of all merchants with more than 1 profession—were all outside the primary food producing or provisioning industry. Ten had occupations that appear to be predominantly urban in locus, 4 had professions which seem characteristically rural, and 3 fit in a miscellaneous category. Unlike the millers, bakers, and *laboureurs*, it appears that most of these 17 merchants had to renounce their second (or rather their first!) professions—with the exception perhaps of the organist who still could find time to play on Sundays or give lessons sporadically and the tavernkeeper whose wife probably tended the bar and the books. Some of the millers, *laboureurs* and bakers may have had experience in the grain trade prior to liberalization, but these 17 merchants are almost certainly all new men.

In relation to the market and to commercial practice, there were three types of traders enrolled at Meaux. The majority—65%—were *blatiers*, ostensibly small dealers operating locally and with very limited means and ambitions among the different markets of the Brie and environs. Only 11% of the entire contingent were exclusively Parisian suppliers, channeling grain or flour from the hinterland to the capital in large doses and on a regular basis more or less without regard for local demand. The remaining traders—24% of the total—ran a mixed commerce, functioning both as *blatiers* and as merchants-for-the-provisioning-of-Paris. It should be noted that in the grain trade, as in many other professions where there are supposed to be clear-cut gradations of scope and rank, the nomenclature is not always precise or reliable. Alfred Cobban cited the case of a self-styled Malouin *négociant* who was said by his neighbors to have earned his living selling fruit in the streets. The works of Paul Bois, Pierre de Saint Jacob, and Pierre Goubert, among others, have taught us how misleading putatively hierarchical nominal typologies of peasants can be. In this same sense it is chastening to note that one Pierre Lefebvre, a trader from Coulommiers who appears to be engaged in *blatier* traffic, at the time of his declaration had a stock of 30 *muids* of grain (probably wheat), an enormous quantity even for a substantial metropolitan-oriented dealer let alone a *blatier* who is supposed to be dealing in a few *septiers* at a time. This case is a useful warning, but in the Meaux context it seems to be exceptional. On the whole the *blatier* traffic in the area was indeed quite modest.

The predominance of *blatiers* obscures the real magnitude of the Meaux-centered contribution to the supply of the capital, for a great deal of the grain resold by the *blatiers* at Meaux and some of the nearby entrepôt markets ended up in the hands of Paris commissioners. At least 7 of the registered Meaux traders served as commissioners, or factors, for Paris-based merchants (5 of them for the river-trading elite of the rue de la Mortellerie). Seven others, all millers, bought grain in behalf of Paris bakers. Twenty-three of the Meaux merchants who were integrated into the Parisian supply network had brokers who managed their business and disposed of their grain and flour in the capital.

Aside from these ties with agents or factors, the vast majority of merchants apparently operated alone. Of 165 merchants, only 6—less than 4%—were "associated" with others: 4 *blatiers*, 1 Paris merchant, and 1 local-metropolitan dealer. Although it is not surprising that a commerce heavily *blatier* in organization did not support more "societies," it is possible that the police actively discouraged the formation of commercial partnerships or groups which reminded them of the "companies" of the late sixties and invariably prompted suspicion of monopoly.

The desire to associate implies a certain amount of sophistication in business and often, but by no means always, a rudimentary education. The mass of the Meaux registrants appear to be literate, though we do not know if they all kept business records as the law now required. Seventeen per cent of the 165 merchants could not sign their names, a figure strikingly similar to the number of zone-based traders in the Paris register who are by this measure presumed unlettered. Of these 28 Meaux merchants, only 1 was a primary Paris supplier; 25 or 93% were *blatier*-types.

All of the merchants except 8 kept or intended to keep grain and/or flour magazines. The mode for the whole universe was 2, though the data on which it is based are not precise. There appears to be no necessary relationship between the number of magazines a trader maintained and the magnitude of his commerce; the dealer with the most storehouses in the listing—6—was a *blatier*-type who bought on a small scale throughout the upper Brie and resold at Meaux. Most traders kept 1 magazine "at home" in a spare room, in the back of a shop, or in a mill and another in or near one of the market-towns on their commercial itinerary. But at least 15 merchants indicated that they stocked their merchandise in various inns or cabarets in the town and the countryside. There is a certain irony in these innocent declarations to the police, for in the days before liberalization the inn had been the most notorious hideout for secret, illicit hordes. Liberalization legitimized this practice and during the sixties the inns did a bustling and open business as grain and flour entrepôts and surrogate marketplaces. When the old rules were restored beginning in 1771 the merchant could still use the inn, but like the prostitute, only on condition that he declared his purpose to the nearby police clerk.

Several registration lists, with scanty information, survive in the records of the intendancies of Flandre-Artois and Hainaut-Cambrésis.[78] Of 58 traders enrolled at Maubeuge, almost 20%, an unusually high proportion, were associated with other merchants. The vast majority had no storehouses outside their own homes. Only 4 had more than 1 magazine; 4 others claimed they did business without storage facilities. Twenty-two of the 23 merchants registered at Avesnes kept a storehouse at home; only 1 had more than 1 magazine. Two traders had associates. Only 1 of the 23 was a woman—a baker's widow. Eight merchants enrolled at Landescq: 2 declared that they had associates and 5 asserted that they maintained no storehouses at all.

---

78 The lists for Maubeuge, Avesnes, and Valenciennes are in C. 5977, A.D. Nord; the Landesq register is C. 6690, *ibid.*; the Lille declarations are in C. 3745, *ibid.*

The Valenciennes register is the only one of this group that contains some details on the professional origin of the merchants. None of the 16 registrants claimed to be a grain merchant by profession. Nine exercised professions which had nothing at all to do with the grain trade; they were clearly new men. The remaining 7—5 millers, a *fermier*, and a starchmaker—practiced trades more or less closely related to grain commerce. Yet they, too, qualify as newcomers since all were legally excluded from dealing in grain before 1763–64. Though 9 of the 16 Valenciennes registrants declared no magazines, it is likely that each maintained a storehouse at home.

It is unfortunate that the huge Lille declaration list recorded virtually no socioprofessional data. We know that 32 of the 225 registrants were millers, confirming a trend noted elsewhere. Strikingly few merchants—4—operated with associates. Only 6 of the 225 were women; 5 of these 6 were widows. At least 74% of the Lille group conducted business "at home"; apparently they had no stocks elsewhere. Thirty-eight dealers reported a single magazine located away from home. Only 7 merchants had more than 1 storehouse away from home. Seven merchants established their granaries in inns or cabarets. As in the other northern cities which left declaration lists, the grain trade in the Lille region was highly fragmented. Most of the traders were of the *blatier*-type, dealing on a small scale within a strictly local context. Though many new men entered the trade, very few appear to have been "capitalists" in the sense that their contemporaries used the term.

IV

The emergence of a plethora of so-called "companies" worried observers even more than the proliferation of individual new faces in the grain and flour trade. It was alarming enough to envision solitary hoarders and monopolists lurking about in the grain trade underground and surfacing to commit occasional crimes against society. But, then as now, it was far more portentous to encounter organized crime, intrigue institutionalized in societies designed specifically to fleece the region or country of its vital supplies. In times of stress in the past, the French had fallen prey to the obsession with invidious "companies" held responsible for a copious array of turpitude, from child-snatching and blood-letting to currency manipulation and various kinds of commercial piracy. The disorder, malaise, and hardship generated in the sixties induced people to think in terms of plots and machinations.

The particular preoccupation with "companies" resulted in part from a confused understanding of the nature of government grain operations and a memory which recalled previous scandals and revived stale but enduring suspicions—the "famine pact" mentality which found its apotheosis in the sixties—and in part from the authorization to form such commercial associations generously accorded by the liberal laws and utilized by a considerable number of entrepreneurs.

These companies were no more imaginary than the strange new traders who scoured the countryside in search of grain. But a fatal combination of public anxiety, local police suspicion, and, on the part of the agents of the companies, accidental indiscretion and short-sighted braggadocio, puffed, distorted, and tainted the image these societies projected.[79] The failure of the government to undertake a vigorous public relations campaign to clear the air reinforced, as we shall see, the fabulous impressions. Pierre Malisset's operation in behalf of the king, to which we shall return, became the popular prototype of the treacherous grain company of the sixties. But far more typical of the kind of commercial venture which resulted in association was the society founded shortly after the promulgation of the first liberal law by François Jausse, Farmer-General and entrepreneur of river transports on the Aisne and Oise, Henry Monginot, écuyer and "secretary of the king," and Daniel Neser, "investor [intéressé] in the affairs of the king." Jausse wanted to expand the scope of his transport activities and place them in the service of a speculative business specialized in the purchase and resale of grain. "Unable by himself to encompass such a vast project," he turned to Monginot and Neser, experienced venture capitalists, who agreed that the moment was ripe, economically and juridically, for such an enterprise and promised to invest in it 50,000 livres apiece. Jausse contracted to provide the capital equipment, the expertise, and the managerial direction. In the first stages of the plan the passenger depots along the boat-routes would conveniently and unobtrusively double as headquarters for the grain commissioners.[80]

Other companies were less successful than Jausse in avoiding notoriety. Reports reached the government that various companies were burning over whole districts in pursuit of grain, driving up prices, establishing secret grain caches, forcing honest men who could not

---

79 See the striking remarks of the philosophe-philanthropist, P. de Chamousset, Œuvres complètes (Paris, 1783), II, 291.

80 30 July 1764, Archives Seine-Paris, D3B⁶ 65.

compete to abandon the trade, and shipping huge stores out of the country. Leclerc, a Poissy flour merchant, purchased and stored grain "for the companies." They offered a wealthy *fermier* in the Ile-de-France a splendid price for his grain provided he agreed to hold it till after the next year's harvest. Barat, the fiscal procurator at St. Denis, reported that it was generally believed in his area that the "dearth" which dried up Gonesse and choked other Paris provisioning markets was the work of "certain companies which undertake exportation." "I do not know if these companies are authorized and if exportation is permitted," he added, betraying his incredulity (and that of so many other police officials) that the law could in a single stroke license both commercial association and exporting, and his perplexity about the applicability of the liberal reform in the Paris area. Barat could provide details only about one of the companies, which operated two "powerful" mills at St. Denis and two others at Dugny. Grinding 14 to 15 *muids* a day, the mills emptied the countryside of "incredible" quantities of grain. Nor did the company return any of the flour it produced to the neighborhood. Packed in heavy-duty casks, all the local flour was intended for sale abroad.[81]

The Controller-General Laverdy felt that it was perfectly normal for prices to be rising and for the traditional configuration of the grain and flour trade to be changing. "As for the establishments which have been formed at Saint Denis for the fabrication of flour," he wrote, "very far from imposing any obstacle on them, they must be accorded every protection; it would be desirable for these sorts of establishments to multiply in all the provinces." Predictably, Laverdy hailed the creation of such flour factories in the Nivernais whence an anonymous remonstrance called his attention to a "society" which builds mills, hoards grain, and exports flour to England while prices skyrocket and the people go without bread. Overwrought and lacking vision, the people complained "by habit of the prohibitive laws and the ancient prejudices against the liberty of the grain trade."[82]

Trennin of Versailles, the outspoken police critic of liberalization, denounced the companies born of the reform legislation in letters to Joly de Fleury and Sartine. As a result of their grain purchases, prices increased by six *livres* in the first year (1765–66) to 25 *livres*, five more

---

81 BN, Coll. Joly 1111, fol. 137; "Cherté du pain," AN, T644[1–2]; Barat to PG, 1 Oct. 1766, Coll. Joly 1134, fol. 93.

82 CG to PG, 17 Oct. 1766, BN, Coll. Joly 1134, fol. 96; CG to PG, 17 Dec. 1766, *ibid.*, fol. 97.

the next year to 30 *livres*, and six more *livres* the following year to the current price of 36 *livres* the *septier*. The companies not only proved that liberalization was socially catastrophic but also illustrated the fallacies of liberal reasoning. Trennin seized upon an apparent contradiction which continued to trouble free enterprise states committed to liberty in later times. On the one hand, the liberals argued that competition was the only form of police appropriate for commerce; on the other hand, they recently began to complain that the liberty accorded by the new laws was insufficient. Yet if the freedom was not as "entire" as the liberals desired, in Trennin's view, it was largely the fault of the very companies spawned by liberalization which choked competition and dominated the trade.[83]

Not sharing Laverdy's faith in progress through liberty, the Procurator General took the news of the maneuvers of companies much more seriously than the minister. In the margin of a denunciation exposing the wiles of a miller named Copérieux, he wrote "notice which merits attention" and instituted an investigation. The informer claimed that in the papers of Copérieux "would be found information and proof of *Monopoly* and would be revealed the names of a Company with which he is associated … and would be discovered many things for the relief of the people." Sartine's researches showed that Copérieux was innocent and that he was not even involved in active grain and flour commerce. Commissioned to mill "by economy" the flour for the bread of the French and Swiss Guard, Copérieux had occasion to make sizeable purchases at the Halles which gave rise to rumors. Sartine conjectured that the real motive for the denunciation was jealousy on the part of one of the bakers who previously supplied the Guard before Copérieux displaced him.[84]

At about the same time, the royal procurator at Montlhéry entertained suspicions which made him tremble, for they implicated highly placed officials in questionable enterprises. He learned that "a company of grain merchants under the name of Ballet" maintained an entrepôt near the Breton coast "which empties and refills every day" as well as magazines in the Brie and elsewhere. An associate of the company told him that "this commerce was known to and protected by Monsieur de Sartine and by Monsieur Trudaine de Montigny" and that, although it seemed to divert grain from the capital, in fact "it tended only to

---

83 Trennin to PG and Sartine, 26 Oct. 1768, BN, Coll. Joly 1142, fols. 162, 164.
84 2 March 1769, BN, Coll. Joly 1147, fols. 47–50; Sartine to PG, 8 March and 5 April 1769, *ibid.*, fols. 52, 53.

place abundance in the city."[85] There is little doubt that the company unearthed by the wary procurator was a more mature version of a provisioning company founded in 1760 with the encouragement of inspector Poussot of the Halles and known variously under the names Mabille; Mabille and Monnerie; Ballet, Mabille and Monnerie associates; and Ballet, Mabille company. Mabille, "one of our young people who furnish flour for retail," courted Poussot's favor by bringing him intelligence from the zone markets and ostentatiously conforming to all the rules established in the Halles. Poussot hailed the "utility" of Mabille's first company venture, an operation involving the supply and storage of secondary grains. Subsequently, Mabille and his partners expanded their affairs, dealing in flour more than in grain and slighting retail in favor of large-scale wholesale dealings. Shrewdly managed, the company flourished in the mid-sixties and survived until 1771. While the charge that the company used its Paris provisioning reputation as a cover to conceal a substantial export business can be neither confirmed nor refuted, it is quite likely that its directors cooperated with and enjoyed the support of highly-placed officials.[86]

The most startling revelations about "company" maneuvers, aside from those associated with Leprévost de Beaumont, came from a Bavarian farm-manager/agronomist who had come to France shortly after the grain trade reform of 1763. In contrast to Leprévost, whose hysterical tone and universal theory of conspiracy undermined his credibility from the very beginning, the Sieur Marnville de la Roque was remarkably self-possessed and restrained. Although he had a monstrous "intrigue" to expose, he treated it simply as a sordid business affair without imputing any responsibility to the government or dramatizing it into an infernal plot. In 1765 a company of agricultural entrepreneurs headed by Billard, *caissier général des postes*, seconded by fifteen or sixteen partners, hired de la Roque to manage a huge estate. The company, in magazines near Dammartin, Dugny and elsewhere, had "huge heaps of grain" representing "the harvests of five or six years." Either poor conservation or natural deterioration resulted in massive spoilage. The Company disposed of the most infected grain by dumping it in the Seine. It produced thousands of *septiers* of flour per month packaged for export. The aim of the

---

85 Desromont to PG, 10 Feb. 1769, BN, Coll. Joly 1146, fols. 154–55.

86 10,16 Dec. 1760, Arsenal, mss. Bastille 10141; 11 Dec. 1767, AN, Y 12616; 24 May 1771, AN, F^{12} 716; 6 May 1766, Archives Seine-Paris, D4B^6 29–1530; 8 Nov. 1771, Archives Seine-Paris, D2B^6 1103.

company, according to de la Roque, was to generate and sustain dearth artificially by cornering supplies, controlling the markets, and halting the mills. It maintained permanent agents in some of the markets and to the others dispatched skilled operatives such as Bar who "traveled day and night in the saddle" in the area around Paris. "To color its deception," the company had one of its associates, Nezet, become a regular supplier for the provisioning of the Halles in flour. De la Roque protested in vain against the strategy and finally "quit this job in order not to cooperate in the ruin of my country for the love of which I had left Germany."

Since he was angling for a job it cannot be said that the motives for de la Roque's petition were entirely altruistic. Moreover, the petition contains a dose of ill-concealed megalomania: de la Roque claimed a fantastic scientific prowess for "the multiplication of grain," having realized yields of 25 to 1 in Germany, and hinted at a master plan which would enable France to export a million *septiers* a year while maintaining the price of 12 *livres*. Yet his disclosures faithfully reflected a strain of contemporary opinion and were not in themselves wholly implausible.[87] The financier Billard was rumored to be involved in all sorts of speculation including grain maneuvers; traces of rotten grain had allegedly been found in the Seine; Nezet, conceivably, was the "investor in the affairs of the king," Daniel Neser, whose interests in Jausse and Company we have mentioned. The absence of corroborative evidence of any sort suggests that the company was considerably less high-powered and oppressive than de la Roque imagined. But there is no reason to believe that the company did not energetically seek to raise prices—after all, the government itself favored a higher grain price and an activist trading class—or that it did not use a network of agents and conduct buying and hoarding operations which convulsed the grain and flour trade. Whatever real effects these new companies of the sixties had upon supply and demand were in part the result of the fears and expectations they inspired. Preceded and shadowed by their stereotyped reputations, these companies committed depredations which were psychological as well as economic.

---

87 18 Dec. 1768, BN, Coll. Joly 1138, fols. 92–93. See also *Conseil Secret*, Paris Parl., 29 Dec. 1769, AN, X^{1a} 8551, fol. 158. Billard's papers were seized on 16 Dec. 1769. AN, Y 11441. In the early seventies he was imprisoned and convicted of malversation and fraudulent bankruptcy. Allegedly as a result of Madame du Barry's intervention, he escaped the extremely harsh sentence which his judges planned to impose. Hardy's Journal, 3, 12 Feb. 1772, BN, mss. fr. 6681, fols. 15, 19; Pidansat de Mairobert, *Journal historique*, II, 373 (13 Feb. 1772).

Much more evidence must be accumulated on the nature of the grain trade before and during liberalization before one can determine with any precision how the liberal laws affected provisioning in the sixties. There is no doubt that the trade was seriously disrupted after the middle of the decade. We know that during other subsistence crises—in 1725 and in 1739–41, for example—many of the same "abuses" and deviations appeared. There were, however, at least three additional factors operating during the experience of the sixties. First, the control apparatus could not respond as it usually did once bad times struck. Merchants clearly had more freedom than ever before to pursue their interests. The government did not attempt to marshal the nation's resources; it left this business to commerce. Second, exportation was not only permitted on a kingdom-wide basis but it was maintained well after the dearth began to make itself felt. The opportunity to export, outside one's own bailiwick or outside the kingdom, encouraged the merchants to venture beyond their traditional avenues of exchange. In this sense, internal liberty and the freedom to export were inextricably linked and their respective effects are impossible to unravel. Third, liberalization cued the public and the police to expect the worst. It generated fears even beyond those that characteristically possessed people's minds during dearth. If we cannot discern whether the disorganization of the grain trade was the product of liberalization or of short crops and their customary sequellae, it is in part because contemporaries could not separate the two elements.

In principle, Paris was not supposed to suffer, or profit from, the changes in the grain trade instigated by the reforms—not at least in the short run. In the next two chapters, we shall take stock of the government's efforts to insulate the capital.

Chapter VII

PARIS

The government felt that it could surmount the crisis provided, above all, that the situation in Paris remained under control. As long as it did not have to face massive disaffection and disorder in the capital, the ministry felt it could win the day in the rest of France, where the mutinies were relatively small and widely scattered and where there was still to be found considerable sentiment in favor of the new regime. In this chapter we shall examine the impact of the crisis upon the capital and the way in which the Paris police tried to deal with it. In the following chapter, we shall consider the extraordinary efforts which the central government made, not without serious reservations and contretemps, to spare the capital the most terrible costs of dearth.

I

The quarantine of Paris proclaimed by the clauses of exception in the liberal laws proved singularly unsuccessful in preserving the capital from fear, dearth, and the disruption of its provisioning trade. Once the rest of France was liberated, the special guarantees regarding Paris provisioning became largely illusory. At the confluence of her great rivers, in the very center of the realm, the capital simply could not be isolated from the rest of France by fiat. Provisioning was a two-way affair. It made little sense to stand on the Port of the Grève or the *carreau* of the Halles and declare that nothing had changed while at the same time telling the rest of the nation that things would never be the same again. The exemption provision created a bizarre disjuncture between the capital and the hinterland, enjoining the police of the latter to conform to the very liberal code which it empowered the police of the former to ignore.

According to the May and July laws Paris was to continue to provision itself as it always had done in the past. The survival of the old way, however, depended upon the preservation of both the traditional regulatory apparatus and the familiar trading patterns. Liberalization, as we have seen, jarred them both mightily, and the disarray of each encouraged the further breakdown of the other. The maintenance of the old Paris police system depended primarily upon the vigorous support of the Controller-General, the freedom of action of the Lieutenant General, and the cooperation, or subjugation, of the officials in the provisioning zones. Traditionally the remedies for dearth, the disorganization of supply lines, and the breakdown of the ordinary structure of controls were massive doses of police, administered by central, Parisian, and hinterland authorities. Now Laverdy's passion was the promotion of the grain trade. Despite the exemption clauses in the laws of 1763–64, he permitted the Paris regulations to lapse or interpreted them in such a restrictive way as to make them impracticable. By compensating the capital with a copious mass of the king's grain, he felt that Paris could remain an island of tranquility in a turbulent sea of riots, speculation, and hoarding. The local police were paralyzed before the crisis made itself felt. Prohibited from enforcing the old regulations and prohibitions, they could neither guarantee their own supplies nor assure the regular shipment of provisions to the capital.

In this situation, the authority of the Paris police chief was severely curtailed. He could neither regulate the activities of merchants for the provisioning of Paris in the countryside nor woo them with the protection against local competition which he had accorded them in the past. Nor was he equipped to intervene on virtually a daily basis in the host of hinterland markets whose own police were forbidden to exercise their powers. In the old days the range of the Lieutenant's jurisdiction used to swell in times of dearth as new areas fell tributary to the capital in its avid search for fresh sources of supply. Now the frontiers of his authority receded as new frontiers were opened to the grain owners and traders; his *droit de suite* shriveled as they found a multitude of unbarricaded freedom roads leading away from the capital. The usual sanctions no longer had any sense because the dealers had new options which mocked the old constraints. In practice if not in law, as a consequence of this new mobility, a Parisian destination no longer ennobled grain, bestowing upon it privileges and immunities of which no common cereal could boast.

Heretofore the vagueness of many of the prescriptions governing Paris provisioning benefitted the police, for it enabled them to
pursue a supple, opportunistic policy attuned to the needs of the
hour. Now the police became victims of their own unorthodoxy,
for it was not clear to anyone precisely what it meant, in scope and
substance, to enforce the traditional regulations, in the murky language of the exemption clause, "as before."[1] The clause was as negative in character as it was terse in expression: nothing ("for the time
being"—a demoralizing threat from the police vantage point) was to
be "changed or innovated" in the old regulations. It established no
concrete guidelines to deal with new circumstances, drew no boundaries—geographical, administrative, or commercial—, and assumed
that two diametrically opposed regimes, each by nature dynamic and
aggressive, could coexist side-by-side without attacking and undermining each other.

With their broad, albeit amorphous, mandate and their considerable skill, the Parisian police won many individual battles. But armed
with conventional weapons there was no question of winning the war.
As a result of the inability of the Parisian police to contain the grain
trade, the eight (later ten) league de-commercialized zone around the
capital became open prey to merchants and companies; "foreign" buyers encroached upon the second and third "crowns" of the Parisian
reserve; *laboureurs* stayed home; traders amassed stocks and diverted
supplies toward domestic outlets free of police influence on pricing
and exchange or toward export entrepôts; the markets dried up; and
all the other activities which the police construed as abuses flowered.

Police confusion and uncertainty, along with the new speculative
climate induced by liberalization, facilitated changes in the methods
and structure of trade in the Paris region. Whether or not they understood the dilemma of the police or the theoretical tenuousness of the
liberty which they could exercise in the Parisian sphere of influence,
grain owners and dealers quickly perceived that the authorities were
unsure of themselves. The discomfiture of the police as much as their
consciousness of the new rules of the game emboldened them. Fear of
entrapment and of heavy penalties was no longer a powerful deterrent
to what had once been sinisterly called "maneuvers." Paris no longer
cast an intimidating and ubiquitous shadow across their path. Nor was

---

1 See, for exemple, the remarks of Cypierre, the intendant of the Orléanais, which included
  part of the Parisian supply zone, who did not know "the regulations whose execution was
  reserved...." To Sartine, 7 Oct. 1768 in C. Bloch, *Correspondance inédite de l'intendant Cypierre*, 112.

it merely a matter of escaping detection, punishment, and regimentation. For liberty also meant alternatives to the Paris system: new commercial opportunities, new clients and connections, new itineraries. The old commercial structure had reflected and in some ways internalized police priorities and procedures. Once the police requirements were annulled, diluted, or blurred, the old structure lost much (though by no means all) of its logic and compulsion. While in some places there was no need for readjustment, in others the trade was reorganized according to a purely commercial calculus. More or less stable relationships linking buyers, sellers, brokers, and commissioners in networks crisscrossing the hinterland were abandoned in favor of new arrangements, often ephemeral or shifting in nature. New names appeared on business registers which had once been inhospitable to strangers. The country traders became less dependent on the Paris merchant barons, millers less dependent on the Paris bakers, and mealmen less dependent on factors.

The "privilege" of serving Paris, once a passport into forbidden territory and a competitive lever outside the markets, no longer carried the same weight. The aim of the exemption clause was to assure the provisioning of Paris by preventing all this from happening. Yet it may have served to hinder the supply of the capital not only as a result of its impotence to stem the tide of liberty but also because it announced that merchants who continued to frequent the capital, unlike traders anywhere else, would still suffer the old servitudes and pressures. Save where they believed that it was in their self-interest or where the empire of habit proved irresistible, merchants were unlikely to rush to bondage.

The Prévôt des Marchands testified bitterly to the impact of liberalization upon Parisian controls. Before 1763 a substantial number of merchants—between 25 and 40—annually applied for commissions from the Bureau de Ville to undertake trade for the benefit of the capital. "By this means," noted the Prévôt Bignon, "our ports were always furnished in grain." "But," he continued, "since the Declaration of 1763 gave them the same privileges as these commissions without any subjection, they were renounced by the majority [of merchants] or the merchants did not renew them, and we have retained but a small number and only by showing them the most careful attention."[2] In addition, the Parisian police lost their indirect dominion over the host of lesser dealers operating in the supply zone because the exemption

___

2 Nov. 1768, *Recueil*, 145–46.

clause did not specifically require them to enroll with local officials and respect the Paris rules in order to remain in the grain trade. By way of authority there was virtually nothing the police could do to retain their fidelity. It is no wonder that the royal procurator of the city government, in anticipation of the erosion of control over the lines of supply, had argued strenuously in January 1764 for increasing the "precautions for Paris rather than destroying those which are already established in the new regime."[3] Ultimately the Parisian counterpoint in the liberal laws revealed itself to be a hollow promise which served as a sop to police anxieties rather than as a basis for a provisioning policy.

Always marked by tensions which reached their peak during shortages, supply relations between the capital and the hinterland were further strained by liberalization. While Paris drained the supply zones with what the consumer population regarded as calculated indifference to their needs, local officials found themselves substantially less capable than usual of defending their interests.[4] Parisian authorities tried to play both sides of the provisioning game: they piously invoked the innovative clauses of the reform laws when liberty seemed to favor the flow of grain to Paris and they flourished the exemption mandate to cover their intervention when liberty appeared to militate against their ambitions. The local police, however, were triply disarmed: vis-à-vis hometown traders, mostly *blatiers*, *laboureurs*, and brokers; vis-à-vis the dealers and commissioners squarely in the Parisian network; and vis-à-vis outsiders from still other regions who came in search of grain.[5] As a result of the liberal laws, these authorities could no longer exercise any police in the grain trade. Legally, they could not oscillate from a permissive to a restrictive posture as it pleased them. On the one hand, they could not control local traders and protect local supply and on the other, without power either to assist or resist Parisian incursions,

---

3 Jollivet to Saint Florentin (?), 29 Jan. 1764, AN, O¹ 361.
4 While the capital drained the countryside dry, the Paris police—measurers and commissaires—did not even allow country folk who marketed their wares at the Halles to fill their empty carts with "Paris grain" for the trip home. Interrogation of Visbec, 16 Oct. 1770, AN, X²ᴮ 1312; Mediator's report, 6 Nov. 1771, Archives Seine-Paris, D5B⁶, carton 6.
5 The capital launched buying expeditions in all parts of the kingdom without seeking any permission, yet Paris took umbrage when outsiders encroached upon its supply reserve. To the extent that they were successful in warding off outsiders—it is my view that "foreigners" made serious inroads in the Parisian provisioning region with the blessing of the central government—the Parisian authorities incidentally rendered service to the local police. See T. de Montigny to Sartine, 8 Aug. 1765, AN, F¹²* 150 and CG to B. de Sauvigny, 5 Dec. 1770, AN, F¹²* 155, fols. 136–37.

and thus without any bargaining counters, they stood helpless before metropolitan exactions.

Although the protest against excessive liberty and the breakdown of order was the major theme of discontent in the Paris hinterland just as it was elsewhere in the kingdom, local authorities felt that Parisian pressure seriously aggravated their difficulties. They resented the cavalier attitude of the Parisian police and the refusal of *soi-disant* Paris merchants to demonstrate self-restraint. Shortly after a raucous market disturbance, the fiscal procurator of Lagny in the Brie complained that the unsettled situation was due partly to the huge purchases made by millers buying "for the provisioning of Paris."[6] His counterpart at Saint Florentin in Champagne deplored the short supply and "excessive" price level caused in large measure by the operations of a Paris merchant. "Must we suffer," he asked, "that strangers continue [to make] these removals?"[7] The fiscal procurator of Châtillon-sur-Loing submitted a stringent objection against the disruptive activities of a Sieur Lenormant who "claims to be licensed and employed for the provisioning of Paris" and who was draining off the "little grain" which remains in the area. (Two years earlier the same trader had aroused similar ill-feeling as a result of large-scale purchases made in the Orléanais.) Since the investigation of this affair was entrusted to the Paris Prévôt des Marchands, who was more than ever interested in cultivating a client-relationship with Paris-suppliers, the Châtillon procurator had little reason to imagine that relief would be forthcoming. Ironically, there was a strong chance that Lenormant cheated Paris even as he plundered the hinterland by failing to deliver his grain to the capital.[8]

Even as they defied the law in order to protect themselves against the depredations of liberalization, so the local police took illegal initiatives in order to ward off Parisian strikes. The procurator at Montereau forced a Paris factor to resell twenty-five *septiers* of grain which he purchased from a local curate for 25 *livres* the measure on the town market at a loss of 3 *livres* per *septier*. The Provins police retaliated against the Paris merchants by excluding them from the market during the prime morning hours. When the police imposed similar constraints

---

6 Gillet to PG, 14 July 1770, BN, Coll. Joly 1150, fols. 39–40.
7 Billebache to PG, 16 July 1770, BN, Coll. Joly 1152, fol. 10. Cf. similar problems at Troyes where the intendant tried to mediate. Jean Ricommard, *La Lieutenance générale de police à Troyes*, 255, 263.
8 Dispatch to Bignon, 16 March 1769, AN O¹* 411, fols. 187–88.

at Lizy, the Paris buyers struck back by diverting the supply to nearby inns where *laboureurs* flocked with pouches of samples on which to base transactions unencumbered by public or official interference.[9] In some instances the campaigns against liberalization and against Paris seemed perfectly coterminous. In these cases Paris was explicitly denounced as the destination point of "removals" or "exports" which the people rose up to intercept or the police requisitioned for distribution at a fixed "just" price. Yet it must be emphasized that the local authorities did not confuse the two issues *causally* even if they appeared to merge in practice. For the officials had lived with Paris in the past; all the *new* and unsettling elements in their situation resulted from liberalization which incidentally made their Paris-problem far more acute than it had been before. Animosity for the capital did not deflect the attention of the local officials from the liberal laws. Many of them understood that Paris, despite the famous exemption clause, was as much a victim of the reforms as the hinterland.

While hoping for a revision of the new laws and without ceasing to rail against Parisian exploitation, a number of officials sought to profit from the "special" relationship which they had with the capital by shrewdly deriving from it a justification for the resuscitation of their traditional police powers. The basic idea was a sort of grain blackmail which the authorities responsible for provisioning Paris might very well be prepared to pay. Dronay, a police magistrate at Vitry, reminded the Procurator General that "the capital of the kingdom during different *chertés* [in the past] drew upon resources in the city of Vitry", but cautioned that the town, "finding itself exhausted," would not be able to "make itself useful" again unless local authorities applied vigorous corrective measures.[10] Historically, observed the procurator Jarry at Bray, this town has been "one of the principal markets on the upper Seine for the provisioning of Paris." To assure this service, the town had always required merchants to make themselves known through formal registration. "Since the Declaration of the King," however, Jarry explained, "which accords the liberty of the grain trade to all persons the inhabitants of our city ... refuse to have themselves received as merchants." As a result, surveillance became impossible and there reigned a terrible "confusion" in the market. To facilitate the flow of grain to the capital, the local police had to be reaffirmed. "I beg you,

---

9 March and May 1768, BN, Coll. Joly 1142, fols. 12–13, 64–65; Petition from Lizy and CG to PG, Aug. 1767, Coll. Joly 1135, fols. 135–141.
10 Dronay to PG, 14 Sept. 1766, BN, Coll. Joly 1134, fols. 187–98.

therefore, Monseigneur," Jarry addressed Joly de Fleury, "to please indicate to me if in spite of the declaration of the King I can *maintain the usage established always* and compel those who do a regular grain trade for the supply of Paris to have themselves received as has *always been practiced....*"[11]

In theory, Jarry could have based his claim on the text of the liberal laws themselves, for they specifically preserved the traditional rules governing the supply of the capital—rules, it could have been argued, which would have no substance unless they were applicable through-out the elastic hinterland where Parisian traders dealt. A local official with a talent for loose construction of the law, who in ordinary times would strenuously resist the tutelage of the capital, might attempt to salvage his police powers by placing them under the shelter of the Parisian exemption. Citing the immunity clause in the May Declaration, the fiscal procurator of Dammartin shared the "hope" with Joly that "the *halle* of Dammartin located eight leagues from the capital is included in the preceding regulations rendered for the provisioning of the city of Paris...."[12] Petit, fiscal procurator of Rambouillet, "pre-sumed" that he could continue to police his merchants and markets as always "... since it is said that nothing will be changed or inno-vated in the Regulations rendered for the Provisioning of Paris."[13] The government rejected these interpretations, for it had no inten-tion of permitting the "provisioning of Paris" to become a pretext for the perpetuation of traditional police habits and the constriction of the spread of liberty.[14] Ambiguous in meaning and inspiration, the exemption clause was no more an invitation to local authorities to evade the liberal reforms than it was a viable program for reconciling the peculiar needs of the capital with the broader requirements of national policy.

Paris began to feel the effects of harvest failure, the disruption of the grain and flour trade, and incipient panic toward the end of 1767. Throughout the previous year prices had remained well within popu-lar reach. The four-pound white loaf sold at 8 *sous* 6 *deniers* from Easter through the summer and only attained 10 *sous* at Christmas. The price dipped slightly during the first half of 1767, but began increasing steadily after the harvest.[15] In September the Procurator General warned

---

11 Jarry to PG, 17 Feb. 1770, BN, Coll. Joly 1148, fols. 199–200. My italics.
12 Noyer to PG, 4 Sept. 1766, BN, Coll. Joly 1133, fol. 149.
13 Petit to PG, 9 April 1766, BN, Coll. Joly 1134, fols. 85–88.
14 CG to PG. 29 Sept. 1766, *ibid.*, fol. 29.
15 See tables 2, 4, 5.

Table 1. Flour and grain arrivals at the Paris ports and halles during 1766 (in *muids* and *septiers*)

Month	Wheat & Wheaten Flour	Rye	Barley
Jan.1766	1,747m.–11s.	33m.	53m.– 1s.
Feb.	1,850 –10	28 – 3	50 –11
March	2,669 – 2	30 – 6	45
April	2,391	34 – 4	48 – 3
May	1,766 – 6	45 – 7	28
June	2,257 – 9	43 – 6	28 – 8
July	2,339 – 8	31 – 4	31 –11
Aug.	1,711 – 5	57 – 1	62 –11
Sept.	1,672	49	80
Oct.	2,262 – 3	49 – 4	49 – 9
Nov.	2,103 – 1	44 – 3	58 – 8
Dec.	2,743 – 9	49 – 7	81
Total 1766	25,515m.– 4s.	495m.– 9s.	618m.– 2s
Cf. Total 1765	22,835m.–11s.	496m.–10s.	596m.–11s.

Source: *Gazette du Commerce, de l'Agriculture et des Finances* (6 Jan. 1767), 12.

Laverdy that the price—11 and 12 *sous*—was "exciting the public" to an uproar. The Controller-General confidently replied that it was normal for the price to swell fleetingly during the harvest-sowing period. "Moreover," he added, rebuffing Parisian self-regard, "the price of bread is less dear in Paris than in all the rest of the king-dom."[16] In December the price rose to 13 *sous*, provoking the ire of the bookdealer Hardy who esteemed that because the harvest had "not been bad" the increase could only be due to the "too great Exportation of grains outside the kingdom." As a symptom of the deteriorating situation, Hardy noted an incident that caused a stir in popular milieus. The police arrested a woman in the Halles quarter for stealing an eight-pound loaf. When asked why she committed the theft, she invited the commissaire to come to her home to observe her husband and four children languishing "in the last misery." The commissaire returned home with her to discover the father dead,

---

16 PG to CG, 16 Sept. 1767 and CG to PG, 24 Sept. 1767, BN, Coll. Joly 1135, fols. 223–24.

Table 2. Quantity and price of flour sold at the Paris halles, 1767–1768

Date	Price (*livres tournois* & *sous*)		Quantity (in sacks of 325 pounds)
	Minimum	Maximum	
Jan. 1767	31– 5	41–10	11,745
Feb.	28– 5	45	10,822
March			12,033
Apr.	31– 5	37	11,825
May	29–10	43–15	12,047
June	31	43–10	11,449
July	29–10	48– 5	12,089
Aug.			
Sept.	31– 5	59–10	12,082
Oct.	30	57–10	12,842
Nov.	36	57–10	13,683
Dec.	44	58	13,965
Jan. 1768	42	58–10	14,148
Feb.	39	59	13,552
March	37	59	14,001
Apr.	36	58–10	12,047
May	40	58–10	11,886
June	40	60–10	12,786
July	38	62–10	12,319
Aug.	40	64	13,337
Sept.	48	74	12,319
Oct.	45	74	8,104

Source: BN, Collection Joly de Fleury 1139, fol. 129.

hanging from a rope behind the door surrounded by the children in a state of horrified shock. The commissaire released the woman from custody and paid for the bread she stole.[17]

In mid-October, in response to worsening conditions, the government had invoked the prerogative, written in its contract with the

---

17 2 and 3 Dec. 1767, BN, mss. fr. 6680, fol. 140.

Malisset company which maintained an emergency reserve for the capital, transforming the enterprise into an exclusively royal venture. Henceforth all the dealings of the company would be for the account of the king and his government; Malisset would be paid for his labor according to the pre-established schedule. Malisset was instructed to provide the grain and flour requested by Sartine. In addition, he was told to provision certain markets in the countryside around the capital, "but you will send there only modest quantities and when you find these markets to be abundantly supplied and the prices reduced to 24 and 25 *livres* the *septier* measure of Paris you will cease to ship them the king's grain." Both Laverdy and Trudaine de Montigny were loathe to resort to this expedient. Trudaine feared that the king's provisions would frighten away the *laboureurs* and, to be effective, would require "sacrifices" on the price which would produce a loss for the royal accounts. They agreed to authorize regular Malisset shipments to Paris only after repeated, insistent demands by Sartine.[18]

Seventeen sixty-eight proved to be, in Trudaine's own words, a "critical" time for Paris.[19] The winter was bitterly harsh; the duc de Croy compared it to the brutal ravages of 1709. At the turn of the year the Seine, littered with huge chunks of ice, rose dangerously high, impeding river transport and threatening bridge residences.[20] The inclement weather, by arresting the mills, generated one of those recurrent flour crises to which pre-industrial Europe was so vulnerable, menacing scarcity even when grain was available. The ice, Malisset reported, stopped all the mills on the navigable rivers and reduced installations on small streams to one-quarter speed. Since windmills could never "be counted upon," he suggested mobilizing the manual mills used in the breweries. If the situation did not improve, Malisset proposed drawing upon the reserves of the religious and hospital communities and flushing out supplies stocked by Paris bakers by checking the records of the measurers for entries registered at the Halles and the barriers during the past two months.[21] An emergency Assembly of Notables at Chartres, in the heart of a major milling center, lamented the "absolute impotence" of the millers to grind grain and warned that the people, already "murmuring loudly," would not

---

18 Courteille to Malisset, 2 Oct. 1767 and Etat, 21 Dec. 1767, AN, F¹¹ 1194.
19 Trudaine to Sartine, 13 Sept. 1768, Archives Seine-Paris, 3 AZ 10 1, pièces 6, 7.
20 Duc de Croy, *Journal*, ed. by de Grouchy and Cottin, II, 296; *Gazette de France*, 18 Jan. 1768, no. 6, 23–24.
21 6 Jan. 1768, AN, F¹¹ 1194.

Table 3. Wheat, flour, and bread prices at Paris halles 1768 (in *livres* and fractions of *livres*)

Date	Flour best 325-pd.sack	Flour white min.	Wheat *septier* min. –max.	Bread 4-pd. white loaf min.–max. (in *sous* & *deniers*)
2 Jan.	58	50	20–25.75	12–13
13 Jan.	58	42	20–26	12–13
3 Feb.	58	42	22–26	12–13
20 Feb.	58	43	19–31	12–13
9 Mar.	59	42	18.25–27.50	12–13
19 Mar.	59	46	23–29	12–13
4 Apr.	58	44	22–30.50	12–13
16 Apr.	58	39	24–31	12–13
7 May	58	44	21–29.75	12–13
18 May	57	46	23–30.50	13
4 June	58.50	43	23–30.75	12–13
22 June	60	44	24.50–30	12–13
2 July	61	40	25–32.50	
20 July	62	43	26–33	12s6d–13
6 Aug.	62.50	40	22–34	12s6d 13
17 Aug.	62	40	25.50–34	12s6d 13
3 Sept.	64	50	26–33.50	13
21 Sept.			27.50–36	13s6d–15
1 Oct.	74	50	25–35	14–15
19 Oct.	74	55	24.50–36.50	14–15
5 Nov.	80	48	25–38.10	15s6d 16
12 Nov.	76		27–41	15–16
16 Nov.	76	55	25.50–37.50	15–16
26 Nov.	76	60	25–35	15s6d–16
3 Dec.	74	55	24–32.50	15–16
10 Dec.	72	50	24–30	14–15s6d
17 Dec.	70	58	21–30	14–15
24 Dec.	69	50	27–31.50	13–14s6d
31 Dec.	69	59	20–31.50	13–14s6d

Source: BN, Collection Joly de Fleury 1137.

tolerate a lack of bread.[22] Though the weather gradually became less rigorous, the mills faced obstruction again in the spring as a result of

---

22 BN, Coll. Joly 1140, fols. 100–101; police ordonnance, 5 Jan. 1768, B. 3958, fol. 47 and police sentence, 2 April 1768, B. 3953, fol. 66, A.D. E-et-L. Cf. similar mill stoppages in lower Normandy: CG to IN. of Alençon, 19 Jan. 1768, C. 90, A.D. Orne.

excessively low waters. The summer was morose: cold and rainy, ominous for the harvest and for the poor who could not afford to heat their homes.[23]

Already in January top flour had commanded 10 *livres* more per sack than it had the winter before. In September the flour merchant Caron sold his dark flour at 60 *livres*, an incredibly high price that the whitest wheaten meal could not have earned even in tolerably bad times.[24] In November, the master baker Tupin paid 77 *livres* for a white sack, the highest price he had seen in his professional life. At that same moment the official *cours* at the Halles posted the best flour at 80 *livres*. Wheat also reached its cyclical zenith in early November, the head bursting over 40 *livres* at the Halles. Miller Philippe Aube found wheat at Congis in the Brie at 36 *livres*; in four other zone markets, Gonesse, Pontoise in the Oise valley, Magny in the Vexin français, and Meulan in the Seine valley, prices reached 34 *livres*, 35, 35½ and 37 respectively.[25] At Brie-Comte-Robert, where "the artisan lacks bread" and "a *journalier* finds no work," wheat had attained 40 *livres* in late September.[26] Yet according to one observer who claimed to have toured the zone, the harvest was excellent in the Aube, Seine, Oise, Aisne, Marne, and Yonne regions as well as in the Beauce, the Orléanais, and the Gâtinais.[27]

As the price of bread increased in the capital, so did the malaise and "murmurings" which bespoke popular fear and misery and acutely worried the police. The four-pound white loaf hovered between 12 and 13 *sous* until the fall. In the course of September, in the shops and markets, it went from 13 to 15 *sous*. In early November, it climbed to 16 sous, almost twice the price considered normal, higher than it had been in over a quarter century. It dipped slightly in December but it did not fall below 13 *sous*, still exorbitant, until the summer of 1769.[28] Aside from occasional eruptions in the bakeries and sporadic brawls at the marketplaces, the capital experienced no serious popular disorders.[29]

---

23 Duc de Croy, *Journal*, ed. by de Grouchy and Cottin, II, 301; 19 Sept. 1768, *Lettres Ossolinski*, BHVP, mss. 627, fol. 167.

24 Caron, registre D5B⁶–5217, Archives Seine-Paris.

25 Miller Aube, registre D5B⁶-2114, Archives Seine-Paris and see Table 4.

26 Fiscal procurator to PG, 24 Sept. 1768, BN, Coll. Joly 1146, fol. 27.

27 Daure, "Mémoire" (ca. 1771), AN, F¹¹ 264.

28 See Table 5. In addition to the sources cited there, for price data see *Hardy's Journal*, BN, mss. fr. 6680, fols. 151, 183ff.; *Lettres Ossolinski*, 21 Nov. 1768; BHVP, mss. 627, fol. 190; *Conseil Secret*, Délibération of 20 Oct. 1768, AN, X¹ᴬ 8545, fol. 462.

29 See, for example, 12 Sept. 1768, AN, Y 12617.

Table 4. Wheat prices in the provisioning zone, 1767–70 (in *livres* and fractions of *livres*)

Date	Gonesse	Magny	Meulan
1767			
Jan.	16–17.75	18.50	18.50–22
Feb.	16.50–18.50	18–21	18.25
Mar.	15–18	18	18.50
Apr.	15–17	18.25	18.25
May	14.50–16.50	18.75	18.25
June	15.50–17.50	20	19.25
July	17–19	21	22.25
Aug.	19–21	23	24
Sept.	20–24.50	24.50	26.50
Oct.	24–28	28	29
Nov.	23.50–28	27	29.50
Dec.	25.50–28	26.50	28
1768			
Jan.	24–26	25	26.50
Feb.	24.50–26.50	26.50	27
Mar.	26–28	28	29
Apr.	24.50–26.50	29	29
May	26–28	29	29
June	25.50–27.50	31.50	31
July	29.50–31.50	32.25	33
Aug.	29–31	31	34
Sept.	29–33	32–33.50	33.50
Oct.	29–31	36.50	35
Nov.	32–34	35.50	37
Dec.	26–28	30.50	34
1769			
Jan.	29.50–31.50	31	33–34
Feb.	28–30	31	30
Mar.	27.25–29.25	29.75	30
Apr.	27.25–29.25	30.50	30
May	26.50–28.50	30	30
June	26–28	28	27.50
July	24.50–26.50	28.75	30
Aug.	21–23	26.50–28.50	28
Sept.	22.50–26	29–31	31.50
Oct.	22.50–26	28.25–31.50	32
Nov.	20–25	25.50–27.50	26.50

(*Continued*)

Table 4. Continued

Date	Gonesse	Magny	Meulan
Dec.	23–25	24.75–26.75	26.50
1770			
Jan.	20.50–22.50	22.75–25.25	26
Feb.	19.50–21.50	21.25–23	25
Mar.	20.75–22.75	22.50–24.50	24.50
Apr.	20.25–22.25	23–25	25.50
May	23–25	28–29.50	30
June	26–28	27–29	30
July	30–32	33–35	36
Aug.	32.50–34.50	34.50–36.50	35
Sept.	34–36	34–36	35
Oct.	34.50–38	33–36.50	34.50
Nov.	27–29	25–27.50	29
Dec.	26–28	26.50–28.50	29

Source: J. Dupâquier, *et al.*, *Mercuriales du Pays de France et du Vexin François*, 196–203.

Table 5. Paris bread prices from baker registers, 1766–69 (4-pound white loaf, in *sous* and *deniers*)

Date	Tayret	Pigeot	Lemerle	Lecocq
1766				
Jan.				
Feb.				
Mar.	8; 8s6d			
Apr.	8s6d			
May	8; 8s6d			
June	8			
July	8			
Aug.	8s6d			
Sept.	8s6d			
Oct.	9; 9s6d			
Nov.	9s6d			
Dec.	9s6d; 10			

(*Continued*)

Table 5. Continued

Date	Tayret	Pigeot	Lemerle	Lecocq
1767				
Jan.	10			
Feb.	9s6d; 10			
Mar.	9s6d; 10			
Apr.	9s6d			
May	9s6d; 9s9d			
June	9s6d			
July	9s6d; 9; 10	9s6d; 10		
Aug.	10	10		
Sept.	11; 12	10s6d; 11; 11s6d		
Oct.	11s6d; 12; 12s6d	11s6d; 12		
Nov.	12s6d	12		
Dec.	12s6d; 13	12s6d; 13		
1768				
Jan.	12s6d; 13	13		
Feb.	12s6d; 13	13		
Mar.	13	13		
Apr.	13	12s6d		
May	13	12s6d		
June	13	13		
July	13	13; 14	13; 13s6d	
Aug.	13	13; 14	13; 13s6d	
Sept.	13; 13s6d; 14; 15	13; 13s6d; 14; 15	13; 13s6d; 14; 14s6d	
Oct.	15	14s6d; 15; 16	14s6d; 15	
Nov.	16	15s6d; 16	15s6d; 16	
Dec.	16; 15s6d; 15	16; 15s6d; 15	15s6d; 15; 14s6d	
1769				
Jan.	15	15; 15s6d	14	
Feb.	14s6d; 14	14s6d	15	
Mar.	14	14s6d; 14	13s6d	
Apr.	14; 13s6d	14; 13s6d	14	13
May	13s6d; 13	13s6d; 13	13	13
June		13; 12s6d; 13	12s6d	13
July		13s6d; 13	11s6d; 12; 12s6d	13
Aug.		14; 13s6d	12s6d; 12	13
Sept.		12s6d; 12	12; 11s6d	12
Oct.		12	12; 12s6d	12
Nov.		12	13	12; 11s6d
Dec.		12	11s6d	12; 11s6d

Source: Archives Seine-Paris, D6B[6], registres: 4118, 4119, 1003, 84, 2619, 4481, 3009, 3760, 3327.

Table 6. Flour prices 1768–1774 from merchant and baker registers: place of transaction unknown (Paris region) (white flour, 325-pound sack in *livres tournois* and *sous*)

Date	Flour Merchant	Baker	Baker
Jan. 1768			
Feb.			
March			
April			
May	58–10		
June	59		
July	62		62
Aug.	62		59
Sept.	66; 72		
Oct.	71		73; 75
Nov.	74		75; 77
Dec.			74

	Flour Merchant	Baker	Baker
Jan. 1769	66	68	68–10
Feb.	64	67	67–10
March	62	67	
April	60		62
May	59	59	64
June	56		
July	55	56	52
Aug.	54	54	55
Sept.		60	
Oct.			60
Nov.		60	54
Dec.		54	53

(Continued)

Table 6. Continued

Date	Baker	Baker
Jan. 1770		52
Feb.		46
March	48	47
April		46; 47
May	51	53
June		
July	69	68-10
Aug.	70	
Sept.	70	70; 72; 76
Oct.	69; 72	71
Nov.	64	64; 60
Dec.	61; 72	62
	Baker	Baker
Jan. 1771	64	63
Feb.	60	62; 51
March	60	59
April	60	59
May	62	60
June	62	62
July	64	60–10
Aug.	62	59–10
Sept.	57–10	61
Oct.	60	61
Nov.		57–10
Dec.	62	56
Date	Baker	Baker
Jan. 1772	57	54
Feb.	60	54
March	54	54
April	49	50
May	51	49
June		
July		49
Aug.	53	
Sept.	51	50
Oct.	51; 54	52
Nov.		49
Dec.		48

(*Continued*)

Table 6. Continued

	Baker
Jan. 1773	52
Feb.	51
March	50
April	50
May	50
June	54
July	54
Aug.	58
Sept.	58
Oct.	60; 61
Nov.	61; 60
Dec.	60
Jan. 1774	59
Feb.	59
March	58; 57
April	57; 56
May	48

Source: Archives Seine-Paris, registres: D5B[6] 5217, 5234, 2532, 2169.

Table 7. Flour and grain arrivals at the Paris ports and halles during 1769 (in *muids* and *septiers*)

Month	Wheat & Wheaten Flour	Rye	Barley
Jan. 1769	3,716m.– 6s.	43m.	109m.–10s.
Feb.	2,993 – 8	67 – 2	121 – 5
March	3,734 – 2	63	84 –11
Apr.	4,258 –11	77 –11	123 – 3
May	3,205	60 – 6	97 – 1
June	4,365 – 5	90 – 8	67 – 8
July	3,579 –11	67 – 1	77 –11
Aug.	3,680 –11	101 – 2	89 – 4
Sept.	4,756 –11	111 – 8	134 – 6
Oct.	4,040 – 4	83 – 9	96 – 9
Nov.	3,320 – 4	74 – 6	98 –10
Dec.	3,456 – 4	91 – 3	138 – 9
Total 1769	45,104m.– 7s.	931m. – 8s.	1,240m.– 3s.
Cf. Total 1768	41,276m.– 9s.	1,251m.– 7s.	1,023m.– 7s.

Source: BN, Collection Joly de Fleury 1143, fol. 166.

II

Authorities were genuinely alarmed, however, by a series of subversive posters which appeared on the walls of various quarters during a twelvemonth period. Parisians, and other city-dwellers during the Old Regime, resorted to placards in times of trouble to express their disaffection.[30] The posters varied in style and scope from simple scurrilous effusions to primitive political manifestoes. Overtly seditious language, whether spoken in a cabaret or conveyed by poster, was generally more harshly punished than the most portentous works of philosophical speculation. It aroused greater immediate fears precisely because of its transparent crudity, because it seemed to emerge from the people whose irascibility enjoyed less indulgence than the more sophisticated spleen of the elite, and because it appeared more likely to infect other people with its bad example. The police regarded the walls of the cities in much the same way that modern governments view the air-waves and it strove with the same urgency to safeguard its monopoly over their use.

"You are doubtless not unaware," Sartine wrote the commissaries in the fall of 1768,

> that from time to time placards are found posted at the corner of the streets. It is your duty to neglect nothing in seeking to discover the authors in your quarter or at least in making in the breadth of your department exact rounds at the break of day in order to take down those that you find and bring them to me immediately.[31]

At the same moment, in letters patent of 12 November, the king alluded to the wave of placarding and instructed the Paris Parlement to take account of it in its investigations of alleged grain monopolies.[32] Ten

---

30 In 1725, a year of serious dearth, at least one placard appeared on the walls of the capital implying that the crisis was the result of a nefarious plot. Arsenal, mss. Bastille 10905. Shortly after mid-century Jean Moriceau de la Motte was hanged for sedition, largely because of the offensive posters he was convicted of having prepared. BN, Coll. Joly 1415, fols. 73–86. The Procurator General characterized the unauthorized posting of bills as "a public crime vis-à-vis all persons." BN, Coll. Joly 2428, fol. 111. See also the resort to posters at Caen in 1764 and 1765 and at Vire in 1775 to protest grain removals and high prices. C. 2598, C. 2664, and C. 2684, A.D. Cal. In 1778 "incendiary" posters appeared on the walls in London. See G. Rudé, "Paris et Londres au 18e siècle: société et conflits de classes," *Annales historiques de la révolution française*, 45 (Oct.-Dec. 1973), 497.
31 Sartine to Goupil, 2 Nov. 1768, Arsenal, mss. Bastille, 10277.
32 *Hardy's Journal*, 12 Nov. 1768, BN, mss. fr. 6680, fol. 186.

months later the Lieutenant General was still exhorting the commissaires to tolerate no manifestations of discontent; anyone "who would
hold indiscreet discourse" was to be peremptorily jailed.[33]

The first poster about which we have substantive information
appeared in late September 1768, although Hardy claimed that others had been previously discovered, in Versailles as well as in Paris,
and "even in the chamber of the King."[34] A commissaire found
it on the rue des Noyers where it attracted a throng of spectators.
It "warned" the King to "get rid of Mssrs Choiseul and Laverdy
who with a troop of thieves cause Grain to be removed outside the
Kingdom" or else "30,000 men" would do the job for him "at an
unexpected moment." In the opinion of the commissaire, the poster
"comes from *Gens de Peu de Chose* because there is no [proper] spelling
and the writing does not at all appear to be dissembled."[35] Several
days later another placard glued with mud to the church of St. André
des Arts raised the most serious of traditional popular urban threats:
"if we go on eating dear bread we will put the torch to the four corners of Paris." Commissaire Leblanc described the placard as "very
badly spelled and written with all sorts of characters."[36] Nor was this
the only poster menacing fire and Parisians were uneasy about it.
Several weeks later, when a fire destroyed a broom factory, a number
of observers linked the blaze directly with the promises to burn the
city contained in the wall messages. During the next two months a
host of similar bills appeared on both the right and left banks and in
the faubourg St. Antoine warning in particular that the houses of the
ministers and the Lieutenant General would be the first to go up in
flames if the price of bread did not recede.[37]

At the end of October commissaire Roland reported "a large poster
badly written containing horrors and imprecations against the King."
Hardy, who must not have been the only Parisian privy to such information, noted its contents in detail. The placard evoked the famine
plot theme, which had wide currency at the time. It expressed profound
disenchantment with Louis XV, sharply reproaching him for abdicat-
ing the traditional paternalistic kingship—at about this time the liberal

---

33 Sartine to Goupil, 4 Sept. 1769, Arsenal mss. Bastille 10277.
34 *Hardy's Journal*, 23 Sept. 1768, BN, mss. fr. 6680, fol. 178.
35 Roland to PG, 21 Sept. 1768, BN, Coll. Joly 1139, fol. 54.
36 Leblanc to PG, 28 Sept. 1768, *ibid.*, fol. 55. Cf. A. Abbiateci, *et al.*, *Crimes et criminalité en France sous l'ancien régime* (Paris, 1971), 13–32.
37 *Hardy's Journal*, 25 Oct., 27 Oct., 13 Nov. 1768 and 28 Jan. 1769, BN, mss. fr. 6680, fols. 183, 184, 190, 210.

Journal économique remarked that Louis' "handsomest title is that of Father of his people"—and darkly hinting that he had a venal interest in prolonging the suffering of his subjects. The substance and style of the poster suggest that it did not emanate from "gens de peu de chose" or at least not from wholly untutored subversives. According to Hardy it said that

> Under Henry IV we suffered a *cherté* of bread occasioned by the wars but during this time we had a King; Under Louis XIV we similarly experienced several other *chertés* of bread, produced sometimes by the war, sometimes by a real shortage caused by the inclemency of the seasons, but we still had a King; in the present time the *cherté* of bread could be attributed neither to wars nor to a real shortage of Grain; *but we didn't have a King for the King was a Grain Merchant.*

The poster concluded by recalling the attempt which Damiens made upon the life of the king in 1757, intimating that such a fate would not be unworthy of the apostate monarch and that men capable of assassination were prepared to act. Commissaire Roland found comfort in the fact that the crowds gathering to read the placard seemed aghast at its insinuations and Hardy reassured himself that "the spirit of fanaticism and revolt" caused "good citizens to shudder." But the Procurator General, who received news of it from Sartine, was sufficiently concerned that he immediately notified the Chancellor, the Controller-General and the Secretary of State for Parisian affairs.[38] Posters such as this confirmed the terrible suspicions of Leprévost de Beaumont, the lay church official who was imprisoned as a result of his efforts to expose what he called the "pacte de famine."[39]

None of the posters subsequently found took aim at the king in such a violent fashion.[40] "Abominable and seditious" though they were, they assailed the government in general terms and complained of "public misery" and excessively dear bread. Nor did the police apprehend any of the "authors" of these written crimes. The authorities had a somewhat better chance to punish verbal sedition which usually took place in bars and marketplaces and left witnesses. Thus, for example, in the countryside, police detained an individual who, "carried away by the heat of wine," uttered "reprehensible remarks against the person of

38 Roland to PG, 31 Oct. 1768, BN, Coll. Joly 1139, fol. 56; *Hardy's Journal*, 31 Oct. 1768, BN, mss. fr. 6680, fol. 183; *Journal économique* (Jan. 1769), 3.
39 J.-C.-G. Leprévost de Beaumont, *Dénonciation d'un pacte de famine générale au roi Louis XV ....* (Paris, n.d.), 28. Cf. his *Le Prisonnier d'état* (Paris, 1791), 25.
40 2 Nov. 1768, AN, Y 12617; Machurin to Joly, 9 Nov. 1768, BN, Coll. Joly 1139, fol. 57; 9 Nov. 1768, *Hardy's Journal*, BN, mss. fr. 6680, fol. 186.

the King" in reference to his grain trade policies. The city police arrested a former notarial clerk charged with turning a cabaret table into a podium for the denunciation of Choiseul's inhumanity which exposed thousands of Parisians to death from extreme misery.[41]

That Paris suffered misery was not a subversive idea invented by the popular underground, nor was the wall-poster the only medium which dealt with it. In the summer of 1768 the Académie Française awarded a prize to an "Epître aux Pauvres" which described the distress of the poor, "hungry in the midst of the harvests," for whom bread remains an inaccessible and "forbidden fruit."[42] In September the administrators of the Hôtel-Dieu worried aloud about the "misery" caused by the dearth, for experience taught them that such episodes always provoked widespread disease and led to an influx of sick admissions straining the chronically distended capacity of the establishment. Seven months later they called attention to "the extraordinary abundance of sick people who arrive daily at the Hôtel-Dieu as a result of the Misery."[43]

The Lieutenant Criminel Testard du Lys took the measure of popular adversity in the upsurge of crime in the late sixties. "Crimes multiply," he said, "not because the human heart is more corrupt but because the social faculties are more constricted." "Verification made" of their cases, Testard concluded that "misery" drove "the majority" of the people filling the prisons to commit crimes.[44] The Paris Parlement shared his view, noting that the jails "overflow" with prisoners in unparalleled numbers, "citizens more wretched than culpable," victims of the *cherté* of bread.[45]

The crisis of the late sixties resulted in a general economic contraction which caused a serious problem of unemployment throughout the kingdom.[46] Inability to find work was one of the chief sources of popular desperation in the flat country and the city. The Bureau de la Ville financed some public works and Sartine stubbornly pressed the Controller-General for funds to expand the hiring of the poor. Obliged

41 St.-Florentin to PG, 12 Dec. 1769, BN, Coll. Joly 2075, fol. 38; Henry to Sartine, 18, 22 Nov. 1768, F. and L. Ravaisson-Mollien, eds., *Archives de la Bastille* (Paris, 1904), XIX, 422–23.

42 *Hardy's Journal*, 25 Aug. 1768, BN, mss. fr. 6680, fol. 177; *Journal encyclopédique*, VI (16 Sept. 1768), 117.

43 Délibérations du Bureau de l'Hôtel-Dieu, 30 Sept. 1768 and 5 April 1769, AAP, numbers 137–138.

44 Nov. 1768, *Recueil*, 133.

45 Sept. 1768, in Flammermont, ed., *Remontrances du Parlement de Paris*, II, 945–8.

46 See Labrousse, *Esquisse*, 531ff.

to turn away many applicants, Sartine was never able to employ more than 500 to 1,000 workers a day on the ramparts, hills, and sewerage basins.[47]

Although he tried to stimulate the organization of charitable activities in the parishes, there is some indication that the Lieutenant General's effort was not brilliantly successful. Despite the attempts of the police to direct the people to their parish priests, the suppli- cants flocked to the commissaires rather than the churches. In the fall of 1768 the rumor was current that the commissaires were regis- tering names for the distribution of assistance. Besieged by visitors, the police assured them "with gentleness and humanity" that they had been misinformed.[48] On a number of occasions in the course of the year the police may have helped the poor in purchasing bread but Sartine pursued no general policy of subsidies to consumers in cash or in bread.[49] Although rice, as always, was available for distri- bution, it does not seem to have won any more favor in the sixties than it had in the forties and Sartine did not count upon it to render major service.[50] On a small scale, private charity contributed to alle- viate the misery of the poor. For example, the duc de Penthièvre, a prince of the blood, arranged for the distribution of cards to the "pauvres honteux"—fallen men of known moral vertebra rather than the entrenched poor—enabling them to purchase bread at two *sous* the pound in certain bakeries in the Saint Eustache quarter.[51]

III

Sartine devoted most of his energies to staving off the spread of hard- ship and tempering its impact by obtaining more supplies of grain and flour and by maintaining tight discipline over the bakers. In September

---

47 Draft memoir, 10 Oct. 1768 and Sartine to CG, 5 Dec. 1768, BN, mss. fr. 6801, fols. 133, 135; *Recueil*, 147.

48 Syndic Chenon to the commissaires, 10 Oct. 1768, AN, Y 13728. Yet in Sept. 1768 Sartine told the commissaires that the king had provided him with "the means" to assist "some honest families in a state of indigence who are not aided by the parish...." Sartine to Mouricault, 26 Sept. 1768, AN, Y 12830.

49 In mentioning the availability of cheaper bread for the "poor" and the "workers," it is not clear whether Hardy meant that the bread was subsidized or that it was of inferior quality. *Journal*, 28 Dec. 1768, BN, mss. fr. 6680, fol. 199.

50 Trudaine to Sartine, 13 Sept. 1768, Archives Seine-Paris, 3 AZ 10 1, piéce 7; *Mercure historique*, CLXV (Oct. 1768), 426–27.

51 *Hardy's Journal*, 23 Nov. 1768, BN, mss. fr. 6680, fol. 190.

he began to call upon the grain stored by the religious communities and hospitals. Although he found them unevenly stocked and ill-disposed, he later wrote that their contribution of several hundred *muids*, intervening at a crucial moment, proved invaluable.[52] The shipment of community grain helped create the impression of abundance at the Halles. Psychological warfare was an important instrument in the campaign against dearth. To heighten the panorama of plenty, the Lieutenant General used other "little ruses of war."[53] He had dummy sacks of what was meant to appear as grain stacked high in front of the Halles and huge piles of flour ostentatiously placed near the streets.

Of much more fundamental importance was the flow of supplies to the capital. In September Sartine submitted a memorandum to the royal council that underlined to what extent the rules governing the provisioning of the capital had fallen into desuetude. He "complained that the markets of the environs of Paris are not sufficiently furnished and that the bakers and merchants supplying the capital have much trouble finding the grain necessary for this important object." The government responded by specifically instructing the intendants of the *généralités* surrounding Paris, for the first time since 1763, to urge (but not require or constrain) the *laboureurs* to bring to the markets "quantities of grain proportional to their exploitations in conformity with the regulations reserved in the Edict of the Month of July 1764 for that which concerns the provisioning of Paris."[54]

Though Sartine had reason to be encouraged by the government's action, for it is unlikely that he could have obtained so much as a hearing on this issue a year earlier, its practical effects were extremely limited. Apart from the strictly *legal* authority of the exemption clause in the liberal legislation which empowered him to enforce the old police code, the Lieutenant General believed that a "reasonable liberty of the grain trade" was "not incompatible" with certain "precautions" such

52 23 Sept. 1768, *ibid.*, fol. 178. The community reserve system, embodying an old idea, took form after the dearth of 1725–26. For a discussion of its origin, organization, and destiny, see my forthcoming article, "Lean Years, Fat Years: the 'Community' Granary System and the Search for Abundance in 18th-Century Paris."

53 "Mémoire" (ca. 1771), AN, F¹¹ 264. Cf. the similar tactics used at Caen. J. -C. Perrot, cited by R. Cobb, "Problèmes de subsistances de l'an II et de l'an III: l'exemple de Honfleur," in *Comité des travaux historiques et scientifiques, Actes du 81ᵉ Congrès national des Sociétés savantes*, Rouen-Caen, 1956 (Paris, 1956), 303n.

54 Dispatches to intendants B. de Sauvigny, Cypierre, Lepelletier, 21 Sept. 1768 and to Sartine, 24 Sept. 1768, AN, O¹ 410; Sartine to commissaire Mouricault, 28 Sept. 1768, AN, Y 12830.

as the regularization of the *laboureur* supply to the capital, which was the logical outlet for their production.[55] The ministry regarded this reasoning as specious and even disingenuous; the only liberty sanctioned by reason was unqualified liberty and the precaution pressed by Sartine was a crude Trojan horse cantering to a police beat. If the ministry could not comfortably refuse Sartine's request for a reaffirmation of Parisian rights, nevertheless it had no intention of putting any teeth into its instructions to the intendants. There was nothing to compel the *laboureurs* to accept the "invitations" issued by the intendants to supply the markets, especially the metropolitan entrepot chain.[56] As Cypierre of Orléans told his Secretary of State, a mobilization of supply required the promulgation of a formal ordinance calling the grain owners to their duty. The government rejected this suggestion out of hand, regarding it as "dangerous and likely to sow anxiety...."[57] While he shared Cypierre's skepticism about the efficacy of remote moral suasion, Sartine personally wrote to the intendants involved, in the hope that he could enlist their aid in resuscitating a few of the most important markets and perhaps also with the idea of feeling them out on their attitude toward liberalization for political rather than for strictly administrative reasons.

Sartine believed that the city could not become fully secure until private commerce resumed its regular service. But in the short run he could not have managed to feed the capital and keep it calm without the extraordinary aid of the king's grain. Every day the commissaire Machurin of the Halles department, specialist in grain and flour provisioning, surveyed the market and decided whether extra help was necessary.[58] Between the end of September 1767 and the end of March 1768, Malisset sent *at least* 8,652 sacks of flour to the Halles (approximately the equivalent of 17,300 *septiers* wheat) from his magazines at St. Charles and Corbeil. Shipments during the winter mill stoppage were especially heavy. Slightly more than 75% of this flour was white,

55 Sartine to Cypierre, 25 Sept. 1768 in C. Bloch, *Correspondance inédite de l'intendant Cypierre*, 94.

56 Cf. the remark which Turgot made to the intendant Taboureau, 13 June 1775: "Whatever polite form one wishes to give it, it is very difficult for the *laboureurs* not to regard an invitation as an order." C. 6691, A.D. Nord.

57 Cypierre to St.-Florentin, 23 Sept. 1768 and to T. de Montigny, 27 Sept. 1768 and St.-Florentin to Cypierre 24 Sept. 1768, in C. Bloch, *Correspondance inédite de l'intendant Cypierre*, 87, 88, 92, 98.

58 Goujet to Trudaine de Montigny (?), 10 Feb. 1768, AN, F¹¹ 1194 and Albert, compte Malisset (1769), AN, F¹¹ 1193.

theoretically of the first grade, and sold to the bakers through ordinary factorage, at an average price of 55.77 *livres*, somewhat below the current. Between April and the end of November, when the government abruptly and unilaterally cancelled the Malisset contract, Corbeil shipped 11,908 sacks to the Halles, 10,766 of which were white and marketed substantially below the current at an average price of 56.47 *livres*. From February to mid-November 1768, the Halles received over 30,000 *septiers* of presumably first-rank wheat from St. Charles which sold at an average of 27.05, markedly below the going levels. From Corbeil between mid-June and mid-November over 9,000 *septiers* arrived, registering an average sale price of 26.31 *livres*. Thus, within a fourteen-month span, Malisset provided the equivalent of *at least* 80,000 *septiers* or approximately 15% of an *average* year's total Parisian consumption.[59]

Now the records which preserved these figures are egregiously incomplete. Surely they do not encompass all the grain and flour emanating from the Malisset operation nor do they indicate the scale and rhythm of shipments made after November by the agents who replaced Malisset in the administration of king's grain. The Malisset invoices suggest the nature of the government's relationship as supplier to the provisioning of Paris, but they do not permit us to measure the precise extent to which it affected the aggregate supply and influenced, psychologically and materially, the *mercuriale*. Moreover, it is certain that in 1768 the government established new connections for supply and tapped fresh sources of domestic and foreign grain and flour which benefitted the capital. We shall return presently to the question of the organization and management of the king's grain and its relation to politics and public opinion.

Despite the steady flow of king's grain, Sartine's relations with the government remained somewhat strained. The liberal group in the ministry identified him with the police reaction and saw him as an enemy of reform. In fact Sartine was the least tradition-bound of all the lieutenants of police of the reign of Louis XV. He kept an open mind on the grain question, consulting on the one side Morellet and on the other Galiani—both of whom were at one time friends of Trudaine de Montigny—and seeking advice as well from professionals of the *métier* like Doumerc who continued to play an expert's part

---

59 Comptes and Etats Malisset, AN, F^{11} 1194.

in provisioning affairs until the Revolution.[60] Sartine's view of things took him beyond the city of Paris. He appreciated the need to regenerate agriculture, to combat old-fashioned prejudices, and to modernize the Delamarist gospel. To be sure, he believed that Paris required special consideration in any general reform project, but he was a man of breadth and imagination with a talent for compromise. He could have rendered the ministerial liberals valuable support had they not contrived to bar him from virtually all top-level discussions on the grain issue. As much as this exclusion annoyed and embarrassed Sartine, it was of much less practical consequence than the government's increasing isolation from reality. The inflexibility of the ministry and its failure to develop a coherent, workable Paris policy drove the Lieutenant General into the opposition camp.

Until the very last moment, Laverdy obstinately refused to admit that there was anything abnormal or ominous in the Paris provisioning situation. He preached time and patience until the fall of 1768 when, on the eve of his disgrace, he finally changed the diagnosis and declared that it was "indispensable" to commit "all of the resources of the king" to the supply of the capital.[61] His chief aide, Trudaine de Montigny, who showed increasing signs of fatigue and sullenness, concurred, but only half-heartedly and with important nuances. He did not believe that it was most useful or wise to succor Paris directly with large, inert masses of grain whose only imprint would be made on consumers' stomachs. If the government intervened at all on the supply side, it should act according to tactical criteria to maximize its impact. The aim should not be to assist the public but to make such assistance unnecessary. While Laverdy resigned himself to a policy of provisioning the capital directly, Trudaine proposed a strategy of rapid thrusts in the supply zone to shake loose hidden grain and flour by "disconcerting the measures of the *laboureurs* and merchants in showing them that we can do without them" in certain markets. Thus, for example, in September he proposed diverting 1,200 to 1,300 sacks of flour from Paris to the Orléans market to parry the "prodigious rise in prices that we suffer in the markets around Paris." "This operation," he claimed, "if it succeeds, will procure us more repose than could the same [amount of] provision" sent to Paris.

---

60 Morellet, *Mémoires*, I, 185; Galiani to Madame d'Epinay, 22 Sept. 1770 and d'Epinay to Galiani, 1 Nov. 1770, in appendices, Galiani, *Dialogues*, ed. by Nicolini, 580–81; Colin des Murs to Sartine, 8 Jan. 1769, AN, Y 12618.

61 CG to PG, 26 Sept. 1768, BN, Coll. Joly 1140, fol. 190.

At bottom Trudaine remained fervently hostile to the use of king's grain, an approach to problem-solving which he believed the new political economy irretrievably discredited. "I desire very much for the Halles to be as furnished in flour as you desire it," he assured Sartine, "... but I find it hard to believe that the means proposed [the king's grain] can be as useful to that end as the free and entire competition that it would be desirable to establish." Trudaine knew that his stance was highly unpopular with Sartine and his subordinates. The attitudes of the commissaires, who were close to the consumer milieus and in a position to influence public opinion, stung deeply. They were in large measure responsible, he hinted, for the persistence of antiliberal prejudices and for the contempt and mistrust which the people felt for the government. "Where did these men [the commissaires] go, then, to acquire their doctrine which they not only allow to become accredited among the people but which they fortify themselves?" Trudaine angrily demanded of the Lieutenant General, adding that it was this "which produces the murmurs much more than the moderate price increase on the four-pound loaf." Begging "pardon for my candor," he wrote to the man responsible for the behavior and reputation of the commissaires, "it is sad that the magistrates of the people in the first city in the world for enlightenment should be so destitute of sense."

Whatever Paris may think, Trudaine protested, I am making "incredible efforts," "the greatest efforts," to assure the supply of the Halles. "If it is believed that the thing is badly run as it is," he told Sartine pointedly, "I am more than ready to abandon a department that I assure you I did not choose by taste."[62] What the Lieutenant General replied to this passionate outburst is not known. Trudaine not only remained in office, but found his authority enhanced by the appointment of his friend Maynon to the Contrôle-Général in October 1768. Once he was sure of a regular supply of king's grain, Sartine spent more time arguing with the bakers than with the ministers.

IV

Beginning in the fall of 1767, Sartine found himself engaged in a long and wearing struggle with the bakers which did not really end until

---

62 Trudaine to Sartine, 13 Sept. 1768, Archives Seine-Paris, 3 AZ 10 1, pièce 6.

the middle of the next decade. To be sure, the police and the bakers always lived in a state of tension or mutual mistrust. But in the normal years the latent frictions rarely surfaced on a scale or rhythm to warrant concern on either side. As long as the prices remained within reasonable bounds, the police generally left the bakers on their own. They continued to search for violations in weight, quality, and grain or flour trading practices, but they did not often intervene in the market or shop nexus which brought buyers and consumers together for the exchange of bread against money (or the promise of money, for sale on credit was widely practiced at all social levels, making the bakers in turn dependent on credit offered by their suppliers). The steep climb in the price of grain and flour, however, made the bakers as well as the consumers restive and forced the police to place the bakery under strict surveillance and tight control. Sartine asked his commissaires and inspectors to report daily on every aspect of baker activity.[63] He wanted to know what bakers were saying to each other, how they were treating their clients, and how the dearth was affecting their commerce. Above all he was concerned to maintain the "ordinary" level of bread furnishing and to temper the bakers' desire to pass the cost of the crisis immediately on to the consumers.

From the point of view of many bakers, these two goals were mutually contradictory, for it was unfair and unrealistic to expect the baker to continue to provide bread at a loss. Not indifferent to the plight of the bakers, Sartine nevertheless insisted on their obedience. Combining cajolery and intimidation, he made it clear that bakers who cooperated would reap long-term benefits while those who resisted would pay dearly for their insubordination. While the Lieutenant General confidentially instructed his commissaires, dispatched to the markets for the purpose of pressuring the bakers, to effect their missions "in a manner so that the public perceived as little as possible"—the police always sought to avoid confrontations at the marketplace that could ignite the crowd—he threatened the defiant bakers with "public judgements," which would expose them to popular wrath by announcing openly which bakers committed what crimes of self-interest.[64] Bakers who failed to conform to the current price or the price proposed by

---

63 Sartine to commissaire Coquelin, 6 Sept. 1768, AN, Y 13728.
64 Sartine to commissaire Goupil, 22 Nov. and 1 Dec. 1768, AN, Y 10277; Sartine to Coquelin, 28 Feb. 1768, Y 13728.

the police were either issued summonses to appear in court or summarily jailed by *lettre de cachet* or mandate of the Lieutenant General.[65]

Sometimes by individual gesture, sometimes by collective petition, the bakers pressed tirelessly for permission to raise the price of bread. Sartine tried to hold them off as long as possible; at the height of the crisis he considered a holding-action of a week or even of a single market day a substantial victory for public order. By preventing the rise in bread price he hoped not only to spare the consumers and facilitate the task of social control, but also to influence the grain price. For he knew that grain responded to bread even as bread depended on grain. There was little prospect of "containing" the grain sellers as long as the baker-buyers could count on a tariff pegged to follow the slightest rise in the price of grain.[66] The first major encounter between the police and the bakers came right after the harvest of 1767. During the summer the four-pound loaf had risen by 2 *sous*. Basing their demand on "the *cherté* of flour at the Halle and on the little grain which they find in the markets of the environs," in September the *jurés* or guild officers requested permission to augment again from 11 to 12 *sous*. Sartine rejected their argument on the grounds that the scarcity of grain was a temporary function of the harvest labors and that flour was in ample supply at the Halle.

Although he was firm in his recommendation to hold the line, he took pains to avoid alienating the bakers. He wanted them to believe that their demands were genuinely negotiable and subject to frank discussion rather than authoritarian disposal. "The *juré* bakers admitted I was right," noted Sartine, "and they gave me reason to hope that they will not carry the four-pound bread to 12 *sous*" at least till the end of next week. But he realized that this self-restraint entailed material "sacrifice" and he felt he could not impose the same burden on the *forain* bakers who commuted from the suburbs and hinterland to supply the bread markets twice a week because "the bulk" of them were "men extremely ill at ease, unable to suffer the least loss" who would "be forced to quit their commerce if we obliged them to give their bread at a price below cost." Thus he decided not to prevent the *forains* from asking 12 *sous*, but reassured himself that if they succeeded in getting this price, "it

---

65 See, for example, bulletins de sûreté, 27 and 28 July 1768, Arsenal, mss. Bastille, 10123; 22 Dec. 1768, AN, Y 14095; 21 Dec. 1769, AN, Y 12618.

66 For the most lapidary statement of the idea that "the increased [price of] bread causes the price of wheat to increase," see Terray to *jurats of Bordeaux*, 16 May 1773, C. 1441, A.D. Gir.

will be the fault of those who buy, for they could have it cheaper by addressing themselves to the bakers of Paris."[67] This solution was hardly satisfactory, for it was bound to cause bitterness among the Paris bakers and confusion and resentment among the poorest consumers who habitually formed the clientele of the *forains* at the markets. Sartine's caveat-emptor stand and his tender manner with the bakers suggest that he felt certain that grain and flour prices would dip significantly in the near future, thereby relieving everyone.

The next few months convinced Sartine to change his posture. As he anticipated, between November and January the price of grain and flour dropped perceptibly. Not only did the bakers refuse to lower their price, but on the pretext of "the slight augmentation" provoked by spring grain planting, "they believed themselves authorized to announce that they will demand 13 *sous* 6 *deniers* for the best four-pound loaf and soon 14 *sous*." Sartine denounced the move as "a nuisance on their part which I will certainly not suffer." He was "all the more discontent" with the bakers because they "owe me gratitude for not even having set the price of bread and for having used until now indulgence in their regard." The Lieutenant General ordered each commissaire to convoke all the bakers in his department to a meeting to inform them of his acute displeasure and to warn them that they risk summonses and condemnation if they exceed the price of 13 *sous* or merely if they "announce" their intention or desire to increase the price.[68]

Faced with the threat of prison or the closing of their shops, the vast majority of bakers appear to have complied. Despite the pronounced increase in grain and flour prices, bread held fast at 13 *sous* until the end of August. Here and there, bakers transgressed the ceiling. Many, like Pigeot of la Courtille, selling on credit to customers who desperately wanted bread, simply went undetected. Of the handful who were arrested for selling above the current tariff, the *forain* Jean-Baptiste Martin of Puteaux, attached to the Carouzel market, faced the heaviest charges for permitting himself to speak his mind to the commissaire on the price situation and the police control. Other violators escaped with a fine in recognition of the "superior quality" of the bread whose price they inflated.[69]

---

67 Sartine to PG, 18 Sept. 1767, BN, Coll. Joly 1136, fol. 12.
68 Sartine to commissaire Grimperel, 28 Feb. 1768, AN, Y 13396; Sartine to commissaire Thierry, 28 Feb. 1768, Y 11255; Sartine to Coquelin, 28 Feb. 1768, Y 13728.
69 Archives Seine-Paris, D5B⁶ 3009; *bulletin de sûreté*, 27 July 1768. Arsenal, mss. Bastille, 10123; Sartine to PG, 25 June 1768, BN, Coll. Joly 1137, fol. 53.

Assessing the situation in the first week of September 1768, Sartine acknowledged the legitimacy of baker grievances but insisted that it was wholly inopportune to permit the price of bread to increase in the capital. "I view with distress, Monsieur," he wrote the commissaires in a circular letter whose mood was solicitous partly because it was to be read aloud to the bakers, "the position of the bakers at the price where grain and flour is, they cannot do their business with profit, some of them must even take losses, which is not Just; I am touched more than I can tell you and although they cannot blame their losses on me, I nevertheless desire to come to their aid." Each commissaire was to summon his bakers to a meeting in which he would explain the Lieutenant's warm sentiments while expressly forbidding the bakers to surpass the 13 *sous* ceiling (which had now been in effect for over half a year) at least until the end of the month. "I have reason to hope," Sartine asserted, "that the grain will diminish before this time." If the price did not fall, he pledged to try to obtain cash compensation from the crown and "if I were not fortunate enough to succeed in this I would not oppose a reasonable augmentation [in the price of bread]." Meanwhile he instructed the commissaires to make sure the bakers continued to stock their shops "as usual" and treat the public with "kindness."[70]

While some bakers promised to obey, a delegation received by Sartine the next day made it clear that they could not accept his decision.[71] Already a large number of bakers had made their anger manifest by raising prices on their own initiative or cutting back production. Confronted with a *fait accompli*, which seemed irreversible and widespread, the Lieutenant General agreed to grant them an augmentation of half of what they desired, from 13 to 13½ *sous* instead of from 13 to 14. The concession was meant to stem the tide of this incipient mutiny. This time the bakers "kept their word"; at the new ceiling "they furnished their places in the principal markets abundantly."[72]

But for the rest of the month, while the "people murmur and protest bitterly against the *cherté*," the bakers continued to complain about the exorbitant price of grain and flour.[73] The upward momentum was too powerful for the police to contain. Although the police did

---

70 Sartine to Grimperel, Coquelin, Mouricault, and other commissaires, 6 Sept. 1768, AN, Y 13396, Y 13728 and Y 12830.
71 Grimperel to Sartine, ca. 7 Sept. 1768, AN, Y 13396.
72 Sartine to PG, 8 Sept. 1768, BN, Coll. Joly 1137, fol. 74.
73 Sartine to PG, 10, 14, 17 Sept. 1768, *ibid.*, fols. 75–77.

not officially relax the maximum—the price schedule reported at the Halle listed 13 *sous* as the going price for September—city and *forain* bakers alike raised it to 14½ and 15 *sous* before the end of the month. In October the price went to 15 *sous* without any opposition on the part of authorities. There were price variations from breadmarket to breadmarket depending upon the afflux of customers, the personal initiative of the commissaires and inspectors, and the solidity of the bakers' positions.[74] Whether these differentials of 6 *deniers* or a *sou* were durable or notorious enough to stimulate important shifts in buying patterns and the invasion of new turf by "strangers" from other quarters is not known. Such a phenomenon of consumer transhumance, in unsettled times, would surely have aroused suspicions and exacerbated tensions around the marketstalls and the bakeries.

In the first few days of November the four-pound loaf reached its crisis apex at 16 and 16½ *sous;* thereafter Sartine successfully resisted any further upward movement. Through the vigorous intervention of the commissaires, the police thwarted a spontaneous baker effort to push to 17 *sous.*[75] By the middle of the month, the Lieutenant General imposed a ceiling of 16 *sous.* For the first time the bakers in the markets and shops received printed notices indicating the official tariff.[76] Sartine asked to be informed each day of the "slightest augmentation." Personally, he reprimanded disobedient bakers and arranged for their punishment. By early December the price of grain and flour had "diminished considerably in the Halles and in all the markets of the environs of Paris where our bakers go for supplies." As a result, Sartine expected an immediate reduction of the four-pound loaf to 15 *sous* 6 *deniers.* "If the bakers object that they have suffered losses and are entitled to indemnify themselves now that their costs are decreasing"—the usual procedure of natural compensation—they were to be told that the time is not yet ripe, that bread is still far too expensive, and that "they must absolutely not envision this at this moment."[77] By the middle of the month bakers who sold above 15 *sous* risked summonses, heavy fines, and jail.[78] Before Christmas the police set the

74 12, 15 Oct. 1768, *ibid.*, fols. 85, 86.
75 Sartine to Goupil, 2 Nov. 1768, Arsenal, mss. Bastille 10277.
76 *Hardy's Journal*, 23 Nov. 1768, BN, mss. fr. 6680, fol. 190.
77 Sartine to Goupil, 22 Nov. 1768, Arsenal, mss. Bastille, 10277; Sartine to PG, 12, 16 Nov. 1768, BN, Coll. Joly 1141, fols. 94–95; Collerot Dutilleul (Sartine's clerk) to Coquelin, 23 Nov. 1768, AN, Y 13728; Sartine to Goupil, 1 Dec. 1768, Arsenal, mss. Bastille, 10277.
78 Sartine to PG, 21 Dec. 1768, BN, Coll. Joly 1137, fol. 105; Sartine to Coquelin,

tax at 14½; although some bakers continued to offer bread at 15 *sous*, others reduced the price to 14 by the first of the new year. For the consumers the worst of the nightmare seemed to have passed.

Even at the height of the price spiral, violence against the bakers was relatively rare, in part because police dispositions (*exempts* in the markets, frequent street patrols) proved effective, but also because of the widespread belief that the bakers, like everyone else, were victims rather than authors of the *cherté*. Nothing even remotely comparable to the massive faubourg Saint Antoine riot of 1725 transpired in the late sixties. Although individual acts of violence were fairly common, they rarely escalated into collective demonstrations. At the Saint Paul market, for example, on 2 November 1768 a man attempted to bargain with the Widow Tressaux for a four-pound bread. The bakeress offered 15 *sous* 6 *deniers* which, if the loaf was white, was a reasonable price. The buyer replied "with a furious air," insulting her and swearing that he would have it "for nothing." A moment later another shopper "inveighed against the same woman," pushed her, punched her in the stomach and cursed her. In neither instance did the large crowd around the stalls respond to the appeals of the irate buyers for assistance.[79]

Consumers collaborated with the police in the effort to control the bakers by filing complaints against bakers who were dealing unfairly. On a Saturday in mid-December Catherine Picot, armed with the knowledge that the Lieutenant General of Police had fixed the price of the best bread at 15 *sous*, went shopping for a four-pound loaf. Four different bakers in her quarter asked 15 *sous* 6 *deniers* for their bread. She reported this violation to the commissaire Grimperel who issued summonses to the offenders.[80] At about the same moment an unemployed postillion entered the shop of the Widow Ferray on the rue de Seine to buy a half-pound of bread for his noon-time meal. He expected

---

13 Dec. 1768, AN, Y 13728; Sartine to Thierry, 15 Dec. 1768, AN, Y 11255; *Hardy's Journal*, 14 Dec. 1768, BN, mss. fr. 6680, fol. 197.

According to the abbé Baudeau—if indeed he is the author of this journal—the bakers reduced prices "very late," well after they received the orders from the police which themselves came "late." Baudeau also hinted that the bakers had an "infallible means" of winning price increases: bribing the commissaires and the inspectors. The first charges are demonstrably false and the second, similar to accusations made in 1725 and 1740, impossible to verify. See the "Chronique secrète de Paris sous le règne de Louis XVI," *Revue rétrospective*, III (1834), 53.

79 Sartine to Goupil, 2 Nov. 1768, Arsenal, mss. Bastille 10277.

80 19, 30 Dec. 1768, AN, Y 13396.

to pay 2 *sous* but the *garçon*, son of the owner, demanded 3 *deniers* more. The postillion, who had placed an *écu* on the counter, refused and asked for his money back. The *garçon* handed him a loaf, disdainfully offering to "make charity" of the extra 3 *deniers*. Affronted, the postillion rejected the offer, asserting that he did not take charity. The *garçon* grabbed the knife used to slice bread and stabbed the postillion in the hand. On the complaint of the wounded buyer, the police arrested the son and also arraigned the mother for violating the price ceiling.[81]

V

The pricing system imposed by Sartine was an improvised, circumstantial expedient fashioned to meet immediate public needs rather than a scientifically-elaborated schedule constructed to anticipate the whole range of conditions that affect supply and demand and the costs of fabrication. It was more like the revolutionary maximums than the "rates for the fixation of the price of bread" utilized by many municipalities in the Old Regime. Sartine's purpose was to contain the upward thrust of prices in a situation viewed as extraordinary and transitory. In ordinary times Paris had no fixed price structure; once the crisis passed, the bread price would once again become largely a matter of market determination. From the beginning of his tenure as Lieutenant, however, Sartine had been passionately interested in the nascent science of provisioning: rationalization of procedures to save money and increase efficiency, technological innovation, in production and conservation, and increased productivity in the bread industry. Under the twin product of the crisis and the wave of interest in "economic" innovations, which had helped to prepare a climate favorable to liberalization, Sartine continued to sponsor experiments—"trials" as they were called in the late sixties—one of whose goals was "to succeed as far as possible in regulating the price of bread with respect to the prices of the production [of wheat and flour] ... in such a way so that the public can find the relief which it must expect and at the same time the baker can find in his situation a means of subsisting."[82]

These were the most imaginative, the most thorough and potentially

---

81 13, 15, 20 Dec. 1768, AN, Y 13540.
82 23 Jan. 1769, AN, Y 12618. Cf. 8 April 1767, Arsenal, mss. 7458. Sartine also sponsored tests of methods for preparing and planting wheat. 14 Aug. 1768, AN, Y 12617.

the most promising trials which had thus far taken place in the Old Regime. Before Sartine's time the police as a rule took little interest in the technological side of the subsistence question, in part because they did not see that it would have important *policy* implications and in part because it was taken for granted that production methods, save where they raised issues of public health or artisanal honesty (*loyauté*), should be left to the men of the *métier*: the miller whose lungs were filled with flour dust and the baker who put his hands in the dough. Before the sixties the police called upon Science (in the institutionalized embodiment of the Academy of Science or the Faculty of Medicine) only in extraordinary circumstances, such as during the great quarrel in the late seventeenth century over *pain mollet*, a highly esteemed fancy bread made with brewer's yeast, which certain bakers and a number of high police officials believed was "noxious to and unworthy of entering the human body." For purposes of verifying the legitimacy of miller and baker fees and prices, until Sartine's time the police relied upon trials which Delamare had conducted in 1700. The aim of those tests was not to introduce or assay improvements, but merely to *register* the results and costs of the commonly used methods of milling and baking. Even before liberalization, Sartine began to question the old standards and the old routines. He tried to establish closer working connections between the police and the Academy of Sciences, he drew upon expertise in the subsistence *métiers* themselves, and he profited from his personal relations with scientists such as Duhamel and patrons of science-in-the-service-of-business such as Pâris-DuVerney to favor the cause of progress in subsistence technology. The subsistence crisis spurred Sartine to accelerate the experimental program.

During the late sixties, under his personal direction, Bricoteau, head baker at the Scipion hospital, and Malisset, manager of the royal grain storehouse at Corbeil, undertook countless tests to compare the productivity of flour ground by "economic" and "gross" (traditional) milling methods and the quality and cost of bread made from the different flours. The work done in the sixties led ultimately to the creation of a School for Baking under the tutelage of Sartine's protégé and successor, Lenoir, which gave the Paris police their own scientific academy devoted to research and education in all aspects of provisioning technology and policy.

The experiments organized by Sartine focussed on the development of a new or newly-perfected flour manufacturing process appropriately called economic milling. It involved multiple stages of bolting and regrinding which enabled the miller to salvage the rich flour of the middlings that had heretofore passed almost completely with the bran into flour byproducts not used in bread-making. Though the reasons that this technique had never been widely used before have much more to do with the skills, attitudes, and ambitions of millers and bakers than with public policy, it is interesting to note that the regrinding of middlings had been officially prohibited by police ordinance on the grounds that it produced an adulterated and potentially dangerous flour. It is fitting, then, at least in a symbolical sense, that economic milling came into its own at the very moment that the old police regime was discarded. Among other advantages, economic milling promised to yield between one-ninth and one-sixth more (good quality) flour than the grain ground by the customary milling procedure. Although it remains to be demonstrated in convincing fashion, I am inclined to believe that in the decade after Sartine's experiments (during which time the central government vigorously promoted the diffusion of the new technique) economic milling was widely adopted in the Paris area, that it resulted in a substantial "savings" or increase in flour yield from the same quantity of wheat, and that this advance in productivity helped significantly to meet the ever-growing demand for bread, which scholars generally suppose to have been met exclusively by increases in agricultural production.[83]

As for Sartine's immediate effort to establish a universally applicable and acceptable bread price schedule, it failed, or at least the implementation of its results had to be postponed. Although the subsistence crisis induced the police to proceed with the tests and to draft reform projects, it was simply not an auspicious moment to attempt to introduce major changes in artisanal and commercial practices. In the late sixties and early seventies the entire provisioning community was mobilized to provide urgently needed supplies for Paris and elsewhere; there was neither time nor capital to invest in these innovations. Even in a less frenetic time it is questionable whether it would have been possible to devise and institute a regular price control system in a huge city serviced by over a thousand bakers of various types drawing their grain and flour from different places and baking different kinds of bread for a broad range of customers. Moreover, there were still technical flaws to be worked out in the "economic" system. Finally, there was

---

83 "Procès-verbal d'expérience sur 2 septiers de bled," AN, F[11] 1194; Sartine to syndics, 12 March 1767, AN Y 13396; 23 Jan. 1769, AN, Y 12618.

the impassioned resistance of the bakers whom Sartine consulted in order to learn about their production methods and costs as well as their attitudes and whom he invited to witness and comment upon the trials.

The bakers detested the idea of price controls in any form, especially controls which would implicitly require them to modify their commercial and manufacturing habits. After the terrible strain of a subsistence crisis, they looked forward avidly to a return to the wide margin of maneuver they enjoyed in ordinary times. Nor is there any doubt that the bakers resented and felt threatened by this intrusion of outside authority into the *métier*. Armed with new technology and irresistible quantitative data, well-funded, and backed by government agencies, the innovators pretended to send the retrograde craftsmen back to school. The bakers entrenched themselves in one redoubt which they still believed to be impregnable, the refuge to which all proud artisans bypassed by time cling: the exclusive and unfailing talent for producing quality goods. They had no interest in endorsing a process which suggested that they could (and, ultimately should be required to) produce and sell *more* bread for *less* money than ever before. The bakers impugned the validity of Sartine's tests on a host of technical grounds. But to avoid the appearance of sacrificing public good to their selfish calculations, they sought to discredit the new process by showing that it made goods of a drastically inferior and unacceptable quality. In addition to other defects in the system, the bread produced by "economic" flour, the bakers claimed, was nutritionally marred, studded with impurities, malodorous, and tinted a dark honey color "which the worker despises" and would refuse to purchase.[84]

At the beginning of the liberal period, the Controller-General had also expressed interest in the price control question. He instructed the intendants to investigate the relation of the price of bread to the price of grain. He claimed to have ordered tests himself which proved that the demands for an upward revision of price schedules by the bakers were unjustified. His liberal scruples did not extend to a desire to protect the right of the bakers to dispose freely of their property as they saw fit. Clearly the social advantages of dear bread were much more difficult to discern than the social benefits of dear grain. Like the physiocrats, the Controller-General did not believe that the former followed

---

84 *Procès-verbal* beginning in Jan. 1769 and Sartine to Machurin, 7 Feb. 1770, AN, Y 12618.

necessarily from and in proportion to the latter.[85] As La Chalotais, the sanguine Breton magistrate-philosophe put it, "if there were a good administration of Police [i.e., revised, parsimonious price schedule], it would not be impossible for the price of grain to rise throughout the kingdom while the price of bread diminished."[86] The liberals believed that a rational, i.e., downward, adjustment of the baker index, achieved either by increasing productivity or reducing costs and/or profits, could serve to *conceal* the grain price rise from the consuming public.[87] Partly in the hope that technical innovations in milling and baking, followed by appropriate administrative action, would compensate consumers for the permanent rise in the level of grain prices (apart from any wage adjustment), the *économistes*, led by Baudeau, became tireless promoters of subsistence reform.[88] While they refused to denounce the police of bakers in the way that they excoriated the police of the grain trade, the liberals nevertheless favored a radical liberalization of the corporate structure of the bakery. In addition to improved technology and a keener police of baker avarice, Turgot argued that a more rigorous competition among bakers would help modulate the rise in the price of bread in relation to the increase in grain.[89]

As for the development of a popular thrift bread—a *pain de ménage* so ardently desired by the *économistes* and the police—no substantial progress was made under the impetus of the crisis of the sixties. Individual bakers experimented with various kinds of dough without marked success. Toward the end of 1767 several bakers in the faubourgs and suburbs developed a dearth bread similar to the kinds which had appeared in 1709 made of a mixture of wheat, rye, and barley and selling for 25 or 26 *sous* the 12 pounds. While it found some favor among the country-folk on the periphery of the city, Parisians spurned it when it was brought to the marketplaces. Similarly, the following year a Montmartre baker produced a "very good" bread of rye to be sold at 2 *sous* 6 *deniers* the pound which found few takers.[90]

---

85 CG to Miromesnil, 20 March 1768, in LeVerdier, ed., *Correspondance Miromesnil*, V, 127: Turgot, *Œuvres*, ed. by Schelle, IV, 494.

86 Address to Parl. of Rennes, 20 Aug. 1764, C. 1648–49, A.D. I-et-V.

87 See Turgot to IN. of Caen, 15 June 1775, *Œuvres*, ed. by Schelle, IV, 492.

88 See, for example, Baudeau's *Avis au peuple sur son premier besoin* (Paris, 1768).

89 Turgot, *Œuvres*, ed. by Schelle, IV, 494.

90 Note to Laverdy, ca. Dec. 1767, AN, F[11] 1194; BN, Coll. Joly 1138, fol. 82. The *économiste* Baudeau personally promoted the development of an "economic" and "popular" bread in the late sixties. See AN, F[11] 1194 and his *Avis au peuple sur son premier besoin*.

VI

Few bakers had the means to experiment with new bread forms in the last years of the sixties. The piquant aphorism "three dear years will raise a baker's daughter to a portion" did not hold true for the bulk of the baking community.[91] Many bakers were caught in the squeeze between soaring grain and flour prices and the slower-paced rise in the price of bread. Others, who operated habitually on a slim margin, found that they lacked the resources to buy supplies in a highly competitive market. Still others complained of the rising cost of goods and services, the evaporation of customary sources of grain and flour, the bitterness of the weather, and the inability to collect considerable sums of money due from customers who purchased bread on credit. Although there are no serial statistical indicators either in the police or consular archives, there is no question that many bakers faced bankruptcy and ruin.

Neighbors described baker Charles Desauze of the faubourg St. Antoine as a "very gallant man" victimized by "the present misfortunes." Inundated by debts and sued by his wife for a property separation aimed at saving what little of her investment in the marriage could be salvaged, Desauze ascribed his agony to "circumstances of the dearth" as well as to the "bad faith" of grain and flour merchants who exploited the bakers by selling poor quality merchandise which produced much less bread than it should have.[92] Baker Jean Simon of La Nouvelle France complained to the commissaire of the Halles that he had no operating cash at all "due to the *cherté* of goods, having earned only enough to support his household and this with much difficulty." Simon profited from the goodwill of the flour broker Widow Delaitre who continued to extend credit to him.[93] Another factor, Delasalle, simply turned away the weak bakers as poor risks.[94] From debtors' prison, René Morin of the rue de Grenelle, whose assets consisted of 24 *livres* in veritable rags and 106 *livres* worth of baking utensils, declared that the "harshness of the times" compelled him to abandon all his

---

91 On "baker" folklore, see Paul Sébillot, *Traditions et superstitions de la boulangerie* (Paris, 1891).
92 16 Dec. 1768, AN, Y 13540.
93 9 Sept. 1768, AN, Y 12617.
94 "Etat des boulangers de ce quartier qui demandent du secours," Sept. 1767, AN, Y 13396.

possessions and sleep "atop his oven."[95] In September 1768 a deputation of 36 guild "ancients" visited Sartine to "represent to him how much they are suffering from the *cherté* of bread and that if things continue to remain on the same footing, many of them will be faced with the necessity of closing shop."[96]

Sartine, too, was caught in a bind. On the one hand, he could not afford to abandon price controls and, on the other, he could not reasonably expect the poorer bakers to continue in these conditions the regular supply which he felt it was imperative to maintain. To avoid erosion of the baker corps, he discreetly offered to provide various kinds of assistance. By means of subsidies to the bakers, he paid a modest ransom for the tax ceiling he fixed on bread and a small compensation for the troubles bakers experienced on their grain and flour trade. Through the commissaires, the Lieutenant General distributed flour and grain in three- or four-sack loads or a cash stipend of 300 *livres*. A single bounty, it was hoped, would set the baker back on course and enable him thereafter to support himself. "It is not at all my intention," noted Sartine, "to give to the same person two times" but exceptions were made in the course of the year.[97]

Not every importunate baker qualified for help. The commissaires examined each request individually and sought to verify the state of need of the supplicant. Pierre Amar, master baker of the rue Montorgueuil, reported commissaire Grimperel, is "very poor and lacking means, is reduced to baking only a half-sack of flour a day." Indigent, he and his sickly wife were obliged to sublet their bedroom and sleep atop the oven in order to pay the rent. The curé of St. Sauveur authenticated their story in a written declaration. Amar received 300 *livres* in cash. Like him, the Widow Provendier, "who passes for an honest woman," has little bread for sale in her shop. "A little boost will enable her to continue her commerce," observed Grimperel. She received three sacks of flour. Pierre Tauvin, a newly-established master who formerly worked in the faubourgs, claimed "to be in a very great need, having been ruined by his reception in the mastership which he said cost him 1,500 *livres* and by the misery of the times." To permit him to furnish his shop and the place he had at the Halles market, the police granted him 21 *septiers* in grain. Cut off by his miller-suppliers at Persan and Versailles, to whom

---

95 15 June 1771, Archives Seine-Paris, D4B⁶ 41–2260.

96 *Hardy's Journal*, 6 Oct. 1768, BN, mss. fr. 6680, fol. 179.

97 Sartine to Grimperel, 14, 16 Sept. and 4 Oct. 1768, AN, Y 13396; Sartine to Thierry, 14 Sept. 1768, Y 11255.

he owed over 1,800 *livres* for flour, Guillaume of the rue aux Ours, an "honest chap," desperately needed the 3 sacks promised by Grimperel. Sartine gave 5 sacks and 70 *livres* to master Labbé who, to everyone's astonishment, received no assistance for his shop and two market-stalls from his relative, the grain and flour entrepreneur Malisset. Much less persuasive was the request from Jean Trouillet who "had quite a comfortable air" and an arrogant manner that annoyed the commissaire. Baker Descosal, a former member of the Paris watch, still wore a sword over his apron and seemed too eccentric to be taken seriously. Grimperel endorsed the application of Sébastien Lapareillé, scion of a huge baker family, who had seven children and was "very ill at ease," but Sartine rejected the request, noting that this master "can very well wait."[98]

After careful investigation and in consultation with a former and a present *juré*, Grimperel estimated that at least forty bakers in the St. Denis quarter alone merited assistance. In most cases the commissaire learned of their need indirectly. Unlike the desperate Amars, who went to see Sartine, the majority of bakers, "despite their misery," still have too much "amour-propre" to step forward. A sense of honor—an alloy of self-esteem and neighborhood reputation—was the pendant to the cupidity for which the baker, like the *bon bourgeois*, was more famous. Although it did not dissuade him from cheating the public on weight or defying the price ceiling, it inhibited him from soliciting or accepting charity. Grimperel proposed that the police should actively seek out the needy instead of waiting for shops to close and bakers to fail. He carefully explained to those whom the police assisted that the bounties were "advances" or "credits" rather than gifts and that the bakers were expected to repay them when they recovered. In return for the advances, the police expected their shops to be "exactly"—amply—furnished in bread.[99]

Several hundred bakers—perhaps as many as 500—benefitted from the distributions and, with remarkably few exceptions, fulfilled their obligations to continue regular supply.[100] The bakers proved less cooperative, however, in meeting their promises of restitution. Except for the very poor, the subsidized bakers were expected to pay a small weekly installment on their advances to enable them to amortize

---

98 Etats, Sept. 1768, AN, Y 13396; Sartine to Grimperel, 21 Sept. 1768, *ibid.*
99 Draft letter, Grimperel to Sartine, mid-Sept. 1768, *ibid.*
100 *Recueil*, 13, 132, 268; Roubaud, *Représentations*, 410–11.

their debts gradually and to permit the police, who had no special budget allotment for this program, to help other bakers. After an initial access of assiduity, many of the bakers began to neglect their payments. Afraid of pressure or reprisals from their bolder colleagues, those docile bakers who paid begged the commissaires not to reveal their names publicly. The police suspected a "cabal" among the bakers to avoid reimbursement, a collective effort on their part to exact damages from Sartine for the difficulties he had imposed. To set an example, Sartine obtained *lettres de cachet* in January 1769 resulting in the incarceration of four of the leaders of this debtors' strike. Chastened by a short sojourn in the Grand Châtelet, they agreed to make good on their debts. The news of their experience spread rapidly, inducing the other bakers to comply as well.[101]

Paris escaped neither the effects of liberalization nor of the subsistence crisis. From the fall of 1767, the capital's supply lines were mangled and its provisioning was in jeopardy. While Sartine labored to repair the channels that linked Paris to the hinterland (without any guarantee, moreover, that the hinterland would have grain to dispatch) and to keep the bakers in line, the city turned increasingly to the central government for direct assistance on the supply side. In the next chapter, we deal with the operation of the king's grain, at once a study in combatting dearth in the traditional style, in managing or failing to manage public opinion, and in the practice of the high and low politics of subsistence.

---

101 Dec. 1768, Arsenal, mss. Bastille, 12334.

Chapter VIII

THE ROYAL TRUMP

In considering, across the long run, the increasing success eighteenth-century society enjoyed in escaping or attenuating the effects of the deadly old-style subsistence crises—an incomplete triumph which we must be careful not to exaggerate—the role played by government in husbanding resources, containing disease, and organizing social services is often overlooked. If Paris was spared a serious "crisis of mortality" and violent sociopolitical disruptions in the late sixties, it was partly due to the efforts the government made—without enthusiasm, it must be noted—to keep the city adequately supplied in the midst of a grave and prolonged dearth. To be sure, it can be, and in fact was, argued that the methods used by authorities were prodigal and inefficient. The king was said to have spent as much as 10,000,000 *livres* in purchasing grain and flour, the bulk of which served the capital.[1] But it remains extremely doubtful, given the harvest failures, the disorganization of the grain trade, the primitive state of communications, and the mood of consumers, that the city could have fared so relatively well without massive governmental assistance. In any case, no one, with the exception of a handful of ideologues and optimists, not even the ministers who fathered the radical program of liberalization, was prepared to court the risks that non-intervention implied.

This chapter examines certain aspects of the king's grain operation in the late sixties. Like the previous interventions of the government on the supply side, it must be seen first of all as an extraordinary measure devised to deal with a critical subsistence problem. Throughout this discussion, it is imperative to keep in mind that the provisioning situation of the capital was grave and that the grain provided by the government, though it could offer nothing more than stop-gap relief,

---

1 "Mémoire" (Aug. 1771), BN, Coll. Joly 1111, fol. 144.

was desperately needed if the bakers were to continue to offer bread for sale in sufficient quantity. Unlike earlier royal victualing enterprises, which did not come into being until after a crisis declared itself, the king's grain operation of the late sixties was prepared well in advance. This point, too, should not be overlooked. On the eve of liberalization, for the first time ever, the central government established an emergency reserve fund for the capital. *Theoretically*, the government was better equipped than it ever had been to deal with potential subsistence difficulties. Liberalization, however, added a new variable whose effects the government could not foresee.

The king's grain system also focuses attention upon administrative practices. It is important to see what the king's grain was: an arm against dearth and for liberty. But it is also revealing to see how it worked or how it was supposed to work. Like tax collecting, victualing, whether for the army, the hospitals, the colonies, or the great cities, was an incredibly difficult task. The more we learn about how it was done, the more we shall know about the aims, the composition, and the operation of the old-regime administration, its relations with business groups, its appetite for change, etc. Unfortunately, we do not have as much information about the details of the king's grain undertaking of the sixties as we do about a similar effort on an even greater scale conducted in the early 1740's. Yet enough evidence emerges to suggest the way the government conceived of the enterprise, the approach it took in launching it, and the fashion in which it tried to liquidate it. It would be useful, in order to take the measure of this administrative experience, to compare it with the provisioning operations which preceded and followed it, with the *étapes* and *vivrier-munitionnaire* operations of the army, with the functioning of organizations of abundance in Lyons, Marseilles, the Lorraine, Geneva, Rome, and even China.

Nor can we ignore the political implications of the king's grain experience. In many ways they are at the very center of our preoccupations. It was, more than anything else, its connection with liberalization that distinguished this episode of royal paternalism and social control from previous ones. The king's grain service, I argue, was the royal trump for liberalization: the final resource on which the government could draw in its efforts to lead the kingdom to a new manner of treating the grain question. A number of factors, however, threatened to blunt the potential effectiveness of this resource. First of all, it is clear that the government hoped it would never have to be used. At worst, from the vantage point of the mid-sixties, the ministry envisioned occasional forays into the Paris markets to reinforce the supply at strategic moments. The government was not prepared, materially, psychologically, or politically, for a subsistence problem of the acuity of the situation which developed in the late sixties, not only in the capital but through much of the rest of the kingdom as well. Second, the ministry was itself divided in opinion. Bits of evidence suggest that Choiseul and Saint-Florentin favored the use of the king's grain on a substantial scale. Trudaine de Montigny, Laverdy's closest adviser, made no pretense about his hostility to this traditional policy. The Controller-General himself hesitated and the operation reflected his uncertainty. Third, there is the question of organization, which we touched upon above. To undertake the extremely complex and delicate provisioning mission, the government relied upon a peculiar old-regime genre of organization located equivocally on the frontier between public and private enterprise. The king's grain operation aroused serious misunderstanding and mistrust. Yet it is arguable that any form of organization would have encountered the same sort of troubles.

The combination of a highly publicized new departure in national grain legislation and the semi-clandestine recourse to "official" grain purchases and sales revived and gave urgency to the old suspicions bequeathed by one generation to the next that powerful men at the summit of authority were speculating for their own purposes on the hunger and misery of the people. The "famine pact" accusations heaped odium on a king whose moral reputation was already sullied and vulnerable. Inept at public relations in ordinary times, the government proved woefully unable to deal with popular credulity and the dearth mentality. On the one hand, it did not know how to address public opinion and, on the other, divided in its own attitudes, it did not know what posture to present. The revolutionaries of '89 believed in the famine pact and placed it prominently on the list of crimes committed by kings and their henchmen. For many nineteenth-century historical commentators, nothing exemplified as well as the pact the discredit and the degeneracy into which the old regime had fallen. After dealing with the operation of the king's grain system, we shall examine the so-called legend of the famine pact, insisting upon its relationship to the liberal reforms and upon the terrible irony through which royal paternalism lost its credibility.

In this chapter we meet a number of extraordinary individuals whose paths cross in a remarkable way: a grain entrepreneur cuckolded by John Paul Jones, an embittered victualer who ended up organizing provisioning for the French expeditionary army in revolutionary America, and, at center stage, two men, strangers to each other, whose destinies were inextricably intertwined: Malisset, the "major-domo" of the king's grain, and Leprévost de Beaumont, the man who first exposed the famine pact. I pay deference to these individuals, especially the last two, not simply because they are engaging, but because they illuminate in striking fashion the ambience and the problems of the late sixties. Malisset and Leprévost were both unusually intelligent, self-consciously "enlightened," and acutely aware that they were living in an age of great ferment and innovation. Both favored liberalization, although both became instruments of its downfall and discrediting. In his own way, each one had a fascinating career, which tells us, in Malisset's case, a good deal about the transformation of the subsistence industry and about changing patterns of social and economic mobility, and in Leprévost's case, a good deal about the experience of politicization and alienation, which many men underwent in the last decades of the eighteenth century. Together, they are the two links that tie together the political, psychological, and administrative elements in the story of a subsistence crisis unlike any other in the Old Regime.

Finally, the last part of this chapter deals with the liberal reaction to the king's grain and famine pact experiences and with the attitudes of supporters and opponents of liberalization to the general question of official victualing. Their commitment to liberalization placed the *économistes* in an intellectually untenable position; like politically engaged intellectuals at any given moment, they had to strain to remain faithful both to their ideas and to their political allies.

I

The immediate origins of the king's grain operations of the sixties are to be found in the ministry of the Controller-General Machault (1745–54), one of the longest and most enterprising in the eighteenth century. Partly in response to immediate needs, partly as a buffer against future uncertainties, Machault decided just after mid-century to set up a grain reserve. Critical of the careless way in which the accounts of previous royal operations had been handled, he assigned Gaudet, senior clerk in the *vingtième* department, the task of collecting and verifying invoices and generally of overseeing the program under the supervision of the intendant of finance, Courteille.[2] Machault believed that precise knowledge of the grain dealings would enable the ministry to control and utilize them more effectively and prevent the long and unseemly squabbles between government and contractors, which frequently arose during or after the operations, poisoning the atmosphere and delaying final settlements.

Ironically, eighteen years later, Gaudet, who had renounced a commission "out of the desire to please M. de Machault and in the hope of an advancement [in the ministry] which I sought to merit," found himself involved in a bitter dispute with superiors over the accounts for the supply operations he directed in the early fifties.[3] In the 1780's, as we shall see, the government was still contesting the claims of the parties who ran the king's grain in the sixties. Grain bred suspicion, not only in the mind of the crowd, but in the cabinets of ministers, even when they could place their own men in charge of the business. The inquisitions which invariably followed grain affairs demoralized experienced middle-echelon managers like Gaudet and made respectable entrepreneurs reluctant to serve the government.[4]

For reasons that apparently had nothing to do with Gaudet's management, Machault's successor, Moreau de Séchelles (1754–56), dissolved the royal grain fund. Earlier in his career Séchelles had directed army provisioning, an experience which may have convinced him that victualing and stockpiling were uneconomical and politically questionable undertakings. Under pressure from Courteille, a convinced reservist who believed in the utility of "always having a million or 1,500,000 *livres* worth of grain in case of need" and in reaction to the war with England which would deprive France of a prime source of imports for emergencies, a new ministry in 1757 charged Gaudet once again with assembling 40,000 *septiers* in the Paris region.[5] Gaudet had no difficulty in constituting the stock, but in the course of the next few years there was little call for supplies from either the capital or the outlying

2 "Réponse du Sieur Gaudet," Jan. 1769, AN, F^{11} 1192; *Almanach royal* (1761), 163 and (1763), 173. For the sort of business which occupied the grain department, see Courteille to IN. of Burgundy, 12 June 1766, C. 77, A.D. C d'O.

3 Gaudet to (?), 16 Jan. 1769, AN, F^{11} 1192. Despite his dispute with the government, Gaudet remained in charge of the *vingtième* department at least until the ministry of Turgot. See *Almanach royal* (1774), 200.

4 Cf. the "Chambre des bleds" of 1709, AN, X^{2B} 1090, and the experience at the local level in Bordeaux, Joseph Benzacar, *Le Pain à Bordeaux* (Bordeaux, 1905), 92–93.

5 Notes of a conversation between Courteille and the Avocat Général Joly, 16 June 1757, BN, Coll. Joly 1130, fol. 21; AN, F^{11} 1191–1192.

area. The reserve became a costly and unwieldy insurance policy—expenses for maintenance alone, not counting granary rental and wages for workers, amounted to over 90,000 *livres*—and the ministry, now directed by the Controller-General Bertin, began looking for a way to enjoy the benefits of security while transferring the burden of maintenance to private hands. In 1760 the government commissioned Pierre Malisset, a Paris master baker, to undertake purchase of replacement grains for the reserve and in 1762 it named him to take charge of the *"régie* of the king's grain for the provisioning of Paris."[6]

II

The eighteenth century was not accustomed to men like Pierre Simon Malisset. An Algeresque figure gifted with extraordinary talent and imagination, he had an entrepreneurial and industrial vision of the future uncommon to his time and inconsonant with his place as a guild artisan, master baker, and son of a provincial baker of no fortune. Installed in a modest shop on the rue Saint Laurent,[7] sweating over the oven, serving a clientele he knew by name, and dealing in *sous* and *deniers*, he became in a short period of time merchant, miller, subsistence engineer, and supplier to masses of consumers, handling accounts of hundreds of thousands of *livres* and counselling members of the Academy of Science and Controllers-General. Bakers and millers felt threatened by his inventions, rivals in commerce resented the advantages which efficient methods and good connections afforded him, and the businessmen and officials with whom he worked scorned him for his lowly origins. They all begrudged his dazzling ascension and lost no opportunity to impugn his honor and the authenticity of his success.

Malisset's participation in the king's grain operations won for him a dubious celebrity beyond the professional milieu. He signed the contract with Laverdy which Leprévost de Beaumont called the "famine pact" and thus became party, so it was claimed, to a horrible crime against mankind. What qualified him to undertake this charge was not his technical expertise, with which Leprévost was unfamiliar, but his "bankrupter's soul."[8] The Paris Parlement, conducting an investigation

---

6 29 Sept. 1760, Arsenal, mss. Bastille 10141; AN, F[11] 1194 (*régie*).

7 16 Feb. 1756, Arsenal, mss. Bastille 10042.

8 Leprévost, Arsenal, mss. Bastille 12353. Cf. Gustave Bord, *Histoire du blé en France. Le Pacte de famine, histoire, légende* (Paris, 1887), 60 and Maxime du Camp, *Paris, ses organes, ses zones et sa vie dans la seconde moitié du XIXe siècle* (Paris, 1869–1875), II, 29.

into "monopoly" in the late sixties, interrogated "this former *garçon* baker [who has] become very rich in a very short time." The lawyer and journalist Linguet used his name metaphorically to evoke the notion of monopoly and hoarding. Manuel, the revolutionary muck-raker, resurrected Leprévost's charges, characterizing Malisset as the "generalissimo" of the famine plot.[9]

Malisset first set up shop in 1748. From the beginning, he con-ducted experiments in bread-making and in the production of flour meant to improve quality and increase yield. More than any other individual, he was responsible for the early development and diffusion of economic milling, a technique which promised enormous benefits to the public.[10] Despite considerable opposition, he stubbornly per-sisted in his efforts to persuade the directors of public assistance insti-tutions to adopt the new methods and drastically modify their flour and bread-making procedures. After initial, hard-won triumphs at the General Hospital, the Controller-General Bertin offered govern-mental patronage and launched a program to promote the technique throughout the kingdom. In 1761, signing himself simply "baker at Paris," Malisset wrote the first widely disseminated piece on the new method for the *Journal économique*, the appropriate organ for Malisset's brand of micropolitical economy.[11]

He also assisted Doctor Malouin, a well-known physician and chemist, in the preparation of his volume on baking and milling for the encyclopedic series on the arts and crafts sponsored by the Acad-emy. The scientist Parmentier and the lawyer-scholar Béguillet, two of the most prolific writers on subsistence questions in the eighteenth century, drew heavily on Malisset's experience.

Economic milling, as Malisset construed it, postulated a whole new approach to the bread industry, not merely a technical modification

---

9   23 Nov. 1768, BN, mss. fr. 6680; Linguet, *Du Pain et du bled*, 59; Manuel, *Police dévoilée*, I, 371.

10 Béguillet, *Traité des subsistances*, part II, 6; Béguillet, *Discours sur la mouture économique* (1775), 184–85; Béguillet (?), "Mémoire sur les avantages de la mouture par économie," Arsenal, mss. 2891, fol. 209; "Mémoire sur l'expérience des bleds" (ca. 1764), BN, mss. fr. 14296, fol. 19; C. 9780, A.D. Nord. For Malisset's contemporary reputation, see also Baudeau, *Avis au premier besoin*, 2ᵉ traité, 28 and P.-J. Malouin, *Description et détails des arts du meunier, du vermicellier et du boulanger*, ed. by J.-E. Bertrand, 50. For a modern view, see Mauguin, *Etudes historiques sur l'administration de l'agriculture en France*, I, 332 and Alfred des Cilleuls, "Rapport sur l'étude de M. Camille Bloch, 'Création par Malisset d'un moulin économique à Châtillon-surLoing en 1776,'" *Bulletin du Comité des Travaux Historiques et Scientifiques*, Section des Sciences Economiques et Sociales (1899), 10–11.

11 *Journal économique* (Aug. 1761), 363–64.

of the grinding and sifting process. He wanted to introduce thrift, efficiency, and the rational use of resources at every stage of production:
from seed to loaf. Deeply interested in techniques of grain and flour
conservation which would eliminate waste, protect consumers from
disease, enhance bread quality, and make the trade more profitable at
all levels, Malisset conducted experiments under the sponsorship of
Pâris-DuVerney, intendant of the Royal Military School and an old
hand in provisioning affairs. Malisset worked directly with the eminent savant Duhamel du Monceau, whose *étuves*, or drying ovens, he
installed in several magazines. He proposed important modifications
in the drying process and developed tests to prove the unquestionable
superiority of grain subjected to treatment.[12] The Paris municipality
engaged him to conduct experiments on the river to develop the best
methods for covering and conserving grain shipped by boat.[13] He
directed numerous trials commissioned by the Paris police to determine more effective ways to prepare bread.

At Corbeil, the center of his operations in the sixties, he established
a complex of six economic mills which were the wonder of the whole
region. There he installed drying chambers, harnessed the energy of
the water-mills to power a pulley-elevator system capable of lifting grain
to seventh-floor granaries, experimented with new baking ovens in the
shape of a parallelogram, and developed molds for baking a form of
bread which many Parisians still prefer today ("une baguette moulée,
pas trop cuite, s.v.p.").[14] Years before the founding of a public bakery
school by Parmentier and Cadet de Vaux, Malisset fixed as his "aim"
at Corbeil "to assemble everything that concerns the preservation and
manufacture of flour and bread, to present models of each machine
and tool suitable for these operations, to train students without neglect-
ing the part for bookkeeping which is so essential in a big business."[15]

Big business was Malisset's dream; he considered the traditional
artisanal style an anachronism. He had a revolutionary vision in which

---

12 AN, 127 AP 6 (Duhamel du Monceau); Pâris-DuVerney to Duhamel, 3 May 1762, cited by
Béguillet, *Traité des subsistances*, 775–78n; Bourde, *Agronomie*, II, 940–41; *Gazette du commerce,
de l'agriculture et des finances* (29 July 1776), 507.

13 14 Oct. 1762, AN, K 1026.

14 Béguillet, *Traité des subsistances*, 520; Malouin, *Description* (ed. 1761), 243, 252; "Mémoire"
(n.d.), AN, F[11] 264. Similar installations, with mechanical elevators, aerating machines, and
more efficient grinding apparatus, apparently existed in England and were familiar to
specialists in France. See Société d'Agriculture de Rouen, "Mémoire sur le commerce des
bleds et des farines," ca. 1763, AN, H 1507.

15 "Mémoire justificatif par le Sr Malisset," 8 Feb. 1771, AN, F[11] 1173.

technology rather than politics was to be the corrosive of the old socioeconomic order. The air at Corbeil today is still thick with flour dust produced by milling factories working for Paris of the sort which Malisset anticipated 200 years ago. In the 1760's he saw millers as "fabriquans" and grain merchants as "négociants."[16] Even while he was employed in the royal service, he prepared to seize the opportunities which liberalization offered the industrial-scale flour trade by creating workshops to construct and repair barrels and packaging material for the transport of flour to the colonies and to foreign countries.[17]

As a result of his innovative spirit and driving energy, Malisset became an adviser to the government. Bertin called upon Malisset for consultation on general questions concerning agriculture—Bertin's specialty—as well as concrete matters pertaining to milling.[18] Malisset enjoyed a long and fruitful collaboration with the police experts in subsistence, Machurin and Poussot, respectively commissaire and inspector in the Halles department. Poussot described him as "one of the men most informed about trade in grain from its birth until it is converted into bread; there is no matter on this commerce, good or bad, that he does not know."[19] The police hoped, through a series of physical improvements and structural reforms, to regenerate the Halles and make it the paramount and perhaps even the exclusive center for grain and flour traffic serving the capital. With Malisset's technical assistance, the police planned to compose a detailed, rigorously exact treatise for "ministers and magistrates" on the problems of provisioning, in effect a much needed revision of parts of Delamare's *Traité*.[20]

Business was the center of Malisset's life. Childless, he and his wife devoted themselves completely to their affairs. Madame, whom he described as "assiduous and intelligent ... [and] extremely thrifty"— the sort of bourgeoise whom Chardin liked to paint—assumed a large share of the burdens of day to day management, freeing her husband for other pursuits. They lived frugally; without taste for ostentation and with no dowries to build, they invested all their earnings in their commerce.[21] There is no evidence, as Malisset's enemies hinted, that

---

16 Malisset, "Observations," (Jan. 1765), BN, mss. fr. 14295, fol. 164.
17 AN, F[11] 1193.
18 Béguillet, *Traité des subsistances*, 87–90n.
19 22 March 1760, Arsenal, mss. Bastille 10141.
20 7 April, 2 Oct. 1760, *ibid.*
21 "Mémoire justificatif par le Sr Malisset," AN, F[11] 1173.

he lived a life of debauchery and dissipation. A curious episode in the fifties does not gainsay his puritanical self-portrait but suggests nonetheless that he was vulnerable to certain worldly vices. On a grain buying expedition in the Oise Valley, he met three "cavaliers" who invited him to join a card game called "the triumph of France." Malisset won handily and refused to continue, claiming that he played too well and would merely be "stealing" their money. Finally he ceded, lost 36 *louis*, a tidy sum, and later discovered that one of the players had emptied his saddle bags of their contents and filled them with hay while he was at the gaming table.[22]

Nor did Malisset have an untarnished police record. On at least one occasion, also in the fifties before he achieved notoriety, the police, at the request of the guild *jurés*, seized 14 *septiers* of flour seconds and a wagon drawn by three horses belonging to Malisset, on the grounds that the corporate statutes prohibited bakers from trading in flour. Malisset insisted that the flour was to be used for dusting his bread and feeding animals.[23] It is quite likely, however, that he purchased seconds specifically for purposes of regrinding and converting into bread-flour according to the principles of economic milling that he would later make famous.

Although it is easy to account for his sinister contemporary reputation on other grounds, it is possible that he owed a portion of the stigma assigned to him to his older brother with whom he was often confused by contemporaries and historians. Antoine-Charles Malisset, who signed his name almost precisely like Pierre-Simon, was a *forain* baker singularly unsuccessful in his business. His wife, the widow of a Paris master baker who brought him a considerable dowry including a house in the faubourg St. Antoine, sued him for separation of property in 1759. Witnesses who knew him well described him as "negligent in his affairs," "deranged in behavior," irresponsible, and heavily indebted to a host of merchants. Pierre came to his brother's rescue, employing him first as a warehouseman, then as a "mealman and miller" for the General Hospital, and finally as a salesman and promoter of Malisset grain and flour in the provinces.[24] An even more

---

22 20 Dec. 1755, Arsenal, mss. Bastille 10041.

23 2 June 1757, AN, Y 12605.

24 23 Aug. 1759, AN, Y 15060; Minutier Central, XXVIII, 290 (13 Feb. 1745); Minutier Central, VII, 349 (15 March 1764); Minutier Central, LXXXV, 583 (23 Nov. 1764).
Arpin noted that there were two Malissets, the older a specialist in milling and the younger an expert in baking. I have found no evidence to support this claim. Marcel

serious blow to family honor and solidarity came from his nephew Jean-Baptiste (the son of Antoine-Charles?) who became his first clerk and heir apparent in the late sixties. Jean-Baptiste betrayed Malisset by joining his rival, enemy, and successor in the management of the king's grain, Doumerc, who allegedly encouraged the nephew's frivolities and alienated him "from the fidelity he owed his uncle in order to draw from him the secrets of the commerce of Sieur Malisset." Later, on his own, Jean-Baptiste became "négociant" in grain and a flour merchant, barely surviving until he filed for bankruptcy in 1779.[25]

Impressed with Malisset's credentials, in the fall of 1760 Gaudet asked him to begin to purchase grain for the king's account. If the arrangement proved satisfactory, Gaudet intended to tranfer the entire operation to private, or rather, semi-private hands. Malisset expressed serious reservations about the proposition, not merely to enhance his bargaining power, but because he knew that there were grave risks involved in such a collaboration. Firstly, he was concerned because Gaudet's affairs "did not pass for being clear," a circuitous way of suggesting that Gaudet was already under suspicion for mismanagement, a charge Malisset himself would later face. Secondly, long before Leprévost de Beaumont ever imagined a famine pact, Malisset fully understood that the administration of the king's grain had never been a wholesome and unblemished enterprise. In studying the government's role as a supplier in the Old Regime, it is extremely important to keep this insight in mind. "In these sorts of purchases and maintenance of grain," he noted, "many things occur which are against the interests of the King and consequently of the State." If the Lieutenant General of Police insisted, he would undertake the mission, but he wanted it known from the beginning that he was entering a sort of Augean stable.

Poussot assured him that Sartine and the intendant Bertier, another of Malisset's patrons, would follow his activities closely and protect

---

Arpin, *Historique de la meunerie et de la boulangerie, depuis les temps préhistoriques jusqu'à l'année 1914* (Paris, 1948), I, 118–19. Lefèvre wrote about a Malisset *père* and a Malisset *fils*. It is almost certain that he mistook Malisset's older brother for his father. P. Lefèvre, *Le Commerce des grains à Lille*, 88n.

An Antoine-Charles Malisset, "associated baker at Choisy-le-Roy," husband of Louise Brive (not the woman from whom our Antoine-Charles separated in 1759) appears in the records in 1781 ceding his property to creditors. 31 March 1781, Archives Seine-Paris, DC 6 24, fol. 12.

25 Archives Seine-Paris, D4B⁶-53-3245, D5B⁶ 531, DC 6 21, fol. 150, D4B⁶-80-5338; "Mémoire justificatif par le Sr Malisset," AN, F¹¹ 1173.

him. The reformist police inspector was elated by Malisset's acceptance, for it would mark a new era, he felt, in the management of
the king's grain. With Malisset there would be no corruption and no
waste; none of the royal stock would henceforth be thrown in the river,
as the public often suspected and as Poussot attested had occurred in
the past. Given the "infallible precautions" he would take, his purchases would be discreet and without effect upon the normal flow of
grain to the capital and his sales would be prompt and strategically
distributed.[26]

As a gesture of good faith and as a reward for his willingness to
cooperate in the king's grain, in November the royal council granted
Malisset a nine-year concession for furnishing all the prisons of Paris
with bread. Prison supply had long been a source of concern to the
government. Prisoners rioted a half dozen times in the course of the
century over bad quality bread. Authorities conceded that the bread
was often "badly manufactured" by bakers "of poor economy" who
tried to squeeze a substantial profit from the six-month contracts they
habitually signed. Malisset promised a bread of at least "one-third"
better quality at a lower price than previously offered.[27] The opportunity to implement his economic milling and baking technique on an
institutional or quasi-industrial scale pleased Malisset enormously. It
would facilitate his role in the king's grain operations, for the prison
concession required him to maintain at all times a full year's advance
supply of grain or flour. Already operating one economic mill on his
own, the contract prompted him to establish a second one. In the
light of similar charges which later arose, it is interesting to note that
his prison bread drew criticism from a jailhouse concierge for poor
quality. Such an opinion deserved no credit, contended Poussot, "for
everyone agrees that it [the bread] is pretty and good."[28]

The exact nature and scope of Malisset's initial activities in the
king's grain is not known. They must have gratified the ministry,
for beginning in 1762 Malisset undertook full responsibility for the
"*régie* of the king's grain for the provisioning of Paris." He inherited
from Gaudet a part of the 40,000 *septiers* fund he was supposed to
maintain. He had complete freedom to make purchases where he
chose as long as he constantly kept the fund at par, but he could only

---

26 29 Sept. 1760, Arsenal, mss. Bastille 10141, fol. 380.
27 *Arrêt du Conseil*, 14 Nov. 1760; 23 Sept. 1760, Arsenal, mss. Bastille, 10141, fols. 377–78.
28 10 Dec. 1760 and 3 Jan. 1761, *ibid.*, fols. 419, 425.

dispose of grain as the government ordered. Between December of 1762 and December of 1764 he bought or replenished 40,424 *septiers* worth 579,107 *livres* at time of purchase. From the beginning of 1763 to August 1765 he sold 34,307 *septiers*. The General Hospital was the largest single buyer. The capital, still amply supplied by the ordinary channels of provisioning, drew less than 8,000 *septiers* in king's grain. Malisset stored his grain in sixteen different magazines, most of which were located in the Brie, a prime theatre for buying. The cost of maintaining the stock was 107,164 *livres*, the bulk of it in warehouse rentals and wages for day-laborers and supervisory personnel. The expenses involved in purchase—transport, loading, duties, etc.—amounted to over 24,000 *livres*. For his labors, Malisset received a commission, based on sales volume and price, of 51,530 *livres*, The royal accountant for the king's grain, Mirlavaud, one-time clerk to the famous financier Bouret who aided Machault in grain purchases, provisionally approved Malisset's calculations on the very day they were submitted. In addition to buying and selling grain, Malisset also manufactured government flour for shipment to the colonies.[29]

Malisset's arrangement with the government does not seem to have prohibited him from undertaking grain trade in his name. It is known, for example, that he sold grain to the hospitals on his own.[30] How carefully he separated, physically and financially, his personal dealings from those in the king's name cannot be determined.

III

In August 1765, Malisset signed the contract with the Controller-General Laverdy, which later put Leprévost de Beaumont on the scent of the famine pact. This contract significantly altered the way

---

29 Comptes and états, AN F[11] 1194; André Cochut, "Le Pain à Paris," *Revue des deux mondes*, XLVI (15 Aug. 1863), 989; Courteille to La Michodière, 25 Jan. 1764, C. 103, A.D. S-M.

30 AAP, 105, liasse 9, #2. Malisset may also have been involved in purchases made by order of Sartine in 1763. *Ibid.*, new series 47 (Scipion accounts). He was also "the *munitionnaire* charged with the supply of bread for the troops of the camp of Compiègne," according to the *Journal encyclopédique*, XVIII (1 Aug. 1764), 131. Malisset's brother Antoine had a share in the enterprise for the supply of bread to the hospitals of the royal army in Germany in the early sixties—a concession he probably obtained through Malisset's influence. 2 April 1769, AN, Y 9086 (I owe this reference to the graciousness of Professor S. Chassagne, currently at the C.N.R.S.). Finally, Malisset organized his own flour exporting venture. See "Observations sur le commerce de bled et de farine," ca. Sept. 1765, C. 9780, A.D. Nord.

in which the government administered the king's grain.[31] In the fifties and early sixties, the king's grain had been a royal operation managed by crown officials with the participation of outside agents working exclusively for the king's account. With the signing of the new agreement, the government diluted its responsibility for the administration of the operation; it lost its quality of *régie*, or more precisely, was to become a *régie* only under certain conditions. Malisset acknowledged receipt of 40,000 *septiers* of "first quality" wheat, which he promised to maintain at all times at the disposition of the government. As long as the price remained below 21 *livres* at the Paris market he could, however, dispose of up to one-third of the stock as he wished provided he replaced it within four months. Once the price attained 21 *livres* the fund was supposed to be "entire", but Malisset still had some latitude for his own dealings, for he had another margin of two weeks to "complete" the stock once the price climbed to 25 *livres*. At that moment, the grain kept by Malisset formally became the king's grain. Malisset could no longer sell for his own purposes; all purchases and sales were to be made for the king's account and all sums received were to be deposited with Mirlavaud's royal grain treasury.

The contract carefully safeguarded royal interests; it was hardly a windfall for Malisset. He assumed all expenses for magazines, mills, transport, labor, and equipment, in return for which he was to receive an annual indemnity of 24,000 *livres* and a 2% commission on the current value of all grain bought and sold for the king's account.[32] In addition to a number of material benefits, such as exemption from the *taille*, the contract afforded Malisset one enormous moral advantage which he cleverly commercialized. Article eleven stipulated that "all the operations relative to the maintenance and provisioning of the magazines of the king will be made in the name of His Majesty and I will be accorded every protection in this respect." This provision enabled Malisset to invoke royal patronage as a lever in all his dealings. Even when he was not acting specifically in behalf of the government, he could use this license to facilitate his business, to win the favor of clients, and to preempt rivals who could not sport a royal imprimatur.

---

31 Malisset Contract, AN, F11 1194.

32 Courteille supported Malisset's request for a 30,000 *livres* indemnity, arguing that it was "much less considerable" than what the government had paid in the past for such services. Mémoire (1765), AN, F[11] 1194. Note, too, that Malisset promised to provide 170 pounds of flour for every *septier* of wheat, at least ten pounds more than commonly offered.

Malisset's liberal use of the royal name was partly responsible for the astonishing proliferation of rumors concerning the operations of a royal "monopoly" or royal "companies" in the late sixties.

In his policy of liberalization, the king's grain served as Laverdy's royal trump card. The availability of a reserve for the capital, he believed, would free him to implement the liberal reforms throughout the rest of the kingdom. If the Paris supply lines became threatened, he could draw upon the king's grain "without," in the words of one of Malisset's associates, "at all altering the liberty of commerce."[33] This was, in any case, the intention and the rationalization. Whether indeed Laverdy genuinely believed that the Company, when called upon to act in a difficult moment, could avoid "altering" the liberty of commerce for many buyers and sellers is an open question. The Controller-General conceived of the grain fund as a tactical *pis aller*, not as a proper granary of abundance charged with responsibility for provisioning the city at all times. There is no doubt that Laverdy felt uneasy about resorting to interventionist practices in virtually the same instant that his ministry formally broke with that traditional style of administration. Nor was he unaware that certain observers would point to the Company as evidence of his hypocritical or luke-warm commitment to liberty. Yet he viewed the king's grain arrange-ment, at least at the start, as a crucial form of insurance and as an integral part of the plan to contain Paris for the sake of liberalization.

Why Laverdy chose to reorganize the reserve system along the lines of the new Malisset contract remains a puzzling question. In other arrangements for institutional provisioning—the army, for example—he prided himself on substituting a *régie*-like operation for the traditional "companies" in order to obtain "economy" and order.[34] In the Mal-isset deal, the government farmed out the management and, despite rigorous checks, inevitably weakened its control. In part, the decision seems to have been motivated by growing dissatisfaction with the old management under Gaudet. The government had never desired nor been equipped to go into the grain business. Gaudet had little difficulty mobilizing the reserve, but during relatively long intervals of quiescence he could maintain it only at great cost and with considerable waste.

---

33 Mémoire to Trudaine, May 1768, AN, F[11] 1193. Malisset himself understood the primacy of liberalization in the Controller-General's mind. "Observations" (Jan. 1765), BN, mss. fr. 14295, fols. 153–54.

34 Laverdy to Miromesnil, 24 April 1768, in LeVerdier, ed., *Correspondance Miromesnil*, V, 157.

He could not sell and renew with the ease and mastery of a merchant. Malisset was a skilled expert with a formidable background in the *métier* and a fetish for economy; given the incentives for private initiative in the contract, it could be expected that he would manage the reserve with greater success. Financially, the arrangement had allure for a government facing chronic deficits. Malisset provided all the capital for construction and upkeep and he paid all current expenses; the government simply deposited in his hands the initial grain fund.

Finally, there seems to have been a political dimension to Laverdy's reckoning. Implicit in the doctrine of liberalization was the idea that once all obstacles and vexations were removed, an uninhibited free trade would assume all the burdens of supply in good times and bad. The government would not only cease to be a policeman, but it would also renounce any entrepreneurial role in the economy. For the moment an exception in favor of Paris had to be tolerated. As a first step in the new direction, however, Laverdy thought it was important to break away from the old style system in which the government itself operated the king's grain. Divesting itself of its managerial and financial interest in the business, the government would give the grain operation an aspect less harshly in contradiction with its liberalizing policies. Whether the resort to a quasi-private company dressed in royal livery was the best way for the government to divorce itself from the association was a question warmly debated within the ministry and in liberal circles.

Although Malisset had full technical control of the operation, he was not the only party to the "submission" of August 1765. While "the experience and fidelity of Sieur Malisset left no fear as regards him," wrote Courteille, the intendant who struggled until his death in 1767 with Trudaine de Montigny for control of the grain department in the ministry, "several inconveniences which it is prudent to prevent gave reason to fear that in the moment of need, the totality of the provision might not be constituted and that the time required for replacement might delay the help that the circumstances might require instantaneously; in consequence, it was judged necessary to ask Malisset for backers."[35] In a word, the government knew that Malisset could convert grain and prepare bread, but he was, after all, merely a master baker recently risen and he had neither the rank nor presumably the wealth to guarantee that he would be in a position to fulfill all his obligations. The convention sought by the government was customary practice in both

---

35 Courteille, 11 Sept. 1765, AN, F[11] 1194.

business and what passed for public affairs in the Old Regime. It wanted men of impeccable credentials and substance to pledge their honor and property along with Malisset in this important venture.

Nor is it likely that Malisset had the opportunity to choose his guarantors and partners. With his consent, the ministry proposed three men who had important positions and connections: Jacques-Donatien Leray de Chaumont, honorary grand master of the Eaux et Forêts of France at Blois; his friend Bernard Perruchot, director of the hospital services of the royal armies, a position which probably gave him some experience in provisioning; and Pierre Rousseau, another friend and business associate of Leray, who had a long career in the finances, most recently as receiver-general of the Domaines in the Orléanais. (Endogamy was not the rule in either the financial or victualing milieu, but in both those places, as in the mafia, it facilitated connections: Rousseau married the sister-in-law of Brochet de Saint-Prest whom we shall meet as manager of Controller-General Terray's grain department in the seventies.)

In a separate contract, the three guarantors joined Malisset in the formation of a "society" for the conduct of the grain and flour business. Each man held four shares for which he paid 10,000 *livres* apiece, forming an investment pool of 160,000 to launch operations. "To excite his zeal," the guarantors bestowed a gift of two extra shares upon Malisset. Malisset retained a large autonomy in day-to-day management, but the associates agreed to appoint a treasurer quartered in offices in Paris, institute a regular accounting and reporting system, and hold a weekly meeting of the shareholders.[36]

Leray de Chaumont was the dominant figure in the triumvirate of backers. In the opinion of Courteille, Leray "can by his fortune and by the range of his commerce render to the State the most essential services in the times of crisis."[37] Son of a prosperous Nantes bourgeois who became a city councillor and chevalier of the order of St. Michel, Leray made the first of his many fortunes in maritime

---

36 J.-C. Colfavru, "La Question des subsistances," *La Révolution française*, V (July–Dec. 1883), 219–26; L. Cahen, "Le Prétendu pacte de famine," *Revue historique*, CLXXXVI (Sept.–Oct. 1935), 180–81. On Rousseau, see Jean-Nicolas Dufort, comte de Cheverney, *Mémoires sur les règnes de Louis XV et de Louis XVI et sur la révolution*, ed. by Robert de Crèvecœur (Paris, 1886), I, 331, 345, 399–400 and II, 23, 145, 371. There is also a brief reference to Rousseau, who acquired an important financial post in Paris toward the end of his career, in J.F. Bosher, *French Finances 1770–1795, From Business to Bureaucracy* (Cambridge, 1970), 339. Without adducing any evidence to back his claim, E. Lavaquery wrote that Necker invested in the Malisset operation. *Necker, fourrier de la Révolution* (Paris, 1933), 29.

37 Courteille, 11 Sept. 1765, AN, F¹¹ 1194.

trade and invested part of it in the purchase of vast manors, including the estate of Chaumont-sur-Loire, which dated from 980 and once belonged to Catherine de Medici. One of his neighbors was Choiseul, who regarded him highly and brought him in touch with other members of the ministry.[38]

Like Malisset, Leray was an innovator, an experimenter, and a gambler, but on a far greater scale. According to a friend, Leray "was mixed up in every possible commercial enterprise."[39] Within several years after the liberalization of the grain trade and the development of economic milling, he established a plant at Blois for the manufacture of economically-ground flour for exportation to the colonies.[40] He was a correspondent and admirer of Duhamel du Monceau whose works on grain conservation had direct bearing upon his commerce. He experimented with various methods of drying and fortifying grain and developed a simple and relatively inexpensive system of *étuves* modeled after Chinese grain saunas.[41] He participated with and advised Sartine on the milling and baking experiments which the police chief sponsored. Later, when Leray became intendant of the Invalides, he encouraged Parmentier in his researches and hired Brocq, a noted experimental baker who later became technical director of the School of Baking.[42]

For Leray, however, subsistence was only a sideline. He established glass and pottery factories and supported several prominent artists, including Nini, the celebrated medallionist.[43] He was a grand speculator, involved before and after the sixties in every sort of overseas traffic. A member of the "reform party," which rebelled against the

---

38 For Leray's background, see J. de Broglie, *Histoire du Château de Chaumont* (Paris, 1944), 181–83 and *passim*.

39 Dufort-Cheverney, *Mémoires*, ed. by Crèvecœur, I, 345. For his comments on Leray's later career, see *ibid.*, I, 174–75.

40 Béguillet, *Traité des subsistances*, 91. Béguillet thought highly of Leray, hailed his great services for provisioning in 1768, but criticized his application of economic milling. *Ibid.*, 669n, 113.

41 C. Bucquet, *Observations intéressantes et amusantes du Sieur César Bucquet, ancien meunier de l'hôpital général, à MM. Parmentier et Cadet* ... (Paris, 1783), 130n; Leray to Duhamel, (n.d.), AN, 127 AP 6 (Duhamel du Monceau).

42 4 May 1769, AN, Y 12618; 22 Jan. 1771, Archives Seine-Paris, D5B⁶ 2169, AN, F¹¹ 1230; Deliberations of Bureau of the General Hospital, 15 Jan. 1787, AAP, new series 47; A. A. Parmentier, *Manière de faire le pain de pommes de terre sans mélange de farine* (Paris, 1779), 23.
     One wonders whether it was his expertise in grain trade and commercial affairs which enabled the economist Forbonnais to win the hand of Leray's daughter. See Claude Lopez, *Mon cher papa, Franklin and the Ladies of Paris*, (New Haven, 1966), 323–24.

43 Broglie, *Château*, 181–82.

directors of the mismanaged Indies Company in 1764, he helped form a giant India-consortium in the seventies that included the nephew of John Law and a number of prominent international bankers.[44] He borrowed heavily and was also the source of huge loans for needy financiers.[45] According to an American correspondent writing in the eighties from "New Haven dans la Nouvelle Yorck," Leray was among "the first and true authors of our glory and of our liberty."[46] Leray became the intimate friend and counselor of Benjamin Franklin, who used his splendid Passy hotel as an American business and propaganda office and salon.[47] Leray served as intermediary between Franklin and the French foreign ministry, won the favor of Sartine who was navy minister in the mid-seventies, helped Franklin procure desperately needed supplies and ships for the American revolutionaries, and personally fitted out several of the vessels with which John Paul Jones made his mark.

A man immersed in such extensive, complex, and delicate dealings was bound to inspire strong feelings among his associates. Franklin regarded him as "the only Person here whom I could rely on for Counsel", but also noted that "his embarrassments have made him say and do things inconsistent with his character...."[48] John Paul Jones, who allegedly seduced Leray's wife, called him a "harebrained man" and accused him of "base conduct."[49] The *Mémoires Secrets* cited his "very equivocal reputation" while the "English Spy" described him as "an ardent, industrious, and greedy man, who would grasp, if he could, the commerce of the 13 united colonies for himself alone."[50]

---

44 Lüthy, *Banque*, II, 384, 452–53, 455–56.

45 See, for example, Bosher, *French Finances*, 106n.

46 Bachaumont, *Mémoires secrets*, XXIX, 136 (25 July 1785).

47 Lopez, "Benjamin Franklin, Lafayette, and the *Lafayette*," *Proceedings of the American Philosophical Society*, 108 (1964), no. 3, 185–87 and *Mon cher papa*, 123–29. On Leray's role as an intermediary between France and America during the revolutionary war, see Lafayette to Leray, 16 April 1779, typescript translation from Louis Gottschalk collection (courtesy of a private collector). On Leray's American connections, also see Beaumarchais to Vergennes, 21 Sept. 1776 and 3 April 1777, in *Beaumarchais Correspondance*, ed. by B.N. Morton (Paris, 1969–72), II, 254 and III, 83.

48 Cited by Lopez, "Benjamin Franklin, Lafayette and the *Lafayette*" *Proceedings of the American Philosophical Society*, 108 (1964), no. 3, 188 and Lincoln Lorenz, *John Paul Jones: Fighter for Freedom and Glory* (Annapolis, 1943), 464. Cf. Franklin's description of Leray as "the first in France who gave us credit" in Lopez, *Mon cher papa*, 324–25.

49 S. E. Morison, *John Paul Jones: A Sailor's Biography* (Boston, 1959), 123, 185; Lorenz, *John Paul Jones*, 456–57.

50 Bachaumont, *Mémoires secrets*, XXX, 249 (28 May 1775); A.O. Aldridge, *Franklin and his French Contemporaries* (New York, 1957), 62. Cf. the stinging assessment ascribed to Baudeau, "Chronique secrète," *Revue rétrospective*, III (1834), 90–91.

Necker saved him from financial failure in 1780, but Leray had to struggle throughout the decade to keep his affairs in order. Necker's daughter, Madame de Staël, helped finance the efforts of Leray's son, who fought in the War of Independence and married an American, to colonize the Ohio Valley.[51] Leray is said to have become the confidant of the duc de Chartes and an active Mason.[52] An enlightened and paternalistic seigneur, he managed to obtain certificates of civism through all the vicissitudes of the Revolution. Astonishingly versatile, thoroughly familiar with every phase of the enterprises he launched, devoted to science, art, and lively conversation, willing to take enormous risks but shrewd enough to invest in land as well as commerce and the bank, officeholder and courtier, philanthropist and robber-baron, Leray was a striking representative of that breed of dynamic businessmen-nobles who rose to prominence in the old-regime equivalent of the industrial-military complex.

Except for the impression made upon the popular imagination—a gauge that is difficult to read—there is little trace of the activities of the Malisset company in the first two years after the signing of the contracts. It seems probable that the company took maximum advantage of the opportunities afforded by the contract to engage in the grain trade, but there is no evidence indicating the magnitude of the operations, the origin and purposes of the buyers, the amount which entered export traffic, or the sources from which replacements were drawn.

The base of the Malisset company was at Corbeil, a town watered by the Seine with a centuries-old milling tradition. The king and the Paris hospitals were among the most noteworthy old-time mill-owners.[53] Corbeil was an ideal entrepôt because its grain- and flour-laden boats could reach the capital in four or five hours and there were seven rivers traversing rich wheat-lands from which one could reach the door of Malisset's magazine without changing boats or using horses. If the weather impeded river navigation, supplies could take the paved road which led from the gate of the company's

---

51 Lescure, ed., *Correspondance secrète inédite sur Louis XVI, Marie-Antoinette, la cour et la ville de 1777 à 1792*.... (Paris, 1866), I, 324–25; Broglie, *Château*, 203–205; Lopez, *Mon cher papa*, 135, 322, 324–25; Robert de Crèvecœur, *Saint John de Crèvecœur, sa vie et ses ouvrages* (Paris, 1883), 187–88.

52 B. Fay, *Louis XVI or the End of a World* (London, 1968), 318; Valentine Thomson, *Knights of the Seas. The Adventurous Life of John Paul Jones* (New York, 1939), 220.

53 Abbé Lebeuf, *Histoire de la ville et de tout le diocèse de Paris*, ed. by Augier and Bournon (Paris, 1883–1893), IV, 312; Y. Bézard. *La Vie rurale dans le sud de la région parisienne de 1450 à 1560* (Paris, 1929), 172; J.-A. Le Paire, *Histoire de la ville de Corbeil* (Lagny, 1902), II, 33, 56.

installations to Paris. The tributary tapped to power the six mills rarely froze or dried up. Malisset boasted that the country was "very salubrious" with "good air" congenial to the conservation of grain and flour.[54]

Visiting the area in 1771, the duc de Croy expressed admiration for the design of the mills, for the soaring seven-story warehouse which loomed like a skyscraper against the flat horizon, and for the mechanized system of cleaning and aerating the grain and loading and mounting the sacks.[55] The mills were engineered with great care to enhance their productivity and durability.[56] The central magazine cost over a quarter of a million *livres* to build, had a capacity of 70,000 *septiers* and was equipped with a "laboratory"; the automatic elevators, sieves, and fans, Malisset claimed, were especially invented to meet his needs. The company utilized thirteen other magazines, including the St. Charles religious house in a Paris faubourg and a storehouse near Nogent rented out by the abbé Terray who lurks about the periphery of the provisioning business throughout the sixties. For buying and selling, Malisset, his brother, and a few trusted aides toured through-out the countryside and relied heavily upon a dozen experienced commissioners widely dispersed to the north and west of the capi-tal who, Malisset said, "have the best reputation and who are in a position to answer for the funds which might be advanced to them." Although Malisset insisted that he enjoyed "the greatest credit and the greatest consideration [everywhere], even abroad," it is likely that he depended upon the contacts of his guarantors for deals that took the company far afield.[57]

In the fall of 1767, as we have seen, the government "royalized" the company and Malisset once again became a mere agent of the ministry. Officials treated Malisset like a minor functionary, not like a farmer of royal interests or a future merchant-prince. Courteille barked instructions to Malisset peppered with admonitions rather

---

54 Malisset, Evaluation (Aug. 1768), AN, F[11] 1194; Lenoir, "Essai," published by R. Darnton, "Le Lieutenant de police J.P. Lenoir, la guerre des farines et l'approvisionnement de Paris à la veille de la Rèvolution," *Revue d'histoire moderne et contemporaine*, XVI (Oct.–Dec. 1969), 619.
55 Duc de Croy, *Journal*, ed. by de Grouchy and P. Cottin, II, 504 (May 1771).
56 The national survey of grain mills conducted in the year ten revealed the Corbeil mills to be among the most productive in France with an output of 75 *septiers* a day. AN, F[20] 294.
57 AN, F[11] 1193–1194; Béguillet, *Traité des subsistances*, 522; *Encyclopédie méthodique*, Jurisprudence, Police et Municipalités (Paris, 1791), X, 35; CG to PG, 7 Nov. 1767, BN, Coll. Joly 1135, fol. 161.

than encouragements. Allowing him little room for maneuver, the intendant of finance elaborated a detailed procedure by which Malisset would have to justify his accounts and remit funds every Saturday.[58] Upon Courteille's death in November, Trudaine de Montigny took over the correspondence and allegedly found reasons to be discontent with Malisset. He rebuked him for tardiness in submitting accounts, questioned his choice of milling techniques, and rejected a plan to accelerate the service of the Halles by mixing different sorts of flour.[59] Malisset defended himself politely but did not at this time make an issue of any of the charges, which seemed to be the standard fare served up to royal contractors to keep them on their toes.

Every week until November 1768 Malisset shipped large amounts of wheat and flour to Paris and lesser quantities to markets throughout the zone. In addition to the six mills at Corbeil, Malisset controlled four others at Robinson and Essonne and utilized the services of a score of mills at St. Denis, Charenton, Nogent, and elsewhere.[60] The government did not fix the price of the grain and flour. In Paris it offered them slightly below the current in order to encourage a downturn and in the zone markets it rarely permitted them to be sold below the "average" going price. As in previous dearths, this cautious price policy was motivated by a desire, on the one hand, to alleviate distress and prevent disorder and, on the other, to normalize trade relations as quickly as possible and to minimize royal losses in the distribution of supplies. It would be "dangerous" to set prices too low, warned the guarantor Rousseau, for that would "drive away" the *laboureurs* and merchants.[61] This last concern was of special importance in the liberal sixties, for unlike earlier times the government refused to accelerate the normalization of trade "by way of authority." Sartine could not, as did the police lieutenants Hérault in 1725 and Marville in 1740, constrain the *laboureurs* and merchants who had grain to come into the open and furnish the markets.

It is not known with certainty how much grain and flour the Malisset company placed upon the market. One invoice, which inspires little confidence but perhaps fairly suggests the general order of magnitude, indicates that sales in the year 1768 accumulated 2,156,191 *livres* in

---

58 See, for example, Courteille to Malisset, 17 Oct. 1767, AN, F[11] 1194.

59 Trudaine de Montigny to Malisset, 8 Dec. 1767, *ibid.*; Malisset to Trudaine, 10 Dec. 1767, *ibid.*; Trudaine to (?), 11 Feb. 1768, *ibid.*

60 Malisset to Courteille (?), 20 Oct. 1767, *ibid.*

61 Rousseau to Trudaine, 23 June 1768, *ibid.*

Mirlavaud's treasury.[62] This amount would represent approximately 180,000 *septiers* worth of grain. Yet another estimate, made by an observer who claimed to be close to the scene, placed the level of king's grain used in Paris and the provinces at 300,000 *septiers*, an extraordinary figure albeit not inconceivable if it embraced conduits other than the Malisset company.[63]

At the very moment that Malisset was engrossed in provisioning the capital, dissatisfaction with his management reached a peak within the ministry and among his associates. Malisset became the protagonist in precisely the sort of drama which he knew had occurred in the king's grain operations before and which had made him reticent about accepting the government's overtures in 1760. On November 1, 1768 the government formally annulled the Malisset contract. The events and maneuvers surrounding the cancellation are extremely difficult to disentangle and reconstruct. Courteille had been brusque with Malisset, but he was a firm believer in a permanent king's grain fund and one of the few men close to the Controller-General who was nostalgic for the days before liberalization. After his death the grain department reverted wholly to Trudaine *fils* who had no sympathy for an institutional reserve of any kind.[64] Late in 1767 Trudaine became convinced, presumably upon the basis of an examination of the accounts—he never enumerated the charges—that there was "prejudice for the king" in the way Malisset handled his responsibilities.[65] Trudaine consulted with Laverdy and probably also with Choiseul and Leray de Chaumont who was already beginning to estrange himself from Malisset and the other guarantors. They agreed to invite Brillon Duperron, an administrator of the General Hospital with special responsibilities for food supply who had worked with Sartine and Malisset in the testing of economic milling, to conduct a discreet but comprehensive investigation.

In January 1768, well before the Duperron report was completed, the Controller-General took the first step toward repudiating Malisset by awarding Leray, under the name Trezel, a secret contract for the supply of replacement grain for the king's Paris fund as well as for

---

62 "Borderau général" (March 1769), *ibid.*
63 "Mémoire" (1771), AN, F[11] 264.
64 For the announcement of Trudaine de Montigny's appointment to head the grain department, see CG to INs. of Burgundy and Champagne, 20 Nov. 1767, C. 78. A.D. C d'O. and C. 379, A.D. Marne.
65 "Mémoire" (July 1768), AN, F[11] 1193.

the provisioning of the provinces in need of assistance.[66] The Malisset contract had reserved for the king the right to choose whomever he desired to replace the stocks used to provision the capital, but it had seemed highly unlikely that the king would not entrust the task to the company in charge of maintaining the reserve. The deal with Leray deprived Malisset and the other guarantors of the opprtunity to earn the 2% commission paid on replacement purchases, thus striking a harsh blow at their sources of revenue and future prospects.

Nor did Laverdy stop with the Trezel-Leray order. Indications are that the Controller-General was sufficiently worried to launch a European-wide search for stocks of grain available for immediate purchase. At Danzig, for example, he placed an order for 50,000 *septiers*.[67] The liberal friends of the Controller-General felt that such purchases were extravagant and needless; it was enough to pay bounties on imports effected by private hands. The critics of liberalization, however, lamented that he had waited so long before taking this emergency action.

IV

What troubled Laverdy most about the Malisset company was not the suspicion that it was mulcting the king, but the fear that it was undermining confidence in the sovereign and his government and discrediting the policy of liberalization. Throughout 1768, the air was thick with the sort of rumor which had once besmirched the duc de Bourbon and Madame de Prie, Samuel Bernard, Dodun, the Pâris brothers, the Indies Company, Cardinal Fleury, and the Orry brothers.

---

66 AN, F^{11} 1173, F^{11} 1193–1194. By the end of the decade, Leray de Chaumont appeared to contemporary observers as the dominant figure in the provisioning business. The parlementaire Baudouin went so far as to describe Corbeil as Leray's own establishment. Baudouin to Galiani, 23 Mar. 1770, in Galiani, *Dialogues sur le commerce des bleds*, ed. F. Nicolini, 570 (appendix 10).

67 "Mémoire particulier," AN, K 908. Cf. correspondance consulaire (8 June 1768), AN, AE B I 480. An anonymous memorialist writing in the early 1770s claimed that Danzig alone supplied 120,000 *septiers* in the late sixties and that Hamburg, Lübeck, and several Dutch ports also provided substantial shipments. "Réflexions sur les principes des parlements de Paris et de Rouen par rapport au commerce de bleds." Arch. AE, France 1375, fol. 301. Yet England, habitually a major source of imports, herself suffered from dearth in 1768. *Gazette du commerce, de l'agriculture et des finances* (5 Jan. 1768), 11. Earlier in the sixties, disastrously short crops plagued both southern and northern Europe. *Ibid.*, (4 Jan. 1766), 2 and (16 Sept. 1766), 647.

The charges were hauntingly familiar: for sordid, venal reasons, the ministers nourished the dearth, mounted horrible maneuvers to deprive people of bread, and extracted huge profits from grain secretly and illicitly bought, stocked and resold. This time, unlike in 1725 when he was judged too young and captive to know better, Louis XV was explicitly said to be a part of the "manège."

The source of these rumors was not merely Porcherons *guinguettes* and Parisian wallposters.[68] *Laboureurs*, farmers, and local officials complained about allegedly "authorized companies" plundering the countryside; the Estates of Languedoc warned against the spoliations of "an Accredited Company";[69] Cypierre, the intendant of the Orléanais, where Leray's brother-in-law, among others, operated what one witness called the "grain shuttle," blamed hoarding, off-market manipulations, and interceptions on a "single Company" which seemed to have a plan and an organization;[70] Leprévost de Beaumont, into whose hands fell some of the documents concerning the grain department of the Contrôle-Général and the Malisset company, began propagating his cry of indignation; and the Rouen Parlement, with which Leprévost may have been in touch, diffused a number of accusatory queries in which it suggested that the king and the ministry were behind the misery of the times.

Beginning with the harvest of 1768, Cypierre bombarded the ministry with protests against the speculations of a company. First he called it a "private Company", but he soon became persuaded that it was a "privileged Company" abusively operating behind a shield of government authority. Its agents appeared throughout the Beauce, the Perche, and the Gâtinais, buying secretly, even before the crop was taken, and constituting hoards. Increasingly, Cypierre came to believe that the Company was itself largely responsible for the *cherté*, at least in his territory. "The price rise, Monsieur, has other causes than the [natural] exhaustion of the old grain," he informed Trudaine de Montigny; "I repeat, it is [the result of] the maneuvers of this Company which has

---

68 Turgot contended that "the outcry of Parisians against the pretended monopolies" was "excited by" the outcry "raised in the provinces on the occasion of the purchases ordered for the provisioning of Paris." "Lettres sur le commerce des grains," 30 Oct. 1770, in *Œuvres*, ed. by Schelle, III, 271. That is to say, Parisians believed that they were being starved by the very companies which were starving the provincials in order to feed the inhabitants of the capital. Turgot claimed that the rumors traveled from the countryside to Paris "from mouth to mouth."

69 Deliberation, Dec. 1768, C. 2411, A.D. H-G.

70 "Première question," BN, Coll. Joly 1111, fols. 154–55; C. Bloch, "Le commerce des grains," *Études sur l'histoire économique*, 32–33.

made itself master [of the supply] ...." What scandalized and frustrated the intendant was that the law—specifically, the liberal laws—prohibited him from taking any action. "These purchases," he complained to Sartine, "were made by agents whom we could not question without appearing to infringe upon the liberty of trade." The ministry scoffed at Cypierre's "vague allegations." They were the product of an overheated imagination or the residue of old-style prejudices; after all, the intendant himself confessed that he learned of the Company "only by the outcry of the People" transmitted by his subdelegates. The government itself could not have invented a better excuse for treating Cypierre's reports with derision.[71]

Meanwhile the magistrates of Rouen picked up the trail of the Company and pursued it with their usual enthusiasm. In April a member of a subcommittee named by the Parlement to investigate the causes of the *cherté* claimed to have discovered that "there was in Paris a society which, under pretext of the provisioning of the capital, has become master of this [grain] commerce in the whole kingdom." The design of the society was to "starve out" whole provinces, such as Normandy, Picardy, and Flanders, by buying up all the grain in the markets and granaries and shipping it abroad to store (even as their counterparts in earlier times had cached their grain in the isles of Guernsey and Jersey proximate to the coast of France), and then reimporting the same grain for a bountiful profit after the prices had skyrocketed. The parlementaire declared that "it would be easy to have proofs of all these facts" and that, accordingly, it was urgent "to supplicate the King to destroy the company of Paris and to prohibit all societies for the commerce of grain." In an effort to counteract the impression this report made upon the subcommittee, the First President Miromesnil vigorously denied that the government "had any part in the grain trade except perhaps to encourage it." He conceded that a Paris company might in fact exist, but if it did it held no "exclusive privilege" for buying and selling and "it could not do any damage to the rest of the kingdom."[72]

Laverdy expressed contempt for the rumors, which implicated himself, Choiseul, and Trudaine de Montigny in a grain trade plot.

---

71 Cypierre to T. de Montigny, 1,7, 11 Sept. 1768 in C. Bloch, *Correspondance inédite de l'intendant Cypierre*, 50, 63, 73–75; Cypierre to CG, 10 Sept. 1768, *ibid.*, 70; Cypierre to Sartine, 27 Sept. 1768, *ibid.*, 97.

72 Miromesnil to Laverdy, 30 April 1768 (two letters), in LeVerdier, ed., *Correspondance Miromesnil*, V, 163–69.

He took the trouble, however, to rebut the charges, without specifically mentioning the Malisset company. "As for the foul remarks concerning the monopoly of the government," he wrote, "I know that to my regret it was necessary to draw 2,400,000 from the royal treasury, and, in stimulating commerce to act, squeeze from that the stuff for a grain operation of 6,000,000 in order to meet our needs; and I would gladly be whipped in the public square of Rouen if I have gotten an *écu* out of it to this day." "In any event," he added, "I am neither so dumb nor so absurd as to place my money in such a job." According to the Controller-General, Trudaine had succeeded marvelously in exciting commerce and, through a combination of private enterprise and royal purchases, the Seine was covered with ships bringing succor to Paris and the surrounding provinces. Choiseul assisted the Controller-General by agreeing to lend civil authorities grain from military reserves and to absorb any foreign grain which the government felt it could not use, thus sparing it the costly burden of disposing of residues after the passing of the emergency.

Laverdy encouraged Miromesnil to share these details with the parlementaires: tell them about our "crimes"—we have nothing to be ashamed of.[73] Shortly after the Rouennais launched their inquiry, their Parisian confreres threatened to come to the charge. Laverdy claimed to welcome their intrusion because it would help clear the air. "Now comes the Parlement of Paris," he noted,

> which undertakes researches, I am gratified, for if it discovers maneuvers on the part of the government or someone dependent upon it, I will give it a *merle blanc*.[74]

The Parlement of Paris backed off, probably because it came to realize that it was not in its interest to unmask an operation devoted to the provisioning of the capital. But the Rouen court continued to press its case even after Laverdy's disgrace. The efforts made by the ministry to quash its investigation merely tended to reinforce its sense of a plot even as the royal orders to suspend judicial procedures instituted in the summer of 1768 against alleged monopolists had confirmed its suspicions that the government was trying to cover-up wrongdoing in which it was involved. Like Cypierre, the Rouen magistrates reached the conclusion that it was no accident that liberalization tied their hands at the same time it afforded immunity and encouragement to a

---

73 Laverdy to Miromesnil, 24 April 1768, *ibid.*, V, 156–57.
74 Laverdy to Miromesnil, 19 April 1768, *ibid.*, V, 151.

band of mighty speculators. In October, in the course of two weeks, the Parlement sent two extraordinarily virulent "letters and supplications" to Louis XV which were illegally published and disseminated. Bluntly condemning the "badly-managed administration" for causing the dearth, the first letter nevertheless mitigated the king's own responsibility by placing the blame with his advisers who "deceived" him with their "badly-wrought systems."[75] But the second letter virtually accused the king of complicity in a "criminal" grain monopoly operating "in the shadow of a law [ostensibly] devised to prevent it."[76] Enormous amounts of grain, wrote the Parlement, have been purchased "for the same account" in many markets. No "private enterprise" could handle such "immense" transactions:

> There is only one Company whose members are powerful in credit which could be capable of such an undertaking ... Here *we have recognized the imprint of power and the trace of authority.*

Inured to personal calumnies, Laverdy worried about charges such as these because they took such striking proportions and because they were clearly linked to the liberalization policy.[77] The liberal reforms were said to be a cunning pretext for the maneuvers of the government monopoly, which used the export authorization in order to store grain in foreign caches for re-entry into France once prices rose enough to assure a grandly usurious profit and the freedom from police control in order to strip the countryside bare and weaken the nation for the kill. The operations of the company and the ministry's refusal to allow police authorities to act seemed to be conclusive proof that the reform and the dearth were not simply coincidences.

How much of this climate of accusation he ascribed to Malisset's doing and how much of it he understood to be the product of a deeply-seated paranoia or the propaganda of the enemies of the ministry is difficult to say. Clearly he felt that Malisset had shown poor judgment in everywhere brandishing the king's name. In skillfully handled operations for the royal account, "the hand of the King

---

75 Letter of 15 Oct. 1768, *Conseil Secret* 1767–68, A.D. S-M.
76 Letter of 29 Oct. 1768, *ibid.* Cf. the severe and horrified reaction of a contemporary observer to the Parlement's hint that the King was an "accomplice" in a "crime" against the nation. (Anonymous), "Réflexions sur les principes des parlements de Paris et de Rouen," Arch. AE, France 1375, fols. 293–304. In a remonstrance drafted in January 1769, the Rouen court piously disclaimed any intention of implicating the king ("God forbid"). Remonstrances, 25 Jan. 1769, Registre St. Martin, A.D. S-M.
77 See, for example, the anonymous letter to Joly de Fleury, 4 Oct. 1768, BN, Coll. Joly 1139, fol. 84.

would be less easily discovered."[78] By incarcerating Leprévost, tearing down placards, and reprimanding parlements, he could not halt the insinuations. Nor could he effectively combat the charges by dismissing Malisset. But the latter gesture, symbolic and perfunctory as it was, might at least reassure the sensible, highly-placed men who had begun to share the popular fears and suspicions. In September he told the intendant Cypierre in an evasive but placatory letter, which was probably a circular meant for other officials as well:

> It has spread among the People and even among the most enlightened persons[79] that different companies, several of which even protected by the government, had a part in this price rise through large purchases indiscreetly made. This fact, hardly likely in itself given the high price of goods and the little evidence that there is that they will remain at such a disproportionate price, has however become so generalized that I believed it necessary to ask you to verify if in fact indiscreet purchases have taken place in your *généralité*, while assuring you that the King has authorized no Company for this badly conceived commerce.

That Laverdy sanctioned such "verifications" suggests how very anxious he was about the rumors and about the willingness of highly placed persons to believe them, for "verifications" smacked of the old police style and doubtless could be used as a pretext to interfere with the liberty of commerce. Moreover, immediately after denying that the king "authorized" any company to engage in this "badly conceived" trade, Laverdy casually announced the decision to terminate the arrangement with a company called Malisset whose object had been to assist in the provisioning of Paris. Anyone who claimed to be buying for this or for any other company was engaging in deceit and merited severe punishment.[80] Apparently, Laverdy had confidence that Leray, functioning through the straw man Trezel, would buy his grain without fanfare.

In a tone blending triumph and irony, Cypierre reminded the Controller-General that he, the intendant, had never doubted for an instant the existence of a Company whose "indiscreet and multiple purchases

---

78 "Mémoire" (ca. Dec. 1767), AN, F[11] 1194. Compare the widespread perception of Malisset-as-villain with Galiani's perspicacious assessment of him as a sort of anti-monopoly warrior. Galiani to Tanucci, 21 Sept. 1767, in Galiani, *Dialogues sur le commerce des bleds*, ed. F. Nicolini, 324 (appendix 4).

79 Cf.: "... those who make the most rumor are the persons above the people whose fear causes them to speak indiscreetly in front of their valets." Miromesnil to Laverdy, 21 March 1768, in LeVerdier, ed., *Correspondance Miromesnil*, V, 129.

80 Laverdy to Cypierre, 26 Sept. 1768, cited by C. Bloch, "Le Commerce des grains," *Etudes sur l'histoire économique*, 46–47.

caused grain prices to rise rapidly." The Company, which Cypierre had repeatedly denounced, whose reality the ministry had reiteratively denied, "is perhaps," noted the intendant, "the very one formed under the name of Malisset ... whose dissolution you have just announced to me, Monsieur." Cypierre relished his revenge: "this Company," he suggested to his superior, "has perhaps exceeded the object for which it was established ...." Laverdy suffered disgrace before he could reply, but his assistant, Trudaine de Montigny, conceded virtually nothing to the intendant of the Orléanais. While he savagely criticized Malisset's management of the government grain operations within the confines of the ministry, Trudaine unblushingly assured Cypierre that the Company had made no purchases in over a year and that "it never did anything which could give rise to the suspicion" of illicit speculations.[81]

Malisset was a victim rather than a cause of the *pacte*-type rumors, which covered the land even as he was a scapegoat for Laverdy's embarrassment. The name Malisset, however, did not become opprobrious only because it was said to represent the monstrous royal monopoly. The quality of his grain and flour inspired criticism repeatedly, arousing suspicion and resentment, which the public passed on to the king and government and interpreted as another manifestation of the plot against the general interest. To be sure, it followed from the belief in the king-as-speculator that the king's grain would be rotten: indifferent to the well-being of his subjects and to the conventions of honest trade, the king would be sure to market only the least valuable and most volatile grain, which could no longer bear storage. Nor was this suspicion about the quality of royal grain unfounded; like the elements of most paranoia, it drew its first breath of life from an unmistakable perception of reality. In 1709, 1725, 1740, and 1752 portions of the grain sold in the king's name had been contaminated.[82] Much of it was foreign grain which arrived "fatigued," received inadequate conditioning, and was stocked in exiguous, fetid, makeshift warehouses which further aggravated its condition. Nor was domestic grain, harvested during inclement times, amenable to easy conservation. The demands of the buyers, who had clienteles to protect, remained rigorous even in periods of crisis.

81 Cypierre to CG, 24 Sept. 1768 in C. Bloch, *Correspondance inédite de l'intendant Cypierre*, 102; Cypierre to bishop of Orléans, 20 Sept. 1768, *ibid.*, 106; T. de Montigny to Cypierre, 14 Oct. 1768, *ibid.*, 131.

82 On the chronic mistrust of king's grain, see Bertin to IN. of Burgundy, 17 Sept. 1760, C. 80, A.D. C d'O.; "Mémoire sur la manière de faire des provisions de bled pour prévenir la famine" (1736), Arch. AE, France 1304, fol. 161.

Not all of the complaints against bad quality in the late sixties struck at Malisset. Sellers, especially the transient ones who had no interest in pleasing their customers, sought to profit from the shortage and the press of buyers by disposing of poor-grade merchandise. A Paris baker protested against mealmen who foisted bad flour on bakers like himself who were desperate to find supplies. "All the merchants," reported the lieutenant general of Provins, "unanimously complain that since the onset of the grain *cherté* the *laboureurs* do not take the trouble to clean it with as much exactitude as when it is at a lower price." A faubourg St. Antoine baker tried to avenge himself against the suppliers and turn a trick by substituting dark for white flour in a sack he bought at the Halles and filing a claim against the flour merchant for fraudulently selling him inferior goods. The flour broker's aide, whom he tried to bribe, exposed his perfidy and reported him to the police.[83] King's grain not emanating from Malisset provoked public anger. Leray de Chaumont's agents sent grain to Orléans under the name of the "Royal Company" which proved to be "absolutely spoiled." The grain specialist Doumerc, who worked at this time for Leray, had a large cache of grain at Pontoise which "smelled of blemish." Royal grain sent to Angers had a bad odor and an offensive taste. Fifteen hundred sacks of wheat which the *négociant* Prémord imported on order of Trudaine arrived "overheated and damaged." The flour that the government commissioned from Bordeaux for Paris was "abominable."[84]

Malisset, however, was especially vulnerable because he was a regular supplier, close at hand, and a known experimenter with flour manufacture and mixture. Predictably, Leprévost de Beaumont charged that his flour, adulterated with beanmeal, "was crawling with worms" and his grain "exhaled infection." Later, when the government wanted to convince itself that Malisset was a sharpster, it gave some credence to these charges by formally accusing him of "negligence" in the preparation of flour and infidelity in failing to replace the king's grain with first quality wheat. Several times in the course of 1768 Trudaine forbade Malisset to market mixed flour under the king's name for fear that it was not of unquestionable

---

83 16 Dec. 1768, AN, Y 13540; Colin des Murs to Sartine, 8 Jan. 1769, AN, Y 12618; 30 June 1767, AN, Y 12613.

84 "Première question," BN, Coll. Joly 1111, fols. 156–57; Forest to Joly de Fleury (?), Coll. Joly 1140, fols. 47–49; petition of bakers of Angers, 28 July 1770, Coll. Joly 1148, fols. 61–63; Archives Seine-Paris, D5B⁶ 284; (?) to PG, ca. Feb. 1769, BN, Coll. Joly 1147, fol. 45.

goodness. Municipal authorities at Lille virtually banned Malisset from the market as a result of several large-scale transactions which raised questions about the soundness of his grain and flour. Encamped in his citadel of abundance, Malisset became an object of hatred to the townsmen of Corbeil. The local police accused him of hoarding all the best wheat in the region and marketing only grain of inferior quality. In a consumer riot which they joined, the police fixed the grain they seized from him at a penalty price because it contained worms and smelled of the boat.[85]

In February 1768 Malisset sold a huge quantity of Breton grain to the Paris bakers which was filled with stones and dirt. "The bakers who purchased it," noted Sartine, "complain that the public does not want the bread which comes from it." He warned that it was dangerous to permit bread of such poor quality to be sold, for the public was in a nasty humor and likely to react with violence if incidents such as this recurred. Trudaine de Montigny ordered Malisset to take back the remaining wheat and indemnify the three dozen bakers involved.[86]

One of Malisset's most ferocious critics went so far as to blame him for "this sad idea which circulates that one wishes to poison the poor people."[87] There is no evidence that Parisians seriously entertained such fears but dreadful rumors reached the capital that rural populations in outlying areas were mortally striken from eating Malisset-brand bread. Duperron, the government's inspector, and one of his agents, investigated the charges. "It is quite difficult," the agent cautiously wrote, "to ascertain if they have some foundation or if they have for basis envy and jealousy or rather the bad mood which the bread *cherté* engenders." In his initial inquiry he could find no one who was made ill by "bad flour." It is true that Malisset mixes barley in his flour (not, however, in the flour destined for Paris), "but does he add other kinds of grain or bad wheat [?] — that remains to be proven."

The investigators visited three villages in the general area of Corbeil. Lisse and Villabbé were in the past "frequently" subject to "epidemics" and "pestilential" maladies. In the summer of 1763 the villagers suffered a "great number" of illnesses which they ascribed to poor bread made

---

85 Arsenal, mss. Bastille 12353; Albert's analysis, AN, F^{11} 1173; AN, F^{11} 1194; P. Lefèvre, *Le Commerce des grains ... Lille*, 88n.

86 Sartine to Trudaine de Montigny, 9 March 1768 and état-général St. Charles (Feb.-Nov. 1768), AN, F^{11} 1194. Cf. the Controller-General's rebuttal of a "bad quality" complaint from Brie-Comte-Robert, 21 Nov. 1768, BN, Coll. Joly 1146, fol. 64.

87 Daure, "Mémoire," (ca. 1771), AN, F^{11} 264.

from Malisset flour. "But," said the report, "those who have reflected on these relations might think quite differently." With few exceptions, all of those who died were chronically miserable, "poor people lacking everything necessary to live, even bread, given the *cherté* of grain." The grain sold to these people by Malisset—"announced," it is significant to note, "under the name of the King's Grain"—"without being of the first quality," nevertheless made good bread. Others who ate it elsewhere suffered no untoward effects. In addition, Malisset sold four qualities of flour. The "firsts" went exclusively to Paris. The villagers could afford to buy only the thirds and fourths and thus ate a bread "browner and of much less quality" than the Parisians, yet without noxious content.

Duperron found the same thing at Limeil, a village he knew intimately because he maintained a country home there. The Malisset-made bread was "extremely dark" and somewhat bitter "but it did no damage to anyone, and I have seen with my own eyes," Duperron wrote, "numerous families who have subsisted on nothing else for the last six months and who are in excellent health." Everywhere the imperfect bread "excited murmurs" but everywhere the poor consumers who had no choice continued to eat it.[88]

Duperron cleared Malisset of the most horrible of the accusations, but he could not purge the stigma attached to the Malisset name. Heir to the dubious reputation which the king's grain always bore, Malisset bequeathed it to his successors in a slightly shabbier condition. The duc de Croy, who praised the Corbeil installation generously, reported in 1771 that it produced mixed and repaired grain of "bad quality about which the people murmured a great deal." Lenoir, Paris police chief in the mid-seventies, noted that "murmurs" against the "rotten" flours of Corbeil were widespread. When a fire erupted at the warehouse in October 1775 the people refused to help extinguish it. The revolutionaries of '89 condemned the Leleu brothers, the last Corbeil victualers of the Old Regime, for the same alleged frauds.[89]

That Malisset, who devoted so much of his professional life to improving the quality of wheat-flour and bread, should stand accused of carelessness, adulteration, and deceit is particularly ironical but not surprising. Although his science, in theory and practice, was far in advance of his times, he was unable to assure the proper conservation

---

88 July-Sept. 1768, BN, Coll. Joly 1140, fols. 180–90.

89 Duc de Croy, *Journal*, ed. by de Grouchy and Cottin, II, 504; Lenoir papers, Bibliothèque Municipale d'Orléans, mss. 1421; *Hardy's Journal*, 21 Oct. 1775, BN, mss. fr. 6681.

of his goods. His technique was imperfect, the cost of global application was prohibitive, and the crisis conditions in which he operated were not conducive to painstaking labor and inspection. Dealing on a wide scale and at a frantic pace, dependent in part on millers for whose expertise he could not vouch and on day-workers in fifteen different magazines, he was not fully in control of the business. The public was not yet accustomed to the flour produced by economic milling or to the dearth-mixtures, which Malisset improvised, nor were the bakers comfortable with much of the grain that he had to bring in from far away sources. Doubtless, too, Malisset also confounded the economy of his own business with the "economy," which he always claimed to seek for the consumer. He had to replenish the stock of king's grain, depleted by at least a third on the eve of the royalization of the company, in highly adverse circumstances. Like all buyers in a *cherté*, Malisset looked for the cheapest possible buy even when it did not fully meet the "first quality" standard established by his contract.

Still, the tableau must not be overdrawn. In a dearth people expected to be force-fed bad quality food. "They cried out against rotten grain," commented an observer, "even as they cried out against [fantom] monopolists."[90] There is only a small grain of truth in the self-serving memory cultivated by the revolutionaries that the Parisians in the late sixties had been nourished on "stinking wheat."[91] In relative terms, the Parisians, as always—at least until the Second World War when the countryside had its revenge—fared reasonably well. Sensibly, Malisset sent them most of his finest goods; save for accidents, he reserved his trimming for the provinces. The most beautiful flour at the Halles, Diderot wrote Sophie Volland in November, is that "called Malicet [*sic*], from the name of he who furnishes it."[92]

V

Even before the ministry decided to abandon the company in 1768, the guarantors, evincing growing dissatisfaction with Malisset and with the terms of their obligations to the government, petitioned for a cancellation of the contract. On the one hand, they claimed

---

90 Anonymous, "Mémoire" (Nov. 1768), Arsenal, mss. Bastille, 12353.
91 R. Le Bon, "Observations sur les subsistances et les moyens d'y remédier à partir de 1770 jusqu'à 1789," AN, F^{10} 226.
92 Diderot to Sophie Volland, 15 Nov. 1768, in *Correspondance Diderot*, ed. by Roth, VIII, 222.

"great losses," which they blamed on Malisset as a consequence of the inopportune deals he "made us" engage in with "faithless correspondents," the bad quality of the merchandise which he procured, and other reverses attributable to his managerial shortcomings. On the other hand, in a much more convincing argument which incidentally flattered Malisset's stewardship, they ascribed their setbacks to the cruel circumstances of the time and to the onerous terms of the contract. At the time of the signing one could still purchase first quality wheat at 14 *livres* the *septier*. Three years later, as a result of an "almost universal dearth" and an "extraordinary" exportation which exhausted national stocks, the price had doubled. "Disconcerted," they nevertheless managed to discharge their obligations "exactly and even beyond." They marshalled 3 to 4,000 *septiers* more grain than required and, in addition to supplying the Halles and the zone markets with king's grain, provided large amounts of flour for the anxious consumers as well.

"But," the guarantors noted, "if they fulfilled this important goal, they did it at their own expense...." They had to replenish their stocks in the midst of the crisis at prices much higher than those at which they previously sold their grain. This "radically unwonted" clause which required them to replace grain at the current price and prohibited them, once the company was royalized, from continuing their own speculations, meant that they could not go on without "ruining themselves." The 2% commission on the sale of the king's grain and the annual subsidy of 24,000 *livres* did not remotely cover their expenses. And, given the policy of liberalization, they contended, it was very unlikely that the price of wheat will drop below the level permitting them to use the stocks for their own commercial purposes. In the present arrangement the "King alone" profited. He had reason to be pleased, for according to the guarantors this was the first time in the history of the king's grain that the administrators of the reserve provided precisely the amount of grain demanded and spared the treasury "immense" outlays.[93]

The guarantors wanted to annul the old contract without, however, losing the opportunity to "repair" their losses. Malisset, who was deeply in debt to them and to others for advances, agreed to step aside and transfer the Corbeil establishment, in return for proper

---

93 Leray de Chaumont and Perruchot to Trudaine de Montigny, 10 May, 17 Aug. 1768 and Trudaine to MM. les intéressés en 'la régie des grains, 24 Oct. 1768, AN, F[11] 1193.

indemnities, to a new company. For reasons that remain obscure, Leray and Perruchot joined forces, to the exclusion of Rousseau, and proposed a "new contract" in mid-August which they implored Trudaine *fils* to "put under the eyes of the Controller-General" as quickly as possible.

It was a provisioner's dream, containing virtually ironclad guarantees against losses, requiring little capital investment, and involving slight risk. The demands made by the new group vividly underline the enormous advantages accorded the government by the Malisset submission. The king would purchase the Corbeil establishment for 700,000 *livres* (not including boats, horses, carts, and sacks, which he would acquire separately) and place it at the disposition of the contractors; remit to them a fund of 40,000 *septiers* of wheat; pay them an annual indemnity of 40,000 *livres* (16,000 more than granted Malisset) and an additional 1,000 *livres* for every extra thousand *septiers* stored; indemnify them fully for losses suffered by riot, fire or other disaster; place a Swiss guard at the door underneath a sign reading "Royal Magazine and Manufactury of Grain and Flour"; and permit them to conduct business "in the name of His Majesty" and under the protection of commandants, intendants, and local magistrates. Unlike Malisset, the contractors would have "complete liberty" to engage in grain and flour trade, inside the kingdom and abroad, in all times regardless of prices "as they will see fit and without restriction of any sort." Upon notification the company would have a month's time to complete its stock. If they were found short they would simply pay a cash penalty equivalent to the current price of the amount of grain that was missing. The company would be prepared at all times to deliver up to 1,000 *septiers* of wheat or 500 sacks of flour (at 160 pounds of flour to the *septier*, or ten pounds less than Malisset had offered) for which they would receive a fee of 4 *livres* per sack of flour and 2 *sous* per *septier* of wheat. The contract would run for twelve years and could not be cancelled without proof of malversation or infidelity.

Aware of its liberalizing ambitions, Leray and Perruchot warned the government against succumbing to the lingering temptation to abandon the provisioning of Paris wholly to private commerce. Liberty has failed to create a corps of rich and well-connected *négociants* capable of nourishing Paris and maintaining stores. Abundance at the Halles, they argued, "can only be physically guaranteed by the vigilance of the government and by means of a bountiful magazine always ready to be opened for the needs of the public." Properly managed, they hastened to reassure the liberals of the ministry, such an operation would not undermine "the spirit and the liberty of the trade."[94]

The government flatly refused these propositions. The new contract excised everything which pleased the government in the old relationship, magnified all of its dubious characteristics, and imposed, in addition, a charter of privileges and prerequisites which would cost the government money, and deprive it of control. In principle, the ministry was more favorably disposed to an idea secretly submitted by the third guarantor, Rousseau, who had been squeezed out of the affair *along* with Malisset by his former partners. Rousseau understood Laverdy's sensitivity to the impact of the Malisset venture on public opinion and the shadow it cast over the liberalization policy. Without explaining how it would work or why it should be expected to prove any more successful than previous undertakings, he recommended a return to the *régie* whose chief merit would somehow be to protect the government against public suspicion.[95]

By early September Laverdy had decided upon a course of action. Until the end of the dearth he would continue to purchase king's grain through the agency of men such as Leray, but he would no longer support an institutionalized company or *régie*. Just at the moment that prices reached their zenith, the Controller-General felt the need for a new beginning. He wanted to clean his hands entirely of the Corbeil affair. Judging the installations there to be "of no utility whatsoever" to the government, he offered them to the General Hospital, which had planned for many years to build a storehouse and mills in the area.[96]

It was, however, too late for Laverdy to make a fresh start. A few weeks later the King dismissed him. Reviled by the people and several of the parlements, challenged by some of his own intendants, and too intimately identified with hard times, he was sacrificed to public opinion much in the same way that he repudiated Malisset. His successor, Maynon d'Invau, had an impressive liberal background; his appointment presaged no change in political orientation. On the contrary, the king detemined to breathe fresh vigor into the liberalization policy and to gird against the forthcoming onslaught of the Paris Parlement.

Maynon, according to the *économiste* Dupont, broke decisively with the king's grain tradition. This thesis served Dupont well, for

94 "Nouveau Traité," May 1768, *ibid.*
95 Rousseau to Trudaine de Montigny (?), 11 May 1768, *ibid.*
96 Laverdy to Duperron (?), 6 Sept. 1768, AN, F[11] 1194. Cf. M.B.D. ***** [probably Brillon Duperron], *Observations sur la mouture d'après l'hôpital général* (Paris, 1768), 2.

it enabled him to depict the abbé Terray as a dark reactionary who "reestablished" the royal grain operation when he replaced the right-thinking Maynon at the end of 1769. In fact, no such brusque rupture in governmental position occurred. Laverdy suppressed the company without ending the system. Maynon "resolved," as Baudeau prudently put it, to stop large-scale provisioning for the account of the king.[97] Given the pressing demands of the capital and the momentum of the grain operations already under way, however, he was unable to realize this aim.

One of his subsistence advisers was Daure, a man with considerable experience in grain affairs and strong convictions about government policy. Rudely treated by men he thought to be his friends, Daure wrote in bitter retrospect about his experience in the corridors of the ministry. Since he is the major source for information about official attitudes in 1768–69, his testimony must be treated with caution. Daure detested Malisset, characterizing him as a venal and "dangerous" schemer responsible for keeping prices high and fomenting popular discontent. Daure also distrusted Leray de Chaumont whom he suspected of desiring to control the grain trade of the entire kingdom. On the basis of extensive visits to the provisioning zones and sober reflection, Daure "believed very positively that if one had the strength and the courage to leave [*laisser faire*] the [grain] trade alone everything would return to a natural state which would content all reasonable persons, and that if on the contrary one wishes to provision Paris like a city in war, one must count on spending an immense sum of money and experience always the greatest anxieties and the greatest alarms." A survey of the harvest of 1769 convinced him that it was "the decisive moment to *trancher au vif*." "I will submit to be jailed for ten years in the Bastille," he averred, "if grain by its own mass does not diminish [in price] by the first of October." According to Daure, the Controller-General "definitely vowed to depend on commerce" and to maintain only a token reserve for dire emergencies.

Not surprisingly, there coursed victualer's blood in the veins of this passionately liberal functionary. Daure proposed to organize this emergency grain fund, which would be concealed behind a contract for the supply of bread to the French and Swiss guards.

---

97 Dupont to Prince Carl Ludwig, (n.d., ca. 1773), in *Correspondance Dupont*, ed. by Knies, II, 142; Baudeau, "Second mémoire à un Magistrat du Parlement de Paris ...," *Nouvelles éphémérides économiques* (1775), I, 42.

The government apparently accepted the conditions he posed for undertaking this mission: that the contract be absolutely secret, that he be considered a consultant rather than an entrepreneur in the style of Malisset, that Malisset be banned from any participation in grain affairs, and that he, Daure, suffer no competition in his service to the crown.[98]

Despite his good will, however, Maynon lacked the energy and the influence to keep his word. He had underestimated the complexity and difficulty of stopping the giant "machine" (Maynon's word) of royal provisioning. More of the king's grain remained in stock and more operations were underway than he had imagined and there were more vested interests to dislodge than he was able to count. Choiseul allegedly pressed the King to continue the provisioning operations. Leray supplied Paris and environs with at least 70,000 *septiers* in 1769. J.-B. Prémord, an *armateur-négociant* from Honfleur with a background similar to Leray's, imported large amounts of grain from Holland "for the account of the king." Some of Malisset's old correspondents continued to supply for the king's account and Malisset himself furnished the Halles and other markets with grain and flour in his own name. With some embarrassment and confusion the government continued to use Corbeil as an entrepôt, under the direction (in *régie* form) of Malisset's former subordinates.[99]

VI

Surrounded by a mass of hungry rivals who undercut his commercial dealings and destroyed his morale, Daure felt himself betrayed. At the end of the year his erstwhile protector left the Contrôle-Général. Maynon's successor, Terray, Daure noted scornfully, believes that "a king must hold the price of this good [grain] in his hand and charge himself with feeding his people." Terray, as we shall see, made extensive use of the king's grain in combatting scarcity and high prices throughout the kingdom. Under Terray, the ministry forced a revision of Daure's contract and refused to honor the promises which Maynon's government allegedly made. They never reconciled their

---

98 Daure, "Mémoire," (1771), AN, F¹¹ 264 and "Mémoire particulier" (ca. 1775), AN, K 908. Léon Cahen incorrectly attributed these essays to Doumerc and as a result made serious errors of comprehension and interpretation. "Le Prétendu pacte de famine," *Revue historique*, CLXXVI (Sept.-Oct. 1935), 173–214.

99 Daure's "Mémoire," AN, F¹¹ 264 and K 908; états et comptes, AN, F¹¹ 1193 and F¹¹ 1173; Archives Seine-Paris, D4B⁶–43–2391 and D5B⁶ 284 and 298.

differences and soon Daure stood accused, as Malisset had been, of misconduct and ineptitude. According to the three bakers who worked for him, Daure did not manage the flour and bread-making company with skill and economy. One of the bakers was completely ruined in the deal, another filed for business failure, and a third fled the capital. Daure blamed his troubles on the ministry and, once again like Malisset, quarreled with the government over the settlement of accounts until the Revolution. His campaign for rehabilitation was interrupted only by a short sojourn he made to America where he organized military provisioning, serving Rochambeau with the same zeal and versatility with which Leray de Chaumont served Franklin.[100]

Uncommonly resilient, Malisset did not disappear from the provisioning arena upon the abrogation of his contract and the liquidation of his company. Public provisioning in the Old Regime was a decentralized, fragmented, and competitive affair. Despite his repudiation by the Contrôle-Général, other officials on various levels of responsibility sought Malisset's services. The intendant of Paris, one of his original sponsors in the early sixties, contracted for his supplies as did the intendant of Auvergne. Malisset furnished grain and flour to "several small cities," to the Depot of the Poor in the Bourbonnais, and to other public assistance facilities called Depots of Mendicancy, and he continued his regular provision of bread for the Paris prisons. Nor did the ministry sever its ties with him completely, for it still needed his Corbeil apparatus and it asked him to collaborate with the new *régisseur* in the storage and conversion of grain to flour.[101]

In January of 1771, Malisset sent the Terray government a blueprint for another full-blown Paris grain fund of 40,000 *septiers* under his direction. He had learned his lessons well. To be sure, he called attention to his experience in the *métier*, to his extensive network of "the most solid

---

100 Daure, "Mémoire," AN, F^{11} 264 and AN, K 908; Daure to St.-Florentin (?), 20 June 1775, AN, O^1 361; Bourgade to Joly de Fleury, 14 March 1782 and Daure to Montaran, 25 May 1768, AN, F^{12} 1299^a. In 1775 Turgot ordered the grain treasury to pay Daure 50,000 *livres*. *Œuvres de Turgot*, ed. by Schelle, IV, 197. According to my calculations, this was approximately the sum which Daure claimed in the early seventies. Given his protracted quarrel with the government, it appears that either Daure never received this payment in full or that he revised his demands for reimbursement.

101 "Mémoire justificatif pour le Sr Malisset," AN, F^{11} 1173; AN, F^{11} 1193; Malisset to Bertier de Sauvigny, 27 May 1771 and Malisset to Rives (one of Bertier's agents), 21 June 1771, AN, 80 AP 19 (Bertier de Sauvigny family papers to which the descendents of the *grands commis* kindly granted me access). Malisset to Monthyon, 6, 9, 14, 18, 21 June 1770, C. 915, C. 917 and C. 918, A.D. P-de-D.

and intelligent" correspondents who know how to keep books, and to his willingness to forego all advances and to settle for a 2% commission on all operations without further compensation. But the leitmotif of the project, which seems so ironical in retrospect, was his emphatic assurance that he would perform the task "without producing any sensation." His normal commercial dealings on the Paris ports and Halles and in the countryside "will serve as a cover for buying without giving rise to any suspicion that his purchases might involve the King."[102] Malisset's pitch failed to arouse enthusiasm in the Terray ministry.

As "miller," "flour merchant," "*négociant*," and "grain merchant for the provisioning of Paris," he expanded his private operations which he always maintained were in the public interest. He invested in the construction of new mills, established business connections in the midi and the southwest, and found it relatively easy to borrow substantial sums of money despite his huge debts. He retained enough moral credit, too, to continue serving as a public commercial mediator in the Consular Courts as he had before his ordeal.[103] The one-time journeyman baker proudly and legitimately styled himself "bourgeois de Paris" when he penetrated the realm of high finance to enter into a partnership with the Swiss banker Ferdinand Grand, later one of the founders of the Caisse d'Escompte, for the importation of foreign grain. Grand, a creditor of Leray de Chaumont, functioned as chief banker for Benjamin Franklin and the American Congress in France.[104] With audacity, a sense of destiny, and visions of Samuel Bernard and the Pâris brothers dancing in his head, Malisset petitioned the king not long after his disgrace to reward him for his achievements with a pension and a promotion in rank:

> The Sieur Malisset asks that for proof of satisfaction with the services that he rendered to His Majesty, & for recompense of his works which were useful to the public and to the hospitals, the King please accord him the cordon of Saint Michel, or letters of Nobility; having need of some mark of distinction to triumph over the Jealousy which has persecuted him in all times and to live with some felicity in the estate to which he shall retire.[105]

---

102 "Mémoire," 26 Jan. 1771, AN, F¹¹ 1194.
103 Archives Seine-Paris, D4B⁶–36–1958, D4B⁶–42–2307, D2B⁶ 1104 (16 Dec. 1771), D2B⁶ 1107 (2 March 1772), D5B⁶ 2532, D4B⁶–64–4161; Malisset to Sartine, 21 Feb. 1771, AN, F¹¹ 1193; 7 July 1767, Archives Seine-Paris, D6B⁶ article 5 and 23 July 1773, Archives Seine-Paris, D6B⁶ article 6.
104 Minutier Central, XIII, 391 (11 May 1776); Lüthy, *Banque*, II, 451–54, 613.
105 Petition, 9 April 1771, AN, F¹¹ 294–295.

Throughout this third phase of his career, Malisset remained a highly controversial figure. Daure charged that the post-company Malisset was just like the old one, buying and selling to prolong rather than combat the dearth. In September 1770 Hardy recorded that Malisset was hoarding oats, depleting the ports, and causing the price to double. He clashed with the grain measurers over fees which they claimed were due.[106] Doumerc, Leray's former aide, who directed Terray's provisioning operations, accused Malisset of stealing the king's flour in the magazine they shared at Corbeil. Malisset indignantly rebuffed Doumerc's "atrocious" imputations. Precisely to avert any confusion, he had installed steel bars and separators to seal windows and to close off communicating doors between the rooms containing royal flour and those harboring his own goods. In a lengthy, semi-autobiographical memoir, Malisset presented himself as a man of unwavering virtue and suggested that Doumerc and his clerk Dure invented these absurd "calumnies" to mask their own "malversations." Dure, he said, lost his last job on suspicion of speculation and spent much of his time in "Dissipation." As for Doumerc, although there were many instances of his misconduct that could be cited, Malisset refused to stoop to the name-calling level of his adversary, adding that "he will not mention the observations that he could make on the habits of this Director [one of Doumerc's titles was "Director of grain coming from abroad"] with a woman of ill-repute."[107] In 1770 Malisset's charges had no credibility. But the situation was different several years later when it became Doumerc's turn to fall into disgrace, allegedly for misappropriating government funds and conducting official business in a dishonest fashion.

In 1772 another ugly affair arose concerning the quality of Malisset's merchandise.[108] He had sold a Lyon client 600 sacks of reputedly "first quality, fresh and well-made" flour through an intermediary who had no experience in the trade. When the client withheld payment of more than half the sale price, Malisset sued him before the Juges-Consuls. The Lyonnais angrily complained that the conditions of the contract had not been fulfilled since the flour contained "everything most defective in quality as well as in bad taste, to the

---

106 Daure, "Mémoire," (1771), AN, F[11] 264; 15 Sept. 1770, *Hardy's Journal*, BN, mss. fr. 6680; AN, F[11] 264; 7 March 1770, AN, H * 1873, fol. 497.

107 "Mémoire justificatif pour le Sr Malisset," AN, F[11] 1173. A Malisset appeared as creditor in the statement of business failure which Dure filed in 1772. Archives Seine-Paris, D4B[6]–50–3037.

108 28 April 1773, Archives Seine-Paris, D6B[6] carton 7.

point that after having delivered it to different bakers ... they made of it such a bad bread ... that he was obliged to take it back." The referee, a Paris *négociant*, assigned by the court to try to settle the case amicably, esteemed that the flour in question, made from "very bad" Picardy wheat harvested in rainy conditions, "could not be compared with that of the third quality." He found Malisset guilty of "abusing the confidence" of the buying agent and reproached him for failing to present the issue honestly. Malisset's deal with the banker Grand also ended in controversy—the parties could agree neither on the interest each had in the enterprise nor on the amount which the sales produced—but they were able to reach an out-of-court convention by which Malisset promised to pay his associate 15,000 *livres*.[109]

The most significant and protracted dispute involving Malisset concerned the settlement of accounts of the contract with the Laverdy government. While Leray remained aloof, Malisset and the other two guarantors were angered by the ministry's refusal to grant them any consideration at the time of cancellation. Although their claims that they were "ruined" by the enterprise were grossly puffed, there can be no question that they lost considerable sums of money in 1767–68. On several occasions the three demanded reimbursement for money they advanced after the company had become royalized, and for indemnities to compensate them for the remaining nine years of the contract, despite the fact that they had all concurred in soliciting cancellation. Perruchot even dared to withhold sums deriving from the sale of the king's grain, which he was supposed to remit immediately to Mirlavaud. Trudaine sternly rebuked him, telling him that it "is against all rules for you to keep the funds of the King in your hands to fulfill your pretensions" and flatly asserting that "the King owes you nothing."[110]

In fact, after a critical inspection of the accounts the following year, Albert, the intendant trained by Trudaine to take over the grain department, concluded that Malisset and the guarantors owed the government over 300,000 *livres*. His report was a *visa*, or a *chambre de justice* in miniature. He clearly began with the conviction that the government had been cheated and he expressed contempt for Malisset's claims and explanations at every juncture. The examination was mercilessly exacting and sometimes quite strained, covering hundreds of items ranging from the purchase of grain to the repair of damaged sacks. Albert

---

109 Minutier Central, XIII, 391, 11 May 1776.
110 Mémoire, March, 1791, AN, F[11] 1193; Malisset, Rousseau and Perruchot to Trudaine de Montigny, 19 Jan. 1769 and Trudaine to Perruchot, Nov. 1768, *ibid.*

contended that the company did not replenish the stock of 40,000 *sep-tiers* in the time specified by the contract and that Malisset "fraudulently" supplied replacement grain of light weight and "bad quality" even though the government's grain expert Duperron suggested that given the harvest conditions the grain "could have been of an inferior quality without any fraud on his part." Albert accused Malisset of systematically falsifying the weight of grain and flour sold, of rendering much less flour per *septier* than promised, of inflating the amount lost due to natural waste (again, despite the opinion of Duperron), of passing on to the king expenses for which the company alone was responsible, and of exaggerating costs legitimately attributable to the king. The intendant categorically denied all the company's requests for compensation for unanticipated expenses or unusual circumstances and refused its claim for a 2% commission on the replacement grains purchased by Leray under the name of Trezel.

Malisset, Perruchot, and Rousseau rightly protested that Albert's accounting was excessively severe. His rectifications were often arbitrary and abstract and on the whole his stance was no less one-sided and self-protective than that of the company. The dispute dragged on for years, during which time the government does not seem to have pressed its case vigorously. In the 1780's Montaran, the new chief of the grain department, reviewed the contest step by step. Although he reduced the government claim substantially, he generally found in favor of Albert. The heirs of Perruchot and Rousseau, on whose estates the government had placed liens, proposed a *quid pro quo* for the termination of the affair. If the government abandoned its quest for restitution, the company would renounce its demands for indemnities. Despite the intercession of Sartine and other men of influence in favor of Malisset and the guarantors, Calonne refused to drop the case and appointed another in a series of extraordinary commissions of the royal council to study the affair. This panel also examined the accounts of Leray de Chaumont and "other commissioners charged with the provisioning of grain for the account of His Majesty." As late as 1791 the case remained unresolved and litigation for recovery may very well have resumed after the Revolution.[111]

Corbeil, Malisset's only durable monument, passed into royal hands, after considerable bickering, in early 1772. Plunged into debt and deprived of the contract at the end of 1768, Malisset had agreed

---

111 AN, F^{11} 1193; AN, F^{11} 1173; AN, V^7 273.

to offer the establishment to the General Hospital. He estimated its worth to be 850,000 *livres*, including a quarter of a million each for the central warehouse and the six mill-installations and 200,000 "for the water" which drives the machinery. He fixed its potential annual income at 48,422 *livres*, encompassing revenue from grain storage, milling, and the rental of houses, boats, and a small vineyard. He was willing to let the Hospital acquire the establishment for a mere 500,000 *livres*, 200,000 in cash (which would cover a large portion of his debts), and 300,000 in "exchanges" for houses in Paris and/or farms in the countryside (which would mark the beginning of a new patrimony). Among the special "advantages" in the bargain, aside from the superb location, capacious quarters and modern machinery, Malisset offered to cede his network of correspondents much as a baker sold his "clients" [*pratiques*] and to refrain from competing against the Hospital for grain purchases in those areas.

The Hospital deal fell through, apparently because the government decided that it still needed Corbeil. By an *arrêt du conseil* of January 1769, the ministry offered to lease the Corbeil mills from Malisset for 12,000 *livres* a year and grant him a ten year loan of 260,000 *livres* to be paid directly to his creditors. Malisset accepted the terms but, for reasons that are obscure, the government fulfilled only a part of its obligations. It paid no rent to Malisset and advanced only 115,000 *livres* of the loan (the bulk of which Leray received), which it tried to recover from Malisset in 1791. In February 1771, Malisset offered to sell the entire Corbeil establishment to the King for 590,000 *livres* plus a pension for himself and a "part" in some royal operation to indemnify a Sieur Demontvallier who had purchased a quarter interest in Malisset's business. In April he reduced the price to 500,000 *livres*. The government approved this arrangement and became proprietor of the establishment.[112]

First under Doumerc and then, in the late seventies and eighties, under the Leleu brothers, Corbeil remained a major entrepôt and the sole reserve for the capital. At the end of 1790, a committee appointed

---

112 Evaluation (Aug. 1768), état (20 April 1769), mémoires (July 1769), *arrêt du Conseil* (Jan. 1769), and Malisset to CG, 20 Feb. 1771, AN, F[11] 1193–1194; "Offre du Sr Malisset," 9 April 1771 and "Mémoire sur l'établissement de Corbeil" (1790), AN, F[11] 294–295. Like many innovative undertakings in the Old Regime, the ultra-modern Corbeil milling establishment was still burdened with the weight of the past. As soon as the sale of Corbeil to the government became official, the Order of Malta rushed to levy its sacrosanct claim to *lods et ventes*. Boscheron to St.-Prest, 6 Mar. 1772, AN, F[11] 1193.

by the Paris municipality urged the city to acquire the Corbeil installation. The provisioning of such a great city must not be "delivered to chance," they warned; "an almost physical certitude is necessary" and Corbeil could help provide this security. The matter was urgent, for a number of "companies of speculators" coveted the establishment for their own purposes. The committee assessed the value at 162,450 *livres*, substantially lower than the most niggardly estimates made twenty years earlier. Through various arrangements, Corbeil remained under government control. Well into the nineteenth century, it continued to serve Paris as a reserve center and a laboratory for testing the merits of different types of grain and flour.[113]

With the transfer of Corbeil, Malisset finally terminated his active role as an "intéressé dans les affaires du Roy," an intentionally vague and portentous title which covered a vast range of activities in the borderland between the public and private sectors of the Old Regime. Malisset emerged from his experience in provisioning with enough funds or enough credit to become a gentleman-farmer: he purchased four *domaines* and operated the duché de Châtillon-sur-Loing, leased from the duc de Luxembourg. But he did not find serenity in retirement. To build this new empire, he had to borrow heavily; in addition, while he insisted with a certain haughtiness that he "no longer engaged in trade of any kind," he still owed money to some of his former business relations. Unable to pay his creditors and either unable or unwilling to liquidate his properties, in March 1781 he filed for failure with the Consular Court. His debts amounted to over 71,000 *livres*; the banker Grand spearheaded the organization of creditors which pressed for recovery. He had substantial assets, including 98,000 *livres* in domain land, a 24,000 *livres* house in Paris, and over 16,000 *livres* in rentes. Nevertheless, he was judged insolvent. According to a government report, he suffered from madness in his declining years.[114]

VII

His was not the most famous case of purported insanity linked to the history of the king's grain in the late sixties. Leprévost de Beaumont,

---

113 AN, F¹²* 1, fols. 11, 32, 161–62, 203, 338; Mémoire, 22 Feb. 1791, AN, F¹¹ 294–295; Nov. 1790 and May 1791, AAP, #105, liasse 10; AN, F¹¹ 1359.

114 Archives Seine-Paris; D4B⁶–80–5338; "Subsistance, 1765–68" (Feb. 1788), AN, F¹¹ 1173; decision of M. Delessart, 8 April 1791, published by Bord, *Histoire du blé*, 228.

who denounced the "pact of famine" in 1768, was described by Sartine as a "dangerous maniac," treated during 21 years of captivity in the Bastille, Vincennes, Bicêtre, and Charenton as a demented subversive, and characterized by modern historians as either a pathetic or a rascally madman.

In a mawkish novel written in the first half of the nineteenth century by Elie Berthet, whose chief fault was his prolificacy, Malisset and Leprévost crossed paths.[115] The "hero of this story," Leprévost, was an intensely earnest and compassionate young man "of noble visage, smooth, full of character and expression," dressed in the simple black of a layman attached to the ecclesiastical bureaucracy. The villain, "so bloated with fat and importance, was named Pierre Malisset: he was a former baker, who, after having become bankrupt, had acquired a fatal celebrity in the grain markets, where he purchased immense quantities of grain for the king's account." This "big financier" had a "proud and disdainful air" with "one of those fresh, round, flowered faces made to reflect a wholly material beatitude." Richly garbed, he wore an elegant wig and diamonds sparkled on his fingers. He lived in a sumptuous house filled with masterpieces of woodwork and sculpture and attended by an army of servants. There he often received his fellow-financiers, to whom he once proposed the toast: "to the health of the people of Paris, this good people whom we nourish so badly and who nourish us so well." This wretched people, suffering the "horrors of dearth," suspected that Malisset's operations, made under the name of the king's grain, were really part of "a vast system of hoarding" authorized by a "secret deal" between the financiers on the one side and the ministers and the court on the other.

To learn more of the plot, the philantropic Leprévost tried to infiltrate the Malisset organization. "He wants to rip the mask from the grain hoarders," sobbed his wife Angèle, who begged her husband to abandon the dangerous plan, "denounce the famine pact in Parlement, and present to the judges documented proof of an execrable convention." "That is to say," commented his aged father, "to attack the government of the king head-on: and, if he does not succeed, or even if he succeeds, to fall into the cells of the Bastille, which will enclose him like a tomb." Leprévost passionately rebuffed these objections: "My father, there is something still more powerful than the voice of the family, it is

---

115 Elie Berthet, *Le Pacte de famine* (Paris, 1857). Cf. Berthet's play, written in collaboration with
      P. Foucher, *Le Pacte de famine* (Paris, 1857).

the voice of a people which is suffering and hungry, this voice calls me, I must obey it."

The denouement was cruel and predictable. One of Sartine's spies exposed Leprévost; the police, accompanied by Malisset, whose face radiated an "infernal joy," arrested him and tossed him in jail where he languished until the 14th of July 1789 when the good people of Paris, led by Leprévost's own son, liberated him.[116] He survived his release only a week but he passed away in peace with the knowledge that a new day had come:

Adieu, my friends; I am able to die. The people will have bread.

Berthet's treacly fiction embodies what historians have come to call the legend of the famine pact. The legend itself is a curious historical reality which survived in scholarly and imaginative literature until the end of the nineteenth century and still occasionally surfaces today.[117] Leprévost invented the highly charged phrase and elaborated the legend, which the revolutionaries of '89 consecrated in the form that we know it. Son of a procurator of the bailliage of Beaumont, he was secretary to the abbé de Broglie, general agent of the clergy of France.[118] Sustained by a modest salary and bits and pieces of land and *rentes*, his expenses appear to have exceeded his income. In July 1768 he fortuitously came across a file of papers concerning the Malisset company and its relations with the government. Convinced that he had found the trace of "an infernal pact of a monstrous league" whose goal it was "to establish famine methodically" in order to reap enormous profits, he felt that it was his obligation to denounce the plot and to force a purge of the malefactors from the seats of power. The police arrested Leprévost in November 1768 at approximately the same moment that bread prices reached their crisis apex

---

116 The real Leprévost in fact was freed more appropriately on the 5th of October, the day the crowd marched to Versailles to retrieve the Baker-King. Leprévost, *Dénonciation, pétition et rogation* (Paris, 1791), 7.

117 See, for example, P. S. Laurentie, *Histoire de France* (Paris, 1845), VIII, 266; G. de Molinari, article "Céréales," in Coquelin and Guillaumin, eds., *Dictionnaire de l'économie politique* (Paris, 1873), I, 305; Cochut, "Le Pain à Paris," *Revue des deux mondes*, LXVI (Aug.-Sept. 1863), 986–89; Mauguin, *Etudes historiques sur l'administration de l'agriculture*, I, 326–330, 340–41; Maxime du Camp, *Paris*, II, 29, 32; Colfavru, "Question des subsistances," *La Révolution française*, V (July-Dec. 1883), 507–508; F. Rocquain, "Le Parti des philosophes," *Séances et Travaux de l'Académie des Sciences Morales et Politiques*, XIV (1880), 102–46; Eugène Bonnemère, *Histoire des paysans* (Paris, 1846), II, 160–61; and most recently Gérard Walter, *Histoire des paysans de France* (Paris, 1963), 308.

118 Arsenal, mss. Bastille 12353. Cf. Jobez who claimed that Leprévost was a relative of the former Lieutenant General of Police of Paris Hérault. *Louis XV*, VI, 401–403.

and that the Paris Parlement subpoenaed Malisset. The interception of a packet of documents and charges, addressed by Leprévost to the Rouen Parlement, led to his apprehension.[119] Sartine at first seems to have treated him sympathetically, to have tried to win his confidence, and perhaps disabuse him of his illusions by explaining in detail the nature of the king's grain system. Not even the prospect of freedom could induce Leprévost to repudiate his charges. "How could one act against one's conscience," he asked, "when it is a question of the fatherland, of the cause of the people, and of that of our monarch?" Morally bound to the heroic course, he later justified his persistence on legal grounds as well, citing an obscure law of 1477 that required citizens to expose plots against the government.[120]

According to Leprévost, the "blackguard" Laverdy was the engineer of the conspiracy on the government's side, assisted by the intendants of finance, tyrannical Sartine ("the most refined knave of his time"), a large contingent from the Paris Parlement, and a host of "pirates," "vultures," "privileged vampires," "millionaires," and "monopolists." Using liberalization as a device to suppress controls without arousing suspicion and the permission to export as a pretext to secrete vast quantities of grain abroad, the conspirators stripped the kingdom bare of subsistence, beginning first around Paris and gradually spreading their net across the rest of the nation. The proof of the crimes was to be found in the correspondence between officials and financiers and in the contracts they signed. There were other "strong indications" of the cabal plain for everyone to read in the unnatural course of events: "the general outcry, the scarcity of goods in the markets, the precipitate removals and concealments, the nocturnal transports by land and sea, the continual *cherté* even in a time *of Abundance*, the sharp lowering and raising of the price against the usual order," in a word the same set of factors which aroused suspicion among local officials and provoked

---

119 It is an interesting reflection on Leprévost's perception of the political divisions at the summit of power to note that he also sent, or intended to send, a denunciation of the famine pact to the Prince de Conti.

120 Arsenal, mss. Bastille 12353; Leprévost, *Le Prisonnier d'état*, 22–23, 52, 86; Leprévost, *Dénonciation d'un pacte de famine générale au roi Louis XV* (Paris, n.d.), 35. Preferring duty to liberty, Leprévost claimed he also lost the love of his life, "a very beautiful, rich girl" whom "he was about to marry." Leprévost, *Dénonciation et pétition aux représentants de l'Assemblée de la seconde Législature* (Paris, 1791), 4. For the official view of Leprévost as a "dangerous" and "totally deranged" man, see Sartine to Jumillac, 17 Nov. 1768 and Florentin to Rougemont, 1 Sept. 1770, F. and L. Ravaisson-Mollien, eds., *Archives de la Bastille*, XIX, 410, 411.

consumer riots. Nor was the Laverdien pact the first of its kind. Leprévost traced the conspiracy back at least as far as Orry. From prison he averred that it was continued by Laverdy's successors.

Leprévost vacillated in his attitude toward the king. Sometimes he depicted the king as an innocent victim of "lèse-majesté and lèse-humanité": "they took special care to hide from the King Louis XV the exercise of the monopoly of grain and all the magazines during his whole reign so that he neither knew nor suspected anything even in the time of the most rigorous *chertés* in the years 1752, 1767 and 1768 though everything was done in his name and at the expense of his finances." But at other times he suggested, like the Rouen Parlement, that the operation was too vast and important for the king to remain unaware and uninvolved and he referred bitterly to "our monarch, merchant of grain." He took refuge, too, like others who had suspected royal complicity in grain speculations in the course of the century but could not bring themselves to believe that the aim was personal aggrandizement, in a middle position which made the king a party to a sort of physiocratic-fiscal plot through which his associates concealed from him their true motives:

> The King knows of the Contract. He has been made to believe that it was the only means to bring back into France all the money which has left his Kingdom, to give back to the *laboureurs* the capacity to extend the cultivation of their lands with their personal fortunes, to force up the price of land in favor of the proprietors, and to succeed in amortizing the debts of the State little by little since no other financial operation revealed the possibility of doing it.[121]

During his long incarceration Leprévost remained defiant. He complained bitterly of the cruel treatment accorded him (1,631 days in solitary and a diet composed of "the bread of suffering and the water of anguish"), yet he rejected numerous offers of accommodation on the grounds that they compromised his integrity.[122] He continued to fashion denunciations, which he cast to the wind over the prison walls in the hope that they would reach and arouse men of good will. He shared his discoveries with fellow prisoners, including

---

121 *Ibid*. Cf. Leprévost, *Dénonciation d'un pacte de famine générale*, 17, 24, 40 and Regnaud, "Histoire des événements arrivés en France ...," BN, mss. fr. 13733, fols. 26–27.

122 See, for example, Leprévost to Lenoir (?), 23 May 1778, Archives Seine-Paris, 4AZ 68, a frenzied but moving cry for justice and liberty. For Leprévost's perception of the treatment he received in the various prisons he inhabited, see A. Arnould, *et al.*, *Histoire de la Bastille* (Paris, 1844), VI, 85–106 and Alboize du Pujol and Auguste Macquet, *Le Donjon de Vincennes* (Paris, 1844), II, 135–56.

one de Sades, until he was placed in solitary confinement. He wrote incessantly and, although most of the essays are quite coherent, they show signs of the strain of isolation and of a febrile and agitated imagination. The rhythm and tone of his rhetoric sometimes became frenzied, he drew increasingly upon apocalyptic religious imagery, and he indulged in escapist fantasies and role-playing. Released in 1789, Leprévost became something of a celebrity, living proof of the perfidy and inhumanity of the Old Regime. His revelations seemed particularly relevant at a time when the people once again lacked bread, and when the intendant of Paris, Bertier de Sauvigny (once a patron of Malisset!) and his father-in-law Foulon were massacred by vengeful mobs who accused them of conspiring to starve the people.[123] No one was surprised to learn in 1789 that the counterrevolutionary conspiracy to starve the nation had deep roots in the prerevolutionary past. Manuel hailed his patriotism in the *Police Unmasked* and the *Moniteur*, and the *Révolutions de Paris* told his story in stilted detail.[124]

On the whole, Leprévost remained faithful to his original scenario, making certain adjustments to accommodate the revolutionary vocabulary (he now called the pact crime "nationicide"), extending the scope of the plot a bit to encompass all the parlements except Rouen and Grenoble and some members of the upper clergy whom he had served in the old days, and abandoning any serious effort to salvage the honor of the king. It is difficult to imagine what an extraordinary experience it must have been for him to witness his own resurrection, vindication, and apotheosis in terms which he had obscurely foreseen in his prison lucubrations.[125] Understandably, prison had nurtured an appetite for vengeance. He testified at the trial that sent Laverdy to the guillotine and he pursued in the courts several of the ministers and officials responsible for his oppression.[126] He became a nuisance as well as a fury, harassing the assembly with requests for indemnities

---

123 In his "revolutionary" writing, Leprévost explicitly connected, in linear fashion, the "pact" of Bertier, Foulon and their associates with the earlier conspiracies of Laverdy, Sartine, etc. *Le Prisonnier d'état*, iii.

124 Manuel, *Police dévoilée*, I 370–71, 375–80; *Révolutions de Paris*, successive numbers beginning with #31 (6–13 Feb. 1790) and concluding with #52 (3–10 July 1790). Cf. Buchez and Roux, *Histoire de l'Assemblée Constituante*, II, 74, 76–78.

125 Leprévost himself reminded his readers that they were "in front of a ghost [returned] from another world...." *Dénonciation et pétition*, 1.

126 On his obsessive demand for vengeance, especially against Laverdy, see *Le Prisonnier d'état*, passim, and *Dénonciation, pétition et rogation*, 8 and *Dénonciation et pétition*, 7.

and recognition, consolation more substantial than the knowledge that the people will at last have bread.

The terrible famine conspiracy, in the extravagant, all-embracing form in which Leprévost presented it, may have been the creation of a spirit touched with madness. But it is well to remember that unless such folly was an epidemic disease, it required no madness to imagine, in less exalted cast, a plot of officials and entrepreneurs contrived to profit from public misery. Viewed in retrospect, the vision is almost trite. What is striking about its reemergence in the sixties is not so much Leprévost's muckraking—which, after all, had no influence until the Revolution when it had to compete for attention with a host of other plots hatched on the left and on the right—but the fact that it was so widely ventilated on so many levels and that in most cases it specifically connected the conspiracy with the broad policy of reform undertaken by the government of Louis XV.

France bristled with talk of speculative conspiracies in the late sixties, as it had in 1725 and 1740. But in the late sixties the talk did not focus on an allegedly depraved minister like the duc de Bourbon, on an ambitious royal mistress like Madame de Prie (although Pompadour did not suffer for lack of abuse), on corrupt hangers-on like Orry's brother, on preeminent court bankers like Bernard and the Pâris brothers, on a grand commercial monopoly like the Company of the Indies, or upon a particularly rapacious Controller-General like the abbé Terray (at least not till later). Although there are many important similarities in the plot conceptions of the sixties and those of earlier periods, the indictment of the sixties fixed not so much upon individuals as upon institutions and policies. The "mark of authority," as the Rouen Parlement said, was everywhere apparent. Even if the government did not itself direct every maneuver, it tolerated, or rather forced local authorities to tolerate, maneuvers which in the past had been strictly forbidden. Leprévost himself had copies of letters from local police complaining against removals of grain made in the name of the king and reports of Sartine's own agents calling attention to suspected maneuvers.[127] The accusations current in the sixties suggested the idea that the government prepared the conditions which made a crisis likely and for reasons of its own—fiscal, venal, economic—made every effort to turn the crisis to advantage.

---

127 Arsenal, mss. Bastille 12353.

These charges, of course, are no less fabulous than the earlier ones. It is worth asking, however, whether they do not betray a significantly different political perspective. To be sure, it would be unwise to strain the point. Not enough is known about the "pact-type" mentality to warrant hasty inferences. But if one contends that it was a sort of recurring *Weltanschauung* characteristic of stressful episodes of scarcity and *cherté*, one is presuming not only a certain collective psychology (or collective psychopathology) but also a number of conscious or semiconscious political choices. For one must explain why the mentality took the peculiar shape that it did. While events and memories may condition people to think about their situation in conspiratorial terms, they must still decide, from a relatively wide range of options, who or what to hold responsible. Traditionally, the king and the people had a special, symbiotic relationship. The father of the people expected his subjects to obey. The people expected the monarch to look out for their welfare. When a dearth came, the people sometimes blamed the king. But there is a considerable difference between reproaching a ruler for his lack of foresight and accusing him of brazenly disregarding and exploiting public misery. Some sort of political consciousness bridges the distance between these two postures.

Activated by the crisis, this political consciousness is the cumulative product of the everyday experiences and perceptions of individuals. The Great Fear of 1789 grew out of a plot mentality triggered by a complex of well-known causes. To explain why it resulted in the burning of some châteaux and not of others, one must consider political variables. I have suggested that the "pact mentality" acquired its special stamp in the sixties as the result of a widely shared political sentiment. A segment of the population, persuaded that there was a causal relationship—a deliberately-engineered connection—between the policy of liberalization and the grain crisis, lost confidence in the government. So profound was their disenchantment that they were prepared to believe that the government and perhaps the king as well, had turned against the nation. Nor was this the only element which could have contributed to political alienation. There were other factors that had nothing to do with the dearth or plot mentality which informed political consciousness. Leprévost's conceptualization of the famine pact, for example, clearly fits into a larger view of the politics of the Old Regime.

Like the marquis d'Argenson, whose idiosyncratic political ideas predisposed him to expect to find evidence of government malfeasance in the dearths of the forties and fifties, Leprévost came to the famine pact with serious reservations about the way in which the government of Louis XV managed the affairs of state and society.[128] Morally and materially, he argued, France was in a state of ruin. Everywhere there were signs that the people no longer believed in the government. The people have been infinitely patient, but the day of reckoning, Leprévost warned, was not far off:

> For some time the evils have been increasing, the complaints have been registered again and again, confidence has been evaporating, desolation has been growing, murmurs follow, succeeded by discouragement, the people become indignant, and the keen and constant love which they have always had for Your Majesty is ready today to pass to hatred; there remains only to dread the Universal Rising of the Kingdom in the train of the local revolts which have already erupted.

The government has only itself to blame, Leprévost contended. Structurally, it was corrupt and defective and its policies perpetuated old abuses and created new problems. The people felt betrayed because the government repeatedly broke its "most sacred engagements."

Fiscality furnished the most egregious example. The government admitted that taxes were oppressively heavy but, despite its solemn promises, the double *vingtième* and the supplementary "sols pour livre" were not abolished and the *taille* was increased. Fraud, theft, and tyranny were rampant in the fiscal system and they spread from there to other domains. Leprévost hated the "maltôtiers" in finance, in the farms, and in other semi-official enterprises who "purchased the right to plunder." He shared the desire of certain reformers and officials to see the General Farms converted into *régies* and the *receveurs* prohibited from using "the people's money" for private purposes. It was no accident that to describe the mechanism of the famine pact he used the vocabulary of fiscality: farms, leases, *croupiers*.

Like the parlements, Leprévost accused the government of promoting or failing to correct "alterations of the fundamental constitutions of the kingdom." He viewed the parlements as "permanent councils" which the king must depend upon and trust. But he did not hesitate to denounce the "odious and shameful venality of offices" and the failure of the courts to provide free and easily accessible justice to everyone. Like Necker, Leprévost viewed "general administration" as a "true science"—an "encyclopedia," he said, in a revealing metaphor—which must be carefully studied. The king, however, treated it casually, like a royal domain, or frivolously, like a game. Without careful consideration,

---

128 For d'Argenson's "pact" charges, see his *Mémoires*, ed. by Rathery, 5, 8 Nov. 1740, III, 213, 219, 223.
    The analysis of Leprévost below is based upon letters, essays, outlines and mss. fragments in Arsenal, mss. Bastille 12353.

he appointed ministers who were not qualified. As a consequence, there were "frequent revolutions" in the government, "instability in its principles," and confusion and consternation on the part of the citizenry, which did not know what to expect.

In this age of vulgar materialism, where "everything is reduced to finance," where luxury and misery coexisted in scandalous counterpoint, not even the church escaped unscathed. Leprévost, who had a professional knowledge of ecclesiastical affairs, criticized the pomp and prodigality of the upper clergy, the general avarice of clerics at all levels, and such abuses as the plurality of benefices, nonresidence of prelates, and inequalities of ecclesiastical jurisdictions. Although he had little to say about the second estate, he did censure nobles for clinging to privileges and dues which retarded the development of commerce, agriculture, and industry.

The fruit of mismanagement and corruption was universal decay and suffering. The cities teemed with beggars, the countryside was "almost deserted," commerce was rife with bankruptcies, old industry languished, and new manufactures were stillborn. Dishonor abroad matched disorder at home. Humiliating defeat in war cost the kingdom its colonies and its "glory." "Never," insisted Leprévost, "yes, never, was misery in France more crushing and more general than during the peace [that followed] and after successive and abundant harvests." The artificial dearth caused by excessive exportation and "the criminal monopoly" produced a general economic crisis, according to Leprévost's analysis, which was not at all far-fetched. The prices of other necessities and of rents and land followed the soaring course of the price of grain while wages lagged far behind. The ranks of the jobless swelled as employers cut back their operations. "Twenty successive years of foreign warfare," he contended, "make less ravage in the kingdom than bread *cherté* during two years."

On the issue of the grain trade, Leprévost did not take a narrowly traditionalist stance. There was a tension in his mind between an ardently physiocratic inclination to liberate commerce from all servitudes and a Delamarist fear that the consumer would suffer unbearably under such a system.[129] He favored an unlimited internal liberty for the grain trade except in times of shortage, but demanded that exportation, which served only to enrich millionaires, be closely controlled.

---

129 See his sympathic remarks about the physiocrats in *Dénonciation d'un pacte de famine générale*, 27.

There is nothing arresting or original in Leprévost's indictment of the Old Regime. He was one of the growing circle of men of disparate backgrounds and interests who wanted to change things. He read the philosophes, he was interested in the Jansenist attack on the church, he knew all the economists from Melon through Mirabeau, and he drew heavily on the spirit and substance of the parlementary opposition to the crown and the government. He saw himself as a philosophe, not the sort given to poetry and abstractions but to practical, urgent matters of state. The police chief Lenoir, his arch-enemy ("the black ogre"), called him "a dangerous writer seeking to arouse [men's] minds through seditious works … an *homme à projets*…."[130] While in prison, Leprévost claimed to have written a twenty volume manuscript called "L'Art de régner," of which only a bare outline survives today.[131] He believed that he had synthesized the "scientific" principles upon which good government should be based. As time passed, he learned with satisfaction of changes taking place in the administration, changes very similar to those which he himself recommended in his writings. He characterized the sweeping reforms of the financial system and the army in the seventies and eighties as "coups d'état" for which, in some sense, he believed he deserved credit. In the year VIII, when he was 75 years old, "seeing the fatherland in the most imminent danger," he published a long critique of the legislative and constitutional record of the Revolution from its inception. He proposed "forty fundamental columns" on which a nation could be solidly built, of which financial order was the most important. Despairing of a solution on the part of the inept Directory, he was prepared to place his confidence, at least provisionally, in a "hero" on horseback.[132]

While there is still a great leap between Leprévost's vigorous criticism of the government and his manic formulation of the famine pact, his overall posture suggests that the denunciation of the plot was not merely a wild-eyed aberration, but a manifestation, albeit grotesquely distorted, of a political attitude. He convinced himself that a government as corrupt and as indifferent to the public good as the one he described was capable of the most diabolical actions. Political alienation is a powerful prism. Present-day Americans who

---

130 Lenoir papers, Bibliothèque Municipale d'Orléans, mss. 1422.

131 He claimed that the manuscript was confiscated by the police when he was transferred from Vincennes to Charenton in 1784. *Le Prisonnier d'état*, 123–24. During the Revolution he referred to himself as the author of "L'art de régner," as if it were, along with the *Spirit of the Laws*, a standard text of political science. *Ibid.*, 102.

132 Leprévost, *Aspect de la France* (Paris, year VIII).

have heard men of goodwill impute the Kennedy assassination to a conspiracy of highly-placed government or military officials and a handful of rightist millionaires know what it can do. For that matter, future Americans, looking back to the Watergate Administration, may well perceive the Russian-American wheat deal of 1972–73 as a sophisticated version of a *pacte de famine*.

VIII

The pact phenomenon placed the liberals in an embarrassing and delicate position. Had it occurred at a different time, before the government instituted the grain reforms, the liberals could have profited from the impact on public opinion, for it underscored one of the lessons that they never tired of preaching: that the government had no business interfering in subsistence matters at any time. But in the sixties the liberals were the servants, not the adversaries, of the party in power. Politically, they had invested all their hopes in the government's liberalization policy. For the sake of solidarity, they had modulated their demands and tempered their criticisms of the government and they tacitly accepted, as part of the global strategy, the recourse to the king's grain, Laverdy's royal trump. So long as the government maintained its commitment to liberalization, they could not afford to question its wisdom or good intentions. The outburst of rumors and suspicions did not startle the liberals—in the fifties Herbert and others had warned that the king's grain invariably provoked popular "insults" and "murmurs" which turned the people against the government—so much as it exasperated them.[133] For it discredited the government with which they were closely associated and it jeopardized the fate of the program they had labored so devotedly to realize.

With deep ambivalence—they could never excuse the ministry for its weakness and stupidity—the liberals came to the defense of the government and provided the only serious public refutation of the charges of Leprévost, the Rouen Parlement, and others. The idea that the ministry was part of a plot against the people's subsistence, the abbé Roubaud argued at the end of the sixties, was absurd, naive, and illogical. There was indeed a Malisset company—he called it by name—which functioned "by order of the Government and under

---

133 Herbert, *Essai*, ed. by Depitre, 55. Cf. *ibid.*, 20 and *Journal économique* (May 1754), 72–73.

the inspection of the Ministry." Like many previous ventures similarly organized following the precepts of "the old system," its purpose was to provide "for the provisioning of the capital, large cities,
and provinces which might have need of assistance." The Malisset
operation, however, Roubaud emphasized, was a temporary measure
meant to last "until commerce was sufficiently free and extensive to
spare the administration this care." "This is," he wrote, "the single and
only enterprise that conjectures have been able to transform into odious and shocking monopoly." What sort of monopoly, he asked, sells
regularly at a loss and conducts its business soberly to avoid "stifling
the competition" and "ruining" the merchants? Malisset did not even
engage in trade, properly speaking; rather he "rendered a service"
to the nation. It was a sad irony (attributable to longstanding "prejudices" and to the panic fears peculiar to dearths), Roubaud concluded,
that the very people who implored the king for food were the ones who
rushed to denounce the activities of the government in their behalf.[134]

In an essay published toward the end of 1768, the abbé Baudeau
joined Roubaud in a warm defense of the integrity and the ideological
commitment of the ministry to liberty and a straightforward explanation of the king's grain operation as an emergency service which the
government construed as a "necessary evil."[135] While liberalization was
still in force, Baudeau regarded "pact" imputations and criticism of
government victualing as direct attacks on the liberal reforms. Yet his
tone changed considerably by the time he treated the question again
in the seventies, well after the government had abjured liberalism. He
was now free to deal with the matter without any political constraints.
"In recent times," Baudeau noted, "the public has been persuaded
that there was exercised in the kingdom a general monopoly on grain
and flour: the public was right." It erred, however, in its conception of
"the nature and the characteristics" of the monopoly:

> It was imagined that the company of commissioners of the King ran a trade for *profit*,
> buying grain *cheaply*, & reselling them *more dearly*. In truth, this company was doing
> quite the contrary: it bought *more dearly*, & sold *more cheaply* ... so that its general com-
> merce was conducted at a loss, but a very great loss for the royal treasury, that is to say
> for the Nation which filled it.

---

134 Roubaud, *Représentations*, 126–32.
135 Baudeau, *Avis aux honnêtes gens qui veulent bien faire* (Paris, 1768), 64–80 and *passim*. The Rouen
   Parlement pointed to the revelations in the *Avis* as a vindicaton of their contention that
   "this famous and protected company" existed and as further evidence that the government
   had lied in its replies to the Parlement's charges. Remonstrance, 25 Jan. 1769, Registre St.
   Martin, A.D. S-M.

The company was not exclusively devoted to the public interest, whatever the intentions of the government, nor did it have any scruples about crushing competition. The "natural goal" of the agents was to become "the only dealers in grain and flour in all the kingdom." "Open warfare" broke out between the company and the ordinary merchants who could not successfully rival an enterprise protected and subsidized by the government.

Baudeau disabused the public of its suspicions in a singularly curious way. He said that it was absurd to imagine a plot against the people, yet he described a system of provisioning whose effect was clearly contrary to the public interest, viewed from the perspective of simple consumer or physiocratic prophet. In the same reassuring, clinical tone, Roubaud wrote that it "had an interest in allowing or even causing local dearths to arise in order to prove its utility." "So as not to accuse anyone," he added mysteriously, "let us not insist on these last points." Roubaud had punctured the pact/plot idea in order to rescue the government's reputation and program; Baudeau refuted it in order to discredit the ministry and its policy on the solid grounds of political economy rather than to exonerate the ministry as a victim of the fantasies of a gullible and insecure public. Baudeau hated the notion of a provisioning company because he believed that it was wholly incompatible with a genuine liberalization and he detested the agents of the company ("they are my known enemies") because he saw them as the most vocal antiliberal, pro-police lobby within the government.[136]

Along with many others, liberals and nonliberals alike, Baudeau felt that any sort of governmental provisioning, even if it were done, as Turgot once said, "by angels," was misconceived, generally deleterious, and doomed to failure. The experience of the late sixties reinforced their belief that all such activities ought to be stopped for reasons that were political as well as doctrinal. The famine pact episode underscored the enormous difficulty of calculating public opinion in the practice of public administration. The king's grain, alleged the Provence Parlement, spread "terror" rather than comfort throughout the realm; the whole pact syndrome could have been averted had Louis XV not turned against his "own principles" in order to satisfy a lingering and misguided paternalistic scruple.[137] The économiste-bureaucrat Dupont took it as a sort of behavioral law that government grain operations provoke "anxieties"

---

136 Baudeau, "Lettres ... à un Magistrat du Parlement de Paris ...," *Nouvelles éphémérides économiques*, I (1775), 1–23.

137 Letter to Louis XV, 10 Nov. 1770, B. 3677, A.D. B-du-R.

and "expose the Ministry to unjust suspicions." Like Turgot, he argued that whatever the design of the government, the people "never see in it anything but crime and monopoly."[138] Turgot's friend Véri discerned the same kind of plot reflex and thought it might have a salutary effect if it taught administrators a lesson: "Anything which might deter them from directing the grain [operations] will seem to me so great a good that I cannot be troubled by the false imputations made to them."[139]

Whereas the liberals claimed that the people were too blind to appreciate the true defects in royal victualing systems, partisans of government intervention maintained that they were too blind to understand its true benefits. Necker deplored the popular tendency to attribute government "beneficence" to "interested views." Acutely sensitive to public opinion, he felt that the political cost of extensive government provisioning was prohibitive: "thus the constant intervention of the Government in the grain trade is contrary to the good of the State; it is especially destructive of that precious opinion, of that tender confidence which must bind the People to its sovereign." On the other hand, in a time of need, the government should not hesitate to come to the aid of the people regardless of what the people thought. Nonintervention cannot be a fixed rule, Necker lectured the *économistes* and especially his rival Turgot, "for in political economy and in administration, there is nothing absolute."[140]

Critics assailed government grain operations such as those of the sixties on very much the same grounds as they had attacked the "Josephist" idea of prophylaxis in any form. *Economistes*, encyclopedists, and parlementaires agreed that government-sponsored enterprises were exorbitantly expensive. With nothing to lose and sometimes a great deal to gain from inflating prices, government agents bought at any price, transported without genuine concern for economy, and conserved with indifference, thus losing considerable amounts of grain and flour or marketing poor quality goods. In addition to absorbing all the losses, the government in some cases had to pay substantial initial advances. Turgot's axiom, that only self-interest could guarantee efficiency and fidelity, was widely shared.[141] Despite government instructions, agents and commissioners were likely to commit abuses.

---

138 Dupont, *Analyse ... rapport*, 96, 106. Cf. Turgot, "Septième lettre sur le commerce des grains," 2 Dec. 1770, in *Œuvres*, ed. by Schelle, III, 323–24.

139 Abbé de Véri, *Journal*, ed. by J. de Witte, I, 150.

140 Necker, *Sur la législation*, 285–96.

141 Turgot, "Septième lettre sur le commerce des grains," 2 Dec. 1770, in *Œuvres*, ed. by Schelle, III, 325–29.

They had no reason to want prices to decrease, remarked a committee of the Paris Enquêtes; they were easily tempted to engage in "culpable maneuvers," Turgot warned; they might themselves become "monopolists," cautioned Clément of the Paris Chambre des Comptes.[142] The most serious charge made against government operations was that they ruined commerce. The marquis d'Argenson vividly described how the specter of government intervention, competition, and constraint paralyzed and demoralized the merchant community.[143] Writing from Rome in the midst of the "famine" of 1764, the abbé Coyer argued that the grain-dealing business of the administration furnished the "infallible means to disgust the *laboureur*, ruin agriculture, and bring on [future] dearths."[144] The Languedoc Parlement complained to the king in the sixties that his goodwill undertaking served only to "intimidate" proprietors of grain and "discourage" traders.[145] "We have never had a grain commerce in full activity," Dupont contended, "because we are accustomed to seeing the Government mix in...."[146]

Every time the government intervened in the course of the century, merchants protested bitterly against the unfair competition. How many of them actually fulfilled their threats to abandon the profession, we do not know. The critics of official provisioning liked to believe that the tale of the Etampes flour merchant at the end of the sixties was typical:

I have two mills, when the public does not occupy them I make flour for my own account which I reserve for the moments when the Halles of Paris are not well furnished [when the price was high], this commerce always brought me a profit; but for some time I have ceased this commerce because the Government made individual deals with several of my confreres to provision the Paris Halles, they were given such a great advantage that 1 would have ruined myself if I had wanted to compete with them. Do you know what happened? These *messieurs* came to me, put me to work for them, had me doing everything which I had so simply done before and surely much

---

142 "Mémoire," Aug. 1771, BN, Coll. Joly 1111, fol. 139; Turgot, "Septième lettre sur le commerce des grains," in *Œuvres*, ed. by Schelle, III, 324–25 and *arrêt du conseil*, 13 Sept. 1774 in Des Essarts, *Dictionnaire*, I, 24; *Recueil*, 176. Cf. Roubaud, *Représentations*, 165–66; Dupont to Prince Carl Ludwig (1773), in *Correspondance Dupont*, ed. by Knies, II, 147; article "disette," *Encyclopédie méthodique*, Jurisprudence, Police et Municipalités, X, 35.

143 D'Argenson, *Mémoires et journal inédit du marquis d'Argenson*, ed. by d'Argenson, V, 361–72.

141 Abbé Coyer, *Voyage d'Italie et de Hollande* (Paris, 1775), 204.

145 Letter from Languedoc to king, published in the *Ephémérides du citoyen* in early 1767 cited by Weulersse, *Mouvement*, II, 617. Cf. *Journal économique* (April 1769), 178.

146 Dupont, *Analyse ... rapport*, 162.

more cheaply than they, so it is the Government which lost and it is in the end the people who will pay.[147]

Implicit in the argument that government commerce crushes private trade is the notion that the latter is infinitely better at performing the services undertaken by the former. Turgot made the case brilliantly, first in his *Letters on the Grain Trade* and then in the preamble to the *arrêt du Conseil* of 13 September 1774, one of the most scathing critiques of government published in the eighteenth century and one of the many examples of the Old Regime doing itself in. Private commerce, with its network of correspondents, its superb intelligence system, and its frugal habits, Turgot argued, was the "surest, quickest and least expensive" means to meet the needs of the people. Merchants knew their business better than anyone else, they did not need a special cue to begin their operations, and they were highly motivated to perform well. Compared with the king's men, Turgot's merchants were of heroic stature, not because they wanted to be, but because the forces of nature and the economy made them so: "Their vigilance, excited by [self-] interest, prevents waste and losses, their rivalry makes any monopoly impossible and the continual need which they have to realize a prompt return on their investments in order to maintain their commerce, engages them to be content with moderate profits." If the "avidity" of the merchant is not "repressed by competition" or if he does not satisfy the demand, the error is not in the model but in the environment (police constraints or government intervention on the supply side) or in the person (unusual ineptitude or knavery). For Turgot, the best and only way to assure subsistence was to maintain rigorously the "legitimate rights of property and liberty."

The striking failure of the governments of the last century to resolve the subsistence imbroglio by following the principles of the old system was more than sufficient reason to abandon that system. It inspired a fatal "illusion" that the government, through its grain operations, could not only succor the people in emergencies, but control the entire distribution process. The government deluded itself and the people if it believed that it could prevent dearths. Let us face reality, Turgot urged: the product of an ordinary harvest was less, not more, than enough; shortages were frequent; price rises were "inevitable"; and *cherté* was the "unique possible remedy for scarcity." Government grain operations were short-run balms which did not deal with the fundamental

---

147 "Cherté du pain," AN, T 644[1-2].

problems. They were bound to fail and to exacerbate the fears they were meant to allay. In the midst of victualing operations, the administrators themselves took alarm and unleashed a sort of "terror" which, as Turgot described it, resembled Jacobinism more nearly than Delamarism. Commerce, "vexed, outraged, denounced to the hatred of the people," virtually ceased; popular clamors became more boisterous; prices continued to soar. The government, concluded Turgot, "cannot, then, reserve to itself the transport and storage of grain without compromising the subsistence and the tranquility of the peoples."[148]

Turgot gave substance to his thesis in the third article of the *arrêt* of 1774 by having the king solemnly renounce any future purchases of grain and flour for his account. The major purpose of this self-righteous declaration of purity was to give commerce this final reassurance and encouragement absent in the liberal laws of 1763–64. Its effect was to confirm the age-old suspicion that there was something profoundly rotten not only in the quality, but also in the administration of the king's grain. Turgot's attack on the government provisioning operations was an admission of guilt; in a very limited but significant way, it was a public vindication of the mission of Leprévost de Beaumont.

To the extent that it provided urgently needed supplies at a critical moment, it would be a mistake to view the king's grain experience as a debacle for the government. Yet there is no doubt that Malisset, despite himself, and Leprévost, as a symptom for a deeper predicament than he himself represented, each helped to undermine the position of the liberal ministry. It was the intervention of the Parlement of Paris, however, upon a background of ongoing subsistence crisis, which forced the issues to a head. Although the king's grain contributed substantially to improve the subsistence situation in the capital, it did not succeed, as the government had hoped it would, in preserving the goodwill or at least the neutrality of the authorities responsible for the police of Paris. Indeed, by the beginning of 1768, it was no longer merely a question of the short-run fate of the capital. Increasingly, it seemed impossible to separate the problem of Paris from the general dilemma which confronted the kingdom as a whole. Increasingly,

---

148 See especially the "Septième lettre sur le commerce des grains," 2 Dec. 1770, in *Œuvres*, ed. by Schelle, III, 323ff. For the *arrêt*, see BN, Coll. Joly 1111, fol. 39; *Journal historique et politique des différentes cours* (Oct. 10, 1774); and Des Essarts, *Dictionnaire*, I, 24. For similar views expressed by a prelate-*économiste* and former classmate of Turgot, see E. Lavaquéry, *Le Cardinal de Boisgelin* (Paris, 1920), I, 126.

attention focused on the meaning and the wisdom of the liberal reform and its social and political implications. The next chapter treats the evolution of the Paris Parlement's attitude from the onset of the crisis until the end of 1768 when it declared its opposition overtly and joined the campaign to quash liberalization in which its sister-court at Rouen had already taken the lead.

Chapter IX

THE GOVERNMENT, THE PARLEMENTS, AND THE BATTLE OVER LIBERTY: I

In the modern scholarly view of the sixties, which has brought considerable order and sophistication to the study of eighteenth-century France, the dominant motif is constitutional, the lingering crisis is the Brittany affair, and the denouement is the stunning coup engineered by Maupeou. I have viewed the decade from a different vantage point. I have suggested that another issue preoccupied Frenchmen in the sixties and in many ways cut more deeply and touched more people than the well-known political confrontation. I have focused upon a social and political crisis concerning subsistence, which set the stage for the outburst of absolutism in 1770–71 by producing widespread economic disruption and recession.

From this perspective, the main themes of parlementary action eddy against the prevailing current. What is striking are not the claims of parlementary union and indivisibility, but the deep divisions among the sovereign courts; not the political pretensions of the parlements, but their vitally important administrative and regulatory responsibilities; not the obscurantist attitudes and obstructionist tactics for which they are famous, but their critique of government mismanagement and royal abuse, which had much in common with what we conventionally call "enlightened"; not their adamantine hostility to change and their persecution of truth, but their inability to decide amongst themselves what changes were best and what opinions were true; not their egotistical defense of privilege, but their discussion of the nature of *la chose publique*; not their desire to curtail royal authority, but their debate on the responsibilities of kingship. The parlements of the grain crisis were the same parlements which thwarted Bertin's intelligent reforms, burned LaBarre, and mercilessly harassed the king. But the view of France from the marketplace differed sharply from the scene perceived from La Chalotais' prison or the *fauteuil* in which Louis presided over *lits de justice,* even as it differed from vantage points in Rouen, Toulouse, Grenoble, and Paris. The issues raised by the grain crisis differed from the problems posed by the constitutional quarrel and elicited different responses from parlements for whom politics was a very complex and subtle business. The constitutional question, as important as it was, must not obscure the existence of other matters of urgent public concern and other dimensions of parlementary behavior.

Chapters IX and X are concerned with the relations between the government and the parlements, especially the Parlement of Paris which became the most prominent adversary of liberalization in 1768. In the past, the Paris court had never seriously quarreled with the king on subsistence affairs. With some hesitation, this Parlement had approved the liberal reforms of 1763–64. It resolved, on the motion of the *grand chambrier* abbé Terray, to give liberalization a proper trial. For almost four years, the Parlement remained silent as the new policy took root. Chapter IX treats the reaction of the court to the deepening subsistence difficulties in its *ressort* and the reawakening of its interest in liberalization. It traces the growing hostility between the Parlement and the ministry and the hardening of positions on both sides. The Parlement understood the motivation for the new departure in grain policy and many of its members sympathized with its goals. But the experience of the sixties convinced the majority of its members that liberalization opened the gates to perils which far outweighed the advantages it could deliver.

This issue became, in the Parlement's view, not only a matter of a subsistence crisis, but also a crisis in the nature of kingship. Through its own offices and by means of an extraordinary representative assembly, the Parlement reaffirmed the traditional values of police and the "well-policed state."

Among the sovereign courts, the Paris Parlement did not stand alone in the struggle against liberalization. Several other courts shared its alarm about the consequences of the reforms. Yet it would be wrong to imagine that their common opposition rested on a self-conscious community of interest. Sympathy for Paris was not, as Chapter X suggests, at the base of the loose antiliberal coalition.

The bulk of Chapter X concerns the liberal effort to mount a counter-offensive. Locked in battle with the most powerful Parlement, the government turned to the nation for support against Paris. Three parlements hastened to the defense of the new grain regime and the liberal style of kingship, giving the lie to the claim of the Parisian court that it spoke for the people of France. The *économistes* publicized the views of the liberal courts and mounted a campaign of their own to prove that liberalization was a salutary undertaking. Strengthened by this support, it was not until the very end of 1769 that the government betrayed any hint of weakening resolve.

I

While the Brittany affair dragged on, the attention of the Paris Parlement turned increasingly to the subsistence problem. It observed with growing inquietude the proliferation of disorder in its *ressort*. Through the Procurator General, the Parlement received first-hand reports of the effects of the dearth and the remonstrances and lamentations of the local authorities. Jurisdictionally, the problem directly concerned the sovereign court in the exercise of its *grande police*. The Parlement did not leap rashly into the affair as it often did with matters which it could exploit to political advantage. It regarded the situation as extremely delicate and it showed uncharacteristic forbearance in its approach and restraint in its language. In December 1767, the Parlement appealed to the king to "take measures to facilitate the subsistence of the poor People" who suffered most from the "excessive *cherté*." It neither raised general questions of royal policy nor attacked liberalization, perhaps partly to avoid a falling out with several of the other sovereign courts, which remained passionately committed to the liberal reforms, but primarily because it saw the issue at this stage in limited terms as one of reestablishing public tranquility.

The king rebuffed this overture and another which the court made the following April: "I love my Peoples; I have no need of being excited to assist and relieve them; the efficacious measures that I have taken have assured their subsistence: they can be upset only by ill-considered démarches [like yours]." The government, even more than the Parlement, wanted to avert a debate on principles and policy. The king treated the *cherté* as a commonplace accident: bad weather produced a bad harvest, which caused a major price rise "that no attention could prevent."

The Parlement responded with an initiative that bypassed the monarch and threatened to provoke the "éclat" which above all he wanted to avoid. The court instructed the Procurator General to ask all the *substituts* to send memoirs on prices, the grain trade and the overall state of local affairs. By this measure, the litany of misery and protests would formally enter the record and become subject to deliberation. The king viewed this action as the first step in going to the country to mobilize opinion for an assault on liberalization. The ministry would not let the Parlement use the *cherté* as a stalking horse; Louis XV brought the issue into the open. Under no circumstances would he compromise "the principles which form the basis" of the May Declaration and the July Edict. "I want to maintain the execution of these two laws," the monarch told the court, and "my Parlement must penetrate itself more and more with their utility and consequently support my views in having them exactly observed." He ordered the court to send the government copies of the country poll and he prohibited it from taking any action before it made known its intentions. The Parlement made no reply; it appointed a watchdog committee and awaited the results of the new harvest and the distribution of the king's grain.[1]

In the fall the crisis deepened; in October, the price of bread in Paris reached 15 *sous*. To appease public opinion as well as an expanding current of opposition in official quarters, Louis dismissed Laverdy, even as he had appointed him five years earlier to placate the parlements. At the same time the First President Maupeou, who had a reputation for devotion to the king and had served fruitlessly as mediator between crown and parlement in the discussion of the *cherté*, succeeded his father as chancellor.[2] His appointment was viewed as a mark of the king's determination to deal more forcefully with the court. Earlier in the year, the king had resuscitated the *Grand Conseil*, rival and bete noire of the parlements, which vehemently protested the decision.[3] This peremptory measure followed hard upon yet another squabble over the extension of the second twentieth tax.[4]

---

1 Parl. of Paris, *Conseil Secret*, 28 March, 18 April, 4 May 1768, AN X^{1B} 8955; *Recueil*, 65–70.
  The *Gens du Roy* instructed the *substituts* to "avoid confounding the rumor of the people with the truth of the facts" and to conduct their investigation with "prudence & discretion" so as not to "interrupt the provisioning of the markets or cause any alarm." *Conseil Secret*, 3 May 1768, AN, X^{1B} 8955 and BN, Coll. Joly 1139, fols. 7, 11, 15; PG to royal procurator of Aurillac, 19 April 1768, C. 7506, A.D. P-de-D.
2 Flammermont, ed., *Remontrances du Parlement de Paris*, III, i–iv. D'Aligre succeeded Maupeou as First President.
3 Glasson, *Parlement de Paris*, II, 222–35, 335–37; *Le Nouvelliste suisse* (June 1768), 139 and (July 1768), 162–166; Bertin to Miromesnil, March 1768. in LeVerdier, ed., *Correspondance Miromesnil*, V, 109; Bertin to Mssrs. du Parlement, 10 Aug. 1768, *Conseil* for 1767 (entry 16 Aug. 1768), A.D. S-M.; Choiseul to Parl. of Dauphiné, n.d. and St.-Florentin to Parl. of Dijon, n.d., Arch. AE, France 1366, fols. 110 and *passim*.
4 Remontrances, 21 Aug. 1767, Conseil 1767, A.D. S-M.; Remontrances, 5 June 1767, Flammermont, ed., *Remontrances du Parlement de Paris*, II, 809ff. Nor did the liberal parlements

The climate was not conducive to conciliation, though Maupeou made a few symbolic gestures meant to relieve the tension.

On October 15 in the *Chambre des Vacations,* a councillor captured the predominant mood when he pronounced the past year's low-key appeals to the king a failure and demanded urgently a full scale debate on the mounting *cherté*.[5] The government frantically tried to have the deliberation, set by the *Chambre* for the 20th, quashed or postponed. Maupeou pressed the presidents who were in Paris and the *Gens du Roi* to lobby among the magistrates for a delay. "Any action," he warned, "can only worsen the situation." He won the support of Sartine, whose voice concerning conditions in Paris would have influence with the *Chambre.* The Lieutenant General agreed to tell the councillors that "precautions" have been taken and needed time—at least until after the return of the whole court following St. Martin's—to take effect.

Speaking for the ministry, St. Florentin, the Secretary of State for Paris, wrote that we applied ourselves "incessantly to procure a diminution on the price of grain." If, "despite all the efforts," it has not come as rapidly as hoped, he argued, it is "because the *causes* of the *cherté* are *physical* and *do not depend on the will of those who govern.*" This confession of quasi-impotence followed logically from the liberal line of the government. Before liberalization, the government had rarely shown much humility vis-à-vis a subsistence crisis. Seldom in the past had it been willing to admit that a crisis was natural and in some fashion ineluctable, rather than the consequence of human error or malevolence. The age of liberalization was a time of candor; the government, like any other mortal, could only operate within the limits of the possible. Although the facts clearly belied his serenity, the Secretary of State insisted that "the spirit of the people is tranquil" and that parlementary action "could only serve to make [it] anxious." After working on the magistrates informally for four days, Maupeou hoped that they would cede to the suggestion of the *Gens du Roi* when they were called to render conclusions at the deliberation of the 20th. Kept waiting for two hours, the Procurator General

---

graciously spare the king on this issue. In a violent tone, the Grenoble court charged the king with lying to the people, violating the constitution, mismanaging finances, and ignoring the "cries of misery and of indigence." At roughly the same moment, in an entirely different humor, the Dauphinais reported the beginnings of a delicious prosperity, which they had not tasted before, consequent upon the introduction of liberty and the promise of more to come. 21 April, 31 Aug. 1769, B. 2314, fols. 77–87, 123–39, A.D. Isère.

5 15 Oct. 1768, AN, X^{1A} 8545, fol. 457.

Joly and the Advocate General Séguier, both of whom sympathized with the magistrates despite their formal expression of loyalty to the chancellor, did not even have a chance to address the *Chambre* when they were finally invited to enter.[6]

The *Chambre* presented them with a fait accompli, an *arrêt* of remonstrance which challenged the entire liberal program. "If obedience and respect have for a long time kept [us] in silence" and limited us to employing the "private offices" of the First President, the Parlement declared, this same fidelity now imposes upon us the obligation to reveal to the king "some important truths" on the state of the nation. To give the new legislation a fair trial and "to allow the promised benefits the time to develop," the nation "endured this long and grievous ordeal." Liberty promised wealth and ease, but it wrought misery, which forced mothers to "deplore their fecundity." It caused hunger, which provoked "peaceful and domiciled citizens"—not the *gens sans aveu* or the rootless rabble, but "citizens whose hearts were naturally faithful and submissive"—into rebellion. For his obliviousness to these "calamities," the Parlement generously afforded the king an excuse. Isolated from reality at Fontainebleau, where bread was fixed at a price below the market value and spared incriminating details by his ministers, Louis could not have been aware of the full gravity of the situation.

Now, said the Parlement, it was time for him to demand "an accounting of the new system of legislation introduced a few years ago on the commerce of grain." He must "compare" the dispositions of these laws "with the events that followed" and ask himself "if these *chertés* of bread, these public alarms, these popular riots do not have their hidden principle in some defect of the new system." Louis must examine "whether an indefinite liberty cannot degenerate into the license of monopoly" which "until now only the inspection of an attentive police was capable of averting." Finally, concluded the *Chambre*, the king must decide whether it would be prudent to "prolong" this system any further.[7]

"Here we are preoccupied with the *cherté* of grain," wrote a Parisian to his provincial correspondent," and it could happen that we end up by

---

6 St. Florentin to PG, 16, 20 Oct. 1768, AN, O¹ 410 and BN, Coll. Joly 1139, fol. 98; Maupeou to PG, 15, 16 Oct. 1768, BN, Coll. Joly 1139, fols. 88–89, 96–97; drafts, PG to Maupeou, 15, 20, 24 Oct. 1768, BN, Coll. Joly 1139, fols. 89, 115–120.

7 *Conseil Secret*, 20 Oct. 1768, AN X¹ᴬ 8545, fols. 460ff.; *Hardy's Journal*, BN, mss. fr. 6680, fol. 180.

[seeing] the export law suspended."[8] This prediction was premature, but the Parlement's bristling remonstrance was not the only sign of government vulnerability. From the time of the grain and bread riots, which erupted throughout Normandy in the spring and summer of 1768, the Rouen Parlement, which had demanded freedom to export with such passion in 1763–64, began to question the virtues of liberalization. The violent uprising in Rouen in March was the catalyst in the court's volte-face; it was as if the mutinous citizenry released the magistrates from their commitment to the reform laws. For Laverdy, it was another example of, on the one side, "the weakness of different police officials" and, on the other, "a blinded people ruining its future subsistence by pillaging and destroying the only thing which can guarantee it [i.e., free trade in private hands]." Hours after the revolt broke out, without any need for a prod from Versailles, the Parlement pledged a swift and terrible repression. But as the rioting intensified in the city and spread throughout the region, the magistrates seemed to lose their taste for punishment and shift their focus of interest from effects to causes. Even as they interrogated suspects arrested by the watch, they listened to reports on "the general state of misery" and discussed ways to alleviate it.[9]

The Rouen Parlement chose to make an example, not of the rioters, but of the dearth and the circumstances that sustained it. As calm returned, the punitive measures taken by the court proved to be much less severe than anyone expected. Its action was meant as a sign that the Parlement did not wish to lay blame on the public for "excesses" which it was driven to commit and as a defiant snub of the Controller-General's express desire for a stern reckoning. While Laverdy dispatched troops to guarantee the maintenance of order, the magistrates issued an *arrêt*, which implicitly held government policy responsible for the disorders. It revived a number of the most important grain trade controls which the liberal laws had abolished including the prohibition against speculative buying and hoarding and the obligation to furnish the marketplaces regularly. In addition, the court promised to appeal to Louis XV "to procure the most prompt and efficient assistance" for the people and to petition the royal council to lower the export cut-off mark from 30 *livres* to 21 *livres* 12 *sous* the *septier* (Paris measure).[10]

---

8 Lettres Ossolinski, 24 Oct. 1768, BHVP, mss. 627, fol. 184.

9 Rouen Parl., *Conseil Secret* (1767–1768), 23 March—15 April 1768, A.D. S-M.; Laverdy to Miromesnil, 23 March 1768 and Laverdy to de Crosne, 10 April 1768, C. 107, *ibid.*

10 Rouen Parl., *Conseil Secret* (1767–1768), 23 March—15 April 1768, A.D. S-M.; Maupeou to Miromesnil, 23 March 1768, C. 107, *ibid.*; Laverdy to Miromesnil, 27 March and

Appalled by the "bad conduct" of the Rouen magistrates, the government labored to minimize the impact of their defection. Though the royal council could have annulled the Rouen *arrêt* in a stroke, Laverdy calculated that such an authoritarian gesture would drive the Rouennais more irretrievably into opposition and focus national attention and debate on the issue at a very inopportune time—precisely the results he wanted to avoid. On the other hand, he felt that to countenance such a flagrant violation of the laws of 1763–64 would undermine the entire reform enterprise. All spring he worked strenuously to induce the magistrates to withdraw voluntarily the reactionary *arrêt*. The Parlement refused, however, to abjure its "errors" and confess to having "been carried away by its own zeal." In a deliberately circuitous manner, the royal council finally promulgated an *arrêt* which ordered the exact execution of the May and July laws in the Normandy jurisdiction, without explicitly quashing the Parlement's *arrêt*. The intendant of Rouen cautioned the ministry against having this legislation cried and posted for fear of arousing the ire of the people of the province, who remained convinced that liberalization was the cause of the ongoing dearth.[11]

The Rouen Parlement clearly indicated that it was not interested in devices for saving face or maintaining convenient fictions. Even before it received the royal *arrêt*, it sent the king a long remonstrance-sermon depicting widespread misery due to soaring prices and massive unemployment. Pointedly, it reminded him that "the most powerful tie of obedience and affection of the subjects is the attention the prince pays to their needs...." In June, the Parlement invited Louis XV to retract the letters patent which contained the royal *arrêt* reaffirming the liberal legislation. Later that summer, in new remonstrances, it developed, with increasing intensity, its objections to the liberal regime. Rejecting the ministry's argument that the subsistence difficulties were due to "accidents" of weather and commerce, the Parlement urged the government to deal with its "true causes," first of all by placing tighter limits on exports. The tone of the ministry's response in late September suggests that it had abandoned hope of recapturing the support of the Rouennais.

---

4 April 1768, in LeVerdier, ed., *Correspondance Miromesnil*, V, 135, 142–44; Floquet, *Parlement de Normandie*, VI. 424–25.

11 LeVerdier, ed. *Correspondance Miromesnil*, V, xxvi–xxx (intro).; Bertin to Miromesnil, 18 April 1768, *ibid.*, V, 149–50; Miromesnil to Bertin, 21 April 1768, *ibid.*, V, 152–55; *Arrêt du Conseil*, 20 June 1768, C. 103, A.D. S-M.; T. de Montigny to La Michodière, 1 July 1768 and La Michodière to Montigny, 3 July 1768, C. 103, *ibid.*

Victim of "a residue of anxiety and prejudice" from earlier days, the Rouen court had lost touch with its own time. Citing the vocal demands of other parlements in the kingdom for the elimination of all restrictions on exportation as evidence of the prevalent state of French opinion, the government pledged that it would take no backward steps along the path to total liberty.[12]

These expressions of mutual hostility led inexorably to open warfare. The Rouen Parlement attacked fiercely in October with two "letter-supplications" addressed to Louis XV, which were illicitly printed and circulated. The sensation these letters provoked as a result of their intimation that the government was involved in a grain speculation conspiracy obscured the fact that they were also a detailed indictment of the liberal laws and no longer a demand for certain modifications, but for a full-scale revision. As a result of irresponsible leadership and of laws that were both ill-conceived and subject to easy abuse, the nation now faced "terrible dangers"—a social and economic "calamity" which deprived people of work at the very moment that it drove prices far beyond reach. Although more than once we called attention to our needs, "we were answered only by vague expressions of efforts and of hopes." Perhaps, suggested the Rouen magistrates, you do not believe us:

> The Courtier swimming in delights cannot imagine the horrors of indigence, then let him descend into the details! let him visit the countryside; let him traverse our cities, depots of human misery! His delicacy will tremble at the spectacles which will present themselves from everywhere to his eyes.

The "theory" of liberalization, the Rouen Parlement contended, "has been contradicted by the practice." As a stimulus for agriculture, the *bon prix* program seemed "on the outside extremely seductive." Had it only produced "a moderate augmentation" it might still be worthy of our suffrage. But the fact that it "plunged an entire people into the most horrible misery and upset the whole commercial economy" is incontrovertible proof of its failure and the best reply to those who "obstinately continue to solicit a total liberty." Yet the Rouen magistrates had no desire to appear as enemies of liberty, of a "true liberty." But a genuine liberty, they insisted, by definition, could never have produced such disastrous results. These very results demonstrated that the liberty of May and July was a deformation, "an illusory liberty."

---

12 Remonstrances of 5 May and 19 Aug. 1768, *Conseil Secret* (1767–68), A.D. S.-M.; Bertin to Parl., 20 Sept. 1768, inserted in *Conseil Secret*, 10 Oct. 1768, *ibid*.

Instead of promoting "competition" and "the division" of the trade in many hands, the laws encouraged monopoly: the concentration of the supply in the hands of a "powerful" few with enormous credit, the hoarding of stocks, and the manipulation of prices for the sake of inflating profits at public expense. This, the Parlement concluded, was "the principal and most important cause" of the present crisis. The facility accorded exportation merely aggravated the evil effects of monopoly; the curtailment of exports would not by itself solve the problem. To save the nation from doom, the government had to rush to the aid of the people and renounce the theory and practice of liberalization.[13]

By the end of October 1768, the government found it increasingly difficult to pretend that there was no really serious opposition to the liberal reforms. Despite considerable differences in their style and emphasis and in their appreciation of the motives of the king and his ministers, the Parlements of Paris and Rouen shared the view that liberalization had produced monopoly and misery and that it could not safely be allowed to endure. The outrageously disrespectful and provocative letters from Rouen merited severe punishment, but the ministry refused to satisfy the magistrates' appetite for a public brawl and a *cause célèbre* which they would use to discredit liberalization. Instead, a secretary of state sent them two wishy-washy rebukes that they treated with a mocking disdain, which barely concealed their deep disappointment.[14] Louis XV addressed himself personally to the Parisian remonstrances, but he had nothing new to say. "I have taken the most efficacious means," the king reiterated, "to fix abundance in the markets and to stop, *insofar as it is possible*, a *cherté* occasioned above all by the circumstance of the season, heightened by the fear of the Public." The Paris Parlement, he added, must make it a duty to "second" my views by "dissipating the anxieties," that is to say, by taking no further action.[15]

A week later the council issued an *arrêt* which could be read either as an expression of weakness or of determination. The king was not, after all, unaware of what was happening in the nation. He publicly acknowledged that "in several provinces" the price of grain had risen considerably faster and higher than wages and thus made it difficult

---

13 *Lettres-Suppliques*, 15 and 29 Oct. 1768, *Conseil Secret* (1767–68), *ibid.*

14 See the references to these letters in *Lettres-Suppliques*, 29 Oct. 1768, *Conseil Secret* (1767–68) and remonstrances, 25 Jan. 1769, Registre St. Martin, *ibid.*

15 BN, Coll. Joly 1139, fol. 116; *Hardy's Journal*, 23 Oct. 1768, BN, mss. fr. 6680, fol. 182. My italics.

for the people to subsist. But having examined the problem carefully, the council concluded that "the most appropriate means to remedy the evil" was to reaffirm the liberal program,

> to recall the dispositions of the Declaration of 25 May 1763, whose effect must be to establish throughout his [the king's] realm a free circulation, by which means there occurs, uniquely by the ordinary operations of a free commerce, transfer [of grain] from the most abundant provinces to those which experienced misfortune in their harvests.

The government added one new dimension to the standard prescription. To assure a more rapid relief and to promote the competition which alone can force down prices, the government decided to offer bounties to importers of all nationalities.[16]

On November 10, the eve of the opening of the new parlementary year, the royal council finally took the offensive with the publication of artfully designed letters patent. Their aim was to fix clearly the responsibility for the ostensible shortcomings of liberalization and to dispel the persistent and injurious rumors that the government was coddling monopolists. Through the voice of Louis XV, the ministry again explained that it had abolished the old legislation which fettered the grain trade because it was inimical to the interests of cultivators and consumers alike. Convinced that it was the "surest means" to satisfy everyone's needs, we embarked on a program "to establish the most absolute and complete liberty and competition." If problems arose, it was not, as several parlements contended, because of too much liberty, but because there was too little. "We have not yet succeeded in implementing this salutary liberty as fully as we would have desired," the king confessed. The government imputed this failure directly to the local police, abetted by the people who knew no better: "our Declaration of 25 May 1763 has not been executed in its entirety in several provinces ... as a result of the fears which swelled in the mind of a large part of our Subjects and principally of those who were specifically charged with its execution." Had the law not been subverted, the letters suggested, commerce would have been strong enough by itself to deal with the predicament caused—it could not be emphasized too much—by the series of unfortunate harvests. The remedy to our problems, then, is not the repudiation or dilution of the liberal theory but

---

16 BN, Coll. Joly 1139, fols. 125–26; *Hardy's Journal*, 5 Nov. 1768, BN, mss. fr. 6680, fol. 185; *arrêt* of 31 Oct. 1768, *Gazette de France* (7 Nov. 1768), 368; C. 848, A.D. Nord.

its universal application, to which end the government renewed its unswerving commitment.

I have been troubled to learn, the king went on to say in a frank allusion to the proliferation of famine-plot rumors, that the notion has "spread among our People that several rich & powerful individuals have formed the plan to turn the general calamity to their profit" by hoarding massively. The government considered these rumors to be nonsense; beyond their source, which should have been sufficient to discredit them, it was clear that such vast maneuvers were logistically, commercially, and financially inconceivable. But these "vague" and "uncertain" reports persisted, and now they worried Maynon as they had Laverdy. The danger was that alarm would continue to spread, alienating public opinion and creating pretexts for precipitate, authoritarian action by parlements or by the local administration.

By not taking any action at all, the ministry realized, it was giving credence to the idea that the government was somehow involved in one or many plots. By taking the initiative, the government calculated that it could appease public opinion, upstage the parlements, and at the same time keep the local authorities in check. Thus, after having dismissed Laverdy, the object of many suspicions, and dissolved the Malisset contract, by these letters patent the king ordered the parlements to investigate the reports of "companies" and "monopolies" (which the government knew to be false), to denounce any "enterprises which might tend to the prejudice of our Subjects" (the ministry expected none to be found, or in any event none with ties to the government), and, most important of all, from the ministry's perspective, to put a stop to the spreading of rumors (including posting of placards), to expose those who (like Leprévost de Beaumont) "wickedly" propagated rumors in order to "excite disorders," and to "convince all our Subjects of the falsity of these rumors."

Nor could the investigation be used as a pretext for a reversion to old police techniques. On the contrary, the letters not only prohibited the parlements from "violating in any fashion" the May Declaration, but enjoined them to suggest the means by which this law could be rigorously and uniformly implemented. In order to prevent a resurgence of local police activity under the aegis of the parlements, the letters explicitly forbad them to "make or renew any prohibitive regulations." Given "the pernicious effects for the liberty of circulation and the operations of a legitimate commerce which might result from the indiscreet zeal of some subordinate officials," the government authorized only the sovereign courts to conduct the inquiry.[17]

The government's new tactics momentarily threw the parlements off balance. How could they reject, in full public view, the ministry's ostensibly hard-line stand against abuses in the grain trade after they had campaigned so vigorously to expose these abuses and to force the government to take action? Would not such a refractory posture suggest that their opposition to the liberal program had been motivated by political considerations rather than a genuine concern for the fate of the reforms and the state of the kingdom?[18] Yet the parlements could not bring themselves to endorse the letters patent, not merely because they viewed them as a cynical political trap, but because the letters presented the issues in what the magistrates regarded as a perverse and misleading manner. Both parlements refused to register the letters on very similar grounds, though the remonstrances of Rouen were at once more sharply worded and wider-ranging.

The remonstrances of both courts criticized the government for underestimating—wilfully—the gravity of the economic and social situation in large segments of the realm.[19] They assailed the letters patent for lumping together the phenomena of monopoly and of rumor, implying that the former was largely the creation of the latter, and treating them both as products of the same aberrant mentality. The Parisian magistrates conceded that the rumors were dangerous and they agreed to look into them, but their Rouen counterparts, convinced that the indictment of rumor-mongering was aimed largely at them, denounced the whole enterprise as a worthless, diversionary ploy. For both parlements, monopoly, "this destructive scourge," was the really urgent affair. Monopoly, the parlements lectured the king, was a very real menace, an enemy of the throne as well as of the people. Operating everywhere, at every level and stage, monopoly struck rapidly and decisively and then concealed itself in the "shadow of mystery" (Paris) or "under the veil of the law" (Rouen). For the Parisians, monopoly was a treacherous and elusive force, fragmented and

---

17 *Recueil*, 77–83; *Hardy's Journal*, 12 Nov. 1768, BN, mss. ft. 6680, fol. 186; St. Florentin to PG, Nov. 1768 and PG to Maupeou, 18 Nov. 1768, BN, Coll. Joly 1139, fols. 100–104; *Le Nouvelliste suisse* (Nov. 1768), 259–61.

18 This was the line promoted by the anonymous author of "Réflexions sur les principes des Parlements de Paris et de Rouen." Arch. AE, France 1375, fols. 293–304.

19 The Paris representations are in *Recueil*, 84–91; the Rouen remonstrances are in Registre St. Martin, 25 Jan. 1769, A.D. S-M.

dispersed in time and space, which would be difficult to uncover and neutralize. The Rouennais had a more immediate and nearly anthropomorphic conception of monopoly: it operated brazenly before their eyes and they suspected that it was the expression of organized, coordinated criminal designs rather than merely the results of autonomous, local abuses. While the Paris magistrates welcomed the opportunity to launch an investigation, the Rouen magistrates claimed that they already had the "proofs" in hand and that they needed, not the condescending and gratuitous grant of authority of these letters patent to prosecute common crimes ("We are no longer in the infancy of the Monarchy; our Criminal Code has long been composed..."), but the government's solemn assurance that it would not interfere with the ordinary judicial process in the Rouen jurisdiction.

Both Parlements scored the letters patent for "debasing" the local police and disqualifying them from participation in local affairs that directly concerned them. Now it is true that the parlements had rarely shown high regard for the authorities in the field. The magistrates scorned their ignorance and pettiness and derided their pretensions. Nevertheless, the sovereign courts depended upon them to maintain order, enforce the law, implement *arrêts de règlement* and parlementary sentences, and provide information on the turn of events. The revolt of the local police against liberalization made a powerful impression on the magistrates; a large majority of them favored a strengthening of local authority to deal with subsistence problems. Liberalization had already severely limited the powers of the local police; now, to protect liberalization, the government wanted to bind them in tighter manacles and stronger muzzles. The Parlement of Paris resolved not to permit the ministry to "tie the hands" and "shut the mouths" of the officials. Such action would serve only to prolong the dearth and "assure impunity" to the monopolists who could only be ferreted out from below by officials with "local knowledge" who stalked the movement of grain. The constraints which the letters patent placed on the police suggested to the Parisians that the government did not seriously mean to uncover monopolistic maneuvers. The Rouennais warned that, by dishonoring the local police in the public eye, in order to destroy their moral authority at the same time that it circumscribed their legal authority, the government was laying waste to the very foundations of law and order.

While the Parisian remonstrances dealt exclusively with the issues raised in the letters of 10 November, the Rouen Parlement moved beyond them to discuss the "theory" on which they were based. "The system called *economic*," the Rouennais charged, was another version of "the republic of Plato, an imaginary speculation." It was flawed in its assumptions about human nature, social organization, and public administration. Obsessed by their concept of the perfect "evidence" and infallibility of natural law, the *économistes* have forgotten the nature of man: "the passions will always resist this evidence." Private interest, the motive force on which the *économistes* built their system, the Rouen Parlement argued, will "perpetually violate" the natural order which it is supposed to guarantee. To establish "self-interest, this violent passion," as "the general law" would be "to cast us into the pure state of nature." It is because experience has taught us the danger of unleashing the passions in society under the name of "total liberty" that our laws must perforce be "restrictions on liberty." Grain liberty conjured for the Rouennais an apocalyptical vision whose horrors went beyond famines and riots to social and political disintegration, the logical consequence of unchecked liberty:

> Suppress all the Regulations, leaving only an unlimited liberty [!] the balance-spring of society will be destroyed; the Peoples will be [indiscriminately] blended; the Sovereign will be nothing more than a magnate distinguished by some sort of mark but without any power to be useful; thus, this system which appears to lay the foundation for everything tends in fact to shake and destroy everything.

"Unlimited liberty" is not only "contrary to the happiness of your subjects," the Parlement informed the king, but it is also "an Alteration of the French Constitution."

Given their past record and style of opposition, it seems hardly surprising that the Rouennais would end on a constitutional note. After all, they fought virtually every other issue on constitutional grounds, for it flattered their self-regard and gave their obstructionism a certain luster of coherence and legitimacy. Yet the argument over grain did not conform to the usual criteria for constitutional bickering.[20] The Rouennais were not trying to place limits on royal power and enhance their own authority in the usual way. The Parlement did not pretend that the king had done something illegal according to its interpretation of fundamental law, the cumulative wisdom which formed the base of its constitutionalism. The grain question ran *deeper* than fundamental law; it raised questions not so much about the legal constitution of the

---

20 Cf. the Rouen remonstrances of 26 Feb. 1771, which suggest the extent to which the critique of liberalism eddied *against* the main currents of eighteenth century parlementary political theory: "Every law which guarantees property is fundamental law, anything which violates it attacks the constitution of your state."

monarchy—the habitual preoccupation of remonstrances—as about the very nature of the social and political structure. Instead of swaggering, the magistrates trembled with fear, even as they admonished. Unlimited liberty, they maintained, was not merely contrary to the French Constitution; it was incompatible with "a monarchical constitution" of any type. In retrospect, the warnings of the Rouen court against the liberal ethic seem much less hysterical and hyperbolic than they must have appeared in the narrow context of the letters patent of November tenth. But even in their own time, as we shall see, they were beginning to gather a worried audience in many quarters.

The Rouen remonstrances, rewritten several times in committee, did not reach the king until several months after the promulgation of the letters patent. By that time, the court had already launched the policy it would pursue for the next two years: a refusal to enforce the liberal laws in its jurisdiction, combined with a discreet effort to assist local authorities who wished to reestablish police controls. This shift from conventional to a sort of guerilla warfare was based on the pragmatic calculation that, while the government would surely reject the proposals to jettison the reforms, it would almost certainly not engage in a costly, raucous campaign to force liberalization down the throats of the Rouennais. The Normandy Parlement correctly supposed that the ministry, in order to devote its energy to enforcing the liberal program in less hostile regions, would tolerate a large measure of *de facto* defiance of the law of the land. With a view toward reconquering the province when more favorable circumstances developed, the government tried to hold some ground in Normandy by continuing to encourage the merchant community, relying on the influence of the intendant, and repairing damages caused by local authorities through direct action of the royal council.

At the very center of things, the Paris Parlement could not turn its back on the government with the ease of the Rouennais. It had no confidence that a strategy of sabotage could work and it feared the confusion and disorder that it would produce, if in fact it could be implemented on the massive scale of the Paris jurisdiction. Moreover, such an approach begged the fundamental questions concerning liberalization and the grave social and economic disorganization which accompanied it. Unlike their Rouen colleagues, the Parisian magistrates responded succinctly and rapidly to the letters patent of November tenth and asked Louis XV to reply immediately to their objections. While waiting, later in the month, in a move meant to underscore its determination to unmask monopoly, the Parlement convoked and interrogated late into the night the baker-entrepreneur Malisset of Paris and Corbeil and a Vaugirard baker named Sauvageot, both "suspected of having a part in the monopoly." If the news of this investigation reached Leprévost de Beaumont in the prison cell which he had occupied now for only a little more than a week, he must have had a tremor of excitement. But it led to nothing; the Parlement accepted Malisset's written commission as agent for the king's grain without probing further and released him immediately. Sauvageot, on the other hand, a pitiful figure who had had the imprudence to make a wager with a *laboureur* that prices would continue to rise, was tossed in prison. The same day the king formally retracted the disputed letters patent and the Parlement sought yet another dramatic way to fortify its case.[21]

II

At the end of November, for the first time in 76 years, the Parlement decided abruptly to convene "all the estates of Paris" to an "Assembly of General Police" (or "General Assembly of Police" as some of the texts call it).[22] Previously convoked only in times of "extraordinary calamity," the function of the gathering was to assess the causes of and seek remedies for the crisis. Delamare traced the custom of holding assemblies as far back as the fourteenth century. They met at least six times in the sixteenth century and eight times in the seventeenth. Usually subsistence problems filled the agenda, though several assemblies dealt with the plague, the floating population, and other issues of public order.[23] The Parlement boasted that these meetings had often succeeded in uncovering

---

21 Draft, PG to Maupeou, 23, 24 Nov. 1768, BN, Coll. Joly 1138, fols. 115, 117; *Hardy's Journal*, 23, 25 Nov. 1768, BN, mss. fr. 6680, fols. 190–92; Lettres Ossolinski, 28 Nov. 1768, BHVP, mss. 627, fol. 193; *Journal encyclopédique* (Dec. 1 1768). The Rouen Parlement also pressed its investigation of monopoly despite the government's efforts to impede it. See, for example, Registre St. Martin, 8 Oct. 1769, A.D. S-M.

22 *Arrêt* of 25 Nov. 1768, *Recueil*, 92–93; Moreau, procurator at the Châtelet, AN, H* 1873, fol. 161; Lettres Ossolinski, 5 Dec. 1768, BHVP, mss. 627, fol. 194.

23 *Recueil*, 94–99; AN, H* 1873; *Hardy's Journal*, 28 Nov. 1768, BN, mss. 6680, fol. 192; Delamare, *Traité de la police*, II. 764, 867; BN, mss. fr. 21639 (Delamare), fol. 342; BN, mss. fr. 21640 (Delamare), fol. 21; BN, mss. fr. 21641 (Delamare), fols. 123–32; ordonnance of 1619, Archives Seine-Paris, mss. 6 AZ 133/2; article "Châtelet," in Diderot, *et al.*, *Encyclopédie*, II, 246; G. de Molinari, "Céréales," in Coquelin and Guillaumin, eds., *Dictionnaire de l'économie politique*, I, 303, 305; Alfred Franklin, *La Vie privée d'autrefois: L'Hygiène* (Paris, 1890), 93; Jacques Saint-Germain, *La Reynie*, 267; P. Bondois, "La Disette de 1662," *Revue d'histoire économique et sociale*, XII (1924), 53–118; Louis Thuillat, *La Reynie, premier Lieutenant Général*, 88.

"maneuvers" and generating recovery "with a surprising rapidity."[24] The bookseller Hardy noted in his journal that immediately after such an assembly in 1676—for which meeting, curiously, there is no documentary record—the price of wheat fell from 44 to 20 *livres* the *septier*.[25]

None of the assemblies seems to have achieved as much as either the magistrates or Hardy pretended. Of the most recent consultations, the one in 1662 failed to arrest the crisis and the one in 1692 merely flattered the reigning wisdom. The Parlement in 1768 did not count upon the Assembly to produce the sort of miracle which the public expected from the procession of the reliquary of Saint Genevieve, another traditional disaster measure. Clearly, the motive of the parlementaires who engineered the convocation was to embarrass the government and broaden the basis of criticism of royal policy. They wanted to demonstrate that the question at hand was not merely another phase in the interminable struggle between king and sovereign court, but a bipartisan issue, political to be sure, but not of the same order of politics, say, as the contemporary d'Aiguillon affair or a fiscal confrontation.

The Assembly did not, however, serve as an inert cipher for a monolithic opposition. There was no disciplined, rehearsed anti-orthodoxy that performed according to cue. The debates revealed a prodigious diversity of opinion; they are of interest precisely because they permit us to follow the lines of argument as we might in the minutes of a representative assembly, rather than simply take note of an impersonal institutional verdict, which conceals differences and creates a misleading impression of uniformity. At the end of the discussion, however, when it became a choice between granting liberty the totally free reign which its proponents claimed it required to be effective or petitioning the crown for a far-reaching revision of the liberal legislation, a large majority of the delegates found themselves in accord. Their agreement embodied a rebuke to the king and a refutation of the new political economy.

Meeting for only a day, the Assembly brought together on Monday, 28 November, almost 200 representatives of "all the companies and diverse orders of citizens" including deputies from the different chambers of the Paris Parlement, the Chambre des Comptes, the Cour des

---

The Procurator General Joly de Fleury consulted Delamare and prepared a complete reconstruction of the Assembly of 1692 which served as model. BN, Coll. Joly 1138, fols. 1–18 and Joly 1139, fol. 131.

24 *Recueil*, 92–93.

25 *Hardy's Journal*, 25 Nov. 1769, BN, mss. fr. 6680, fol. 192.

Aides, the Bureau des Finances, the Châtelet, the Hôtel de Ville, the six great guilds, the major religious communities and hospitals, and a number of "notables," four of whom were singularly equipped to proffer technical advice: the academician-agronomists Duhamel du Monceau and Fougeroux, the chief of the grain measurers, and a leading financier.[26] The Parlement had voted to call the Assembly on Friday afternoon, 25 November. The Procurator General issued most of the invitations on Sunday, the day before the meeting; some of the delegates did not learn that they were to take part until early Monday morning.[27] It is likely that the Parlement acted so brusquely in order to preclude governmental pressure and avoid charges of sensationalism. The government apparently did not learn of the court's intention until after passage of the *arrêt*.[28] Maupeou expressed concern about the authority that such a body could exercise; Joly assured him that it could not render *arrêts* or *arrêtés* but only "plans of conduct" and "plans of démarche."[29] Only the commonly felt urgency of the situation can explain the relative facility with which the Parlement got the highly status-conscious, proudly independent companies to meet under its aegis on such short notice. Nor were they able completely to avert squabbles over such matters—not mere formalities for the parties involved—as precedence and procedure.[30]

The First President D'Aligre, known for his extraordinary wealth and his ability to get on with the magistrates despite his devotion to

---

26 There is unfortunately no information regarding the process of selection of the deputies. In view of the persistence of a liberal element within the Paris Parlement, it would be particulary interesting to know how that body chose its delegates. See the address of the First President, *Recueil*, 104.

The physiocratic president of the Rouen Parlement, Bigot de Sainte-Croix, criticized the presence in the Assembly "d'un grand nombre d'ecclésiastiques et de religieux auxquels leur état semble interdire toutes spéculations politiques." Cited by Jean Egret, *Le Parlement de Dauphiné*, I, 185.

Galiani, who began to compose his *Dialogues* at the time of the Assembly and who may very well have used its *procès-verbaux* as a reference work, had the Chevalier remark: "Assemblez quelques Magistrats, quelques intendants, hommes de vertu et de génie... Priez-les de composer un nouveau code de police des bleds." *Dialogues*, ed. by Nicolini, 292.

27 BN, Coll. Joly 1138, fols. 43–51; extraordinary Sunday deliberation of the Bureau of the Hôtel-Dieu, 27 Nov. 1768, AAP, Hôtel-Dieu, #137; Deliberations of the Bureau of the Hôtel de Ville, AN, H* 1873, fols. 70ff.

28 Draft, PG to Saint-Florentin and Maupeou, 25 Nov. 1768, BN, Coll. Joly 1138. fol. 118. Cf. Roubaud, *Représentations*, 283.

29 PG to Maupeou, 26 Nov. 1768, BN, Coll. Joly 1138, fol. 133.

30 *Recueil*, 99–101, 155–57, 247; AN, H*1873, fols. 70ff; Deliberation of the Bureau, 7 Dec. 1768, AAP, Hôtel-Dieu, #137.

the government, opened the assembly with an address which betrayed strained loyalties, but nevertheless put the issue in clear terms.[31] "We have lived under two very different and very contrary jurisprudences," he said. In the old system "everything was anticipated," monopoly was "severely prohibited," and each local police official had "the most ample power to do everything which he believed useful for the provisioning of the markets of the areas of his territory." The liberal laws changed everything and for the first two years there were "no regrets." Prices rose with "just moderation," helping cultivators without harming consumers. Then we suffered bad weather, bad harvests, and widespread social disorder. Now grain is "dear and far beyond the faculties of the people." Yet D'Aligre refused to draw any explicit causal links between liberalization and the grave problems of the hour: that was for the assembly to decide. Although the "bitter pleas" of the people could not be ignored, D'Aligre reminded the delegates that the nation was divided on the issue: certain parts of the kingdom still favored the new system, "numerous writings" have appeared for and against, and within the Parlement of Paris itself voices have differed sharply.

Significant differences in tone and attitude emerged at the Assembly. A number of deputies openly despaired of the prospects of redressing the supply situation and restoring public order in the near future. Another group, nervous about the impact which the meeting would have upon public opinion and anxious to avoid debating in a crisis atmosphere, deprecated the gravity of the situation. "The misfortune is not as great as we feared," noted the President Lepelletier, who was not in the least sympathetic with liberalization.[32] Still others denounced this posture of restraint as a liberal trick to make everyone forget how bad things really are. Hocquart of the *Requêtes* believed it "indispensable to state by an Article that the whole Assembly unanimously thinks that grain was too dear, that this proposition simple in itself still seemed to be doubtful in the minds of the authors of the new system of the

---

31 Henri Carré, *La Fin des parlements, 1788–1790* (Paris, 1912), 2, 9–11, 47 for D'Aligre's background and *Recueil*, 102–110 for his speech.

32 *Recueil*, 223 (Lepelletier), 192–204 (Murard), 132–33 (Sartine), 157 (Levasseur d'Hérouville); AN, H* 1873, fols. 100–103 (Moreau). For Lepelletier's background, see François Bluche, *L'Origine des magistrats du parlement de Paris au 18ᵉ siècle* in *Mémoires de la Fédération des Sociétés Historiques et Archéologiques de Paris et de l'Ile de France*, V–VI (1956 for 1953–54), 273. On Murard, see J. Flammermont, *Le Chancelier Maupeou et les parlements*, 2nd. ed. (Paris, 1885), xvi.

unlimited liberty of the grain trade."[33] There was something tragi-comic in a request for a formal declaration of unequivocal *cherté* at a time when bread had passed four *sous* in the capital and reached even higher elsewhere, yet it bespeaks the conviction of these magistrates that the liberal ideology still had powerful influence.

Testard du Lys, the Lieutenant Criminel, underlined the "urgency" of popular needs and flatly blamed liberalization for producing the hunger and misery, which were driving increasingly large numbers of innocent people to commit crimes. His colleague Moreau, the Châtelet's procurator, who was not a partisan of the liberal reforms, nevertheless briskly rebutted Testard's contention. "There were never fewer major crimes," he claimed, and those who invoke high prices and suffering as an excuse seek "a pretext for slothfulness or libertinage."[34]

---

33 *Recueil*, 183. On Hocquart, see Bluche, *L'Origine des magistrats*, 214. Michau de Montblin, an influential young counselor in the First Enquêtes and the son of a *maître des requêtes* and intendant of commerce, took a similar, uncompromising position. *Recueil*, 189. On his family, see Bluche, *L'Origine des magistrats*, 313. Turgot acknowledged Montblin's growing prominence in the parlement but expressed contempt for his subsistence politics. Turgot to Dupont, 4 Jan. 1769, in *Œuvres*, ed. by Schelle, III, 53. It is interesting to note that Montblin and the liberal parlementaire Chavannes, who were bitterly divided on the grain issue, fought side by side against the Maupeou purge and suffered particularly harsh exiles. See Flammermont, *Maupeou*, 81, 220–21 and Pidansat de Mairobert, *Journal historique*, III, 237 (23 Aug. 1772).

34 *Recueil*, 133–41; AN, H* 1873, fol. 102: remonstrances of 19 Aug. and 4 Sept. 1768, in Flammermont, ed., *Remontrances du Parlement de Paris*, II, 944–48. Cf. similar sentiments in the representations of 22 March 1769, *ibid.*, III, 32.

The philosophes debated the question of crime specifically in its relation to misery. Mercier insisted on the need "to make a distinction" between theft motivated by hunger on the one hand and avarice or libertinage on the other. *Tableau de Paris*, XI, 311. Cf. *ibid.*, VI, 232 and Mercier's *L'An 2440*, I, 143n. Yet the *économiste* Condorcet insisted that "need does not give them [the people] any more [than other motives] the right to steal grain and money." *Lettre d'un laboureur de Picardie à M. N. auteur prohibitif à Paris* (1775), in E. Daire and G. de Molinari, eds., *Collection des principaux économistes*, XIV, 487. See also the exchange between D'Alembert and Frederick and the views of Brissot cited by A. Lichtenberger, *Le Socialisme au XVIII* siècle (Paris, 1895), 259–260, 414.

We need a serious study of criminality and criminology, based in part on the Y and X series at the Archives Nationales. The team study directed by F. Billacois is a step in that direction. See A. Abbiateci, *et al.*, *Crimes et criminalité en France sous l'ancien régime, 17e–18e siècles*, Cahier des *Annales*, #33 (Paris, 1971). Albeit suggestive, Arlette Farge's *Le Vol d'aliments à Paris au 18e siècle* (Paris, 1974) rests on a precarious source base and a simplistic conceptual foundation. There are many stimulating notions in Yves Castan's *Honnêteté et relations sociales en Languedoc* (Paris, 1974). The discussion has been recently enriched by the publication of a special number of the *Revue d'histoire moderne et contemporaine*, XXI (July-Sept. 1974) devoted to "marginality and criminality."

These and still other points of contention proved that the deputies did not all see things in the same manner and enabled the *économiste* Roubaud to remark, with ironic satisfaction, that they could not even agree whether the widely proclaimed dearth was a dearth after all.[35] The crucial question before the Assembly concerned the merits and defects of the liberal laws. It was believed that an emergency assembly meeting under the standard of "police" and dominated by men from institutions of a regulatory character and tradition would take a stand violently opposed to exportation, the issue on which so much public attention had been focused.[36] As expected, a number of deputies maintained that the liberals had exaggerated the decadent state of agriculture and belittled the real magnitude of exports, that exportation was one of the chief causes of the *cherté*, and that it was perverse and wasteful for the government to encourage the export of wheat needed by the nation while it paid bounties on imports of foreign grain.[37] But an influential bloc of deputies claimed to understand and sympathize with the July Edict and a far larger group criticized it constructively and with moderation. Although they felt that exports were presently inopportune or even dangerous and that the cut-off ceiling should have been lower (Sartine proposed 24 *livres* instead of 30, an idea which Miromesnil, Laverdy's friend, had proposed a year before), they agreed that exportation was "absolutely essential" for the reinvigoration of a

---

Modern criminologists have been impressed by the relationship which Testard suggested. See Y.M. Bercé, "Aspects de la criminalité au XVIIe siècle," *Revue historique*, 92nd year, CCXXIX (Jan.–March 1968), 35.

R. Cobb has written about the confluence of crime and dearth during the Revolution. *The Police and the People*, 271. See also the case of the citizen of Saumur, sentenced to death for theft but pardoned when "il fut reconnu qu'il avait volé pour manger" (1700). André Alem, *Le Marquis d'Argenson et l'économie politique* (Paris, 1900), 59n.

35 Roubaud, *Représentations*, 408–09. In fact, virtually no one doubted that there was a dearth situation. The question they pondered was whether the dearth was "real" or "artificial." See, for example, *Recueil*, 116, 162. For the significance of these distinctions, see above, chapter two. The deputies who emphasized the importance of exports tended to argue that the dearth was indeed real as a result of this drainage. The deputies who focused on the disruption of internal trade were more inclined to see the dearth as "artificial." Their point was to highlight an ominously paradoxical situation in which high prices subsisted despite the availability of relatively ample supplies.

36 Lettres Ossolinski, 5 Dec. 1768, BHVP, mss. 627, fol. 194.

37 *Recueil*, 39–40, 136–37, 140, 189, 219–23, 230–31, 233–35; AN, H*1873, fol. 108. Galiani, Chamousset, and later Malthus warned against the "imbecility" of those who count on compensating exports with imports. Galiani's phrase, in a letter to Madame D'Epinay, 1 Sept. 1770, in Asse, ed., *Lettres*, I, 131; Chamousset, *Œuvres*, II, 282; Malthus, *On Population*, ed. by G. Himmelfarb (New York, 1960), 421.

"lethargic" agriculture.[38] In the end, to be sure, the assembly decided "almost unanimously," in the words of one observer, that continued exporting was contrary to "the interests of the people," but it would be misleading to ignore the ambivalence of many deputies.[39]

It is equally important, however, to remember that the bulk of the deputies did not regard exportation, despite its salience in the public mind, as the most delicate and decisive issue. In the last analysis, whatever its magnitude and psychological impact, exportation was a "secondary cause" of the troubles, as a magistrate later remarked.[40] The Parlement of Paris had acted on this premise from the very beginning; it agonized over the May Declaration, but once it agreed to concede internal liberty, it readily approved the July Edict. On this point the deputies agreed with the ministry's position, for the letters patent of early November clearly argued that May, not July, cut to the heart of the quarrel. President Murard of the *Enquêtes* spoke for a large portion of the assembly when he said that monopoly was "infinitely more dangerous" than free exporting.[41] The fundamental questions raised by the May Declaration, as the assembly saw it, were the nature of the grain trade, the meaning of liberty, and the responsibilities of the governors to the governed.

The permissive conception of the grain trade aroused little support from the majority of delegates. A handful, led by the leading liberal in the Paris Parlement, the *grand'chambrier* Chavannes, argued for a totally untrammelled freedom for merchants to operate "as it will please them," viewed stockpiling, off-market transactions, and secrecy as absolutely necessary for the proper functioning of commerce, and defended the right of the merchants to a "very considerable profit" for their services.[42] But most of the deputies believed that grain, as an article of vital necessity, had to be treated differently from all other goods in commerce. "Obstruction is the destruction of trade," Lebegue, a secretary of the king, readily admitted. "But," he

---

38 *Recueil*, 130–31,148–49,154,192–97; Miromesnil to CG, 21 Dec. 1767 in LeVerdier, ed., *Correspondance Miromesnil*, V, 67.

39 Desaubiez, *Le Bonheur public*, 66.

40 BN, Coll. Joly 1109, fol. 215. The magistrates of the Provence Parlement observed that it was not against exports, but "against the free circulation [of grain] that the principal effort is directed." Letter to king, 21 Nov. 1768, B. 3677, A.D. B-du-R. Cf. also Moreau's letter of 2 Oct. 1768, AN, F[11] 1179.

41 *Recueil*, 192–204.

42 *Ibid.*, 166–172, 192–204, 206–212. The *Ephémérides du citoyen* later hailed Chavannes' speech and Baudeau praised his "enlightenment," "probity," and "patriotism." *Ephémérides* (1769), II, 122–25; *Nouvelles éphémérides* (1775), I, 115–124. The liberal press published parts of Chavannes' speech; manuscript copies also circulated in liberal milieu. C. 2420, A.D. B-du-R.

went on to say, "when it is a question of grain, primary matter of the food of men, one will not think that liberty is obstructed when it is subjected to laws which oppose avidity and illicit gains."[43] "What will the merchant regard as a sufficient profit?" asked President Lefebvre, one of the leading figures of the Parlement. It is in the nature of commerce, he answered, to seek greater and greater profits. Without police controls "all the speculations of the merchant tend to produce *cherté*, to sustain it, & to increase it."[44] All of these speakers rejected the liberal-utilitarian notion of a happy convergence of private and public interest.[45] Unchecked self-interest betrays the public good, according to the Advocate General Séguier, and "sacrifices everything to the inordinate desire to make a fortune and rapidly amass riches." The lesson was clear: the government must not, in Lepelletier's words, "abandon the consumer, who could not do without bread, to the law that the cupidity of the merchant would impose upon him."[46]

Liberty, in Séguier's traditional police view, authorized a man to work for his happiness only in ways which did not "trouble" that of other men. What we see now, another parlementaire contended, is "a liberty unfortunately degenerated into license."[47] This of course was the great fear of the police, what they had always predicted would happen were liberty unleashed. The rest of the causal chain was simple to follow: license engendered monopolies, which plunged the nation into crisis. On the basis of "personal" observations in the Beauce during the past three years, a *maître des comptes* affirmed that the present "disorder" had no other cause than "monopolies and evil maneuvers," none of which could have occurred had not the reform legislation "tied the hands" of the local police.[48] Lefebvre used the same image, a staple in the protest refrain from the local officials and one of the keys to understanding the problem of liberalization: "the police, the administration itself, have their hands tied." We find ourselves, Lefebvre went on, in an absurd situation in which "the merchant can do

---

43 *Recueil*, 151.
44 *Ibid.*, 237, 239. On Lefebvre, see Bluche, *L'Origine des magistrats*, 261.
45 Cf. Grimm's *Correspondance littéraire*, ed. by Tourneux, X, 516–17 (Dec. 1774): "... the experience of every day and the history of all times, doesn't it prove that private interest and the public interest have almost always a very different course... and that the greatest art of the legislator is to force them to come together or to support each other."
46 *Recueil*, 115.
47 *Ibid.*, 190–91 (Hocquart).
48 *Ibid.*, 248.

anything to the people & neither the Judge *nor even the Sovereign* can do anything to the merchant to whom the law has given immunity."[49] Even Sartine, who was closer to Chavannes than to the parlementary presidents on many issues, defined the grain trade, as the police always had, in terms of a public service, as "a tribute that society is empowered to demand."[50]

It followed that the state's highest interest was to assure the subsistence of the people. It was "infinitely more important for the State," Lepelletier maintained, to "give an entire people the means to feed itself" than "to enrich a few individuals."[51] On other issues—fiscality is the most prominent—when it became a question of choosing between the interest of the many and that of the few, magistrates like Lepelletier were less avidly self-denying. Moreover, Lepelletier and many of the other deputies were landowners who stood to profit from the *bon prix* which liberalization sought to produce. What caused them to demur on liberalization was neither a paroxysm of altruism or statesmanship on the one hand, nor a wile of demagogy on the other, though their enemies accused them of the latter and their friends congratulated them for the former. Rather, it was a sense of fear or alarm, more sophisticated and less visceral than the sensation experienced by the people, but not unlike it. "In these moments of crisis," the *économiste* Dupont scornfully noted, "... the Magistrates ... become *people* themselves."[52] "Everyone is *people*" said Joly de Fleury, "when they lack bread."[53]

Now the deputies did not lack bread, but they were frightened by the effects of scarce and dear bread upon the social order. For the state and the estates to survive, they had to pay a certain price for social peace. "Our predecessors," Séguier asserted, were always prepared to pay this price: "all their policy on this matter was to give to the most considerable portion of the state, to the People, bread at the lowest possible price."[54] Like Necker and the other theorists of social equilibrium in a society rent with inequality, Séguier saw it as part of the tacit bargain by which the rulers assumed responsibility and the ruled submitted. A policy of government which ignored this responsibility and made turbulence endemic, he suggested, would undermine the political and

---

49 *Ibid.*, 238–39.
50 *Ibid.*, 130–31.
51 *Ibid.*, 226.
52 Dupont to Prince Carl Ludwig, 1773, in Knies, ed., *Dupont Correspondence*, II, 146.
53 Speech of 5 July 1763, *Recueil*, 48.
54 *Ibid.*, 112.

social structure. Few of the deputies could listen with equanimity to *maître des comptes* Clement's analysis—strikingly like Necker's reaction to Turgot in the next decade—of "this combat" between rich and poor for wealth on the one side and subsistence on the other.[55]

Lepelletier understood that the purpose of the liberal program was not merely to "enrich a few individuals." He knew that it aimed at economic growth and agricultural renewal. To achieve this end, the liberals wanted to raise prices. They not only "fulfilled their goal," he argued, "but they overshot it." Give "him who cultivates grain & him who sells it the liberty to draw a profit," he allowed, "up to the point which will not reduce to famine or indigence those who must nourish themselves on it." On balance, the social trade-off realized by liberalization was disastrous. "The people cannot live at the price to which bread has risen," Lepelletier told the assembly.[56] Not even good citizens could be expected to forbear infinitely. Clement frankly accepted the prospect that many of the poor would perish in their struggle "to wring" wages commensurate with the price rise from their employers. In the end, by the "commiseration of the proprietors"—that is, as a result of their fear of insurrection and turmoil—the workers will win the new subsistence minimum.[57] The Malthusian prospect, with its peril to the social order, horrified the other deputies. Nor were they optimistic about a short-run accommodation between workers and employers, in the countryside (where the *économistes* wrongly predicted these pressures would not exist) as well as the cities. Lepelletier and Montblin of the *Enquêtes* foresaw more and more unemployment and a widening of the fatal wage lag. Experience, they declared, has revealed the speciousness of the physiocratic assurances to the people and underlined the urgency of returning to the "judicious spirit of the old police."[58]

---

55 *Ibid.*, 161–64.

56 *Ibid.*, 226, 228.

57 *Ibid.*, 161–64.

58 *Ibid.*, 183, 228. Like Joly in 1763 and Necker in 1775, the critics of the physiocratic wage theory rejected the suggestion that only urban workers—not the rural laboring force—would suffer from a price-wage lag. See *ibid.*, 37; remonstrances of Rouen Parl., 25 Jan. 1769, Registre St. Martin, A.D. S-M.; and Necker, *Sur la législation des grains*, 179–180. Cf. J.-B. Briatte's blistering refutation of the *économistes'* "horribly cruel assertion" that wages kept pace with commodity prices. *Offrande à l'humanité* (Amsterdam, 1780), 159–60.

The failure of wages to keep pace with prices was one of the major items of criticism from field administration. Even where bread was in relatively plentiful supply, the loaf "cost more than the day [of labor]." This, said an intendant, was the "crisis of the people." The "number and the competition of unemployed hands diminishes the price of the day," even as

A revival of the old police spirit, these critics of liberalization insisted, did not mean a return to the dark ages. They refused to be constrained by the liberal formulation of the question which allowed, as a matter of principle, no middle ground. "It has been presented in this manner in several writings by the Authors of the new system," said Lepelletier, "because the idea of liberty, always being agreeable, & that of prohibitions always being repugnant, they believed that many persons, without examining further, would decide for that which one covered with the name of liberty." (The parlements, of course, to capitalize upon the fashion of the age, had used the same ploy countless times on other issues.) Lepelletier spoke for what he called "a legitimate, honest, moderate liberty," between what he admitted had sometimes been "excessive prohibitions," on the one hand, and "an absolute license, exempt from all rules, shielded from all inspection," on the other.[59] Pursuing the same theme, Séguier claimed that a return to the old laws did not mean strict adherence to legislation, such as the 1723 Declaration on mandatory market exchanges, which everyone considered overdrawn.

In anticipation of some of the severest antiphysiocratic criticism of the seventies, Séguier emphasized the contrast between his relativism and the absolutism of the *économistes*. He did not find it strange that the leading voices in "several provinces" praised liberalization. He accepted the thesis that "the most entire liberty" was a "genuine good" in the seaports and especially in the Mediterranean provinces, but, he insisted, "what is good in one place becomes harmful or dangerous in another."

---

grain prices continued to rise or remain high. Cypierre to bishop of Orléans, 23 Sept. 1768 and to CG, 9 Oct. 1768 in C. Bloch, *Correspondance inédite de l'intendant Cypierre*, 85–86, 123; SD at Dourdan to Cypierre, 24 Sept. 1768, *ibid.*, 100; état de la situation actuelle (1768), C. 81, A.D. Somme; état des Récoltes, St. Quentin, C. 82, A.D. Somme; état des Récoltes, Mondidier and état des Pertes, Ponthoile, *ibid.*; IN. of Lorraine to CG, 30 Dec. 1771, AN, F[11] 223; Anon., "Mémoire sur l'exportation des grains," Oct. 1768, Arch. Armée, Al/3677, no. 113. Nor did the situation appear to improve in the early seventies; on the contrary, it seemed even more acute than before. In the north, a subdelegate reported that the competition for jobs "forces the workers to decrease the price of their days even as that of grain increased...." Belterre to IN. of Picardy, 27 Jan. 1772, C. 84, A.D. Somme. Cf. the similar appraisal which the subdelegate of Alençon made for the intendant of that generality, 22 Oct. 1773, C. 89, A.D. Orne. In the south, a correspondent depicted for the intendant of Languedoc "a tableau too frightening for humanity" in which employers "profit from the hard necessity" of the worker by forcing them to work for wages (15 *sous* in the cities, 10 *sous* in the countryside, 5 *sous* for women) too low to enable them to buy bread. 28 April 1773, C. 2914, A.D. Hér.

59 *Recueil*, 225–26.

Liberty worked well in England, but its success there was of no relevance for France because the two nations were not at all comparable in character, laws, and physiognomy. Similarly, the Advocate General reasoned, it would be a "dangerous evil" to impose this complete liberty upon Paris, whose geographical position and needs differed so markedly from those of the maritime provinces.[60] Séguier followed Lefebvre's premise—widely and instinctively shared by a great many Frenchmen— that provisioning questions were "in the moral order" where they depended on changing circumstances, rather than in the natural or "physical" order of the physiocrats, where they depended on fixed, universal relationships. As a result, it made sense to think of such matters as liberty in relative terms, in terms of good and bad in relation to time, place, and dose.[61]

The spokesmen of the movement against liberalization assailed the mainsprings of its ideology as well as its policies. Corrosive philosophical speculations produced abusive grain speculations. The new political economy was not merely erroneous; venturing into the realm of everyday material life, it became a public menace. For President Lefebvre, the liberty of the *économistes* was atavistic and antisocial. It implied a chaotic state of nature in which strife replaced structure and private interests crushed the public good. Just as the king, in the famous castigation of the Paris Parlement known as the *séance de flagellation*, depicted himself as a bulwark against "all new systems and all these expressions invented to accredit the most false and dangerous idea," so Lefebvre saw it as "the most urgent duty" of the magistrates to "defend the State against novelties," which threatened "the conservation of the inhabitants of France."[62]

President Lepelletier frankly characterized the *économistes* as enemies of the public good. The liberal ideologues, he charged, preached the seditious and "inhuman" dogma of constant *cherté*, equating the *bon prix* with an "excessive" price beyond the reach of the people. He intimated that publicists who promoted such a program of exploitation

60 *Ibid.*, 114–16, 123, 225. Cf. the similarities between the arguments of Séguier and Galiani: Galiani to Suard, 7 Sept. 1770 in Asse, ed., *Lettres*, I, 140 and *Dialogues*, ed. by Nicolini, 13.
61 *Recueil*, 243.
62 *Recueil*, 241–42; 3 March 1766, in Flammermont, ed., *Remontrances du Parlement de Paris*, II, 559. Cf. the attitude of the Dijon Parlement: "all the reasonings of the speculatives run aground against the facts." Remonstrances of 14 Aug. 1770, cited by Parmentier, *Recherches sur les végétaux nourrissans qui, dans les temps de disette, peuvent remplacer les alimens ordinaires* (Paris, 1781), 343–44.

and extravagant profits probably had a venal interest in it.[63] Lepelletier denounced them for the same kind of crime for which the king dissolved the parlements two years later. In the preamble of the famous Maupeou edict, Louis XV condemned their *"esprit de système*, as uncertain in its principles as it is bold in its undertakings" and the "new ideas … capable of troubling the public order." The economic liberalism and the pretensions of the *économistes* were as abhorrent to the leaders of the Paris Parlement as the constitutional liberalism and pretensions of the parlements were to the monarch. "A crowd of writers without mission & without power to express the public wish," said Lepelletier, "had pretended to be its organs in extolling the wildest systems on this subject [of subsistence]." Henceforth, however, he declared, the *économistes* "will no longer be able to present, as the public desire, false & dangerous views, against which, on this day, has risen the general wish of the citizens of all the orders."[64]

If the assembly had been convened, however, simply to excoriate another dangerous intellectual "system," it would have been a commonplace affair, like the numerous judicial, ecclesiastical, and university assemblies which periodically banned and burned books. Without overlooking their significance, it must be emphasized that the assembly was only incidentally concerned about the peril of ideas. This was not an airy debate about political and economic theory. The "system" in question, or at least significant parts of it, had been made the law of the land. It was defended not only by professional colporteurs of ideas but by ministers and royal councillors. The debate in the assembly turned on concrete matters of policy and practical details of administration. The deputies addressed themselves not to vague potential threats to the public order but to the sources of damage already done and likely to be done in the immediate future. At the end of the day, when the deputies were asked to formulate a set of collective recommendations, which would ultimately be presented to the king, it was this pressing question of police, not theory, which was uppermost in their minds.

---

63 Cf. the Intendant Cypierre's remark on the *économiste* Letrosne "… who is known to be engaged in grain commerce, and so hated, not to say scorned, in this city [Orléans] that the people, seeing him return from Paris at the moment when grain went up in price, cited him in the middle of the market as the principal author of their misery." To T. de Montigny, 7 Sept. 1768 in C. Bloch, *Correspondance inédite de l'intendant Cypierre*, 63.

64 *Recueil*, 224–25; Edict of Dec. 1770, cited by Flammermont, *Maupeou*, 116. Cf. Galiani to d'Epinay, 22 Dec. 1770, in Asse, ed., *Lettres*, I, 192; Linguet, *Réponse aux docteurs modernes* (Paris, and London, 1771), part III, 73.

Despite their disagreements on the meaning of liberty, the success of the old prohibitions, the necessity of reform, the rights of commerce, and the claims of agriculture upon the nation, the majority of deputies obviously felt that liberalization had wrought infinitely more harm than good and that the government was set upon a disaster course. The government's intransigent program for the rigorous application of the liberal laws as they were originally conceived, presented to the assembly by Chavannes, won no support. A single deputy voted for an equivocal, unwieldy compromise devised by Murard and Clément to salvage the core of liberalization, while meeting some of the major objections of its critics.[65] In the final roll call of the session, the deputies gave "almost unanimous support" to a tough proposal sponsored by Lepelletier which clearly called for a repudiation of the liberal system.[66] His projected *arrêt* would beseech the king to issue new legislation "modifying" the laws of 1763–64 by "renewing the dispositions of the old ordinances which for such a long time assured to the citizens a subsistence in proportion to their faculties and to the State a happy tranquility." Specifically, it asked for obligatory declarations of name, address, stocks, and destinations by the merchants, for the restriction of all transactions to the public marketplace, for a buying schedule which would favor consumers and bakers over traders, for police authority to constrain merchants and owners of grain to provision markets "in case of necessity," and for a complete suspension of all exports for at least a year—in a word, a return to "the spirit of the old police." Drafted as a political program of action, the recommendations of the assembly allowed for no nuances. Séguier had characterized the triumph of liberty as a "revolution" in politics and in ideas. The final report of the Assembly of General Police was forthrightly counter-revolutionary.

III

Virtually to the letter, the Paris Parlement embodied the assembly's project in an *arrêt* on December 2, which it hoped would make a special impression on the monarch. If "tears" and "lamentations" did not reach the crown, the magistrates wrote, surely the king would hear the "voice of the people" expressed by the recent assembly, which had drawn together "the Noble and the Commoner, the

---

65 *Recueil*, 166–76, 202–210.
66 *Ibid.*, 229–33, 251; *Hardy's Journal*, 28 Nov. 1768, BN, mss. fr. 6680, fols. 192–193.

Bourgeois and the Merchant, the Poor and the Rich, the Proprietor of real estate and the businessman, the Private Person and the Public Man, the Ministers of Religion and those of Justice." And the "voice of the people," the Parlement reminded God's viceroy, "... in this matter more than any other, is the voice of God, that is, the expression of the truth itself." ("Who is this people whose voice is the voice of God?" asked Roubaud, sometime cleric and full-time *économiste*, "is it the people of the cities or the people of the countryside, the people of the capital or the people of the provinces, an educated people or an ignorant people?") The chastening idea that the Parlement was trying to convey through the *vox populi* invocation was as much political as it was moral. It meant not that the people's instinct was wiser or holier than the king's, but that it was in this affair *irresistible*.

The Parlement claimed that there was overwhelming evidence, not the neo-Cartesian variety favored by the *économistes*, but the kind measured in terms of prices and disorders, that liberalization had worked a disaster. It was unimaginable that the king would knowingly perpetuate "a system so harsh" to the poor who could not procure bread "enough for their subsistence" at the current levels. Though flawed by "some excessive prohibitions," the old legislation "contained nothing that was not prudent and equitable" for the cultivators and the consumers. The new system had turned "the balance" drastically against the latter, "authorizing a license without limits," assuring "impunity to all sorts of frauds [and] to the most odious maneuvers," favoring the greedy grain barons over the small traders who used to swarm in the markets, and "exposing the people ... to perish of hunger." Liberty was "legitimate," contended the Parlement, to the extent that it was "compatible with the public interest"; it lost legitimacy the moment it clearly began to ravage that interest. By instituting the new system, the king showed that he misconceived the public interest. By maintaining it, Louis placed the kingdom in jeopardy and failed in his primary responsibility to his subjects: to make it possible for them to find bread sufficient to meet their needs and commensurate with their means. Ultimately, the question concerned the legitimacy of the king as much as that of his liberal policy. Would the monarch who had, in a sense, desacralized bread by abandoning the stewardship of subsistence recognize the voice of God?[67]

---

67 *Recueil*, 252–54, 260; *Conseil Secret*, 13 Dec. 1768, AN, X^{lb} 8957; Roubaud, *Représentations aux magistrats*, 385–86. On the tradition of invoking the Vox populi, see George Boas' *Vox*

The king rejected the assembly's recommendations in a mild and evasive reply, which Turgot considered "weak and without dignity." The government attributed the *cherté*, as it had before, to bad harvests and "the anxieties of weak and prejudiced spirits," but for the first time it also blamed the problem on the maneuvers of "interested persons" and on the "prosperity" of *laboureurs* who had profited from the price rise and were now in no hurry to supply the markets. The government envisaged no changes in policy to combat the *cherté*. It would continue to provide king's grain and it would enforce the liberal legislation. Louis chided the Paris Parlement for pretending to speak for the whole nation. He boasted that he had allies among its own sister courts, several of which construed the public interest differently from the Parisians. "All my Subjects are equally dear to my heart," averred the king—a claim which the Rouen magistrates had bitterly contested several months earlier.[68]

The Parlement planned to express its unhappiness in "iterative remonstrances" after the Christmas recess. Meanwhile another of the periodic clashes over finances strained relations further between the crown and the sovereign court. In a strongly worded remonstrance attributed to the abbé Terray, copies of which were "allowed to leak out" to the public, the Parlement painted a "sad tableau of the misfortunes of France and of the disorder of her finances" and protested against the extension of the second *vingtième* and certain indirect taxes and the issue of a new loan. In early January 1769, the king forced registration in a *lit de justice* and contemptuously rebuffed the worn and deficient remedies which Terray proposed, some of which he would bring with him to the Contrôle-Général a year later.[69] The conduct of another future member of the triumvirate, D'Aiguillon, whose ministerial destiny was no more likely than Terray's at the end of 1768, was also the subject of parlementary remonstrances.[70]

Populi. Essays in the History of an Idea (Baltimore, 1969). See also Rousseau's remark: "often injustice and fraud find protectors; they never have the public on their side; in this way the voice of the people is the voice of God." C.E. Vaughan, ed., *Political Writings of Rousseau* (Cambridge, 1915), II, 256.

68 *Conseil Secret*, 19 Dec. 1768, 17 Jan. 1769, AN, X^{1b} 8957; AN, O^1 pièce 349; *Recueil*, 261–62; Lettres Ossolinski, 26 Dec. 1768, BHVP, mss. 627, fol. 202; *Hardy's Journal*, 13, 19 Dec. 1768, BN, mss. fr. 6680, fols. 196–97; Turgot to Dupont, 4 Jan. 1769, in Turgot, *Œuvres*, ed. by Schelle, III, 53.

69 *Conseil Secret*, 20–21 Dec. 1768 and 11 Jan. 1769, AN, X^{1b} 8957; *Le Nouvelliste suisse* (Jan. 1769), 25–28; Bachaumont, *Mémoires secrets*, ed. by P.-L. Jacob (Paris, 1883), 330 (14 Jan. 1769); *Mercure historique* (Jan. 1769), CLXVI, 55–57. Cf. the similar complaints drawn up by the Parl. of Metz, 27 Feb. 1769, B. 467 (registre secret) and the remonstrances prepared by Malesherbes in *Le Nouvelliste suisse* (Feb. 1769), 41–43.

70 Lettres Ossolinski, Dec. 1768, BHVP, mss. 627, fol. 196.

On Friday, 20 January, after preparing another remonstrance asking the king to revise the liberal laws, the Parlement passed a spectacularly defiant *arrêt* in which it took it upon itself to legislate the revisions which it had vainly urged the king to make.[71] After a sarcastic preface ("in order to conform to the known intentions of the said Seigneur King ..."), the *arrêt* ordered all those who wished "to make use of the liberty" to enter the grain trade—the irony was either unconscious or heavy-handed—to file the very sort of declaration with the local police from which the May Law explicitly dispensed them. In addition, the *arrêt* enjoined the Procurator General to open a formal investigation into grain trade maneuvers in the hinterland of the jurisdiction. The Parlement voted to publish the *arrêt* that very day and post it that night so that Parisians could see it before, as expected, the royal council quashed it. The aim of the magistrates was to dramatize the stalemate between king and court and to enlist the full weight of public opinion against the government, implicitly depicted as the villain, the defender of *cherté*.

Eighteen months earlier, the Parlement had launched its campaign for a reassessment of liberalization in a low-key, unpublicized manner precisely because it understood the grave danger of stirring the apprehensions of people who were already uneasy and volatile in mood. Indeed, throughout the political wars of the Old Regime, it was tacitly agreed to suspend public hostilities during such general emergencies as dearths when they were likely to enhance anxieties and contribute to disorder. After repeated failures to influence the king through diplomatic channels, the Parlement turned to the Assembly of Police as a safe surrogate for public opinion and as a warning to the government that it was prepared to escalate its attack. Still, the Assembly was organized without fanfare and the deputies consciously kept their voices down so that only the ministers and not the public would hear them. When it became clear that the king had no intention of honoring any of the Assembly's recommendations, in frustration, the magistrates decided to take the issue outside the Palais, to the people, where they had often found favor in the past, albeit in situations less fraught with risk. They hoped that this act of impudence would somehow provoke the king to assume his responsibilities.

The *arrêt* infuriated the king and his ministers; Sunday, approximately thirty-six hours after its passage, the council annulled it, save

---

71 *Conseil Secret*, 20 Jan. 1769, AN, X[1b] 8957; *Recueil*, 263–65; *Hardy's Journal*, 20 Jan. 1769, BN, mss. fr. 6680, fols. 208–209; Lettres Ossolinski, 23 Jan. 1769 BHVP, mss. 627, fol. 209.

for the clause launching an investigation into maneuvers.[72] The Parlement knew very well, the king was made to say in the accompanying message, that "His intention was to change nothing" in the liberal laws. The parlementary *arrêt* would have done nothing less than "destroy the liberty of this commerce." Deftly, the king refused to be drawn into a discussion of the merits of his subsistence policy and the effects of the *cherté*, turning the issue instead into one of obedience. Once again the Parlement had dared to deliver a "stroke against the legislative power of His Majesty." The king sought to discredit the sovereign court by explaining its opposition to liberalization in terms of its notorious record of resistance to the will of the government on a host of important matters. It was hardly surprising that a company of magistrates which had systematically obstructed reform during a half century would place "obstructions" in the way of commerce. On the liberty issue as on all the others, the king implied, the motive of the Parlement was political self-aggrandizement and its intention was to undermine the power of the throne.

Whether or not this charge was generally true across the century is a question which merits re-examination; in this instance at least, it was patently spurious. Far from seeking to limit the authority of kingship, the Parlement sought to prevent its erosion. The Parlement was concerned with its own destiny only indirectly, to the extent that it perceived that a diminution of royalty meant a loss, not a gain, in influence for the sovereign courts. The determination of the king to regard the quarrel as merely another partisan political confrontation made it less likely than ever that the government would relent on liberalization. For if the king deserted liberalization he would appear to be ceding, not to good sense, but to parlementary pressure. It was precisely to spare the king this embarrassment that the Parlement had convoked the Assembly of Police, an institution which historically had played a non-partisan role.

Nor was disobedience the only misconduct of which the Parlement was guilty. The king sharply condemned it for demagogy and agitation, for recklessly affecting "expressions tending to interest the People [in the affair], to excite their minds, and to augment their anxieties about the present and the future."[73] Similar charges were levelled in

---

72 Conseil Secret, 23 Jan. 1769, AN, X[1b] 8957; *Hardy's Journal*, 24 Jan. 1769, BN, mss. fr. 6680, fol. 209; *arrêt du Conseil*, 22 Jan. 1769, BN, Coll. Joly 1111, fol. 25.

73 An anonymous contemporary writer went a step further accusing the Parlements of Paris and Rouen of using "grand words of public welfare" and passing measures likely "to worry,

1775 by the friends of Turgot when his effort to reintroduce liberalization encountered difficulties not unlike those faced by the government at the end of the sixties. The "aim' of the Parlement's "bread
assemblies," warned Condorcet, "is to please the populace."[74] The
"motive" of the Parlement, wrote the abbé de Véri in reference to
an *arrêt* which asked the king to take steps to place bread at a price
within the reach of the consumers, was "a corporate interest: the
desire to inveigle the good will of the people in presenting itself as
their father."[75]

There is no question that the Paris Parlement assiduously cultivated
its popularity in the eighteenth century, a practice which the government naturally resented and feared. But one must not assume that its
popularity was either insidiously acquired or easily retained, or that
the Parlement embraced the subsistence issue merely to enhance its
prestige. All the evidence indicates that the magistrates were genuinely
concerned for the safety of the social and political order; if they had
been motivated exclusively or even primarily by a lust for acclaim from
below, they would not have approved the liberal innovations in 1763–
64, they would not have waited so long before speaking out or initiated their protests with such restraint, and they would not have been
divided amongst themselves on the issues. That, in fact, the Parlement
was popular suggests either that the public was stupid and gullible, as
the king's party liked to believe, or that it had a fairly clear idea of its
interests. In 1768–69, as in 1775, the "people" did not await a signal
from the sovereign court to become "interested" and involved in a question which concerned their material life. If the magistrates became the
"fathers" of the people, it was because the people had been orphaned;
the Parlement had no need to "inveigle" favor. "All Paris is parlementaire," Mercier later remarked. Since they had "no other organs," he
continued, "the people thus see in the parlement the assembly of magistrates ready to speak for them & to defend them."[76]

---

embitter, provoke the people to rise" at a time when they were "already only too disposed
to revolt." Instead of attempting to "calm" and "control" the people as they were supposed
to do, the Parlements manipulated them for political advantage, "inciting them indirectly to
commit acts of violence." "Réflexions sur les principes des parlemens de Paris et de Rouen
par rapport au commerce des bleds," Arch. AE, France 1375, fols. 293–304.

74 Condorcet to Turgot, 1775, in Henry, ed., *Correspondance Condorcet-Turgot*, 211. Cf. Arthur
   Young's admonition in his *Travels*, ed. by J. Kaplow, 386.

75 Abbé de Véri, *Journal*, ed. by J. de Witte, I, 293 (26 May 1775).

76 Mercier, *Tableau*, X, 281–82, 288. On the souvereign courts as "protectors of the people,"
   see the remarks of Malesherbes, a friend of the liberals who did not share their opinion on

At the end of January 1769, Hardy noted in his journal that the royal reply to the parlementary *arrêt* "excited the murmurs of the People" who believed that liberalization—they subsumed everything under the term "exportation"—was the source of the crisis and that the council's firm support for this policy meant that hard times would continue. Hardy also reported the rumor—another avatar of the famine pact persuasion, tailored to fit the needs of the moment—that Trudaine de Montigny composed the reply and that he put so much fervor into it because because he had a large share in the clandestine export enterprise, which sustained and profited from the *cherté*.[77]

Another observer, who had been sanguine about the prospects for a change in government policy in December, wrote in early February that it was certain that "nothing will be altered."[78] In a bitter rejoinder redolent of the tone of the remonstrances of the early sixties, written not by a young Turk from the *Enquêtes,* but a distinguished jurist of the *grand chambre,* Gars de Frémainville, dubbed "the Roman," the Parlement denounced liberalization as "a badly conceived and dangerous system" and promised to wage a relentless struggle for the application of its *arrêt.*[79] Repulsing the charges of inciting popular passions, the Parlement contrasted its "language of truth and humanity" with the king's lack of compassion and his unwillingness to examine the facts. Despite the government's campaign against the local police reaction and its solemn warning that it would not tolerate any official interference with the freedom of trade, the magistrates announced that they would encourage the officials within their jurisdiction to take firm action to unmask and repress "the odious maneuvers which tend to procure or maintain the *cherté* of grain and bread."

New representations submitted in mid-March developed the Parlement's thesis that the king had abdicated his leadership.[80] Instead

---

this matter. Remonstrances of the Cour des Aides, 18 Feb. 1771, cited by Flammermont, *Maupeou,* 269. Cf. on this point the *Mémoires du Baron de Besenval,* ed. by Berville and Barrière (Paris, 1821), 348.

77 *Hardy's Journal,* 24 Jan. 1769, BN, mss. fr. 6680, fol. 209.

78 Lettres Ossolinski, 13 Feb. 1769, BHVP, mss. 627, fol. 215. Cf. the *Mercure historique* (Feb. 1769), CLXVI, 191 : "It appears more and more that despite the representations that the Parlement has made, and that it might yet make to the King, His Majesty will change nothing in the Edicts...."

79 BN, Coll. Joly 1111, fols. 37–39; *Hardy's Journal,* 31 Jan. 1769, BN, mss. fr. 6680, fols. 211–212; Lettres Ossolinski, 9 Feb. 1769, BHVP, mss. 627, fol. 213; Délibérations du Bureau de la Ville, AN, H * 1873, fol. 256. Cf. Pidansat de Mairobert, *Journal historique,* IV, 342–343 (16 Oct. 1773).

80 *Conseil Secret,* 18 March 1769, AN, X[1B] 8957.

of asserting his authority and presence in matter of subsistence and grain commerce, he averted his eyes; he established neglect and non-vigilance as a fixed "principle of administration." Liberty seemed to have imposed more imperious inhibitions on the exercise of king-ship than police ever placed on the movement of grain. Instead of formulating a supply policy geared to meet the needs of the people, the government left all the choices to the proprietor of grain, "under the illusory pretext"—the keystone of the liberal arch—"that his pri-vate interest, properly understood, must lead him to the common good...." Instead of insisting upon publicity, the king invited the merchants to cloak their operations in a "veil" of "mystery," even as he shrouded the management of his own finances in secrecy. For the Parlement, the "principle" and "end" of the grain trade was "to assure the subsistence of the people," but for the government it was to create wealth—wealth which the court considered "absolutely fic-tional," for its counterpart was widespread misery. The Parlement took a stand that we would call populationist, arguing, as Mirabeau had before his conversion to physiocracy, that population, not wealth, was the true measure of a nation's "force and its power."

Like the government, the Parlement hardened its position. Whereas before it had been willing to accept the notion that liberalization might very well have made sense in the context of the years 1763–64 and that the origins of the crisis were, as the ministry insisted, "physical" and psychological, now it regarded the reforms as fatally flawed from the beginning and the great misfortunes that followed as the direct "result," not of the weather or of "weak spirits," but of the "new system." Even the king's grain distribution for which the Parlement had always expressed effusive gratitude—and which more than any other single factor spared the government a major upheaval in the capital—no longer escaped criticism. The court considered it a contradictory and prodigal policy to expend enormous resources from the public treasury to buy foreign grain, while letting national grain find vent abroad. This time the king did not bother to reply to the parlementary barrage and the Parlement, convinced that it was hopeless to pursue the matter in further remonstrances, abandoned its public campaign.

IV

In 1763, the government appeared to be politically as well as economi-cally bankrupt. It had just suffered at the hands of the parlements a defeat as humiliating as the one it sustained in the foreign war ending

that same year. Despite many encouraging signs of expansion—easier
to perceive in retrospect than they were for contemporaries to see—
important sectors of the economy languished. In the preceding decade
the Contrôle-Général had changed hands a half-dozen times. The
parlements quite rightly accused the government of ineptitude, arbitrariness, and corruption in management, and the government no less
persuasively charged the sovereign courts with self-regarding obstruction of urgently needed reforms. It often appeared that both sides were
resigned to the well-rehearsed impasse. Successive ministers followed
the routine of submitting substantially the same proposals, with slight
cosmetic disguises, time and again and the parlements responded
reflexively with the familiar shibboleths. The parlements were obdurate
and irascible, but the government behaved almost as perversely, refusing to accept the magistrates, in fact if not in right, as serious political
interlocutors, despite their obvious ability to thwart government initiatives, and preferring on many occasions confrontation and stalemate
to negotiation and transaction. Royal prestige was at a low ebb, as the
reactions to the Damiens affair and to the end of the war and as the
vignettes of the diarists testified. In 1763, the government of Louis XV
desperately needed a new beginning, a breath of fresh life.

Liberalization provided the government with the opportunity to
strike out on a new course. It had the merit not only of addressing
itself directly to a number of pressing problems, but of being politically viable. It had the prestige of scientific formulation; it was not a
brusque improvisation. It drew its sanction from nature's law; it was
not the product of ministerial opportunism. It was not an incidental
or short-run reform with a fixed expiration date or a mere technical
adjustment in commerce; liberalization was a major, drastic reform,
unprecedented in the cast which it took and meant to be permanent.[81]
None of the other "economic" reforms to which the government
turned after mid-century—land reclamation, enclosure, the easing of
restrictions on manufactures, etc.—had the extraordinary resonance
and the sweeping multiplier effects of liberalization. Geared specifically to promote agriculture and revitalize the economy, liberalization
marked the first triumph of the new political economy, whose logic
portended further changes in the approach to public administration.
The government believed that success in economic reform would
help clear the way for fiscal and institutional reforms. In any event,

---

81 Liberalization was, as the Parlement of Provence noted, a "coup d'état." Remonstrances,
26 June 1769, B. 3677, A.D. B-du-R.

a generous increase in national wealth would improve the financial situation of the government and give it greater freedom of action. The new political economy staked out an untouched, neutral ground for cooperation between crown and constituted bodies. By framing reform in terms of liberal discourse, the government hoped to avoid fatal squabbles over authority and constitutional law. The liberal laws had an immaculate conception and pointed the way towards a new relationship between king and parlements, provided both were willing to cede to the arbitration of natural law and utility.

Over the years, albeit usually for different reasons, parlementaires and reformers had assailed the excesses of the administrative monarchy: its proliferation of controls and controllers, its relentless officiousness, its rapacity, its subordination of a vast range of public and private activities to proto-bureaucratic regulation. The decision to renounce the old grain police was the most radical and significant departure from the mold of the administrative monarchy made in the Old Regime. Liberalization inverted the old priorities and redefined the traditional idea of responsibility. Provisioning was no longer the business of government; and business, not provisioning, was the chief purpose of agriculture.

The government was not oblivious to the perils of the liberal policy. That it was willing to risk so much suggests how important it regarded the reforms. Anticipating some difficulties, it took certain precautions where it felt most vulnerable. The ministry exempted Paris from the liberal legislation and readied the king's grain machinery in case of emergency. It could not, however, foresee a series of short harvests and it did not expect that liberalization would arouse such bitter and widespread opposition from below and from above. Yet the government refused to make any concessions. There were few major issues on which it showed such grim determination to prevail virtually at any cost. The king and his ministers had found a reform in which they believed and they clung to it longer than anyone could have predicted.

If the liberal approach, in a sense, took public policy out of the sphere of politics, the renunciation of traditional royal paternalism and state intervention politicized the subsistence question. Grain scarcity and high prices, which might have passed in other times as disruptive but inevitable facts of life, became widely associated with royal policy. In a similar conjuncture in the mid-seventies, after Turgot reintroduced the liberal measures and the Paris area was convulsed with the chain of subsistence mutinies known as the Flour War, the Paris Parlement told the king:

It was, Sire, in envisioning this system ... as destructive of all police that it was easy to see why the dearths anterior to liberty were accompanied by almost no trouble, while the recent *chertés* had successively occasioned movements in all your provinces; the peoples, tranquil then under the protection of the regulations, blamed only the seasons for the misfortunes, which they have believed since they should blame on the rules of the new administration.[82]

To be sure, the Parlement's analysis was tendentious; dearths often caused popular disturbances and the people were never tranquil about their bread. But the incidence of disorder was incomparably greater in the sixties (and in the seventies) than during any other time in the reign of Louis XV, and the government was implicated in a way that it never had been before. What distinguished the famine pact or plot persuasion of the sixties from earlier conspiratorial visions was precisely the political element, the formal complicity of the government. The mobilization of the people and the police into a powerful force of outraged and puzzled opposition graphically illustrated the sense of betrayal they felt. Turgot scoffed at the credulity and paranoia of the feeble-spirited, but he himself ascribed the Flour War to a sinister and venal plot involving the police and the people.[83] To vindicate liberalization, he became, in Linguet's harsh words, "the calumniator of his own subjects."[84]

In the sixties the government explained popular upheavals and police malaise in terms of "prejudices," which it chose to see as a form of ignorance rather than a way of life. To account for the police attitude, there is no need to impute either sordid or high-minded motives. They simply could not deal with the situation according to the instructions which the government gave them. On the one hand, they felt that those instructions were ill-advised and unwarranted and, on the other, they could not hold the people responsible, morally or criminally, for their expressions of fear and frustration. The

---

82 Remonstrances, 2–4 March 1776, in Flammermont, ed., *Remontrances du Parlement de Paris* III, 300. Cf. the municipality's critique of Turgot's policy, deliberations, 3 May 1775, AN, H* 1876, fols. 127–129 and Bachauraont's remark: "... many people attribute [the *cherté*] to the entire and unlimited liberty with respect to this commerce." *Mémoires secrets*, XXX, 212 (1 May 1775).

83 On the plot thesis, see Dupont to Prince Carl Ludwig, 15 Jan. 1783, in Knies, ed., *Correspondance Dupont*, 357–62; Bachaumont, *Mémoires secrets*, XXX, 217 (5 May 1775); Marmontel, *Mémoires*, ed. by M. Tourneux (Paris, 1891), III, 95; Véri, *Journal*, ed. by J. de Witte, I, 286 (26 May 1775); Coquereau, *Mémoires concernant... l'abbé Terray*, 286. Galiani hoped that the Flour War "will have taught M. Turgot and M. l'abbé Morellet to know Men and the world, which is not that of the works of the economists." Galiani to Epinay, 27 May 1775, in Asse, ed., *Lettres*, II, 197.

84 Linguet, *Annales*, VI, 305–306.

permissive father offered his people a *roi-laboureur*, but they demanded a *roi-boulanger*. The paternal king had been cruel in his punishment of subsistence usurers and magnanimous in his assistance to the needy innocent. The permissive monarch seemed to indulge the malefactors and even his charity was suspect. When he distributed the king's grain, he was called *roi-marchand de blé* and accused of speculating on the people's hunger.

In 1763–64 the Paris Parlement gave its approbation to liberalization, albeit with less enthusiasm than some of the other sovereign courts. For more than four years after the May Declaration, it made no public statement or private overture concerning liberalization. It withdrew its support for the reforms as a result of the prolonged subsistence crisis which began in 1765 and which provoked serious disruptions throughout its jurisdiction. The course of events persuaded the Parlement that the liberal reforms were largely responsible for the acuity, the breadth, and the persistence of the crisis. Charged with the execution of the "grand police" and the maintenance of law and order, the court was deeply impressed by the general outcry of the local officials. It regarded the popular revolts not as criminal outbreaks, but as legitimate and inevitable consequences of suffering and anxiety and as signs of a grave flaw in the public administration.

In reference to the grain riots of the mid-seventies, Condorcet wrote contemptuously of the people who "removed wheat by force, paid for it the price they desired, and believed their expedition legitimate because they had the *Right to Live*."[85] To be sure, the Parlement did not condone collective consumer extortion any more than it did extortion by individual grain dealers. But, implicitly, it recognized that the people had a right to existence—not Morelly's sociopolitical right to a portion of the commonwealth, but Montesquieu's moral right to a reasonable chance for survival. The right to existence was not a meal ticket, but the right to compete for subsistence in a situation in which there was a rough proportion between the means and the elementary needs of most of the people. The vast majority of consumers were poorly armed for this struggle. The government's task was to assure their competitiveness by protecting them against the avarice and spoliations of the owners and traders. The government itself was to be victualer only in the last resort; indirectly, however, to prevent

---

85 Condorcet, *Lettre d'un laboureur de Picardie à M. N.****, *auteur prohibitif* (Paris, 1775), in E. Daire and G. de Molinari, eds., *Collection des principaux économistes*, XIV, 487.

catastrophes, it had to play an active distributing role by managing scarcity and regulating the allocation of supplies.

The government guaranteed the right to existence in return for the submission of the citizenry. The government had an obligation to honor this right, not only for the sake of justice, but to assure the survival of the society as a whole. In the Parlement's conception, social life was not founded on an underlying harmony of interests, but on a delicate balance of conflicting and contradictory interests, needs, and ambitions which could be kept in uneasy equilibrium only by the mediation of an agency hostage to no single party. Harmony was neither natural nor ineluctable; the government had to arrange it. In the Parlement's view, the public interest could not be defined and realized through the concourse of a multitude of private interests. It was the function of the public interest to channel the private interests in a direction that was generally useful. The Parlement believed that the highest public interest was subsistence because it was the precondition for social cohesion. The experience of the sixties seemed to be a graphic illustration of this lesson. In other matters, the court vigorously defended the sovereign claims of private property, especially against the aggrandizement of the state. It refused, however, to accept an unqualified and absolute idea of property when that idea clashed with the exigencies of provisioning. It tacitly rejected the notion that property was a natural right anterior to all forms of social organization and superior to the claims of society as a whole. It stood as the defender of what we have called the police tradition. Nor did it stand there alone. The Paris Parlement's analysis, if not all its specific recommendations, could have served as a platform for the whole antiliberal movement of the sixties and seventies.

Lofting a trial balloon for Herbert's liberalization scheme in 1755, a reviewer in the *Journal de Trévoux* had written: "It is not incompatible, this liberty, with the monarchical government." Fifteen years later, Galiani told his friend Suard: "In every government, the grain legislation gives the tone of the spirit of the government ... if you tamper too much with the administration of grain in France, if you succeed, you alter the form and the constitution of the government."[86] The Paris magistrates did not perceive liberalization, like their Rouen

---

86 *Journal de Trévoux*, (Oct. 1755), 2601–02; Galiani to Suard, 8 Sept. 1770, in Asse, ed., *Lettres*, I, 138–39. For an analysis of Galiani's view, see below, chapter 12. On the relationship between liberty and monarchy, see also Linguet's *Réflexions des six corps de la ville de Paris sur la suppression des jurandes* (N.p., 1776), 2 and L. Beffroy, *Rapport fait au nom de la Section des Subsistances chargée de combattre les économistes* (Paris, 1792), 3–4.

colleagues, as a threat to the form or constitution of the government, at least not in the short run. But they did believe that liberalization fundamentally changed the relationship between state and society, estranging the one from the other and placing them both in jeopardy. In the Parlement's view, state and society were interdependent and intertwined. In the liberal conception, the state functioned on the margin of society, abandoning it largely to its own devices. By instituting liberalization, the Parlement alleged, the state renounced its responsibilities to society. Liberalization upset the balance of society and at the same time announced that it was no longer the duty of the government to maintain this balance. The Parlement decried the advent of the spectator-state because the magistrates believed that it would lead to chaos and social disintegration. By abrogating all the rules of conduct, the government lost view of its very purpose; laissez-faire, the court argued, was ultimately an anti-social policy.

Although it had fiercely combatted the bloated king of the administrative monarchy, the Parlement rejected the lean king of liberalism. For years and years it had relentlessly tried to limit the power of the king. Now it exhorted the monarch to exercise his authority with vigor. In this sense, the Assembly of General Police stands as a *séance de flagellation* in which the king and the deputies switched roles.

Chapter X

THE GOVERNMENT, THE PARLEMENTS, AND THE BATTLE OVER LIBERTY: II

I

Unlike most of the great political battles of the Old Regime, the struggle over the liberal reforms did not find the government on one side and the parlements on the other. There were parlements on both sides of the question. Nor were the courts that took a stand against liberalization along with the Paris Parlement united in their views or bound by a sense of common interest. There is no evidence that the opposition companies of Dijon, Bordeaux, Rennes, Rouen, and Paris coordinated their attacks or corresponded, as they did on many other issues, to plan strategy and exchange ideas. Each parlement was concerned specifically about the fate of its own *ressort*. The Breton magistrates appear to have calculated their policy without regard to the situation of the other courts. Liberalism had deep roots in the Rennes Parlement and it was vigorously seconded by the Estates of Brittany, which had close ties with the court and which remained committed to the reforms at least until 1770.[1] The Parlement hesitated a long while before moving against liberalization, and then tried to take a position which would not foreclose the possibility of a return to liberty when conditions improved. The Bordeaux court oscillated between liberal and police positions, depending far less on a global conception of political economy and administration than on short-term factors which affected the supply situation of the territory.[2] If the Paris Parlement struck a more universal pose, it was because it habitually pretended to speak for the whole nation,

---

1 On Brittany, see Letaconnoux, *Commerce des grains en Bretagne*, 41, 87–88, 91, 194–95, 197 and Bachaumont, *Mémoires secrets*, XIX, 74 (19 May 1769).

2 See, for example, a magistrate's letter to the Bordeaux IN., 23 Sept. 1766, C. 1425, A.D. Gir.; Terray to First President, 26 July 1773, C. 1441, *ibid.*; M.-F. Pidansat de Mairobert, *Journal historique de la révolution opérée dans la constitution de la monarchie françoise* (London, 1776), IV, 401 (14 Dec. 1773).

to the chagrin of its sister-parlements, and because the provisioning of Paris depended upon circumstances throughout the kingdom.

The case of Rouen best illustrates the contradictions and the brittle solidarities which characterized inter-parlementary relations and grain policies. In the course of the public debate, the courts at Rouen and Paris became allies in the struggle against liberalization. Indeed, the Rouen Parlement launched the early assault with its usual vivacity and in a sense prepared the ground for Parisian intervention. Yet there were important differences in outlook between the parlements which should not be obscured by their common hostility to the liberal reforms. While they assailed liberalization, the Rouennais also attacked the policy by which the ministry systematically favored Parisian provisioning as if no one else had to fear or suffer the consequences of scarcity and steep prices. This was an old but smoldering issue, fanned by the subsistence crisis and left to burn itself out by the liberal ministry.

We have already shown what deep resentment the primacy which the central government gave to Paris provisioning aroused in the rest of France. In 1773, well *after* the liberal reforms were abrogated, upon a continuing background of serious revolts especially in the south and southwest, the minister of war solemnly warned the royal council against "a fatal principle of government which seems unfortunately to gain credit more and more and which appears capable of igniting the four corners of the kingdom, to wit, that we worry very little about the provinces provided the capital is provisioned."[3] This "fatal principle of government" had thrived during the liberal period despite the fact that it ran counter in every respect to the spirit of the reform. To be sure, the government would have liked to subjugate the capital to the common law of the market. But the Laverdy ministry rested its whole strategy for phase one of liberalization upon its ability to insulate and contain Paris while the rest of the kingdom adjusted to the liberal regime. Throughout the liberal period and especially after 1767, the government made a point of treating Paris more or less in the traditional way. Although the liberal parlements denounced Parisian egotism in vitriolic terms, the most resounding expression of rancor and indignation came from Rouen, a sovereign court in the opposite camp.

For centuries Paris and Rouen had been rivals in the competition for subsistence and the contest for staking out hinterland. Although the Rouennais could not arrest Parisian aggrandizement, its access to

---

3 *Hardy's Journal*, 19 May 1773, BN, mss. fr. 6681, fol. 192.

the sea and to coastwise and foreign trade gave the Norman city options and advantages which the capital could not easily usurp. One can find instances in which the Rouen municipality importunately solicited grain supplies from Paris, but far more frequently the capital had to rely on Rouen's willingness to serve as entrepôt for the massive supplies imported in time of dearth.[4]

Rouen profited materially from this role until the moment when her own supplies became short, at which time the city became nervous and resentful of its semi-colonial status. The central government, viewing the provisioning of the capital as a national responsibility of the utmost urgency, sternly reproved Rouen's repeated desire to give first priority to its own needs. In 1725, for example, the Controller-General did not hesitate to argue that Paris was simply more important than Rouen, while the Procurator General of the Paris Parlement badgered the intendant of Normandy to accelerate transshipments and rebuked him for countenancing diversions.[5] In 1752 Rouen suffered a subsistence revolt during which crowds of insurgents pillaged boats loaded with grain marked "for the provisioning of Paris."[6] Four decades later, Parisian revolutionaries denounced the "bad will" of the Rouennais whom they accused of hoarding grain expressly to deny the capital.[7]

Toward the end of March 1768, as we have noted, subsistence troubles convulsed a large area of Normandy. Although the exact path of contagion is not clear, the riots seem to have spread from place to place, infecting a different town every day, in the kind of pattern which the Flour War later made famous. Elbeuf, Darnétal, La Bouille, Marmomme, Gournay, Bourgthéroulde, and Louviers were among the major points of disorder. In their genesis and their modes of action, these riots were no different from the scores of others that buffeted the kingdom during this time. The populace rose in order

---

4 Usher, *Grain Trade*, 50, 53–55; E. Boutaric, *Actes du Parlement de Paris* (Paris, 1863), I, lxiin (25 May 1522). Cf. the Controller-General's warning to the Rouen intendant against encroaching upon the Parisian supply area during a time when Normandy was experiencing serious shortages. Moras to de Brou, 31 Jan. 1757, C. 104, A.D. S-M.

5 CG to Duc de Luxembourg, 4 Aug. 1725, AN, G⁷ 34; De Gasville, IN. of Rouen, to PG, 21 Aug. 1725, BN, Coll. Joly 1117, fols. 82–83.

6 E.J. F. Barbier, *Journal d'un bourgeois de Paris sous le règne de Louis XV*, ed. P. Bernard (Paris, 1963), 251 (May 1752).

7 R. Cobb, "Les Disettes de l'an II et de l'an III dans le district de Mantes et la vallée de la Basse-Seine," *Mémoires de la Fédération des Sociétés Historiques et Archéologiques de Paris et de l'Ile-de-France*, III (1951), 240. Cf. M. Levainvillain, "Rouen et la région rouennaise," C. Bloch, *et al., Les Divisions régionales de la France* (Paris, 1913), 236–38.

to protest against exorbitant prices, and penury and inconsistency of supply, and in order to stem the outflow of grain from the community. For weeks, there had been premonitions of trouble at Rouen, the provincial capital. At every level of society, men were "murmuring" against "exportation," by which they meant the removal of grain for shipment elsewhere, whether in France or abroad.[8]

Miromesnil, the First President of the Rouen Parlement, lamented the burgeoning misery and the persistent upward spiral of bread prices. That city dark bread (*pain bis*) had risen to 3 *sous* the pound was surely an ominous sign. In a tone of stoic resignation rather than outrage, Miromesnil wrote his friend Laverdy, the Controller-General: "I see that there arrives every day [quantities of] grain at Rouen of which in truth the greatest part is destined for Paris."[9] Although he personally considered the grumblings from below to be innocuous, the chief magistrate observed that an intense social fear and expectation of violence gripped the upper elements of Rouen society:

> The people are tranquil enough but the big merchants [*négocians*], the persons of distinction, and especially quite a large number of Messieurs of the Parlement tremble; they still remember the riot of 1752, and you know that one is not easily cured of fear.

He dismissed reports of imminent insurrection and popular movements as false alarms and idle rumor.[10] Certainly he was surprised several days later when a fierce riot broke out at Rouen lasting for almost a week. Large crowds pillaged grain storehouses and bakeries and engaged the forces of order in several bloody encounters.[11]

If there is little evidence to suggest that the mutineers specifically felt themselves to be victims of Parisian colonialism, there is no doubt that the Rouen magistrates blamed their troubles in large measure on the policies of the liberal ministry. We have already traced the path which led from the Parlement's illegal regulatory *arrêt* immediately following the riots through a spring and summer of increasingly vehement opposition. In October the Rouennais vented their rage in two extraordinary letters to the king which revealed just how poisoned the

---

8 Miromesnil to Laverdy, 2 Feb. 1768, in LeVerdier, ed., *Correspondance Miromesnil*, V, 79. Cf. Trudaine's characterization of popular attitudes toward "exportation." Trudaine to Miromesnil, 13 May 1768, *ibid.*, V, 200.

9 Miromesnil to Laverdy, 23 Feb., 1768, *ibid.*, V, 96.

10 Miromesnil to Laverdy, 18 March 1768, *ibid.*, V, 122.

11 Rouen Parl., Conseil Secret (1767), 23 March to 1 May, 1768, A.D. S-M.; *Hardy's Journal*, 28 March 1768, BN, mss. fr. 6680, fol. 152; *Lettres Ossolinski*, 28 March 1768, BHVP, mss. 627, fol. 127.

atmosphere had become. In addition to ascribing the social and economic crisis that afflicted Normandy directly to liberalization, the letters gave voice to the kind of charges which Leprévost de Beaumont
would soon immortalize as the *pacte de famine*. Indeed, according to Leprévost, the news of the Rouen accusations quickened his determination
to expose the plot and helped convince him that he could safely share
his suspicions with the civic-minded Norman magistrates.[12]

If Rouen, like Paris, had been the beneficiary of large injections
of the king's grain, perhaps the Rouen magistrates, like their Parisian colleagues, would have been less avid to find clues of criminal
maneuvers in royal conduct. In any event, by these sensational imputations, the Rouen court underscored how urgently a change in policy was needed. The crucial matter for these magistrates was that
liberalization, with or without illicit activities secretly undertaken by
royal agents, was a calamity, responsible for the dearth and the social
troubles. On this fundamental point they shared the view of their
counterparts in the capital. But there is no doubt that the discrimination practiced by the royal government in favor of Paris envenomed
the attitude of the Rouennais. Liberalization had failed to free the
provinces from the Parisian grip and, in addition, it made them even
more vulnerable than before by abolishing the police powers which
they once used to defend themselves. The odor of a plot merely confirmed other evidence that the king was not meeting his responsibilities toward his subjects.

Rouen, more than other places and certainly more than Paris,
seemed to be victim of royal negligence. To be sure, the Norman Parlement acknowledged that Rouen was a commercial city which derived
its reputation and much of its wealth from serving as a place "of passage
and of entrepôt." But were there no limits, the Parlement wondered, on
the duties which this trading vocation imposed? For over a year, since
the beginning of 1767, the inhabitants of the city have suffered hunger, deprivation, and uncertainty. Everyday they witnessed the arrival of

---

12 It is interesting to note that Léprevost considered the ultraliberal Dauphiné Parlement
   to be the only court besides Rouen which merited his confidence. Like the Rouennais,
   the Dauphinais had given a prominent place in their declarations to the denunciation of
   officially fostered monopoly. For Leprévost this was obviously *the* crucial issue. Apparently
   it did not matter for him that the Norman Parlement blamed these illicit operations on
   the general abandonment of the police regime while the Dauphiné magistrates blamed
   them on its persistence in many quarters. Though it is misinformed, Leprévost's perception
   suggests another dimension of ambiguity in the alignment of the parlements on the grain
   issue. *Dénonciation, pétition et rogation du sieur Leprévôt de Beaumont*, 2–3.

grain which remained only long enough for conditioning and transfer to boats bound for Paris. It was proper, the magistrates allowed, to ask the city to serve as a granary for Paris, "but, Sire," they addressed the king,

> to strip her bare of what is physically necessary, to reduce her to dearth in order to procure abundance elsewhere, to make her the Magazine of the most essential of goods without regard for her needs, to refuse her the Natural Right to share in her warehouse deposits [similar to the natural right which consumers claimed to grain "born" in their "place"] is to act against the intentions of Your Majesty.

It is "so difficult" for those of us in the provinces to get your ear, the magistrates protested. Why do you ignore our pleas? "All the subjects of your empire are equally dear to you," they felt obliged to remind the monarch.[13]

This pathetic complaint made no impression upon the government, which had become inured to such effusions in times of stress. Within a week of the March 1768 riot, Laverdy had reiterated that his priorities were immutable: "Above all it is necessary to assure us the passage of the Seine: otherwise Paris will lack."[14] Several times in the course of the next few months the government either authorized the city to draw on Paris-bound stores or dispatched boats downstream from the capital to Rouen. Miromesnil expressed gratitude, but made it clear that "we understand perfectly the importance of supporting the provisioning of Paris." A nearly perfect king's man with a great talent for obedience and self-abnegation, the First President could not contain his irritation when the Controller-General suggested in mid-May that Rouen was abusing Parisian largesse. "… Never was any shipment for Paris ever held back, even during the riot," he wrote indignantly; "pardon this little apology but you must see that I am far removed from discouraging the commerce, crossing your operations, or hindering the subsistence of Paris."[15]

Despite his protestations of fidelity, Miromesnil endured another

---

13 *Lettres et suppliques* to the king, 15 and 29 Oct. 1768, *Conseil Secret* (1767–1768), A.D. S-M.; *Mercure Suisse* (Oct. 1768), 241–245.

14 Berulle to Choiseul and Laverdy, 13 June 1768, B. 2316, fol. 123 and Dauphiné Parl. to Louis XV, 12 July 1768, Recueil Giroud, XXV, 47, A.D. Isère; Laverdy to Miromesnil, 29 March 1768, in LeVerdier, ed., *Correspondance Miromesnil*, V, 138. Even as the Parlement insisted on the prosperity wrought by liberalization, in another letter to the king it asked for an easing of the fiscal burden on the province as a result of a succession of mediocre-to-bad harvests. 13 May 1767, B. 2313, fol. 296, A.D. Isère.

15 Miromesnil to T. de Montigny, 10 May 1768, in LeVerdier, ed., *Correspondance Miromesnil*, V, 191. Miromesnil to Laverdy, 16 May 1768, *ibid.*, V, 207–208.

scolding in August, this time from Trudaine de Montigny, chief of the provisioning department, who lectured in terms ill-becoming an outspoken liberal, on the necessity of "preventing the particular interest" of Rouen from "being preferred" to the interest of the capital. Any impediment placed in the way of the flow of grain to Paris, Trudaine explained, would be "a true disaster for the *chose publique*," the commonweal:

> We find ourselves, my dear colleague, in a cruel fix for the provisioning of Paris. We are told that the Chamber of Commerce of Rouen wishes to purchase by act of authority [a sort of eminent domain] two cargoes of Danzig wheat destined for the supply of the capital... which we cannot deny ourselves without the greatest harm.

What is interesting about Trudaine's letter is that he tried to make his case *not* on the basis of the traditional primacy of Paris in the Delamarist scheme of things, but on the grounds of liberty of trade. On the one hand, he half-implored, half-commanded Miromesnil "in the name of God" not to "suffer that the precautions taken for the capital be disrupted." On the other, he contended that the grain in question was the private property of merchants who would surely discontinue the service if they could not dispose of their goods as they pleased. Neither argument, the one from necessity and solicitude or the one from liberty, had any merits in the eyes of the Rouen Parlement, or indeed any other police authority constrained to martyr itself for the sake of the capital. For Trudaine and the government, however, it was crucial to sustain the idea that it was not so much for Paris as for the successful prosecution of the liberal reforms that the capital's old privileges were maintained. If the provinces persisted in their age-old complaints against the tyranny of Paris, the government wanted them to know that their sacrifices were worthier than ever before, for they were made not on the discredited altar of prejudice and police, but in honor of freedom and nature.[16]

II

On the other side, in the liberal camp, stood the Estates and the Parlement of Languedoc and the Parlements of Provence and Dauphiné, hailed by the *économistes* as "illustrious defenders of the Fatherland" for their "striking and reasoned positions." In the midst

---

16 T. de Montigny to Miromesnil, 9 Aug. 1768, *ibid.*, V, 230–31.

of the Paris onslaught against liberalization, when the government felt beleaguered and the *économistes* felt demoralized, these *corps* publicly and effusively expressed their gratitude to the monarch for his commitment to the reforms and exhorted him "to cede to none of the [antiliberal] demands."[17] Though little prodding was needed, the ministry itself solicited at least some of these declarations of fidelity.[18] There is some evidence to suggest that the liberal parlements, on their own account, coordinated action or at least exchanged ideas and information.[19]

Precisely why these parlements chose *and were able* to support liberalization so vigorously and consistently is a question that merits careful local study.[20] Although it is well-known that the magistrates of these courts invested heavily in agriculture and were actively involved in the grain trade, there is no reason to believe that a differential analysis of personal fortune would be any more helpful in explaining their attitudes than those of the officers of the other sovereign courts whose socioeconomic interests appear to be quite similar. A more fruitful line of inquiry would lead to an examination of regional economic, geophysical, and climatological differences.[21] Each of the

---

17 *Ephémérides du citoyen* (1769), I, 69, 197, 198; *Journal économique* (April 1771), 179. Cf. Bachaumont, *Mémoires secrets*, XIX, 73–74 (19 May 1769).

18 See, for example, de Latour to CG, 8 July 1768 and T. de Montigny, 16 July 1768, C. 2420, A.D. B-du-R. Cf. P.-Albert Robert, *Les Remontrances et arrêts du Parlement de Provence au dix-huitième siècle* (Paris, 1912), 588n.

19 See, for example, the démarches of Louis de Sausin, counselor in the Dauphiné Parlement, described by the historian of that court as "one of the most refined and cultivated minds in the Company." In August 1768, he congratulated the First President of the Aix court on the eloquence of his letter to the Controller-General. Citing an "urgent need" for a further statement by the liberal forces, he sent his Provence counterpart a copy of the Dauphiné July letter to Louis XV. He continued to exchange information and invite comment on the grain issue until December, when he made a trip to Avignon apparently to consult with representatives of the Provence Parlement. There is some indication drawn from earlier experiences that Sausin regularly consulted sister-courts on major affairs of the day. Sausin to First President of Aix (?), 6 Aug. and 23 Dec. 1768, C. 2420, A.D. B-du-R.; Egret, *Parlement de Dauphiné*, I, 32, 135, 203, 207 and II, 29–30.

20 One of the outspoken antiliberals at the Assembly of General Police, the parlementaire Hocquart, intimated that soaring prices would soon make the liberal parlements less enthusiastic for the new regime. *Recueil*, 191.

21 See Galiani's geopolitical explanation of parlementary divisions. *Dialogues*, ed. by Nicolini, 249. It is interesting to note that in 1740 D'Argenson reported that while the rest of France suffered misery, there was abundance in Languedoc, Provence, and Dauphiné. *Mémoires*, ed. by Rathery, III, 221 (10 Nov. 1740). In 1768, the Dauphiné Parlement readily admitted to having suffered "three consecutive years" of harvests

liberal provinces, bordering the sea or the frontier, seems genuinely to have benefitted from liberalization. Future investigation must discover precisely how widely and how unevenly the gains were shared—socially, politically, and geographically. The persistent friction between the municipality and the Parlement of Toulouse suggests one collective line of cleavage.[22] Whatever pattern of distribution emerges, it is significant that the three regions were generally spared the turmoil endemic in the northern half of the kingdom since 1765–66.[23]

The public pronouncements of the liberal parlements were a compound of physiocratic doctrine and regional economic pride. In the summer of 1768, the First President of the Dauphiné Parlement, speaking for the entire court, told the king that the reforms had brought agricultural and commercial prosperity and abundance and asked him to lift the remaining restrictions on the grain trade, especially those concerning exports, so that the full effects of an "unlimited" liberty could be enjoyed. The Dauphiné magistrates were not oblivious to all the talk of monopoly in the air. Like their colleagues in Paris and Rouen, they considered monopoly to be the great "enemy" and the chief cause of past dearths. But unlike its sister courts, the Dauphiné Parlement viewed monopoly as a product of the police regime, which only "a general, total and protected liberty could uproot forever." The irreversible export suspension mechanism in the July Edict, the court told the king, encouraged manipulative practices—"interior monopoly"—which paralyzed the trade. If the government could not remove all the "barriers" to freedom at once, then at least it should modify the law to permit exports to begin again automatically from an embargoed station once the price dropped for three consecutive markets below the cut-off ceiling. The *Ephémérides* published the Dauphiné letter with an enthusiastic endorsement.[24]

"worse than they have been for a long time." But it insisted that the prices nevertheless remained below the prices characteristic of "the time of prohibitions." *Arrêté*, 12 July 1768, C. 2420, A.D. B-du-R.

22 L. Viala, *La Question des grains et leur commerce à Toulouse au 18ᵉ siècle*, 72–75. Cf. M. Bordes, *L'Administration provinciate et municpale en France au dix-huitième siècle*, (Paris, 1972).

23 That is not to say that there were not "local crises" in these regions. See, for example, J. Godechot and S. Moncassin, "Démographie et subsistance en Languedoc du XVIIIᵉ siècle au début du XIXᵉ siècle," *Bulletin de l'histoire économique et sociale de la révolution française* (1964), 35–36. In Languedoc, too, there were *anti-cherté* and anti-export riots in 1765 at Montpellier, Pezenas, Agde and Béziers and in 1766 at Narbonne. C. 2908, A.D. Hér. and (?) to IN., 10 May 1767, C. 117, A.D. H-G.

24 Berulle, First President, to CG, 13 June 1768 and Dauphiné Parl. *arrêté* and letter to king, 12 July 1768, C. 2420, A.D. B-du-R.; *Journal économique* (Aug. 1768), 352;

Shortly after the Assembly of General Police and in stark contrast to its recommendations, the same Parlement reiterated its plea for an extension of liberalization in an *avis* ghost-written by a Rouen magistrate-*économiste* named Bigot de Sainte-Croix, who also wrote essays against the dangers of Colbertism and the abuses of the guilds.[25] Dupont called it "one of the best conceived, best thought out, best written treatises ever made," and the *Éphémérides* found "three centuries of distance between this memoir of the Parlement of Grenoble and those published by the adversaries of liberty."[26] The magistrates of Grenoble proudly characterized their stand as "modern" and inveighed against the "erroneous" precedents invoked to justify a stultifying and anachronistic policy of prohibitions. Champions of law and tradition in so many bitter struggles waged against the government, these parlementaires discovered that the "order of nature" was an infinitely better guide than the "order of purely factitious legislation."

Liberty was not merely a matter of convenience. Both social and political organization derived from the laws of nature. "There is a law, Sire," the Parlement declared, "anterior to civil laws, a law founded immediately by Nature, whose maintenance must be the single end of all social institutions, a law by which and for which you reign, it is the sacred law of property." Since property was an empty right unless owners had the freedom to dispose of it as they pleased, it was the duty of the government, through the person of the king, to guarantee the "liberty" as well as the "security" of property.

So confident were the magistrates in these fundamental, unimpeachable axioms, from which everything necessarily had to follow, that they were willing to concede, unlike many of their fellow liberals, that the kingdom was actually plunged into crisis, an inevitable "crisis of passage" from a prohibitive to a permissive regime. But they were determined not to allow the crisis, which was accidental and ephemeral

---

Bachaumont, *Mémoires secrets*, XIX, 9 (3 Aug. 1768); *Mercure historique* (Sept. 1768), vol. 165, pp. 281–295; *Éphémérides du citoyen* (1768), VII and (1769), VI.

25 The *avis* took the form of a letter addressed to Louis XV dated 26 April 1769. Citations below are from the manuscript copy in the parlementary registers, B. 2314, A.D. Isère. It was published in the *Éphémérides du citoyen* (1769), VII, 109–256. The Dauphiné court also addressed an *arrêté* to Louis XV on 20 Dec. 1768 importuning him to make no changes in the liberal laws before consulting with "the people of the kingdom" through the Parlement. Sausin to (?), 23 Dec. 1768. A.D. B-du-R.

26 Dupont, "Discours prononcé à la clôture de la huitième année des assemblées économiques chez M. le Marquis de Mirabeau," 13 May 1774, in Knies, ed., *Dupont Correspondance*, II, 199. See also *Éphémérides du citoyen* (1769), V, 236–39 and J. Egret, *Le Parlement de Dauphiné*, I, 161–85.

in nature and scattered in incidence, to be used to impugn the eternal truths which formed "the essential and constitutive principle of society."[27] First of all, "the evils" of the crisis were far more likely "the product of the old Regulations still subsisting," rather than of the liberal legislation. Moreover, the magistrates did not regard the ascription of responsibility as the crucial matter. It was the function of the king to "judge" positive laws "by their conformity to the natural order and to the essential laws of justice," rather than "by confronting ... positive laws with the facts [of daily life]." A wise monarch, therefore, would not hesitate in choosing his course, for a wise monarch understood that he had no choice. He would not be deterred by the crisis. Committed to govern according to nature's laws, he would support the liberal laws because they approximated the laws of nature; indeed, he would even try to make these positive laws conform more rigorously to nature's model by liberalizing them further.

Viewed in this light, the liberal laws were unassailable. "Should the social order be contrary to the order of nature?" asked the parlementaires of Grenoble. Since their answer was a resounding no, there was no need for them to entertain the claims of "different policed societies," which sought to "restrict" natural rights "on the pretext of removing a dangerous liberty from individuals." Nothing was more dangerous than trifling with natural law. The only "limits" on the rights of property were formed by the property rights of others. But consumer "need," the Parlement pointed out in a phrase which captures the essence of liberalism, "is not a title of property." The empty stomachs of the people did not entitle public authorities, as Linguet later contended, to infringe upon the property rights of grain owners. For grain was the same as any other property, undistinguished by the fact that it was universally needed. "It is only in the case of the Cultivator [read grain owner as well as tiller of the soil]," complained the magistrates, "that the empire of Justice ceases, giving way to oppression and to violence." The paradoxical idea that "the citizen who is most useful to society" should become "the victim of the social order" horrified them. They viewed the violation of natural law by the police, who turned flawed positive laws against property, with as much alarm as they had regarded the king's violation of constitutional law. Despite the apparent tranquility which such action might procure, for

---

27 Elsewhere in the *avis* the Parlement averred: "Local and transient disadvantages disappear before the sublime eye of the Legislator which embraces the universality of places and times...." B. 2314, fol. 91, A.D. Isère.

the Parlement of Dauphiné this policed "social order" was chaos: "confusion and disorder." Whereas the Parlement of Paris assailed liberty for introducing war between owners and consumers, the court at Grenoble contended that they fell into "a state of war" only when liberty was suppressed. A "happy harmony" would prevail in society when "each individual enjoyed the greatest possible liberty in the exercise of his property rights" and when socioeconomic relations were mediated exclusively through the "purely natural" workings of competition, a "stronger and surer" protector of the public interest "than all the prohibitive regulations."

The order of nature, in the view of the Parlement, delimited the power of the ruler, even as it defined the rights of the citizens. The enormous merit of these natural limits, unlike those drawn from the controversial archive of fundamental law, was that the king graciously accepted them. Unlike positive law, which could be made to rationalize any act of sovereign power, a commitment to natural law precluded "arbitrary" actions of any sort. Without renouncing the classical parlementary arguments against royal despotism, on the liberty issue the Dauphiné court came close to accepting the new contractual relationship proposed by Louis XV.

While the Paris Parlement censured the monarch for failing to fulfill his fundamental duties, the Grenoble Parlement retorted that those pretended duties were in fact abuses of power, or "arbitrary institutions." The traditional brand of royal paternalism and interventionism was no less contrary to the natural order than the "barbarous" style of the old police. It was not within the province of the king to be victualer or price regulator to the nation. The Grenoble magistrates considered such a conception of kingship as "impossible," "unjust," and "ruinous." The monarch's authority and his responsibilities stopped with the protection of the sacred rights of liberty and property. The efforts of their adversaries to "arouse the paternal heart of Your Majesty ... by the touching depiction of the misfortunes that the *cherté* causes" deeply alarmed the Dauphinais. Louis XV must resist "a false commiseration," inspired by "prejudice" rather than a genuine "sentiment of humanity," even as he rejected the "false combinations" of the police sophists. Though the king did not foresee "the dangerous consequences," already his "tenderness" for his subjects has led him astray. In the guise of a "welfare" project, the distribution of royal grain has resulted in the restriction of trading freedom, the violation of the property rights of many owners and traders, the disruption and in some places the

paralysis of commerce, the pillage of whole provinces, and the prop-
agation of rumors and suspicions of maneuvers, which tarnished
the reputation of the government and the reforms. The King's grain
itself was the source of the biggest monopoly afield in the late sixties,
"a double monopoly [directed] against the people and against the
Sovereign himself." Though they did not cite it by name, when the
magistrates mentioned the "legal monopoly" in the Paris area they
meant the Malisset company and they charged that it had turned
(inevitably) against the public interest because it ran against the natural order. By driving off competition, interrupting circulation, and
hoarding, the company became itself "the principal cause" of the
dearth rather than its remedy. Even as it aggravated the dearth, royal
intervention continued to teach "the people to hold the government
responsible for the dearth"—a doubly disastrous policy. Thus the
"crisis of passage" from police to liberty had urgent lessons in kingship for Louis XV to assimilate. For royal intervention was not only
morally and politically wrong—the distribution of king's grain was
no less arbitrary and deplorable than the issuance of *lettres de cachet*—
but it was also pointless and deleterious. If liberty were to survive
the crisis, the interlude of "tenderness" had to give way to a time of
realpolitik.

Above all, suggested the Grenoble magistrates, the antiliberal
movement must be placed in proper perspective. First of all, it was
centered in the Paris region and in Normandy, areas which had never
really implemented the liberal legislation or given the liberal idea a
chance.[28] It was no wonder that the capital took the lead in the campaign against liberty, for its inhabitants, who lived in a sordid and useless world of luxury, *rentes, tontines*, offices, lotteries, stocks, and paper
wealth, were "accustomed from infancy to the yoke of regulations and
nursed, as it were, at the breast of prohibitions"; as a result of their
bad "education," they can see the liberty of the grain trade only as
a "frightening novelty." But there was no need for France to tremble
merely because Paris raised its voice. Like the federalists of the Revolution and the "regionalists" of the 1970's, the Dauphiné magistrates
rejected the pretension of the capital to impose its will upon the nation.
To the demands of the Assembly of Police, they opposed "the wishes
of all the Provinces of Your Kingdom, of all the owners of land, of
all the cultivators and the inhabitants of the countryside, 10,000,000

---

28 Note the way in which the *avis* attempts to explain away the Normand case and thus isolate
   Paris as if it were not only the symbol but also the only genuine and ineluctable source of
   antiliberalism. See, for example, *ibid.*, fol. 118.

men...." These men pointed to the true moral and economic character of the nation, which was primordially agricultural. Agricultural France was the exclusive source of the nation's real wealth and its real virtue as well. To the mercantilism which denatured state and society by trying to make France "an industrial and commercial nation," the Grenoble Parlement opposed a rural fundamentalism, an alloy of the old-style Christian agrarianism and the new mood of agrarian capitalism, which perceived the "true manufacture" of the nation in "the cultivation of its lands."

The prohibitive regime, based on a low price policy, had led to "the total decay of agriculture." Liberalization "restored hopes," gave "a new life" to the rural economy, and signified the beginning of "the regeneration of the body politic." It marked "the most memorable epoch of your reign," the magistrates told the king. No one should underestimate its importance in terms of its long-run implications, as well as the immediate rush of prosperity which it generated. For, the Parlement reminded the reformer-monarch, "*everything* is intimately linked to this vast operation whose consequences embrace the [entire] social order and without which there is *no reform possible*, either in the physical or the moral sphere." This of course was precisely the wager which Louis XV had made in the dismal years at the beginning of the decade; no one knew better than he how much was riding upon the success of liberalization. As a solid sign of his good faith, at the very moment when the liberal regime seemed most imperilled, the Dauphiné magistrates asked the king, for his own hopes as well as for the sake of the ten million faithful, to demolish all the relics of the Old Regime and "to build upon the ruins of the prohibitive laws a simple and general law which establishes in Your Kingdom the absolute and unconditional liberty of the grain trade."[29]

The Assembly of Police made the Estates of Languedoc extremely anxious about the future of liberalization. Proud to have been "the first to solicit" the reforms, they had waited patiently for the government to give liberty its fullest expression by removing all limits in the grain trade. Exactly a year ago, the Estates, through their permanent agents at Versailles, mounted a concerted effort to induce the government to quash the restrictions on exportation. Now the syndic general reported, not only that he had failed to win an extension of liberty,

---

29 Clever, vigorous, and brilliantly written, the Dauphiné *avis* was generously plundered by the *économiste* Roubaud for his refutation of the arguments of the Assembly of Police, *Représentations aux magistrats* (Paris, 1769).

but that "on the contrary what is taking place in Paris at this moment in regard to this matter gives us reason to fear that circumstances peculiar [to Paris] which should have absolutely no bearing on this province are leading up to [the announcement of] some new general police regulation which will be extremely harmful [to us]." Though they had never been happy with an "incomplete" liberty, the sudden prospect of losing everything terrified the deputies. The aim of the "supplications," which the Estates addressed to Louis XV in December, was not to win more liberty, but to preserve at all costs what had already been obtained.

The Estates urged the government not to succumb to the pressure to judge liberalization from the Parisian vantage point. The situation was far less critical, they claimed, in the rest of the kingdom where prices were "honest." Moreover, the Parisians were the authors of their own distress. By insisting on the maintenance of the police regime with the "thousand obstacles" it placed in the way of commerce, they assured themselves of dearth and high prices. What enraged the Estates was that the Parisians now "dare accuse the liberty which they did not practice and impute to it the effects which it could have prevented." This argument, though it completely misapprehended the Paris situation, had great allure for the liberals because it enabled them to believe that liberty had not been given a fair chance. By conserving "the old regulations," the Estates intimated, Paris not only wounded itself, but it also prevented the implementation of liberty in a vast area in the interior of the kingdom. Paris served as an alibi for the liberals (especially for Turgot a few years later), just as liberty served as a scapegoat for Paris. In this whole affair, the Parisians were the real provincials, for the "desire of the nation," the Estates informed the government, was for an extension, not an abridgement, of liberalization.

The traditional solutions proposed by the Parisians, besides threatening the interests of the kingdom as a whole, were themselves contradictory and doomed to failure, the Estates pointed out. The Parisians said they wanted to make the markets abundant, yet they made the markets as attractive to frequent as the state prisons. They desired to promote the grain trade, yet they subjected the merchants to harassment and dishonor. They wanted to prohibit exports, yet at the same time they refused to tolerate domestic stockpiling. They railed against monopoly, yet they created conditions which made commercial competition impossible and thus rendered monopoly inevitable. The very notion of police was "odious" to the deputies of the Estates. It bespoke privilege, corruption, favoritism, tyranny, and the transgression of the most sacred rights, especially "the inviolable right of property." The king, concluded the Estates, had a clear choice to make: between freedom and oppression, nature and artifice, prosperity and stagnation, real wealth and the superficial glitter of luxury, the economy of non-intervention and the ruinous waste of paternalism, a self-sufficient people and a helpless, dependent people, France and Paris. Nor should the government forget how much its own needs were bound up in the grain question. If Languedoc were "deprived" of the "natural right" of liberty, the Estates bluntly threatened, "it would not be able to pay the [fiscal] impositions which become more onerous each day."[30]

In a separate address to the king, the Parlement of Languedoc emphasized the practical advantages of liberalization.[31] Before the reforms, the magistrates wrote, our people were burdened with a chronic surplus, which they could not dispose of profitably. As prices lagged, agriculture stagnated and the countryside lost population. Liberalization had a remarkably tonic effect. "Serenity" replaced "misery," agriculture flourished, and—a result to which the king could hardly be indifferent and one which parlements were usually loathe to admit—it became easier to collect taxes.[32] To give us the reform measures, the king had to brave an infinity of "prejudices, ancient maxims, interested sophisms." Be as courageous now as you were then, implored the Languedoc Parlement, stand your ground firmly, for "the suppression [or] the least suspension of the liberty of the grain trade would be [for our people] the most deadly blow, the most terrible of punishments."

Like the other liberal corps, the Provence Parlement viewed with

---

30 Deliberations of the Estates, 3 Dec. 1767, C. 2410 and 13 Dec. 1768, C. 2411, A.D. H-G. The "supplications" were published in the *Ephémérides* (1769), I, 199–212. The fiscal threat became increasingly prominent in the liberal argument as the risk of a royal volte-face burgeoned. "If exportation had not taken place during the past three years," the archbishop of Narbonne reminded the Controller-General, "Languedoc, Guyenne, and all the neighboring provinces which comprise more than half of the realm would surely not have been able to pay their impositions." 16 Dec. 1768, AN H 887. Cf. the "Lettre d'un gentilhomme des états de Languedoc à un magistrat de Rouen sur le commerce des bleds." (1768), C. 774, A.D. L-A.

31 "Lettre du Parlement de Toulouse au Roi ...," *Ephémérides du citoyen* (1769), III, 182–98.

32 Cf. the remark of the Procurator General of the Dauphiné Parlement to the intendant of the province: "The Controller-General must have observed that despite the *cherté* of grain, despite the mediocrity of the harvests, the king's revenues have come in much more readily than in the years during which a sterile abundance made the multitude of grain harvested useless." Vidaud to Pajot, 29 June 1770, Q 4 (2), fol. 59, Bibliothèque municipale de Grenoble.

mounting alarm the gathering momentum of the antiliberal campaign. In the spring of 1767 the magistrates worried about the impact which the "accidents" suffered by a number of provinces would have upon royal policy.[33] A little over a year later, the First President, in response to a ministerial request for a public expression of support, wrote an open letter to the Controller-General emphasizing Provence's attachment to the liberal reforms.[34] We cannot remain silent, the letter stated, when "a law so long solicited by our very humble prayers is [so sharply] attacked." The Provençal magistrates understood that Louis XV was in a bind. Tremendous pressure, generated in the name of compassion and humanity, was building up for a change in policy. Normally, it is true that "authority is too solidly entrenched in France to cede to popular impressions." It was, however, extremely difficult to resist these "clamors" on "such a delicate matter as subsistence." Prejudice and passion clouded the merits of the issue and cast a shadow over the remarkable accomplishments of liberalization. Representing the enlightened and productive part of the nation, the Parlement of Provence spoke up to tip the scales back into balance.

In this same letter, the First President also sought to reach the members of the sovereign courts who opposed liberalization. He recalled to them how useful parlementary solidarity had been in the past in exposing "the error" to which even "the greatest monarchs" were susceptible. We have not forgotten that it is the duty of the parlements to criticize aberrations in royal policy: "God forbid that we should [appear to] combat this maxim...." But it is also the responsibility of the parlements, continued the First President, "to assure the stability of the laws when they have been meditated and examined with the greatest care." The May and July reforms were just such laws. Because they broke so radically with tradition, they required the most energetic application in order to win public confidence. Since "nothing was more capable of fixing ideas than *the concert of all the magistrates,*" the fissures in parlementary solidarity wrought by liberalization were especially lamentable. Communicate to us the specific objections of the parlementary critics of liberalization, the First President told the Controller-General, and we will work to change their minds.

The more the Provence Parlement learned about the opposition, however, the more pessimistic it became about the prospects for conciliation and the more militant a posture it took. Provided by the government

---

33 Parlementary deliberation, 27 April 1767, B. 3676, A.D. B-du-R.
34 Letter of 8 July 1768, C. 2420, A.D. B-du-R.

with a list of "questions," which the antiliberal courts had raised regarding the reforms, the Provençaux replied in a long letter addressed to the king, just at the time that the Assembly of Police convened in Paris.[35] They reported grimly that the "principles" of the critics were "directly contrary to our own" and beyond accommodation. "They see it as an interest of state to keep grain below the natural price [while] we believe that Justice and Political wisdom require that property be respected and that the trade be left free," wrote the Provençal magistrates; "they wish to put us back under the yoke of prohibitive laws [while] we bless the moment that the nation was freed from them." Not only were the liberal and antiliberal parlementaires "divided on principles in a speculative sense," but in addition "they viewed the observable facts with a different eye." The magistrates "who are prejudiced against the new police believe that it is condemned by experience itself, they see misery spread by it and the population diminished day by day [while] the others insist on the contrary that its success has met the expectations of the Sovereign Legislator, that it has prepared the way for the prosperity of this Empire...."

With no hope of bridging the enormous gulf that separated it from its adversaries, the Provence Parlement turned instead to the attack in order to show the king that there were no legitimate grounds for retreating from liberalization. The Rouen and Paris accusations were false, the Parlement asserted; the price rise was not "the work" of liberal policy. It resulted rather from "accidents" of international incidence which brought dearth to Spain, Portugal, and Italy, reduced the northern European and American harvests to mediocrity, and forced the British to import on massive scale for the first time in almost a century. Moreover, "it was always anticipated that the passage from prohibitions to liberty would be a time of crisis" for segments of the population. This crisis was seriously and unexpectedly aggravated by these accidents of weather and circumstance "that no human prudence could have foreseen." (Unlike their confreres in Grenoble and Toulouse, the magistrates of Aix seemed satisfied with a naturalistic explanation; they did not lay stress on the "artificial" quality of the crisis and account for it by means of a police-remnants thesis.) Nor should the long-term promise of liberalization be misconstrued. On this matter the Provençaux took

---

35 Letter to the king, 21 Nov. 1768, B. 3677, A.D. B-du-R. (dépôt Aix). There is also a copy in the Marseilles dépôt, C. 2420. The *Ephémérides du citoyen* published the letter in (1769), II, 138–96. On the liberalism of the Provence court, see P.-A. Robert, *Remontrances ... Provence*, 351, 502–503, 585–608.

a more sober and candid stand than many other liberal apologists. It was never claimed that the new system would "guarantee" us against scarcities. It assured us only that the inevitable crises would be attenuated and that we would be far better protected than we had been under the police regime, which inhibited both production and distribution. Accidents, which in the past produced dearths, partly as a consequence of police mediation, would in the liberal world result in nothing more serious than *chertés*. Unlike their critics, the magistrates of Provence considered *cherté*, in the light of the advantages of the system which engendered it, to be a "tolerable" social burden.

The advantage of liberalization, which they extolled above all others, was "the universal resurrection of agriculture," marked by a major increase in production and income. This vision of rural regeneration, the magistrates suggested, must temper our grief for urban distress. Let us be realistic social engineers, they proposed: would it be "so great an evil if the excessive number of useless artisans who escape farming in order to corrupt themselves in the cities suffered some reduction?" It was high time to teach urban consumers that "the privilege of having cheaper bread" than their fellow citizens living elsewhere was not an "unquestionable right" of the cities. Arrogant even in misery, Paris acted as if only its poor counted. Now it was time to take pity on the "cultivator-people" who had experienced "the most horrible misery" for years and years under the old system, but whose suffering was "less visible and less well-known" than the occasional hardships of the capital. The Provence Parlement did not strain, like many of the partisans of liberty, to show that the new system would be universally beneficent. It was not embarrassed to see liberalization as a policy strictly cast to stimulate agriculture and to regard it as the rightful vengeance of the countryside upon the city.[36] Every law had its unfortunate effects, argued the parlementaires, utilitarians in the circumstance. The business of government was to choose the laws which do the most good for the most people. Liberty was bound to do the most good because it sprung from the dictates of nature. By far the most numerous group, its chief beneficiaries, "the owners and the cultivators," were also those who form the nation properly speaking"; the others were "merely hired hands."

---

36 The Provençaux also regarded liberalization as the proper vengeance of agriculture upon industry, although this theme was much less salient in liberal literature than one might have been led to expect. See the deliberations of the Parl. of 26 June 1769, B. 3677, A.D. B-du-R.

Politically, the liberal regime suited the Provençaux because it reduced the margin for arbitrary royal action, a goal which parlementaires everywhere had pursued single-mindedly during the whole century. The laissez-faire doctrine meant that there were certain things which it was not within the power or right of government to do. The government must remain at all times *"neutral between the seller and the buyer."* The nation had far more to gain than to lose if the king abstained from interfering with subsistence matters. By recognizing the natural limits of governmental activity, the Provence Parlement absolved the king of the responsibilities which the Paris magistrates, among others, insisted he must fulfill. "The government," declared the Provence court, "is much more responsible for the evil that it does by arbitrary institutions than for those which it cannot prevent or anticipate in letting things go following the natural course." *Cherté*, as Louis XV had told the Parlement of Paris, had "physical" causes; it was susceptible to natural, not political, remedies.

To be sure, the tough-minded Provençaux understood that enlightenment did not come easy, especially to the blind: "up to a point it was necessary to treat popular opinion on the subsistence question with extreme care like the eyes from which cataracts have just been removed." Yet "this system of condescension" developed by the ministry—the limits built into the reform laws, the distribution of king's grain, and, most recently, the *arrêt* of October 1768 offering bounties on imports—had dangerous implications. For one thing, it interfered with private speculation and the workings of the market, the only arbitration on which the kingdom should rely. Worse were its psychological and political consequences, for it "accustoms the people to believe following the old prejudice that the government has some sort of obligation" to intervene. Each concession, the Provence Parlement warned, emboldened the critics of liberalization and made it easier for them to extort another. This is not the time, the magistrates conceded, for us to make further demands for more liberty; though this and other reforms are necessary to assure the "prosperity of the State," they must await the passing of the "ferment." By the same token, however, it is not the time for the government to show weakness. Show us, the Provençaux exhorted, "a judicious steadfastness."

The expressions of parlementary support buoyed the confidence of the government. From its inception, the king had insisted that liberalization was a popular program, instituted in response to the demand of the nation; he had no intention of conceding the battle for public opinion to the Paris magistracy. Implicitly, the king recognized the liberal parlements as spokesmen for the interests of the people residing in their jurisdictions, a political relationship between constituted bodies and constituents which he had never before admitted and which he contined to contest in the case of Paris. From the vantage point of 1762–63, when Toulouse and Grenoble took the lead in fiercely defying the royal will, it would have been hard to imagine that the King would publicly seek the measure of his government's popularity and wisdom in the acclaim of these same sovereign courts. To be sure, all the issues of the time were not of a piece; there was nothing monolithic about eighteenth century politics. A parlement could praise the king in an *avis* and revile him in a remonstrance bearing the same date. But there was an unusually warm feeling between the king and the liberal parlements. The earnest desire of these courts to preserve liberalization made them unwilling to risk a falling out with the government.

Nothing more effectively undermined the Paris Parlement's position than the refusal of its sister-courts to confirm its analysis of the public interest, the causes of the crisis, the mechanism of liberalization, the purpose of the grain trade, the subversiveness of the new political economy, the boundaries between public and private responsibilities, and the nature of kingship. The collective appeal of the Assembly of Police was meant to isolate the king, but the solidarity of three of the most important judicial companies with the government tended instead to isolate the Paris Parlement, to give its angry complaints a parochial air, and to reduce the Paris problem to smaller proportions. The deep discord among the parlements, and the extremely harsh posture taken by the liberal courts toward the capital, aggrieved the Paris magistrates as much as it delighted the ministry. The Parisians anticipated the liberal dissent but they expected that it would be more restrained. They were shocked that the liberal magistrates so warmly embraced not a number of specific reform clauses, but the entire system which their Paris confreres had found so detestable and dangerous. It was hardly a propitious sign for inter-parlementary relations that the Paris court tried to suppress the public distribution of the Dauphiné *avis*.[37]

---

37 Bachaumont, *Mémoires secrets*, XIX, 143 (22 Dec. 1769).

III

Along with the liberal parlements, the économistes, the leading propagandists and theoreticians of liberalization, raised their voices in
support of the government. For several years after the triumphs of
1763–64 they had conducted a low-key campaign in favor of a vigorous implementation of the reform laws. They had also asked for
new measures in the direction of an even greater liberty, but they
had not pressed the matter too insistently in order not to embarrass the government during the delicate transitional period.[38]
While awaiting the opportunity to chronicle the felicitous results
of liberalization, the économistes turned to other aspects of political
economy.

During this time Letrosne was the only major figure who wrote
extensively about the grain trade. His The Grain Trade, Always Useful, Never Harmful (1765) was ambivalent in mood, on the one
hand, sublimely confident of the scientific validity of the physiocratic doctrine and of the universal social utility of the bon prix
(the people may have to pay a little more for their bread, but they
will be "richer" and it will be a "better bread") and, on the other,
deeply pessimistic about the prospects of convincing "the people" to
share his understanding or his faith. The people, "blinded by prejudice," could not be reached "by way of education," but only through
"example." Letrosne was worried that the public officials at the local
level who had to set the example would themselves turn against liberty, either because they, too, had "a blindfold across their eyes" or
because they had a vested stake in the old system: "But if these persons who are supposed to reassure them [the people] by their words
and examples are themselves People in this matter, isn't it to be feared
that they will spread alarm instead of dissipating it?" Letrosne hoped
that public men would find in his combative essay compelling reasons
for resisting the impulse to become "People" and for embracing the
liberty doctrine.[39]

---

38 A number of économistes criticized the limits placed on liberty but their manner was
extremely sober and reserved. See, for example, Dupont's "Au sujet du cabotage," Journal de
l'agriculture, du commerce et des finances (July 1766), 187–204 and Anon., "Quatrième mémoire
pour la concurrence dans le fret," ibid. (Sept. 1766), 116–117, 132–133.

39 G.-F. Letrosne, La Liberté du commerce des grains, toujours utile et jamais nuisible (Paris,
1765), 8–19, 39, 47, 91–92. In the same year Letrosne published several other
pieces in which he denounced "the malady ... of wishing to regulate everything." See

It was not until the middle of 1767, however, that the *économistes* became genuinely alarmed by the turn of events.[40] Mirabeau and Baudeau joined Letrosne in writing major essays on liberty and the state of the kingdom for the *Ephémérides*.[41] The common themes were the idea that the reform laws were not the cause of rising prices and subsistence disorders, a plea against ceding to "panic terrors" echoing Letrosne's earlier warnings, and an argument in favor of a stronger dose of liberty to counteract the remnants of the police system which still obstructed circulation. The following year the physiocratic journal bulged with articles defending liberalization and calling upon the ministry to hold the line in face of the growing opposition.[42] Shortly before the Assembly of General Police, in a piece meant to reinforce the morale of the liberals, Letrosne quite rightly pointed to the serious divisions of opinion in the antiliberal camp which, he hinted, would result in their ruin by their own hand.[43]

At about the same time the abbé Baudeau wrote a series of *Avis* in which, interspersed between recipes for a hearty bread of the people and an essay in which he gave the dubious physiocratic cachet to the process of economic milling, he launched a violent attack on the police for its failure to execute the liberal laws. The time of relative moderation in public discourse had passed. Baudeau carefully developed the line which the government had already pointed to in its exchanges with the Paris Parlement and which Roubaud, Dupont, Turgot, and other liberals further embroidered in the next few years. Baudeau urged "the people" not to be "deceived" about the real causes of the subsistence difficulties. It could not be the fault of liberty because we have never enjoyed more than "a half-liberty." Much of the problem

---

"Sur les avantages de la concurrence des vaisseaux étrangers pour la voiture de nos grains," *Journal de l'agriculture, du commerce el des finances*, I (July 1765), especially 106–107, 114–115 and "Réponse à la lettre de M. Girard," *ibid.*, III (Nov. 1765), 43–48, 72–73.

40 In fact the attitude of many liberals remained astonishingly serene and confident despite burgeoning social unrest and economic dislocation. See, for example, the *Gazette du commerce, de l'agriculture et des finances*, 28 June and 5 July 1766.

41 N. Baudeau, "Recherches politiques sur les terreurs populaires que cause le bon prix des grains …," *Ephémérides du citoyen*, II (1767), 19–48; [Mirabeau], "Lettre sur l'entière liberté du commerce des grains," *ibid.*, VIII (1767), 102–32; LeTrosne, "Lettre sur l'entière liberté du commerce des grains," *ibid.*, XI (1767), 119–33. See also the call upon liberals to close ranks in "Lettre de M.D. à un Magistrat du Parlement de Bourgogne," *ibid.*, XI (1768), 7, 15–16, 26–27.

42 See all twelve volumes of the *Ephémérides* for 1768.

43 Letrosne, *Lettres à un ami sur les avantages de la liberté du commerce des grains, et le danger des prohibitions* (Amsterdam, and Paris, 1768), 10–11.

results simply from bad harvests but much of it was also the fruit of police subversion and "the lack of liberty, the remnants of regulations, conditions, vexations, and contraints...."[44] According to Bachaumont's *Mémoires Secrets*, the abbé sent a copy of his *Avis* to every member of the Paris Parlement toward the end of October 1768.[45] We have seen how little impression it seems to have made on their way of thinking about the crisis.

The *économistes* bitterly resented the Assembly of General Police, which occurred the following month. The assembly marked the beginning of the end of physiocracy in its first life, for from the end of 1768 until the ascension of Turgot to the Contrôle-Général the school was in decline and disfavor. Until the meeting of the assembly, lamented Mirabeau, "We had been the friends of men [the title of one of Mirabeau's best-known works was *L'Ami des Hommes*] ... and suddenly we were denounced as agents of authority and of monopoly [and] someone called us corrupt and mercenary...."[46] The broader political implications of the assembly troubled Turgot more than the attack on the *économistes*: "I cannot understand how the police could have the

---

44 Baudeau, *Avis au peuple sur son premier besoin* (Amsterdam, and Paris, 1768), and *Avis aux honnêtes gens qui veulent bien faire....* (Amsterdam, and Paris, 1768).

For the argument that the source of the problem in France in the late sixties was too little liberty or an imperfect liberty, see also [Baudeau], *Lettre sur les émeutes populaires* (Paris, 1768), 43; Dupont to Prince Carl Ludwig, *Correspondance Dupont*, ed. by Knies, II, 141; "Avis des Députés du Commerce," Oct. 1769, AN, F¹¹ 715; Roubaud, *Représentations*, 49, 210–211; "De la liberté du commerce des grains," *Ephémérides du citoyen*, I (1769), 62–64; Turgot, "Septième lettre sur le commerce des grains," 2 Dec. 1770, in *Oeuvres*, ed. by Schelle, III, 341.

For the insistence that bad harvests were the major "physical" cause of the troubles, see: Roubaud, *Représentations*, 106–107, 114–15, 118; Roubaud, *Récréations économiques....* (Amsterdam, and Paris, 1770), 190; *Journal économique* (April 1769), 177; Turgot, "Cinquième lettre sur le commerce des grains," in *Oeuvres*, ed. by Schelle, III, 298; [Dupont], "Observations sur les effets de la liberté...," *Journal économique* (July 1770), 333–34; Suard to Galiani, 6 Aug. 1770, "Lettere inedite di G.B. Suard all'abate Galiani," ed. by F. Nicolini, in *Mélanges de philologie, d'histoire et de littérature offerts à Henri Hauvette* (Paris, 1934), 465; St.-Florentin to PG, 16 Oct. 1768, AN, O¹ 410; Anon., "Réflexions sur les principes des parlements de Paris et de Rouen ...," Arch. AE, France 1375, fols. 293–304.

Linguet energetically disputed what he considered to be a self-serving contention: "It is false that from 1764 through 1768 there were three bad harvests." *Du Pain et du bled*, 164–65.

45 Bachaumont, *Mémoires secrets*, XIX, 27–29 (20 Oct. 1768) and XIX, 31 (Dec. 1768). Cf. Galiani to d'Epinay, 27 July 1770, *Lettres*, ed. by Asse, I, 117.

46 Discours de Rentrée (1776–77), cited by Weulersse, *Mouvement physiocratique*, I, 183–84n. Cf. the remarks of the subdelegate of Avesnes in the Hainaut who reviled the physiocrats as "certain mercenary writers" bent on deceiving the public. "Réflexions sur l'édit du mois de juillet 1764" (ca. Oct. 1770), C. 6690, A.D. Nord.

stupidity to confirm the prejudices of the people."[47] At first the Parlement planned to keep the minutes of the Assembly secret. Once it became clear, however, that the government would make no concessions, the court apparently authorized publication. By the early spring, the minutes and other antiliberal propaganda in book form were distributed in Paris. According to Baudeau, it was soon in "everyone's hands."[48]

The Assembly of General Police elicited an elaborate refutation from a leading *économiste*, as well as public expressions of solidarity with the government from the liberal parlements. Roubaud's *Representations to the Magistrates* remains the most comprehensive statement on liberalization that the physiocrats made.[49] Although none of the arguments was fresh, they were written with a sense of political urgency and with specific reference to the events of the past few years. Roubaud denounced the "spirit of the old administration" which dominated the police Assembly. Everyone should know that the "old regime" which it "exalted" was responsible for destroying agriculture, depopulating the countryside, diminishing public revenues, hampering commerce, dividing the nation into "enemy peoples," and causing and prolonging dearths. ("Yes, every time that the police reached out its hand to restore abundance by force, subsistence faded away and the dearth increased.") Yet Roubaud saw signs in the assembly that "light" was gradually breaking through: "It seems that, in this Assembly, the prohibitive regime was praised only as the past is often praised, without a desire, at least not a manifest one, to see it reborn, at least not completely." After all, there was a general awareness of the need to "repair" agriculture and a general willingness to abandon "a great part of the old Regulations." For Roubaud, the striking "diversity" and "contrariety" of opinion at the Assembly was a clue to the fundamental defect in the police system as well as a source of encouragement to the liberal camp.[50]

The lack of unity at the assembly underlined the intellectual barrenness of the police system. The assembly reflected the characteristics of the

47 Turgot to Dupont, 4 Jan. 1769, in *Oeuvres*, ed. by Schelle, III, 54.
48 *Hardy's Journal*, 10 May 1769, BN, mss. fr. 6680, fol. 233; Baudeau, "Lettres ... à un Magistrat du Parlement de Paris," *Nouvelles éphémérides*, I (1775), 23. On the transmission of news of the Assembly, see also: C. 2420, A.D. B-du-R.; (?) to First President, Bordeaux Parl., 17 Dec. 1768, C. 1427, A.D. Gir.
49 See the celebration of Roubaud's work and further criticism of the Assembly of General Police in *Ephémérides du citoyen*, II (1769), 122–25 and VI (1769), 210–11.
50 Roubaud, *Représentations*, 16, 283–84, 391–93. Cf. *ibid.*, 466–68.

system: "capriciousness," "variability," "vacillation," and recourse to "arbitrary" solutions for want of principles. What the police system lacked most of all, in Roubaud's view, was "fixed and certain principles" which would have spared the Assembly lengthy debates and anguished hesitation.[51] For the police, government was a complex, difficult, and approximate affair, but for the *économistes*, because they had self-evident principles (revealed and "determined by their evidence"), it was "easy, simple, natural." The "science of government" was the "science of the natural order." The natural order was founded upon the "laws of nature," the first of which was the "inviolable and imprescriptible" right of property "instituted by God when he created man." While the police claimed that the right of property and the corollary right of liberty sometimes threatened the right to exist, from an entirely different perspective Roubaud argued that the property right "is identical to the right to exist." The "purpose" and the "aim" of "all human societies," as Dupont maintained, was to protect property.[52]

Nor could liberty be divided or compromised. Roubaud scorned the notion, reaffirmed by the assembly, that police and liberty were compatible: "the liberty of commerce is reconcilable with the Regulations as personal liberty is reconcilable with slavery." If the government followed the "original" and scientific principles of administration, it would acknowledge that "the full, entire, general, unlimited and indefinite liberty of the grain trade is uniquely and sovereignly just, useful and necessary in perpetuity." Without any foundations in nature and without any immutable guidelines, Roubaud concluded, the recommendations of the assembly would merely reestablish the "violence and tyranny" of the Old Regime.[53]

From this analysis, it followed that grain was simply another object

---

51 See the very similar view of the Dauphiné Parlement, *avis* and letter to king, 26 April 1769, B. 2314, fol. 100, A.D. Isère.

52 Dupont, "Vrais principes du droit naturel," *Ephémérides du citoyen*, III (1767), 167; Dupont, ed., *Physiocratie* (Paris, 1767–68), I, xc; Dupont, "Observations sur les effets de la liberté ...," *Journal économique* (Aug. 1770), 348.

  For similar views on the rights of property and liberty, see: J.-P.-L. Luchet, *Examen d'un livre qui a pour titre: "Sur la législation et le commerce des bleds"* (N.p., 1775), 17, 40–41; Baudeau, *Avis au premier besoin*, 72–73; Condillac, *Le Commerce et le gouvernement* in *Collection des principaux économistes*, ed. by Daire and Molinari, XIV, 421; *Journal helvétique* (June 1768), 605; *Mercure de France* (Aug. 1769), 132; Lemercier de la Rivière, *L'Intérêt général de l'état*, 64–65, 290–91, 377–78; Condorcet, *Sur la liberté de la circulation des subsistances* (1792) in *Oeuvres de Condorcet*, ed. by A.E. O'Connor and M.F. Arago, X, 363–64; G.-J.-B. Target, *Observations sur le commerce des grains* (Amsterdam, 1775), 26–27.

53 Roubaud, *Représentations*, 7–8, 363, 379, 392–95, 398–400.

of property without any special burdens or privileges as the police contended. Grain, Letrosne had written, must be considered "like every other merchandise" (like cloth, said St. Mars; like wool or shoes, Benjamin Fanklin wrote). "The property of grain," Turgot complained, "is regarded as less sacred than that of any other goods." From the police point of view, however, it was precisely because they considered grain *more sacred* than any other good that they could not allow its disposition to be decided purely in terms of individual rights and interests. Nothing more clearly marks the chasm between the liberal world of the future and the corporate world of the past. Only a vigorous and substantial grain trade, argued Roubaud, can distribute grain in deficit areas and equalize and stabilize prices, in time and across space. But, he cautioned, unless grain is given the status of an ordinary good and the merchant allowed to do with it what he pleases the commerce will remain small, local, and undependable. The police not only deprived the merchant of his rights; they also ruined his reputation by treating him publicly as "a brigand and an executioner" and teaching the people to distrust and hate him. "Instead of begrudging the merchant his profits, interfering with his speculations ... anathematizing his so useful and so honorable profession," Roubaud contended, "a wise, just and good Government" would not fail to "protect, encourage, reassure [and] favor" him. For all its well-known disdain for commerce, physiocracy reserved a special place for "this class of subjects so salutarily situated" between the producer and the consumer of grain.[54]

Implicitly, the Assembly reaffirmed the old police idea that the government owed the consumers their subsistence. Nothing could be more erroneous and more dangerous, the *économistes* charged. Like the liberal parlements, Roubaud argued that "the Government owes the people" nothing but "good laws." When they lacked bread, the people

---

54 *Ibid.*, 19–21, 112–13, 396, 451–54; Roubaud, "De l'histoire des subsistances," *Journal de l'agriculture, du commerce, des arts et des finances* (Jan. 1772), 64; Letrosne, *Lettres à un ami*, 15; Saint-Mars, *Le Spéculatif, ou dissertation sur la liberté du commerce des grains* (Amsterdam, and Paris, 1770), 37; B. Franklin, "Sur le prix du blé et sur l'administration des pauvres," from the *London Chronicle* (1766) in *Collection des principaux économistes*, XIV, 659–61: Turgot, "Septième lettre sur le commerce des grains," 2 Dec. 1770, in *Oeuvres*, ed. by Schelle, III, 323.

For similar views see *Journal économique* (May 1754), 66–67 and (Sept. 1770), 388; Condillac, *Le Commerce et le gouvernement* in *Collection des principaux économistes*, ed. by Daire and Molinari, XIV, 421; *Journal encyclopédique* (15 April 1775), 228; *Encyclopédie méthodique* (Paris, 1793), Agriculture, III, 370.

Lemercier de la Rivière conceded that grain was unlike any other commodity, but made his case for a total liberty of trade precisely on the grounds of the urgency of distributing it rapidly and efficiently. *L'Intérêt général*, 164–65.

should turn their heads to God; instead, the police taught them to look to the government "as if it made abundance or dearth to its liking; as if it were cultivator or merchant; as if it had to furnish wood and clothing when people suffered from cold." (The *économistes* lauded God the father in approximately the same proportion that they reviled the paternal state.) In this fashion the police aroused false hopes and assumed responsibilities which they had no right or mandate to undertake. What the government must do as a general rule in dealing with social problems and specifically in coping with a subsistence crisis is nothing—nothing at all.[55]

The revolt of the local police and the convocation of the Assembly of General Police provided compelling evidence, in the view of the *économistes*, that the authorities, "frightened by the cries of the people," had panicked. Instead of combatting "popular fears," Roubaud claimed, the police "shared them and erected them into Regulations." As Condorcet later remarked, "fear is at the origin of almost all human stupidities, especially political stupidities." If the authorities themselves did not resist these "vain terrors," what chance could there be of re-educating the people, a process which Baudeau, most forcefully among the physiocrats, insisted was necessary in order to modernize the society and the economy.

The point was not to be indifferent to popular outcries. The same Roubaud who emphasized that "needs were not rights" took umbrage at the Assembly's insinuation that the physiocrats were cruel and heartless. We have pity for the people, but a "thoughtful and enlightened pity," he explained. "In sharing and relieving their troubles, let us beware of their prejudices," he added; "suffering leads them astray." If you want to be "the fathers" of the people, Roubaud urged the parlementaires, "well then! treat them like children who are dear to you but who do not know what is best for them." Unschooled in political economy, the people cannot know "what their true interests" are. It is up to the magistrates to "disabuse" them of "false opinions"

---

55 Roubaud, *Représentations*, 7, 34, 44–46, 428; Weulersse, *Mouvement physiocratique*, I, 528. See also Weulersse, *La Physiocratie sous Turgot et Necker*, 109, 310 and *La Physiocratie ... Louis XV*, 84, 86, 91; Baudeau, "Suite des avis au peuple," *Ephémérides du citoyen*, X (1769), 19; Condorcet, *Le Monopole et le monopoleur*, in *Collection des principaux économistes*, ed. by Daire and Molinari, XIV, 463. Cf. Gournay's disdainful attitude toward "la bureaumanie" or "la bureaucratie" which has a strikingly modern ring. Grimm, *Correspondance littéraire*, ed. by Tourneux, VI, 30 (July 1764). The lawyer Target also had a horror for administration. G.-J.-B. Target, *Observations sur le commerce des grains* (Amsterdam, 1775), 43 and *passim*.

and "enlighten them." Teach them, for example, as Baudeau suggested, that what the "vulgar uninformed" called *cherté* was really the
"bon prix," the salvation of agriculture and the guarantee of future
subsistence. As for wages, Roubaud, following Quesnay, had nothing
to offer the people but the iron law of subsistence level adjustment
and the vague reassurance (about which Turgot and Condorcet were
less optimistic) that wages would promptly follow prices.[56]

Of course there were people and there were *people*, or so at least
the *économistes* tried to suggest. While on one level they preached a
universal solidarity of interests among all people in all places, on
another they divided the people, for polemical purposes, into camps
of different interests. Like the liberal parlements, first they divided
them into the people of the countryside (solid, forbearing, productive, austere, and submissive) and the people of the cities (generally
useless, often indolent and dissolute, spasmodically turbulent, and in
any case less precious than their cousins in the flat country). Then,
in the hope of laying claim to a larger universe of support and for
the sake of focusing upon a more manageable enemy, they divided
the people into the people of France, i.e., the provinces, the overwhelming bulk of the kingdom, and the people of Paris (parasitical,
spoiled, self-regarding).

The themes in both cases were very much the same; it was merely
a question of redrawing the boundaries. One is no more likely, said
Roubaud, to "find the sources of joy in tombs than one is to find

---

56 Roubaud, *Représentations*, 44–46, 104, 272, 368, 381–82; *Mercure de France* (Aug. 1769), 129;
   Baudeau, *Avis au premier besoin*, 123–29; Baudeau, "Sur les terreurs populaires," *Ephémérides
   du citoyen*, II (1767), 22, 33, 48; Condorcet, *Le Monopole et le monopoleur* in *Collection des principaux
   économistes*, ed. by Daire and Molinari, XIV, 463, 468; Quesnay, "Grains," in Diderot, *et al.*,
   Encyclopédie, VII, 831; Weulersse, *Mouvement physiocratique*, II, 327; Turgot, "Septième lettre
   sur le commerce des grains," 2 Dec. 1770, in *Oeuvres*, ed. by Schelle, III, 346–48.
       On the *économiste* attitude toward the people, see also: Letrosne, *La Liberté toujours utile*, 19,
   84–85, 89 and *Lettres à un ami*, 17–18; Mirabeau, cited by Weulersse, *La Physiocratie ... Louis
   XV*, 67–68; Dupont, "Observations sur les effets de la liberté," *Journal économique* (July 1770),
   333; Abbé Morellet, *Théorie du paradoxe* (Amsterdam, 1775), 109. Cf. Diderot to Necker,
   10 June 1775, *Correspondance Diderot*, ed. by G. Roth, XIV, 144–45; "Lettre de M.D. à un
   Magistrat du Parlement de Bourgogne," *Ephémérides du citoyen* XI (1768), 26–27.
       On the "right to exist," see Condillac, *Le Commerce et le gouvernement* and Condorcet, *Le
   Monopole et le monopoleur*, both in *Collection des principaux économistes*, ed. by Daire and Molinari,
   XIV, 421, 487.
       On the physiocratie wage theory, see also Letrosne's remarks in *Journal de l'agriculture, du
   commerce et des finances*, I (Aug. 1765), 80; Spengler, *French Predecessors*, 202–209; René Savetier,
   La Théorie du commerce chez les physiocrates (Paris, 1918), 199; J. F. Faure-Solet, *Economie politique
   et progrès au siècle des lumières* (Paris, 1964), 129, 133, 136.

the sources of prosperity in cities." Composed of "the excrement of the countryside," "eternally sterile" but "forever devouring," the city was an aberration in the national scheme of things and it was no accident that police was essentially an urban contrivance. "By what right," asked Condorcet, "is the inhabitant of the countryside sacrificed to the one of the big cities?" Under the cover of what they call police, the *économistes* charged, the cities exploit and oppress the productive heartland of the nation. Parisians were especially guilty of tyranny and egotism but, just as the state is not composed exclusively of cities, so the capital, Roubaud assured the bone and sinew of France, "is not our universe." The Assembly of General Police could fool no one by trying to pass off the voice of Paris as the "voice of God." It was hardly surprising that an assembly representing the capital would reach such false and vicious conclusions, hostile to the development of agriculture, the true source of national wealth and well-being. "If there was one place in the kingdom," wrote Baudeau, "from which it was difficult to see liberty act & justify the new laws, it was the capital, constantly subjected to the old Regulations, infested with passions ardent and contrary to the national interest...." If Paris suffered now it was because the capital enjoyed too little, not too much, liberty in the provisioning trade; indeed, as a result of the special "condescension" it demanded in the reform laws, it caused neighboring provinces to suffer as well. As Mirabeau was said to have remarked some years later, "Paris will be fed when Paris will pay."[57]

---

57 Roubaud, *Représentations*, 48, 52–53, 61–63, 73, 88, 105, 380, 385–86, 436–37; Condorcet, *Le Monopole et le monopoleur* in *Collection des principaux économistes*, ed. by Daire and Molinari, XIV, 465; Mirabeau, cited by Weulersse, *La Physiocratie ... Louis XV*, 158–59. See also Letrosne, *Réflexions sur les mœurs* (Orléans, ca. 1765); "Lettre de Mr. Dupont ...," *Journal de l'agriculture, du commerce et des finances*, VII (Nov. 1766), 207–208; Parl. of Provence, letter to king, 10 Nov. 1770, B. 3677, A.D. B-du-R.; *arrêt* of Parl. of Languedoc, 14 Nov. 1772, AN, AD XI 39; G.-J.-B. Target, *Observations sur le commerce des grains*, 33; Arthur Young, *Travels*, ed. by Kaplow, 389; Voltaire to M. de la Harpe, 10 March 1769, in *Oeuvres complètes de Voltaire*, ed. by Moland, XIV, 283; letter from Voltaire "à l'Auteur des Représentations aux Magistrats," 1 July 1769, published in *Mercure de France* (Aug. 1769), 134; Dupont, "Observations sur les effets de la liberté," *Journal économique* (Aug. 1770), 341; *Ephémérides du citoyen*, VI (1769), 222; Anon., "Mémoire sur l'exportation des grains," (1764), BN, mss. fr. 14296, fol. 18; Turgot, "Lettre circulaire aux officiers de police," 15 Feb. 1766, C. 479, A.D. Haute-Vienne; Baudeau, *Avis au premier besoin*, 94–95; Antoine Rivarol, *Oeuvres complètes*, ed. by Chênedollé and Fayolle (Paris, 1808), IV, 80n.

Note how dramatically the revolutionary experience transformed Condorcet's view of Paris and its place: *Sur le préjugé qui suppose une contrariété d'intérêts entre Paris et les provinces* (1790) in *Oeuvres de Condorcet*, ed. by A. C. O'Connor and M.F. Arago (Paris, 1847), X, 134, 147.

Illustration 6. Grain and Bread: 1. farmer. 2. harvesters. 3. threshers. 4. miller. 5. baker. Deutsches Brotmuseum, Ulm/Donau.

Illustration 7. Bakeshop. Note devices for sale on credit: the "tailles" in the hand of the baker-boy and the register kept by the baker's wife. *Encyclopédie.*

The *économiste* argument was tenuous but the syllogism rang true, especially in a time of dearth when feelings were raw and vulnerable: the interests of Paris are contrary to those of the nation at large; Paris hates liberty and loves police; therefore, liberty is in the national interest and police is contrary to it. The premises of the syllogism were politically attractive not only to the liberals but to the antiliberals like the Rouennais as well. For the latter, however, the conclusion was utterly unpalatable.

Like the liberal parlements, the *économistes* at the end of 1768 aimed to counteract the impression which the Assembly of General Police made on opinion and identify the opposition with urban and especially Parisian interests. But whereas their allies in the magistracy generally agreed that it was an inauspicious moment to make further demands upon the ministry, they stressed the urgency of moving into the second phase of liberalization even while the results of the first phase were under attack. The stroke of bad harvest luck could not continue indefinitely, so their argument went, and the best way to protect ourselves against future problems would be to make liberty more "perfect" and more "complete" than it had been under the 1763–64 reforms. Roubaud's book was also meant to defend the honor of the physiocratic school. We are not subversives or system-mongers, the abbé wrote indignantly, but scientists devoted to the public good, "philosophes who profess only one science, the science par excellence, it is true, the science proper to man, the science of kings and of subjects, the science of the social order." The "regulatory code" put forth by the Assembly of General Police was the real incarnation of "system, that is to say, a corpus of arbitrary combinations disposed to give to things a forced course."[58]

Roubaud wrote his five hundred page book in a remarkably short time and had the satisfaction of seeing it appear only a few weeks after the published minutes of the Assembly began to circulate.[59] For the moment there was a truce in the war of words, though in the background the abbé Galiani was busy finishing his devastating *Dialogues on the Grain Trade*, a work which may have been partially inspired by the Assembly of General Police. While they anxiously awaited the 1769 harvest, the *économistes* placed all their hopes in the liberal parlements, the royal council whose majority they believed still regarded liberalization with favor, and the determination of Louis XV to "stand firm."[60]

58 Roubaud, *Représentations*, 24, 437–48.
59 St.-Florentin to Roubault [*sic*], 9 June 1769, AN, O¹ 411.
60 Bachaumont, *Mémoires secrets*, XIX, 31 (Dec. 1768).

IV

The government drew encouragement from the staunch public declarations of the liberal parlements and the press campaign in its favor, but it found a more palpable source of strength in the apparent reversal of the upward price movement.[61] Even as the Parlement of Paris was translating the recommendations of the Assembly into formal remonstrances, the prices of bread, flour, and wheat had begun to drop. From the apex of 16½ to 17 *sous* the four pound loaf in November 1768, bread fell to 14½ in January, 14 in late March, 13 in May, 12 in July, and 10½ in January 1770, the lowest it had been since the summer of 1767. Between January 1769 and January 1770, the common price of wheat dropped from 27 *livres* the *septier* to 21 and the best white flour slipped from 68 *livres* the sack to 50 *livres*. The downward course appears to have resulted from the continuing distribution of king's grain, the prospect of a return to the old grain legislation spurred by the Paris Parlement's campaign which frightened hoarders into releasing supplies, the expectation of an excellent harvest produced by the "fine appearances" in early spring, and, finally, the harvest itself which, albeit far from a triumph, was nevertheless the best in the recent past. The government believed that the worst was over and the diminution of the prices blunted the urgency of the antiliberal parlementary appeal. With an air of extraordinary self-assurance and optimism that was not destined to last, the Controller-General Maynon d'Invau wrote the First President of the Parlement of Dauphiné that "the good effects that this liberty has produced … confirm His Majesty more and more in the firm resolution to maintain it … and even to extend it as soon as the circumstances appear favorable...."[62]

This fresh burst of confidence induced the new ministry to make claims for the first stage of liberalization which the government had never made before. "These laws [of 1763–64] rendered the grain trade an *absolute liberty*," the ministry informed its correspondents.[63] In letters to intendants the Controller-General Maynon and his aides Trudaine de Montigny and Albert continued to insist that dearth could be conquered only through "the natural path of commerce."[64]

---

61 See tables 1, 2 and 3 below.

62 Maynon to Berulle, 22 May 1769, B. 2314, fol. 121, A.D. Isère.

63 CG to de Fontette, IN. of Caen, 1769, AN, F[12]* 153, fols. 48–52.

64 See, for example, CG to DuCluzel, IN. of Tours, 10 Sept. 1769, *ibid.*, fol. 59 and C. 96, A.D. I-et-L.; Maynon d'Invau to Monthyon, 30 Oct. 1769, C. 906, A.D. P-de-D.

When local officials took measures that infringed upon the liberty, the central government acted quickly to quash them. A Rouen merchant successfully appealed a 500 *livres* fine imposed upon him by the Rouen police for buying in a market that used to be off limits to dealers. Since the "abolition of the prohibitive regime," Maynon reminded the police, you may no longer interfere with "the natural activity" of commerce.[65] The bailliage of Coutances condemned a grain merchant for depriving the community of grain by making purchases on the highway instead of in the public purview at the market. The Controller-General condemned the procedure as a "formal violation of the laws of the Kingdom," which

do not distinguish purchases made on the highways from those made in the granaries or marketplaces ... [the liberal laws] have solemnly proscribed all

Table 1. Wheat, flour, and bread prices 1769 Paris (Halles)

Date	Wheat *(septier)* in *livres* and *sous*			White flour (325 *livres* sack) in *livres* and *sous*		Best loaf (4 *livres*) in *sous* and *deniers*	
	Min.	Max.	Common	Min.	Max.	Min.	Max.
11 Jan.	22	32–10	27	48	68	14	14–6
28 Jan.	24	32–10	28	60	67	14	14–6
8 Feb.	26	32	29	50	66	14	14–6
25 Feb.	22	33	28–10	55	66	13–6	14–6
8 Mar.	24	30–10	28	44	65	13–6	14–6
25 Mar.	22	32	28	40	64	13–6	14
22 Apr.	22	30	26	43	63	13	14
10 May	16	27	22–10	50	62	13	13–6
24 May	21	26–10	24	40	58	12–6	13
7 June	23	28–5	25–10	40	57	12–6	
24 June	23	28–15	26	37	55–10	11–6	12–6
5 July	20	25	22–10	36	55	11	12–6
22 July	20	25	23	32	55	11	12
26 Aug.	22	28–15	26	36	55	11	12
6 Sept.	22–5		25	43	58	11	12
11 Oct.	22	28	25–10	40	57	11–6	12
8 Nov.	19	26–5	25	44	56	11–6	12
25 Nov.	20	27	23	44	55–10	11	11–6
6 Dec.	20–5	25–5	22	36	54	11	11–6
30 Dec	19	24	21	32	51	11	11–6

Source: B.N., Collection Joly de Fleury, 1143.

65 CG to de Crosne, 5 Nov. 1769, C. 103, A.D. S-M.

the obstacles and all the regulations which by preventing the circulation [of grain] halted the reproduction of subsistence and which in the false idea of preventing short-age led necessarily to establish it forever in the kingdom and to cast the people into famine.[66]

While the Paris Parlement characterized liberalization as the out-rider of famine, Maynon's government warned that it was the police

Table 2. Wheat, flour and, bread prices 1770 Paris (halles)

Date	Wheat *(septier)*			White flour (325 *livres* sack)		Best loaf (4 livres) in *sous* and *deniers*	
	Min.	Max.	Common	Min.	Max.	Min.	Max.
3 Jan.	20–10	23–5	21	40	51	10	11
13 Jan.	20	25	22–10	35	50	10–6	11
24 Feb.	26–10	22	20	36	45	10	10–6
24 Mar.	18	24	20–10	39	48	10	10–6
21 Apr.	20	23	21–10	36	47	10	10–6
12 May	23–10	28	25–10	40	56	11	11–6
9 June	26	28–5	27	39	56	11	11–6
30 June	25	31–5	28	43	60	12	12–6
11 July	25	34		61	68	13	13–6
21 July	27	32–10		60	67	13–6	14
1 Aug.	29–10	33		59	66	13–6	14
22 Aug.	30	35		62	67	13–6	14
1 Sept.	29	35–10		64	70	14–6	14–6
12 Sept.	30	36–10		64	70	14–6	15
19 Sept.	28	37		64	73	15	15–6
10 Oct.	25	34–10		68	74	15	15–6
31 Oct.	26	31		62	68	14–6	15
7 Nov.	20	29		62	66	14	14–6
14 Nov.	26	36		55	62	13–6	14
28 Nov.	24	29–10		57	62	12–6	13–6
5 Dec.	25	30		57	62	12–6	13
26 Dec.	25	31		58	63	13	
1771							
26 Jan.	26	30–10		58	63	13	
27 Feb.	26	30		56	60	12–6	13
23 Mar.	28	29–10		55	60	12–6	

Source: B.N., Collection Joly de Fleury, 1428, 1429.

---

66 CG to de Fontette, 1769, AN, F^{12}* 153, fols. 48–52.

Table 3. Paris bread prices from baker registers 1770–1774 (4 pound white loaf in *sous* and *deniers*)

Date	Pigeot	Houdart	Lecocq	Bernier
Jan. 1770			11–6, 11	
Feb.	10–6		11	
March	10–6		10–6	
April	10–6		11	
May	10–6, 11, 11–6		11, 11–6	11–6
June	11–6, 12	12	12, 13, 13–6	12–6
July	12–6, 13–6	13	12–6, 13, 13–6	13, 13–6, 14
Aug.	14	14	14, 14–6	14–6, 15
Sept.	15	15, 16	15, 15–6, 16	15–6
Oct.	15, 15–6	16, 15	15–6, 16	16
Nov.	14–6, 14, 13–6	16, 15, 14	15, 14–6, 14	15–6, 14–6
Dec.	13	14	14, 13–6	14

	Pigeot	Houdart		Chantal
Jan. 1771	13	14		13–6, 14
Feb.	13	13–6		13–6, 14
March	13	13–6		13
April	12–6	13		13
May	12–6	13		13
June	12–6	13		13
July	13	13		13
Aug.				13
Sept.				13
Oct.				13
Nov.				13
Dec.				12–6

	Garmont		Lecocq	Chantal
Jan. 1772			12	12–6
Feb.			11–6, 12	12
March	12		11–6, 12	12
April	12		11–6	12, 11–6
May	12		11	11–6, 11
June	11		10–6, 10	10–6, 10
July	10–6		10–6	
Aug.	10–6, 11		10–6	
Sept.	10–6, 11			
Oct.				
Nov.				
Dec.				

(Continued)

Table 3. Continued

	Garmont	Avé	Lecocq	Morin
Jan. 1773	10–6, 11			
Feb.	10–6, 11			
March	10–6, 11			
April				
May				
June			11	
July		11–6	11–6	12
Aug.		11–6, 12	11–6	12–6
Sept.		12, 12–6, 13	12, 12–6	12–6, 13
Oct.		13	13	13
Nov.		13	13	13
Dec.		13	13	13

	Lecocq	Morin
Jan. 1774	12–6	13, 12–6
Feb.	12–6	12–6
March	12–6	12–6
April	12–6	12–6
May	12	12–6
June	12	12, 11–6
July	11–6	11–6
Aug.		
Sept.		
Oct.		
Nov.		
Dec.		

Source: Archives Seine-Paris, registres: D5B[6] 4481, 1647, 1829, 84, 4837, 82, 3064, 1939.

actions tending "to alter the liberty of commerce" which threatened "to starve the people."[67] The Controller-General urged police officials to do everything in their power to facilitate and protect the "speculations" of the merchants, for they were the only source of salvation. It was neither wise nor "necessary," he maintained, for the government to undertake supply operations. "Only commerce can and must furnish," he wrote; "any provisioning made by authority would only drive it off, exclude competition, and augment the dearth." Not only did Maynon refuse to provide government subsistence aid to the provinces but he made it clear that the government discountenanced any local

---

67 CG to de Crosne, IN. of Rouen, 9 Aug. 1769, *ibid.*, fols. 54–55.

Table 4. Paris wheat prices, 1760–1780 (per *septier*, in *livres tournois* and fractions)

Years	Average Annual Wheat Prices, Contrôle-Général (AN, F[20] 105)	Chapitre de Paris table of Halles price at Martinmas (Nov.) every year (AN, L530)	A. Arnould, *De la balance du commerce* (Paris, 1791), III, Table 16
1760	17.85	18.00	19.80
1761	13.75	13.50	15.90
1762	13.80	17.00	16.05
1763	13.05	13.00	15.90
1764	12.30	15.25	15.55
1765	16.00	20.00	18.30
1766	16.85	19.50	20.40
1767	20.75	26.00	22.05
1768	27.50	37.50	32.80
1769	24.10	25.50	32.40
1770	26.55	30.00	29.05
1771	25.70	29.50	33.45
1772	21.55	26.75	28.20
1773	24.60	29.00	29.50
1774	22.20	26.00	26.55
1755	27.55		29.50
1776	22.65		24.95
1777	21.95		23.20
1778	19.65		22.45
1779	19.25		20.40
1780	17.35		19.20

self-help enterprises in which public officials played a role. Limit your activities, he told them, to "exciting and encouraging the *négociants* so that they bring their speculations your way."[68] To promote these speculations, the Controller-General asked the intendants to publicize widely the schedule of import bounties established at the end of October 1768.[69] Though he preached strict execution of the law, Maynon himself groped for loopholes in order to postpone the closing

---

68 CG to Dupleix, IN. of Amiens, 9 Aug. 1769 and to Monthyon, IN. of Auvergne, 10 Sept. 1769, *ibid.*, fols. 52–53, 57; CG to DuCluzel, 2 Nov. 1768, C. 94 and 10 Jan. and 10 and 17 Sept. 1769, C. 96, A.D. I-et-L.

69 CG to IN. of Champagne, 4 Nov. 1768, C. 418, A.D. Marne; CG to DuCluzel, 5 Nov. 1768, C. 94, A.D. I-et-L.; intendant's notes, ca. Nov. 1768, C. 81, A.D. C d'O.

of ports where prices had passed the export ceiling.[70] Since both policies sought to bolster a free grain trade, Maynon saw no inconsistency
between subsidizing imports and fostering a continued drain of domestic supplies.

For those who looked at France through the eyes of Paris, the
recoiling of prices in 1769 masked the fact that almost everywhere
else in the kingdom the crisis was expanding and deepening. In the
classical mechanism of this cereals-dominated economy, what began
as a subsistence crisis swelled, unevenly but implacably, into a general
economic crisis.[71] Unequal in bad times as in good, the rhythm of
the cyclical price rise varied from place to place. Measured against
the national mean, the Parisian maxima were precocious. Even as
the spiral seemed to taper off in the Paris area (and to some extent
in Normandy as well), the prices in other regions climbed steeply.
On a national scale, 1770 marked the height of the crisis. In many
places the plateau of high prices persisted until the middle of the
decade. The immediate cause of the crisis in most places was a series
of harvest failures, but other long-term factors such as demographic
expansion, monetary inflation, climatological change, and pressures
of international scope seem to have come into play.

Directly and indirectly, liberalization nurtured and exacerbated
the crisis by creating a feverish climate of speculation, opening
new commercial outlets, disorganizing the distribution system, and
spreading fear and uncertainty. Everywhere the grain price served
as the "barometer" for the whole economy. The precipitous decline
in cereal production led to a severe contraction in purchasing

---

70 CG to IN. of Bordeaux, 31 March 1769, C. 1427, A.D. Gir.

71 See Labrousse, *Esquisse*, his *La Crise de l'économie française*, especially the preface, and the
sections he contributed to F. Braudel and E. Labrousse, eds., *Histoire économique et soeiale*, II,
385ff. For the "general crisis" of 1770, see *Histoire économique et sociale*, II, 408, 414–16, 489,
536–555. The "flare-up of prosperity" discerned by Goubert, Tarrade, and other scholars
in the years following the end of the Seven Years' War must have been short-lived in many
places and sectors. See Goubert in *Histoire économique et sociale*, II, 76 and Jean Tarrade, *Le
commerce colonial de la France à la fin de l'ancien régime* (Paris, 1972), I, 7–8. Though Marseille
suffered a severe crisis in the early seventies, according to Charles Carrière it was "financial" in nature, without any clearcut relation to the grain question. *Négociants marseillais au
XVIIIᵉ siècle* (Aix-Marseille, 1973), I, 455. Carriére is reacting against the almost irresistible
historiograph-ical propensity for a quasi-grain-determinism in explaining eighteenth century economic history. But it seems to me that the case for sectorial autonomy is overdrawn
when it leads to a sort of causal compartmentalization. On the international dimensions of
the crisis, see W. Abel, *Massenarmut und Hungerkrisen im vorindustriellen Deutschland* (Göttingen,
1972), 46–54 and *Crises agraires en Europe* (Berlin, 1935; Paris, 1973), 25, 286, 339, and *passim*.

power, widespread unemployment in the countryside and in the cities, lagging wages, serious indebtedness, an extraordinary wave of business failures affecting petty artisans as well as great financiers, and an industrial recession, most acute in the pilot textile sector. Second in severity only to the disasters of 1788–89, the general economic crisis of 1770 inaugurated a troubled "intercyclical" period of almost two decades bringing a half century of expansion to a close on a note of recurring agricultural and industrial adversities. In the early years of the seventies, the rest of the kingdom suffered the same sort of misery and disorder of which Paris and Rouen had been complaining since the late sixties. The *curés* and intendants in many parts of France recorded a sharp increase in the mortality rate.[72]

Just as the economic crisis was reaching a crescendo, the government faced a grave fiscal crisis. Unwilling to believe that the economic situation was as bad as the reports indicated—it tended to regard them as products of antiliberal propaganda—the government nevertheless could not avert its eyes from the fiscal predicament which threatened to paralyze its operation. The financial problem was not a cyclical counterpoint to a prevailing trend. It was chronic, built-in to the political and administrative institutions of the monarchy and to the social structure.[73] The parlements thwarted the efforts of the government to rationalize the fiscal system, extend the tax base, impose the burden equitably, and establish uniform and efficient collection procedures. The government itself, at least until the last third of the century, made little effort to

---

72 See P. Goubert's analysis in Labrousse and Braudel, eds., *Histoire économique et sociale*, II, 76–78. It is of course extremely difficult to date with precision the onset, apex, and passing of this crisis. It manifested itself in many different ways, without concern for logic or consistency, in different places. Administrators sometimes announced its arrival or celebrated its departure prematurely. In some instances—one thinks especially of parts of Normandy—the crisis appeared to make two or three visitations. Obviously a great deal of research must be undertaken at the local as well as the regional level before the character of the crisis or crises is fully known to us. For a beginning, see Masson to IN., 5 July 1770, C. 299, A.D. Aube; état d'apparences, 5 July 1771, C. 84, A.D. Somme; Monteymard to IN., 25 Oct. 1771, C. 423, A.D. Marne; Geslin to IN., 8 May 1772, C. 1726, A.D. I-et-V.; Ateliers de Charité, C. 591, A.D. Aisne; de Vandoul to IN., 21 April 1773, C. 2914, A.D. Hér.; Auron to IN., 5 July 1773, C. 1440, A.D. Gir.; de Badoine to IN., 22 Oct. 1773, C. 89, A.D. Orne; Toulouse municipal accounts, 1773, C. 412, A.D. H-G.; C. 2626, A.D. Cal.; Letaconnoux, *Le commerce des grains en Bretagne*, 140–141; J. Godechot and S. Moncassin, "Démographie et subsistances en Languedoc," 34, René Baehrel, *Une croissance: la Basse-Provence rurale* (Paris, 1961), 75–76.
73 See, for these questions, Marcel Marion, *Histoire financière*, I; René Stourm, *Les Finances de l'ancien régime*, I; and J.F. Bosher, *French Finances*.

adapt the fiscal administration to its needs. With few exceptions, the government fell back upon short-term, flimsy solutions, which sustained it by postponing the reckoning to another time. Periodically, the government found itself in desperate straits and had to seek a new accommodation or invent new expedients. The last major revision of fiscal affairs occurred in 1763. It was meant to circumvent an impasse, not to be durable. Another crisis was in the making as soon as the preceding one had been quelled.

That it erupted, however, in 1770 and proved to be so violent seems to be directly related to the general economic crisis. Business distress and uncertainty made money, like grain, scarce. The financiers suffered setbacks and the government found it difficult to obtain large doses of fresh credit. Measured against the claims on the treasury— one should say, more precisely, treasuries—the increased revenue which Laverdy said liberalization produced was a mere trifle. Maynon D'Invau had a 55,000,000 *livres* deficit, eighty millions in arrears, and was meeting the needs of 1769 with the anticipated receipts of 1770. "The finances of Your Majesty," the Controller-General confessed to the king, "are in the most horrible state of ruin."[74] Facing imminent bankruptcy, Maynon resigned in December 1769. With him passed the last hope of liberalization.

---

74 Marion, *Histoire financière*, I, 246. Several contemporary observers depicted Maynon as a simple tool or "creature" of Choiseul and attributed his downfall to the machinations of Maupeou, who was determined to purge the ministry entirely of Choiseul's influence. Pidansat de Mairobert, *Journal historique*, 389–90; Moreau, *Mes souvenirs*, ed. by C. Hermelin, I, 187; Lebrun, *Opinions*, 27.

Chapter XI

FROM POLITICAL ECONOMY TO POLICE: THE RETURN TO APPREHENSIVE PATERNALISM

The government's inability to stem the generalization and deepening of the crisis at the very end of the decade doomed liberalization. The new Controller-General, Terray, metaphorically portrayed the liberal experience as "the flood" and imagined his responsibility, in part, as channeling the waters back into their natural reservoirs and building dikes capable of withstanding future inundations of any sort. But he did not take a nostalgically antediluvian approach to the task—at least he tried not to. The problem was that de-liberalization did not bring instant recovery. Terray enjoyed virtually no respite from subsistence troubles during his four-year tenure and the subsistence troubles generated other political and economic problems which compounded the difficulty for him.

The discussion of his administration is divided into three parts which mark the boundaries of this and the following two chapters. The first concerns the return to a police regime, a transition not easily effected, and the nature of Terray's short- and long-term goals. The second examines the Controller-General's efforts to apply his subsistence policy throughout the kingdom during the years 1771–74 and the reactions of a broad spectrum of opinion to it. The third explores Terray's use of the king's grain, a vital instrument in his attempt to parry the ongoing dearth, and the political costs of government intervention on the supply side.

I

The abbé Joseph Marie Terray, "the best mind in the parlement," a fifty-five year old clerical counselor from a modest bourgeois family which ascended slowly into the Robe during the last part of the reign of

Louis XIV, became the new Controller-General.[1] The departure of Maynon, a friend of the physiocrats and a stout defender of the liberal reforms, did not signify a determination within the royal council to change the grain policy. It was motivated by the financial imbroglio, not the subsistence crisis, two problems whose relationship at this point in time the king's advisers did not clearly perceive. Although Terray had expressed serious doubts about the May Declaration at the time of registration, he had asked his colleagues to give it a fair chance. He had not taken an active role in the parlementary campaign against liberalization. Throughout his career as rapporteur of royal legislation he had shown singular talent for mediating between the desires of the sovereign court and those of the king. At the end of 1769 it was expected that he would devote all of his energies to the herculean task of restoring a semblance of order to the crown's finances, leaving the subsistence question in the hands of the liberals Trudaine de Montigny and Albert who remained in charge of the grain department. Choiseul, whose influence in the council had not yet been undercut by Maupeou, detested the *économistes* but remained a partisan of liberalization.[2] At the moment Terray came to power, prices in Paris were still declining and the Parlement had lapsed into silence.

In the provinces, however, there was little warrant for subsistence optimism. A new wave of grassroots reaction against liberalization broke over the kingdom, reaching from Normandy across the heart of France to Franche-Comté and touching large areas of the center, the southwest, and the south. Exasperated by years of unremitting pressure and uncertainty, the local police groped desperately to uncover supplies and unmask "infamous monopoly." In violation of the national laws, authorities in many towns and bourgs issued sentences and ordinances prohibiting the removal of grain or allowing removals only upon the award of a special license, denying outsiders the right to purchase, banning all off-market exchanges, requisitioning supplies and obliging merchants to furnish quotas, imposing fixed

---

1 *Gazette de France* (23 Dec. 1769), 418; Lebrun, *Opinions* cited by Girard, *L'Abbé Terray*, 30; M.-F. Pidansat de Mairobert, *L'Observateur anglois, ou Correspondance secrète entre mylord all'eye et mylord all'ear* (London, 1784), I, 89. See also Marmontel, *Mémoires*, ed. by Tourneux, III, 91 and Jobez, *La France sous Louis XV*, VI, 460–61.

2 I share Weulersse's view of Choiseul's general attitude. *Mouvement*, I, 225–26. For an opposing view, see Girard, *Terray*, 70n.

    While he seemed to defer to Trudaine de Montigny's judgment on grain affairs, Terray labored from the beginning to force him out of office. See J.-M. Augeard, *Mémoires secrets de J.-M. Augeard*, ed. by E. Bavoux (Paris, 1866), 66.

buying priorities, forcing dealers to relax their price demands by refusing them the right to withdraw unsold grain, forbidding stocking, and making inspections and inventories of private granaries. As usual, the liberal press exaggerated and distorted the picture for political reasons, but there was nevertheless an element of truth in the shrill outcry of the *Gazette de l'Agriculture, du Commerce, des Arts et des Finances* that everywhere "commerce is hampered, proscribed, repelled" by the resurgence of "high police."[3]

In response to the protests against the *cherté* several parlements took measures aimed at provisioning the towns and preventing the drainage of grain from their regions. In January 1770 the Bordeaux court ordered all grain owners in the provinces of Limousin and Périgord to bring grain to market and banned all transactions in the granaries or the countryside. Determined to close loopholes, several months later the council acting as a parlement in Alsace ordered, in addition to requisitions and mandatory market exchanges, searches, and inventories. During the course of the year, without authorization from the central government, the Parlements of Dombes, Alsace, Lorraine, and Metz segregated their jurisdictions from the rest of the kingdom by unilaterally imposing embargoes on the departure of any grain from within their boundaries. An *arrêt* of the Besançon court, though it ostensibly forbad only exports abroad, had the same effect. Like its eastern neighbors, Burgundy was the scene of frequent popular disorders. In an effort to stem the price rise and restore tranquility, the Parlement forbad grain to leave the capital city of Dijon, required merchants wishing to deal there to register with the municipality, banned certain speculative practices such as trading in futures, and imposed a form of requisition. All these measures, in turn, encouraged (indeed, in some cases enjoined) local authorities to resurrect old controls. At the same time, a number of intendants, especially in the eastern provinces, began to press for a modification of the liberal laws.[4]

---

3 See, for example, the cases in Sermaize-les-Bains, Caen, Bayeux, Angoulême, Fontenay-le-Comte, Tours, Amboise, Orléans, Saumur, St. Dizier, Joinville, Rodez, and in towns in the Poitou, Guyenne, Auvergne, Berry, and Lorraine. Royal council *arrêts de cassation* 12, 19 Aug. 1770, AN, F^{12} 6; CG to Turgot, 10 April 1770, AN, F^{12} 154; royal council *arrêts de cassation*, 9, 28 May and 24 June 1770, C. 774, A.D. L-A.; CG to IN. of Champagne, 10 July 1770, AN, F^{12} 153; CG to IN. of Champagne, 24 May, 2 June 1770, C. 417, A.D. Marne; DuCluzel to officers of Amboise, 11 May 1770, author's private collection; CG to La Galaisière, 10 July 1770, AN, F^{11} 153; C. 908 and C. 910, A.D. P-de-D.; *Gazette de l'agriculture, du commerce, des arts et des finances* (7 July 1770), 506, (10 July 1770), 517–18, and (26 Jan. 1771), 59.

4 *Arrêts du Conseil*, 19 Feb., 4 Aug., 31 Oct., 4 Dec, 1770, AN, F^{12} 6; CG to

In dealing with each of these cases, the Controller-General maintained a staunchly liberal posture. In part this was the result of the presence of Trudaine de Montigny and Albert who ran the grain department. Yet, even after Terray forced them out of the ministry in the summer of 1770, the government continued to take what passed for a liberal stand in response to specific instances of police reaction. From the beginning it is clear that he did not share the all-embracing faith of Trudaine and Albert in the efficacy of liberty. On strictly practical grounds, however, he consistently favored the freest possible movement of grain within as well as among different provinces. In order to enable surplus areas to succor deficit areas and deficit areas to unburden surplus areas, it was necessary to guarantee open circulation in the interior. Though the family image habitually used to describe the fraternal relations which were supposed to exist between the various parts of the kingdom had an old-fashioned ring, the aim of this policy was wholly modern: the interdependence of the components of the realm was a measure of its unity, its political coherence, and its national strength. Indeed, one of the liberal arguments pitched to appeal to statemakers was the idea that liberalization would create stronger ties of national unity even as government played a far less prominent role in mediating between regions, between cities, and between town and country. Terray, to be sure, did not associate unification with nonintervention, but the prospect of watching the kingdom disintegrate into myriad quasi-autonomous, enemy camps under the impact of dearth and doubt made him shudder along with the most unblenching liberals.

Unlike the liberals, Terray believed that, on many occasions, it was in the general interest for a province or an area to be closed or for trading relations to be artificially modified in some other fashion. But, he insisted, only the central government was in a position to determine when such steps were expedient. Nor was this only a matter of reserving the decision to the central government because it was infinitely better informed than anyone else and thus in a position to make a better decision. Terray was as much concerned about settling the crucial political question of the competence to make decisions as about

---

Bertin, 10 June 1770, AN, F¹² 153; Dijon Parl. *arrêts*, 4, 18 July 1770, C. 81, A.D. C d'O.; Girod, "Les Subsistances en Bourgogne à la fin de l'ancien régime," *Revue bourguignonne de l'enseignement supérieur*, XVI (1906), viiin; CG to Amelot, 1 Aug. 1770, AN, F¹² 155; *Mercure de France* (July 1770), 195–97; Besançon Parl. *arrêts*, 10 May and 20 Nov. 1770, B. 2174 and 20 Aug. 1770, B. 3270, A.D. Doubs; de la Corée to Terray, Sept. 1770, C. 844, A.D. Doubs.

assuring the quality of decisions. The police reaction might very well constitute evidence that there was something very wrong with the law but it was not the prerogative of parlements or local authorities (or, for that matter, of the consumer-people) to abjure or remake the law on their own initiative and by their own devices. Regardless of the circumstances, the Controller-General could not afford to give the impression that the government would tolerate local and regional particularism, vigilantism, or other forms of subsistence home rule; to the government, administrative and political anarchy, whatever its causes, was as abhorrent as social anarchy was frightening. Liberalization, incidentally, became an awkward and inopportune test of the political system. Terray could not ignore the oft-repeated liberal charges that the government had lost control of the situation, that it was not able (not merely unwilling) to command obedience, that it was reckless. (In retrospect the liberal accusation seems both ironic and true: the government of Louis XV was not strong enough to govern absolutely or, what amounted to the same thing, it was not strong enough absolutely not to govern.) Thus Terray had to teach the rebel parlements and local authorities a lesson even as he had to administer a lesson to rebel consumers. But that did not mean that he was prepared to cling to a grain policy in which he did not believe merely because it was the government's inherited legal responsibility; unlike many of the enlightened ministers of the eighteenth century, Terray had no taste for pyrrhic victories.

On the grounds that they were contrary to the May and July laws, illegitimate assertions of power, and, in addition, likely to do more bad than good, Terray had the council annul the measures taken by local authorities (that is to say, the local measures which were denounced formally to the government—which surely represented only a small portion of the illegal acts of local authority). They were "dangerous examples" certain to "intensify the dearth" by driving off suppliers, further alarming the public, and encouraging competition and strife between neighboring communities.[5] "Instruct your *substituts*," the Controller-General wrote the Paris Procurator General,

---

5 CG to IN. de Pont (Moulins), 23 June 1770 and to IN. Cypierre (Orléans), 29 May 1770, AN, F^{12}* 153, fols. 303, 327; CG to IN. Amelot (Dijon), 5 Aug. 1770 and to IN. of Metz, 25 April 1770, AN, F^{12}* 155, fols. 6, 30–31; and the references in the preceding note. Even after he moved to an overtly antiliberal position, Terray continued to demand the annulment of police measures which he judged inappropriate. In June 1772, for example, the Nantes municipality, which had battled so passionately for total liberty in the sixties, forbad the "export" of any grain from the city and

that they must leave to the grain trade all liberty, that if they should alter it they would drive away the very commerce upon which they must count in this moment for all their subsistence and which flees the places where it sees obstacles or blows of authority.[6]

Terray also pressed the intendants to enjoin municipal officials "to protect the liberty of trade and circulation." Yet while the intendant of Tours gently consoled the town fathers of Amboise with the assurance that the ministry has taken "the most effective measures for the provisioning of the provinces," the Contrôle-Général reiterated the theme upon which Maynon had dwelled: the people and the police must learn to understand that private commerce, not government, supplies grain. Less than a year before Terray began a massive expansion of the king's grain operations, his office told the intendant of Brittany that it was the intention of the king to "cease all provisioning operations made by the efforts of the government."[7] The new Controller-General inspired little confidence on the local level, at least in the beginning. Nor is it surprising to discover instances where the authorities openly defied the council by reissuing the cancelled sentences and ordinances in slightly altered form. To discourage police recidivism, the council added to its *arrêts* of invalidation a clause holding the chief police officer personally responsible in his private capacity for costs, damages, and interest arising from further repetitions.[8]

The government rebuked the parlements in similar fashion. The royal council quashed the "embargo" *arrêts* of the courts of Lorraine, Dombes, Alsace, Metz, and Burgundy on the grounds that they were illegal, ill-conceived, and inopportune, tending "directly to destroy the liberty of circulation in all the extent of the kingdom," to cut "the ties which unite all the subjects" of France, and "to authorize in the mind of the people ... the prejudice against liberty of shipments." Charging that its intervention had already driven up prices "considerably" in less than a month's time and carried the people to the brink of panic, the government suppressed the marketing controls revived by the Alsace court. Similar regulations reimposed by the Bordeaux Parlement

---

hinterland to other areas. The council quashed the measure on the grounds that it was an "abuse of authority" contrary to the interests of both the king and his people. *Arrêt* of 17 June 1772, C, 774, A.D. L-A.

6 Terray to Joly, 5 May 1770, BN, Coll. Joly 1148, fols. 22–23.

7 CG to DuCluzel, 9 May 1770 and DuCluzel to officials of Amboise, 11 May 1770, author's private collection; CG to D'Agay, 10 Feb. 1770, AN, F^{12}* 153, fol. 108. Cf. CG to Juges-Consuls of Nantes, 27 May 1770, *ibid.*, fol. 267.

8 See, for example, *arrêt du conseil*, 19 Aug. 1770, AN, F^{12} 6.

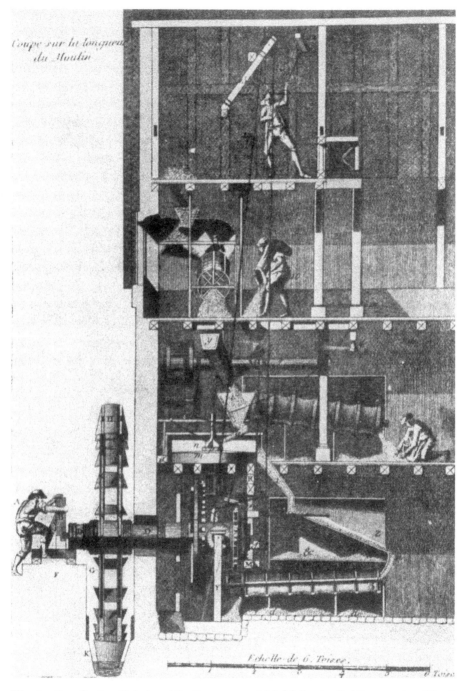

Coupe sur la longueur du Moulin

Echelle de 6. Toises.

Illustration 8. A mill designed for the process which Malisset called "economic milling." P.-J. Malouin, *Descriptions et détails des arts du meunier,* du *vermicellier, et du boulanger* (Paris, 1767).

Illustration 9. Leprévost de Beaumont, the citizen who denounced the "famine plot," languishing in prison. Bibliothèque Nationale.

were annulled for "spreading alarm and terror and inciting the owners of grain to use all the means and detours to hide their grain," that
is, for causing the very hoarding which the magistrates claimed they
wanted to prevent.[9]

Instead of taking "dangerous" and "useless" measures on their own
account, the Controller-General urged the parlements to apply directly
to the central government for advice and remedies. Terray protested
vehemently when the Besançon court named a special commission to
deal with grain affairs. He asked the First President to do everything in
his power to make sure that the commission "sits in *inaction* and that it
takes no act of authority: otherwise you will see the price increase still
more and the grain flee, go into hoards, or perhaps lack totally." Yet,
in return for the quiescence he sought, it is not at all clear that Terray
was able to deliver the help he pledged, at least not until he began
to back his promises with the distribution of government grain. One
of the grievances of the Besançon magistrates was that grain purchased for the urgent provisioning needs of Franche-Comté was being
intercepted in Burgundy and allocated for local use there. Committed
to the principle of free internal circulation, the Controller-General
assured the Besançon Parlement that he would take steps to guarantee
the movement of grain into their province. But would the Dijon court
agree to honor the principle and to aid in supplying Franche-Comté
at the risk of depleting its own jurisdiction? Parlementary solidarity
stopped short of sharing scarce subsistence.[10]

II

A torrent of riots heralded the *soudure* despite excellent portents of
the coming harvest.[11] The "whole town" of Herman in Auvergne

---

9 *Arrêts du conseil*, 4 Aug., 31 Oct., 4 and 21 Dec. 1770, AN, F^{12} 6; CG to Bertin, 10 June 1770,
   F12* 153; *arrêts du conseil*, 19 Feb. and 27 July 1770, AN, AD XI 39; *Gazette de l'agriculture, du
   commerce, des arts et des finances* (10 July 1770), 518 and (28 Aug. 1770), 629.
10 CG to Grosbois, 29 May 1770 and CG to Amelot, La Galaisière, Rouillé and Maupeou, 24
   May 1770, AN, F^{12} 153; de la Porte to de la Corée, 2 Dec. 1770, C. 844, A.D. Doubs. Cf.
   Directeur des vivres at Besançon to IN. of Champagne, 11 May 1770, C. 299, A.D. Aube.
   The Parlement of Metz, on two different occasions, tried to set up permanent subsistence
   commissions, similar in structure and function to the Parisian assemblies of police, to deal
   with all matters concerning provisioning. Deliberations (*registres secrets*), 23 July 1770, B. 469,
   fol. 37 and 17 June 1771, B. 470, fol. 65, A.D. Moselle.
11 The *Gazette de l'agriculture, du commerce, des arts et des finances* reported an expectation of a

assembled, armed with rocks, to prevent the removal of 40 *septiers* of grain in March. At Mauriac in the same province, consumers also tried to stop "the export of their subsistence." Though the market was allegedly "well-furnished," large numbers of Dijonnais were in a violent and defiant mood in mid-May. Wandering bands ambushed grain wagons while others threatened to burn the city hall and pillage the marketplace. People at nearby Auxonne made similar efforts to block the outflow of grain and force more of it on the market. With tacit assistance from the police, a crowd at Tours attacked a passing grain boat. In an attempt to prevent grain removals, consumers transformed the marketplace at Tulle in the Limousin into a battleground, one of many which scarred the jurisdiction of the Bordeaux Parlement that summer. "Furious" that prices continued to rise, consumers at Cambrai demonstrated in the streets. To defend their grain against outsiders, the inhabitants of Loing, near Gray, turned to violence. Enraged that "their provisions were being taken away," a part of the Besançon citizenry rose up in the market. Later in the year the people of Besançon rioted again, shouting "they want to starve the city, we must not let one single grain wagon leave." For almost three days crowds roamed the streets carrying sticks and pitchforks, insulting the police, and hunting for grain. The people treated those who were arrested as heroes and martyrs; they organized alms collections to help those "who were detained for having intercepted grain for the public good."[12]

In August bread rioting buffeted Lyons. The Lyons experience illustrated why consumers had recourse to violence: because it worked, or at least appeared to work. Immediately after the ferment, the bread price in France's second city declined, probably as the result of administrative action. Terray understandably wanted the rioters to draw a different moral from their experience. At Lons-le-Saunier (Franche-Comté), for example, after a crowd pillaged the town's storehouses, the Controller-General called for "an example capable

---

"quite generally abundant harvest." (24 July 1770), 547. Though he was less sanguine about the prospect for real abundance, the intendant of Picardy foresaw a crop comfortably sufficient to meet needs. Draft to CG, 24 Sept. 1770, C. 83, A.D. Somme.

12 Chaumeit to IN. (?), 26 March 1770, C. 908, A.D. P-de-D.; SD to IN. (?), 12 March 1770, C. 907, A.D. P-de-D.; CG to First President, Dijon, 19 May 1770 and to Amelot, 20 May 1770, AN, F¹² 153; *arrêt du conseil*, 9 May 1770, C. 774, A.D. L-A.; *arrêts* of Bordeaux Parl., 11 Aug. 19 Sept. 1770, uncatalogued, A.D. Gir.; Taporten to IN., 15 July 1770, C. 5976, A.D. Nord; Deliberations, Besançon Parl., 31 Aug. and 20 Nov. 1770, B. 3270, A.D. Doubs; *Lettres Ossolinski*, 6 Aug. 1770, BHVP, mss. 628, fol. 67.

of containing the people and preventing them from resorting in the future to such excesses." Yet he viewed the motives of the insurgents with far more sympathy than had Laverdy and he did not press with his predecessor's zeal for pitiless repression. Terray hesitated between sending king's grain and king's troops to troubled areas; in the end, in many instances, he seems to have dispatched both.[13]

During the course of the summer and early fall disturbances marred the peace in Upper and Lower Normandy, the Hainaut, Picardy, Anjou, the Touraine, Auvergne, the Nivernais, Alsace, and Lorraine.[14] Some of the most serious rioting occurred in Champagne. Alarmed at the prospect of seeing their market depleted, consumers at Troyes demonstrated in order to prevent further removals, force the price down, and settle a score with a prominent dealer on whom they blamed much of their distress. At St. Dizier a trader known for siphoning grain out of the community was forced to "abandon [his] grain to the discretion of the people" when they attacked his drivers and threatened to burn his granaries. Crowds prevented the departure of grain wagons from Joinville. At Sainte-Menehould the "lowly people promised to let no grain go." The police took note of similar threats at Chaumont. The consumers at Bar-sur-Seine won a victory when the police, in order to dissipate a swelling riot, passed measures guaranteeing consumers first access to the market and ordered the sale of stored grain at a fixed price below the current. Here, as in Dijon, the people rose up to prevent the removal of grain not by greedy speculators but by "the people of the countryside" who came to the city in search of subsistence. With nowhere to turn, the country folk felt increasingly desperate.

---

13 CG to First President, Dijon Parl., 19 May 1770 and to Amelot, 20 May 1770, AN, F^{12} 153; *arrêts* of Bordeaux Parl., 11 Aug., 19 Sept. 1770, uncatalogued, A.D. Gir.; *Lettres Ossolinski*, 6 Aug. 1770, BHVP, mss. 628, fol. 67; CG to de Flesselles and to de la Verpillière, 23 Aug. 1770, AN, F^{12} 155, fols. 27–29; CG to PG of Besançon Parl., 9 Sept. 1770, AN, F^{12} 155.

14 CG to Dupleix, 16 Aug. 1770 and CG to Jullien, 28 Aug. 1770, AN, F^{12} 155, fols. 20, 38; lieutenant of police of Caen to Miromesnil, 20 July 1770 and Fontette to Terray, 21 July 1770, C. 2653, A.D. Cal.; Dehauld to IN., 19 Dec. 1770, C. 5976, A.D. Nord; *Gazette de l'agriculture, du commerce, des arts et des finances* (3 July 1770), 500–501; François Lebrun, *Les Hommes et la mort en Anjou*, 139–40; C. 908, C. 910, A.D. P-de-D.; *Journal politique* (July 1770, second quinzaine), 55–56; *Lettres Ossolinski*, 23 July 1770, BHVP. mss. 628, fol. 65; Daniel Mornet, *Les Origines intellectuelles de la révolution française* (Paris, 1954), 445.
  On the disorders, subsistence difficulties, and "mortalités" in eastern France in 1770–1771, see; C. Pfister, "Le Magasin de blé à Nancy et la révolte de 1771," *Revue historique de la Lorraine* (1906), 77–92 and F.Y. Lemoigne, "La Crise frumentaire de 1770–71 à Metz, Nancy et Strasbourg," *Bulletin de la Société d'Histoire Moderne* (71st year, 15th series, number 3), 305.

A delegation of thirty "workers" [*ouvriers*]—future rioters—from a hamlet near Bar visited the fiscal procurator to complain that no one would sell them grain or bread. The procurator asked for authority to search local homes and storehouses with a brigade of the constabulary. At Reims, in July, "troops of people" intercepted grain traffic on the roads and raided convents and other places suspected of keeping grain stocks. Continued violence obliged Choiseul to send troops, who remained in garrison for several weeks. To placate consumers, the municipal authorities agreed to review all grain transactions and to buy grain for resale to the public, presumably at discount. Not long afterward, the police at Vitry, in the aftermath of a price-fixing and grain-blocking riot, began purchasing grain in the countryside for sale on the Vitry market below the current.[15]

Nor was the Paris region spared social conflagration.[16] Price-fixing mutinies erupted throughout the Brie. At Coulommiers "the populace, after many tumultuous remarks, on its own authority fixed the price of wheat at 2 *livres* 10 *sous* the bushel and forced the *fermiers* to give it at this price instead of at 3 *livres* several *sous* which was the going rate." At nearby Faremoutiers, after imposing a price on the *laboureurs*, a crowd rampaged through the streets and invaded the houses of persons suspected of hoarding grain. According to the fiscal procurator, it might have become a "bloody revolt" if the Mother Superior of a local convent had not distributed a copious quantity of wheat "to this starved people for a price much below that at which it was sold at the last market." At Meaux, as in the rest of the Brie, the *cherté* was crushing, there was a gaping "disproportion" between the

---

15 C. 1908, A.D. Aube; CG to Rouillé d'Orfeuil, 10 July 1770, AN F¹² 153; Mathieu to Goutier, 16 July 1770, C. 414, A.D. Marne; Masson to IN., 5, 17 July 1770 and IN. to CG, 28 July 1770, C. 299, A.D. Aube; Reims municipality to IN., 12 July 1770 and Choiseul to IN., 2 Sept. 1770, C. 414, A.D. Marne; *Lettres Ossolinski*, 29 Oct. 1770, BHVP, mss. 628, fol. 93; Heuvrard to IN., 3 Oct. 1770 and CG to IN., 14 Oct. 1770, C. 416, A.D. Marne.

16 For the next four paragraphs: Farquel to PG, 20 July 1770, BN, Coll. Joly 1157, fols. 80–81; Cordenier to PG, 23 July 1770, *ibid.*, 1151, fols. 52–53; Canelle to PG, 21 July 1769, *ibid.*, 1151, fols. 55–56; CG to Bertier de Sauvigny, 1, 9 Aug. 1770, AN, F¹²* 155, fols. 1, 10; memoir to PG from Lagny, July 1770, BN, Coll. Joly 1150, fols. 33–36, 47, 51; Petition of Simon Lenormand, *et al.* to PG, July 1770, *ibid.*, 1150, fol. 44; Ganneron to PG, 18 June and 23, 27 July 1770, *ibid.*, 1149, fols. 118–19, 123–24, 126; petition of "laboureurs et fermiers de la province du Mulcien," 27 July 1770, *ibid.*, 1151, fol. 61; Canelle to PG, 23 July 1770, *ibid.*, 1151, fol. 59; CG to Chancellor Maupeou, 26 July 1770, AN, F¹²* 153, fol. 375; CG to Bertier de Sauvigny, 10, 26, 30 July 1770, *ibid.*, fols. 353, 375–76, 380; CG to duc de la Vrillière, 28 July 1770, *ibid.*, fol. 377; Beaufils to PG, 22 July 1770, BN, Coll. Joly 1149, fols. 112–113; "Grains," July 1770, AN, 80 AP 19 (Bertier de Sauvigny papers).

needs of the consumers and the available supplies, and unemployment and mendicancy were swelling the floating population. Toward
the end of July, a large band of frustrated buyers "made themselves
masters of the sale and of the price of grain" at the market. Although
they had sufficient force on hand to suppress the uprising, the authorities deemed it more prudent not to intervene.

At Lagny, "furious" consumers who "seemed to have concerted
among themselves before the opening of the market" attacked the
laboureurs and then decided "to fix by private authority the price of
grain" at 26 to 28 *livres* when the current was 35 *livres* the *septier*, Paris
measure. On the day of the riot the royal procurator managed to be
absent and the *maréchaussée* refused to act on the strange and spurious
grounds that "these facts were not of its competence." The citizens
who denounced the revolt to the Procurator General—probably a
group of *fermiers*—explained it in terms of the sort of plot thesis which
Turgot embellished and made famous several years later. The rebels
were "of the scum of the people"—a phrase the police authorities
usually avoided, partly out of compassion, partly because subsistence
riots were hardly ever the work of the totally downtrodden or devi-
ant—and since they obviously could not afford to pay for grain even at
fixed prices, it was safe to "presume" that "this money was furnished
by other more wealthy individuals" who had some sinister interest in
disturbing the social order. Among those arrested for the Lagny rising
were several wine-growers who blamed the malaise of the consumers
on a different kind of conspiracy, a local famine plot mounted by the
producers and the notables against the people: "It is the *fermiers*, millers
and bakers of Lagny and the officers of police who by a reprehensible
concert will cause the little people to die of hunger." The week after
the revolt, grain again was "prodigiously dear," almost provoking "a
second riot." An atmosphere of calm did not return until the lieutenant general of Lagny officially fixed the grain price at the end of July.

To prevent a throng of angry women from assaulting the *laboureurs*
and pillaging their supplies, the royal procurator at Dammartin fixed
the price at 22 to 24 *livres*, 8 to 10 *livres* below the current. He ascribed
the agitation in his market to the "long *cherté*," the responsibility for
which he assigned squarely to the *laboureurs* who "believe themselves
to be authorized in virtue of the Declaration of the King of 1763" to
withhold grain from the market, sell on samples, and introduce secret
agents to bid against the bakers and consumers in order to drive the
price higher.

The *laboureurs* supplying Meaux and Dammartin bitterly protested in a collective petition against the arbitrary and violent reception which greeted them at the markets and threatened not to return there again. They were frightened by rumors, of the kind which would later mark the Great Fear, that bands of "leagued persons" would terrorize them at home, rob them, and even burn them out. The thought of the approaching season heightened their apprehensions, the fears of the haves against the rootless have-nots:

> ... being near harvest-time, their Province will [soon] be filled with Strangers who come from the provinces of Brie, Champagne, Lorraine, Burgundy and other places to *work* here, and a part of whom would be capable of joining this [local] populace and together cause the greatest disorders.

The *laboureurs* demanded that the government assure their liberty and, above all, their security. Faced with the threat of empty markets, the royal procurator at Meaux implored the Procurator General to call upon "superior" authorities to assure the provisioning of the markets.

The harvest, judged to be "excellent" in the Paris region, did not check the upward course of prices. Between two market-days in September, the *laboureurs* at Brie-Comte-Robert raised the price from 36 to 41 ½ *livres* the *septier*. Although they were known to have ample supplies, they brought to offer for sale less than half of what they usually displayed in a "mediocre" year. An angry crowd at the grain stalls spat and cursed at the *laboureurs*, assaulted them, and tried to take their sacks. The feeling in the area, transmitted by the royal procurator, was that the augmentation would continue unabated so long as the *laboureurs* were allowed to buy and sell freely. Authorities in the Beauce and the Pays Chartrain, where transactions and prices followed the same pattern, expressed similar sentiments.[17]

In many places outside the Paris region, the harvest was insufficient or worse. Reports of "terrible maladies," "the appalling mortality rate," and "extreme misery" circulated throughout the kingdom. Like their fathers and grandfathers in 1740–41 and 1709–10, the most impoverished *journaliers*, unable to obtain secondary grains, were forced to eat stuffs that one dares not call ersatz: "grass like the animals," roots, various forms of bark. Bitter weather, following a succession of bad harvests, deprived the people of Alsace of their last resources. In

---

17 Procurator of Brie-Comte-Robert to PG, 13 Sept. 1770, BN, Coll. Joly 1153, fols. 8–9 and 1154, fols. 43–44; B. 3989, A.D. E-et-L.

the first eight months of 1770 the price of wheat doubled at Nancy.[18] In the generality of Caen, the ever-widening disparity between prices and wages reduced the people to desperation. "The price of our labor is no longer enough to buy bread," wrote the subdelegate of Cambrai in the summer of 1770. "All goods have increased in price following the price of grain," observed another subdelegate in the same generality, "while the wage of the workers has remained, in our region, at the level it was before the [liberal] Edict." The result was a sort of class struggle between "the most wealthy but at the same time least numerous portion of the nation," which supported and profited from liberalization and the impoverished majority who "detested" the rich and "cried out passionately against the [liberal] law."[19]

In a tone at once lugubrious and indignant, a subdelegate in Auvergne urgently requested assistance:

> We are on the eve of witnessing one of the most horrible famines; there will be risings against the rich. I am doing everything in my power to pacify as much as I am able but the dearth is too violent; a host of people in this area have died and are dying every day for want of food.... While so many of the miserable perish in the countryside, luxury and self-indulgence go on just the same in the big cities.

Elsewhere in the province municipal officials and curates announced that "whole families were dying of hunger." The subdelegate at Riom warned that, given their "state of weakness," the people would surely succumb to "maladies." "It is the most fatal misery that man has ever known," wrote a sergeant, "the men are beginning to emigrate and the women and children to die." "Three quarters of the inhabitants of this community can no longer provide for their subsistence," wrote the city fathers of Maurs. Another subdelegate reported that desperate people were abandoning their children: "I found one exposed at my door yesterday and the number increases every day." While certain Auvergnats turned *in extremis* to infanticide, in the Hainaut, according to the subdelegate of Valenciennes, the poor began to imitate the rich

---

18 *Journal politique* (July 1770, second *quinzaine*), 55; Malyot to PG, 20 Dec. 1770, BN, Coll. Joly 1157, fol. 92; Regnaud, "Histoire des événemens arrivés en France," BN, mss. fr. 13733, fol. 27; SD of Haguenau, état de récolte, 1770, C. 391, A.D. Bas-Rhin; C. 364, A.D. Meurthe-et-Moselle.

19 First échevin of Caen to Miromesnil, 21 July 1770, C. 2653 and Besnardière of St.-Lô to Malafart, 28 July 1770, C. 2673, A.D. Cal.; Buillaboz to IN., 22 July 1770, C. 5976, A.D. Nord; SD of Avesnes, "Réflexions sur l'édit du mois de juillet 1764," ca. Oct. 1770, C. 6690, A.D. Nord.

by seeking to avoid having children, "so miserable" did this life on earth appear to them in the years around 1770. The intendant of Auvergne estimated, at different moments during the course of the summer, that between 150,000 and a half-million people in the province needed assistance in order to survive. At Riom there were 3,500 beggars; one third of the population of Giat was reduced to mendicancy; charity alone sustained 2,000 "impoverished" at Aurillac.[20] Encouraged by Terray, who provided substantial sums from the royal treasury, intendants in Auvergne, Burgundy, Champagne, the Soissonnais, and elsewhere organized public works projects and opened "ateliers de charité" to provide employment.[21] Nor were the poor always consoled by the offer of assistance, for they did not always understand it. Traditionally suspicious of the far-off government, the people and the village priests of the mountain country of Auvergne were terrified by the administrative questionnaires which the intendant circulated in order to learn more about the state of their existence. They were "persuaded that all the needy families would be sent to Guiana" as punishment for having fallen into misery.[22]

Voltaire deplored the onset of "famine": "I have a desire to carry my protests to the *Ephémérides des Citoyens*."[23] Madame d'Epinay and other friends of Galiani kept the abbé, disconsolate since his recall from France, informed on the details of the "very great dearth" spreading across the kingdom.[24] "It is no longer time to descant, it is

20 Rynet to IN., 4 May 1770, and IN. to CG, May 1770, C. 912, A.D. P-de-D.; Dubat to IN., 27 June 1770, C. 918, *ibid.;* curé of St. Priest to IN., 7 July 1770, C. 920, *ibid.;* Destait to IN., 2 July 1770, C. 919, *ibid.;* Chevalier de Manoux (Combraille) to IN., 9 July 1770, C. 920, *ibid.;* municipality of Maurs to IN., 12 April 1770, C. 911, *ibid.;* Verdier (Aurillac) to IN., 20 March 1770, C. 908, *ibid.;* Monthyon to Terray, 15 March 1770, C. 912, *ibid.;* SD of Valenciennes to IN. of Hainaut, Oct. 1773, C. 6690, A.D. Nord.

21 Monthyon to CG, 14 May and 14 Aug. 1770, C. 924, P-de-D.; CG to Amelot, 4 Nov. 1770, C. 3363, fols. 71–72 and Amelot to *élus des Etats de Bourgogne* 17 Nov. 1770, C. 3355, fol. 107, A.D. C d'O.; C. 591, A.D. Aisne; *Gazette de l'agriculture, du commerce, des arts et des finances* (12 Jan. 1771), 26; municipality of Troyes to Rouillé d'Orfeuil, 1 July 1770, C. 1909, A.D. Aube. See also J.-L. Harouel, *Les Ateliers de charité dans la province de Haute-Guyenne* (Paris, 1969).

22 Bugnet to first secretary of IN., 30 March 1770, C. 909, A.D. P-de-D.

23 Voltaire to comtesse d'Argental, 7 Dec. 1770, in *Correspondence*, ed. by Besterman, vol. 77, pp. 135–36 (# 15782); Voltaire to Louis Gaspard Faliz, 7 Dec. 1770, *ibid.*, vol. 77, p. 137 (# 15783). Cf. Voltaire to comte de Schomberg, 6 Jan. 1771, *ibid.*, vol. 78, p. 14 (# 15917) and Voltaire to Mme. d'Epinay, 16 Jan. 1771, *ibid.*, vol. 78, p. 32 (# 15938).

24 Mme. d'Epinay to Galiani, 30 June and 22 July 1770, in *La Signora*, ed. by Nicolini, 71, 75; d'Epinay to Galiani, 29 Oct. 1770 in *Mémoires et correspondance de Madame d'Epinay*, ed. by J.P.A. Parison, (Paris, 1818), III, 382–84.

time that you [begin] thinking about bread and the cruel dearth which threatens you by retracting a bad law that you have made," the Neapolitan wrote to Suard and, beyond him, to the French nation. "Ah! I was a Cassandra," he added, "I was not believed and my prophecies are [now] accomplished."[25] "M. the intendant Turgot is very disconcerted," the baron d'Holbach related, after describing the "dreadful dearth" in the center and southwest, "and I do not doubt that he will renounce the beautiful theory of exports without limits." The philosophe-impresario woefully underestimated Turgot's ideological tenacity, though he rightly pointed out that the situation in the Limousin embarrassed the intendant and taxed his energy and resources. Despite his scruples, Turgot sponsored official supply operations in his *generalité*, partly with funds which the government, despite its solemn commitment to discourage public sector provisioning, provided for many intendants.[26]

Parisians once again saw the *mercuriale* reverse itself, reflecting the unrest in the hinterland. The new price spiral caused bitter disappointment, for 1769 had ended on a note of relative optimism. For the first time in over two years, Hardy had noted in December, the consumer paid less than 3 *sous* the pound for the four-pound loaf.[27] Between February and June 1770, however, the common price of wheat at the Halles rose from 20 to 28 *livres* the *septier*. The best white flour increased 20 *livres* from 45 to 65. At Gonesse wheat went from 19½—21½ *livres* in February to 34½—38 *livres* in early October. Beginning in late April, bread began inexorably to follow the course of wheat and flour. At the end of August, Hardy recorded the four-pound loaf at 15, the level of December 1768, an inexplicable and unwarranted augmentation, for the harvest was "abundant ... much prettier this year than it has been seen for almost ten years."[28] The police noted with concern the reappearance of seditious placards on the walls. ("If bread is not diminished and if the affairs of State are not put in order, we are twenty against one bayonet.")[29]

---

25 Galiani to Suard, 14 July 1770, in *Correspondance*, ed. by Perey and Maugras, I, 193. Cf. Galiani to Holbach, 31 July 1770, in *Lettres*, ed. by Asse, I, 113.

26 Holbach to Galiani, 3 June 1770, in *Amicie Corrispondenti Francesi dell' abate Galiani*, ed. by Nicolini, (Naples, 1954), 198; CG to Turgot, 5 Aug. 1770, AN, F¹²* 155, fols. 7–8; L. Cahen, "Le Prétendu pacte de famine," *Revue historique*, 176 (Sept.–Oct. 1935), 209. Cf. Linguet's attack on Turgot's ostensibly inconsistent position on government provisioning operations. *Annales*, VI, 304–305.

27 *Hardy's Journal*, 13 Dec. 1769, BN, mss. fr. 6680, fol. 276.

28 *Ibid.*, 28 April, 5 May, 14 July, 19 Aug. 1770.

29 *Ibid.*, 11 Sept., 26 Dec. 1770.

Albert, in a letter to Sartine in early May, insisted that the price increase was due merely to "a transient cause" and must occasion "no uneasiness." He attributed it to bad weather, heavy seas, and flooding on the rivers, which impeded navigation and delayed the arrival of foreign grain. As a result, Albert maintained, a number of deficit provinces were obliged to seek grain within the Parisian provisioning crowns, thus momentarily forcing the price up. His argument is rather strained, for it is unclear how these unnamed provinces could have managed to direct their buyers on such short notice and in such large numbers into the Paris zone. Nevertheless, the letter is revealing, for it gives some indication of the magnitude of foreign purchases made either by private speculators or by government, local and regional, or by a combination of private enterprise and public backing. In the last two weeks of April, 27,000 *septiers*, Paris measure, reached Nantes. On a single day in May a fleet of 25 large ships arrived with 75,000 *septiers* of Baltic grain. Another 200,000 *septiers*, mostly from Danzig, were expected imminently at Nantes and still more grain was en route to St. Malo and Rouen.

"It is thus certain," Albert assured Sartine, "that the subsistence for Paris will increase as a function of the diminution of the demand made by the other regions, and that the price will diminish in the same proportion." In addition to the increased pressure on Paris supplies, the inclement weather had resulted in an acute short-term flour shortage, exposing the capital to suffer despite the availability of wheat. Flooding waters halted the operation of the mills and the conversion of flour. Bakers bid the price of flour out of proportion to the price of wheat. With the return of temperate weather, the mills could be expected to resume normal production and the price of flour to fall in line with wheat.[30]

If one trusts Mercier, the habit of "placarding" seems to have been lost after the seventies: "Formerly, it was common enough to find some critical placards on the affairs of the day. So much surveillance was put into the pursuit of the bill-posters that this usage has become impracticable." Untroubled by a major subsistence problem after 1775, the vast majority of Parisians remained indifferent to public affairs, according to Mercier. *Tableau de Paris*, VI, 85–87.

30 Albert to Sartine, 10 May 1770, AN, F[12]* 153, fols. 201–205. According to the "*négotiants de Nantes*," almost 400,000 *septiers* of grain plus hundreds of thousands of pounds of rice entered Nantes between January and June 1770. See their mémoire, ca. Oct. 1772, C. 774, A.D. L-A. Lassalle, a Nantes trader, told the intendant of Auvergne that 18 large grain vessels arrived in the first three weeks of April and 50 more ships in the last 2 weeks of May. Lassalle to Monthyon, 23 April 1770, C. 911 and 30 May 1770, C. 915, A.D. P-de-D. Albert's report of Nantes' arrivals was also confirmed by the intendants of Tours and Brittany. DuCluzel to CG, 9 May 1770, author's personal collection and d'Agay to CG, 10 May 1770, C. 1718, A.D. I-et-V. Cf. also Paul Jeulin, *L'Evolution du port de Nantes* (Paris, 1929), 241.

Parisian authorities were less confident about the immediate future than the co-director of the grain department. The "subsistence of Paris" did not increase as Albert promised, not even after the harvest. The *Prévôt des Marchands* Bignon and Sartine both expressed their alarm to Terray. The Lieutenant General denounced "maneuvers" and "removals" which diverted supplies from the capital and suggested the need for police intervention.[31] Cautiously, without sanctioning recourse to the "authoritarian way," Terray, in September, asked the intendants of the five generalities surrounding the capital to "invite the *laboureurs*" to supply the markets that formed the chain of the Parisian supply system, markets which were not attracting enough grain to satisfy the demands of the bakers and traders. "You must not act towards them by constraint," the Controller-General instructed, "but only by the method of invitation." Invitation, however, in this instance clearly meant pressure, a form of moral intimidation. The subdelegates were to speak personally to the *laboureurs*, make lists of the names of those who agreed to cooperate, and keep a record "of the success which they will have had" to be transmitted to the central government.[32]

At the same time Sartine called upon the government to increase the dose of foreign grain to be placed at the Paris market. Terray agreed to provide from foreign and domestic sources enough grain to "fill the vacuum" left by the failure of private commerce.[33] In the course of the next year the king's grain operations grew even larger than they had been at the end of the sixties. Major Paris area traders like Malisset, who had clients throughout the realm, were suddenly obliged to suspend all their provincial shipments in order to concentrate their supplies in the capital.[34]

While awaiting an injection of fresh supplies, Sartine tried to shield the public from the full impact of the price rise by rigidly controlling the price of bread. Controls had remained in force throughout 1769 despite the marked improvement in the price situation and the bakers had continued to protest bitterly against the injustice of the constraint. They felt that they should be permitted to compensate for

---

31 Sartine to Joly, 26 Sept. and 4, 10 Oct. 1770, BN, Coll. Joly 1109, fols. 206–208; Sartine to CG, 10 Nov. 1770, AN, F^{12*} 155, fol. 89; CG to Bignon, 29 Oct. 1770, *ibid.*, fol. 69.

32 CG to intendants of Amiens, Soissons, Orléans, Champagne and Paris, 21 Sept. 1770, AN, F^{12*} 155, fol. 47.

33 Sartine to Joly, 30 Aug. 1770, BN, Coll. Joly 1428, fol. 240.

34 J.-B. Malisset to Monthyon, 16 July 1770, C. 921, A.D. P-de-D.

the sacrifices they made in 1768 by selling at a price slightly higher than the level warranted by the downturn of the following year. The police, on the contrary, believed it was imperative to enable the consumers to profit materially from the remission of the *cherté* after two years of constantly high prices.

As the grain price dropped in the spring of 1769, Sartine instructed the commissaires to require the bakers to reduce bread in proportion. In May, with the ceiling set at 13 *sous*, the vast majority of bakers conformed, but not without expressing their resentment. In the district of the commissaire Coquelin, for example, 25 bakers offered their four-pound loaves between 12 and 13 *sous* while four claimed that "the merchandise was still rising" and thus it was "impossible to give it at 13 *sous*." Although the top flour price momentarily rose from 55 to 58 *livres* the sack in early September before turning downward again in October, Sartine rejected the bakers' demand for an adjustment, fixing the ceiling at 12 *sous* and arresting three bakers who vociferously contested his decision and increased the price without his authorization. "My intention," he told the commissaires, "is that the bakers of your market be informed of this punishment which awaits them if they are as audacious as the others."

The Lieutenant General ordered the commissaires to be at the markets beginning at dawn and to remain there until after the "principal sale" was completed at mid-day. If any bakers attempted to raise the price, they were to be arrested "after the market"—Sartine did not want to risk provoking an incident while the crowds of consumers thronged the bread-stalls. Another arrest took place toward the end of October when a faubourg St. Antoine bakeress selling at the Halles rejected a buyer's bid of 12 *sous*—the maximum—and demanded an extra six *deniers* for the four-pound loaf. On the whole, however, Sartine reported that "everything is tranquil" at the end of the year.[35]

Save for an episode of recalcitrance at the very beginning of the new year, the police encountered little resistance from the bakers during the first four months of 1770.[36] Wheat continued to decline and Sartine gently scaled the price of bread down to 10½ *sous*. In May, the *mercuriale* bounded upward and the bakers vehemently demanded

---

35 Sartine to Goupil, 6 April 1769, Arsenal, mss. Bastille 10277; Sartine to Coquelin, 29 May 1769, AN, Y 13728; Sartine to Grimperel, 29 May 1769, AN, Y 13397; Sartine to Goupil, 4 Sept. 1769, Arsenal, mss. Bastille 10277; procès-verbal, 21 Oct. 1769, AN, Y 12618.

36 Sartine to Goupil, 4 Jan. 1770, Arsenal, mss. Bastille 10277.

redress. Albert, despite his hardline liberalism and his abhorrence of commercial controls, urged Sartine to "contain" the bakers. While Albert regarded the cupidity of grain merchants as the proper source of commercial motivation, he denounced the "avidity" of the bakers as the "moral cause" of the upturn in flour prices. (Five years later, when the Controller-General Turgot named him to the Lieutenant General of Police in the aftermath of the Flour War, Albert threatened to hang the first baker who stopped making bread out of dissatisfaction with the draconian price maximum he imposed.)[37] Sartine rejected Albert's analysis and considered his advice to be wholly unrealistic. "The progressive augmentation which makes itself felt on wheat and flour," wrote the police chief, "forces me to permit the bakers to increase their bread by two *liards* [one-half *sou*] for the four pounds at the first market."

For the remainder of the year, Sartine found himself compelled to retreat.[38] "It appears to me more than impossible to prevent an increase of two liards per four-pound bread at the next market," he wrote at the end of August when the price had already climbed to 14 *sous*. In mid-September, he informed his commissaires that he could not "dispense with according to those bakers who demanded it permission to raise their price another two *liards*" in view of the "continuing" increase in the prices of wheat and flour. "If the bakers of your department have not asked for an augmentation," he added, somewhat quixotically, "you will tell them nothing." At the end of the month, bread climbed to 15½ and 16 *sous*, skidding off to 13 *sous* at Christmas, the level around which it was to remain during the next year. The conduct of the bakers generally pleased Sartine. The only trouble he had with them in the second half of 1770 occurred in December when a number of market bakers sold above the price ceiling and "excited" their confreres to emulate their defiance of the police will. They received remarkably light punishments—verbal reprimands and 200 *livres* fines—either because Sartine no longer regarded their disobedience as a serious threat or because he sympathized with their difficulties.[39]

---

37 Albert to Sartine, 10 May 1770, AN, F¹²* 153, fol. 205; Bachaumont, *Mémoires secrets*, XXX, 292 (22 July 1775). Nicknamed "Albert Honni," he was not a popular police chief. Moreau, *Mes souvenirs*, II, 257.

38 Sartine to PG, 9, 13 June 1770, BN, Coll. Joly 1428, fols. 227–28; Sartine to Goupil, 10 June 1770, Arsenal, mss. Bastille 10277; Sartine to PG, 22 Aug. 1770, BN, Coll. Joly 1428, fol. 308; Sartine to Goupil, 17 Sept. 1770, Arsenal, mss. Bastille 10277.

39 Sartine to Trudon, 29 Dec. 1770, AN, Y 15114; *Chambre de Police* (Châtelet),

III

Pointing to the proliferation of disorders throughout the kingdom and the aggravation of the *cherté*, Terray asked the royal council in mid-July 1770 to indicate publicly its concern over the deteriorating situation.[40] By an *arrêt* of the fourteenth of the month, the council reaffirmed the controversial liberal Edict of July 1764 and in the same breath formally prohibited the export of any wheat, rye, or barley outside the realm on the grounds that the price of grain had surpassed throughout the kingdom the suspension point specified in the 1764 law. The fact that the council took pains to complicate and obscure a relatively simple matter suggests that there was still an influential party in its midst prepared to accept a momentary setback, but unwilling to repudiate the new regime and the law that spawned liberalization. Without this pressure, the government could have merely declared the suspension *sine die* of exportation without reference to the earlier legislation. On the other hand, if it desired nothing more than to stem the actual drainage of supplies outside the kingdom, an *arrêt du conseil* was superfluous, for the prohibitive clause in the Edict of July 1764 had already automatically stopped exports in every part of the kingdom save for some outposts in the east.[41]

The primary purpose of the *arrêt* was political and psychological. In Terray's reading, public opinion held exports responsible for the prolonged distress. Although they did not understand precisely how it worked, the people—not only the little people, for educated observers like Hardy and more than a handful of magistrates and police officials shared their view—believed that the dearth would continue as long as the government refused to pronounce formally on the export

---

ca. Jan. 1771, AN, Y 9474. Cf. the similarly indulgent treatment accorded refractory bakers in 1771: *Chambre de Police*, ca. Oct. 1771, AN, Y 9474 and Sartine to Trudon, 14 Nov. 1771, AN, Y 15114.

40 *Gazette de France* (20 July 1770), 238; *Gazette de l'agriculture, du commerce, des arts et des finances* (24 July 1770), 548; there are copies of the *arrêt* in C. 2592, A.D. Cal. and C. 6689, A.D. Nord. Cf. Girard, *Terray*, 38ff. and Musart, *Réglementation du commerce des grains*, 129. Exportation of flour was not officially suspended by the central government until the end of November, several weeks after it prohibited the outflow of oats and legumes. CG to farmers-general, 12 Aug., 5, 22 Nov. 1770, AN, F[12]* 155, fols. 12, 73, 81.

41 In fact there is evidence to suggest that there were numerous exceptions to this putatively universal export embargo. See, for example, *officiers de l'amirauté* to IN. (?), 15 Dec. 1770, B. 5646, A.D. C-M.

question. "The principal good that this prohibition will produce in the provinces of the interior," explained the Controller-General, "will be to console the people and to make them see that the *cherté* does not come from the exports to which they attribute it."[42] By removing the ostensible root-cause of the alarm, Terray hoped to calm public anxieties, convince the public that the government was not (or at least no longer) party to a plot to profit from their suffering, and to placate the critics of liberalization. In order to reach the public, he repeatedly urged the intendants to give the *arrêt* the widest possible publicity.[43] Terray also calculated that the *arrêt* would discourage speculators and grain owners from withholding their stocks in the hope that the ports and export stations would soon reopen. With no other prospective outlets, he told a provincial magistrate, they will now shift their attention to the provisioning of the interior.[44]

If Hardy bespoke a widespread sentiment, then Terray could take satisfaction. "Perhaps they [the ministers] have begun to see the disastrous consequences and results of Exportation," commented the book-seller in recording the news of the *arrêt*.[45] Yet the reaction of the subdelegate at Valenciennes suggests that a good deal more was expected from the Controller-General. "At first," the subdelegate told his intendant, the *arrêt* "raised a sensation and appeared surely to mean the return of abundance at the *halle*." But once it was "closely examined" by the speculators, they realized that "at bottom it placed no obstacle in the way of their cupidity." By the end of July the halle was less well supplied than before the *arrêt*. The only way to restore order, concluded the subdelegate, was for the king to restore the "regulations" governing internal trade.[46] Other officials, in the royal administration and the parlements, similarly urged the Controller-General to prepare an all-embracing regulatory law moving far beyond the confines of the July *arrêt*.[47]

---

42 Terray to Turgot, 5 Aug. 1770, AN, F¹²* 155, fol. 8.
43 Terray to IN. of Tours, 15 July 1770, C. 94, A.D. I-et-L.; Terray to IN. of Champagne, 15 July 1770 and IN. to Terray, 2 Aug. 1770, C. 418, A.D. Marne.
44 Terray to First President of the Sovereign Court of Nancy, 30 July 1770, AN, F¹²* 153.
45 *Hardy's Journal*, 18 July 1770, BN, mss. fr. 6680, fol. 172.
46 SD to Taboureau, 26 July 1770, C. 6690, A.D. Nord. If one is to believe Fontette, intendant of Caen, the July suspension ban did not succeed in "tranquilizing the people." "Réflexions," ca. Oct. 1770, C. 2523, A.D. Cal.
47 See, for example, the magistrates of Schlestatt to the IN. of Alsace, 22 Nov. 1772, C. 390, A.D. Bas-Rhin and the deliberations of the Metz Parl., 9 Aug. 1770, B. 469, fol. 42 (registre secret), A.D. Moselle.

Turgot, the intendant at Limoges, vainly sought permission *not* to publish the *arrêt* in his *généralité* for fear that it would inspire a frenzy of xenophobia, blocking not the flow of grain abroad, but circulation within the interior. Turgot's fears, though doctrinaire in spirit, were by no means groundless. In the popular mind, export meant the removal of grain anywhere outside its immediate sphere of origin, and a number of local judges and sovereign courts had already taken measures to place an embargo on the transport of grain outside their jurisdictions. Deeply committed to the principle of free internal circulation, Terray understood the risk and promised to act vigorously to prevent the paralysis of circulation: "one cannot abuse this *arrêt* to place obstacles to the outflow of grain from each *généralité*, article two expressly consecrating the liberty of movement throughout the interior of the kingdom."[48]

Yet Turgot was perfectly correct in interpreting the *arrêt*, despite its formal concessions to the liberals, as a victory for reaction. Now that the ministry had officially banned exportation it would be virtually impossible to reestablish it on a national scale in the foreseeable future by means of a global permissive law. If exportation was indeed the towering symbol of liberalization, the way seemed to be practically clear for a further shrinkage of liberty. "It is full of respect for the [law of] 1764," Madame d'Epinay told Galiani in reference to the *arrêt du Conseil* of July 1770, "and when you come down to brass tacks it destroys it from top to bottom."[49]

There is no doubt that Terray was already contemplating a more fundamental de-liberalizing measure aimed not so much at reassuring the public as at re-equipping the police to assume responsibility for the orderly provisioning of the markets. Shortly before the *arrêt* of 14 July, Trudaine de Montigny and Albert left the government. Their relations with the Controller-General had become strained over the management of subsistence affairs and their departure increased Terray's freedom of action. Terray personally assumed the direction of the grain

---

48 Terray to Turgot, 5 Aug. 1770, AN, F^{12}* 155, fol. 8. On Terray's concern to prevent the export ban from serving as a pretext for stifling liberty in the interior, see CG to La Galaisière, 1, 10 July 1770 and CG to First President of Metz Parl., 30 July 1770, AN F^{12} 153.

49 Mme. d'Epinay to Galiani, 22 July 1770, in *La Signora*, ed. by Nicolini, 75. Cf. the attitude of the Provence Parlement which fully understood the psychological aim of the *arrêt* ("the uselessness of this *arrêt* renders it suspect") and which understood that, by reaffirming the July 1764 Edict, "the way was found to destroy it under the guise of executing it." Letter to Louis XV, 10 Nov. 1770, B. 3677, A.D. B-du-R.

department. In an exchange with the Paris Parlement at the end of July, the government indicated that a "new regulation" was being prepared. The council continued to quash the ordinances and *arrêts* issued by local officials and the sovereign courts, which it regarded as infringements on royal authority and impediments to the free circulation of grain within the realm. But, at the same time, Terray made clear in his correspondence with provincial magistrates that the grain legislation was under review.

At the end of August, just a few weeks before Terray completed his grain project, the Parlement of Paris promulgated a regulatory *arrêt* which the council did not annul. It seems certain that the Parlement knew that the *arrêt* would pass unopposed and it is probable that Terray gave it his blessing in draft if he did not in fact collaborate in its composition. Smoothly and without éclat, the Parlement achieved everything for which it had battled so ferociously and abortively in 1768–69. Arguing that the "excessive *cherté* of grain perpetuates and renews itself each day" and that it was the "result of monopolies and hoarding [which] continue in the midst of the most favorable harvest," the Parlement considered it "indispensable" to intervene "to prevent the present crop from being taken away from the People, reducing them to the harshest extremities in depriving them of their subsistence."

Although it did not effect a total return to the old police regime— both the Assembly of General Police and the Parlement had decried the occasional excesses of the traditional system—the *arrêt* specifically abrogated many of the liberties granted by the Declaration of May 1763 and unleashed the local police by restoring their generous discretionary powers. Anyone, regardless of profession or status, could still enter the grain trade, but henceforth he or she would be required to register with the local police name, "quality" (socio-professional rank), address, places of storage, and the same information regarding any associates with whom the prospective merchant shared the business. In addition, the trader would be obliged to keep a record-book, "in good and due form," of all purchases and sales of grain and flour, a requirement which a number of registrants found difficult to fulfill given their inability to read and write.

The thesis that the grain merchant was in some sense a public servant triumphed in the *arrêt*: it enjoined him to bring "a sufficient quantity" of grain regularly to the market(s) he furnished. "In case of necessity," it empowered the police to "force" the merchants with magazines in their jurisdictions to supply the marketplaces.

Nor could dealers buy or *laboureurs* sell grain futures, grain still in the ground, or grain not yet placed in the barns or storehouses; all contracts made to these ends were pronounced void. The parlementary *arrêt* did not, however, restrict all transactions to the public markets, the constraint which the merchants in the days before liberalization found more vexatious than any other. Presumably, the magistrates felt that the local officials would have enough leverage over the merchants without a formal off-market ban. Such a restriction, in any event, would not have applied to merchants serving the capital who had always been permitted to scour the countryside and buy in the granaries.

Finally, as Terray would have wished, the *arrêt* instructed the police to "maintain, with the greatest care, the free circulation of grain in the kingdom." The phrase "in the kingdom" rather than the more legally accurate "in the *ressort* of the Parlement of Paris" was not merely a tiresome emblem of the court's overmighty pretensions. The latter formula might have been construed as an invitation to obstruct the free passage of grain on the suspicion or pretext that it was destined for shipment outside the Paris boundaries. If for no other reason than to protect the supply lines of the capital, which depended upon resources within and outside the ressort, the Parlement wanted to prevent interference with grain movement.[50]

The government's failure to quash the Paris *arrêt*, following hard upon its formal suspension of exports, plainly signalled the direction in which royal policy was moving. During the next five months at least two other parlements passed regulatory *arrêts* fashioned after the Paris model. Though the government did not relish this proliferation of parlementary intervention, it did not annul the *arrêts* in question. Instead Terray urged the magistrates to delay execution and "to defer taking precautions which might perhaps be necessary to take concerning the grain trade" in anticipation of a general regulatory law dealing with all aspects of the grain problem which the king pledged to issue shortly.[51] A major reversal in public policy was imminent. The new policy promised to bring order not only to the grain trade but to the

50 BN, Coll. Joly 1109, fols. 184–85; *ibid.*, 1111, fol. 144; *Hardy's Journal*, 29 Aug. 1770, BN, mss. fr. 6680, fol. 179; *Lettres Ossolinski*, 6 Aug., 3 Sept. 1770, BHVP, mss. 628, fols. 67, 77; *Journal politique* (Sept. 1770, first quinzaine), 50; Des Essarts, *Dictionnaire*, I, 22–23.

51 Amelot to Mesnard de Cornichard, 20 Dec. 1770, AN, H 187; *Gazette de l'agriculture, du commerce, des arts et des finances* (12 Jan. 1771), 27; CG to First President of *Conseil Supérieur d'Alsace*, 21 Sept. 1770, AN, F¹²* 155, fols. 46–47.

police of the grain trade as well. In the future, parlementary and local initiatives would be politically superfluous as well as unwelcome.[52]

The local police welcomed the Paris *arrêt* with enthusiasm. For years they had been lobbying for a revival of their authority. In violation of the law and the express prohibitions of the king, many of them had taken action on their own account, in the course of the past several years, in order to provision their markets and to restrict the freedom of the dealers. In the late sixties, they implored the Procurator General to seek a modification of the liberal reforms. In the months before the August *arrêt*, when prices soared and riots erupted throughout the Paris region, they again besieged Joly de Fleury with letters groping for authorization and encouragement to take measures which they believed to be urgently necessary, but which they knew to be against the law. His town in a "critical" situation in mid-July, the fiscal procurator of Saint Florentin in Champagne asked: "Could I, My Lord ... prohibit individuals from selling to others than the inhabitants and bakers of this city, have inspection visits made in all the granaries, reduce everyone to his provision, and constrain them to expose and sell the rest on the market?"[53] Similarly, the royal procurator at Tonnerre, "fearing some outbreak," inquired if he could "as he did in 1740 and 1742," compel all the *laboureurs, fermiers* and bourgeois owners in the radius of three leagues around the town to bring their grain to market.[54]

Before the August *arrêt* Joly could not tell them what they wanted to hear, at least not frankly and confidently. In September, however, when the royal procurator at Gallardon complained that the *laboureurs* were buying in the markets for regrate or hoards instead of supplying grain and justifying their conduct "on the pretext of the free trade in grain," Joly told him to announce that the trade was no longer free, at least not in the sense that they understood it.[55] In response to other reports of *laboureur* and merchant maneuvers from Montlhéry, Rambouillet, Sézanne, Méry, Meulan, Sens, Charly, Brie-Comte-Robert, and elsewhere, the Procurator General urged repression.[56] In October,

52 See, for example, Terray's hostility to the initiatives taken by the Besançon court to intensify the grain police. Terray to First President, 10 Dec. 1771, B. 2850 and Terray to. IN., 22 Aug. 1772, C. 354, A.D. Doubs.

53 Billebaute to PG, 16 July 1770, BN, Coll. Joly 1152, fol. 10.

54 Heuvrard to PG, 11 July 1770, *ibid.*, fol. 75.

55 Royal procurator of Gallardon to PG, 29 Aug. 1770, *ibid.*, 1153, fol. 73.

56 Prévôt of Montlhéry to PG, 8 Sept. 1770, *ibid.*, 1153, fol. 13; royal procurator of Rambouillet to PG, 1 Sept. 1770, *ibid.*, fol. 14; officers of the bailliage of Sézanne to PG, 4 Jan. 1771, *ibid.*, 1155, fol. 23; royal procurator of Brie-Comte-Robert to PG, 13 Sept. 1770,

when the Tonnerre procurator again asked permission to coerce the suppliers, Joly cheerfully authorized him "to force the *laboureurs* to furnish the market."[57] To deal with refractory merchants, Joly instructed the police to use fines and threats of arrest, confiscation, and exclusion from the trade.

To depict the police campaign against the traders after the August *arrêt* as a sort of grain terror would be to misrepresent its nature and exaggerate its scope and aims. Most of the local officials appear to have acted with moderation. Yet it is clear that in some places, the police struck out mercilessly against the suppliers. After years of eclipse and frustration, the police seemed to relish their revenge. At Mantes, for example, the officials conducted an anti-monopoly inquisition, making numerous seizures and arrests, investigating the most trivial complaints with unwonted assiduity, and resuscitating sixteenth and seventeenth century prohibitive legislation which the law of May 1763, still operative albeit modified, had abrogated.[58]

The Paris Parlement set the example in the hunt for monopolists. Even before the August *arrêt*, it had opened an investigation—its third major probe since 1768—and had made several arrests. Monopoly of course embraced an extraordinarily wide range of offenses, from petty regrate and rumor-mongering to large-scale international speculation. The king and the Parlement disputed the existence of monopoly in 1768 because they did not subscribe to the same definition of the notion. From the liberal perspective, almost everything which had once been stigmatized as monopoly was a legitimate manifestation of self-interest. In good times, the authorities tolerated many of the practices which they vilified as monopoly in periods of stress and shortage.

The singularity of the Paris situation, since the late sixties, according to many of the critics of liberalization, was that there were adequate supplies available—supplies which were diverted from the markets for criminal motives. If natural failure by itself was insufficient to account for a dearth, then it must be considered the work of monopoly. Witness the reasoning, in October 1770, of Rolland de Challerange, a sixty-nine year old counselor in the Paris Parlement promoted to the *Grand'-Chambre* a year earlier, in his interrogation of a suspected grain monopolist:

---

ibid., 1153, fol. 8; royal procurator of Charly to PG, 14 Sept. 1770, *ibid.*, fol. 9; PG to judges and procurators of Méry and Meulan, Sept. 1770, *ibid.*, fol. 13; royal procurator at Sens to PG, 29 Sept. 1770, *ibid.*, fol. 15.

57 PG to procurator of Tonnerre, 21 Oct. 1770, *ibid.*, 15.

58 *Ibid.*, 1151, fols. 7–49.

Represented to him [the accused] that the persistent *cherté* of grain after a harvest which everyone agrees to be of good quality and which would be sufficient to put bread at a price much below its present level can only come from illicit and secret maneuvers to keep grain forever at a very high price in order to make a greater profit at the expense of the people who lived much more easily without the monopolists and other merchants who made a commerce that can be regarded as murderous. That it is these clandestine purchases which have given rise in many places to murmurs of the people to these complaints against the merchants and to riots which can have the most disastrous consequences.[59]

The Procurator General repeatedly asked his *substituts* to report evidence of maneuvers to his office. In September 1770, Sartine prepared a questionnaire for the royal and fiscal procurators in the Paris supply crowns in which he asked them, "to what do you attribute the present *cherté?*" and hinted that he would not be surprised if the answer were "monopoly."[60]

The records of at least one parlementary monopoly case have survived. The "monopoly," first detected at Mantes but encompassing a much larger area, involved at least six different dealers based at Poissy, St. Germain-en-Laye, Houdan, LaRocheguyon, and Mantes. The Parlement had reason to believe that there existed "a society of persons who bought as much grain as they could and at a higher price than it should have been selling and this in the hope that by making the price of grain rise it would make more considerable profits...."[61] One of the accused was a 26 year old retail grain dealer who exercised certain police functions at the Mantes market, including the inspection of entering grain, ringing the bell for the opening and closing of business, and short-term storage of unsold merchandise. The examining magistrates charged him with collaborating with the monopolists, permitting them access to the market before other traders, and accompanying them on *sub rosa* buying missions. The accused firmly denied that he was part of any conspiracy "to deprive the people of its subsistence." When asked if he had heard of the parlementary *arrêt* of August, he replied affirmatively, but claimed that it did not apply to him because he was not a wholesale grain trader or an associate of one.

Another suspect had entered wholesale grain trading shortly after the passage of the liberal laws in the mid-sixties with a 300 *livres* advance from his father. The accusation that he was "one of the

---

59 Interrogation, 24, 25 Oct. 1770, AN, X^{2B} 1312. On Rolland, see Bluche, *Origine des magistrats*, 374.
60 Sartine to Joly, 20 Sept. 1770, BN, Coll. Joly 1109, fols. 195–96.
61 "Affaire des bleds," 13, 20, 27 Oct. 1770, AN, X^{2B} 1312.

principal authors of the augmentation of grain and of the continued *cherté* of bread" he characterized as neither "true nor plausible." While the indictment charged that he had, in concert with others, purchased more than 6,000 sacks of grain from *laboureurs* and hoarded them in secret caches during the past six months, the merchant pictured himself as a petty, *blatier*-type trader whose operations were neither "mysterious nor clandestine." He insisted that he never sought more than "a small profit" from the rapid turnover of small quantities exchanged "at the current price" and that since his commerce was "so imperceptible" he could not possibly have caused the "sensation" for which he is held responsible. Are you aware, the magistrate queried him, of the August *arrêt* devised

> in order to halt the progress of the illicit paths by which the price of grain was maintained much higher than it should have been ... and in order to give the grain merchants rules to conduct their commerce and make it impossible for them to abuse it to the detriment of the people?

The merchant replied that "he had heard that an *arrêt* of the court of parlement was cried out but that he does not know what it contains not knowing how to read and no one having read it for him." His commerce was so small that he esteemed that it "does not merit that he be given or take the quality of grain merchant" and thus he had not registered like the others. In any case, the defendant added, the *arrêt* no longer applied to him because he had decided to renounce the grain trade in order to deal in apple cider.

It hardly seems accidental that this trader embraced the grain business when the government abolished the rules of conduct and abandoned it when they were reimposed. Whether this means that he had an abject and dishonest character, as the police suggested, or a shrewd mind and a sensitive nature, as the liberals might have contended, is subject to dispute. Nor do we know if many other liberty-made merchants left the trade at the end of 1770 in disgust with the police revival. Despite their zeal and bravado, the magistrates do not seem to have been able to marshal sufficient evidence to make a formal case against any of the putative monopolists, although many of them languished in prison while the investigation continued.

At the very moment that the Paris Parlement issued the August *arrêt*, its sister court at Besançon launched a furious onslaught against "monopoly," "hoarding," and other "odious crimes" which denied the people "life's first substance." Merchants who withheld grain "in the hope of making themselves masters of the price and of making great profits before the next harvest" would no longer be able to find protection in the right of property. Such trading practices were nothing less than "theft and usury." To stamp out such abuses, the Parlement published an *arrêt* voiding all sales of futures and ordering an all-out campaign against monopolists. A companion *arrêt* sought to prevent illicit exports undertaken on the pretext of provisioning the frontier regions. The millers in particular were stigmatized for practicing this fraud. Numerous arrests were made in the next few months.[62]

The Parlement at Metz organized a similar campaign. Already in May it had convoked an "assembly of general police" to consider ways to quiet the "spirit of rebellion" which possessed the people as their subsistence became less and less certain. Given the "excessive price" of grain and its rarity, one magistrate told the assembled chambers, the people had "*just* worries" which it was the duty of the court to assuage. The people blamed their misery on "monopoly"; the "great rumor" in the summer of 1770 was that the "hoarders" would devour the whole crop before it reached the markets. The Parlement adopted this analysis, at first in order to placate public opinion, but later because the evidence seemed to show that it corresponded to reality. Resuscitating legislation which had been abrogated by royal decree, toward the end of July the court banned all purchases of grain futures and ordered the Procurator General to open a broad inquiry into the phenomenon of "monopoly." In the fall the *Chambre des Vacations* stepped up the investigation in the hope of securing exemplary indictments. On the motion of a magistrate who was shocked by signs of monopoly, which he perceived at the Metz city market, the Parlement convoked the municipal authorities just before Christmas in order to impress upon them the urgency of "preventing maneuvers" and repressing socioeconomic crime.[63]

IV

At the end of December, the government finally issued its long awaited grain *arrêt* which, in the words of Hardy, "ordered nothing

---

62 Deliberation of Besançon Parl., 20, 21 Aug. and 7 Dec. 1770, B. 2174 and B. 3270, A.D. Doubs. Cf. Supplique Forquenot, Jan. 1772, B. 4463, *ibid.*

63 Deliberations, (registres secrets), Metz Parl., 17 May, 12, 19, 20 July, 17 Oct. and 22 Dec. 1770, B. 469, fols. 22–23, 33, 36, 37 and Vacations, fol. 2 and B. 470, fol. 24, A.D. Moselle. Nor did the Parlement's anti-monopoly energy flag with the passage of time. See, for example, 17 June 1771, B. 470, fol. 65, *ibid.*

other than the confirmation of everything which the Parlement of Paris had decreed by its *arrêt* rendered on the same subject in the month of August last."[64] A draft version of the new law had been ready as early as mid-September. Terray needed time to circulate the project to solicit the reactions and recommendations of magistrates and intendants, but there was no doubt in his mind about the substance of the changes to be made—they had already been foreshadowed in August—and it is reasonable to assume that he would have wanted the law to take effect rapidly in view of the continued disorders throughout the kingdom, especially in the east and northeast.[65]

It seems probable that the delay between the elaboration and the promulgation of the de-liberalizing law was linked to the acute tensions between the crown and the parlements over the D'Aiguillon affair and the internal struggle for power between Maupeou and Choiseul. Precisely what the relationship was between Terray's law and the burgeoning political crisis is difficult to determine. Was it merely a coincidence, in the complex flurry of great events which marked the turn of the year, that the king submitted the letters patent destroying liberalization to the Paris Parlement only a few days before he issued *lettres de cachet* which destroyed the Parlement as it had been traditionally known? Was there political significance as well as poetic justice in this double climax: a striking triumph for the Parlement followed immediately by a staggering defeat? The sovereign court had campaigned passionately for a restoration of the old-fashioned monarchy of authority, and Louis XV, casting aside his drab liberal vestments, offered the Parlement resounding proof—far more than it had bargained for—that the old-style monarch, paternal and despotic, had returned. Could it be argued that the government timed the two events to deprive the Parlement of the fruits of its victory, to emphasize to the public that the repudiation of liberalization was a decision judiciously reached by the council rather than an act of weakness and a concession to the court? Yet the Parlement had already won its point in August and the other sovereign courts, including those which sided with the king on liberalization, also reeled under Maupeou's coup. Was the double climax orchestrated to strike a double blow against

---

64 *Hardy's Journal*, 29 Dec. 1770, BN, mss. fr. 6680, fol. 197.

65 The draft version of the new ban reached all the intendants by the first week of October. Terray urged them to rush their comments to him in order to enable him to present a law for registration in the parlements immediately upon the *rentrée* in early November 1770. For copies of the draft and covering letters, see C. 417, A.D. Marne; C. 1431, A.D. Gir.; C. 89, A.D. Orne; C. 94, A.D. I-et-L.; C. 844, A.D. Doubs.

Choiseul, who was believed to favor liberalization and to be a supporter of the parlements? Choiseul played an ambiguous role in the early days of both the Brittany affair and liberalization: both questions merit further investigation. Yet it is hard to grant much weight to the claim, alleged by some contemporaries, that Choiseul incited parlementary resistance to royal policy on many different issues in the sixties.[66] The parlements needed no prod to oppose the policies of the government. Nor was it in the foreign minister's interest to weaken the authority of the government, especially if he hoped to restore French fortunes abroad. On the other hand, as we shall see in a moment, Maupeou tried to profit from the subsistence crisis by blaming it on the liberal ministries in which Choiseul was believed to have played a leading role. According to Hardy, the *arrêt* of December 1770 by which the government repudiated liberalization "is regarded as a political tactic of the council to induce the public to believe that the duc de Choiseul Minister newly disgraced *had the greatest responsibility for the grain cherté.*"[67]

It could be argued that the de-liberalizing law was a cynical political measure meant to appease the public and put it in a more hospitable mood to receive the news of the stroke against the sovereign courts. Sartine warned the Chancellor against preparing "a storm at this most untimely moment." The Lieutenant of Police intimated that he could not answer for the reaction of the people "who were already in misery from the *cherté* of bread" and who were now "going to see their suffering brought to the limit" by the projected coup.[68]

If other Parisians shared Hardy's view, then it appears that observers

---

66 On Choiseul's special relation with the parlements, see Besenval, *Mémoires*, I, 366; Mercy to Marie-Thérèse, 23 Jan. 1771 in *Correspondance secrète entre Marie-Thérèse et le comte de Mercy-Argenteau*, ed. by A. d'Arneth and A. Geoffroy, (Paris, 1875), I, 126–27; Flammermont, *Maupeou*, 173, 109, 153, 187–89, 228; Charles Vatel, *Histoire de Madame du Barry* (Versailles, 1883), I, 444; abbé Georgel, *Mémoires*, I, 199.

67 *Hardy's Journal*, 29 Dec. 1770, BN, mss. fr. 6680, fol. 197 (my italics).

68 Cited by Flammermont, *Maupeou*, 110n.

There was considerable tension between Sartine and Maupeou. The Lieutenant General opposed the coup and refused to appear with other councillors of state before the new Parlement. Later we shall see that he also had serious flare-ups with Terray. According to Moreau, it was only "the confidence of the public which kept him in place." If Maupeou did not dare discard him, he nevertheless cast him in a "sort of disgrace." That he ascended to the ministry along with Turgot after the death of Louis XV suggests that his differences with the triumvirate were well known in political circles. See Moreau, *Mes souvenirs*, ed. by C. Hermelin, I, 262, 422; Pidansat de Mairobert, *Journal historique*, VI, 54 (10 June 1774) and VI, 61 (18 June 1774); Pidansat de Mairobert, *L'Espion anglais*, I, 286–87; and Flammermont, *Maupeou*, 284–85.

began to make a connection between the subsistence question and the Triumvirate's political plans by the late fall of 1770. Throughout the sixties, Hardy had never questioned the motives of public authorities who labored so zealously to lower the price of bread in the capital. But on Saturday, 17 November 1770, after noting that "the *exempts* [police agents] roam the markets and arrange for the bread to be put at 13½ instead of 14 *sous*," Hardy wrote:

> it is feared, however, that this diminution was only momentary and … that it had for its aim the project formed by the chancellor to bring violent blows against the parlement upon its return [from recess] and to deprive it of the resource of the discontent of the people occasioned by the *cherté* of bread.[69]

It would have been perfectly reasonable for any government, including one which did not intend to bring the Parlement down, to try to "deprive" it of an issue which gave it great leverage and which was in any case an embarrassment to the administration. Yet it seems quite plausible that Maupeou pressed Sartine to make extraordinary efforts to reduce the bread price in preparation for his coup.

In Paris the dearth was a political onus to the government, for it was well known that the Parlement had for several years vigorously opposed the liberalization policy in the name of cheaper bread. In certain of the provinces, however, especially at the seats of the liberal parlements, Maupeou could exploit the dearth to political advantage. There is some indication that the chancellor launched a propaganda campaign meant explicitly to portray the parlementaires as the authors of the subsistence crisis, as men who sacrificed the public interest to personal greed on the solemn grain question as blithely as they had on other matters of general concern. In a letter written in the spring of 1771, the President de Brosses of the Burgundy Parlement, one of the most distinguished provincial magistrates in the kingdom, asked: "What do you have to say about the fabrication [by which the government] persuaded the people throughout the whole kingdom that the parlements had caused the famine, having been the promoters of the grain export edict [of 1764]?" Maupeou's tactic alarmed the President. "You could not believe," he continued, "how much this innocent artifice is used in order to win support for our destruction, *and it does not work badly.*" Elsewhere he referred to the "ridiculous" and "base" rumor spread by "emissaries dispatched throughout the kingdom" that the "parlements run the grain monopoly.…" The charge was bitterly ironic to

---

69 *Hardy's Journal,* 17 Nov. 1770, BN, mss. fr. 6680, fol. 188.

de Brosses because he was sure that, if anyone practiced grain maneuvers ,it was the government itself. Maupeou was trying to deflect the famine plot suspicions away from the government and towards the parlements and he was successful, de Brosses esteemed, because "the people of the cities," who "abhor exportation," are ready to believe anyone who promises that the dearth will soon end.[70]

"To prepare the Provinces for the commotion," claimed one of the leading anti-Maupeou "journals" of the seventies, "emissaries of the Chancellor have for some time been spreading the rumor that it was the parlements which were the cause of the *cherté* of grain in the provinces." The word was spread that it was "in part to punish them for the Monopoly which a great many of their members secretly operated that they were being suppressed." What worried the parlementary party was that "these insinuations had taken deeply in the minds" of the people. "Far from expressing the least attachment to these Magistrates, whom they once regarded as their Fathers," the people "ardently wish a change which they hope will result in their happiness." Everywhere the people were ready to "abuse" and "insult" the exiled parlementaires, as in fact they did at Besançon.[71]

"The people could not conceive that the dearth was due to accidental causes," noted an observer in Franche-Comté; "they blame it on the grain monopoly and on the export of grain to Switzerland." Already in 1770 a councillor in the Besançon Parlement had stood accused before his colleagues of hoarding grain and promoting higher prices for speculative purposes. Maupeou, assisted by the First President of the court, allegedly turned the climate of opinion to political advantage by fostering the idea that the magistrates were "the authors of the monopoly and of the *cherté* in the City and the Countryside." After the departure of the exiled parlementaires, lamented only by the wealthier elements of the population, the issue continued to agitate the citizenry. A pitched battle erupted between the sons of the exiled magistrates and the sons of the Maupeou surrogates. The latter renewed the "atrocious charge" that the old court had caused the dearth while the former denounced a conspiracy to besmirch the old court involving, *inter alia*, "a momentary maneuver" by which prices were lowered to smooth

---

70 Letters of de Brosses, 16 May and Sept. 1771, cited by J.-T. Foisset, *Le Président de Brosses, histoire des lettres et des parlements au 18ᵉ siècle* (Paris, 1842), 315–16, 321–22. On de Brosses' cautious attitude toward liberalization, see *ibid.*, 378–79. On Maupeou's use of the *cherté*, see also Flammermont, *Maupeou*, 425–26.

71 Pidansat de Mairobert, *Journal historique*, II, 147 (24 Sept. 1771). Cf. *ibid.*, II, 146 (23 Sept. 1771) and II, 194 (25 Oct. 1771).

Maupeou's assault on a once popular institution.[72] Though it is possible that individual members were implicated in speculative activities, directed against the court as a corporate body the charge seems strangely awry, especially in light of the Besançon Parlement's critical posture toward liberalization.

Objects of the same accusation, the Rouen parlementaires must have viewed it with utter incredulity, for no corps had cried out earlier or more violently against the liberal reforms, the dearth, and the crimes of monopoly. The people of Rouen apparently had a nuanced and selective memory and a taste for scapegoats. According to Terray, the people remembered "that it was this Company [the Rouen Parlement] which addressed the first representation demanding the unlimited export of grain"—it was true, in the exuberant wake of the Edict of July 1764—and thus "the people rejoiced publicly" when Maupeou struck at the Rouen court, "believing that this Company earned it as a consequence of the excessive *cherté* of bread which the new form of administration [i.e., liberalization] had occasioned." It was the Chancellor, of course, who had coached the people's memory by organizing a propaganda campaign on the eve of his coup aimed at discrediting the magistrates.[73] At the same moment, an observer at Grenoble noted that "our Poor Parlement is in Extremis and by its own fault (if the sentiments of the People should prevail), for, according to them, it is the Parlement which is the cause of the grain cherté ...."[74]

On the eve of the Maupeou coup, the Parlement of Aix detected a plot linking Terray's projected new grain law and the struggle over the Brittany affair. Though their suspicions lacked the concreteness of the charges later formed at Dijon, Besançon, and Aix, they turned on the same basic notion: that there was a ministerial conspiracy afoot to win over public, especially popular, opinion and neutralize it politically at a very crucial juncture in royal-parlementary relations by discrediting and dismantling the liberal system and introducing a new law that carried the explicit promise of lower prices. "It is not possible to doubt, Sire," the Aix magistrates told Louis XV, "that some hidden interest which we have not yet unraveled presides over this maneuver." In a rare moment of generosity, the Parlement intimated that sincere concerns

---

72 *Ibid.*, II, 116–17 (5 Sept. 1771); A. Estignard, *Le Parlement de Franche-Comté* (Paris, 1892), I, 380–81 and II, 211–13.

73 Terray to the comte de Périgord, 25 Nov. 1772, C. 2912, A.D. Hér.; Floquet, *Histoire du parlement de Normandie*, VI, 422, 638–39.

74 Mélanges Letourneau, June 1771, IV. 1458, Bibliothèque Municipale de Grenoble.

inspired some of the critics of liberalization. But what distinguished the promoters of Terray's de-liberalizing campaign was precisely the fact that they were "partisans of *bad faith* who know the truth and who wish to stifle it...." Though they knew that liberty was not really at fault, for iniquitous political reasons they made it "odious" by blaming it for the dearth and for public misery. If things work out as the Terray-Maupeou faction hopes,

> the Regulation [Terray's forthcoming December law] will have the merit of having lowered prices in a year of abundance. The vulgar imbecile [the people, especially the urban crowd] will not perceive the maneuver at all, they will attribute the *cherté* to the new police [i.e., to liberalization] and abundance to the restoration of [police] regulations.[75]

We cannot say with confidence whether Maupeou's campaign was really of the scope that de Brosses and others suggested and whether it had the effects they indicated. Surely it was a cunning idea, for no issue was more explosive than the grain issue, especially among the urban people.

It may indeed have been partly responsible for the fact that Maupeou's parlementary suppressions and reforms were received with such relative tranquility by most of the provincial populations.[76] But the royal de-liberalizing legislation was the necessary concomitant to Maupeou's propaganda campaign, the proof of the government's good faith. For if the government had not issued Terray's new law at the moment of the parlementary reforms, the public might have connected the Maupeou coup with grain maneuvers and continued subsistence distress even as the Chancellor tried to link the parlements with dearth and monopoly. Without the December de-liberalizing law the Maupeou coup might have been seen, especially in the cities which sheltered antiliberal parlements, as a new, more insidious phase of the vicious plot symbolized by the famine pact. Although this argument, like the suspicions of the Provence Parlement, has the merit of drawing a direct

---

75 Letter to Louis XV, 10 Nov. 1770, B. 3677, A.D. B-du-R.

76 Bastard-D'Estang, *Parlements*, II, 492. Cf. *ibid.*, II, 446–47.

    If one is to judge by the efforts of the Metz court, the parlementaires were determined not to allow the subsistence issue to be turned against them again. Positing a subsistence mentality which will always cause the people to react to stress in the same fashion, one of the presidents proposed a plan aimed at shielding the Parlement from any "pact" suspicions. By demonstrating to the people through repeated public actions (inquiries, regulatory *arrêts*, etc.) that "you are taking care of their Subsistence," he told his colleagues, you will be "blessed" by public opinion. See deliberations, 17 June 1771, B. 470, fol. 65 (registre secret), A.D. Moselle.

connection between the grain and the constitutional crisis, it can do no more than help to explain the timing of de-liberalization. Regardless of the outcome of the parlementary question, Terray was planning to repudiate the liberal reforms. After the August 1770 *arrêt* it was merely a matter of time before the era of liberalization formally came to an end.

It should be noted that the Paris Parlement, in its last hours, also tried to make political capital out of the grain question.[77] Understandably, the court did not want to be deprived, as Hardy put it, of an issue on which it had expended so much energy and which had served to reaffirm its popularity with the people of the capital. But the Parlement itself had dampened the issue with its *arrêt*. When, in early December 1770, in response to Maupeou's disciplinary edict, it raised the question of the prolonged dearth, the misery of the people, and the failure of the government to publish its long-promised general de-liberalizing law, the court's position was no longer credible. It was too late. It was widely known that Terray's measure was forthcoming. The parlementary maneuver was a transparent diversionary ploy. It warned the government that it still faced serious subsistence problems, but Terray knew very well what he had to do to deal with the situation. It reminded the government that the Parlement commanded a devoted following, but the ministry refused to be intimidated by the vague threat of a popular disturbance in favor of the court.

Theoretically, conditions were favorable for a popular demonstration. The price of bread was still high in the beginning of 1771 and the Maupeou reforms were decried everywhere in the capital. A poster found on walls in various parts of the city captured the general mood: "Bread at two *sous*.—Chancellor hanged or Revolt in Paris."[78] It is often alleged, somewhat smugly, that people do not revolt for bread alone. In this instance, they had a political issue as well as a material or economic one. Sometimes it is more difficult to explain why a revolt did not take place than to explain why one did occur. As a deterrent, Maupeou organized a fairly massive display of force in the capital. Doubtless many persons did not know exactly what to make of Maupeou's actions. In the past, after all, the Parlement had always been recalled after exile. It was not entirely implausible to imagine that an accommodation would be reached. The parlementaires themselves were unprepared to invite

77 Flaramermont, *Maupeou*, 135.
78 Poster cited by *ibid.*, 425–26 and Vatel, *du Barry*, II, 43.

the population to revolt violently. Discontent with Maupeou was rife in the capital, but there was no leadership to mobilize it and give it direction. Finally, it is possible that the affections of Parisians for the Parlement did not run as deeply as I have suggested or that after more than three years of acute subsistence distress and anxiety the people were emotionally and physically drained.[79]

Although the Parlement raised the grain smokescreen in a desperate effort to gain some time, liberalization was no longer really a matter of concern to the magistrates. From September 1770 onwards, the parlements were fighting for their survival over a different matter. Maupeou hinted broadly that he would settle for nothing less than total submission and the sovereign courts rediscovered the pressing need for solidarity.[80] In the polarization generated by the Maupeou offensive, attitude toward liberty was no longer a mark of party. Choiseul, who had supported liberalization, stood as the champion of the Paris Parlement.[81] The liberal Trudaine de Montigny, like many others associated with the community of philosophes, deplored the coup, despite his disdain for the antiliberal parlementaires.[82] Voltaire energetically backed the government against the sovereign courts, although he had become increasingly skeptical of liberalization. The debate over liberalization was a question of how to rule; the debate over the liquidation of the D'Aiguillon quarrel quickly became a question of who was to rule. The Parlement of Paris, in the battle over the liberal reforms, had never challenged the right of the king to change the grain laws; it challenged his wisdom and warned that he was undermining his authority. The D'Aiguillon affair raised fundamental constitutional questions about the location and exercise of authority.

If liberalization cannot be considered a cause of the Maupeou coup, it nevertheless helped create the conditions which prepared the way for the rupture between crown and sovereign courts. Firstly, it

---

79 On the discontent in Paris and the fear of revolts, see Besenval, *Mémoires*, I, 376 and Flammermont, *Maupeou*, 216–17, 250–52. Cf. Mercier, *Tableau de Paris*, VI, 27.

80 Cf. in this regard the militantly liberal Parlement of Provence's pointed admonition to the government in November 1770: "that His [the King's] Parlements, animated by the same zeal, can be divided on a political question concerning the interest of the state without prejudicing the essential union formed among them by the identity of functions, the link of the same sentiments, common ground and solidary duty...." Alluding to the Brittany affair, the court warned that, when "the laws [are] in danger and the Constitution of the State threatened by a fatal change," the parlements will always stand together. Deliberation, 10 Nov. 1770, B. 3677, A.D. B-du-R.

81 Flammermont, *Maupeou*, 153ff.

82 *Ibid.*, 235–36.

rekindled a climate of acrimony between the government and several of the parlements. The goodwill earned by the liberal courts could not purchase redemption for the Parlements of Paris and Rouen, which engaged the monarch in a vituperative debate for several years. Although they advanced no constitutional claims in these exchanges, they pretended to speak for and represent the will of the people, a pretension which the crown rightly found offensive and threatening.

Secondly, the prolonged grain crisis provoked a general economic crisis which caused serious and widespread social disorder and placed great strain on the finances of the government. Liberalization had begun on a sanguine note. The government had hoped that it would generate a wave of prosperity which would relieve some of the political and financial pressure it felt and clear the path for further reforms. Liberalization did not cause but it ended in economic disaster. The government was deeply disappointed with the results and resentful of the parlements' charges that it was responsible for the misery of the people and the recession of the economy. Faced with subsistence disorders throughout the kingdom, in 1770, the government also had to deal with the question of its own solvency. The parlements had already expressed their hostility to Terray's initial financial measures and they were certain to resist any serious effort to reform the fiscal structure.[83] The anticipation of parlementary resistance to the Controller-General's program helped to seal the fate of the sovereign courts. Maupeou would have had more difficulty and less support in seeking to provoke a confrontation with the parlements had there not occurred an economic crisis of great magnitude and had liberalization fulfilled the ambitions of its architects.

If the socioeconomic disorder associated with liberalization facilitated Maupeou's drive against the sovereign courts, there is also some evidence that the prolonged *cherté* reinforced the parlementary will to resist in the provinces. The Brittany Affair (1765–70) began after an extended period of low and/or declining cereal prices. Low prices meant diminishing income for a substantial bloc of the nobility. Just as the Brittany Affair began to take shape, the short-term price trend sharply reversed itself: from the subsistence point of view we saw the consequences as early as 1765. Even as rising prices hurt the bulk of the population, they enhanced the economic position of the Breton nobles

---

83 C.F. Lebrun, *Opinions, rapports,* cited by John Rothney, ed., *The Brittany Affair and the Crisis of the Ancien Régime* (New York, 1969), 272.

who controlled the Rennes Parlement and dominated the Estates. Liberalization gave them solid grounds to anticipate a continuing upward price-movement or at worst a stabilization around a new high level (the *bon prix* of the *économistes*). By strengthening the fortunes and the prospects of the noble political elite, liberalization may have helped to sustain the Brittany Affair and encourage hard-line parlementary opposition.[84] This argument, it should be emphasized, does not explain parlementary attitudes. The attitudes themselves cannot be understood in terms of a short-run model of material betterment leading to rising expectations and growing pugnacity. The argument can, however, help to explain why the climate was favorable for political resistance in Brittany as well as in some of the other provinces.

There is still another connection between liberalization and the Brittany Affair, which inspires less confidence because it is serpentine and strained.[85] It is more a personal than a political link, joining two of the most prominent figures of the decade of the sixties, Doctor Quesnay, the physiocratic founding father, and La Chalotais, the Procurator General of Rennes, the one known for his intellectual contribution to the liberty movement and the other for his central role in the Brittany

---

84 This tack is suggested by Meyer, *Noblesse de Bretagne*, I, 513. See also on the relationship between the economic crisis and the Maupeou coup, the luminous remarks of P. de St.-Jacob, "Histoire économique et sociale dans les archives de la Juridiction-Consulaire de Dijon," *Bulletin de la Société d'Histoire Moderne*, 56th year (Oct. 1957), 7.

85 This argument is drawn from the fragmentary memoirs of Lenoir, who succeeded Sartine as Parisian Lieutenant General of Police. Lenoir's recall of detail is remarkable, for he wrote years after the fact. Even more striking is his extraordinary insight: he understood the politics of the Old Regime, both high and low. Though he had strong feelings about the conduct of affairs in the last decades before the Revolution, his presentation was on the whole fair-minded. It was marred less by a lack of balance or a desire to settle scores than by an abiding sense of discretion about what he observed and overheard. Just as he did not spend his tenure as Lieutenant General collecting *chronique scandaleuse*, so he did not spend his retirement recollecting it. It is worth emphasizing that he did not consider the La Chalotais-Quesnay episode as *petite histoire*. He suspected that it may have been of enormous importance, though he cautiously avoided a full-blown interpretation of its relationship to the Brittany Affair, perhaps because he felt he did not possess all the necessary information. Lenoir, it must not be forgotten, played an important role as a special royal commissioner in the persecution and prosecution of La Chalotais. See mss. 1423, piéces 34ff., Bibliothèque Municipale d'Orléans. This episode is the subject of a recent article by Michel Antoine, "En Marge ou au cœur de l'affaire de Bretagne? Intrigues et cabales de M. de la Chalotais," *Bibliothèque de l'Ecole des Chartes*, CXXVIII (July–Dec. 1970), 369–408. Antoine is a remarkably erudite and perspicacious historian, but his analysis is flawed by a bitterly anti-parlementaire bias—not surprising from the leading authority on royal government in the eighteenth century. On the Quesnay-La Chalotais link, see also Henri Carré, *La Chalotais et le duc D'Aiguillon* (Paris, 1893), 21–22, 67, 173n.

Affair.[86] In the early sixties La Chalotais frequented Quesnay's apartment at Versailles. Politically ambitious, the parlementaire also thought of himself as a philosophe, a title to which his part in the campaign against the Jesuits and his celebrated essay on education gave him a genuine claim. An established philosophe, Quesnay, perhaps under the tutelage of Madame de Pompadour, developed a keen interest in politics. It is well known that at various times he promoted Mirabeau and Lemercier for ministerial posts.

Now it appears that Quesnay decided to invest all his hope in La Chalotais; at about the time of liberalization, the two men began to talk seriously about ways to make La Chalotais a minister. Their maneuvers are said to have aroused the ire of Choiseul, who already disliked Quesnay (and was much less discreet about his feelings after the death of their mutual protectress, Pompadour, in 1764) and who felt threatened by La Chalotais' political ambitions. In order to displace Choiseul and catapult La Chalotais to the head of a new ministry, Quesnay and La Chalotais allegedly tried to win Louis XV's favor through the good offices of a new mistress. After that failed, they purportedly attempted to pressure the monarch—indeed, to blackmail him—by threatening to reveal parts of an intimate correspondence between Louis and his lover, which would have seriously embarrassed the crown.[87] Fortunately for the king, the plot was uncovered and an early analogue to the "affair of the Diamond Necklace" averted.

This story, embedded in the interstices between the great events of the sixties, is intriguing, though the evidence and the interpretation are by no means wholly convincing. If it is true, it could help explain Louis XV's personal appetite for punishing La Chalotais and his decision to quash the case entirely without, however, clearing the Procurator General's reputation or releasing him from detention.[88] It

---

86 As we have indicated, La Chalotais was one of the leading spokesmen for the liberal movement; in fact, he was more widely identified with liberalization in the public view than was Quesnay. See, in this regard, the testimony of a Paris merchant who was "convinced that the nation owes the first rays of [grain] liberty" to La Chalotais. "Lettre d'un négociant de Paris à un commercant de Nantes," 15 July 1768, C. 775, A.D. L-A.

87 On several occasions, La Chalotais suggested that he did not collaborate in the plot but that it was the idea of Quesnay alone and the work of one Sieur Reynie, chef des gobelets du Roi, "one of these low intriguers, of whom there are so many at Versailles." Reynie, remarked the Procurator General, is one of the valets used by the *Economistes*." Though he equivocated on this point, Lenoir seemed inclined to believe that *if* there was a plot to catapult La Chalotais to power, then the Breton magistrate was personally involved. Mss. 1423, pieces 34ff., Bibliothèque Municipale d'Orléans.

88 In the campaign of support for the Brittany court, the liberal parlements pictured

would also help account for Choiseul's willingness to force the issue against La Chalotais and the Breton court despite the fact that he despised D'Aiguillon, who was as menacing a political rival as the Procurator, detested the Jesuits, who were D'Aiguillon's friends and La Chalotais' enemies, and sympathized with the parlements, all of which supported La Chalotais.

Viewed upon this background, it could be argued that two of the most important leaders of the liberty lobby, Quesnay and La Chalotais, motivated by a desire for political power (presumably to use in the service of the new political economy), were responsible not for creating the Brittany Affair but for giving it the peculiar form it took. In this same light there are several conjectures one could make about the impact of the cabal upon the liberalization experience. It is possible that Choiseul's failure to play a major role in the execution and defense of the liberal reforms was related to his fear and dislike of the two intriguers. He might have calculated that a successful liberalization program would jeopardize his position by enhancing Quesnay's influence with the king and thus La Chalotais' chances of entering the government. The exposure of the plot might have cooled Louis' ardor for the liberal policies so closely associated with the Quesnay faction. Unlike his collaborator, Quesnay was not punished for his part in the conspiracy, but he did lose favor with the king. Although he was the likely candidate to succeed to the vacant post of first royal physician in 1770, he was passed over for the honor. The intrigue proves that at least one of the "speculative" *économistes* was perfectly capable of practicing hard-nosed, earthy politics.

All of this is rather far-fetched; it reads too much like *A Glass of Water*. A good deal of clarification will be required before the cabal thesis can be fairly assessed. Yet between Pompadour on the one side and Du Barry and the Cardinal de Rohan on the other, the rudiments of the story do not seem implausible. There are of course far more compelling reasons for the repudiation of liberalization and for the constitutional crisis to which the Brittany Affair led. But, without restoring court politics to center stage, it is perhaps worthwhile to remember that the events of the sixties and seventies were not always the product of prices and principles.

La Chalotais not only as a martyr-victim of royal oppression but as a philosopher-statesman who served the king and the nation zealously by taking the lead of the liberty movement in the early sixties. See, for example, the Dauphiné Parl. to Louis XV, 26 April 1769, B. 2314, fol. 115, A.D. Isére.

V

Terray's grain law, rendered public in December and submitted to the parlements in January, was considerably more restrictive of liberty than the August *arrêt* of the Paris Parlement whose dispositions it confirmed.[89] It was not a minimal offering grudgingly designed to mollify the critics of liberalization. Terray voluntarily renounced more than they demanded. For all practical purposes, the new regulatory law effected a complete return to the old police regime. To be sure, Terray retained the freedom of internal circulation, yet this principle was not in itself alien to the police tradition. In two separate articles (numbers eight and nine), he forbade "all individuals from placing obstacles in the way of the free circulation of grain and flour from one place to another, or from province to province, in the interior of our kingdom ... on pain of being pursued extraordinarily as a perturber of the public peace," and he prohibited all police officers, including seignorial judges, from opposing "the free circulation of grain from province to province on any pretext whatsoever." Translated into functional terms, the first of these articles, vague and prolix, declared that collective actions to prevent the removal of grain from a given place or to intercept convoys were against the law. This was not a legislative milestone. Riots had always been against the law, even in the dark ages before liberty. Surely Terray did not imagine that he could deter by proclamation frightened and frustrated people from attempting to capture fleeing grain supplies in a time of dearth. It appears that this clause was meant primarily to reassure merchants that the retreat from liberalization did not give consumers the license to spoliate dealers any more than the freedom of trade gave traders the right to abuse consumers.

The second of these free trade articles, even more nebulous than the first, prohibited the police from obstructing traffic. Ostensibly the aim of this clause was to prevent local officials from making policy on their own initiative as they had frequently done during the course of 1770 and before—that is, to prevent them from committing in the name of law and order actions which, if undertaken by simple citizens, would result in their condemnation as "perturbers" of order. Convinced that it was

---

89 For the text of the *arrêt* and the accompanying *lettres patentes* of 11 Jan. 1771, see AN, H* 1874, fols. 106–107; BN, Coll. Joly 1111, fols. 31–34 and 1109, fols. 241–242; C. 81, A.D. C d'O.; Arch. AE, France 1368, fols. 302–303.

necessary for the well-being of the nation, Terray moved to restore the old police regime without, however, turning it over completely to the local authorities for their use. He harbored "the fear"—it was not an exclusively liberal anxiety—"of re-animating the pretensions of the officers of police whose indiscreet zeal causes bad more often than it operates good." The Controller-General did not want de-liberalization to foster an epidemic mood of decentralization or revive and legitimize habits of particularism, though he knew that a deal of this was inevitable. Controlling the police concerned him even as the business of controlling grain and grain merchants preoccupied him. Indeed, the Procurator General of the Paris Parlement sternly reproached Terray for adding a clause to the draft version of the article regarding the police which would have held local authorities financially responsible, in their private persons, for any losses or damages caused by "illegal" sentences rendered by them. The Procurator complained that Terray treated the police in harsher and "more rigorous" terms than he treated the profit-hungry traders and the monopolists. "The laws of honor and obedience to the Sovereign are laws which seem sufficient" to contain the police, he concluded. Terray remained skeptical of this curiously idealized conception, not in the least perhaps because it seemed to protect the freedom of action of local authorities who were more nearly integrated into the parlementary network of parallel administration over which the Procurators General presided than into the royal provincial administration. But he did not wish to stigmatize or demoralize the local police upon whom, after all, he would have to depend. The offending clause did not appear in the final version which became the December law.[90]

The spirit of this police containment article ran counter to the tenor and the substance of the other seven articles of the law which reimposed controls on the grain trade. These other articles gave the police a thousand pretexts to hamper the movement of grain for the sake of provisioning; indeed, in a number of instances, the royal *arrêt* positively enjoined them to channel the flow in useful directions. Moreover, it is significant that the article on the police forbade them to obstruct interprovincial trade, not circulation "from place to place." Now the only authorities actually in a position to impede interprovincial circulation

---

90 Terray to IN. of Burgundy, 22 Sept. 1772, C. 81, A.D. C d'O.; BN, Coll. Joly 1109, fols. 222–27.

were the intendants, creatures of the Controller-General, and the parlements, all of which paid at least lip service to the ideal of free internal
movement, not the horde of local officials whose caprice and impetu-
osity worried liberals and nonliberals alike. It was not Terray's purpose
to obscure the sense of the regulatory law by taking away from the
police with one hand what he gave them with the other. The police
article was meant as a cautionary note to local officials to mind their
own business, follow the lead of the ministry in grain affairs, and use
their authority frugally and temperately.

Only constant attention to subsistence affairs by the Controller-
General could make this moral restraint effective. Terray did not
believe that the task of the government ended with the publication
of the grain law. It was clearly his intention, henceforth, to play a
major role in determining grain policy. This was the real significance
of his commitment to freedom of internal trade. Terray viewed subsistence as a national problem. Within the severe limits imposed by
the rudimentary nature of transportation and communication and
the labyrinthine administrative structure which could not pass for
a bureaucracy, Terray planned to deal with subsistence *as if* there
were a national market. Free trade was neither an invitation to a Brie
trader to divert his grain to Lyons while the demands of the capital
were still not satisfied nor to a Brie procurator to harass merchants
in a time of plenty: both procedures were illogical and gratuitous,
counter-productive in the jargon of our own time. Free trade did not
mean trade free of controls; it meant facilitating the distribution of
supplies by the simplest and most efficient course. Free trade did not
mean freeing the government from responsibility; it was Terray's way
of declaring that subsistence was preeminently a matter of public
rather than private interest, central rather than exclusively local concern. It was an assertion of national unity and purpose as well as an
affirmation of economic and social solidarity among the constituent
parts of the kingdom.[91]

Terray's liberty was not, as the Provence Parlement charged, simply a

---

91 Cf. the passionate pleas of the Bordeaux intendant to protect internal liberty ("which has
saved so many parishes from the horror of famine") from the onslaught of both "the people
and the officers of justice or police." To Terray, 16 Oct. 1770, C. 1431, A.D. Gir.

It is also worthwhile noting the intendant's argument that, regardless of the law, free
internal circulation will not really come about and produce salutary results by linking the
different parts of the kingdom in a truly national market and equalizing prices across space
and time until the state undertakes an enormous effort to improve navigation and build
and repair roads.

hollow rhetorical phrase meant to sustain a useful fiction.[92] Yet liberty just as surely was not the leitmotif of the December law. On the contrary, its aim, Louis XV was made to say in the pithy introduction which took the place of a preamble, was "to repress the abuses which trouble this [grain] commerce by renewing certain dispositions of the old regulations which concern it." Terray distinguished sharply between two kinds of liberty: a liberty accorded grain to circulate freely throughout the kingdom, which he consistently demanded and defended, and a liberty granted traders to deal as they pleased, which he considered dangerous and unacceptable. On countless occasions the Controller-General warned intendants and lesser officials that "obstructions" placed in the way of commerce would produce "difficulties" in provisioning and lead to "misery." His repeated protestations that "it was never our intention to hamper trade" as a consequence of the restoration of controls were sincere.[93] But Terray feared the power which ownership of grain bestowed and he could never overcome (though he tried) a deep Delamarist distrust for all those who dealt in this commerce.

The grain trade, in Terray's estimation, inevitably generated abuses. It was fatuous to imagine that it could or would police itself. Given their control over subsistence, dealers exercised an extraordinary sort of authority over society, which had no means to call them to account. Left to themselves, Terray felt, they would press their advantage to disastrous extremes. Even as the liberals argued that police by its nature was incapable of moderation, so the Controller-General maintained that grain dealers, unless checked, ineluctably damaged the public interest. "Only surveillance can stop Monopoly," the gravest abuse, he contended. Grain could not be allowed to become "an object of speculation for the rich"—precisely the liberal goal, from Boisguilbert to Turgot. The problem with the reforms of 1763–64, in Terray's view, was that they "opened up an excessively great cupidity, they stirred the desire to get rich on the traffic of a commodity of indispensable necessity," an enterprise which he regarded as morally wrong and politically untenable. Since it had lost "the spirit of purity" the grain trade could not post its own guarantees of good conduct.[94]

92 Provence Parlement to Louis XV, 10 Nov. 1770, B. 3677, A.D. B-du-R.

93 Terray to Dupleix, 9 Sept. 1771, C. 84, A.D. Somme; Terray to St.-Priest, 21 Oct. 1772, C. 2912, A.D. Hér.; Terray to Rouillé d'Orfeuil, 10 Nov. 1772, C. 416 and 29 May 1773, C. 417, A.D. Marne; Terray to Amelot, 1 Aug. 1772, C. 81, A.D. C d'O.; Terray to Esmangart, 12 June 1773, C. 1441 and 1 March 1774, C. 1442, A.D. Gir.

94 Terray to Rouillé d'Orfeuil, 27 Sept. 1772, C. 417, A.D. Marne; Terray to

Through the reestablishment of a control system, backed by stringent penalties, the Controller-General hoped to force the trade into
the open and dissuade the grain owners and dealers from practicing
tyranny, extortion, or fraud. Four of the first seven articles reiterated
points of the parlementary *arrêt* of August with only minor modifications. The first three concerned general conditions of admission to the
trade. All persons entering the trade were required to register on pain
of 500 *livres* fine which "cannot be forgiven or reduced" as such penalties often were in the old regime. Dealers forming "societies" had to
draw up contracts before notaries or other public officials and register
them along with the standard information, or else face the same fine.
Though Terray claimed that he wished "to dispel the idea of what is
called inquisition" in police matters and to allay "the fear of infringement upon individual liberty," he insisted that "the public interest"
demanded "vigilance" and "precautions." The "first substance" of the
popular diet "had to be, as it were, continually under the eye of the
People and under those of the Administrators." In order to assure this
visibility, the dealer and his business had to be "known."[95]

Two other articles dealt with trading practices. Liberalization had
legitimized *enarrhement*, an extremely difficult transaction for the police
to unmask, which enabled traders to gain control of a portion of the
winter market by making downpayments on future harvests in the preceding spring and thus exercise an inflationary influence on prices the
year round. Article seven once again made it a crime, which, along
with the purchase of grain that was en route to market for public
sale, was punishable by a 3,000 *livres* unnegotiable fine, annulment
of the deals contracted with loss of advances paid out, deprivation of
the right to continue to engage in grain commerce, and even corporal punishment. Unlike the parlementary *arrêt*, Terray's law did not
explicitly empower the police to compel dealers and cultivators to
supply the markets. But article six restricted all business to the public
marketplaces, *implicitly* requiring traders and *laboureurs* to furnish those
markets and authorizing the police to make certain that they were
appropriately provisioned.

INs. of Amiens and Brittany, 1 Aug. 1773, C. 86, A.D. Somme and C. 1653, A.D. I-et-V.;
Terray to archbishop of Toulouse and to comte de Périgord, 25 Nov. 1772, C 2912 A.D. Hér.
95 Terray to IN. of Amiens, 1 Aug. 1773, C. 86, A.D. Somme. Protests from intendants
persuaded Terray to exclude from the final version of the registration article the obligation
to keep formal business ledgers subject to police inspection. See "Observations sur le projet
de déclaration," C. 1431, A.D. Gir.

The mandatory market clause was the most important article in Terray's law. During liberalization, the market had become merely an arena of convenience with no institutional status, an unpredictable bivouac rather than a sacred meeting ground. For the sake of the supply system, as a means of control, and in deference to popular habits, Terray restored the market to its traditional dignity as sole concourse of buyers and sellers. In principle, the concentration of supplies on the market would assure a regular, predictable, visible supply, facilitate exchanges between buyers and sellers, and expose them to constant scrutiny. Without a fixed market system, the police could not possibly wage a successful war against monopoly. Moreover, once grain was at the market the owners were subject to myriad pressures from the public and the police, which tended to limit considerably their opportunities for committing "abuses." The mandatory market clause aroused considerable controversy in 1770, as it had before and as it would continue to do, within the police camp itself. For the intendant of Champagne it was the very heart of things, without which the police of provisioning could not operate. Concern for the "invincible repugnance" it would inspire in the grain-owning community, however, caused the intendant of Bordeaux to have serious reservations about its wisdom. Liberty and the obligation to furnish the market, Fontette of Caen categorically averred, could not be reconciled in practice: they were "absolutely contradictory" demands.[96]

Terray himself had equivocal feelings about the market article. The draft version of the article specifically required grain owners to supply the nearest markets on a regular basis, but it did not proscribe off-market transactions. The Controller-General included the ban in the law as the result of pressure from administrators such as the intendant of Champagne. To preserve a measure of flexibility, he did not fix mandatory and crushing penalties as he did in article seven; violators were to be pursued according to the seriousness of the case, to be defined locally and circumstantially. In addition, this restriction to the market would not affect "merchants for the provisioning of Paris" who had

---

96 IN. of Champagne to CG, 22 Oct. 1770, C. 417, A.D. Marne; "Observations," C. 1431, A.D. Gir. Cf. the critical posture of the juges-consuls of Nantes, "Mémoire," Oct. 1770, C. 774, A.D. L-A. Since the interdiction of *enarrhement* was implicit in the prohibition of all off-market transactions, it is not clear why Terray insisted on a separate article seven. See the shrewd remarks of the police of Chaumont who interpreted Terray's tactics to mean that he would tolerate *certain kinds* of off-market business. "Résultat des observations ...," C. 417, A.D. Marne; Fontette, "Observations," Oct. 1770, C. 2623, A.D. Cal.

always enjoyed a "tolerance," written into law in 1737, to canvass the countryside and buy in the barns and granaries. Although it was phrased in general terms, it seems likely that the market requirement was aimed at the merchants who bought for purposes of resale, the real operators of the grain trade, not the little men, the modest cultivators whose plight Voltaire exposed in the *Quarante Ecus*. It is significant that the market restriction was not demanded by the Parlement, but by the procurators of the marginal hinterland towns who feared they would be bypassed if they had to depend on mere commercial magnetism rather than coercion in order to attract supplies.[97]

Whereas the parlementary *arrêt* did not challenge anyone's freedom to enter grain commerce, article four of the December law expressly forbad all police and judicial officers, all farmers, receivers, clerks, cashiers, and "other interested parties having the management of our finances" to engage directly or indirectly in grain traffic on penalty of confiscation of the merchandise, 2,000 *livres* fine and, should the case merit it, corporal punishment. The aim, of course, was to try to reduce corruption, eliminate conflicts of interest, and inspire public confidence in the public administration as well as the trade. The Paris Procurator General, a sharp critic of the excessive power and independence of the financial milieu, persuaded Terray to exclude all persons involved in "finance."[98] Either because he simply did not think it was necessary or because he did not wish to exclude men with considerable amounts of liquid capital from engaging in legitimate grain commerce, the Controller-General had not mentioned the *gens de finance* in the draft article. On the other hand, the intendant of Alençon argued boldly, albeit without success, in favor of permitting all police officials to enter the trade on the pragmatic grounds that they would do it surreptitiously

---

97 See the appeals of the procurators of Chevreuse and Angerville-la-Gaste who felt that the August parlementary *arrêt* did not go far enough. They demanded a renewal of the Royal Declaration of 1723 whose main purpose was to concentrate exchanges on the public markets. Letters to PG, 14 Sept. 1770, BN, Coll. Joly, 1157, fol. 75 and (?), 1770, *ibid.*, 1148, fols. 65–66. At the Assembly of General Police, Séguier explicitly stated that it was not necessary to resurrect the 1723 Declaration in its entirety. See his frequent interventions in the *Recueil*.

98 BN, Coll. Joly 1109, fols. 222–27. The intendant of Lille favored a total exclusion of public officials from the grain trade in order to restore public confidence in local administration: "It is not enough that they [local authorities] are not allowed to abuse their functions; it is even more important that they not be suspected of doing so by the people in order not to lose the people's confidence." Taboureau to Terray, 27 Oct. 1770, C. 6690, A.D. Nord.

despite the law if they could not do it openly and legally and that in some places the officials were the only persons with sufficient funds and ability to undertake this commerce.[99]

Finally, another article resurrected a heavily dated model of police-defined commercial roles which had not been widely respected even in the days before liberalization. Article five prohibited *laboureurs* and *fermiers* from buying grain for purposes of stockage or resale (as cultivators their vocation was to sell their own produce, not to traffic) and bakers and millers from selling grain (as artisans, their task was to transform grain into flour and bread, not to deal as merchants). More than ever before, this rigid categorization of function no longer fitted the facts of commerce, at least in the Paris region. The lines separating the professions of grain merchant, mealman, and miller had become blurred: millers found that they could not survive unless they speculated in grain; grain merchants increasingly had to turn to flour processing in order to retain their clienteles; certain *fermiers* made more money as traders than as planters and it was no longer an absolute rarity to find a *laboureur* or a baker who owned a mill. To be sure, the Controller-General had no intention of dismantling the commerce of the Paris area, but if he succeeded in enforcing these restrictions elsewhere the effect would be to retard the rationalization and modernization of the trade. In their comments on the draft project, several intendants pointed out that this article would jeopardize the well-being of a host of petty *laboureurs* who needed to buy grain not for speculation but for their own subsistence.[100]

VI

While the December law unequivocally indicated what the government's new policy would be, its sure and stringent cast obscured the way in which the Controller-General conceived the grain problem. Though he took a starkly antiliberal position, he did not arrive there in a heedless, reflexive manner. In the eighteenth century, the preamble of laws often served as

---

99 Jullien to CG, Oct. 1770, C. 89, A.D. Orne. The intendant of Champagne and the juges-consuls of Nantes took similar positions. Rouillé to Terray, 22 Oct. 1770, C. 417, A.D. Marne and "Mémoire," Oct. 1770, C. 774, A.D. L-A. Cf. Fontette's sanguine argument that the police "are too afraid of the people to undertake this [grain] trade...." "Observation," Oct. 1770, C. 2623, A.D. Cal.

100 "Observations," C. 1431, A.D. Gir.; Rouillé d'Orfeuil to CG, 22 Oct. 1770, C. 417, A.D. Marne; Fontette, "Observations," Oct. 1770, C. 2623, A.D. Cal.

a sort of philosophical declaration in which the government explained the genesis and purpose of its policy. Terray's successor Turgot made the genre famous, though he was hardly the first to use it. To introduce the December law, Terray drafted a free-speaking preamble which caused him considerable trouble and which clearly reveals that he did not regard the police solution as a panacea.[101] Persuaded that de-liberalization was politically necessary, nevertheless he was not certain that it would really work in the long run, nor was he oblivious to the damage that it might do. "We shall not dissimulate," Terray wrote in the preamble, "that we hesitated on the precautions to take."

> If we have reason to believe that too great a liberty in the interior grain trade is one of the principal causes in the extreme variation of the grain price, and affords too great a facility to hoarding, monopolies, and sequestration of the said grain, we also fear that hindrances [*la gêne*] placed in the way of commerce will cause the grain price to fall to a level capable of discouraging the owners and cultivators by depriving them of the means to make the expenditures necessary not only for the improvement but for the simple cultivation of their lands.

The "example of past centuries"—the terrain of precedent and history which had been violently contested by the liberals and their critics—served only to reinforce the Controller-General's doubts. Failures and inconsistencies marred the records of both liberal and prohibitive regimes in past time. "Thus we cannot be assured," concluded Terray forthrightly, "that the law which we have prepared will be able fully to remedy the disadvantages and procure all the advantages of the one side and of the other."

The Controller-General's access of candor provoked trenchant criticism, which induced him to drop the preamble from the final version of the December law. Afraid that the preamble would "inspire anxieties in the people," DuCluzel, intendant of Tours, recommended "that it would be better to be silent on the disadvantages of badly run administration in previous centuries [and] to speak in a tone that was affirmative and full of confidence." The intendant of Bordeaux reproached Terray for dealing too frankly with monopoly. By presenting monopoly as one of the chief causes of the ongoing dearth and by admitting that the government had done nothing till now to combat it, the intendant feared that Terray would encourage "the people" (already "too inclined" to think in these terms) to believe in some sort

---

101 Draft preamble, Oct. 1770, C. 94, A.D. I-et-L.

of famine plot involving public authority. The "uncertainty" of the preamble, warned Fontette of Caen, would "increase anxieties." By acknowledging that the measure was historically and economically bound to be inadequate, the ministry "in a way justifies in advance the excesses to which it is to be feared the people will resort."[102]

The Procurator General Joly de Fleury also insisted upon the enormous significance of language and mood in the law. The preamble undermined the aim of the December law, which was "to reassure and give confidence to the consumers." It is "dangerous," Joly continued, to present "the regulations whose object is to guarantee subsistence to everyone at a just and moderate and accessible price" as "laws of hindrance [*gêne*] and constraint." It is "the consumers ... who must be consulted to learn if they call these regulations by the name of hindrance and constraint." Only "the smallest number" of citizens is interested in promoting the idea that police regulations are "hindrances" and thus ought not to exist. Joly solemnly advised Terray to offer no encouragement to this elite of cultivators, owners, "spéculateurs de cabinet," and "spéculateurs de pratique" who "coolly conceive in their imaginations plans for increasing the wealth of the State by means which cause their fellow men to perish from hunger and which [in truth] impoverish the kingdom...."[103]

Despite the reproaches of the Procurator General, who gently accused him of internalizing *économiste* propaganda, Terray continued to think of the police controls that he believed were necessary as *gênes*, hindrances, or constraints, which unquestionably inconvenienced the grain owners and interfered with their freedom to dispose of their property. He believed that the liberals had an argument of substance and he put their case as fairly and objectively as was possible in the climate of 1770. Yet in the final analysis Terray shared Joly's populistic view, his "hesitation" to the contrary notwithstanding. At the end of the draft preamble he made the choice from which he recoiled at the beginning: "the number of consumers being greater and less well-off than that of the proprietors and cultivators, our paternal solicitude

---

102 "Réflexions sur la loi...," ca. Nov. 1770, *ibid.*; IN. of Bordeaux to CG, 16 Oct. 1770, C. 1431, A.D. Gir.; Fontette, "Observations," Oct. 1770, C. 2623, A.D. Cal. The intendant of Lille also criticized the preamble for its "diffuseness" and lack of "clarity." Taboureau to Terray, 27 Oct. 1770, C. 6690, A.D. Nord. Cf. the intendant of Champagne's apparent satisfaction with the preamble. To CG, 22 Oct. 1770, C. 417, A.D. Marne.

103 BN, Coll. Joly 1109, fols. 211–212.

must make us incline rather in their favor."[104] Though he continued to worry about its economic implications, all things considered he felt that it was the right choice, not merely one that was circumstantially expedient.

Terray justified his choice of the consumers over the producers in terms of both the *salus populi* ethic and the doctrine of *raison d'état*, two political conceptions that clashed more often than not, but which converged on the grain question. He rejected the idea that wealth could be calculated without regard to the social costs of amassing it. The liberals failed utterly to take account of the people in making their policy. Ultimately what mattered for Terray was less the fact that the people were "the most necessitous of the King's subjects" than the fact that they were "unfortunately the most numerous."[105] Like Joly de Fleury, the Controller-General believed that the French monarchy, unlike a military despotism, simply could not function when the majority of citizens were not only reduced to a chronically miserable and precarious existence, but also alienated from authority on the grounds that it was improvident, unjust, and perhaps evil. Like Necker, Terray had no illusion about the resilience of the social structure or the immutability of social relations. For the sake of social and political stability, the government had to consider the interests of the people.

The people "reason little and badly," but they had a lucid sense of their chief interest—subsistence. Terray understood the subsistence mentality, its expectations, its propensity to view the world conspiratorially, the limits of its patience, and its potential explosiveness. It was folly for the government to think that it could turn its back upon the people and disqualify itself from dealing with provisioning, the most sensitive of all social operations. The sign of flaw or failure in grain policy was when the price became "too dear for the people." Administrative distinctions between *cherté* and famine made no difference to consumers: "it is all the same to the people whether grain is [too] dear or whether it is completely lacking." The people were unwilling and unequipped to deal with prolonged bouts of *cherté*, whether they were the consequence of government policy, monopoly, or natural disaster. Such *cherté* generated a vicious circle of disorders, which became greater in intensity and incidence the longer they persisted: a sharp rise in prices stimulated panic fears which in turn helped make grain

---

104 In addition to the preamble, see Terray's "Mémoire" in AN, K. 908.
105 Terray to comte de Périgord, 25 Nov. 1772, C. 2912, A.D. Hér.

more scarce which led to "seditious movements" which launched the cycle again unless the government intervened decisively.[106]

Liberalization, in Terray's view, produced just such a vicious circle. It threw the old trading system into chaotic disarray, increased the leverage of the rich over the poor whose wages tended to decline even as prices rose spectacularly, and at the same time paralyzed the administrative apparatus which in similar crises in the past had come to the aid of the majority. Because normally everything favored the producers, Terray argued that the normal policy of the government had to favor the consumers. By taking measures to "conserve the commodity of first necessity for the people," the Controller-General hoped to restore order; by convincing the people "that the King is incessantly working for their relief by continually overseeing its subsistence," he hoped to restore confidence along with tranquility.[107]

Asked "at what price should wheat be set for the common interest of the *laboureurs* and the inhabitants," the procurator of Crépy-en-Valois replied that there was *no* common interest, thus underscoring a dilemma almost as familiar and intractable for us as it was for Old Regime administrators:

> The price of wheat could not be fixed at the same level for the common interest of the *laboureurs* and inhabitants because the *laboureurs* have an interest different from that of the inhabitants, especially of the workers [*ouvriers*] charged with family who prefer to buy wheat at 12 *livres* the *septier* or 15 1. at most; whereas the *laboureur* who has always until now sold his grain at 24, 28, and 29 1. the *septier* [Paris measure] would not find his interest in selling it at only 12 or 15 *livres*, which means that one cannot fix a price for the interest of the two.[108]

Despite the distance and the level of sophistication which separated them, the Controller-General saw the problem in very much the same light as the local police official. "One party, wrote Terray,

> proposed to abolish all the laws and to leave everything to the free will of the proprietors of grain. Grain, they say, is their possession, they must be masters to sell it when, where, how and at the price they wish. The other demands the rigorous execution of the hindrances [*gênes*] established by the old laws, because, they retort, grain cannot be compared to any other good or merchandise.

106 Terray to jurats of Bordeaux, 16 May 1773, C. 1441, A.D. Gir.; Terray to IN., 28 Sept. 1773 and memoir, probably by St.-Prest, ca. Sept. 1770, *ibid.*; Terray to IN. of Champagne, 28 Sept. 1773, C. 419, A.D. Marne.

107 Terray to IN. of Brittany, 1 Aug. 1773, C. 1653, A.D. I-et-V.; memoir by St.-Prest (?), Sept. 1770, C. 1441, A.D. Gir; Terray to IN. of Brittany, 26 Feb. 1773, C. 1684, A.D. I-et-V.; Terray to IN. of Amiens,? Aug. 1773, C. 86, A.D. Somme.

108 Second Tableau, BN, mss. fr. 8128, fol. 60.

Man needs bread every day. Thenceforth, the grain owner, if he holds it hoarded away, becomes too much the master of the price, he can and he is tempted to abuse it. It is thus that the most antithetical maxims are often founded in good reasons and that the disputes become interminable and the discussions unsolvable.[109]

The "opposition of interests" between consumers and grain owners, each of whom had their own "justice," impressed Terray deeply. So fundamental was it that he despaired of effecting a genuine reconciliation. Instead of reconciliation, the Controller-General talked a great deal about "*balancing*" interests, even as we discuss balancing the different interests of rival nations in raw terms of power adjustment and stabilization. From Terray's perspective, however, balancing, in the nature of things, meant favoring the people-consumers, given their inherent disadvantages in the struggle with producers and owners. (Remember that it was also in the name of "balance" that Louis XV gave liberty to the owners and cultivators in 1763–64 against whom the old-fashioned paternal monarchy was said to have systematically discriminated.) As a general rule, Terray rejected any grain policy which was "useful to a small number [but] fatal to the majority of inhabitants."[110]

Yet Terray was a realist and a finance minister very much concerned about creating wealth and expropriating as much of it as possible for the government. Moreover, with a few exceptions, he revered property rights, he felt that owners should be properly compensated for their goods (he always insisted that he sought the "moderation" of prices, not their "dirt-cheapness"), and he wanted to encourage investment, especially in agriculture, not only for the sake of subsistence requirements, but because agriculture held the key to the expansion of the entire economy. In this regard he was a confirmed Sullyist. The problem was to find a way to promote agriculture without jeopardizing the well-being of the consumers and the tranquility of society. Liberalization and the high price program were unacceptable, not as growth stimulants (unlike many critics of liberalism, Terray readily conceded that the high price incentives of liberalization had in fact been a boon to agriculture,) but as political and social policy because of their disastrous

---

109 Terray papers, cited by Jobez, *Louis XV*, VI, 405–406.
110 Terray, "Mémoire," 1 Aug. 1773, C. 1653, A.D. I-et-V.; Terray to Monthyon, 1 Aug. 1773, C. 181, A.D. P-de-D.; Terray to comte de Périgord, 25 Nov. 1772, C. 2912, A.D. Hér. Cf. D'Agay to Turgot, 20 Sept. 1774, C. 87, A.D. Somme and L.-J. Bourdon des Planches, *Projet nouveau sur la manière de faire utilement en France le commerce des grains* (Brussels, 1785), 12.

side-effects. Terray groped for the developing nation's elixir: a growth strategy requiring only limited sacrifices. The king had already "given different laws in favor of land drainage and clearing" and the Controller-General pledged, in earnest but vague words, "to employ all the means possible to support the cultivation of the lands." Preoccupied with one crisis after another, Terray never managed to elaborate a systematic policy of agricultural development geared to a regime of moderate-to-low prices.[111]

To afford the consumers protection, in Terray's estimation, it was not enough to repudiate liberalization and restore the police. To meet immediate needs, he believed that it was urgent to mount a major government-sponsored and administered victualing effort, the organization and operation of which we shall examine shortly. For the long run, it would be necessary to establish a system of planning the allocation of scarce supplies and of dealing with shortages. In Terray's view, the central government had to commit itself to an unwavering policy of subsistence management instead of spasmodic and sensational interventions in emergencies. Logistically and financially, he felt it would be impossible to erect "abundance" organizations on the model of Joseph's Egypt or contemporary Geneva.[112] Commerce, as always, would retain first responsibility for provisioning the nation. Nor would it be possible, no matter how deeply government became involved, to avert catastrophes brought on by unpredictable and unavoidable harvest accidents. But if the government could not prevent dearths, it could prepare ahead to combat them and it could attempt to place the whole structure of provisioning on a more solid foundation.

It is not too much to say that Terray's long-term ambition was to *control* the grain trade and the provisioning system throughout the realm. This idea preoccupied him not only because he viewed subsistence as the most important single business of administration, but also because he believed, no less intensely than the *économistes*, that "all the other branches of political economy are intimately tied to it."[113] To become

---

111 Draft preamble, C. 94, I-et-L.; Terray to comte de Périgord and to archbishop of Toulouse, 25 Nov. 1772, C. 2912, A.D. Hér.; Terray to IN. of Tours, 18 Sept. 1773, C. 95, A.D. I-et-L. On Terray's "physiocratic" enthusiasm for agricultural development, see P. de St.-Jacob, *Les Paysans de la Bourgogne du nord*, 347ff.

112 Though Terray did not pursue the notion systematically, at one point he proposed resuscitating the plan requiring every religious house in the realm to stock an extra year's grain which would serve as an emergency civil reserve. See Terray to de la Corée, 15 July 1772, C. 354, A.D. Doubs.

113 Terray to First President, Bordeaux Parl., 21 Dec. 1773, C. 1441, A.D. Gir.

master of subsistence was to gain control over the entire economy; such mastery, joined to the political stability it would assure, would give the government extraordinary opportunities for shaping the course of the kingdom's future. This prospect intoxicated Terray; though he ordinarily had a healthy sense of his administrative limitations, when he thought about grain he often succumbed to an all-embracing vision of bureaucratic rationalism and centralism. He had a notion of "the general subsistence," a fresh and rather daring conception, at least for an administrator.[114] By this he meant that he viewed the burden of provisioning as a whole, as a national enterprise. He thought of subsistence in terms of an aggregate supply pool susceptible to manipulation from the center. "General subsistence" required a general subsistence policy which depended not merely upon uniform national laws, but also upon an unremitting effort at the center to control and coordinate provisioning operations. Instead of waiting passively for subsistence needs to present themselves, the Controller-General proposed an ongoing provisioning offensive which would insert the government squarely into the day-to-day business of monitoring grain movement, allocating supplies, supervising, adjusting, and planning. Ultimately, Terray's goal was the same which the liberals assigned to laissez-faire: the equalization of prices across time and space (for Terray the "just price," for the liberals the "bon prix") and the stabilization of supply in relation to local demand.

In some ways Terray's notion of control was as far removed from the traditional police way as it was from the liberal system. Previous ministers had assumed, understandably, that control, and thus any truly systematic program of prophylaxis, was beyond their grasp. Subsistence was a matter of state, to be sure, but it was to be worked out as a general rule on the local level. Characteristically, the central government intervened fitfully, by convulsion, rather than regularly, by habit or plan. Often high officials hesitated, lapsing into what I have called the paralysis of discretion and postponing action until it was too late. In the field there were practically as many different "police" as there were different communities, different regions, and different administrative institutions. The field police operated on the same laissez-faire principle which was denied to commerce, presumably according to the logic that each police, left to pursue its own interest, would contribute to the general subsistence interest.

---

114 Terray to INs. of Brittany and Bordeaux, 26 Feb. 1773, C. 1684, A.D. I-et-V. and C. 1447, A.D. Gir.

Terray reacted with equal horror to commercial and to police laissez-faire, though he was politically astute enough to realize that the latter would be far more difficult to curtail than the former. He groped for a *third* way, an alternative both to the chaos of liberty and to the babel of police. This third way—Terray's vision of control—implied not a repudiation of the police ideology—the Controller-General remained a Delamarist in outlook—but rather a far-reaching rationalization of operation, which both the merchants and the local authorities were bound to find distasteful. Strictly local traders were unlikely to be affected by Terray's scheme, save to the extent that it insulated them a bit against police harassment. Merchants who dealt on a wider scale, however, would have to resign themselves to a quasi-partnership with the central government which they would surely find constrictive, and probably profitable as well. Police would begin at the top. Local action would not be forbidden, but in theory police from above would gradually obviate police from below. A sort of Copernican revolution would transform the police of provisioning. The local police would acknowledge that their community was not at the center of the universe, that there were other communities in a similar situation linked together as interdependent parts of a single whole, and that they were all dependent on the government in the center of the universe. The enormous moral and administrative onus of provisioning would no longer remain almost exclusively in the hands of local and regional authorities. Terray would stand as a sort of guarantor of just and efficient distribution in ordinary times as well as an unfailing victualer of last resort in emergencies.

Terray argued that he was "the only one" who could conduct a "general subsistence" policy because only the Controller-General "sees the whole picture" and "holds the reins" of authority capable of commanding action throughout the realm. No one was better placed than he to determine the "general interest" and the best means of serving it. Given his vantage point, he believed that he was well-equipped to channel the flow of grain from surplus to deficit areas, to "direct speculations" in the most useful and efficient fashion, to manipulate buyer and seller psychology (generally to "calm" anxious consumers and "frighten" and "demoralize" hoarders), and to plan for contingencies. Though Terray's scheme implied a permanent commitment to government intervention on the supply side (the king's grain), he insisted that his first aim was to cooperate with private commerce and facilitate its mission.[115] He would alert merchants to opportunities they could not see for themselves and he would dissuade them from undertaking fruitless or redundant operations.[116]

This was in part the rationale the Controller-General used when he sought to increase his control over interprovincial (especially coastwise) trade in 1772 and 1773. "The *négociant* of Languedoc who wishes for example to make a shipment to Provence," Terray asked, "is he sure that there are not traders in other ports who have already launched and executed the same speculation?" "If I allow him to go ahead with his project," Terray reasoned, "I expose him to a certain loss." But, by requiring all merchants to seek a license from him, the Controller-General claimed that he could guarantee them all a profit and at the same time arrange for the efficient distribution of supply.[117] In fact, from the end of 1770, well before he entertained the idea of imposing new kinds of licenses, Terray tried to orchestrate private speculations according to a more or less global provisioning plan. In order to emphasize the ways in which his type of control differed from the old-style police, the Controller-General pointedly remarked that his decisions to promote this or that speculation would be based on objective indicators rather than on privilege, patronage, or favoritism. So important were all these matters that Terray promised that he would deal with them personally, entering "all the details … despite the extent of my occupations." Not only did Terray pledge to "take care of everything," but he asserted that he would do it better than anyone else because, given his grasp of "the ensemble," he knew more about the real needs and resources of the different places of the kingdom than their own regional and local officials:

> I know how much grain can [safely] be drawn from your province, how much its surplus might amount to. I know the areas toward which commerce should be directed, don't worry, I will prevent glut and price stagnation … as well as dearth.[118]

---

115 On this commitment to a permanent king's grain operation, see below, chapter thirteen and also Terray to IN. of Brittany, 26 Feb. 1773, C. 1684, A.D. I-et-V.

116 Terray to archbishop of Narbonne and Toulouse, 25 Nov. 1772, C. 2912, A.D. Hér.; Terray to IN. of Bordeaux, 4 May 1773, C. 1441, A.D. Gir.

117 Terray to archbishop of Narbonne, 25 Nov. 1772, C. 2912 and Terray to IN. of Languedoc, 20 Nov. 1772, C. 2911, A.D. Hér.

118 Terray, "Mémoire," 1 Aug. 1773, C. 1653, A.D. I-et-V.; Terray to IN. of Burgundy, 1 Sept. 1772, C. 81, A.D. C d'O.; Terray to IN. of Languedoc, 20 Nov. 1772, C. 2911, A.D. Hér.; Terray to archbishop of Toulouse and Narbonne, 25 Nov. 1772, C. 2912, A.D. Hér.

For Terray, *savoir* was *pouvoir.* "It is only through *knowledge* of the ensemble of resources and needs that one can direct operations to advantage," the Controller-General wrote. The key element in his strategy was control through the collection, centralization, and analysis of information, from every corner of the kingdom and from certain foreign quarters as well. The refrain of letter after letter emanating from his bureaus was that good data was the best police. He envisaged something approaching a total tracking system dealing with demand as well as supply. He wanted constantly "to be in a position to follow grain from the place of its departure [after harvest] to that of its consumption" and to follow the demographic vicissitudes of every area of France. The very concept of conducting a "general subsistence" policy would founder without the regular and prompt arrival of reliable, homogeneous, comparable, and comprehensive information. With this data, Terray believed that he would be able to make the right decisions, to direct transfers from places of glut to places of penury without arousing panic fears and in the shortest possible time, to project a map of likely crisis areas and scenarios of relief, to avoid misplaced speculations, and to determine quickly whether extraordinary (public rather than commercial) supplies would be necessary and through what channels they could most efficiently and economically be arranged.[119]

Remembered today as one of the founders of modern French statistical surveying and data-management, Terray vigorously sought to improve both the system of information-gathering and the quality of the intelligence. He regarded the old collection procedures as deeply flawed. No one, save the clerks in the Contrôle-Général, seemed to take the matter seriously and the clerks, for their part, did not always ask the right questions. Very often information on harvest prospects, on the crops, and on prices was inaccurate, incomplete, or it arrived too late to enable the government to take the "necessary precautions." Shortly after taking office, the Controller-General asked the intendants to provide more detailed information on expectations (*espérances*) including quality differentiation and price projections. Mere statistics on the market reports did not satisfy him: "the price accounts ... must

119 Terray to archbishop of Toulouse, 25 Nov. 1772, C. 2912, A.D. Hér.; Terray to Rouillé d'Orfeuil, 28 Sept. 1773, C. 419, A.D. Marne; Terray to IN. of Brittany, 22 Feb. 1774 (second letter that day), C. 1684, A.D. I-et-V.; Terray to Amelot, 18 May 1773, C. 77, A.D. C d'O.; Terray to Chazerat, 9 Sept. 1773, C. 181, A.D. P-de-D. Cf. Terray to de Crosne, 6 Aug. 1770, AN, F¹²* 155, fol. 19; R. Mols, *Introduction à la démographie historique des villes d'Europe du XIVe au XVIIIe siècles* (Gembloux, 1954–56), I, 56; P. Clément, *Portraits historiques*, 380.

always contain observations on the *causes* of price variations." In fact, he was avid to know "everything concerning the grain trade." In addition to the regular harvest and price information, in the spring of 1770 he asked the intendants for "statements of the subsistence necessary for life" in each generality, accompanied by "statements of the comparison of the persons who must consume it." The intendants, for the most part, ignored his request, "doubtless," he surmised, "because they took it for the expression of a passing interest" linked to continuing provisioning difficulties. The next year he devised a "new model" for harvest reporting, more detailed, more exigent, more demographic in content than ever before. Repeatedly, he complained that he was poorly informed and that he lacked "precious details" of both a quantitative (production-consumption) and qualitative (state of the grain trade) data and he rebuked intendants and subdelegates for their slovenliness and procrastination.[120]

In the second half of 1773, at a time when he felt he was on the brink of restoring subsistence stability to the kingdom, Terray proposed a comprehensive new plan for collecting data which he hoped would lay the foundation for a successful general subsistence policy. "My idea," he wrote, "was to learn on the one side the production of all the generalities and on the other the population in order to know each year, by a comparison of [the aggregate of] subsistence with the number of consumers, what the status of each generality would be in terms of its needs or its surplus." This was a more elaborate version of the request he had vainly made in 1770, this time in the form of a detailed memoir endorsed by the hand of Louis XV and submitted to the intendants as a formal administrative directive to be implemented immediately. In the past, the Controller-General explained, we have settled for muddled, misleading, and truncated intelligence. The accounts of harvest expectations and of the crop yields, for example, have always been reported in nebulous terms of "half years," "three-quarter years," "good years," etc. "But," asked Terray,

what is the quantity of grain indicated by these denominations? We don't know. What is the proportion between the harvest and the consumption needs of the generalities? We know even less about this.

---

120 Terray, "Mémoire," 1 Aug. 1773, C. 86, A.D. Somme; Terray to Amelot, 31 May, 14 June 1770, C. 77, A.D. C d'O.; Terray to Rouillé d'Orfeuil, 2 July 1771, C. 379, A.D. Marne; IN. of Languedoc to SDs, 8 July 1771, C. 119, A.D. H-G.; Terray to Sénac de Meilhan, 5 March 1771 and 26 May 1772, C. 196, A.D. C-M.; Terray to Taboureau, 17 Dec. 1771 and 18 Feb. 1772, C. 8277, A.D. Nord; Terray to Monthyon, 30 June, 12 Aug. 1772, C. 2445, A.D. B-du-R.; Terray to Rouillé d'Orfeuil, 27 Sept. 1772, C.417, A.D. Marne; Terray to Fontette, 27 Feb. 1771, C. 2624, A.D. Caen.

Habitually, we have relied upon the price as a surrogate indicator both of the supply and of the relationship between supply and demand. In Terray's view, however, the price was a poor "barometer" because the price changed not only with changes in supply and demand, but as a result of "fears, hopes, sales, purchases." Since bad information has often misled us, the Controller-General argued, "it is thus time now for us to make things clear and for that two bases are necessary, the first the population or the number of consumers and the second the quantity of productions."[121]

Through their subdelegates and other trusted agents, the intendants were to launch two sorts of perennial inquiries. Since an annual "arithmetical census" was a practical impossibility, the registration of vital events would serve as a substitute indicator of population changes. Production figures, Terray conceded, would be more difficult to procure. Officials could construct an index based on the tithe return (very much as historians trying to determine production do today) or they could use a measure based upon "charrues," or ploughs, the practice the Controller-General preferred, but which depended on normative "common year" estimations of yield-to-seed likely to flaw comparisons and translate rather crudely into numbers. Though officials were bound to encounter many difficulties at first, Terray assured them that assiduity and experience would enable them to improve their techniques and to advance "by degree to the point of precision and perfection that is possible to attain." Think, he marveled, how much better we will come to know the kingdom and how much this knowledge will enhance our ability to "direct subsistence aid according to needs that we will have foreseen in advance."

Though it may strike our computer-dulled imagination as a bagatelle, Terray's project was a prodigious undertaking in his time. Not only did it raise complex technical and logistical problems, but it also sparked administrative and political controversy. The parlements and the provincial estates, under whose gaze functioned many of the local officials upon whom would devolve the responsibility for data collection, were hostile to any extension of royal control in the provinces. This allergy to centralization even seemed to affect some intendants, who felt uneasy about the intrusion of the Controller-General into the intimate life of their jurisdictions. They understood that the better informed the central government was, the fewer decisions would be left for

---

121 This and the following paragraph are based upon Terray's "Mémoire," 1 Aug. 1773, which can be found in A.D. Somme (C. 86), A.D. I-et-V. (C. 1653), and A.D. P-de-D. (C. 181).

them to make. They complained that Terray's project demanded more sophistication than they could muster among their subordinates, that it required a great deal of data that could not be obtained, and that its problematic results would not be able to justify the investment necessary to operate it. Or, like the intendant of Bordeaux, they objected on the grounds that "detailed researches" would arouse the "mistrust of the owners and cultivators" and provoke "sensations" in the public mind.[122] Nor did the precedents for energetic execution by the intendants augur well. A royal Declaration in 1736 requiring civil registration of baptismal, nuptial, and burial data produced extremely disappointing results. More recently, Terray himself witnessed the insouciance with which intendants were capable of regarding instructions.[123]

Prominent among the critics of Terray's plan were the partisans of liberalization. When one of their leading spokesmen, Turgot, succeeded Terray as Controller-General, one of his first acts was to suspend sine die the collection of all production data (he continued to solicit population information because "it did not cause the same difficulties"). Officially, he justified his repudiation of the Terray system on the grounds that it was too "complicated," that the information it yielded inspired "no confidence" and was of "little utility," and that the procedures employed were "dangerous," presumably because they "cast alarm among the people." Turgot's real motive, however, had nothing to do with the allegedly bad quality data or the troubles of collection. He rightly understood that information implied control and that in certain circumstances information might even compel action. Since the liberals decried any sort of governmental involvement in grain affairs at any time, they regarded Terray's intelligence system as a trap. Information collection itself was intervention. If it was of "little utility," it was because the liberals did not want to use it; if it was "dangerous," it was because it threatened to ensnare them in problems about which they wanted to know nothing.[124]

Since Terray survived as Controller-General for less than a year

---

122 Terray to Esmangart, 12 Nov. 1773, C. 1439, A.D. Gir. Cf. the similar position of the intendant of Brittany, reinforced by the peculiar political circumstances of this pays d'état in the early seventies. To Terray, 8 Oct. 1773, C. 1653, A.D. I-et-V.

123 Terray, "Mémoire," 1 Aug. 1773, C. 86, A.D. Somme.

124 Turgot to Amelot, 21 Sept. 1774, C. 77, A.D. C d'O; Turgot to Taboureau, 27 Sept. 1774, C. 8273, A.D. Nord; Turgot to Chazerat, 27 Sept. 1774, C. 181, A.D. P-de-D; Rey, Du Commerce des bleds (Paris, 1775), 55–57. Cf. the similar attitude of the Estates of Languedoc, deliberations, Dec. 1768, C. 2411, A.D. H-G.

following the introduction of his data project, it is extremely difficult to determine the degree of execution it actually began to enjoy.
For every intendant like Esmangart of Bordeaux who delayed and
obstructed, there were others such as the Bertier de Sauvigny of
Paris, Julien of Alençon, and Amelot of Burgundy who cooperated
fully. One would like to imagine, too, that there were a number of
subdelegates like Gehier of Bar-sur-Aube who shared Terray's vision
of a comprehensive statistical network and information organization
capable of forecasting difficulties, matching supply and demand, and
assisting in other administrative matters. Gehier proposed his own
data collection plan which he called "the dream of an *homme de bien*"
and he likened his motivation to the reformist-humanitarian zeal
which inspired his hero, the abbé de St.-Pierre.[125]

The subdelegates, of course, were crucial intermediaries in the collection process, for they linked the syndics of rural communities and
the municipalities of the towns with the intendant. In Burgundy they
received a printed instruction sheet from the intendant outlining the
procedure in copious detail, stressing the importance and the *novelty*
of rigor and precision (the crop indicators, for instance, "will not be as
they have been heretofore, vaguely designated in ideal fraction...."),
and insisting upon the urgency of acting with dispatch ("The King
gave the order to do this in *his own hand.*"). Calling upon them to practice prudence and discretion, the intendant warned them to be prepared to face "obstacles" and "infidelities" from the "inhabitants of
the countryside," who were "always disposed to suspect evil" and who
might view the inquiries as "dangerous investigations into their tax-
paying capacities."[126]

The subdelegates in turn prepared instructions for the syndics and
other local agents who would actually gather much of the data. Pitched
on a far simpler plane than the intendant's directive, they are interesting for the trouble they take to discuss the government's motives. The
syndics were told that the ministry's aim, on the one hand, was "to prevent grain from [ever again] rising to a price which exceeds the faculties of the poor Journalier [the rural analogues to the urban consumers
whom the liberals pretended did not exist]" and, on the other, "to favor
agriculture." In other words, interests would somehow be balanced. In
addition, the subdelegates promised the syndics "unequivocally" that

---

125 Gehier to IN. of Champagne, 23 Oct. 1773, C. 299, A.D. Aube.
126 "Mémoire sur les états à former...," Nov. 1773, C. 77, A.D. C d'O.

the data collection had absolutely no fiscal purpose. Unfortunately, we do not know how convincing the syndics found this presentation.[127]

The merits of Terray's idea, its modernity and its breadth, were also its chief shortcomings. Partly because of the severe limitations of communications and partly because of the insufficiently national and bureaucratic nature of the administration implanted throughout the realm, his government was simply not equipped to execute the information-gathering task as he imagined it. Terray's enthusiasm gave him the illusion that his data system could conquer time as well as space and will. Once the collection machinery was in place, the Controller-General boasted to Louis XV, "Your Majesty will then be able to command reports *from one moment to another* regarding each part of the Administration of his Kingdom and evaluate them with confidence."[128] To be sure, Terray did not remain in office long enough to give the system a proper trial. Moreover, it was hardly auspicious to introduce it in the midst of grave social, political, economic, and fiscal disorders. The Controller-General never had in hand the amount and quality of data which might have given him a commanding edge in dealing with dearth. The claim Terray made that "I see the ensemble of the movement of grain" was a bit of wishful thinking and a bluff designed to increase his administrative leverage.

Moreover, the Controller-General underestimated the problem of establishing effective regulatory mechanisms and enforcing distribution decisions made at the center. The short-term exigencies of crisis management in some ways eddied against his control ideal. The same structural factors that impeded information-collection made it extremely difficult to integrate local communities into a global interest system. Terray could never convince an intendant or a local official that he knew more about their needs than they did. When it affected their freedom of action, intendants and the field police did not like "gênes" any more than did the merchants and *laboureurs*. The Controller-General, I have suggested, viewed subsistence as a national problem, but he was, alas, probably the only administrator in France to see it in these terms.

---

127 SD to syndics, 20 Dec. 1773, C. 81, A.D. C d'O.
128 Terray, "Mémoire," 1 Aug. 1773, C. 86, A.D. Somme.

Chapter XII

POLICING THE GENERAL SUBSISTENCE, 1771–1774

I

Many monographs will have to be written before one can properly assess the impact of Terray's policy. De-liberalization wrought no miracles. It did not herald the general return of abundance and it did not restore universal social tranquility. Even in those places which enjoyed a marked change of fortune after the end of 1770, it would be difficult to *show* that the improvement in conditions was due to the reinstitution of controls. Yet there is no question that Terray's law buoyed the morale of the police, infusing them with a sense of confidence that they had not felt for years. There were still frequent denunciations of "disorders" and "monopolies" in the trade, but the police no longer complained that they were impotent to act; they once again located the source of the vice in the malice and greed of the dealers rather than in the laws, and they resorted to "the usages of authority" when necessary to furnish their markets.[1] There is some evidence that consumers in parts of the Hainaut and the Paris region received the news of the government's regulatory law with enthusiasm.[2] An observer in Champagne reported that the break with liberalization helped to "revive" the "courage" of the people.[3] Large numbers of merchants began to register with the police in order to secure permission to traffic in grain.[4]

As always, execution of the law depended heavily upon the parlements; in this regard the Maupeou purge changed very little. It was

---

1 See, for example, *Dépêches*, 16 June 1771, AN O^{1*} 413, fol. 393; 19 Sept. 1772, AN, O^{1*} 414, fols. 853–55; and 26 June 1774, AN, O^{1*} 416, fols. 407–408.
2 Terray to Taboureau, 16 Jan. 1771, C. 5977, A.D. Nord.
3 "Administration des grains," BN, mss. fr. 11561, fol. 6.
4 AN, Y 9648. Cf. 8 March 1771, Archives Seine-Paris, D5B^6 4910.
   The Paris municipality reconstituted its clientele of licensed suppliers. It issued new credentials to qualified merchants and their hinterland commissioners and no longer had cause to bemoan defections from the ranks. See *Ordonnance de Police, Bureau de Ville*, 21 Feb. 1771, AN, F^{11} 264; deliberations of the Bureau, 21 Feb. 1771, AN, H* 1874, fols. 116–17.

precisely in order to assure the widest possible diffusion and enforcement that Terray had the December law enveloped in letters patent requiring registration. Though a number of courts, such as the Parlements of Paris and Metz, gave their approbation without difficulty, it should not be imagined that registration was either universal or uncontested. None of the liberal parlements endorsed the letters patent. By not insisting on registration at the beginning of 1771, the government, after a fashion, discharged its debts to these courts for having supported the king's position on the grain question so fervently in the sixties. Aware that it would take a "combat of authority" to secure registration and convinced that a forced registration would serve no purpose, Terray decided to wait for the evolution of events and opinion to cause the liberal courts to gravitate toward the police system on their own.[5]

Yet the liberal parlements, which behaved predictably, were not the only ones which failed to comply amiably with Terray's wishes. The increasingly tense political climate may have encouraged recalcitrance. After the experience of the sixties, when the central government revealed that it could not be counted upon in a subsistence crisis, a number of courts may have felt that they could deal with the problems more efficiently on a regional scale without formal collaboration or coordination with the ministry. The Brittany court refused registration until February 1774, when it accepted a diluted version. Nevertheless, in November 1771, the Parlement issued a regulatory *arrêt* purely on its own authority which bore a striking resemblance to Terray's December law. Presented as an antidote to "monopoly," which perpetuated a dearth that threatened the well-being of the people, the *arrêt* reserved even less freedom for commerce than the royal measure. It provoked violent opposition throughout Brittany from the spokesmen of the powerful liberty lobby, which united the land and the sea. The *négociants* of Nantes warned that if they were subjected to police constraints, particularly the obligation to keep books (these international merchants claimed to do business on good faith, *sans écrits!*) and to deal on the public markets, they would quit the grain trade and deprive the kingdom of a "precious subsistence entrepôt." It appears doubtful that this parlementary *arrêt* was vigorously enforced. Nor did Terray press the matter of registering the royal Declaration with the Parlement. In his

---

5 Terray to St.-Priest, 26, 28 May 1771, C. 2909, A.D. Hér.; Terray to Pajot, 31 Oct. 1771, AN, F[11] 223; Terray to Sénac de Meilhan, 21 Dec. 1773, C. 2421, A.D. B-du-R.

correspondence with the intendant, the Controller-General acted *as if* the provisions of the December law were applicable in Brittany as in any other part of the realm.[6]

Similarly, while he asked the intendant of Bordeaux to assess the prospects for enforcing a simple *arrêt du conseil* without registration, Terray began long and sometimes strained negotiations with the Parlement for a text which it would find acceptable. In the beginning, in return for their cooperation, he was willing to allow the magistrates a wide latitude to "reform" and interpret the law as circumstances required. But over the next several years, as the subsistence situation in the south of France got worse rather than better, Terray became increasingly adamant that the Bordeaux court conform exactly to the December law and the magistrates became increasingly unhappy with the Controller-General's management of provisioning affairs. Attacked by the Parlement repeatedly in 1773 for allegedly "blocking the free circulation of grain" and "destroying" the grain trade in order to protect a "privileged" band of government-backed speculators—Bordeaux's version of the eternal famine plot!—Terray grew impatient and angry. Announcing that he would henceforth deal "specially" with the intendant regarding subsistence matters, the Controller-General decried the Bordeaux magistrates' "desire to play a role" as astringently as Laverdy had denounced the Rouen and Paris initiatives in the late sixties.[7]

The Rouennais themselves, both despite and because of their anti-liberal zeal, also managed to vex Terray. In the *arrêt* by which they registered the law shortly after their Parisian colleagues in January 1771, they proposed certain "modifications," at least one of which the ministry found wholly unacceptable. Despite their obsession with commercial "abuses," the Rouen magistrates wanted *laboureurs* to have authorization to engage in trade, ostensibly in order to promote *blatier*-style, small-scale provisioning. Though Terray became increasingly disillusioned with the role of the *laboureurs* over the next few years, the demand for this indulgence was so widespread in the

---

6 "Arrêt et règlement de la police générate," 5 Nov. 1771, C. 774, A.D. L-A.; "Mémoire des juges-consuls de Nantes," *ibid.*; Terray to IN. of Brittany, 30 Sept. 1772, C. 1691, A.D. I-et-V.; Genard to IN., 25 Feb. 1772, C. 1725, *ibid.*; IN. to Terray, June 1774, C. 1653, *ibid.*

7 Terray to Esmangart, 22 Oct. 1771, C. 1432, A.D. Gir.; Terray to Esmangart and First President of Bordeaux Parl., 21 Dec. 1773, C. 1441, *ibid.*; Terray to First President, 26 July 1773, C. 1441 and 5 Nov. 1773, C. 1442, *ibid.*; Pidansat de Mairobert, *Journal historique*, IV, 401–404 (14 Dec. 1773).

beginning of 1771 that he ceded to it. The Rouen court also demanded the legal abolition of the flour trade, save for the colonies, on the grounds that it encouraged fraud in quantity and quality and that it had even caused disease and death in the way it had been practiced in the sixties. The flour trade, however, had grown enormously during the previous decade, especially in the Paris area. Terray bluntly told the Rouen court that he would do nothing to stifle it, though he remained uneasy about miller involvement in grain traffic.[8]

While he plainly did not relish them, the Controller-General did not challenge the modifications instituted by the Dijon Parlement in the act by which it endorsed the letters patent in early February. Like the Rouennais, the Dijon magistrates reserved the right of *laboureurs* and *fermiers* to engage in trade (presumably with grain of their own cultivation, a condition which would be practically impossible to enforce) and, in addition, it stipulated that cultivators and proprietors would be able to sell their *own* grain off the market in their barns and granaries.[9] The Parlements of Besançon and Metz made their registration contingent upon the government's acceptance of very similar changes in the law.[10] Allowing for these modifications, which did not radically alter the character of the law, Terray secured registration for a vast part of the kingdom comprising all of France north of the Loire and the large segment of central France which belonged to what used to be, *ante*-Maupeou, the Paris jurisdiction.

Though he was anxious to establish clearly a new national law which would define the government's attitude toward grain and help create a new psychological climate, it was not Terray's intention at the beginning of 1771 to demand an exacting, rigorous execution of every clause, at all times, in all places. First of all, he knew that this could be impossible: "a general law," he wrote, "cannot be enforced with precision in all the provinces ... in all circumstances...." Furthermore, an inflexible approach would be undesirable. In order to make the law effective, the king's agents had to be in a position to adjust the "disadvantages" of the law, apply it "more or less strictly" as their "prudence" dictates, and "repair the abuses which could arise from a false interpretation."[11]

---

8 18 Jan. 1771, Rouen Parl., Conseil 1770, fols. 60, 63, and remonstrances, 25 Jan. 1771, fols. 65–82, A.D. S-M.; C. 103, *ibid.* Cf. *arrêt*, conseil supérieur of Bayeux, 24 Nov. 1772, C. 2600, A.D. Cal.

9 B. 12 138, fol. 64, A.D. C d'O.

10 Deliberations, 20 March 1771, B. 2174, fol. 21, A.D. Doubs; deliberation, 19 Jan. 1771, Metz Parl., B. 40 and B. 470, fol. 31 (registre secret), A.D. Moselle.

11 Terray to DuCluzel, 28 Jan. 1771, C. 94 and 25 Feb. 1771, C. 95, A.D. I-et-L.;

The Controller-General was not indifferent to the wave of criticism which certain provisions of the law provoked, especially those concerning mandatory market sales and the interdiction of *laboureurs*. Certain objections could perhaps be discounted, for they came from political and ideological adversaries: Turgot's, for example, or those of his colleague Pajot, the intendant of Dauphiné, who shared the liberal stance of that province's parlementaires. It was less easy, however, to dispose of the reservations of friends such as Cypierre, the strong-willed intendant of the Orléanais, who had militated so vigorously for a police revival in the late sixties.[12] "It seems to me," Cypierre wrote,

> that it is appropriate to follow the spirit of this law [of December 1770] rather than sticking to the letter: its spirit is very just; taken at the letter, however, it goes too far, hampers and fails to meet the goal that it set.

Only a few years after his campaign to unmask those who veiled their monopolies in the sacred garb of property rights, Cypierre was not embarrassed to speak in defense of owners and cultivators who sold their *own* grain (rather than grain belonging to commerce, i.e., acquired second-hand through purchase) off market on the grounds that to do so was "a natural right attached to property, [a] legitimate right in the social order." Nor did it require the large vistas of an intendant to make this analysis of the December law and this distinction between right and abuse. A minor police official at Reims later remarked that he had systematically "closed his eyes" upon the mandatory market clause because it was "contrary to the natural right of property."[13]

In opting for a supple, conditional application of the market clause in the law, Terray inclined less to these theoretical arguments than to their practical concomitants: the claim that there were no markets nearby and that "the little people would die of starvation" if country sales were all forbidden; the appeal to local history and customary usage which proved that such transactions had commonly occurred before

---

Terray to Rouillé d'Orfeuil, 14, 28 Jan. 1771, C. 417, A.D. Marne; Terray to Jullien, 7, 28 May 1771, C. 89, A.D. Orne; Terray to Blair de Boisement, 20 Feb. 1771, C. 553, A.D. Bas-Rhin.

12 Turgot, "Lettres sur le commerce des grains," in *Oeuvres*, ed. by Schelle, III, 265ff; Pajot to Terray 31 Oct. 1771, AN, F[11] 223; Cypierre, *Réflexions* and Terray to Cypierre, 7 May 1771, published by Louis Guérin, *L'Intendant Cypierre et la vie économique de l'Orléanais*, 199, 207. Cf. the intendant of Picardy whose past record and present attitudes were similar to Cypierre's. To Terray, Oct. 1773, C. 86, A.D. Somme.

13 "Résultat des observations des officiers de police des différentes villes … sur l'exécution," C. 417, A.D. Marne.

liberalization without precipitating trouble; and the contention that the law should aim specifically at policing "professional traffickers" rather than all grain holders. On the basis of this last idea the Controller-General tentatively agreed to "tolerate" (by which he explicitly meant provisionally "closing one's eyes" rather than "authorizing formally") small-scale commerce by *laboureurs*, many of whom purchased grain for their own subsistence or for seed. Nor was he willing to make exceptions only for marginal buyers and sellers. When two international traders from Caen complained that they could not successfully conduct their import operations if they were obliged to rush their grain straight to market, the Controller-General assured them, albeit cautiously, that they could count on a generous measure of freedom to delay marketing provided no supply emergencies developed.[14]

Finally, as the text of the law itself suggested, Terray was worried about "resuscitating the pretentions of the [local] officers of police." His "fear" of provoking them to take "excesses" encouraged the Controller-General not to insist upon an unbending execution. "I think that it might be necessary," he instructed the intendant of Tours, "to remind the police officials of the motives which should determine them *not* to enforce the new grain regulation rigorously." When the police of a Champagne town halted a convoy and set a price below the current for public sale on the market, the Controller-General condemned them as vigorously as Laverdy had ever denounced local authorities at the height of their reaction against liberalization. Nor did he hesitate to ask the royal council to quash a brutal Caen police sentence which unfairly fined and dishonored a local *laboureur* and tithe-farmer who had in fact been supplying the market regularly. On the other hand, the Controller-General rushed to back up local authorities when they fell victim to what he considered to be unjust criticism for applying the law.[15]

It is difficult to make a general assessment of police conduct vis-à-vis the December law. For each case of overzealousness—in the Bordeaux

---

14 *Ibid.*; Terray to DuCluzel, 7 May, 15 Oct. 1771, C. 95, A.D. I-et-L.; Taboureau to SDs of Hainaut, 28 March 1771, C. 6689, A.D. Nord; memoir of Burgundy IN. to SDs, ca. Oct. 1771, C. 81, A.D. C d'O; Terray to Fontette, 7 May 1771, C. 2624, A.D. Cal.; Terray to IN. of Bordeaux, 28 Jan. 1771, C. 1432, A.D. Gir.; Moisson and Le Cavelier fils to Terray, 16 March 1771 and his reply of 26 March, C. 1653, A.D. Cal.

15 Terray to Amelot, 22 Sept. 1772, C. 81, A.D. C d'O.; Terray to Rouillé d'Orfeuil, 28 Jan. 1771, C. 417, A.D. Marne; Terray to DuCluzel, 30 April 1771, C. 94, A.D. I-et-L.; Esmangart to Terray, 2 Nov. 1771, C. 1432, A.D. Gir.; Terray to Rouillé d'Orfeuil, 26 March 1771, C. 421 and 29 May 1773, C. 417, A.D. Marne; *arrêt du conseil*, 18 Aug. 1772, C. 2601, A.D. Cal.

area, for example, where the intendant appears to have lost control of the local police once they were unleashed—there seems to be a case of overindulgence—in Alençon, for instance, where a subdelegate rebuked the royal procurator for "tolerating" secret deals or in Champagne where another subdelegate blamed continuing subsistence difficulties on the indifference of the local police and the *maréchaussée* to the December law. The Champenois called for a multiplication of "ad hoc police commissions" not only in order to increase surveillance of the grain trade, but also in order to assign "watchdogs to watch the watchdogs."[16] In other parts of Champagne, however, the local authorities regularly "shut their eyes" to violations of the law with the approval of the intendant, for the violations in fact facilitated local provisioning. In these places it was clear that police aims were best achieved by "allowing the freedom of buying and selling grain to subsist as before."[17]

In one town in the Hainaut, the police and the merchants entered into a mutually profitable accord which put them both outside the law. The police tolerated private sales in granaries; in return the traders supplied the town with sufficient amounts of grain to meet its needs. Taboureau, the intendant, strongly disapproved such transactions; few intendants enforced the December law with such determination. Convinced that the "crushing misery" suffered by his province was the result of commercial maneuvers, he urged his subdelegates to "worry the monopolists" by "an indefatigable surveillance." Taboureau personally pronounced judicial sentences against law-breaking merchants in his campaign to suppress all off-market dealings.[18]

In several towns in Alençon and Champagne, fiscality and venality rather than concern for provisioning inspired police rigor. In order to maximize the opportunity for collecting fees charged for all transactions on the marketplace, authorities vigorously prosecuted the clause banning off-market business. Here the law was executed in exacting fashion for the wrong reasons.[19] Yet in their reports to the

---

16 Intendant's circular, 5 June 1773, C. 1439, A.D. Gir.; Soalhat to IN. of Alençon, 31 Oct. 1773, C.89, A.D. Orne; Gehier to IN. of Champagne, 29 Oct. 1773 and 4 Jan. 1774, C. 299, A.D. Aube.

17 "Résultat des observations ...," C. 417, A.D. Marne.

18 Contamine (Givet) to Taboureau, 29 Dec. 1773, C. 6690, A.D. Nord; Taboureau to SDs, 19 Dec. 1771, C. 5977, *ibid.*; ordonnances of IN., 23 Dec. 1771 and 3 Feb. 1772, C. 6689, *ibid.*; Taboureau to Hennet, 7 Nov. 1773, C. 6690, *ibid.*

19 *Ibid.*; état, Nogent-le-Rotrou, C. 90, A.D. Orne.
    A great deal of local level work will have to be done before we can evaluate the importance of fiscality, in commercial as well as political terms, at the marketplace.

ministry, the intendants of Brittany, Picardy, Hainaut, and Caen had high praise for the performance of the local police in their generalities. In Burgundy, where the intendant educated local authorities with detailed instructions explaining the operations of the regulatory law and the measure of severity to apply in different situations, the results also appear to have been favorable.[20]

If Terray had had his way, every local official would have acted more or less in the style of Trippier, royal procurator of Bar-sur-Aube:

> Here is how I interpret and execute the letters patent. I have the prévôtal clerk keep a register containing the declarations of those in the grain business in order to be in a position to oblige them, in a time of pressing need and absolute necessity, to provision the market.
>
> I prevent as much as I can illicit transactions made before the opening of the market, this Monopoly of those who buy and resell immediately and at a higher price without even removing the grain they first bought. I have it announced by the beat of the drum that it is forbidden to buy grain for commerce in the villages and hamlets of the countryside where there are neither markets nor fairs.

Nevertheless, Trippier allowed the *laboureurs* to sell to consumers for their subsistence needs in villages outside the market nexus. As long as merchants waited until consumers and bakers had satisfied their needs, the procurator allowed merchants to buy and remove as much grain as they wished provided they indicated the places of storage in their declarations to the police. Trippier seemed to understand the Controller-General's conception of and expectations for the December law. Remarkably, hardly a month after the law went into effect, this official was able to pretend that it "has produced abundance in our markets and some diminution in the prices of grain which [nevertheless] remain very expensive."[21] Not all local and regional reports, to be sure, were so sanguine. The overall picture is checkered. But there seems to have been a general satisfaction on all levels of police with the flexible, empirical approach which Terray took.

In 148 marketplaces in Brittany, for which an annual "produit" was recorded, the total of fees collected for marketing and measuring "rights" was 52,395 *livres*. Nobles comprise the largest single social group among the holders, followed by members of the royal household, including the king, and by ecclesiastics. See the appendices of Letaconnoux, *Le Commerce des grains en Bretagne*.

20 IN. of Brittany to Terray, ca. May 1774, C. 1653, A.D. I-et-V.; Reply to Terray's inquiry, ca. Oct. 1773, C. 86, A.D. Somme; Taboureau to Terray, 4 Aug. 1774, C. 6690, A.D. Nord; Fontette to Terray, 14 Oct. 1771, C. 2624, A.D. Cal.; Amelot, "Mémoire concernant les grains," Oct. 1771, C. 81, A.D. C d'O.

21 Trippier to Rouillé d'Orfeuil, 19 Feb. 1771, C. 299, A.D. Aube.

II

In the spring of 1771 Terray himself was cautiously optimistic about the prospects for bringing subsistence problems under control. Though he worried that the circumstantial, uneven application of the law could cause confusion, the reasonably smooth transition back to the police system encouraged him. There were few reports about panic in the merchant community and the consumer-public seemed calmer than it had been in quite a while. If prices remained high, despite a harsh winter and a busy spring sowing, many places reported a marked attenuation in the amplitude of market-to-market variation. All of this led Terray to claim, only months after the promulgation of the December law, that it "was working," even as the liberals had rushed to celebrate the swift accomplishments of the reforms of 1763–64.[22]

Yet events during the course of the next few years forced Terray to revise his estimation and to reconsider his attitude toward the execution of the regulatory measures. For there were still hard times to come. Mediocre to bad harvests in much of the kingdom belied the hopes raised by propitious spring appearances, which themselves had helped to reinforce the mood of confidence inspired by the return to regulation. The tableau of "the most horrible misery" painted by Fontette, intendant of Caen, could have applied to a dozen other generalities.[23] Assisted by instructions and funds from the central government, intendants in the stricken areas opened *ateliers de charité* and expanded other public works projects.[24] In Paris wheat prices rose sharply during 1771 and police reported considerable ferment in the bread markets. In May Hardy noted that a thirty year old pregnant woman cut her own throat when a baker refused to give her credit.[25] A riot at Nancy sent shock tremors throughout Lorraine.[26] In Brittany the situation deteriorated dramatically between the fall of 1771 and the spring of 1772.

---

22 Terray to INs. of Caen, Tours, and Bordeaux, 7 May 1771, C. 2624, A.D. Cal.; C. 95, A.D. I-et-L.; C. 1432, A.D. Gir.

23 Fontette to Terray, 14 Oct. 1771, C. 2624, A.D. Cal. Cf. Monteymard to IN. of Champagne, 25 Oct. 1771, C. 423, A.D. Marne and état de récoltes, 1771, C. 84, A.D. Somme.

24 C. Bloch, *L'Assistance et l'état à la veille de la Révolution* (Paris, 1908), 201–202.

25 *Hardy's Journal*, 1 May 1771, BN, mss. fr. 6680, fol. 256. On Paris prices see M. Baulant, "Le Prix des grains à Paris," *Annales: E.S.C.*, XXIII (May–June 1968), 520–40. For a different index, see Labrousse, *Esquisse*, 113.

26 Deliberation of Metz Parl., 17 June 1771, B. 470, fol. 65 (*registre secret*), A.D. Moselle.

"The misery of the people is very great," the subdelegate of Qui-mper informed the intendant. "Almost all [the peasants] are spec-ters ready to expire," wrote the substitut of a parish near Rennes.[27] During this same period a series of riots aimed at preventing grain removal and forcing down the price of bread broke out in the gener-alities of Brittany, Caen, and Tours.[28]

Though prices remained dear, a relatively good harvest in 1773 brought a measure of tranquility to Picardy, Champagne, and neigh-boring areas in the north and northeast.[29] But from Alençon came grisly reports of "starvation," "epidemic and popular diseases," record "mortalities" (seven heads of family allegedly "died of misery" during the year in one village), persistently high prices, and lagging wages—eight to ten *sous* a day—insufficient to support the smallest and most frugal families.[30] Massive unemployment due to the col-lapse of the silk-lace and other textile industries compounded the continuing subsistence crisis in Caen and surrounding areas.[31] After a year during which the four-pound loaf in Paris fluctuated around ten *sous*, a price which authorities considered manageable, cold and wet weather in the late spring and early summer of 1773 menaced the harvest and caused the bread price to mount. Though not a disaster, the crop proved to be disappointing and bread soared to thirteen *sous* in late September. Large doses of king's grain helped to bring down the prices by the end of the year.[32]

---

27 DuRun to IN., 11 Feb. 1772, C. 1725 and Geslin to IN., 8 May 1772, C. 1726, A.D. I-et-V.
28 C. 1653, A.D. I-et-V.; C. 2665 and C. 2684, A.D. Cal.; Terray to DuCluzel, 24 Sept., 10 Dec. 1771 and 12 Aug. 1772, C. 97, A.D. I-et-L. There was also *at least* one major uprising in the generality of Champagne during this time. Terray to Rouillé d'Orfeuil, 9 Oct. 1772, C. 109, A.D. Meuse.
29 Paillot (?) to IN. of Champagne (?), 6 June 1773, C. 1179, A.D. Aube; reply to *enquête*, Oct. 1773, C. 86, A.D. Somme. On the eve of the harvest, however, the intendant of Champagne reported that acute subsistence "anxiety" was widespread in his jurisdiction. Several grain riots flared up, the most serious in the town of Vaucouleurs where bands of soldiers from the army garrison, seconded by local women, prevented the removal of several grain wagons and forced market sales of the grain at a fixed price below the current. Rouillé to Terray, 20 May 1773 and Rouillé to police of Vaucouleurs, 24 May 1773, C. 109, A.D. Meuse. The current of grain riots affected neighboring areas as well. See, for instance, the *arrêt* of the *cour souveraine* of Lorraine, 4 Dec. 1773, A.D. Moselle. Less than a year before, the town of Vaucouleurs had experienced a similar upheaval which was allegedly led by the mayor and an officer of the maréchaussée. Lieutenant general of police to SD (?), 21 Sept. 1772, and mayor to IN., 21 Sept. 1772, C. 109, A.D. Meuse.
30 DeBadoire to IN. of Alençon, 22 Oct. 1773, C. 89, A.D. Orne.
31 C. 2626, A.D. Cal.
32 Sartine to Trudon, 14 Nov. 1771,13 March, 13 April, 14, 22 Sept. 1772, AN, Y 15144;

During the course of 1773 the major center of subsistence difficulties shifted southward. The Poitou suffered "extreme misery" and popular disorders, provoked, according to one observer, by mysterious "removals" of grain from the province. In order to communicate to the king the degree of their hardship, a group of peasants is said to have sent Madame du Barry a sample of the awful substance that passed for their daily bread. The "specter of famine" terrorized Provence. Throughout Guyenne prices surged, supplies were impossible to procure through normal channels, and consumers everywhere were near panic. "No work and no bread" was how one official characterized the situation in Languedoc; the subsistence crisis triggered a more general economic crisis: "the dearness of all goods prevents the consumption of our cloths."[33]

The Midi had its Flour War in the spring of 1773. A blaze of riots scorched the entire area from the Mediterranean to the Atlantic. "We learn from all sides," wrote the Toulouse subdelegate, "that the people are rising because of the grain *cherté*." The process of "contagion" impressed observers everywhere. "Begun at Aix, imitated at Toulouse and other cities of Languedoc," noted Terray, the riots "moved on from place to place" until they reached Bordeaux.[34] At Toulouse the people—predominantly women, many of them armed with 3-feet long poles—pillaged the marketplace for grain. The merchants, "seized with fear, fled and barricaded themselves in their houses." Municipal officials reestablished calm by fixing the price of grain at 16 *livres*, six *livres* below the current price.[35] There were other outbreaks at Albi, Castres, and Montpellier. Troops were called to quell several of the risings; at Montauban alone, eight people were killed and at least a dozen

---

procès-verbal, Machurin, 25 April 1772, AN, Y 12622; *Hardy's Journal*, 7 July, 29 Sept. 1773, BN, mss. fr. 6681, fols. 208, 229; Anon., "Mémoire," (8 Aug. 1773), AN, F[11] 265.

33 Pidansat de Mairobert, *Journal historique*, IV, 186 (31 May 1773); *ibid.*; IV, 162–63 (4, 7 May 1773); René Baehrel, *Une Croissance: La Basse-Provence rurale* (Paris, 1961), 75–76; Esmangart to Terray, 10 June 1773, C. 1435 and Aurou to Esmangart, 5 July 1773, C. 1440, A.D. Gir.; de Vandoul (?) to St.-Priest, 21 April 1773, C. 2914, A.D. Hér.; C. 412, A.D. H-G.; J. Godechot and S. Moncassin, "Démographie et subsistances en Languedoc du XVIIIe siècle au début du XIXe siècle," *Bulletin de l'histoire économique et sociale de la Révolution française* (1964), 34.

34 Terray to St.-Priest, 5 May 1773, C. 2914, A.D. Hér.; Raynal to St.-Priest, 19 May 1773, *ibid.*; Marquis de Bertand to St.-Priest (?), 1 Aug. 1773, C. 2915, *ibid.*; Terray to First President, Bordeaux Parl., 5 Nov. 1773, C. 1442, A.D. Gir.; BN, mss. n.a. 4389, fol. 1527 (Albertas).

35 Raynal to St.-Priest, 28 April 1773 and de Vandoul to St.-Priest, 21 April 1773, C. 2914, A.D. Hér.; *Journal historique et politique des principaux événements* (20 May 1773), 55.

wounded.[36] Beginning in May there was what one official called a "revolutionary" situation in the Guyenne. The city of Bordeaux experienced, in Voltaire's words, "a murderous sedition."[37] The news surprised as well as horrified Terray, for he believed, on the basis of his own calculations, that the city had ample provisions for several months.[38] A "spirit of vertigo" seized people along the Garonne and in other areas in the generality. At least twenty-three separate riots erupted between May and August, many of them spreading from one town or village to another in a snakedance of violence and pillage.[39] The Bordeaux Parlement demanded troops and Terray called for a "severe" punishment of the leading mutineers but a lieutenant of the *maréchaussée*, on duty at Bergerac, scene of a tumultuous uprising, warned that repression was not the answer to the problem: "10,000 armed soldiers will never have as much effect here as 5,000 sacks of grain, and I repeat to you aloud, we need grain, grain, grain, and with grain peace will be made, for otherwise you will never make peace with the people...."[40] Terray's colleague Monteynard, the war minister, shared this view:

36 SD at Albi to St.-Priest, 27 April 1773, C. 2914, A.D. Hér.; Terray to St.-Priest, 10 May 1773, *ibid.*; La Vrillière to St.-Priest, 15 May 1773, *ibid.*; Pidansat de Mairobert, *Journal historique*, IV, 180 (26 May 1773); *Hardy's Journal*, 29 April, 19 May, 1 June 1773, BN, mss. fr. 6681, fols. 185, 195–98; Dupont to Prince Carl Ludwig, 1773 in Knies, ed., *Dupont correspondance*, II, 147.

37 Voltaire to duc de Richelieu, 4 June 1773 in Besterman, ed., *Correspondence*, vol. 85, p. 119 (# 17331). Cf. P. Caraman, "La Disette des grains et les émeutes populaires en 1773 dans la généralité de Bordeaux," *Revue historique de Bordeaux*, II (1910), 297 and *passim*.

38 Terray to Esmangart, 16 May 1773, C. 1441, A.D. Gir. Terray's surprise temporarily shocked him into considering a plot thesis to explain the Bordeaux risings similar to the one which Turgot made into a veritable principle of government after the Flour War. Terray to First President, 19 May 1773, C. 1441. Turgot later blamed the agitation in the Guyenne in 1773 on the "false measures" taken by Terray. Turgot to Esmangart, 24 May 1775, C. 1448, A.D. Gir.

39 All the archival references that follow are from A.D. Gir.: Casteljaloux municipality to SD, 18 May 1773, C. 1435; Robert to Esmangart, 18 May 1776, C. 1446; Dumogues to Esmangart, 8, 15 July 1773 and Bonner to Esmangart, 9 July 1773, C. 1437; Municipality of Bergerac to Esmangart, 23 May 1773, C. 1437; Terray to Esmangart, 27 April 1773, C. 1441; Esmangart to mayor of St. André, 16 May 1773, C. 1436; Affonen (Moissac) to Esmangart, 11 May 1773, C. 1437; municipality of Cenac, 25 July 1773, C. 1437; officiers of Libourne to Esmangart, 19 May 1773, C. 1435; Esmangart to chevalier de Ferrette (Langon), 20 May 1773, C. 1435. Cf. Pidansat de Mairobert, *Journal historique*, IV, 172, 175 (18, 20 May 1773) and Caraman, "Disette," *Revue historique de Bordeaux*, III (1911), 299ff.

40 Terray to First President, 19 May, 1 June 1773, C. 1441, A.D. Gir.; lieutenant de la maréchaussée to Esmangart, 25 May 1773, C. 1437, *ibid.* Terray was accused—unfairly, I think—of being more interested in repression than "in procuring bread for the malcontents." Pidansat de Mairobert, *Journal historique*, IV, 176–77, 180 (23, 26 May 1773). Though it is true that the Bordeaux contagion angered him more than any other episode of insurgency during his ministry, he labored strenuously, after as before

"It was not troops," he advised the king, but *bread* which ought to be sent "to the riot areas."[41] Meanwhile a rumor circulated in Paris that the Controller-General would be disgraced as a result of these farflung disorders.[42]

Had Terray been able to persuade himself that the subsistence troubles and the unrest of 1771–73 were primarily the result of harvest failures, and thus beyond government prevention or remedy, in all likelihood he would not have abandoned his moderate stand on the interpretation and execution of the regulatory law of December 1770. But the news of misery, shortage, and riots was accompanied by ominous reports, from a plethora of sources, of "abuses" in the grain trade and "violations" of the law. Grain owners everywhere practiced "maneuvers" with impunity, profiting from the indulgence of officials who did not enforce the law rigorously and "deceiving" authorities who had tried to remain vigilant. Dealers were making false declarations or failing to register the names of associates. Individuals "claiming to be *blatiers*, most of them unknown," were stripping the markets bare, without bargaining for price and apparently with the intention of holding the grain in storage until the prices mounted further. More substantial merchants were making huge purchases, both on and off market, and placing the grain in secret storehouses. Buying and selling in their granaries and on the road, trading on samples, and taking payment for futures, the *laboureurs* were said to be in the forefront of illicit operations. Terray had no doubt that the dearths signalled in many places were "artificial" rather than "real." A nightmarish vista of chaos rudely interrupted his dream of eventual control of the provisioning trade.[43]

Nor did the Controller-General escape criticism for what some observers regarded as a policy of excessive leniency. Less than a

---

the riots, to find supplies for the Guyenne. Terray to Esmangart, 25 May 1773, and Terray to First President, 26 July 1773, C. 1441, A.D. Gir.

41 *Hardy's Journal*, 19 May 1773, BN, mss. fr. 6681, fol. 192.

42 *Ibid.* Though the Midi experience of 1773 was the last great wave of riots Terray encountered, it should be mentioned that there were scattered outbreaks the following year in many places in the south and at Tours, Cherbourg, etc. See, for example, *Hardy's Journal*, 2 March 1774, BN, mss. fr. 6681, fol. 303; *Journal historique et politique* (10, 30 March 1774), 415, 446 and (10 April 1774), 57; Terray to Esmangart, 29 April, 3 May 1774, C. 1442, A.D. Gir.; C. 2681, A.D. Cal.

43 Terray to Esmangart, 7 May 1771, C. 1432, A.D. Gir.; Trippier to Rouillé d'Orfeuil (?), 12 Aug. 1771, C. 299, A.D. Aube; Terray to Dupleix, 9 Sept. 1771, C. 84, A.D. Somme; Amelot, memoir to SDs, Oct. 1771, C. 81, A.D. C d'O; Genard to IN., 25 Feb. 1772, C. 1725, A.D. I-et-V.; Terray to Rouillé d'Orfeuil, 9 Nov. 1772, C. 1179, A.D. Aube; Terray to IN., 20 Nov. 1772, C. 106, A.D. S-M.

year after he had destroyed the liberal reforms, even as his enemies assailed him as a ruthless tyrant, Terray found himself charged by some administrators with tolerating too much liberty. A committee of inquiry composed of four members of the Enquêtes section of the Paris Parlement made the most striking statement of this position. The fact that subsistence difficulties persisted despite the return to controls could only mean, in their view, that the restored police was too flaccid and unexacting, not only in execution but in conceptualization as well. Demanding new legislation better suited to combat *cherté*, these parlementaires attacked not only the abuses of liberty but the principle of free internal circulation itself, "perhaps the primary cause of the misfortunes that France has suffered for such a long time." Their specific recommendations, some of which curiously mimicked Terray's own view of control, were neither fresh nor compelling; the Parlement as a whole refused to join the issue by adopting the committee report.[44] But the general theme of the Enquêtes' protest, in large part because it echoed sentiment held by field officials at all levels of administration, clearly made an impression upon the government. Just as the liberals had called for more and better liberty when liberalization began to founder toward the end of the sixties, so these magistrates cried out for more and better police in the aftermath of the police reaction.[45] Even as this and other demands were being registered, the Controller-General, under the pressure of events, was moving toward a policy of ever-expanding rigor and regulation.

Terray made his new goal "the general and literal execution" of the law, especially the controversial articles regarding market transactions and *laboureur* trade. Immediately after the promulgation of the December law, wrote the Controller-General, "I insisted with less force upon the necessity of selling grain on the markets" because I then thought that "this was the best means to use for reestablishing order and

---

44 BN, Coll. Joly 1111, fols. 144–46 (Aug. 1771).

45 Among the demands for a more rigorous and comprehensive police, see DuCluzel report. ca. June 1771, C. 94, A.D. I-et-L.; Rouillé d'Orfeuil to Terray, 14 May 1772, C. 418, A.D. Marne; SD of Châlons and Châteaupotier, "Résultat des observations des subdélégués...," C. 417, A.D. Marne; SDs Champassais and Bond to IN. of Alençon, 13 Oct. 1773, C. 89, A.D. Orne; SD of Valenciennes to IN. of Hainaut, ca. Oct. 1773, C. 6690, A.D. Nord; *arrêt du 12 Sept. 1772, Cour souveraine* de Lorraine, C. 38, A.D. Moselle; deliberations, Metz Parl., 17 June 1771, B. 470, fol. 65 (registre secret), A.D. Moselle; deliberations, Feb. 1771, *Conseil supérieur* d'Alsace, C. 553, A.D. Bas-Rhin.

police in this sphere." In many areas, however, this toleration resulted in confusion and monopoly instead of order and police. Owners hoarded instead of coming to market or dealt clandestinely "and in the midst of abundance or at least of sufficiency [of supply] we heard the cries of need." The lesson was clear: the mandatory market clause was the keystone of the provisioning and control systems; without it, they broke down. In letter after letter the Controller-General insisted upon "the absolute necessity of executing article six [i.e., the market clause] rigorously" and of subjecting dealers who defied the law to "severe punishment." So serious was the Controller-General about making the market the unique theatre of commercial transactions that he tried to deny the Paris merchants their "time-immemorial right," written into law in the 1730's, to buy in the countryside.[46]

By their abuse of the law and indifference to their public responsibilities, Terray suggested, the grain dealers had in a sense forfeited their claim to liberty. The purpose of the "liberty of the grain trade" was to encourage agriculture and to enable the producers to draw a return "proportional" to their investment. Now "if they had conducted themselves in a manner exclusively to fulfill this goal, no one would have anything to complain about," the Controller-General allowed. But the problem was precisely that "they veered far away from this goal." Fascinated by the prospects for self-aggrandizement, they "were guided only by their personal interest," a state of mind and business as alarming to Terray as it would have been reassuring to a Laverdy or a Turgot. In Terray's view the grain trade was above all a public service, a subsistence service. The turn to rigor made it plain that the government did not intend to allow grain to become "an object of speculation for the rich because it must be employed first in [meeting the needs of] consumption." The obligatory market clause would enable the "people to stand witness" to all provisioning transactions but "the eye of the government" would also roam the countryside to uncover "monopolies."[47]

---

46 Terray to IN. and to First President of Bordeaux, 21 Dec. 1773, C. 1441, A.D. Gir.; Terray to IN. of Provence, 18 Sept. 1773, C. 2421, A.D. B-du-R.; Terray to IN. of Tours, 18 Sept. 1773, C. 95, A.D. I-et-L.; Terray to IN. of Franche-Comté, 18 Sept. 1773, C. 354, A.D. Doubs; Terray to Rouillé d'Orfeuil, 30 Oct. 1772, C. 299, A.D. Aube; Terray to Rouillé d'Orfeuil, 7 March 1774, C. 419, A.D. Marne. Not long after it modified the December law to enhance the freedom of dealers, especially *laboureurs*, the Dijon Parlement found it necessary to pass an *arrêt* banning all off-market transactions, 25 March 1771, C. 81, A.D. C d'O.

47 Terray to IN. of Alençon, 2, 18 Sept. 1772, and 10 Nov. 1773, C. 89, A.D. Orne; IN. of Alençon to SDs, 9 Sept. 1772, *ibid.*; Terray to Amelot, 2 Sept. 1772, C. 81,

Terray's concern about the grain trade overshadowed his fears about the excesses of the local police. He ordered local and regional authorities not merely to give the December law "the severest execution" but to step beyond its specific injunctions in order to ferret out those who "would deprive the public of its subsistence." The Controller-General also tried to involve himself personally in the details of enforcement: he wanted to know of instances of enormous purchases, "multiple sales" of the same grain, and hoarding; he denied the request of an Anjou official to permit trading on samples; he inquired into the activities of regraters in a small town in the Hainaut; he proposed a buying schedule for the tiny market of Richelieu in order to prevent merchants from removing all supplies before consumers could buy.[48]

The dealers who emerged as the chief villains in Terray's campaign for rigor between 1771 and 1773 were not the "merchants"— ostensibly because they registered with the police and were subject to more or less constant scrutiny—but the *laboureurs* and *laboureur-fermiers* who were legally prohibited from engaging in grain trade and who were more difficult to police given their amphibious role as producers and distributors. Liberalization, according to Terray's analysis, had transformed the *laboureurs*, economically and psychologically, from simple suppliers to professional traders. "Enriched by high prices," the *laboureurs* "became more avid for gain" than ever before and more interested in grain maneuvers. Their wealth emboldened them by sparing them of the urgent need for cash, thus enabling them to hoard grain until prices climbed to "exorbitant" levels. Moreover, these *laboureurs* bought grain from other cultivators and dealers on the pretext that they needed grain for seed or subsistence.[49] Aiming at making themselves "masters of the good and thus of the price," they practiced "a veritable

A.D. C d'O.; Terray to archbishop of Narbonne, 25 Nov. 1772, C. 2912, A.D. Hér.; Terray to IN. of La Rochelle, 1 July 1772, C. 196, A.D. C-M. Though he tended increasingly to view the grain merchants in adversary terms, the Controller-General was never indifferent to their well-being. He demanded, for example, a thorough investigation of charges made by a Champagne merchant that townspeople, inspired by a "feeling of impunity," vandalized his house, threatened the lives of his children, interrupted his trade, and confiscated his grain. Petition of Louis Carmouche, Sept. 1772 and CG to IN., 4 Oct. 1772, C. 109, A.D. Meuse.

48 Terray to Cluzel, 10 March 1772 and 28 Sept. 1773, C. 95, A.D. I-et-L.; (?) to Terray, 10 March 1771, C. 94, *ibid.;* Terray to Taboureau, 2 Sept. 1772, C. 5977, A.D. Nord; Terray to Rouillé d'Orfeuil, 27 Sept. 1772, C. 417, A.D. Marne; Terray to Taboureau, 15 July 1772, C. 8277, A.D. Nord; Terray to IN. of Alençon, 15 Oct. 1771, and IN. to SDs, 18 Oct. 1771, C. 89, A.D. Orne.

49 Terray to IN. of Alençon, 18 Sept. 1773, C. 89, A.D. Orne; Amelot, "Mémoire concernant les grains," ca. Oct. 1771, C. 81, A.D. C d'O; Terray to Rouillé d'Orfeuil, 18 Sept. 1773, C. 419, A.D. Marne; Paillot to Rouillé d'Orfeuil, 23 Oct. 1773, C. 1179,

monopoly." As a result of lax execution in the beginning or the exceptions which certain Parlements imposed upon the December law, the *laboureurs* believed or pretended that the law did not apply to them. Terray held the *laboureurs* responsible for much of the *cherté* which plagued the kingdom between 1771 and 1773 as well as the popular disorders "which would not have taken place" if the suppliers had not forced the consumers "to pay an excessive price for the commodity of first necessity."[50] In his call for rigor the Controller-General emphasized the need not only to repress their illicit dealings and flush the *laboureurs* out of the trade but also to discipline them to supply the nearby markets on a regular basis. In addition, he recommended fiscal pressure to force the *laboureurs* onto the markets by having the receivers of the *taille* press for exact, punctual payments. Finally, he hoped to be able to increase the share of the *taille* to be paid by the "rich" *laboureurs* who "have profited excessively from the sale of their grain" and to reduce the obligation of the poor rural day-workers. It is a revealing mark, however, of the administrative and social organization of the Old Regime that the finance minister was not in a position to effect such a change in the allocation of taxes on his own.[51]

It is difficult to determine exactly whom he meant when Terray inveighed against the rich *laboureurs*. Despite requests from subordinates for a criterion of identification ("what quantity of land under cultivation can imprint the quality of *laboureur?*" asked the police officials of Sézanne), the Controller-General never defined the term.[52] A *laboureur* represented anyone from the countryside who produced some grain of his own and acquired other grain from purchase, rents, fees, etc. Surely in some instances those who passed as "*laboureurs*" must have been tithe collectors or farmers of ecclesiastical and/or seigneurial dues or seigneurs of one kind or another. It is striking that in assailing

---

A.D. Aube; Terray to Fontette, 9 Sept. 1771, C. 2624, A.D. Cal. Cf. the complaints of local police against *laboureur* abuses. For example, Guerin at Bonnet to SD of Joinville, 26 Nov. 1773 and SD at Vaucouleurs to IN., 8 March 1774, C. 110, A.D. Meuse.

50 Terray to Fontette, 7 May 1771, C. 2624, A.D. Cal.; Terray to Esmangart, 18 Sept. 1773, C. 1441, A.D. Gir.; Terray to IN. of Alençon, 10 Nov. 1773, C. 89, A.D. Orne. Cf. the Lieutenant of Police of Caen's description of the rich *laboureurs-fermiers* as "bloodsuckers." To Miromesnil, 20 July 1770, C. 2653, A.D. Cal.

51 Terray to Rouillé d'Orfeuil, 28 Sept. 1773, C. 419, A.D. Marne; Terray to DuCluzel, 15 Oct. 1771, C. 94, A.D. I-et-L.; Terray to Esmangart, 5 Sept. 1770, C. 1431, A.D. Gir.; Terray to Monthyon, Sept. 1770, C. 925, A.D. P-de-D.; Terray to Fontette, 8 Sept. 1770 and Fontette's reply, 16 Sept. 1770, C. 2623, A.D. Cal.; Terray to Taboureau, 7 April 1772, C. 8277, A.D. Nord.

52 "Résultat des observations des officiers de police …," C. 417, A.D. Marne.

the landed and producer interests, Terray never referred specifically to the great *rentiers* of the land—many of whom were involved in the grain trade, albeit often indirectly—save in his bitter clashes with the liberals of the south and southwest.

Nor are we yet equipped to take the measure of Terray's claim that the *laboureurs*, as a whole, benefitted enormously from the high prices of the period 1764–74. He was neither the only nor the first administrator to call attention to the secondary effects of *laboureur* "opulence." Under the liberal ministry, in the exchanges with the Paris Parlement on the grain question between the fall of 1768 and the summer of 1769, Louis XV alluded several times to the newly-acquired "affluence" which induced the *laboureurs* to suspend provisioning. The *laboureurs* of course denied that they gained nearly as much as certain officials suggested from liberalization and its aftermath. They blamed the *cherté* of the seventies on "the excessive price to which the leases have been carried"—the consequence of the sharp rise in prices of the mid-sixties—and on the general inflation of costs which they argued outstripped grain in many instances.[53] There is no doubt that leases rose substantially in most places, in some cases by more than 50 percent, in the years following the liberal reforms and that high prices encouraged "the *laboureurs* who had enriched themselves" to undertake what one subdelegate called the "réunion des fermes."[54] The subdelegate of Avesnes in the Hainaut urgently called for the "division of the *fermes*" throughout northern France. "Most of these *fermes*," he claimed, were "too rich [and] too closely linked with unions cemented both by interest and by family ties." Given the ease with which they could "form among themselves societies, systems,

---

53 Borondon, SD of Lisieux, to IN. of Alençon, 17 Nov. 1773, C. 89, A.D. Orne.
54 Crosne to Terray, 26 Jan. 1772, AN, F^{11} 223; Dupleix to Terray, 28 Jan. 1772, *ibid.*; reply to Terray *enquête*, Oct. 1773, C. 86, A.D. Somme; SDs of Bernay, Billesuche, and Nogent-le-Rotrou to IN. of Alençon, 12, 13 Oct. 1773, C. 89, A.D. Orne; C. 3215, fols. 622–25, A.D. C d'O.; Flesche to Taboureau, 28 Sept. 1770, C. 6690, A.D. Nord.

I have encountered only one instance in which an official denied that leases have risen and he himself prefaced his remarks by admitting that this would "appear incredible." Revanoc (St.-Malo) to Fontette, 1 May 1770, C. 2673, A.D. Cal. The subdelegates of Cambrai and Valenciennes claimed that "the *cherté* ruined the *fermiers* more than it enriched them." The owners were the real benefactors of the price and lease rise. Reports to the IN., ca. Oct. 1773, C. 6690, A.D. Nord. Cf. the retrospective view that the *laboureurs* were "duped" and ultimately "ruined" by the liberal experience. L.-J. Bourdon-Desplanches, *Projet nouveau sur la manière de faire utilement en France le commerce des grains* (Brussels, 1785), 34–36.

or monopolies," the *fermiers* were in a position to "reduce the poor people to die of hunger."[55]

A number of officials described a vicious circle, from which they perceived no issue, in terms sympathetic to the cultivator-lessees:

> The great evil was done in the first years of the export system. The land increased in value, the price of leases followed the same progression; during this time royal taxes increased considerably and the price of foodstuffs and other merchandise became excessive ... The *cherté* of grain coming [today] from the dearness of leases, the first cannot be checked while the second persists.[56]

Though it appears that in some areas the upward revision of leases was made contingent upon the maintenance of liberalization, many local officials agreed with the Toulouse Parlement that the *laboureur-fermiers* signed long-term leases "on the faith of the stability of the Declaration of 1763 and the Edict of July 1764" and warned that the *laboureurs-fermiers* would neither be able to pay their rents nor their taxes if prices fell back to "the old level."[57] Preoccupied with the provisioning side of the matter, the Controller-General did not pay enough attention to the squeeze that threatened many cultivators. But before we can evaluate Terray's attitude toward the *laboureurs* and make sense of the constraints which operated on them, we need systematic local studies of leases and land transactions of all sorts as well as socially and economically differential analyses of the so-called *laboureur* universe.

Unlike the committee of the *Enquêtes*, the Controller-General did not believe that the December law was "insufficient" to deal with provisioning problems provided that it was energetically and intelligently applied. In the hope of making the law more efficient, in the fall of 1773 Terray introduced a significant modification concerning enforcement procedure. An *arrêt du conseil* invested the intendants with a major part of the *legal* responsibility for the execution of the regulatory law.[58] Heretofore the participation of the intendants was exclusively administrative and political: they supervised local management, explained

---

55 Report to IN., ca. Oct. 1773, C. 6690, A.D. Nord. Most of the other subdelegates here perceived a tendency toward continuing subdivision rather than concentration of *fermes*.

56 Reply to Terray *enquête*, Oct. 1773, C. 86, A.D. Somme.

57 *Arrêt*, Parl. of Toulouse, 14 Nov. 1772, AN, AD XI 39; SDs of Argentau, Lisieux and de Mortagne, 13, 14, 28 Oct. 1773 to IN. of Alençon, C. 89, A.D. Orne. Not surprisingly, the magistrates of Aix saw things in the same fashion as their Languedoc confreres. Letter to Louis XV, 10 Nov. 1770, B. 3677, A.D. B-du-R.

58 *Arrêt du Conseil*, 29 Oct. 1773, AN, AD, XI 39.

the law to subordinates, and transmitted orders and information, but they had nothing to do with the disposition of cases arising from the violation of the law, a judicial matter devolving upon the conventional institutions of local justice. Henceforth, however, the intendants were to indict and *judge* persons accused of violations of the December law, thereby circumventing the entire judicial apparatus, with appeals receivable only by the royal council. Yet the wording of the *arrêt* was ambiguous on certain counts. It was not clear whether intendants would have jurisdiction over all such offenses and, more important, whether they would exercise not merely preemptive but also exclusive jurisdiction. In explanatory letters Terray insisted that the *arrêt* neither encroached upon parlementary justice nor "stripped local and royal judges of the jurisdiction over offenses which might be denounced before them," but he did not provide any machinery for a division of authority.[59] As in many other domains of old-regime public life, there were now to be ordinary and extraordinary channels for the execution of the law: a regular, front-line system absolutely vital for the maintenance of order in the grain trade and an alternate, shadow system enabling high officials to intervene locally at their discretion without regard to form.

Terray's aim was to escalate the war against grain maneuvers. Though it is extremely tempting to read the *arrêt* as a censure of the local police, the evidence suggests that the Controller-General was relatively pleased with their performance, all things considered.[60] Surely he had no interest in alienating them, for he recognized that the role that they played in provisioning was crucial. He believed, however, that local authorities were simply incapable of dealing with certain kinds of "abuses," especially those committed by traders who

---

59 Terray to IN. of Alençon, 10 Nov. 1773, C. 89, A.D. Orne; Terray to IN. and First President of Bordeaux, 21 Dec. 1773, C. 1441, A.D. Gir.

60 A month before the promulgation of the *arrêt*, Terray launched a searching and imaginative inquiry concerning every aspect of the subsistence situation. It is possible that the *arrêt* was partly inspired by the findings of this *enquête*. Yet the extant answers submitted by intendants and lesser officials do not suggest that Terray had cause for serious misgivings about the local police. On the contrary, their conduct was more often praised than reproached. The *enquête* clearly emphasized, however, that the "speculative system" still existed and that prices were still "higher than they should be." There are copies of the questionnaire addressed to the intendants, 28 Sept. 1773, in: C. 1441, A.D. Gir.; C. 95, A.D. I-et-L.; C. 86, A.D. Somme; C. 89, A.D. Orne; C. 419, A.D. Marne; C. 1653, A.D. I-et-V. There are scattered answers in the same places. Biollay's conspiratorial interpretation of the *arrêt* seems to me to be utterly unfounded in fact and mistaken in the assumptions about local and regional administration on which it is based. Biollay, *Pacte*, 191–92.

operated in several different jurisdictions at once, playing one off against the other.[61] The intendants clearly had more power and range; a number of them were anxious to become more directly involved in grain police in order to be in a better position to deal with subsistence questions and probably urged Terray to accord them jurisdiction.[62] Theoretically, in addition to reducing the opportunity for offenders to escape apprehension, the intendants would limit their chances of evading serious punishment by simplifying and speeding up the indictment and trial procedures. The prospect of pursuit across juris-dictional lines and of stiff, summary sentences in a Star Chamber ambience, Terray calculated, might have a deterrent effect upon speculators and monopolists. The intendants' jurisdiction would also enable the Controller-General to exercise far more direct influence on repression than he was equipped to do before.[63] Finally, by arous-ing the jealousy of local officials—a risky business, to be sure—the *arrêt* might make them more alert and assiduous.

We do not know how well the new procedure worked or exactly how much it was used. In practice, everything depended upon the initia-tives taken by the intendants whom Terray exhorted to action. Sev-eral intendants expressed enthusiasm for it. D'Agay of Picardy had no doubt that it would permit him to expose the frauds of "eager specula-tors" who have hitherto succeeded in "eluding the law." Four days after the issuance of the *arrêt*, Amelot of Burgundy pronounced a crush-ing sentence condemning a *fermier* to a 2,000 *livres* fine for engaging in the trade, the first of many sentences which were to appear under his name. Terray himself claimed that the attribution of jurisdiction to the intendants resulted in a significant curtailment of off-market trading and *laboureur* speculation. Yet several intendants opposed the Control-ler-General's strategy because they felt it was needless and overbearing. And although we have testimony from only one court, it is extremely doubtful that the other parlements welcomed another arbitrary and irregular alteration of the existing judicial system.[64]

---

61 Cf. the remark of the subdelegate of Valenciennes that merchants managed to elude and confound local judges by manipulating "the rules of procedure." To IN., ca. Oct. 1773, C. 6690, A.D. Nord.

62 See, for example, Taboureau to Terray, 4 Aug. 1774, *ibid.*, A.D. Nord.

63 See, for instance, Terray's effort to increase the fine imposed on a merchant judged "guilty of monopoly." To de la Corée, 3 Feb. 1774, C. 355, A.D. Doubs.

64 IN. of Picardy to Terray, ca. Oct. 1773, C. 86, A.D. Somme; Terray to Taboureau, 10 Nov. 1773, C. 6690, A.D. Nord; *ordonnance*, Nov. 1773, C. 81, A.D. C d'O.; Terray to IN., of Brittany, 26 Dec. 1773, C. 1671, A.D. I-et-V.; Terray to First President, Bordeaux,

Among the "abuses" or "maneuvers" which most preoccupied the Controller-General between 1771 and 1773 were illicit exports. Legally, all exports were forbidden after the *arrêt* of July 1770, yet myriad reports reached the government of secret grain outflow. In addition to its intrinsic importance—after all, France was short of grain at this time—the export issue concerned Terray because of the enormous sway it had over public, especially popular, opinion.[65] Nothing frightened the people more than the idea of exportation of their subsistence and they were quick to seize upon the slightest and most dubious sign as proof that illegal and immoral maneuvers were being practiced. The Controller-General admitted that many accounts of clandestine exports were unfounded, the product of popular fear and an unwillingness or inability to distinguish between large-scale internal traffic and shipment abroad. Yet Terray had convincing evidence in hand that export fraud was rampant. Coastal and frontier traders used "every imaginable practice" to evade the law.[66] To combat this drain, he asked for more exacting surveillance by the intendants, the subdelegates, and the clerks of the General Farm bureaus. In August 1771, by an *arrêt du conseil*, he renewed the July suspension and ordered the establishment of day and night patrols along the borders of the eastern provinces. At the end of the year he asked the intendants for detailed information on all grain leaving their generalities, especially grain headed towards the ports or frontiers, grain allegedly of foreign origin and thus subject to legal re-export, and grain which had to travel in ships along

---

21 Dec. 1773, C. 1441, A.D. Gir.; IN. of Brittany to Terray, May 1774, C. 1653, A.D. I-et-V. Compare the latter's pretext for not executing this *arrêt*—because the Parlement had *not registered* the antecedent law of 23 Dec. 1770—with the pretext adduced by Fontette, intendant of Caen, for not executing the December law itself—because it *was registered* by the Parlement and therefore its enforcement had nothing to do with him. Fontette to Terray, 14 May 1771 and Terray to Fontette, 7, 28 May 1771, C. 2624, A.D. Cal.

65 For Terray's preoccupation with public opinion and exports, see his revealing letter to Taboureau, 10 March 1772, C. 3745, A.D. Nord.

66 Terray to de la Corée, 10 Nov. 1770, C. 844, A.D. Doubs; Terray to Rouillé d'Orfeuil, 28 Nov. 1770, C. 418, A.D. Marne; Terray to Dupleix and to Fontette, 9 Sept. 1771, C. 84, A.D. Somme and C. 2624, A.D. Cal.; Terray to DuCluzel and to Jullien, 15 Oct. 1771, C. 95, A.D. I-et-L. and C. 89, A.D. Orne; Terray to Esmangart, 10 March 1772, C. 1434, A.D. Gir.; Terray to First President, Besançon Parl., 14 April 1772, B. 2850, A.D. Doubs; Terray to Lefèvre de Caumartin, 9 Sept. 1771, C. 5977 and 9 Nov. 1772, C. 3745, A.D. Nord. One of the indirect techniques used by Terray to discern illicit exportation was the study of prices. A sharp disparity between interior and port prices especially at the full moon when "contrebandiers" could work most effectively raised suspicions of fraudulent export. Terray to Fontette, 12 Nov. 1771, C. 2624, A.D. Cal.

the coasts in order to reach putative destinations in the interior of the kingdom.[67]

Persuaded that coastal trade was the greatest source of export fraud, Terray imposed a series of rigorous controls meant not only to keep him abreast of the flow of grain, but also to empower him to *determine* where it would go. The regulation of coastwise trade reflected Terray's long-run desire to impose control and collect data as well as his immediate interest in repressing a dangerous trading abuse. In the spring of 1771 he asked maritime intendants to impose a visa on grain leaving their ports for domestic destinations which could be verified upon arrival.[68] So long as a merchant applied to a sub-delegate or a clerk of the Farm for a certificate of transit, or *acquit à caution*, he received it automatically. Claiming that this method lacked sufficient rigor to guarantee against fraud, the following year Terray introduced a drastic change requiring coastwise traders to apply for individual licences directly to the intendant. In principle, the Controller-General said, he expected the intendants to refuse "no permits solicited" in this fashion. In each instance, however, the intendant had to inform the Controller-General of the request.[69] Though it was not certain that the intendant would have to await the minister's opinion in every single instance before granting the permit, there is no doubt that Terray now had the means to deny requests, assess their utility upon a background of the "ensemble" of the trade, and "direct," or rather redirect, shipments toward destinations designated with a high priority. "By this means," wrote the Controller-General, "I will know those who are in the commerce [and] it will be easier for me to handle fraud." While he was quite earnest in his desire to eliminate fraud, the goal of preventing illicit exports was partly a pretext for the Controller-General to centralize real decision-making authority and reduce the gap between his ambition of control and his actual power to influence private provisioning operations.[70] In addition to arming him against fraud, "this police [of permits] has another advantage," Terray conceded: "it puts me in a position to supervise the operations

---

67 *Arrêt du Conseil*, 24 Aug. 1771, AN, AD XI 39; Terray to Fontette, 17 Dec. 1771, C. 2624, A.D. Cal. Cf. Terray to IN. of Alençon, 1 Sept. 1772, C. 89, A.D. Orne.

68 Terray to Fontette, 5 March 1771, C. 2624, A.D. Cal.

69 Terray to Amelot, 1 Sept. 1772, C. 81, A.D. C d'O.; Terray to Taboureau, 1 Sept. 1772, C. 3745, A.D. Nord; de Boynes to *officiers de l'amirauté*, La Rochelle, 20 Sept. 1772, B. 5646. Cf. C. 2625, A.D. Cal.

70 On Terray's abiding fear of illegal exports, see his letter to the IN. of Bordeaux, 25 Jan. 1774, C. 1447, A.D. Gir.

of the *négociants* whose badly organized speculations were an evil that it was necessary to destroy and still more to enlighten the *négociant* and to help him succeed in his enterprises by indicating to him the places where supplies were most needed."[71]

The Controller-General correctly predicted that the introduction of "this formality which appears perhaps constrictive to commerce" would cause widespread "umbrage." The most virulent protests came from Languedoc, for whose large-scale grain-traders coastwise "internal" commerce was a matter of economic survival, now that exports were no longer permitted. Given the obligation to reveal all the details of "our speculations" and to await the issuance of licenses, our commerce "will fall into a sort of inaction," the Narbonne *négociants* complained. In the wake of our ruin, agriculture will be crippled again, they pointedly warned the finance minister, "depriving the cultivators of the means of paying their taxes ...." The archbishop of Narbonne bitterly reproached Terray for failing to appreciate the needs and interests of his province. Practically speaking, he asked, "how do you expect a businessman to make the least useful speculation when he must wait at least 21 days for a license that he is not even sure will be granted in whole or in part?" With Voltairean acerbity, the archbishop of Toulouse mocked the system, which required a trader desiring to transport "several bushels of tare to feed pigeons" to seek a permit. Striking at the very core of Terray's program and his pretensions, the archbishop questioned the minister's ability to grasp and to manage the ensemble of things: "We are a bit far removed for you to be able to direct the speculations of our commerce." Perhaps because they knew from their own professional experience how pernicious administrations governed by favoritism, privilege, and patronage were, both prelates made a point of denouncing the licensing system for its inevitable corruption: "Angels would not be immune and there is nothing further removed from angelic purity than the bureaux of any intendant." Since Terray was not famous for his cherubic qualities, it is doubtful that his reply that *he* and not subordinate officials would make all decisions reassured the archbishops. Similar protests were addressed to the ministry by the Estates of Brittany.[72]

---

71 Terray to comte de Périgord and to archbishop of Narbonne, 25 Nov. 1772, C. 2912, A.D. Hér.

72 Petition of Narbonne *négociants* to Terray, ca. Nov. 1772, C. 2912, *ibid.*; syndic of merchant community of Béziers, 4 Oct. 1772, C. 2917, *ibid.*; archbishops of Narbonne and Toulouse (separately) to Terray, 12 Nov. 1772 and Terray to Archbishop of Toulouse, 25 Nov. 1772, C. 2912, *ibid.*; Etats de Bretagne, "Mémoire," ca. Oct. 1772, C. 774, A.D. L.-A.

The Controller-General rejected this criticism as an expression of a parochial and crudely selfish viewpoint. Moreover, he claimed that the other interested provinces "complied with the new police" without suffering any commercial penalties.[73] Yet the fact that the Controller-General substantially modified this new police less than half a year after he instituted it indicates that opposition was fiercer than he admitted and that execution was difficult. Whereas the licensing method introduced in 1772 derived simply from an administrative instruction sent to the intendants, by an *arrêt du conseil* of February 1773 Terray gave it formal legal footing with precise procedural stipulations and a hierarchy of penalties for violations. Henceforth coastwise trade could only take place between ports possessed of admiralty courts. An elaborate double certification and inspection system would theoretically keep the intendants and the ministry alerted to all grain movements by sea and reveal any fraudulent maneuvers.[74]

Terray apparently backed off from his demand that all applications for permits be submitted to him for approval. The text of the *arrêt* seemed to indicate that a subdelegate could deliver an *acquit à caution* on his own authority. There was no question, however, about the Controller-General's power or willingness to block the issuance of permits when he desired. For example, toward the middle of 1773 he prohibited traders in Rouen or Le Havre from engaging in any coastwise trade at all for fear that such a permission would entice them to buy in the Parisian provisioning zone and thus bring "*cherté*, desolation, and trouble to the capital."[75] Though he was concerned about illicit exports, Terray's main aim again was control: "to reconcile the liberty of trade with the security of public subsistence." Once again, critics, this time most vocally from Bordeaux and Brittany, protested that the constraints placed upon commerce made business virtually impossible.[76] Terray's repeated demands for "the most literal execution

73 Terray to archbishop of Toulouse, 25 Nov. 1772, C. 2912, A.D. Hér. As a concession to the traders, Terray permitted unlicensed albeit certified coastwise trade within the *same* province of shipment up to 100 charges, measure of Marseille. To St.-Priest, 19 Oct. 1772, *ibid.*

74 *Arrêt du Conseil,* 14 Feb. 1773, C. 1649, A.D. I-et-V. and B. 5646, A.D. C-M. As in 1772, Terray exempted traders shipping within the same province from the full burden of the control system. Terray to INs. of Bordeaux and Brittany, 9 March 1771, C. 1441. A.D. Gir. and C. 2582, A.D. I-et-V.

75 Memoir, probably by St.-Prest, ca. Sept. 1773, C. 1441, A.D. Gir.

76 Reply to remonstrances of Bordeaux Parl., Oct. 1773, C. 2915, A.D. Hér.; *négociants* of Tréguier to IN., 1773, C. 1675 and officiers of Cordemais to IN., 20 Oct. 1773, C. 1684, A.D. I-et-V.; memoirs of the *négociants* of Nantes to Boynes and to Terray, April–May 1773, C. 774, A.D. L-A.

of this *arrêt* and his frequent complaints that the "essential formalities" were not faithfully practiced suggests once more that he did not obtain universal compliance.[77]

Opposition to illegal exports did not necessarily bespeak an irreducible hostility to the idea of allowing exportation at a future time. In 1771 Terray sent a circular letter-questionnaire to the intendants which was voluntarily ambiguous in intention.[78] On the one hand, he wanted to dissipate any fears which subsisted on the part of the consumers and any illusions which traders still entertained that exports might soon be permitted again. Disabused of misleading notions, the people would have faith in the government and dealers would abandon the hoards they formed in the hope of future high-price outlets. On the other hand, though the day when exportation would again be authorized might be "far off," the Controller-General made a point of *not* intimating that it was unlikely that exports would ever be allowed. His purpose was to avoid providing the liberals with incentives for further demoralization and alienation. He believed, as the intendant of Brittany later remarked, that "the announcement of a perpetual prohibition would have managed needlessly to inspire terrors and strike a fatal blow against agriculture and the clearings that it is in the greatest interest of the State to multiply."[79] To make it clear that he still had an open mind, Terray asked the intendants to indicate the ceiling price limit at which it would be wise to suspend exports when the freedom to trade abroad was reestablished.[80] During

---

77 Terray to IN. of Brittany, 22 Feb. 1774, C. 1684, A.D. I-et-V.; Terray to IN. of Bordeaux, 25 Jan. 1774, C. 1447, A.D. Gir.; Terray to IN. of La Rochelle, 25 Jan., 8, 22 Feb. 1774, C. 191, A.D. C-M. On the failure of officials to send the "discharges" of the *acquits* to the Contrôle-Général, see also C. 193, A.D. C-M. Criticized by certain regions and interests for stifling interprovincial trade by excessive regulation, Terray was implicitly reproached by others for failing to put a halt to illicit exports. See, for example, the efforts of the Cour souveraine de Lorraine to stem fraudulent grain drain. *Arrêt*, 26 Nov. 1773, C. 38, A.D. Moselle.

78 Terray to INs., 1 Oct. 1771, C. 84, A.D. Somme; C. 418, A.D. Marne; C. 1432, A.D. Gir.; C. 3745, A.D. Nord.

79 IN. to Terray, ca. May 1774, C. 1653, A.D. I-et-V. Cf. the plea of the intendant of Hainaut to "destroy all hope of exportation." Taboureau to Terray, 4 Aug. 1774, C. 6690, A.D. Nord.

80 Of the fifteen intendants whose responses to Terray's query I have, seven favored or acquiesced in the idea of allowing future exports up to a ceiling cut-off price of eight *livres* or less the quintal, approximately one-third below the 1764 mark. The intendants of Bordeaux and Dauphiné saw nothing wrong with resurrecting the July Edict as it was written. The intendants of Languedoc and Brittany were willing to compromise on the ceiling, fixing it at ten *livres* or ten *livres* ten *sous*. The intendant of Alençon proposed a supple tariff system which would preserve grain necessary for subsistence while

the next few years, however, Terray's attitude toward exportation evolved in the same unsparing sense as his view of the police of internal trade and his conception of subsistence control. By 1773, he had virtually ruled out the possibility of passing a general permissive law, regardless of the ceiling price and regardless of economic conditions, and he said as much to the intendants without concern for offending liberal sensibilities. Given the burden and uncertainty of provisioning, our chief responsibility, he maintained, we should face up to the fact that exportation will be "forever prohibited" save in the fleeting aftermath of a gargantuan harvest when France choked on her surfeit.[81]

III

Though the record is not without blemishes and ambiguities—Terray was the first to admit that the situation was still "dangerous" and that bread was still "too dear for the people"—by the middle of 1773 his ministry succeeded, through a combination of police activism, massive government supply intervention, and improving weather, in bringing subsistence peace, if not subsistence security, to a large part of the realm. The south and southeast, including the provinces of Aquitaine, Languedoc, Provence, and Dauphiné, were the major exceptions. None of the parlements which operated in these jurisdictions had registered the December regulatory law when it was first promulgated. The Controller-General was tempted to believe that the grave provisioning difficulties each suffered was directly the result of the failure of the province to adopt the police line and submit to his subsistence management.

In the sixties the Bordeaux Parlement had taken a generally cautious yet opportunistic stand on the grain question. Responding warmly to liberalization, the court quickly manifested prohibitionist feelings once the provisioning situation began to worsen. Alternately concerned about public opinion and the general welfare on the one side and regional economic interests on the other, the Parlement tended to avoid

---

allowing exports. All of these replies are in AN, F[11] 223 with the exception of the following: Fontette to Terray, 14 Oct. 1771, C. 2624, A.D. Cal.; IN. of Amiens to Terray, 18 Feb. 1772, C. 84, A.D. Somme; Rouillé d'Orfeuil to Terray, 14 May 1772, C. 418, A.D. Marne. Cf. the attitudes of a group of subdelegates in C. 89, A.D. Orne.

81 Terray to Rouillé d'Orfeuil and to Esmangart, 28 Sept. 1773, C. 419, A.D. Marne and C. 1441, A.D. Gir.

ideological commitments. [82] As we have seen, it refused to adopt the December law in 1770–71, though later it praised its general purposes. Relations between the Controller-General and the court approached the breaking point in the summer of 1773 at the very moment that the province reeled under the impact of one of the most serious subsistence crises it had known in generations. Although neither underestimated the suffering and dislocation that it caused, both Terray and the Parlement characterized the problem as "a sort of artificial famine," a needless crisis, objectively unwarranted. Perceiving things in the manner of their confreres at Toulouse or Aix, the Bordeaux magistrates blamed the troubles upon Terray's administration which "hypocritically" refused to honor its pledge to promote free internal circulation. Hampered by a "host of formalities" and by Terray's refusal to grant all the coastwise permits sought by local merchants, commerce could not perform its central function of transferring grain from surplus to deficit areas. Not unlike the Rouennais in 1768, the Bordelais magistrates hinted that the ministry favored its own merchant "protégés" who sent the province only small doses of high-priced and often "corrupted" grain.

The Parlement's position infuriated Terray, not in the least because he had labored earnestly to provide Bordeaux with large amounts of grain from domestic and foreign sources. For him, the dearth was "factitious" because of "general apprehensions" and "false ideas which have won over minds" which in turn were the fruit of parlementary bumbling and local police miscalculation. In blistering language he warned the magistrates to leave subsistence policy to him and provisioning policy to royal officials. Reminding them that when they implored him for king's grain not long ago, he supplied it promptly, he threatened that future "royal graces," if "unmerited," would be denied. If you fail to obey,

> I will publicize throughout the province the examples of benevolence that the King has shown for his people [i.e., king's grain], the immense sacrifices he has assumed in his charity in order to procure them relief; the impossible situation in which the ill-considered steps of your Company has placed him; and finally the people will be told that if from now on they have any [subsistence] needs, they must address themselves to the Parlement.

Lacking the wherewithal and the experience to play the fatherly role, the Bordeaux Parlement lowered its voice. Terray continued to supply

---

82 See, for example, First President to IN., 23 Sept. 1766, C. 1425 and intendant's marginal note, 31 Oct. 1768, C. 1427, A.D. Gir.

grain through the second part of 1773 and dealt exclusively with the intendant on matters concerning the police of the grain trade.[83]

The relations between the central government and the three "liberal" provinces are perhaps more interesting because of the role their parlements had played in the preparation and implementation of the reform laws of 1763–64. Of the three sovereign courts, only the Grenoble Parlement betrayed signs of weakening resolve in the first years of Terray's ministry. A disappointing harvest in 1770 and a short crop in 1771—estimated by the intendant at "one-half a common year"—combined with growing evidence of public disenchantment with its attitude induced the court to modify its stance.[84] Vidaud, the Procurator General of the court, was a strong supporter of liberalization whose ideas resembled those of his Breton counterpart, La Chalotais. The business of government, in economic matters, was "the encouragement of liberty." "I find in the silence of the whole province on the [question of] free [grain] circulation," he wrote confidently in June 1770, "the most complete proof of its utility." Convinced that a "prohibitive law" would be "dangerous," he vigorously opposed the *arrêt du conseil* by which Terray suspended exports the following month.[85] Yet Vidaud found himself obliged to cede to pressure from local police authorities, who claimed that they could not provision their towns without resorting to certain constraints. I understand "your difficult situation," he wrote one local official, on the one hand the law [i.e., the liberal legislation of 1763–64] wishes that you give the grain trade the greatest freedom and on the other this very liberty snatches away at the gate of your city the grain that is supposed to supply the market." On the one hand, he continued, you want "to procure for the people a necessary subsistence" and, on the other, "you are afraid of measures which will be disapproved by your superiors or which will tend to drive the grain merchants away." If you are desperate—if your market, that is, suffers "total dearth," Vidaud authorized him and other officials to "force the hoarders to furnish

---

83 Pidansat de Mairobert, *Journal historique*, IV, 401–405 (14 Dec. 1773); Terray to the First President, 26 July 1773, C. 1441 and 5 Nov., 7 Dec. 1773, C. 1442, A.D. Gir.; Terray to Esmangart, 12 Nov. 1773, C. 1439, *ibid.*

84 On the harvest situation, see II. C. 51, A.D. Isère. For an example of the criticism aimed at the court, see 26 June 1771, Miscellanea Letourneau, IV, fols. 14, 59–60, Bibliothèque Municipale de Grenoble.

85 Vidaud to Pajot de Marcheval, 29 June 1770, Q 4 (2), fols. 58–59, Bibliothèque Municipale de Grenoble.

the markets," to fix the sale of their grain at the current price, and to ban regrating.[86]

In September 1771, upon the request of the Procurator General, the Parlement ordered the execution of the July 1770 *arrêt* which Vidaud had denounced fifteen months earlier.[87] Though the magistrates declined to approve the major regulatory law of December 1770, Vidaud indicated that the court would be willing to seek a compromise which would reconcile what he called "the usages of the province" with the exigencies of police control.[88] By the beginning of 1774, the intendant Pajot, who shared the liberal posture of the Parlement, began to call for the enforcement of the regulatory laws of 23 December 1770 and 29 October 1773.[89]

In a desperate effort to forestall the promulgation of Terray's regulatory law, the magistrates of Aix had written a long and passionate letter to Louis XV in November 1770.[90] None of the arguments was fresh but they were given a more doctrinaire cast and a more systematic expression than ever before. Having "seen the dawn of a new day," the parlementaires begged the king not to "enslave" them again. They reassured Louis XV that his reform policy was not the cause of the troubles that the kingdom has had to face. These were the product of natural, ephemeral causes, aggravated by the bad faith of the "subaltern" police who conspired with the cowardly populace to violate and discredit the liberal laws. Liberalization made economic and political sense. The magistrates tantalized the king with the prospect of royal fiscal recovery, which the agricultural prosperity engendered by liberty would make possible. To favor consumers over producers and the cities ("scourges of society") over the countryside in "the conflict of interest" which opposed them was "to invert the essential order of Societies and the Constitution of the State in particular."

---

86 Vidaud to the juge d'Embrun, 29 Oct. 1770, Q4 (2), fol. 137, Bibliothèque Municipale de Grenoble. Cf. Vidaud to Berlet, 31 Dec. 1770, *ibid.*, fol. 158.

87 *Arrêt*, 7 Sept. 1771, Recueil Giroud, XXV, 97, A.D. Isère.

88 Vidaud to Maupeou, 8 Sept. 1771, Q 5, fol. 2, Bibliothèque Municipale de Grenoble. Cf., in this same spirit, the *arrêt* of the Parl., 23 March 1774, Recueil Giroud, XXVI, 14, A.D. Isère.

89 Intendant's note, 17 Feb. 1774, C. 48, A.D. Isère. The same year also witnessed the first serious effort of the central government to execute the December regulatory law in the generality of Auch. The government must have enjoyed some success, for the liberal militants of the Société d'Agriculture d'Auch complained bitterly that the enforcement of the legislation struck a "mortal blow" against agriculture and the grain trade. "Observations,", 24 Aug. 1774, AN, H 72–73. Ironically, just as he was completing the reconquest of the "south," Terray suffered disgrace.

90 Letter to Louis XV, 10 Nov. 1770, B. 3677, A.D. B-du-R.

The Parlement stressed the political lessons to be learned from this conflict and from the liberalization experience. The duty of the state was to enforce the laws of nature, the foremost of which guaranteed the rights of property and liberty. It was *not* up to the state to provide subsistence: "this is the personal care of each individual." It was not legitimate for the state to violate property rights on "moral" grounds because moral principle "has little application in politics and commerce." A political philosophy bred of "this sort of communion of goods and needs" led straight to "the reign of the arbitrary." Nothing was more dangerous in the eyes of the magistrates, not only of Aix but of all of the parlements, who had made this the theme of remonstrances on every subject of public life. The more responsibility the state assumed, the bigger it got and the further it reached in social and economic life, the more arbitrary and the more dubious its authority became. To prevent the monarchy from degenerating into abuse and corruption, the king had to resist the pressure of the people who understood nothing in politics save that the government was accountable for everything and the pressure of the administrators who were interested only in "extending their authority" and placating their constituents.

If Terray were permitted to impose his regulatory legislation, the Parlement of Provence solemnly warned Louis XV, the kingdom could look forward only to "universal disorder." Presumably, then, the events of the next few years did not surprise the liberals. While the Controller-General blamed the disorders in part on the abuses and excesses of liberty, Dupont found their origin "in the public prohibition of exportation with all the clauses which accompanied it," in the xenophobia of intendants who obstructed the circulation of supplies, and in the futile and wasteful operations of the king's grain company which frightened away or ruined the private grain speculators who were the only reliable source of relief.[91] At one time the return of tranquility had seemed to be the prerequisite for a return to liberalization. Now it was the vista of persistent turmoil that buoyed liberal hopes, for it was bound to discredit the ministry. The magistrates of Aix continued to criticize Terray's restrictive measures and to demand a new, "perpetual" law authorizing exportation without which internal liberty was "illusory." Even as the Controller-General poured huge amounts of the king's grain into the region in 1773–74 in an effort to parry

---

91 Dupont to Prince Carl Ludwig, 1773 in Knies, ed., *Dupont correspondance*, II, 147.

the dearth, the Parlement reproached Louis XV for sponsoring measures "contrary to your own principles."

Certain practical matters, however, induced the Aix magistrates to bargain with Terray even as they eagerly awaited his fall. They were anxious to preserve the "foreign port" status of Marseilles, which had been threatened by the December law and subsequent *arrêts*. Marseilles' freedom to export and import regardless of the national law had always been a key element in the regional grain trade, both as an outlet for domestic production and a source of foreign supplies, and in the fabrication of Mediterranean fortunes. In return for concessions meant to preserve Marseilles' character, the Parlement apparently agreed not to contest the rules Terray established for internal trade and the efforts he made through the royal administration to keep markets supplied.[92]

In the spring of 1771, Terray was hopeful that the force of circumstances would gradually bring the Parlement of Toulouse around to his way of thinking about grain police, because it was already clear that the jurisdictions in which the courts had registered the December law "suffered fewer abuses in the grain trade" than the others.[93] The magistrates were, however, unyielding; the more demanding the Controller-General became in his insistence that Languedoc conform to his instructions, the more combative they became in their resistance. Like the other spokesmen for regional economic interests, the parlementaires regarded Terray's coastwise trading regulations of 1772 as a virtual act of war. As if nothing had transpired in the previous eight years and the will of the royal government were unknown, in November the Parlement issued an *arrêt* not only ordering the most vigorous execution of the Declaration of May 1763 and the Edict of July 1764, but also asking the king to "suppress the limitations" included in those laws in order to render liberty "invariable and unconditional."[94] The *arrêt* covered a great deal of ground, appealing on the one side to the "sacred law" of property sprung "immediately from nature" and threatening on the other a sort of fiscal blackmail which had become a staple of

92 Deliberation of Parl., 20 Oct. 1770, B. 3677, A.D. B-du-R; *arrêt du Conseil*, 12 Sept. 1773, AN, AD XI 39; Terray to IN., 21 Dec. 1773, C. 2421, A.D. B-du-R.

93 Terray to St.-Priest, 26 May 1771, C. 2909, A.D. Hér.

94 *Arrêt* of Toulouse Parl., 14 Nov. 1772, AN, AD XI 39. There are also copies in C. 89, A.D. Orne and C. 2912, A.D. Hér. In fact, the merchants of Languedoc, till the end of 1772, seem to have acted exclusively "on the faith of the disposition of the Edict of July 1764 registered in all the courts." See the petition of the Narbonne *négociants* to Terray, ca. Nov. 1772, C. 2912, A.D. Hér.

Languedocian liberalism.[95] Since the only laws it recognized as valid expressions of the royal will were the reforms of 1763–64, the Parlement regarded Terray's measures as "illegal steps" contrary both to positive law and the "solemn laws" of the "essential order" of things. It denounced the consumerist policy which favored the parasitical urban-dwellers over the cultivator who "because of his utility [was] more worthy of the beneficence ... of the Sovereign King." Decrying the renascent paternalism of the government, the court went on to state the liberal doctrine in its starkest form:

> The King only owes liberty, security and protection to His peoples ... he owes them no subsistence whatsoever: this must be the price of their work and their industry.

Within two weeks, Terray had the *arrêt* quashed, rebuking the Parlement sternly for its haughtiness and its lack of social conscience.[96] Now the monarch was not to be denied the role that he had so vehemently rejected only three years earlier. The Toulouse Parlement, Terray declared, had no right "to deprive His Majesty of the happy advantage which his supreme authority gives him to watch over the subsistence of the subjects." To be sure, it was "the duty" of the monarch "to maintain [his subjects] in the free usage of their properties" but not at the cost of "exposing the indigent portion of his subjects to lack the food of first necessity ...." The king could not regard *cherté* as the *bon prix*, the right price, because, for the mass of poor people, there was no difference between famine and *cherté*. Like the *économistes*, the Toulouse magistrates made "incredible assertions" and broadcast "dangerous" principles such as the notion that "the more grain exported abroad the greater will be the abundance in the interior." Surely Terray understood that the idea was not at all farfetched in the long-run perspective. But the implications of this policy for consumers here and now were catastrophic. In a moral sense the magistrates were just as guilty as the grain manipulators who contrived speculations and monopolies in the pursuit of exorbitant profits gained at the expense of the consumers. The magistrates, charged Terray, let themselves "be seduced by avid proprietors who will never find their grain sold dearly enough." Merely to espouse

---

95 For other examples of fiscal blackmail, see archbishops of Narbonne and Toulouse to Terray, 12 Nov. 1722 and *négociants* of Narbonne to Terray, ca. Nov. 1772, C. 2912, A.D. Hér.
96 *Arrêt du Conseil*, 29 Nov. 1772, AN, AD XI 39.

liberty in the absolute manner of the Toulouse Parlement was, in this view, tantamount to signing a famine pact.

There should be no question about the nature of royal politics, the Controller-General told the Parlement: they are interventionist and paternalistic. They follow not from natural laws and theories of government but from the king's perception, through the control and data-collecting apparatus, of "the ensemble of the general needs of his State." No one else was in a position to determine "the general good." Nor was any "individual tribunal" equipped to tell him what he could or could not do to deal with any given problem. The only principle that governed the king's action was his commitment to the public interest. Not long before Louis XV had been made to take a very different stance. In the liberal sixties he had reviled the example of his predecessors in the name of a higher truth and "denounced the "hindrances" which fettered freedom as violations of inviolable rights and laws. In the *arrêt* annulling the Toulouse action Louis promised, "following the example of his august predecessors … to place hindrances upon the grain trade whenever the hindrances are [considered] indispensable." Nor would Terray allow the magistrates to nourish the self-serving illusion that the king had two political bodies, an immutable one committed to high principles and solemn laws and an inconstant and vulnerable one which lent itself to arbitrary actions effected by his unscrupulous ministers. Speaking for Louis XV, the Controller-General made it clear that the "King administrator" and the "King legislator" were one in thought and action. The government's brisk and forceful reply to the Toulouse *arrêt*, according to one report, "caused the greatest ferment" in the Parlement and throughout the province.[97]

In correspondence with the leading figures in Languedoc, Terray reiterated the rebuke. In his view, there were two camps confronting each other: the party of "cupidity" and "self-interest" on the one side and the party of "the general well-being" and "the love of the people" on the other. The magistrates, he wrote the archbishop of Narbonne, "let themselves decide by the desire to see their revenues increase rather than by the dread of seeing the misery of the people increase." "One would believe," he told the archbishop of Toulouse, "that they prefer the increase of the income of the rich to the subsistence faculty of the poor."[98] All the other arguments the Controller-General

---

97 Pidansat de Mairobert, *Journal historique*, III, 372–73 (18 Dec. 1772). Cf. Viala, *La Question des grains à Toulouse*, 82–83.

98 Terray to the archbishops of Toulouse and Narbonne and the comte de Périgord, 25 Nov. 1772, C. 2912, A.D. Hér.

dismissed as rhetorical devices designed to mask parlementary greed. Not only was this greed morally despicable; it was also politically shortsighted. For the people, Terray hinted, would one day exact their revenge. In subsistence affairs, for Terray as for Necker, and for other officials who felt tremors from below, there was one prudent rule to follow: "I will always favor in this matter," Terray declared, "the interests of the multitude for whom grain is the principal and often the sole food and whose uprisings when bread is lacking can dissolve empires." The magistrates of Toulouse deluded themselves into believing that the inhabitants of their province were better off than Frenchmen in the parts of the kingdom subjected to the police regime. If they could not hear the "groaning" of their own people it was because their cupidity had dulled their sensibilities. Social conflict would probably one day prove to be sharper in Languedoc than in other places because "the inhabitant of the countryside in this province is rarely a landowner and [he is] more subordinated and more dependent than in any other province."[99] The parlementaires, for their part, took Terray's moralizing no more seriously than he took their theorizing. Even as he denounced them for greed, so they intimated that the government's policy was devised to serve the interests of an officially-backed "Monopoly." From their perspective, all the talk about the consumer interest was meant to veil these maneuvers.

Terray claimed that he "foresaw" the dearth which became critical in Languedoc the following year, though it is not certain if he managed to foresee it because he was so well informed or because he knew that it was bound to occur as a sort of retribution for a refractory province. Like the shortages in other parts of the south, he viewed this dearth as largely artificial: "Subsistence is not at all lacking in your province," he wrote the somewhat skeptical intendant in May 1773 on the eve of the Midi's Flour War. The cause of the problem was "avidity": first the avidity of the magistrates who had refused to arm the province against subsistence dangers and then the avidity of the "*négociants*"—the very ones who had complained so vociferously about Terray's "formalities"—and other dealers who hoarded in an attempt to drive up prices.[100]

---

99 Terray to comte de Périgord, 25 Nov. 1772 and Terray to archbishop of Narbonne, 5 Dec. 1772, C. 2912, *ibid.*

100 Terray to St.-Priest, 5, 10, 11 May 1773, C. 2914, *ibid.* Cf. Terray's warnings the year before against allowing too much grain from leaving the province. To St.-Priest, 19 Oct. 1772, C. 2912, *ibid.*

In the eyes of the Toulouse parlementaires, the Controller-General's way of dealing with the dearth must have seemed at best ambiguous and at worst incoherent. On the one hand, he proposed a Delamare-type investigation by local police to discover the names of the principal hoarders and the location of their storehouses. Presumably the purpose was to put the authorities in a position to requisition supplies and set the rhythm of the trade. On the other hand, in a letter to the Procurator General, Terray solemnly condemned municipal officials who interrupted "the free circulation of grain ... on the pretext of assuring the subsistence of their city" and asked that orders be given to the *substituts* "to favor and even excite this free circulation." Nor did the supply operations conducted by the agents of the central government inspire confidence, though they did provide huge amounts of urgently needed grain. Once again the Controller-General found himself suspected of giving orders to obstruct the speculations of Languedoc's own merchants in order to promote the enterprises of his protégés.[101] Relations remained strained between the Parlement and the Controller-General. Hard times did not sap liberal ardor in Languedoc. Like their colleagues at Aix and Grenoble, and the *économistes* who believed they glimpsed the end of the desert on the horizon in 1773–74, the magistrates of Toulouse anxiously awaited the next ministerial turnover in anticipation of another round of liberty.

IV

Although its voice was never completely silenced and it retained enough vitality to achieve a remarkable comeback several years later, the physiocratic movement was deeply wounded during the retreat from liberalization.[102] The advent of Terray, marking the end of a decade of liberal ministries, and the persistence of the subsistence crisis, set in a broader context of socioeconomic disarray, encouraged the development of a vocal "philosophical" countercurrent, an antiphysiocracy untainted with ordinary Delamarism or parlementarism. To be sure, physiocracy had been criticized from within the philosophical

---

101 Terray to St.-Priest, 26 April and 11, 15, 19 May 1773, C. 2914, *ibid.*; Terray to PG, 18 May 1773, C. 2914, *ibid.*

102 On the decline of the physiocrats, see the works of Weulersse; in particular, his *Mouvement physiocratique*, I, 241.

camp before, but never so widely, so acrimoniously, and with such merciless concreteness as in the seventies. For the experience of liberalization enabled the anti-*économistes* to attack physiocracy not only for its theories but for its *policies* and its politics as well, not for fanciful blueprints to the future but (fairly or unfairly) for tangible results already registered.

Now it is true that the *économistes* had an astonishing variety of interests and the range of their genius made them vulnerable to attack on many grounds. They were assailed for their conception of productive activity and the net product, for their single tax plan, for their vision of "legal despotism," for their insufferable manner. ("Crush them, and pound them, and reduce them to dust and ashes!" exhorted Hume; they are "the most chimerical and most arrogant [set of men] that now exist, since the annihilation of the Sorbonne.")[103] But the other matters of political economy, though they inspired lively polemics and contributed eventually to the justly deserved reputation of the physiocrats for intellectual audacity and originality, paled in significance next to the grain question. It was "the fermentation excited in France for the last two years on the occasion of the *cherté* of grain," as the *Mémoires Secrets* noted in 1770, which propelled the *économistes* from relative obscurity to notoriety. (Was Mirabeau merely flattering himself when he wrote that "invoking my name in the streets of the city Rouen was the secret of getting stoned [by the crowd]"?)[104] It was the grain issue that observers continued to consider "the principal object" of the physiocratic group.[105] In the years following liberalization, a growing band of anti-physiocrats denounced the *économistes* not simply for being pretentious, ridiculous, or wrong—commonplace accusations in the Enlightenment—but for being dangerous, for having caused damage, for preaching a philosophy of famine and disorder.

Jarred by the Assembly of General Police, the *économistes* were routed, in their own estimation as well as in the eyes of other contemporaries, by a single "bomb," as its creator called it, launched by the abbé Galiani.[106] The bomb was the *Dialogues sur le commerce*

---

103 Hume to Morellet, 10 July 1769, in *The Letters of David Hume*, ed. by J. F. Y. Grieg (Oxford, 1932), II, 205.
104 Bachaumont, *Mémoires secrets*, XIX, 171 (18 April 1770); Mirabeau's "discours de rentrée" for 1776 in G. Weulersse, ed., *Les Manuscrits économiques de Quesnay et de Mirabeau* (Paris, 1910), 132.
105 F. Métra, *Correspondance secrète*, I, 323 (20 April 1775).
106 Galiani to d'Epinay, 18 Nov. 1769 in *Correspondance*, ed. by Perey and Maugras, I, 36.

des blés, a series of eight sprightly dialogues, set in Paris beginning in mid-November 1768, between the Chevalier de Zanobi, through whom the author speaks, and the Marquis de Roquemaure and the President, who are tempted by the fashionable liberalism of the day.[107] Composed in the months following the Assembly of Police, corrected and prepared for publication by Diderot, endorsed by Sartine but delayed by Maynon's ministry which appointed a zealous Quesnayite as censor, the *Dialogues* appeared almost immediately after the nomination of Terray to the Contrôle-Général. (The *économistes* promoted the idea that Terray ordered them to measure for the price of 100 louis.)[108] Galiani, an Italian classicist, political economist, and diplomat, whose wit and effervescence had made him the toast of the Parisian salon circuit, was not in the capital to witness the explosion he anticipated. For a diplomatic matter apparently unrelated to the grain question, Choiseul had demanded his recall in 1769.[109]

The *Dialogues* were not Galiani's first encounter with grain affairs. In the fifties he had translated an Italian work on grain conservation technology and, while in service at Paris at the very time France inaugurated liberalization, he was deeply involved in efforts to find grain supplies for his famine-stricken homeland. During his sojourn in France he became a friend of Trudaine de Montigny and frequented other liberals. It is not impossible that Galiani sympathized with liberalization at the beginning, but there is no hard evidence to prove it.[110] Writing in

---

107 Although the first edition sold out rapidly, the *Dialogues* did not have a second edition until 1795. Brunetière, who seems to miss the whole point of the work, takes this as evidence that Galiani's "success was not so striking after all." *Etudes critiques sur l'histoire de la littérature française*, 2nd series (Paris, 1897), 241.

108 Bachaumont, *Mémoires secrets*, VII, 252 (20 Dec. 1774); Pidansat de Mairobert, *Journal historique*, VI, 376 (21 Dec. 1774). Voltaire also alluded to this possibility. Voltaire to Turgot, 12 Jan. 1770 in *Correspondence*, ed. by T. Besterman, vol. 74, p. 28 (# 15100).

109 On Galiani's background, his relations in Paris, and the origins of the *Dialogues*, see: the introductions and commentary in the edition of the *Dialogues* edited by F. Nicolini and the edition of the autograph manuscript entitled *Dialogues entre M. le Marquis de Roquemaure, et Ms. le Chevalier Zanobi*, ed. by Philip Koch in *Analecta Romanica*, XXI (1968); P. Koch, "The Genesis of Galiani's *Dialogues sur le commerce des blés*," *French Studies*, XV (Oct. 1961), 314–23; Maria Valania, *L'Abbé Galiani et sa correspondance avec Madame d'Epinay* (Milan, n.d., ca. 1932), 11–13; Henri Valentino, *Une Femme d'esprit sous Louis XV: Madame d'Epinay* (Paris, 1952), 300; L. Perey and G. Maugras, *Une Femme du monde* (Paris, 1883), 394. *Diderot Correspondance*, ed. by Roth, V, 31 and IX, 54; *Mercure de France* (June 1771), 169–71; d'Epinay to Galiani, 26 July 1769 in *La Signora d'Epinay*, ed. by Nicolini, 19; d'Epinay to Galiani, 4 Nov. 1769 in Nicolini, "Lettere inedite," *Mélanges Hauvette*, 469; Galiani to Suard, 15 Dec. 1770 in *Lettres*, ed. by Asse, I, 188; Galiani to d'Epinay, 18 Sept. 1769 in *Lettres*, ed. by Asse, I, 13.

1770, Galiani himself claimed that he had presented his "system" to Choiseul and Trudaine de Montigny as early as 1763–64.

The *Dialogues* did not affect the *mercuriale* but they had a profound impact on the philosophical community. Celebrated in the salons for his "gaiety," it is not surprising that Galiani's book seemed to be as much admired for its style as for its substance.[111] Nor did the inevitable comparison with the turgidity and ponderousness of the physiocratic style turn to his disadvantage. "But more than 300 pages in little print on the grain trade!" exclaimed Suard,

> That struck me as frightening. I have been so disgusted by the jargon and the tiresome repetitions of the *économistes*, the exportists, the libertyites, etc.! But having barely finished the first 4 pages [of the *Dialogues*] I was swept up till the very end without being able to do anything else. I found the question presented with wholly new viewpoints .…[112]

Voltaire, Madame d'Epinay assured her "little abbot," was "intoxicated with your book." Indeed, the Patriarch told Diderot that he found in it a mixture of Plato and Molière: "No one has ever reasoned better nor more amusingly."[113] Turgot lamented that Voltaire was "talking complete nonsense about economics and given up to all the sophistries of Galiani."[114] *Economistes* disdainfully greeted the "comic" elements as proof that the abbé was not serious and that he was incapable of treating "profound" questions.[115]

One has the impression that the intellectual community and the political class which had followed the grain question with interest and then with alarm were waiting for a book like Galiani's *Dialogues*. What accounted for the success of the book was neither the wit, though

---

110 P. Koch makes the case for Galiani's early liberalism. "Genesis," *French Studies*, XV (Oct. 1961), 314–23. Cf. Galiani to Tanucci 13 Aug. 1764 in *Lettere di F. Galiani al marchese B. Tanucci*, ed. by A. Bazzoni (Florence, 1880), 128.

111 D'Epinay to Galiani, 11 May 1771 in *La Signora d'Epinay*, ed. by Nicolini, 173; Diderot to Mme. de Maux, April or May 1769, *Correspondance*, ed. by Roth, IX, 46; Diderot to Sophie Volland, 25 Nov. 1760, *ibid.*, III, 268.

112 Suard to Galiani, 6 Aug. 1770 in Nicolini, "Lettere inedite," *Mélanges Hauvette*, 464. Cf. Suard's critique of Galiani's political conservatism, Suard to Galiani, 14 Oct. 1770, *ibid.*, 467.

113 D'Epinay to Galiani, 25 Oct. 1770 in *Mémoires et correspondance de Madame d'Epinay*, ed. by J.-P.-A. Parison, III, 381; Voltaire to Diderot, 10 Jan. 1770, *Correspondance Diderot*, ed. by Roth, X, 18–19. Cf.: Voltaire to Turgot, 12 Jan. 1770, *Voltaire's Correspondance*, ed. by Besterman, vol. 74, p. 28 (# 15100); Voltaire to d'Argental, 24 Jan. 1770, *ibid.*, vol. 74, p. 47 (# 15116); Voltaire to Suzanne Necker, 6 Feb. 1770, *ibid.*, vol. 74, p. 81. (# 15144). Yet Voltaire was a bit troubled by Galiani's penchant for "despotism." Voltaire to d'Alembert, 25 Jan. 1770, *ibid.*, vol. 74, p. 51 (# 15120).

114 Turgot to Dupont, 5 July 1771 in *Oeuvres*, ed. by Schelle, III, 491.

115 *Ephémérides du citoyen*, IV (1770), 177–84.

it eased the burden of argument considerably, nor the freshness of the content, for most of Galiani's conclusions and caveats could be found in the minutes of the Assembly of General Police or in the parlementary papers. Rather it was the fact that the case against liberalization was made, with exquisite timing, not by a police official or an administrator or a magistrate, not even by a renegade or eccentric philosophe, but by a philosophe who spent Wednesday evening at Geoffrin's, Fridays at the Neckers', and Thursday and Sunday with the Encyclopedist circle at d'Holbach's or d'Epinay's, and by a philosophe known to have had warm relations with the liberals. It was, in addition, the confidence inspired by his tone, which was on the whole quite moderate vis-à-vis the *économistes*, and by his obvious familiarity with many of the technical aspects of the grain problem. It was also the clarity and persuasiveness with which he crystallized the issues, not for the profane, but for people like Voltaire and Diderot who were very well informed but genuinely perplexed by the grain question. Galiani enabled his readers to despise Terray while generally approving his grain policy and to love liberty while reproving the liberals. Finally, as Galiani knew better than anyone, it was the *cherté* itself which brought him converts.[116]

To be fully understood, the *Dialogues* must be viewed in the context of the ongoing crisis and its political and economic origins, not as a round in a salon feud. They were a response to the crisis; it was in this vein that readers appreciated them and reacted to them. In addition to hinting at its causes, Galiani suggested how it could have been avoided and what might be done to combat it. But, despite his boast, he had no "system." Or rather, like Necker, who later drew heavily on his work, Galiani found his system in an Antisystem. He liked to say that "I am for and not against... yes, I am for and my whole book aims at this for," but it is always what he was against which surges forth. He was against "this spirit of enthusiasm and system which spoils everything," the "fanaticism" in public administration which was good only for "starting riots," and any policy which declared itself absolute and universal. He spoke for what the *économistes* not unreasonably regarded as the traditional and arbitrary approach to government: for empirical, flexible, cautious, and contingent administration.[117] He was deeply

---

116 Galiani to d'Epinay, 13 Nov. 1770 in *Lettres*, ed. by Asse, I, 174. But Galiani was afraid that the praise, like the bite, of such supporters as Fréron could be fatal. *Ibid.*, and *Année littéraire*, I (1770), 291–300.

117 Galiani to Sartine, 27 April 1770, in *Lettres*, ed. by Asse, I, 63–64; Galiani to Morellet, 26 March 1770, *ibid.*, I, 81–83. Cf. Galiani to Baudouin (after whom the

suspicious of general principles, the search for which the *économistes* rightly regarded as one of the distinctive features of the Enlightenment. Grimm correctly saw that the major point of the *Dialogues* was that "a *general rule* could not be established for so complicated a question as that of the grain trade...."[118]

On virtually every important question, Galiani took issue with the *économistes*. The President, taking the physiocratic stance, says that "it is necessary to let nature act." The Chevalier sternly warns him against "trusting her." Nature is immense, infinite, omnipotent; we are "insects, atoms, nothings." Instead of trying to conform to Nature, "our job down here is to combat her." Indeed, the Chevalier claims, everything we achieve and enjoy in life is a product of a hard-won triumph in this struggle. But, objects the President, I thought that "nature left to herself would bring everything into equilibrium." What you say, retorts the Chevalier, is wonderfully true in theory but woefully wrong in practice. The natural equilibrium theory does not take account of the time dimension; it works by balancing inequalities by theoretical compensations and it uses "average terms which never exist except in meditation." For man who is small and frail and whose needs require immediate gratification, what matters is the "short space of his life" during which he cannot count on uncertain compensations if he is to survive.

Now let us apply this theory to the grain trade, says the Chevalier. Nothing is truer than that prices left to adjust themselves in liberty will tend toward equilibrium even as free circulation will diffuse grain wherever there are consumers with money. But beware, the Chevalier warns, that it takes time to send word from a deficit town to a surplus town that grain is lacking and still more time for this grain to arrive. "The theory goes well but the problem goes badly," for after a week of waiting "this insect called man" will die of hunger. Nature "is too great a Lady" to have to bother with the care of our tattered bodies: "Let's leave to her the care of great movements, the great revolutions of empires, the long run [even] as she has that of the stars and the elements." Our business, concludes the Chevalier, is "politics [which]

President in the *Dialogues* was modelled), 20 April 1770, *ibid.*, I, 53 and Galiani to d'Epinay, 6 Nov. 1773 in *Galiani Correspondance*, ed. by Perey and Maugras, II, 274–76.

118 Grimm, *Correspondance littéraire*, ed. by Tourneux, X, 515 (Dec. 1774), my emphasis. Cf. Galiani to d'Epinay, 6 Nov. 1773, *Galiani Correspondance*, ed. by Perey and Maugras, II, 274: "Now, general theories and nothing are approximately the same thing."

is nothing other than the science of preventing or parrying short-run movements set in motion by extraordinary causes...."[119]

Galiani's conception of political economy as a "science of administration" was closer to the police than to the physiocratic view. First of all there was nothing at all "evident" about how to conduct public administration. The goal of political economy was to "do good for men" but to every good there is attached some evil and man himself is an unpredictable variable: there is no "fixed and constant" element in the equation. Rather than the application of absolute principles, political economy is always a task of "approximation," of "finding the greatest possible good with the least possible evil." To strike the right mark, this approximation has to be based on a precise knowledge of the circumstances peculiar to a given problem. "The science of details," Galiani told Madame d'Epinay, "is the only useful one." In the *Dialogues* the Chevalier remarks that police is an affair of detail." When it sticks to "particulars," it is effective; when it "becomes universal, it is converted into a hindrance."[120]

Implicit in Galiani's view of public administration was a conservative idea which was inherent in the traditional notion of police. Ultimately the public good was defined as the preservation of society or the mitigation of those strains which are built-in and constantly threaten the structure of society. Thus, Galiani, like the police, accepted the notion that "liberty and property are sacred rights"—by itself this was hardly a revolutionary conception in the Old Regime. Unlike the *économistes*, however, who insisted that these rights could never legitimately and usefully be violated, the Chevalier said: "nothing must

---

119 Galiani, *Dialogues*, ed. by Nicolini, 221–23. For a similar view, see Necker, *Sur la législation et le commerce des grains*, 393–94. Cf. Galiani's letter to Madame d'Epinay in which he wrote scornfully of the *économistes* who have "so often said that nature left to herself was so beautiful, worked so well, put things in balance, etc." 23 June 1770, in *Lettres*, ed. by Asse, I, 92.

Einaudi argues that the *économistes* and Galiani shared the same goal of a progressive society and saw the relation between man and nature in very much the same way. But to make his case he is obliged to diminish the physiocrats in a curious way: "But it happened only too often that the physiocrats ... forgot about the fundamental principles of their methods." L. Einaudi, "Einaudi on Galiani," in H.W. Spiegel, ed., *The Development of Economic Thought: Great Economists in Perspective* (New York, 1952), 67–68.

120 Galiani, *Dialogues*, ed. by Nicolini, 215–220, 291; Galiani to d'Epinay, 6 Nov. 1773 in *Galiani Correspondance*, ed. by Perey and Maugras, II, 274. Cf. F. Nicolini, ed., *Il Pensiero dell'abate Galiani* (Bari, 1909), 149. For a strikingly similar conception of good public administration, see Necker, *Sur la législation et le commerce des grains*, 210, 237–38, 303–405. Cf. Linguet, *Canaux navigables* (Amsterdam, 1769), 154–55 and *Du Pain et du bled*, 215; Grimm, *Correspondance littéraire*, ed. by Tourneux, X, 516–17 (Dec. 1774).

trouble them, save for the bonds which tie us to society." For the sake of the general interest, for example, for the maintenance of social stability and the prevention of general disaster—indeed, for the sake of property itself in the long run—the government could interfere with these rights whenever necessary.[121]

Provisioning was one of those urgent matters of public interest. Like the police, Galiani believed that private commerce must assume the major burden of distribution and that internal trade should be unencumbered by restrictions on circulation. Like the physiocrats, and a number of police officials as well, he favored the development of a community of powerful grain merchants who dealt on a large scale. But he was deeply impressed with the technical difficulties and the uncertainties of the grain trade and he was not confident that merchant cupidity, if it triumphed over nature's obstacles, would always serve the general interest. Like the President d'Aligre at the police Assembly, the Chevalier distinguished two vastly different, rival approaches to the subsistence question: the one of "our ancestors" who "envisaged grain as an *object of administration*" and the one recently in favor by which grain was made into "an *object of commerce.*" Grain, Galiani felt, could not be treated as an object of commerce because it was different from any other item in trade. His reasoning followed the traditional police line: grain was a matter of life and death; demand for it was inelastic and always urgent; "as the matter of first necessity and the first concern in the civil order of societies," argued the Chevalier, "it belongs to politics and to reason of state." The government, through its police, had to intervene as often as necessary to assure the regularity and adequacy of provisioning.[122]

---

121 Galiani, *Dialogues*, ed. by Nicolini, 199–200. For similar views on the limitations of the rights of private property and their relation to the rights of society as a whole, see Necker, *Sur la législation et le commerce des grains*, 362–63, 381–89; Béguillet, *Traité des subsistances*, 805; Desaubiez, *Le Bonheur public*, 10; *Journal économique* (April 1, 1775), 52–54; Diderot, *Apologie de l'abbé Galiani*, in *Oeuvres politiques*, ed. by P. Vernière (Paris, 1963), 85, 118; and especially Linguet who moved even closer to the police view than Galiani in *Réponse aux docteurs modernes*, part III, 63–64 and *Annales*, VII (Nov. 1779), 229–30.

122 Galiani, *Dialogues*, ed. by Nicolini, 30, 170, 172–74. "Bread is something else," Galiani told Madame d'Epinay, "it belongs to police and not to commerce." 7 Aug. 1773, in *Lettres*, ed. by Asse, II, 77. For similar views on the special nature of grain and bread, see: Mably, *Du Commerce des grains*, in *Collection complète des œuvres de l'abbé Mably*, ed. by G. Arnoux (Paris, 1794–95), XIII, 262–63; Béguillet, *Traité des subsistances*, 804–805; Linguet, *Réponse aux docteurs modernes*, part III, 52–56; Linguet, *Du Pain et du bled*, 54; Linguet in *Annales*, VII (Nov. 1779), 226–28, 232–33; Aubert, "Réflexions simples et pratiques sur le commerce des grains" (1775), BN, mss. n.a. 4433,

Now Galiani was not an apologist for every police practice allegedly devised to promote provisioning. He was hostile to price controls and generally discountenanced any infringements upon liberty at the marketplace. He claimed to share the *économiste* horror of "the arbitrary" in government. He did not trust local police officials whom he believed were characteristically excessive in zeal and unreliable in judgment. He disapproved of the stigmatization of the grain merchant. He detested absolute prohibitions as much as he loathed absolute liberty. Though Galiani insisted upon the need for wide discretionary latitude, he favored "fixed" laws over the "variable" legislation, special derogations, and individual authorizations on which the old police had depended. On the crucial question, however, of the relationship of government to the provisioning process there was no ambiguity in Galiani's position. The government should involve itself as often as necessary and without a guilty conscience. Indeed, in regard to preventing or combatting dearth through victualing or stocking operations, Galiani was a less inhibited Josephist than the French police.[123]

Ideally, of course, the need for spectacular governmental interventions, Galiani believed, would be infrequent in a well-policed state. Such a state would never have followed the liberalization policy adopted by France in 1763–64. Galiani viewed the July law as one of the major causes of the subsistence crisis. Like the police, he was skeptical about the possibility of separating the "superfluous" from the "necessary" in the grain supply for a given time. The 1764 law permitted France to be "plundered" and, given the facility of foreign outlets, drained grain from the interior and halted internal circulation. The experience of the sixties, moreover, exposed as a myth the idea that France could depend on speedy and generous distress-assistance from her neighbors. As for agriculture, Galiani argued somewhat tortuously that it would not truly benefit from the export price and market incentives. The export-related profits would be siphoned off by a host of non-producing intermediaries while the resultant "dear bread" policy would "starve the people" and "harm industry," which Galiani believed to be as real a source of national wealth as agriculture.

---

fols. 10–12; remonstrances of the Paris Parl., March 1776, in Flammermont, ed., *Remontrances*, III, 304.

123 Nicolini, ed., *Il Pensiero dell'abate Galiani*, 202; Galiani, "Mémoire to Sartine" (1770) in *Lettres*, ed. by Asse, I, 411–15; Galiani to d'Epinay, 13 Nov. 1773, in *Lettres*, ed. by Asse, II, 102–103; Galiani, *Dialogues*, ed. by Nicolini, 279–80.

"Everything is linked" in a "political state" as in a machine, Galiani liked to say. Above all, wise administrators had to avoid "sudden jolts and movements"—the political consequences of ideological absolutism and fanaticism—because they "break the links and the springs and the machine is destroyed." "Do you know," asked the Chevalier, "that I regard this sudden steep increase in the value of grain as the most violent and dangerous shock that one can give to the state?"[124]

"Their system," wrote Galiani in reference to the *économistes*, "produced a famine that my book could have prevented."[125] But liberalization had other implications, more subtle and equally as perilous. For Galiani, liberalization itself represented a profound political transformation and portended an even more sweeping kind of political change. By liberating grain, the government also gave the people the freedom, and thus the responsibility, to look out for their own subsistence. "The liberty of providing for one's food brusquely given to someone long accustomed to not having to worry about it," remarked the Chevalier, "is a deadly gift." Historically, Galiani contended, the extent of a monarch's responsibility for provisioning has varied roughly in proportion with the amount of civil liberty his system of rule afforded his subjects. Thus it was no surprise, for example, that the despots were the great victualers, assuring cheap abundance for ultimately ignoble ends. "And what do you conclude from this?" asked the Marquis. "I conclude," said the Chevalier sarcastically,

that we must bless heaven and judge ourselves fortunate to have seen with our own eyes the time where in a monarchical country the confidence between the Sovereign and the subjects has reached such a point that this Sovereign, cheerfully, voluntarily with satisfaction and complaisance discharges himself from the most delicate and sensitive care...The French have for too long been treated like all the other peoples. They enjoyed a more gentle fate in other centuries, they were the children of a good father but they were minor children whom it was necessary to think about feeding.

---

124 Galiani, *Dialogues*, ed. by Nicolini, 169, 186–88, 244–63, 282; Galiani, "Mémoire to Sartine" (1770), in *Lettres*, ed. by Asse, I, 411–15. Galiani, it should be noted, favored the maintenance of the legal right to export on a permanent basis but through a law which helped render it relatively unattractive for economic reasons. See *Dialogues*, 254–61. Later Galiani protested that his proposition to subject exports to a duty had been misunderstood. He claimed that he envisaged the duty as a temporary expedient. See Galiani to Baudouin, 23 April 1770 and to Suard, 8 Sept. 1770, in *Lettres*, ed. by Asse, I, 70, 138–43. Yet his attitude toward exportation was not clear even to his close friends. See Diderot to Sophie Volland, 12 Nov. 1768, *Diderot Correspondance*, ed. by Roth, VIII, 216.
125 Galiani to Caraccioli, 15 July 1773, in *Lettres*, ed. by Asse, II, 69.

"Medals, statues and triumphal arches" should mark the legislation by which the people were declared "major," "emancipated," and thus free to assume responsibility for their subsistence. Like the Paris Parlement, Galiani interpreted liberalization as the renunciation by the king of his traditional role. The new policy radically altered the relationship between government and people. "Peoples," the Chevalier imagined the liberal monarch to proclaim to his subjects, "your fidelity has so deeply merited my confidence that no suspicion will henceforth upset it and the precautions will become superfluous for me [to take]...." Whatever the consequences, the king went on to say, I will not take responsibility for them:

> I feel that if you see the price of food rise, you will not blame me. You will recognize in it the inevitable effect of the contrariety of seasons, or even the felicitous increase in your wealth and the circulation of money.[126]

The question for Galiani was whether this new "mutual confidence" based on liberty was appropriate in a monarchy like France and whether indeed it could sustain the royal system as it had heretofore been known. For "in every government," he told Suard, "grain legislation takes the tone of the spirit of the government." Thus grain liberalism in England seemed as reasonable to Galiani as it had to the Advocate General Séguier, given the constitution peculiar to England. The relationship between grain police and politics posited by Galiani had a corollary which he viewed as cause for genuine alarm: "he who dares to change entirely the administration of grain in France, if he succeeds, will have changed at the same time the form of government." Like the Paris Parlement, Galiani questioned whether liberty was compatible with the French system and with French society as it was structured. Without any preparation, in the early sixties, the king repudiated obligations which in the past he had always assured, less in deference to the people than in the interest of his own rule. The immediate result was chaos, confusion, resentment, and misunderstanding. In the long run, liberty presaged further "upheaval," which Galiani did not discuss in the *Dialogues* but promised facetiously to treat in a new dialogue to be appended to a new edition of his book "in the form of apocalypse."[127]

---

126 Galiani, *Dialogues*, ed. by Nicolini, 229–33, 237–242.

127 Cf. the Prince de Conti's apocalyptical allegory on the vogue for and risks of liberty. A dog dirtied the floor of the salon where the Prince was receiving at tea. When a *huissier* rushed in to chase away the dog before the beast had finished its business, the Prince interceded: "Stop, liberty, liberty, totál liberty." Cited by A. Neymarck, *Turgot et ses doctrines* (Paris, 1885; Geneva, 1967), II, 193n.

His description of this process of further upheaval was extremely sketchy but it suggested a view very much like the one developed at length by Necker several years later in his *On the Legislation and the Commerce of Grain*. The monarchy, Galiani reasoned, "depends essentially on the inequality of ranks [*conditions*], the inequality of ranks upon the low price of foodstuffs, the low price on [police] constraints." Liberty would upset the existing constitution of France in two ways, both of which involved social conflict. The first, upon which Necker insisted more heavily than Galiani, would result from the hatred of the have-nots, who suffered from high prices, for the haves. The second would result from the capitalist ethos which liberty inculcated. Liberty would eventually enrich the peasantry, which would develop confidence in itself and revolt against an oppressive, arbitrary and discriminatory social and political system. The upshot would be "the republican form [of government] and the equality of ranks which it cost us six thousand years to destroy." Galiani's vision was indeed apocalyptic, overdrawn, and unsophisticated in its socioeconomic analysis but in its most general outlines it was not entirely removed from the kind of world which the physiocrats themselves dreamed of making.[128]

Galiani's *Dialogues* inaugurated a decade of sustained criticism of liberalization and of what the Neapolitan called "economystification."[129] Many of the ideas he developed or touched upon reappeared in works by more than a dozen different authors: his repugnance for *économiste* absolutism and universal speculation, the conviction that grain had to retain a special status, his sense of the fragility of society and the interdependence of its parts, the belief that equilibrium was

---

128 Galiani to d'Epinay, 3 June 1775, in *Galiani Correspondance*, ed. by Perey and Maugras, II, 409; Galiani to the comte de Schomberg, 19 May 1770, in *ibid.*, I, 139; Galiani to Suard, 8 Sept. 1770 and Galiani to d'Epinay, 2 Jan. 1773 and 22 Jan. 1774, in *Lettres*, ed. by Asse, I, 138–39 and II, 2–3, 109–110. In the letter to Schomberg cited above, Galiani alluded to the revolts of the late sixties, the *pacte de famine*, and the alliance between people and parlements who together appealed for "despotism" to come to their assistance. In a letter to Morellet, Galiani insisted on the importance of the question of "the relations between the form of government and the manner of provisioning." 26 May 1770, in *Correspondance*, ed. by Perey and Maugras, I, 159.

On the abdication of kingly responsibility, see also: Necker, *Sur la législation et le commerce des grains*, 134–35; Linguet, *Du Pain et du bled*, 81; Séguier's remarks in *Recueil*, 114–15 and as cited by Weulersse, *La Physiocratie sous Turgot et Necker*, 214–15; and De Maistre's comments cited by A. Boland, *Traité pratique de boulangerie* (Paris, 1860), 128.

129 Galiani to d'Epinay, 23 Sept. 1780, in *Galiani Correspondance*, ed. by Perey and Maugras, II, 600.

neither inevitable nor natural but had to be battled for, and his view of the multiple sources of national wealth. Each of the critics, of course, had his own special concerns. Linguet and Mably emphasized the question of social justice and the rights of the dispossessed; Diderot, Mercier, and Briatte stressed the moral rather than the political side of the subsistence issue; Necker devoted most of his attention to the political and administrative dimensions; Grimm never tired of pointing to the philosophical flaws in the way the *économistes* looked at the world; Béardé de l'Abbaye insisted on economic matters while Béguillet focussed on technical as well as social considerations.[130]

Virtually all of them, however, shared Galiani's view that physiocracy was dangerous, that it was "a Mississippi, a Jansenism, a Fronde, a crusade, even one of those epidemic diseases of the spirit by which the French nation is sometimes attacked and which causes cruel ravages until the calm of reason returns."[131] For Linguet, their most ferocious and relentless scourge, the *économistes* were a "dangerous sect" whose "murderous" goal was to institute the reign of "dear bread" and to "make gold from human blood."[132] Diderot admired them for their insatiable curiosity and their intellectual courage in 1769 but by the early seventies he denounced them for a cruel conception which exposed the nation to misery and famine.[133] Béguillet considered them "dangerous" for defying "the first law of all societies," the *salus populi*.[134] Briatte, whose book on eighteenth century poverty deserves to be better known, assailed the "preachers of the dangerous system

---

130 For the full references to these works, see Institut National d'Etudes Démographiques. *Economie et population: les doctrines françaises avant 1800, bibliographie générale commentée* (Paris, 1956). There is unfortunately no first-rate study of the so-called anti-physiocrats. Jean Airiau's *L'Opposition aux physiocrates à la fin de l'ancien régime* (Paris, 1965) is superficial and unreliable. Two of the major figures. Linguet and Necker, have very recently been studied by D. G. S. Levy (forthcoming) and H. Grange, *Les Idées de Necker* (Paris, 1974). In some ways the angry condemnation of the physiocrats by lower level field administrators is more impressive than the more elegant and articulate onslaught of the "professional" critics. See, for instance, the "réflexions" of the SD of Avesnes, ca. Oct. 1770, C. 6690, A.D. Nord.

131 Galiani, "Mémoire to Sartine" (1770) in *Lettres*, ed. by Asse, I, 412; Galiani to Sartine, 27 April 1770, *ibid.*, I, 63. Galiani also referred to the *économistes* as "bloodsuckers of hemorrhoidal veins." Galiani to Suard, 8 Sept. 1770, *ibid.*, I, 142.

132 Linguet, *Réponse aux docteurs modernes*, part III, 80 and part II, 110, 112–13. Cf. his *Du Pain et du bled*, 213–14 and *Canaux navigables*, 156–57.

133 Diderot in Grimm, *Correspondance littéraire*, ed. by Tourneux, VIII, 373–74 (15 Nov. 1769); Diderot to Sartine, 10 March 1770, in *Diderot Correspondance*, ed. by Roth, X, 32–33; Diderot, *Apologie de Galiani*, 17 and *passim*.

134 Béguillet, *Traité des subsistances*, 838n.

of dear bread."[135] For their arrogance, for having given "the most unbridled cupidity the signal to starve the kingdom," and for having "struck the people with a calamity," Mercier felt confident that "equitable history" would "punish" the *économistes*.[136] Although we cannot follow here the thread of the post-Galiani criticism and its relationship to changing political and economic conditions—specifically to the ministries of Turgot and Necker which in a sense mimicked the experience of 1763–74–it is important to note its virulence, its continuity, and its scope.[137]

Of the physiocratic replies and defenses, which were just as impassioned and equally as prolific, we can deal only with those pertaining specifically to Galiani's work. So alarmed were the *économistes* by the positive impression they feared the *Dialogues* made on the public that they sent forth three of their leading spokesmen to refute them.[138] Roubaud conceded that his *Récréations Economiques ou Lettres ... à M. le Chevalier Zanobi* were really superfluous since he had "refuted in advance" all of Galiani's feeble and familiar objections in his *Réprésentations aux Magistrals* of the previous year. With this attitude, it is not surprising that the *Récréations* turned out to be tiresome and uninspired. Roubaud reaffirmed the claims that liberty would prevent dearth and would eventually assure a cheap as well as a regular bread supply, that a child could govern with a single law of nature as guide, and that property by definition could not conflict with the

---

135 J.-B. Briatte, *Ofrande à l'humanité*, 161.

136 Mercier, *Tableau de Paris*, VIII, 162 and VI, 232.

137 Turgot's advent brought a temporary truce, for he had devoted friends in both the *économiste* camp and among its enemies. Galiani predicted disaster for Turgot's "system" in September 1774 and eight months later thanked God that he was not in Paris during the Flour War: "I would have perhaps been put in prison as the author of the Revolt." Galiani to d'Epinay, 17 Sept. 1774, in *Lettres*, ed. by Asse, II, 150–51; Galiani to d'Epinay, 27 May 1775 in *Galiani Correspondance*, ed. by Perey and Maugras, II, 406. Another abbé, named Saury, was in fact arrested on Turgot's orders (along with a number of other clerics who allegedly stirred up their flocks) for having written a pamphlet in which he warned that if the liberal system were reinstituted "it could happen that the people would revolt." F. Métra. *Correspondance secrète*, I, 362–63 (24 May 1775) and Jean Saury, *Réflexions d'un citoyen sur le commerce des grains* (Paris, 1775). Necker, whose book on the grain trade appeared opportunely at the very moment that the Flour War erupted, was not disturbed by the authorities, though they regarded him as an agitator.

138 Roubaud, *Récréations économiques, ou lettres de l'auteur des "Représentations aux magistrats" à M. le Chevalier Zanobi, principal interlocuteur des "Dialogues sur le commerce des blés"* (Amsterdam and Paris, 1770), iii, vi; Grimm, *Correspondance littéraire*, ed. by Tourneux, IX, 81–82 (July 1770); *Ephémérides du citoyen*, IV (1770), 177–84; Bachaumont, *Mémoires secrets*, XIX, 168–69 (18 March 1770).

general interest. He denied responsibility for the crisis that accompanied liberalization, arguing that liberty never really had a chance in
the adverse circumstances of the late sixties. Galiani, in his estimation, was a derivative thinker, a Delamarist and mercantilist bedecked
in modern dress. Roubaud stressed a theme which echoed through
all the replies to the *Dialogues*: that Galiani was an apostate to the
Enlightenment, not merely an enemy of the new political economy;
that he deserved to be banished from philosophical circles for seeking
only to "deepen prejudices and increase fears."[139]

Infuriated by this "atrocious calumny," Galiani vainly asked Sartine to suppress Roubaud's book. The Lieutenant General consoled
Galiani with the assurance that it was not worth the trouble, for no
one was reading it.[140] Nor did the refutation prepared by the other
économiste abbé, Baudeau, stir much interest. Though less tedious than
Roubaud's, it did nothing more than rehearse the points the author
had already made in his *Avis* of 1768.[141]

The third major refutation of the *Dialogues* from within the physiocratic school was contributed by Lemercier de la Riviére, a former
parlementaire and intendant whom Quesnay regarded as a genius
capable of becoming prime minister and whom Diderot at one time
compared favorably to Montesquieu.[142] The ample title of Lemercier's work betrays its argument: *The General Interest of the State, or the
Liberty of the Grain Trade demonstrated as being in conformity with natural
law, with the Public Law of France; with the fundamental laws of the kingdom;*

---

139 Roubaud, *Récréations*, xiv, 13, 16, 58, 97n, 147, 161, 185, 190.

140 Galiani to d'Epinay, 27 July and 4 Aug. 1770, in *Lettres*, ed. by Asse, I, 116, 120; d'Epinay
   to Galiani, 24 Aug. 1770 in *La Signora d'Epinay*, ed. by Nicolini, 89; d'Epinay to Galiani, 22
   July 1770, cited by Koch in his edition of the *Dialogues*, 321.

141 Baudeau, "Lettres de M. l'abbé Baudeau ... à M. l'abbé G*** sur ses dialogues anti-
   économistes," *Éphémérides du citoyen*, XII (1769), 107–28. It is possible that Baudeau prepared
   a more substantial refutation which the government suppressed, though the evidence for
   this rests uniquely on Bachaumont, *Mémoires secrets*, VII, 252, (20 Dec. 1774). Doubtless it
   would have pleased Galiani to know in advance that both the *économiste* abbots, Roubaud
   and Baudeau, would be exiled for seditious writings in August 1776. See Arsenal, mss.
   Bastille 12448.

142 On Lemercier de la Rivière, see Charles de la Rivière, "Mercier de la Rivière à St.
   Petersbourg en 1767," *Revue d'histoire littéraire de France*, 4th year (15 Oct. 1897), 581–
   602; Bluche, *L'Origine des magistrats*, 268; Weulersse, *Mouvement physiocratique*, I, 103, 127;
   Lermercier de la Riviére, *L'Ordre naturel et essentiel des sociétés politiques*, ed. by E. Depitre (Paris,
   1910), introduction. On Diderot's enthusiasm for Lemercier, see Diderot to Damilaville,
   July 1767 and Diderot to Falconet, July 1767, in *Diderot Correspondance*, ed. by Roth, VII,
   75–77, 94. For Voltaire's demurrer, see Voltaire to Damilaville, 16 Oct. 1767, *Voltaire's
   Correspondence*, ed. by Besterman, vol. 67, p. 101 (# 13584).

with the common interest of the Sovereign and of his subjects in all times; with the Refutation of a new system published in the form of "Dialogues on the Grain trade." Far more than a rebuttal of Galiani, the essay was a synthesis of all the basic *économiste* propositions with an effort to integrate such rich ideas as absolute freedom of the grain trade and a single land tax into a unitary, coherent design.

The aim of the entire scheme was to increase national wealth and the proofs Lemercier adduced for its validity were almost theocratic in mood and method. The physiocratic touchstone of "evidence," disdained by Galiani, was in Lemercier's perception God-given and available for everyone to grasp. His starting point was natural law, which he saw as the "immutable laws of divine justice," the first of which was the right of property, "sacred" and "inviolable." He denounced Galiani's view of conditional property and his suggestion that private property and the general interest could be in conflict. "Anything which disturbs property and liberty," Lemercier maintained, "attacks the essence of society [itself]." Galiani was dishonest, naive, and wishy-washy; he was an enemy of the countryside and agriculture and a partisan of manufactures; worst of all, he was intellectually a dwarf next to the *économistes*, a man of levity rather than of science, utterly ignorant of the "first truths" and the "immutable principles of the social order." Lemercier felt confident that philosophes would have no trouble unmasking Galiani as an imposter. Beyond them, he addressed his appeal to the magistrates of the kingdom, his confreres. He deplored the fact that the different parlements were "not in agreement" on liberalization. He hoped that once the foundations of the new political economy were made clear to them they would unite behind liberty in the name of the general interest.[143]

Galiani deeply resented the *General Interest* for its innuendoes and insults.[144] It is not clear whether he envisioned some sort of riposte from the time when the first *économiste* refutations began to appear. But in June 1770 he learned of an event which stirred his imagination as well as his horror and provided him with the allegorical substance for a reply to Lemercier. The event was the Parisian catastrophe of 30 May 1770 which occurred in the midst of an official celebration in the royal square in honor of the marriage of the dauphin. A sudden

---

143 Lemercier de la Riviére, *L'Intérêt général*, 1–16, 21–22, 64–65, 163n, 286, 290–91, 306–17, 322, 326–27, 330–31, 356–57, 367, 373–78, 402.
144 Galiani to d'Epinay, 5 Jan. and 6 March 1771 in *Lettres*, ed. by Asse, I, 196, 219–20. Cf. Galiani to d'Epinay, 5 May 1770, *ibid.*, I, 68–69.

stampede for place sent waves of panic through a crowd estimated at 400,000 people; at least 133 people were crushed or stomped to death; hundreds of others were wounded.[145] Galiani trembled at the news. It was less a mark of his wit than of the depth of outrage at *économiste* doctrine and style that he wrote d'Epinay immediately upon learning of the disaster:

> I accuse, Madame, the *économistes*. They have preached property and liberty so much, they have criticized the police, order, the rules so much; they have said so often that nature left to herself was so beautiful, worked so well, put herself in equilibrium, etc. that finally, convinced that they were proprietors of the pavement and that they had the liberty to walk, everyone wanted to profit from [these rights].[146]

That, for Galiani, was where "the long preaching" of the *économistes* had led. "In truth," he added, "were I in Paris ... this event would have sufficed as my reply to the *économistes*." The lesson he drew was that any place offering "full liberty" would attract a great crowd including "crooks, grand monopolists in watches and snuff-boxes," who would conspire "to profit from the free-for-all [*bagarre*]." "What I tell you is not a joke," Galiani insisted : "Meditate and you will find the exactitude of the comparison."[147]

The phrase *bagarre*—brawl or free-for-all—from this letter became the working title for short satire of Lemercier's *General Interest* which Galiani promised to publish but which he never completed. Long assumed lost and only recently recovered, the *Bagarre* (or a large fragment of it) is a raw verse-by-verse parody with the text of Lemercier on one side of the page and Galiani's burlesque on the other.[148] It is sometimes strained and heavy-handed and frequently hilarious but its most striking quality is a certain viciousness of attitude. The real *bagarre* was social disorganization, social dissolution, chaos; it erupted in the markets and towns in the sixties and seventies in response to grain shortage, high prices and terrible fears; it threatened not merely the public order in a multitude of scattered places but the very essence of the social order. Liberty, the brand of liberty promoted by the *économistes*, was the cause of *bagarres*.

---

145 AN, Y 15707; J.-B. Dénisart, *Collection de décisions nouvelles*, III, 530; Holbach to Galiani, 3 June 1770 in *Amici e Corrispondenti francesi dell'abate Galiani*, ed. by F. Nicolini, 199.

146 Galiani to d'Epinay, 23 June 1770 in *Lettres*, ed., by Asse, I, 92.

147 Galiani to d'Epinay, 25 Aug. and 13 Oct. 1770, *ibid.*, I, 126–27, 155.

148 Galiani to d'Epinay, 16 March 1771 and 24 June 1775, *ibid.*, I, 219–20 and II, 205. On the "lost" *Bagarre*, see Koch's edition of the *Dialogues*, 332–33.

The government itself commissioned a refutation of Galiani's *Dialogues* by the abbé Morellet. It caused a stir because the author was an intimate friend of Galiani and because Terray ordered its suppression immediately after its publication in 1770, probably as a slight to Choiseul, one of its sponsors.[149] Substantively, the work was unworthy of the tempest it excited. It was a faithful rendition of the physiocratic theses with the standard emphasis on the primacy of property in the social and natural orders. Whereas Galiani argued that a rigorous and unconditional application of property rights could threaten social stability, Morellet maintained that "everything becomes arbitrary and changeable and society tends towards dissolution" when the rights of property were placed in doubt. Morellet bluntly denied that the government had any responsibility for assuring subsistence and criticized the king's grain operations as excessively costly, wasteful, and inimical to commerce. Disdainful of Galiani's relativism, his empiricism, and his insistence upon detail, which, like Lemercier, he attributed to Galiani's lack of true principles, Morellet claimed that liberty must be operative in all circumstances.

As a corollary to this proposition, in the most original part of his essay, Morellet vigorously denied that there was a direct relationship between a nation's political system and its social structure on the one hand and its grain administration on the other. He accused Galiani of "apologizing" for the police resistance to liberalization and for the brutal and backward style of administration associated with the police regime. In Morellet's assessment, Galiani revealed himself to be not merely an anti-*économiste* but an anti-philosophe as well.[150] When he became Controller-General in 1774 Turgot avenged Terray's blow against Morellet. With an enthusiastic covering letter endorsing Morellet's "very solid" position and urging its

---

149 Morellet, *Mémoires*, ed. by Lemontey, 2nd edition, I, 191–92, 194; Condorcet to Turgot, 10 March 1770 and 10 May 1770 in *Correspondance inédite de Condorcet et de Turgot, 1770–79*, ed. by C. Henry, 2, 13; Diderot, *Apologie de Galiani* in *Oeuvres politiques*, ed. by Vernière, 69n, 71; Diderot to Sartine, 10 March 1770 in *Diderot Correspondance*, ed. by Roth, X, 32–33; Arthur Wilson, *Diderot* (New York, 1972), 555; Grimm, *Correspondance littéraire*, ed. by Tourneux, X, 514 (Dec. 1774); Bachaumont, *Mémoires secrets*, VII, 252 (20 Dec. 1774). Cf. Turgot's decision to distribute the refutation to all the intendants, circular, 10 Dec. 1774, *Oeuvres*, ed. by Schelle, IV, 228–29.

150 Morellet, *Réfutation de l'ouvrage qui a pour titre: "Dialogues sur le commerce des bleds"* (London, 1770), 49–50, 69–71, 106–111, 240–49, 254–56, 319–20. Morellet claimed that Galiani's *Dialogues* were aimed not at development of principles of political economy but at settling a score with Choiseul for having expelled him from France. *Mémoires*, ed. by Lemontey, 2nd edition, I, 192.

dissemination throughout the realm, Turgot sent hundreds of copies of the *Refutation* to the intendants. It thus became one of the most widely distributed tracts of liberal propaganda of the seventies, serving not only as a belated rejoinder to Galiani but as an apology for Turgot's own liberalization program.[151]

Either because he was enraged by Morellet's foray against a mutual friend or because he wanted to test out on paper the solidity of his own intellectual conversion to an anti-*économiste* posture, Diderot wrote a refutation of Morellet's refutation entitled *Apology for the abbé Galiani* which was not published during his lifetime. The issues as well as the persons involved moved Diderot deeply; his tone was pitilessly cruel and ironical. It was Morellet, not Galiani, who was "no philosophe." He was a "man sold to the ministry," a "vile and low rogue." His chief defect was his reasoning: it was "abstract," "utopian," and indifferent to social realities and human needs. In Diderot's view, Morellet, and through him the *économistes*, suffered from many of the flaws with which the Taines, the Faguets, and the other modern enemies of the Enlightenment have taxed the philosophes in general. On socioeconomic and political questions, at least, Diderot felt safer with Galiani's uncertain and variable empiricism than with the *économiste* search for a "general principle" from which to deduce everything else. Diderot found "in the sciences, in the *métiers* a method which is precisely the opposite of yours." He would begin with "individual cases" and after accumulating, comparing, and evaluating different cases arrive at "more or less general notions" or "theories." But it is "the facts ... which serve as stages for climbing, and not abstract speculations as steps for descending."[152]

A methodology totally unfitted to the social sciences led the *économistes* dangerously astray even as it had led France to near-disaster in the late sixties. It beckoned Morellet to write reassuringly about a "possible" or potential surplus as justification for allowing exportation. But, remarked Diderot, "I eat badly when I have only potential bread." It led Morellet to an utterly abstract, arithmetic conception of dearth as if dearth were an orderly, predictable process, as if one dearth were like all the others. "You don't have the first notion of what happens in a dearth time," Diderot charged, for dearth was "a tumultuous conflict

---

151 Turgot to INs., 10 Dec. 1774 in C. 2420, A.D. B-du-R.; C. 1442, A.D. Gir.; C. 2916, A.D. Hér.; C. 2627, A.D. Cal. Cf. Pidansat de Mairobert, *Journal historique*, VI, 376 (21 Dec. 1774).
152 Diderot, *Apologie de Galiani*, 78, 97, 113.

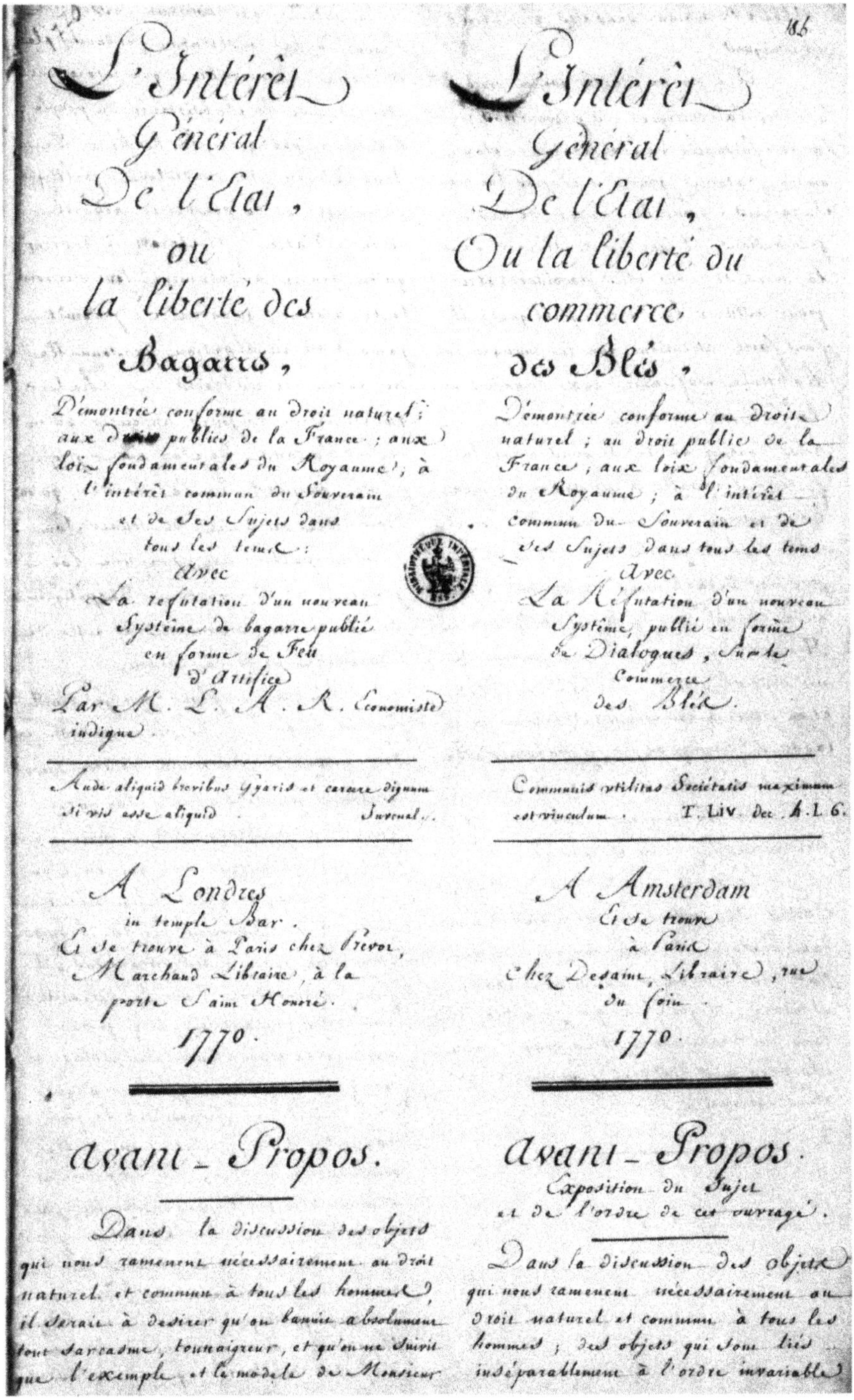

Illustration 10. Manuscript page of Galiani's "lost" work, *La Bagarre*, a parody of Lemercier de la Rivière's *L'Intérêt général*. Bibliothèque Nationale.

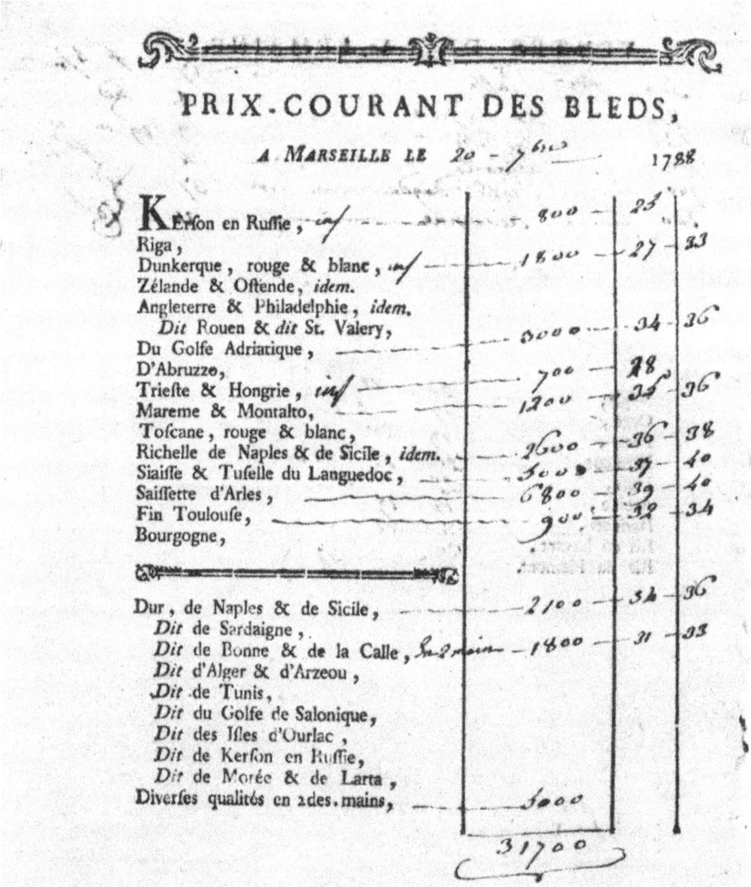

PRIX-COURANT DES BLEDS,

A Marseille le 20 – 7bre 1788

Kerson en Russie, inf	800	25	
Riga,			
Dunkerque, rouge & blanc, inf	1800	27	33
Zélande & Ostende, *idem.*			
Angleterre & Philadelphie, *idem.*			
Dit Rouen & *dit* St. Valery,	3000	34	36
Du Golfe Adriatique,			
D'Abruzzo,	700	28	
Trieste & Hongrie, inf	1200	35	36
Mareme & Montalto,			
Toscane, rouge & blanc,			
Richelle de Naples & de Sicile, *idem.*	2600	36	38
Siaisse & Tuselle du Languedoc,	5000	37	40
Saissette d'Arles,	6800	39	40
Fin Toulouse,	900	32	34
Bourgogne,			
Dur, de Naples & de Sicile,	2100	34	36
Dit de Sardaigne,			
Dit de Bonne & de la Calle, 2e main	1800	31	33
Dit d'Alger & d'Arzeou,			
Dit de Tunis,			
Dit du Golfe de Salonique,			
Dit des Isles d'Ourlac,			
Dit de Kerson en Russie,			
Dit de Morée & de Larta,			
Diverses qualités en 2des. mains,	5000		
	31700		

Illustration 11. Current price listing illustrating the international character of the grain trade at Marseilles. Private collection.

of fear, of avidity, or cupidity." Morellet's fine principles led him to a contempt for the people and for "the notions of the people." After all, asked Diderot, "isn't it their instinct for what is advantageous to them which should be at the base of your sermons on liberty?" It is true, Diderot conceded, that Galiani "fears the people", but when "it is a question of bread, only a drunkard would not be afraid of them."

In a passage in which he came close to justifying popular subsistence violence, Diderot likened grain to air or water as an article of elemental necessity. He also compared it to a case of quinine hoarded by an owner who refused to sell except at a price above popular means, despite the fact that a dangerous epidemic fever raged at the moment. In an allegory strikingly redolent of many grain and bread riots which had taken or were to take place in the eighteenth century, Diderot wrote that the people would break down the hoarder's door, take the drug they needed to save themselves, and leave a reasonable amount of money in exchange. "What?" asked Diderot, "Is an epidemic fever a more dangerous disease than dearth and hunger?"[153]

Nor would Diderot accept the *économiste* argument for the inviolability of property. "Isn't the sentiment of humanity more sacred than the right of property?" he wondered. None of the public authorities responsible for provisioning would have disputed Diderot's claim that the absolute physiocratic concept of property was "a Tartar principle, a cannibal [principle] and not [the principle] of a policed man [*un homme policé*]." [154]

Product of a grave subsistence crisis, Galiani's *Dialogues* questioned some of the basic assumptions and called attention to some of the ominous implications of liberalization and of the new political economy. Before 1770, the voices of opposition to the new system were the voices of the past, of the police, the magistracy, and the people—not the voice of philosophy. For the philosophes, unity of purpose, at least on major questions, had been of the utmost importance in the campaign against the tyranny of authority and tradition. Galiani sounded the alarm within the philosophical community at a critical moment when a group of philosophes called *économistes*, who had managed for the first time in the eighteenth century to have an important part of their program adopted by the government, came under severe attack from

---

153 *Ibid.*, 75–76, 84, 115, 117–21. Cf. *Journal économique* (1 April 1775), 57–59.
154 Diderot, *Apologie de Galiani*, 85, 87, 90, 99, 118–19.

a coalition of interests which the philosophes had always distrusted. Instead of rushing to the aid of the embattled champions of liberty— not the old-style liberty, which was still used to defend encrusted privilege, but a vision of liberty that was very much in the mainstream of Enlightenment thought—Galiani repudiated them. Galiani assailed their science and their politics, not through occasional sallies but in a full-scale frontal assault and not in rarefied terms of theory but upon a background of a national crisis. The *économistes* took pride in moving the Enlightenment a giant step closer to the everyday reality of social and economic problems, in radiating light into the marketplaces and farms, and in founding what one close observer of the republic of letters called "a practical Politics." Galiani confronted them on their own terrain and found a gaping incongruity between their broadest aims and their means. The *Dialogues* helped to open a breach in the philosophical party, to make the crisis of liberalization into a crisis of the Enlightenment as well.

Diderot's *Apologie de l'abbé Galiani* is a symbol and a symptom of that breach. The liberalization experience transformed his warm sympathy for physiocracy into deep skepticism and intellectual and moral distaste. The grain issue was important enough on its own to give the debate enormous significance. But for Diderot, it opened a larger question which had far-reaching implications: what were to be the foundations of the political science and the social science of the future? Were a political science and a social science possible? How were the needs of a capitalist economy to be reconciled with the humane ideals which the Enlightenment embodied?

The appearance of Galiani's *Dialogues* brought something of the disarray of society into the salons. A Diderot-Grimm-Necker group, frequently supported by Holbach and Voltaire, opposed a Turgot-Condorcet-Dupont branch of the philosophical family. To be sure, the division was not always clear-cut. If Diderot remained cool to Turgot, Voltaire welcomed his rise to power with genuine enthusiasm. Moreover, the other great issue of the hour, the constitutional struggle, resulted in another split which did not follow the same lines. Voltaire wrote Maupeou's apology even as Diderot composed Galiani's, while a number of liberals and anti-*économistes* deplored the despotic fashion in which the parlementary problem was handled. If we are to make sense of the underlying unity of the Enlightenment, it will be necessary to look more closely at the fissures in the philosophical party which developed in the seventies and at the impact of social, economic, and political crisis on the thinking of the established leaders and of the coming men of the post-Ferney generation.[155]

V

Though Galiani told a correspondent that he was sure of "the hatred of M. Turgot for my *Dialogues*," the intendant of Limousin took no direct part in the controversy over the work.[156] Even as the public debate raged, however, Turgot made his views known to the Controller-General through administrative channels in a series of unusually frank and detailed letters written in the fall of 1770, which began as a point-by-point critique of Terray's proposed regulatory law, but developed imperceptibly into a brilliant essay on the theory and practice of grain administration. Turgot's purpose was to warn Terray against pursuing a reactionary course. He analyzed the nature of national wealth, examined the basic principles of political economy, used historical and comparative examples, adduced price and harvest statistics, and assessed the policies of previous regimes in order to invest his conclusions with "the evidence of a mathematical demonstration."

---

155 On the connection between the encyclopedist and the *économiste* branches and the idea of "stages" of the Enlightenment, see the suggestive remarks attributed to Pidansat de Mairobert, *Avertissement* to Bachaumont's *Mémoires secrets*, ed. by P.-L. Jacob (Paris, 1883), 11. On the "confusion" in the public mind between the different "philosophical sects" and especially between the encyclopedists and the *économistes*, see Weulersse, *La Physiocratie sous Turgot et Necker*, 15–16. Many philosophes were both encyclopedists and *économistes*; the confusion reached its zenith at the ascension of Turgot to the ministry. On the careful and petulant distinction Mirabeau always drew between these two groups and for the dislike he had for philosophes in general, see his "Discours de rentrée" (1776) in Weulersse, ed., *Manuscrits économiques de Quesnay et Mirabeau*, 138–39. Writing on the causes of the French Revolution, the administrator-writer Sénac de Meilhan insisted upon the common goals of the *économistes* and the philosophes. In an important argument which merits careful consideration. Sénac de Meilhan assimilated the struggle for liberty of the press to the campaign for liberty of the grain trade, viewing both as manifestations of the same subversive spirit. *Des Principes et des causes de la révolution en France* (Paris, 1790), 28.

156 Galiani to d'Epinay, 24 Sept. 1774, in *Lettres*, ed. by Asse, II, 152. Cf. Galiani's remarks after learning of the Flour War: "I hope that this event will have taught M. Turgot and M. l'abbé Morellet to know men and the world...." to d'Epinay, 27 May 1775, in *Galiani Correspondance*, ed. by Perey and Maugras, II, 406. It was precisely for this knowledge of "the world and men, the human heart [and] the nature of society" that Diderot admired Galiani. Diderot to Sartine, 10 March 1770, in *Diderot Correspondance*, ed. by Roth, X, 32–33. In a circular to the intendants on 10 Dec. 1774 Turgot characterized Galiani's arguments as "objections that little-educated persons make against the liberty of the grain trade." C. 2916, A.D. Hér.

Total liberty, Turgot argued, served the interests of the State and of every section of the citizenry. It meant prosperity for the entire agricultural nation, not merely an elite of rich owners as Terray charged. With liberty, agriculture would thrive, expand, create new jobs, circulate new wealth, and increase the fund of subsistence and the revenue of the government. Liberty was "the only preservative against dearth, the sole means of establishing and conserving between the prices of different places and different times this just level incessantly troubled by the inconstancy of the seasons and the unevenness of the harvests." The people would discover a new security, a certainty, and predictability of subsistence which they had never before known. In 1740 as in 1768 and 1770, it was "lack of liberty and not liberty" which produced the dearths.

"If there has ever been a time," Turgot intoned, "when the most entire, the most absolute liberty, the liberty most unencumbered with any sort of obstacle was necessary, I daresay it is now." Given the psychology of human motivation, the vast size of the kingdom, and the futility and extravagance of government intervention, commerce was the only dependable and efficient source of supply. Terray's planification and allocation scheme was a chimera, materially and morally incapable of realization. Already the limitations placed on trade have prevented merchants from concentrating capital, establishing networks of correspondence, and forming the private hoards which are the only true granaries of abundance. To place further restraints on the trade would be to paralyze it completely. To brand the merchants as monopolists, "to denounce them to the people as the authors of the dearth," and to "deliver them to a terrible inquisition" instituted by an "ignorant or ill-intentioned" police was a foolish, demagogic, and vain policy which would merely serve to perpetuate the crisis and reinforce the "blind" prejudices which united consumers and officials.

The Paris Parlement along with the Controller-General on the one side and the liberal parlements on the other both had assumed that there was a fundamental disjuncture between the interests of consumers and proprietor-dealers. Each party called for the sacrifice of the interests of the other on the grounds that the interests it represented were of a higher order and of greater utility to the state. Rejecting their common premise, Turgot took a more politic position, consistently maintaining the view that there was an ineluctable, underlying harmony of interests which liberty could actuate and through which advantages would result for all.

Yet, in the end, he demanded the greater sacrifice of the people. For even if he could sincerely promise that they would not starve—at least not in the long run, one must add—he still asked them to abandon a way of thinking and a system of values through which they made sense of their uncertain lives. The foremost "prejudice" of the people was the expectation that the government would in the last resort provide for their subsistence. According to Turgot, the Controller-General ceded to the popular demand, proclaiming a policy by which he "personally engaged himself to procure abundance no matter what happens." In deference to the popular mentality, Terray made the government hostage for a ransom it could never pay or which it would have to pay forever. In his place, Turgot would have shown the people the naiveté and the sophistry of their ideas. He would have taught them the laws of nature and the limits of public administration. He would have reminded them that "the government is not the master of the seasons" and that "it does not have the right to violate the property of the *laboureurs* and the grain merchants." He would have told them in 1770, as in fact he later did in 1774–75: "What you ask me for is an injustice." The "Letters on the Grain Trade" adroitly restated the liberal case and announced, four years in advance, the program of Turgot's ministry and another chance for liberalization.[157]

---

157 Turgot to Terray, "Lettres sur le commerce des grains," 30 Oct., 2 Dec. 1770, in Turgot, *Oeuvres*, ed. by Schelle, III, 266–354. On Turgot's view of the "blindness" of the people, see also his letter to the IN. of Toulouse, 19 Sept. 1774, C. 2916, A.D. Hér. and his more nuanced "lettre circulaire aux officiers de police," 15 Feb. 1766, C. 479, A.D. Haute-Vienne.

Chapter XIII

THE KING'S GRAIN AND THE RETREAT FROM LIBERALIZATION

Whereas Laverdy used the king's grain to facilitate the transition from a police to a liberal regime, Terray used it to facilitate the transition from a liberal to a police regime. There are of course other important differences and many striking similarities between the government grain operations of the sixties and of the seventies: we explore some of them in the pages that follow.

This chapter begins with an examination of the situation inherited by Terray when he replaced Maynon d'Invau at the end of 1769. It considers the broad outlines of the new Controller-General's strategy before turning to several case studies of victualing enterprises. The operations launched under Terray's aegis were far greater in scale and ambition than the provisioning activities undertaken in the sixties in the shadow of liberalization. The men involved were in the main much more like Leray de Chaumont than Pierre Malisset, bankers and *négociants* rather than bakers and millers. Instead of signing a contract with a group of suppliers, Terray created a quasi-governmental organization called a *régie*. This chapter focuses on the practices and problems of the *régie*. Of the many troubles encountered or generated by the *régie*, the most serious concerned its reputation in the eyes of the public: we shall see that the famine pact persuasion did not die with the demise of the liberals, even if it changed somewhat in tone and emphasis. The last third of the chapter is devoted to denouement—not only the outcome of the king's grain administration under Terray, but in a more general sense the unraveling of some of the questions which have preoccupied us from the outset.

I

Maynon d'Invau passed the king's grain operation to Terray in a highly equivocal state. Maynon, as we have seen, would have liked to abjure the government supply role completely. Like the *économistes*, he regarded official grain dealings as improvident, unavailing, and inimical to the development of a powerful, autonomous grain trading community serving the general interest according to the laws of nature. He warned his intendants that they could not count on the central government for assistance and he announced that he would not renew the provisioning connections with several provinces which the ministry had arranged.

But the operations of Leray de Chaumont (under the names of several straw men) and of a handful of Atlantic *armateurs* and Mediterranean *négociants* had proceeded too far to permit a brusque liquidation of their affairs. More king's grain had been purchased, was en route, or was already in public magazines than Maynon had anticipated. The government felt obliged to honor the contractual commitments its agents had made in the interior and abroad. Moreover, as a result of his own fears and pressure from his colleagues (probably Choiseul and Saint-Florentin), Maynon was unwilling to raze entirely the Parisian reserve structure and abandon the capital to the fate of the marketplace.

Throughout 1769 foreign and domestic grain and flour continued to reach Paris from Corbeil and its affiliated entrepôts, now placed directly under the control of Trudaine de Montigny's grain department and managed for the king by Doumerc, a grain merchant who had worked for Leray. In principle Corbeil was to be phased out as a Paris storehouse once its current sources of supply had dried up. To replace Corbeil as an emergency Paris provisioning fund, Maynon signed an agreement with Daure, an experienced victualing hand and aspiring minor functionary, to establish a grain and bread supply system for the *Gardes Françaises* and other troops garrisoned in the capital which would be capable, on very short notice, of diverting substantial amounts of its stocked grain and flour to the Halles in a moment of urgent need. By the time Terray arrived at the Contrôle-Général, Daure had already launched his enterprise and the Corbeil provision had begun to dwindle, though we do not know (and Terray may not have known precisely) how much king's grain remained in its magazines or what quantities, ordered long before, had yet to arrive there. Nor is it clear what interest the government may have had in the large quantities of foreign grains which Albert announced were reaching Nantes in the first half of 1770.[1]

---

1 For these cargo arrivals, see C. 775, A.D. L-A.

The abrupt deterioration of the subsistence situation towards the end of the spring persuaded Terray to take a more active part in the provisioning process. It was too late in the harvest year to mount a full-scale victualing campaign. Compelled to improvise, Terray later openly regretted that he had not acted sooner; he regarded the 1770 experience as irrefragable proof of the necessity of planning well in advance. Terray pressed Daure to increase his reserve and accelerate his shipments to the market. Daure bitterly resented the stiff conditions which the new ministry imposed. When he had stocked a considerable surplus in 1769, the Parisian police had not called upon him for aid. Now at an extremely difficult moment he would be required to buy in competition with a host of merchants all claiming authority from the government. Daure deplored the revival of official buying operations which, he admonished, would dissuade independent suppliers from furnishing the capital and which, incidentally, ravished his special privilege.[2] If Daure did not become the Malisset of the seventies, however, it was less because of his ideological reservations than his managerial ineptitude. Terray had no confidence in his ability to assume major responsibilities.

The Controller-General turned instead to Daniel Doumerc, a 33 year old native of Montauban. Son of a businessman, he arrived in Paris in 1766, established himself as a merchant on the make for any lucrative affair, and joined the service of Leray de Chaumont, which brought him in close touch with royal provisioning affairs. In the late sixties, while serving as secretary to Leray and advising Sartine on provisioning matters, he conducted his own grain commerce. One finds him exporting wheat from the port of Dieppe and importing rye, at the government's request, for sale at Caen. In 1770, after the royal council removed onerous import duties, Doumerc speculated in the purchase of Carolina rice, perhaps in expectation that the king, who maintained rice in a magazine at St. Germain for distribution to the poor in time of dearth, would buy it from him for public use. After Malisset's disgrace, Trudaine placed the Corbeil installation under Doumerc's management as agent of the government. In June or July 1770, Terray invited Doumerc to make large-scale grain purchases in behalf of the government.[3]

---

2   For Daure's agreement, see above: Chapter 11. Also, AN, F^{12} 1299^a; Daure to St.-Florentin (?), 20 June 1775, AN, O^1 361; Daure, "Mémoire" (1771), AN, F^{11} 264; "Accounts," AN, F^{11} 1195.

3   BN, Coll. Joly 1140, fols. 47–49; Roubquin to Sartine, 16 Jan. 1769, AN, Y 12618; CG to Doumerc, 1 May 1770, AN, F^{12*} 153; CG to farmers-general, 5 Nov. 1770,

Years later, when it was his turn to come under fire for alleged fraud and malversation, the fate of virtually all official entrepreneurs, Doumerc denied that he had solicited the place as royal grain broker or that he had promised *croupes* to influential courtiers. According to Doumerc, the operation began initially as a semi-private affair, funded by himself and a single associate, Sorin de Bonne, a 45-year-old Dauphinois who conducted a vast array of business interests from a superb Parisian mansion once owned by the Joly de Fleury family. Unlike Doumerc, who came from a modest family and who married a wood merchant's daughter, Sorin appears to have married into wealth and status and to have been enmeshed in the elite world of finance from the beginning of his career. He had relations with the Pâris brothers, the great victualing and banking family, an interest in military provisioning (food, fodder, clothing, and powder), a share in several tax farms, and a large portfolio of *rentes*. In 1771 he placed a million florin loan in Holland for the government upon Terray's request. To Doumerc's grain expertise, Sorin joined the prestige, the international connections, and the practical experience of a financier with one foot planted in the public domain and the other in the private sector.[4] It is unclear how he came into contact with Doumerc, who certainly frequented a different milieu. It is possible that Terray fused the connection even as Laverdy had attached Malisset to Leray de Chaumont.

Shortly after Terray first asked Doumerc and Sorin to undertake grain purchases, he converted their affair into a *régie* in order to keep a tight rein on their activities and spare them the dilemma of having to choose between protecting their investment and serving the interests of the government. Although they were to make advances when Terray lacked liquidity, all their dealings would be for the king's account. Doumerc acquired the title of "Director of grain coming from abroad."[5] In addition to arranging the purchase and distribution of all foreign grain, he and Sorin also managed domestic buying operations in the

---

AN, F¹²* 155, fol. 72; CG to duchesse d'Aiguillon, 12 Dec. 1770, *ibid.*, fol. 141; interrogation, 5,9 May 1775, Arsenal, mss. Bastille 12447; IN. of Rouen to (?), 8 June 1767 and Laverdy to IN., 7, 22 June 1767, C. 103, A.D. S-M.; Trudaine de Montigny to Fontette, 26 July 1768, C. 2652, A.D. Cal.; C. 921, A.D. P-de-D. Doumerc began supplying Auvergne with rice as early as 1768; he continued to furnish rice until mid-1773. C. 1095, C. 916, C. 921 and C. 1131, A.D. P-de-D. The inventory of *régie* papers seized in September 1774 records 5 July 1770 as the date of Doumerc's initial "soumission" to Terray. AN, Y 15383.

4 Saisie, Commissaire Chenon, May 1775, AN, Y 11441; interrogation, May 1775, Arsenal, mss. Bastille 12447.

5 Malisset, "Mémoire Justificatif," AN, F¹¹ 1173.

king's name. To provide a base for these dealings, the government became proprietor of the entire Corbeil establishment in 1771.

II

In the early stages, during the summer and fall of 1770, Terray could not depend on the nascent Doumerc and Sorin enterprise to conduct all public operations. The directors of the *régie* brimmed with confidence. They offered to contract with local governments for the supply of grain at "moderate" prices and they pledged "to try to satisfy everybody." They could not, however, promise delivery until the spring of 1771 at the earliest.[6] Meanwhile, for the provisioning of the capital and adjacent areas, the ministry continued to issue small commissions, many of which were filled by local merchants who had been part of the Malisset network. Leray de Chaumont provided several large shipments until he had completed his obligations by early 1771.[7] The government offered extraordinary bonuses to *négociants* throughout the realm who undertook imports on their own initiative. In May 1770 Louis XV issued a special declaration of gratitude to honor the community of Nantes traders for their service to the cause of national subsistence.[8]

Though later he would ruthlessly insist on centralizing purchasing for the sake of efficiency and economy, for the moment Terray encouraged local and regional officials to contract on their own with merchants to supply grain for a commission and a guarantee against loss. Turgot made wide use of this option, relying less on Limousin merchants than on international traders based at Nantes. While he, too, turned to the Nantes import specialists, the intendant of Auvergne also sought to stimulate local initiatives by offering a 600 *livres* bonus for every 400 *septiers* of wheat or rye brought in from

---

6 Sorin and Doumerc to IN. of Champagne, 21 Dec. 1770, C. 416, A.D. Marne.

7 "Mémoire en défense de Brochet de St.-Prest," ca. Oct. 1774, *Oeuvres de Turgot*, ed. by Schelle, IV, 191.

8 Contrôle-Général to juges-consuls of Nantes, 27 May 1770 and to IN. of Bretagne, 10 Feb. 1770, AN, F[12]* 153, fols. 267, 108; Mémoires des négociants de Nantes, Oct. 1772 and March 1773, C. 774 and C. 775, A.D. L-A.; d'Agay to Terray, 10 May 1770, C. 1718, A.D. I-et-V. Terray continued to offer incentives to *négociants* who undertook provisioning operations on their own even after he had organized the governmental victualing system. See Terray to IN. of Languedoc, 28 May 1771, C. 2909, A.D. Hér.; Terray to IN. of Provence, 28 May 1771, C. 2433, A.D. B-du-R.; Terray to IN. of Rouen, 18 Sept. 1771, C. 106, A.D. S-M.; Terray to First President, Bordeaux Parl., 19 July 1772, C. 1441, A.D. Gir.

outside the generality. The merchants who responded to the urgings of Taboureau, the intendant of the Hainaut, ran enormous risks in their buying operations, for they sought supplies in the low countries where exports had recently been forbidden. Taboureau also received permission from Choiseul to "borrow" grain in emergencies from the military stores in the frontier garrisons. The intendant of Poitiers commissioned a Mortellerie grain trader and a broker at the Halles to procure grain for his jurisdiction. The municipality of Troyes borrowed 30,000 *livres* to finance purchases. The mayor of Saintes personally managed the grain-buying expeditions for his town and later obtained authorization to impose a tax on all persons, including the "privileged" and "exempt," in order to reimburse the municipality's advances. The assembly of notables at Amiens offered cash incentives to *laboureurs* who furnished the market. *Négociants* at Nantes revived the patriotic society, which had mobilized a fund of 240,000 *livres* for the purchase of grain for the needy in 1768. Though they did not institutionalize their activities in the manner of their Breton counterparts, the merchants of La Rochelle assisted the city government in similar fashion. Besides contributing a portion of their judicial income for poor relief, the Rennes parlementaires announced a loan "in the name of the court" for 90,000 *livres* to buy grain and empowered localities to purchase grain with public revenues. At Dijon, the magistrates appointed commissioners to buy grain for public distribution.[9]

Inevitably, buying agents working for different governmental and institutional units found themselves in competition for limited resources. Deploring this fratricidal rivalry, which led buyers to "outbid one another without limit," Terray urged them to buy with care and preferably to buy abroad where their confrontations would have a less direct impact on domestic markets. The Controller-General blamed the *cherté* which afflicted the Lyonnais, Franche-Comté, and Burgundy toward the end of 1770 on the insouciance of the agents who had purchasing commissions "in behalf of the different cities." It is interesting to note that Terray criticized these official purchases in exactly

---

9 Lasalle to Monthyon, 23 April 1770, C. 911 and SD of St.-Flour to Monthyon, 23 June 1770, C. 918, A.D. P-de-D.; Terray to Taboureau, 23 June 1770 and Choiseul to Taboureau, 26 July 1770, C. 6690, A.D. Nord; C. 189 and C. 191, A.D. C-M.; *Gazette d'agriculture, du commerce et des finances* (7 July 1770), 507 and (24 July 1770), 547; Maynon d'Invau to Durat, 26 Oct. 1768 and *arrêt* of Brittany Parl., 3 May 1770, C. 775, A.D. L-A.; IN. of Brittany to CG, ca. June 1774, C. 1653, A.D. I-et-V. Cf. the purchases of Châlons-sur-Marne, HH.2 and HH.3, A.D. Marne.

the same terms that Turgot and the *économistes* criticized royal grain operations: "their commissioners, having no interest in the thing, buy [grain] for governmental corps which themselves have no interest in it." Without "interest," or some form of investment in the affair, to restrain them and give them the right incentives, these buyers were unlikely to function with frugality and efficiency. Obviously the Controller-General felt confident that *he* could have done better had he managed the purchasing operations. Unlike the liberals, he did not believe that public buying was inherently and universally flawed. "The abuse," he maintained, was peculiar to "this sort of [local] administrations."[10] Terray asked the intendants to attempt to coordinate public purchasing within each generality in order to reduce the incidence of conflicts between cities or hospitals or other corps.

Sometimes the intendants themselves clashed. The most curious instance involved two of the most vehemently liberal confreres, Monthyon of Auvergne and Turgot of the Limousin. Monthyon complained that he had information that Turgot was launching official buying expeditions in Auvergne. With considerable irritation, Turgot denounced this as "an absurd tale."

> I would have to be quite an imbecile to use government money so badly, in the way that your Auvergnats suppose. It is in Danzig, in Holland, in Nantes, in Marans, and in Bordeaux that our merchants buy and not in Auvergne.

To be sure, Turgot added, it is quite likely that traders from the Limousin in their "private" capacity have been buying in Auvergne just as it is probable that certain Auvergnats have been hunting grain in the Limousin. This is perfectly proper, concluded Turgot: "Liberty and God for all."[11]

During this difficult time Terray never turned his back on a request for aid. While he urged officials to "make do" on their own until he could organize a provisioning system, the Controller-General engaged the central government to help those authorities who could not make satisfactory arrangements, "my intention being to assure the subsistence of the people ...."[12] He flooded the kingdom with copies of the

---

10 Terray to IN. of Champagne, 5 Nov. 1770, C. 416, A.D. Marne; Terray to First President, Parl. of Besançon, 5 Dec. 1770, B. 2850, A.D. Doubs. On the Controller-General's irritation with internecine grain warfare, see also his rebuke of the Lyonnais. Terray to Amelot, 22 Sept. 1770, C. 81, A.D. C d'O. Cf. the intendant of Burgundy's bitter complaint that Albert had sabotaged or at least impeded the provisioning of his generality. Amelot to Mesnard de Cornichard, 13, 22, 26 Dec. 1770, AN, H 187.

11 Turgot to Monthyon, 13 April 1770, C. 910, A.D. P-de-D.

12 Terray to DuCluzel, 3 May 1770, C. 96, A.D. I-et-L.; Terray to Bertin, 4 Oct., 5

curé of St. Roch's recipe for an "economical rice soup" along with vast amounts of imported rice. It is difficult to say just how effective this rice assistance was. At Montpellier and in parts of the Dauphiné, for example, it was consumed without hesitation. In Auvergne, however, one subdelegate characterized it as a "foreign foodstuff which was not to the taste of our inhabitants" and another suggested that it would work only if it were prepared and distributed in immediately edible form to the people. In the countryside the suspicion lingered that rice was "too light" and not nourishing enough to "put the peasants in shape to work."[13] Terray also encouraged the substitution of the potato for grain consumption. He circulated instructions on its proper use, urged that it be sold on the market right alongside grain and flour, and later prohibited its export. Of limited diffusion, the potato seems to have won more favor in the northern than in the southern part of the kingdom.[14] When royal grain supplies were available, the Controller-General directed them to the places where the need was greatest. Thus king's grain from Corbeil brought a measure of relief to remote Auvergne. Despite resistance within his own grain department, Terray pledged to find supplies for Burgundy and Champagne. In addition, he provided substantial sums of money for the expansion of public works projects which sprung up throughout the realm in the next few years. In the first half of 1770, for instance, Monthyon received 75,000 *livres* for the creation of jobs in Auvergne. For a day's labor men received 12 *sous*, women 10 *sous*, and children 6 to 8 *sous*.[15]

Opportunities on foreign markets where the French usually procured grain in hard times were extremely limited. The grain crisis of 1770 had international dimensions. The harvests in Poland and lower Germany ranged from mediocre to catastrophic. Prices at Danzig, one of the major entrepôts, were soaring. The spread of plague in Poland seriously

Dec. 1770, AN, F¹²* 155, fols. 49, 136–37; C. 915, A.D. P-de-D.; *élus* to Amelot, 26 Nov. 1770, C. 3363, A.D. C d'O.; Amelot to Mesnard de Cornichard, 17,22 Dec. 1770, AN, H 187; Terray to Rouillé, 5 Nov. 1770, C. 416, A.D. Marne.

13 Terray to Monthyon, 4 Jan. 1770, C. 906, A.D. P-de-D.; C. 47, A.D. Isère; Pages to Monthyon's secretary, 13, 20 May 1770, C. 913, A.D. P-de-D.; Ruynet to Monthyon's secretary, 5 June 1770, C. 917, A.D. P-de-D.

14 Bacalan, "Observations," (1768), AN, F¹² 650; Monluc to Monthyon, 17 March 1770, C. 908, A.D. P-de-D.; Taboureau to SD, 15 Nov. 1772, C. 6689 and SD at Quesnoy to Taboureau, ca. Oct. 1773, C. 6690, A.D. Nord.

15 *Elus* to Amelot, 26 Nov. 1770, C. 3363, A.D. C d'O; Amelot to Mesnard de Cornichard, 17, 22 Dec. 1770, AN, H 187; Terray to Rouillé d'Orfeuil, 5 Nov. 1770, C. 416, A.D. Marne; Terray to Monthyon, 28 Feb. 1770, C. 907 and 8 June 1770, C. 915, A.D. P-de-D.; Monthyon to Terray, 14 Aug. 1770, C. 924, A.D. P-de-D.

impeded circulation. In September, a Rouen merchant reported that Holland, where Doumerc and Sorin initiated their first purchases in the summer, had prohibited the export of grain. The King of Prussia followed suit. The English market was still closed and Italy had not yet fully recovered from several years of penury.[16] When Sartine presented to the government a merchant named Pascaud, who claimed that he could procure more than 3,000 sacks of flour on short notice in the La Rochelle-Bordeaux area for the provisioning of Paris, the king's council did not hesitate to give its approval. Pascaud's dealings, undertaken independently of the Contrôle-Général, led to serious tensions between the Lieutenant General of Police and the grain department and reinforced Terray's desire to concentrate all the purchases in a single *régie*.

Like Leray de Chaumont, whose path he crossed several times, Antoine Pascaud had an adventurous and controversial career in public and private commerce in both the old and the new worlds. In the fifties Pascaud lived in Canada where he acted as royal agent for the supply of cod and wood for the French colonies. Uprooted by the Seven Years' War, he moved briefly to New England before settling temporarily in the Caribbean whence he contracted to supply the royal plantation with slaves and other goods. Accused of accounting irregularities and fraud in the estimation of the "quality" of the slaves he furnished, Pascaud returned to France where he was arrested, presumably as a result of these charges. After a sojourn of seven months in the Bastille, which completed the "ruin" of his business, he was exiled, in 1768, to familial lands in southwest France. Sartine apparently was instrumental in effecting Pascaud's rehabilitation. It is quite possible that Pascaud's provisioning offer was part of an effort to win grace and to reestablish his credit in both the private and public sectors.[17]

Pascaud found conditions to be less propitious for grain and flour purchases than he had imagined when he arrived at La Rochelle in September 1770. He encountered a host of prospective buyers and learned, with some consternation, that a number of *négociants* who

---

16 Turgot to Terray, 25 Oct. 1770, in *Oeuvres de Turgot*, ed. by Schelle, III, 144–45; CG to Garriez, 9 Sept. 1770, AN, F^{12}* 155, fols. 40–41. Nor, according to Terray, did the situation improve dramatically the following year: floods in Germany, "mediocre" harvests in Italy, excessively high prices in Holland, export embargo in Poland. Terray to IN. of Rouen, 18 Sept., 15 Oct. 1771, C. 106, A.D. S-M.

17 AN, E 330 (colonies). One wonders whether Pascaud was related to the Pacaud (Pascaud according to the archives de la *Chambre du Commerce* of La Rochelle) who sat as a député de commerce in the 1760's. See the *Almanach royal* (1766), 171.

had conducted foreign operations for the king's account had been waiting a long time to be paid. Instead of committing himself personally to make the promised flour purchases, Pascaud arranged to receive what we might call a finder's fee and contracted with a leading local *négotiant*, Sieur Goguel, a secretary of the king and president trésorier de France at the La Rochelle bureau, to supply the flour, not in the king's name, but on his own account, with royal guarantees against loss and a commission.

To avoid causing alarm, which might be reflected in unfavorable price fluctuations, Goguel kept the purpose of his mission secret. Since Terray had not yet begun to coordinate buying on the national scale, Goguel faced competition from other public buyers, from private businessmen like himself discreetly acting for intendants, municipalities, or public assistance institutions, and private speculators masquerading as legitimate victualers. Pascaud related that another prominent *négociant*, in a "malicious coup," almost ruined Goguel's chances by announcing his intention of buying 10,000 sacks of flour just when Goguel was about to place his orders. Goguel managed to purchase 3,354 sacks, more than half of which was shipped to Paris by water via Rouen in October and the rest in February 1771.

The odyssey of this flour thrusts into relief the perils and difficulties of subsistence commerce in the pre-industrial age.[18] Bad winds and weather delayed the ships for five to seven months. The quality of the flour deteriorated radically during the long transit, obliging Sartine to dispose of some of it to starchmakers and the rest to bakers at a price consonant with its "very inferior" value. Goguel lost over 66,000 *livres*, for which he sought reimbursement along with payment of his commission. Ascribing the fatal delay in arrival to "diverse unfortunate events," Sartine exonerated Goguel in generous terms, praising his spirit of public service ("his only motive") and vouching for his "good management." Despite the Lieutenant General's recommendation for a prompt settlement of the account, Terray ordered an investigation, calling into question Goguel's honesty as well as his commercial acumen. Eventually the account went for expert evaluation to Leray de Chaumont who knew as well as anyone the pitfalls of the victualing business. Leray found a "prejudice" of only 3 *livres* 19 *sous* 7 *deniers* against the

---

18 On the overwhelmingly complex problems of provisioning logistics and the uncertainties of transportation, see, for example, d'Agay to Terray, 10 May 1770, C. 1718, A.D. I-et-V. and Terray to First President, Bordeaux Parl., 5 Nov. 1773, C. 1442, A.D. Gir.

crown and concluded that the money claimed by Goguel was "quite legitimately due him."[19]

While Goguel took charge of the domestic flour deal, Pascaud obtained approval, through Sartine's patronage, to make purchases for the provisioning of Paris in Naples and in the Papal States where he claimed grain was "abundant" in contrast to its penury in northern Europe.[20] He was to start buying immediately, in September and October 1770. Beginning in March of the following year, 10,000 *septiers* were to reach Paris each month for five months, from the time when old grain began to be scarce through the critical *soudure* period. The arrangement seemed at this time to be attractive to the government, for Doumerc and Sorin had not yet organized their buying network and Pascaud agreed to make all the advances in an engagement similar to the one accepted by Goguel. To facilitate Pascaud's mission, Sartine personally requested the intendant of Provence to assist him ("I take a special interest in everything concerning him"), without revealing the nature of Pascaud's business. Also upon the Lieutenant General's request, Choiseul instructed French diplomats in Italy and Sicily to second Pascaud's dealings in every way possible.[21]

As often happened in foreign buying campaigns, Pascaud fell far behind schedule. At the end of May 1771, Sartine and Saint-Florentin (now the duc de La Vrillière), Secretary of State for Paris affairs, asked the naval minister Boynes to dispatch four ships from the royal navy to Civitavécchia to accelerate the shipment of Pascaud's grain to the capital. Boynes cheerfully agreed to provide the transport but then countermanded his order after receiving a raging letter from Philippe Brochet de Saint-Prest, the intendant of commerce named by Terray to replace Trudaine and Albert in the grain department.[22]

---

19 AN, H 1669.
20 St.-Prest to Boynes, 4, 18 June 1771 and "Réponse du Sr Pascaud," ca. end of June, 1771, AN, F¹¹ 265.
   Is it possible that Galiani, who sent Sartine a memoir on subsistence management and kept in touch from Naples through Madame d'Epinay, assisted the Paris Police chief in arranging grain purchases in Italy? In September 1770, he wrote from Naples: "I am engaged here trying to persuade [the government? the merchant community?] to give help in grain to France this year, better, more extensive, and more efficient than that which she furnished us in 1764 ...." To D'Epinay, 1 Sept. 1770, in *Lettres*, ed. by Asse, I, 130. Cf. Galiani to same, 22 Sept. 1770, *ibid.*, I, 148.
21 C. 2452, A.D. B-du-R.; France, 1366, fols. 246–50, Arch. AE.
22 Boynes to St.-Prest, 31 May, 3 June 1771, AN, F¹¹ 265.

Saint-Prest attacked Pascaud for abusing the terms of his contract, but the real reason for his opposition to the extraordinary naval assistance seems to be the fact that Pascaud operated outside the system that the ministry had begun to erect around Doumerc and Sorin and that his interests clashed with those of the *régie*'s correspondents. Saint-Prest charged that Pascaud's grain would not reach the capital in "useful time" before the harvest. He claimed that Pascaud had purchased 200,000 charges of grain (the charge, 250 pounds, was slightly bigger than the Paris *septier*), 150,000 more than he was authorized to provide, and that the navy would have to equip a veritable fleet of 12 frigates at tremendous cost to transport them. Reports from the scene indicated that Pascaud had bought low quality grain; shipped in the hot summer months, it would rot in the hold and arrive at Paris "burning" and in urgent need of repair. On this enormous provision, "without having been useful to the State," Pascaud would enjoy an "exorbitant" profit of 2,083,330 *livres*. By rescuing him with naval vessels, Saint-Prest continued, the government would become his accomplice and undermine its right to challenge his accounts and penalize him for his extreme tardiness. "If you persist in sending ships to Italy," the intendant of commerce warned the minister, "you will perpetuate and accredit the indiscreet rumors that this man spread there upon his arrival [when] he announced himself as the necessary man who was sent abroad to save his country from inevitable famine." His braggadocio caused the price to rise and discouraged other French merchants from seeking supplies in the same areas. These merchants, all of whom came from Marseilles, would view the dispatch of ships as "a mortification" and "an affliction" and would surely lose interest in gathering further provisions.[23]

This was the heart of Saint-Prest's case, and unless it is assumed that he was secretly protecting a number of Doumerc-Sorin's allies— the Guys Company, for instance—it was wholly inconsistent with the government's provisioning policy and the kingdom's grain requirements. Saint-Prest took the side of the "merchants of Marseilles" who were not in the government's service against a man commissioned by the government to buy grain for the capital. If Paris urgently needed grain, and other parts of France clamored for assistance, it made no sense to try to sabotage a provisioning mission in mid-course even if the merchant in charge revealed himself to be inept or dishonest. A minister with no ulterior motives would have first made every

---

23 St.-Prest to Boynes, 4, 18 June 1771, *ibid.*

effort to facilitate the delivery of the grain and then, as the government had often done in the past, subjected the merchant to a decade of inquisition and reproach. Allegedly demoralized by Pascaud's dealings, Saint-Prest's Marseillais had nevertheless been able to buy and ship home some 200,000 charges of grain. Unless they could dispose of their grain, he feared, their commerce would stagnate. The government could buy their grain for far less money than Pascaud's venture would ultimately cost and distribute it more rapidly and effectively. What seems extraordinary in Saint-Prest's letters is the suggestion that the Marseilles merchants could not find an outlet at a time when the central government was besieged with requests for supplies. Why it should not have been possible to use both the Marseilles grain and Pascaud's provision he did not say. Nor did the intendant of Provence, who also urged Terray to give preference to the merchants of Marseilles who were "choking" on the abundance of their grain holdings.[24]

Sartine, as Pascaud's sponsor, understandably took umbrage at Saint-Prest's attack. But he replied in remarkably sober terms, ignoring the implicit censure of his judgment and emphasizing what he felt to be the real issue. Although he has always been "exact" in his dealings with me and he received excellent references from French diplomats in Italy who watched him at work, said the Lieutenant General, Pascaud's fate is not what concerns me. "The only thing that interests me," he wrote, "is our provisioning." Quite rightly, Sartine believed that his assessment of the Paris situation should be valued more than that of anyone else. As a result of the acute dearth in Burgundy and other provinces, which forces us to share our supplies with them, the price at the Halles "increases every day." There is absolutely no question that Pascaud's grain "will be extremely useful to us. Even if the last of his provision did not reach us until November, it would still be of great assistance because the new grain of the harvest always reaches us very late and the old grain will surely be exhausted long before then. "In urgent terms, Sartine pressed Boynes to reverse himself again and send the four ships "without delay."[25]

---

24 De La Tour to Terray, 30 Jan. 1771 and to Amelot, 10 April, C. 2452, A.D. B-du-R.

25 Sartine to Boynes, 15 June 1771, AN, F¹¹ 265. A year later Sartine wrote that Pascaud "has conducted himself with all the intelligence, zeal, and disinterest possible [and] that it is partly to him that we owe the current diminution in the price of bread." To Boynes, 9 May 1772, AN, E 330 (colonies).

Pascaud defended himself in a detailed rebuttal which Sartine circulated through the ministry. His provision would not arrive too late to be useful. Twenty-five thousand *septiers* from Naples, already at sea, would arrive in July and August, "epoch when the provisioning of Paris is the most difficult." Grain departing from Rome would be on the Paris market by September, "time when the sowing prevents the *laboureurs* from threshing and frequenting the markets." He had purchased, as commissioned, 50,000 charges, not 200,000 as Saint-Prest pretended. He would need 4 rather than 12 ships and he would help defray the freight costs by paying the government 50 *livres* the tonneau, approximately 15 *livres* less than he would ordinarily have to pay for private transit. He appealed to the navy for transport only because of "the penury of merchant shipping." His profit, Pascaud insisted, would be "very modest," 64,000 *livres*, or less than 4 percent of the anticipated revenue from sales, "barely enough" to cover his expenses. The accusations that he had behaved indiscreetly in his Italian purchases he characterized as premeditated calumnies. He hinted that he was the victim of a plot inspired by jealous rivals and orchestrated by Saint-Prest. To mask their own avarice and enhance their commercial position, they contrived to embarrass him and ruin his operation.[26]

The outcome of the Pascaud affair remains obscure. Boynes told Saint-Florentin, who favored Pascaud, that he would not make a final decision until he had consulted the other ministers. Sartine and Saint-Prest both appear to have courted D'Aiguillon, minister for foreign affairs, even as they had sought the protection of D'Aiguillon's predecessor and rival, Choiseul. Pascaud's grain eventually reached Paris, though it is not clear if he used government or private shipping.[27] His patrons were sufficiently powerful to assure him a continued, albeit subordinate, role in the king's grain operations. In late 1771 and early 1772 Pascaud helped to provide supplies for Rouen, working in collaboration with the powerful Feray merchant family and with the intendant. Between 1772 and 1773 he returned to Italy several times to purchase grain "for the account of the government," perhaps now under the direction of Sorin and Doumerc.[28] According to Pascaud, these operations were not "grain speculations": "I never practiced commerce in grain nor surely will I ever in the future." Surely all

---

26 "Réponse du Sr Pascaud," AN, F[11] 265.
27 The *Journal politique* (Aug. 1771, second *quinzaine*), 61 reported "many boats" on the river between Rouen and Paris bearing king's grain in August 1771.
28 See Pascaud to IN. of Rouen, 7 July 1771 and Sartine to IN., 19 Jan. 1772, C. 106, A.D. S-M.

the great old-regime victualers—Samuel Bernard, Isaac Thellus-son, the Pâris brothers—conceived of their role in the same way. What Pascaud did was "to execute the orders of the ministry" for the "relief of the people." Invited by a Breton correspondent to par-ticipate in an illegal export venture under the cover of the king's grain enterprise, Pascaud rejected the suggestion without flinch-ing: such a scheme was "against my fashion of thinking" as well as "far removed from the ministry's line of thinking."[29] In May 1774, Pascaud's "intimate friend" and business associate, Verdil-hon, who had served as an intermediary between Sartine and Pas-caud in 1771, suffered a massive 4,000,000 *livres* bankruptcy which allegedly brought 24 other major commercial houses down with it. The litigation provoked by the affair tied up a large quantity of grain which Pascaud and Verdilhon had imported.[30]

The quarrel over Pascaud strained relations between Terray and Sartine. Despite the Lieutenant General's endorsements, the Control-ler-General refused to settle the accounts from Pascaud's Paris opera-tions on the grounds that Pascaud had not adequately explained the disposition of "enormous sums." Terray made his displeasure with Sartine public, intimating that the Lieutenant General was more deeply and suspiciously involved in the grain dealing than he cared to admit. Rumor implicated Terray himself in numerous grain specula-tions and he was not, remarked the abbé de Véri, "unhappy to spread the veil of monopolist which covers him in the eyes of the public to M. de Sartine, reputed to be an honest man."[31] Doubtless the Controller-General's offensive pleased Maupeou, who could never forgive Sar-tine for his failure to cooperate in the parlementary purge. Curiously enough, the *économiste* abbé Baudeau, one of Terray's severest critics, helped to spread the charge that the Lieutenant General of Police had a hand in "the grain monopoly."[32] In the spring of 1775, at the very

29 Pascaud to Desruisseaux, 1 July, 5 Aug. 1772 and 29 June, 8 Sept. 1773, II B 53, A.D. Morbihan. (I am deeply indebted to Professor T. Le Goff of York University for all the Morbihan references.)

30 "Chronique," 18 April 1774 and Guys (?) to Sorin (?), 27 May 1774, AN, F¹¹ 1191; Boynes to St.-Prest, 31 May 1771, AN, F¹¹ 265.

31 Véri, *Journal*, ed. by J. de Witte, I, 151. Cf. J.-N. Moreau, *Mes souvenirs*, ed. by Hermelin, II, 187–89 and *Oeuvres de Turgot*, ed. by Schelle, IV, 17.

32 F. Métra, *Correspondance secrète*, II, 17 (1 July 1775); Moreau, *Mes souvenirs*, ed. by C. Hermelin, II, 17, 209–10; Galiani to d'Epinay, 27 July 1770, *Lettres*, ed. by E. Asse, 1,116–17. Baudeau was also reported to have accused Sartine of helping to plan the anti-Turgot Flour War. Pidansat de Mairobert, *Journal historique*, VII, 332.

moment that he ordered the arrest of Doumerc and Sorin and the "purification" of their accounts, the Controller-General Turgot instructed the treasurer of the grain department to pay Pascaud 300,000 *livres*, without, however, indicating which operations the payment was meant to cover.[33]

The American war opened for Pascaud, as it did for Leray de Chaumont and Daure, a whole vista of fresh opportunities. Sartine's appointment to the key post of naval and colonial secretary assured Pascaud many lucrative commissions. Beginning in 1774–75, "he was charged with buying ships, arming them, stocking others, having them disguised under neutral colors, and taking responsibility for the transmission of supplies and food for the colonies." Sartine assigned him a number of extremely delicate missions involving the introduction of funds into England "for secret expenses" and the supply of French colonial ports with foreign monies and with gold and silver for commercial and military needs. Pascaud continued these massive banking operations, involving scores of millions of dollars, into the 1780's. One is not wholly surprised to discover that Leray was one of his partners in this venture for several years. In addition to all this, Pascaud conducted a provisioning operation from the leading Atlantic and Mediterranean ports of the kingdom to keep French colonies supplied with flour, beef, and other goods.[34] In the mid-eighties Pascaud allegedly helped Calonne to place a major government loan and collaborated with this minister in an international conspiracy aimed at toppling some of Europe's most powerful banking and mercantile houses. According to this same source, Pascaud died in 1786 in bankruptcy.[35] That was not, however, the opinion of the government auditors responsible for verifying a decade's tangled accounts. Though they reproached Pascaud for careless bookkeeping, they praised the general conduct of his affairs, his zeal, and his discretion, and declared his estate creditor of 2,951,642 *livres*. What sweet revenge for the calumnies of 1770–71![36]

---

33 Compte, April–May 1775, AN, F^{11} 1195. Elsewhere the sum in question is said to have been 240,000 *livres*. *Oeuvres de Turgot*, ed. by Schelle, IV, 196–97.

34 AN, E 330 (colonies).

35 J. Bouchary, *Les Manieurs d'argent à Paris à la fin du 18ᵉ siècle* (Paris, 1939–40), I, 156–57.

36 AN, E 330 (colonies).

III

By the beginning of 1771, Terray had concentrated the bulk of royal purchases in the hands of Doumerc and Sorin. Although he formed a special council to advise the ministry on subsistence affairs and oversee the operations of the *régie*, he did not convoke it often nor did he bother to keep its members well-informed.[37] Nor did the Controller-General reorganize the grain department to adapt it more efficiently to the task of determining and verifying needs, controlling distribution, and reviewing accounts. Despite the magnitude of the operations and his intention to continue procuring supplies on an occasional basis after the crisis passed, Terray made no effort to give the grain administration a bureaucratic structure. Whereas in finances he labored to establish a rational division of labor and accountability, in grain he left the lines of responsibility blurred. Theoretically, the grain bureau, headed by the 34 year old ex-parlementary counselor Saint-Prest, and composed of a handful of clerks, had charge of the day-to-day victualing business as in the time of Machault and Laverdy.[38] But Terray often bypassed it, personally handling many of the details of the purchases and sales and dealing directly with Doumerc and Sorin. His relationship with them was remarkably informal. Frequently he gave them verbal instructions which were never confirmed in writing. He does not appear to have harassed them incessantly for explanations of their actions. Unlike the Controller-General Orry, who managed the government's grain dealings on the assumption that everyone would try to cheat him, or Trudaine de Montigny, who treated Malisset as a delinquent, Terray seems to have trusted Doumerc and Sorin.

Immediately after the crop was taken each year, the Controller-General and his advisers analyzed the results, projected likely supply against demand, and designed the overall subsistence strategy for the

---

37 "Mémoire en défense de B. de St.-Prest," ca. Oct. 1774, *Oeuvres de Turgot*, ed. by Schelle, IV, 191; Pidansat de Mairobert, *Journal historique*, IV, 204–205 (22 June 1773).

38 Trudaine de Montigny allegedly "asked the king to be discharged in the future from the grain department" in June. Terray to IN. of Bordeaux, 11 June 1770, C. 1431, A.D. Gir. Terray dismissed him sometime before autumn and personally assumed control of the department. St.-Prest did not become titular head until early 1772. Amelot to Mesnard de Cornichard, 22 Dec. 1770, AN, H 187; Terray to INs. of Champagne and Provence, 18 Feb. 1772, C. 379, A.D. Marne and C. 2445, A.D. B-du-R.; IN. of Languedoc to Toulouse SD, 26 Feb. 1772, C. 2063, A.D. H-G.; Terray to IN. of Bordeaux, 14 Oct. 1773, C. 1442, A.D. Gir.

harvest year—concrete measures to be taken immediately and flexible contingency plans to be implemented in case of necessity. In August 1772, for example, given the generally good harvest in the north and east, it was expected that direct supply intervention would be necessary only in the south, the southwest, the Lyonnais, Brittany, and as always, for safety's sake, the Paris region. A year later, the grain department drew up an elaborate provisioning plan based upon an evaluation of the previous year's efforts, an assessment of international as well as domestic market factors, and an examination of political and psychological as well as technological variables that affected grain distribution. The forecast resembled the predictions of 1772: Burgundy, part of Normandy, and the Dauphiné joined the Paris area and the provinces of the south and west as likely candidates for subsistence support. The plans paid more attention to charting out a geography of demand than to mapping out sources of supply. The assumption seemed to be that if a region genuinely needed grain somehow the grain would be procured. Nevertheless, the planners made an effort to appraise supply alternatives, to rank them in terms of economic and political cost, and to match them with specific areas of need. The instructional outlines addressed to the victualers were supple; they gave Doumerc and Sorin considerable autonomy in executing their mission. As a rule the directors of the *régie* decided where to buy (though Terray told them where to sell), they chose their own agents, and they made their own financial arrangements.

The plans were noteworthy for their imagination and their ambition but overall resource planning—the construction of hypotheses rather than of granaries—was of limited use in dealing with subsistence uncertainties. Indeed, the very notion of planning, as we understand it, was an anachronism in an age before bureaucracy and easy long distance communication. Victualing tended to degenerate into a highly empirical operation under the pressure of changing circumstances and fresh information. This tendency was reinforced by a desire to avoid irrevocable commitments until the last possible moment in order to test their relevance. Nor did Terray's staff, like some of our modern planners, stubbornly cling to the plan well after it was clear that it could not work, as if to show displeasure with reality for not conforming to their scenario. They simply abandoned it in practice, though Terray found it politically useful to sustain the illusion of a plan in order to create the impression of control where in fact there was confusion.

The extreme paucity of extant papers precludes a searching examination of the operations of the *régie*. Between 1771 and 1774, Doumerc and Sorin spent approximately 15,000,000 *livres* on grain purchases for the government. We do not know how much money the government received from the sales of the king's grain but it is certain that its losses were in the millions. The *régie* paid a 2 percent commission on the purchase price to an original buying agent, say Francois Rottenburgh at Danzig, and a further 2 percent on the value of the merchandise plus expenses incurred to a commercial house which received and processed the grain or flour in France, say Plantes at Rouen or Feray or Baudry and Boulongne at Le Havre. In addition, the *régie* covered the costs of shipping, insurance, conditioning, and storage of the merchandise. Like the Malisset company Doumerc and Sorin were entitled to a 2 percent commission for their services, though it is not clear whether they earned it twice, once on the purchase and again on the sale.[39]

There is no satisfactory way to appraise the grave charges, which Turgot later made, that most of the king's grain was purchased in the interior rather than abroad, thus driving up prices, destroying local commerce, and aggravating the *cherté*.[40] Pascaud claimed that the ministry wanted its victualers to do their shopping abroad and that he never made any purchases in the interior. But Pascaud did not speak for the *régie*.[41] Fragments of correspondence in the papers of the Bertier de Sauvigny family (intendants of the *généralité* of Paris) give numerous examples of domestic purchasing operations. In the fall of 1770 or in early 1771, Doumerc wrote to one Noireau, an innkeeper in a Burgundy hamlet where the Bertier family owned considerable amounts of land, that the *régie* had "a continual need of grain for the upkeep of the King's Magazines and I would like to be able to draw some from your area provided the prices allow it." He offered to absorb all the grain that Noireau could procure and he promised to send replacement grain from the *régie's* stock if the area should suddenly find itself short. The manner in which the arrangement actually worked out is not entirely clear. We know for certain that Doumerc sent government

---

39 According to their critics, Sorin and Doumerc not only claimed a double commission on sale as well as on purchase but, as a result of phantom companies they created and named as intermediaries in their bookkeeping, they actually collected as much as 8% commmission on many transactions. See "Réponse au mémoire des Sieurs Sorin et Doumerc," ca. 1774–75, AN, K 908.

40 *Oeuvres*, ed. by Schelle, IV, 188.

41 Pascaud to Desruisseaux, 8 Sept. 1773, II B. 53, A.D. Morbihan.

grain for sale in the local markets upon the request of Bertier on a number of occasions between 1771 and 1773. It cannot be determined, however, how much grain Noireau bought for Doumerc and whether his instructions to buy remained in effect even after the *régie* began to send grain into his area. In a letter addressed to Bertier in June 1771 Doumerc complained that local inhabitants were inhibiting the efforts of his agents to buy grain in other areas of Burgundy.

More than two years later, in a note meant for himself, or his secretary, the substance of which we know reached Doumerc, Bertier wrote:

> Grain is diminishing in price a great deal in these areas [presumably near his Burgundian estates]. It would appear useful to make purchases there. Speak to Doumerc about this.

Had a note such as this fallen into the hands of a Leprévost de Beaumont or of anyone else who had reason to distrust the government or its grain operations, it would have been taken as evidence of a famine-pact plot or at least of a highly suspect form of speculation. On the surface, such an inference is not wholly implausible, though, to be sure, one would need to marshal a great deal more proof before drawing up an indictment. On the other hand, it is possible to explain Bertier's remark in terms that are not incriminating. It may have been "useful" to force the price up in order to reduce losses on the sale of the king's grain. Or it may have struck Bertier as a propitious moment to replenish the stock of the royal magazines now that prices were falling. In whatever way one interprets Bertier's note, however, it does lend some credence to Turgot's critique of the *régie's* operation.[42]

On a partial accounting register of the 1772 operations, a great many purchases appear to have been made within the kingdom. Grain and flour procured at Soissons, Châlons, Etampes, Bray, Presle, and Amiens surely were of French origin.[43] Malisset is listed for selling 80,000 *livres* worth of flour to the government in 1772, probably only a small part of what he supplied during the lifetime of the *régie*. Dure, one of Malisset's former commissioners, also bought for

---

42 All the following references are from AN, 80 AP 19 (Bertier de Sauvigny papers): Doumerc to Noireau, Sept. 1770 or early 1771; Doumerc to Rives, 19 Jan. 1772; Doumerc to B. de Sauvigny, 5 Sept. 1772; Terray to B. de Sauvigny, 4 June 1771; Doumerc to B. de Sauvigny, 3 June 1771; memo by B. de Sauvigny, 11 Sept. 1773.

43 AN, F11* 5. According to this register, during the course of 1772 the *régie* expended 4,092,359 *livres* in the purchase of grain and flour. From the sale of this merchandise, the *régie* realized 2,550,019 *livres*.

the *régie* in the interior.[44] But we cannot be certain that grain purchased at St. Malo, Nantes, Bordeaux, and Marseilles did not come from abroad in private hands. The same recordbook indicates grain purchases at Danzig and several hundred thousand *livres* worth of flour imported from "Nouvelle-York," "Balthimore," and "Philadelphie." The *régie* conducted extensive buying operations in Italy, North Africa, and the Levant assisted by the French diplomatic and consular corps. Doumerc and Sorin charted the availability of supplies on the international market in detailed "tableaux" for the "north," the "ocean," and the Mediterranean.[45]

The fact is that the government had to intervene much more massively on the supply side than it had anticipated during the year following the 1772 harvest. Though every effort was made to procure grain abroad, unfavorable political and economic conditions in the leading foreign markets compelled the government to order purchases throughout the interior in a desperate effort to transfer the "national" surplus from the north, northeast and east to the south, southwest, and west.[46] The *régie*'s correspondents interfered with internal grain circulation in countless ways. They scoured the kingdom for supplies, arousing resentment all along their path. "We cannot deny all the difficulties that had to be overcome in order to make purchases in the interior of the kingdom," conceded a report drafted by the grain department;

the people became alarmed [and] even the courts and administrators complained and failed to cooperate; the precautions taken by the government were seen merely as an exclusive privilege accorded to individuals; justice was not done to the views which inspired the officials in charge; monopoly! was cried out, [though] unjust and without foundation these cries produced fermentation which once born is very difficult to check.

---

44 Archives Seine-Paris, D5B⁶ 531; AN, F¹¹* 5 (Feb. 1772). See, for other commercial relations in the Paris region, the *faillite* of Louis Leroy, 26 May 1773, Archives Seine-Paris, D4B⁶ 47–2845.

45 Guys (?) to Sorin and Doumerc (?), 23 May 1774, AN F¹¹ 1191; "Instructions," 8 Sept. 1773, *ibid.*; Sorin and Doumerc to Guys, Dec. 1773, *ibid.*

Two of the merchant-brokers used by Sorin and Doumerc for foreign purchases, Montaudouin, liberal militant, polemist, and international trader of Nantes, and Drouin of Saumur, had supplied grain for the *généralité* of Limoges at the request of its intendant Turgot in 1770. See Turgot to CG, 9 March 1770 and Turgot to Bertier de Sauvigny, 13 Jan. 1770, in *Oeuvres de Turgot*, ed. by Schelle, III, 137, 253. Cf. Dumas, *Tours*, 347–48.

46 St.-Prest (?), "Mémoire," Sept. 1773, C. 1441, A.D. Gir.; Anon., "Mémoire," 20 April 1773, AN, K 908. Despite adverse circumstances, the government managed to buy large quantities of grain and flour in Sicily, the Baltic, and New England. St.-Prest to d'Aiguillon, 21 Dec. 1772, France 1740, fols. 56–57, Arch. AE; Terray to IN. of Rouen, 9 Jan. 1772, C. 106, A.D. S-M.

This climate of fear and uncertainty paralyzed private commerce. Merchants protested that they were denied access to their ordinary sources of supply and that they were driven away from their usual outlets by unfair outside competition. The *régie*'s buying agents created in their wake a current of "artificial dearth" that aggravated real distribution difficulties. At the time it seemed clear that those purchases *had* to be made and they were justified by the crucial services they rendered in many places. They proved, however, to be costly in every sense, the grain department report concluded frankly, and, ultimately, "the kingdom suffered more than its position should have caused us to fear."[47]

The indiscretions and incompetence of some of the *régie*'s agents, as a number of officials charged, probably were responsible for some of the disorders that accompanied the grain purchases. But given the enormous scale and range of the operations and the recent history of subsistence problems, it is hard to imagine how the *régie* could have avoided causing ferment. In the end what mattered above all was Terray's fierce determination to provide urgently needed supplies whatever the risks and difficulties involved. Without any precise notion how he would fulfill his pledge, the Controller-General guaranteed the Toulouse *capitouls*, the Bordeaux intendant, and other deficit-area officials in the course of 1772–73 that "you will not lack subsistence." He assured the administrators of surplus regions that they had nothing to fear from buying incursions into their territory. Indeed, he promised he would authorize such purchases only so long "as they did not trouble public order" or cause "price rises." Yet the Controller-General pressed intendants unremittingly to assist the *régie*'s commissioners regardless of short-term consequences, vaguely promising recompenses for compliance and menacing retribution for disobedience. Only when complaints threatened to have major repercussions—such as in Burgundy in March 1773—did Terray have the *régie* recall its agents. When he could not count on the protection of the intendant or some other highly placid provincial official, he ordered the secret dispatch of buyers with instructions to effect their purchases rapidly without revealing their aims to anyone. Nor did the Controller-General shrink from lying in the name of public good. He categorically disavowed, in a letter to one intendant, anyone who claimed to be "charged with

47 St.-Prest (?), "Mémoire," Sept. 1773, C. 1461, A.D. Gir.; St.-Prest, "Mémoire en défense de B. de St.-Prest," in *Oeuvres de Turgot*, ed. by Schelle, IV, 190–94; AN, F¹² 727; interrogation of Doumerc, May 1775, Arsenal, mss. Bastille 12447; Doumerc to Rives, 18 June 1773, AN 80 AP 19 (B. de Sauvigny papers).

undertaking a grain operation for the king's account." Only when that same intendant surprised Terray with irrefutable proof that a *négotiant* was maintaining a royal flour stock did the Controller-General, without apology and with obvious annoyance, acknowledge "that I had hoped to keep that secret...."[48]

The experience of 1772–73 left its mark upon the grain department and the *régie* as well as on public opinion. In the planning scenario composed in September 1773 for the following harvest year, the government explicitly renounced "official" grain purchasing in the interior (save for the constitution of the Paris safety-valve stock) in order to "avoid fermentation." Though such a procedure was contrary to Terray's desire for control, the plan envisaged "charging the intendants to find [their own] merchants to draw the necessary grain from the interior" if private commerce fell short of the task. As if to repent for having brutalized commerce in 1772–73, the plan took as its leitmotif the need to maintain, "with the greatest care and by all available means, free circulation in the interior." To be sure, the government would intervene, as circumstances required, on the supply side, but only with the stocks of foreign grain—projected at 700,000 *septiers*—stored in the principal ports.[49] At about the time that the grain department approved the plan, Terray personally addressed himself to the merchant community which remained hesitant to launch grain speculations "for fear of being undermined in their operations by individuals claiming to be under orders of the administration...." The Controller-General promised that "no order from me will be given which concerns the acquisition of grain in your province." Reiterating his non-intervention pledge, several months later Terray assured the intendant of Languedoc of his desire to see "commerce regain full confidence."[50] When the secretary to the intendant of Burgundy proposed that the central government take complete charge of the distribution of royal grain in that province, Terray uncharacteristically refused. Given the state of public opinion, he preferred to see local brokers assume the task of marketing the foreign grain which the king would deliver.[51]

48 Terray to Toulouse *capitouls*, 26 April 1773, C. 2914, A.D. Hér.; Terray to Esmangart, 31 March 1773, C. 1441, A.D. Gir.; Terray to Amelot, 6 Oct., 8 Dec. 1772 and 9 March 1773, C. 81, A.D. Cd'O.; Terray to Esmangart, 25 Nov. 1773, C. 1442, A.D. Gir. On the persistence of administrative suspicion of the Controller-General's buying plans, see IN. of Hainaut to Terray, 4 Aug. 1774, C. 6690, A.D. Nord.

49 C. 1441, A.D. Gir.

50 Terray to Chambers of Commerce of Marseilles and Montpellier, 1 Sept. 1773, C. 2915 and Terray to IN., 3 Feb. 1774, C. 2916, A.D. Hér.

51 Contrôle-Général to Robert, 18 June 1773, C. 81, A.D. C d'O.

Terray honored the spirit of his pledge if not the letter. *Régie* agents did make domestic purchases, more or less clandestinely, in the course of the year.[52] The scale of their operations, however, was far more modest than it had been in 1772–73. More favorable conditions on some of the major European grain markets following the harvest of 1773 encouraged the government to eschew domestic buying. Still, the government did not escape the sort of reproaches it had elicited at the zenith of its internal purchasing activities. Terray's pious renunciations did little to dissipate the fund of suspicion which he developed over the previous few years. For certain critics it made no difference whether the provenance of the bulk of the king's grain was national or foreign: one form of intervention was virtually as pernicious as the other. Nor was it always clear whether the grain which the government moved from one part of the kingdom to another was domestic or foreign. If merchants could be relatively sure that they would not have to compete with government commissioners for the purchase of grain, nevertheless they still had to worry about encountering king's grain when they were ready to market their stocks.

Fragments of surviving correspondence suggest that Doumerc and Sorin planned their missions carefully and kept in regular contact with their key representatives. For the 1773 provisioning operation in the Midi each agent had precise instructions on the course to follow. The directors insisted on the need for discretion, to avoid arousing the suspicions of the public and the outcries of private dealers. Four different agents at Marseilles were to distribute the first shipment of 20,000 charges. The prime agent, Bourguignon, was to "give the impression" that the grain was his personal "speculation" rather than the property of the government. Through "simulated sales," he would pass it on as circumstances required to the other Marseilles commissioners and to agents of Aix and other areas in the interior.[53] To meet unanticipated needs, Doumerc and Sorin told the buyers at home and abroad to neglect no attractive source of supply: "it is better to have 10,000 charges more than 5,000 less."[54] No other instruction could have better captured Terray's victualing ambitions nor better demonstrated the fidelity with which the *régie* directors implemented the Controller-General's conception.

---

52 See, for example, *procès-verbal* drawn by Toulouse SD, 2 Oct. 1774, C. 2916 and Béziers SD to Languedoc IN., 31 Oct. 1774, C. 2917, A.D. Hér.

53 "Instructions," 8 Sept. 1773, AN, F[11] 1191.

54 Sorin and Doumerc to Guys, 10 Aug. 1773, *ibid.*

While they placed no formal ceiling on the price which the buyers could pay for prospective king's grain, in the selling phase they insisted on economy and prudence. The aim of the operation was to provide help, without, however, destroying independent dealers or convulsing the market. The gradual return of abundance would gently depress prices. The king's grain was not to be used in a blitzkrieg maneuver to restore prices to pre-dearth levels overnight. Victualing may have been incompatible with grain liberation but Sorin and Doumerc were not oblivious to the political and economic implications of governmental intervention. "By marching alongside commerce," wrote Doumerc and Sorin, "we have reason to hope that the prices of the sales will answer for the prices of the purchases: the contrary would announce that there is no need and it would be necessary to cease or suspend shipments to the places which promise losses."

While the *régie* directors kept close watch on all the aspects of the mammoth provisioning operation, not all the agents who comprised the network knew in fact that they were working for Sorin and Doumerc. In the hope of simplifying their dealings and making them appear as inconspicuous and innocuous as possible, Sorin and Doumerc purposely kept a considerable number of their agents at the base in the dark about the specific nature of the business. This was a calculated risk founded on the premise that news of government involvement usually had adverse commercial and political effects. Besides promoting discretion, the tactic of secrecy enabled the *régie* to manipulate its unknowing agents with greater ease, to appeal strictly to their interest without encumbering the profit incentive with extraneous considerations which could lead them astray, and to make communications between the center and the field more efficient by rationalizing the lines of authority.

On the other hand, this disingenuousness had disadvantages. Lack of information about the purposes of their task handicapped the agents in buying and selling at certain junctures, forcing them to pay more and accept less than they could have done. It is hard to believe that the instructions they received did not raise suspicions in the minds of some of the agents, thus causing them to act with less zeal than they might have otherwise. Finally, this practice clearly attenuated the amount of direct control which Sorin and Doumerc could exercise, especially in the auditing of accounts. The *régie* became dependent on a number of middle-level brokers who were generally neither wealthy enough to answer for the failures or infidelities of the agents at the base nor cunning enough to prevent them. The *régie*'s use of blind commissions resulted in considerable embarrassment and anguish for many of the agents when Turgot came to power and set about investigating and closing down the victualing organization. The *régie*'s papers revealed that Embry of Agde, Liron of Lunel, Gottis of Béziers, and Mergue of Montpellier, among others, were all part of the network. Yet each faced perjury charges when he vigorously—and truthfully!—denied ever having heard of or dealt with Sorin and Doumerc of Paris.[55]

The *régie*'s commissioners varied widely in background, wealth, range, and size of business. At the bottom of the hierarchy were myriad humble brokers—not *blatiers* by any means but not imposing entrepreneurs either. The "blind" agents fell into this category along with the local commissioners who supplied Paris from domestic sources. An intermediate rank was held by the chief regional correspondents who managed the blind commissions at the same time that they bought and sold in their own right for the *régie*. The agent responsible for domestic operations in Languedoc, for example, was Perrouteau, a very substantial merchant from Montauban. While he conducted the *régie*'s distribution and stockage program, Perrouteau engaged in grain commerce on a grander scale than ever before. Expanding his dealings to include flour production and trade, he established a quasi-industrial milling operation geared for colonial as well as high-grade domestic provisioning and magazines throughout the province. Like Malisset, whom he resembled in a number of ways, Perrouteau did not bother to distinguish carefully between royal grain and flour and the stocks with which he dealt in his own name. The fact that his agents were not aware that they were more often than not operating for the *régie* facilitated and compounded the confusion. Ultimately it invited charges of fraud and malversation.[56]

The third general type of commissioner employed by the *régie* was the international trader or banker. In its most prestigious embodiment, this type of agent would resemble a Leray de Chaumont drawn by the lure of adventure and profit or a Samuel Bernard, more or less earnestly responding to a call to civil charity. It could hardly be said that agents of this sort worked for the *régie*. In fact, Terray himself seems

---

55 See, for example, Embry to St.-Priest, 30 Sept. 1774, C. 2916, A.D. Hér.; Liron to same, 17 Nov. 1774, C. 2916, *ibid.*; Gottis to same, 2 Oct. 1774, C. 2917, *ibid.*; Mergue to same, 8 Nov. 1774, C. 2916, *ibid.*

56 Gorsse to Turgot, 3 Oct., 15 Dec. 1774, C. 2916, *ibid.*; Turgot to St.-Priest, 26 Nov. 1774, C. 2916, *ibid.*; Etat Perrouteau, 30 Sept. 1774, C. 2917, *ibid.*

to have been responsible for recruiting the handful who participated in the victualing operations of his ministry. Bethmann of Bordeaux played such a role in the 1770's. Member of a German banking family at Frankfurt and represented in the principal European trading cities, Bethmann used his ability to marshal huge amounts of capital and his international connections to launch a diversified import-export business centered at Bordeaux. During the Seven Years' War Bethmann earned the gratitude of the French government for his banking services, a debt which the government partially repaid by favoring the commercial ventures of the Bethmann company, several of which involved grain and flour exportation. Honored with consular titles from Russia and Austria, Bethmann had links with the philosophical community through Grimm, an old friend from Germany, and Madame d'Epinay, whose feckless son he briefly received as a clerk in his office. Though commerce was said to be his all-consuming obsession and profits and losses his overriding preoccupation, there is no reason to doubt his contention that his house accepted the *régie*'s commission to import flour and grain "to respond to the views of humanity which appear to me to be the soul of this operation." Like Bernard, Thellusson, and Necker, Bethmann knew that philanthropy was good business as well as good works in a society where so much depended on favor, privilege, and reputation. He himself had learned the lesson in 1749 when he imported English grain in the midst of a terrible dearth upon the request of the Bordeaux town fathers.[57]

Except for special situations, the king's grain had never been envisioned, with Samuel Bernard in 1725, with Orry and Isaac Thellusson in 1740, or with Machault and Courteille in the fifties, as an eleemosynary undertaking. The government became victualer to fill the gap which private production and distribution could not cover. Habitually, the king's grain was marketed at or just below the current price. Offers significantly below "the current" usually meant that the government's grain was of inferior quality. In the fifties and sixties, local officials complained that the king's grain was not used more decisively to combat the *cherté*. The unwillingness of the government to dispose of the extraordinary supplies with greater abandon reinforced suspicions that the king's grain

---

57 Bethmann to Terray, 25 May 1773, C. 1441, A.D. Gir.; Bethmann to Courteille, s.d. [1758], C. 1666, A.D. I-et-V.; G. Maugras and L. Perey, *Une femme du monde au 18ᵉ siècle*, 270–71, 274; J. Tarrade, *Le Commerce colonial*, I, 307; Herbert Lüthy, *La Banque protestante*, II, 114–15, 355, 720; Alfred Leroux, *La Colonie germanique de Bordeaux* (Bordeaux, 1918), I, 63–64.

was a speculative, money-making enterprise. For the distribution of the king's grain in parts of Burgundy, the *régie* instructed the local agents to sell slightly below the current, the "unique object" of the operation being "to remedy the dearth." The current price in this instance was itself quite high and the yield from the sale of king's grain probably covered its cost.[58]

"Try not to lose," Doumerc and Sorin urged the agents. The *régie* directors were not blithely indifferent, as Turgot claimed, to the burdens of the public treasury. But, they added, "not making money must not drive you away: we make a case for the cost margins only to parry the inevitable losses but we can also do without profits."[59] If the actions of the Toulon agent were not atypical, it appears that the policy of parsimony was respected. "We are not selling," he reported in April 1774, "because the prices are low with respect to what the grain costs and because we have no grain which is likely to spoil."[60] At Bordeaux, despite their experience in international trade, the *régie*'s agents Bethmann and Desclaux made no decisions concerning marketing without contacting the Contrôle-Générale.[61]

In the name of economy, the directors of the *régie* demanded that their agents submit detailed financial accounts promptly and at regular intervals. "We live in a time which demands the greatest exactitude [even] from the most orderly persons," they wrote their Marseilles correspondent.[62] When he recruited the innkeeper Noireau to serve as a buying and selling agent, Doumerc imposed only one condition: "You must keep accounts in the greatest detail and the greatest order so that I can always be in a position to judge the purposes of your expenses and the amount of grain you measure out." From his relations with the intendant Bertier we know that Doumerc was insistent that the *régie* be paid rapidly for grain that it provided. "I am in the most pressing need [of cash]," he wrote one agent, "my bookkeeping languishes, my money-box awaits your assistance."[63] Once they justified

---

58 The following letters are all from AN, 80 AP 19 (Bertier de Sauvigny papers): B. de Sauvigny to Rives, 10, 17 July 1770; B. de Sauvigny to Baudot, 17 Sept. 1770; *régie* to Baudot, 20 July 1770. Cf. Sorin and Doumerc's instruction to an agent at Vannes to sell "always following the current price." To Desruisseaux, 29 Feb., 20 March, 26 April 1773, II B. 53, A.D. Morbihan.

59 Sorin and Doumerc to Guys, 10 Aug. 1773, AN, F¹¹ 1191. Cf. Sorin and Doumerc to Guys, 18 Sept. 1773, *ibid.*

60 "Chroniques," 25 April 1774, *ibid.*

61 See Terray to Esmangart, 14 Oct. 1773, C. 1442, A.D. Gir.

62 Sorin and Doumerc to Guys, 23 Oct. 1773, AN, F¹¹ 1191.

63 The following references are all from AN, 80 AP 19 (Bertier de Sauvigny

their accounts and honored their obligations, the *regie's* correspondents received their 2 percent commission plus costs. A Breton agent who persistenly demanded 3 percent found his billing reduced every time. Nor did he succeed in persuading the directors to join with him in, and thereby in a sense legitimize, a project for exporting grain—a project devised at the very time the government was engaged in an all-out war against dearth. Though they were later accused of certain illicit activities, in this instance Sorin and Doumerc were unequivocal: "We reiterate to you that we will have nothing at all to do with an operation in the style of the one you spoke to us about."[64]

IV

The *regie's* most important correspondent in the south, Guys and Company, was one of the most prominent commercial establishments in Marseilles.[65] Scion of a family-based trading empire with interests in shipping, banking, textile manufacturing, and commerce of all sorts stretching from Cairo and Constantinople to Amsterdam and Copenhagen, Pierre Augustin Guys was a 51-year-old former deputy of the Chamber of Commerce and first *échevin* of Marseilles, his native city. In the sixties, he joined forces with Pierre Rémuzat, whose family had settled in Marseilles in the seventeenth century, and enjoyed a meteoric rise to wealth, status, and local political power, in part as a result of successes in grain importing.

In November 1764, on Laverdy's orders, Sartine dispatched two inspectors of the Paris police to Marseilles to arrest Guys and his brother-in-law and sometimes partner, Etienne-Baltazar Gautier, a *négociant* with forty years experience, on suspicion of illicit and abusive export of grain. Under any circumstances it would have been unusual to *embastiller* two highly esteemed business and civic leaders. It was especially striking at the end of 1764, for Laverdy had just promulgated

---

papers): Doumerc to Noireau, n.d. (1771); état, 20 Aug. 1771; Doumerc to Rives, 1 Aug. 1771; Doumerc to B. de Sauvigny, 5 Sept. 1772; Doumerc to B. de Sauvigny, 3 June 1771.

64 Sorin and Doumerc to Desruisseaux, ? July, 25 Aug., 4 Sept. 1773, II B. 53, A.D. Morbihan.

65 The following paragraph is based on the interrogation, Arsenal, mss. Bastille 12223 and Gaston Rambert, *Histoire du commerce de Marseille* (Paris, 1954–1966), IV, 363–64, 380–82, 509–10. Cf. the erratic piece by H. Pellissier-Guys, "Le Séjour d'un négociant marseillais à la Bastille," *Provincia*, III (1923), 18–34.

the law authorizing exporting, a law motivated in part by his desire to induce men of substance like Guys and his associates to undertake grain speculations.

The interrogation of the prisoners revealed that the ministry suspected them of hoarding, lying, maneuvering to keep grain from the public, and attempting to suborn and bribe public officials. Gautier, later joined by Guys, was one of approximately thirty Marseilles *négociants* who sought to profit from the grave scarcity and astronomically high prices, which afflicted Italy in the early sixties, by provisioning its major cities with grain from the interior of France. He gathered thousands of charges of grain from as far away as Brittany and Normandy, not, he insisted, from the areas which normally supplied the markets of Provence.

To export grain from Marseilles, which had a special commercial regime vis-à-vis the rest of France and foreign nations, the trader had to solicit the approval of the intendant and the city's granary-victualing organization, the bureau of abundance, half of whose members were "notable *négociants*." "In order not to obstruct commerce in a free city," the bureau, according to Guys and Gautier, "shut its eyes to the outflow of grain." Guys claimed that the intendant De La Tour never denied permission for export to businessmen who had in the past rendered the province useful services. Gautier, however, reported that the intendant initially refused to sanction the exports.

Finally, after intense pressure from the *negociants*, De La Tour agreed to grant a limited number of authorizations. He declined several exotic gifts, including 100 bottles of fine Malaga wine, which Guys and Gautier offered for his consideration and he would not allow his wife to accept a share in one of the ships destined for Italy (his subdelegate, however, took a thousand-charge portion in the speculation). The other *négociants* turned to Gautier and Guys for help in securing one of the few export licenses to be issued. Though they insisted that permits were not sold, Gautier and Guys admitted that they were "borrowed and exchanged" among the *négociants*. Gautier readily confessed that he followed the common practice of loading one-fifth to one-quarter more grain than the permits allowed by bribing the official measurers. The final accounting, Gautier maintained, will show that he and Guys will have lost money despite their "infinite care and attention," for they appear to have purchased more grain than they could profitably sell. The government apparently decided that it did not have sufficient material to prosecute the two *négociants*.

Sartine released them from jail after less than two weeks but required them to remain in Paris while the investigation continued through the beginning of the new year.

Seven and a half years later, the Terray *régie* entrusted Guys and Company with the delicate task of arranging the importation and the distribution of large quantities of grain in the Midi.[66] On the whole the Guys connection seems to have worked admirably. Guys arranged for the purchase of grain throughout the Mediterranean—surely no one had better contacts in the area—found capable men to take charge of the reception and marketing of the grain, and advised the directors of the *régie* on the peculiarities of the subsistence situation in the Midi. In 1772 Guys personally visited Italy to assure the buying operations would proceed "without noise." Fearing that the Italian authorities would soon ban exports as a result of burgeoning subsistence problems of their own, Guys purchased as much grain as he could locate. In a letter to the grain department, he promised to arrange the sale of the grain in France "so as not to frighten or deter the individual speculator whose collaboration is so necessary to keep up the distribution of supplies." Hailing the undertaking as a model of its kind, Saint-Prest praised the "intelligence" and "honesty" of the Marseilles businessman.[67] One of the Guys-directed operations, however, went awry and provoked a scandal which seriously tarnished his company's reputation and gave credence to doubts about the entegrity of Doumerc and Sorin.

Guys commissioned a Sieur Feraud, an old Levant hand, to buy at least 10,000 charges of grain in Greece and Turkey in the fall of 1773. To facilitate his dealings, the government was to give him a vice-consul's post. Guys claimed that in order to guarantee Feraud's discretion, he did not inform him that the purchases were to be made for the government. On the basis of the testimony of the French ambassador at Constantinople, the government later contended that Feraud knew precisely the true nature of his mission. Guys advanced funds to Feraud for the grain purchases, partly, it appears, in the form of goods that he was to market at the ports where he debarked. For political and

---

66 Sorin and Doumerc to Guys, 10 Aug. 1773 and "Instructions," 8 Sept. 1773, AN, F[11] 1181; "Observations sur la correspondance du Sr Guys & Cie ... compte actuellement en discussion" (dossier containing material compiled between 1774 and 1781) and "Mémoire pour les Srs Guys et Cie," *ibid.* Rambert's treatment of the *régie* is highly unreliable and misinformed. *Commerce de Marseille*, IV, 364–65.

67 Guys to d'Aiguillon (?), 14 Dec. 1772 and St.-Prest to d'Aiguillon, 21 Dec. 1772, France 1740, fols. 54–56, Arch. AE.

commercial reasons, Feraud found the conditions for grain purchase highly unfavorable. While he waited for a change in fortune, Guys suggested that he invest the grain money in other goods for shipment to France rather than "keep the funds inertly in the cashbox." Feraud appears to have followed Guys' advice. Ultimately, he sent only one shipload of grain to Marseilles.

Guys claimed to have suffered huge losses in what the *régie* recognized from the beginning to be a high-risk undertaking. He insisted that the government should assume responsibility for the deficit. Albert, who returned to power with Turgot in mid-1774, refused to compensate Guys. Indeed, he demanded that the Marseillais reimburse the government for sums improperly spent or unaccounted for.[68] There is little doubt that Guys used the Feraud expedition for his own commercial purposes. Even if he did not use royal funds to finance his non-grain speculations, he entangled his public charge and his private business, a practice that was extremely common among financiers and *armateurs*, but which undercut his moral position when he sought financial relief.

It is interesting to note that, at several junctures during their collaboration in 1773–74, Guys passed speculative tips on to Doumerc and Sorin and invited them to join ventures which he promised would be lucrative. In August 1774, they rejected a Guys proposition to invest in the purchase of Dutch and Austrian wheat for private import and distribution. (Obviously Guys the trader was not afraid to compete against Guys the government agent/victualer!) "At any other time we would come in with pleasure," they wrote apologetically, "but until we have finished the accounts we have with the Government, we do not permit ourselves any personal speculation on this article."[69] Guys continued to seek vindication and compensation for the Levant operation through the next decade. The head of the grain department in the early eighties, Montaran, who also inherited the Malisset accounts, determined that Guys owed the king 64,082 *livres*. Shortly afterward, Guys and Company filed bankruptcy papers.[70]

---

68 "Chronique," 22 April 1774, AN, F[11] 1191. Albert accused Sorin and Doumerc of conspiring with Guys to divert government funds from grain buying to speculation in sugar, foreign currency and other commodities. Memoir to the king, 16 Oct. 1774, *Oeuvres de Turgot*, ed. by Schelle, IV, 187.

69 Sorin and Doumerc to Guys, 23 Aug. 1774, AN, F[11] 1191.

70 "Subsistances," (1788), AN, F[11] 1173. In the 1780's the government tried to recover other funds which remained due as a result of the *régie's*, sales (for example, the Ursulines of Vézelay and the municipality of Châlons-sur-Marne both owed sums for grains purchased) and advances (several Marseilles merchants). "Etats de Recette de Rouillé de l'Estang," AN, F[11] 1195.

V

Terray's *régie* differed in many ways from the provisioning apparatus that Laverdy fashioned. The Malisset operation was established in a time of relative serenity as a reserve fund to meet the emergency requirements of the capital. Malisset created the Corbeil establishment with the idea of making it the center of a vast industrial-commercial complex serving public and private needs. The government planned to utilize it during a transitional period for specific, limited ends. From the beginning, the ministry viewed the enterprise with ambivalence. On the one hand, it could be justified as a political device contrived to buffer the capital against the dislocating effects of liberalization, compounded by the uncertainties caused by harvest failure. On the other hand, it was a source of embarrassment, a reflection of the minister's own doubts about the viability of his program, and a lode-stone for popular fears and scurrilous innuendo. Malisset never enjoyed the full confidence of the government, even after Leray and the other guarantors joined the organization. A hybrid creature, part company, part *régie*, its structural ambiguities inspired distrust and resentment on all sides. The enormous strain of trying to sustain liberalization, combat the hostile parlements, and deal with disaffected police officials and an anxious public prevented the government from making the Malisset enterprise an effective arm in the service of its own policy.

In contrast, the Doumerc-Sorin operation had a less anguished beginning, though it was launched at the peak of the crisis. Terray did not rush impulsively into the king's grain business, but neither did he ulcerate about the legitimacy or wisdom of his decision to move ahead. It seemed to him perfectly proper and necessary for the state to intervene; for Terray, there was no disjuncture between his general grain policy and his resort to the king's grain. He launched the operation not in anticipation of future needs but to cope with pressing demands. For the provisioning of Paris he inherited a superb installation at Corbeil, along with its branch magazines, as well as a network of agents who had previously worked for Malisset. Doumerc himself had an intimate knowledge of the merits and defects of the Malisset system and of the characteristics of the Parisian supply lines. Infinitely greater in scope than the Malisset affair, the Doumerc-Sorin design stretched across the entire breadth of the kingdom. Paris remained privileged, but no areas were off limits, for purchases or for sales.

The organization was unequivocally a *régie*, a wholly public affair, or rather as exclusively public as such undertakings outside the normal bounds of administration could be in the Old Regime. The directors advanced no money and were permitted to derive no profit except through commission. Unlike Malisset, they had no personal investment to protect. Nor did the management of the *régie* suffer the internal jealousies and dissension that characterized the Malisset company. Throughout their operations, Doumerc and Sorin enjoyed the full confidence of the Controller-General.

There were, to be sure, certain similarities between the experiences of the Malisset company and Terray's *régie*. Buyers complained about the quality of the *régie* grain just as they had questioned the "goodness" of Malisset's merchandise, though the incidence and intensity of protests appear to have diminished. A shipment of 300 sacks sent to Beauvais emitted an offensive odor. On the basis of an "essay," or test, the police of the comté-pairie concluded that the bread produced by the suspicious grain, "without being as good as local wheat, would not be harmful to the people and would bring abundance to the area." A rival police authority, the officers of the royal bailliage of Beauvais, conducted their own essay which revealed the grain to have been improperly stored and the bread to have a "bad taste" and, far more ominously, properties likely to generate "epidemic illnesses."[71] The Procurator General polled the parish priests of the capital to investigate charges that bad grain was provoking such diseases in the capital. The curé of St. Sauveur reported an extraordinary number of pleurisy attacks and putrid fevers, but he had no grounds for ascribing them to "bread of bad quality." While the curé of St. Roch found bread to be "less good than usual," he saw no evidence of grain-induced illness in his circumscription.[72]

Throughout the seventies, rumors persisted that Corbeil specialized in supplying rotten or defective grain under the cover of the king's name.[73] "I will not conceal from you," the intendant of Champagne

---

71 BN, Coll. Joly, 1158, fols. 81–96. In Aug. 1770, the doctors at the Hôtel-Dieu found the bread disagreeable but not deleterious to health. Deliberations of the Bureau of the Hôtel-Dieu, 8 Aug. 1770, AAP, # 139. For a later episode concerning grain quality not directly related to the king's supply, see *Hardy's Journal*, 16 June 1774, BN, mss. fr. 6681, fol. 363.

72 PG to curé of St. Sauveur, 24 May 1771 and PG to curé of St. Roch, 22 May 1771, BN, Coll. Joly 1111, fols. 131–32. Cf. Daure, "Mémoire," 8 Aug. 1773, AN, F¹¹ 265.

73 Lenoir, "Essai," published by R. Darnton, "Le Lieutenant de police J.-P. Lenoir ...," *Revue d'histoire moderne et contemporaine*, XVI (Oct.–Dec. 1969), 618–19.

wrote Sorin and Doumerc, "the fact that the people have worries about the quality of your flour." Although a local apothecary pronounced it harmless, consumers suspected that the bread's "crackling" texture resulted from adulteration of the flour with sand or chalk. Since we use only "very pure" wheat, replied Sorin and Doumerc, the defect must be the result of an accident in conservation or fabrication for which we are not responsible. "Furthermore, Monsieur," they declared, "our Storehouses are open to the Public and to the Administration, and, we daresay, they are in very pure hands."[74]

Nor did Terray's grain operations escape the suspicions and accusations of speculations and monopoly which had discredited the provisioning enterprise of Laverdy. Even if he had not inherited the treasury of stigma and mistrust traditionally associated with the king's grain and replenished in the time of Malisset and Leprévost, Terray, on his own, would have succeeded in sullying the reputation of the *régie*. Politically, he did not reap great profit from the restoration of the regime of police paternalism. Although he unequivocally repudiated liberalization, he did not make an effort to show the nation how completely he had broken with the policies which many Frenchmen felt were responsible for the disasters of recent years. Terray's grain policy was in large measure a response to public pressures and demands but he did not for a moment consider acknowledging publicly the influence that the people had exercised on the decisions his ministry had made. Until the very end, Old Regime administrators maintained the fiction—necessary, to be sure, to preserve the face and the self-confidence of a system both monarchical and absolutist—that government was the exclusive business of the king and the council, not the concern of the citizenry. Necker, the last Controller-General, was the first one bold (or reckless) enough to dabble in popular politics and to view the public, in the manner of the parlements, as his constituency. Instead of undertaking a campaign to clear the air on an issue which had preoccupied everyone for almost a decade, and demanding credit for renouncing a highly unpopular policy, Terray announced the change in a brief and arid ukase which had no further development. He allowed doubts to persist concerning his intentions, doubts which crystallized around his use of the king's grain.

Moreover, other factors seriously militated against an entente between the ministry and the public. Who (besides Voltaire and one

---

74 IN. to Sorin and Doumerc, 31 Dec. 1770 and Sorin and Doumerc to IN., 12 Jan. 1771, C. 416, A.D. Marne.

branch of the divided party of reform) could trust the motives of the government which struck the deadly blow against the sovereign courts? Who could have faith in the integrity of a Controller-General, obsessed with fiscality, whose policies appeared to violate sacred agreements and to promise heavier tax burdens? (Not even Voltaire himself, who claimed that the abbé's measures cost him some two millions.)[75] Given Terray's personal reputation for debauchery and avidity and his well-publicized, brutal steps to bring order to the finances—contemporaries called him "Cartouche," the "hangman," "bloodsucker," "cannibal," "bankrupter," and "improbity personified"—it required little imagination to believe that he carried over these same qualities and appetites to the management of the king's grain.[76] "Under Monsieur the abbé Terray," wrote Choiseul, "one had the idea of working the matter of grain *en finances*," a cryptic description of an administration which seemed to lend itself to *double entendre*.[77]

So long as the king's grain operations remained shrouded in secrecy, the shift from a company to a *régie* form of administration had no effect upon public opinion. With few exceptions, contemporaries perceived no discontinuity between the operations of Malisset and those of Doumerc-Sorin. At Beauvais the bailliage police believed that the "company" which provided grain in 1771 was the "same company" which had furnished supplies in 1768. The Paris bakers buying at the Halles in 1773 referred to the "flour of the company" in the same terms as they had five years before. The abbé de Véri, who had little sympathy for Terray's policies, was one of the few commentators to take the trouble to insist on the differences between the government's relationship with Malisset and its association with Doumerc-Sorin. The *régie* was not conceived as a private enterprise, he emphasized; there was "no company" and "no contract."[78]

---

75 Voltaire to Mme. d'Epinay, 6 Nov. 1770, in *Correspondence*, ed. by Besterman, vol. 78, (# 15727).

76 See, for example, Charles Collé to M de V***, 7 Aug. 1780, in *Correspondance inédite de C. Collé*, ed. by H. Bonhomme (Paris, 1864), 205; Bachaumont, *Mémoires secrets*, IX, 109 (13 May 1776) and XI, 79 (31 Jan. 1778); Monthyon, *Particularités et observations sur les ministres des finances les plus célèbres depuis 1660 jusqu'en 1791* (Paris, 1812), 150–53, 169. Cf. Afanassiev, *Commerce des céréales*, 254; Clément, *Portraits historiques*, 415; Augustin Challamel, *Mémoires du peuple français depuis son origine jusqu'à nos jours* (Paris, 1873), VIII, 355–57; E. Levasseur, *Histoire des classes ouvrières*, II, 549.

77 Choiseul, *Mémoires*, ed. by Soulavie, I, 42.

78 BN, Coll. Joly 1158, fols. 81–96; Letter of mediator (*arbitre*) to juges-consuls,

The *économistes*, no longer inhibited by their alliance with the ministry, made no effort to dispel the rumors and uncertainties surrounding the *régie*'s operations. Dupont depicted a vast, ubiquitous company with emissaries in every province and foreign market, stifling all competition from the private sector.[79] That is to say, he pictured an operation of a scope and magnitude which his colleagues-in-arms Roubaud and Baudeau had derided as inherently absurd and inconceivable when they undertook to defend Laverdy against similar charges in the sixties. In his letters to Terray in 1770, Turgot had warned that it was impossible to manage an honest, efficient victualing enterprise compatible with the functioning of private trade and free of the odor of monopoly. When he became Controller-General in 1774, as we shall shortly see, he did everything in his power to prove that his predictions had been well founded. After Terray's fall, Condorcet openly accused the government's agents of having provoked the very dearths which they were supposed to combat.[80] Condillac discerned no material difference between the old style monopoly "born of the rules made for the grain police" and the "agiotage" of the government's commissioners. Both operations were fiscal and venal in nature and both exploited the public on the pretext of serving its needs.[81]

Coquereau, one of Terray's most vitriolic critics, imagined a scenario less elaborately staged but not vastly different from Leprévost's.[82] The Controller-General "fomented" an "artificial famine" which lasted the whole time he was in office. While Terray manipulated prices by alternately permitting and prohibiting exports, Coquereau alleged, his agents purchased grain at low prices and resold it for "enormous profits." "By the most criminal abuse of the confidence of his Master," Terray "made the King a monopolist and associated him with his infamous traffic." Fascinated by the "little details," Louis XV

---

29 March 1773, Archives Seine-Paris, D6B⁶ carton 6; Véri, *Journal*, ed. by J. de Witte, I, 150.

79 Dupont to Prince Carl Ludwig, 1773, in Knies, ed., *Dupont Correspondance*, II, 47. Later Dupont charged that it was "the former agents of the company" who "spread the rumor" in 1774–75 that "the system of M. Turgot would make Paris die of hunger," thereby preparing the way for the Flour War uprising. Dupont to Carl Ludwig, 15 Jan. 1783, *ibid.*, II, 356.

80 Condorcet, *Lettre d'un laboureur de Picardie*, in *Collection des principaux économistes*, ed. by Daure and Molinari, XIV, 485.

81 Condillac, *Le Commerce et le gouvernement*. in *ibid.*, XIV, 417–19.

82 Coquereau, *Mémoire concernant ... l'Abbé Terrai*, 158–59. For a similar representation, see "Tableau du gouvernement intérieur de la France du 1 octobre 1771," France 1366, fol. 233 and *passim*, Arch. AE.

sat in his office, according to Cocquereau, charting the price fluctuations in the markets throughout the kingdom. Characterizing Terray as the "master monopolist" of France, another journalist charged that the "company" functioned with the blessing and "concert" of the king himself.[83] In 1789, the *Moniteur* took note of the two techniques that Terray had employed to balance his budget: "bankruptcy" and "the grain monopoly."[84]

Not all the charges against Terray were made after the fact, though many of them had the transparent character of political polemic and rationalization. "It is said," Hardy related in his journal in May 1773,

> that the sieur abbé Terray, Controller-General of finances, suspected perhaps rightly of favoring the Monopoly and the Exportation of grain which occasioned the dearth and the *cherté* in different provinces, could very well suffer a disgrace....[85]

Nor were the accusations of exclusively (and suspiciously) Parisian provenance. Like the famine plot charges of the sixties, they circulated throughout the realm and in many instances took on a peculiarly local character. "It is true, Monsieur," one subdelegate declared to the intendant of Alençon, "that the people attributed the grain *cherté* to the ridiculous idea that there existed a company exclusively charged with the provisioning trade of the entire kingdom." "But," he added, as if to reassure, "the people who suffer are always quick to judge." More circumspect in his analysis, another subdelegate in the same generality denied that "there even appeared in my district the least appearance of the reality of this company," but he had no doubt that certain individuals "with evil intentions" spread "various seditious absurdities which insult the government [and] give rise to [popular] murmuring."[86] The intendant of Brittany reported the existence of "rumor," which "wins credence easily" concerning the operation of "a company which has the exclusive privilege to engage in grain commerce in the interior of the kingdom" and which organizes

---

83 Pidansat de Mairobert, *Journal historique*, III, 278 (9 Oct. 1772), IV, 278–79 (24 Aug. 1773), V, 97 (2 March 1774), VI, 17 (22 May 1774), and VI, 40 (1 June 1774).
84 Buchez and Roux, *Histoire parlementaire de la révolution française*, II, 74–75.
85 *Hardy's Journal*, 19 May 1773, BN, mss. fr. 6681, fol. 192. Cf. *ibid.*, 27 Sept. 1774 and H. Martin, *Histoire de France*, XVI, 298.
86 SD at Argentau to IN., 13 Oct. 1773 and SD Bernay to same, 12 Oct. 1772, C. 89, A.D. Orne. A number of other delegates were less impressed by the diffusion of the conspiratorial rumor among the people. See the SDs of Nogent-le-Rotrou and Billesuche to IN., 13, 25 Oct. 1773, C. 89, *ibid.*

surreptitious exporting.[87] Though similar rumors traveled through the Hainaut, according to the intendant they "were not widely accredited."[88] In Bordeaux "there is open talk of a Company of Monopolists who maneuver for their own account and for that of the government which seeks to fatten itself by starving the people."[89] The specific character that public suspicions took worried the Metz Parlement less than the underlying process of thought of which they were an expression. Regardless of the evidence, the people "will never believe that the high cost and scarcity of a commodity of first necessity is the result of [genuine] dearth." They will "always attribute it" to some sort of "roguery."[90]

"Popular rumors" were worrisome but they were after all commonplace in the sociopolitical history of the Old Regime and usually harmless provided they remained crude in conception and isolated in terms of social incidence. What alarmed Terray in 1773, even as it had preoccupied Laverdy in 1767–68, was that "the Bourgeoisie of the cities and even distinguished persons" as well as "the people" were "imbued with the false idea that there exists a company exclusively appointed to undertake the provisioning of the kingdom and the grain trade."[91] Events at Bordeaux provided the Controller-General with the most striking examples of this phenomenon. The Parlement of Bordeaux, like the Rouen court several years earlier, repeatedly denounced the existence of "a pretended Company in Paris which had an exclusive privilege for the grain supply of the kingdom." The denunciations of the magistrates reached a fever pitch at the moment that the rhythm of delivery of *régie* grain to the Bordeaux area was most intense—that is to say, from Terray's point of view, the Parlement evinced the meanest possible spirit at the very moment it should have

---

87 IN. to SD at Nantes, 15 Sept. 1773, C. 774, A.D. L-A. and IN. to Terray, ca. May-June 1774, C. 1653, A.D. I-et-V.

88 IN. to Terray, 4 Aug. 1774, C. 6690, A.D. Nord.

89 Bethmann to Terray, 25 May 1773, C. 1441, and Terray to First President, Bordeaux Parl., 5 Nov. 1773, C. 1442, A.D. Gir.

90 Deliberations, Metz Parlement, 17 June 1771, B. 470, fol. 65 (registre secret), A.D. Moselle. Cf. the desire of the Troyes municipality in 1789 "to avoid as much as possible [the] buying and selling [of] grain for the city because, if it becomes known, this would bring the people to rise up against us because they would think that we were in this commerce to make money on them...." Letter to CG (?), 10 May 1789, C. 1909, A.D. Aube. Surely many other town fathers and police officials drew similar lessons from the "pact" experience. Given the popular subsistence mentality, action and inaction seemed to be equally parlous options.

91 Terray to IN. of Picardy, 28 Sept. 1773, C. 86, A.D. Somme.

expressed the warmest gratitude. He warned the court not to allow itself "to be caught up by the charges of the vulgar [people]; do not, like them, see monopoly in the help which has been sent to you by His Majesty." There was "no company authorized to engage in a grain trade harmful to the king's subjects" but only "a few persons charged with the task of meeting your needs [with grain] … which the Beneficence of His Majesty caused to be brought from abroad at great expense and distributed at great loss for the assistance of the people." If "you shout Monopoly and complain that private commerce is destroyed" when the government intervenes to help you, Terray admonished, then in the future the government will stay out of your affairs and you will have relinquished your right to protection against dearth.[92]

Silencing the Parlement, however, was only one part of the problem at Bordeaux. Though a number of different versions circulated, most of the plot scenarios pointed to the distinguished international merchant-banker and local philanthropist, Bethmann. Accused of belonging to "the company of Monopolists" which masterminded the terrible dearth that afflicted the Bordelais in 1773, Bethmann was obliged to hire twenty armed guards to protect his life and property, which were repeatedly menaced. The charges and threats jarred Bethmann profoundly, for he saw himself as a public benefactor who merited acclaim rather than obloquy. After all, he had agreed to participate in the *régie* in order to serve the king and the general interest without any view toward speculative profits and he felt that he had fulfilled his mission with "zeal" and "precision." "If it were only the transient outcry of an aroused populace, I would let them shout," wrote Bethmann, "I would have wrapped myself up in my innocence, in the esteem of honest persons, in the confidence with which the government honors me, and I would have hoped that the people themselves would have rendered me justice once they had the time to calm down." But what horrified the *négociant* above all was that "the charges against me come from higher up and find supporters in all social ranks." The "general prejudice" was that Bethmann was "a monopolist": "on this point even some parlementaires were people."

---

92 Terray to First President, 19 July 1772 and 5 Nov. 1773, C. 1441 and 1442, A.D. Gir.; "Réponse aux remontrances du Parlement de Bordeaux," Oct. 1773, C. 2915, A.D. Hér. The grain-plot mentality had an almost traditional place in the history of the Bordeaux Parlement. See the court's representations to Louis XV, ca. fall 1748, C. 1439, A.D. Gir.

The "calumny," its provenance, and its dissemination troubled
Bethmann far more than the threats against his well-being. Though
the phrase invites derision today, there is no reason to doubt the sincerity of this *négociant's* impassioned claim that "my honor is dearer
to me than my fortune and my life … it is impossible for me to live
dishonored." In "an instant" the famine plot accusation cost him an
impeccable reputation that he had worked forty years to attain. Since
his honor was stained "only for having served the state," he turned to
the state to assist him in salvaging it. "I must cleanse myself in the eyes
of all Europe of the crimes of which I am accused," wrote Bethmann
to the Controller-General, and in order for me to do so you must lead
the way. Though he did not specify exactly what he wanted—perhaps
he himself did not precisely know what would be necessary—it was
clear that Bethmann would not stop until he felt himself properly
vindicated. He hinted that he would accept nothing short of a full
public disclosure and explanation of the *régie* system and his role in
it. If the government failed to take the first step, Bethmann threatened that he would—"by filing suit against his defamers, presenting
to the courts *and to the public* the tableau of the operations of which
I was head, proving the exactitude of the tableau of the correspondence of my firm with Messieurs Sorin de Bonne and Doumerc, and
of the testimony of agents and brokers that I employed in the sale of
the grain I received." In effect, what Bethmann proposed was to create another scandal to eclipse his own—a prospect that Terray was
bound to find repugnant.

Yet there was a very instructive lesson for the Controller-General
to learn in Bethmann's argument that his own rehabilitation had
important political implications. By responding positively to his
demands, Bethmann suggested, the state would not simply be serving an individual: "perhaps the *interest* of the government, properly
understood, should convince it to accord me in this unfortunate affair
all the help, all the clarification which I might need." For, the *négociant*
emphasized, "this affair, to tell the truth, is an *affair of state.*" Beyond
Bethmann, trader and banker, the famine plot rumors directly implicated the government. Regardless of the outcome of the Bethmann
case—a single episode in an elaborate drama—sooner or later the
government would have to face up to the "humiliating suspicions"
which the citizenry entertained. By using his case as a vehicle, Bethmann reasoned, the government could offer a full explanation which
would restore its credit in the public mind. "I know," Bethmann

hastened to add, "that His Majesty does not owe any account of his conduct to his peoples but

> if without compromising Himself, without lowering Himself to the point of justifying Himself; if through my personal justification the people could be made to see that the Government that they slander, that they accuse of monopoly, made the grain trade a ministerial affair only in order to assure subsistence to the unfortunate people in all parts of the kingdom and to prevent individual monopolies from taking place; if it were demonstrated that far from profiting, the Government has almost always lost on the sale of grain of which my firm handles [a part], and that nevertheless the losses did not stop it from sending everyone assistance in proportion to the need; Do you think, my lord, that that will not produce a good effect? Do you think that the people will not blush for having held an unjust prejudice against a beneficial and protective authority?[93]

Terray was much less sanguine about the blushing power of the people; it was partly for this reason that he rejected the Bethmann plan. If he had announced publicly that the government was in fact deeply involved in grain distribution for the sake of the general interest, there was a strong likelihood that no one would have believed him. Terray feared that such frankness would have promoted suspicions instead of dissipating them. Nor was the Controller-General comfortable with the idea of appealing to the people to believe in the king and his ministers. Terray's conception of paternalism was no less generous than Bethmann's but, by its very nature, it precluded a dialogue between father and children. In addition to its unsettling political effects, nationwide publicity, in Terray's view, would have made it more difficult for the *régie* to buy and sell economically and deterred independent suppliers from furnishing the market. Even as the plot rumors gained greater and greater currency, Terray clung to the idea that there was something to be gained from not officially acknowledging their existence. It was for this reason that he was extremely anxious to preempt Bethmann's "démarches d'éclat." Though he knew better, the Controller-General tried to persuade the *négociant* that the rumors and accusations were of minor significance, ephemeral "popular rumblings" not worthy of his anxiety. Praising him warmly for his services and promising "tokens of special protection" from the royal council, Terray nevertheless warned him not to make the issue a cause célèbre.[94] At the same time the Controller-General enjoined

---

93 Bethmann to Terray, 25 May 1773, C. 1441, A.D. Gir.
94 Terray to Bethmann, 5 June 1773, C. 1441, *ibid.*

the First President ("for the sake of the general good") to try to stifle the anti-Bethmann sentiment in the Parlement and he urged the
intendant to use his influence to reassure Bethmann.[95]

Apparently a bargain was struck. In return for choosing the path of
discretion, Bethmann was rewarded by the royal council, though in precisely what way we do not know. To restore Bethmann's standing in the
business community, Terray enlisted the cooperation of the Bordeaux
Chamber of Commerce.[96] Just as he was beginning to regain confidence,
Bethmann suffered another rude blow upon Turgot's rise to power. In a
series of legal actions that were widely publicized, the government subpoenaed the papers and sealed the warehouses of all of the agents of
the *régie*. From Bethmann's perspective these moves must have seemed
calculated to prove that the suspicions against him had been exactly on
the mark. Turgot assured him, however, that his management was not
at all in question and his firm continued to engage—for its own account
henceforth—in grain commerce and the myriad other exchanges which
befitted an internationally known establishment.[97]

If the Bethmann affair ended well from the government's point
of view, nevertheless it offered no solution to the problem of dealing
with public opinion on the subsistence question. The problem disturbed Terray deeply, even as it had disconcerted Laverdy six years
earlier. Though he was ideologically more inclined to sympathize with
the people in their subsistence terrors than his predecessor had been,
Terray was no better prepared to deal with the subsistence mentality
in political rather than purely humanitarian and moral terms. The
plot persuasion was "making the government odious" in everyone's
eyes. Terray did not know how to convince "the people [who] attribute the high price of grain to a scheme devised to force them to pay
dearly for their food" that such reasoning was utterly false. The fact
that "they saw Monopolists everywhere, even in the help which they
received," stupefied him.[98]

The attitude of the public struck the Controller-General as bitterly
and tragically ironical. For "on the one hand, the government is condemned for causing the price to rise in order to profit by means of an

---

95 Terray to Esmangart, 21 June 1773 and to First President, 5 June 1773, C. 1441, *ibid.*

96 Terray to Chamber of Commerce, 26 June 1773, C. 1441, *ibid.* Cf. the sarcastic commentary
    of Pidansat de Mairobert, *Journal historique*, IV, 280–84 (24 Aug. 1773).

97 Turgot to Esmangart, 23 Dec. 1774, C. 1442, A.D. Gir. Cf. *Oeuvres de Turgot*, ed. by Schelle,
    IV, 227.

98 Terray, "Mémoire", 1 Aug. 1773, C. 86, A.D. Somme and C. 1653, A.D. I-et-V.

odious monopoly and, on the other, it is said that the government blocks [private] commerce by taking voluntary losses that individual dealers cannot bear." If we are accused at once of "desiring to profit and consenting to lose" when we send help, "soon we will be accused of negligence and of abandoning the people to the greed of the merchants if we make no effort to provision." In this situation it was extremely difficult to continue to govern. Though "it acts only for the good of the people," the government "is criticized on all sides for its activities." No matter what we do for the people, Terray noted, "they always believe that we wish to do them harm or that we neglect them." Yet the Controller-General did not reproach the people for their caprice or their ingratitude; he merely lamented it. Nor did he try to fix the blame for the plot rumors on a small band of villains even as his successor would ascribe the Flour War to a mischievous cabal. Terray understood that the suspicions came from the people, from their daily experience; though there were "evil-intentioned persons"—the *économistes*, for example, who labored to ruin Terray—they could do no more than "second the people's way of thinking on this matter."[99]

His inability to find a clear way out frustrated and pained the Controller-General. Yet he resisted the temptation to abandon his subsistence policy in order to avoid casting further discredit on the government. "It would be an inexcusable weakness," Terray wrote, "if the fear of evil gossip stopped the administration from acting for the public good as it can and as it must act." In September 1773, in a circular letter which resembled the one Laverdy composed on a similar occasion in the fall of 1768, the Controller-General formally alerted the intendants to the danger of the famine-plot-monopoly rumors (as if they needed to be warned) and exhorted them not to be intimidated into inaction by public opinion.[100] "It is your duty," he instructed, "to undeceive those who are in the error" of believing that the government is sponsoring a company" to control national provisioning for its own ends. But he could not tell the intendants *how* to do this. Those who "spread rumors with evil intentions" could be punished but what about all the others who gossiped and suspected innocently or instinctively? The Controller-General promised the intendants that he would cut back drastically on domestic purchases, which led to many disturbances and appeared to give credence to the rumors.

---

99 Terray to INs. (circular), 28 Sept. 1773, C. 86, A.D. Somme; C. 1441, A.D. Gir; C. 95, A.D. I-et-L.; C. 419, A.D. Marne.

100 *Ibid.*

By a kind of negative reinforcement, Terray hoped that he could reduce the propensity to believe in the plot.[101] Terray's strategy hardly went to the core of the matter. Following his lead, the intendant of Brittany enjoined his subdelegates to "announce that the Council will not vary in the slightest in its commitment to the liberty of grain circulation in the interior of the kingdom...."[102] This was not the sort of announcement that Bethmann had proposed and it was not the kind of message which many people were likely to hear or heed.

The following year a trivial incident swelled into a major embarrassment illustrating the danger of a policy of candor or, rather, of incomplete candor. In the *Almanach Royal* of 1774, the yearbook of administrative and judicial organization and information, following the list of the members of the Royal Society of Agriculture and preceding the enumeration of the *jurés crieurs*, an ostensibly innocent entry read:

> Treasurers of Grain, for the Account of the King, M. Demirlavaud rue St. Martin vis-à-vis la Fontaine Maubué.[103]

Ordinarily no one read the *Almanach*; it was used, like a phone directory, as a reference of occasion. The word spread, however, that page 553 contained an extraordinary revelation. Overnight, for the first time in its history, the *Almanach* became a best-seller and a cause célèbre. "This commission, found for the first time in this Catalogue, excited a great commotion in Paris," Cocquereau noted with relish; "it was concluded that the rumors current for some time on the monopoly of grain by the government, that were rejected as odious & absurd, were only too well established, & that one must no longer hope to see this commodity fall to the [price] level where it had been."[104]

Cocquereau was a hostile observer, but Linguet, a witness friendly to Terray, confirmed his testimony. Once the news of the *Almanach* became known, "terrible cries arose: it was clear that the king was trafficking in grain, it was clear that the stooge of finance [Terray] was also the agent of this infernal commerce...." Linguet blamed the *économistes* for distorting the significance of the *Almanach* entry and puffing it into scandalous proportion to discredit the Controller-General.[105]

---

101 Cf. Terray to Chambers of Commerce of Marseille and Montpellier, 1 Sept. 1773, C. 2915 and Terray to IN. of Languedoc, 3 Feb. 1774, C. 2916, A.D. Her.
102 IN. of Brittany to Ballaye, 15 Sept. 1773, C. 774, A.D. L-A.
103 *Almanach royal* (1774), 553.
104 Cocquereau, *Mémoires concernant ... l'Abbé Terrai*, 198. Cf. Pidansat de Mairo-bert, *Journal historique*, V, 44 (30 Jan. 1774).
105 Linguet, *Annales*, VI, 302.

Mirlavaud was indeed the treasurer of the king's grain; he had held this post for many years.[106] To administrators and others who dealt with the ministry he was well known, but as long as the king's grain remained an official secret he was not supposed to celebrate his position publicly. How his name and title infiltrated the pages of the *Almanach* remains an enigma—an horrendous gaffe committed by a functionary not familiar with government policy or perhaps the fruit of a plot or prank engineered to bedevil the ministry. The government reacted in characteristically ponderous fashion: it fired the censor charged with verifying the proofs and it punished the printer by closing his shop for three months. It could not, however, prevent Parisians from reciting the sprightly and subversive lines which commemorated the episode:

> Ce qu'on disoit tout bas est aujourd'hui public;
>
> Des présents de Cérès le maître fait traffic,
>
> Et le bon Roi, loin qu'il s'en cache,
>
> Pour que tout le monde le sache,
>
> Par son grand *Almanach* sans façon nous apprend,
>
> Et l'adresse et le nom de son heureux agent.[107]

In May 1774, not long after the affair of the *Almanach*, Louis XV died. The nation, it appears, did not deeply mourn his passing. "The King had irretrievably lost the affection of his peoples," wrote the *nouvelliste* Métra. "Never was a prince less regretted than poor Louis XV," commented Moreau, the royalist lawyer-writer.[108] A torrent of abusive epitaphs, some of which circulated even before his death, took the king's alleged grain speculations as one of their leitmotivs and one of the chief marks of royal infamy. In prose: "here lies a King who gave us the system [of John Law] in his infancy, war as he grew up, famine as he grew old, and the plague in his death."[109] In verse:

---

106 Mirlavaud symbolized the close connection between liberalization on the one hand and perceptions of the famine plot on the other, for his post was created in 1764 specifically for "the collection of duties imposed on the export of grains" according to the July Edict. See Terray to INs. of Brittany and Bordeaux, 26 Feb. 1773, C. 1684, A.D. I-et-V. and C. 1447, A.D. Gir. Turgot dismissed Mirlavaud in Nov. 1774. Turgot to St. Priest, 23 Nov. 1774, C. 2916, A.D. Hér.

107 Bachaumont, *Mémoires secrets*, VII, 121 (1 Feb. 1774). Cf. *Révolutions de Paris* (30 Jan. 1790), 34; Félix Rocquain. *L'Esprit révolutionnaire avant la révolution* (Paris, 1879), 309; Pierre Foncin, *Essai sur le ministère de Turgot* (Paris, 1877), 72; Pierre Clément and Alfred Lemoine, *M. de Silhouette; Bouret; les derniers fermiers-généraux, étude sur les financiers du dix-huitième siècle* (Paris, 1872), 161–62.

108 F. Métra, *Correspondance secrète*, I, 16 (7 July 1774); Moreau, *Mes Souvenirs*, ed. by C. Hermelin, I, 379.

109 In two slightly different versions, F. Métra, *Correspondance secrète*, I, 2 (4 June 1774) and Moreau, *Mes Souvenirs*, I, 379.

Ci-gît le bien-aimé Bourbon,
Monarque d'assez bonne mine,
Et qui paye sur le charbon
Ce qu'il gagne sur la farine.[110]

Shortly after his demise, someone put a sign on the new grain and flour building in the central markets of the capital reading: "Storehouse for the king's grain for rent."[111]

VI

There is no doubt that Louis XV's inglorious end and the circumstances surrounding it made a profound impression on his successor. The decline in royal prestige deeply worried Louis XVI. At his accession to the throne, he nurtured one overriding ambition: "I would wish to be loved."[112] To Sartine he confided the wish that "the poor always be able to eat bread at two *sous* [the pound]."[113] The events of the past few years—indeed, of the past decade, gave these royal fancies a significance which ordinarily such hackneyed pieties would not warrant. To his shock, only weeks after he became king, Louis XVI found himself accused by "the people" of "having part like his grandfather" in the illicit profits of the official grain monopoly. Stung by an anonymous letter informing him of the existence of a "contract" authorizing the speculations, he demanded clarification from his ministers. "This investigation," wrote the abbé de Véri "will make him penetrate into the previous administration of grain...."[114] Meanwhile Maurepas, his chief counselor, had received at least one memoir denouncing Terray's unspeakable operations. If Maurepas encouraged the new king to pursue his inquiry it was purely for reasons of court politics, for he himself had served in the ministry many years before when Orry and his brother fell victim to the same sort of charges now leveled against Terray and he must have known how groundless they really were.

---

110 Cited by Bastard-d'Estang, *Parlements*, II, 508–509. Reviled for speculating on grain when he was prime minister during the dearth of 1725, the duc de Bourbon elicited a strikingly similar epitaph upon his demise in 1740. Gazetins de la police, 13–15 Feb. 1740, Arsenal, mss. Bastille 10167.

111 F. Metra, *Correspondance secrète*, I, 5 (4 June 1774).

112 Michelet, *Histoire de France*, XVI, 200.

113 Moreau, *Mes Souvenirs*, ed. by C. Hermelin, II, 2. Cf. Pierre, Marquis de Ségur, *Au Couchant de la monarchie* (Paris, 1909), I, 6.

114 Véri, *Journal*, ed. by J. de Witte, I, 150–51. Cf. Mornet, *Origines intellectuelles*, 402.

Schooled by her mother and by the Austrian ambassador Mercy-Argenteau, Marie-Antoinette pressed the king to give the new reign an auspicious beginning by breaking decisively with the suspect ways of Louis XV. She had a personal taste of the popular mood at approximately the same time the king began to ask questions about grain policy. Promenading in the capital in July, she encountered a stark silence instead of the huzzahs she wanted to hear. One person cried out: "Long live the King, provided that the price of bread diminishes."[115] In a letter he wrote to Maria-Theresa in August 1774, Mercy-Argenteau explained one of the steps taken by the queen to enhance her popularity. Perhaps the most striking thing about his remarks is the extent to which he subscribed to the current version of the famine pact persuasion:

> The monopoly of the provisioning of grain had raised this good to an excessively high price and occasioned some tumult. Yet this monopoly was going to be accorded again to the Company which profited from it and which paid quite a large retribution to the Royal Treasury. The King having consulted the Queen on this affair, ... [he] prevented the renewal of the monopoly, and when the public learns the source of this decision [circumstance that I will have the means to make known], it is certain that that will have a great effect and infinitely increase the attachment of the public for the queen.[116]

There were, to be sure, other matters of great urgency facing the king. But it seems reasonable to contend that his desire to purge the government of the stigma of grain speculation was one of the factors which persuaded him to accept Turgot, whose reputation as a bold spirit caused him some hesitation, as Controller-General. According to one source, when Louis XVI reached his decision toward the end of August, he wrote the secretary of state for the royal household:

> Inform M. Turgot immediately that I appoint him Comptroller-General of my finances. I place the greatest hopes on this choice for the welfare of my people, whom the disastrous administration of Abbé Terray has so much alarmed. Let M. Turgot come to see me tomorrow morning and *bring with him the memoir on grains...* [117]

The new monarch's decision suggests that he did not understand Terray's methods and goals and perhaps, too, that he believed the gossip about Terray's culpability to be true. It also indicates that he did not grasp the implications of Turgot's program, especially in the short run. For contemporary observers tell us that it was Louis'

---

115 *Hardy's Journal*, 21 July 1774, BN, mss. fr. 6681, fols. 384–85.
116 Mercy-Argenteau to Marie-Thérèse, 15 Aug. 1774, in *Correspondance secrète entre Marie-Thérèse et le comte de Mercy-Argenteau avec les lettres de Marie-Thérèse et de Marie-Antoinette*, ed. by Alfred d'Arneth and A. Geoffroy, II, 221.
117 Cited by S.K. Padover, *The Life and Death of Louis XVI* (New York, 1963), 53.

widely-publicized ambition to lower the price of bread quickly and durably and that he was no less disappointed than were his subjects when that diminution did not come about.[118] It was wholly gratuitous to presume that because Turgot was determined to undo Terray's work he was thus committed to a policy of cheap bread. It remained possible, however, for many months to come to ascribe persistently high prices to the continuing ill-effects of Terray's four-year tenure as grain minister.

Virtually the moment he took office, Turgot set out to dismantle the *régie* and discredit, with éclat, the policy behind it and the men who fashioned and executed that policy. The measures he took were widely publicized for maximum impact on opinion. Though Turgot himself had warned countless times against the dangers of giving credence and authority to popular prejudices, his actions served to confirm the worst suspicions about Terray's ministry. At the end of August, the new Controller-General suspended Brochet de Saint-Prest from the post of intendant of commerce and chief of the grain department. Hardy viewed this act as Turgot's message to the public that he was determined to expose "the cabal formed to make the poor people eat dear bread."[119]

Rumors of the day accused Saint-Prest of skimming a fortune from the grain speculations which he managed. His lifestyle provided the circumstantial evidence that convicted him in the public mind. Known once as a man of modest means who had been obliged to borrow heavily in order to purchase his post, he was now said to keep lavish train in a sumptuous townhouse staffed with a host of domestics and to spend vast sums on his wife's wardrobe and his guests' fantasies. Although there was no evidence that Saint-Prest actually profited from the *régie*'s operations, Turgot's auditors allegedly found proof that he had received or perhaps extorted a number of gifts and a loan of 50,000 *livres* from Doumerc and Sorin, which he was not expected to repay. St. Prest, in a word, lacked "purity."[120]

In a "memoir in defense of himself," Saint-Prest insisted that he played a relatively minor role in the grain affairs, that he performed his work sedulously and scrupulously, and that he had a "stainless reputation."

---

118 *Hardy's Journal*, 10 Aug. 1774, BN, mss. fr. 6681, fol. 394; Pidansat de Mairobert, *Journal historique*, VI, 17 (22 May 1774); Bourdon-Desplanches, *Projet nouveau*, 4.

119 *Hardy's Journal*, 28 Aug. 1774, BN, mss. fr. 6681, fol. 407.

120 *Oeuvres de Turgot*, ed. by Schelle, IV, 41–42, 194–95. Cf. Baudeau (?), "Chronique Louis XVI," *Révue rétrospective*, III (1834), 40, 403 (14 May, 27 Aug. 1774); Coquereau, *Mémoires concernant … l'Abbé Terrai*, 223, 228; Véri, *Journal*, ed. by J. de Witte, I, 156; Foncin, *Turgot*, 71–72; F. Métra, *Correspondance secrète*, I, 200–201 (18 Feb. 1775); Pidansat de Mairobert, *Journal historique*, VI, 162 (1 Sept. 1774).

As head of the grain department, he supervised "the correspondence relative to subsistence," centralizing statistical data, assessing requests for assistance from intendants, and preparing status reports for the ministry. Concerning the management of the *régie*, Saint-Prest claimed that "M. le Contrôleur-Général gave his orders directly to the commissioners: I had responsibility uniquely for the precautions taken for Paris," an "immense" task but one which supposedly did not involve him in decisions to buy foreign grains. "On the basis of these details, justified by documentary proofs, how is it possible for me to demonstrate more convincingly the falseness of the rumor which has been spread that I arranged for the renewal of the grain contract?" he asked. Contrary to what people imagined, there was no company, no monopoly, no "contract":

> Orders were given to individuals to buy; they executed the orders; they accounted for their mission; on the presentation of invoices, they received 2% commission on the purchase and as much on the sale; it was thus practiced during the administration of Messrs. de Machault, de Courteilles, de Trudaine, and D'Albert.[121]

Saint-Prest may very well have been as much a "scoundrel" as Mademoiselle de Lespinasse pretended.[122] There is no doubt that he minimized the role he actually played in grain management, in the access of humility provoked by Turgot's indictment. His part in the Pascaud affair alone belies his contention that he had nothing to do with grain purchases abroad. Guys reported to "Mr. de St. Prest who is in charge of this important mission" during his Italian grain-buying expedition in 1772. Though he was often obscured by Terray, who immersed himself in every aspect of victualing operations, Saint-Prest's correspondence reveals that he was the man to whom provincial administrators first looked when they sought to acquire more king's grain or modify distribution procedures.[123] It seems quite possible—it was after all not so unusual in the Old Regime or afterward—that he capitalized upon his public position for private advantage. But he did not participate in a nefarious conspiracy, inspired by

---

121 "Mémoire en défense de Brochet de St.-Prest," in *Oeuvres de Turgot*, ed. by Schelle, IV, 190–94; Pidansat de Mairobert, *Journal historique*, VII, 166 (13 March 1775).

122 Lespinasse to Guibert, 27 Aug. 1774, in *Lettres de Mademoiselle de Lespinasse*, ed. by E. Asse, (Paris, 1876), 93. Alluding to the dismissal of St.-Prest and several others, Madame du Deffand wrote: "M. Turgot sweeps away all the garbage." To Voltaire, 29 Aug. 1774, in *Correspondance complète de la Marquise du Deffand*, ed. by Lescure (Paris, 1865), II, 429. Cf. Sorhuet to Maupeou in Pidansat de Mairobert (?), *Maupeouana*, II, 102.

123 Guys to d'Aiguillon (?), 14 Dec. 1772, France, 1740, fol. 54, Arch. AE; St.-Prest to Robert, 18 June 1773, C. 81, A.D. C d'O.

the Controller-General, to speculate with the king's grain, for no such plot existed. Saint-Prest passed rapidly into disgrace and oblivion. Even before he had a chance to vacate his splendid home, a prankster placed a sign over his door reading "Flour Mansion for rent."

In early September, Turgot issued a momentous royal *arrêt* based upon his belief in the natural and social primacy and the efficacy of the rights of property and liberty. By this legislative act, he reestablished liberalization along the principles set forth in the Declaration of May 1763, decried the grain policies of his predecessors, and solemnly renounced government intervention in the provisioning of grain. This *arrêt* was, as one observer put it, "a bitter satire of the old administration."[124] At approximately the same moment, the story began to circulate in Paris that two fishermen residing on the outskirts of the capital at Boulogne fished out of the Seine one or two large packages of documents wrapped in cloth and bound with rope weighted with a large stone to make them sink. Another package, similarly destined for the river bottom, was reported to have been dredged up near Passy. Somehow all these papers found their way to the Contrôle-Général. Allegedly, they concerned the grain operations of the *régie* and contained highly incriminating evidence of mismanagement, malversation, and illicit speculation; according to one observer, Sorin had them tossed in the Seine in anticipation of a police search of his offices.[125]

What extraordinary good fortune for Turgot to come into possession of such evidence just two weeks after he discharged Saint-Prest on suspicion of corruption and just days after he publicly denounced officially-sponsored victualing operations in the *arrêt du conseil*! In terms of their impact on public opinion, it made little difference whether or

---

124 Pidansat de Mairobert, *Journal historique*, VI, 189 (21 Sept. 1774). The Paris Parlement registered it after considerable debate and with serious reservations. The Rouen court added modifications, salvaging for the police the authority to intervene when necessary. In a remarkable piece of casuistry, utterly demolished by Turgot with a few pithy marginal comments, Miromesnil, once the First President of the Rouen company but now Keeper of the Seals and Turgot's colleague, tried to justify the Parlement's modifications on the grounds (a.) that they were harmless and (b.) that, without them, the Parlement would be alienated, the people alarmed, and the traders frightened into hiding by the prospect of having to face a united front of magistrates and consumers. *Ibid.*, VI, 361–62 (17 Dec. 1774) and 381–82 (24 Dec. 1774); Moreau, *Mes Souvenirs*, ed. by Hermelin, II, 187; *Oeuvres de Turgot*, ed. by Schelle, IV, 217–19.

125 *Hardy's Journal*, 30 Sept. 1774, BN, mss. fr. 6681, fol. 423; F. Métra, *Correspondance secréte*, I, 84 (29 Sept. 1774). According to another source, one set of papers was found by several journeymen butchers and another by two ferrymen. Pidansat de Mairobert, *Journal historique*, VI, 205 (2 Oct. 1774).

not these episodes really took place, for by the end of the month they were generally known and believed to be true. (Although it admittedly "looked very much like a popular fairy tale," one writer insisted that the story was "exact" in its facts.)[126] In the subsequent investigation of the *régie*, no mention was ever made of the fishy packages. But a ledger in the records of the treasurer of the grain department plainly records that Turgot ordered Albert, whom he had recalled to replace Saint-Prest, to pay a "gratification" of 100 *livres* to the two Boulogne fishermen who had discovered "the two certain packages of papers."[127] In their testimony, Sorin and Doumerc indirectly confirmed the existence of these packets of papers but they claimed that they had been planted by Albert in a maneuver designed to frame the directors of the *régie*.[128]

Either on the pretext of this discovery or as a result of the leads it provided, the ministry issued *lettres de cachet* authorizing the search of and the placing of seals upon all the grain installations maintained by the *régie* in the Paris area and in the provinces as well. Between midnight and 1 A.M. on 24 September, a police team began its inspection at one of the Paris convents used as a warehouse. They examined "papers, books, journals, letters, bills, registers ... and generally all documents concerning the provisioning of grain." They were to try to learn where other records and other supplies of grain and flour might be stored and they were "to have care to prevent any furtive removal of papers, monies, or other active effects." For some reason the police did not visit Sorin's house and seize his personal papers until 5 October.[129] Presumably, Doumerc suffered the same treatment. Although a number of their subordinates were arrested, neither Doumerc nor Sorin, despite the report of several observers, appears to have been detained or interrogated at this juncture.[130] As a

126 Pidansat de Mairobert, *Journal historique*, VI, 202 (29 Sept. 1774).

127 21 Nov. 1774, AN, F[11] 1195. On Albert's recall, his devotion to Turgot, and his militant liberalism ("great friend of the sect"), see Turgot to Bordeaux IN., 21 Sept. 1774, C. 1442, A.D. Gir.; "Relation historique de l'émeute arrivée à Paris le 3 mai 1775," in Pidansat de Mairobert, *Journal historique*, VII, 299; Alfred Neymarck, *Turgot et ses doctrines* (Paris, 1885), II, 154.

128 "Réponse au Mémoire des Srs Sorin et Doumerc," ca. Sept. 1774, AN, K 908; Pidansat de Mairobert, *Journal historique*, VI, 247–48 (3 Nov. 1774).

129 23, 24, 28 Sept., 5 Oct. 1774, AN, Y 12624; *Hardy's Journal*, 27 Sept. 1774, BN, mss. fr. 6681, fol. 422; Regnaud, "Histoire des événements ... depuis 1770 concernant les parlements," BN, mss. fr. 13755, fol. 132; 23–24 Sept. 1774, AN, Y 15383 (scellé).

130 Hardy and Monthyon both suggest that the directors of the *régie* were jailed in the fall of 1774. *Hardy's Journal*, 30 Sept. 1774, BN, mss. fr. 6681, fol. 423 and Monthyon, *Particularités*, 175–76.

result of these events, noted a commentator, " the public is extremely satisfied with the vigilance of the new Controller-General."[131]

In the provinces, Turgot instructed the intendants to move with the utmost "celerity and secrecy" against the *régie*'s agents to make sure that they had no opportunity to destroy documents or conceal grain and flour stocks. In Languedoc, all the commissioners were taken by surprise; the authorities confiscated their papers and sealed their storehouses. Save in one instance, these merchants were cooperative, albeit baffled and worried about the government's keen interest in their affairs.[132] In La Rochelle, Moheau, the intendant's first secretary, personally led the expedition against Jean Perry, a prominent *négociant* who held at least 300,000 *livres* worth of *régie* grain. Preliminary inspection convinced Moheau that Perry's books were "perfectly in order." Worried about the effect that the news of this inquiry would have upon his business, Perry pressed for a rapid hearing and discharge. "I worked uniquely in the capacity of a simple agent, having *no* knowledge of the reasons behind the operations," Perry wrote, and "I filled the duties that my position imposed with integrity and precision."[133]

While the investigation proceeded, Turgot officially "suspended" all activities of the *régie*.[134] To give substance to the promises of the September *arrêt*, he immediately began to dispose of the grain and flour holdings of the *régie*, which, in the various depots throughout the kingdom, amounted to between 150,000 and 177,000 *septiers*. As a further gage of his good faith and his devotion to the rule of non-intervention in subsistence affairs, the new Controller-General named a second-rank career public servant to manage the dismantling of the victualing system: "Sieur Lentherie [Turgot's nominee] is not a *négociant* who, as a function of his fortune or the breadth of his connections, might raise suspicions that he will be secretly charged with some new provisioning mission; he is a simple clerk delegated to *terminate* an operation that His Majesty has resolved not to renew."[135] This was a lesson that Turgot

---

131 Pidansat de Mairobert, *Journal historique*, VI, 197 (25 Sept. 1774).
132 Turgot to St.-Priest, 22 Sept., 23 Nov. 1774, C. 2616, A.D. Hér.; St.-Priest to SD at Agde and subdelegate's *procès-verbal*, 30 Sept. 1774, C. 2616, *ibid.*; Giristy to St.-Priest, 19 Oct. 1774, C. 2616, *ibid.*; Turgot to IN. of Montauban, 25 Sept. 1774, C. 118, A.D. H-G. Cf. Turgot to Esmangart, 23 Nov. 1774, C. 1442, A.D. Gir.
133 Turgot to Monthyon, 23 Sept. and 23 Nov. 1774, C. 189, A.D. C-M.; Moheau to Turgot, 29 Sept. and 1 Oct. 1774, C. 189, *ibid.*; Perry to Monthyon (?), 1 Oct. 1774, C. 189, *ibid.*
134 "Observations sur la correspondance des Srs Guys et Cie ... compte actuellement en discussion," (ca. 1780), AN, F[11] 1191.
135 Turgot to Monthyon, 6 Oct. 1774, C. 189, A.D. C-M.

took pains to make in numerous letters to administrators, magistrates, and businessmen. He wanted to "persuade all of France" that the king "would never again violate the liberty [of the grain trade]...."[136] Nor was Turgot content to place full responsibility for the purging of the *régie* in the hands of subordinates. He crusaded for details as well as for principles. Personally supervising the audit and sale of royal grain and flour, he vigorously challenged not only the accounts and final balance sheets of former *régie* agents, but the pound-per-*septier* claims they made for losses due to aging, evaporation, over-heating, rotting, etc.[137]

In several memoirs written later in the fall, probably by Albert, the ministry accused Doumerc and Sorin of having committed "malversations and maneuvers." Through a series of banking and exchange devices, it was charged, the directors of the *régie* diverted royal funds into private, unspecified speculations. Instead of directly utilizing the 12,000,000 *livres* they received from the treasury to pay for the grain they bought, they drew letters of exchange on financial and commercial houses in the major cities of France and in London, Amsterdam, Danzig, and elsewhere in Europe, thereby freeing the royal advance for their own purposes. By a process of "successive and perpetual renewal," they drew new letters to pay for the old ones. They charged the burden of interest and the costs of these operations to the king. In addition, the memoirs alleged, Doumerc and Sorin extorted a sort of kickback from their correspondents by asking them, in effect, to lend their own money for the payment of the grain they were commissioned to buy. At the present time, many thousands of *livres* of letters had not yet been paid. In principle, the report contended, the government *should* refuse to honor them and thus force Doumerc and Sorin into the ruin and disrepute they so richly deserve. But such a step would generate a chain reaction of business failures, which would compromise many honest men and further taint the credit of the government at home

---

136 Turgot to Bordeaux Chamber of Commerce, 19 Sept. 1774, C. 1441, A.D. Gir.; Turgot to IN. of Bordeaux, 19 Sept. 1774, C. 1442, *ibid.*; Turgot to same, 24 May 1775, C. 1448, *ibid.*; Turgot to IN. of Alençon, 19 Sept. 1774, C. 89, A.D. Orne; Turgot to Chambers of Commerce of Toulouse and Montpellier, 2 Oct. 1774, C. 2916, A.D. Hér.; Turgot to IN. of Languedoc, 19 Sept. 1774 and IN. to SDs, 30 Sept. 1774, C. 2916, *ibid.*; Turgot to IN. of Brittany, 19 Sept. 1774, C. 1673, A.D. I-et-V.; C. 6691, A.D. Nord.
137 Mergue to St.-Priest, 1 Dec. 1774, C. 2916, A.D. Hér.; Delon to St.-Priest, 27 June 1775, C. 2917, *ibid.*; Turgot to St.-Priest, 4 April, 3 June 1775, C. 2917, *ibid.* Cf. Faure, *Disgrâce de Turgot*, 220–21 and Foncin, *Turgot*, 75.

and abroad.[138] It was charged that the *régie* directors may have siphoned off into their own pockets millions of the king's *livres*, though no effort was made to justify this estimate.

In other aspects of the *régie* administration, the directors were said to be guilty "of yet more intolerable abuses." Using royal funds, they mounted a private flour manufacturing venture—a "secret company" involving some of their southern contacts—aimed at supplying the colonies. The Albert memoirs hinted that they had a share in the sugar and spice trade conducted by the Guys company in the Levant under the guise of buying grain for the government. Instead of purchasing the king's grain abroad as they were commissioned to do, they procured most of their supplies in France at extortionate prices and at the cost of aggravating the *cherté* and driving off private trade. The ministry depicted the 1773 operation in the Midi as a fraud. The *régie* purchased grain in Marseilles and instead of transferring it to the interior for distribution, sold it indifferently to anyone who would pay the price. Some of this so-called foreign grain, it was intimated, actually was shipped to Spain, Portugal, and Italy. In still other instances, Sorin and Doumerc were said to have arranged or participated in fraudulent exporting. They diverted royal grain for their own needs, emptying storehouses that were supposed to be ready for emergency allocation and ultimately replenishing them with inferior quality goods. The government indictment accused them of fabricating pretexts for assigning excessive commissions to themselves or their nominees. In a word, the *régie* was nothing more than a racket, though one of Albert's clerks conceded that "it is rare to meet such refined thievery." Had not Turgot come to power, it was likely that Sorin and Doumerc would have taken over military provisioning in 1774. By combining military and civilian supply into a single system, the government charged, they would have become "the absolute masters of all the grain in the kingdom and the most despotic of monopolists."[139]

---

138 Cf. the spate of Marseilles bankruptcies in the spring and summer of 1774 linked to unhappy grain speculations. Pidansat de Mairobert, *Journal historique*, VI, 53 (10 June 1774).

139 "Mémoire au roi sur la conduite des Srs Sorin et Doumerck...." in *Oeuvres de Turgot*, ed. by Schelle, IV, 185–90; and the memoirs and replies (1774–75) drafted by Albert's office and by experts commissioned by Albert in AN, K 908. For the accusation that Terray furtively arranged to export grain under the cover of his supply operations, see "Questions importantes relativement à l'affaire des bleds," AN, K 908 and *Oeuvres de Turgot*, ed. by Schelle, IV, 43. Albert scoffed at the *régie*'s claim that some national grain was diverted to Switzerland in repayment of earlier grain "loans" for the provisioning of Franche-Comté and the Pays de Gex. Yet there is some evidence which

Albert and his clerks made a number of very grave charges against Sorin and Doumerc and, implicitly, against Terray, who was directly responsible for their actions. The most striking thing about them, however, was their vagueness and imprecision. Although Albert's assessment of the Malisset accounts had been excessively harsh and vengeful in spirit, it had been based on a painstaking, detailed examination and it had been abundantly documented with specific examples. The analysis of the *régie*'s operations was incomplete, superficial, and largely rhetorical. It appears certain that Albert could not marshal the hard evidence necessary to substantiate his accusations. Whereas Malisset had kept his accounts badly and thus was vulnerable when he demanded to be judged on his record, the *régie*'s accounts were "too neat." They frustrated Albert's clerks who insisted that "the interests of His Majesty demand that we not content ourselves with an arithmetic operation but that we go *to the principle*, to the source of the purchases and sales...." After all, there "was an art to drawing up [false] balance sheets" and Sorin and Doumerc were master craftsmen. Yet "the principle" had to be quantified and documented if it were to serve to convict as well as to discredit.

The presumptions against Doumerc and Sorin were doctrinal and heuristic as well as circumstantial. For the memoirs condemned not only the "abuses which resulted" in fact from the *régie*'s operations, but also "the abuses ... which *will always result from any provisioning* undertaken for the account of His Majesty: it will tend only to burden his finances, do harm to his peoples, raise the price of their subsistence, corrupt it and lose it, and occasion dearth."[140] From this perspective, Sorin and Doumerc would have been guilty no matter how they managed the *régie* because victualing "obstructed the liberty of trade" and only this liberty could have performed the services which Sorin and Doumerc pretended to render. After having investigated the Malisset enterprise, Albert had concluded that he and his guarantors owed the government a certain amount of money; after investigating the *régie*, he drew a general moral and political lesson, which could not be translated in *livres* and *sous*. Apparently for lack of a persuasive case—surely not for want of desire—the government took no action,

---

suggests that the *régie*'s claim was plausible. See Edouard Chapuisat, *Necker* (Paris, 1938), 37, 49–51 and J. Flammermont, ed., *Les Correspondances des agents diplomatiques étrangers en France avant la Révolution* (Paris, 1896), 288.

140 "Mémoire au roi sur la conduite ...," in *Oeuvres de Turgot*, ed. by Schelle, IV, 185–90 and "Réponse au mémoire des Srs Sorin et Doumerg [*sic*]," AN, K 908.

police or judicial, against Doumerc and Sorin. Finally, in early May 1775, long after it seemed that the affair had been buried, they were arrested, along with the now-celebrated ex-treasurer of the king's grain, Mirlavaud.

What was singular about the arrest was that it transpired only a few days after the outbreak of the Flour War, the chain of major subsistence riots that erupted in the hinterland and the capital in reaction to yet another serious current of shortages and high prices.[141] Unlike the Paris Parlement, observers such as Necker and Linguet, local police officials, and many parish priests, Turgot rejected the idea that they were spontaneous risings of an alarmed people. He sensed a plot, some sort of machination, though he was not certain precisely how it was organized.[142] Years later Dupont wrote that the "former agents of the Company which had engaged in the grain trade" led the uprising against Turgot by "spreading the rumor" everywhere that "the system of Mr. Turgot would cause Paris to die of hunger.[143] Another writer interested in grain questions viewed the Flour War as "the last convulsions of monopoly."[144] Either because he suspected they may have had some hand

---

141 On the Flour War, see: G. Rudé, "La Taxation populaire de mai 1775 à Paris et dans la région parisienne," *Annales historiques de la révolution française*, 28th year (April–June 1956), 139–79; Rudé, "La Taxation populaire de mai 1775 en Picardie, en Normandie, et dans le Beauvaisis," *ibid.*, 33rd year (July–Sept. 1961), 305–26; Rudé, *The Crowd in History, 1730–1848* (New York, 1964), 19–32; V. Lublinsky, "Voltaire et la guerre des farines," *Annales historiques de la révolution française*, 31st year (April–June 1959), 127–45; Lublinsky, "Les Nouvelles données sur les troubles de mai 1775 à Paris, lettres et notices," *Voprosy Istorii*, no. 11 (1955), 113–17; Faure, *Disgrâce de Turgot*, 195–318. Though generally viewed as an eruption in the Paris region, the Flour War threatened to break out or spread to Flanders, Hainaut, Lorraine, and elsewhere. See the concern evinced by military and civilian officials: "Mémoire pour le maréchal de Muy," 7 May 1775, A1/3701 and Bertier de Sauvigny to Turgot, 9 May 1775, A1/3694, pièce 107 bis, Arch. Armée. On a modest scale, there was a harbinger of and a dress-rehearsal for the Flour War at Metz in the fall of 1774. See Pidansat de Mairobert, *Journal historique*, VI, 215 (10 Oct. 1774), 235 (26 Oct. 1774), and 335 (7 Dec. 1774).
142 For contemporary evidence of Turgot's "plot thesis," see: Bachaumont, *Mémoires secrets*, VII, 123 (22 July 1775); F. Métra, *Correspondance secrète*, I, 351 (9 May 1775), and II, 302 (1 Jan. 1776); J.G. Marmontel, *Mémoires*, ed. by M. Tourneux, III, 94–96; Moreau, *Mes Souvenirs*, ed. by C. Hermelin, II, 191–92; A1/3694, pièces 18, 86, and 105, Arch. Armée. The efforts of Turgot's supporters to show that the rioters were mob rather than "people" is particularly interesting. F. Métra, *Correspondance secrète*, I, 345 (3 May 1775). Turgot expected trouble; in anticipation, he had a ready-made, universally-applicable plot thesis prepared from the time he took office. See his fear of "maneuvers from all those who have an interest in preventing the success of the principles of liberty...." To Esmangart, 30 Sept. 1774, C. 1442, A.D. Gir.
143 Dupont to Prince Carl Ludwig, 15 Jan. 1783, in Knies, ed., *Dupont Correspondance*, II, 356.
144 Rey, *Du Commerce des bleds* (Paris, 1775), 82.

in the revolts, or much more likely in order to mount a diversion, find a scapegoat, remind the public of his dedication to honesty in grain policy, and strengthen his hand at an extremely critical moment, Turgot ordered the incarceration of the leading figures of the disbanded *régie*. On 7 May the *Mémoires Secrets* observed that "the detention of these messieurs, who regarded themselves as already exonerated, undertaken at such a critical moment, would seem to indicate that they are suspected of having some role in the present troubles."[145] Less than two weeks later, the same *Mémoires* noted that "there is grand appearance that the Sieurs Saurin and Daumer [*sic*] were put in the Bastille only for form's sake, & to show the people that [the ministry] was busy trying to discover the authors of the public calamities."[146] Another observer was struck by the government's frenzied efforts to prove the existence of "a plot," by its frustration at not finding "any trace of evidence," and by its unwillingness to see that "the instigators are only common men" and that the "real causes" are to be found in "misery, hunger, and despair carried to the extreme."[147]

Albert, on the eve of his nomination to the Parisian Lieutenance of Police in a reorganization provoked by the flour riots, personally interrogated the imprisoned directors of the *régie*. The record of his strained exchange with Doumerc has survived.[148] Albert asked him about the management practices he used and criticized his laxity in verifying the delivery of supplies and the accounts of his agents. In only one instance—an apparent discrepancy of 1,000 *livres*—did Albert challenge him on concrete grounds. Doumerc replied that he could not explain the matter without reference to his papers. "Did they not sometimes

145 Bachaumont, *Mémoires secrets*, XXX, 225 (7 May 1775).

146 *Ibid.*, XXX, 242 (19 May 1775).

147 "Relation historique de l'émeute …," in Pidansat de Mairobert, *Journal historique*, VII, 315. Cf. the verses which circulated in the aftermath of the Flour War (*ibid.*, VII, 329–30):
Est-ce Maupeou tant abhorré
Qui nous rend le bled cher en France?
Ou bien est-ce l'abbé Terrai?
Est-ce le Clergé, la Finance?
Des Jésuites est-ce vengeance,
Ou de l'Anglois un tour falot?
Non, ce n'est point-là le fin mot.
Mais voulez-vous qu'en confidence
Je vous le dise? … C'est Turgot.

148 Arsenal, mss. Bastille, 12447. Cf. yet another "perquisition et saisie" of the *regie*'s papers, AN, Y 11441.

employ authoritarian measures [i.e. the government's authority] to prevent private traders from buying grain in order to reserve it all for themselves?" queried Albert. No, said Doumerc, we were not empowered to do that. Did they not export certain quantities of grain and flour? No, rejoined Doumerc. How, then, asked Albert, attacking, can you account for the turning away of three ships of American flour in June 1772 and another flour-laden vessel in June 1774? We had orders from the minister, explained the prisoner, adding that in the latter case it was because the foreign correspondent had not delivered the merchandise within the pre-arranged time limit. Doumerc did not satisfy Albert in answering the charge that he and Sorin had used the royal grain fund to launch a private banking and commercial affair. He refused to answer a question about an alleged secret contract with Guys of Marseilles on the grounds that he had already fully explained the *régie*'s relations with its agents. At no point in the encounter did Albert ask Doumerc about anything pertaining to the Flour War.

A large part of the interrogation focussed on the *régie*'s role in a private grain and flour trading company based in Montauban and operated by Perrouteau in association with Doumerc's father. Clearly this was Albert's strongest point and the issue which most disconcerted Doumerc. Doumerc claimed that he could not "recollect" many of the details. Nor could he explain exactly what links the Perrouteau company had with the *régie* and what tasks it performed for it. Although he admitted that he lent his "credit" to the operation, he indignantly denied that he had funded it with the king's money or that it functioned clandestinely for the personal profit of Doumerc and Sorin. The Perrouteau affair seemed to offer Albert the sort of lever he had been so anxiously trying to find.

In the end, however, Albert could still not make a case that would stick against the *régie* directors. Despite repeated requests, Doumerc and Sorin could not obtain a formal statement of the charges against them. Nor could their wives, who petitioned minister after minister for their release, win permission to visit them.[149] Turgot did not concede defeat until a committee of members of the royal council, chosen by himself, determined that there were no grounds to hold them. They left the Bastille at the end of June. According to one report, upon regaining their freedom Doumerc and Sorin demanded still another

---

149 See the letters and petitions of the wives in Arsenal, mss. Bastille 12447. Cf. Bachaumont, *Mémoires secrets*, XXX, 249 (28 May 1774). On their conditions of imprisonment, see Charpentier, *La Bastille dévoilée* (Paris, 1789), IV, 44–48.

investigation of all their accounts in order to clear their names completely. Apparently, they received formal vindication the following year.[150]
The confrontation with Turgot did not leave a permanent stain
on their reputation. Though Sorin disappeared from view, Doumerc
enjoyed a successful career in private commerce as well as public service.[151] Béguillet, the subsistence commentator and crusader for modernization in the bread industry, praised him as a "good citizen" and
"enlightened businessman" for developing a portable market scale
capable of measuring 1/192nd of a Paris *septier* and thus assisting the
buyer in determining the quality of the grain. Doumerc continued
to advise the government on provisioning affairs. On his suggestion,
in 1784, the ministry began to build a "vast" grain magazine at Auxonne for military and civil grain storage. Throughout the eighties, he
counseled the Paris Parlement, the Procurator General and the Controllers-General on grain operations. He claimed a large share of the
responsibility for dealing successfully with a threatening subsistence
situation in the Paris area in 1788. Yet he insisted on the need to look
"to the future," beyond "the palliatives of the moment." His experience under Terray had made him an avid planner. In 1789, on the eve
of the Revolution, he had the title of "general administrator of subsistence," serving probably in the grain department of the Contrôle-
Général. In the estimation of Bailly, Paris' first revolutionary mayor,
no one was better equipped to administer the subsistence department.
But the volatility of opinion in the capital in the early months of the
Revolution drove Doumerc into hiding. Like other officials and dealers
associated with provisioning affairs, he was terribly frightened by the
executions of Bertier de Sauvigny and Foulon and by the talk of famine plot vengeance for the people. In 1791 he quietly re-emerged to
become one of the "general administrators of military subsistence."[152]

---

150 Lenoir papers, Bibliothèque Municipale d'Orléans, mss. 1421; Bord, *Histoire du blé*, 41.
Bachaumont, *Mémoires secrets*, XXX, 284 (13 July 1774).

151 A police "scandal" report casts a curious sidelight on Doumerc's private life, confirming
Malisset's charge that Doumerc had a considerable appetite for pleasure: "M. Doumergue
[*sic*], courtier of M. Trudaine de Montigny for the grain department [here the observer is
using dated intelligence], has just received a lesson from the demoiselle Daguin who arranges
for a part of his great profits to flow back into commerce. This demoiselle, after having pinched
him for some very fine furniture, a wardrobe closet, a great many jewels and a contract for
a 600 *livres* rent, has given him notice and immediately replaced him with Sieur de Patarin,
Spaniard, said to be a *négociant*, lodged in Paris, rue de Marl." 20 Sept. 1771, in Camille Piton,
ed., *Paris sous Louis XV, rapports des inspecteurs de police au roi* (Paris, 1910), 343.

152 Béguillet, *Traité des subsistances*, 164–65; "Mémoire sur l'approvisionnement

Doumerc's one-time patron, the abbé Terray, enjoyed no such rehabilitation after his disgrace. According to Marie-Antoinette, the "people" could not contain their "extravagances of joy" upon notification of his dismissal in the summer of 1774.[153] It is difficult to sort out and weigh the elements which conspired to discredit him: his association with Maupeou, scourge of the parlements; his fiscal reforms; the revulsion (and jealousy) that his personal life inspired; and his management of the grain question. Obsessed themselves with the subsistence problem, the revolutionaries remembered him not as the minister who spoke for the consumer interest against the aristocracy of wealth, but as the Controller-General who turned provisioning into a lucrative business affair. For Camille Desmoulins, Terray was a Judas clothed in the motley robe of Joseph, using the "same methods" the son of Jacob employed to nourish Egypt in order "to starve France."[154] Modern historians have challenged the Terray stereotypes and have generally viewed him, as a public man, in a highly favorable light.[155]

Historians were not the first, however, to undertake the task of revision. In Terray's own time, a number of commentators made a serious effort to render a balanced judgment of his administration, an assessment which has strong claims to scholarly endorsement today. "In the epoch when the abbé Terray was a simple counselor in the Grand'Chambre," wrote Moreau, "he drew attention by carrying the sacraments himself to those Jansenists to whom the Archbishop of Paris, Beaumont, refused them." Not long after, he became a shameless "libertine"; the "details" of his debauchery horrified Moreau. "But if he was one of the worst priests that I ever knew," added Moreau, "he was also one of the best Controllers-General of the reign of Louis XV...." He sought to "make himself master of the grain price" for the sake of the public interest:

I do not know if he was the inventor of the depots established at Corbeil amidst the numerous mills which surround this city and which never cease to

de réserve ou greniers d'abondance," AN, F¹¹ 222; Doumerc to Joly, 17 Feb. 1789, BN, Coll. Joly, 1111, fols. 198–205; AN, F¹¹ 1173–74; "Mémoire concernant la cultivation d'un grain dit Seigle de Russie," AN, F¹⁰ 226; Bailly, *Mémoires*, ed. by Berville and Barrière (Paris, 1822), II, 71, 136.

153 Marie-Antoinette to Marie-Thérèse, 7 Sept. 1774, in *Correspondance secrète*, ed. by d'Arneth and Geoffroy, II, 229.

154 C. Desmoulins, *Les Insignes meuniers de Corbeil* (Paris, 1789), 2.

155 See, in addition to Marion's *Histoire financière*, Faure, *Disgrâce de Turgot*, 216–23; Cahen, "Prétendu pacte," *Revue historique*, CLXVI (Sept.–Oct. 1935), 195; and Girard, *Terray, passim*.

function: what I know is that he used them to great advantage to set up a salutary equilibrium between the disadvantages of sterility and of abundance; in this respect, I considered him as one of the good servants of the King.[156]

Simon Linguet, defender of pariahs and friend of the underdog, viewed Terray's achievements in a similar light. The abbé assumed his post at a time when the finances suffered "a disorder of which it is impossible to form an idea." Against enormous odds, in the face of "frightening" difficulties, without concern for his own reputation, he implemented many important reforms. Heir to an immense deficit, "the abbé Terray, so decried, burdened with so many insults and public execration, regarded as an avid man, liar, odious, even criminal in all the senses," left the Treasury in a remarkably good state of health. His grain operations, which gave rise to further calumnies and legends, were sound and necessary measures devised to correct the damage done by the "flour fanaticism" of the liberals. Terray "imagined that prudent purchases and sales made with discretion could achieve the effect on the markets which one had been falsely led to expect from a [liberalizing] law." Aiming at a more viable "balance" of interests, he used the weight" of the government to curtail and contain price "oscillations." Linguet suggested that Terray may have used wrong methods and that some of his subordinates may not have conducted themselves in irreproachable fashion. On the whole, however, he merits our gratitude, for he spared us from suffering a famine "as cruel" as there was reason to fear.

Ironically, after reviling Terray, Turgot found himself obliged to imitate him. "After having so haughtily, so viciously, so cruelly, so unjustly censured his regime," wrote Linguet, "it was necessary to return to it: solemn laws were promulgated to dispense grain from coming to the markets: it was necessary [afterwards] to force it there by secret orders...." Not long after the Flour War, Turgot signed a contract—which Linguet interpreted as an indirect vindication of Terray—with the Leleu brothers, merchants who had assisted Albert

---

156 Moreau, *Mes Souvenirs*, ed. by C. Hermelin, II, 34. For a similar evaluation, see Besenval, *Mémoires*, ed. by Berville and Barrière, I, 380.

157 On the Leleu arrangement, see Taboureau, *Rapport au Roi (1777)* (Paris, 1789); Accounts, AN, F[11] 1195; James Rutledge, *Second mémoire pour les maîtres boulangers* (Paris, [1789]), 10, 22–23; Archives Seine-Paris, DC [6]25, fol. 118; *Révolutions de Paris*, (9–16 Jan. 1790), 16–17; Musart, *Réglementation du commerce des grains*, 135; F. Vincent, *Histoire des famines à Paris* (Paris, 1946), 84–85; Faure, *Disgrâce de Turgot*, 412–14.

in his investigation of the *régie*, for the maintenance of a flour stock at Corbeil for the service of the Paris Halles.[157] "From everything which precedes," Linguet asked, "what is the result?"

> That the abbé Terray was a prodigy of virtue? I do not say that. That his administration was a model to propose to all of his successors? Even less ... I say simply that he was very badly judged ... he had some talents and some defects: one has prodigiously exaggerated the latter and not rendered justice to the former.[158]

---

158 Linguet, *Annales*, VI, 157, 285–88, 298, 301–05.

CONCLUSION

Like many parts of the Third World today, old-regime France was obsessed with subsistence—and for good reasons. Dependent for the most part on a single foodstuff whose production and distribution were hostage to a host of uncertainties, it is no wonder that the people of this society agonized over their material life. They had no sense of control over their environment—either the sociojuridical structure around which their lives were organized or the economic and physical circumstances in which they lived. Nor could the Enlightenment provide a dose of confidence and courage powerful enough to reach the bulk of the population. Not all the philosophical tracts on man's earthly potential, nor all the manuals on the application of vetch or the use of sainfoin, nor all the inoculations practiced on the children of princes could convince the "little people" of the eighteenth century that they lived in a world on the verge of mastering, or at least reaching an accord with, nature. Subsistence, of course, was not the whole story of man's predicament, but preoccupation with it was sufficiently universal and relentless to remind men every day of the precariousness of their situation and of their relative helplessness to change it.

Even as the marketplace, like the cemetery, was at the center of popular life in the Old Regime, so subsistence was always at the center of public concern. In the crudest terms, it can be said that fear of the people commanded attention to the people's fears. Subsistence uncertainty and anxiety impelled government to give the highest priority to provisioning. But government intervened in the first instance not so much to reassure the people as to reassure itself. From top to bottom, officials believed that the social and political structures could not passively bear the strain or tolerate the risks of scarcity. Subsistence was the precondition to social order. Their assumptions about the psychology of human motivation, the nature of commerce, and the habits of cultivators and suppliers convinced authorities that grain distribution could not safely be left entirely to private initiative and the arbitration of free market forces.

What nourished this ideology of fear and mistrust, what made the governors, like the governed, timid and conservative, what made intervention necessary and inevitable, was above all the nature of pre-industrial society itself. Grain made a victim of the government, just as it made a victim of the people. Total dependence on the vagaries of the harvest left government little margin in which to function. The myth of abundance (which, to be sure, was not always and in all places a myth) could not alter the fact that deficits occurred frequently and that they often had an impact wholly out of proportion to their real importance. Rampant particularism and primitive means of transportation and communication reinforced this tyranny of grain. If the police were often rigid and brutal and unpredictable, it was in large part because the material world with which they tried to deal, without the help of what we call technology, was rigid and brutal and unpredictable.

The point is that the police had no choice. With few exceptions, public authorities did not seek out responsibility for provisioning, say, as the central government sought to extend its exercise of justice and fiscality. Imperiously, the need to intervene imposed itself; the government used controls because it saw no other way to assure subsistence and thus obtain the relative stability without which it feared it could not survive. It would be a mistake, in my view, to envision the police of provisioning as a product of statemaking or as a function of absolutism. Rather, statemaking and the development of absolutism were themselves limited and conditioned by the exigencies of subsistence management. It is tempting to assimilate provisioning controls to other authoritarian, arbitrary and oppressive expressions of absolutist rule, but the bastilles and the grain regulations of the Old Regime, though they ended up serving many common ends, were very different kinds of institutions. While the government had a number of reasons for wanting to control the food supply, feeding the people was not one of its deliberate totalitarian ambitions. On one level, then, police controls translated a political design: an unwillingness to court the risks of disorder. On another even more rudimentary level, however, the controls appear as consequences of material conditions and social constraints which were to some degree independent of political will. Doubtless, the reformers were right in condemning the controls as impediments to growth or modernization. But they were in large measure the result, not the explanation, of what we have come to call backwardness.

Nor was the provisioning policy exclusively the product of an urban consciousness peculiar to the large cities and divorced from the realities and needs of an overwhelmingly agrarian world. In some cases, it was easier to supply the great cities than other areas and it was often possible to do so with greater reliance upon the open market. The subsistence preoccupation reached deeply into the countryside; the police of provisioning in small towns, *bourgs*, and many villages was as vigorous as in the urban agglomerations. Moreover, there was no brusque discontinuity between urban and rural, non-agrarian and agrarian in old-regime France, not even in the major cities.

We have had occasion to examine, in considerable detail, the organization of police and the control apparatus it elaborated in order to assure provisioning. We have noted, too, the difficulty of generalizing about the operation of the police. It varied enormously from time to time, place to place, and hand to hand. The police were extremely parochial because subsistence was primarily a local matter. More often than not, police operations were not well coordinated. Structural incoherence and communications gaps exacerbated the inevitable rivalries over hinterland and jurisdiction. The grain police was a preeminently circumstantial affair. There were certain controls built into the grain trade, but a large part of the regulatory machine tended to lie dormant until activated by menacing supply, price, or weather conditions.

On the whole the grain police seems to have been more supple than is generally assumed. There is evidence that there was a generous tolerance of officially prohibited trading practices in many places and perhaps even a growing climate of de facto liberalization in the quarter century before 1763, especially around the large urban centers and ports where grain and flour increasingly bypassed local markets en route to their final destination. There is little doubt that the police apparatus militated against the emergence of large-scale trade concentrating vast amounts of capital and dealing across great distances of time and space. But there are also strong indications that the trade would have remained fragmented and relatively modest in magnitude regardless of the police system, as a result of the modes of production, deeply-rooted local habits, and technological factors, which made grain and flour commerce extremely risky, costly, and cumbersome. In some ways, the police regime inhibited the development of a more responsive market system, but in other ways it promoted the rationalization and integration of the markets where the suppliers themselves resisted fresh currents of commercialization. The police encouraged, for example, the expansion of credit facilities and the development of factorage systems at the larger markets.

Nevertheless, as I attempted to show earlier, it would be absurd to pretend that the police system was genuinely hospitable to commerce. In many of its particulars, the liberal bill of indictment was well founded. It would not be hard to demonstrate that police controls and interventions violated property rights, demoralized and confused traders, jeopardized wide-ranging speculations, encouraged particularism, and led to inefficient and expensive distributive practices. It is true that police action often forced or induced grain to flee and thus drove prices up (though it is also true that on other occasions the same actions smoked grain into the open and depressed prices). It is true that the police style, in a sense, invited public disorder and helped to make the riot or demonstration a very effective consumer weapon. And it is true, as the liberals charged, that the police regime failed to prevent the recurrence of dearths, though it must be added that the authorities never pretended that it could achieve this goal.

In response to cues from the police, and as a result of their own instincts of justice and survival, the consumers developed attitudes that helped them deal with subsistence uncertainties. These beliefs — about the duties of government, the wealth of France, the motives of merchants, the causes of dearth—served them in much the same way that myths, rites of propitiation, and collective defense mechanisms helped other societies cope with chronic or extraordinary threats. This subsistence mentality taught the consumers how to interpret supply and price indicators in various circumstances, when to be suspicious and when to be patient, whom to blame and upon whom to rely. Naturally, it varied in its particular manifestations from place to place, but like the different brands of police, the subsistence mentality took its general coherence from a number of commonly held assumptions. The most important concerned claims of the people upon public authority—ultimately upon the king—and their expectation, repeatedly authorized and encouraged by officials at all levels of administration, that government would intervene when popular subsistence was menaced in any prolonged or unusual fashion.

Over time, the provisioning policy acquired not merely conventional sanction, but a sanction that one is tempted to call sacrosanct. The consumers embraced it with ferocity, for it was vital to their existence. The liberals quite rightly perceived this subsistence mentality as an enormous obstacle to change. They denounced its components as so many "prejudices" in very much the same way that critics of traditional religious practices decried widespread "superstitions." The prospects for freeing men from superstitions of the spirit may have been better than for persuading them to abandon instincts concerning their material lives, if only because spiritual surrogates were easier to come by in eighteenth-century France than ersatz for bread (though, to be sure, for most people, rationalism was no more palatable or filling than rice).

In general, it is difficult to take issue with the liberal charge that the consumerist viewpoint perpetuated misleading and vicious stereotypes about commerce, nurtured dangerous hopes among the people, and imposed enormous demands upon the government; that it was timorous, selfish, xenophobic, and anti-economic. Nor were the liberals wrong in pointing out the existence of a powerful tacit alliance between the police and the people. Dupont was right: under stress the police "became people," that is to say, evinced unmistakable traces of the subsistence mentality. Although it was not a genuinely comfortable or willingly acknowledged relationship for either, the alliance nevertheless served both their interests.

The subsistence problem was a powerful political force in the shaping of the Old Regime. It placed constraints upon government at all levels, especially the central government, and it mediated relations between the governors and the governed. Moreover, it was construed as a political question, dimly and crudely by consumers who depended upon the government to heed its contract and more explicitly by the authorities who worried about containment and social control. Consumers never perceived subsistence as an economic problem; for the police, it was a concern of economic policy only incidentally and accessorily, in reluctant deference to the fact that grain was not the product of spontaneous generation.[1] (The wage side of the equation had little bearing in this matter for either the active population of consumers or for the authorities.) Finally, subsistence was a political question which stood outside the arena of what we ordinarily call politics. Provisioning policy was not something to be defended, praised, or criticized. It was supposed to be beyond debate; it had a consensual, quasi-institutional status.

Against this background, I stressed the radicalism of the grain reform.

---

1 See, in this connection, Turgot's wry reminder to the local police that "the cobblestones of the cities do not produce any [grain]." "Lettre circulaire aux officiers de police," 15 Feb. 1766, C. 479, A.D. Haute-Vienne.

It is hardly surprising to discover in the corpus of eighteenth-century thought a number of ideas that were profoundly subversive of the old-regime way of life; the Enlightenment is replete with them. But it does seem to me remarkable that a few of these ideas, affecting the most delicate, most traditional, and, next to religion itself, the most sacrosanct sphere of public and private life, passed into law.

The grain reforms were a devastating critique of the police practices we have discussed. But they were not concerned, as royal reforms often were, with remedying specific defects. Ultimately, it is fruitless to confront the police and liberal arguments in these terms. The liberal legislation demanded nothing less than a *tabula rasa* in subsistence affairs; it was an indictment of the whole subsistence past, of the provisioning policy, of the way in which the problem was posed.

A vast gulf separated the new and the old ways. Laissez-faire meant the end of subsistence primacy as a national goal and the end of the special relation it implied between the government and the people. The new focus was on agriculture, the chief source of national wealth as well as the source of the kingdom's food. Provisioning was to be reduced to its proper status, as an offshoot of agriculture, and the producer was to replace the consumer as most-favored-subject. To be sure, the consumers were not entirely ignored, for the new policy offered them the prospect of an expanded agriculture, which would theoretically make dearth less likely, and a revitalized commerce, which would theoretically distribute grain more evenly, equalizing prices across time and space and attenuating their oscillations.

But the crucial fact for consumers was that prices would rise practically by royal declaration and that it was officially no longer to be the business of government to assure their subsistence by the police of provisioning. The entire police apparatus was to be dismantled, for it was now superfluous as well as vexatious. Commerce was to assume exclusive responsibility for provisioning, not as a service it owed society, but purely as a function of its quest for profits, and it would police itself through the purgative action of competition. Imbalances would no longer be subject to administrative adjustment; as a result of the underlying harmony of interests, they would correct themselves naturally. In virtually every respect, the new way differed from the old—in its conceptions of nature, liberty, property, competition, human motivation and the psychology of interest, the proper role of the state, and so on.

The liberals tended to ignore the political aspects of the subsistence question, even as the police tended to neglect the economic ones. Implicit in the police view was the idea that there was only one meaningful time dimension, the short run—the dimension of political time—and that all decisions had to be made within this framework. The liberals, on the contrary, averted their eyes from the present and immediate future in order to focus on long-range goals in the economic dimension of time. Persuaded that their principles were true, the liberals proceeded in the confidence that things would work out in the end, and that the end would justify the means. For reformers, the short run is often a trap. To break out of the police cast of mind, the liberals were obliged to look beyond. To do so required courage and resolution, though it may very well have been based upon serious miscalculations.

The government apparently presumed that it could disestablish the police and unilaterally disavow its traditional covenant with the people by a sweeping set of laws. It explained and justified its action in simple terms (though, as we have seen, its motives in fact were highly sophisticated and ambitious): the old system was no longer useful and the old promises no longer binding because they had been founded on utterly false premises. The liberal king pretended to be accountable only to nature; natural law declared that subsistence could not be an affair of state. But would the nation understand this reasoning? Would not the transition from bloated interventionist state to lean spectator state be extremely difficult and costly?

There is no question that the government expected certain problems of transition and acclimatization. Nevertheless, it had no strategy for dealing with them, except perhaps in the capital. By its own design and doctrine, provisioning was out of its control. It would use authority only to force grain to be free, not to force it to market on grounds of social justice or expediency. Yet the government was determined to repress (it could no longer think in terms of preventing) disorders, for it had not lost its taste for tranquility along with its appetite for the police of subsistence. Repression, by itself, was hardly a durable principle of social stability. During the Old Regime the stick had almost always been accompanied by the carrot; the one was usually not effective without the other. What after repression? The dilemma can be epitomized by the instructions that Turgot as Controller-General gave to the Lieutenant General of Police at the time of the Flour War, instructions which struck the police as mutually contradictory. On the one hand: "Tend to the security of the capital" and on the other: "Do not meddle with [the question of] bread."[2]

As it turned out, the incidence and intensity of popular unrest in the aftermath of liberalization stunned the ministry. Even more shocking was the *frondeur* spirit it encountered in the local administration. Local authorities had to answer for subsistence problems after 1763 as before, even as they had to answer for public order; vis-à-vis their constituents and their superiors, liberalization did not free them from their traditional responsibilities. At Versailles, the king could turn spectator imperceptibly, but in the field it was far more difficult for officials to remain on the sidelines. Liberalization by itself elicited a wide range of reactions from the local police: some were pleased, others indifferent, still others puzzled, startled, or horrified. But the subsistence crisis put the squeeze on all of them and placed many of them in a wholly untenable position. The government could provide them with little in the way of concrete support, save for the occasional dispatch of a *maréchaussée* or an army unit lodged in the area. Nor had the ministry consulted widely with local authorities before the promulgation of the reforms in order to smooth the path for implementation. From the point of view of the grassroots police, this was liberalism by absolutist swagger. The government commanded and exhorted, but the incongruity between its instructions and local exigencies forced or prompted many officials to disobey, usually with reluctance and trepidation. Its estrangement from its own infrastructure of local authority gradually placed the liberal ministry, too, in an untenable situation.[3]

The government knew that the reforms would have a deep impact on the popular milieu since they affected daily life so directly, but it did not know how to deal with popular opinion or with what we have called the subsistence mentality. It was not that the government was indifferent to public relations. On the contrary, it orchestrated the preparation of the reforms to derive maximum political advantage from the idea of associating the king with the nation. Though the monarchical system was not well suited for this kind of politics, when liberalization came under attack, the king and the ministry appealed

---

2 J.-N. Moreau, *Mes Souvenirs*, ed. by C. Hermelin, II, 190.

3 It would be worth investigating whether there was any connection, intended or coincidental, between Laverdy's municipal reform of 1764–65 and liberalization, whether this administrative reform facilitated or hindered the dismantling of the police of provisioning, etc. The answer doubtless lies in departmental and communal archives, but the point of departure would be Maurice Bordes, *La Réforme municipale du Contrôleur-général Laverdy et son application (1764–71)* (Toulouse, 1968).

directly to the nation for support. But the nation which it addressed was not the bone and sinew that the government pretended it to be; the opinion which it cultivated and with which it felt at ease, the opinion which was acknowledged to be "queen" in the century of Enlightenment, was naturally an elite opinion, the opinion of the educated, the men of substance. This opinion was informed, it was accessible, especially through the written word, and in a number of ways it was easier to manipulate or to influence than inarticulate and elusive popular opinion. It would have been pointless for the liberal government to have hired a band of Voltaires to write essays or grain catechisms promoting its policy, for they would not have reached the formless public of consumers.

But suppose the government had found a way to address this public: What could it have said? That natural law could be counted on? That higher prices would make the world safer for their children and their children's children? That self-restraint under stress was a virtue? That the king, as a sign of his confidence, had declared his children emancipated or major? The problem, from the liberal standpoint, was that the people "did not reason" on subsistence questions. Thus there was no easy way to discredit their old assumptions and to invite belief in a new approach, which sprung from nature, but required a sophisticated, multivariate, rational analysis of economic and social activity. The fact that the people clung to "prejudices" frustrated the liberals, but it reassured them at the same time, for it justified their unwillingness to give serious consideration to popular attitudes. These prejudices were unfounded, rationally and objectively. Popular fears, like many so-called dearths, were "artificial" and "unreal."

There was a brutal edge to grain liberalism; perhaps there had to be. Pitted against the massive inertia of tradition and the deeply-ingrained habits of the people, it had to be unflinching and it was bound to seem cruel. Grain liberalism was founded on an ethos hostile to the dominant values of the society and it involved abrupt and jolting changes. Doctrinally, its own logic gave it an intransigent and cold-hearted cast. There was no place for old-style moral reckoning in the new political economy. The discovery of a social and economic science stood between the liberalism of the sixties and the diffuse humanitarianism of the Enlightenment of the abbé de Saint-Pierre. Faith in the scientific basis of their analysis relieved the liberals of a potential moral dilemma (though it did not resolve the political one). The prescriptions of liberalism were not moral choices; they were *imposed* by the physical laws of nature, laws which were by definition just and inexorable and which were perforce anterior to any conception of morality. The liberals were men of charity, but they believed that compassion had to be subordinated to the first principles around which society was organized. They warned against succumbing to sentimentality in dealing with the fundamental questions of social and economic life. Sentimentality was the ally of and the alibi for tradition and timidity. Good government had to be strong in self-restraint; it could not take its lead from the people.

The doctrine of grain liberalism provoked a considerable amount of criticism; we have had the occasion to examine some of it in detail. The reproaches that stung the liberals most deeply were those which charged that they were indifferent to popular suffering, that they were inhumane. Whatever their doctrine later became, the leading theorists were not inspired by mean or unworthy motives. There is no reason to doubt the sincerity of their commitment to human progress and their belief in the capacity of man to fashion a better world. It is easier for many of us to sympathize with the poor of the consumer army and with harried officials than with salon or state ideologues; it is easy to forget that the latter were locked in a struggle, aimed, in their view, at freeing man from the shackles of the past, and that their doctrine was a program of combat. It was not, however, liberalism's attitude toward the people nor its apparent ferocity which troubled most contemporary critics. Nor was it the doctrine's refusal to recognize a social justice apart from the justice of natural law which was stacked against the people or its allegedly scientific rationalization of what we would call class interests. Lurking in the shadows of the progress and prosperity which liberalism promised to generate, these critics sensed chaos. It was not so much that the liberal program could pass only at the expense of the people than that it would subject the whole society to progress by ordeal. The critics feared that the liberal future would be less desirable than the past, not only for the people but for everyone.

The range of this criticism was enormous; on one point or another, it united men of vastly different views. They included administrators who were primarily concerned about social equilibrium and writers who were interested in what later became called social and political science. At one extreme were old-fashioned conservatives, frightened by the spectre of change, who assimilated grain liberalism to the broader quest for liberty undertaken by the Enlightenment in myriad other domains and denounced all of them in one shrill cry. At the other extreme were critics at home within the Enlightenment whose reactions were more arresting because they were far less predictable.

In this respect the attitude of Diderot seems especially significant to me, though it would be wrong to make any flat claim for its representativeness in the philosophical community as a whole. In the early days of physiocracy—the theoretical days—Diderot shared the enthusiasm of the *économistes* for their exciting enterprise. Unlike his friend Grimm, who expressed contempt for their pomposity and dogmatism, Diderot admired their critical pugnacity, their boundless curiosity, and their search for universality. In the end, however, after the crisis of the sixties, he recoiled in horror from their social program. The prospect of a society operating strictly according to the absolute laws of property and liberty repelled Diderot because it was politically brittle and morally objectionable. What bothered him about physiocracy was not its legal despotism nor its single tax, but its underlying principles as they figured in its grain policy, its laissez-faire complaisance, its capitalist ethos. Although Diderot's position is not without ambiguities, it is safe to say that the encounter between liberal theory and old-regime habits in the late sixties and early seventies severely jarred him. Grain liberalism was too radical for one of the most radical of philosophes.

The remarkable thing about grain liberalism, I have argued, was its radicalism. It broke violently with tradition and it crystallized, in embryo, many of the powerful psychological, political, and socio-economic forces which in the next three generations would drastically change France and much of the Western world. Yet the radicalism of this liberalism depends to a large degree on the perspective of the beholder. For it must not be forgotten that the liberal program drew its support from some of the most reputedly traditional and conservative-minded elements in French society: the major land- and grain-owners, including important segments of the nobility, sword and robe. It was able to do this, not because it preached an enlightened, progressive philosophical doctrine—utilitarianism, individualism, the laws of nature, the worth of liberty and the power of evidence—but because it defined its liberalism in terms of grain. In other forms, the liberalism of physiocracy, like the ideas of other philosophes, would have frightened the proprietors and grain holders, not to mention the members of the royal council and of the sovereign courts. The political triumph of grain liberalism was precisely its ability to link its fate to a powerful, traditional, and resurgent economic (and political) interest.

The proprietors and grain owners, unlike the *économistes* and some of their critics, did not believe that "tout se tient"—"everything is linked together." They were not interested in systems nor did they worry about intellectual coherence. Grain liberalism for them meant, above all, higher prices and a better return. It had no universal dimension of truth, no complex ideological content. Nor did it portend for them the revolt of the police and the people, the dismantling of corporate bonds, the ascendency of merit and parvenu wealth, the dislocation of the traditional corporate structure, or any other nightmare of social upheaval. Grain liberalism meant that they could have the best of both worlds. It meant, for example, that the Parlement of Toulouse could have liberty of trade as sanctioned by nature, while retaining the liberty to extirpate heresy as sanctioned by God. The socioeconomic elites were prepared to join in a movement profoundly subversive of their world because they did not understand it or because they did not take seriously its far-reaching implications.

Moreover, it is virtually certain that the theorists themselves did not foresee the violent shocks that liberalism would produce in years to come. Galiani's charges to the contrary notwithstanding, the leading *économistes* were not *enragés*—far from it. In their view society was stalemated, its development blocked by the bonds that tied it to the past. Were there compelling reasons for them, from a vantage point within the stifling atmosphere of the Old Regime, to anticipate how dramatically laissez-faire would change, not only the rules of the game, but the game itself? Was there any reason for them to suspect how corrosive their brand of liberty could or would become? Their adventure was so parlous and so exciting precisely because they did not know where it would lead, though they undertook it, I think, with the belief that it would not turn the world upside-down. For lack of better models, there was always the example of England, a nation which seemed at first glance to have reconciled and integrated the goals of stability and growth along lines not completely foreign to the liberal vision.

The liberals were groping for a formula for what we have come to call modernization. Indeed, from their standpoint, unlike other reformers, they were not groping—on the contrary, they had found in nature the philosopher's stone, which some had sought in magic potions that made base metal glitter (or more recently made seed grain multiply prodigiously) and which others had sought in piecemeal schemes of innovation. The peculiar merit of grain liberalism was that it proclaimed that the road to modernization passed first through economic expansion, that this was the only way to remove the social and political blockages which clogged the channels of the Old Regime. Superficially, the idea bears a certain resemblance to mercantilist doctrine, but the goals and methods of liberalism and its conceptions of the relation of state and society and of the functions of wealth were vastly different and its socioeconomic model infinitely more supple and dynamic.[4] It is of at least symbolical significance that when the government of 1770–71 repudiated grain liberalism and the economic road to modernization, it turned again to the war against the parlements and to the worn political-institutional road to modernization, a road more familiar to the ministers of the Old Regime than the uncertain path of liberalism, but one which proved time and again to be a cul-de-sac.

Thus it would be wrong to claim categorically that the liberals did not understand their society and attempt, in this fashion, to explain liberalization as an aberration, one of those geometrical and abstract reforms which eighteenth century government produced in its stuporous cups after having imbibed too many drafts of (bad) philosophy. This was the view of some of the police apologists; later it became the standard interpretation of many nineteenth- and twentieth-century writers on the Enlightenment and the Old Regime. In the eyes of its partisans, liberalization was politics geared to both profits and principles. One can hardly imagine, it seems to me, a doctrine that could better serve the restlessness of the economic and intellectual elites of the time than the new political economy, nor a program more neatly tailored to satisfy certain of the economic needs of pre-industrial France. If the liberals, as I have tried to suggest, were unwilling or unable to deal with some realities, nevertheless they had an ingenious plan for dealing with others. The prescription seemed to fit; that is why the government invested so much hope in it and transformed it into policy and law. But that does not mean, as we have seen, that the medicine did not have ominous contraindications.

Liberalization was short-lived; whether it did not survive because it did not work or for other reasons was hotly debated by contemporaries and is still subject to controversy. I am inclined to believe that it could not have worked in eighteenth-century France; that France was not yet ready for laissez-faire. Liberalization was bound to founderevery

---

4 The antithesis mercantilism-liberalism is extremely misleading. The two doctrines had a great deal in common and many points of intersection in old-regime policy and literature. An economist like Véron de Forbonnais, for example, served as a bridge between the two approaches and exerted considerable influence. Although the context is rather narrow, see the useful remarks of Paul H. Beik, *A Judgment of the Old Regime* (New York, 1941) 266ff.

time it came under stress and it was bound to come under stress frequently, given the tyrannical hold of grain, the inelasticity of demand and the continued increase in population, the narrow aggregative margin between production and consumption and the frequent cases of regional or local disproportion between them, the acute vulnerability of the whole production-distribution nexus to myriad accidents, the implacable constraints of time and space, the disunity of France as reflected in the persistence of legal, commercial, administrative, and folk particularisms, the rigidity of foodways, the uncertainty of international economic relations, and so on. The liberals argued that liberty could have progressively created the conditions prerequisite for its own success. In some ways I think they were right. Laissez-faire, for example, would ultimately have forced a unification of weights and measures and could probably have produced the sort of market organization and the trade factors equipped to respond effectively to supply and demand pressures. Whether by itself, however, it could have overcome the other obstructions or the fresh barriers that it was likely to generate as it gained momentum seems highly doubtful to me. For laissez-faire to have solved the subsistence problem, major technological changes would have been necessary on both the production and distribution sides. All these elements remain apart from the short-term political, social, and psychological considerations, which proved to be decisive in the sixties and again in the seventies.

Although in the early stages the liberals rushed to catalogue the putative achievements of the reforms in stimulating agriculture and reinvigorating the grain trade, in the end they argued that the reforms had not received a fair trial. They claimed first that liberalization had been thwarted by a stroke of bad luck: a series of bad harvests. There is no doubt that there were short crops throughout the late sixties, though the opponents of the reforms insisted, not implausibly, that the failures were not as bad or as general as the liberals claimed. Yet, given past experience, it was not unreasonable to expect that the kingdom, or large parts of it, would have to face harvest failures sooner or later. The constant threat of meteorological accident had to figure in the liberal design, even as it weighed heavily on police thinking. Second, the liberals maintained that the reforms had been undermined by bad faith, that they had not been vigorously executed in many areas, and that they had been actively subverted in others. The evidence suggests that the laws, at least in the beginning, were widely implemented. The police did not brazenly refuse to execute royal will. Their revolt took shape slowly, spasmodically, and painfully. Moreover, the reforms were permissive, enabling laws; their success depended in considerable measure on the initiatives and the aggressiveness of the traders and grain-owners. Indications are that they took advantage of the new conditions on a broad scale. Still, it is clear that as the subsistence crisis worsened, the local authorities became increasingly unwilling to abide by the reform constraints and in some fashion or other many of them violated the liberal laws. At the very moment the government declared that it was most urgent to execute the reform laws rigorously, the police refused to stand aside.

Third, the liberals claimed that the reforms themselves were incomplete and thus that liberal theory had been improperly served. This line permitted the *économistes*, after the fall of the liberal ministry, to hold the government partly responsible for the failure of the reform and to argue that a larger dose of liberty would have done the job. Total liberty, however, was more a battle cry than a program. In terms of domestic traffic, the law could not have granted a more perfect liberty, save for its failure to assure the elimination of all customs and fees barriers in and en route to markets. Moreover, the liberals made far too much of the restrictions that the government deliberately imposed on liberty. The Paris exemptions purchased some time for the government, but they failed utterly to insulate the capital or its hinterlands and they did not prevent the traders in the Paris region from responding to the blandishments of liberty. The export ceiling never choked off exportation completely; at many outlets it never came into play. Nor did it prevent the price from reaching and maintaining (in many areas surpassing) the international par sought by the liberals or dampen the optimistic commercial mood which the July Edict was intended to create. If anything, the ceiling was higher than it needed to be to achieve the aims of the government; a lower cut-off point would have made the law politically more palatable at no real cost.

The government, as I have tried to demonstrate, had a great stake in the success of the reform. It showed remarkable nerve in undertaking it and it defended it stubbornly in the face of increasingly serious disaffection and opposition. There are very few examples of such determination in the history of the eighteenth-century ministries. The government refused to compromise, nor was there any room for compromise. For there was no middle ground to occupy between police and liberty; or rather, the police regime had already appropriated whatever terrain lay between controls and freedom. Liberalism was perforce extremism in the old-regime context.

The Paris reserve operation was a very reasonable gamble to take. Had the ministry used it more decisively and managed it with greater care, it might have rendered the liberal cause a major service—at the price, to be sure, of offending its liberal scruples. As it turned out, the king's grain was of vital importance to the Parisian supply system. Politically, the operation proved disastrous; it alienated an important segment of public and police opinion, on the one hand, and liberal opinion, on the other. It did not, however, as certain liberal writers claimed, paralyze or undermine private commerce throughout the kingdom.

The subsistence crisis, which began in some places as early as 1765, interrupted the process of liberalization and eventually led to its abandonment. It breached the gap between theory and fact, thrust the liberals on the defensive, and welded a strong opposition coalition. It was one of the most severe crises of this kind which the eighteenth century experienced; indeed, for most areas, it was the most catastrophic since 1709, and in some it was considerably worse than the situation proved to be in 1788–89. Eventually, it engulfed almost the entire kingdom; while it did not reach many areas of the South and Southeast until the seventies, in certain portions of the North it persisted or recurred in one form or another for almost a decade.

The crisis was characterized by serious shortages of grain, violent disruptions in the supply trade, and a doubling of the price level (in some places a tripling), accompanied by wild oscillations around the new level. It was a political crisis from below and from above, in terms of the repeated eruptions of popular protest of an incidence and intensity without parallel in the reign of Louis XV and as a result of the challenge which the emergence of a powerful opposition force posed to the ministry. It was a socioeconomic crisis for vast numbers of the laboring poor in cities and in the countryside, who suffered at best from belt-tightening and anxiety and at worst from hunger, panic, unemployment, uprooting, disease and death. Recent investigation intimates that mortality and morbidity, the most dramatic instances of the horrors of dearth, may have been greater than usually supposed. Yet these are not the sole and perhaps not the best indicators of grave social troubles; more research will be necessary before we can measure the full disorganizing impact of the crisis on daily life. Nor were the laboring poor the only segment of society affected. By 1770–71, the grain crisis had provoked a general economic crisis, which dislocated business life of all kinds through a large part of the kingdom.

I have suggested that this subsistence crisis was in many ways similar to others which preceded it. Leaving aside the question of scale and intensity, there are familiar patterns of genesis, spontaneity and contagion, protest and accommodation, commercial fever and stagnation, market disorganization, seasonal price fluctuations, urban-rural and market-hinterland tensions, and so on. The major difference, again leaving aside the question of magnitude, between this crisis and the others was that this dearth was preceded by a comprehensive grain reform. After the dearth began to make itself felt, the government did nothing to contain it and tried to prevent other authorities from combatting it with traditional methods—not as a result of what I have called the paralysis of discretion, nor because it could not determine whether it was a "real" or an "artificial" dearth, nor because it lacked the resources or information to take measures, but because of a conscious decision by which it had drastically altered its policy. The point, let me stress, is not that the government could have stemmed the crisis; one of the themes of this study is the tragic disproportion between the means at the disposal of the police and the gravity and complexity of the problems with which they had to deal. Rather, it is that for the first time in the Old Regime the government chose to play a passive role.

Both in terms of causes and effects, it is extremely difficult to disentangle the reforms and the grain crisis. I have argued that liberalization did not cause the dearth, but that it helped, directly and indirectly, to transform it into a crisis. The liberals denied any responsibility for it. They steeled themselves for the test; they felt, quite rightly within the terms of their doctrine and policy, that whatever the consequences, they could not give ground or they would lose everything. They called for more liberty to fight the dearth and for more authority to contain the police and the people. Officially, the liberal line was that there was no crisis. Yet others traced the origins of the dearth directly to the reforms; the longer subsistence difficulties persisted and the longer the government refused to acknowledge the gravity of the situation in the classical police fashion, the more convincing this analysis appeared, even to those who were disinclined to cast blame.

It required neither sophistication nor credulity to hold liberalization at least partly responsible for the subsistence difficulties. For one thing, higher prices were one of the announced goals of the reform and their consequences were supposed to be salutary for the whole nation. For another, liberalization, even without the burden of short crops, by its very nature mimicked many of the effects of a traditional subsistence crisis. As a result, it was almost inevitable that some observers would mistake the one for the other. Historically, at least from the police perspective, subsistence crises were times when the ordinary supply organization broke down, when human vice preceded or compounded nature's ravages, when license created or aggravated the problem of scarcity. Before harvest shortages declared themselves in many regions in the second half of the sixties, grain appeared to be rare and prices began to mount as traders and owners began to reassess their options in the light of new opportunities. The market structure was not strong or supple enough to accommodate shifting patterns of commerce without serious supply and price disturbances. Nor were the early signs of uncertainty or trouble without disquieting effects on the attitudes of police and consumers. These fears themselves began to act like self-fulfilling prophecies.

A great deal more must be learned about the operation of the grain and flour trades in ordinary times before we can take stock of the real influence of liberalization from place to place. Among the developments which are likely to be discerned and connected with the reforms are the entry of new persons into the trade, including, on the one extreme, a horde of micro-traders and, on the other, a handful of men concentrating uncommon amounts of capital and business expertise; the establishment of regional markets bypassing local demand or new lines of supply for metropolitan centers; and the elaboration of new marketing facilities and new trading practices. Apart from these "real" influences, we must take acount of psychological factors which have a reality of their own. There was, for example, the new spirit of independence and confidence evinced by owners and traders, as well as the buoyant expectations of cultivators, which the liberal writers celebrated.[5] Nothing better illustrates the antiliberal state of mind than

---

5 I have pointed out above how impatient the liberals were immediately after the promulgation of the liberal reforms to find evidence of its beneficent effect on agriculture—as a prod to clearing land, improving cultivation and increasing productivity. Baudeau suggested that the owners, *fermiers* and cultivators were keenly aware of the influence liberalization was likely to have on land revenues in particular and on the rural economy in general. He cited an as example the fact that "shrewd *fermiers*" stipulated in writing that the conditions of their new or revised leases would be binding only so long as liberty prevailed as the law of the land. As a measure of the psychological as well as the economic impact of liberalization, it would be worthwhile testing Baudeau's claim in the notarial and registration records. See N. Baudeau, *Avis aux honnêtes gens qui veulent bien faire* (Amsterdam, and Paris, 1768), 37. There are also interesting indications in a major study which unfortunately reached me after completion of the present work: Georges Frêche, *Toulouse et la région Midi-Pyrénées au siècle des lumières* (Paris: Cujas, 1974–75), 567. Cf. above, chapter 12 and P. de Saint-Jacob, *Les Paysans de la Bourgogne du Nord*, 347–95.

the export question. For many officials and consumers, the permission to export was synonymous with the abolition of all controls, and the removal of any grain from the local environment meant export regardless of the destination of the commodity. Whether or not liberalization in fact drained a huge amount of grain from France, as many critics claimed, became from this perspective immaterial, a superfluous refinement of analysis.

The evidence suggests that the nation was deeply divided over liberalization. I have tried to chart some of the lines of division—political, regional, social, economic, philosophical, administrative—but it would be worthwhile to explore these divisions more closely in future inquiry. I have depicted the popular and the police revolts as a grassroots movement for the recall of the liberal reforms and for the restoration of traditional subsistence relations, but a good deal more must be learned about politics and, indeed, about government at the local level before we can be satisfied with this view. The composition of the liberal lobby, both before and after the promulgation of the reforms, is not well known. To a considerable extent, the lines of division cut across the conventional sociojuridical cleavages of the Old Regime. Past political record was not a reliable predictor of attitude toward the reforms or toward the government. Nor was economic interest always a determining factor. Liberal theory focussed attention on the hiatus between city and countryside, but liberalization and the crisis built many bridges between urban and rural interests.

The experience of the sixties and seventies casts light upon regional life and regional conflicts, subjects which have been neglected in studies of old-regime political history. It is not easy to say what constitutes a regional interest or what renders it peculiar and it would be presumptuous to imagine that a parlement or an estate or a chamber of commerce or a society of agriculture spoke for the interest of a whole region rather than for corporate or privileged interests similar to others to be found throughout the kingdom. Yet these institutions were self-consciously regional bodies; I think it would be a mistake to submerge their attitudes in an interpretive scheme which associated them with their counterparts elsewhere in France without any consideration of regional idiosyncracies or identification. In the same way, it would be a mistake to tax as parochialism every instance of local or regional deviation from some standard set by modernizing, rationalizing *commis* in the bureaus of the Contrôle-Général. Nor should the divisions wrought by the grain issue remain obscured by the conventional sociopolitical frames in which we view the "age of reform," the "age of enlightened despotism," or the royal-parlementary struggle featuring the *union des classes*.

Another aspect of center-periphery relations illuminated by the grain crisis was the hostility of the provinces to Paris—the hostility not only of the liberal regions, but of such pillars of antiliberalism as the Norman Parlement. While it did not take an explosive turn until after 1789, the hatred that parts of France felt for Paris was not an invention of the Revolution, nor was this hatred during the Old Regime purely a matter of anti-urban moralizing or jealousy of the capital's prestige. Paris weighed heavily upon the rest of France long before the Revolution. It would be worth-while to examine systematically the ways in which the provinces defended themselves. Many provincials had the impression that the government could not see beyond Paris. The attitude of Rouen suggests that hostility to Paris was not a veiled expression of antagonism towards absolutism and centralization—a nostalgic affirmation of provincialism—but a protest against the ineffectiveness of centralization and the failure to integrate the provinces into a united kingdom on a level of equality.

All these matters are closely connected with the question of the parlements. The parlements were, on occasion, spokesmen for regional concerns which transcended or had nothing to do with their corporate solidarities. They were, at least in some instances, capable of treating political, social, and economic questions without reference to the narrow range of motives usually ascribed to them. The parlements played an administrative and a local and regional political role which is easy to overlook in the national context. I have tried to suggest not that the parlements did not merit their reputation for egotism and obstructionism, but that parlementary politics were much more nuanced than is generally supposed. Despite the kilometers of shelves of parlementary records and the scores of studies devoted to the courts, we know remarkably little about them as work-a-day institutions and about the magistrates as working members of these institutions rather than as representatives of a so-called social group. It seems to me that we must be more cautious in dealing with the parlements than we have been and more skeptical of the slogans used in contemporary debate to describe them. The grain affair is perhaps the exception which confirms the rule. But it is also possible that the grain affair is only the most notable of many exceptions.

In any event, as I argued at some length above, I think that the conventional view of the sixties, which focuses almost exclusively on fiscality, the constitutional and political struggle between crown and courts, and the preparation for the Maupeou coup by way of the Brittany Affair must be substantially revised to take account of liberalization and the general crisis associated with it, which was in the foreground of local and national preoccupations throughout the realm. I have tried to point out some of the political consequences and implications of this crisis; doubtless there are other paths to follow, especially in relation to the Maupeou coup, in regard to the pressures that came into play on the regional plane, and in terms of the reputation of the king, attitudes toward kingship, and the effects of the experience of 1765–75 on local administration and on what we might tentatively call popular political consciousness.

It would also be fruitful to reexamine Turgot's ministry in the light of the crisis spawned in the sixties. Viewed upon this background, the Flour War is something of an anticlimax. Rather than a new beginning, Turgot's ministry marks the resuscitation and extension of the reform spirit of the sixties. I have tried to sketch the way in which Turgot attempted to turn the subsistence difficulties and especially the discredit of the government of Louis XV to his advantage in preparation for the next phase of liberalization.

The crisis of the sixties also left a deep imprint on the thinking of Necker, Turgot's outspoken critic and his most influential successor. Necker, too, we are beginning to remember, was a philosophe, in the sense that contemporaries understood that word, and a reformer. Though the Turgot-Necker dichotomy, like the Sully-Colbert opposition, drastically oversimplifies the issue, it does portray the broad range of policy options available to the government in the last decades of the Old Regime. But the choice between them was not a choice between light and darkness, the modern and the gothic, and so on. Finally, both the crisis of the sixties-seventies and the Turgot-Necker tension suggest the need to reexamine, first, the notion of enlightened despotism and, second, the political and social ideas of the philosophes and their relation to the politics of the last quarter of the Age of Enlightenment.

The economic impact of the crisis, apart from the subsistence element, deserves more careful attention than I could give it. Surely it is not sufficient to characterize it simply as a cyclical setback in a long-term upswing, as has often been done, without undertaking a more patient assessment of its significance. In addition to a socially differential evaluation of the consequences of the economic crisis, with special emphasis on the price-wage lag and the employment situation, we must have a regionally differential picture as well. We also need a sharper sense of the schedule and rhythm of recovery, by sector as well as by place and by socioprofessional category. It would be worthwhile to examine the bearing of the economic dislocation of the late sixties and early seventies on the Maupeou reforms, especially in reference to their implementation in the provinces. Terray's brutality, too, would make more sense when viewed upon a background not only of fiscal emergency, but of severe economic crisis of a broader nature.

De-liberalization marked a great moral and political triumph for the critics of the reforms. It did not, however, bring an immediate end to the crisis, as many Frenchmen had been led to expect it would. Ironically, the result was to cast suspicion on Terray's policy and intentions, despite the fact that he was a staunch exponent of consumerism, and to salvage a glimmer of hope and a measure of grim satisfaction for the liberals, who were defeated, but not totally crushed.

Controls proved to be no more a panacea than liberty, especially since they were not accompanied by copious harvest surpluses. Recurrent short crops remained the chief source of the problem (which was international in dimension), but it was aggravated by the continued disruption of the grain and flour trade. Not even grain dealers were immune to the effects of the general economic crisis, which created an environment highly unfavorable to commercial exchanges, especially those involving risks, requiring credit, or covering large spans of time and distance. In some places, the process of reimposing controls was hardly felt, but in others it buffeted or paralyzed the trade. De-liberalization enhanced the climate of economic uncertainty. At the same time, riots and demonstrations continued to reflect consumer dissatisfaction, frustation, and fear.

Yet, from the police-consumer standpoint, there were positive signs associated with the restoration policy. Public disorder was less widespread than it had been in the sixties and it tended to be most serious in those areas which were just beginning to feel the full intensity of the subsistence crisis and, to some extent, in those areas which were slowest to subject trade to regulation. De-liberalization filled the local authorities with confidence and gave them a sense of mastery over the situation which they had not felt for years. There is evidence in some places that the public consciously joined in a sigh of relief. Still, we must await further research before we can discern patterns and assess the consequences of de-liberalization on the local plane. In some areas, the police appear to have been successful in reorganizing the trade, reestablishing the centrality and the reliability of the market, locating supplies, and quieting anxieties. In some places police restoration involved only minor adjustments, while in others it took the form of a St. Bartholomew's massacre. Nor is it clear that those authorities who practiced the restraint that was supposed to be the mark of administrative wisdom enjoyed better results than those who bludgeoned.

Restraint, nevertheless, was Terray's watchword. While he had no inhibitions about public intervention, like other leading police figures, he believed that an authoritarian grain policy could do as much harm as it did good. The problem was to know when, where, and how to intervene most effectively and to prevent miscalculations or excesses on the part of the police as well as the traders and owners. Implicit in Terray's view was the idea that subsistence could not be considered from a strictly local perspective. It implied central control, over local administration as well as over the distributive mechanisms. In the end, as I attempted to show, Terray was unable to realize either aim, for similar reasons. He was the first Controller-General to think in terms of a national subsistence policy, but it remained nothing more than a vision, buttressed by a little more data than his predecessors had at their disposal. Beyond the desire to centralize decision making in the hands of the royal government, Terray suggested nothing new: no long-term schemes for dealing with lean and fat years, no innovation in the strategy and tactics of short-term regulatory or preventive policies, except perhaps in the use of the king's grain.

There are strong hints that Terray envisaged the king's grain as a permanent, ongoing adjunct to central subsistence policy. In the past, after dearths, the government had hurried to rid itself of the king's grain as rapidly as possible in order to recover as much of its investment as possible, to save on maintenance costs, to avoid giving credence to suspicions of maneuvers, and to remove royal supplies from competition with private commerce. Machault, followed by the liberal ministers of the sixties, kept a permanent reserve, but it was of modest proportions and it was destined exclusively for the capital. Terray's operations were, of course, undertaken in the midst of dearth, not prophylactically, and they knew no geographical bounds, albeit the capital continued to be favored. Despite the financial and political burden, Terray considered the royal grain operations to be extremely useful. They allowed him to give substance to his desire to view the kingdom's supply problem as a whole and they permitted him to intervene tactically, to borrow from one place in order to assist another, and to support local police in a decisive fashion. Like his predecessors, he relied wholly on commerce for ordinary provisioning, but he wanted to be prepared to take direct action when difficulties arose. He played the role of Joseph to the king's desultory Pharaoh with less uneasiness than any other Controller-General.

I have characterized the grain victualer's world in the eighteenth century as the counterpart of our military-industrial complex (to be sure, the bankers, and before them the financiers, also had serious claims to this title). The "milieu" is not well known; it needs to be carefully studied, if not as Lüthy did the Protestant banking establishment, for want of documentation, then as Mathiez exposed the revolutionary profiteers. The Bernards, Thellussons, Pâris brothers, Leray de Chaumonts, Sorins, and Doumercs comprise only the tip of the iceberg. Moreover, their operations are clouded in the mysteries and the highly-charged atmosphere of famine plots and other machinations. The result is that we know little about their networks of correspondence in France and in Amsterdam, Danzig, London, the Levant, Africa, and America; we do not know to what extent they really perturbed domestic trade; we do not know about the relations among different victualers, dependent on different (sometimes rival) institutions or assigned to different regions; we cannot gauge what share of the provisioning burden they assumed. Victualing was an immensely complicated and onerous business. In retrospect, it seems less remarkable that the king's grain operations were so badly managed in the sixties and seventies (and in 1725–26 and the early forties), than that they rendered as much service as they did. On a relatively large scale, during the short term, and without any substantial institutional framework, they were the most effective disaster-relief agencies in the Old Regime.

It is impossible to deal with the king's grain without touching upon the "famine pact." From our perspective today, it is less important to debunk the "legend," as historians have come to style it, than to understand how it took root and what sustained it. I have tried to show that it was an integral and predictable part of what I have called the subsistence mentality and the dearth syndrome, and that it was of great political as well as psychological significance. It required no particular gift for credulity to believe in the pact idea in its most rudimentary form. Nor is it wholly inexact to contend that the government did indeed speculate on grain, directly and indirectly, though always in the context of a victualing operation and never for exclusively fiscal or venal motives. Through the stories of Malisset and Leprévost de Beaumont, I indicated how liberalization gave the pact idea a special political meaning. These charges contributed mightily to discredit Louis the Beloved. I suggested that they may also have had political implications which transcended the reputation of the king. Ironically, de-liberalization did not purge the government of the stain; the government continued to inspire deep mistrust, even as it restored the police, extended victualing operations, and fulfilled its paternalistic obligations. Before it became legend, the *pacte de famine* was a brutal fact of life for kings, ministers, and consumers.

The experience of the sixties and seventies did nothing to resolve or alter the subsistence problem in any fundamental way. Subsistence continued to be an object of worry and sometimes of terror for many years to come. For those who believed in the efficacy of police, the restoration of the old system was a source of reassurance. It represented, however, a return to the *status quo ante* rather than an advance on a new front of attack. There are some vague signs that the crisis might have had a chastening effect on the police. It did compel the police to take a serious look at themselves and to acknowledge certain excesses and absurdities in organization and operation. But it led to no formal reform effort, and it is clear that the police continued to cling to the same assumptions and techniques upon which they had relied for the past half century. Indeed, in some cases, the vivid memory of the sixties led to a hardening rather than a softening of attitudes on controls.

As a result of the crisis, of the sixties and seventies the subsistence question became a major issue of political debate; it would never again fall under the hushed silence of taboo or consensus. Liberalization, I argued, desacralized grain; de-liberalization, for all the clamor it made, did not succeed in restituting to subsistence its once-sacrosanct status. The subject remained embroiled in controversy; the suspicions and the sensitivities, which usually abated as good times superseded dearth, persisted. Although the government reaffirmed its old commitments, they no longer had the same axiomatic value. The eerily familiar replay of events during Turgot's ministry graphically underscored the realization that subsistence was not to be one of the absolutes of absolute monarchy in its old age.

Before the sixties, there was a kind of subsistence unconsciousness: a dread fear of the problem, but a sense of resignation, a feeling that nothing could be done about it—at least nothing that had not been done before. The liberalization episode helped fashion a subsistence consciousness—not only a political one, but a scientific one as well. Directly and indirectly, the crisis gave impetus to research on subsistence problems, to studies of foodways and ersatz possibilities, and to the introduction of reform in the trade (a new emphasis on flour as opposed to grain commerce), in conservation of grain and flour for the sake of quality and productivity, in fabrication of bread (new forms and new recipes), and especially in milling technology (the perfecting and the dissemination of economic milling, which had a direct bearing on efforts to transform the provisioning trade and the bakery). To the chagrin of the professionals of the *métier*, the idea developed among savants and economic commentators that subsistence-making was too important to be left to the merchants, millers, and bakers, even as the police believed that distribution of grain, flour, and bread was too important to be left to commerce on its own.

BIBLIOGRAPHY

I. PRIMARY SOURCES

A. Archival Sources

The documents consulted are too numerous and dispersed to enumerate individually. For sources cited, the precise *cotes* are given in the notes. Here I shall indicate the categories of materials I used in the various depots.

Archives Nationales (by series):

Y. Police archives including minutes and registers of the audience of the Chambre de Police; reports and *procès-verbaux* of summonses, arrests, violations, etc.; visits, searches, and seizures; complaints of citizens and of tradesmen; guild papers; correspondence of police officials; the papers and logs of commissaires and inspectors of police; criminal and police investigations and interrogations; market and price data; sentences and ordonnances; reports of the *maréchaussée*; appraisals of the state of public opinion.

   X. Archives of the Paris Parlement including remonstrances, sentences, appeals, and especially the minutes and the registers of the Conseil Secret.

   F. Especially F^{10}, F^{11}, F^{12}, which concern police, subsistence, agriculture, commerce, industry, and elements of the correspondence between the Contrôle-Général and the intendants. There are also pertinent materials in F^7.

   G^7. Correspondence between the Contrôle-Général and the intendants.

   O^1. Papers of the royal household, dispatched from the Secretary of State to officials in the field, administrative correspondence.

   H. Deliberations of the Bureau of the Hôtel de Ville as well as other materials concerning the administration of the capital.

   K. Memoirs and papers concerning subsistence questions, dearths, the grain trade, etc. Series KK contains the important correspondence between Orry and his buying and distributing agents during the dearth of 1738–42, which proved useful to me for comparative purposes.

   AP. I used a half-dozen "private papers" collections deposited in the AN, the most important of which were the papers of Maurepas, Duhamel du Monceau, and Bertier de Sauvigny.

   Miscellaneous materials including certain marine colonial and consular papers and elements in the series AD, E, T, V, W, and Z were useful in a limited fashion.

   Minutier Central (Notarial archives). Research in the *inventaires après décès*, marriage contracts, leases, apprenticeship contracts, constitution of loans, divisions of estates, business partnership agreements, and acknowledgement of debts of bakers, mealmen, millers, and traders led me to important materials bearing on the bread industry in the sixties and seventies.

Bibliothèque Nationale:

The material here is less easy to describe because it is not organized in logical series. The two most important and coherent "fonds" are the Joly de Fleury papers (arranged in a separate "Collection") which I used extensively for the whole eighteenth century and the Delamare papers which are integrated in the *manuscrits français*. Composed of administrative correspondence reaching from the top to the bottom of public life, market reports, investigations, *procès-verbaux* of riots and disturbances, legislation in draft and final form, discussion of public events, etc., the Collection Joly de Fleury was of invaluable assistance to me. The Delamare papers are a rich adjunct to the published *Traité de la police*, a guide to the evolving police tradition, and a source for the study of subsistence problems between 1685 and 1730.

Of the scores of other documents in the BN which rendered service, the most important are the minutes of the assemblies of police (generally convoked by the First President), diaries and journals, miscellaneous market and price data, and several dozen *mémoires* written on the question of the liberty of the grain trade. All of these are catalogued in the *manuscrits français* and in the *nouvelles acquisitions*.

Although they are located in the "imprimés" section (because they are "printed" or published materials), hundreds of sentences, ordonnances, arrêts, declarations, and letters patent which bear on subsistence questions deserve to be cited under archival holdings. A manuscript index, still far from complete, is available in the hemicycle of the main reading room.

Bibliothèque de l'Arsenal:

The material here, especially in the Bastille mss., is an indispensable complement to the police archives in the Y series of the AN, in the Delamare and Joly de Fleury papers of the BN, and in the Archives de la Préfecture de Police (which yielded little directly relevant to this study). The Bastille papers contain correspondence of the Lieutenants General of Police, reports and logs of commissaires and inspectors, a multitude of *procès-verbaux* of crimes of various kinds, reports on public opinion in Paris, interrogations of suspects and *saisies* of papers, and information on the structure and operation of the police. Outside the Bastille *fonds*, the Arsenal also has several important *mémoires* on grain questions as well as contemporary "histories" of the leading events of the reign of Louis XV.

Bibliothèque Historique de la Ville de Paris:

I used a great many documents scattered through the manuscript collection, the most pertinent of which were the "gazetins" and letters of several private or semi-public individuals writing from Paris in the sixties and seventies. For an earlier period, the part of the Marville papers which Boislisle did not publish are an invaluable guide to police activities. I also used the file of legislation and sentences to complement the holdings of the BN and the AN. I found valuable material in the papers of several eminent historians of Paris which the BHVP now holds. The map collections of this library are a precious source.

Archives de l'Assistance Publique:

These materials are extremely difficult to use because of the lack of adequate, up-to-date catalogues and a muddled system of classification. I used the deliberations of the bureau of the Hôtel-Dieu, administrative correspondence emanating from the Hôtel-Dieu and the Hôpital-Général, records of admissions, the archives of the *paneterie* and other data concerning grain purchases, bread-making and experiments with grain and flour.

Archives du Département de la Seine et de la Ville de Paris:

This is an extremely rich and intelligently organized depot which contains a vast amount of material that has so far escaped systematic scrutiny by historians of Paris and the Old Regime.

I used a wealth of miscellaneous family and administrative materials, correspondence, legislation, etc. But the most important materials are the registration archives and the consular documents, especially the *faillites* of bakers, millers, and merchants, the ledgers and business registers of tradesmen of all sorts, the reports of *arbitres* in commercial disputes, the complaints of merchants against other tradespeople, and the decisions of the *juges-consuls*. These materials, in conjunction with notarial archives and the documents in the civil series of the Châtelet, the Parlement, and the Parisian municipality (series Z in the AN), provide the basis for studying the "business" history of the Paris region in the Old Regime.

Archives des Affaires Étrangères:

The Mémoires et Documents : France series contains a considerable amount of legislative and administrative data, most of which can be found in the other depots cited above. There are also specialized kinds of administrative correspondence and occasional commentaries on public policy and current events which proved useful.

Archives Historiques de l'Armée:

Fragmentary information on the relations between civil and military provisioning, on the coordination of government purchasing, on the dispatch of troops to quell grain riots and protect convoys and markets, etc.

Archives Départementales:

The major series of interest in all these depots are B and C. B is the judicial series. It is comprised of *informations*, depositions, briefs, petitions, appeals, trials and decisions, background data on civil as well as police and criminal matters, correspondence with the government and with other jurisdictions, documents concerning the registration and the application and enforcement of legislation, etc. Virtually all the parlementary papers, including the extant secret registers of deliberations and decisions, are found in the B series.

C is the administrative series, an omnicompetent, residual category which seems to touch upon every aspect of life in the Old Regime. The most useful materials here are the correspondence which links, on the one hand, the intendants to the central government and, on the other, the intendants to local government. The series C is often bursting with information on agriculture, industry, commerce, market organization, and the economy in general; on the execution of legislation, the local and regional police, the *maréchaussée*, and jurisdictional disputes; on public assistance, public order, and public opinion. One frequently encounters *enquêtes* of various sorts, in unequal stages of perfection, some of which provide invaluable quantitative data as well as insightful commentary on the state of local affairs.

In addition to the B and C series, in several of the depots listed below I examined parts of D, E, notarial documents, and unclassified holdings. Once again, for specific *cotes*, readers are referred to the references in the footnotes.

The following departmental archives were consulted:

Aisne	Loir-et-Cher
Aube	Loire-Atlantique
Bas-Rhin	Loiret (most of C. destroyed)
Bouches-du-Rhône (Marseilles and Aix)	Manche
Calvados	Marne

Charente-Maritime
Côte-d'Or
Doubs
Eure
Eure-et-Loir
Gironde
Haute-Garonne
Haute-Vienne
Hérault
Ille-et-Vilaine
Indre-et-Loire
Isère

Meurthe-et-Moselle
Meuse
Moselle
Nord
Oise
Orne
Puy-de-Dôme
Rhône
Seine-et-Marne
Seine-et-Oise
Seine-Maritime
Somme
Vienne

Other Provincial Depots:

The Bibliothèque Municipale and the Archives Municipales of Bordeaux contain extremely important parlementary papers as well as administrative correspondence and miscellaneous information about the institutions and the social life of the city and region.

The Bibliothèque Municipale of Orléans houses the papers of the Parisian Lieutenant General of Police Lenoir. They provide a rich source of information on the organization and operation of the police of the capital, on the provisioning tradition, and on the attitude of highly placed royal officials toward liberty and liberalization.

The Bibliothèque Municipale of Grenoble conserves the papers of the Procurator General of the Dauphiné Parlement in the sixties and seventies. They complement and help elucidate the parlementary records in the departmental B series. In addition, this library has several illuminating contemporary diaries.

B. Contemporary Periodicals

Année littéraire. Amsterdam, 1754–1769; Paris, 1770–1775.
Ephémérides du citoyen, ou bibliothèque raisonnée des sciences morales et politiques. Paris, 1776–1772.
Gazette de France. Paris 1725–1775.
Gazette de l'agriculture, du commerce, des arts et des finances. Paris, 1769–1783.
Gazette du commerce. Paris, 1763–1765.
Gazette du commerce, de l'agriculture et des finances. Paris, 1763–1768.
Journal de commerce. Brussels, 1759–1762.
Journal de l'agriculture, du commerce, des arts et des finances. Paris, 1765–1783; also, *Journal de l'agriculture, du commerce et des finances.*
Journal de physique. Paris, 1773–1793.
Journal de politique et de littérature. Brussels, 1774.
Journal des sçavans. Amsterdam and Paris, 1725–1775.
Journal économique, ou Mémoires, notes et avis sur les arts, l'agriculture, et tout ce qui peut avoir rapport à la santé ainsi qu'à l'augmentation des biens de famille. Paris, 1751–1772.
Journal encyclopédique ou universel. Liège, 1756–1759; Bouillon, 1760–1780.
Journal historique et politique [Journal de Genève]. Geneva [Paris], 1772–1776.
Journal politique, ou Gazette des gazettes. Bouillon, 1765–1780.
Mémoires pour servir à l'histoire des sciences et des beaux-arts [Journal de Trévoux]. Paris, 1750–1767.
Mercure de France. Paris, 1725–1775.

Mercure historique et politique contenant l'état présent de l'Europe, ce qui se passe dans toutes les cours, l'intérêt des princes, et généralement tout ce qu'il y a de plus curieux ... le tout accompagné de réflexions politiques pour chaque état. The Hague, 1725–1775.

Nouvelles éphémérides économiques, ou bibliothèque raisonnée de l'histoire, de la morale et de la politique. Paris, 1774–1788.

Nouvelliste suisse. Neufchâtel, 1732–1769.

Révolutions de Paris, dédiées à la nation et au district des Petits Augustins. Paris, 1789–1793 [1794].

C. Anonymous Primary Works

L'Art de battre, écraser, piler, moudre et monder les grains avec de nouvelles machines. Paris, 1769.

Détail sur quelques établissements de la ville de Paris demandé par sa majesté impériale la reine de Hongrie à M. LeNoir. Paris, 1780.

Du Pain ou coup d'œil sur les moyens les plus sûrs et les plus prompts d'approvisionner Paris de grains et de farines comme d'entretenir un rapport constant entre ses marchés et ceux qui y correspondent ordinairement sans nuire aux travaux de la campagne. Paris: Blanchon, 1789.

Guide des corps des marchands et des communautés des arts et métiers tant de la ville de Paris que du Royaume. Paris: Duchesne, 1766.

"Le Journal d'un bourgeois de Corbeil." *Bulletin de la Société historique et archéologique de Corbeil, d'Etampes et du Hurepoix,* 4th year (1898), 33–42, 86–101.

Mémoire important par rapport au bien public et à la provision de farine pour la ville de Paris. Paris, 1733.

Moyens sûrs et infaillibles de ne payer le pain que deux sols la livre en tout temps par l'établissement de greniers publics ou approvisionnement de blé pour la ville de Paris. Paris, n.d.

Nouveau stile du Châtelet de Paris ... tant en matière civile, criminelle que de police. New ed., rev. Paris: Knapen, 1762.

Projet de magasins nationaux ou moyens d'éviter la disette des villes. Paris: Imprimerie Didot l'aîné, n.d. (ca. 1789–1790).

Recueil de pièces concernant le tribunal du Châtelet. N.p., n.d.

Recueil des édits, déclarations, arrêts et règlemens concernant les arts et les métiers de Paris et autres villes du Royaume. N.p., 1701.

Relation de l'assassinat commis en la personne du sieur François, maître-boulanger, 21 octobre 1789. Paris: Imprimerie Lottin l'aîné, 1789.

Statuts et lettres patentes pour les maîtres boulangers de la ville et les faubourgs de Paris. Paris, 1721.

D. Primary Works by Author

Abeille, Louis-Paul. *Corps d'observations de la Société d'agriculture, de commerce et des arts établie par les Etats de Bretagne.* By L.-P. Abeille et Jean-Gabriel Montaudouin. For 1757 and 1758. Rennes: J. Vatar, 1760.

———. *Lettre d'un négociant sur la nature du commerce des grains* (1763). *Collection des économistes et des réformateurs sociaux de la France.* Ed. Edgar Depitre. Paris: P. Guethner, 1911.

Académie des Sciences. Paris. "Eloge de Monsieur d'Argenson." *Eloges des académiciens, avec l'histoire de l'Académie royale des sciences en MDCXCIX avec un discours préliminaire sur l'utilité des mathématiques par Mr. de Fontenelle, secrétaire perpétuel.* Vol. II: Eloges des académiciens ... morts depuis l'an 1717. The Hague: chez Isaac van der Kloot, 1740. Reprint edition, Brussels, 1969.

———. "Eloge de M. Malouin." *Histoire de l'Académie royale des sciences de Paris* (1778), 94–109.

———. "Eloge de M. Trudaine." *Histoire de l'Académie royale des sciences de Paris* (1769), 261–91.

———. *Les Membres et les correspondants de l'Académie royale des sciences, 1666–1793.* Paris: au palais de l'Institut, 1931.

————: *Nouvelle table des articles contenus dans les volumes de l'Académie royale des sciences de Paris, depuis 1666 jusqu'en 1770*. Ed. Rozier. 4 vols. Paris: Ruault, 1775–1776.

Alfieri, Victor. *Mémoires de Victor Alfieri*. Ed. F. Barrière. Paris: Didot frères, 1882.

Andrews, John. *Letters to a Young Gentleman on his setting out for France: containing a survey of Paris....* London: J. Walter & W. Brown, 1784.

Arbuthnot, John. *An Essay Concerning the Nature of Aliments and the Choice of Them, According to the Different Constitutions of Human Bodies*. 2nd ed. London: J. Tonson, 1732.

Argenson, Marc-René de Voyer, Cte. d'. *Notes de René d'Argenson, lieutenant-général de police, intéressantes pour l'histoire des mœurs et de la police de Paris à la fin du règne de Louis XIV.* Paris: Imprimerie E. Voitelain et Cⁱᵉ, 1866.

————: *Rapports inédits du lieutenant de police René d'Argenson (1679–1715)*. Ed. Paul Cottin. Paris: E. Plon et Nourrit et Cⁱᵉ, 1891.

Argenson, René-Louis de Voyer, Mis. d'. *Journal et mémoires du marquis d'Argenson; publiés pour la première fois d'après les manuscrits autographes de la bibliothèque du Louvre pour la Société de l'histoire de France....* Ed. E.-J.-B. Rathery. 9 vols. Paris: Mme. J. Renouard, 1859–1867.

————: *Mémoires et journal inédit du marquis d'Argenson, ministre des affaires étrangères sous Louis XV, publiés et annotés par M. le Mis. d'Argenson*. 5 vols. Paris: P. Jannet, 1857–1858.

Arnould, A.-M. *Histoire générale des finances de la France*. Paris: Imprimerie du corps législatif, 1806.

Augeard, Jacques-Mathieu. *Mémoires secrets de J.-M. Augeard, secrétaire des Commandements de la reine Marie-Antoinette (1760–1800), documents inédits*. Ed. Evariste Bavoux. Paris: H. Plon, 1866.

Bachaumont, Louis Petit de. *Mémoires secrets pour servir à l'histoire de la République des Lettres en France depuis 1762 jusqu'à nos jours; ou Journal d'un Observateur....* 30 vols. London: John Adamson, 1780–1786.

————: *Mémoires secrets de Bachaumont....* Ed. P.-L. Jacob [pseud.]. Paris: Garnier frères, 1883.

Bailly, J.-S. *Mémoires de Bailly*. Ed. B. Barrière, 2 vols. Paris: Baudouin, 1822.

Barbier, Edmond-Jean-François. *Chronique de la régence et du règne de Louis XV (1718–1763), ou Journal de Barbier*. 8 vols. Paris: Charpentier, 1857.

————: *Journal d'un bourgeois de Paris sous le règne de Louis XV.* Ed. Philippe Bernard. Paris: Union générale d'éditions, 1963.

Baudeau, Abbé Nicolas. *Avis au peuple sur l'impôt forcé qui se percevoit dans les halles et marchés sur tous les bleds et toutes les farines*. N.p., 1774.

————: *Avis au peuple sur son premier besoin, ou Petits traités économiques, par l'auteur des "Ephémérides du citoyen."* Amsterdam and Paris: Hochereau jeune, 1768.

————: *Avis aux honnêtes gens qui veulent bien faire*. Amsterdam and Paris: Desaint, et al., 1768.

————: "Chronique secrète de Paris sous le règne de Louis XVI (7 June 1774)." *Revue rétrospective*, 1st. ser., III (1834), 29–96, 262–96, 375–415.

————: *Idées d'un citoyen sur les besoins, les droits et les devoirs des vrais pauvres*. Amsterdam; and Paris: B. Hochereau le jeune, 1765.

————: "Lettres et mémoires à un magistrat du parlement de Paris sur l'arrêt du 13 Septembre 1774." *Nouvelles éphémérides économiques* (1775), I, 1–146.

————: *Première introduction à la philosophic économique ou Analyse des états policés (1767)*. Ed. A. Dubois. Paris: P. Guethner, 1910.

Beardé de l'Abbaye. *Essays in Agriculture, or a Variety of Useful Hints for its Improvement*. London: T. Carnan, 1776.

Beaumarchais, Pierre-Augustin baron de. *Correspondance*. Ed. B.N. Morton. 3 vols. Paris: A.-G. Hizet, 1969–72.

Beausobre, Louis de. *Introduction générale à l'étude de la politique, des finances et du commerce*. New ed. 2 vols. Amsterdam: J. H. Schneider, 1765.

Beckmann, John. *A History of Inventions and Discoveries*. Trans. by William Johnston. 3rd ed. 4 vols. London: Longman, et al., 1817.

Béguillet, Edme. "Abondance." *Supplément à l'Encyclopédie ... mis en ordre et publié par m****....
Vol. I. Amsterdam: M.M. Rey, 1776, pp. 30–32.

―――――*: Description historique de Paris et de ses plus beaux monuments.* 3 vols. Paris: n.p., 1779–81.

―――――*: Discours sur la mouture économique.* Paris: Panckoucke, 1775.

―――――*: Manuel du meunier et du charpentier de moulins, ou Abrégé classique du traité de la mouture par économic* Paris: Panckoucke, 1775.

―――――*: Manuel du meunier et du constructeur de moulins à eau et à grains, par M. Bucquet* [E. Béguillet]. Rev. ed. Paris: Onfroy, 1790.

―――――*: Mémoires sur les avantages de la mouture économique et du commerce des farines, par M.B., de la Société d'agriculture de Lyon.* Dijon: Imprimerie de L.-N. Frantin, 1769.

―――――*: Traité de la connoissance générate des grains et de la mouture par économie.* 2 vols. Paris: Panckoucke, 1775.

―――――*: Traité de la connoissance générate des grains et de la mouture par économie.* Dijon: Imprimerie de L.-N. Frantin, 1778.

―――――*: Traité des subsistances et des grains qui servent à la nourriture de l'homme.* Paris: Prault fils, 1780.

Bellepierre de Neuve-Eglise, Louis-Joseph de. *L'Agronomie et l'industrie, ou les Principes de l'agriculture, du commerce et des arts réduits en pratique par une société d'agriculteurs, de commerçants et d'artistes.* 6 vols. Paris: Despilly, 1761.

Benoiston de Châteauneuf, Louis-François. *Recherches sur les consommations de tout genre de la ville de Paris en 1817, comparées à ce qu'elles étaient en 1789.* 2nd. ed. Paris by the author, 1821.

Besenval, Pierre. *Mémoires de M. le Baron de Besenval ... contenant beaucoup de particularités et d'anecdotes sur la cour, sur les ministres et les règnes de Louis XV et Louis XVI, et sur les événements du temps, précédés d'une notice sur la vie de l'auteur.* Ed. A.-J. de Ségur. 3 vols. Paris: F. Buisson, 1805.

―――――*: Mémoires du Baron de Besenval.* Ed. Berville and Barrière. 2 vols. Paris: Baudouin frères, 1821.

Bielfeld, S.F. von. *Institutions politiques.* The Hague: P. Gosse, 1761.

Bigot de Sainte-Croix. *Essai sur la liberté du commerce et de l'industrie.* Paris: Lacombe, 1775.

Boesnier de l'Orme. *De l'Esprit du gouvernement économique.* Paris: Debure, 1775.

Boisguilbert, Pierre LePesant de. *Le Détail de la France, la cause de la diminution de ses biens, et la faculté du remède, en fournissant en un mois tout l'argent dont le roi a besoin, et enrichissant tout le monde. Economistes financiers du XVIIIe siècle.* Ed. Eugène Daire. Paris: Guillaumin et Cie, 1851.

―――――*: Factum de la France, ou Moyens très faciles de faire recevoir au roi quatre-vingts millions par-dessus la capitation.... Economistes financiers du XVIIIe siècle.* Ed. Eugène Daire. Paris: Guillaumin et Cie, 1851.

―――――*: Traité de la nature, culture, commerce et intérêt des grains. Economistes financiers du XVIIIe siècle.* Ed. Eugène Daire. Paris: Guillaumin et Cie, 1851.

Boislisle, Arthur Michel de, ed. *Correspondance des contrôleurs généraux des finances avec les intendants des provinces.* 3 vols. Paris: Imprimerie nationale, 1874–1897.

Bonnardot, François; Tutey, A.; *et al.*, eds. *Registres des délibérations du Bureau de la Ville de Paris.* 17 vols. Paris: Imprimerie nationale, 1883–1948.

Bourdon Des Planches, L.-J. *Du pain, du pain, et moyen d'en avoir. Lettre sur la subsistance et sur les impositions et finances* (19 pluviose an III). N.p., n.p.

―――――*: Lettre à l'auteur des observations sur le commerce des grains.* Amsterdam: n.p., 1775.

―――――*: Mémoire sur les subsistances.* Paris: Imprimerie de la Société des jeunes Français. N.p.: n.p., n.d.

―――――*: Projet nouveau sur la manière de faire utilement en France le commerce des grains.* Brussels; and Paris: Veuve Esprit, 1785.

Briatte, Jean Baptiste. *Offrande à l'humanité.* Amsterdam; and Paris: Noyon, 1780.

Brodin de la Jutais, Pierre. *L'Abondance ou Véritable pierre philosophale, qui consiste seulement à la multiplication de toutes sortes de grains, de fruits, de fleurs, et généralement de tous les végétatifs.* Paris: Delaguette, 1752.

Bucquet, César. *Observations intéressantes et amusantes du Sieur César Bucquet, ancien meunier de l'Hôpital Général, à MM. Parmentier et Cadet.* [Under the pseudonym of Michel Morin.] Revised by E. Béguillet. Paris: chez les marchands de nouveautés, 1783.

Cadet de Vaux, Antoine-Alexis. *Avis sur les blés germés par le comité de l'école gratuite de boulangerie.* Paris: Imprimerie de P.-D. Pierres, 1782.

_____. *Discours prononcés à l'ouverture de l'école gratuite de boulangerie, le 8 juin 1780.* Paris: l'Imprimerie P.-D. Pierres, 1780.

_____. *Moyens de prévenir le retour des disettes.* Paris: C. Colas, 1812.

Caraccioli, Louis-Antoine de. *Paris, métropole de l'univers.* Paris: Le Normant, 1802.

Charpentier. *La Bastille dévoilée.* 9 vols. Paris: Desenne, 1789.

Chevalier, Etienne. *Mémoire sur les moyens d'assurer la diminution du pain, de prévenir les disettes, et de tenir les grains à un prix qui soit tout à la fois avantageux au peuple, sans être nuisible à l'agriculture.* Paris: Imprimerie de Chaudrillie, n.d. [ca. 1793].

Choiseul, Etienne-François, duc de. *Mémoires de M. le duc de Choiseul, ... écrits par lui-même et imprimés sous ses yeux, dans son cabinet, à Chanteloup, en 1778.* Ed. Soulavie. Chanteloup; and Paris: Buisson, 1790.

Collé, Charles. *Correspondance inédite de Collé faisant suite à son journal, accompagnée de fragments également inédits de ses œuvres posthumes.* Ed. Honoré Bonhomme. Paris: H. Plon, 1864.

_____. *Journal et mémoires de Charles Collé sur les hommes de lettres, les ouvrages dramatiques et les événements les plus mémorables du règne de Louis XV, 1748–1772.* Ed. Honoré Bonhomme. 3 vols. Paris: Firmin-Didot frères et fils et Cie, 1868.

Condillac, abbé Etienne Bonnot de. *Le Commerce et le gouvernement considérés relativement l'un à l'autre* (1776). *Collection des principaux économistes.* Ed. E. Daire and G. de Molinari. Vol. XIV. Reprint of 1847 edition. Osnabrück: Otto Zeller, 1966.

Condorcet, Jean-Antoine-Nicolas de Caritat, marquis de. *Correspondance inédite de Condorcet et de Turgot, 1770–1779.* Ed. Charles Henry. Paris: Charavay frères, 1883.

_____. *Lettre d'un laboureur de Picardie à M.N**** [*Necker*] *auteur prohibitif* (Paris, 1775). *Collection des principaux économistes.* Ed. E. Daire and G. de Molinari. Vol. XIV. Reprint of 1847 edition. Osnabrück: Otto Zeller, 1966.

_____. *Réflexions sur le commerce des bleds.* London: n.p., 1776.

_____. *Le Monopole et le monopoleur* (n.d.). *Collection des principaux économistes.* Ed. E. Daire and G. de Molinari. Vol. XIV, Reprint of 1847 edition. Osnabrück: Otto Zeller, 1966.

_____. *Sur le préjugé qui suppose une contrariété d'intérêts entre Paris et les provinces* (1790). *Œuvres de Condorcet.* Ed. A. Condorcet O'Connor and M.F. Arago. Vol. X. Paris: Firmin-Didot, 1847.

Coquereau, Jean-Baptiste-Louis. *Mémoires concernant l'administration des finances sous le ministère de M. l'abbé Terrai....* London: J. Adamson, 1776.

_____. *Mémoires de l'abbé Terrai, contrôleur-général des finances, avec une relation de l'émeute arrivée à Paris en 1775, et suivis de quatorze lettres d'un actionnaire de la Compagnie des Indes.* London, 1776.

Coyer, abbé Gabriel-François. *Développement et défense du système de la noblesse commerçante.* Amsterdam; and Paris: Duchesne, 1757.

_____. *La Noblesse commerçante.* London; and Paris: Duchesne, 1756.

_____. *Voyage d'Italie et de Hollande.* Paris: Veuve Duchesne, 1775.

_____. *Essai sur la prédication.* Paris: Veuve Duchesne, 1781.

_____. *Chinki, histoire cochinchinoise.* London: n.p., 1768.

Creuzé-Latouche, Jacques-Antoine. *Rapport des députés de la convention ... en faveur de la liberté entière du commerce des grains.* 8 décembre 1792. Paris: Imprimerie nationale, n.d.

Croy, Emmanuel, maréchal, duc de. *Journal inédit du duc de Croy, 1718–1784.* Ed. Vte. de Grouchy and Paul Cottin. 4 vols. Paris: E. Flammarion, 1906–1907.

D.***, M.B. [Brillon Duperron?]. *Observations sur la mouture des bleds et sur leur produit d'après les expériences de l'Hôpital général de Paris.* Paris: chez Lacombe, 1768.

D.-Z. [Desaubiez, Vatar]. *Le Bonheur public*, [etc.]. Vol. III: *Conciliation des droits de l'Etat, des propriétaires, et du peuple, sur l'exportation des grains*. London: T. Hookham, 1782.

Delamare, Nicolas. *Traité de la police*. 4 vols. 2nd. ed. Amsterdam; and Paris, 1729.

Denisart, Jean-Baptiste. *Collection de décisions nouvelles et de notions relatives à la jurisprudence actuelle*. 9th ed. 48 vols. Paris: Desaint, 1777.

Des Essarts, Nicolas-Toussaint Lemoyne. *Dictionnaire universel de police*. 8 vols. Paris: Moutard, 1786–1790.

Desbordes, Jean-Michel, ed. *La Chronique villageoise de Varreddes (Seine-et-Marne): un document sur la vie rurale des XVII* et *XVIII* siècles*. Paris: Editions de l'Ecole, n.d.

Desmoulins, Camille. *Les Insignes meuniers de Corbeil, ou la Compagnie des famines découverte, en présence de M. Necker, accusé, par M. Desmoulins*. Paris: Lefèvre, 1789.

Dictionnaire universel françois et latin, vulgairement appellé Dictionnaire de Trévoux. New ed., rev. and augm. 5 vols. Paris: chez F. Delaulne [*et al.*], 1721.

Diderot, Denis. *Apologie de l'abbé Galiani* (1770). *Œuvres politiques*. Ed. Paul Vernière. Paris: Editions Garnier frères, 1963.

———. *Correspondance*. Ed. Georges Roth. 16 vols. Paris: les Editions de Minuit, 1955–1970.

———. "Essai historique sur la police rédigé pour Catherine II." Ed. Maurice Tourneux. *Revue historique*, XXV (1884), 298–321.

———. *et al. Encyclopédie, ou Dictionnaire raisonné des sciences, des arts et des métiers, par une société de gens de lettres*. Ed. Diderot and D'Alembert. 35 vols. Paris: Briasson, David l'aîné, LeBreton, Durand, 1751–1765.

Dionis du Séjour, Louis-A. *Mémoire pour servir à l'histoire de la Cour des Aides ... jusqu'à 1791*. Paris: Knapen, 1792.

Dubuisson, Simon-Henri. *Mémoires secrets du XVIII* siècle. Lettres du commissaire Dubuisson au marquis de Caumont, 1735–1741*. Ed. A. Rouxel. Paris: P. Arnould, [1882].

Duchesne. *Code de la police ou analyse des règlements de police*. 2 vols. Paris: n.p., 1767.

Du Deffand, Marie de Vichy-Chamrond, marquise. *Correspondance complète de la Marquise du Deffand*. Ed. M. de Lescure. 2 vols. Paris: Henri Plon, 1865.

Dufort, Jean-Nicolas, comte de Cheverny. *Mémoires sur les règnes de Louis XV et Louis XVI et sur la révolution*. Ed. Robert de Crèvecœur. 2 vols. Paris: E. Plon, Nourrit et Cⁱᵉ, 1886.

Dugas de Bois St. Just, J. L. M. *Paris, Versailles et les provinces au 18ᵉ siècle*. 3 vols. Paris: Le Normand, 1809–1817.

Duhamel du Monceau, Henri-Louis. *Ecole d'agriculture*. Paris: Frères Estienne, 1759.

———. *Eléments d'agriculture*. 2 vols. Paris: H.-L. Guérin et L.-F. Delatour, 1762.

———. *Traité de la conservation des grains et en particulier du froment*. Paris: H.-L. Guérin et L.-F. Delatour, 1753.

———. *Traité de la culture des terres, suivant les principes de M. Tull, Anglois*. 6 vols. Paris: H.-L. Guérin et L.-F. Delatour, 1750–1761.

Du Hausset. *Mémoires de Madame Du Hausset.... Bibliothèque des mémoires relatifs à l'histoire de France pendant le XVIII* siècle*. Ed. F. Barrière. Vol. III. Paris: F.-Didot frères, 1846.

Dulaure, Jacques-A. *Histoire physique, civile et morale de Paris*. Ed. J.-L. Belin. 7th ed. 4 vols. Paris: Bureau des publications illustrées, 1842.

Dupin, Claude. "Mémoire sur les blés, avec un projet d'édit pour maintenir en tout tems la valeur des grains à un prix convenable au vendeur et à l'acheteur." Paris: n.p., 1748.

Dupont de Nemours, Pierre-Samuel. *Analyse historique de la législation des grains depuis 1692 à laquelle on a donné la forme d'un rapport à l'Assemblée nationale*. Paris: Petit, 1789.

———. *Carl Friedrichs von Baden Brieflicher Verkehr mit Mirabeau und Dupont*. Ed. Carl Knies. 2 vols. Heidelberg: C. Winter, 1892.

———. *De l'exportation et de l'importation des grains*. (Paris, 1764). *Collection des économistes et des réformateurs sociaux de la France*. Ed. Edgar Depitre. Paris: P. Guethner, 1911.

———. *Objections et réponses sur le commerce des grains et des farines*. Amsterdam; and Paris: Delalain, 1769.

Dupré d'Aulnay, Louis. *Traité général des subsistances militaires.* Paris: Imprimerie de Prault père, 1744.

Dupré de St-Maur, Nicolas-François. *Essai sur les monnaies, ou Réflexions sur le rapport entre l'argent et les denrées.* Paris: J.-B. Coignard, 1746.

Encyclopédie méthodique. 185 vols. Paris: Panckoucke, 1782–1832.

Epinay, Louise-Florence-Pétronille Tardieu d'Esclaves, marquise d'. *Mémoires et correspondance de Mme d'Epinay.* Ed. J.-P.-A. Parison. 2nd ed. 3 vols. Paris: Volland, 1818.

Evans, Oliver. *The Young Mill-Wright and Miller's Guide* (1975). 5th ed. Ed. T. P. Jones. Philadelphia: Carey, Lea, and Banchard, 1836.

———. *Guide du meunier et du constructeur de moulins.* Trans. by P. M. N. Benoît. Paris: Mahler, 1830.

Evelyn, J. *An Account of Bread Panification....* (1681). *A Collection of Letters for the Improvement of Husbandry and Trade.* Ed. John Houghton. Vol. I. London: Printed for J. Lawrence, 1681.

Félibien, Michel. *Histoire de la ville de Paris.* 5 vols. Paris: G. Desprez, 1725.

Foisset, Thomas, ed. *Voltaire et le Président de Brosses. Correspondance inédite.* Paris: Didier et Cⁱᵉ, 1858.

France. *Actes du Parlement de Paris.* Ed. Edgard Boutaric. 2 vols. Paris: H. Plon, 1863–1867.

———. *Almanach royal.* Paris, 1700–1775.

———. *Archives parlementaires de 1787 à 1860. Recueil complet des débats législatifs et politiques des chambres françaises.* First Series. Paris: Librairie administrative de P. Dupont, 1879–1894.

———. *Conseil de commerce et Bureau de commerce, 1700–1791. Inventaire analytique des procès-verbaux.* Ed. Pierre Bonnassieux. Paris: Imprimerie nationale, 1900.

———. *Les Correspondances des agents diplomatiques étrangers en France avant la révolution.* Ed. J. Flammermont. Paris: Imprimerie nationale, 1896.

———. *Recueil des principales lois relatives au commerce des grains avec les arrêts, arrêtés et remontrances du Parlement sur cet objet et le procès-verbal de l'assemblée générate de police, 28 novembre 1768.* Paris: n.p., 1769.

———. *Recueil général des anciennes lois françaises depuis l'année 420 jusqu'à la révolution de 1789.* Ed. François-A. Isambert, *et al.* 29 vols. Paris: Belin-LePrieur [etc.], 1821–1833.

———. *Remontrances du Parlement de Paris au dix-huitième siècle.* Ed. Jules Flammermont [Vol. II: ed. J. Flammermont and Maurice Tourneux]. 3 vols. Paris: Imprimerie nationale, 1888–1898.

Fréminville, Edme de la Poix de. *Dictionnaire ou traité de la Police générate des villes, bourgs, paroisses et seigneuries de la campagne.* Paris: Gissey, 1758.

Furetière, Antoine. *Dictionnaire universel, contenant généralement tous les mots français, tant vieux que modernes, et les termes des sciences et des arts.* New rev. ed. Ed. Butel de la Rivière. 4 vols. The Hague: P. Husson, 1727.

Galiani, abbé Ferdinando. *Amici e corrispondenti francesi dell'abate Galiani. Notizie, lettere, documenti.* Ed. Fausto Nicolini. Naples: Arte tipografica, 1954.

———. *Correspondance.* Nouvelle édition. Ed. Lucien Perey and Gaston Maugras. 2 vols. Paris: Calmann-Lévy, 1881.

———. *Dialogues sur le commerce des bleds* (1770). Ed. Fausto Nicolini. Milan: R. Riccardi, n.d.

———. *Dialogues entre M. Marquis de Rocquemaure, et Mˢ. le Chevalier Zanobi.* Ed. Philip Koch. *Analecta Romanica,* XXI (1968).

———. *Lettere di Ferdinando Galiani al marchese Bernardo Tanucci.* Ed. A. Bazzoni. Florence: G. Pietro Vieusseux, 1880.

———. "Lettere inedite di G.B. Suard all'abate Galiani." Ed. Fausto Nicolini. *Mélanges de philologie, d'histoire, et de littérature offerts à Henri Hauvette.* Paris: Les Presses françaises, 1934.

———. *Lettres de l'abbé Galiani à Madame d'Epinay.* Ed. Eugène Asse. 2 vols. Paris: G. Charpentier, 1882.

———. *La Signora d'Epinay e l'abate Galiani lettere inedite, 1769–1772.* Ed. Fausto Nicolini. Bari: Laterza & Figli, 1929.

———. *Il pensiero dell'abate Galiani. Antologia dei suoi scritti editi e inediti.* Bari: Laterza, 1909.

_____· F. Nicolini, ed. "Un Inedito dell'abate Galiani," *Biblion*, I (June 1959), 139–56.

Gazier, A., ed. "La Police de Paris en 1770, mémoire inédit, composé par ordre de G. de Sartine sur la demande de Marie-Thérèse." *Mémoires de la Société de l'Histoire de Paris et de l'Ile-de-France*, V (1878).

Georgel, abbé J.-F. *Mémoires pour servir à l'histoire des événemens de la fin du dix-huitième siècle*. 6 vols. Paris: A Eymery, 1820.

Gerbaux, Fernand, and Schmidt, C, eds. *Procès-verbaux des comités d'agriculture et de commerce de la Constituante, de la Législative et de la Convention. Collection des documents inédits sur l'histoire économique de la Révolution française*. 4 vols. Paris: Imprimerie nationale, 1906–1910.

Goudar, Ange. *Les Intérêts de la France mal entendus, dans les branches de l'agriculture, de la population, des finances, du commerce, de la marine et de l'industrie*. 3 vols. Amsterdam: J. Cœur, 1756.

Goyon de La Plombanie, Henri de. *L'Unique moyen de soulager le peuple et d'enrichir la nation française*. Paris: A. Boudet, 1775.

_____· *Vues politiques sur le commerce, ouvrage dans lequel on traite particulièrement des denrées, et où l'on propose de nouveaux moyens pour encourager l'agriculture et les arts, et pour augmenter le commerce général du royaume*. Amsterdam: aux dépens de la compagnie, 1759.

Grenus, Jacques. *Essai sur les ressources de la France, ou Développement de quelques branches d'industrie et de commerce, etc*. Paris: Dufart, 1796.

Grimm, Friedrich Melchior. *Correspondance littéraire, philosophique et critique par Grimm, Diderot, Raynal, Meister, etc....* Ed. Maurice Tourneux. 16 vols. Paris: Garnier frères, 1877–1882.

_____· *Correspondance inédite de F. M. Grimm*. Ed. J. Schlobach. Munich: W. Fink, 1972.

Guérineau de St.-Péravi, Jean-Nicolas M. *Principes du commerce opposé au trafic*. N.p.: n.p., 1787.

Guyot, Pierre-Jean-Jacques-Guillaume. *Traité des droits, fonctions, franchises, exemptions, prérogatives et privileges annexés en France à chaque dignité, à chaque office....* 4 vols. Paris: Visse, 1786–1788.

Herbert, Claude-Jacques. *Essai sur la police générale des grains, sur leurs prix et sur les effets de l'agriculture* (London, 1755). *Collection des économistes et des réformateurs sociaux de la France*. Ed. E. Depitre. Paris: P. Geuthner, 1910.

Jackson, H. *An Essay on Bread; wherein the bakers and millers are vindicated from the aspersions contained in two pamphlets; one entitled "Poison Detected"; and the other "The Nature of Bread honestly and dishonestly made."* London: J.Wilkie, 1758.

Jones, William. *Observations on a Journey to Paris by Way of Flanders in the month of August 1776*. 2 vols. London: G. Robinson, 1777.

Laborde, J.-J. de. *Mémoires de Jean-Joseph de Laborde, fermier général et banquier de la Cour*. Ed. Y.-R. Durand. *Annuaire-Bulletin de la Société de l'histoire de France* (1968–69).

Laboulinière, Pierre. *De la disette et de la surabondance en France, des moyens de prévenir l'une, en mettant l'autre à profit, et d'empêcher les trop grandes variations dans les prix des grains*. 3 vols. Paris: Imprimerie de Le Normant, 1821.

Lacombe, François (d'Avignon). *Le Mitron de Vaugirard, dialogues sur le bled, la farine et le pain*. Amsterdam: n.p., 1777.

Larchey, Loredan, ed. *Journal des inspecteurs de M. de Sartines*. Brussels; and Paris: n.p., 1863.

Lavoisier, Antoine-Laurent. *De la richesse territoriale du royaume de France. Collection des principaux économistes*. Ed. E. Daire. Vol. XIV. Paris: Guillaumin et Cⁱᵉ, 1847.

_____· *Mémoires et rapports sur divers sujets de chimie et de physique pures ou appliquées à l'histoire naturelle, à l'administration et à l'hygiène publique. Œuvres de Lavoisier*. Vol. IV. Paris: Imprimerie impériale, 1868.

Lebeuf, abbé Jean. *Histoire de la ville et de tout le diocèse de Paris*. (15 vols., 1754–1758). Ed. A. Augier and F. Bournon. 7 vols. Paris: Fechoz, 1883–1893.

Lebrun, Charles-François. *Opinions, rapports et choix d'écrits politiques de Charles-F. Lebrun*. Ed. by his son [A.-C. Lebrun]. Paris: Bossange père, 1829.

Legrand d'Aussy, Pierre-Jean-Baptiste. *Histoire de la vie privée des François ...* (1783). New ed. Ed. J.-B.-B. de Roquefort. 3 vols. Paris: Laurent-Beaupré, 1815.

Lemercier de la Rivière, P.-P.-F.-J.-H. *L'Intérêt général de l'Etat: ou, La Liberté du commerce des blés, démontrée conforme au droit naturel, au droit public de la France, aux lois fondamentales du royaume, à l'intérêt commun du souverain et de ses sujets dans tous les temps, avec la réfutation d'un nouveau système publié en forme de dialogues sur le commerce des blés.* Amsterdam; and Paris: chez Desaint, 1770.

———. *L'Ordre naturel et essentiel des sociétés politiques* (1767). *Collection des économistes et des réformateurs sociaux de la France.* Ed. Edgar Depitre. Paris: P. Guethner, 1910.

Lémery, Louis. *Traité des aliments.* 3rd ed., rev. and augm. Ed. Jacques-Jean Bruhier. 2 vols. Paris: Durand, 1755.

Lenoir, Jean-Charles-Pierre. "Essai sur la guerre des farines." "Le Lieutenant de police J. P. Lenoir, la guerre des farines et l'approvisionnement de Paris à la veille de la révolution." Ed. R. Darnton. *Revue d'histoire moderne et contemporaine.* XVI (Oct.-Dec. 1969), 611–24.

———. "The Memoirs of Lenoir, Lieutenant de Police of Paris, 1774–1785." Ed. Robert Darnton. *The English Historical Review.* LXXXV (July 1970), 532–59.

Le Paige, Louis-Adrien. *Lettres historiques sur les fonctions essentielles du Parlement, sur le droit des Pairs et sur les loix fondamentales du royaume.* 2 vols. Amsterdam: n.p., 1753.

Leprévost de Beaumont, J.-C.-G. *Aspect de la France, actuellement, et depuis dix mois, dans un péril qui s'accroît de plus en plus, jusqu'à l'an VIII.* Paris: n.p., an VIII.

———. *Dénonciation d'un pacte de famine générale au roi Louis XV.* Paris: n.p., n.d.

———. *Dénonciation et pétition du sieur Le Prévôt de Beaumont... prisonnier d'Etat en cinq prisons ... pour avoir découvert ... les quatrième et cinquième pactes de famine générale.* Paris: n.p., 1791.

———. *Dénonciation, pétition et rogation du sieur Le Prévôt de Beaumont.* Paris: n.p., 1791.

———. *Le Prisonnier d'Etat, ou Tableau historique de la captivité de J.-C.-G. Le Prévôt de Beaumont. ...* Paris: n.p., 1791.

Lescure, Adolphe Maturin de, ed. *Correspondance secrète inédite sur Louis XVI, Marie-Antoinette, la cour et la ville de 1777 à 1792.* 2 vols. Paris: H. Plon, 1866.

Lespinasse, Julie [Jeanne-Julie-Eléonore] de. *Lettres de Mlle de Lespinasse.* Ed. Eugène Asse. Paris: Charpentier et Cⁱᵉ, 1876.

Lespinasse, René de. *Les Métiers et corporations de la ville de Paris.* Vol. I: *Ordonnances Générales, Métiers d'Alimentation.* Paris: Imprimerie nationale, 1886.

Letrosne, Guillaume-François. *De l'Administration provinciale et de la réforme de l'impôt.* 2 vols. Basel; and Paris: P.-J. Duplain, 1788.

———. *Discours sur l'état actuel de la magistrature et sur les causes de sa décadence.* N.p.: n.p., n.d.

———. *Lettres à un ami sur les avantages de la liberté du commerce des grains, et le danger des prohibitions.* Amsterdam; and Paris: Desaint, 1768.

———. *La Liberté du commerce des grains, toujours utile et jamais nuisible.* Paris: n.p., 1 Nov. 1765.

———. *Mémoire sur les vagabonds et les mendiants.* Paris: Simon, 1764.

———. *Réflexions sur les mœurs.* Orléans: Couvet de Villeneuve, n.d.

Linguet, Simon-Nicolas-Henri. *Annales politiques, civiles et littéraires du dix-huitième siècle, ouvrage périodique.* 19 vols. London; and Paris: chez l'auteur, 1777–1792.

———. *Canaux navigables, ou Développement des avantages qui résulteraient de l'exécution de plusieurs projets en ce genre pour la Picardie, l'Artois, la Bourgogne, la Champagne, la Bretagne.* Amsterdam; and Paris: L. Cellot, 1769.

———. *Du Pain et du bled. Œuvres.* Vol. VI. London: n.p., 1774.

———. *Histoire des révolutions de l'empire romain.* 2 vols. Paris: Desaint, 1766.

———. *Réponse aux docteurs modernes, ou Apologie pour l'auteur de la "Théorie des loix," et des "Lettres sur cette théorie," avec la réfutation du système des philosophes économistes.* 2 vols. London and Paris: n.p., 1771.

———. *Réflexions des six corps de la ville de Paris sur la suppression des jurandes.* N.p.: n.p., 1776.

Luchet, Jean-Pierre-Louis de la Roche Du Maine. *Examen d'un livre qui a pour titre: "Sur la législation et le commerce des bleds."* N.p.: n.p., 1775.

Mably, Gabriel Bonnot, abbé de. *Du Commerce des grains. Collection complète des œuvres de l'abbé de Mably.* Ed. G. Arnoux. Vol. XIII. Paris: Ch. Desbrières, l'an III (1794–1795).

Macquer, Philippe. *Dictionnaire portatif des arts et métiers, contenant l'histoire, la description, la police des fabriques et manufactures de France et des pays étrangers.* 2 vols. Paris: chez Lacombe, 1766.

———. *Dictionnaire raisonné universel des arts et métiers, contenant l'histoire, la description, la police des fabriques et manufactures de France et des pays étrangers.* New edition, rev. Ed. Pierre Jaubert. 4 vols. Paris: P.-F. Didot jeune, 1773.

Malouin, Paul-Jacques. *Description et détails des arts du meunier, du vermicelier et du boulanger, avec une histoire abrégée de la boulangerie et un dictionnaire de ces arts, par M. Malouin.* Paris: Saillant et Nyon, 1767.

———. *Description et détails des arts du meunier, du vermicelier et du boulanger.* N.p: n.p., 1779.

———. *Description des arts du meunier, du vermicellier et du boulanger.* Nouvelle édition, publiée avec des observations et augmentée de tout ce qui a été écrit de mieux sur ces matières, en Allemagne, en Angleterre, en Suisse, en Italie. Ed. Jean-Elie Bertrand. Neufchâtel: Imprimerie de la Société typographique, 1771.

Malthus, Thomas Robert. *On Population.* Ed. Gertrude Himmelfarb. New York: Modern Library, 1960.

Manuel, [Louis-] Pierre. *La Police de Paris dévoilée.* 2 vols. Paris: J.-B. Garnery, an II.

Marais, Mathieu. *Journal et mémoires ... sur la régence et le règne de Louis XV (1715–1737).* Ed. M. de Lescure. 4 vols. Paris: Firmin-Didot frères, fils et Cⁱᵉ, 1863–1868.

Marie-Thérèse. *Correspondance secrète entre Marie-Thérèse et le Cte de Mercy-Argenteau avec les lettres de Marie-Thérèse et de Marie-Antoinette.* Ed. Alfred d'Arneth and M.A. Geoffroy. 3 vols. Paris: Firmin-Didot frères, fils et Cⁱᵉ, 1874.

Marmontel, Jean-François. *Mémoires de Marmontel.* Ed. Maurice Tourneux. 3 vols. Paris: Librairie des bibliophiles, 1891.

Marville, F. de. "Chronique du règne de Louis XV, 1742–1743." *Revue rétrospective*, 1st. ser., IV (1834), 438–73; V (1834), 24–80, 213–76, 376–468.

———. *Lettres de M. de Marville, lieutenant général de police, au ministre Maurepas (1742–1747).* Ed. A. de Boislisle. 3 vols. Paris: H. Champion, 1896–1905.

Mathon de la Cour, C.-J., ed. *Collection de Comptes-rendus ... concernant les finances de France.* Lausanne: n.p., 1788.

Melon, Jean-Francois. *Essai politique sur le commerce (1734). Economistes financiers du XVIIIᵉ siècle.* Ed. E. Daire. Paris: Guillaumin et Cⁱᵉ, 1843.

Mercier, Louis-Sébastien. *L'An deux mille quatre-cent quarante, Rêve s'il en fût jamais.* New ed. 2 vols. London: n.p., 1785.

———. *Tableau de Paris.* New ed. 12 vols. Amsterdam: n.p., 1782–1788.

Méry de la Canorgue, abbé Joseph. *L'Ami de ceux qui n'en ont point ou système économique, politique et moral.* Paris: P. Prault, 1767.

Messance. *Recherches sur la population des généralités d'Auvergne, de Lyon, de Rouen et de quelques provinces et villes du royaume, avec des réflexions sur la valeur du bled, tant en France qu'en Angleterre, 1674 jusqu'en 1764.* Paris: Durand, 1766.

Métra, François. *Correspondance secrète, politique et littéraire, ou Mémoires pour servir à l'histoire des cours, des sociétés et de la littérature en France, depuis la mort de Louis XV London, 1787–1790. 18 vols. in 3 vols.* Geneva: Slatkine reprints, 1967.

Mildmay, William. *The Police of France, or an Account of the laws and regulations established in that kingdom for the preservation of peace and the preventing of robberies, to which is added a particular description of the police and government of the city of Paris.* London: E. Owen and T. Harrison, 1763.

Mirabeau, Victor de Riquetti, marquis de. *L'Ami des hommes, ou Traité de la population.* 5 vols. Avignon: n.p., 1756–1758.

———. *Lettres sur le commerce des grains.* Amsterdam; and Paris: Desaint, 1768.

———. *Philosophie rurale, ou économie générale et politique de l'agriculture, réduite á l'ordre immuable des loix physiques & morales, qui assurent la prospérité des Empires.* 3 vols. Amsterdam: chez les Libraires associés, 1763.

Miromesnil, Armand-Thomas Hue. *Correspondance politique et administrative de Miromesnil, premier président du Parlement de Normandie.* Ed. P. LeVerdier. 5 vols. Rouen; and Paris: A. Picard et fils, 1899–1903.

Moheau. *Recherches et considérations sur la population de la France* (1778). *Collection des économistes et des réformateurs sociaux de la France.* Ed. René Gonnard. Paris: P. Geuthner, 1912.

Montaudouin de La Touche, Jean-Gabriel. *Supplément à "l'Essai sur la police générale des grains"* (The Hague, 1757). *Collection des économistes et des réformateurs sociaux de la France.* Ed. E. Depitre. Paris: P. Geuthner, 1910.

Monthyon, Antoine-J.-B.-R. Auget, baron de. *Particularités et observations sur les ministres des finances les plus célèbres depuis 1660 jusqu'en 1791.* London; and Paris: LeNormant, 1812.

Moreau, Jacob-Nicolas. *Mes Souvenirs, par Jacob-Nicolas Moreau, né en 1717, mort en 1803.* Ed. Camille Hermelin. 2 vols. Paris: E. Plon, Nourrit et Cie, 1898–1901.

Morellet, abbé André. *Analyse de l'ouvrage intitulé: "De la législation et du commerce des grains."* Paris: Pissot, 1775.

————· *Mémoires inédits de l'abbé Morellet, de l'Académic française, sur le dixhuitième siècle et sur la révolution, précédés de l'éloge de l'abbé Morellet par M. Lemontey.* 2 vols. Paris: Ladvocat, 1821.

————· *Réfutation de l'ouvrage qui a pour titre: "Dialogues sur le commerce des bleds."* London: n.p., 1770.

————· *Théorie du paradoxe.* Amsterdam: n.p., 1775.

Morelly. *Code de la nature.* Paris: n.p., n.d.

Moréri, Louis. *Le Grand dictionnaire historique, ou le mélange curieux de l'histoire sacrée et profane.* New ed. Ed. M. Drouet. 10 vols. Paris: Les Libraires associés, 1759.

Narbonne, Pierre de. *Journal des règnes de Louis XIV et Louis XV de l'année 1701 à l'année 1744 par Pierre Narbonne, premier commissaire de police de la ville de Versailles.* Ed. J.-A. LeRoi. Versailles: Bernard, 1866.

Necker, Jacques. *Sur la législation et le commerce des grains.* 2 vols. Paris: Pissot, 1775.

————· *Eloge de Jean-Baptiste Colbert.* Paris: Brunet, 1773.

————· *De l'Administration des finances de la France.* 3 vols. N.p.: n.p., 1784.

O'Heguerty, Pierre-André [Cte. de Magnières]. *Essai sur les intérêts du commerce….* The Hague: n.p., 1754.

————· *Essai de finances sur les droits des aides.* Paris: Bastien, 1775.

Parmentier, Antoine-Auguste. *Avis aux bonnes ménagères des villes et des campagnes sur la meilleure manière de faire leur pain.* Paris: Imprimerie royale, 1772.

————· *Expériences et réflexions relatives à l'analyse des blés et des farines.* Paris: Monory, 1776.

————· *Manière de faire le pain de pommes de terre sans mélange de farine.* Paris: Imprimerie royale, 1779.

————· *Mémoire sur les avantages du commerce des grains et des farines.* Paris: n.p., 1785.

————· *Mémoire sur les avantages que la province de Languedoc peut retirer de ses grains, avec le mémoire sur la nouvelle manière de construire les moulins à farine par M. Dransy.* Paris: L'Imprimerie des Etats de Languedoc, 1787.

————· *Le Parfait boulanger, ou Traité complet sur la fabrication et le commerce du pain.* Paris: Imprimerie royale, 1778.

————· *Recherches sur les végétaux nourrissans, qui, dans les temps de disette, peuvent remplacer les aliments ordinaires, avec des nouvelles observations sur la culture des pommes de terre.* Paris: Imprimerie royale, 1781.

Pattullo, H. *Essai sur l'amélioration des terres.* Paris: n.p., 1758.

Paucton, A.-J.-P. *Métrologie, ou traité des mesures, des poids et des monnoies des anciens peuples et des modernes.* Paris: Desaint, 1780.

Pellissery, R.-A. de. *Le Caffé politique d'Amsterdam.* 2 vols. Amsterdam: n.p., 1776.

Peuchet, Jacques, ed. *Collection des lois, ordonnances et règlements de police depuis le XIIIe siècle jusqu'à l'année 1818.* 2nd. ser.: Police moderne, 1667 à 1789. 8 vols. Paris: n.p., 1818–1819.

————· ed. *Mémoires tirés des archives de la police de Paris pour servir à l'histoire de la morale et de la police, depuis Louis XIV jusqu'à nos jours.* 6 vols. Paris: Bourmance, 1838.

Piarron de Chamousset, Claude-Humbert. *Œuvres complètes de P. de Chamousset, ... précédées de son éloge par l'abbé Cotton des Houssayes.* 2 vols. Paris: P.-D. Pierres, 1783.

Pidansat de Mairobert, Mathieu-François. *L'Observateur anglois, ou Correspondance secrète entre Milord All'eye and Milord All'ear.* 10 vols. London: J. Adamson, 1778–1786[?].

———. *Journal historique de la révolution opérée dans la constitution de la monarchie françoise.* 6 vols. London: n.p., 1776.

———. [?]. *Maupeouana.* 5 vols. Paris: n.p., 1775.

———. *L'Observateur anglois....* 4 vols. London: J. Adamson, 1777–1778.

Piganiol de la Force, Jean-Aymar. *Description historique de la ville de Paris et de ses environs.* New ed. 10 vols. Paris: G. Desprez, 1765.

Pigeonneau, H. and Foville, A. de, eds. *L'Administration de l'agriculture au contrôle général des finances. Procès-verbaux et rapports.* Paris: Librairie Guillaumin et Cie, 1882.

Pilati. *Voyages en differens pays de l'Europe en 1774–76.* The Hague: C. Plaat, 1777.

Pinczon du Sel des Monts. *Considérations sur le commerce de Bretagne.* [Rennes]: Imprimerie de J. Vatar, [1756].

Piton, Camille, ed. *Paris sous Louis XV. Rapports des inspecteurs de police au Roi.* 5 series. Paris: Société du "Mercure de France," 1908–1914.

Plumart de Dangeul, Louis-Joseph. *Remarques sur les avantages et désavantages de la France et de la Grande Bretagne par rapport au commerce et aux autres sources de la puissance des états.* Leyden, 1754.

Pluche, abbé Antoine. *Le Spectacle de la nature, ou Entretiens sur les particularités de l'histoire naturelle qui ont paru les plus propres à rendre les jeunes gens curieux et à leur former l'esprit.* 9 vols. Paris: Veuve Estienne, 1732–1750.

Poncelet, Polycarpe. *Histoire naturelle du froment.* Paris: Imprimerie de G. Desprez, 1779.

Quesnay, François. "Fermier." *Encyclopédie, ou Dictionnaire raisonné des sciences, des arts, et des métiers, par une société de gens de lettres.* Ed. Diderot, *et al.* Vol. VI. Paris: Briasson, David l'aîné, LeBreton, Durand, 1756. Pp. 528–40.

———. "Grains." *Encyclopédie, ou Dictionnaire raisonné des sciences, des arts et des métiers, ...* Ed. Diderot, *et al.* Vol. VII. Paris: Briasson, David l'aîné, LeBreton, Durand, 1757. Pp. 812–31.

———. Dupont; *et al. Physiocratie, ou constitution naturelle du gouvernement le plus avantageux au genre humain.* 2 vols. Paris: Dupont, 1767–1768.

Raunié, Emile, ed. *Recueil Clairambault-Maurepas. Chansonnier historique du XVIIIe siècle.* 10 vols. Paris: A. Quantin, 1879–1884.

Ravaisson-Mollien, F. and L., eds. *Archives de la Bastille. Documents inédits.* Vol. XIX. Paris: C. Pedone, 1904.

Reneaume, M. "Sur la manière de conserver les grains." *Mémoires de l'Académie des Sciences, 1708.* Paris, 1709.

Restif de la Bretonne, Nicolas-Edme. *Les Nuits de Paris. L'Œuvre de Restif de la Bretonne.* Ed. Henri Bachelin. Vol. I. Paris: Editions du Trianon, 1930.

Rey. *Du Commerce des bleds. Pour servir à la réfutation de l'ouvrage sur la législation et le commerce des grains.* Paris: Grange, 1775.

Richelet, Pierre. *Dictionnaire de la langue française ancienne et moderne.* Rev. ed. Ed. abbé Goujet. 3 vols. Lyon: Duplain frères, 1759.

Richer, Adrien. *Vies des surintendans des finances et des contrôleurs-généraux, depuis Enguerrand de Marigny, jusqu'à nos jours.* 3 vols. Paris; Debray, 1790.

Rivarol, Antoine, Cte de. *Œuvres complètes d'Antoine Rivarol.* Ed. Chênedollé and F.-J.-M. Fayolle. 5 vols. Paris: Léopold Collin, 1808.

Roland, C.N. *Recueil d'idées patriotiques.* N.p.: n.p., 1769.

Roland de la Platière, J.-M. *Voyages en France 1769.* Ed. C. Perroud. Villefranche: Auray fils, 1913.

Roubaud, abbé Pierre-Joseph-André. *Récréations économiques, ou Lettres de l'auteur des "Représentations aux Magistrats" à M. le Chevalier Zanobi, principal interlocuteur des "Dialogues sur le commerce des blés."* Amsterdam; and Paris: Delalain, 1770.

————. *Représentations aux magistrats, contenant l'exposition raisonnée des faits relatifs à la liberté du commerce des grains, et les résultats respectifs des règlemens et de la liberté.* London; and Paris: Lacombe, 1769.

Rousseau, Jean-Jacques. *Œuvres complètes.* 4 vols. Paris: A. Houssiaux, 1852–53.

Rozier, abbé François. *Cours complet d'agriculture théorique, pratique, économique, et de médecine rurale et vétérinaire, suivi d'une méthode pour étudier l'agriculture par principes.* 9 vols. Paris: Hôtel Serpente, 1781–1796.

Rossi, A.-J.-L.-P. de. *Considérations sur les principes politiques de mon siècle et sur la nécessité indispensable d'une morale politique [sic] à l'occasion de l'ouvrage intitulé: Sur la législation des grains....* London: A. Grant, 1776.

Rutledge, Jean-Jacques [James Rutlidge]. *Mémoire pour la communauté des maîtres boulangers de la ville et faubourgs de Paris, présenté au Roi, le 19 février 1789.* N.p.: n.p., 1789.

————. *Second mémoire pour les maîtres boulangers, lu au bureau des subsistances de l'Assemblée nationale, par le chevalier Rutledge.* Paris: Baudouin, [1789].

Sage, Balthasar-Georges. *Analyse des blés.* Paris: Imprimerie royale, 1776.

Saint-Lambert, François de. "Les Saisons, Poème (1769)." *Saint-Lambert, Scienza e paesaggio nella poesia del Settecento.* Ed. Luigi de Nardis. Rome: Edizioni dell'Ateneo Roma, 1961.

Saint-Priest, François-Emmanuel Guignard, Cte de. *Mémoires....* Ed. Baron de Barante. 2 vols. Paris: Calmann-Lévy, 1929.

Saint-Simon, Louis de Rouvroy, duc de. *Mémoires de St. Simon.* Ed. A. de Boislisle. 41 vols. Paris: Hachette, 1879–1928.

Saury, abbé Jean. *Réflexions d'un citoyen sur le commerce des grains.* Paris: Ruault, 1775.

Sauval, Henri. *Histoire et recherches des antiquités de la ville de Paris.* 3 vols. Paris: C. Moette, 1724.

Savary, Jacques. *Le Parfait négociant.* 8th ed. Ed. P.-L. Savary. 2 vols. Paris: Claude Robustel, 1721.

Savary des Bruslons, Jacques. *Dictionnaire portatif de commerce.* 7 vols. Copenhagen, 1761–1762.

————. *Dictionnaire universel de commerce.* Ed. P.-L. Savary. 3 vols. Paris: J. Estienne, 1723–30.

Sénac de Meilhan, Gabriel. *Du Gouvernement, des mœurs, et des conditions en France avant la Révolution.* Paris: Maradan, 1814.

————. *Des Principes et des causes de la révolution en France.* Paris: n.p., 1790.

Smith, Adam. *Lectures on Justice, Police, Revenue and Arms....* Ed. E. Cannon. Oxford: Clarendon Press, 1896.

Taboureau. *Rapport fait au Roi par M. Taboureau, contrôleur-général, le 23 février 1777.* [Au sujet de l'approvisionnement de Paris.] Paris: Imprimerie de Demonville, 1789.

Talbot, Robert. *Letters on the French Nation Considered in the Different Departments.* 2 vols. London: n.p., 1771.

Target, Guy-Jean-Baptiste. *Observations sur le commerce des grains, écrites en décembre 1769.* Amsterdam; and Paris: L. Cellot, 1775.

Tessier, Henri-Alexandre. "Commerce des grains." *Encyclopédie Méthodique. Agriculture.* Vol. III. Paris: Panckoucke, 1793.

Thicknesse, Philip. *Useful Hints to Those Who Make the Tour of France.* London: R. Davis, et al., 1768.

Tickell, Richard [Mlle. Duthé]. *La Cassette verte de M. de Sartines trouvée chez Mlle Duthé.* The Hague: chez la Veuve Whiskerfeld, 1779.

————. *A Year's Journey Through France and Part of Spain.* 2 vols. London: R. Cruttwell, 1777.

Thiéry, Luc-Vincent. *Almanach du voyageur à Paris... année 1783.* Paris: Hardouin, n.d.

Tillet, Mathieu. *Dissertation sur la cause qui corrompt et noircit les grains de bled dans les épis, et sur les moyens de prévenir ces accidens.* Bordeaux: Veuve de P. Brun, 1775.

_____. *Expériences et observations sur le poids de pain, au sortir du four et sur le règlement par lequel les boulangers sont assujettis à donner aux pains qu'ils exposent en vente un poids fixe et déterminé....* Paris: Imprimerie de P.-D. Pierres, 1781.

Turgot, Anne-Robert-Jacques. *Œuvres de Turgot et documents le concernant, avec biographie et notes.* Ed. Gustave Schelle. 5 vols. Paris: F. Alcan 1913–1923.

Vaudrey, de. *Considérations sur la cherté des grains et tableau de la valeur du marc d'argent et du prix du bled depuis 1304 jusqu'en 1770, avec distinction des années abondantes, médiocres et insuffisantes.* Dijon: n.p., 1789.

Véri, abbé Joseph-Alphonse de. *Journal de l'abbé de Véri.* Ed. Bon. Jehan de Witte. 2 vols. Paris: J. Tallandier, 1928–1930.

Véron de Forbonnais, François. *Considérations sur les finances d'Espagne.* 2nd ed. Paris: les frères Estienne, 1755.

_____. *Principes et observations économiques.* 2 vols. Amsterdam: Marc Michel Rey, 1767.

_____. *Recherches et considérations sur les finances de France depuis 1595 jusqu'en 1721.* 6 vols. Liège: n.p., 1758.

Vivens, François de. *Observations sur divers moyens de soutenir l'agriculture, principalement dans la Guyenne: où l'on traite des cultures propres à cette province.* N.p: n.p., 1756–1761.

Voltaire, François-Marie Arouet de. *The Age of Louis XIV.* Trans. Martyn P. Pollack. New York: E.P. Dutton & Co., Inc., 1962.

_____. *Correspondence.* Ed. Theodore Besterman. 107 vols. Geneva: Institut et Muséee Voltaire, 1953–1965.

_____. *Œuvres complètes de Voltaire.* Ed. L. Moland. 52 vols. Paris: Garnier frères, 1877–1885.

_____. *Œuvres complètes de Voltaire.* Ed. Beaumarchais, *et al.* 70 vols. Kehl: Société littéraire-typographique, 1784–89.

Walpole, Horace. *The Letters of Horace Walpole.* Ed. Paget Toynbee. 16 vols. Oxford: Clarendon Press, 1903–1905.

Weber, Max. *The City.* Trans. and ed. Don Martindale and Gertrud Neuworth. Glencoe, Ill.: Free Press, 1958.

Weulersse, Georges, ed. *Les Manuscrits économiques de François Quesnay et du marquis de Mirabeau aux Archives Nationales.* New York: B. Franklin reprint, 1968; original edition: Paris, 1916.

Young, Arthur. *Political Arithmetic, containing observations on the present state of Great Britain....* London: W. Nicoll, 1774.

_____. *The Question of Scarcity plainly stated and remedies considered. With observations on permanent measures to keep wheat at a more regular price.* London: MacMillan, 1800.

_____. *Travels in France during the years 1787, 1788, and 1789.* Ed. Jeffry Kaplow. Garden City, N.Y.: Doubleday, 1969.

II. SECONDARY WORKS

Abbiateci, André, *et al. Crimes et criminalité en France sous l'ancien régime: 17ᵉ–18ᵉ siècles.* Cahiers des Annales, no. 33. Paris: A. Colin, 1971.

Abel, Wilhelm. *Crises agraires en Europe (XIIIᵉ–XXᵉ siècle).* Paris: Flammarion, 1973.

_____. *Massenarmut und Hungerkrisen im vorindustriellen Deutschland.* Göttingen: Van den Hoeck & Ruprecht, 1972.

Acomb, Frances, *Anglophobia in France, 1763 to 1789; An Essay in the History of Constitutionalism and Nationalism.* Durham, N. C.: Duke University Press, 1950.

Afanassiev, Georges. *Le Commerce des céréales en France au XVIIIᵉ siècle.* Trans. from the Russian by Paul Boyer. Paris: A. Picard et fils, 1894.

_____. "Le Pacte de famine." *Séances et travaux de l'Académie des sciences morales et politiques.* 50th year, n.s., XXXIV (1890), 569–93, 740–69.

Airiau, Jean. *L'Opposition aux physiocrates à la fin de l'ancien régime*. Paris: Pichon et Durand-Auzias, 1965.

Albaum, Martin. "The Moral Defenses of the Physiocrats' laissez-faire." *Journal of the History of Ideas*, XVI (April 1955), 179–97.

Alboize du Pujol, J.-E., and Macquet, A. *Le Donjon de Vincennes*. 2 vols. Paris: Administration de librairie, 1844.

Aldridge, Alfred Owen. *Franklin and his French Contemporaries*. New York: New York University Press, 1957.

Alem, André. *D'Argenson économiste*. Paris: A. Rousseau, 1899.

————. *Le Marquis d'Argenson et l'économie politique au début du XVIIIe siècle. Pratiques mercantiles et théories libérales*. Paris: A. Rousseau, 1900.

Amin, Galal A. *Food Supply and Economic Development, with Special Reference to Egypt*. London: Frank Cass & Co., 1966.

Ammann, Louis. *Meunerie et boulangerie*. Paris: J.-B. Ballière et fils, 1925.

André, Louis. *Michel le Tellier et l'organisation de l'armée monarchique*. Paris: F. Alcan, 1906.

Andrieux, Charles. *Trudaine; sa vie, son œuvre, ses idées*. Clermont-Ferrand: Raclot frères, 1922.

Anglade, Eugène. *Coup d'oeil sur la police depuis son origine jusqu'à nos jours*. Paris: Martinon, 1847.

Antoine, Michel. "Les Comités de ministres sous le règne de Louis XV." *Revue historique de droit français et étranger*, 4th ser., 29th year (1951), 193–230.

————. "Le Conseil des Dépêches sous le règne de Louis XV." *Bibliothèque de l'Ecole des Chartes*, CXI (1953), 158–208; CXII (1954), 126–81.

————. "Le Conseil des Finances sous Louis XV." *Revue d'histoire moderne et contemporaine*, V (July–Sept. 1958), 161–200.

————. "Le Discours de la flagellation." *Recueil de Travaux offert à M. Clovis Brunel*. Vol. I. Paris: Société de l'Ecole des Chartes, 1955.

————. "En Marge ou au cœur de 'l'affaire de Bretagne'? Intrigues et cabales de M. de La Chalotais." *Bibliothèque de l'Ecole des Chartes*, CXXVIII (July–Dec. 1970), 369–408.

————. "Les Remontrances des cours supérieures au XVIIIe siècle. Essai de problématique et d'inventaire." *Comité des travaux historiques et scientifiques. Bulletin de la section d'histoire moderne et contemporaine* (Paris: Bibliothèque Nationale, 1971), fasc. VIII, 7–81.

————. "Une Séance royale au conseil d'état privé sous le règne de Louis XV." *Revue historique de droit français et étranger*, 4th ser., 28th year (1950), 413–25.

————. *Le Conseil du Roi sous le règne de Louis XV*. Geneva. Droz, 1970.

————. Buffet, H.-F.; *et al. Guide des recherches dans les fonds judiciaires de l'ancien régime*. Paris: Imprimerie nationale, 1958.

Araskhaniantz, Awetis. *Die französische Getreidehandelspolitik bis zum Jahre 1789, in ihrem Zusammenhange mit der Land-, Volks-, und Finanzwissenschaft Frankreichs*. Leipzig: Duncker & Humblot, 1882.

Ardashev, *Les Intendants de province sous Louis XVI*. Trans. L. Jousserandot. Paris: Alcan, 1909.

Arias, Gino. "Ferdinando Galiani et les Physiocrates." *Revue des sciences politiques*, 37th year, XLV (July–Sept. 1922), 346–66.

Ariés, Philippe. *Histoire des populations françaises et de leurs attitudes devant la vie depuis le XVIIIe siècle*. Paris: by the author, 1948.

Arnould, A.; Alboize du Pujol, J. E.; and Macquet, A. *Histoire de la Bastille*. 6 vols. Paris: Administration de librairie, 1844.

Arpin, Marcel. *Historique de la meunerie et de la boulangerie, depuis les temps préhistoriques jusqu'à l'année 1914*. 2 vols. Paris: Le Chancelier, 1948.

Ashley, W. *The Bread of Our Forefathers*. Oxford: Clarendon Press, 1928.

Ashton, John. *The History of Bread from Prehistoric to Modern Times*. London: Brooke House, n.d.

Attman, Artur. *The Russian and Polish Markets in International Trade, 1500–1650*. Gothenburg: Publications of the Institute of Economic History of Gothenburg University, 1973.

Aubert, Felix. *Histoire du parlement de Paris de l'origine à François Ier, 1250–1515.* 2 vols. Paris: A. Picard et fils, 1894.

———. *Le Parlement de Paris, de Philippe le Bel à Charles VII (1314–1422).* 2 vols. Paris: A. Picard, 1886–1890.

Avenel, Georges, Vte. d'. *Histoire économique de la propriété, des salaires, des denrées et de tous les prix en général, depuis l'an 1200 jusqu'en l'an 1800.* 7 vols. Paris: Imprimerie nationale, 1894–1926.

Babeau, Albert. *La Lutte de l'état contre la cherté en 1724.* Paris: E. Leroux, 1892.

———. *Paris en 1789.* New ed. Paris: Didot, 1892.

———. *La Ville sous l'ancien régime.* 2 vols. Paris: Didier et Cie, 1884.

Baehrel, René. "Épidémie et terreur: histoire et sociologie." *Annales historiques de la révolution française,* XXIII (1951), 113–46.

———. "La Haine de classe en temps d'épidémie." *Annales: économies, sociétés, civilisations,* VII (1952), 351–60.

———. "La Mortalité sous l'ancien régime: remarques inquiètes." *Annales: économies, sociétés, civilisations,* XII (1957), 85–98.

———. *Une Croissance: la Basse-Provence rurale (fin XVIe siècle—1789); essai d'économie historique statistique.* Paris: S.E.V.P.E.N., 1961.

Baker, G.W. and Chapman, D.W. *Man and Society in Disaster.* New York: Basic Books, 1962.

Baldwin, John W. "The Medieval Theories of the Just Price." *Transactions of the American Philosophical Society,* XLIX, part 4 (1959), 1–92.

Balland, Joseph-Antoine-Felix. *La Chimie alimentaire dans l'œuvre de Parmentier.* Paris: Baillière, 1902.

———. "La Légende de Parmentier." *Revue scientifique,* XCVIII (Jan. 1918), 19–26.

Baltard, Victor, and Callet, F. *Monographie des Halles centrales de Paris.* 2nd ed. Paris: Librairie générale de l'architecture et des travaux publics, 1873.

Bamford, Paul W. "Entrepreneurship in 17th Century and 18th Century France: Some General Conditions and a Case Study." *Explorations in Entrepreneurial History,* IX (April 1958), 204–13.

Barnes, Donald G. *A History of the English Corn Laws from 1660 to 1846.* London: G. Routledge & Sons, Ltd., 1930.

Barrabé, E. *Le Pain à bon marché; meuneries-boulangeries, nécessité de leur création.* Paris: E. Plon, 1876.

Barrey, P. "Le Havre maritime: la batellerie et les transports par terre du 16e au 19e siècle." *Mémoires et documents pour servir à l'histoire du commerce et de l'industrie en France.* Ed. J. Hayem. 6th series. Paris: Hachette, 1921.

Barroux, Maurius. *Le Département de la Seine et de la ville de Paris; notions générates et bibliographiques pour en étudier l'histoire.* Paris: Champion, 1910.

———. *Essai de bibliographie critique des généralités de l'histoire de Paris.* Paris: Champion, 1908.

Bastié, Jean. *La Croissance de la banlieue parisienne.* Paris: Presses universitaires de France, 1964.

Baudrillart, Henri. *Histoire du luxe privé et public, depuis l'antiquité jusqu'à nos jours.* 2nd ed. 4 vols. Paris: Hachette, 1880–1881.

———. *Les Populations agricoles de la France.* 3 vols. Paris: Hachette (et Guillaumin), 1885–1893.

Baulant, Micheline. "Le Prix des grains à Paris de 1431 à 1788." *Annales: économies, sociétés, civilisations,* 23rd year (May–June 1968), 520–40.

———. and Meuvret, J. *Prix des céréales, extraits de la Mercuriale de Paris (1520–1698).* 2 vols. Paris: S.E.V.P.E.N., 1960–1962.

Baumont, Maurice. *Le Blé.* 5th ed. Paris: Presses universitaires de France, 1967.

Beauroy, Jacques. "The Pre-revolutionary Crises in Bergerac, 1770–1789." *Proceedings of the First Annual Meeting of the Western Society for French History,* March 1974. Ed. E. Newman. New Mexico State University (Mimeograph-Offset), 75–97.

Beer, Max. *An Inquiry into Physiocracy.* London: G. Allen and Unwin, Ltd., 1939.

Beik, Paul H. *A Judgment of the Old Regime.* New York: Columbia University Press, 1944.

Bellanger, Claude, *et al. Histoire générale de la presse française des origines à 1814*. Paris: Presses universitaires de France, 1969.

Beloff, Max. *Public Order and Popular Disturbances, 1660–1714*. London: Oxford University Press, 1938.

Bennett, Richard, and Elton, John. *History of Corn Milling.* 4 vols. London: Simplin, Marshall and Company, 1898–1904.

Bennion, Edmund Baron. *Breadmaking, Its Principles and Practice*. 3rd ed. London: Oxford University Press, 1954.

Benot, Yves. "Un Inédit de Diderot." *La Pensée*, LV (May–June 1954), 3–11.

Benzacar, Joseph. "La Disette de 1747–1748." *Revue philomathique de Bordeaux et du Sud-Ouest* (Nov. 1904).

―――. *Le Pain à Bordeaux (XVIIIe siècle)*. Bordeaux: Gounouilhou, 1905.

―――. "La Question du pain sous l'ancien régime et la Révolution." *Revue économique de Bordeaux* (March 1904).

Bercé, Yves-Marie. "Aspects de la criminalité au XVIIe siècle." *Revue historique*, 92nd year, CCXXXIX (Jan.–March 1968), 33–43.

―――. *Croquants et nu-pieds*. Paris: Gallimard-Julliard, 1974.

Bergeron, Louis. "Approvisionnement et consommation à Paris sous le premier Empire." *Mémoires de la Fédération des Sociétés historiques et archéologiques de Paris et de l'Ile de France*, XIV (1963), 197–232.

Bernard, Leon. *The Emerging City. Paris in the Age of Louis XIV.* Durham, N.C.: Duke University Press, 1970.

Bernard, Michel. *Introduction à une sociologie des doctrines économiques des physiocrates à Stuart Mill*. Paris: Mouton, 1963.

Berthet, Elie. *Le Pacte de famine*. 2 vols. Paris: G. Roux et Cassanet, 1847.

―――. *Le Pacte de famine*. Ed. B.B. Dickinson. Boston: D.C. Heath & Co., 1893.

―――. and Foucher, Paul. *Le Pacte de famine, drame historique en 5 actes* (Paris, Porte-Saint-Martin, 17 juin 1839). Paris: Imprimerie de Dubuisson, [1857].

Bertin, Jacques; Hemardinquer, J.-J.; *et al. Atlas of Food Crops*. Paris: Mouton, 1971.

Bézard, Yvonne. *La Vie rurale dans le sud de la région parisienne de 1450 à 1560*. Paris: Firmin-Didot & Cie, 1929.

Bickart, Roger. *Les Parlements et la notion de souveraineté nationale au XVIIIe siècle*. Paris: Felix Alcan, 1932.

Bienaymé, Gustave. "Le Coût de la vie à Paris à diverses époques." *Journal de la Société de statistique de Paris*, 36th year (Feb. 1895), 57–68; (Oct. 1895), 355–60; 37th year (Oct. 1896), 375–90; 38th year (March 1897), 83–90; 39th year (Nov. 1898), 369–82.

―――. "La Fiscalité alimentaire et gastronomique à Paris." *Journal de la Société de statistique de Paris*, 31st year (1890), 40–60.

―――. and St. Julien, A. de. "Les Droits d'entrée et d'octroi à Paris depuis le XIIe siècle." *Bulletin de statistique et de législation comparative*, XVII (Jan.–June 1885), 42–79, 193–211, 323–33, 549–59, 641–49; XVIII (July–Dec. 1885), 211–23, 346–61, 477–87, 563–85, 705–13.

―――. and St. Julien, A. de. *Histoire des droits d'entrée et d'octroi à Paris*. Paris: P. Dupont, 1887.

Binet, Pierre. *La Réglementation du marché du blé en France au XVIIIe siècle et à l'époque contemporaine*. Paris: Librairie sociale et économique, 1939.

Biollay, Léon. "Les Anciennes halles de Paris." *Mémoires de la Société de l'histoire de Paris et de l'Ile-de-France*, III (1876), 293–355.

―――. *Un Episode de l'approvisionnement de Paris en 1789*. Paris: Imprimerie P. Dupont, 1878.

―――. *Etudes économiques sur le XVIIIe siècle. Le Pacte de famine; l'administration du commerce*. Paris: Guillaumin, 1885.

―――. *Etudes économiques sur le XVIIIe siècle. Les Prix en 1790*. Paris: Guillaumin, 1886.

―――. *Origines et transformations du factorat dans les marchés de Paris*. Paris: Berger-Levrault & Cie, 1880.

Biot, Jean-Baptiste. *Lettres sur l'approvisionnement de Paris et sur le commerce des grains*. Paris: Bachelier, 1835.

Birembaut, A. "Le Problème de la panification à Paris en 1790." *Annales historiques de la Révolution française*, XXXVII (1965), 361–67.

Bisson de Barthélemy, Paul. *L'Activité d'un procureur général au parlement de Paris à la fin de l'ancien régime: les Joly de Fleury*. Paris: Société d'édition d'enseignement supérieur, 1964.

Blanc, Hippolyte. *Bibliographie des corporations ouvrières avant 1789*. Paris: Librairie de la société bibliographique, 1885.

Bloch, Camille. "Le Commerce des grains dans la généralité d'Orléans (1768)." *Etudes sur l'histoire économique de la France (1760–1789)*. Paris: Picard et fils, 1900.

––––––. *Le Commerce des grains dans la généralité d'Orléans d'après la Correspondance inédite de l'intendant Cypierre*. Orléans: H. Herluison, 1898.

––––––. *L'Assistance et l'état en France à la veille de la révolution*. Paris: Picard et fils, 1908.

––––––. *et al. Les Divisions régionales de la France; leçons faites à l'Ecole des Hautes Etudes Sociales*. Paris: Fèlix Alcan, 1913.

Bloch, Marc. "Les Aliments du Français." *Encyclopedic française*. Ed. Gaston Berger. Paris: Société nouvelle de l'Encyclopédie française, 1955, Vol. XIV, chap. V, no. 1, 14.42–7-14.42–10.

––––––. "Avènement et conquêtes du moulin à l'eau." *Annales d'histoire économique et sociale*, VII (1935), 538–63.

––––––. *L'Ile de France*. Paris: Cerf, 1913.

––––––. "La Lutte pour l'individualisme agraire dans la France du XVIIIᵉ siècle." *Annales d'histoire économique et sociale*, II (July–Oct. 1930), 329–81, 511–56.

––––––. "La Morale économique: le droit et la pratique: actions et réactions." *Annales d'histoire économique et sociale*, V (1933), 295–99.

––––––. "Le Ravitaillement d'une capitale d'empire à travers les siècles." *Annales d'histoire économique et sociale*, IV (1932), 408.

––––––. "La Segregation alimentaire dans la France ancienne." *Encyclopédic française*. Ed. Gaston Berger. Paris: Société nouvelle de l'Encyclopédie française, 1955. Vol. XIV, chap. IV, no. 3, 14.40–2-14.40–3.

Block, Maurice. *Administration de la ville de Paris et du département de la Seine*. Paris: Guillaumin, 1884.

Bloomfield, Arthur I. "The Foreign Trade Doctrine of the Physiocrats." *American Economic Review*, XXVIII (December 1938), 716–35.

Bluche, François. *Les Magistrats du Grand Conseil au XVIIIᵉ siècle, 1690–1791*. Paris: Les Belles Lettres, 1966.

––––––. *Les Magistrats du Parlement de Paris au XVIIIᵉ siècle (1715–1771)*. Paris: Les Belles Lettres, 1960.

––––––. "L'Origine des magistrats du Parlement de Paris au XVIIIᵉ siècle." *Mémoires de la Fédération des Sociétés historiques et archéologiques de Paris et de l'Ile-de-France*, V–VI (1956 for 1953–54).

Boas, George. *Vox Populi: Essays in the History of an Idea*. Baltimore: Johns Hopkins University Press, 1969.

Bois, Paul. *Paysans de l'Ouest. Des Structures économiques et sociales aux options politiques depuis l'époque révolutionnaire*. Paris: Mouton, 1960.

Boislisle, Arthur-Michel de. "Le Grand hiver et la disette de 1709." *Revue des questions historiques*, LXXIII (1903), 442–509; LXXIV (1903), 486–542.

––––––. "Nicolas Delamare et 'Le Traité de la police.'" *Bulletin de la Société de l'histoire de Paris et de l'Ile-de-France*, III (1876), 79–85.

Boissonnade, P. *Le Socialisme d'état: l'industrie et les classes industrielles en France pendant les deux premiers siècles de l'ère moderne (1453–1661)*. Paris: H. Champion, 1927.

Boland, A. *Traité pratique de boulangerie*. Paris: E. Lacroix, 1860.

Bondois, Paul. "Le Commissaire Nicolas Delamare et le 'Traité de la police.'" *Revue d'histoire moderne*, X (Sept.–Oct. 1935), 313–51.

_____. "Les Difficultés du ravitaillement parisien. Les projets de nouvelles halles de 1663 à 1718." *Revue d'histoire moderne*, XI (1936), 295–322.

_____. "Un Essai de culture exotique sous l'ancien régime: la 'Peste du riz' de Thiers (1741)." *Revue d'histoire économique et sociale*, XVI (1928), 586–655.

_____. "La Misère sous Louis XIV: la disette de 1662." *Revue d'histoire économique et sociale*, XII, no. 1 (1924), 53–118.

Bonnassieux, Pierre. "Note sur l'ancienne police de Paris." *Bulletin de la Société de l'histoire de Paris et de l'Ile-de-France*, XXI (1894), 182.

Bonnemère, Eugène. *Histoire des paysans*. 2 vols. Paris: Chamelot, 1856.

Bord, Gustave. *Histoire du blé en France. Le Pacte de famine, histoire, légende*. Paris: A Sauton, 1887.

Bordes, Maurice. "Les Intendants de Louis XV." *Revue historique*, CCXXIII (1960), 45–62.

_____. "Les Intendants éclaires de la fin de l'ancien régime." *Revue d'histoire économique et sociale*, XXXIX (1961), 57–83.

_____. *La Réforme municipale du contrôleur général Laverdy et son application (1764–1771)*. Toulouse: Association des Publications de la Faculté des lettres et sciences humaines, 1968.

_____. *D'Etigny et l'Administration de l'Intendance d'Auch, 1751–67*. 2 vols. Auch: F. Cocharaux, 1957.

_____. *L'Administration provinciale et municipale en France au dix-huitième siècle*. Paris: S.E.D.E.S., 1972.

_____. "Le Rôle des subdélégués en France au 18ᵉ siècle." *Provence Historique*, XXIII (July–Dec. 1973), 386–403.

_____. "Les Survivances du régime féodal et la réforme municipale du contrôleur général Laverdy." *L'Abolition de la féodalite dans le monde occidental*. Colloque, Toulouse, Nov. 1968. Ed. J. Godechot, *et al*. Vol. I. Paris: C.N.R.S., 1971.

Borie, Victor. *Le Pain*. Paris: Dentu, 1863.

Boscheron des Portes, C.-B.-F. *Histoire du Parlement de Bordeaux, 1451 à 1790*. 2 vols. Bordeaux: C. Lefebvre, 1877.

_____. "Les Registres secrets du Parlement de Bordeaux," *Revue historique de droit français et étranger*, XIII (1867), 142–68.

Bosher, J.F. *French Finances 1770–1795: From Business to Bureaucracy*. Cambridge: Cambridge University Press, 1970.

Bouchard, Marcel. *De l'Humanisme à l'Encyclopédie: l'esprit public en Bourgogne sous l'ancien régime*. Paris: Hachette, 1930.

Bouchary, Jean. *Les Manieurs d'argent à Paris à la fin du XVIIIᵉ siècle*. 3 vols. Paris: M. Rivière et Cⁱᵉ, 1939.

Bouchel. "Le Grand hiver de 1709 à Serval et dans le Soissonnais." *Bulletin de la Société archéologique, historique et scientifique de Soissons*, 3rd ser., XII (1907 [1903–1904]), 133–35.

Bourde, André J. *Agronomie et agronomes en France au XVIIIᵉ siècle*. 3 vols. Paris: S.E.V.P.E.N., 1967.

_____. *Deux registres (H. 1520–H. 1521) du contrôle général des finances aux Archives nationales, 1730–1736. Contribution à l'étude du ministère d'Orry*. Aix-en-Provence: Editions Ophrys, 1965.

_____. *The Influence of England on the French Agronomes, 1750–1789*. Cambridge: Cambridge University Press, 1953.

Bourderon, H. "La Lutte contre la vie chère dans la généralité du Languedoc au XVIIIᵉ siècle." *Annales du Midi*, (1954), 155–70.

Bourdon, J. "Psychosociologie de la famine." *Annales de démographie historique* (1968), 10–27.

Bourne, Henry E. "La Fixation des prix et le contrôle alimentaire sous la révolution." *Annales révolutionnaires*, XI (1919), 565.

Boutroux, Léon. *Le Pain et la panification; chimie et technologie de la boulangerie et de la meunerie*. Paris: J.-B. Baillière et fils, 1897.

Bouvet, M. "Le Testament de Parmentier." *Revue d'histoire de la pharmacie*, 49th year (Jan.–March 1961), 1–3.

Brandenburg, David J. "Agriculture in the *Encyclopédie*: An Essay in French Intellectual History." *Agricultural History*, XXIV (April 1950), 96–108.

Braudel, Fernand. *Civilisation matérielle et capitalisme (XVe-XVIIIe siècles)*. Paris: A. Colin, 1967.

———, and Labrousse, Ernest, eds. *Histoire économique et sociale de la France*. Vol. II: *Des derniers temps de l'âge seigneurial aux préludes de l'age industriel (1660–1789)*. Paris: Presses universitaires de France, 1970.

———, *et al.* "Vie matérielle et comportements biologiques. Bulletin no. 1." *Annales: économies, sociétés, civilisations*, 16th year (May–June 1961), 545–74.

Briaune, M. *Du Prix des grains, du libre échange et des réserves*. Paris: Firmin Didot, fils et Cie, 1857.

Brochin, Maurice. *Les Règlements sur les marchés des blés de Paris sous l'ancien régime*. Paris: n.p., 1917.

Broglie, Jacques de. *Histoire du Château de Chaumont (980–1943)*. Paris: Editions Balzac, 1944.

Brunetière, Ferdinand. *Etudes critiques sur l'histoire de la littérature française*. 2nd ser. 5th ed. Paris: Hachette, 1897.

Brunot, Ferdinand. *Histoire de la langue française des origines à 1900*. 13 vols. Paris: Armand Colin, 1905.

Brunschwig, Henry. *Les Subsistances à Strasbourg pendant les premières années de la révolution française*. Strasbourg: Imprimerie alsacienne, 1932.

Brust, P. A. "The Roman Mob." *Past and Present*, no. 35 (Dec. 1966), 3–27.

Brutails, J.-A. "Contre la vie chère à Bordeaux au XVIIIe siècle." *Revue historique de Bordeaux et du département de la Gironde*, XVIII (1925), 169–75.

———, "Tourny et Machault et une crise de subsistances." *Revue historique de Bordeaux*, VIII, no. 2 (1915), 68–71.

Buchez, Philippe-Joseph-Benjamin. *Histoire de l'assemblée constituante*. 2nd ed., rev. by P.-J.-B. Buchez, Jules Bastide, *et al.* 5 vols. Paris: Hetzel, 1845.

———, and Roux, P.-C. *Histoire parlementaire de la révolution française*. 40 vols. Paris: Paulin, 1834–38.

Buisson, Henry. *La Police: son histoire*. Paris: Nouvelles éditions Latie, 1958.

Burnett, John. *Plenty and Want. A Social History of Diet in England from 1815 to the Present Day*. London: Thomas Nelson and Sons Ltd., 1966.

Busnelli, Manlio D. *Diderot et l'Italie*. Paris: Librairie Ancienne Edouard Champion, 1925.

Bussière, G. "Bertin." *Bulletin de la Société historique et archéologique du Périgord*, XXXII (1905), 216–44, 381–418; XXXIII (1906), 72–113, 211–43, 311–31; XXXIV (1907), 53–83, 272–314, 373–88, 451–66; XXXV (1908), 274–313, 437–64; XXXVI (1909), 133–62, 210–81.

Cabasse, Prosper. *Essais historiques sur le parlement de Provence, 1501–1790*. 3 vols. Paris: Delaforest, 1826.

Cahen, Léon. "Une Affaire d'accaparement au début du XVIIIe siècle." *Bulletin de la Société d'histoire moderne* (Dec. 1910), 143–44.

———, "L'Approvisionnement en pain de Paris au XVIIIe siècle et la question de la boulangerie." *Revue d'histoire économique et sociale*, XIV (1926), 458–72.

———, "A propos du livre d'Afanassiev. L'Approvisionnement de Paris en grains au début du XVIIIe siècle." *Bulletin de la Société d'histoire moderne*, 22nd year (5 March 1922), 162–72.

———, "Ce qu'enseigne un péage du XVIIIe siècle: la Seine entre Rouen et Paris et les caractères de l'économie parisienne." *Annales d'histoire économique et sociale*, III (1931), 487–517.

———, "L'Idée de lutte de classes au XVIIIe siècle." *Revue de synthèse historique*, XII (1906), 44–56.

———, "Les Lieutenants de police et les municipalités dans le ressort du parlement de Paris au début du XVIIIe siècle." *Revue des études historiques*, I (1899), 19–34.

———, "Le Pacte de famine et les spéculations sur les blés." *Revue historique*, 51st year, CLII (May-June 1926), 32–43.

———, "La Population parisienne au milieu du XVIIIe siècle." *Revue de Paris*, 26th year (1 Sept. 1919), 146–70.

_____· "Le Prétendu pacte de famine. Quelques précisions nouvelles." *Revue historique*, 60th year, CLXXVI (Sept.-Oct. 1935), 173–216.

_____· "La Question du pain à Paris à la fin du XVIIIe siècle." *La Révolution française*, LXXX-VII (1934), 92–93.

_____· "La Répartition de la population à Paris au milieu du XVIIIe siècle." *Bulletin de la Société d'histoire moderne*, no. 6 (28 May 1911), 54–55.

_____, and Bondois, P. "Le Dossier Delamare." *Bulletin de la Société d'histoire moderne*, 31st year, 7th ser., no. 4 (April–May 1933), 26–29.

Cahn, Kenneth S. "The Roman and Frankish Roots of the Just Price of Medieval Canon Law." *Studies in Medieval and Renaissance History*, VI (1969), 1–52.

Caire, Guy. "Bertin, ministre physiocrate." *Revue d'histoire économique et sociale*, XXXVIII (1960), 257–84.

Callery, Alphonse. *Histoire des attributions du parlement, de la cour des aydes et de la chambre des comptes depuis la féodalité jusqu'à la révolution française*. Paris: E. Thorin, 1880.

Calvet, Henri. *L'Accaparement à Paris sous la terreur*. Paris: Imprimerie nationale, 1933.

Cannon, Walter B. *Bodily Changes in Pain, Hunger, Fear and Rage; an account of recent researches into the functions of emotional excitement*. New York and London: D. Appleton and Company, 1915.

Caraman, P. "La Disette des grains et les émeutes populaires en 1773 dans la généralité de Bordeaux." *Revue historique de Bordeaux*, III (1910), 297–319.

Caron, Pierre, and Raulet, L. *Le Comité des subsistances de Meulan et l'approvisionnement de Paris (1789–1791). Bulletin d'histoire économique de la Révolution française*. [Commission de recherche et de publication des documents relatifs à la vie économique de la Révolution française. Bulletin trimestriel.] Nos. 1–2 (1907–1908), 21–67.

Carré, Antonio. *Necker et la question des grains à la fin du XVIIIe siècle*. Paris: H. Jouve, 1903.

Carré, Henri. *La Chalotais et le duc d'Aiguillon ... [followed by the] Correspondance du Chevalier de Fontelle*. Paris: Librairies-imprimeries réunies, 1893.

_____· *La Fin des parlements (1788–1790)*. Paris: Hachette et Cie, 1912.

Carrière, Charles. *Négociants marseillais au 18e siècle*. Marseille-Aix: Institut historique de Provence, 1973.

_____· "Le Problème des grains et farines à Marseille pendant la période du maximum." *Conférences de l'Institut historique de Provence*, (1958).

Cépède, Michel, and Lengellé, Maurice. *Economie alimentaire du globe; essai d'interprétation*. Paris: Librairie de Médicis, [1953].

_____; Houtart, F.; Grond, L. *Population and Food*. New York: Sheed and Ward, 1964.

_____; Gounelle, Hugues. *La Faim*. Paris: Presses universitaires de France, 1967.

Chabert, Alexandre de. "Rousseau économiste." *Revue d'histoire économique et sociale*, XLII (1964), 345–56.

Chagniot, J. "Le Problème du maintien de l'ordre à Paris au 18e siècle." *Bulletin de la Société d'Histoire Moderne*, 73 (1974), 32–45.

Challamel, Augustin. *Mémoires du peuple français depuis son origine jusqu'à nos jours*. 8 vols. Paris: Hachette et Cie, 1866–1873.

Chambers, J.D. *Population, Economy and Society in Pre-Industrial England*. Ed. W.A. Armstrong. Oxford: Oxford University Press, 1972.

Chapuisat, Edouard. *Necker*. Paris: Sirey, 1938.

Charbonnaud, Roger. *Les Idées économiques de Voltaire*. Angoulême: n.p., 1907.

Charlot, E., and Dupâquier, J. "Mouvement annuel de la population de la ville de Paris de 1670 à 1821." *Annales de démographie historique* (1967), 511–19.

Chassaigne, Marc. *La Lieutenance générale de police de Paris*. Paris: A. Rousseau, 1906.

_____· "Essai sur l'ancienne police de Paris. L'Approvisionnement." *Revue des études historiques*, LXXII (1906), 225–56, 377–99.

Chaunu, Pierre. *La Civilisation de l'Europe des lumières*. Paris: Arthaud, 1971.

————· *Histoire, science sociale*. Paris: S.E.D.E.S., 1974.

Cherrière. *La Lutte contre l'incendie dans les halles, les marchés et les foires de Paris sous l'ancien régime*. Mémoires et documents pour servir à l'histoire du commerce et de l'industrie en France. Ed. J. Hayem. 3rd ser. Paris: Hachette et Cⁱᵉ, 1913.

Chevalier, Pierre. "Diderot et le lieutenant de police LeNoir." *Bulletin mensuel de la Société académique d'agriculture, des sciences, arts et belles-lettres du département de l'Aube*, 34th year, no. 9 (1963), 94–100.

Christ, Yvan. "Le Président de Brosses à Paris [et lettres à son frère, le comte de Tournay]." *La Revue de Paris*, 72nd year, no. 8 (1965), 38–55.

Clément, Pierre. *Histoire du système protecteur en France depuis le ministère de Colbert jusqu'à la révolution de 1848*. Paris: Guillaumin, 1854.

————· *La Police sous Louis XIV.* Paris: Didier, 1866.

————· *Portraits historiques: Suger, Sully, le président de Novion, le Cte de Grignan, le garde des sceaux d'Argenson, Jean Law, Machault d'Arnouville, les frères Pâris, l'abbé Terray, le duc de Gaëte, le comte Mollien*. Paris: Didier, 1855.

————; and Lemoine, Alfred. *M. de Silhouette; Bouret; les derniers fermiers généraux, études sur les financiers du XVIIIᵉ siècle*. Paris: Didier, 1872.

Cobb, Richard C. *Les Armées révolutionnaires; instrument de la terreur dans les départements, avril 1793 (floréal an II)*. 2 vols. Paris: Mouton, 1961–1963.

————· "Les Disettes de l'an II et de l'an III dans le district de Mantes et la vallée de la Basse Seine." *Mémoires de la Fédération des Sociétés historiques et archéologiques de Paris et de l'Ile-de-France*, III (1951), 227–51.

————· *The Police and the People: French Popular Protest, 1789–1820*. Oxford: Clarendon Press, 1970.

————· "The Police, the Repressive Authorities and the Beginning of the Revolutionary Crisis in Paris." *Welsh History Review*, IV (Dec. 1967), 427–40.

————· "Quelques aspects de la crise de l'an III en France." *Bulletin de la Société d'histoire moderne*, 65th year, 13th ser. (Jan.–March 1966), 2–5.

————· "Le Ravitaillement des villes sous la terreur; la question des arrivages (septembre 1793, germinal an II)." *Bulletin de la Société d'histoire moderne*, 53rd year, 2nd ser. (April–June 1954), 8–12.

————· *Terreur et subsistances 1793–1795. Etudes d'histoire révolutionnaire*. Paris: Clavreuil, 1965.

Cobban, Alfred. *The Social Interpretation of the French Revolution*. Cambridge: Cambridge University Press, 1964.

Cochut, André. "Le Pain à Paris (I: La Meunerie et la boulangerie sous l'ancien régime; II: La Réglementation moderne et la liberté)." *Revue des deux mondes*, 33rd year, 2nd period, XLVI (15 Aug. 1863), 964–95; XLVII (15 Sept. 1863), 400–35.

Cole, Arthur Harrison, and Walts, George B. *The Handicrafts of France as recorded in the Descriptions des arts et métiers, 1761–1788*. Boston: Baker Library, Harvard Graduate School of Business Administration, 1952.

Coleman, Earle F. "*Ephémérides du citoyen*, 1767–1772." *The Papers of the Bibliographical Society of America*, LVI (1962), 17–45.

Colfavru, J.-C. "La Question des subsistances en 1789." *La Révolution française*, V (July–Dec. 1883), 127–36, 219–29, 321–31, 385–93.

Conan, Jules. "Les Débuts de l'école physiocratique. Un faux départ: l'échec de la réforme fiscale." *Revue d'histoire économique et sociale*, XXXVI (1958), 45–63.

Conte, Robert. *L'Administration de la généralité de Paris à la fin du règne de Louis XIV, 1681–1715*. Lille: L. Danel, 1926.

Coornaert, Emile. *Les Corporations en France avant 1789*. Paris: Gallimard, 1941.

Coquelin, Charles, and Guillaumin, eds. *Dictionnaire de l'économie politique*. 2 vols. Paris: Librairie de Guillaumin et Cⁱᵉ, 1873.

Coyecque, Ernest. *L'Hôtel-Dieu de Paris au moyen âge, histoire et documents.* 2 vols. Paris: H. Champion, 1889–1891.

Crawford, William, and Broadley, H. *The People's Food.* London and Toronto: W. Heinemann Ltd., [1938].

Crousaz-Crétet, Paul de. "La Question du pain à Paris en 1709." *La Revue hebdomadaire,* XI (Nov. 1917), 451–79.

Cruickshanks, Evelyn G. "Public Opinion in Paris in the 1740's: The Reports of the Chevalier de Mouchy." *Bulletin of the Institute of Historical Research* (London University), XXVII (1954), 54–68.

Cuisine, E.F. de la. *Le Parlement de Bourgogne.* 3 vols. Dijon: Rabutot, 1880.

Curmond, Henri, *Le Commerce des grains et l'école physiocratique.* Paris: A. Rousseau, 1900.

Curtis-Bennett, N. *The Food of the People; Being the History of Industrial Feeding.* London: Faber and Faber, 1949.

Daire, Eugène. "La Doctrine des Physiocrates." *Journal des économistes,* XVII (1847), 349–75; XVIII (1847), 113–40.

D'Arbois de Jubainville. *L'Administration des intendants.* Paris: H. Champion, 1880.

Dardel, Pierre. *Commerce, industrie et navigation à Rouen et au Havre au XVIIIᵉ siècle, rivalité croissante entre ces deux ports, la conjoncture.* Rouen: Société libre d'émulation de la Seine-Maritime, 1966.

_____. *Navires et marchandises dans les ports de Rouen et du Havre au XVIIIᵉ siècle.* Paris: S.E.V.P.E.N., 1963.

_____. *Le Trafic maritime de Rouen aux XVIIᵉ et XVIIIᵉ siècles; essai statistique.* Rouen: Imprimerie Laine, 1946.

Daudet, Alphonse. *Lettres de mon moulin.* Paris: Bibliothèque Charpentier, 1907.

Daumard, Adeline, and Furet, François. *Structures et relations sociales à Paris au milieu du XVIIIᵉ siècle.* Cahiers des *Annales,* no. 18. Paris: Armand Colin, 1961.

Davies, C.S.L. "Les Révoltes populaires en Angleterre (1500–1700)." *Annales: économies, sociétés, civilisations,* 24th year (Jan.–Feb. 1969), 24–60.

Debien, Gabriel. *En Haut-Poitou: Défricheurs au travail.* Cahier des *Annales,* no. 7. Paris: A. Colin, 1952.

Defresne, A., and Evrard, F. *Les Subsistances dans le district de Versailles de 1788 à l'an V. Collection des documents inédits sur l'histoire économique de la révolution française.* Vol. I. Rennes: Imprimerie. Oberthur, 1921.

Delaunay, J.B. "La Question des céréales en France." *Journal des économistes,* XXV (Dec. 1849–March 1850), 274–79, 368–79.

Delorme, Suzanne. "Une Famille de grands commis de l'état, amis des sciences, au XVIIIᵉ siècle: Les Trudaine." *Revue d'histoire des sciences,* III (April–June 1950), 101–09.

Dempsey, B.W. "Just Price in a Functional Economy." *The American Economic Review,* XXV (Sept. 1935), 471–86.

Denière, G. *La Juridiction consulaire de Paris 1563–1792.* Paris: Henri Plon, 1872.

Derathé, Robert. "Les Philosophes et le despotisme." *Utopie et institutions au XVIIIᵉ siècle: le pragmatisme des lumières.* Ed. Pierre Francastel. Paris: Mouton, 1963.

Des Cilleuls, Alfred. *L'Approvisionnement de Paris en céréales dans le passé et dans le présent.* Nancy; and Paris: Imprimerie et Librairie Berger-Levrault, 1910.

_____. "Enquêtes sur les céréales au XVIIIᵉ siècle." *Revue générate d'administration,* III (1897), 129–47.

_____. *Le Prix de la vie en France du XVIᵉ siècle à 1789.* Paris: Berger-Levrault, 1887.

_____. "Rapport sur l'étude de M. Camille Bloch, *Création par Malisset d'un Moulin économique à Châtillon-sur-Loing en 1776.*" *Bulletin du comité des travaux historiques et scientifiques. Section des sciences économiques et sociales,* (1899), 8–11.

_____. *Le Socialisme municipal à travers les siècles.* Paris: A. Picard et fils, 1905.

Deslandres, Paul. "Sébastien Mercier (1740–1814)." *Bulletin de la Société de l'histoire de Paris et de l'Ile-de-France,* 58th year (1931), 129–41.

Desmarest, Charles. *Le Commerce des grains dans la généralité de Rouen à la fin de l'ancien régime.* Paris: Jouve et Cⁱᵉ, 1926.

Desmaze, Charles. *Le Châtelet de Paris, son organisation.* 2nd ed. Paris: Didier, 1870.

Desaive, J.-P., *et al. Médecins, climat et épidémies à la fin du 18ᵉ siècle.* Paris: Mouton, 1972.

Desnoireterres, Gustave. *Tableau de Paris; étude sur la vie et les ouvrages de Mercier.* Paris: Pagnerre, 1853.

Desnoyers. "Saint Firmin, Patron des Boulangers d'Orléans." *Mémoires de la Société archéologique et historique de l'Orléanais,* XXVII (1898), 155–168.

Dessables, A.-M. *Manuel du boulanger et du meunier.* Paris: Roret, 1825.

Deyon, Pierre. *Amiens, capitale provinciale—étude sur la société urbaine au XVIᵉ siècle.* Paris; and the Hague: Mouton, 1967.

Dionnet, Georges. *Le Néo-mercantilisme au XVIIIᵉ siècle et au début du XIXᵉ siècle.* Paris: V. Giard et E. Brière, 1901.

Dockes, Pierre. *L'Espace dans la pensée économique du XVIᵉ au XVIIIᵉ siècles.* Paris: Flammarion, 1969.

Dolléans, Edouard. *De l'accaparement.* Paris: L. Larose, 1902.

Dommanget, Maurice. "La Carte de pain à Beauvais en l'an II." *Annales révolutionnaires,* IX (1917), 248–51.

Doyle, William O. "The Parlements of France and the Breakdown of the Old Regime." *French Historical Studies,* VI (1970), 415–58.

Dubédat, Jean-Baptiste. *Histoire du parlement de Toulouse.* 2 vols. Paris: A. Rousseau, 1885.

Dubois, Auguste. "Quesnay anti-mercantiliste et libre-échangiste." *Revue d'économie politique,* XVIII (1904), 213–29.

Dubois, Jean. *Le Vocabulaire politique et social en France de 1869 à 1872.* Paris: Librairie Larousse, 1962.

Du Camp, Maxime. *Paris, ses organes, ses fonctions et sa vie dans la seconde moitié du XIXᵉ siècle.* 6 vols. Paris: Hachette, 1869–1875.

Dufey, Pierre-Joseph-Spiridon, and Béraud, Antony. *Dictionnaire historique de Paris ....* 2nd ed. 2 vols. Paris: J.-N. Barba, 1828.

Duffor, J. "La Question du pain en Gascogne au XVIIIᵉ siècle." *Revue de Gascogne* [Bulletin de la Société historique de Gascogne], XVI (1921), 145–62, 207–18.

Dufour, E. *Traité pratique de panification française et parisienne.* Château-Thierry: Imprimerie moderne, 1937.

Dujarric de la Rivière, René. *Lavoisier économiste.* Paris: Masson et Cⁱᵉ and Librairie Plon, 1949.

Dumas, Alexandre, père. *Louis XV et sa cour.* 2 vols. Paris: Michel Levy, 1866.

————· *Mémoires d'un médecin, Joseph Balsamo.* 5 vols. Paris: C. Levy, 1878–1883.

Dumas, Auguste. "L'Action des secrétaires d'état sous l'ancien régime." *Annales de la Faculté de Droit d'Aix-en-Provence,* n.s., no. 47 (1954), 5–92.

Dumas, François. *La Généralité de Tours au XVIIIᵉ siècle; administration de l'intendant Du Cluzel (1766–1783).* Paris: Hachette, 1894.

Dumay, Gabriel, ed. *Une Emeute à Dijon en 1775.* Dijon: Darantière, 1886.

Dupâquier, Jacques. "Croissance démographique régionale dans le Bassin parisien au XVIIIᵉ siècle." *Hommage à Marcel Reinhard, Sur la population française au XVIIIᵉ et XIXᵉ siècles.* Paris: Société d'histoire démographique, 1973.

————· "Le Peuplement de l'élection de Paris à la fin du XVIIᵉ et au début du XVIIIᵉ siècle." *Bulletin de la Société de l'histoire de Paris et de l'Ile-de-France,* XCIV–XCV (1967–1968), 141–56.

————· "Sur la population française au XVIIᵉ et au XVIIIᵉ siècles." *Revue historique,* CCXXIX (Jan.–March 1968), 43–79.

————; Lachiver, M.; and Meuvret, J. *Mercuriales du pays de France et du Vexin français, 1640–1792.* Paris: S.E.V.P.E.N., 1968.

Dupieux, Paul. "Les Attributions de la juridiction consulaire de Paris (1563–1792)." *Bibliothèque de l'Ecole des Chartes,* XCV (1934), 116–46.

Egret, Jean. *Le Parlement de Dauphiné et les affaires publiques dans la deuxième moitié du XVIII* siècle*. 2 vols. Grenoble: Imprimerie Allier père et fils, 1942.

———. *Louis XV et l'opposition parlementaire*. Paris: A. Colin, 1970.

Einaudi, Luigi. "Einaudi on Galiani." [Extracted from *Schweizerische Zeitschrift für Volkswirtschaft und Statistik*, LXXXI, no. 1 (1945)]. *The Development of Economic Thought: Great Economists in Perspective*. Ed. H.W. Spiegel. New York: J. Wiley and Sons, 1952.

Eisenstadt, Samuel Noah. *Modernization: Protest and Change*. Ed. W.E. Moore and N.J. Smelser. Englewood Cliffs, N.J.: Prentice Hall, 1966.

El Kordi, Mohamed. *Bayeux aux XVII* et XVIII* siècles*. Paris: Mouton, 1970.

Englinger, Albert. *L'Origine de la police administrative, les villes à police d'Etat*. Paris: Librairie du Recueil Sirey, 1939.

Esmein, Adhémar. *Cours élémentaire d'histoire du droit français, à l'usage des étudiants de première année*. 3rd ed. Paris: Librairie de la Société du recueil général des lois et des arrêts, 1898.

———. "La Science politique des physiocrates." *Congrès des Sociétés savantes, 1904. Bulletin du Comité des travaux historiques et scientifiques. Section des sciences économiques et sociales.*

Espinas, Georges. "La Vie d'un moulin." *Annales d'histoire économique et sociale*, X (1938), 357–58.

Estignard, A. *Le Parlement de Franche-Comté*. 2 vols. Paris: A. Ricard, 1892.

Euvrard, F. *Historique de l'institution des commissaires de police, son origine, leurs prérogatives*. Montpellier: Imprimerie de Firmin, Montane et Sicardi, 1911.

Everitt, Alan. "The Food Market of the English Town, 1660–1760." *Third International Conference of Economic History*, Munich, 1965. Paris: Mouton, 1968.

Evrard, Femand. "Une Enquête du parlement de Paris sur la récolte de 1788." *La Révolution française*, LXXII (1919), no. 1, 38–53; no. 2, 135–70; no. 3, 221–30.

———. *Les Subsistances en céréales dans le département de l'Eure de 1788 à l'an V*. Paris: E. Leroux, 1910.

———. *Versailles, ville du Roi (1770–1789). Etude d'économie urbaine*. Paris: E. Leroux, 1935.

Facque, Robert. *Les Halles et marchés alimentaires de Paris*. Paris: Librairie du Recueil Sirey, 1911.

Faucher, D. "La Révolution agricole du XVIIIᶜ–XIXᵉ siècle." *Bulletin de la Société d'histoire moderne*. 11th ser., 55th year (Nov. 1956), 2–11.

Faure, Edgar. "Les Bases expérimentales et doctrinales de la politique économique de Turgot." *Revue historique de droit français et étranger*, 4th ser., 39th year (April–June 1961), 255–95; (July–Sept. 1961), 382–447.

———. *La Disgrâce de Turgot*. Paris: Gallimard, 1961.

Faure-Solet, J. F. *Economie politique et progrès au siècle des lumières*. Paris: Gauthier-Villars, 1964.

Faÿ, Bernard. *Louis XVI, or the End of a World*. Trans. Patrick O'Brian. London: W.H. Allen, 1968.

Febvre, Lucien. "Une Monographie (Jules Ricommard, 'La Lieutenance générale de police à Troyes au XVIIIᵉ siècle')." *Annales d'histoire économique et sociale*, VII (1935), 517.

———, and Berger, G., eds. *Encyclopédie française*. 21 vols. Paris: Société de Gestion de l'Encyclopédie Française, 1935–66.

Feillet, Alphonse. *La Misère au temps de la Fronde et saint Vincent de Paul, ou Un Chapitre de l'histoire du paupérisme en France*. Paris: Didier, 1862.

Festy, Octave. "Un Projet d'association coopérative pour l'approvisionnement de Paris en l'an II." *Annales historiques de la révolution française*, XXII (1950), 163–66.

Filion, Maurice. *Maurepas. Ministre de Louis XV.* Montreal: Editions Leméac, [1967],

Flammermont, Jules. *Le Chancelier Maupeou et les parlements*. 2nd ed. Paris: A. Picard, 1885.

Fleurent, Emile. *Le Pain de froment. Etude critique et recherches sur la valeur alimentaire selon le blutage et les systèmes de mouture*. Paris: Gauthier-Villars, 1911.

Floquet, Amable-Pierre. *Histoire du parlement de Normandie*. 7 vols. Rouen: E. Frère, 1840–1842.

Foiret, F. "Deux marchés de 1644 pour la fourniture du pain de Gonesse." *Bulletin de la Société historique du VIᵉ arrondissement de Paris*, XXIV (1923), 85–87.

Foisset, Joseph-Théophile. *Le Président de Brosses, histoire des lettres et des Parlements au XVIIIe siècle.* Paris: Olivier-Fulgence, 1842.

Foncin, Pierre. *Essai sur le Ministère de Turgot.* Paris: Germer-Baillière et Cie, 1877.

Food and Agriculture Organization of the United Nations. Committee on Calorie Requirements. *Besoins en calories; rapport du deuxième comité des besoins en calories.* Rome: Organisation des Nations Unies pour l'alimentation et l'agriculture, 1957. (Etudes de nutrition de la FAO, no. 15.)

Ford, Franklin. *Robe and Sword; the Regrouping of the French Aristocracy after Louis XIV.* Cambridge, Mass.: Harvard University Press, 1953.

Forster, Robert. *The Nobility of Toulouse in the 18th Century: A Social and Economic Study.* Baltimore: Johns Hopkins University Press, 1960.

————. "Obstacles to Agricultural Growth in 18th Century France." *American Historical Review,* LXXV (Oct. 1970), 1600–15.

Fosseyeux, Marcel. *Une Administration parisienne sous l'ancien régime: l'Hôtel-Dieu aux XVIIe et XVIIIe siècles.* Paris: Berger-Levrault, 1912.

Foster, C.A. "Honoring Commerce and Industry in 18th Century France: A Case Study of Change in Traditional Social Function." Unpublished doctoral dissertation, Harvard, 1950.

Fournière, G. de la. "Les Comités d'Agriculture de 1760 et de 1784." *Bulletin du comité des travaux historiques et scientifiques. Section des sciences économiques.* Paris, 1909, 94–121.

Fourastié, Jean. *Machinisme et bien-être.* 3rd ed. Paris: Editions de Minuit, 1962.

————, and Grandamy, René. "Remarques sur les prix salariaux des céréales et la productivité du travail agricole en Europe du XVe au XXe siècle." *Third International Conference of Economic History,* Munich, 1965. Paris: Mouton, 1968. pp. 647–56.

Francastel, Pierre, ed. *Utopie et institutions au 18e siècle; le pragmatisme des lumières.* Paris: Mouton, 1963.

France. Conseil d'Etat. *Enquête sur la boulangerie du département de la Seine.* Paris: Imprimerie impériale, 1860.

France. Institut national d'études démographiques. *François Quesnay et la physiocratie.* 2 vols. Paris, 1958.

France. Ministère de l'Intérieur. *Encyclopédie nationale de la police.* Paris: distribuée par la compagnie nationale de diffusion du livre, 1955.

Franklin, Alfred. *Les Corporations ouvrières de Paris du XIIe au XVIIIe siècle.* Paris: Firmin-Didot, 1885.

————. *Dictionnaire historique des arts, métiers et professions exercés dans Paris depuis le XIIIe siècle.* Paris: H. Welter, 1906.

————. *La Vie privée d'autrefois.* Vol. VII: *L'Hygiène.* Paris: E. Plon, Nourrit et Cie, 1890.

————. *La Vie privée d'autrefois.* Vol. XXVI: *La Vie de Paris sous Louis XV.* Paris: E. Plon, Nourrit et Cie, 1901.

————. *La Vie privée d'autrefois.* Vol. XXVII: *La Vie de Paris sous Louis XVI.* Paris: E. Plon, Nourrit et Cie, 1902.

————. *La Vie privée d'autrefois.* Vol. XXI: *La Vie de Paris sous la Régence.* Paris: E. Plon, Nourrit et Cie, 1897.

Frêche, Georges. "Etudes statistiques sur le commerce céréalier de la France méridionale au XVIIIe siècle." *Revue d'histoire économique et sociale,* 49th year, (1971), no. 1, 5–43; no. 2, 180–224.

————. *Histoire des prix des céréales à Toulouse (1650–1715).* Paris: Presses universitaires de France, 1964.

————. "La Conjoncture des prix céréales dans le Midi de la France du 16e–18e siècle." *Revue historique du droit français et étranger,* 49th year, 4th ser. (1971), 224–77.

Frégier, H. A. *Histoire de l'administration de la police de Paris, depuis Philippe-Auguste jusqu'aux Etats-généraux de 1789, ou Tableau moral et politique de la ville de Paris durant cette période, considérée dans ses rapports avec l'action de la police.* 2 vols. Paris: Guillaumin, 1850.

Fréville, H. *L'Intendance de Bretagne*. 3 vols. Rennes: Plihon, 1953.

Fridrichowicz, Eugen. *Die Getreidehandelspolitik des ancien régime*. Weimar: E. Felber, 1897.

Furet, François. "Pour une définition des classes inférieures à l'époque moderne." *Annales: économies, sociétés, civilisations*, 18th year (May–June 1963), 459–74.

Galante Garrone, Alessandro. *Gilbert Romme: Histoire d'un révolutionnaire*. Paris: Flammarion, 1971.

Ganzin, Michel. "Le Parlement de Provence, la physiocratie, et la police des grains (1760–1770)." *Annales de la Faculté de Droit et des Sciences Economiques de l'Université d'Aix-Marseille*, LVIII, 1–57.

Garden, Maurice. *Lyon et les Lyonnais du XVIIIᵉ siècle*. Paris: Société d'Edition "les Belles-Lettres," 1970.

Gaudemet, Eugène. *L'Abbé Galiani et la question du commerce des blés à la fin du règne de Louis XV.* Paris: A. Rousseau, 1899.

Gautier, Etienne, and Henry, Louis. *La Population de Crulai, paroisse normande*. Paris: Presses universitaires de France, Institut national d'études démographiques, 1958.

Gay, Jean-Lucien. "L'Administration de la capitale entre 1770 et 1789, la tutelle de la royauté et ses limites." *Mémoires de la Fédération des Sociétés historiques et archéologiques de Paris et de l'Ile-de-France*, VIII (1956), 299–370; IX (1957–1958), 283–363; X (1959), 181–247; XI (1960), 363–403; XII (1961), 135–218.

————. "Observations sur le recrutement et la composition du bureau de la ville de Paris de 1770 à 1789." *Revue historique de droit français et étranger*, 4th ser., 36th year, no. 2 (1958), 313–14.

Gay, Peter. *The Enlightenment, an Interpretation*. 2 vols. New York: Alfred A. Knopf, 1966–1969.

Gazier, A. "La Guerre des farines (mai 1775)." *Mémoires de la Société de l'histoire de Paris et de L'Ile-de-France*, VI (1879), 1–23.

Generas, M.-C. *Les Marginaux dans les environs de Paris, 1768–72*. Unpublished mémoire de maîtrise, Université de Paris I, 1971–72 (directed by P. Goubert).

Geoffroy, R. *Le Blé, la farine, le pain*. Paris: Dunod, 1939.

George, Pierre. *La Ville; le fait urbain à travers le monde*. Paris: Presses universitaires de France, 1952.

Gérard, Constantin. *Histoire du Châtelet et du Parlement de Paris, leur fondation, leurs juridictions*. Paris: Librairie historique, [1844].

Gide, Charles, and Rist, Charles. *A History of Economic Doctrines*. Trans. R. Richards, from the 2nd rev. ed. of 1913. London: G.G. Harrap, 1915.

Gignoux, C.-J. "L'Abbé Galiani et la querelle des grains au XVIIIᵉ siècle." *Revue d'histoire économique et sociale*, X (1922), 17–37.

Gille, B. *Les Sources statistiques de l'histoire de France des enquêtes du XVIIᵉ siècle à 1870*. Geneva: Droz, 1964.

Ginsberg, Robert. "The Argument of Voltaire's 'L'homme aux quarante écus': a Study in Philosophic Rhetoric." *Studies on Voltaire and the Eighteenth Century*, LVI (Geneva, 1967), 611–57.

Girard, René. *L'Abbé Terray et la liberté du commerce des grains 1769–1774*. Paris: Presses universitaires de France, 1924.

Girod, P.-E. "Les Subsistances en Bourgogne et particulièrement à Dijon à la fin du XVIIIᵉ siècle, 1774–1789." *Revue bourguignonne de l'enseignement supérieur*, XVI, no. 4 (1906), i–xxiii, 1–145.

Glasson, Ernest-D. *Le Parlement de Paris, son rôle politique depuis le règne de Charles VII jusqu'à la révolution*. 2 vols. Paris: Hachette, 1901.

Godechot, Jacques, and Moncassin, S. "Démographie et subsistances en Languedoc du XVIIIᵉ siècle au début du XIXᵉ siècle." *Bulletin de l'histoire économique et sociale de la Révolution française* (1964), 23–63.

Gohin, Ferdinand. *Les Transformations de la langue française pendant la deuxième moitié du XVIIIᵉ siècle (1740–1789)*. Paris: Belin frères, 1903.

Gomel, Charles. *Les Causes financières de la révolution française*. Vol. I: *Les Ministères de Turgot et de Necker*. Paris: Librairie Guillaumin et.Cⁱᵉ, 1892.

Gomont, H. "La Guerre des farines." *Journal des économistes*, X (Feb. 1845), 279–89.

Gonnard, René. *Histoire des doctrines économiques*. 3 vols. Paris: Nouvelle librairie nationale, 1921–1922.

———. *Histoire des doctrines monétaires dans ses rapports avec l'histoire des monnaies*. Paris: Recueil Sirey, 1936.

Gosset, P. *La Boulangerie régénérée. Le Pain à un prix toujours invariable!!* Paris: A. Goin, 1854.

Goubert, Jean-Pierre. "Le Phénomène épidémique en Bretagne à la fin du XVIIIᵉ siècle (1770–1787)." *Annales: économies, sociétés, civilisations*, 24th year (Nov.–Dec. 1969), 1562–88.

Goubert, Pierre. *Beauvais et le Beauvaisis de 1600 à 1730, Contribution à l'histoire sociale de la France du XVIIᵉ siècle*. 2 vols. Paris: S.E.V.P.E.N., 1960.

———. "Historical Demography and the Reinterpretation of Early Modern French History." *Journal of Interdisciplinary History*, I (Autumn 1970), 37–48.

———. "Un quart de siècle de démographie historique: bilan et réflexions." *Hommage à Marcel Reinhard*. Paris: Société de démographie historique, 1973.

———. "Recent Theories and Research in French Population Between 1500 and 1700." *Population in History*. Ed. D. V. Glass and D.E.C. Eversley. London: Edward Arnold, 1965.

Goulier, Lucien. *Le Commerce du blé, et spécialement de son organisation en France*. Poitiers: Imprimerie de M. Bousrez, 1909.

Gout, Simone. *Henri de Goyon de la Plombanie, économiste périgourdin. Ses idées, sa place dans l'histoire des doctrines économiques*. Poitiers: Imprimerie moderne, 1933.

Goy, Joseph, and Le Roy Ladurie, Emmanuel, eds. *Les Fluctuations du produit de la dîme: conjoncture décimale et domaniale de la fin du moyen âge au XVIIIᵉ siècle*. (Association française des historiens économistes. 1ᵉʳ Congrès national. Paris, Jan. 11–12, 1969.) Paris: Mouton, 1972.

Grange, H. "Turgot et Necker devant le problème du salaire." *Annales historiques de la révolution française*, XXIX (1957), 19–33.

———. *Les Idées de Necker*. Paris: L. Klincksieck, 1974.

Greer, Sarah. *A Bibliography of Police Administration and Police Science*. New York: Columbia University Institute of Public Administration, 1936.

Griffuel, Albert. *La Taxe du pain*. Paris: L. Larose, 1903.

Grosclaude, Pierre. *Malesherbes et son temps*. Paris: Fischbacher, 1964.

Gruder, V. R. *The Royal Provincial Intendants: A Governing Elite in 18th Century France*. Ithaca: Cornell University Press, 1968.

Guérin, Louis. *L'Intendant de Cypierre et la vie économique de l'Orléanais 1760–1785*. Mayenne: Floch, 1938.

Guérrin, André. *Humanité et subsistances*. Paris: Dunod, 1957.

Guérrini, Maurice. *Napoléon et Paris: trente ans d'histoire*. Paris: P. Tequi, 1967.

Guillaumat-Vallet, Maurice. *Le Contrôleur-général Silhouette et ses réformes en matière financière*. Paris: Librairie générale de droit et de jurisprudence, 1914.

Gutton, Jean-Pierre. "Les Mendiants dans la société parisienne au début du XVIIIᵉ siècle." *Cahiers d'histoire*, XIII, no. 2 (1968), 131–41.

———. *La Société et les pauvres. L'Exemple de la généralité de Lyon 1534–1789*. Paris: Société d'édition "les Belles Lettres," 1971.

Harouel, Jean-L. *Les Ateliers de charité dans la province de Haute-Guyenne*. Paris: Presses universitaires de France, 1969.

Harsin, Paul. *Les Doctrines monétaires et financières en France du XVIᵉ au XVIIIᵉ siècle*. Paris: Alcan, 1928.

———. "La Théorie fiscale des physiocrates." *Revue d'histoire économique et sociale*, XXXI (1958), 7–17.

Hecht, Jacqueline. "Trois précurseurs de la sécurité sociale au 18ᵉ siècle," *Population*, XIV (Jan.–March 1959), 73–88.

Heckscher, Eli Filip. *Mercantilism*. Trans. M. Shapiro. 2 vols. London: George Allen and Unwin, Ltd., 1935.

Hemardinquer, Jean-Jacques. "En France aujourd'hui: données quantitatives sur les consommations alimentaires." *Annales: économies, sociétés, civilisations, 16th year* (May–June 1961), 553–64.

_____, ed. *Pour une histoire de l'alimentation.* Cahiers des *Annales,* no. 28. Paris: A. Colin, 1970.

Henry, Louis. "Historical Demography." *Daedalus,* XCVII (Spring 1968), 385–96.

_____. "The Population of France in the Eighteenth Century." *Population in History.* Ed. D.V. Glass and D.E.C. Eversley. London: E. Arnold, 1965.

_____, and Courgeou, Daniel. "Le Volume de l'immigration à Paris de 1740 à 1792." *Population,* XXVI (1971), 1073–92.

_____, and Lévy, Claude. "Quelques données sur la région autour de Paris au XVIIIᵉ siècle." *Population,* XVII (April–June, 1962), 297–326.

Herlaut. "La Disette de pain à Paris en 1709." *Mémoires de la Société de l'histoire de Paris et de l'Ile-de-France,* XLV (1918), 5–100.

Higgs, Henry. *The Physiocrats, Six Lectures on the French "Economistes" of the 18th Century.* London, and New York: Macmillan and Co., Ltd., 1897.

Hillairet, Jacques. *Connaissance du vieux Paris.* 3 vols. Paris: Gonthieu, 1963.

_____. *Dictionnaire historique des rues de Paris.* 2 vols. Paris: Editions de Minuit, 1960.

Hirschman, Albert O. *The Strategy of Economic Development.* New Haven, Conn.: Yale University Press, 1958.

Holt, Robert T., and Turner, J.E. *The Political Basis of Economic Development: An Exploration in Comparative Political Analysis.* Princeton, N.J.: Van Nostrand, 1966.

Horcher, T., et al. *Bread: The Chemistry and Nutrition of Flour and Bread.* London: Constable, 1954.

Horn, J.E. *L'Economie politique avant les physiocrates.* Paris: Guillaumin et Cⁱᵉ, 1867.

Hoselitz, B.F. "Agriculture in Industrial Development." *Foods, One Tool in International Economic Development.* Ames, Iowa: Iowa State University Press, 1963.

Hoskins, W.G. "Harvest Fluctuations and English Economic History, 1620–1759." *Agricultural History Review,* XVI (1968), 15–31.

Hours, Henri. "Emeutes et émotions populaires dans les campagnes du Lyonnais au 18ᵉ siècle." *Cahiers d'histoire,* IX (1964), 137–53.

Hudson, David. "The Parlementary Crisis of 1763 in France and its Consequences." *Canadian Journal of History,* VII (Sept. 1972), 97–117.

Huntington, S.P. *Political Order and Changing Societies.* New Haven: Yale University Press, 1968.

Husson, Armand. *Les Consommations de Paris.* 2nd ed. Paris: Librairie Hachette, 1875.

Husson, G. [Camilleu fils]. *Histoire du pain à toutes les époques et chez tous les peuples.* Tours: A. Cattier, 1887.

Institut National d'Etudes Démographiques. *Economie et Population: Les Doctrines françaises avant 1800. Bibliographic générate commentée.* Cahier No. 28, Travaux et documents. Paris: Presses universitaires de France, 1956.

Jacob, H.-E. *Histoire du pain depuis six mille ans.* Trans. from the German by M. Gabelle. Paris: Editions du Seuil, 1958.

Jeulin, Paul. *L'Evolution du Port de Nantes.* Paris: Presses universitaires de France, 1929.

Jobert, Ambroise, *Magnats polonais et physiocrates français.* Paris: 'les Belles Lettres,' 1941.

Jobez, L.-E.-Alphonse. *La France sous Louis XV, 1715–1774.* 6 vols. Paris: Didier, 1864–1873.

Johnson, Edgar Augustus Jerome. "Just Price in an Unjust World." *International Journal of Ethics,* XLVIII (Jan. 1938), 165–181.

Jones, Eric L. *Seasons and Prices: The Role of the Weather in English Agricultural History.* London: George Allen and Unwin Ltd., 1964.

Jorré, Georges. "Le Commerce des grains et la minoterie à Toulouse." *Revue géographique des Pyrénées et du Sud-ouest,* IV (1933), 30–72.

Joubleou, F. "Notice sur P.-P. Lemercier de la Rivière." *Séances et travaux de l'Académie des sciences morales et politiques,* 3rd ser., XXVI (1858), 439–55; XXVII (1859), 121–50, 249–65.

Jouvencel, Henri de. *Le Contrôleur-général des finances sous l'ancien régime.* Paris: L. Larose, 1901.

Kaplow, Jeffry. "The Culture of Poverty in Paris on the Eve of the Revolution." *International Review of Social History,* XII (1967), 277–91.

————· "Sur la population flottante de Paris à la fin de l'ancien régime." *Annales historiques de la révolution française,* XXXIX (Jan.–March 1967), 1–14.

Kauder, Emil. *A History of Marginal Utility.* Princeton: Princeton University Press, 1965.

Koch, Philip. "The Genesis of Galiani's *Dialogues sur le commerce des blés.*" *French Studies,* XV (Oct. 1961), 314–23.

Labiche, E. *Les Sociétés d'agriculture au XVIIIe siècle.* Paris: F. Pichon et Durand-Auzias, 1908.

Laborde, Léon-E.-S.-J., Cte de. *Le Parlement de Paris, sa compétence et les ressources que l'érudition trouvera dans l'inventaire de ses archives.* Paris: H. Plon, 1863.

Labrousse, Ernest. *La Crise de l'économie française à la fin de l'ancien régime et au début de la Révolution.* Paris: Presses universitaires de France, 1944.

————· *Esquisse du mouvement des prix et des revenus en France au XVIIIe siècle.* 2 vols. Paris: Presses universitaires de France, 1933.

————; Romano, R.; and Dreyfus, F. G. *Le Prix du froment en France au temps de la monnaie stable 1726–1913.* Paris: S.E.V.P.E.N., 1970.

Lachiver, Marcel. "Projet de création d'un marché de grain à Vigny en 1771–78." *Mémoires de la Société historique et archéologique de Pontoise, du Val d'Oise et du Vexin,* LXIV (1972), 65–78.

Lacombe, Paul. *Bibliographie parisienne. Tableaux de mœurs (1600–1880).* Paris: P. Rouquette, 1887.

Lacretelle, Charles-Jean-Dominique de. *Histoire de France pendant le XVIIIe siècle.* 5th ed. 6 vols. Paris: Delaunay, 1830.

Lafue, Pierre. *Louis XV, la victoire de l'unité monarchique.* Paris: Hachette, 1952.

Landes, David. "The Statistical Study of French Crises." *Journal of Economic History,* X (May 1950), 195–211.

Landry, Adolphe. "La Démographie de l'ancien régime: Paris." *Journal de la Société de statistique de Paris,* LXXVI (1935), 34–45.

Lanzac de Laborie, Léon de. *Paris sous Napoléon.* Vol. V: *Assistance et bienfaisance. Approvisionnement.* Paris: Plon-Nourrit et Cie, 1908.

LaPalombara, Joseph, ed. *Bureaucracy and Political Development.* Princeton, N.J.: Princeton University Press, 1963.

La Riviére, Charles de. "Mercier de la Rivière à St. Petersbourg en 1767." *Revue d'histoire littéraire de la France.* 4th year (15 Oct. 1897), 581–602.

Larrère, C. "L'Analyse physiocratique des rapports entre la ville et le campagne." *Etudes rurales,* 49–50 (Jan.–June 1973), 42–68.

Laslett, Peter. *The World We Have Lost.* London: Methuen, 1968.

Las Vergnas, Raymond. *Le Chevalier Rutlidge "gentilhomme anglais," 1742–1794.* Paris: Ancienne Librairie Honoré Champion, 1932.

Latouche, R. "Le Prix du blé à Grenoble du XVe siècle au XVIIIe siècle." *Revue d'histoire économique et sociale,* XX (1932), 337–51.

Laurentie, Pierre S. *Histoire de France.* 8 vols. Paris: Lagny frères, 1839–1845.

Lavaquery, E. *Le Cardinal de Boisgelin.* 2 vols. Paris: Plon-Nourrit et Cie, 1920.

————· *Necker, fourrier de la Révolution.* Paris: Plon, 1933.

Lavedan, Pierre. *Histoire de Paris,* [new ed.] Paris: Presses universitaires de France, 1960.

Lavergne, Pierre S. *Les Economistes français du XVIIIe siècle.* Paris: Guillaumin et Cie, 1870.

————· *La Société d'agriculture de Paris.* Paris: Imprimerie de J. Claye, 1859.

Lazare, Louis. "La Halle au blé." *La Revue municipale,* 2nd year (1 May 1849), 195–96.

Lebeau, Auguste. *Condillac économiste.* Paris: Guillaumin et Cie, 1903.

Leblanc, Marguerite. *De Thomas More à Chaptal. Contribution bibliographique à l'histoire économique.* Paris: Editions Cujas, 1961.

Leblond, Paul. *Le Problème de l'approvisionnement des centres urbains en denrées alimentaires en France*. Paris: Garnier, 1926.

Lebrun, François. *Les Hommes et la mort en Anjou aux 17e et 18e siècles*. Paris: Mouton, 1971.

_____· "Les Intendants de Tours et d'Orléans aux 17e et 18e siècles." *Annales de Bretagne*, LXXVIII (June 1971), 287–305.

_____· "Les Soulèvements populaires à Angers aux XVIIe et XVIIIe siècles". Actes du 90e *Congrès national des Sociétés Savantes*. Vol. I. Paris: Bibliothèque Nationale, 1966.

LeCaron, Frédéric. "Les Origines de la Municipalité Parisienne." *Mémoires de la Société de l'histoire de Paris et de l'Ile-de-France*, VII (1880), 79–174 and VIII (1881), 161–272.

LeClère, Marcel. *Histoire de la police*. Paris: Presses universitaires de France, 1947.

Lefèvre, Pierre. *Le Commerce des grains et la question du pain à Lille de 1713 à 1789*. Lille: C. Robbe, 1925.

Lefort, Antonin. *La Taxe du pain et la liberté de la boulangerie*. Beauvais: Drubay, 1886.

Le Goff, Jacques. *La Civilisation de l'occident médiéval*. Paris: Arthaud, 1967.

Leibenstein, Harvey. *Economic Backwardness and Economic Growth; Studies in the Theory of Economic Development*. New York: J. Wiley, 1957.

Lelièvre, Jacques. *La Pratique des contrats de mariage chez les notaires au Châtelet de Paris de 1769 à 1804*. Paris: Editions Cujas, 1959.

Lemaire, André. *Les Lois fondamentales de la monarchie française d'après les théoriciens de l'ancien régime*. Paris: A. Fontemoing, 1907.

Lemarchand, Guy. "Les Troubles de subsistances dans la généralité de Rouen." *Annales historiques de la révolution française*, XXXV (Oct.–Dec. 1963), 401–27.

Le Mercier, E. *Le Prévôt dit de Beaumont*. Bernay: Miaulle-Duval, 1883.

LeMoigne, F.-Y. "La Crise frumentaire de 1770–1771 à Metz, Nancy et Strasbourg." *Bulletin de la Société d'histoire moderne*, 71st year, 15th ser., no. 3 (1972), 3–5.

LeMoy, A. *Le Parlement de Bretagne et le pouvoir royal au XVIIIe siècle*. Angers: Burdin et Cie, 1909.

Léon, Pierre. "La Crise des subsistances de 1810–1812 dans le département de l'Isére." *Annales historiques de la révolution française*, XXIV (July–Aug. 1952), 289–309.

_____· *Economies et sociétés préindustrielles, 1650–1780*. Paris: A. Colin, 1970.

LePaire, Jacques-Amédée. *Histoire de la Ville de Corbeil*. 2 vols. Lagny: E. Colin, 1901–1902.

Le Play, Frédéric. *Conseil d'Etat … Enquête sur la boulangerie, du département de la Seine*. Paris: Imprimerie impériale, 1860.

Leroux de Lincy, Antoine-Jean-Victor. *L'Histoire de l'Hôtel de Ville de Paris, suivie d'un essai sur l'ancien gouvernement municipal de cette ville*. Paris: J.-B. Dumoulin, 1846.

Le Roy Ladurie, E. *Les Paysans de Languedoc*. 2 vols. Paris: S.E.V.P.E.N., 1966.

_____· "L'Aménorrhée de famine (XVII–XXe siècles)." *Annales: économies, sociétés, civilisations*, 24th year (1969), 1589–1601.

_____· *Histoire du climat depuis l'an mil*. Paris: Flammarion, 1967.

_____· "L'Histoire immobile." *Annales: économies, sociétés, civilisations*, 29th year (May–June 1974), 673–92.

_____· "Révoltes et contestations rurales en France de 1675 à 1788." *Annales: économies, sociétés, civilisations*, 19th year (Jan.–Feb. 1974), 6–22.

_____· *Le Territoire de l'historien*. Paris: Gallimard, 1973.

Lerner, D. *The Passing of Traditional Society*. New York: Free Press of Glencoe, 1958.

Lescure, Jean. "La Liberté du commerce des grains et le parlement de Paris (1763–1768)." *Revue d'économie politique*, XXIV (1910), 451–70.

Letaconnoux, J. "La Navigation intérieure et les transports par eau en France au XVIIIe siècle." *Bulletin de la Société d'histoire moderne*, 8th year, 2nd ser. (Nov. 1908), 46–51.

_____· "La Question des subsistances et du commerce des grains en France au XVIIIe siècle. Travaux, sources, questions à traiter." *Revue d'histoire moderne et contemporaine*, VIII (1906–1907), 407–45.

_____· "Les Subsistances et le commerce des grains en Bretagne au XVIIIe siècle." *Annales de la Faculté de Rennes*, XX (1904–1905), 126–35.

————· *Les Subsistances et le commerce des grains en Bretagne au XVIIIe siècle, essai de monographic économique.* Rennes: Imprimerie Oberthür, 1909.

————· "La Transformation des moyens de transport." C. Bloch, *et al.*, *Les Divisions régionales de la France.* Paris: Félix Alcan, 1913.

————· "Les Transports en France au XVIIIe siècle." *Revue d'histoire moderne et contemporaine,* XI (1908–1909), 97–114, 269–92.

————· "Les Voies de communication en France au XVIIIe siècle." *Vierteljahrschrift für Sozial- und Wirtschaftsgeschichte,* VII (1909), 94–141.

Levasseur, Emile. "Des progrès de l'agriculture française dans la seconde moitié du XVIIIe siècle." *Revue d'économie politique,* XII (Jan. 1898), 1–29.

————· *Histoire des classes ouvrières et de l'industrie en France avant 1789.* 2nd ed. 2 vols. Paris: A. Rousseau, 1900–1901.

————· *La Population française: histoire de la population avant 1789....* 3 vols. Paris: A. Rousseau, 1889–1892.

————· *Les Prix. Aperçu historique de l'histoire économique de la valeur et du revenu de la terre en France.* Paris: Typographie Chamerot et Renouard, 1893.

Levron, Jacques. "Pierre Narbonne, commissaire de police à Versailles." *Revue des deux mondes,* no. 21 (1965), 60–72.

Lévy-Bruhl, Henri. "La Noblesse de France et le commerce à la fin de l'ancien régime." *Revue d'histoire moderne,* n.s., VIII (March–July 1933), 209–35.

Lhéritier, Michel. *L'Intendant Tourny (1695–1760).* 2 vols. Paris: Librairie F. Alcan, 1920.

————· "Le Pain à Bordeaux de 1789 à 1796." *Assemblée générale de la commission centrale et des comités départementaux. Commission d'histoire économique et sociale de la Révolution,* II (1939), 187–213.

Lichtenberger, André. *Le Socialisme au XVIIIe siècle: étude sur les idées socialistes dans les écrivains français du XVIIIe siècle avant la Révolution.* Paris: F. Alcan, 1895.

————· *Le Socialisme utopique.* Paris: F. Alcan, 1898.

Liebel, Helen P. "Enlightened Bureaucracy Versus Enlightened Despotism in Baden, 1750–1792." *Transactions of the American Philosophical Society,* n.s., LV (1965) part 5.

Lodge, E.C. *Sully, Colbert, and Turgot. A Chapter in French Economic History.* London: Methuen and Co., 1931.

Logette, Aline. *Le Comité contentieux des finances près le Conseil du Roi (1777–1791).* Nancy: Société d'impressions typographiques, n.d.

Lopez, Claude Anne. "Benjamin Franklin, Lafayette, and the *Lafayette.*" *Proceedings of the American Philosophical Society,* CVIII (June 22, 1964), 181–223.

————· *Mon cher papa, Franklin and the Ladies of Paris.* New Haven, Conn.: Yale University Press, 1966.

Lorain, Charles. *Les Subsistances en céréales dans le district de Chaumont, de 1788 à l'an V.* 2 vols. Chaumont: Imprimerie de R. Cavaniol, 1911–1912.

Lorenz, Lincoln. *John Paul Jones. Fighter for Freedom and Glory.* Annapolis: U.S. Naval Institute, 1943.

Loua, T. "De l'influence des disettes sur les mouvements de la population." *Journal de la Société de statistique de Paris,* 8th year (April 1867), 95–97.

————· "L'Approvisionnement de Paris." *Journal de la Société de statistique de Paris,* 15th year (March 1874), 78–82.

Louandre, Charles. *De l'Alimentation publique sous l'ancienne monarchic française.* Paris: Imprimerie de P. Dupont, 1864.

Louis, Paul. *Histoire du socialisme en France ... 1789–1936.* 3rd ed. Paris: M. Riviere, 1936.

Loutchisky, I. "Régime agraire et populations agricoles dans les environs de Paris à la veille de la Révolution." *Revue d'histoire moderne,* n.s., VIII (March-April 1933), 97–142.

Lublinsky, V.S. ["Les nouvelles données sur les troubles de mai 1775 à Paris. Lettres et notices."] *Voprosy Istorii,* no. 11 (1955), 113–17.

———· "Voltaire et la guerre des farines." *Annales historiques de la révolution française*, XXXI (April-June 1959), 127–45.

Luçay, Cte. Helion de. *Des Origines du pouvoir ministériel en France: les secrétaires d'état jusqu'à la mort de Louis XV.* Paris: M. Tardieu, 1881.

Lupo, Larry W. "The Abbé Ferdinando Galiani in Paris, 1759–69." Unpublished doctoral dissertation, University of Georgia, 1971.

Lüthy, Herbert. *La Banque protestante en France de la révocation de l'édit de Nantes à la révolution.* 2 vols. Paris: S.E.V.P.E.N., 1959–1961.

Lurine, Louis. *Histoire secrète et publique de la police ancienne et moderne.* 3 vols. Paris: G. Havard et Bry aîné, 1847.

Lutfalla, Michel. "L'Evidence, fondement nécessaire et suffisant de l'ordre naturel chez Quesnay et Morelly." *Revue d'histoire économique et sociale*, XLI, no. 2 (1963), 213–49.

MacCance, R. A., and Widdowson, E. M. *Breads White and Brown, Their Place in Thought and Social History.* London: Pitman, 1956.

McCloy, Shelby T. *Government Assistance in Eighteenth Century France.* Durham, N.C.: Duke University Press, 1946.

———· *The Humanitarian Movement in Eighteenth Century France.* Lexington: University of Kentucky Press, 1957.

Magnier, Achille. *Le Pain, son rôle, son histoire, sa technique.* Paris: G. Roustan, 1907.

Maire, Louis; Debré, Robert; Dunot, René; *et al. La Faim.* Texte des conférences et des entretiens. [Rencontres internationales. 15th, Geneva, 1960.] Neufchâtel: La Baconnière, 1960.

Mamet, Henri. *Le Président de Brosses. Sa Vie et ses ouvrages.* Lille: A. Masart, 1874.

Mandrou, Robert. *Introduction à la France moderne: essai de psychologie historique, 1500–1640.* Paris: Albin Michel, 1961.

———· *La France aux 17e et 18e siècles.* Nouvelle Clio. Paris: Presses universitaires de France, 1967.

Marchal, André. "Les Doctrines économiques de Necker." *Revue d'histoire économique et sociale*, XXI (1933), 237–54.

Marczewski, J. "Some Aspects of the Economic Growth of France, 1660–1958." *Economic Development and Cultural Change*, IX (1961), 369–96.

Marion, Marcel. *La Bretagne et le duc d'Aiguillon 1753–1770.* Paris: Fontemoing, 1898.

———· *Dictionnaire des institutions de la France aux XVIIe et XVIIIe siècles.* Paris: A. & J. Picard, 1969. (Orig. ed. 1923.)

———· "Une Famine en Guyenne (1747–1748)." *Revue historique*, XLVI (May–Aug. 1891), 241–87.

———· "Le Grand exil du Parlement de Besançon (1759–61)." *Revue des questions historiques*, L (1913), 65–93.

———· *Histoire financière de la France depuis 1715.* 6 vols. Paris: A. Rousseau, 1914–1927.

———· *Machault d'Arnouville. Etude sur l'histoire du contrôleur général des finances de 1749 à 1754.* Paris: Hachette et Cie, 1891.

Maroussem, Pierre du, and Guérie, Camille. "Une Grande cité et son marché central: le carreau des halles de Paris et sa réglementation traditionnelle." *Revue d'économie politique*, VIII (1894), 364–83.

Marsy, Cte. de. "L'Approvisionnement de Paris sous Louis XII, difficultés au sujet d'acquisition de blé faites à Noyon, au détriment des habitants de Compiègne et des environs (1501–1503)." *Bulletin de la Société de l'histoire de Paris et de l'Ile-de-France*, IV (1877), 138–45.

Martin, Germain. "Les Famines de 1693 et 1709 et la spéculation sur les blés." *Bulletin du Comité des travaux historiques et scientifiques. Section des sciences économiques et sociales* (1908), 150–71.

———· *Les Associations ouvrières au 18e siècle.* Paris: Rousseau, 1900.

Martin, [Bon-Louis-] Henri. *Histoire de France.* 4th ed. Vols. XV–XVI. Paris: Furne, 1860.

———· *Martin's History of France. The Decline of the French Monarchy.* Trans. Mary L. Booth. 2 vols. Boston: Walker, Fuller and Company, 1866.

Mathiez, Albert. "Les Réquisitions de grains sous la Terreur." *Revue d'histoire économique et sociale*, VIII, (1920), 231–54.

————. "La Révolution et les subsistances: L'Agitation sectionnaire à Paris en août 1793." *Annales révolutionnaires*, XIV (Jan.–Feb. 1922), 27–54.

————. "La Révolution et les subsistances: La Dictature économique du Comité de salut public." *Annales révolutionnaires*, XV (Nov.–Dec. 1923), 457–81.

————. *La Vie chère et le mouvement social sous la Terreur.* Paris: Payot, 1927.

Maugis, Edouard. *Histoire du Parlement de Paris de l'avènement des rois Valois à la mort d'Henri IV.* 3 vols. Paris: A. Picard, 1913–1916.

Maugras, Gaston. *La Disgrâce du duc et de la duchesse de Choiseul.* Paris: Plon, 1903.

Mauguin. *Etudes historiques sur l'administration de l'agriculture en France.* 3 vols. Paris: Jules Tremblay, 1876–1877.

Maurizio, A. *Histoire de l'alimentation végétale depuis la préhistoire jusqu'à nos jours.* Trans. F. Gidon. Paris: Payot, 1932.

Mauzi, Robert. *L'Idée du bonheur dans la littérature et la pensée françaises au XVIIIᵉ siècle.* Paris: A. Colin, 1960.

Maverick, Lewis A. *China, A Model for Europe.* 2 vols. San Antonio, Texas: Paul Anderson Company, 1946.

————. "The Chinese and the Physiocrats." *Economic History*, IV (1940), 312–19.

————. "Chinese Influence Upon the Physiocrats." *Economic History*, IV (1938), 54–64.

May, Louis-Philippe. *L'Ancien Régime devant le mur d'argent.* Paris: F. Alcan, 1935.

————. "Le Mercier de la Rivière, intendant des îles du vent (1759–1764)." *Revue d'histoire économique et sociale*, XX (1932), 44–74.

Meek, Ronald L. *The Economics of Physiocracy: Essays and Translations.* Cambridge, Mass.: Harvard University Press, 1963.

Merton, Robert K. "Role of the Intellectual in Public Bureaucracy." *Studies and Essays in the History of Science and Learning Offered in Homage to George Sarton.* Ed. M. F. Ashley Montagu. New York: H. Schuman, [1946?].

Meuvret, Jean. "Le Commerce des grains et des farines à Paris et les marchands parisiens à l'époque de Louis XIV." *Revue d'histoire moderne et contemporaine*, III (July–Sept. 1956), 169–203.

————. "Les Crises de subsistance et la démographie de la France d'ancien régime." *Population*, I (Oct.–Dec. 1946), 643–50.

————. "Demographic Crises in France from the Sixteenth to the Eighteenth Century." *Population in History.* Ed. D.V. Glass and D.E.C. Eversley. London: Edward Arnold, 1965.

————. "La Géographie des prix des céréales et les anciennes économies européennes; Prix méditerranéens, prix continentaux, prix atlantiques à la fin du XVIIᵉ siècle." *Revista de Economia* (Lisbon), IV (June 1951), 63–69.

————. "L'Histoire des prix des céréales dans la seconde moitié du XVIIᵉ siècle: sources et publication." *Mélanges d'histoire sociale*, V (1944), 27–44.

————. "Les Mouvements des prix de 1661 à 1715 et leurs répercussions." *Journal de la Société de statistique de Paris*, LXXXV (May–June 1944), 109–19.

————. "Les Oscillations des prix des céréales aux XVIIᵉ et XVIIIᵉ siècles en Angleterre et dans les pays du Bassin parisien." *Revue d'histoire moderne et contemporaine*, XVI (Oct.–Dec. 1969), 540–54.

————. "Les Prix des grains à Paris au XVᵉ siècle et les origines de la mercuriale." *Mémoires de la Fédération des Sociétés historiques et archéologiques de Paris et de l'Ile-de-France*, XI (1960), 283–311.

Meyer, Jean. *La Noblesse bretonne au XVIIIᵉ siècle.* 2 vols. Paris: S.E.V.P.E.N., 1966.

————. *L'Armement nantais dans la deuxième moitié du 18ᵉ siècle.* Paris: S.E.V.P.E.N., 1969.

Michaud, Guy, ed. *Paris, croissance d'une capitale.* Paris: Hachette, 1961.

————. *Paris, fonctions d'une capitale.* Paris: Hachette, 1962.

Michel, Georges, and Liesse, André. *Vauban économiste*. Paris: Plon, Nourrit et Cie, 1891.

Michelet, Jules. *Histoire de France. Louis XV. Louis XV et Louis XVI. Oeuvres complètes de J. Michelet*. Vols. XV–XVI. Paris: E. Flammarion, 1897.

Modeste, Victor. *De la cherté des grains et des préjugés populaires qui déterminent des violences dans les temps de disettes*. 3rd ed. Paris: Guillaumin, 1862.

————. *De la taxe du pain*. Paris: Imprimerie de Hennuyer, 1856.

Moiset, C. "Jacob Moreau, historiographe de France." *Bulletin de la Société des sciences historiques et naturelles de l'Yonne*, XLII (1888), 351–72.

Molinari, Gustave de. *Conversations familières sur le commerce des grains*. Paris: Guillaumin et Cie, 1855.

Mols, Roger. *Introduction à la démographie historique des villes d'Europe du XVIe au XVIIIe siècle*. 3 vols. Gembloux: J. Duclot, 1954–1956.

Monbeig, Pierre. "La 'géographie de la faim,' de Josué de Castro." *Annales: économies, sociétés, civilisations*, 3rd year (1948), 495–500.

Monin, Hippolyte. *Essai sur l'histoire administrative du Languedoc pendant l'intendance de Basville (1685–1719)*. Paris: Hachette, 1884.

————. *L'Etat de Paris en 1789, études et documents sur l'ancien régime à Paris*. Paris: Jouaust, 1889.

————. "Le Pacte de famine." *La Grande encyclopédie*. Vol. XVI. Paris: H. Lamirault, 1895.

Montbas, Hugues de. *La Police parisienne sous Louis XVI*. Paris: Hachette, 1949.

Moreau, Henri. "Le Rôle des subdélégués au 18e siècle: justice, police et affaires militaires." *Annales de Bourgogne*, XXIX (1957), 225–56.

Moreau de Jonnès, A. "Statistique des céréales de la France. Le Blé. Sa Culture, sa production, sa consommation, son commerce." *Journal des économistes*, IV (Jan.–March 1843), 129–66, 309–19.

Morel, Ambroise. *Histoire abrégée de la boulangerie en France*. Paris: Imprimerie de la Bourse du commerce, 1899.

Moreu Rey, Enric. *Un Barcellini a la corte de Maria-Antonieta: Sartine (Barcelona 1729-Tarragona 1801)*. Barcelona: Editorial Selecta, 1955.

Morineau, Michel. "Budgets populaires en France au dix-huitième siècle." *Revue d'histoire économique et sociale*, L (1972) no. 2, 203–37; no. 4, 449–81.

————. *Les Faux-semblants d'un démarrage économique: agriculture et démographie en France au XVIIIe siècle*. Cahiers des *Annales*, no. 30, Paris: A. Colin, 1971.

————. "La Pomme de terre au XVIIIe siècle." *Annales: économies, sociétés, civilisations*, 25th year (Nov.–Dec. 1970), 1767–85.

————. "Y a-t-il eu une révolution agricole en France au XVIIIe siècle?" *Revue historique*, CCXLII (April–June 1968), 299–326.

Morison, S.E. *John Paul Jones, A Sailor's Biography*. Boston: Little, Brown and Co., 1959.

Mornet, Daniel. *Les Origines intellectuelles de la révolution française, 1715–1787*. Paris: A. Colin, 1954.

Muret, P. "Les Mémoires du duc de Choiseul." *Revue d'histoire moderne et contemporaine*, VI (1904–1905), 229–48, 377–99.

Musart, Charles. *La Réglementation du commerce des grains en France au XVIIIe siècle: la théorie de Delamare, étude économique*. Paris: E. Champion, 1922.

Naude, Wilhelm. *Die Getreidehandelspolitik der europäischen Staaten vom 13. bis zum 18. Jahrhundert, als Einleitung in die preussische Getreidehandelspolitik*. Berlin: P. Parey, 1896.

Needler, Martin C. *Political Development in Latin America: Instability, Violence and Revolutionary Change*. New York: Random House, 1968.

Neymarck, Alfred. *Turgot et ses doctrines*. Geneva: Slatkine reprint [Paris, 1885], 1967.

Nicolas, Jean. "Pour une enquête sur les émotions populaires au 18e siècle: le cas de la Savoie." *Annales historiques de la révolution française*, XLV (Oct.–Dec. 1973), 593–607 and XLVI (Jan.–March 1974), 111–153.

Nio, Joseph. *Turgot et la liberté du commerce.* Bordeaux: Imprimerie de J. Bière, 1928.

Noussanne, Henri de. *Paris sous Louis XVI et Paris aujourd'hui.* Paris: Firmin-Didot, 1900.

Oestreicher, Jean. *La Pensée politique et économique de Diderot.* Vincennes: Rosay, 1936.

Olivier-Martin, François. *Cours d'histoire du droit public. La police économique sous l'ancien régime.* Paris: n.p., 1944–1945.

————. *Cours d'histoire du droit public. Les Cours de droit.* Paris: n.p., 1945–1946.

————. *L'Organisation corporative de la France d'ancien régime.* Paris: Librairie du Recueil Sirey, 1938.

Padover, Saul K. *The Life and Death of Louis XVI.* New York: Pyramid Books, 1963. (Orig. publ. 1939).

Palgrave, Robert Harry Ingles, ed. *Dictionary of Political Economy.* 3 vols. London: MacMillan and Co., 1894–1899.

Pallard, Jules. *La Liberté du commerce extérieur au XVIIIᵉ siècle.* Rennes: Caillot et fils, 1904.

Palmer, Robert R. *The Age of the Democratic Revolution: A Political History of Europe and America, 1760–1800.* 2 vols. Princeton, N.J.: Princeton University Press, 1959–1964.

Parturier, Louis. *L'Assistance à Paris sous l'ancien régime et pendant la révolution.* Paris: L. Larose, 1897.

Passy, Louis. *Histoire de la Société nationale d'agriculture de France.* Vol. I: 1761–1793. Paris: Imprimerie de P. Renouard, 1912.

————. "Napoléon, l'approvisionnement de la ville de Paris et la question des subsistances sous la révolution et l'empire." *Mémoires de la Société nationale d'agriculture,* CXXXVII (1896), 233–344.

Paultre, Christian. *De la répression de la mendicité et du vagabondage en France sous l'ancien régime.* Paris: L. Larose et L. Tenin, 1906.

Pelatant, Léopold. *De l'organisation de la police, étude historique, théorique et pratique.* Dijon: J. Berthaud, 1899.

Pellissier-Guys, H. "Le Séjour d'un négociant marseillais à la Bastille." *Provincia, Revue d'histoire et d'archéologie provençales,* III (1923), 18–34.

Perey, Lucien, and Maugras, Gaston. *Une Femme du monde au XVIIIᵉ siècle. Dernières années de Mme d'Epinay, son salon, et ses amis, d'après des lettres et des documents inédits.* Paris: C. Lévy, 1883.

Permezel, Paul. *Les Idées des physiocrates en matière de commerce international.* Lyon: J. Poncet, 1907.

Perrot, J.-C. "Note sur l'utilisation des dossiers de la lieutenance de police pour l'étude de la vie urbaine et des structures sociales (à propos de Caen au XVIIIᵉ siècle)." *Actes du 82ᵉ Congrès des Sociétés Savantes.* Bordeaux, 1957. Paris: Imprimerie nationale, 1958.

Petot, Jean. *Histoire de l'administration des ponts et chaussées 1599–1815.* Paris: M. Rivière & Cⁱᵉ, 1958.

Peyre, Roger. *La Question des subsistances et des approvisionnements en France à la fin du XVIIᵉ siècle, pendant la guerre de la Ligue d'Augsbourg.* Paris: A. Picard et fils, n.d.

Pfister, Charles. "Le Magasin de blé à Nancy et la 'révolte' de 1771." *Revue historique de la Lorraine* (1906), 77–92.

Philippe, Robert. "Une Opération pilote—l'étude du ravitaillement de Paris au temps de Lavoisier." *Annales: économies, sociétés, civilisations,* 16th year (May–June 1961), 564–68.

Phytallis, Jacques, *et al. Questions administratives dans la France du 18ᵉ siècle.* Paris: Presses universitaires de France, 1965.

Picard, Roger. "Etude sur quelques théories du salaire au XVIIIᵉ siècle." *Revue d'histoire des doctrines économiques et sociales,* III (1910), 153–68.

Pichon, Paul. *Histoire et organisation des services de police en France.* Issoudun: Laboureur et Cⁱᵉ, 1949.

Pigeonneau, Henri. *Histoire du commerce de la France.* 2 vols. Paris: L. Cerf, 1885–1889.

Pillorget, René, and Viguerie, Jean de. "Les Quartiers de Paris aux XVIIᵉ et XVIIIᵉ siècles." *Revue d'histoire moderne et contemporaine,* XVII (April–June 1970), 253–77.

Pinot, Virgile. "Les Physiocrates et la Chine au XVIIIᵉ." *Revue d'histoire moderne et contemporaine,* VIII (1906–1907), 200–14.

Piotrowski, Roman. *Cartels and Trusts, Their Origin and Historical Development from the Economic and Legal Aspects.* London: G. Allen and Unwin Ltd., 1933.

Piton, Camille. *Comment Paris s'est transformé. Histoire de Paris....* Paris: J. Rothschild, 1891.

Pitsch, Marguerite. *La Vie populaire à Paris au XVIII⁵ siècle d'après les textes contemporains et les estampes. Essai de catalogue sur l'iconographie de la vie populaire.* Paris: Picard, 1952.

Piuz, Anne-Marie. *Affaires et politique. Recherches sur le commerce de Genève au XVII⁵ siècle.* Geneva: Kundig, 1964.

Plantefol, Lucien. "Duhamel du Monceau." *Revue du dix-huitième siècle*, no. 1 (1969), 123–37.

Pocquet du Haut-Jussé, Barthélemy-A. "La Chalotais: Essai de biographie psychologique." *Annales de Bretagne*, LXXII (1965), 263–98.

Pocquet du Haut-Jussé, Barthélemy-A.-M. *Le Duc d'Aiguillon et La Chalotais.* 3 vols. Paris: Emile Perrin, 1900–1901.

————. *Les Origines de la révolution en Bretagne.* 2 vols. Paris: Emile Perrin, 1885.

Poète, Marcel. *Une Vie de cité. Paris, de sa naissance à nos jours.* 3 vols. Paris: Picard, 1924–1931.

Poisson, Charles. *Les Fournisseurs aux armées sous la révolution française. Le Directoire des achats (1792–1793).* Paris: A. Margraff, 1932.

Poitrineau, Abel. *La Vie rurale en Basse-Auvergne au XVIII⁵ siècle.* 2 vols. Paris: Presses universitaires de France, 1965.

Poizot, Edmond. *Le Commissaire de police.* Paris: L. Arnette, 1922.

Porter, Richard L., S.J. "'Scarcity' in Economic Theory and Policy." *Social Science*, XL (Jan. 1965), 22–30.

Poussou, Jean-Pierre. "Les Mouvements migratoires en France et à partir de la France de la fin du XV⁵ siècle au début du XIX⁵ siècle: Approches pour une synthèse." *Annales de démographie historique* (1970), 11–78.

Prentice, E. P. *Hunger and History. The Influence of Hunger on Human History.* New York: Harper and Brothers, 1939.

Prevost, M. "Bertin." *Dictionnaire de biographie française.* Ed. M. Prevost and R. d'Amat. Vol. VI. Paris: Letouzey et Ane, 1954.

Prévost de Lavand, Etienne. *Les Théories de l'intendant Rouillé d'Orfeuil.* Rochechouart: Dupanier frères, 1909.

Prost, François. *Les Remontrances du Parlement de Franche-Comté au 18⁵ siècle.* Lyon: Bosc and Riou, 1936.

Proteau, Pierre. *Etude sur Morellet considérée comme auxiliaire de l'école physiocratique et examen de ses principaux ouvrages économiques.* Laval: Imprimerie de L. Barneoud, 1910.

Rabatel, Pierre. *Le Parlement de Grenoble et les réformes de Maupeou (1771–1775).* Grenoble: E. Allegde. 1912.

Raisson, Horace. *Histoire de la police de Paris.... (1667–1844).* Paris: A. Levavasseur, 1844.

Rambaud, Adrien. *La Chambre d'abondance de la ville de Lyon (1643–1677).* Lyon: Imprimerie de J. Poncet, 1911.

Rambaud, Joseph. *Histoire des doctrines économiques.* Paris: L. Larose, 1899.

Rambert, Gaston, ed. *Histoire du commerce de Marseille.* Vol. IV–VII. Paris: Plon, 1954–1966.

Raynaud, B. "Les Discussions sur l'ordre naturel au XVIII⁵ siècle." *Revue d'économie politique*, XIX (1905), 231–48, 354–73.

Regnault, Emile, S.J. *Christophe de Beaumont, archevêque de Paris (1703–1781).* 2 vols. Paris: V. Lecoffre, 1882.

Reinhard, Marcel. *La Légende de Henri IV.* St. Brieuc: Les Presses bretonnes, 1935.

————. *Nouvelle histoire de Paris. La Révolution.* Paris: Association pour la publication d'une histoire de Paris, diffusion Hachette, 1971.

————. "Les Répercussions démographiques des crises de subsistances en France au 18⁵ siècle." *Actes du 81⁵ Congrès des Sociétés Savantes*, Rouen and Caen, 1956. Comité des travaux historiques et scientifiques. Paris: Presses universitaires de France, 1956.

————; Armengaud, André; and Dupâquier, Jacques. *Histoire générale de la population mondiale.* Paris: Editions Montchrestien, 1968.

Reith, Charles. *The Police Idea.* London: Oxford University Press, 1938.

Renner, H. *The Origin of Food Habits.* London: Faber and Faber, 1944.

Reverdy, Antony. *Morelly: idées philosophiques, économiques, et politiques.* Poitiers: Imprimerie de M. Bousrez, 1909.

Rich, E.E., and Wilson, C.H., eds. *The Economy of Expanding Europe in the 16th and 17th Centuries.* Vol. IV of *The Cambridge Economic History of Europe.* Ed. M. Postan and H.J. Habakkuk. Cambridge: Cambridge University Press, 1967.

Richet, Charles, and Mans, Antonin. *La Famine.* Paris: Centre de recherches, Charles Richet, 1965.

Richner, Edmund. *Le Mercier de la Rivière, ein Führer der physiokratischen Bewegung in Frankreich.* Zurich: Girsberger, 1931.

Ricommard, Jean. *La Lieutenance générale de police à Troyes au XVIIIe siècle.* Troyes: Imprimerie de J. L. Paton, 1934.

————. "Les Rapports du subdélégué de Marseille avec les maires et échevins de la ville." *Revue historique de droit français et étranger,* 4th ser., 43rd year (1965), 409–57.

————. "Les Subdélégués des intendants aux XVIIe et XVIIIe siècles." *Information historique,* 24th year (Sept.–Oct. 1962), 139–48; (Nov.–Dec. 1962), 190–95; 25th year (Jan.–Feb. 1963), 1–8.

————. "Les Subdélégués des intendants jusqu'à leur érection en titre d'office." *Revue d'histoire moderne,* XII (Sept.–Dec. 1937), 338–407.

————. "Les Subdélégués en titre d'office dans les Flandres et en Hainaut." *Revue du Nord,* XLII (Jan.–March 1960), 27–62.

————. "Les Subdélégués en titre d'office en Provence (1704–15)." *Provence historique,* (July–Sept. 1964), 242–71; (Oct.–Dec. 1964), 336–78.

————. "Les Subdélégués des intendants en titre d'office et leurs greffiers dans le 'département' de Metz (1704–1714)." *Revue historique de droit français et étranger,* 4th ser., 31st year (1953), 521–58.

————. "Les Subdélégués en titre d'office et leurs greffiers dans l'intendance de Bretagne." *Annales de Bretagne,* LXIX (Sept. 1962), 305–41.

Robert, P.-Albert. *Les Remontrances et arrêts du Parlement de Provence au XVIIIe siècle.* Paris: A. Rousseau, 1912.

Roberts, Hazel van Dyke. *Boisguilbert, Economist of the Reign of Louis XIV.* New York: Columbia University Press, 1935.

Rocquain, Félix. *L'Esprit révolutionnaire avant la révolution 1715–1789.* Paris: Plon, 1878.

————. "Le Parti des philosophes." *Séances et Travaux de l'Académie des Sciences Morales et Politiques,* XIV (1880), 102–46.

Rollet, Augustin. *Mémoire sur la meunerie, la boulangerie et la conservation des grains et des farines....* Paris: Carilian-Goeury, 1846.

Roover, R. de. "The Concept of the Just Price: Theory and Economic Politics." *Journal of Economic History,* XVIII (Dec. 1958), 418–34.

————. "Monopoly Theory Prior to Adam Smith. A Revision." *Quarterly Journal of Economics,* LXV (Nov. 1951), 492–524.

————. "The Scholastic Attitude Toward Trade and Entrepreneurship." *Explorations in Entrepreneurial History,* n.s., I (Fall 1963), 76–87.

————. "Scholastic Economics: Survival and Lasting Influence from the 16th Century to Adam Smith." *Quarterly Journal of Economics,* LXIX (1955), 161–90.

Roscher, Guillaume [Wilhelm]. *Du Commerce des grains et des mesures à prendre en cas de cherté.* Trans. from the German by Maurice Block. Paris: Guillaumin, 1854.

Rose, R. B. "Eighteenth Century Price Riots and Public Policy in England." *International Review of Social History*, VI (1961), 277–92.

———. "Eighteenth Century Price Riots, the French Revolution, and the Jacobin Maximum." *International Review of Social History*, IV (1959), 432–45.

———. "The French Revolution and Grain Supply." *Bulletin of the John Rylands Library*, XXXIX, no. 1 (1956–1957), 171–87.

Rosen, George. *Madness in Society*. New York: Harper and Row, 1969.

Rostow, Walt Whitman. "Business Cycles, Harvests and Politics: 1790–1850." *Journal of Economic History*, I (Nov. 1941), 206–21.

Rothkrug, Lionel. *Opposition to Louis XIV; The Political and Social Origins of the French Enlightenment.* Princeton, N.J.: Princeton University Press, 1965.

Rothney, John, ed. *The Brittany Affair and the Crisis of the Ancien Régime.* New York: Oxford University Press, 1969.

Rudé, George F. *The Crowd in History: A Study of Popular Disturbances in France and England, 1730–1848.* New York: Wiley, 1964.

———. "Paris et Londres au XVIIIᵉ siècle: société et conflits de classe." *Annales historiques de la révolution française*, XLV (Oct.–Dec. 1973), 481–502.

———. "Prices, Wages and Popular Movements in Paris during the French Revolution." *Economic History Review*, 2nd ser., VI (1954), 246–67.

———. "The Study of Popular Disturbances in the 'Preindustrial' Age." *Historical Studies, Australia and New Zealand*, X (May 1963), 457–69.

———. "La Taxation populaire de mai 1775 à Paris et dans la région parisienne." *Annales historiques de la révolution française*, XXVIII (April–June 1956), 139–79.

———. "La Taxation populaire de mai 1775 en Picardie, Normandie et dans le Beauvaisis." *Annales historiques de la révolution française*, XXXIII (July–Sept. 1961), 305–26.

Ruwet, Joseph, *et al. Marché des céréales à Ruremonde, Luxembourg, Namur et Diest aux XVIIᵉ et XVIIIᵉ siècles.* Recueil de travaux d'histoire et de philologie. Louvain: Publications universitaires de Louvain, 1966.

Sagnac, Philippe. "La Crise de l'économie française à la fin de l'ancien régime et au début de la révolution." *Revue d'histoire économique et sociale*, XXVIII (1950), 225–42.

Saint-Germain, Jacques. *La Reynie et la police au grand siècle, d'après de nombreux documents inédits.* Paris: Hachette, 1962.

———. *La Vie quotidienne en France à la fin du grand siècle d'après les archives … du lieutenant général de police Marc-René d'Argenson.* Paris: Hachette, 1965.

———. *Samuel Bernard, Le Banquier des rois.* Paris: Hachette, 1960.

Saint-Jacob, Pierre de. *Les Paysans de la Bourgogne du Nord au dernier siècle de l'ancien régime.* Paris: Société d'édition "les Belles Lettres," 1960.

———. "Histoire économique et sociale dans les archives de la juridiction consulaire à Dijon." *Bulletin de la Société d'histoire moderne*, 56 (Oct. 1957).

———. "La Question des prix en France à la fin de l'ancien régime d'après les contemporains." *Revue d'histoire économique et sociale*, XXX (1952), 133–46.

Sala, F.R. "The Influence of Physiocracy on the Programme of Reform Instituted by the National Assembly of France, 1789–91." Unpublished doctoral dissertation, University of California, 1943.

Salaman, Redcliffe N. *The History and Social Influence of the Potato.* Cambridge: Cambridge University Press, 1949.

Samaran, Charles, ed. *L'Histoire et ses méthodes.* Encyclopédie de la Pléiade. Paris: Librairie Gallimard, 1961.

Saricks, Ambrose. *Pierre Samuel DuPont de Nemours.* Lawrence, KS: University of Kansas Press, 1965.

Sars, Maxime, Cte. de. *LeNoir, lieutenant de police 1732–1807.* Paris: Hachette, 1948.

Saulnier, Frédéric. *Le Parlement de Bretagne 1554–1790.* 2 vols. Rennes: J. Plihon et L. Hommay, 1909.

Sauvy, Alfred. "La Pensée économique en France sur l'idée d'abondance et de besoin." *History of Political Economy*, I (Fall 1969), 279–305.

————, and Hecht, J. "La Population agricole française du XVIIIe siècle et l'expérience du marquis de Turbilly." *Population*, XX (1965), 269–86.

Savatier, René. *La Théorie du commerce chez les physiocrates*. Paris: Société française d'imprimerie et de librairie, 1918.

Say, Léon. *Nouveau dictionnaire d'économie politique*. 2 vols. Paris: Guillaumin, 1891–1892.

Schatz, A. *L'Individualisme économique et social, ses origines, son évolution, ses formes contemporaines*. Paris: A. Colin, 1907.

Schelle, Gustave. *Dupont de Nemours et l'école physiocratique*. Paris: Librairie Guillaumin et Cie, 1888.

————. "Notes sur la statistique en France au milieu du XVIIIe siècle." *Journal de la Société de statistique de Paris*, LI (Jan. 1910), 6–10.

————. "Quesnay avant d'être économiste." *Revue d'économie politique*, XVIII (1904), 177–212.

————. "Sur les physiocrates." *Journal des économistes*, 6th series, XXXI (July–Sept. 1911), 231–43.

————. "Turgot et le pacte de famine." *Séances et travaux de l'Académie des sciences morales et politiques*. 70th year, n.s., LXXIV (Aug. 1910), 189–217.

————. *Vincent de Gournay*. Paris: Guillaumin et Cie, 1897.

Schmidt, C. "Le Fonds de la police générale aux Archives nationales [F⁷]." *Revue d'histoire moderne et contemporaine*, IV (1902–1903), 313–27.

Schultz, Theodore W. *Transforming Traditional Agriculture*. New Haven, Conn.: Yale University Press, 1964.

Schumpeter, Joseph A. *History of Economic Analysis*. New York: Oxford University Press, 1954.

Sébillot, Paul. *Traditions et superstitions de la boulangerie*. Paris: Lechevalier, 1891.

Sée, Henri. "Les Classes ouvrières et la question sociale à la veille de la révolution." *Annales révolutionnaires*, XIV (Sept.–Oct. 1922), 373–86.

————. "La Doctrine politique des parlements du XVIIIe siècle." *Revue historique de droit français et étranger*, 4th ser. III (1924), 287–306.

————. *Histoire économique de la France*. 2 vols. Paris: A. Colin, 1939.

————. "La Mise en valeur des terres incultes. Défrichements et dessèchements à la fin de l'ancien régime." *Revue d'histoire économique et sociale*, XI, no. 1 (1923), 62–81.

————. "Quelques aperçus sur le transit des marchands au XVIIIe siècle." *Revue d'histoire économique et sociale*, XIV (1926), 27–31.

Ségur, Pierre, marquis de. *Au Couchant de la Monarchie*. 2 vols. Paris: Calmann-Lévy, 1909–1913.

Séta, Paul. *Les Huissiers et sergents sous l'ancien régime*. Paris: M. Giard et E. Brière, 1913.

Shennan, J.H. *The Parlement of Paris*. Ithaca: Cornell University Press, 1968.

Shepard, William Finley. *Price Control and the Reign of Terror 1793–1795*. Berkeley, California: University of California Press, 1953.

Sheppard, Ronald, and Newton, Edward. *The Story of Bread*. London: Routledge and Kegan Paul, 1957.

Silvestre, A.J. *Histoire des professions alimentaires dans Paris et ses environs*. Paris: Dentu, 1853.

Simiand, François. *Recherches anciennes et nouvelles sur le mouvement général des prix du XVIe siècle au XIXe siècle*. Paris: Domat Montchrestien, 1932.

Simoons, Frederick J. *Eat Not This Flesh; Food Avoidances in the Old World*. Madison, Wisc.: University of Wisconsin Press, 1961.

Siron, Jean. *Les Problèmes français du blé*. Toulouse: Imprimerie de Berthoumieu, 1933.

Sjoberg, Gideon. *The Preindustrial City: Past and Present*. New York: The Free Press, 1960.

Slicher Van Bath, B.H. *The Agrarian History of Western Europe A.D. 500–1850*. Trans. O. Ordish. London: Arnold Ltd., 1963.

————. "Eighteenth Century Agriculture on the Continent of Europe: Evolution or Revolution?" *Agricultural History*, XLIII (Jan. 1969), 169–79.

Small, Albion W. *The Cameralists. The Pioneers of German Social Polity.* Chicago: University of Chicago Press, 1909.

Soboul, Albert. "Aux Origines de la classe ouvrière parisienne (fin XVIIIe siècle—début XIXe siècle)." *Third International Conference of Economic History.* Munich, 1965. Paris: Mouton, 1968.

Soltau, Roger Henry. *The Duke of Choiseul.* Oxford: B.H. Blackwell, 1909.

Sorokin, Pitrim A. *The Sociology of Revolution.* Philadelphia and London: J.B. Lippincott Company, 1925.

Spengler, Joseph John. *French Predecessors of Malthus: A Study in Eighteenth-Century Wage and Population Theory.* Durham, N.C.: Duke University Press, 1942.

_____. "Mercantilist and Physiocratic Growth Theory." *Theories of Economic Growth.* Ed. Berthold Hoselitz, *et al.* Glencoe, Ill.: Free Press, 1960.

Spooner, F. "Régime alimentaire d'autrefois: Proportions et calculations en calories." *Annales: économies, sociétés, civilisations,* 16th year (May–June 1961), 568–74.

Stead, Philip John. *The Police of Paris.* London: Staples Press, 1957.

Storck, John, and Teague, Walter D. *Flour for Man's Bread—A History of Milling.* Minneapolis: University of Minnesota Press, 1952.

Stouff, Louis. *Ravitaillement et alimentation en Provence aux XIVe et XVe siècles.* The Hague; and Paris: Mouton, 1970.

Stourm, René. *Bibliographie historique des finances de la France au XVIIIe siècle.* Paris: Guillaumin et Cie, 1895.

_____. *Les Finances de l'ancien régime et de la révolution, origine du système financier actuel.* Vol. I. Paris: Guillaumin et Cie, 1885.

Strauss, Anselm. "The Literature on Panic." *Journal of Abnormal and Social Psychology,* XXXIX (1944), 317–20.

Strenski, Ellen M. "Diderot, For and Against the Physiocrats." *Studies on Voltaire and the Eighteenth Century,* LVII (1967), 1435–55.

Tagliacozzo, G. "Economic Vichianism: Vico, Galiani, Croce—Economics, Economic Liberalism." *Giambattista Vico: An International Symposium.* Ed. G. Tagliacozzo. Baltimore: The Johns Hopkins University Press, 1971.

_____, ed. *Economisti napoletani dei sec. XVIIe XVIII.* Bologna: L. Cappelli, 1937.

Talbot, Albert. *Les Théories de Boisguilbert et leur place dans l'histoire des doctrines économiques.* Paris: A. Rousseau, 1903.

Tarde, Alfred de. *L'Idée du juste prix.* New York: Burt Franklin, 1971. (Orig. Paris, 1907).

Tardif, Joseph. *Des pouvoirs de police municipale en matière de commerce.* Caen: Imprimerie de H. Delesques, 1917.

Tarrade, Jean. *Le Commerce colonial de la France à la fin de l'ancien régime.* Paris: Presses universitaires de France, 1972.

Taylor, Overton H. *A History of Economic Thought.* New York: McGraw-Hill, 1960.

Temple, Nora. "The Control and Exploitation of French Towns During the Ancien Régime." *History,* LI (Feb. 1966), 16–34.

Terr, S. D. "Grain Trade Legislation in France during the French Revolution (1789–92)." Unpublished doctoral dissertation, The Ohio State University, 1937.

Thompson, E. P. "The Moral Economy of the English Crowd in the Eighteenth Century." *Past & Present,* 52 (Feb. 1971), 76–136.

Thomson, Valentine. *Knights of the Seas. The Adventurous Life of John Paul Jones.* New York: Liveright Publishing Corp., 1939.

Thrupp, Sylvia. *A Short History of the Worshipful Company of Bakers of London.* London, 1933.

Thuillat, Louis. *Gabriel Nicolas de la Reynie, premier lieutenant général de police de Paris.* Limoges: Imprimerie générale, 1930.

Thuillier, Guy. "Comment les Français voyaient l'administration en 1789; Jacques Peuchet et la 'burocratie'." *La Revue administrative,* XV (July–August 1962), 378–83.

Tilly, Charles. "Collective Violence in European Perspective." *Violence in America, Historical and Comparative Perspectives.* A Report to the National Commission on the Causes and Prevention of Violence, June 1969. Ed. H. D. Graham and T.R. Gurr. New York: New American Library, 1969.

Tilly, Louise A. "La Révolte frumentaire, forme de conflit politique en France." *Annales: économies, sociétés, civilisations,* 17th year (May–June 1972), 731–57.

Tourneux, Maurice. *Bibliographie de l'histoire de Paris pendant la Révolution française.* 4 vols. Paris: Imprimerie nouvelle, 1890–1906.

Toutain, Jean-Claude. "La Consommation alimentaire en France de 1789 à 1964." *Cahiers de l'I.S.E.A.* [Institut de science économique appliquée], V (Nov. 1971).

———. "La Population de la France de 1700 à 1959." *Cahiers de l'I.S.E.A.* [Institut de science économique appliquée] Supplement no. 133 (Jan. 1963), ser. AF, no. 3.

———. "Le Produit de l'agriculture française de 1700 à 1958. I: Estimation du produit agricole du XVIIIᵉ siècle. II: Le Produit de l'agriculture française 1700–1750: La Croissance." *Cahiers de l'I.S.E.A.* [Institut de science économique appliquée. Paris.] Supplement no. 115, nos. 1–2 (1961).

Tulard, Jean. "La Police de Paris sous la révolution." *Information historique,* 24th year (May–June 1962), 113–18.

———. *Nouvelle histoire de Paris. Le Consulat et l'empire.* Paris: Association pour la publication d'une histoire de Paris, diffusion Hachette, 1970.

Usher, Abbot P. "The General Course of Wheat Prices in France, 1350–1788." *Review of Economic Statistics,* XII (1930), 159–69.

———. *The History of the Grain Trade in France, 1400–1710.* Cambridge, Mass.: Harvard University Press, 1913.

Valania, Maria. *L'Abbé Galiani et sa correspondance avec madame d'Epinay.* Milan: Edizioni commerciali, n.d. [ca. 1933].

Valentino, Henri. *Une femme d'esprit sous Louis XV: Madame d'Epinay.* Paris: Librairie Académique Perrin, 1952.

Valery, Lucien. *Les Idées économiques de Dutot.* Ligugé: Imprimerie de E. Aubin, 1920.

Valmont, Gustave. *Le Commerce des grains dans la généralité de Rouen au XVIIIᵉ siècle.* Paris, n.p., 1908.

Vatel, Charles. *Histoire de Madame du Barry.* 3 vols. Versailles: L. Bernard, 1883.

Vergne, Julien. *Gabriel Nicolas de La Reynie, premier lieutenant général de police de Paris, 1667–1697.* Paris: n.p., 1953.

Vexliard, Alexandre. *Introduction à la sociologie du vagabondage.* Paris: Rivière, 1956.

Viala, Louis. *La Question des grains et leur commerce à Toulouse au dix-huitième siècle (de 1715 à 1789).* Toulouse: E. Privat, 1909.

Vidalenc, Jean. "L'Approvisionnement de Paris en viande sous l'ancien régime." *Revue d'histoire économique et sociale,* XXX, no. 2 (1952), 116–32.

Vignes, J.-B.-Maurice. *Histoire des doctrines sur l'impôt en France.* Paris: V. Giard et E. Brière, 1909.

Vigoureux, C. *Le Commerce des grains à Paris au temps jadis.* Rodez: extrait du *Bulletin du Centre de Paris,* n.d.

Villers, Robert. *L'Organisation du parlement de Paris et des conseils supérieurs d'après la réforme de Maupeou (1771–1774).* Paris: Recueil Sirey, 1937.

Villey, Edmond. "La Taxe du pain et les boulangers de la ville de Caen en 1776." *Revue d'économie politique,* II (1888), 178–92.

Vincent, François. *Histoire des famines à Paris.* Paris: Editions politiques, économiques et sociales, 1946.

Viollet, P. *Le Roi et ses ministres pendant les trois derniers siècles de la monarchie.* Paris: n.p., 1912.

Vovelle, Michel. "Les Taxations populaires de février-mars et novembre-décembre 1792 dans la Beauce et sur ses confins." *Actes du 82ᵉ Congrès national des Sociétés Savantes,* Bordeaux 1957. Mémoires et Documents, XIII. Commission de recherche et de publication des documents relatifs à la vie économique de la Révolution. Paris: Imprimerie nationale, 1958.

Wada, Tomi. *An Experimental Study of Hunger in Its Relation to Activity.* Archives of Psychology. Ed. R.S. Woodworth. No. 57. New York, 1932.

Walford, Cornelius. *The Famines of the World: Past and Present.* London: E. Stanford, 1879.

Wallon, Henri Alexandre. *Histoire du Tribunal révolutionnaire de Paris avec le journal de ses actes.* 6 vols. Paris: Hachette, 1880–1882.

Walter, Gérard. *Histoire des paysans de France.* Paris: Flammarion, 1963.

Ware, Norman J. "The Physiocrats: A Study in Economic Rationalization." *American Economic Review,* XXI (Dec. 1931), 607–19.

Weulersse, Géorges. *Le Mouvement physiocratique en France de 1756 à 1770.* 2 vols. Paris: F. Alcan, 1910.

————. "Les Physiocrates et la question du pain cher au milieu du XVIIIᵉ siècle, 1756–1770." *Revue du dix-huitième siècle,* I (Jan.–March 1913), 175–92.

————. "Les Physiocrates sous le ministère de Turgot." *Revue d'histoire économique et sociale,* XIII, no. 3 (1925), 314–37.

————. *La Physiocratie à la fin du règne de Louis XV, 1770–1774.* Paris: Presses universitaires de France, 1959.

————. *La Physiocratie sous les ministères de Turgot et de Necker (1774–1781).* Paris: Presses universitaires de France, 1950.

————. "Sully et Colbert jugés par les Physiocrates." *Revue d'histoire économique et sociale,* IV (1922), 234–51.

Wilson, Arthur. *Diderot.* New York: Oxford University Press, 1972.

Witte, J. de. "Un Prélat du XVIIIᵉ siècle: l'abbé de Véri." *Revue des deux mondes,* XXIII (1924), 116–29.

Wolfenstein, Martha. *Disaster: A Psychological Essay.* Glencoe, Ill.: The Free Press, 1957.

Wrigley, E.A. "A Simple Model of London's Importance in Changing English Society and Economy 1650–1750." *Past and Present,* no. 37 (July 1967), 44–71.

————. *Population and History.* New York: McGraw-Hill, 1969.

Zaretti, Dante. "L'Approvisionnement de Pavie au 16ᵉ siècle." *Annales: économies, sociétés, civilisations,* 18th year (Jan.–Feb. 1963) 44–62.

Zola, Emile. *Le Ventre de Paris.* 15th ed. Paris: G. Charpentier, 1880.

Zolla, Daniel. *Les Industries agricoles; le blé et les céréales.* Paris: O. Doin et fils, 1909.

Works received after the completion of this book

Adams, Thomas M. "An Approach to the Problem of Beggary in Eighteenth Century France: the dépots de mendicité." Unpublished doctoral dissertation, University of Wisconsin, 1972.

Antoine, Michel. "La Notion de subdélégation dans la monarchie d'ancien régime." *Bibliothèque de l'Ecole des Chartes,* CXXXII (July–Dec. 1974), 267–87.

Baudot, Marcel. "Un Ministre champenois méconnu: le comte Saint-Florentin, secrétaire d'état et ministre de Louis XV durant cinquante ans." *Actes du 95ᵉ Congrès National des Sociétés Savantes,* Reims, 1970. Paris: Bibliothèque Nationale, 1974.

Blayo, Yves. "La Mortalité en France de 1740 à 1829." *Population,* XXX (Nov. 1975), 123–142.

Braeuner, Gabriel. "La Crise de subsistances 1770–1771 à Colmar." *Annuaire de la Société historique et littéraire de Colmar,* XXII (1972), 67–82.

Castan, Yves. *Honnêteté et relations sociales en Languedoc, 1715–1780.* Paris: Plon, 1974.

Coulet, H., ed. *La Ville au XVIIIᵉ siècle.* Colloque d'Aix-en-Provence, 1973. Aix: Edisud, 1975.

Doyle, William. *The Parlement of Bordeaux and the End of the Old Regime, 1771–1790.* New York: St. Martin's Press, 1974.

Dupâquier, Jacques. *Introduction à la démographie historique.* Paris: Gamma, 1974.

————. "De l'Animal à l'homme: le mécanisme autorégulateur des populations traditionnelles." *Revue de l'Institut de sociologie* (1972), no. 2, 177–211.

Egret, Jean. *Necker, ministre de Louis XVI.* Paris: H. Champion, 1975.

Farge, Arlette. *Délinquance et criminalité: le vol d'aliments à Paris au 18ᵉ siècle.* Paris: Plon, 1974.

Fossier, Robert, ed. *Histoire de la Picardie.* Toulouse: E. Privat, 1974.

Frêche, Georges. *Toulouse et la région Midi-Pyrénées au siècle des lumières.* Paris: Editions Cujas, 1974–1975.

Goubert, Jean-Pierre. *Malades et médecins en Bretagne, 1770–1790.* Rennes: Institut armoricain de recherches historiques, 1974.

Henry, Louis and Blayo, Yves. "La Population de la France de 1740 à 1860." *Population,* XXX (Nov. 1975), 71–122.

Hufton, Olwen H. *The Poor of Eighteenth Century France, 1750–1789.* Oxford: Clarendon Press, 1974.

Laugier, Lucien. *Un Ministère réformateur sous Louis XV. Le Triumvirat (1770–1774).* Paris: La Pensée universelle, 1975.

Lavedan, Pierre. *Nouvelle histoire de Paris. Histoire de l'urbanisme à Paris.* Paris: Association pour la publication d'une histoire de Paris, diffusion Hachette, 1975.

Le Roy Ladurie, E. "Pour un modèle de l'économie rurale française au 18ᵉ siècle." *Cahiers d'histoire,* XIX (1974), 5–26.

Morineau, Michel. "A la Halle de Charleville: fourniture et prix des grains ou les mécanismes du marché (1647–1821)." *Actes du 95ᵉ Congrès National des Sociétés Savantes,* Reims, 1970. Paris: Bibliothèque Nationale, 1974.

———. "Révolution agricole, révolution alimentaire, révolution démographique." *Annales de démographie historique* (1974), 335–71.

Perrot, Jean-Claude. *Genèse d'une ville moderne. Caen au XVIIIᵉ siècle.* 2 vols. Lille: Service de reproduction des thèses. Université de Lille III, 1974.

Revel, Jacques. "Le Grain de Rome et la crise de l'annone dans la seconde moitié du 18ᵉ siècle." *Mélanges de l'Ecole française de Rome,* LXXXIV (1972), 201–81.

Trenard, Louis. "Les Intendants et leurs enquêtes." *L'Information Historique,* 38th year (Jan.–Feb. 1976), 11–23.

Vilar, Pierre. "Motín de Esquilache et crises d'ancien régime." *Historia Iberica,* (1973), 11–33.

Virieux, Maurice. "Une Enquête sur le Parlement de Toulouse en 1718." *Annales du Midi,* LXXXVII (Jan.–Mar. 1975), 37–65.

INDEX

Abbeville, 188 n, 190, 193, 217

Abeille, Louis-Paul, 113, 124, 131, 168, 244

absolutism, 6, 91, 154, 228, 678

abundance, xix n, 10, 110, 116, 135, 137, 168, 177–79, 183, 392, 405, 678

—as burden, 133, 177–78

Académie Française, 322

Academy of Sciences, 336, 349 administrative monarchy, 148–49, 155

—bureaucracy, 446, 478 n, 546, 554 advocate general, of the Paris Parlement, *see* Omer Joly de Fleury *and* Séguier

Africa, 634, 700

Agay de Mutigny, François-Marie-Bruno d',

—intendant of Brittany 1767–71, 226 n, 496

—intendant of Picardy 1771–89,179, 559 n, 562, 575

Agde, 459, 639

agriculture, xxv–xxvi, 94–96, 98, 102, 104, 112, 116, 119–20, 125–27, 130, 132, 137, 139, 141, 152, 168–69, 172, 174–78, 186, 206–07, 240 n, 246, 257, 259, 263–66, 327, 398, 404, 429, 433, 437, 445–46, 458–59, 464, 466, 469, 475, 479–80, 489, 540, 544–45, 553, 569, 578, 580, 584, 598, 605, 612, 682, 688, 690, 694

—enclosure, 445

—land reclamation, 263 n, 445, 580, 694 n

—leases, 122, 572, 573, 694 n

—production, 337, 550–51, 690

—rural depopulation, 475

—societies of, 119, 121, 123–24, 137, 157, 584 n, 658, 695

agronomy and agromania, 119, 120

Aiguillon, Emmanuel-Armand d', 244, 250, 439, 520, 527, 531, 627

Aix–en–Provence, 75, 256, 524, 565, 637

—Parlement of, *see* Provence

Albert, Joseph–François-Ildefonse-Rémand, lieutenant general of police 1775–76 and intendant of finance, 386–87, 482, 492, 494, 506, 509, 512, 615, 620 n, 645, 663, 665, 667–69, 671–72

Albi, 565

Alembert, Jean Le Rond d', 428 n

Alençon, 134, 275, 538

—intendants of, 74, 134, 263–64 n, 538, 553, 580 n, 651

—subdelegates of, 135, 207, 501

Aligre, d', 426, 427

Almanach royal, 658, 659

Alsace,

—Parlement of, 493, 496, 499, 514

Amar, Pierre, 341–42

Amboise, 493 n

—municipality of, 496

Amelot de Chaillou, Antoine-Jean, intendant of Burgundy 1764–76, 504, 553, 562, 575, 620 n, 636

America, 468, 672, 700

Amiens, 128, 188 n, 190, 619, 633

Amsterdam, 642, 667, 700

Angers, 188 n, 277, 374

—municipality of, 204

Angerville-la-Gaste, royal procurator of, 538

Angoulême, 493 n

Anjou, 499, 570

Antifinancier, 176

anti-mercantilism, 97

Antoine, Michel, 250 n, 529 n

Arcis-sur-Aube, 212, 270

Argenson, Marc-René de Voyer, comte d', lieutenant general of police 1697–1718, 38, 45, 89

Argenson, René-Louis de Voyer, marquis d', 26, 27 n, 105–160, 396, 404, 458 n

Argentan, 134

Arpajon, 271

arrêt de réglement, 22

arrêt du conseil of 1754, 106–07, 125–26, 127, 129

arrêt du conseil of 14 July 1770, 510–12, 576, 583–84

arrêt du conseil of 23 December 1770, 283, 519–21, 525, 532–90

—flexible execution of, 558–63

—registration in parlements, 556–58
—rigorous execution of, 568–81
—special jurisdiction of intendants, 573–75
arrêt du conseil of 13 September 1774, 179,
    405–06, 664, 666
Assembly of General Police (Paris, November
    1768), 157, 424–41, 463–64, 468, 471, 473–76,
    478, 480–82, 513, 538 n, 591–92, 594
—projected *arrêt*, 437
—recruitment, 426
—*see also* police of Paris
Aube, Philippe, 311
Aubert, Jean-Honoré, 285
Aubry, 275
Auray, 190, 193
Aurillac, 504
Austria, 640, 645
Auvergne, 269, 493 n, 499, 503–04, 617 n,
    620, 621
—intendants of, 230, 235, 383, 504, 618,
    620, 621
—subdelegates of, 503
Auxonne, 190, 498
Avesnes, 206
—dealer registration list, 292
—subdelegates of, 474 n, 572, 602 n
Avoise, 188 n

Bacalan, André-Timothée-Isaac de, 282
Bacquencourt, Guillaume-Joseph Dupleix de,
    intendant of Brittany 1771–74, 75, 214,
    552 n, 557, 562, 576 n, 580, 651 n, 658
Bagarre, La, 606
Bailly, Jean-Sylvain, 673
bakers, 22, 37, 47–48, 68, 71, 72, 85, 90, 197,
    272–75, 287, 290–91, 323, 324, 326,
    328–43, 345, 349, 355, 374–75, 424, 437,
    501, 506, 507–09, 539, 562, 563, 614, 623,
    649, 702
—failure, 340
—*forains*, 330–31, 353
—guild, 341
—in hard times, 340–43
—*jurés*, 330, 353
—master, 311, 341, 342
—public assistance for, 341–43
—sales on credit, 331, 340
Balinvilliers, Bernard de, intendant of
    Auvergne 1757–67, 235
Baltic, 634 n
Baltimore, 634

Barat, 295
Barbier, Edmond-Jean-François, 26
barley, 339, 375, 510
Bar-sur-Aube, 188 n, 195, 222, 277, 553
—royal procurator of, 562
—subdelegate of, 553
Bar-sur-Seine, 499, 500
Bastille, 390, 622, 642, 671, 672, 678
Baudeau, Nicolas, 17, 114, 131, 178, 223,
    339, 401–02, 473–75, 478–79, 480, 604,
    628, 650, 694 n
Baudouin, 367 n, 594
Baudry, 632
Bayeux, 493 n
Beard, Charles, 181
Beardé de l'Abbaye, 602
Beauce, 202, 269, 277, 286, 311, 368, 431,
    502
Beaufort, 188 n, 193
Beaumarchais, Pierre-Augustin Caron de,
    362 n
Beauvais, 647
—royal bailliage of, 647, 649
Béguillet, Edme, 146, 179, 260, 350, 361 n,
    602, 673
Belleville, 188 n, 190, 275
Belly, 221, 278–79
Bergerac, 566
Bernard, Samuel, 58, 156, 367, 384, 395,
    628, 639, 640, 700
Berry, 493 n
Berthet, Elie, 390, 391
Bertier de Sauvigny, Louis-Jean, intendant of
    the generality of Paris 1744–76, 4 n, 20 n,
    74, 80, 88, 168, 178, 200, 354, 383
Bertier de Sauvigny, Louis-Bénigne-François,
    intendant of the generality of Paris
    1776–89, 394, 673
Bertin, Henri-Léonard-Jean-Baptiste, con-
    troller–general 1759–63, 74, 118, 128,
    130–33, 135–42, 148, 150, 158, 167, 183,
    249, 279, 349–50, 352, 408, 417
—disgrace of, 140
—draft proposal for reform of grain laws,
    131–39
—fiscal reforms of, 140, 180
Bertinière, 205
Besançon, 195, 277, 523, 524
Bethmann, 640, 641, 653–56, 658
Béziers, 459 n, 639
Bicêtre, 200, 390

Bignon, Armand-Jérême, 507
Bigot de Sainte-Croix, Louis-Claude, 426 n, 460
Billacois, François, 428 n
Billard, François-Pierre, 297–98
blatiers, 40, 196, 204, 239, 269, 290–93, 304, 518, 557, 567, 639 ; see also grain trade and merchants
Bléré, 188 n, 190, 193, 200, 269
Blois, 188 n
Blois, Paul, 291
Boisguilbert, Pierre Le Pesant de, 98, 110
Boismont Louis-Guillaume de Blair de, intendant of Hainaut 1754–64, 133 n
bon prix, 239, 405, 432, 435, 468, 472, 479, 529, 546, 587, 612, 687, 691, 693; see also économistes and physiocracy
Bonaparte, Napoléon, 91
Bonhommet, 275
Bordeaux, 185 n, 560, 565–66, 579, 620, 622, 634, 640, 641, 652, 656
—chamber of commerce, 656
—intendants of, 133, 216, 534 n, 537, 540, 552–53, 557, 561, 580 n, 583, 635
—municipality, 640
—Parlement of, 183, 235, 248 n, 451, 493, 496, 498, 557, 566, 581–83, 652–53, 655–56
Bossuet, Jacques-Bénigne, 6
Boulanger, 274
Boulogne, 664
Boulongne, 632
Bourbon, Louis-Henri, duc de, 367, 395, 660 n
Bourdon, 134
Bourdon-Desplanches, L.-J., 265–66 n
Bouret, 356
Bourg-la-Reine, 278
Bourges, 188 n, 193, 226
Bourgthéroulde, 188 n, 453
Bourguignon, 637
Boutin, intendant of Bordeaux 1760–66, 133, 216
Boynes, Pierre-Etienne Bourgeois de, 624–27
Bray, 633
—procurator at, 306
bread, xx, 104, 120, 169, 172, 192, 202, 203, 233, 238 n, 255, 279, 311, 321–23, 328–43, 345, 350–53, 355, 375–77, 413, 431, 432, 438, 443, 447, 473, 477, 505, 526, 539, 544, 564–65, 567, 589, 598, 603, 608, 609, 647, 648, 660, 662, 673, 681, 684, 702

—fabrication, 335–39, 350–51
—"fantasy," 336
—price fixation, 335–39
—prices, 340, 341, 411, 428, 432, 433, 472, 482–87, 498, 507–09, 517, 518, 521, 522, 524, 526, 564, 581, 626, 661, 662
—quality, 338, 375–77
—thrift, 339
Bretoncelle, 275
Brevant, 188 n
Briare, canal of, 270
Briatte, Jean-Baptiste, xxiv n, 433 n, 602
Bricoteau, 336
Brie, 193, 198, 270, 271, 277, 280, 286, 287, 288, 290, 296, 356, 500, 502
Brie-Comte-Robert, 195, 311, 375 n, 502, 515
Brissot de Warville, Jacques-Pierre, 428 n
Brittany, 123–24, 204, 209, 225, 230, 269, 277, 296, 529, 556, 557, 563, 564, 579, 619, 631, 643
—Estates of, 451, 529
—intendants of, 75, 133, 214, 226 n, 230, 496, 552 n, 557, 562, 576 n, 580, 651, 658
—nobility of, 528–29
—Parlement of, 154, 159, 183, 184, 451, 529, 530 n, 556, 558, 619
Brittany Affair, xxix, xxxi, 154, 408, 410, 425, 521, 524, 527, 528, 697
—constitutional crisis, 153, 526, 610
Brocq, 361
Brasses, Charles de, 522, 523, 525
Brunetière, Ferdinand, 592
Buquet, César, 285
Bureau of Commerce, 137, 167, 244
Burgundy, 285, 493, 497, 502, 504, 553, 575, 619, 620, 626, 631, 632, 633, 635, 641
—intendants of, 107 n, 504, 553, 562, 575, 620 n, 636
—Parlement of, 493, 496, 497, 514, 558, 569 n, 619

Cadet de Vaux, Antoine-Alexis, 351
Caen, 188, 319, 493, 503, 560, 564, 616
—intendant of, 511 n, 537, 541, 561, 562, 563, 576 n
—police of, 560, 571
Cahen, Léon, xxvi n, 382 n
Cairo, 642
Caisse d'Escompte, 384

Calas, Jean, 154
Calonne, Charles-Alexandre de,
—intendant of Metz 1768–78, 191
—controller-general 1783–87, 387, 629
Cambrai, 498
—subdelegate of, 503
Canada, 622
Carentan, 188 n
Caron, 311
Caribbean, 622
Carrière, Charles, 488 n
Castres, 565
Châlons-sur-Marne, 188 n, 190, 193, 200,
    277, 633, 645 n
—municipal officers of, 202, 227
chambers of commerce, 121, 123, 133, 165,
    457, 622 n, 656, 695
Champagne, 204, 210, 221, 269, 271, 277,
    282 n, 285, 499, 502, 504, 555, 560, 564,
    570, 621
—intendant of, 194 n, 226 n, 230, 264 n,
    504, 537, 541 n, 561, 564 n, 647–48
—subdelegates of, 561
Champassais, 207
Charenton, 365, 390
charity, 323, 504
Charly, 288, 51 5
Chartres, 195, 209, 310
Châteauneuf, dealer registration list, 285 n
Châtelet (Paris), 66, 74, 268, 426, 428; see also
    police of Paris
Châtellerault, 188 n
Châtillon-sur-Loing, 201
—fiscal procurator of, 305
Chaumont, 270, 499
—police of, 537 n
Chaunu, Pierre, xxiv n
Chavannes, 428 n, 430, 432, 437
Cherbourg, 188, 567 n
cherté, 102, 104, 204–06, 208, 211, 222, 230,
    235, 237, 253–54, 267–68, 270, 274, 281,
    322, 330, 341, 368, 374–77, 392–93, 396,
    398, 405, 410, 412–13, 417, 428–29,
    439–41, 443, 447, 462, 470, 479, 493, 510,
    513, 517–18, 521, 523, 528, 542, 571–73,
    587, 594, 619, 632, 651, 668
—definition of, 87
Chevalier, Antoine, 274
Chevreuse, royal procurator of, 538
China, 345

Choiseul, Etienne-François, duc de, 130, 142–
    43, 234, 250, 261, 320, 322, 346,361, 366,
    369, 370, 382, 492, 500, 520, 527, 530–31,
    592–93, 607, 615, 619, 624, 627, 649
Christian-agrarianism, 97
cities, 2, 31, 438, 463, 466, 469, 479–80, 481,
    523, 525, 584, 587, 679, 695–96
—versus country, 172, 182
Civitavecchia, 624
class struggle, 3, 259, 433, 449, 462, 503,
    542, 589, 601, 610
Claye, 287
Clément, 404, 433, 437
clergy and church, 398, 399, 647, 670, 671 n
coastwise trade, 138–39, 548, 577–79, 582,
    586
—admiralty courts, 579
Cobb, Richard, xxiii n, 429 n
Cobban, Alfred, 291
Code Duchesne, 68, 88
Cognac, 188 n
Colas, Jean-Claude, 288
Colbert, Jean-Baptiste, 1, 2, 38, 98, 112, 170,
    260, 697
—Colbertism, 460
commercial associations, 67, 285, 291–94, 536
companies, 247 n, 272, 291, 293–99, 302,
    358, 368, 419
competition, 96, 103, 462, 465, 682; see also
    laissez-faire and liberal theory
Compiègne, 188 n, 190
Condillac, Etienne Bonnot de, 650
Condorcet, Jean-Antoine-Nicolas de Caritat,
    marquis de, 88, 177 n, 222–24, 428 n, 442,
    448, 478–80, 610, 650
Congis, 311
Constantinople, 642, 644
consumer rights, 135, 169, 192–93, 198,
    208–11, 215, 437, 444, 448–49, 461, 476,
    479 n, 680–81
consumers, xxx, xxxi, 3, 66, 70–71, 94–95,
    104, 111, 125, 153, 156, 165, 172, 187,
    189, 192, 206, 209, 218, 221, 226, 231,
    254, 258–60, 267–68, 271–72, 283, 299,
    323, 329, 333–34, 339, 344, 351, 378, 398,
    413, 418, 431–33, 438, 448, 462, 467, 470,
    477, 495, 498, 500–01, 508, 532, 541–45,
    547, 550–51, 553, 555, 562–63, 565, 571,
    584, 587, 589, 599, 612–13, 621, 664 n,
    680–81, 685–86, 690, 694–95, 698, 701

Conti, Louis-François de Bourbon, prince de, 392 n, 600

Contrôle-Général 549

—bureaus of, 148, 206, 695

controllers-general, 15, 17, 24, 27, 42, 156; see also Dodun; Orry; Machault; Moreau de Séchelles; Moras; Silhouette; Bertin; Laverdy; Maynon d'Invau; Terray; Turgot

Copenhagen, 642

Copérieux, 296

Coquelin, commissaire of police of Paris, 508

Coquelin, Henry, 278–79

Coquereau, Jean-Baptiste-Louis, 249 n, 650, 651, 658

Corbeil, 188 n, 197–98, 221, 325–26, 336, 351–52, 363, 365, 367 n, 375–76, 378–80, 382–83, 385, 387–89, 424, 615, 621, 646–47, 674–75

Cosne, 188 n

Coulommiers, 188 n, 288, 291, 500

Courteille, 216, 244, 348, 357, 359, 364–66, 640, 663

Coutances, bailliage of, 483

Coyer, Gabriel-François, 32, 54, 112, 404

Craon, police of, 227

Crécy-en-Brie, 188 n, 197

Creuze-Latouche, Jacques-Antoine, 60, 73 n, 161–62

criminality, 192, 198, 205, 322, 428 n

Crosne, Louis Thiroux de, intendant of Rouen 1767–85, 423

Croy, Emmanuel, maréchal, duc de, 148, 210, 310, 364, 376

cultivators, 112, 120, 122, 137, 153, 172, 206, 237, 418, 438, 461, 463, 469, 540–41, 544, 558–59, 570, 572–73, 578, 587, 694; see also producers

Cypierre, Jean-François-Claude Perrin de, intendant of Orleans 1760–85, 196, 205, 214, 230–35, 250, 368–70, 372–73, 434 n, 559

Daguesseau, Henri-François, 79

Damiens, Robert-François, 131, 321, 445

Dammartin, 190, 204–05, 272, 287, 288, 297, 501

—fiscal procurator of, 307

Dampierre de la Salle, Picot de, 280

Dantzig, 367, 457, 506, 620, 621, 632, 634, 667, 700

Darnétal, 188 n, 453

Dauphiné, 188, 277, 281, 458 n, 621, 631

—intendant of, 466 n, 559, 580 n, 584

—parlement of, 154, 159, 177 n, 183, 222, 226 n, 247 n, 256, 264, 266 n, 281 n, 282, 394, 409, 412 n, 455 n, 457, 458 n, 459–64, 466 n, 468, 471, 476 n, 482, 524, 532 n, 583–84, 590

Daure, 381–82, 383, 385, 615–16, 629

dearths, 125, 344–45, 365, 396, 404–05, 429, 447, 463, 469, 475, 486, 491, 495, 502, 505, 523, 525, 540, 583, 589, 603, 608, 612, 626, 641, 652, 680, 692–93, 699, 701

—"artificial," 69, 88, 208, 217, 298, 429 n, 567, 582, 589, 650, 652, 685, 693

—definition of, 86–87

—of 1692–93, 55

—of 1709–10, 79, 86, 210, 310, 339, 373, 502, 692

—of 1725–26, 25, 81, 83–84, 86, 87, 89, 299, 319 n, 334, 373, 395, 453, 700

—of 1739–41, 26, 86–87, 89, 210, 299, 345, 373, 395, 458 n, 502, 700

—"real," xxi, 88, 693

debtors' prison, 340

Declaration of April 1723, 73, 76, 173, 204, 538 n

Declaration of May 1 763, 90–93, 96, 137–39, 141, 164, 173, 180, 184, 186, 187, 201, 203–04, 209, 225, 227, 233, 252, 268, 276, 282 n, 301, 303, 306–07, 411, 416, 418–19, 430, 448, 467, 492, 495, 513, 516, 573, 586, 664

—registration by parlements, 183, 185

de-commercialized zone, 71, 302

De Gourgues, see Gourgues

Delaitre, 340 53 n, 55, 62 n, 63, 67, 69 n, 71–72, 79, 82–83, 86, 88, 90, 98, 101–02, 173, 256, 327, 336, 352, 398, 406, 424, 457, 535, 547, 590, 604

Delasalle, 340

de-liberalization, xxxii, xxxiii, 491, 525–26, 532–90, 698–99

—balancing interests, 544, 553, 675

—"general subsistence," 546–49, 554

—the majority, 542–45, 589

—project for a new regulatory law, 515, 519–20, 533, 536 n, 539–41, 611–13

—savoir equals pouvoir, 549–54, 577–79, 699

—search for control, 554, 567–68, 577–81, 636, 699

demographic crises, xxiii, xxiv, xxvii, 344, 489, 502, 564, 692

—historiography of, xxiii, xxiv, xxv

Demolle, Antoine, 278
Demontvallier, 388
Deniloy, 206
depots of mendicancy, 383
deputies of commerce, 124, 159, 177 n, 261, 282
Desauze, Charles, 340
Desclaux, 641
Descosal, 342
Desmoulins, Camille, 674
Desruisseaux, 628 n, 641 n, 642
Dezobry, 288
Dialogues sur le commerce des blés, 591–611 ; see also Galiani
diamond necklace affair, 530
Diderot, Denis, 194, 257, 272 n, 377, 592, 594, 602, 604, 608–11, 687
Dieppe, 616
Dijon, 190, 493, 498, 499, 524, 619
disease, 207, 344, 351, 375–77, 424, 502, 564, 647, 692
Dodun, Charles-Gaspard, marquis d'Herbault, controller-general 1722–1726, 30, 38, 79, 81, 84, 89, 367, 453
Dombes, Parlement of, 493, 496
Doumerc *(père)*, 672
Doumerc, Daniel, 326, 354, 374, 385, 388, 615–18, 632–33, 646, 665, 671, 673, 700
Doumerc and Sorin, 618, 622, 624–25, 627, 629, 630–49, 667–73
—arrest of, 670–73
—indicted, 667–70
Dreux, 204, 272
Dronay, 306
Drouin, 634 n
Du Barry, Jeanne Bécu, comtesse, 298 n, 531, 563
DuCluzel, François–Pierre, intendant of Tours 1766–83, 226 n, 496, 540, 560
Dugny, 295, 297
Duhamel du Monceau, Henri–Louis, 112, 119, 177 n, 336, 351, 361, 426
Dupâquier, Jacques, xxiii, xxiv, xxvii
Duperron, Brillon, 366, 375, 387
Dupin, Claude, 9, 99, 105
Duplessis, 83, 84
Dupont de Nemours, Pierre-Samuel, 1, 33, 88, 106 n, 115, 131, 141–43, 146, 152, 188, 190, 220, 223–24, 255, 263, 380–81, 402, 404, 432, 460, 473, 476, 610, 650, 670, 681
Dupré de St.-Maur, Nicolas-François, 102
Dure, 385, 633

economic crisis, xxx, 322, 408, 488–89, 528, 529 n, 564–65, 692, 697–98
economic development, 150, 181, 433, 445, 464, 466, 480, 544–46, 681, 688–89
—"economic years," 117–18, 120–21
—economic assemblies, 121
—economic knowledge, 110
—economic press, 121, 137
économistes, 98, 114, 116–17, 121, 142–43, 146–47, 149, 150, 152–53, 161, 171, 176, 182, 220, 222–23, 225, 235, 237, 239, 244, 254–55, 258–60, 263, 265, 282, 338–39, 347, 380, 400, 403, 410, 422, 433–36, 457–58, 460, 472–74, 476, 478–81, 492, 529, 531, 541, 587, 590–99, 601, 603, 605–06, 608–10, 611 n, 615, 620, 650, 657, 675, 687–88, 691; see also physiocracy
Edict of July 1764, 90, 93–96, 139, 142, 164, 186, 205–06, 211, 227, 235, 242–43, 246–48, 257–58, 268, 301, 324, 411, 41
429–30, 459, 467, 495, 510, 573, 586, 598, 659 n, 691
—registration by parlements, 184, 185
Egypt, 674
Ehrard, Jacques, 97
Einaudi, Luigi, 596 n
Elbeuf, 188 n, 453
Embry, 639
enarrhement, 233, 240–41, 271, 289, 514, 536, 537 n; see also grain trade, abuses
Encyclopédie and encyclopedists, 101, 112, 113, 118, 403, 594, 611 n
engagistes, 28
England, 102, 118, 124, 150, 170–71, 351 n, 367 n, 435, 468, 600, 622, 629, 640, 671 n, 688
—anglomania, 118
Enlightenment, 6, 13, 89, 97, 102, 104, 107–08, 118, 140, 147–49, 151, 153, 216, 347, 397, 408, 591, 595, 604, 610, 611 n, 677, 682, 685–87, 689, 697
—*salons*, 147, 148, 206
—see also philosophes
Ephémérides du Citoyen, 122, 223, 255, 430 n, 459, 460, 466 n, 473, 475 n, 504
Epinay, Louise-Florence-Pétronille Tardieu d'Esclaves, marquise d', 504, 512, 593, 594, 596, 606, 624 n, 640
Esmangart, Charles-François-Hyacinthe, intendant of Bordeaux 1770–75, 534 n, 537, 540, 552–53, 557, 561, 580 n, 583, 635

Essonne, 365
Estates,
—of Brittany, 451
—of Languedoc, 160, 224, 368, 457, 464, 465–66
Etampes, 270–71, 276, 285, 404, 633
exportation, 64, 93, 104, 110–11, 124, 127, 132, 134,136–39,141–43, 146,156, 159–61, 164, 168, 170, 185–86, 188, 193, 200, 202, 206, 211, 227, 230, 242, 245–48, 254–56, 259–61, 266–69, 295, 297–99, 308, 352, 392, 398, 414–15, 417, 429–30, 437, 443–44, 454, 464–65, 488, 493, 498, 505, 510, 519, 523, 573, 580–81, 583, 585–86, 598, 599 n, 619, 642–43, 651–52, 659 n, 668 n, 691, 695
—and internal circulation, 266, 267, 268, 269
—confusion with removals and internal circulation, 19, 189, 255 n, 267 n
—export accounts, 260–63
—export ceiling, 167, 211, 242, 243, 245, 247, 414, 429, 459, 488, 510, 580, 691
—illicit, 138, 139, 261, 519, 576–81

factors and brokerage system, 90, 196, 275, 287, 291, 304, 305, 326, 340; see also flour merchants and grain trade
Faguet, Emile, 608
famine, 86, 87, 205, 542, 565, 587, 659
famine plots, xx, xxxii, 26, 49–50, 96, 160–62,247 n, 251, 293–94, 321, 346–47, 349, 354, 356, 367–77, 390–406,416, 419,443, 447–48, 455, 501, 522–26, 541, 557, 588, 590,601 n, 614, 628–29, 633–35, 640–41, 648–76, 700–01
—rumors, 419–20, 463, 516, 519, 650–52, 657–58
—Russian-American wheat deals of 1972–73, 400
Faremoutiers, 198, 500
Fécamp, 188 n
Feraud, 644, 645
Feray, 627, 632
fermiers, 67, 94, 153, 288, 293, 500, 501, 515, 539, 558, 570; see also cultivators and laboureurs
Ferray, 334
Feuquières, marquis de, 285
Feydeau de Brou, Charles-Henri, intendant of Rouen 1757–62, 128–30, 136, 453

—fiscality and fiscal reform, 2, 81–85, 118, 1 26, 140, 145, 150–52, 158–59, 169, 172–73, 182, 187, 258, 286, 397, 432, 439, 445–46, 456 n, 466, 477, 554, 561, 571, 573, 584, 649–50, 674–75, 678, 697
—fiscal crisis, xxviii, 489–90, 528
—see also liberalization, thesis of fiscality Flanders, 369, 670 n
—intendant of, 267 n
—Parlement of, 18p n
Fleury, Andre–Hercule, Cardinal de, 367
floating population, 2, 424, 50l ; see also population and mendicancy
flour, xx, 335, 337, 340, 352, 353, 365, 376, 379, 506, 508, 510 n, 539, 558, 622, 623, 639, 648, 668, 702
—flour crises, xx, 310–11
—productivity of, 337
—quality of, 254 n, 337, 338, 374–77, 386
—seconds, 353
—trade in, 90, 275, 279, 297
—see also millers and milling
flour merchants and mealmen, 47, 84, 85, 195, 275, 276, 285, 287, 295, 311, 340, 374, 404, 539
Flour War, xxx, 7, 446–47, 453, 509, 566 n, 603, 628 n, 650 n, 657, 670, 672, 675, 683, 697
Fontenay-le-Comte, 493 n
Fontette, Jean-François d'Orceau de, intendant of Caen 1752–75, 511 n, 537, 541, 561–63, 576 n
foodways, xx
—ersatz, xx, 502, 621, 681, 702
—see also potato and rice
Forbonnais, François Vèron Duverger de, 111, 175, 361 n, 689 n
forestalling, 68; see also grain trade, abuses
Foucaud, Charles, 45, 77
Fougeroux, 426
Foulon, Joseph-Frantçois, 394, 673
France, rural, 152, 153, 172–74, 182
Franche-Comté, 270, 492, 497, 498, 619, 668 n
—intendant of, 230
—Parlement of, 184, 185 n, 493, 517–19, 523–24, 558
Frankfurt, 640
Franklin, Benjamin, 362, 383, 384, 477
frontier trade, 138, 139

Fréche, Georges, xxvi, xxix, xxvii, 694 n
freemasonry, 363
fundamental law, 154, 155, 187, 422, 462
futures, 68, 211, 271, 289, 493, 514, 519,
    536; see also grain trade, abuses

Galiani, Ferdinando, 88, 92 n, 146, 157,
    171, 175, 179, 187, 257–59, 265–68, 326,
    426 n, 429 n, 447 n, 449, 458 n, 474 n,
    504–05, 512, 591–611, 624 n, 688
Gallardon, royal procurator of, 515
Ganneron, 204–05
Gamier, 244, 245
Gars de Frémainville, 443
Gasville, de, intendant of Rouen, 453
Gâtinais, 311, 368
Gaudet, 347–48, 354–55, 358
Gautier, Etienne–Balthazar, 642–44
Gazette de l'agriculture, du commerce, des arts et des
    finances, 493
Gazette du commerce, de l'agriculture, et des finances,
    235
Gehier, 553
General Farm, 94, 156, 261, 294, 397, 576,
    577
General Hospital, 145, 350, 353, 356, 366,
    380, 388
Geneva, 345
Geoffrin, MarieTherese Rodet, 594
Germany, 621, 622
Giat, 504
Gibert, François, 273–74
God, 438, 476, 478, 480, 605, 620, 688
Goguel, 623–24
Gonesse, 34–35, 273, 287, 295, 311, 505
Goriot, 275
Gottis, 639
Goubert, Pierre, xx, xxi n, xxiii, 91 n, 291,
    488 n
Goudar, Ange, 113
Gourgues, de, intendant of Montauban, 134,
    214, 230
Gournay, Vincent de, 106, 113–14, 133, 148,
    478 n
Gournay, 188 n, 453
grain, xix n, 103, 209, 340, 365, 379, 476–77,
    535, 543, 597, 599, 626, 673, 678, 681,
    683, 690, 694, 701–02
—cereal-dependence, xx, xxi
—conservation, xxii, 68, 335, 351, 361, 364,
    373

—passports, 578–79, 580 n; see also lettres de
    voiture
—price of, 145, 412, 417, 427, 435; see also
    prices
—quality of, xx, 156, 197, 198, 254 n,
    374–77, 386
grain department, 16, 156, 366, 386–87, 494,
    512, 615, 630–31, 635–36, 645, 662–63
grain trade, xxvii, 52, 65, 68, 70, 1 33, 135,
    344, 352, 398, 430–32, 437, 444, 448, 463,
    465, 468, 471, 476–77, 482–83, 493, 496,
    514–16, 519, 532, 534–37, 540, 550, 555–
    58, 569–70, 572, 574, 582, 586, 588, 595,
    597, 611 n, 615, 635, 652, 668, 679–80,
    690–91, 694, 698–700, 702
—abuses, 269–71, 276, 420, 438, 448, 515,
    519, 535, 537, 557, 561, 567, 574–76, 583,
    586
—and capitalist entrepreneurs, 133, 280, 293
—and nobles, 277
—commissioners, 66, 71, 291
—earnest money, 271
—new faces in, 201, 205, 276–93
—promotion of, 238–41, 246
—regulations, 52, 65–66, 70; see also police of
    provisioning
—sale on samples, 570
Graisivaudan, dealer registration List, 285 n
granaries,
—private, 138, 193, 197, 211–12, 227,
    268–69, 271, 277, 286–87, 290, 292–93,
    465, 513, 515, 538, 561–62, 567,–612
—private, visits to, 195, 197
—public, 9, 89, 170, 245, 260, 324 n, 345,
    403, 598, 673, 699
Grand, Ferdinand, 384, 386, 389
Grand Conseil, 411
"grand hiver" of 1709, 87; see also dearths
Grange, Henri, 602 n
Greece, 644
Grenoble, 524, 583, 584
—Parlement of, see Parlement of Dauphiné
Gréve, port of the, 90; see also Paris, ports of
Grimm, Friedrich Melchior, 105, 168, 595,
    602, 610, 640, 687
—Correspondance littéraire, 431 n
Grimperel, 334, 341–42
Guard, French and Swiss, 275, 296, 381, 615
Guernsey, Isle of, 369
Guillaume, 342
Guillot, Urbain, 278

Guyenne, 466 n, 565, 566
Guys, Pierre-Augustin, 642–45, 663, 672
Guys and Company, 625, 642–45, 668

Hainaut, 202, 206, 230, 277, 474 n, 503,
    555, 560, 570, 670 n
—intendants of, 133 n, 230, 247, 538 n, 541
    n, 561, 562, 619, 652
—subdelegate of, 281 n, 284 n
Halle, Claude, 275
Halles, 66, 83, 90, 191, 197, 274–75, 285–87,
    296–98, 300, 304 n, 310–11, 324–26, 328,
    330, 333, 340–41, 352, 365, 374, 377–78,
    382, 384, 404, 619, 626, 649, 675
Hamburg, 367 n
Hardy, 308, 320–21, 323 n, 425, 443, 505,
    510–11, 519, 521–22, 527, 563, 651, 662
harvests, xx, 192, 200, 205, 207–08, 241,
    245, 253–54, 307, 344, 367 n, 381, 398,
    427, 439, 446, 456 n, 458 n, 466 n, 468,
    474, 481–82, 488, 497, 502, 505, 513,
    517, 549–50, 563–64, 567, 611–12, 621,
    622 n, 626, 631, 634, 637, 690, 693–94,
    698
—appearances and espérances, 141, 549, 563
Henri IV, 93, 165, 321
Henry, Louis, xxiii
Hérault, René, lieutenant general of police
    1725–1739, 39, 48, 84, 365
Herbert, Claude-Jacques, 92 n, 101–111,
    117, 121, 124, 134, 177 n, 400, 449
Herman, 497
Hettard, 275
hoarding, 68, 204–05, 212, 240, 268–69,
    271, 293, 295, 301–02, 385, 414, 417,
    419, 482, 497, 500, 513, 515, 517–19,
    540, 544, 547, 567, 569–70, 580, 583,
    609 Hocquart, 157, 427, 458 n
Holbach, Paul-Henri-Dietrich, baron d', 594,
    610
Holland, 367 n, 382, 617, 619, 620, 622, 645
Hôpital General, see General Hospital
Hôtel de Ville (Paris), 66, 74, 90, 168–71,
    174, 272, 322, 351, 389, 426, 555; see also
    prévôt des marchands
Hôtel-Dieu (Paris), 322, 426, 647 n
Houdan, 517
Hume, David, 591
Hurepoix, 286
importation, 95, 429, 470, 487–88, 618, 644

Indies Company, 58, 362, 367, 395 industry,
    259, 260, 398, 445, 464, 469 n, 489, 564,
    598, 605
infanticide, 503
inns and cabarets, 197, 202, 292, 293, 306
inspections and inventories of grain, 212,
    493, 515; see also granaries, private and pro-
    visioning by constraint
Institut National d'Etudes Démographiques,
    xxviii n, xxix
intendants, 2, 16, 18, 19, 42, 65, 106, 123,
    126, 128, 150, 156, 203, 229, 324–25, 348,
    386, 493, 496, 507, 511, 520, 534, 535,
    536 n, 539, 549–52, 554, 573–77, 579,
    585, 615, 620, 657, 663, 666
—of Alençon, see Levignen and Jullien
—of Auvergne, see Balinvilliers and Monthyon
—of Bordeaux, see Boutin and Esmangart
—of Brittany, see Lebret, Agay de Mutigny,
    and Bacquencourt
—of Burgundy, see Jean-François Joly de
    Fleury and Amelot de Chaillou
—of Caen, see Fontette
—of Champagne, see Rouille d'Orfeuil
—of Dauphiné, see Pajot de Marcheval
—of Flanders, see LeFevre de Caumartin
—of Franche–Comté, see La Corée
—of Hainaut, see Boismont and Taboureau
    des Reaux
—of Languedoc, see Saint-Priest
—of Limousin, see Turgot
—of Lorraine, see La Galaizière
—of Metz, see Calonne
—of Montauban, see Gourgues
—of Orléans, see Cypierre
—of Paris, see Louis-Jean Bertier de Sauvigny and
    Louis–Bénigne–François Bertier de Sauvigny
—of Picardy, see Agay de Mutigny
—of Poitou, see La Bourdonnaye de Blossac
—of Provence, see La Tour
—of Rouen, see Gasville, Feydeau de Brou,
    La Michodière, and Crosne
—of Soissons, see LePeletier de Morfontaine
—of Tours, see Lescalopier and DuCluzel
internal grain circulation, liberty of, 64–65,
    100, 103, 106, Il l, 127, 133–34, 136–38,
    141, 173, 186, 209, 232, 257, 261–62, 267,
    299, 398, 430, 494–97, 511–14, 532–35,
    541, 548, 557, 568, 580–81, 585–86, 595,
    597–98, 634, 638, 658, 691

internal grain embargoes, 493, 495 n, 496, 513

Italy, 262, 468, 622 n, 625–26, 634, 643–44, 668

Jacobinism, 406
Jansenists, 674
Jarry, 306–07
Jausse, François, 294, 298
Jersey, Isle of, 161, 369 786
Jesuits, 163, 180, 530, 531, 671 n
Joigny, 188 n
Joinville, 493 n, 499
Joly de Fleury, Guillaume-François, procurator general of the Paris Parlement 1717–1746, 39, 41, 50, 83, 453
Joly de Fleury, Guillaume-François-Louis, procurator general of the Paris Parlement 1746–1771, 46, 73–74, 202–03, 205, 207, 218–19, 221, 226, 229, 238, 268–69, 271, 272, 295–96, 306, 307, 321, 410, 412, 426, 440, 495, 501–02, 515–16, 533, 538, 541–42
Joly de Fleury, Jean-François, intendant of Burgundy 1749–1760, 1 07 n
Joly de Fleury, Omer, advocate general of the Paris Parlement, 1746–68, 171–76, 178, 180, 186, 225, 432
Joly de Fleury, Omer-Louis-François, procurator general of the Paris Parlement 1771–74, 80, 647
Jones, John Paul, 346, 362
Jourdain, Catherine, 272
Journal d'agriculture, du commerce, des arts et des finances, 60
Journal de commerce, 112
Journal de commerce et d'agriculture, 167
Journal de Trévoux, 61, 105–06, 109, 449
Journal des sçavans, 108
Journal économique, 61, 62, 105, 109, 117, 164, 175, 187, 277, 321, 350
Jullien, Antoine-lean-Baptiste, intendant of Alençon 1766–90, 263–64 n, 538, 553, 580 n, 651
just price, 58–59, 202, 306, 546, 612

Kennedy, John F., 400
king's grain, xxx, xxxi, xxxii, 86, 89, 90, 95, 197, 248–49, 301, 325–26, 343–407, 424, 439, 444, 446, 448, 455, 462–63, 470, 482,

491, 496, 499, 507, 547, 548 n, 564, 582, 585–86, 607, 614–76, 692, 699–700
—quality of king's grain and flour, 373–77, 625, 647
—*see also* public provisioning
kingship, xxx, 6, 15, 91, 152, 154–55, 202, 396, 408–09, 430, 438, 440, 443–44, 446, 448–50, 456, 461–62, 470–71, 478, 520, 542–43, 585, 587–88, 599–600, 601 n, 613, 650, 664, 680–84, 686, 697, 699–700; see also paternalism
Koch, Philip, 593 n, 606 n

La Barre, Jean-François Lefèvre, 408
Labbé, 342
LaBouille, 188 n, 453
La Bourdonnaye de Blossac, Paul-Esprit-Marie de, intendant of Poitou 1751–84, 619
laboureurs, 40, 67–69, 71–72, 76, 82–83, 85, 135, 153, 164, 169–70, 173, 196, 198, 204, 218, 269–71, 288, 290, 302, 304, 306, 325, 327, 368, 374, 404, 439, 500–02, 507, 514–16, 518, 536, 539, 543, 557–60, 562, 568, 570–73, 613, 627; see also cultivators *and* fermiers
Labrousse, Ernest, xxiv, xxv, xxix, 263 n
La Chalotais, Louis–René de Caradeuc de, 21, 93 n, 124 n, 147 n, 154, 159, 164–65, 339, 409, 583
La Corée, Charles-André de, intendant of Franche-Comte 1761–84, 230
La Ferté-Bernard, 188 n
La Ferté-Gaucher, 188 n, 190, 196, 288
La Ferté-sous-Jouarre, 286, 288
La Flèche, 188 n
La Galaizière, Antoine Chaumont de, intendant of Lorraine 1766–77, 230
Lagny, 190, 288, 501
—fiscal procurator, 305
laissez-faire, xxviii, xxx, 95, 103, 125, 133, 225, 450, 470, 478, 487, 546–47, 552, 612, 664, 682, 687–91; see also competition *and* liberal theory
Lambert, 276
La Michodière, intendant of Rouen 1762–67, 415
La Mortellerie, rue de (Paris), 291
Landescq, dealer registration list, 292
Langres, 270

Languedoc, 264, 277, 458 n, 466, 548, 565, 586–90, 666
—Estates of, 160, 224, 368, 457, 464–66, 552 n
—intendant of, 231 n, 580 n, 636
—parlement of, 154, 160, 404, 457, 466, 573, 582, 586–90
La Nouvelle France (Paris), 340
Lapareillé, Sébastien, 342
Laperde, 278
La Place, 276
La Reynie, Gabriel-Nicolas, lieutenant general of police 1667–1697, 57, 89
Larocheguyon, 51 7
La Rochelle, 619, 622, 666
—Chamber of Commerce, 622 n
La Tour, Charles-Jean-Baptiste des Gallois de, intendant of Provence 1744–71, 126, 624, 626, 643
Laverdy, Clément-Charles-François de, controller–general 1763–1768, 142, 158, 168–69, 180, 185–86, 215–19, 221, 225–41, 243–48, 295–96, 301, 308, 310, 320, 327, 338–39, 346, 349, 356, 358–59, 366–67, 369–73, 386, 392–94, 400, 411, 414–15, 419, 452, 454, 456, 467, 490, 499, 557, 560, 569, 614, 630, 642, 646, 648, 650, 652, 656–57, 685
—background and appointment, 140
—disgrace of, 249
—execution of, 25 1
—his liberalism, 241–45, 249
Law, John, 98, 277, 362, 659
Lebeque, 430
Leblanc, 320
Lebret, intendant of Brittany 1753–65, 230
Lebrun, Charles-François, 249 n
Leclerc, 295
Lefebvre, 262, 431, 435
Lefebvre, Pierre, 29 1
Le Havre, 170, 243, 262, 579, 632
LeFèvre de Caumartin, Antoine-Louis-François, intendant of Flanders 1756–78, 267 n
Leleu brothers, 376, 388, 675
Lelievre, Antoine, 271
Lemaire, 13
Lemercier de la Rivière, Pierre-Paul-François-Joachim-Henri, 73 n, 87, 114, 152, 477 n, 530, 604–07

Lenoir, Jean-Charles-Pierre, lieutenant general of police 1776–85, 35 n, 336, 376, 399, 529 n, 530 n
Lenormant, 305
Lentherie, 666
LePeletier de Morfontaine, Louis, intendant of Soissons 1765–84, 504
Lepelletier, 157, 427, 431–34, 437
Leprévost de Beaumont, Jean–Charles Guillaume, 160–61, 247 n, 251, 297, 321, 347, 349–50, 354, 356, 368, 372, 374, 389–406, 424, 455, 633, 648, 650, 701
Leray de Chaumont, Jacques–Donatien, 245–46, 262, 282, 360–63, 366, 368, 372, 374, 377–84, 387, 614–18, 624, 629, 639, 646, 700
Leroi, 112
Le Roy Ladurie, Emmanuel, xxviii n, xxix
Lescalopier, Gaspard-César-Charles de, intendant of Tours 1756–66, 158, 216
Lespinasse, Julie-Jeanne–Eieonore de, 663
Letrosne, Guillaume–François, 114, 122, 141, 177 n, 222–23, 244, 472–73, 477
letters patent of November 1768, 225, 319, 418–24
lettres de cachet, 330, 343, 463, 665
lettres de voiture, 69, 200; *see also* grain, passports
Levant, 634, 645, 668, 700
Levignen, Louis–François Lallemant de, intendant of Alençon 1726–1 766, 74, 134
Levy, Darline G. S., 602 n liberalism, 91, 148, 150, 153
—definition of, 97
—*see also* liberal movement; liberal theory; parlements, libera l
liberalization, xxx, 97, 116–17, 123, 142–43, 149–51, 213, 217, 252–99, 358–59, 378, 392, 396, 412, 418, 427, 441, 443, 445–46, 451–52, 464, 471, 490–91, 495, 503, 521, 527–29, 531, 543–44, 570, 572, 591–92, 594, 599, 604, 607, 609, 648, 664, 684, 689–90, 692–95, 701–02
—early critique of, 167–78
—explanations of, 144–62
—political implications of, 155, 171, 449–50, 599–601, 607–08
—reform laws of 1763–64, 154, 157, 161, 183, 202, 249, 406, 415, 437, 455, 482, 535, 583, 587, 682, 690–91, 693; *see also* Declaration of May 1763 *and* Edict of July 1764

liberal movement, 107, 111, 1 21–24, 137–38, 163, 166, 169, 243–44, 252, 400, 409–10, 481, 529, 530 n, 556, 680–81, 683, 686, 689, 693, 695
—fiscal blackmail, 160, 466, 578, 586, 587 n
—liberal press, 482–83
—see also liberalism and parlements, liberal
liberal theory, 416, 418–19, 421–22, 435, 605, 686–87, 691, 695; see also economistes and physiocracy
liberty, xxxi, xxxii, 61–63, 96, 97, 100, 104, 137, 405, 413, 416, 425, 430–31, 433–35, 437–38, 462–63, 465–66, 469–70, 472–73, 480–81, 486, 496, 518, 525, 534–37, 540, 547, 568–69, 579, 583, 585, 587, 590, 595–96, 600–01, 603–05, 609–12, 620, 664, 669, 670 n, 682, 687–89, 691, 693
—total, 110, 115, 133, 135, 141, 164, 169, 234, 416, 418, 422–23, 425, 430, 434, 447, 459, 464–65, 476, 477 n, 482, 495, 586, 588, 598, 600 n, 605, 612, 688, 691
Libourne, 195
Lille, 375
—dealer registration list, 293
Limeil, 376
Limousin, 493, 505, 618, 620
—intendant of, 133, 141, 146, 222, 230, 368 n, 505, 512, 611–13, 618, 620, 634 n, 650, 681 n
Linguet, Simon-Nicolas-Henri, 6, 33, 87, 92 n, 146, 179, 265, 350, 447, 449 n, 461, 474 n, 602, 658, 670, 675
Liron, 639
Lisieux, 134
Lisse, 375
Lizy, 288, 306
Locke, John, 101, 112
Loing, 498
Loire (River), 170
London, 319 n, 667, 700
"long run," xxiv–xxv, xxxiii, 595
—the event, xxiv
Lons-le-Saunier, 498
Lorraine, 230, 282 n, 345, 493 n, 499, 502, 563, 670 n
—intendant of, 230
—Parlement of, 493, 496, 564 n
Louis XIV, 6, 321, 492
Louis XV, xxiv, xxv, xxx, xxxi, xxxii, 7, 90, 96, 146–47, 151–53, 162, 164–66, 183, 202, 225, 234, 320–22, 344, 368–69, 371,

380, 393, 395, 397, 401–02, 410–11, 413, 415, 417–19, 423, 425, 436–41, 443–45, 458 n, 462–68, 470–71, 481–82, 495, 514–15, 520, 521 n, 528, 530–31, 535, 545, 550, 553–54, 565, 567, 571, 583, 584–86, 588, 618, 650–51, 655, 659–61, 674, 692, 697, 701
—public relations of, 346, 445, 648, 684–85, 701
—see also kingship and paternalism
Louis XVI, 660–61
Louviers, 453
Lübeck, 367 n
Lüthy, Herbert, 700
Lunel, 639
Lyonnais, 619, 631
Lyons, 345, 385, 498, 620 n

Mabille, 285, 297
Mably, Gabriel Bonnot de, 6, 146, 157, 602
Machault, Jean–Baptiste, sieur d'Arnouville, controller general 1745–54, 26, 89–90, 99–100, 106 n, 118, 127–28, 249, 347–48, 356, 630, 640, 663, 699
Machurin, 325, 340, 352
Magny, 188 n, 311
Malesherbes, Chrétien-Guillaume de Lamoignon de, 188 n, 443 n
Malisset, Antoine-Charles, 353–54, 356 n, 364
Malisset, Jean-Baptiste, 354
Malisset, Pierre-Simon, 262, 294, 310, 325–26, 336, 347–89, 390–92, 394, 400–01, 406, 419, 424, 463, 507, 614, 616–18, 630, 632–33, 646–49, 669, 673 n, 701
Malouin, Paul-Jacques, 32, 350
Malthus, Thomas R., 429 n, 433
Mamers, 188 n, 193
Mantes, 203, 272, 278, 516–17
Manuel, Louis-Pierre, 350, 394
Marans, 620
maréchaussée, 198, 221, 229, 271, 273, 280, 501, 561, 566, 684
Maria-Theresa, 660–61
Marie-Antoinette, 661, 674
Marion, Marcel, 250 n
marketing obligations, 68–70, 74–77, 128–29, 136, 138, 173, 201–02, 204, 212, 223, 437, 493, 514, 437, 493, 514, 536–38, 556, 559, 560–62, 568–69

—market organization, 534, 679–80, 690, 694

—*see also* grain trade

Marnville de la Roque, 297–98

Marseilles, 125, 345, 488 n, 586, 625–26, 634, 637, 641–45, 668

—bureau of abundance of, 643

—chamber of commerce of, 133

—merchants of, 625–26

—*négociants* of, 643

Martin, Henri, 249 n

Marville, Claude–Henri Feydeau de, lieutenant general of police 1739–47, 89, 365

Masson, 212

Mathiez, Albert, 700

Maubeuge, dealer registration list, 292

Maupeou, René-Nicolas-Charles-Augustin de, xxxi, xxxiii, 321, 408, 411–13, 426, 428 n, 436, 520–23, 525–28, 610, 628, 671 n, 674

—"coup d'état" of, 155, 520–31, 558, 697–98

Maupertuis, Pierre-Louis-Moreau de, 101

Maurepas, Jean-Frédéric Phélypeaux, comte de, 17 n, 660

Mauriac, 498

Maurs, municipality of, 503

Mauzi, Robert, 97

Maynon d'Invau, Etienne, controller general October 1768–December 1769, 234, 250, 321, 328, 380–83, 419, 482–84, 486–88, 490, 492, 496, 592, 614

measurers of grain, 28, 47–48, 69, 274, 304 n, 310, 385, 426

Meaux, 198, 253 n, 275, 285, 289, 500–02

—dealer registration list, 288–93

—royal procurator, 502

Mediterranean, 634, 644

Melon, Jean-François, 98, 399

Melun, 205, 253 n

Mémoires secrets, by Bachaumont, etc., 671

mendicancy, 198, 207, 398, 501, 504

—*see also* floating population

mercantilism, 2, 98, 464, 689

—neo-mercantilism, 110

—*see also* Colbertism

merchants, 53–55, 66–67, 69, 71–73, 75, 83, 85, 103, 122, 133, 170, 192–96, 204, 211, 220–21, 224, 226, 240, 267, 269, 275, 280–81, 284–85, 289–91, 299, 303–05, 324, 327, 340, 352, 374, 405, 430–31, 437, 444, 457, 462, 465, 477, 483, 513–19, 532, 535–37, 547–48, 555, 560–63, 567, 570, 574–75, 578, 580, 582–83, 590, 597–98, 612–13, 615, 618–19, 622, 635–36, 639, 666, 680, 691, 694, 698, 702

—"for the provisioning of Paris," 37, 39, 67, 70, 76–77, 285, 287, 291, 301, 537–38, 555 n, 569

—police view of, 54–55

—registration and declaration, 66–72, 211–12, 513, 536, 562

—rehabilitation, 238–41

—reputation, 53–54

—*see also* flour merchants; millers; grain trade

Mercier, Louis-Sébastien, 32–34, 35 n, 56, 92 n, 146, 191, 260, 428 n, 442, 506 n, 602–03

Mercure de France, 185

mercuriale, 326, 508, 593

Mercy-Argenteau, Florimond-Claude, comte de, 660–61

Mergue, 639

Méry-sur-Seine, 270, 515

Metz, 519, 499 n, 670 n

—intendant of, 191

—Parlement of, 184, 439 n, 493, 497, 511 n, 519, 525 n, 556, 558, 652

Meulan, 207, 311, 515

—procurator of, 237

Meuvret, Jean, xxiii

Meyer, Jean, 529 n

Michelet, Jules, xxvii, 92 n

Midi, xxxii, 452, 459, 557, 565–67, 572, 581, 589, 637, 644, 668, 692

—"Flour War" of 1773, 565–67, 589

military provisioning, 2, 345, 356 n, 358, 617, 619, 668, 673

millers, 40, 47, 54, 68, 84, 195–96, 275–76, 285, 287–88, 290–91, 293, 295–96, 305, 310–11, 336–37, 341, 349, 352, 377, 501, 539, 558, 614, 702

milling, 120, 364–65, 388, 506, 639

—bolting, 336

—economic, 276, 279, 296, 336–38, 350–51, 353, 355, 357 n, 364, 366, 473, 702

—gross, 336–37

—middlings, 337 n

—regrinding, 337, 353

—*see also* flour

Mirabeau, Victor de Riquetti, marquis de, 113–14, 152, 182, 399, 444, 473–74, 480, 530, 591, 611 n

Mirlavaud, 356–57, 366, 386, 658–59, 670

Miromesnil, Armand-Thomas Hue, marquis de, 21, 186, 248, 273, 369–70, 429, 454, 456–57, 664 n

misery, 198, 200, 207, 209–10, 231, 413, 416, 433, 448, 455, 468, 502–04, 513, 525–27, 561, 563–65, 580, 671, 692, 697

Missonnet, 77

modernization, xxviii, 678, 688–89

Moheau, 192, 666

Molière, Jean-Baptiste Poquelin de, 593

Monginot, Henry, 294

Moniteur, 157, 394, 651

monopoly and monopolists, 26, 56, 57, 59–63, 67, 75, 77, 95, 100, 109, 125, 173, 204, 209, 211, 231, 244, 247 n, 248, 268, 272, 293, 296, 319, 350, 377, 392, 398, 401, 403, 413, 417, 419, 420–21, 423–24, 427, 430–31, 438, 443, 459, 463, 465, 492, 513, 516, 522–26, 535, 537, 540, 542, 555–56, 562, 567, 569, 571, 573, 575, 587, 589, 612, 628, 634, 648, 650–53, 655–58, 660–61, 668, 670

Montaran, 387, 645

Montargis, 195, 202, 272

Montauban, 214, 230, 565, 639, 672
—intendant of, 134, 214, 230

Montaudouin de la Touche, Jean-Gabriel, 110–11, 124, 245, 634 n

Montblin, Michau de, 428 n, 433

Montereau, 188 n, 193, 221, 273
—procurator at, 305

Montesquieu, Charles de Secondat, baron de, 6, 101, 448, 604

Monteynard, marquis de, 567

Montgolfier, 220–21, 224

Monthyon, Antoine-Jean–Baptiste-Robert Auget de, intendant of Auvergne 1767–71, 230, 383, 504, 618, 620, 621

Montlhéry, 188 n, 190, 276, 515
—royal procurator at, 296

Montpellier, 459 n, 565, 621, 639

Montrésor, 188 n, 212

moral economy, 194 n

Moras, Franoçois-Marie Peirenc de, controller-general 1756–57, 126, 453 n

Moreau, 268–69, 428, 674

Moreau, Jacob-Nicolas, 131, 659

Moreau de Séchelles, controller-general 1754–56, 106 n, 348

Morellet, André, 131, 143, 265, 326, 447 n, 601 n, 610

Morelly, 448

Morin, René, 340

Morineau, Michel, xxvi, xxviii, xxix

Murard, 430

Nancy, 499 n, 503, 563

Nantes, 170, 206, 243–47, 495 n, 506, 615, 618, 620, 634
— juges-consuls of, 537 n
—*négociants* of, 556, 618–19, 634 n

Naples, 624, 627

Narbonne, 459 n
—archbishop of, 578, 588
—*négociants* of, 578, 586 n

Narbonne, Pierre de, 30

nature and natural law, 111, 115–16, 150, 152, 155, 209, 215, 224, 265, 422, 435, 445, 449, 457, 460–63, 470, 476, 585–86, 588, 595, 603, 605, 607, 613, 615, 683, 685–88

Necker, Jacques, 1, 3, 92 n, 179, 210, 258–59, 260, 263, 265, 280, 360 n, 362–63, 397, 403, 432–33, 542, 589, 594, 596, 601–03, 610, 640, 648, 670, 697

Needler, Martin, 194 n

négociants, 112, 221, 238–39, 240 n, 243, 248, 282, 285, 287, 352, 374, 379, 382, 548, 556, 560, 577–78, 586 n, 589, 618–19, 622, 634, 636, 639–40, 642–43, 666

Neser, Daniel, 294, 298

New England, 634 n

New York, 634

Newton, Issac, 101, 112

Nivernais, 295, 499

nobility, 67, 277, 398, 528–29, 687

Nogent-le-Rotrou, 212

Nogent-sur-Seine, 364, 365

Noireau, 632, 633, 641

Noirot, 277

Normandy, 368, 414, 463, 488, 489 n, 492, 499, 631, 643
—Parlement of, 21, 25, 136, 154, 157, 182, 185–86, 214, 235–36, 368–71, 392–95, 400, 401 n, 407, 409, 414–17, 420–23, 424 n, 439, 442 n, 449, 451–57, 463, 468, 481, 488, 489 n, 492, 499, 524, 528, 557–58, 631, 643, 652, 664 n

Normant, 272

owners (of grain), 497, 511, 515, 536–37, 540, 544, 559–60, 572 n, 612

O'Heguerty, Pierre-Andre, 113

Orléans, 188 n, 244, 277, 327, 374, 493 n
—bishop of, 231 n, 233–34
—dealer registration list, 285 n
—intendants of, 80, 196, 205, 214, 230–35, 250, 368–70, 372–73, 434 n, 559

Orléanais, 188 n, 311, 360

Orry, Philibert, controller-general 1740–45, 31, 38, 99, 249, 367, 395, 630, 640, 660

Pajot de Marcheval, Christophe, intendant of Dauphiné 1761–84, 466 n, 559, 580 n, 584

Papal States, 624

Parc aux Cerfs, 161

Paris, xxxii, xxxiii, 18, 20, 25, 32–35, 66, 145, 154, 163, 170, 197, 236, 238, 245–46, 272–73, 299, 300–44, 346, 355, 358, 365–66, 368 n, 369, 372, 374, 376–77, 379, 381, 389, 392, 406, 411, 426, 438, 440, 442, 446, 452–53, 456–57, 463, 465, 468–69, 471, 475, 479–81, 488, 492, 502, 505–06, 514–16, 521–22, 526–27, 539, 555, 558, 564, 579, 592, 606, 615, 623–27, 631, 644, 646–47, 650 n, 652, 658–59, 663–64, 691–92, 696
—catastrophe of 30 May 1770 of, 605–06
—Chambre des Comptes of, 404, 425
—Cour des Aides of, 425, 443 n
—exempted from liberalization, 95, 137–38, 183, 300–303, 306–07, 446, 691
—Faculty of Medicine of, 336
—hinterland and supply crowns of, 36, 71, 76, 85, 300–02, 304–05, 307, 324 168, 178, 354, 383, 394, 553, 632–33, 641, 673
—Juridiction Consulaire of, 384–86, 389
—municipality of, see Hôtel de Ville and prévôt des marchands
—police of, see police of Paris
—population of, 33–34
—ports of, 66, 90, 286–87, 300, 384
—prisons of, 200, 343, 355, 383, 390, 622, 642, 671–72, 678
—versus France, 465–67, 469, 479–81, 696
—versus provinces, 31–33, 35–41, 76, 153, 438, 452–57, 696

Pâris brothers, 367, 384, 395, 617, 628, 700
—Pâris-DuVerney, Joseph, 10, 177 n, 257, 336, 351

Parlement [conseil souverain] of Alsace, 493, 496, 514

Parlement of Franche-Comté (Besançon), 184, 185 n, 493, 518–19, 523–24, 558 Parlement of Bordeaux, 183, 235, 248 n, 451, 493, 498, 557, 566, 581–83, 652–53, 656
—first president of, 655

Parlement of Brittany (Rennes), 154, 159, 183–84, 451, 529, 530 n, 556

Parlement of Burgundy (Dijon), 22, 107 n, 183–84, 451, 493, 496–97, 514, 558, 569 n, 619

Parlement of Dauphiné (Grenoble), 154, 159, 177 n, 183, 222, 247 n, 256, 264, 266 n, 281 n, 282, 394, 409, 412 n, 455 n, 458 n, 459–64, 468, 471, 476 n, 524, 532 n, 583–84, 590
—first president of, 482
—procurator general, 466 n, 583–84

Parlement of Dombes, 493, 496

Parlement of Flanders, 183, 185 n

Parlement of Languedoc (Toulouse), 154, 160, 181, 183, 404, 409, 459, 466, 468, 471, 573, 582, 586–90, 688
—arret of November 1772, 586–88
—procurator general, 590

Parlement of Lorraine, 493, 496, 564 n, 580 n

Parlement of Metz, 184 n, 439 n, 493, 496–97, 525 n, 556, 558, 652
—procurator general, 519

Parlement of Normandy (Rouen), 21, 25, 136, 154, 157, 182, 185–86, 214, 235–36, 368–71, 392–95, 400, 401 n, 407, 409, 414–17, 420–23, 424 n, 439, 442 n, 449, 451–57, 463, 468, 481, 488, 489 n, 492, 499, 524, 528, 557–58, 631, 643, 652, 664n 664 n
—arrêts of March-April 1768, 414–15, 454
—first president of, 21, 186, 248, 273, 369–70, 429, 454, 456–57, 664 n
—October 1768 "letters," 416, 454

Parlement of Paris, 21, 22, 25–27, 79, 140, 153–54, 157, 180, 1 85, 236, 250, 274–76, 319, 322, 349, 370, 392, 404, 406–07, 409–11, 413–14, 417, 420–21, 423–52, 462, 468, 471, 473–75, 482, 513, 520, 522, 526–28, 532, 538, 556–57, 572, 600, 612, 664 n, 670, 673, 696
—advocate general, see Omer Joly de
—Fleury and Séguier

—*arrêt* of 20 January 1 769, 440–43
—*arrêt* of August 1770, 51 3–20, 526, 532, 536, 538 n
—Chambres des Enquêtes, 428 n, 443, 568
—Chambre des vacations, 412–13
—first president of, 24, 219, 426, 427 procurators general, 203, 229, 453: *see also* Guillaume–François–Louis Joly de
—Fleury *and* Omer–Louis–François Joly de
—Fleury
—liberalism within, 171
—popularity of, 441–43, 526
—*séance de flagellation*, 435, 450
Parlement of Provence (Aix), 75, 183, 224, 232, 256, 263 n, 264, 402, 430 n, 445 n, 457, 458 n, 466–70, 512 n, 524–25, 527 n, 534, 573, 582, 584–86, 590
—status of Marseilles, 586
parlements, xxxi, 20, 74, 121, 123, 132, 137, 140, 152–55, 158, 164–66, 169, 175, 180–82, 185–87, 192, 224, 229, 283, 380, 394, 397, 408–09, 411, 416, 418–20, 434, 436, 439, 446, 451–52, 467–68, 478, 495–97, 511, 514, 520–21, 523, 527–28, 534, 551–52, 556, 571, 574–75, 601 n, 605, 649, 687, 689, 695–96
—"authors" of famine, 522–26
—constitutional issues, 408–09, 412 n, 422, 527, 697
—constitutional liberalism, 155, 436
—*gens du roi*, 20, 23, 412
—liberal, 412 n, 458–72, 479, 481–82, 522, 528, 530 n, 556, 583–90, 612: *see also* liberal movement *and* individual parlements
—*lits de justice*, 25, 180, 409, 439
—quarrels with the crown, 21, 409, 422, 425, 439, 441, 444–45, 451, 462, 470, 527–28, 585, 696–97
—*union des classes*, 154, 408, 527 n, 696
Parmentier, Antoine–Auguste, 177 n, 350, 351, 361
Pascaud, Antoine, 622–29, 632, 663
Passy, 664
paternalism, 346, 446, 448, 450, 462, 466, 541–42, 544, 587–88, 598–600, 607, 655, 664, 680, 682–83, 699; *see also* kingship
pauvres honteux, 323; *see also* misery *and* poverty
Pavie, Jacques, 275
Pays Chartrain, 286, 502
Pays de Gex, 668 n

Penthièvre, Louis-Jean-Marie de Bourbon, due de, 323
people, the, xxviii, xxxi, 3, 87, 104, 139, 169, 187, 197, 204, 207–09, 215, 218, 220, 222, 224, 227, 231–35, 258, 261, 272, 279, 332, 369, 372, 377, 380, 396, 401–03, 405–06, 409, 412, 414–15, 418–20, 427, 430, 432, 435–39, 441–44, 447–48, 466, 469–73, 475, 477–79, 486, 496, 498–99, 501, 510, 513, 517, 518–19, 521, 523–28, 534 n, 536, 538 n, 540–44, 555–56, 559, 564, 566, 569, 573, 576, 581–85, 587–89, 598, 600–01, 609, 612–13, 634–35, 651–53, 655–57, 659–60, 662, 670 n, 674, 677–78, 680–83, 685–88, 693, 701; *see also* consumers; prejudices; public opinion
Perche, 368
Perigord, 493
Perrouteau, 639, 672
Perruchot, Bernard, 360, 377–80, 386–87
Perry, Jean, 666
Persan, 275, 341
Petit, 307
Pezenas, 459 n
Pharoux, 274
Philadelphia, 634
philosophes, xxxi, 169, 527, 605, 607–09, 649, 687; *see also* Enlightenment
physiocracy, xxxiii, 88, 112, 115, 122, 149, 152, 160, 208, 261, 426 n, 477, 590–91, 596, 605, 607, 610, 687
—evidence, 422, 438, 476, 605
—*see also economistes*
Piarron de Chamousset, Claude–Humbert, 113, 429 n
Picardy, 206, 269, 285, 369, 386, 499, 564
—intendant of, 179, 559 n, 562, 575
Pidansat de Mairobert, Mathieu-François, 249–50 n, 611 n
Pinczon du Sel des Monts, 113
Pithiviers, 188 n
Plantes, 632
Plato, 422, 593
plot mentality, 390–406, 566 n, 670–71; *see also* famine plot
Plumart de Dangeul, Louis-Joseph, 113, 131
Poilly, 286
Poissy, 272, 295, 517
Poitou, 493 n, 565
—intendant of, 619

Poland, 621, 622
police, and the people, 104, 129, 194–96,
198–99; *see also* the people
—criticism of, 44–47, 49, 59, 220–25
—benign neglect, 72
—"hands tied," 201, 205, 213–14, 232,
421, 431
—idea of, 1–14, 224, 436, 449, 465–66, 543,
596, 597–98, 607, 678, 683, 701
—local level administration, 19, 28–30,
40–41, 43, 50–51, 76, 85, 106, 127,
182, 220, 225, 229–30, 284, 302, 304–
07, 368, 375, 395, 410, 414, 418–21,
423, 427, 443, 448, 472, 475, 483–86,
492, 495–96, 511, 513–16, 532–36,
538–39, 543, 546–47, 551–55, 560–61,
568, 570–71, 574–75, 583–84, 590,
598, 634, 670, 679, 681, 684, 690–92,
694–95, 697–701
—of Paris, *see* police of Paris
—of provisioning, 14, 28, 72–86, 89
—paralysis of discretion, 78, 546, 693
—police of the, 225–29
—reaction to liberalization, 166, 200, 220,
225, 228–29, 231, 414, 421, 423, 447–48,
473–74, 495, 516, 518, 555, 568, 607,
690–92, 695, 698–99
—view of liberty, 62–63, 83, 128–130, 431
police of Paris, 24, 36, 43–44, 69, 71,
75–77, 82, 90, 273–74, 285, 287, 300–02,
304 n, 322, 329, 335–36, 351, 406, 616,
642
—assemblies of police, 24, 76 n, 77 n, 79–80;
see also Assembly of General Police
—commissaires, 83–84, 319, 320–21, 323,
325, 328–29, 332–34, 341–42, 508–09
—*droit de suite*, 301
—*exempts*, 334, 522
—inspectors, 285, 297, 333
—*lieutenants criminels*, 167, 256–57, 322, 428;
see also Châtelet
—*lieutenants généraux*, 24, 38, 45, 48, 57, 74,
374, 386; *see also* La Reynie; Marc-Rene
de Voyer de Paulmy d'Argenson; Herault;
Marville; Sartine; Lenoir
political economy, 97, 118, 140, 151–52,
155, 171, 181, 215, 232, 237, 425, 435–36,
445–46, 471–72, 478, 591, 596, 605, 609,
611, 613, 685, 689; *see also economistes;* liberal theory; physiocracy

Pompadour, Jeanne-Antoinette Poisson, marquise de, 131, 141, 143, 147, 395, 530, 531
Pompiez, 212
Pont-l'évêque, 188 n
Pontoise, 275, 276, 311, 374
Pont Sainte-Maxence, 285
population, 488, 550, 551–52, 690
—populationism, 444
—*see also* demographic crises *and* floating
population
Portugal, 262, 468, 668
posters, 319–21, 368, 372, 419, 505, 506 n,
526
potato, 621; *see also* foodways
Poussot, 48, 83, 285, 297, 352, 354–55
poverty, xxiv, xxvi n, 308–09, 322–23, 376,
398, 416, 573; *see also* misery
prejudices, 110, 112, 129, 130, 136, 149, 186,
216–17, 221, 232–33, 237, 267, 295, 328,
369, 401, 416, 439, 447, 466–67, 470, 472,
475, 478, 496, 604, 613, 681, 685; *see also*
the people *and* public opinion
Prémord, J. B., 374
prévôt des marchands, of Paris, 24, 66, 303, 305,
507; *see also* Hôtel de Ville (Paris)
price fixation *(taxation)*, 81–85, 190, 196–200,
212, 226, 499–501, 506, 584, 598
prices, 95, 98, 116, 123, 141–42, 145, 165,
170, 172, 181, 186–87, 189, 196,200,207,
209, 236–38, 244, 246, 258–59, 307, 311–
18, 329, 340, 398, 405, 410–12, 417, 427,
432–33, 435, 439, 468, 472, 482–88, 496,
505–06, 519, 528, 543, 564, 572–73, 598–
99, 635, 691–94; *see also* bread *and* grain
Prie, Agnès Berthelot de Pléneuf, marquise
de, 367, 395
procurators general, 23, 284
—of the Parlement of Dauphine, 466 n,
583–84
—of the Parlement of Languedoc, 590
—of the Parlement of Metz, 519
—of the Parlement of Paris, *see* Daguesseau;
—Guillaume-François Joly de Fleury;
—Guillaume-François-Louis Joly de Fleury;
and Omer-Louis-François Joly de Fleury
producers, 104, 111, 125, 543–44, 569, 584,
612; *see also* cultivators
prohibitive laws, 414–15, 423, 437–38, 468,
475, 493, 543, 583, 680; *see also* police
categories

property, xxx, 115, 194, 196, 240, 259, 422 n, 449, 477, 544, 586, 603, 605, 607, 613, 682
—laws of, 460–61, 687
—propertyless, 209
—rights of, 181–82, 209, 405, 466, 476, 559, 585, 596–97, 609, 664, 680
proprietors (of land), 94, 95, 98, 122, 153, 206, 208, 259, 433, 444, 460–63, 469 n, 477, 541, 543, 558, 587, 606, 612, 687, 691, 694, 699
Provence, 21, 126, 282 n, 548, 565, 643
—Parlement of, 154, 183, 224, 232, 264, 402, 430 n, 445 n, 457, 458 n, 466–70, 512 n, 524, 525 n, 527 n, 534, 573, 582, 590
—intendant of, 126, 624, 626, 643
Provendier, 341
provincial estates, 121, 123, 551, 552, 578, 695
Provins, 190, 288
—police of, 305
—lieutenant general of, 374
provisioning by constraint, 73, 136, 190, 193, 195, 197, 210, 212, 242, 414, 493, 513, 516–19, 536, 583, 675
Prussia, 622
porters of grain, 28, 274
public opinion, 104, 108, 111, 130, 132, 132, 144, 150, 162–63, 215, 219, 227, 234, 343, 346, 380, 400–06, 411, 417, 419, 427, 440, 444, 470–71, 510–12, 519–20, 523–24, 525 n, 541, 549, 552–53, 576, 580–82, 584, 634–35, 648–76, 654, 656–58, 660–62, 664, 666, 671, 684–85, 692, 694, 698–99; see also consumers; the people; prejudices
public provisioning, 2, 195, 241–49, 345, 347, 354, 402–06, 449, 462, 486, 497, 500, 505, 547, 557, 581, 585, 590, 612, 614–15,618–30,635, 664, 669, 675, 699; see also king's grain and granaries, public
—competitive institutional victualing, 619, 620, 623
—distribution problems, xvi, xxiii
public tranquility, 410, 437, 442, 543, 555, 688; see also social control
public works, 322–23, 621
—ateliers de charité, 504, 563

Quesnay, François, 88, 113–15, 117, 121, 124, 131, 133, 143, 146–47, 149–50, 152, 158, 177 n, 178, 182, 265, 479, 529, 604
Quimper, 209
—subdelegate, 564

Raison d'etat, 542
Rambouillet, 237, 271, 277, 285, 515
—fiscal procurator of, 269, 307
Rebais, 188 n, 200, 218, 288
Regency, the, 98
régie, 614, 617, 618, 622, 625, 630–49
—agents, 634–45, 666, 671
—domestic purchasing, 633–37
—grain and flour stocks, 666
—planning allocation, 630–32, 636–37
—selling, 640–42
—Turgot's critique, 632–33
—under attack, 667–73
regionalism, 483, 581, 586, 695–96
—center versus periphery, 554, 578, 696
registration lists of grain and flour dealers, 283–93
registration lists, of Avesnes, 292; of Chateauneuf, 285 n; of Graisivaudan, 285 n; of Landescq, 292 ; of Lille, 293; of Maubeuge, 292; of Meaux, 288–93; of Orléans, 285 n; of Paris, 284–88; of Valenciennes, 292
regrating, 69, 204, 211, 269, 273–74, 289, 515–16, 562, 570, 584: see also grain trade, abuses
Reims, 193, 195, 500, 559
relativism, 434–35, 607
religious communities, 89, 287, 310, 324, 426, 500
removals (enlèvements), 189, 193, 195, 200, 213, 220, 306, 392, 492, 498–99, 565
Remuzat, Pierre, 642
Rennes, Parlement of, see Parlement of Brittany
repression, 218, 219, 227, 499–500, 566, 575, 683: see also riots
Revolution, French, xxiii, 7–8, 14, 36, 56, 161, 179, 335, 346, 363, 377, 383, 387–89, 394–96, 399, 453, 463, 480 n, 529, 651, 673–74, 692, 696, 700
Révolutions de Paris, 394
Reynie, 530 n
rice, 323, 616, 617 n, 621, 681; see also foodways and dearth
Richelieu, 570
Riom, 504
—subdelegate, 503
riots, xxxi, 165–66, 168–69, 188–200, 217–20, 225, 226 n, 227, 230, 267 n, 270, 273, 275, 279, 301, 334, 375, 414, 422, 447–48, 453–54, 459 n, 497–502, 520,

528, 532, 563–67, 601 n, 609, 670, 680, 683–84, 692, 695, 698
—pre-riot, 195–96
—women in, 190–92
Rivarol, Antoine, 33
Robinson, 365
Rochambeau, Jean-Baptiste-Donatien de Vimeur, comte de, 383
Rodez, 493 n
Rohan, Louis–René-Edouard, prince de, 531
Roland, 320–21
Rolland d'Erceville, Barthélemi-Gabriel, 262
Rolland, Nicolas, 285–86
Rolland de Challerange, 516
Rome, 345, 627
—Roman precedents, 224
Rottenburgh, François, 632
Roubaud, Pierre-Joseph-André, 61, 87, 147, 222, 224, 261, 400–02, 429, 438, 464 n, 473–81, 603–04, 650
Rouen, 170, 188 n, 190, 218, 230 n, 262, 269, 285, 370, 506, 524, 579, 591, 622–23, 627, 632
—chamber of commerce of, 457
—intendants of, 128–30, 136, 415, 423, 453 n
—Parlement of, see Parlement of Normandy
—police of, 483
—riot at, of 1752, 453–54
—riots at, March–April 1768, 414, 453–54
Rouillé d'Orfeuil, Gaspard-Louis, intendant of Champagne 1764–90, 194 n, 226 n, 230, 264 n, 504, 537, 541 n, 561, 564 n, 647–48
Rousseau, Jean-Jacques, 101, 439 n
Rousseau, Pierre, 360, 365, 377–80, 387
Roux, Cadet, 278
royal councils, 15, 22, 137, 140, 143, 162, 228–29, 324, 355, 417–18, 423, 441, 452, 495–96, 510, 513, 560, 574, 616, 622, 656, 659, 672, 687
Rozoy, 188 n, 288
Russia, 400, 640
rye, 339, 618

Sablé, 188 n
Sade, Donatien-Alphonse-François, comte, called marquis de, 393
Saint-Antoine, faubourg (Paris), riot in 1725, 334
Saint-Brieuc, 190
Saint-Charles, 325–26, 364

Saint-Denis, 188 n, 287, 288, 295, 365
—fiscal procurator of, 227, 295
Saint-Dizier, 188 n, 193, 493 n, 499
Saint-Florentin (Champagne), 305
—fiscal procurator of, 515
Saint-Florentin, Louis Phélypeaux, comte de, 131, 234, 321, 325, 346, 412, 615, 624, 627
Saint-Germain-en-Laye, 190, 198, 272, 517, 616
Saint-Jacob, Pierre de, 291, 529 n
Saint-Lambert, François de, 264
Saint-Malo, 124, 139, 506, 634
Saint-Mars, de, 477
Saint-Pierre, Charles-Irénée Castel, abbé de, 553, 685
Saint-Prest, Philippe Brochet de, 360, 624–27 630, 644, 662–65
Saint-Priest, Jean–Emmanuel de Guignard de, intendant of Languedoc 1751–85, 231 n, 580 n, 636
Sainte-Geneviève, 25, 425
Sainte-Menehould, 499
Saintes, municipality of, 619
salus populi, 39, 125, 542, 602
samples, 69, 202, 273, 289, 306; see also grain trade, abuses
Sancerre, 188 n
Sartine, Antoine-Raymond-Jean-Gualbert de, lieutenant general of police 1759–1774, 89, 234, 262, 275, 295–96, 310, 319–26, 328–37, 341–3, 354, 356 n, 361–62, 365, 369, 387, 390–92, 395, 412, 432, 506, 520, 522, 592, 604, 616, 622–24, 626, 628–29, 642, 644, 660
Saumur, 493 n, 634 n
Saury, (abbé), 603 n
Sausin, Louis de, 458 n
Sauvageot, 424
Schlestatt, 511 n
School for Baking, 336, 361
Scipion, hospital, 336
Sées, 135
Séguier, Antoine-Louis, 412–13, 431–32, 434–35, 437, 538 n, 600
seigneurial dues, 571
Séine (River), 170, 363, 456, 664
self–interest, 102–03, 110, 128, 171, 201, 205, 405, 422, 431, 435, 444, 449, 516, 569, 682; see also liberal theory
Sénac de Meilhan, Gabriel, 611

Sens, 188 n, 217, 515
Sermaize-les-Bains, 493 n
Serres, Olivier de, 119
Seven Years' War, 125, 132, 167, 398,
    444–45, 488 n, 622, 640
Sézanne, 277, 515
shipowners, 122, 124, 382
Sicily, 634 n
Silhouette, Etienne de, controller-general
    March–Nov. 1759, 107 n, 118, 126, 128,
    130–32, 249
Simon, Jean, 340
Simonneau, 272
slave trade, 622
social control, 3, 4, 33–35, 128, 168, 170,
    194, 208, 210, 432, 435–36, 442, 449–50,
    542–43, 589, 596, 601, 683–84, 688; see
    also public tranquility
Soissonnais, 280, 633
Soissons, 280, 633
—intendant of, 504
Sorbonne, 591
Sorin de Bonne, 617, 664–65, 673, 700
soudure, xxi, 624
Spain, 262, 468, 668
speculation and speculators, 193, 238–41,
    246, 254, 301–02, 431, 435, 470, 477, 487,
    488, 511, 516, 547–49, 569, 575, 577–78,
    587, 589–90, 627, 633, 636, 648, 662, 680
Staël, Anne-Louise-Germaine Necker, bar-
    onne de, 363
Stains, 288
starchmakers, 623
state-of-the-nation issue, 174–77, 179, 182,
    186; see also agriculture
Strasbourg, 499 n
Suard, Jean-Baptiste-Antoine, 449, 474 n,
    505, 593
subdelegates, 18, 134–35, 150, 198, 202, 204,
    206–07, 210, 229, 235, 281 n, 284, 474 n,
    503, 507, 511, 551, 553–54, 561, 564, 572,
    576, 579, 602 n
subsistence, science of, 335–39
subsistence mentality, 200, 215, 217, 231,
    346, 377, 396, 405–06, 525 n, 542–43,
    576, 613, 652, 656, 677–81, 684, 700: see
    also consumers; the people; prejudices;
    public opinion
substituts, 23, 205, 229, 411, 495, 538

Sully, Maximilien de Bethune, baron de
    Rosny, due de, and Sullyism, 125, 141,
    161, 1 65, 170, 544, 697
surplus, 168–69, 206, 256–58, 260, 466, 549,
    581, 598, 698; see also abundance: exporta-
    tion ; liberal theory
Switzerland, 523, 668 n
syndics of rural communities, 553, 554

Taboureau des Réaux, Louis-Gabriel, in-
    tendant of Hainaut 1764–75, 230, 247,
    538 n, 541 n, 561, 562, 619, 652
taille, 156–57, 250, 397, 571
Taine, Hippolyte, xxv, 608
Tallard, 188, 226 n
Target, Guy-Jean-Baptiste, 60, 478 n
Tarrade, Jean, 488 n
Tauvin, Pierre, 341
Terray, Joseph-Marie, controller general of
    finance 1769–74, xxxii–xxxiv, 187, 200,
    225, 280, 287, 360, 364, 381–85, 395, 409,
    439, 491–676, 698–99
Testard du Lys, 256–57, 322, 428
Thellusson, Isaac, 58, 156, 628, 640, 700
Thompson, E. P., 194 n
tithe, 551, 566, 571
tolls and duties, internal, 28, 92, 133, 138,
    184, 185 n
—market fees, 28, 76
Tolosan, Jean-François de, 179 n
Toulon, 641
Toulouse, 123–24, 164–65, 177 n, 277, 565
—archbishop of, 578, 588
—capitouls, 459, 635
—Parlement of, see Parlement of
    Languedoc
—subdelegate of, 565
Tonnerre, 190
—royal procurator, 515–16
Touraine, 188 n, 192, 269, 499
Tournan-en-Brie, 188 n, 204, 288
Tours, 230 n, 493 n, 498, 564, 567 n
—intendant of, 158, 216, 226 n, 496, 499,
    540, 560
transportation and communications, xx, 262,
    344, 534, 554, 623, 678, 690
Tréguier, 124
Trennin, 210–11, 295–96
Tressaux, 334

Trezel, 366–67, 372, 387: *see also* Leray de Chaumont
Trippier, 562
triumvirate, 522, 649; *see also* d'Aiguillon; Maupeou; *and* Terray
Troyes, 188 n, 190–91, 197, 219, 221, 225, 230 n, 277–79, 499
—municipality of, 619, 652 n
Trudaine, Daniel-Charles, 113, 131, 148
Trudaine de Montigny, Jean-Charles-Philibert, 148–50, 226–27, 229, 232–33, 235–36, 244, 250, 253 n, 273, 296, 310, 326–28, 346, 359, 365–66, 368–70, 373–75, 379, 386, 443, 454 n, 457, 482, 492, 494, 512, 527, 592–93, 615–16, 630, 663, 673 n
Tulle, 498
Tupin, 311
Turgot, Anne-Robert-Jacques, xxix n, xxxii, 114, 116–17, 149, 339, 368 n, 402–06, 428 n, 439, 473–75, 477, 479, 569, 610
—intendant of Limousin 1761–74, 133, 141, 146, 222, 230, 368 n, 505, 512, 611–13, 618, 620, 634 n, 650, 681 n
—controller-general 1774–76, 148, 157, 179, 216, 220, 222–23, 240 n, 325 n, 383 n, 404–06, 433, 442, 446–47, 465, 509, 521 n, 552, 559, 566 n, 603, 607–08, 613, 629, 632–33, 639, 641, 645, 661–76, 683, 697, 701
Turkey, 644

unemployment, 207, 231, 322, 398, 433, 489, 501, 564–65, 692, 697
Unigenitus, 27
urbanization, 31 n
utilitarianism, 98; *see also économistes;* physiocracy ; liberal theory

Valenciennes,
—dealer registration list, 292

—subdelegate of, 503, 511, 575 n
Vannes, 124, 193
Vauban, Sébastien Le Prestre, seigneur de, 177
Vaucouleurs, 564 n
Vaugirard, 424
Verdilhon, 628
Véri, Joseph-Alphonse de, 24, 60, 224, 403, 442, 628, 649, 660
Verneuil, subdelegate of, 135
Versailles, 210, 286, 295, 320, 341
Vexin, French, 286
Vézelay, 645 n
Vilar, Pierre, xxix n
Villabbe, 375
Villaines-le-Jubel, 188 n
Vincennes, 390
vingtième, 140, 157, 347, 397, 411, 439
visibility, of supply, 70, 173, 217, 536–37
Vitry-le-François, 188 n, 190, 203, 237, 277, 306, 500
Vivens, François de, 113
Volland, Sophie, 377
Voltaire, François-Marie Arouet de, xxiv n, 35, 54, 92 n, 118–19, 177, 255, 527, 538, 566, 592 n, 593–94, 610–11, 685

wages, 172, 207, 210, 417, 433, 479, 489, 503, 543, 564, 681, 697
war, 126, 136, 140, 145, 163, 174, 176, 180, 187; *see also* Seven Years' War
Watergate, 400
weather, xxii n, xxii, 192, 310–11, 340, 410, 415, 427, 444, 468, 502, 506, 564, 581, 623, 679, 690; *see also* harvests
Weulersse, Georges, 429 n
wheat, 325, 339, 505–06, 510, 618, 648; *see also* grain

Young, Arthur, 179 n

Lightning Source UK Ltd.
Milton Keynes UK
UKHW010635280220
359497UK00004B/757